MW01152327

INTELLIGENT TESTING WITH THE WISC®–V

Alan S. Kaufman, Susan Engi Raiford, and Diane L. Coalson

WILEY

Copyright ©2016 by John Wiley & Sons, Inc. All rights reserved.

Published by John Wiley & Sons, Inc., Hoboken, New Jersey.
Published simultaneously in Canada.

No part of this publication may be reproduced, stored in a retrieval system, or transmitted in any form or by any means, electronic, mechanical, photocopying, recording, scanning, or otherwise, except as permitted under Section 107 or 108 of the 1976 United States Copyright Act, without either the prior written permission of the publisher, or authorization through payment of the appropriate per-copy fee to the Copyright Clearance Center, Inc., 222 Rosewood Drive, Danvers, MA 01923, 978-750-8400, fax 978-646-8600, or on the Web at www.copyright.com. Requests to the publisher for permission should be addressed to the Permissions Department, John Wiley & Sons, Inc., 111 River Street, Hoboken, NJ 07030, 201-748-6011, fax 201-748-6008, or online at www.wiley.com/go/permissions.

Limit of Liability/Disclaimer of Warranty: While the publisher and author have used their best efforts in preparing this book, they make no representations or warranties with respect to the accuracy or completeness of the contents of this book and specifically disclaim any implied warranties of merchantability or fitness for a particular purpose. No warranty may be created or extended by sales representatives or written sales materials. The advice and strategies contained herein may not be suitable for your situation. You should consult with a professional where appropriate. Neither the publisher nor author shall be liable for any loss of profit or any other commercial damages, including but not limited to special, incidental, consequential, or other damages. Readers should be aware that Internet Web sites offered as citations and/or sources for further information may have changed or disappeared between the time this was written and when it is read.

This publication is designed to provide accurate and authoritative information in regard to the subject matter covered. It is sold with the understanding that the publisher is not engaged in rendering professional services. If legal, accounting, medical, psychological or any other expert assistance is required, the services of a competent professional should be sought.

For general information on our other products and services, please contact our Customer Care Department within the U.S. at 800-956-7739, outside the U.S. at 317-572-3986, or fax 317-572-4002.

Wiley publishes in a variety of print and electronic formats and by print-on-demand. Some material included with standard print versions of this book may not be included in e-books or in print-on-demand. If this book refers to media such as a CD or DVD that is not included in the version you purchased, you may download this material at **http://booksupport.wiley.com**. For more information about Wiley products, visit **www.wiley.com**.

Library of Congress Cataloging-in-Publication Data

Names: Kaufman, Alan S., 1944- | Raiford, Susan Engi. | Coalson, Diane L.
Title: Intelligent testing with the WISC®-V / Alan S. Kaufman, Susan Engi
   Raiford, and Diane L. Coalson.
Description: Hoboken : Wiley, 2015. | Includes index.
Identifiers: LCCN 2015028406 | ISBN 9781118589236 (hardback) | ISBN 9781119176732 (epdf) | ISBN 9781119176749 (epub)
Subjects: LCSH: Wechsler Intelligence Scale for Children. | BISAC: PSYCHOLOGY
   / Assessment, Testing & Measurement.
Classification: LCC BF432.5.W42 K38 2015 | DDC 155.4/1393–dc23 LC record available at http://lccn.loc.gov/2015028406

Cover design: Wiley
Cover image: © traffic_analyzer/iStockphoto

Printed in the United States of America

FIRST EDITION

HB Printing 10 9 8 7 6 5 4 3 2
PB Printing 10 9 8 7 6 5 4 3 2 1

For Nadeen, My Sweet Lady,
Alan

> When you are old and grey and full of sleep,
> And nodding by the fire, take down this book,
> And slowly read, and dream of the soft look
> Your eyes had once, and of their shadows deep;
> How many loved your moments of glad grace,
> And loved your beauty with love false or true,
> But one man loved the pilgrim soul in you,
> And loved the sorrows of your changing face …

From "When You Are Old"
By William Butler Yeats

• • •

For Robert, whose love is patient, kind, not envious, not boastful, not proud, not rude, not easily angered, keeps no record of wrongs, always protects, always trusts, always hopes, always perseveres, and never fails.
For George, my beloved son, with whom I am well pleased.
For God, I can do all this through you, you strengthen me.
Susie

• • •

For David,
We need one another, not to fill an emptiness, but to grow from our fullness together. We embrace but do not encircle the other. We succeed in all the important ways and do not fret about the small stuff. We have happiness and find it in making one another happy. We have love, and we find it in loving one another. As promised, now and forever.
Diane

CONTENTS

Foreword   xi
   Alan S. Kaufman

Preface   xv

Acknowledgments   xvii

PART I
INTRODUCTION TO INTELLIGENT TESTING AND THE WISC–V   **1**

CHAPTER 1
INTELLIGENT TESTING   5

PART II
ADMINISTRATION AND SCORING   **35**

CHAPTER 2
INTELLIGENT WISC–V ADMINISTRATION: TEST KIT VERSION   37

CHAPTER 3
WISC–V SCORING: TEST KIT VERSION   91

CHAPTER 4
WISC–V DIGITAL ADMINISTRATION AND SCORING   139

PART III
BASIC WISC–V TEST INTERPRETATION   **157**

CHAPTER 5
WISC–V SEX, ETHNIC, AND SOCIOECONOMIC STATUS (SES) DIFFERENCES   159

CHAPTER 6
THE CREATION OF NEW RISK SCALES FOR SCHOOL FAILURE AND JUVENILE DELINQUENCY: THE CHILD AND ADOLESCENT ACADEMIC AND BEHAVIOR QUESTIONNAIRES   **175**

Jennie Kaufman Singer, Alan S. Kaufman, Susan Engi Raiford, and Diane L. Coalson

CHAPTER 7
DOES WISC–V SCATTER MATTER?   **209**

Troy Courville, Diane L. Coalson, Alan S. Kaufman, and Susan Engi Raiford

CHAPTER 8
BASIC STEPS FOR WISC–V INTERPRETATION   **227**

PART IV
THEORETICAL FRAMEWORKS FOR WISC–V INTERPRETATION   249

CHAPTER 9
INTERPRETING THE WISC–V FROM THE PERSPECTIVE OF CATTELL-HORN-CARROLL THEORY   **251**

Case 1—Liam, age 9: Emotionally Intelligent Testing with the WISC–V and CHC Theory   **265**

W. Joel Schneider

Case 2—Alicia, Age 13: Looking Under the Hood   **283**

Jill Hartmann and John Willis

Case 3—Luke, Age 9: A CHC-Based Cross-Battery Assessment Case Report   **304**

Jennifer T. Mascolo and Dawn P. Flanagan

CHAPTER 10
INTERPRETING THE WISC–V FROM A COGNITIVE NEUROSCIENCE PERSPECTIVE   **331**

Case 4—Josh, Age 8: A Neurodevelopmental Processing "No Numbers" Approach to Case Report Writing   **348**

Elaine Fletcher-Janzen and Elizabeth Power

Case 5—Tawna, Age 13: Eighth-Grade Girl with ADHD Struggling with Processing Speed, Sustained Attention, and Emotional Functioning   **362**

Michelle Lurie and Elizabeth Lichtenberger

Case 6—Tom, Age 8 (Digital Administration): Evaluation of a Twice Exceptional Child: Gifted with Dyslexia and Symptoms of Inattention and Social-Behavioral Issues   **372**

Kristina Breaux

CHAPTER 11
INTERPRETING THE WISC–V FROM A NEUROPSYCHOLOGICAL PERSPECTIVE   405

Case 7—Jaime, Age 10: A Fourth-Grade Boy on the Autism Spectrum Struggling with Behavioral and Learning Problems   425

Jennie Kaufman Singer

Case 8—Christopher, Age 11: Phonological Dyslexia in Child with Visual Perceptual Disorder   437

Marsha Vasserman

Case 9—Isabella, Age 13: Teenage Girl with Low Cognitive Ability, ADHD, and Emotional Issues   448

Michelle Lurie

CHAPTER 12
INTERPRETING THE WISC–V FROM DAN MILLER'S INTEGRATED SCHOOL NEUROPSYCHOLOGICAL/CATTELL-HORN-CARROLL MODEL   459

Daniel C. Miller and Alicia M. Jones

Case 10—John, Age 12: A Neuropsychological Case Study Using the WISC–V with a 10-Year-Old Boy with a Suspected Specific Learning Disability in Written Expression   471

Daniel C. Miller and Alicia M. Jones

CHAPTER 13
INTERPRETING THE WISC–V USING GEORGE MCCLOSKEY'S NEUROPSYCHOLOGICALLY ORIENTED PROCESS APPROACH TO PSYCHOEDUCATIONAL EVALUATIONS   493

George McCloskey, Emily Hartz and Jaime Slonim

Case 11—Colin, Age 8: An Eight-Year-Old Boy with Mild Executive Function Difficulties but No Specific Learning Disabilities   497

George McCloskey

Case 12—Derek, Age 13: A Teenage Boy Exhibiting Phonological Dyslexia and Executive Function Difficulties   523

George McCloskey

CHAPTER 14
INTERPRETING THE WISC–V FOR CHILDREN WITH READING OR LANGUAGE PROBLEMS: FIVE ILLUSTRATIVE CASE REPORTS   549

Introduction to the Five Case Reports on Children with Reading or Language Problems   549

Diane L. Coalson and Nadeen L. Kaufman

Conceptual and Clinical Integration of All 17 Case Reports in the Book   **550**

Nadeen L. Kaufman and Diane L. Coalson

Case 13—Ellie, Age 10: Complexity in Diagnosis: Neuropsychological Assessment of a
    Chinese Adoptee   **557**

Michelle Lurie

Case 14—Jordan, Age 15: Cognitive Development in a Child Who Is Hard of Hearing: Is It
    More than Just Hearing?   **568**

Marsha Vasserman

Case 15—Jane, Age 8: Consumer-Responsive Approach to Assessment Reports   **578**

Robert Lichtenstein and Joan Axelrod

Case 16—Lizzie, Age 8: Low Cognition, Low Achievement—Still With a Learning Disability   **587**

Carlea Dries and Ron Dumont

Case 17—Patrick, Age 9: Does My Son Have a Reading Disability?: Application of the
    WISC–V and WJ IV   **600**

Nancy Mather and Katie Eklund

PART V
INDEPENDENT WISC–V TEST REVIEWS   613

CHAPTER 15
OUR WISC–V REVIEW   **615**

Matthew R. Reynolds and Megan B. Hadorn

CHAPTER 16
REVIEW OF THE WISC–V   **637**

Ron Dumont and John O. Willis

CHAPTER 17
REVIEW OF THE WISC–V   **645**

Daniel C. Miller and Ryan J. McGill

CHAPTER 18
INDEPENDENT WISC-V TEST REVIEW: THEORETICAL AND PRACTICAL CONSIDERATIONS   **663**

Jack A. Naglieri

CHAPTER 19
SOME IMPRESSIONS OF, AND QUESTIONS ABOUT, THE WISC–V   669

George McCloskey

CHAPTER 20
*REVIEW OF THE WECHSLER INTELLIGENCE SCALE FOR CHILDREN–FIFTH EDITION: CRITIQUE,
COMMENTARY, AND INDEPENDENT ANALYSES*   683

Gary L. Canivez and Marley W. Watkins

CHAPTER 21
OVERVIEW AND INTEGRATION OF THE INDEPENDENT REVIEWS OF WISC–V   703

PART VI
AFTERWORD: ALAN KAUFMAN REFLECTS ON DAVID WECHSLER
AND HIS LEGACY   713

Dr. Wechsler Remembered, Part I (1992)
Dr. Wechsler Remembered, Part II (2015)

References   725

About the Authors   771

About the Contributors   773

About the Online Resources   781

Author Index   785

Subject Index   795

APPENDIXES
AVAILABLE AT DOWNLOADABLE RESOURCES: WWW.WILEY.COM/GO/ITWISCV

FOREWORD ON THE ORIGINS OF "INTELLIGENT TESTING"

Alan S. Kaufman

When I started working at The Psychological Corporation in 1968, I was 24, a father of a 2-year-old girl, Jennie (and Nadeen was about to deliver number 2, David), and I was 2 years away from earning my PhD at Columbia. I was also 2 years away from starting a 4-year apprenticeship with David Wechsler that began with an item-by-item critique of the 1949 WISC and ended with the publication of the WISC–R in 1974. Post-Wechsler, I left The Psychological Corporation for the University of Georgia, where I began my academic career. (Paul Torrance was the chair of the department and, like Dr. Wechsler, was a mentor who had a profound influence on the direction my career would take.)

And 1968 was also when I met Dr. Alexander Wesman, director of Psych Corp's Test Division. He was a gentle-speaking and humble man, in his mid-50s (who would never reach 60 because of a sudden heart attack), with a wealth of wisdom and a lifetime of experience working side by side with Dr. Wechsler and all other authors who published their tests with his beloved Psych Corp. His office lined the east wall, facing the UN Building, and he was my first real boss. The first time I entered his office he handed me a reprint of an article that he had just published in *American Psychologist*. He didn't say much about it, just asked me to read it when I had the time. I was intrigued by the title —"Intelligent Testing"—and read it on the train ride home that night.

Dr. Wesman's premise was that a test's classification—as a test of aptitude, intelligence, or achievement—was unimportant. Every test was a measure of what each of us has learned, whether formally or informally, intentionally or by accident. What mattered was *how* the test was interpreted, how it was used to change people's lives. Test scores must make a difference. If the test scores just sit inertly in someone's file, then that is stupid testing. Intelligent testing became my credo, though I didn't really know it at the time. It did not become apparent until I had served most of my clinical apprenticeship with Dr. Wechsler and finally had internalized his assertion—often said with exasperation—that his tests were *clinical* tools that went way beyond Terman's psychometrics. The Wesman-Wechsler combination gave me a philosophy. But I still lacked a methodology.

The method came from Nadeen, courtesy of her doctoral program in the emerging field of learning disabilities at Columbia University. Nadeen had a brilliant mentor in the Special Education Department, Margaret Jo Shepherd. At the psychoeducational clinic the doctoral students would do an intake with parents in the morning, then test the child, come up with hypotheses and new strategies for assessment during lunchtime, continue the testing in the early afternoon, score and interpret the data in the late afternoon, and give the parents a feedback conference—with a list of intervention strategies—before the sun had set. But the interpretive approach was totally different from what I had learned in the neighboring Psychology Department. I was taught reliability, validity, norms, standard error of measurement, factor analysis by Robert Thorndike in one IQ course; in my other IQ course I was taught about the powerful influence of personality on test scores. What did they teach me? If you see a higher backward span than forward span—that is undoubtedly due to "negativism." If you observe a substantially higher P-IQ than V-IQ in a person of average or above-average intelligence—watch out for hysteria, narcissism, or psychopathic character disorder.

Nadeen was taught about strengths and weaknesses in the cognitive profile. About looking for consistencies across subtests to uncover hypotheses about a person's *relative* assets and deficits and to focus on how to best capitalize on the assets to ameliorate deficits in cognition as well as in reading, math, and writing. She was taught to operate out of the "learning disabilities" model of input-integration-storage-output. To think in terms of various perceptual-motor and psycholinguistic models to pinpoint where the student's learning was going wrong, and to try to fix it. To focus on the child's or adult's behaviors during the evaluation and to use those behaviors as linchpins for test interpretation and interventions.

It was not what I was taught. And I don't think I gave her methods much credence while I was working with Dr. Wechsler to develop the WISC–R. But when I started training school psychologists at the University of Georgia, I suddenly realized that my background in IQ testing, even the articles I had published on WISC–R factor analysis and scatter, did not tell me how to teach profile interpretation or how to grade case reports. And Dr. Wechsler provided me with the knowledge that the WISC–R and Stanford-Binet were first and foremost clinical instruments, and I knew that *he* was a master clinician, who could gain great meaning from a person's verbal responses to his Vocabulary or Comprehension items. But I didn't know how to operationalize his philosophy. Nadeen did.

What became the "Kaufman method" of interpreting the WISC–R, the veritable backbone of the intelligent testing philosophy, was a merger of the psychometrics I had learned in my psychology courses and the clinical applications that Nadeen had internalized from her learning disabilities clinic with Jo Shepherd. The method indeed had problems, flaws that critics would enjoy pointing out over the next couple of decades. The "shared abilities" that emerged were not validated. They were based on theories that were popular at the time but didn't have staying power. Sam Kirk's psycholinguistics model, derived from Osgood's theory of communication, yielded shared abilities like "visual perception of meaningful stimuli" and "verbal expression."

Alex Bannatyne's system for reorganizing the WISC subtests ("sequential," "spatial") was enormously popular among reading disabilities specialists, but his categories would first drop out of sight completely and then be reincarnated into the more sophisticated model of Luria's neuropsychological processing approach. And J. P. Guilford's Structure of Intellect (SOI) model was embraced by gifted assessment in the 1970s and produced numerous shared abilities in the original WISC–R model such as convergent-production of figural implications. But Guilford's popularity in the field of IQ testing plummeted with the rise of Horn's expansion of the Horn-Cattell *Gf-Gc* theory in the 1980s and 1990s. Guilford had too many abilities to consider, well over 100, whereas the growing number of Horn abilities could be counted on the fingers of first one hand and then two. Dr. Wechsler was not overly impressed by the clinical or practical value of Guilford's theory of intelligence. In 1958 he noted that some 40 different SOI factors had been identified. But Wechsler dismissed them as trivial because "most of these would hardly occur in any standard test of intelligence."

So the building blocks of the first intelligent testing interpretive methodology were derived from popular theories in the 1970s, none of which had staying power. The multitude of shared abilities encouraged examiners to identify strengths and weaknesses that relied on statistical procedures (not just the popular "eyeballing" that characterized methodologies of the 1960s). They encouraged examiners to think of all of the possible reasons why a child or adolescent had an asset or deficit in a particular grouping of subtests, and whether that strong or weak area was due to a problem in taking in the stimuli, processing them, storing them, or expressing them manually or verbally.

But the shared abilities were based mostly on theories that would soon be outdated. They were not empirically validated or even relevant for the theories that would take the place of Kirk-Osgood, Guilford, Bannatyne, and others. In effect, they were *placeholders* until John Carroll, Raymond Cattell, J. P. Das, Dawn Flanagan, John Horn, Edith Kaplan, Marit Korkman, Alexander Luria, Kevin McGrew, Jack Naglieri, Richard Woodcock, and other notable clinician-theorists came along. Those placeholders allowed a generation of examiners to formulate hypotheses using the methodology that had its origins in Alan's psychometrics, Dr. Wechsler's clinical approach, Alexander Wesman's principles of intelligent testing, and Nadeen's clinically oriented psychoeducational training. The *process* of intelligent testing has remained virtually intact over generations, as is evident in all of the state-of-the-art chapters on clinical applications that comprise Part IV of this book. The intelligent testing process is evident in the 17 case reports that are featured in that part. But the unvalidated shared abilities from the original book on the WISC–R have given way to contemporary, theory-based, empirically validated abilities and processes. The field of intelligent testing has grown and evolved to the "genius" level, a level that I wasn't even close to being able to visualize in the late 1970s. I learned so much this past year by collaborating with Susie Raiford and Diane Coalson, each bringing special gifts to the task of moving intelligent testing into today and tomorrow. It makes me feel good to have been so wrong in some ways and so right in other ways, and to be awed by the interpretive acumen of the intelligent testers who pervade this book. They run rampant in the case reports in Part IV—all of which demonstrate detective work with $n = 1$; all of which were written by innovative scientist-practitioners who bring theoretical, clinical, and research-based expertise to the table when translating clinical observations, referral information, and the child's profile of scores to real-life, empirically validated interventions. This elite group includes our daughter, Jennie Kaufman Singer, who has used her clinical psychology training to energize and add a new dimension to the field of criminal justice.

And intelligent testing is demonstrated just as effectively in the articulate independent reviews of the WISC–V in Part V of the book. It is simply daunting to read the incisive analyses of the pros and cons and clinical intricacies of the test from as many diverse perspectives as there are reviews. In 1979 I was sure I knew what intelligent testing was. Basically, it was interpretation the way I delineated it, illustrated in the various case reports, all written by Nadeen. I am now older and wiser. Intelligent testing is captured by diversity and eclectic perspectives. Gary Canivez and Marley Watkins, who review the WISC–V in Chapter 21, have spent a chunk of their careers disagreeing with my "intelligent testing" approach. I have argued back. Neither side will ever convince the other, but we won't stop trying!

Ultimately, I am so proud of the students I have touched as a mentor who have helped change the field of assessment. Their number is too great to list, but I will mention the international leaders who have truly changed the shape of intelligent testing: Jan Alm, Bruce Bracken, Jack Cummings, Abdalla El-Mneizel, Patti Harrison, Randy Kamphaus, Toshinori Ishikuma, Elizabeth Lichtenberger, R. Steve McCallum, Soo-Back Moon, Jack Naglieri, and Cecil Reynolds. And I am continually amazed by James Kaufman's application of intelligent testing principles to transform the field of creativity, worldwide, with his groundbreaking theories, research, and assessment tools. But I can't take credit as James's primary mentor; he had the wonderful mentors of John Horn and T. C. Boyle at the University of Southern California and Robert Sternberg at Yale University (and ever since). Thank you, James, for suggesting that I write this foreword.

And thanks also to the late Thomas Oakland for all of his vital contributions to the field of assessment. You are missed, Tom. There is a huge hole in the field of international school psychology that cannot be filled.

And to Nadeen Laurie, Jennie Lynn, James Corey (Jamie), and Nicole Alaina—without all of you, my world would cease to spin on its axis.

PREFACE

When *Intelligent Testing with the WISC–R* was published in 1979, the field of intellectual assessment was in its veritable infancy regarding the reliance on theory and sound psychometric practices for profile interpretation. The WISC–R had just established its supremacy over the Stanford-Binet as the children's test of choice, thanks, in part, to the emergence of the fields of learning disabilities and neuropsychology. Both fields hit the ground running and transformed the assessment scene: Each demanded a profile of scores rather than a single intelligence score; and the one-score Binet didn't help its chances when it opted to restandardize without revising its content (so the 6-year level was passed by the average $5\frac{1}{2}$-year-old).

Today the field of IQ testing is sophisticated, psychometrically and theoretically, and there are many theory-based intelligence tests available to clinicians. There are literally tens of thousands of empirical research investigations on the array of intelligence instruments, past and present, yet the Wechsler scales remain dominant worldwide. The WISC–V represents the greatest height to which any Wechsler scale has dared climb in the realms of psychometric foundation and theory-based development.

Like the 1979 and 1994 version of this book, we have targeted this 2016 text to psychologists, special educators, educational diagnosticians, and graduate students everywhere in diverse disciplines—in short, to anyone who administers and interprets the WISC–V and to anyone who is required to understand the case reports they write and to apply the results to the real world. As with earlier versions of *Intelligent Testing*, this edition emphasizes simplicity in the interpretive approach. The WISC–V yields a wealth of scores, and the test manual's approach to interpretation has been criticized by some as cumbersome. (See the test reviews in Part V of this book.) To assist examiners in the task of profile interpretation, we provide a system that is built on rules of thumb and simple arithmetic (Chapter 8) and that revisits the clinical application of scatter (Chapter 7, with Troy Courville as first author).

Intelligent testing in the 21st century depends on the examiner being as sharp as a tack—no less important to theory-based profile assessment than the tools themselves. However, with the increased maturity of intellectual ability theories and testing approaches, we believe that there are multiple paths to becoming an intelligent tester and numerous methodologies that can be employed successfully. There is no single step-by-step interpretive approach that is best. We invited many experts to contribute to this book—including some who disagree strongly with each other and, often, with us—to allow readers the opportunity to embrace divergent perspectives and decide for themselves which one or two work best for them or best for a particular referral or a child of a particular age. We achieved this diversity of perspective in ways such as the following:

- *Case reports:* *Intelligent Testing with the WISC–V* includes 17 clinical case reports of children and adolescents with a variety of disorders, written by international leaders in the field of assessment (Part IV of this book). These reports reflect an incredible variety of theoretical perspectives, writing styles, and clinical approaches to understanding children—with every report focused on the translation of test scores and behaviors to effective educational and clinical interventions. These reports demonstrate the multifaceted real-life ways that intelligent testing can impact the lives of children and their families.

- *Independent test reviews:* Prominent experts in the field of intellectual assessment contributed objective, unedited reviews of the WISC–V, written to be comparable to Buros reviews in terms of thoroughness and scope. Like the case reports, these reviews represent a huge diversity of theoretical and clinical perspectives and contribute to the understanding and application of intelligent testing principles to psychoeducational and neuropsychological evaluations.
- *Theory-based interpretation:* Consistent with earlier editions of *intelligence testing*, the interpretive system is built on theory. Whereas the math for interpreting the scores remains simple, the theories that underlie interpretation reflect the breadth and depth of state-of-the-art approaches to intelligence. These approaches include cognitive neuroscience models, neuropsychological processing theory, and Cattell-Horn-Carroll (CHC) theory. Chapter 10 on cognitive neuroscience reflects the theory that guided the development of the WISC–V, just as it guided the development of the WISC–IV and WAIS–IV. This chapter highlights the impressive research results and speculations about brain functioning that are springing from laboratories around the world. In addition, separate neuropsychological chapters written by Dan Miller (Chapter 12), George McCloskey (Chapter 13), and their colleagues hammer home the message that intelligent testing embraces multiple technologies and takes many forms.
- *Development of rating scales:* To diversify the tools discussed in this book, we developed two new home-environment rating scales, based on questions administered to the parents of the children and adolescents in the WISC–V standardization samples that dealt with topics like the child's homework and TV habits, the number of high-tech devices in the home, types of discipline, and the nature of family activities. One scale was designed to predict academic failure, the other to predict delinquency (Chapter 6, with Jennie Kaufman Singer as first author).

The very first chapter, on the intelligent testing philosophy, includes thoughtful quotes from about a dozen experts on what contemporary intelligent testing means to each of them. From the first chapter to the next-to-last chapter—an independent review of the WISC–V by Gary Canivez and Marley Watkins, who champion *g* and are generally opposed to profile interpretation—the book gives a clear message: Intelligent testing can best be understood by being exposed to strikingly different theory-based, clinical, and psychometric perspectives espoused by an array of experts. For experienced clinicians, gravitate to the perspectives that match your ideology. For new psychologists and graduate students, learn what is out there by studying the array of theories and clinical methodologies that are presented throughout this book. Try them out. See what works and what doesn't. Then decide which approach is the most intelligent for you.

Alan S. Kaufman, Susan Engi Raiford, and Diane L. Coalson

ACKNOWLEDGMENTS

The preparation, organization, statistical analyses, writing, and editing of *Intelligent Testing with the WISC–V* was a massive effort that could not have been accomplished without the collaboration of a dedicated, amazing, brilliant team of professionals throughout the United States who helped us understand the true and multifaceted meaning of intelligent testing, as it exists in real time on the contemporary assessment scene in schools, clinics, school psychology and clinical neuropsychology training programs, hospitals, and private practices.

We are hugely indebted to many psychologists, special educators, and graduate students.

Nadeen Kaufman worked closely with us at every stage of this project, providing essential commentary on each chapter and, especially, making vital contributions to the 17 case reports that appear in Part IV of the book. Nadeen coauthored, with Diane, two sections of Chapter 14, one that introduces the chapter and the other that integrates all of the case reports, with a special focus on the reports in that chapter that emphasized children with reading or language problems.

Kristina Breaux was Janie-on-the-spot throughout the book writing and editing process. Whenever we ran into a snag, one of us suggested, "Ask Kristina." And she always delivered, especially with her expertise on the KTEA–3, WIAT–III, and translating cognitive profiles to educational interventions.

Jennie Kaufman Singer (Chapter 6, on two new rating scales), Troy Courville (Chapter 7, on scatter), Dan Miller (Chapter 12), and George McCloskey (Chapter 13) were all lead authors of brilliant chapters that expanded the scope, breadth, and context of our intelligent testing message. They each brought unique areas of expertise to the table, as did Dan's coauthor, Alicia Jones, and George's coauthors, Emily Hartz and Jaime Slonim; we are the lucky beneficiaries.

The following master clinicians provide remarkable case reports from divergent theoretical and clinical perspectives: Joan Axelrod, Kristina Breaux, Carlea Dries, Ron Dumont, Katie Eklund, Dawn Flanagan, Elaine Fletcher-Janzen, Jill Hartmann, Alicia Jones, Elizabeth Lichtenberger, Michelle Lurie, Jennifer Mascolo, Nancy Mather, George McCloskey, Dan Miller, Elizabeth Power, Joel Schneider, Jennie Kaufman Singer, Marsha Vasserman, and John Willis. Collectively, they illustrated intelligent testing from almost as many vantage points as there are reports. Joel Schneider and the team of Robert Lichtenstein and Joan Axelrod articulated their intelligent report-writing philosophies with clarity and insight. Michelle Lurie, Marsha Vasserman, and George McCloskey contributed multiple reports. It is not possible to overstate the value of these 17 case reports as hands-on illustrations of the intricacies and far-reaching boundaries of the intelligent testing approach.

We sought and received objective, thorough, incisive, state-of-the-art, Buros-like, independent test reviews of the WISC–V. The content of these reviews was completely unedited by us, other than routine grammatical changes or typos. We considered these objective reviews an essential component of the book: (a) in view of the prominent roles that Susie and Diane played in the development, standardization, and validation of the WISC–V and numerous other Wechsler scales (Susie was the primary author of the WISC–V manuals and continues to serve as a senior research director at Pearson, publisher of Wechsler's scales); and (b) to avoid the customary time lag between publication and independent reviews of major tests of intelligence. We are deeply indebted to the thoughtful and innovative approaches that the following assessment leaders brought to the task of reviewing the WISC–V: Matt Reynolds and

Megan Hadorn (Chapter 15), Ron Dumont and John Willis (Chapter 16), Dan Miller and Ryan McGill (Chapter 17), Jack Naglieri (Chapter 18), George McCloskey (Chapter 19), Gary Canivez and Marley Watkins (Chapter 20), and Joel Schneider (a "mini-review" appended to his case report in Chapter 9).

We are inordinately grateful to the insightful and generous responses about the meaning of "intelligent testing" in 2015, all of which were incorporated into Chapter 1. Thank you: Ron Dumont, Elaine Fletcher-Janzen, Nadeen Kaufman, Jennifer Mascolo, George McCloskey, Jack Naglieri, Nancy Mather, Kevin McGrew, Dan Miller, Cecil Reynolds, Joel Schneider, and John Willis. All comments were far-reaching and insightful, with a special note of thanks to Jennifer Mascolo and Nancy Mather, whose extensive commentary added an extra dimension to the intelligent translation of test scores and behaviors to educational interventions.

We are indebted to John Wasserman for sharing his historical expertise and in-depth knowledge of Wechsler's life; to Caroline Scheiber for her invaluable research assistance; to Peter Melchers for enhancing our cross-cultural understanding of cognitive assessment; to Mitchel Perlman, Carol Schmitt, and Jennie Kaufman Singer for graciously sharing their expertise on clinical assessment; to Rebecca O'Brien for her vital last-minute contributions to enable us to meet our deadline for delivering the manuscript; and to James Kaufman for his wise counsel.

We wish to acknowledge the support of some outstanding colleagues at Pearson, without whom this book would not have been possible. Ou Zhang and Xuechun Zhou developed the norms for the additional scores that appear in the book and on the *WISC–V Interpretive Assistant 1.0*, and Jianjun Zhu reviewed and confirmed the quality of their work. We are grateful to Larry Weiss for granting access to the standardization data and for reading and commenting on the content. We thank William Schryver, senior licensing specialist at Pearson, for his speedy, expert handling of the numerous permissions requests we submitted.

We are also grateful to Marquita Flemming, Senior Editor Professional Development and her remarkable staff at John Wiley & Sons for bringing *Intelligent Testing with the WISC–V* to rapid publication and supporting this project from start to finish. Marquita has been inspiring in her close collaboration with Alan and Nadeen on Wiley's *Essentials of Assessment* series and supervised the present book project with true excellence. Melinda Noack, Senior Editorial Assistant, deserves recognition for her expertise and guidance in manuscript preparation, and we are extremely grateful to Elisha Benjamin, Production Editor, and Brian Grimm, Community Marketing Manager, for their great contributions to the publication of our book.

We are also indebted to the Italian psychologist Professor Arturo Orsini for his contributions to the field of Wechsler interpretation. His publications in Italy have been extremely influential in promoting intelligent testing worldwide. In January 2014 he emailed Alan regarding the rule Alan and his colleagues had used in several books to determine whether IQs had too much variability to be interpreted. Alan and colleagues had stipulated that if the range between a person's highest and lowest index scores was 1.5 standard deviations (23 points) or greater, then the global score should not be interpreted. Professor Orsini sent Alan analyses that demonstrated that about 50% of normal individuals in Italy and the United States had differences of 23 points or greater; therefore, such differences are "normal" and should not denote uninterpretable IQs. In part because of Professor Orsini's contributions (Orsini, Pezzuti, & Hulbert, 2014), we do not use a child's Index variability to declare any WISC–V global scores uninterpretable. Sadly, Arturo Orsini died at age 67 in 2014. His death is a huge loss to the field.

On another personal note, we wish to thank our loving spouses— Nadeen Kaufman, Robert Raiford, and David Shafer—for their enduring support. Susie is especially grateful to Robert for the many evenings and weekends he cared for their son, George, so Susie could work on the book.

Finally, we wish to thank Dr. David Wechsler. We hope that he would be proud of this book and of his enduring legacy, living on in all of us who seek to use the Wechsler scales intelligently.

PART 1

INTRODUCTION TO INTELLIGENT TESTING AND THE WISC–V

TWO VERSIONS OF THE WISC–V

The Wechsler Intelligence Scale for Children–Fifth Edition (WISC–V; Wechsler, 2014) comes in two formats: the traditional "test kit" format and the Q-interactive iPad to iPad format (digital). In Part II of the book, Chapter 2 and Chapter 3 deal with administration and scoring of the traditional test kit format. Chapter 4 tackles both topics, with numerous illustrations of the digital format. For both formats, the structure of the test is the same. The first chapter of the book, on intelligent testing, applies to both versions of the WISC–V, and to all clinical tests everywhere.

WISC–V Test Structure

The WISC–V subtests are grouped at four levels of interpretation: Full, Primary Index, Ancillary Index, and Complementary Index. The levels each contain one or more scales. Each scale (e.g., Full, Verbal Comprehension, Nonverbal, Symbol Translation) consists of a combination of subtests that are used to obtain a composite score. Figure 1.1 shows the WISC–V test structure.

Full Scale

Five domains containing the 16 primary and secondary subtests are included at the Full scale level: Verbal Comprehension, Visual Spatial, Fluid Reasoning, Working Memory, and Processing Speed. There are seven Full Scale

IQ (FSIQ) subtests (shown in Figure 1.1). The subtests that may be used as substitutes are shown in black italics.

Primary Index Scales

Five scales exist at the primary index scale level: Verbal Comprehension, Visual Spatial, Fluid Reasoning, Working Memory, and Processing Speed. The five primary index scores obtained from each scale at the primary index scale level are the Verbal Comprehension Index, Visual Spatial Index, Fluid Reasoning Index, Working Memory Index, and Processing Speed Index. Figure 1.1 indicates the primary subtests that are required to obtain each primary index score. Most evaluations include the primary index scores and the FSIQ. *Subtest substitution is no longer permitted for any index score.*

Ancillary Index Scales

Five scales make up the ancillary index scale level: Quantitative Reasoning, Auditory Working Memory, Nonverbal, General Ability, and Cognitive Proficiency. The ancillary index scores obtained from each scale at the Ancillary Index scale level are the Quantitative Reasoning Index, Auditory Working Memory, Nonverbal Index, General Ability Index, and Cognitive Proficiency Index, respectively. The five ancillary index scores are obtained by summing the scaled scores from primary subtests or primary and secondary subtests. They are designed to provide additional information about the child's cognitive abilities and performance on the WISC–V. Figure 1.1 indicates the subtests that are required to obtain each ancillary index score.

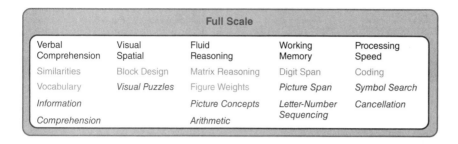

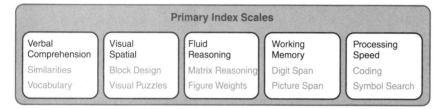

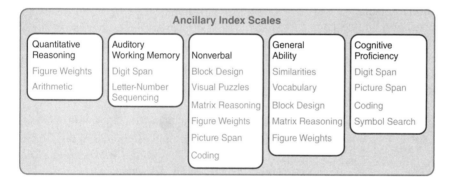

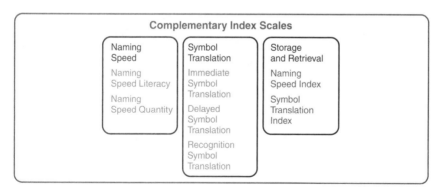

Figure 1.1   WISC–V Test Structure *Wechsler Intelligence Scale for Children, Fifth Edition* (WISC–V). Copyright © 2014 NCS Pearson, Inc. Reproduced with permission. All rights reserved. *"Wechsler Intelligence Scale for Children"* and *"WISC"* are trademarks, in the US and/or other countries, of Pearson Education, Inc. or its affiliates(s).

Complementary Index Scales

Three scales make up the complementary index scale level: Naming Speed, Symbol Translation, and Storage and Retrieval. The complementary index scores obtained from each scale at the Complementary Index scale level are the Naming Speed Index, Symbol Translation Index, and Storage and Retrieval Index. Figure 1.1 indicates the subtests that are required to obtain the Naming Speed Index and the Symbol Translation Index. The Naming Speed Index and the Symbol Translation Index are required to derive the Storage and Retrieval Index. The Storage and Retrieval Index is derived from index scores rather than subtest scores.

Scores

The WISC–V consists of a variety of scores on different metrics. The primary and secondary subtests are on a scaled score metric (1–19) with a mean of 10 and a standard deviation of 3. The complementary subtests are on a standard score metric (45–155) with a mean of 100 and a standard deviation of 15.

All composite scores are on a standard score metric. The range for the Full Scale IQ, Nonverbal Index, General Ability Index , and Cognitive Proficiency Index is 40 to 160; the range for all other index scores is 45 to 155.

There are various process scores included in the WISC–V, and many are new. A total of 10 scaled or standard process scores (e.g., Block Design No Time Bonus, Block Design Partial, Digit Span Forward, Backward, and Sequencing, Naming Speed Letter–Number) are available to examine performance more closely for four subtests: Block Design, Digit Span, Cancellation, and Naming Speed Literacy. Several raw process scores for which base rates can be obtained are also included. These consist of longest span and sequence scores (e.g., Longest Digit Span Forward, Longest Picture Span), error scores (e.g., Block Design rotations), and process observations (e.g., the number of times the child said "Don't know" as a response to Comprehension items).

New experimental scores called contrast scores that provide information about performance on a task given their performance on a related task are available. For example, the child's performance on Digit Span Backward, given his or her performance on Digit Span Backward, can be examined. These are on a scaled score metric. An appendix in the *WISC–V Technical and Interpretive Manual* describes the proposed use and interpretation of the contrast scores.

CHAPTER 1

INTELLIGENT TESTING

This is a book about the Wechsler Intelligence Scale for Children–Fifth Edition (WISC–V; Wechsler, 2014), which, as almost any graduate student in education or psychology knows, is an IQ-yielding intelligence test. But neither the IQ nor the concept of intelligence is the focus of the chapters that follow. The focus is the child, with interpretation of the WISC–V and communication of the test results in the context of the child's particular background, behaviors, and approach to the test items as the main goals. Global scores are deemphasized, flexibility and insight on the part of the examiner are demanded, and the test is perceived as a dynamic helping agent rather than as an instrument for placement, labeling, or other types of academic oppression. In short, *intelligent testing* is the key, and the WISC–V is the vehicle.

The preceding paragraph introduced Alan's 1979 *Intelligent Testing with the WISC–R* (A. S. Kaufman, 1979), with the single change being the substitution of WISC–V for WISC–R. That paragraph also summarized Alan's beliefs about the value of intelligence tests in the 1990s when he wrote *Intelligent Testing with the WISC–III* (A. S. Kaufman, 1994a), even though the field of intellectual assessment had undergone turbulent changes during the 1980s and the "Kaufman method" had been the target of direct attack (e.g., McDermott, Fantuzzo, & Glutting, 1990). And it continues to summarize Alan's current views, even while staring in the face of the post–Individuals with Disabilities Education Act (IDEA) tsunami of anti-IQ-testing sentiment that makes the controversies of the 1980s and 1990s seem like a mild family feud.

Further, that first paragraph is endorsed by Susie Raiford and Diane Coalson, even though these coauthors of *Intelligent Testing with the*

WISC–V were in elementary school when Alan first formulated the philosophy and they cut their teeth as fledgling psychologists on the 1994 edition. For over 15 years, Susie and Diane have been on the firing line and in the trenches as the heirs apparent to David Wechsler, with one or both serving as research directors for every U.S. publication of a Wechsler intelligence scale since 2000, including the WPPSI–III, WISC–IV, WISC–IV Integrated, WAIS–IV, WPPSI–IV, WISC–V, and WISC–V Integrated. Thus, they have weathered the variety of IQ storms as teammates and close colleagues throughout this time. At the core of Susie's and Diane's approaches to cognitive assessment (Raiford & Coalson, 2014) is an intelligent testing philosophy that extends back to David Wechsler, the clinician, but is simultaneously mindful of what assessment is all about in the middle of the second decade of the 21st century:

> *Diane*: With every revision, my appreciation of Wechsler's genius is again renewed. By distinguishing his definition of intelligence from the cognitive abilities he used to measure it, he avoided all of the pitfalls so many of us seem to experience when we align too closely with this theory or that assessment method. He knew his tests were, most importantly, *clinical* instruments, designed to measure key, but not all, aspects of an individual's intelligence. Only in the hands of a skilled clinician (i.e., an intelligent tester), does the instrument become a powerful tool, yielding much more than a handful of scores. This is still true today.
>
> *Susie*: Intelligent testers answer the question that is asked and, where necessary, provide the referral source with the answers to some other questions maybe they should have asked. They select measures that are engaging

to the child, efficient, and reliable; they assess all relevant areas of the child's functioning and avoid the irrelevant. Intelligent testers stay current on issues in the field (listservs), adapt on the fly as the picture of results become clearer, and use the most relevant and current theoretical models, neurocognitive research, and clinical research findings to understand the data as a whole.

Diane: Regardless of your choice of test kit or digital administration, your theoretical orientation to assessment and interpretation, or your approach to intervention, intelligent testing is an ongoing, dynamic process. It involves an active interchange between examiner and child, yielding rich, clinical information as it progresses. Modifications or additions to the assessment plan should be expected and welcomed, as clinical hypotheses are accepted or rejected.

Susie: Perhaps most importantly, intelligent testers present results as a clear description of the living, breathing child—as opposed to providing tables full of scores that are of no use in the real world—and translate results into recommendations that parents, teachers, and other associated professionals can use and that are effective.

Diane: Isn't Wechsler's way still the best way for intelligent testing? I think he would have been so interested in everything going on but quickly gotten back to how it helps the child (or adult).

In fact, David Wechsler—one of the first American clinical psychologists and among the first to open up a private practice—was likely the first intelligent tester within the field of clinical assessment. (Actually, there wasn't even a field of clinical assessment until Wechsler, single-handedly, converted the Binet-Terman tradition of *psychometric testing* to the field that still reigns supreme more than 75 years later.) Witness Wechsler's (1939) caution to clinicians when the first form of the Wechsler–Bellevue was published:

> The kind of life one lives is itself a pretty good test of a person's intelligence. When a life

history (assuming it to be accurate) is in disagreement with the "psychometric," it is well to pause before attempting a classification on the basis of tests alone. Generally it will be found that the former is a more reliable criterion of the individual's intelligence. (p. 48)

Wechsler's elegant wisdom embodies clinical insight, humanism, and, without question, the epitome of *intelligent testing*.

Importantly, Wechsler viewed intelligence as a component of personality, as something inseparable from a person's affect. Drawing from Aristotle's perception of mental faculties, popularized by Kant, Lohman (1989) stated:

> By this account, a complete theory of mind must explain not only the cognitive dimension but also the emotional and intentional dimensions as well. . . . Thus, one direction research on intelligence seems to be taking is to expand its horizons to include affective dimensions long recognized as central to intelligence (e.g., Wechsler, 1939) but rarely combined with the systematic study of the cognitive dimensions. (p. 360)

Putting that concept in simple structure is Dr. Wechsler's credo, spoken to Alan with various degrees of exasperation when he had to deal with Alan's psychometric tendencies: "The Wechsler scales are, first and foremost, *clinical* instruments."

But Dr. Wechsler was far more than a clinician who interpreted intelligence as an aspect of personality. As Alan wrote a few years ago:

> Though I worked with Dr. Wechsler for nearly 5 years in the early 1970s during the process of revising the 1949 WISC and developing and standardizing the WISC–R—which was called the WISC (Rev.) in the manual's page proofs until a last-minute decision by an executive rewrote history—I never knew of his psychometric background. To me, Dr. Wechsler was the consummate clinician who deferred to my statistical expertise because I trained at Columbia with Robert Thorndike, Edward's son. I found out a few years later

about his work with psychometric pioneers just after World War I, but during the time Dr. Wechsler mentored me, he never let on about his statistical savvy. I wanted to include, directly in the 1974 WISC–R test manual (Wechsler, 1974a), the exploratory factor analyses of the WISC–R that I later published for normal children (Kaufman, 1975) and individuals with mental retardation (Van Hagen & Kaufman, 1975), and to have examiners compute three factor scores in addition to the three IQs, but he calmly said, "No, not yet; it isn't time." (A. S. Kaufman, 2013a, p. 225)

Our continued advocacy of an intelligent testing approach to IQ assessment—even tracing it back to the methods that David Wechsler favored almost a century ago—does not imply that we haven't changed, because we have, and it doesn't suggest that the field is static because it is as volatile and energetic and innovative as ever. The three of us retain our beliefs about how to assess intelligence in general and how to interpret the WISC–V in specific. The key is still intelligent testing, as opposed to the mindless testing that never quite disappears. But the context of the IQ construct, both societally and professionally, has altered with time.

IQ TESTING IN THE 1970s

The field of intelligence testing is nearly unrecognizable as the field that Alan entered nearly a half century ago as a student of the brilliant-but-distant Robert L. Thorndike at Columbia University. Alan was hired by the Psychological Corporation's Test Division in late 1968 as a young, idealistic, not-yet-dissertationed, psychologist. Sure the IQ test was at the center of heated controversy—hasn't it always been?—but the issues and the antagonists were different, and the arguments were more emotional than empirical. When Alan was getting his feet wet in the early 1970s as Dorothea McCarthy's and David Wechsler's

right-hand person (though he is left-handed), he began to understand the depth of the feelings of the anti-testing people. At that time, the opponents of the IQ, and of the tests that served this unholy purpose, were mostly enraged about test bias, especially against African American children. They were social psychologists and African American psychologists and sociologists and civic leaders. Some words were tossed around—like "biased," "unfair," "middle class," "discriminatory," and "racist"—while other words were best tossed away, like "immutable," "innate," and "Jensen."

Within the field of the clinical assessment of intelligence in the late 1970s, the WISC–R was virtually the *only* well-normed, psychometrically sound IQ test for children. "Stupid testing" was rampant at that time. Clinicians interpreted small differences between scaled scores as meaningful and tended to interpret "high" and "low" scores in isolation: A scaled score of 8 on Picture Completion meant that the child had trouble distinguishing essential from nonessential details, an 11 on Comprehension meant good social maturity. Psychoanalytic overinterpretation of Wechsler profiles was popular in the early 1950s: Failing easy Comprehension items conceivably reflected schizophrenia or psychotic depression; decrements in Information, contrasted with adequate Comprehension, indicated a hysteric reaction; increments in Picture Completion suggested a possible paranoid trend (Mayman, Schafer, & Rapaport, 1951; Rapaport, Gill, & Schafer, 1945–1946). Yet this type of nonsensical interpretation remained popular throughout the 1970s: Allison, Blatt, and Zimet (1968), for example, claimed that high Digit Symbol (Coding) and low Digit Span characterizes a person

> who seems to be controlling strong and
> pressing anxiety by excessive activity....
> When we find the reverse pattern, a high
> Digit Span and a low Digit Symbol, we are
> usually confronted with an essentially
> depressed person who is attempting to ward

off recognition of depressive affect perhaps in a hypomanic way, usually via denial, but not necessarily through acting and acting out behavior. (p. 32)

A major purpose of *Intelligent Testing with the WISC–R*—and of other landmark 1970s texts written by special educators (Bannatyne, 1971; Bush & Waugh, 1976; Myers & Hammill, 1976) and psychologists (Lutey, 1977; Matarazzo, 1972; Sattler, 1974)—was to impose some empirical order on profile interpretation; to make sensible inferences from the data with full awareness of errors of measurement; and to steer the field away from the psychiatric couch.

IQ TESTING IN THE 1980s AND EARLY 1990s

When Alan revised his 1979 text on the WISC–R and wrote *Intelligent Testing with the WISC–III* (A. S. Kaufman, 1994a), the opposition to IQ tests was no longer so intensely focused on the unfairness of the tests to ethnic minorities. In the 1970s there was talk of "black intellectual genocide" and "the silent mugging of the black community" (R. L. Williams, 1974a, 1974b). In the 1980s and 1990s, the IQ testing opponents were no longer primarily from outside the field. Now many resided within the field: trainers of school psychologists, developers of new approaches to intellectual assessment, cognitive theorists, psychometricians, and neuropsychologists. The people who viewed the IQ test as an instrument of torture for minority group members were still around, but they spoke with quieter voices. By the early 1990s—and still true today—the critics offered few concessions, and the venom applied to everyone, regardless of socioeconomic or ethnic background.

Whereas the 1970s produced an array of innovative textbooks on IQ assessment, such as Matarazzo's, Bannatyne's, Sattler's, and Kaufman's original *Intelligent Testing*, the 1980s

witnessed the first group of individually administered tests built from the foundation of *theory*. Theory-based test construction started in the 1980s with the split-brain/Luria foundation of the Kaufman Assessment Battery for Children (K–ABC; A. S. Kaufman & Kaufman, 1983), the Cattell-Horn fluid-crystallized framework of the Stanford Binet Intelligence Scale–Fourth Edition (SB IV; Thorndike, Hagen, & Sattler, 1986) and the Woodcock-Johnson Tests of Cognitive Ability–Revised (WJ–R; Woodcock & Johnson, 1989). These newcomers on the block aroused both interest and controversy, but they did not knock the king of the hill—Wechsler's scales—off the front pages.

There were two specific key targets of the 1980s and 1990s anti-IQ forces: subtest profile interpretation (especially the "Kaufman method") and Wechsler's children's scales, notably the 1991 Wechsler Intelligence Scale for Children (WISC–III; Wechsler, 1991).

Criticisms of Subtest Profile Interpretation

Some researchers and clinicians argued that using any type of subtest or profile interpretation was like taking illegal drugs: "Such approaches essentially violate primary principles guiding valid test interpretation" (McDermott, Fantuzzo, Glutting, Watkins, & Baggaley, 1992, p. 522); "we are compelled to advise that psychologists just say 'no' to subtest analysis" (McDermott et al., 1990, p. 299). These psychologists based their conclusions on a variety of psychometric analyses that they believed proved their points beyond dispute. They represented the new breed of anti-IQ testing professionals—with a link to the past—Hirshoren and Kavale (1976); but despite their strong words, they were perhaps the mildest of the species. They wanted to kick out subtest interpretation (a practice that Wechsler was devoted to and that the so-called Kaufman method endorsed), but they were okay with keeping the IQ test and even Wechsler's three IQs.

First they put the Kaufman method securely under the blade of the guillotine:

> Perhaps most popular among contemporary practices is the method of ipsative ability assessment advocated by Kaufman (1979) … He cautioned practitioners not to overvalue IQ scores…. A major aspect of this interpretation process is the discovery of children's intellectual strengths and weaknesses by studying the magnitude and direction of each subtest score's deviation from a child's average subtest score. (McDermott et al., 1992, p. 506)

Then they damned his method with faint praise:

> The Kaufman method is presently a common element in university curricula for preparing professional psychologists, with the ipsative procedure now generalized to many other ability tests. (p. 506)

And, finally, they interpreted their data with no mercy, letting the blade drop:

> Thus we cannot recommend either ipsative or normative approaches for subtest interpretation. Such approaches essentially violate primary principles guiding valid test interpretation. (p. 522)

The *ipsative* interpretation that they criticized refers to an axiom that is implicit in any interpretive system that Kaufman has advocated from 1977 (A. S. Kaufman & Kaufman, 1977) through the present (A. S. Kaufman, 2013a; Lichtenberger & Kaufman, 2013): Identify the child's or adult's *relative* strengths and weaknesses (relative to the person's own level of ability, whether high or average or low).

The McDermott-Glutting critique of the Kaufman method was harsh, but you did not need to look too far to find stronger opposition. D. W. Macmann and Barnett (1994) shared the same psychometric tree as the McDermott-Glutting team, but they went farther out on the

limb. They used exploratory and confirmatory factor analysis to conclude that the Wechsler scales measured little more than *g*, or general intelligence. They weren't content to toss out subtest profile interpretation; Macmann and Barnett (1994) also wanted to discard the Verbal and Performance IQs because the separate factors that underlie these IQs were really nothing more than degraded versions of *g*. They then rode the steam of their empirical argument a little further and decided to chunk the Full Scale IQ (FSIQ) as well. They sought alternative types of assessment but saw no useful role for the measurement of *g* within their system.

McDermott and his colleagues shunned subtest analysis in favor of the global IQs. Macmann and Barnett first flushed the Verbal and Performance IQs and then tossed the FSIQ into the bowl for good measure. In fact, these traditions live on today in the middle of the second decade of the 21st century, with passionate fervor. Gary Canivez, Marley Watkins, and Joe Kush continue to argue that clinicians must say no to profile interpretation (Canivez & Kush, 2013; Canivez & Watkins, 2010a), including interpretation of the factor indexes that have replaced the Verbal and Performance IQs; but they show great respect for FSIQ and the *g* that it measures. Regarding WAIS–IV interpretation, for example, Canivez and Watkins (2010a) concluded from their analyses "that the WAIS–IV provides strong measurement of general intelligence, and clinical interpretation should be primarily at that level" (p. 827). By contrast, advocates of Response to Intervention (RTI) as the sole method for identifying children with specific learning disabilities (e.g., Gresham, 2002; VanDerHeyden & Burns, 2010) are entirely comfortable in relegating IQ tests to the historical relic section of museums.

Not all that much has changed since the early 1990s regarding antagonism against Kaufman's method of profile interpretation. Also contemporary in its flavor is the hold-no-prisoners approach to reviewing IQ tests. Wechsler's 1974 and 1991 versions of the WISC were not exempt.

Criticisms of the WISC–R and the WISC–III

Witt and Gresham (1985) spoke metaphorically in their Buros test review:

> The WISC–R is an anachronistic albatross which hangs gamely around the necks of applied psychologists.... Using the WISC–R to assess intelligence in light of the surge of information in [the fields of cognitive psychology and neuroscience] is analogous to applying Newtonian formulae to modern physics problems.... The WISC–R lacks treatment validity in that its use does not enhance remedial interventions for children who show specific academic skill deficiencies. In this sense, the WISC–R is biased for all children and for this reason should be replaced with assessment procedures which have greater treatment validity. (pp. 1716–1717)

Edwards and Edwards (1993) ended their very favorable WISC–III review by extending the metaphor: "Individuals who viewed the WISC–R as burdening our profession (Witt & Gresham, 1985) will probably see the WISC–III as nothing more than an albatross that has molted and grown a few new feathers" (p. 149).

Neuropsychologist Muriel Lezak (1988) also took her own potshots at IQ tests, especially Wechsler's scales ("IQ: R.I.P."). But she was not concerned about treatment validity and argued the opposite perspective of the proponents of *g*:

> When the many and various neuropsychological observations elicited by so-called "intelligence" tests are lumped and leveled into a single IQ score—or even three—the product of this unholy conversion is a number that, in referring to everything, represents nothing ... [W]e need to conceptualize [mental abilities] in all their multivariate complexity and report our examination findings in a profile of test scores. (pp. 352, 358)

From the vantage point of cognitive psychology, the news still wasn't so good. John Carroll (1993b) reviewed the WISC–III and rejected it on empirical grounds. Carroll resurrected Frank's (1983) diatribe against "the Wechsler enterprise" and did not dispute Frank's proclamation that it is time for Wechsler's scales "to become extinct." Carroll (1993b) concluded, "One can raise the question of whether the revisions and improvements introduced in the WISC–III justify a more favorable judgment of the validity and usefulness of this test" (p. 142). But Carroll was not condemning just the WISC–III; like many cognitive psychologists, he'd vote for extinction of all conventional intelligence tests.

Sternberg (1993) was kinder in his WISC–III review, stating "I do not share the view of some contemporary theorists that the conventional tests are worthless or worse" (p. 163). But he criticized the WISC–III for remaining too static ("Recycling is no longer the exclusive province of environmentalists," p. 162). And, in his analogy of the WISC to *Rocky*, Sternberg said, "Eventually, we hope, Hollywood will stop recycling material and instead will retire Rocky in favor of a new shining light. Let's also hope the same happens with the WISC series" (p. 164).

Directly within the field of clinical assessment, the theory-based Kaufman Assessment Battery for Children–Second Edition (KABC–II; A. S. Kaufman & Kaufman, 2004), WJ-R, and the SB-4 began to find supporters, but, on the whole, IQ testing remained a Wechsler establishment. Naglieri (1993) said, "[S]chool psychology in particular, and psychology in general, has relied too much on the Wechsler series and techniques that encourage overinterpretation of scale and subtest variation[;] ... traditional IQ measures will need to be replaced by more modern ones" (pp. 14–15). The seriousness of these rumblings within the field of school psychology prompted Shaw, Swerdlik, and Laurent (1993) to warn that "the WISC–III could be rendered irrelevant in the schools in a short time" (p. 158).

Where do we stand today regarding the criticisms of 25 years ago leveled at Kaufman's method of subtest profile interpretation and at

Wechsler's children's scales? What is our stance on intelligent testing with the latest version of the WISC as we approach 2020? The answers to those two questions frame the remainder of this chapter and, in fact, the remaining chapters of this book.

IQ TESTING TODAY

Even though the critics of IQ testing in the 21st century are speaking virtually the same words spoken by the critics of yesteryear, the cognitive ability measures of today are not your grandparents' IQ tests. By now, astute readers will have noted the variety of terms for these measures (e.g., IQ test, cognitive ability test, intelligence test) and how they often are used interchangeably throughout this text. Regardless of the term used to describe a particular measure, they are all measures of cognitive abilities that have been shown to be critical aspects of intelligence. However, in the authors' opinion, it takes an intelligent tester to translate results from such an instrument into a meaningful estimate of an individual's *intelligence*. An adequate description of an individual's intelligence requires much more than a description of cognitive abilities—a recurring theme in intelligent testing today, as well as in the past. Relative to the psychologists of yesteryear, clinicians of today are armed with a plethora of reliable and valid cognitive ability measures as well as an increased understanding of the complex nature of intelligence.

The role of theory has escalated exponentially in the development and interpretation of cognitive ability tests during the past generation. Following the K–ABC, WJ-R, and SB-4 in the 1980s was a proliferation of instruments and techniques that continued nonstop during the 1990s and early 2000s. The 1990s featured Colin Elliott's (1990) Differential Abilities Scale (DAS)—an American version of his popular British Ability Scales (BAS; Elliott, 1983)—and Jack Naglieri's Cognitive Assessment System

(CAS; Naglieri & Das, 1997). The 2000s produced a flurry of high-quality revisions, each founded in well-researched and clinically important theory: the Woodcock-Johnson–Third Edition (WJ III; Woodcock, McGrew, & Mather, 2001), the Stanford-Binet Intelligence Scales, Fifth Edition (SB5; Roid, 2003), the Wechsler Intelligence Scale for Children–Fourth Edition (WISC–IV; Wechsler, 2003), the Reynolds Intellectual Assessment Scales (RIAS; C. R. Reynolds & Kamphaus, 2003), the KABC–II (A. S. Kaufman & Kaufman, 2004), and the DAS–II (C. D. Elliott, 2007). The year 2014 was marked by publication of three major revisions to comprehensive cognitive ability measures: namely the CAS2 (Naglieri, Das, & Goldstein, 2014), the WJ IV (Schrank, McGrew, & Mather, 2014), and the WISC–V (Wechsler, 2014). These three cutting-edge tests are built on separate but clearly intertwining theoretical foundations.

Applying Theory to Test Construction

Before describing the role of theory in test construction, it is helpful to be reminded of the definition and nature of theory, in general. As with *intelligence*, the term *theory* has many definitions, depending on the context and field of study. Kerlinger's (1986) oft-cited and generally accepted definition describes theory as "a set of interrelated constructs (concepts), definitions, and propositions that present a systematic view of phenomena specifying relations among variables, with the purpose of explaining and predicting the phenomena" (p. 9). Thus, theory provides important descriptive, organizational, and predictive functions. Theories are often represented by (and confused with) *models*, which are simplified graphical or figural representations of key theoretical concepts and relationships.

Since the time of Aristotle, theory has been contrasted with practice and appreciated as a close partner to research. The complex, interactive nature among theory, research, and practice was eloquently described by Schneider and Flanagan (2015):

> Research can be particularly cruel to theory, theory makes impossible demands of practice, and practice can go for long stretches acting as if research is not even in the room. Yet, they are family and they need each other. Research surprises theory with thoughtful gifts, theory gives sound advice when practice is troubled, and practice helps research to get out of the lab and meet people. (p. 317)

Despite the obvious necessity of theory, it is wise to remember some of its troublesome characteristics as it applies to test construction. Theories are never proven: They are ever-changing. Definitions (i.e., terminology and nomenclature) and relations among the concepts are continually revised according to ongoing research and practice. Examples of these ongoing terminology changes are evident in both the WISC–V (e.g., the Perceptual Reasoning Index has been separated into the Visual Spatial Index and the Fluid Reasoning Index) and the WJ IV (e.g., *Gsm* renamed as *Gwm*). Despite attempts to describe these changes in test manuals, they often cause confusion to users, especially during the transitional period after a newly released revision.

There are many types of theories related to cognitive ability and intelligence. Sternberg refers to five types of intelligence theories in the human intelligence entry he authored for *Encyclopædia Britannica* (2015), including psychometric theories (e.g., Cattell-Horn-Carroll [CHC] theory), cognitive theories (e.g., information-processing and working memory theories), cognitive contextual theories (e.g., Gardner's [1983] multiple intelligences theory), biological theories (e.g., neuroanatomical and behavioral genetics theories), and developmental theories (e.g., neurodevelopmental theory and Piaget's development theory). The sheer number of theory types (each with one or more theories as exemplars) attests to the fact that the study of intelligence and cognitive abilities continues to be of critical importance across a number of related fields. Just as intelligent testing demands that clinicians stay abreast of theoretical changes and advances in areas of related research and clinical practice, intelligent test construction demands the same.

Applying Theory to WISC–V Construction

As research directors for the most recent revisions of the Wechsler intelligence scales, Susie and Diane did not have the good fortune to work directly with Dr. Wechsler. The weight of this responsibility was keenly felt, especially considering the numerous assaults on IQ testing in general and, in particular, on the "antiquated" and "atheoretical" Wechsler scales. This perception has been difficult to overcome in some circles, despite substantial revisions to his scales in response to ongoing advances in intelligence theory, research, and clinical practice.

> ***Diane***: Wechsler was not atheoretical: He was all-theoretical. He was well aware that his tests were used by an increasingly diverse group of clinicians to address an ever-growing menagerie of referral questions. He was familiar with the intelligence theories of his time, as well as advances in psychometrics and relevant areas of research. Just as he was throughout his lifetime, I believe he would have been fascinated by and responsive to contemporary advances in psychometrics, intelligence theory, and neuropsychology, as well as the explosion of converging research in such areas as cognitive neuroscience, gene mapping, and brain imaging—but then quickly narrowed his efforts to incorporating in his scales those aspects that provided the most clinically relevant information for evaluating an *individual's* intelligence.

Confirmation of Wechsler's open-mindedness to competing intelligence theories was directly expressed in transcripts from a 1975 interview with David Wechsler conducted by Roger

Lennon and Jerome Doppelt of The Psychological Corporation at Wechsler's apartment in New York City. When asked to describe conversations regarding the definition of intelligence held at a 1921 symposium with such illustrious attendees as Thorndike, Terman, and Thurstone, Wechsler recalled:

> the interesting thing is that there were 14 different opinions. So people got very scared. But I wasn't scared, I wasn't even hurt by it. It simply proved to me that intelligence is a multi something, it isn't one thing. And as you discovered, depending on your area of interest or specialization, you favor one or another definition … I think they're all right, but not a single one suffices. (Wechsler, Doppelt, & Lennon, 1975, pp. 30–31)

At the time Dr. Wechsler developed his first intelligence scale in 1939, the primary theoretical controversy involved the historical debate between Spearman, a proponent of g, a general factor of intelligence, and Thorndike, who denounced g in favor of distinct types of intelligence. Dr. Wechsler's (1939) definition of intelligence, which remains unchanged in the WISC–V, specifically supports the idea that intelligence is composed of both global and distinct abilities. This idea is entirely consistent with contemporary CHC theory, which did not exist in its current form until almost 50 years after Wechsler penned his time-tested definition of intelligence as:

> the aggregate or global capacity of the individual to act purposefully, to think rationally, and to deal effectively with his [or her] environment. It is global because it characterizes the individual's behavior as a whole; it is an aggregate because it is composed of elements or abilities which, though not entirely independent, are qualitatively differentiable. (p. 3)

It should not be surprising that the hierarchical WISC–V structure aligns closely with some of the broad and narrow domains of intelligence as categorized by CHC theory. Subtests with long, preexisting histories on the Wechsler scales had previously been categorized according to the CHC model of intelligence (Flanagan & Kaufman, 2009; Flanagan, Ortiz, & Alfonso, 2013). Subtests were specifically revised (e.g., Digit Span), created (e.g., Matrix Reasoning), or replaced (e.g., Object Assembly replaced with Visual Puzzles) to improve or extend measurement of those CHC domains with the most clinically relevant evidence of validity for the numerous purposes of the test. Measures that look very similar to subtests selected for Wechsler's original (1939) intelligence scale (e.g., Information, Block Design, Digit Span) continue to appear in more recent intelligence measures with reports of closer ties to specific theory (e.g., KABC–II, CAS2, WJ IV).

Like Wechsler, the research directors responsible for the posthumous revisions of his intelligence scales are cautious about introducing revised or new content until its inclusion is supported by theory, research, and practice. The contributions of CHC theory cannot be understated: It is clearly the most comprehensive *structural* theory of cognitive abilities at the time of this writing. However, it is not the sole or primary driving force behind revisions of the Wechsler scales. To construct the most clinically useful measure of intelligence, it is, in our opinion, important to consider other theories related to intelligence and cognitive ability, especially those that are more *functional* in nature, including processing theories from the fields of cognitive psychology and neuropsychology, as well as various theories related to more specific aspects of cognitive ability, such as working memory, attention, and executive function. The importance of understanding how the components of intelligence function together was noted by Wechsler (1975):

> [T]he attributes and factors of intelligence, like the elementary particles in physics, have at once collective and individual properties, that is, they appear to behave differently when alone from what they do when operating in concert. (p. 138)

A closer look at the three most recent publications of comprehensive intelligence measures reflects this shift in emphasis from structure to function—one that is moving beyond the impossible and unfruitful task of attempting to build a usable, completely comprehensive measure of cognitive abilities toward one that focuses on how these components are functionally interrelated when processing information and how this information can be used to develop effective interventions. Construction of the CAS2 (as well as its predecessor) was guided by the Luria-based PASS model of intellectual functioning, which focuses on measurement of cognitive processes (i.e., planning, attention, simultaneous processing, and successive processing) rather than specific broad or narrow cognitive abilities. A growing body of clinical evidence for the CAS and CAS2 suggests that an evaluation of cognitive processes may be sensitive to such conditions as attention-deficit/hyperactivity disorder (Naglieri, Goldstein, Iseman, & Schwebach, 2003; Van Luit, Kroesbergen, & Naglieri, 2005), in which the processing of information may be disrupted despite adequate cognitive abilities. Previous research using the CAS also supported interpretation from a CHC perspective (Keith, Kranzler, & Flanagan, 2001). Based on the relatively minor changes in the CAS2, it is likely that CHC-oriented clinicians will continue to be comfortable using the CAS2. The move from a structural to a more functional emphasis is also evident in the WJ IV (albeit more subtle than that of the CAS2 or WISC–V), which notes the influence of "other venues of research" on test development, including research from the field of neuroscience and on working memory (LaForte, McGrew, & Schrank, 2014, p. 2). This recent change to the WJ IV theoretical foundations makes it remarkably similar to that described in recent revisions of the Wechsler intelligence scales (i.e., WAIS–IV, WPPSI–IV, and WISC–V).

The most recent revisions of Wechsler's intelligence scales have also been influenced by the exponential increase in research from the related fields of cognitive neuroscience and functional brain imaging (see Chapter 10 for additional information). Additionally, intelligent test construction demands an ongoing evaluation of research related to the primary uses of the test (e.g., identification of specific learning disorder (SLD) or intellectual disability; developmental and socioeconomic risk factors for low cognitive ability or achievement; age, gender, and cultural differences in intelligence). Thus, the theoretical basis for development of the Wechsler intelligence scales (as well as the theoretical foundations for the WJ IV) would be more correctly termed a *theoretical framework*, with content reflecting aspects of both structural (e.g., CHC theory) and functional (e.g., neuropsychological processing theory) theories of intelligence or cognitive ability as well as current, relevant research related to theory and practice.

Anyone who develops psychological tests knows that construction is also guided by practical issues, such as psychometric qualities, examiner and examinee preference, testing time, and clinical utility. With so many interacting factors influencing development, test construction can be a humbling experience. Many subtests, scores, and other seemingly novel ideas must be abandoned on the road to publication, for any one or more of these reasons. It is tempting for intelligence test publishers, authors, developers, researchers, and even practitioners to emphasize the differences among the tests' content or theoretical foundations rather than their similarities. We are all attempting to measure cognitive abilities, more specifically, those comprising intelligence. In addition to the wide variety of currently available intelligence measures, numerous other instruments are also available to appraise intelligence-related constructs, including executive function, attention, memory, and language development. Thus, the field of clinical assessment abounds with reliable and valid measures of intelligence and related cognitive abilities. Regardless of the underlying theory or theories that serve as the basis for test construction, or the reported nature of a test's measured constructs, it is the intelligent testers' responsibility to truly know the "tools" they are using.

Applying Theory to Profile Interpretation

Just as impressive as theory-based test construction has been the emergence of theory-based profile interpretation during the past two decades. Most prominent have been the birth and expansion of the innovative cross-battery assessment technique, steeped both in CHC theory and the intelligent testing tradition (Flanagan, Alfonso, & Ortiz, 2012; Flanagan et al., 2013; McGrew & Flanagan, 1998); and the clinical and educational applications of neuropsychological processing theories to cognitive assessment (Kaplan, 1990; Korkman, Kirk, & Kemp, 1998, 2007; McCloskey, Whitaker, Murphy, & Rogers, 2012; Naglieri & Das, 1997; Naglieri et al., 2014).

Certainly theory was prominent from the time Alfred Binet first developed his test in Paris in 1905, almost synchronously with Spearman's (1904) emphasis on g theory. Opposite Spearman were the well-reputed, highly publicized "multiple abilities" research and theory by Thurstone (1938; Thurstone & Thurstone, 1941) and Guilford (1956, 1967). But these multiple ability theorists made their mark only in group-administered IQ tests, never managing to cross the clinical barrier and failing to make a dent in how clinicians interpreted the WISC and WAIS. Far more influential than Thurstone and Guilford was Jacob Cohen's groundbreaking factor-analytic research on Wechsler's scales (Cohen, 1952a, 1952b, 1957a, 1957b, 1959). Cohen shifted focus from subtest analysis to the interpretation of a few specific abilities; he demonstrated that the verbal comprehension and perceptual organization abilities did *not* correspond to Verbal and Performance IQs; and he emphasized the importance of a third factor, which he variously called memory or the infamous freedom from distractibility. As Alan wrote,

"Cohen's factor analyses in the 1950s—endorsed by Wechsler and integrated into his own clinical approach to interpretation—changed the way clinicians viewed subtest profiles and provided the foundation for present-day analyses" (A. S. Kaufman, 2013b, p. 228).

If theory-based test interpretation of Wechsler's scales began to take form with Cohen's empirical research, Matarazzo (1972) clearly gave wings to the movement by recognizing the analog between Wechsler's Verbal and Performance scales and the Cattell-Horn constructs of crystallized (Gc) and fluid (Gf) intelligence. That simple beginning led to more complex interpretation systems based in CHC theory, which underlies cross-battery assessment (Flanagan et al., 2013) and most contemporary IQ tests; and neuropsychological processing theories (McCloskey, 2009b; McCloskey et al., 2012), which have provided the foundation for other widely used tests (Korkman et al., 2007; Naglieri et al., 2014). And the blend of CHC theory, processing theories (e.g., neuropsychological processing theories; working memory, executive function, and fluid reasoning theories; as well as Edith Kaplan's process approach to interpretation), plus relevant research from related fields (e.g., cognitive neuroscience and clinical applications) together form the theoretical framework of the WAIS–IV, WPPSI–IV, and WISC–V (Wechsler, 2008, 2012, 2014; Weiss, Saklofske, Coalson, & Raiford, 2010).

Cohen's pioneering research was oddly prescient of the five CHC-based factors that state-of-the-art confirmatory factor analysis (CFA) has identified for the WISC–IV and WAIS–IV (Keith, Fine, Taub, Reynolds, & Kranzler, 2006; Niileksela, Reynolds, & Kaufman, 2012; Ward, Bergman, & Hebert, 2012; Weiss, Keith, Zhu, & Chen, 2013a, 2013b), and which correspond to the five indexes yielded by the WISC–V. Cohen's factors were: Verbal (Vocabulary, Similarities, Information, Comprehension), Nonverbal or Perceptual Organization (Object Assembly, Block Design, Mazes), Memory or Freedom from Distractibility (Arithmetic, Digit Span),

Picture Completion, and Coding/Digit Symbol. In CHC language, these factors measure *Gc*, *Gv*, *Gsm*, *Gf*, and *Gs*. In the WISC–V vernacular, the old Cohen factors reflect Verbal Comprehension, Visual Spatial, Working Memory, Fluid Reasoning, and Processing Speed. A bull's-eye for probably the least appreciated pioneer in mental testing.

The field of clinical assessment has come full circle, forming a rising spiral that continues to ascend. Yet while this ascent in the field of IQ testing has been steady for 30 years and has achieved heights not even dreamed about in the past (when the hue and cry was to ban IQ tests, not improve them), the IQ test has never before been so easily disposed of by a segment of society. It seems unconscionable to eliminate IQ from the diagnosis of an SLD when the essence of SLD, conceptually, is a discrepancy between a child's potential to learn and that child's school achievement. Yes, state departments of education misused IQ tests, and they glorified formulas that had no place in psychology or education. But RTI is an overreaction to the problem. We are at a point in time that some states are RTI only, and many others are trying to establish sensible guidelines about determining a child's pattern of strengths and weaknesses (PSW). Intelligent testing is all about PSW and putting that information about a child's profile into action to determine the best educational interventions. The WISC is no longer *Rocky*; the WISC–IV was a giant step forward from its earlier editions, and the WISC–V has raised the bar once again.

THE WISC–IV AND THE WISC–V

Unlike the WISC–R and the WISC–III, the WISC–IV abandoned the age-old Wechsler distinction between the Verbal and Performance IQs and relied solely on the FSIQ as a measure of *g*. Four factor-based indexes, two composed of Verbal subtests and two of Performance subtests, replaced the Verbal–Performance IQ discrepancy, and a new WISC age dawned.

The WISC–IV represented "the most substantial revision of any Wechsler scale to date ... Many of the ways in which the instrument has been altered and restructured are considered strengths" (Flanagan & Kaufman, 2009, p. 202). The most notable strengths were inclusion of better measures of fluid reasoning and working memory, elimination of complex and unwieldy composites (like the Verbal and Performance IQs and the Freedom from Distractibility factor) that defied easy interpretation, and emphasis on constructs that were in lockstep with contemporary research and theory. Even the FSIQ, which traditionally was composed of the same basic 10 or 11 subtests that made up the Wechsler-Bellevue Form I (and every WISC or WAIS FSIQ since 1939) had a new look on the WISC–IV. "The FSIQ has changed dramatically in content and concept and barely resembles the FSIQ of previous WISCs. It includes only 5 of the traditional 10 subtests" (Flanagan & Kaufman, 2009, p. 30).

But if the WISC–IV left a lot of its historical roots behind, then the WISC–V is a game changer. Availability of digital administration format using Pearson's Q-interactive™ (Qi) platform and an iPad-to-iPad Bluetooth connection affirms Wechsler's posthumous entry into the digital-technology generation. A seven-subtest FSIQ. Five indexes that match five key CHC abilities. An ancillary global index, the five-subtest General Ability Index, which greatly reduces the working memory and processing speed demands from the *g* equation for children who, for example, have behavioral issues such as anxiety or distractibility or cognitive difficulties in these areas (e.g., many children with SLD). Four other ancillary index scores to measure quantitative reasoning, auditory working memory, nonverbal ability, and cognitive proficiency. Three complementary index scores to measure diverse aspects of the CHC ability Long-term Retrieval (*Glr*): the Naming Speed Index, the Symbol Translation Index, and the Storage and Retrieval Index. The Symbol Translation subtests, which resemble the Woodcock and

Kaufman measures of paired-associates learning, answer the question that has often been leveled at Wechsler's scales: Why do the most popular IQ tests in the world fail to measure something as basic and essential as a person's ability to learn new material?

And the list of subtests is Woodcockian and Reitanian in scope: 21 subtests, eight of them new to the WISC; 10 Kaplanesque process scores; 10 error scores (e.g., errors made on Coding while rapidly copying symbols). Picture Completion is gone (joining Wechsler's favorites, Object Assembly and Picture Arrangement, which disappeared when the WISC–IV was published). Clinicians will need to be intelligent, indeed, to interpret the WISC–V intelligently!

BASIC TENETS OF THE NEW INTELLIGENT TESTING APPROACH

The tools are in place, whether clinicians are oriented toward the WJ IV, the CAS2, the WISC–V, or any other intelligence measure. The theories are in place. Wisdom abounds in the domains of cognitive assessment and educational intervention from a CHC framework (Flanagan et al., 2013; Mather & Wendling, 2012; Schneider & McGrew, 2012; Wendling & Mather, 2009) and from neuropsychological viewpoints (Fletcher-Janzen & Reynolds, 2008; Shaywitz & Shaywitz, 2013). Despite the movements to eliminate IQ tests from the diagnostic process, the ongoing attempts to integrate iPad technology with intelligence testing (e.g., Pearson's Q-i system or PAR's iConnect), and the inevitable time when someone important decides that clinicians are irrelevant, intelligent testing needs to stand tall for contemporary psychologists. The philosophy needs to be reconceived for the present, consistent with the mandates and implications of IDEA (McBride, Dumont, & Willis, 2011), taking into account the needs of unique learners (Mascolo, Alfonso, & Flanagan, 2014), and with an eye on the changing landscape of the future.

Like the theories that guide test construction and interpretation, the basic tenets of intelligent testing cannot remain static. They changed from Alan's 1979 WISC–R text to his 1994 WISC–III text and continued to evolve as the WISC and WAIS were transformed into their fourth editions (Flanagan & Kaufman, 2009; Lichtenberger & Kaufman, 2013). That evolution continues in this WISC–V text.

Certainly the leaps in theory-based models of test construction and profile interpretation rendered certain aspects of Alan's intelligent testing approaches for the WISC–R and WISC–III obsolete. Alan's notion of grouping subtests according to their "shared abilities"—when some of those abilities were armchair concoctions like "visual perception of complete meaningful stimuli" or "integrated brain functioning" or "culture-loaded knowledge"—is fanciful. So, too, is listing the so-called influences that affect children's performance on each subtest, such as "ability to respond when uncertain" or "alertness to environment" or "negativism" or "outside reading." These abilities and influences filled a gap during the last generation but are hopelessly naive and devoid of research support as we approach 2020. Joel Schneider (2013a) expressed these sentiments kindly:

> It is important to group subtests by theory, not by intuition. As brilliant as Kaufman's (1994a) Intelligent Testing system was, there is little evidence that any of the hundreds of subtle influences on test performance he lists has ever been measured with any reliability … Stick with a well-validated interpretive framework such as CHC theory. (p. 314)

Schneider (personal communication, October 20, 2014) expanded on his quote about the Kaufman intelligent testing system in an email to Alan:

> As is often the case, I have a more nuanced opinion about that quote than a literal reading of my words would suggest…. I believe that it is possible to go well beyond a cookbook interpretation of scores, but different cooks

will produce results of widely varying quality once they stray from the recipe. Since we have a profession in which we rarely experience any consequences for producing incorrect interpretations, it is hard to give clear advice on how to deviate from the cookbook. I think that *I* can ... but then everyone else does too.

While in graduate school, I made spreadsheets that automate your interpretative approach. The spreadsheets calculate the dozens of composite scores suggested by your 1994 *Intelligent Testing* book. I quickly came to appreciate how easy it was to get lost in the data. Using the spreadsheet, I found that a post-hoc discovery of which cognitive processes were shaping the cognitive profile was both too easy and too difficult. It was easy to find pairs of contrasting scores that were significantly different but it was difficult to find ways of convincing myself that I had found an explanation that was trustworthy.

My position is evolving on this issue. When I wrote the chapter (Schneider, 2013a) ... my own process was too prone to error and led to too many wild speculations. I needed to fly lower to the ground. Later I invested time and effort to producing methods that would give me a better balance of liberties and constraints .... These methods help me feel a little surefooted about my interpretations and a greater awareness of when I should be appropriately uncertain. Even so, I would like to learn about (or develop) much better methods than the ones I use now.

Schneider and Flanagan (2015) put the original intelligent testing approach to theory into an appropriate time capsule, in view of the great theoretical advancements in the 1990s and 2010s:

The early writings of Sattler (1974) and Kaufman (1979) were extremely persuasive in showing that it was worthwhile to use psychometrics to extract meaningful information from test scores beyond the *g* factor. Not only were Sattler and Kaufman persuasive and practical, their comprehensive and "intelligent" approach to intelligence test interpretation made the process interesting and meaningful to practitioners. Sattler's and

Kaufman's early writings were not purely psychometric, nor were they atheoretical, but compared to later efforts (including their own), they were less theoretically driven. (p. 320)

CONTEMPORARY THOUGHTS ABOUT INTELLIGENT TESTING

Consistent with these sensible criticisms of the original intelligent testing method of profile interpretation, and with a continued search for improved methodologies, the authors sought to create an intelligent testing philosophy that was more compatible with the new wave of well-validated theoretical models, current research related to intelligence, and the contemporary assessment scene. Alan reached out to about a dozen highly respected experts in the field. He wrote in a group email dated October 7, 2014:

I am about to start writing the first chapter on the intelligent testing philosophy and I realize that I am no longer certain what best defines that philosophy in 2015, as the field of assessment is so in flux. It has been much influenced by RTI, PSW, blogs like the CHC and NASP listservs, and the field must now accommodate to the unknown potential of the computer's impact. Pearson's Q-Interactive is available for a number of their instruments, but many practitioners and school systems are still deciding when to turn digital.

I would very much like for each of you to send me sentences, paragraphs, bullet points, PowerPoint slides, or anything that communicates your notion of the most salient aspects of intelligent testing, both for today and "tomorrow." Although the book is about the WISC–V, chapter 1 is a philosophy that applies just as well to the WJ IV or the KTEA–3 or any individual test of intelligence or achievement.

The personal communications of these experts were highly influential in refining and illustrating the specific tenets of the intelligent testing philosophy presented in this WISC–V text, modifying and expanding on previous sets of guidelines (A. S. Kaufman, 1979, 1994a; Lichtenberger & Kaufman, 2013, pp. 119–127). Despite significant advances in the study of intelligence and cognitive abilities, these communications revealed that the intelligent testing philosophy of today is remarkably consistent with that described in the past, due to its child-centered focus. Thus, the tenet revisions are relatively minor, primarily consisting of clarifications based on interim research findings and an increased emphasis on the importance of linking theory, research, and practice to effective interventions. *The core concept of intelligent testing continues to rest on the notions that test interpretation is complex and subtle, that sound theory must underlie profile interpretation, that interventions should walk hand in hand with theory-based interpretation, and—bottom line—that the burden is on test users to be "better" than the tests they use.*

Concern about the present state of intelligence testing and uncertainty about its future produced cautionary words from some of the experts. (These unreferenced personal communications are from email communications with Alan between October 2014 and March 2015.)

Ron Dumont—The debate over IQ testing and its utility seems to me to be not about the tests themselves, but in how they are used or misused, and your book is addressing just those issues. I see many folks who give the tests but totally misuse them. It is unfortunate, but many don't understand the basics of good, intelligent testing.

Cecil Reynolds—I am just not sure what to say about the intelligent testing philosophy at this point given the tremendous flux in the field. I think it will easily be 2 years or so to see where the field is trending—RTI has been a huge drag on everything in standardized assessment and neuropsychologists in private practice are very frustrated about their evaluations being essentially turned away as irrelevant to a lot of RTI-adopting school districts.

Jack Naglieri—I am convinced by recent papers showing WJ is a one-factor test, the lack of evidence for cross battery assessment, the

expansion of the number of subtests in WISC–V, the over-emphasis on subtest analysis, the illusion that subtests can be combined across tests without regard for differences in standardization samples, the view that someone can look at a subtest and decide what it measures, the misuse of factor analysis of WISC subtests old and new to decide the structure of intelligence, and the over-interpretation of tests from a "neuropsychological" perspective that our field has gone down a path that will not help children.

Dan Miller—I believe the field of school psychology is at a perilous crossroads due to the push towards computerized assessment. I must first say that I am a "techie" and I love all of my gadgets (e.g., tablet, smart phone, etc.) so I have a natural affinity for the idea of computerized assessment. However, I am concerned that the current implementation of computerized assessment will hurt the practice of psychology in general, and the practice of school psychology in particular.... My first and foremost concern is that [in my opinion] the major test publishers have all adopted propriety software that work on tablets or cloud-based servers which are mutually exclusive to their own product lines and do not communicate with each other....

As an example, Pearson has developed their Q-interactive platform that allows practitioners to administer and score many of their assessment instruments using two iPads, one for the examiner and one for the examinee. This includes the ability to administer and score a complete WISC–V test of intelligence using the iPads. From a technological standpoint the Q-interactive product has a strong "cool factor" and ease of use. The WISC–V subtests look great on the iPad and the developers have done an excellent job of using the iPad features to facilitate administration and scoring.... [However], the cost factor is a major concern for users of the Q-interactive system....

In summary, school psychologists run the risk of having their professional judgment further constrained because of budgetary constraints related to the costs of computerized assessment. School psychologists and school neuropsychologists who are taught to use cross-battery assessment are the biggest risk of having their skills underutilized in the future.

Diane Coalson—With regards to the computer/digital transition on intelligent testing: Personally, I am still a little nervous about the digital transition. I think we need additional evidence of clinical validity for special groups. I am concerned that the field is prematurely enamored by the medium, similar to results from a recent study in which increased ratings of credibility resulted when bogus brain images were imbedded in a research article. Other research indicates that the mere mention of cognitive neuroscience (as in brain-training commercials) also increased participants' judgment of credibility. Despite such reservations, I believe that the integration of technology and psychological assessment ultimately will lead to substantial improvements in clinical utility and ease of use.

Ron Dumont—I think the future will include much more technology. The iPad versions are certainly taking steps to change how we administer tests, but I imagine a whole new set of test measures designed specifically for the technology. I imagine a test that has algorithms that branch to items depending upon the answer/response to each single item. This will create a fine-tuned assessment that is time efficient and very specific to the individual.

With these cautions in mind, with an eye on where the intelligent testing philosophy began, and with great reliance on the ideas and opinions articulated by brilliant clinicians, here are the latest tenets of intelligent testing.

1. Intelligent Testing with the WISC–V Requires Training, Experience, and Flexibility

This seemingly obvious statement represents a new addition to the intelligent testing tenets. The subject matter of this tenet was addressed in previous versions of the intelligent testing philosophy, but the number of expert comments on this topic suggested it had earned its place as the first tenet of intelligent testing. Therefore, it seems most appropriate to begin this new tenet with a favorite quote by Meyer and colleagues that was submitted by Kevin McGrew in response to Alan's query about intelligent testing:

> Tests do not think for themselves, nor do they directly communicate with patients. Like a stethoscope, a blood pressure gauge, or an MRI scan, a psychological test is a dumb tool, and the worth of the tool cannot be separated from the sophistication of the clinician who draws inferences from it and then communicates with patients and professionals. (Meyer et al., 2001, p. 153)

There's no question, individualizing WISC–V interpretation requires effort. It is fairly easy to look at the array of indexes and scaled scores and come up with some predictable statements about the child's general intellectual functioning and specific strengths and weaknesses (well, maybe not so easy with the bucket-load of scores yielded by the WISC–V). This type of cookbook interpretation is not compatible with the intelligent testing approach or intent of federal legislation, and has led to the insistence on accountability (in the form of treatment validity) by school psychology trainers, state education departments, and IDEA in general (McBride et al., 2011).

John Willis—Just as we claim to believe that each examinee is unique, each evaluation should be unique, driven not only by characteristics of the examinee but also by the examinee's circumstances and by referral questions. Intelligent testing is not just a matter of administering, scoring, and reporting the results of a test or battery of tests, but a thoughtful analysis of the findings within the broader context of the examinee's history and the referral questions. For me, intelligent testing demands heightened mindfulness in planning, conducting, interpreting, and reporting an evaluation.

Joel Schneider—A favorite quote from William Stern, who coined the term "IQ": Every individual is a singularity, a one-time existing being, nowhere else and never before present . . . . In this sense, the individual is a limiting concept, toward which theoretical investigation strives but can never reach; it is, one could say, the asymptote of science.

A child-centered focus drives all aspects of intelligent testing. Individualization demands a flexible examiner, one who is not wedded to just one assessment approach that is applied indiscriminately to all children. If an interpretive approach relies strictly on one view of the world, no matter how theoretically or psychometrically defensible that view may be, it is doomed to fail for some children. The CHC approach, for example, does not deal as effectively with executive functions as does a neuropsychological processing approach. And none of the contemporary models applied to the development and interpretation of IQ tests handles creativity particularly well (J. C. Kaufman, Kaufman, & Lichtenberger, 2011). Concerns with "same-old, same-old" report writing were specifically noted as problematic:

John Willis—In addition to writing a few thousand evaluation reports and receiving feedback from parents, teachers, and adult examinees, I have occasion to read many evaluation reports written by graduate students and by practicing psychologists and other evaluators and to provide my own feedback to those examiners. Even when the testing, scoring, and transcriptions of scores have been competent, many examiners appear to have selected a consistent battery of tests for most or all purposes (perhaps with some variation to accommodate the age of the examinee) and to have settled on an unvarying format for presenting the results with little regard for the audience or the circumstances. That autopilot approach is neither intelligent nor mindful.

Elaine Fletcher-Janzen—I am going rogue right now with report writing style and organization—I believe that because psychologists have written the psychometric test results as they have done for years—the public, special education personnel, parents,

and legal professionals have come to think of us as "testers" and that the numeric test scores trump the clinical judgment of the clinician (who interprets all scores in relation to the whole evaluation—not in isolation)—and worse—that they are entitled to interpret the numerical scores and have just as much insight as the clinician. So . . . I believe that psychologists should write a narrative report (and leave tables of the numeric results in the back of the report).

John Willis—Too often, the history section of an evaluation report seems to be a careful, accurately typed, but thoughtless exercise in summarizing data without considering the implications of those data. The referral questions and intended outcomes need to be considered in the context of the examinee's personal, familial, social, emotional, medical, educational, and vocational history.

Intelligent testing requires the adaptability to be eclectic. In this book, we present interpretation from several clinical and theoretical viewpoints and provide an array of approaches to report writing in the 17 illustrative case reports that are included in Part IV. We provide a similar array of intelligent (but widely varying and often contradictory) WISC–V test reviews in Part V of the book. Thorough knowledge of many techniques for interpreting the WISC–V is important, as is mastery of the core areas of psychology, since these are the inputs necessary for interpreting a child's test profile. Of course, experienced clinicians and trainers can be flexible while staying within a single theoretical model, such as the neuropsychological processing approach (Fletcher-Janzen & Reynolds, 2008; McCloskey et al., 2012) or the CHC-based Cross-Battery Assessment approach (Flanagan et al., 2012; Flanagan, Alfonso, & Reynolds, 2013; Flanagan et al., 2013; Ortiz, Flanagan, & Alfonso, 2015; Schneider & Flanagan, 2015). New examiners, however, should explore a variety of models of profile assessment before determining a priori which methodology is right for them.

Regarding the notion that intelligent testing in the second decade of the 21st century means the ability to respect different methodologies and divergent voices:

> **George McCloskey**—*Intelligent Testing with the WISC–R* was the first book on test interpretation that I read during my internship year (December 1979). Your thoughts about test interpretation and your writing style have influenced everything that I have written since.... Regarding the presentation of diverse approaches in *Intelligent Testing with the WISC–V*, I think this is a good direction to take for the rebirth of the *Intelligent Testing* book given the availability of the *Essentials* series books for handling much of what you might have originally included in the spirit of the *WISC–R* and *WISC–III* editions. I like the fact that multiple perspectives will be provided on test interpretation; this harkens back to your original groundbreaking ideas in the *WISC–R* book about looking at the WISC from multiple interpretive perspectives and with new statistical techniques but with a big twist—a major focus on actual case studies showing how it is done. I know you had case studies in the earlier *Intelligent Testing* books, but they were not the major emphasis the way they are here in the *WISC–V* book. I believe that beyond the *WISC–R* book, I have refined most of my ideas about test interpretation and report writing from reading other clinician's reports (both good and bad).... Thanks so much for including me on this book project; I am confident the content will provide food for thought to many practitioners and scholars.

Ideally, with experience, well-trained examiners will be able to shift from one approach to another to find the best explanations for the observed fluctuations in a particular child's profile and to infer cause-effect relationships between behaviors and test performance. Or, if they are most comfortable with a particular theoretical perspective, then they can be flexible within their preferred discipline. However, experience and good intentions are sometimes not enough in the real world.

> *Joel Schneider*—I struggle with teaching assessment. I only have a semester to teach students about something that takes years to master. I usually give students the advice to fly low to the ground until they have been given excellent supervision and have had the experience of their initial hunches being proven wrong a few times so that they acquire the appropriate level of humility and prudence.

The approach to interpretation advocated in this book may be impractical for some practitioners in the field. School psychologists who practice in states that embrace IQ tests for SLD diagnosis (even if reluctantly) are often faced with long waiting lists and inordinate numbers of cases that must be tested each week; they cannot usually administer very many tests as supplements to the WISC–V. Psychologists or learning disabilities specialists in a clinic have to assess an urban bilingual Korean child referred for evaluation whether or not they speak Korean or have any knowledge whatsoever of the child's subculture. These realities force evaluations of school-age children to be less than ideal in some instances, but they should not be used as excuses for fostering inadequate test interpretation or other types of test abuse.

For new psychologists, including graduate students who are in the process of becoming intelligent testers, here are some tips for use before, during, and after the evaluation.

Before the Evaluation

John Willis

- I require my students to actively solicit and quote referral questions from parents, teachers, specialists, and the examinee and then to copy and paste those questions into the Conclusions section of their report and attempt to answer each one (even if the answer is "I don't know").
- Referral "concerns" are helpful, but genuine, potentially answerable questions are even

better. The questions may, if we really think about them, inspire additional questions that we can add to the collection. The questions can then help drive our choice of evaluation instruments and procedures. For example, if the referral question is the reason the student has difficulty comprehending full chapters in science or social studies texts, then a brief reading comprehension test consisting of very short passages may rule out sentence-reading weakness as a cause of the chapter-reading problem but will not otherwise answer the question.

Nadeen Kaufman

- Select tests to give that have the best chance of providing you with the information you need to both answer referral questions and devise a plan for treatment, amelioration, and other interventions.
- Make sure you are trained and experienced enough (even if it means role play to learn) on every test you give so you can be the most efficient and fluid tester.
- Always select the appropriate, current tests with the correct record forms completely filled out and scored accurately: Always imagine that these forms can be required to be court doc uments that you will need to defend as an examiner. Know the child's birth date before the day of testing, as well as detailed referral questions.
- Get as much of an idea as possible of *exactly* what is wanted by referral source—don't just do a test evaluation based on "updated status needed." On this point, Joel Schneider (2013a) remarked: "You would think that being mindful of the purpose of an assessment is so obvious that it need not be stated explicitly. Unfortunately, it has too often been my experience that I am asked to give a child an assessment and no one involved with the child has a well-articulated understanding of why an assessment is needed" (p. 322).

During the Evaluation
Nadeen Kaufman

- The individual you see the day of testing may not reflect who you prepared the evaluation for; be adaptable and flexible enough to change your plans—even midway—so you can deal with the person in front of you emotionally, physically, and cognitively.
- Understand the importance of rapport, and work to maintain it throughout the entire evaluation. Attend to the child and respect him or her as a participant in this case study. An unhappy or partially cooperative examinee is making test interpretation open to more error.
- Only take breaks when needed; don't interrupt flow because it's longer than you thought appropriate. Take breaks, keep them short, and don't talk about the test during break. Younger children may need some physical action during the break, or bathrooming. Regain rapport once the evaluation has resumed. If you have observed any new information about the child's abilities during the break (e.g., she knew her way back through the winding hallways to lead the examiner to the distant waiting-room area), include it as observation or corroborating hypothesis information.
- Perceive the evaluation as a case study experiment, $n = 1$, where you are incorporating all the psychology, neurology, cognitive processing information, developmental theories, etc., as additional tools you take with you into the test session.

Jennifer Mascolo   Target your observations:

- Observe how the child responds to *qualitative features* of the test (e.g., on a math test, how does the child respond to items that demand mental computation versus those that allow for use of paper and pencil?).
- *Contemplate the interaction between the child's performance and item difficulty* (e.g., at what point

does the child begin to experience difficulty—such as when the guided line structure is removed from a Block Design task).

- Consider the *reasoning* behind the child's responses (e.g., is a child selecting responses for a matrix reasoning task based on location of the option—such as selecting a multiple-choice response that is directly below the "blank" space of the matrix?).
- Evaluate the *child's verbalizations* during testing (e.g., are they productive comments reflecting attempts to problem solve, are they bids for help from the examiner, are they self-evaluative remarks?).
- Note the *child's ability to shift within and between tasks* (e.g., Are children frequently self-correcting/changing responses? Do they want to refer back to check answers? Do they move on when prompted?).
- As clinicians, we need to actively consider these and other behaviors and maintain a close watch over them and record them (either manually or mentally) so that we can begin to see what themes emerge and can begin to build a picture of how this child likely responds and/or reacts to his or her learning environment.

After the Evaluation

Nadeen Kaufman

- Don't let numbers make conclusions for you. Keep the gestalt in mind, and see the test scores as good evidence from one source of information. Factor in the child's behaviors, environment, and so on, to help readers understand the test scores more accurately, including the error inherent in measurement. Look for consistencies and inconsistencies across tests and within tests. Go outside the tasks and include behavioral responses to verbal or nonverbal activities and make comparisons.
- Be prompt in getting information back to referral sources and family. Things are requested for a need and things change; you don't need

to be a part of their problems when you can help solve their problems.

Joel Schneider

- When writing case reports, make every sentence worth reading.

2. The WISC–V Measures What the Individual Has Learned *and* Predicts Future Learning

Subtests measure what the individual has learned. This is a point stated simply, but elaborated cogently, by Wesman (1968) in his seminal article on intelligent testing. The content of all tasks, whether they measure a CHC ability or neuropsychological process, is learned within a culture. The learning may take place formally in the school, casually in the home, or incidentally through everyday life. As a measure of past learning, the IQ test is best thought of as a kind of achievement test, not as a simple measure of aptitude. That contention is supported by the interesting finding that the *g* measured by intelligence tests is essentially the same *g* that underlies tests of academic achievement (reading, math, and writing), across all childhood and adolescent age groups studied (S. B. Kaufman, Reynolds, Liu, Kaufman, & McGrew, 2012). Thus, the strong relationships between cognitive tests and achievement measures (Naglieri & Bornstein, 2003) are inevitable. Plain and simple, cognitive tests measure prior learning.

But not so fast. Cognitive tests also have ample, long-standing evidence of clinical utility for predicting future learning in terms of academic achievement. As Schneider (2013a) articulated, the issue of aptitude-achievement is more complex, circular, and, ultimately, depends on the way the tests are used:

> Most the time, aptitude is assessed by measuring abilities that are considered to be necessary precursors of achievement. For example, children who understand speech have greater aptitude for reading comprehension

than do children who do not understand speech. Such precursors may themselves be a form of achievement.... If we use a test to measure current mastery of a culturally valued ability, it is an achievement test. If we use a test to explain or forecast mastery of a culturally valued ability, it is an aptitude test. IQ tests are primarily used as aptitude tests. However, an inspection of the contents of most IQ tests reveals that many test items could be repurposed as items in an achievement test (e.g., vocabulary, general knowledge, and mental arithmetic items). Sometimes the normal roles of reading tests and IQ tests are reversed, such as when neuropsychologists estimate loss of function following a brain injury by comparing current IQ to performance on a word-reading test. (pp. 286–287)

Theories and research related to cognitive processing also describe a more circular relationship between crystallized and fluid intelligence. According to this line of research, learning occurs when the novel content of fluid reasoning becomes more crystallized, with transfer to long-term memory. The now-crystallized intelligence then serves to strengthen future fluid reasoning ability through increased associations between information in long-term storage for use in subsequent situations requiring fluid reasoning with novel content. Related investigations of the neuroanatomical and neurophysiological correlates of cognitive abilities seem to be zeroing in on this transitional process in the brain (Barbey, Colom, Paul, & Grafman, 2014; Hunt & Jaeggi, 2013).

Although the predictive validity of cognitive test scores is strong, the relationship between cognitive test scores and school achievement need not indicate a predetermined fate for an individual. That is, if results from a cognitive test are appropriately interpreted and translated into helpful recommendations, then positive change in academic achievement may occur, thereby changing one's IQ-determined "destiny."

The interaction between learning potential and availability of learning experiences is too complex to ponder for any given person or subculture, making the whole genetics–environment issue of theoretical value but limited in terms of interpreting an individual's test profile. Issues of heredity versus environment and the validity of the IQ construct have been meaningful for understanding the multifaceted intelligence construct (A. S. Kaufman, 2009, chap. 6), and more recent efforts to evaluate the interaction of heritability and environmental influences on intelligence may shed additional light on this complex subject (Z. Wang, Katz, & Shaw, 2014). Regardless, the accumulating research helps test developers, practitioners, and theoreticians appreciate the relationships between genetic and environmental influences on the development of intellectual abilities as well as their interacting effects. The IQ tests are vehicles for the research, serving as essential sources of group data for use in the scientific study of these topics.

3. The WISC–V Subtests Are Samples of Behavior and Are Not Exhaustive

This tenet is relevant to the generalizability of the test findings. Because test results usually are obtained within 1 or 2 hours and include samples of behavior from a select set of tasks, caution needs to be exercised in generalizing the results to other behaviors in different circumstances. Even though there are 21 separate WISC–V subtests, and an array of subtests that compose the WJ IV, CAS2, DAS–II, and the Kaufman tests, the sum of these parts does not reflect the essential ingredients of intelligence whose mastery implies some type of ultimate life achievement. They, like tasks developed originally by Binet, are more or less arbitrary samples of behavior, even if they are driven by CHC or neuropsychological processing theory or by other research and theories related to cognitive structure, development, and function. Teaching people how to solve similarities, assemble blocks to match abstract designs, or repeat randomly presented digits in sequential order will not make them smarter in any broad or generalizable way. What we are able to infer from the person's success on the tasks and style of responding to them is important; the specific, unique aspect of intellect that each subtest measures is of minimal consequence.

John Willis—Thoughtful consideration of referral questions, intended outcomes, and the examinee's history should be used to guide the selection of instruments and procedures. The referral may include specific desired outcomes, such as a *DSM–5* diagnosis, an IDEA disability identification, a recommendation for an educational or therapeutic placement, determination of legal competence, or prescription for a specific remedial reading program. The intended outcomes can then help drive the choice of evaluation instruments and procedures. A long history of difficulties in reading and spelling should inspire us to include adequate tests of word recognition, phonetic word attack, phonology, rapid naming, reading vocabulary, reading comprehension, oral vocabulary, and listening comprehension.

We can select formal or informal interview techniques, questionnaires, and rating scales; observations; and formal and informal tests that take into account what is already known about the examinee and that can be expected to provide the requested information. If we find ourselves administering the same procedures over and over again, we are probably not engaging in intelligent testing.

True to form, John concluded with a witty remembrance:

History may even guide the choice of examiners. I am a short, fat, homely, older man. When I used to work with a tall, slim, beautiful, young woman, we had the opportunity to accommodate examinees' fears and prejudices.

Limitations in the selection of tasks necessarily mean that one should be cautious in generalizing the results to circumstances that are removed from the one-on-one assessment of a

finite number of skills and processing strategies. Theoretical models of intelligence should be used as a guide for selecting cognitive tasks to administer during an evaluation, and examiners should not be wedded to a single instrument, even one as popular as the WISC–V. The need to use multiple measures was humorously emphasized by Kevin McGrew in his response to Alan's request for expert views on intelligent testing: "Moses may have gone to the mountain to get the Ten Commandments, but where is it written that David Wechsler went to the mountain to get the 12 subtests?"

To the degree that supplementary tasks and tests are chosen to meet theoretical and research-based constructs, the array of cognitive subtests chosen for a comprehensive test battery is systematic and not arbitrary. Dawn Flanagan's cross-battery assessment provides a user-friendly methodology for ensuring that any comprehensive evaluation of a person's intelligence measures a diversity of key broad and narrow CHC abilities (Flanagan et al., 2013). Jack Naglieri's PASS model (Naglieri et al., 2014), Sally Shaywitz's approach to diagnosing dyslexia (Shaywitz & Shaywitz, 2013), and George McCloskey's interpretive system via process analysis (McCloskey, 2009b; McCloskey, Whitaker, Murphy, & Rogers, 2012) are also useful frameworks for choosing the best supplementary measures to administer.

Nonetheless, even when using cross-battery assessment or a thorough neuropsychological processing analysis, neither a global IQ nor a comprehensive profile of CHC abilities should be interpreted as an estimate of a person's "total" or "complete" level of intellectual functioning. Examination of one's individual cognitive strengths and weaknesses obtained from IQ test data is more fruitful when combined with supportive data from other samples of behavior such as those data obtained from supplemental measures. These measures might include behavioral assessment, personality assessment, neuropsychological assessment, adaptive behavior assessment, and even informal assessment of abilities that are not easily tested by standardized instruments, such as measures of the creative and practical intelligence components of Sternberg's triarchic theory of successful human intelligence (J. C. Kaufman, in press; Sternberg, Kaufman, & Grigorenko, 2008).

4. The WISC–V Assesses Cognitive Functioning Under Fixed Experimental Conditions

Jennifer Mascolo—In my view, intelligent testing, as it applies to today and tomorrow, involves the clinician maintaining very *active, purposeful involvement* in the assessment process. While it will remain absolutely essential to familiarize oneself with key administration and scoring features of new and revised tests in any medium (e.g., paper-and-pencil or digital), these basic requirements of assessment must be mastered quickly so that the clinician can focus his or her attention on the child's interaction with the task at hand.

The standardized procedures for administration and scoring of the WISC–V help ensure objectivity in evaluating a child, but they sacrifice the in depth understanding of a youngster's cognitive processing that may be obtained from a technique such as Jean Piaget's probing *methode clinique*, Reuven Feuerstein's test-teach-test dynamic assessment approach (Tzuriel, 2000), Lev Vygotsky's zone of proximal development (Rutland & Campbell, 1996), or Edith Kaplan's (1990) process approach. The rigidity of test instructions, the use of materials such as a stopwatch, and the recording of most words spoken by a child add to the artificial nature of the situation and make the standardized intelligence test scores comparable to data obtained in a psychological experiment. Do *not* deviate from required administration procedures or add nonpermissible probes to elicit a correct response from the child (except when testing the limits). Strict adherence to standardized procedures is essential, for otherwise the obtained scores—derived from

normative data collected painstakingly—are utterly meaningless. But interpretation is another matter, one that demands an awareness of the limitations of the standardized procedures so as to make the most sense out of the numerical scores. That is the time for a clinician's acumen and flexibility to be displayed.

Consider the finding by Hardy, Welcher, Mellits, and Kagen (1976) that urban children really "know" the answers to some WISC questions they get wrong, based on a testing-the-limits procedure. Their conclusion that "a standardized test, in this instance the WISC, may not be a valid estimate of the intellectual capabilities of inner-city children" (p. 50) follows logically only if the intelligence test is viewed as a criterion-referenced measure rather than as a sampling of abilities assessed under carefully specified conditions. Testing the limits on a subtest often can give valuable insight into the reasons for failure or confusion, so long as this flexible, supplemental testing occurs after the score has been recorded under appropriate conditions. Realization of the experimental nature of the testing process will prevent an examiner or researcher from interpreting a child's IQs as evidence of maximum performance or capacity.

Jennifer Mascolo—I firmly believe that with the drive to link assessment results to intervention, we must begin to meaningfully evaluate the child's response to testing of limits in the context of our evaluations. A very basic example might be a child who is administered an audio-recorded sound blending task and has difficulty. An informal testing of limits might involve forgoing the audio recording and, instead, having the child focus on the examiner as he or she is "saying" the sounds to be blended. If the testing of limits reveals that the provision of visual support (e.g., being able to "see" the speaker) improves performance, this recommendation can be carried over to the child's real instructional setting.

In an experiment, the empirical results are of limited value until they are interpreted and discussed in the context of pertinent theory and research by a knowledgeable clinician. By the same token, the empirical outcomes of an IQ test are often meaningless until put into context by the examiner. Interpreting test scores in the context of observed behaviors can aid in the appropriate interpretation of the scores. For example, when an adolescent's oppositionality during testing has led to a low level of motivation on timed tasks, this behavior is crucial to understanding that the obtained scores may be a gross underestimate of the adolescent's abilities. When an examiner is able to relate observations of the child's behaviors in the testing situation to the profile of obtained scores (e.g., by noting that the child's anxiety disrupted test performance on all timed tasks), two things occur: (a) The examiner learns important information about the child that can be translated to practical educational suggestions, thereby enhancing the value of the intelligence test; and (b) The actual IQs earned by the child may represent gross underestimates of his or her real intellectual abilities.

In general, standardized test scores are valuable because they provide evidence of a child's mental functioning under a known set of conditions and permit comparison with youngsters of a comparable age. The value of the scores increases when the examiner functions as a true experimenter and tries to determine *why* the child earned the particular profile revealed on the record form; the scores become harmful when they are unquestioningly interpreted as valid indicators of intellectual functioning and are misconstrued as evidence of the child's maximum or even typical performance. For example, a person with excellent visual-spatial and manipulative skills might perform slowly and ineffectively on Block Design because of anxiety caused by the time pressure; or a person with a good commonsense understanding of social situations (coupled with limited word knowledge) may fail several Comprehension items because of a failure to understand some of the key words used in the questions. It is tempting to give credit to a design solved "just 2 or 3 seconds overtime" or to simplify the

wording of a question that the person "certainly knows the answer to." But the good examiner will resist these temptations, knowing that the people in the reference group did not receive such help.

Truly, standardized administration and scoring makes it imperative for examiners to function as scientist-practitioners and conduct an experiment with $n = 1$ every time they administer a clinical test of intelligence. Only a competent clinician, armed with cutting-edge theory and research findings, can make sense of a person's profile of test scores. Intelligent testers must be exceptional clinicians to establish and maintain rapport and to weave the standardized administration into a natural, pleasant interchange between examiner and subject. Clinical skills are also essential when observing and interpreting a person's myriad behaviors during the examination and when integrating all available information and data to give meaning to the myriad numbers that are yielded by every administration of the WISC–V.

5. The WISC–V Is Optimally Useful When It Is Interpreted from a Theoretical Basis

The theoretical models that began to influence the development of IQ tests in the 1980s and continue to drive both test construction and profile interpretation more than a generation later have reshaped the field of cognitive assessment. CHC theory, neuropsychological processing models, neurodevelopmental, and a variety of other approaches have been researched extensively and applied intelligently to the clinical assessment of mental abilities (Flanagan & Harrison, 2012; Lichtenberger & Kaufman, 2013; Schneider, 2013a).

The need to interpret the WISC–V from theory is axiomatic, is illustrated throughout this book, and requires no elaboration here. Of great interest, though, is the interface between the growth of theory and the development of theory-based IQ tests. Cause and effect is hard to determine.

Still awed by a momentous 1986 meeting in Dallas, **Kevin McGrew** said

> … that this moment—a moment where the interests and wisdom of a leading applied test developer (Woodcock), the leading proponent of Cattell-Horn *Gf-Gc* theory (Horn), and one of the preeminent educational psychologists and scholars of the factor analysis of human abilities (Carroll) intersected—was the *flash point that resulted in all subsequent theory-to-practice bridging events that led to today's CHC theory and related assessment developments.* A fortuitous set of events had resulted in the psychometric stars aligning themselves in perfect position to lead the way for most all subsequent CHC assessment related developments.

Further, Alan has written about a second crucial meeting that took place in 1999 in Chapel Hill:

> That meeting was attended by authors of the WJ III (Dick Woodcock, Kevin McGrew) and Binet-5 [SB5] (Gale Roid), two theorists (John Horn and John Carroll), and staff members from Riverside. The goal was "to seek a common, more meaningful umbrella term that would recognize the strong structural similarities of their respective theoretical models, yet also recognize their differences" (McGrew, 2005, p. 149). The net result of that meeting was the merger of the Cattell-Horn and Carroll systems into CHC theory. Talk about the tail wagging the dog! What had begun back in the late 1970s and early 1980s as a search for the best theories on which to build an IQ test had come full circle: Two decades later, the needs of test publishers and test authors forged the theory that underlies almost all current-day IQ tests. (A. S. Kaufman, 2009, p. 99)

No matter how much a theory such as the CHC theory has been validated and used to inform test development, profile interpretation, and educational interventions, Schneider and Flanagan (2015) remind us that the individual, not the theory, is the bottom line:

> Although classifying tests can be fun, it is a stale enterprise when it becomes an end in itself. It is easy to lose sight of the fact that whether a test measures lexical knowledge, perceptual speed, memory span, and the like cannot be our ultimate concern. What matters is what each test can tell us about individuals. If we do not know what a low score on the WJ III Visual Closure subtest means for the future well-being of an individual, the test's place in a taxonomy is of minor importance. (p. 335)

As previously noted in this chapter and elaborated in the following chapters, the study of intelligence today spans several fields, including clinical psychology, school psychology, cognitive psychology, neuropsychology, cognitive neuroscience, brain imaging, and gene mapping. Increasingly, experts from these different disciplines are joining forces to conduct collaborative research with the common goal of improving outcomes for individuals experiencing difficulties with mental functioning. In light of this trend, it is very likely that the next "meeting of the minds" will require a larger round table and a longer invitation list to forge the next important steps of uniting theory, research, and practice toward that goal. We sincerely hope that is the case.

6. Hypotheses Generated from WISC–V Profiles Should Be Supported with Data from Multiple Sources

Test score profiles are optimally meaningful when interpreted in the context of known background information, observed behaviors, approach to each problem-solving task, and scores on related tasks. Virtually any examiner can figure out that the WISC–V Verbal Comprehension Index is not a very good measure of *Gc* for a child raised in a foreign culture, a child who understands Spanish or Tagalog far better than English, or a child with a hearing impairment; that the WISC–V Processing Speed Index or Block Design (*Gv*) scaled score does not measure its designated CHC ability very well for a child with cerebral palsy or a visual handicap. Intelligent testers must try to deduce when one or more subtests or indexes may be an invalid measure of a child's intellectual functioning for more subtle reasons: distractibility, subcultural differences in language or custom, emotional content of the items, suspected or known lesions in specific regions of the brain, fatigue, boredom, extreme shyness, bizarre thought processes, inconsistent effort, and the like.

> *John Willis*—If we have been asked to measure a person's intelligence, then we should not use an intelligence test that, for that person, measures abilities and disabilities that are not related to that individual's intelligence. Many intelligence tests include, for example, subtests that require motor speed and precision, adequate visual acuity, good auditory acuity and perception, and lifelong exposure to United States culture. If none of those issues represents a disability or disadvantage for the examinee, then those subtests may serve as valid measures of intelligence. However, if one or more of those issues is a disability or disadvantage for the examinee, then the test measures that issue, not intelligence. Similarly, a test of oral reading fluency does not measure the automaticity of reading decoding, recognition, and comprehension for a student with a severe stutter. We should not copy down the information that the examinee has convergence insufficiency or severe fine-motor coordination weaknesses and then measure intelligence with a score that includes such subtests as the Wechsler Coding or Woodcock-Johnson Cross Out.

As samples of behavior obtained under conditions that resemble psychological experiments, test scores can mislead just as easily as they can lead. An investigation of peaks and valleys in WISC–V profiles might yield a relatively high Quantitative Reasoning Index and a low Processing Speed Index. That profile suggests hypotheses of good quantitative reasoning ability, a measure of a CHC narrow ability within the *Gf* domain, and poor processing speed (*Gs*). Even though this combination of strong and weak areas is based on reliable, theory-based indexes, clinicians cannot automatically assume that they have identified the child's precise strength and weakness. The labels given each index must be thought of as *hypotheses*, nothing more. And these hypotheses must be translated to educational interventions for any child referred for a learning problem (or they must help pinpoint processing deficits) or they are of limited value. Experts elaborated further on the important role of intelligent testing in evaluating a child's pattern of cognitive strengths and weaknesses:

> *Nancy Mather*—Essentially, intelligent testing involves an appreciation that the test instruments are only tools that help a clinician validate the specific factors that enhance and impede performance. By obtaining a deeper, more nuanced understanding of both a person's strengths and weaknesses, an evaluator can determine appropriate individualized, targeted interventions and therapies. A skilled clinician uses the results from intelligent testing to weave together a tapestry that depicts all important facets of performance, addresses the individual's current challenges and needs, and presents solutions designed to enhance a person's life.
>
> Another important aspect of intelligent testing is the uncovering and documentation of an individual's areas of strength on the various abilities and factors that facilitate performance. Howard Gardner (1999) clearly made this point when he advised, "We shouldn't ask how smart you are, but rather how are you smart?" The results from intelligent testing can be used to help an individual deepen self-understanding, consider or reconsider scholastic and vocational opportunities, and increase appreciation of his or her own unique talents and abilities.
>
> *Ron Dumont*—The use of IQ testing has changed over the years and continues to evolve. It needs to be viewed, in my opinion, as a

snapshot of differing abilities (maybe the IDEA psychological processes) or the CHC broad abilities. These abilities all have complete test batteries available to assess the separate abilities, and no one seems to be damning or downplaying those tests' importance. The trouble seems to come because modern IQ tests attempt to incorporate the separate abilities all into the "global aggregate." We have to resist the thought that that single score is some sort of be-all and end-all number.

I believe IQ testing has an important place in the diagnosis of certain issues, learning problems included. It isn't the overall global score that makes much sense, but the underlying skills assessed.

Elaine Fletcher-Janzen—I must admit that there is less need for an emphasis on the FSIQ and much more need for determining strengths and weaknesses that must be deconstructed and validated with further testing. The "further testing" does not rely on what test publishers purport the tests to measure but more on the clinician's understanding of the processes needed to succeed on the test at various levels of difficulty throughout the test—the process approach if you will. The "further testing" does not rely on arbitrary rules, such as needing two subtests in any given processing area. The analyses go until the clinician understands the construct boundaries—and also the context of how the process develops in different settings (e.g., testing room with one-on-one examiner versus classroom with teacher and 25 students).

How should one best interpret a particular profile of WISC–V indexes? Are the supposed strengths or weaknesses repeatable, or a one-time phenomenon? Both of these questions can be answered, with varying degrees of confidence, by using multiple sources of information and diverse pieces of data. Some of these bits of evidence come from diligent observation during the WISC–V administration and careful scrutiny of response patterns; others come from the background information provided by referral sources, including previous test data, and from the administration of additional subtests and tests.

Nancy Mather—In the case of an individual suspected of having a reading disability, the evaluator would want to consider:
(a) background information, including a family history of reading difficulties; (b) educational history, including prior services, tutoring, and accommodations that the student received; (c) performance on different facets of reading performance, including word reading accuracy, reading rate, and comprehension; (d) performance on relevant oral language measures (e.g., listening comprehension) versus their performance on reading measures; (e) performance on higher-level cognitive tasks (e.g., language and reasoning measures) and how these abilities compare to performance on lower-level more perceptual tasks (e.g., processing speed, working memory, and phonological awareness); and (f) qualitative information, such as the reader's ability to pronounce multisyllabic words, as well as the types of errors he or she makes, such as having difficulty pronouncing medial vowel sounds. After this information is gathered and analyzed, the evaluator then attempts to determine the exact nature of the reading problem in order to recommend appropriate accommodations and interventions.

Consider the child with WISC-inspired hypotheses of weak processing speed and strong quantitative reasoning (an aspect of the broader domain of fluid reasoning). The processing speed hypothesis is based on a WISC–V grouping of two subtests, Coding and Symbol Search. Those low scores might be due to poor processing speed. However, they also might be due to poor visual-motor coordination (an aspect of output), visual-spatial ability, visual perception (an aspect of input); or to low motivation, reflectiveness, distractibility, or obsessiveness; and so forth. What was the child like during the entire evaluation? Did he or she handle the pencil and blocks awkwardly and appear uncoordinated? Was the child unusually reflective or unmotivated? Was it possibly an attentional problem? What picture was painted of the child by parents or teachers? Did the child score low on other tests of processing speed given sometime in the past, or administered as part of the present evaluation (the secondary Cancellation subtest or even the complementary measures of Naming Speed)? What about the error scores? Did the child make rotation errors on Coding and Symbol Search (if so, the low score might be due to a visual-perceptual input problem)?

Similarly, good quantitative reasoning ability would automatically be hypothesized from high scores on Figure Weights and Arithmetic, the two WISC–V subtests that compose this ancillary index. But to truly test this hypothesis, examiners should check out the child's performance on Coding B (for children ages 8 and above), because that task also involves numbers, and on Letter–Number Sequencing. They might also examine the child's scores on Items 18 to 40 on the Information subtest: Five of these items require numerical answers or knowledge of number concepts—did the child or adolescent pass these number items while failing items of comparable difficulty (i.e., items just before or after the number items)? Children with good quantitative reasoning ability also might have unusually good longest spans on Digit Span Backward and Sequencing, perhaps relative to that of Forward, because the ability to repeat numbers *backward* or in *sequence*—unlike the more mindless task of mimicking a forward span—is aided by a child's facility in handling numbers. The WISC–V process scores are helpful in this regard, providing scaled scores on each separate component of Digit Span and offering invaluable contrast scaled scores to permit direct comparisons (Wechsler, 2014, Appendix C).

Other checks on hypotheses of good quantitative reasoning might come from scores on Mathematics achievement subtests in group or individual batteries that were included on the child's record or administered as part of the evaluation; report card grades in arithmetic; statements by a referral source, or by the child, that he or she is good at math; performance on cognitive or achievement subtests from other batteries that demand quantitative reasoning, such

as Sequential and Quantitative Reasoning on the DAS–II (C. D. Elliott, 2007), Number Series on the WJ IV Cognitive, Applied Problems and Number Matrices on the WJ IV Achievement, and KTEA–3 Math Concepts & Applications (A. S. Kaufman & Kaufman, 2014).

7. Results from WISC–V Profiles Must Be Tied to Educational Interventions

In the olden days of assessment, profile interpretation might have stopped with an incisive understanding of the child's pattern of strengths and weaknesses, but that is no longer the case. If the RTI movement and the passage of IDEA have taught us anything, it is that examiners must translate the test profile to action, especially empirically based educational interventions (McBride et al., 2011). The mandate for making meaningful recommendations that will potentially change a child's life warrants inclusion of this aspect as a new tenet of the intelligent testing philosophy. The increased emphasis on linking practice to intervention was addressed by almost every expert, attesting to the importance of its inclusion in the intelligent testing philosophy of today:

> ***Nancy Mather***—Intelligent testing needs to lead to intelligent decision making. Typically, the central purpose of an assessment is to derive solutions for some type of concern or problem. Thus, the results when combined with other relevant data and observations must be used to diagnose specific conditions, as well as address and hopefully answer the referral question. As Cruickshank (1977) advised: "Diagnosis must take *second* place to instruction, and must be made a *tool of instruction*, not an end in itself" (p. 193). Essentially, intelligent testing involves an appreciation that the test instruments are only tools that help a clinician validate the specific factors that enhance and impede performance. By obtaining a deeper, more nuanced understanding of both a person's strengths and weaknesses, an evaluator can determine appropriate individualized, targeted interventions and therapies.

Jennifer Mascolo—If a child is consistently shutting down or becoming tentative in his or her responding after corrective feedback in an assessment situation, and continues to demonstrate this reaction/response throughout tests involving feedback, we have at least initial support that corrective feedback in learning situations needs to be carefully designed so as to not "close off" the child's attention to the task at hand. In building this picture, I believe that we can use such information to inform instructional efforts.

Nancy Mather—Intelligent testing is not synonymous with the interpretation of an intelligence test; it is the process of using test instruments as tools for helping to understand an individual's unique abilities and then developing recommendations that will result in positive outcomes. The essential focus is upon problem solving for each individual who is evaluated. In many cases, the results from intelligent testing are used to confirm or negate the existence of a specific disability. Intelligent testing, however, goes way beyond the identification of disabilities, or compliance with eligibility requirements that only require the simple calculation of scores. As aptly noted by Willis and Dumont (2002), the determination of a disability involves more than "an exercise in arithmetic" (p. 173). In order to make an accurate diagnosis, an evaluator considers information from a variety of sources, including actual classroom performance, educational history, and behavioral observations. The results then provide important information that helps the evaluator explain the nature and severity of a problem and then determine the most appropriate treatment options.

Jennifer Mascolo—We need to begin to evaluate response to strategy instruction. For example, when we offer the child additional real-time support or model ways to re-approach a task, does the child's performance improve? The degree of responsiveness can inform intervention efforts and potentially inform the level of support that might be required (e.g., a highly responsive child might need basic strategy instruction, whereas one with more significant difficulties might require more intensive remediation and/or accommodations).

So, in short, I think that targeted observations that focus on the child, the interaction of child and task, and the child's response to testing of limits/instructional scenarios are all important to consider and represent "intelligent testing" in the context of assessment.

Nancy Mather—The goals of intelligent testing are to identify the person's strengths and weaknesses, attempt to understand the relationship between and among his or her abilities, and then translate these findings into meaningful intervention plans. Thus, the crux of intelligent testing is the translation of an individual's test results into meaningful recommendations that will produce positive outcomes. Dr. Herman Hall, regarded as an expert in the interpretation of standardized tests, demonstrated how the interpretation of test results could directly help educators, parents, and students find success in their lives. In describing Hall's insights, Shapiro (2004) explained: "the diagnosis could lead to the implementation of a program to help the child—whether formally through a tutor, quietly through a teacher's enhanced awareness of what would work best for the child, indirectly through the ebbing of parents' anxiety or simply by the student gaining a better understanding of himself as a learner, and to some degree, as a person. All of these great things could happen." (pp. 15–16)

And where do we see intelligent testing heading in the future? Here are some closing predictions from experts of today:

Alan Kaufman (in 2009, *regarding the future of IQ testing*)—If IQ tests virtually disappear from the school scene in many districts throughout the nation and in some states altogether, how big a dent will that make in IQ test use? Big, in terms of *quantity*, little in terms of *quality*.

In fact, the quality of test use will increase. The identification of children with SLD has provided a prominent role for IQ tests for more than 30 years. But because of the discrepancy formula that loomed over every child referred for possible SLD, IQ tests were often given for the wrong reasons (to plug a number into a formula) by the wrong people (those who found no use for IQ tests *except* to plug into a formula). That will stop.... But most states, I believe, that opt to use IQ tests will do so to identify the child's pattern of strengths and weaknesses. That approach will help identify a processing disorder as well as cognitive strengths for the purpose of individualizing educational planning. And that is intelligent testing. (pp. 296–297)

Ron Dumont—I see tests being held to higher standards. I see many new tests continually changing to incorporate the science. How long did it take the Wechsler scale to finally divide the Performance/Perceptual Reasoning factor into *Gv* and *Gf*? There seems to be expectations from users for more validity evidence. This will continue I believe.

Diane Coalson—To take things a step further in the future, I think we need well-designed research that integrates improved digital assessments, brain-imaging techniques, "brain-training" interventions, with real-life results to see what type of intervention actually helps (i.e., improved function indicated in a brain scan may not correlate well with improved performance in a real-life task).

I also think that we now know enough about some of the brain's processing system maps to hypothesize about additional problem areas a child may have, based on ongoing test results—something a digital environment may do with more ease than hand scoring. For example, the brain areas indicated in working memory, fluid reasoning, and executive function overlap. Can a combined knowledge of function in these areas lead us to more targeted assessment (something like subtraction-based hypothesis testing) and subsequent interventions?

Joel Schneider and Dawn Flanagan (2015)—It is likely that cognitive ability test interpretation will be directly incorporated into academic progress monitoring. That is, traditional cognitive ability assessments and the Response to Intervention (RTI) approach will become integrated into a coherent and unified interpretive framework. Complex prediction equations involving cognitive and academic abilities will include important covariates such as past performance, time on task, task persistence, and quality of instruction. This framework is likely to be increasingly informed by dynamic brain imaging techniques and well-developed cognitive information processing models. That is, we will be able to observe information processing deficits and abnormalities in real time as evaluees perform academic tasks. Furthermore, we will be able to monitor directly whether interventions succeed in normalizing the processing deficits we identify. (p. 337)

We eagerly await the future events that will support or refute these predictions.

PART 2

ADMINISTRATION AND SCORING

CHAPTER 2

INTELLIGENT WISC–V ADMINISTRATION: TEST KIT VERSION

Intelligent testing begins with accurate and standard administration. Adherence to the established administration procedures outlined in the *WISC–V Administration and Scoring Manual* is **critical** when using the scale. Scores derived from these procedures are used to understand a child's cognitive ability in relation to the normative sample, for which the same procedures were followed. Conscientious use of these procedures boosts the applicability of results to the individual child and helps to prevent data loss at the item and subtest level.

There are important reasons for both novice *and* seasoned practitioners to attend to the information in this chapter. The WISC–V represents a major revision of the prior edition. There are eight new subtests to learn to administer. A variety of changes have been made to the administration procedures for the retained subtests. Substantive changes to the test model impact which subtests are selected and administered to obtain the desired composite scores.

Our own extensive experience reviewing test protocols as well as substantial empirical evidence indicates that both graduate student trainees and experienced examiners are prone to administration errors. For more than a combined quarter of a century we have overseen data collection, examined tens of thousands of research phase and final publication test protocols, and responded to questions about the Wechsler intelligence scales that are submitted to Pearson by practitioners and students.

These experiences have revealed to us the huge potential for data loss due to administration errors. Studies conducted on Wechsler intelligence protocols completed by experienced practitioners and by graduate students validate our impressions and reveal that neither novices nor seasoned examiners are exempt from vulnerability to administration errors and data loss and that almost all administrations contain at least some errors (e.g., Blakey, Fantuzzo, Gorsuch, & Moon, 1987; Blakey, Fantuzzo, & Moon, 1985; Franklin, Stillman, Burpeau, & Sabers, 1982; Moon, Fantuzzo, & Gorsuch, 1986; J. J. Ryan, Prifitera, & Powers, 1983; Slate & Jones, 1990a, 1990b). A close review of and increased attention to the procedures documented in the *WISC–V Administration and Scoring Manual* and related information highlighted in this chapter can decrease this vulnerability.

Whether examining a massive number of protocols during Wechsler scale development or reviewing protocols of trainees or practitioners for a research publication, certain types of errors emerge repeatedly as most prominent. Table 2.1 summarizes the findings of studies that detail the frequency of administration error types on Wechsler intelligence scale protocols.

As Table 2.1 indicates, failure to query when necessary is listed consistently across studies as one of the most common errors. In our extensive experience, the failure to query is pervasive, the most frequent of all errors, and at the root of a great deal of lost data. Other common errors observed in studies include querying when unnecessary; failure to record a response, time, or score; awarding too few or too many points to a response (which affects scoring but can also result in incorrect application of reverse and discontinue rules); and incorrect application of start, reverse, and discontinue rules. Our experiences with research protocol review are consistent with these findings as well.

Table 2.1   Most Frequent Types of Administration Errors Observed in Selected Wechsler Intelligence Scale Protocol Studies

Authors and Year	Fail to Query	Query When Not Needed	Fail to Record Response or Score	Awarding too Many or Few Points to Response	Start, Basal, Ceiling, or Discontinue Problems
Belk, LoBello, Ray, & Zachar (2002)	✓	✓		✓	✓
LoBello & Holley (1999)	✓	✓		✓	✓
Loe, Kadlubek, & Marks (2007)	✓		✓	✓	✓
Moon, Blakey, Gorsuch, & Fantuzzo (1991)	✓		✓		
Mrazik, Janzen, Dombrowski, Barford, & Krawchuk (2012)	✓	✓			✓
Slate & Jones (1990a)	✓	✓	✓	✓	✓
Slate, Jones, & Murray (1991)	✓	✓	✓	✓	
Slate, Jones, Murray, & Coulter (1993)	✓	✓	✓	✓	✓

The errors are numerous and have serious consequences. Studies consistently find an average of about eight administration and scoring errors on Wechsler intelligence scale protocols (Alfonso, Johnson, Patinella, & Rader, 1998; Slate & Chick, 1989; Slate & Jones, 1990a, 1990b; Warren & Brown, 1972). After the combined administration and scoring errors (e.g., adding up item scores for a subtest total raw score incorrectly, transferring information to the summary page incorrectly, or using the wrong norms tables) are corrected, the Full Scale IQ (FSIQ) can change in 50% to 80% of cases by 4 points or less, depending on the study (Alfonso et al., 1998; Slate & Jones, 1990a, 1990b; Warren & Brown, 1972). Practitioners (who are not as frequently studied as students) are not above administration errors; they appear to make about twice as many errors as graduate students make, even when failures to record are not counted as errors (Slate, Jones, Coulter, & Covert, 1992; Slate, Jones, Murray, & Coulter, 1993).

Anyone administering a Wechsler intelligence scale should be mindful of the common administration and scoring errors. This chapter provides a subtest-by-subtest overview of administration procedures, reviews the frequent administration errors made on each subtest, offers responses to the most frequently asked questions about subtest administration, and lists behavioral observations to note during administration that are helpful for interpretation. Special focus should be given to the highlighted information in the Remember and Attention boxes. Tables provide a comparison between the Wechsler Intelligence Scale for Children–Fourth Edition (WISC–IV; Wechsler, 2003) and WISC–V administration rules of retained subtests; these tables will be of particular interest to examiners experienced with the WISC–IV.

PRE-ADMINISTRATION CONSIDERATIONS

Test Materials

Become familiar with the WISC–V test materials before beginning your first administration, and closely read the sections in this chapter titled "Common Errors in WISC–V Subtest Administration" and "Frequently Asked Questions: Subtest Administration." If you administer all subtests, everything except the *WISC–V Administration and Scoring Manual Supplement*, the *WISC–V Technical and Interpretive Manual*, and the scoring templates and key are required for administration. If you do not administer the complementary subtests, Stimulus Book 3 also is not required. If the test kit is not new, ensure that all materials are present and in order well in advance of the testing session.

The materials necessary vary according to which subtests you plan to administer. All kit materials are listed next.

WISC–V Test Kit Materials

Administration and Scoring Manual

Block Design Blocks (9)

Administration and Scoring Manual
    Supplement

Coding Scoring Template

Technical and Interpretive Manual

Symbol Search Scoring Key

Record Form

Cancellation Scoring Template

Stimulus Books 1–3

#2 Pencil without Eraser

Response Booklets 1–2

Red Pencil without Eraser

You should gather a few additional items prior to testing. A stopwatch and two extra #2 pencils (for your own recording purposes) are essential. Use the stopwatch discreetly, and ensure the pencils you will use are sharpened and have proper erasers. We also recommend you have available an extra #2 pencil and extra red pencil without erasers, as sometimes pencil tips break or can become dull. A clipboard can be a useful

addition, although the correct responses and notes on the Record Form can be concealed behind the *WISC–V Administration and Scoring Manual* to ensure the child does not become distracted with attempts to see what you have written. The Remember box lists materials to gather that are not in the kit.

> **Remember**
>
> ### *Materials Not in the Test Kit*
>
> - Stopwatch
> - Pencils with erasers (2)
> - Extra #2 pencil without eraser
> - Extra red pencil without eraser
> - Clipboard

The stimulus books should lay flat on the table. To administer a subtest, position the appropriate stimulus book faceup on the table with the binding toward the child. Grasp the tab and open the book toward the child. Turn the pages toward the child to advance through the items.

On Block Design, do not cover the 7 inches between the stimulus book and the edge of the table with the stimulus book page as you open it: Pull the stimulus book toward you so that there remains 7 inches of space between the edge of the stimulus book and the child's edge of the table. Before the child arrives, ensure all pencils are sharp. Check the length of the pencils, and replace them if they become too short. Check the stimulus books to ensure that prior administrations have not resulted in visible fingerprints on the page, as this can be a cue to the correct answer or may lead a child astray in some cases.

Physical Environment

Before the testing session begins, identify a room well suited to administration. A room with adequate lighting that is most likely to remain quiet

Figure 2.1 Proper Positioning of the Crackback Administration and Scoring Manual *Wechsler Intelligence Scale for Children, Fifth Edition* (WISC–V). Copyright © 2014 NCS Pearson, Inc. Reproduced with permission. All rights reserved. *"Wechsler Intelligence Scale for Children"* and *"WISC"* are trademarks, in the United States and/or other countries, of Pearson Education, Inc. or its affiliates(s).

---

throughout the session is best. If necessary, place a sign on the door indicating that testing is taking place and that you should not be disturbed. Alert others who work or may walk through the area that you will be testing and the child needs an environment that is as quiet and calm as possible. Make attempts to accommodate the child's comfort, size, and developmental level. Find or (at least temporarily) create an uncluttered, clean testing area. Remove extraneous items (e.g., jackets, snacks, drinks, waste receptacles, books, toys, and papers) from the child's view and reach, as some children may become distracted easily and the testing can be disrupted.

Arrange the test materials and seating to optimize efficiency and minimize distractions. Place unnecessary test kit items (e.g., unnecessary stimulus books or response booklets) on a chair or on the floor. Plan the seating arrangement carefully. If there is a window in the testing room, it is best if the child sits with his or her back to it. If the child is small in stature and child-sized furniture

---

Attention

Correct responses appear on the Record Form and in the *WISC–V Administration and Scoring Manual*. Shield the Record Form behind the free-standing manual. Do not lay the manual flat. Stand it upright by pushing back the bottom portion of the "crackback" hardcover until it bends along the crease to create a base, as illustrated in Figure 2.1.

---

is not available in the testing room, a booster seat can be used for smaller children so that they will not slide low in the chair and be unable to see or reach the stimuli. If the child is larger, provide a chair that is comfortable for an individual of that size. Avoid using a chair with wheels, as some children easily can become distracted by or begin to play with and fidget in the chair. Sit directly across the table from the child. The WISC–V does not utilize easel-based stimuli, and all of its test materials are designed to be used from across a table rather than from a 90-degree angle next to the child. Figure 2.1 shows the proper positioning of the crackback manual.

Establishing and Maintaining Rapport

The examiner's approach to establishing and maintaining rapport is a critical factor in keeping the child's interest and cooperation and obtaining maximum effort. Rapport is maximized if the examiner has received specialized training in child and adolescent assessment, is familiar with models of cognitive development for this age range, and can apply that knowledge.

Become familiar with all materials and administration procedures before the testing session so you can focus on the child and he or she will not be distracted by awkward fumbling or pauses during or between subtests. Tailor your initial approach to the child and your continued interactions. Consider developmental level, the setting of the testing, the child's familiarity with you, and the child's attitude toward testing in general. Carefully monitor the child's attitude and effort throughout the testing session, so that you obtain the best estimate of the child's intellectual ability.

Your initial approach to the child should focus on putting him or her at ease. Engaging the child in conversation about his or her interests often can accomplish this goal. If not, shift the child's focus to some feature of the present environment and encourage him or her to talk about it (e.g., the furnishings, a picture, an interesting item in the room). When the child is comfortable enough with you, shift your focus to the testing situation.

Introduce the test using the verbatim directions provided in the *WISC–V Administration and Scoring Manual*. Vary your introduction to the test according to the child's developmental level. For younger children, you might describe the test as a series of special games for the child to play. For children who ask if they will be taking a test, it is acceptable to explain that it will not be like the tests at school. When the child is sufficiently comfortable with the testing situation, begin subtest administration.

Feedback can help to maintain rapport and motivation. As you administer the items and subtests, praise the child's effort and thereby encourage the child to do his or her best. Do not give feedback about performance (e.g., "Good" or "Right") unless instructed to do so in the item administration directions. Record every item within a subtest in a similar manner. Recording only incorrect responses can cue the child to his or her performance, which is to be avoided unless prescribed. Sample items allow for an explicit statement about the child's response accuracy as well as to provide the correct response, but teaching items and items with two trials only permit provision of the correct response. Other test items do not allow for any feedback

beyond praise of the child's effort. However, children sometimes still have a sense of poor performance. Monitor the child's awareness of his or her own successes and difficulties. If a child appears discouraged, reassure him or her that the other parts of the test may be easier, or remind him or her of a subtest that he or she appeared to enjoy.

When administered in the standard order, the subtests provide varied stimuli and task demands to ensure variety and sustained engagement. Nevertheless, the child may become bored or restless. Monitor the child's effort level and engagement closely, and look for signs of cooperation. If the child responds "I don't know" excessively or states that he or she cannot complete a task, it may indicate he or she is discouraged, anxious, or doesn't wish to continue. Be careful to note such occurrences, as they can be relevant to interpretation of scores and performance on the current item or subtest. The converse can also occur: A child may not understand a task or may be unable to complete an item correctly but may hesitate to admit as such and act out his or her frustration.

In these situations, it may be necessary to give breaks, to suspend a subtest and return to it, to vary subtest order, or to continue testing in another session. Do not hesitate to allow a discouraged, tired, or fidgeting child to take breaks as needed. Multiple breaks are acceptable and may be necessary both for young children and children with clinical or medical conditions that limit their ability to sit and concentrate for sustained time periods. If a child refuses to perform a particular task, you may temporarily suspend administration and move to the next subtest, returning later when the child appears engaged again. If necessary, mention an interesting task within the test that is yet to come. Doing so may pique the child's interest in continuing after a break or on another day (e.g., some special codes to write, some "secret messages" to read).

Use your judgment to decide if testing should continue in another session. Multiple sessions are sometimes necessary and are acceptable. In this situation, test the child as soon as possible, preferably within a week. Note and evaluate the impact on test results of significant occurrences in the child's life and changes in mental status between sessions.

Standard Subtest Administration Order

Generally, the subtests are administered in a standard order that alternates selected subtests from originating scales (e.g., one from Visual Spatial, then one from Verbal Comprehension, then one from Fluid Reasoning, then one from Working Memory, then one from Processing Speed, etc.). First, the primary subtests used to derive the FSIQ are administered. Next, the remaining primary subtests used to obtain all primary index scores are given. Last, secondary subtests are administered with complementary subtests interspersed to accommodate necessary time intervals between the Immediate Symbol Translation and Delayed Symbol Translation subtests. Table 2.2 lists the standard subtest administration order, along with the subtests' domain memberships. When discussed in this chapter and in Chapters 3 and 4, the subtests always appear grouped by domain membership (i.e., Verbal Comprehension, Visual Spatial, Fluid Reasoning, Working Memory, Processing Speed, and Complementary), then in standard administration order within each domain.

While some variation is acceptable based on the child's needs, subtests should be administered in the standard order whenever possible. If the standard order is not used, note the altered order on the Record Form and consider it when interpreting results. Table 2.2 provides subtests' domain membership as a quick reference if flexibility in administration order becomes necessary. For example, suppose a child has a

Table 2.2 Standard Subtest Administration Order and Domain Membership

Subtest	Domain Membership
1. Block Design	Visual Spatial
2. Similarities	Verbal Comprehension
3. Matrix Reasoning	Fluid Reasoning
4. Digit Span	Working Memory
5. Coding	Processing Speed
6. Vocabulary	Verbal Comprehension
7. Figure Weights	Fluid Reasoning
8. Visual Puzzles	Visual Spatial
9. Picture Span	Working Memory
10. Symbol Search	Processing Speed
11. Information	Verbal Comprehension
12. Picture Concepts	Fluid Reasoning
13. Letter–Number Sequencing	Working Memory
14. Cancellation	Processing Speed
15. Naming Speed Literacy	Complementary
16. Naming Speed Quantity	Complementary
17. Immediate Symbol Translation	Complementary
18. Comprehension	Verbal Comprehension
19. Arithmetic	Fluid Reasoning
20. Delayed Symbol Translation	Complementary
21. Recognition Symbol Translation	Complementary

condition associated with weaknesses on tasks from a particular primary index scale and appears discouraged or agitated immediately prior to a subtest from that scale. In this situation, it may be necessary to quickly select a different subtest to administer that may be less frustrating for the child.

Selection of Subtests

The WISC–V offers a variety of composite scores and discrepancy analyses that can be used to address referral questions. Not every subtest or composite score is relevant to every referral question. Before testing with the WISC–V, consider which scores are most useful for the situation and plan to administer the appropriate subtests. If all 10 primary index subtests are administered, the FSIQ, all primary index scores, and three ancillary index scores can be obtained. Following administration of the 10 primary subtests, the two remaining ancillary index scores (i.e., the Quantitative Reasoning Index and the Auditory Working Memory Index) can be obtained with administration of one secondary subtest each (Arithmetic and Letter–Number Sequencing, respectively). The additional index scores that appear only in this book often require administration of one or more secondary subtests.

To obtain the complementary index scores (i.e., the Naming Speed Index, Symbol Translation Index, and Storage and Retrieval Index), complementary subtests must be administered. Naming Speed Literacy and Naming Speed Quantity are both necessary in order to derive the Naming Speed Index. Immediate, Delayed, and Recognition Symbol Translation must all be administered to obtain the Symbol Translation Index. If both the Naming Speed Index and the Symbol Translation Index are available, the Storage and Retrieval Index can be derived.

Norms and discrepancy analyses for additional index scores are provided in the appendices and the *WISC–V Interpretive Assistant 1.0*, both of which appear in the downloadable resources: www.wiley.com/go/itwiscv. These additional index scores are provided for specific purposes. Some are available for a Cattell-Horn-Carroll (CHC) theory-based approach to examination of results and interpretation. These index scores are theoretically consistent with various narrow abilities described for the CHC model (J. B. Carroll, 2012; Horn & Blankson, 2012; Schneider & Flanagan, 2015; Schneider & McGrew, 2012). Others facilitate interpretation or hypothesis generation from a neuropsychological perspective. Other index scores are included that, in our clinical judgment, prove useful for new discrepancy analyses with the published composite scores or for other practical purposes. Interpretation of the additional index scores developed for readers of this book is discussed in Chapters 9 and 11.

Fairness

Assessing Children at the Extremes of the Age Range

Examiners testing children at the younger and older extremes of the age range (6:0–7:7 and 16:0–16:11, respectively) can select between the WISC–V and alternate measures of intellectual ability. Although the WISC–V items are unique, other tests contain tasks that are similar to those of the WISC–V. Repeated administration effects (e.g., procedural learning) can therefore impact scores on the second measure. Optimally, the selection between measures should be made based on estimated ability level of the child, referral question, and the presence of special considerations. At times, a battery other than the WISC–V may be preferable.

When testing children at the younger extreme of the age range (6:0–7:7), the Wechsler Preschool and Primary Scale of Intelligence–Fourth Edition (WPPSI–IV; Wechsler, 2012) is a likely alternative. The WPPSI–IV is the more likely choice for a younger child suspected of below-average or average intellectual ability. If there are concerns about the child's visual working memory, the WPPSI–IV might be selected. The WPPSI–IV may be a more appropriate choice for children with fine motor skill delays if the referral question involves processing speed. If intellectual ability is estimated as above average, the WISC–V should be considered. The WISC–V might also be selected if auditory working memory is of concern or if a mixed-modality (i.e., auditory and visual) Working Memory Index is desired.

Regardless of the intellectual ability measure selected (i.e., WPPSI–IV or WISC–V) for children aged 6:0 to 7:7, portions of the other measure may be administered following completion of the first instrument to augment results and provide a multimodal assessment of working memory. For example, if the referral question involves low working memory ability or a clinical condition usually characterized by diffuse working memory deficits, the differences between the child's auditory and visual working memory can be evaluated using the WISC–V Auditory Working Memory Index and the WPPSI–IV Working Memory Index (which measures visual and visual-spatial working memory) to inform interventions targeted to meet the individual child's needs. Table 2.3 provides a summary of the intellectual ability battery to select for children at the extremes of the WISC–V age range. The WISC–V Picture Span subtest may be used with the WISC–V Integrated Spatial Span subtest to derive a Visual Working Memory Index that can serve a similar purpose.

When testing children at the older extreme of the age range (16:0–16:11), the Wechsler Adult Intelligence Scale–Fourth Edition (WAIS–IV; Wechsler, 2008) is a likely alternative. The WISC–V is the more likely choice for a 16-year-old child suspected of below-average or average intellectual ability. If there are concerns about the child's visual working memory or a potential specific learning disorder, the WISC–V might be selected. If intellectual ability is estimated as above average, the WAIS–IV should be considered. The WAIS–IV might also be selected if there are emergent concerns

Table 2.3 Selecting between the WISC–V and Other Batteries When Testing Children at the Extremes of the Age Range

Age	Estimated Ability Level	Intellectual Ability Battery to Select
6:0–7:7	Below Average	WPPSI–IV or an appropriate alternative battery
	Average	WPPSI–IV
	Above Average	WISC–V
16:0–16:11	Below Average	WISC–V
	Average	WISC–V
	Above Average	WAIS–IV or an appropriate alternative battery

about an older child's memory, because of the WAIS–IV link with the Wechsler Memory Scale–Fourth Edition (WMS–IV; Wechsler, 2009). For 16-year-old children with a traumatic brain injury or an autism spectrum disorder, the WAIS–IV may also be selected because of its links with Advanced Clinical Solutions for the WAIS–IV and WMS–IV (Pearson, 2009a). This collection of additional measures provides demographically adjusted norms for both intellectual ability and memory, premorbid prediction of intellectual ability and memory, measures of social cognition, measures of change across multiple administrations, and assessments of executive function and effort.

Assessing Children with Special Needs

Children with special physical, language, or sensory needs are often referred for intellectual ability testing. According to Chapter 10 of the *Standards for Educational and Psychological Testing* (*Standards*; American Educational Research Association, American Psychological

Association, & National Council on Measurement in Education, 2014), caution must be exercised when interpreting intellectual ability test results in these situations, as low test scores may in fact be attributed to the special needs. For these children, it is especially important to supplement the WISC–V with measures tailored to each child's issues. It may be necessary to modify the WISC–V procedures to gain the best understanding of the child, and these modifications or accommodations should be noted on the Record Form and considered when interpreting results. Although norms may be less applicable in some of these cases, individualized accommodations and testing of limits can help you to gain a wealth of information about the child's strengths as well as areas that may benefit from intervention.

Prepare for testing a child with special needs through learning more about the accommodations in general and about the child specifically. Refer to comprehensive references on the subject of testing accommodations in these situations (Braden, 2003; Decker, Englund, & Roberts, 2012; Gordon, Stump, & Glaser, 1996). Also refer to Chapter 10 of the *Standards* for guidelines pertaining to testing children in need of accommodation due to special needs. Gather information about the child's special needs and his or her preferred means of communicating. Review records from prior testing, if any. Interview parents/guardians, and obtain consent to speak with teachers or other professionals involved with the child as appropriate. Seek to learn more about how to obtain the best information and performance in light of his or her limitations. Consider extending testing over multiple sessions if quicker fatigue may be an associated feature of the child's needs. Use what you learn to plan accommodations or modifications to standard administration procedures and to select subtests that are most appropriate.

Consider the next general recommendations for modifications and their impact on the applicability of scaled and composite scores.

Limited Motor Skills

- Do not administer Block Design or Coding.
- Administer the Verbal Comprehension subtests, Visual Puzzles, the Fluid Reasoning subtests, and the Working Memory subtests.
- Consider carefully if the remaining Processing Speed subtests, Symbol Search and Cancellation, are appropriate. If the child is aged 6:0 to 7:7, consider administering the WPPSI–IV Processing Speed subtests instead and using the WPPSI–IV norms to obtain a Processing Speed Index (being sure to note this in the report). The WPPSI–IV subtests can be helpful in some situations because an ink dauber is used to respond. Responding with the ink dauber places relatively light demands on motor performance relative to subtests that use pencils. If the child is 7:8 or older, or if use of the WPPSI–IV ink dauber is not appropriate, administer Naming Speed Literacy and Naming Speed Quantity to gain some insight into the child's speed of information processing. If the child's motor skills do not allow him or her to use a finger to track the stimulus that is currently being responded to, watch closely and query as necessary to ensure you are tracking responses together.

Serious Language Difficulties, Children Who Are Deaf or Hard of Hearing, and Children Who Are English-Language Learners

- Administer the Visual Spatial and Processing Speed subtests as well as all of the Fluid Reasoning subtests (except for Arithmetic from the Fluid Reasoning domain) and administer Picture Span from the Working Memory domain. If it is apparent that the child does not comprehend instructions for a specific task, discontinue administration of the subtest.

- For children who are English-language learners, consider if the use of an interpreter or an adapted or translated version is appropriate.
- Use established procedures for intellectual assessment of children who are English-language learners, such as those outlined by Ortiz, Ochoa, and Dynda (2012). Remember that assessment of children who are English-language learners is a complex process that requires information about the child's English and native-language proficiency and facility with a number of models used to tailor evaluation of these children to the situation.
- Consider using the Nonverbal Index with children who are English-language learners. Remember that the Nonverbal Index is not language-free; it is merely language reduced because the subtests used to derive it require comprehension of instructions in English.
- For children who are deaf or hard of hearing, refer to the guidelines published in the previous edition (WISC–IV; Wechsler, 2003). Similar guidelines are forthcoming in a technical report for the WISC–V that is not available at the time of this writing.

Children with Visual Impairment

- Administer Similarities, Vocabulary, Information, and Comprehension. Do not administer the picture items for Vocabulary. Administer Arithmetic without the picture items.
- Administer Digit Span and Letter–Number Sequencing. Derive the Auditory Working Memory Index (available in the published test).
- Consider using the Verbal (Expanded Crystallized) Index discussed in this book and provided with the online resources as the global intellectual ability score.
- Derive other additional index scores available in this book if possible, in addition to the Verbal Comprehension Index (available in the published test).

GENERAL ADMINISTRATION INFORMATION

A number of standard administration procedures are common to some or most of the WISC–V subtests, including start points and discontinue rules, prompts, and recording responses. These general administration guidelines are described in the next sections.

Start Points, Reverse Rules, and Discontinue Rules

Start points, reverse rules, and discontinue rules are used to ensure the child is not administered unnecessary items. These administration guidelines are described in Chapter 3 of the *WISC–V Administration and Scoring Manual*. Abbreviated descriptions also appear on the Record Form.

Start Points
Item administration generally begins at the start point and proceeds in forward sequence if the child receives perfect scores on the first two items administered. Start points are designated with arrows on the Record Form and in the *WISC–V Administration and Scoring Manual*, and often vary based on the child's age. Start-point items are selected to ensure almost all children (i.e., 90%–95% of the normative sample for a given age group) receive full credit on the first few items administered. The age-appropriate start point should be used in most situations. However, if the child is suspected of having an intellectual disability or low cognitive ability, administration should begin with Item 1.

Some subtests contain demonstration and sample items that are administered prior to the start point. These items are not scored, nor are they included in the total raw score, although the child's responses for sample items should be recorded where appropriate.

Remember to award full credit for items prior to the start point if administration begins with Item 1 and the child then obtains perfect scores on the age-appropriate start-point item and subsequent item. Application of this rule thus overrides scores of 0 points on items prior to the start point. Refer to Figure 2.5 in the *WISC–V Administration and Scoring Manual* for an illustrated example. Examiners commonly draw a slash mark through unadministered items (e.g., items prior to the start point) on the Record Form to indicate that those items were not administered. It is helpful to record the sum of credit for unadministered items next to the last item prior to the start point. Table 2.4 provides a summary of the subtest start points.

Reverse Rules

Reverse rules are criteria that indicate when the items prior to the start point should be given if administration of a subtest did not begin at Item 1. If the child does not receive a perfect score (i.e., all possible points for a given item) on the first two items (i.e., the start point and subsequent item), reverse rules require a decision about which item should be administered next. The term *appropriate* is used in the administration instructions to cue examiners that item administration may proceed forward or backward in the order, depending on the child's performance.

It is important to note that Figure Weights Sample Item A and Picture Span Sample Item A are given only if administration starts at Item 1. If administration does not begin at Item 1, then the reverse rules never result in the respective Sample Item A being administered; do not administer Sample Item A even if administration continues in reverse all the way back to Item 1. Table 2.5 provides a summary of the subtest reverse rules.

Discontinue Rules and Stop Points

Discontinue rules provide criteria to indicate when subtest administration should stop, generally after scores of 0 on a certain number of consecutive items. Scores of 0 that the child earns while reversing count toward the discontinue rule. If the discontinue criterion is met

Table 2.4 Subtest Start Points

Subtest	Start Point by Age
Similarities	Ages 6–7: Sample Item, then Item 1
	Ages 8–11: Sample Item, then Item 5
	Ages 12–16: Sample Item, then Item 8
Vocabulary	Ages 6–7: Item 1
	Ages 8–11: Item 5
	Ages 12–16: Item 9
Information	Ages 6–8: Item 1
	Ages 9–16: Item 8
Comprehension	Ages 6–11: Item 1
	Ages 12–16: Item 3
Block Design	Ages 6–7: Item 1
	Ages 8–16: Item 3
Visual Puzzles	Ages 6–8: Demonstration Item, Sample Item, then Item 1
	Ages 9–11: Demonstration Item, Sample Item, then Item 5
	Ages 12–16: Demonstration Item, Sample Item, then Item 8
Matrix Reasoning	Ages 6–8: Sample Items A & B, then Item 1
	Ages 9–11: Sample Items A & B, then Item 5
	Ages 12–16: Sample Items A & B, then Item 9
Figure Weights	Ages 6–8: Sample Item A, then Item 1
	Ages 9–16: Sample Item B, then Item 4
Picture Concepts	Ages 6–8: Sample Items A & B, then Item 1
	Ages 9–11: Sample Items A & B, then Item 4
	Ages 12–16: Sample Items A & B, then Item 7
Arithmetic	Ages 6–7: Item 3
	Ages 8–9: Item 8
	Ages 10–16: Item 11

(continued)

Table 2.4   *(Continued)*

Subtest	Start Point by Age
Digit Span	Forward: Ages 6–16: Item 1 Backward: Ages 6–16: Sample Item, then Item 1 Sequencing: Ages 6–7: Qualifying Item, Sample Items A & B, then Item 1 Ages 8–16: Sample Items A & B, then Item 1
Picture Span	Ages 6–16: Sample Items B & C, then Item 4
Letter–Number Sequencing	Ages 6–7: Qualifying Items, Demonstration Item A, Sample Item A, then Item 1 Ages 8–16: Demonstration Item A, Sample Items A & B, then Item 1
Coding	Ages 6–7: Form A Demonstration Items, Sample Items, then Test Items Ages 8–16: Form B Demonstration Items, Sample Items, then Test Items
Symbol Search	Ages 6–7: Form A Demonstration Items, Sample Items, then Test Items Ages 8–16: Form B Demonstration Items, Sample Items, then Test Items
Cancellation	Ages 6–16: Demonstration Item, Sample Item, then Item 1
Naming Speed Literacy	Age 6: Demonstration Item A, Sample Item A, then Item 1 Ages 7–8: Demonstration Item B, Sample Item B, then Item 2 Ages 9–16: Sample Item C, then Item 3
Naming Speed Quantity	Age 6: Sample Item A, then Item 1 Ages 7–16: Sample Item B, then Item 2
Immediate Symbol Translation	Ages 6–16: Item 1

Table 2.4   *(Continued)*

Subtest	Start Point by Age
Delayed Symbol Translation	Ages 6–16: Item 1
Recognition Symbol Translation	Ages 6–16: Item 1

Source: From the *Administration and Scoring Manual* of the *Wechsler Intelligence Scale for Children–Fifth Edition.* Copyright © 2014 Pearson. Adapted and reproduced by permission. All rights reserved.

Table 2.5   **Subtest Reverse Rules**

Subtest	Reverse Rule by Age
Similarities	Ages 8–16: Imperfect score on either of the first 2 items given, administer preceding items in reverse order until 2 consecutive perfect scores are obtained.
Vocabulary	Ages 8–16: Imperfect score on either of the first 2 items given, administer preceding items in reverse order until 2 consecutive perfect scores are obtained.
Information	Ages 9–16: Imperfect score on either of the first 2 items given, administer preceding items in reverse order until 2 consecutive perfect scores are obtained.
Comprehension	Ages 12–16: Imperfect score on either of the first 2 items given, administer preceding items in reverse order until 2 consecutive perfect scores are obtained.
Block Design	Ages 8–16: Imperfect score on either of the first 2 items given, administer preceding items in reverse order until 2 consecutive perfect scores are obtained.
Visual Puzzles	Ages 9–16: Imperfect score on either of the first 2 items given, administer preceding items in reverse order until 2 consecutive perfect scores are obtained.

Table 2.5 (*Continued*)

Subtest	Reverse Rule by Age
Matrix Reasoning	Ages 9–16: Imperfect score on either of the first 2 items given, administer preceding items in reverse order until 2 consecutive perfect scores are obtained.
Figure Weights	Ages 9–16: Imperfect score on either of the first 2 items given, administer preceding items in reverse order until 2 consecutive perfect scores are obtained.
Picture Concepts	Ages 9–16: Imperfect score on either of the first 2 items given, administer preceding items in reverse order until 2 consecutive perfect scores are obtained.
Arithmetic	Ages 6–16: Imperfect score on either of the first 2 items given, administer preceding items in reverse order until 2 consecutive perfect scores are obtained.
Digit Span	Do not reverse
Picture Span	Ages 6–16: Imperfect score on either of the first 2 items given, administer preceding items in reverse order until 2 consecutive perfect scores are obtained.
Letter–Number Sequencing	Do not reverse.
Coding	Do not reverse.
Symbol Search	Do not reverse.
Cancellation	Do not reverse.
Naming Speed Literacy	Do not reverse.
Naming Speed Quantity	Do not reverse.
Immediate Symbol Translation	Do not reverse.

Table 2.5 (*Continued*)

Subtest	Reverse Rule by Age
Delayed Symbol Translation	Do not reverse.
Recognition Symbol Translation	Do not reverse.

Source: From the *Administration and Scoring Manual* of the *Wechsler Intelligence Scale for Children–Fifth Edition.* Copyright © 2014 Pearson. Adapted and reproduced by permission. All rights reserved.

while reversing, points are not awarded for items beyond the discontinue point, even if they were originally earned by the child.

The discontinue rules for the primary and secondary subtests are easily committed to memory. Subtests that involve using either of the pencils (the Processing Speed subtests) have discontinue rules that involve stopping administration after a specified amount of time has elapsed. Block Design has a discontinue rule of 2 consecutive scores of 0. The Auditory Working Memory subtests (i.e., Digit Span on the Sequencing task and Letter–Number Sequencing) have qualifying items for ages 6–7 and discontinue rules after missing all trials of an item (within each task for Digit Span and within the subtest for Letter–Number Sequencing). All other primary and secondary subtests have discontinue rules of 3 consecutive scores of 0.

The Symbol Translation subtests (i.e., Immediate, Delayed, and Recognition Symbol Translation) have somewhat unusual discontinue rules. Immediate Symbol Translation can be discontinued at one of three decision points (A, B, or C) or at the end of the subtest, depending on whether the child's cumulative raw score meets or exceeds a specified value at the decision point. The discontinue rules for Delayed and Recognition Symbol Translation are linked to the child's performance on Immediate Symbol Translation. These subtests are discontinued at the same decision point (A, B, or C) as Immediate Symbol Translation or administered in their entirety.

The Naming Speed subtests have stop points. Stop points are an alternative to discontinue rules, and merely designate the items that are administered to a child according to his or her age. Table 2.6 provides a summary of the subtest discontinue rules. Quick Reference 2.1 summarizes the discontinue rules across different types of subtests.

Timing

Some subtests have strict time limits, whereas others have no time limits and are merely subject to a 30-second guideline. Strict time limits are just that. If a subtest has a strict time limit, do not stop or pause the stopwatch for any reason. If administration is disrupted by extraneous noise or activity, note this on the Record Form but instruct the child to keep working. If repetition of instructions or items is permitted or if prompts are given, do not stop timing.

The 30-second guideline is not strict and should not be rigidly applied, and a stopwatch should not be used to mark response time. Merely estimate the time that has passed. If the child's performance on a 30-second guideline subtest is waning, and he or she is spending an inordinate amount of time considering responses without benefit to performance, encourage the child to respond. This practice maintains administration pace, diminishes the potential for fatigue, and may result in the child being able to move to another task to experience more success. In this situation, if about 30 seconds have passed, you may ask the child if he or she has an answer. If he or she doesn't respond, initiate a transition to the next appropriate item. If a child is performing well and taking extra time to

Table 2.6   Subtest Discontinue Rules

Subtest	Discontinue Rule/Stop Point
Similarities	After 3 consecutive scores of 0
Vocabulary	After 3 consecutive scores of 0
Information	After 3 consecutive scores of 0
Comprehension	After 3 consecutive scores of 0
Block Design	After 2 consecutive scores of 0
Visual Puzzles	After 3 consecutive scores of 0
Matrix Reasoning	After 3 consecutive scores of 0
Figure Weights	After 3 consecutive scores of 0
Picture Concepts	After 3 consecutive scores of 0
Arithmetic	After 3 consecutive scores of 0
Digit Span	Forward: After scores of 0 on both trials of an item Backward: After scores of 0 on both trials of an item Sequencing: Ages 6–7: After an incorrect response to Qualifying Item OR after scores of 0 on both trials of an item Ages 8–16: After scores of 0 on both trials of an item
Picture Span	After 3 consecutive scores of 0
Letter–Number Sequencing	Ages 6–7: After an incorrect response to either Qualifying Item OR after scores of 0 on all 3 trials of an item Ages 8–16: After scores of 0 on all 3 trials of an item
Coding	After 120 seconds
Symbol Search	After 120 seconds
Cancellation	After 45 seconds for each item
Naming Speed Literacy	Age 6: Stop after Trial 2 of Item 2 is administered Age 7–16: Stop after Trial 2 of Item 3 is administered

(continued)

QUICK REFERENCE 2.1: REMEMBERING DISCONTINUE RULES

- Block Design: Discontinue after 2 consecutive scores of 0.
- Subtests involving use of a pencil: Discontinue after a specified amount of time has elapsed.
- Digit Span and Letter–Number Sequencing: Discontinue after missing all trials of an item.
- Naming Speed and Symbol Translation subtests: Stop points (i.e., a.g., age-based item administration) or unusual, linked discontinue rules.
- All other subtests: Discontinue after 3 consecutive scores of 0.

Table 2.6 *(Continued)*

Subtest	Discontinue Rule/Stop Point
Naming Speed Quantity	Age 6: Stop after Trial 2 of Item 1 is administered Age 7–16: Stop after Trial 2 of Item 2 is administered
Immediate Symbol Translation	If the cumulative raw score is less than or equal to a specified value at a decision point A, B, or C
Delayed Symbol Translation	At the same decision point as Immediate Symbol Translation (e.g., A, B, or C)
Recognition Symbol Translation	At the same decision point as Immediate Symbol Translation (e.g., A, B, or C)

Source: From the *Administration and Scoring Manual* of the *Wechsler Intelligence Scale for Children–Fifth Edition.* Copyright © 2014 Pearson. Adapted and reproduced by permission. All rights reserved.

consider responses, be more generous with the time you allow before offering these prompts.

For some subtests, a stopwatch is required to mark the stimulus exposure time or to determine when the time limit has expired. Good stopwatch management and use ensures that standard administration procedures can be followed and reduces the likelihood of administration errors. For most subtests, timing starts immediately after the verbal instructions are completed. In general, for these subtests keep the stopwatch in your

nondominant hand or on the table behind the *WISC–V Administration and Scoring Manual* as you give verbal instructions or present stimulus materials. Table 2.7 summarizes the timing rules by subtest.

Remember

- Review Table 2.7 to become familiar with the subtests that require use of a stopwatch.
- The exposure of stimuli is timed on Picture Span.

Qualifying, Demonstration, Sample, and Teaching Items

Some subtests have qualifying, demonstration, sample, and/or teaching items. These are included based on research phase data indicating that they are necessary. Proper administration of these items can improve understanding of a novel task or portion of a subtest.

Qualifying items help you to ensure that the child has the necessary skills to do a given task. Digit Span Sequencing requires the child to count to 3 successfully, and Letter–Number Sequencing requires the child to do the same and to recite the alphabet correctly through the letter C. If the child does not perform the qualifying items correctly, subtest administration

Table 2.7 Subtest Timing Rules

Subtest	Stopwatch Required	Stimulus Exposure Timed	Strict Time Limits	30-Second Guideline
Similarities				✓
Vocabulary				✓
Information				✓
Comprehension				✓
Block Design	✓		✓	
Visual Puzzles	✓		✓	
Matrix Reasoning				✓
Figure Weights	✓		✓	
Picture Concepts				✓
Arithmetic	✓		✓	
Digit Span				✓
Picture Span	✓	✓		✓
Letter–Number Sequencing				✓
Coding	✓		✓	
Symbol Search	✓		✓	
Cancellation	✓		✓	
Naming Speed Literacy	✓		✓	
Naming Speed Quantity	✓		✓	
Immediate Symbol Translation				✓
Delayed Symbol Translation				✓
Recognition Symbol Translation				✓

is discontinued. Qualifying items do not contribute to the total raw score of a subtest.

Demonstration items allow you to demonstrate and explain how to respond to a task. Sample items allow the child to practice completion of an item before transitioning to test items. Neither demonstration nor sample items contribute to the total raw score of a subtest.

Teaching items are scored test items that contribute to the total raw score of a subtest. They permit you to offer feedback about an incorrect response on initial items of a novel task or about items that involve a change in response requirements as you proceed through a subtest. They are designated with a dagger symbol (†) in the *WISC–V Administration and Scoring Manual* and on the Record Form. Remain aware that teaching sometimes occurs on items that are not the first ones administered. For example, because Vocabulary Items 5 and 6 are the first that involve defining a word rather than naming a picture, all children who take these items receive teaching for incorrect responses, even if teaching was previously provided on Item 1.

Repetitions, Prompts, and Queries

Repetitions, prompts, and queries serve to facilitate comprehension of items, reinforce directions, redirect attention, and clarify responses. It is important to familiarize yourself with their prescribed uses across subtests.

Repetitions
Subject to some restrictions, task and item-level instructions generally can be repeated. Do not repeat instructions if the child is concentrating or still working. If permitted, a good practice is to repeat item instructions after about 5–10 seconds if the child has not responded.

If the subtest does not require use of a stopwatch (see Table 2.7), repeat instructions upon request by the child and at your discretion, as many times as necessary. For these subtests, you may readminister items to which a child responded "I don't know" if later performance on the subtest indicates the child might respond correctly to those items. Assign appropriate credit if the child's response is improved upon readministration.

If the subtest requires the use of a stopwatch, the following guidelines apply. You may not readminister items. For those with strict response time limits (see Table 2.7), repeat instructions as many times as necessary, but do not stop timing during repetitions. ***The lone exception to this is Arithmetic:*** *Item repetition is not permitted on Items 1 to 19, but* **a single repetition is permitted on Items 20 to 34 and the stopwatch is paused for the repetition.** For Block Design, you may repeat verbal instructions, but do not model correct assembly a second time during the child's allotted time to respond.

For some subtests that involve recall of auditory or visual stimuli (i.e., Digit Span, Picture Span, Letter–Number Sequencing, and the Symbol Translation subtests), repetition of items is not permitted (i.e., trials **cannot** be repeated, stimuli **cannot** be reexposed or repeated unless explicitly directed, and reminders of the meanings of visual-verbal pairs **cannot** be given unless explicitly instructed); however, subtest *instructions* (not items or trials) can be repeated upon request. As noted, for Arithmetic, Items 1 to 20 **cannot** be repeated, but Items 21 to 37 **can** be repeated one time, subject to constraints specified in the subtest instructions.

If a repetition is requested on a subtest that does not permit repetition, the request is typically noted by recording **RR** on the Record Form. Items that are repeated are denoted by recording **IR**

Prompts

Standard subtest-specific prompts are used as necessary to teach or remind the child of the task instructions. They are listed in the General Directions sections for each subtest. During subtests that have strict time limits (see Table 2.7), do not stop timing to give necessary prompts. For your convenience, all subtest-specific prompts are reproduced in Appendix A in the downloadable resources: www.wiley.com/go/itwiscv. The subtests are organized in administration order in Appendix A. You may print Appendix A and place it next to the *WISC–V Administration and Scoring Manual* for use during administration until you commit the prompts to memory, so you do not need to turn the pages back to the General Directions sections during item administration. Prompts are typically noted with **P** on the Record Form.

Queries

Queries are used as necessary to gather additional information about the child's response if it is incomplete or unclear. In most cases, queries merely involve asking the child what he or she means, or to tell you more about it, or some other phrase that does not lead the child to any particular answer. Sample responses indicated with a **Q** in the *WISC–V Administration and Scoring Manual* should be queried. Some specific sample responses to items require a special query; these are noted with an asterisk (*). For these items, an asterisk also appears next to the item number in the *WISC–V Administration and Scoring Manual* and on the Record Form. Queries are typically noted with **Q** on the Record Form.

Remember

- Don't query a response just to improve a low score or a clearly incorrect response.
- An asterisk (*) next to an item number indicates a special query might be necessary.

Behind the Scenes

Sample responses are selected for the manual based on accumulated evidence throughout all research phases. Every verbatim response is reviewed and evaluated to determine its final point value and whether or not additional query is necessary. If a **Q** follows a sample response, data suggest that additional inquiry often improved the item's discrimination of ability level.

Recording Responses

Thorough recording of responses is in the best interest of the child for a number of reasons. Good records ensure more accurate scoring, facilitate interpretive observations and thus understanding of performance. Detailed recording also enhances communication with other professionals who may gain access to the test protocol in a transfer of records. Administered items should be distinguished from unadministered items with some notation that indicates that they were administered. The Record Form provides areas to circle or record verbatim responses, to indicate item- and/or subtest-level scores, and to note completion times or other subtest-specific information or behaviors. Repetitions, prompts, queries, nonverbal responses, and other behaviors can also be noted. Examiners use commonly understood abbreviations to indicate their own test administration behaviors (e.g., queries, prompts) as well as to record various types of responses and behaviors by the child. A list of these common abbreviations appears in Quick Reference 2.2.

QUICK REFERENCE 2.2: COMMONLY USED RECORDING ABBREVIATIONS

Abbreviation	Meaning
@	At
ABT	About
B	Be or Both
BC	Because
C	See
DK	Child indicated he or she did not know the answer
-G	-ing
INC	Response was incomplete at the time limit
IR	Item was repeated
LL	Looks like
NR	Child did not give a response
P	Prompt administered
PC	Pointed correctly
PPL	People
PX	Pointed incorrectly
Q	Query administered
RR	Child requested repetition, item was not repeated
SO	Someone
ST	Something
SV	Child was observably subvocalizing
W/ or $\bar{c}$	With
W/O or $\bar{s}$	Without
U	You
Y	Why

Source: Adapted from A. S. Kaufman and E. O. Lichtenberger, *Essentials of WISC–III and WPPSI–R Assessment*. Copyright © 2000 John Wiley & Sons, Inc., and from J. E. Exner, Jr., *The Rorschach: A Comprehensive System, Volume 1: Basic Foundations Third Edition*. Copyright © 1993 John Wiley & Sons, Inc. Expanded based on occurrence in standardization test protocols. Table appeared in a similar form in S. E. Raiford and D. L. Coalson, *Essentials of WPPSI–IV Assessment*. Copyright © 2014 John Wiley & Sons, Inc.

Some types of WISC–V testing behaviors can yield data-based process observations for certain subtests. These are discussed further in Chapter 3. To obtain the data for a process observation that corresponds to a given testing behavior, record the appropriate abbreviation (e.g., IR, DK, RR, SC) on the Record Form next to the appropriate items and trials each time the testing behavior is observed.

SUBTEST–BY–SUBTEST ADMINISTRATION

Verbal Comprehension Subtests

Similarities

The child is required to describe how two common objects or concepts are similar. Necessary materials include the *WISC–V Administration and Scoring Manual* and the Record Form.

Similarities start points vary by age. Children aged 6 to 7 start with the sample item then Item 1. Children aged 8 to 11 start with the sample item then Item 5, and children aged 12 to 16 start with the sample item then Item 8. Remember to administer the sample item to all children. If a child aged 8 to 16 does not obtain a perfect score on **either** of the first 2 items administered, give the preceding items in reverse sequence until 2 consecutive perfect scores are obtained.

The discontinue rule is 3 consecutive scores of 0. Be careful not to discontinue too early. If you are unsure about a child's score on one of the items that may count toward the 3 consecutive scores of 0, administer more items until you are positive a proper discontinue has been reached.

Items 1, 2, 5, 6, 8, and 9 are teaching items. The teaching items correspond with the age-appropriate start points. For these items, corrective feedback is given if the child does not receive a perfect score even if the item in question is not one of the first items administered to a particular child.

You may repeat items as often as necessary. Do not use an alternate word or synonym, or

attempt to explain. If multiple pronunciation options exist for a word, pronounce the word using the local pronunciation or the pronunciation you believe is most familiar to the child.

Before administering the items, become familiar with the sample responses. Both the sample responses and the general scoring principles are used to determine item scores, so you must ensure you are familiar with the general scoring principles prior to administration. Review the section on "Using Sample Responses, General Scoring Principles, and General Concepts" in Chapter 3 of this book for more information.

For some of the most difficult items, the two words represent opposite ends of a continuum, with the best responses describing them as extremes of a specified dimension. However, some children are unable to describe the continuum's dimension and merely state how the two words are different. After all subtests have been administered, you may return to the item(s) and test the limits. At that time, point out that the child's previous response specified how the two objects or concepts were different, then ask the child to explain how they are alike or the same. Following this additional administration procedure, you may describe the additional support and explanation in the psychological report, but do not modify the score.

Table 2.8 provides a comparison of Similarities administration procedures across the WISC–IV and WISC–V. The Remember box lists behavioral observations that the examiner should note during administration.

> **Remember**
>
> ***Behavioral Observations for Similarities***
>
> **Note if the child:**
>
> - Initially appears to not understand the task and responds incorrectly to the sample item or a teaching item. Note whether
>
> *(Continued)*

(Continued)

or not the child appeared to benefit from the feedback provided.

- Responded more readily to Block Design, which involves pictorial stimuli and manipulatives and can be responded to nonverbally, and then has more difficulty with Similarities, which involves only verbal stimuli and requires a verbal response. Because this is the first subtest with expressive requirements, it can provide important cues about the child's ability to respond verbally.
- Provides complete responses or must be repeatedly queried as a cue to give all pertinent information.
- Provides additional information about responses upon query, or tends to say he or she does not know any more.
- Consistently states that the two objects or concepts are not alike or are opposites.
- Seems to not know answers to items that might be more closely related to cultural opportunities and educational background (e.g., Items 12, 14, 15, 18, and 23). Utilize this information in interpretation.
- Performs better on Similarities than on Picture Concepts. This comparison can provide clues about the child's reasoning ability from the perspective of different stimulus modalities and response formats.

Vocabulary

Picture items require the child to name a depicted object. Verbal items require the child to define words read by the examiner. Necessary materials include the *WISC–V Administration and Scoring Manual*, the Record Form, and Stimulus Book 1.

Vocabulary start points vary by age. Children aged 6 to 7 start with the picture items (i.e., Item 1). Children aged 8 to 11 start with the

Table 2.8   Comparison of WISC–IV and WISC–V Similarities Administration

WISC–IV	WISC–V
Start points:	Start points:
Ages 6–8: Sample Item, then Item 1	Ages 6–7: Sample Item, then Item 1
Ages 9–11: Sample Item, then Item 3	Ages 8–11: Sample Item, then Item 5
Ages 12–16: Sample Item, then Item 5	Ages 12–16: Sample Item, then Item 8
Discontinue after 5 consecutive scores of 0.	Discontinue after 3 consecutive scores of 0.
23 test items	23 test items: 8 new, 7 retained, and 8 modified. Retained and modified items have revised scoring criteria and sample responses
	1 new sample item

verbal items (i.e., Item 5), and children aged 12 to 16 start with Item 9. If a child aged 8 to 11 does not obtain a perfect score on *either* of the first two items administered, open the stimulus book and give the preceding picture items in reverse sequence until two consecutive perfect scores are obtained. If a child aged 12 to 16 does not obtain a perfect score on *either* of the first two items administered, give the preceding verbal items (and picture items if necessary) in reverse sequence until two consecutive perfect scores are obtained.

The discontinue rule is 3 consecutive scores of 0. Carefully monitor item scores to prevent discontinuing too early. If you are unsure about a child's score on one of the items that may count toward the 3 consecutive scores of 0, administer more items until you know that a proper discontinue has been reached.

Items 1, 5, 6, 9, and 10 are teaching items. The teaching items correspond with the age-appropriate start points. As with Similarities, teaching items involve giving corrective feedback if the child does not receive a perfect score, even if the teaching item is not one of the first items administered to a particular child.

You may repeat items as often as necessary. Do not use a synonym or attempt to explain anything about the word. If multiple pronunciation options exist for a word, pronounce the word using the local pronunciation or the one you believe is most familiar to the child. Do not spell a word, either in an attempt to clarify or in response to a request from the child.

Ensure you are familiar with the sample responses for picture items before administration begins. During picture item administration, four general response situations can arise in which the child's response is not incorrect but fails to provide the common name of the pictured object. You should give these verbatim queries, which are listed in the *WISC–V Administration and Scoring Manual*, as often as necessary. A hypothetical item with a depicted "moon" is used for the sake of illustration. For a marginal but appropriate response (e.g., the child responds "planet"), the examiner would agree but ask the child what the picture is called. The same verbatim query is given if the child provides an appropriate function, such as responding "it shines," or uses appropriate hand gestures, such as holding up his or her hands and pantomiming holding up a spherical object. If a child gives an appropriate but too general response (e.g., the child responds "a thing in outer space"), ask him or her to clarify the response by asking what kind.

Before administering the verbal items, you should also become familiar with their sample responses and the general scoring principles. Both the sample responses and the general scoring principles are used to determine item scores. Read the section on "Using Sample Responses, General Scoring Principles, and General Concepts" in Chapter 3 of this book for more information.

It is important to note that research has demonstrated examiners are prone to more frequent scoring errors on Vocabulary protocols of children in the extremely low and superior

Table 2.9 Comparison of WISC–IV and WISC–V Vocabulary Administration

WISC–IV	WISC–V
Start points:	Start points:
Ages 6–7: Item 5	Ages 6–7: Item 1
Ages 8 to 11: Item 7	Ages 8 to 11: Item 5
Ages 12 to 16: Item 9	Ages 12 to 16: Item 9
Discontinue after 5 consecutive scores of 0.	Discontinue after 3 consecutive scores of 0.
4 picture items	4 picture items: 2 new, 2 retained
32 verbal items	25 verbal items: 12 new, 13 retained with revised scoring criteria and sample responses
36 total test items	29 total test items

ranges of the IQ distribution (Erdodi, Richard, & Hopwood, 2009). Pay special attention to ensure that you query properly and obtain adequate information about each item so that the scores can be properly computed, particularly if the child has very high or very low cognitive ability.

Table 2.9 provides a comparison of Vocabulary administration procedures across the WISC–IV and WISC–V. The Remember box lists behavioral observations that the examiner should note during administration.

Remember

Behavioral Observations for Vocabulary

Note if the child:

• Requires repeated use of the specific query on the picture items to encourage him or her to provide the name of the object rather than describe its function

(Continued)

(Continued)

or to clarify marginal responses. This pattern suggests word-retrieval difficulties or poor object recognition.

- Responds more readily to the picture items, which require only 1-word verbal responses, then has more difficulty with Items 5 and 6, which require more lengthy verbal responses (for younger children or children who begin with Item 1).
- Appears to benefit from the feedback provided on teaching items, giving correct responses after learning the task.
- Provides complete definitions or must be repeatedly queried as a cue to give all pertinent information.
- Provides additional information about responses upon query or tends to say he or she does not know any more.
- Continues to provide complete answers throughout the subtest, or if responses become briefer or vaguer as the subtest progresses.
- Seems to not know answers to items that might be more closely related to cultural opportunities and educational background (e.g., Items 10, 14, 17, and 25). Utilize this information in interpretation.

Information

The child answers verbally presented questions about a general-knowledge topic. Necessary materials include the *WISC–V Administration and Scoring Manual* and the Record Form.

Information start points vary by age, as follows. Children aged 6 to 8 start with Item 1, and children aged 9 to 16 start with Item 8. If a child aged 9 to 16 does not obtain a perfect score on **either** of the first two items administered, give the preceding items in reverse sequence until two consecutive perfect scores are obtained.

The discontinue rule is 3 consecutive scores of 0. Be cautious not to discontinue too early. If you are unsure about a child's score on one of

the items that may count toward the discontinue criterion, proceed by administering more items until you are confident a proper discontinue has been reached.

Items 1, 2, 8, and 9 are teaching items. The teaching items correspond with the age-appropriate start points. For teaching items, corrective feedback is given if the child does not receive a perfect score, even if the item in question is not one of the first items administered to a particular child.

You may repeat items as often as necessary, but do not reword the item. You may readminister items to which a child responded "I don't know" if later item performance on the subtest indicates correct responses to those items might be possible. If multiple pronunciation options exist for a word within an item, pronounce the word using the local pronunciation or the pronunciation you believe is most familiar to the child.

Before administering the items, become familiar with the sample responses, which are organized to facilitate accurate and quick scoring. Also, read the section on "Using Sample Responses, General Scoring Principles, and General Concepts" in Chapter 3 of this book. Clarify contradictory verbal and nonverbal responses (e.g., the child says "Four" but holds up three fingers) by asking the child which one he or she means.

Table 2.10 provides a comparison of Information administration procedures across the WISC–IV and WISC–V. The Remember box lists behavioral observations that the examiner should note during administration.

Remember

Behavioral Observations for Information

Note if the child

- Responds more readily to Items 1, 2, 4, and 5, which require only nonverbal responses, and has more difficulty with items that require a verbal response.

- Appears to benefit from the feedback provided on teaching items, giving correct responses after learning the task.
- Provides complete responses or must be repeatedly queried as a cue to give all pertinent information about the response.
- Provides additional information about responses upon query or tends to say he or she does not know any more.
- Continues to provide complete answers throughout the subtest, or if responses become briefer or vaguer as the subtest progresses.
- Provides multiple correct answers for items where this is appropriate (e.g., Items 3, 6, 8, 10, 11, 12, 15, 16, 19, 24, 25, 26, 28), versus only the single requisite answer.
- Does not know answers to items that might be more closely related to cultural opportunities, geographical location, and educational background (e.g., Items 4, 6, 8, 10, 11, 12, 14, 16, 18, 19, 20, 21, 22, 23, 24, 25, 26, 27, 29, 28, 30, 31). Utilize this information in interpretation.
- Demonstrates developing verbal reasoning abilities and prerequisite knowledge acquisition across Similarities and Information. First, examine the child's responses to Information items that provide a superordinate category and request an example(s) (especially Items 3, 8, 10, 11, and 14). Compare those responses to the child's responses on Similarities items where he or she must describe the superordinate category when provided two examples of the category.

Comprehension

The child is required to respond to questions about general principles and social situations. Necessary materials include the *WISC–V*

Table 2.10   Comparison of WISC–IV and WISC–V Information Administration

WISC–IV	WISC–V
Start points:	Start points:
Ages 6–8: Item 5	Ages 6–8: Sample Item, then Item 1
Ages 9–11: Item 10	Ages 9–16: Sample Item, then Item 8
Ages 12–16: Item 12	
Discontinue after 5 consecutive scores of 0.	Discontinue after 3 consecutive scores of 0.
33 items	31 items: 19 new, 8 retained with little or no change in wording, and 4 modified; revised scoring criteria and sample responses for all retained and modified items

Administration and Scoring Manual and the Record Form.

Comprehension start points vary by age. Children aged 6 to 11 start with Item 1. Children aged 12 to 16 start with Item 3. If a child aged 12 to 16 does not obtain a perfect score on **either** of the first two items administered, give the preceding items in reverse sequence until two consecutive perfect scores are obtained.

The discontinue rule is 3 consecutive scores of 0. Carefully monitor item scores to prevent discontinuing too early. If you are not sure of a child's score on one of the items that may count toward the 3 consecutive scores of 0, administer more items until you know that a proper discontinue has been reached.

Items 1 to 4 are teaching items. The teaching items correspond with the age-appropriate start points. As with the other Verbal Comprehension subtests, teaching items involve giving corrective feedback if the child does not receive a perfect score, even if the teaching item is not one of the first items administered to a particular child.

You may repeat items as often as necessary. Do not reword items or expand upon them in any way. If multiple pronunciation options exist for a word, pronounce the word using the local pronunciation or the pronunciation you believe is most familiar to the child.

Before administering the subtest, become familiar with the sample responses and the general concepts. Both the sample responses and the general concepts are used to determine item scores, so try to become familiar with the general concepts prior to administration as well.

The general concepts provide the major theme associated with responses that receive credit. Either one or two multiple concepts govern each item. For items with two general concepts (i.e., Items 5, 7, and 18), 2 points are not awarded unless the response describes both general concepts. If the initial response is incorrect, it is not queried unless indicated in the sample responses (i.e., designated with a **Q**). If the child supplies a response that refers to only one of the two general concepts for these items, rephrase the item as specified in the *WISC–V Administration and Scoring Manual* to allow the child to supply a response that describes the other general concept. If the second response refers to the same general concept as did the first, do not query a second time. Review the section on "Using Sample Responses, General Scoring Principles, and General Concepts" in Chapter 3 of this book for more information.

Three items (i.e., Items 11, 15, and 19) involve sayings and proverbs from other cultures that have long fallen out of use in their culture of origin and were adapted for the WISC–V. Concrete responses are regarded as incorrect, with more abstract proverb interpretations receiving increasingly more credit. Although some believe these items represent a different ability than the other types of items on Comprehension, they require familiarity with general principles and social situations and correlate highly with the remaining items on the subtest.

Table 2.11 provides a comparison of Comprehension administration procedures across the WISC–IV and WISC–V. The Remember box lists behavioral observations that the examiner should note during administration.

Table 2.11 Comparison of WISC–IV and WISC–V Comprehension Administration

WISC–IV	WISC–V
Start points:	Start points:
Ages 6–8: Item 1	Ages 6–11: Item 1
Ages 9–11: Item 3	Ages 12–16: Item 3
Ages 12–16: Item 5	
Discontinue after 4 consecutive scores of 0.	Discontinue after 3 consecutive scores of 0.
21 items	19 items: 13 new, 2 modified, and 4 retained; all modified and retained items have revised scoring criteria and sample responses

Remember

Behavioral Observations for Comprehension

Note if the child:

- Appears to benefit from the feedback provided on teaching items, giving correct responses after learning the task.
- Provides complete responses for verbal items or must be repeatedly queried as a cue to give all pertinent information.
- Provides responses that address both of the general concepts for Items 5, 7, and 18 without requiring additional query; in contrast to giving responses that address only one general concept, then requiring query before giving a second response that addresses the second general concept. Note if the child learns from initial requests to provide more complete information for these items.
- Provides additional information about responses to verbal items upon query or

tends to say he or she does not know any more.

- Continues to provide complete answers throughout the subtest, or if responses become briefer or vaguer as the subtest progresses.

Visual Spatial Subtests

Block Design

For easier items, the examiner constructs designs that match pictures and then provides blocks for the child to attempt building the same model. More difficult items require the child to use only the picture in the stimulus book when constructing the block design. Necessary materials include the *WISC–V Administration and Scoring Manual*, the Record Form, Stimulus Book 1, the Block Design blocks, and a stopwatch.

Block Design start points vary by age, as follows. Children aged 6 to 7 start with Item 1, and children aged 8 to 16 start with Item 3. If a child aged 8 to 16 does not obtain a perfect score on *either* of the first two items administered, give the preceding items in reverse sequence until two consecutive perfect scores are obtained.

The discontinue rule is 2 consecutive scores of 0. Items 1 to 3 require administration of a second trial if the child does not receive a perfect score on the first trial. These items are the age-appropriate start point items for children aged 6 to 7 (Item 1) and children aged 8 to 16 (Item 3), and the second item for children aged 6 to 7 (Item 2).

Proper Block Design administration requires attention to a number of details. If the child attempts to match all sides of his or her construction to your model, tell the child only the tops need to match. Although you may repeat verbal directions, do not reconstruct your model if it has been disassembled or reexpose stimulus pages of test items that are complete. If the child begins to build his or her construction on top of the stimulus book, point to the correct area specified in

Table 2.12 Comparison of WISC–IV and WISC–V Block Design Administration

WISC–IV	WISC–V
Start points:	Start points:
Ages 6–7: Item 1	Ages 6–7: Item 1
Ages 8–16: Item 3	Ages 8–16: Item 3
Discontinue after 3 consecutive scores of 0.	Discontinue after 2 consecutive scores of 0.
14 test items	13 test items: 8 new and 5 retained

the diagram in the *WISC–V Administration and Scoring Manual* and instruct the child to make it there. Correct only the first rotation error; however, do not award credit for that item.

Be sure to accurately record completion times. The completion times are needed to determine if the response was given within the time limit for all items and to determine if time-bonus points are awarded for Items 10 to 13.

Table 2.12 provides a comparison of Block Design administration procedures across the WISC–IV and WISC–V. The Remember box lists behavioral observations that the examiner should note during administration.

> **Remember**
>
> *Behavioral Observations for Block Design*
>
> **Note if the child:**
>
> - Initially approaches the items by studying the model or picture or immediately begins working with the blocks.
> - Reliably sets an initial anchor block (e.g., always works on the lower right corner first), then builds from it.
> - Learns from trial and error on early items or approaches every item haphazardly.
>
> *(Continued)*

(Continued)

- Finishes items relatively quickly or slowly, frequently and repeatedly studies the stimuli to confirm the construction, or rarely glances at the model or picture then checks after the construction to confirm. These observations can be informative about visual memory as well.
- Displays motor movements and skills that appear clumsy or skilled and smooth.
- Displays signs of nervousness or agitation, such as trembling or shaking hands or clutching the blocks tightly.
- Commits a break-in-configuration error at any time, or seems to understand that items are constrained within a predictable structural matrix. A break-in-configuration error occurs when the maximum dimension of the design is exceeded while assembling a construction. For example, if the child aligns 3 blocks in a row while constructing a 2×2 design, a break-in-configuration error has occurred.
- Commits an uncorrected rotation error (i.e., the construction remains rotated upon completion).
- Performs better on items with model and pictorial stimuli as compared to items with pictorial stimuli only.
- During Items 1 to 3, which use the model and the pictorial stimuli, displays a preference to use the model or picture as a guide.
- Is overly concerned about gaps between the blocks or about aligning the design perfectly with the edge of the table or stimulus book.
- Attempts to rotate the stimulus book or model or to change perspective on the stimulus by standing or twisting his or her head.
- Appears to recognize incorrect constructions upon comparison with the stimuli, and attempts to correct them.

Visual Puzzles

The child views a puzzle and selects from among six response options the three that can be combined to recreate the puzzle within a time limit. Necessary materials include the *WISC–V Administration and Scoring Manual*, the Record Form, Stimulus Book 1, and a stopwatch.

Visual Puzzles start points vary by age. Children aged 6 to 8 start with Item 1. Children aged 9 to 11 start with Item 5; and children aged 12 to 16 start with Item 8. If a child aged 9 to 16 does not obtain a perfect score on *either* of the first two test items administered, give the preceding items in reverse sequence until two consecutive perfect scores are obtained. The discontinue rule is 3 consecutive scores of 0.

Administer the demonstration and sample items to all children, regardless of their age. Ensure you provide both the verbal and the gestured instructions as described. If the child appears confused, you may use the demonstration and the sample item to clarify that the pieces need to fit next to each other and should not be stacked on top of one another to create the puzzle.

You may repeat item instructions as often as necessary. You may also readminister items to which a child responded "I don't know" if later item performance on the subtest indicates correct responses to those items might be possible.

The child must indicate response choices by pointing to or saying the number of the selections. If the child responds by naming a pictured option or with any other verbal response, ask the child to show you his or her selections.

Although the child must provide a response with exactly three selections, they need not be provided in numerical order. If the child asks, you can clarify this point by telling him or her that the responses don't have to be chosen in order. If the child indicates fewer or more than three selections, provide the appropriate prompts until he or she selects exactly three choices.

If a child indicates a piece is rotated in the wrong direction for a given puzzle, explain to the child that he or she might have to mentally rotate a piece for it to fit, using the appropriate prompt from the manual.

Timing is an essential part of subtest administration, because responses are counted as correct only if they are provided within the time limit. The time limit for each item is 30 seconds. Start timing immediately after you complete the instructions for an item. Do not pause or stop timing to provide necessary prompts. If the child has not indicated a response after 20 seconds, ask if he or she has an answer. Stop timing when the child has indicated three selections or that he or she doesn't know the answer.

Be sure to accurately record completion times, which are used to determine if the response was given within the time limit and is therefore creditable. The child must indicate all three selections before the time limit expires, or the response is incomplete.

The Remember box lists behavioral observations that the examiner should note during administration.

> ## Remember
>
> ### Behavioral Observations for Visual Puzzles
>
> #### Note if the child:
>
> - Initially approaches the items by studying the pieces or immediately begins attempting to solve the puzzle with them.
> - Asks if a piece can be flipped, indicating creativity but perhaps also faulty assumption that the back side of a piece mirrors the same color and/or pattern as appears on the faceup side.
> - Selects responses impulsively, based on color or shape, but misses other important features that make the response incorrect.
> - Frequently self-corrects on items initially responded to correctly. This pattern of responding may indicate nervousness or anxiety.
> - Finishes items relatively quickly or slowly. Note if the child frequently and repeatedly studies the pieces and complete picture at the top of the page to confirm an answer or rarely glances at the complete picture then checks after selecting responses to confirm. These observations can be informative about visual memory.
> - Gives up easily on more difficult items or persists in studying them and appears determined to respond correctly.

Fluid Reasoning Subtests

Matrix Reasoning

The child selects among visually presented response options the one which best completes a matrix or a series. Necessary materials include the *WISC–V Administration and Scoring Manual*, the Record Form, and Stimulus Book 1.

Matrix Reasoning start points vary by age. Children aged 6 to 8 start with Sample Items A and B, then Item 1. Children aged 9 to 11 start with Sample Items A and B, then Item 5. Children aged 12 to 16 start with Sample Items A and B, then Item 9. If a child aged 9 to 16 does not obtain a perfect score on *either* of the first two test items administered, give the preceding items in reverse sequence until two consecutive perfect scores are obtained. The discontinue rule is 3 consecutive scores of 0.

Administer the sample items to all children regardless of their age. Ensure you provide both the verbal and the gestured instructions as described.

You may repeat item instructions as often as necessary. You may also readminister the previous item if a child responded "I don't know" and responded correctly to the next item, thus indicating correct responses to the prior item might be possible. The child must indicate a response option by pointing to or saying the number of the selection. If the child responds by naming

Table 2.13 Comparison of WISC–IV and WISC–V Matrix Reasoning Administration

WISC–IV	WISC–V
Start points:	Start points:
Ages 6–8: Samples A–C, then Item 4	Ages 6–8: Samples A–C, then Item 1
Age 9–11: Samples A–C, then Item 7	Age 9–11: Samples A–C, then Item 5
Ages 12–16: Samples A–C, then Item 11	Ages 12–16: Samples A–C, then Item 9
Discontinue after 4 consecutive scores or 4 scores of 0 on 5 consecutive items.	Discontinue after 3 consecutive scores of 0.
3 sample items	2 sample items, both new
35 test items	32 test items: 20 new, 12 retained with a number of modifications to color and/or item content

a pictured option or with any other verbal response, ask the child to show you his or her selection.

Table 2.13 provides a comparison of Matrix Reasoning administration procedures across the WISC–IV and WISC–V. The Remember box lists behavioral observations that the examiner should note during administration.

Remember

Behavioral Observations for Matrix Reasoning

Note if the child:

- Initially approaches the items by studying the matrix or series or immediately begins searching the response options and comparing with the matrix or series.
- Selects response impulsively, based on color or shape, but misses other

important features that make the response incorrect.
- Frequently self-corrects on items initially responded to correctly. This pattern of responding may indicate nervousness or anxiety.
- Finishes items relatively quickly or slowly. Note if the child frequently and repeatedly studies the matrix or series to confirm an answer or rarely glances at the matrix or series then checks after selecting a response to confirm. These observations can be informative about visual memory.
- Gives up easily on more difficult items or persists in studying them and appears determined to understand the item and respond correctly.
- Shows different performance and response times on the matrix items than on the series items. Both item types require the child to track a greater number of rules as the subtest progresses. However, the series items provide multiple examples of the rules in play, whereas the matrix items provide fewer examples of correct answers or the rules followed across the dimensions. Preference for the series items may indicate a greater comfort with increasing confirmation of hypotheses or anxiety. Preference for the matrix items may indicate efficient reasoning ability or a preference for fewer examples in problem solving and tasks.

Figure Weights

The child selects among visually presented response options the one which keeps a scale with missing weight(s) balanced. Necessary materials include the *WISC–V Administration and Scoring Manual*, the Record Form, Stimulus Book 1, and a stopwatch.

Figure Weights start points vary by age. Children aged 6 to 8 start with Sample Item A, then Item 1. Children aged 9 to 16 start with Sample Item B, then Item 4. If a child aged 9 to 16 does not obtain a perfect score on *either* of the first two test items administered, give the preceding items in reverse sequence until two consecutive perfect scores are obtained. Do not administer Sample Item A in this situation. Be sure to administer Sample Item B before Item 4 to children aged 6 to 8 who do not discontinue after Item 3. Ensure you provide both the verbal and the gestured instructions as described. The discontinue rule is 3 consecutive scores of 0.

Timing is an essential part of subtest administration, because responses are counted as correct only if they are provided within the time limit. The time limit is 20 seconds for Items 1 to 18 and 30 seconds for Items 19 to 34. Start timing immediately after you complete the instructions for an item. Do not pause or stop timing to provide necessary prompts. If the child has not indicated a response when 10 seconds remain within the time limit, ask if he or she has an answer. Stop timing when the child has indicated a response or that he or she doesn't know the answer.

You may repeat item instructions as often as necessary. Because there is a time limit on all items, do not readminister or reexpose items to which the child responds incorrectly, even if the child responds correctly to later items.

Do not provide a pencil or paper to the child during item administration. The child may write on the testing surface with his or her finger, but do not prompt the child to do so.

Be sure to accurately record completion times, which are used to determine if the response was given within the time limit and is therefore creditable. The child must indicate all three selections before the time limit expires, or the response is incomplete.

The child must indicate a response option by pointing to or saying the number of the selection. If the child responds by naming a pictured option or with any other verbal response, ask the child to show you his or her selection.

Before you administer Item 27, remember to give the required verbal instruction to introduce the three-scale items. The Record Form and the *WISC–V Administration and Scoring Manual* identify this item with a double asterisk (**). It is helpful to highlight the prompt in your manual to assist you with remembering to provide the required instruction.

The Remember box lists behavioral observations that the examiner should note during administration.

Remember

Behavioral Observations for Figure Weights

Note if the child:

- Initially approaches the items by studying the scales or immediately begins searching the response options and comparing with the final scale.
- Selects response impulsively, based on color or shape, but misses other important features that make the response incorrect.
- Frequently self-corrects on items initially responded to correctly. This pattern of responding may indicate nervousness or anxiety.
- Finishes items relatively quickly or slowly. Note if the child frequently and repeatedly studies the scales to confirm an answer or rarely glances at the scales then checks after selecting a response to confirm. These observations can be informative about visual memory.
- Gives up easily on more difficult items or persists in studying them and appears determined to understand the item and respond correctly.

Note that:

- The items progress in difficulty and cognitive requirements across the subtest.

(Continued)

(Continued)

The point at which the child begins to respond incorrectly can provide insight into the developmental level of the child's reasoning abilities.

- Items 1 to 4 consist of items that require simple matching of the shapes on the scale with the correct response within the response options.
- Items 5 to 8 require the child only to match the shapes on the second scale with the correct response within the response options while ignoring the first scale.
- Items 9 to 12 require simple substitution in position relative to the first scale, where the shapes swap sides and the child must locate the shapes that were swapped and appear in a response option.
- Item 13 requires the child, for the first time in the subtest, to understand that an established relationship between different quantities of shapes applies in a new example.
- Items 14 to 19 and 21 to 23 require simple multiplication and division and application of basic algebraic principles and rudimentary understanding of the concept of a variable.
- Item 20 is similar to Items 5 to 8 but requires an understanding that the shapes, when rearranged, still represent the correct response. Item 14 also may require an understanding of conservation.
- Items 24 to 34 represent more complex polynomials and slightly more advanced understanding of algebraic principles.

Picture Concepts

The child is required to form a group with a shared element by selecting one picture from each of either two or three rows. Necessary materials include the *WISC–V Administration and Scoring Manual*, the Record Form, and Stimulus Book 2.

Picture Concepts start points vary by age. Children aged 6 to 8 start with Sample Items A and B, then Item 1. Children aged 9 to 11 start with Sample Items A and B, then Item 4; and children aged 12 to 16 start with Sample Items A and B, then Item 7. If a child aged 9 to 16 does not obtain a perfect score on *either* of the first two test items administered, give the preceding items in reverse sequence until two consecutive perfect scores are obtained. The discontinue rule is 3 consecutive scores of 0.

You may repeat item instructions as often as necessary. You may also readminister items to which a child responded "I don't know" if later item performance on the subtest indicates correct responses to those items might be possible. The child must indicate response options by pointing to or saying the number of the selections. If the child responds by naming a pictured option or with any other verbal response, ask the child to show you his or her selections.

Table 2.14 provides a comparison of Picture Concepts administration procedures across the

Table 2.14 Comparison of WISC–IV and WISC–V Picture Concepts Administration

WISC–IV	WISC–V
Start points:	Start points:
Ages 6–8: Samples A & B, then Item 1	Ages 6–8: Sample Items A & B, then Item 1
Ages 9–11: Samples A & B, then Item 5	Ages 9–11: Sample Items A & B, then Item 4
Ages 12–16: Sample Items A & B, then Item 7	Ages 12–16: Sample Items A & B, then Item 7
Discontinue after 5 consecutive scores of 0.	Discontinue after 3 consecutive scores of 0.
Two sample items	Two retained sample items with slight modifications
28 test items	27 test items: 7 new, 16 revised substantively, and 4 retained

WISC–IV and WISC–V. The Remember box lists behavioral observations that the examiner should note during administration.

Remember

Behavioral Observations for Picture Concepts

Note if the child:

- Frequently requests the names of objects.
- Selects responses impulsively but misses other important features that make the responses incorrect.
- Repeatedly selects options from a single row and does not appear to respond to the corrective feedback to choose one from each row.
- Frequently self-corrects on items initially responded to correctly. This pattern of responding may indicate nervousness or anxiety.
- Finishes items relatively quickly or slowly, frequently and repeatedly studies all options to confirm an answer, or glances at the rows initially then rechecks them after selecting a response to confirm.
- Gives up easily on more difficult items or persists in studying them and appears determined to understand the item and respond correctly.

To gain further understanding about the child's reasoning ability:

- Compare performance on Picture Concepts and Similarities. This comparison can provide clues about the child's reasoning ability when different stimulus modalities and response formats are employed.
- Consider returning to items with incorrect responses after all subtests have been administered, and query the child about the rationale for his or her selection by asking "Why do they go together?" This procedure permits observations about the sophistication of the child's reasoning ability. Frequently, responses of young children or children with low cognitive ability indicate that options on difficult items are related merely by color or location (e.g., "They are both red," or "They both can be outside.")

Behind the Scenes

- During research phases, examiners intentionally tested the limits of the child's performance to assist with item development by asking for the child's rationale for responses to administered items with scores of 0.
- This method also can be used following a standard administration of the test battery to determine if responses scored 0 were guesses or if the child had a logical but uncreditable reason for the selections.

Arithmetic

Arithmetic problems are read aloud, and the child is required to solve them mentally and provide a response. Necessary materials include the *WISC–V Administration and Scoring Manual*, the Record Form, Stimulus Book 2, and a stopwatch.

Arithmetic start points vary by age. Children aged 6 to 7 start with Item 3. Children aged 8 to 9 start with Item 8; and children aged 10 to 16 start with Item 11. If a child aged 8 to 16 does not obtain a perfect score on *either* of the first two test items administered, give the preceding items in reverse sequence until two consecutive perfect scores are obtained. The discontinue rule is 3 consecutive scores of 0.

For picture items, visual stimuli are presented using the stimulus book. In addition to reading the items, you must point to the visual stimuli as specified. For verbal items, the items are read aloud from the *WISC–V Administration and Scoring Manual*.

Items 1, 2, and 3 are teaching items. The teaching items correspond with the first three picture items. As with all teaching items, they involve giving corrective feedback if the child does not receive a perfect score, even if the teaching item is not one of the first items administered to a particular child.

In contrast to previous editions of this subtest, explicit instruction is now given to all children about repetition. You may not repeat Items 1 to 19. If the child asks for a repetition of any of these items, tell the child you cannot say them again. Before administering Item 20, remember to give the child instruction that he or she may now ask for one repetition. You may repeat Items 20 to 34 *one time only* at the child's request. Repeat the entire item, do not change the wording in any way, and pause timing for the repetition. Immediately start timing again after you have said the last word of the repeated item. Item 31 contains the subtest's only specific query for a given response. Do not stop timing to provide this query.

Table 2.15 provides a comparison of Arithmetic administration procedures across the WISC–IV and WISC–V. The Remember box lists behavioral observations that the examiner should note during administration.

> ### Remember
>
> *Behavioral Observations for Arithmetic*
>
> **Note if the child:**
>
> - Frequently requests repetition of Items 20 to 34.
> - Draws on the table with a finger when solving the mental arithmetic problems.
> - Reasons aloud or silently.
> - Finishes items relatively quickly or slowly.
> - Methodically rechecks his or her response to confirm.

> - Gives up easily on more difficult items or persists in attempting them and appears determined to respond correctly.

Consider returning to items with incorrect responses after all subtests have been administered, rereading them and showing the child a printed version of the problem. Next, readminister items that are still not answered correctly using the same procedures, but provide a paper and pencil with which to work. If the child still does not respond correctly, write the arithmetic calculation on the paper and see if he or she can respond correctly. This procedure will permit observations about the reasons behind the incorrect response and can inform intervention. Consider administering Arithmetic Process Approach and Written Arithmetic from the WISC–V Integrated. These are normed subtests that utilize the procedures described to permit these observations and provide scores relative to those of other children.

Table 2.15   Comparison of WISC–IV and WISC–V Arithmetic Administration

WISC–IV	WISC–V
Start points:	Start points:
Ages 6–7: Item 3	Ages 6–7: Item 3
Ages 8–9: Item 9	Ages 8–9: Item 8
Ages 10–16: Item 12	Ages 10–16: Item 11
Discontinue after 4 consecutive scores of 0.	Discontinue after 3 consecutive scores of 0.
34 test items	34 test items: 10 new, 6 unchanged, and 18 revised substantively but with the same numerical calculations as WISC–IV items
Repetition permitted on all items one time only	Repetition not permitted on Items 1–19 and permitted on Items 20–34 one time only

Working Memory Subtests

Digit Span
The examiner reads a sequence of digits, then the child recalls the digits in the same (Forward), backward (Backward), or ascending (Sequencing) order. Necessary materials include the *WISC–V Administration and Scoring Manual* and the Record Form.

Digit Span Forward and Digit Span Backward have a single start point for children aged 6 to 16: Digit Span Forward begins with Item 1, and Digit Span Backward begins with the sample item, then Item 1. Digit Span Sequencing start points differ by age: Children aged 6 to 7 begin with the qualifying item, Sample Items A and B, then Item 1; however, children aged 8 to 16 start with Sample Items A and B, then Item 1.

Administer all three tasks (Forward, Backward, and Sequencing) regardless of the child's performance on any preceding tasks. All test items have two trials. However, the trials do not operate as do the multiple-trial items on Block Design: That is, you must administer both trials of each item. The second trial must be administered regardless of the child's performance on the first trial, because the trials are not of equal difficulty. Discontinue Forward only after the child obtains a score of 0 on both trials of a Forward item. Discontinue Backward only after the child obtains a score of 0 on both trials of a Backward item.

For children aged 6 to 7, discontinue Sequencing only after the child responds incorrectly to the Qualifying item *or* obtains a score of 0 on both trials of an item. For children aged 8 to 16, discontinue Sequencing only after the child obtains a score of 0 on both trials of an item.

Do not discontinue Backward or Sequencing based on the child's sample item performance alone. Administer Item 1 regardless of sample item performance on these tasks.

You should practice reading the trials before you administer Digit Span. One of the most common examiner errors is reading the trials too quickly. Read one digit per second, and slightly

drop your voice inflection on the last digit of each trial.

On Digit Span Backward and Digit Span Sequencing, be very cautious not to read the digits out of the correct response column inadvertently. This is an easy mistake to make, because the correct response column is directly to the right of the actual trials on both tasks.

At times, children begin to respond before a trial is completely presented (i.e., while you are still reading more digits). If this occurs, you should not pause: Continue reading the sequence, let the child respond, assign the proper score to the trial. Then give the prompt to inform the child to wait until you have stopped before responding.

For Sequencing, a digit may be included in a trial more than once. If a child notices this and asks if a digit should be repeated more than one time, give the appropriate prompt to indicate that the correct response might need to include repeated digits.

You may repeat item instructions as often as necessary. However, do *not* readminister trials under any circumstances. If the child asks for you to repeat any trial, give the prompt that informs the child that a trial can be read only once.

Table 2.16 provides a comparison of Digit Span administration procedures across the WISC–IV and WISC–V. The Remember box lists behavioral observations that the examiner should note during administration.

> **Remember**
> *Behavioral Observations for Digit Span*
>
> **Note if the child:**
>
> • Attempts to use a problem-solving strategy such as "chunking" from the beginning of the task, or as he or she progresses through the task.
>
> *(Continued)*

(Continued)

- Responds incorrectly due to transposing numbers or by completely forgetting them.
- Shows lapses in attention or anxiety that negatively impact his or her score.
- Shows any difficulty hearing the stimuli being read aloud.
- Repeats digits rapidly or before the stimuli has been read completely. Both behaviors may be indicators of impulsivity.
- Shows a pattern of failing the first trial of a given span length and then correctly responding to the second trial, which may indicate learning or a warm-up effect. If this occurs, consider interpreting the Longest Span scores for this subtest.
- Easily learns the Digit Span Forward task but has more difficulty with the Digit Span Backward and/or Digit Span Sequencing tasks, which are more cognitively complex and require resequencing of the stimuli to provide a response.

Picture Span

The child is shown stimulus picture(s) in the stimulus book and then selects (preferably in the sequential order presented) the stimulus picture(s) from a number of response options on a page. Necessary materials include the *WISC–V Administration and Scoring Manual*, the Record Form, Stimulus Book 2, and a stopwatch.

Picture Span has a single age-based start point. Children aged 6 to 16 start with items that require recognition of multiple pictures: Sample Items B and C, then Item 4. Sample Item A and Items 1 to 3 are administered to children who may have an intellectual disability or low cognitive ability. These items require recognition of a single picture. Sample Item A introduces the task of remembering the single picture and selecting it from among the array of response options. Sample Items B and C introduce the child to

Table 2.16   Comparison of WISC–IV and WISC–V Digit Span Administration

WISC–IV	WISC–V
Start points:	Start points:
Forward: Item 1	Forward: Item 1
Backward: Sample Item, then Item 1	Backward: Sample Item, then Item 1
	Sequencing:
	Ages 6–7: Qualifying Item, Sample Items A & B, then Item 1
	Ages 8–16: Sample Items A & B, then Item 1
Forward: Discontinue after scores of 0 on both trials of an item.	Forward: Discontinue after scores of 0 on both trials of an item.
Backward: Discontinue after scores of 0 on both trials of an item.	Backward: Discontinue after scores of 0 on both trials of an item.
	Sequencing:
	Ages 6–7: Discontinue after incorrect response to the Qualifying Item or after scores of 0 on both trials of an item.
	Ages 8–16: Discontinue after scores of 0 on both trials of an item.
Backward: 1 sample item	Backward: 1 sample item
	Sequencing: 2 sample items
Forward: 8 test items	Forward: 9 test items
Backward: 8 test items	Backward: 9 test items
	Sequencing: 9 test items
Total test items: 16	Total test items: 27

the task of remembering and selecting multiple pictures in the order they were presented.

If a child aged 6 to 16 does not start with Item 1 and does not obtain a perfect score on *either* of the first two test items administered, give the preceding items in reverse sequence until two consecutive perfect scores are obtained. Do not administer Sample Item A in this situation. The discontinue rule is 3 consecutive scores of 0.

Exposure of the stimulus pages is timed. For items that require recognition of a single picture (i.e., Sample Item A to Item 3), the stimulus page should be exposed for only 3 seconds. For items that require recognition of multiple pictures (i.e., Sample Items B and C and Item 4 to 26), the stimulus page is exposed for 5 seconds. You must use a stopwatch to ensure accurate exposure time. Do *not* shorten or eliminate the verbatim prompt that is given before you start the stopwatch to time the stimulus page exposure. Doing so will reduce the allotted exposure time.

You may repeat item instructions as often as necessary. However, do *not* readminister items under any circumstances. Items 1, 2, 4, and 5 are teaching items. Only reexpose stimuli as instructed for sample and teaching items to provide the prescribed corrective feedback.

Do not permit the child to turn the stimulus book pages before the exposure time expires. Provide the verbatim prompt from the manual if the child attempts to do so.

Except for the sample and teaching items, do not expose the stimulus page a second time. If the child asks to see the stimuli again, tell the child you can only show it once and encourage a guess, as specified in the general directions.

The child must indicate a response by pointing to or saying the letter(s) of the selection(s). If the child responds by naming pictured options or with any other verbal response, ask the child to show you his or her selection(s).

Watch the child as a response is given to ensure you see the entire response. It is preferable that you practice writing responses without looking at the Record Form before you administer your first WISC–V so that you will not miss any part of the child's response. Recording the response as it is given will ensure that you accurately capture the child's performance: Some items require lengthier responses than others, and portions of the response could be missed or forgotten if you do not record during the response.

If it appears the child is memorizing the pictures in reverse order, allow him or her to complete the entire response and assign the appropriate score. Then provide the appropriate prompt given in the manual to remind the child to start with the first picture.

Remember

Behavioral Observations for Picture Span

Note if the child:

- Displays wandering attention during the brief stimulus exposure time, leading to a lower score.
- Gives up easily or responds impulsively on more difficult items, or appears determined to respond correctly.
- Hesitates to respond resulting in decay of the encoded memory and increased errors. These are qualitatively different errors than those due to inattention during stimulus exposure.
- Scores 1 point on items scored 2, 1, or 0 points because he or she swaps the order of only two pictures or chooses the correct responses in the incorrect order more haphazardly.
- Frequently self-corrects on items initially responded to correctly. This pattern of responding may indicate nervousness or anxiety.
- For items with multiple responses necessary to obtain credit, neglects to choose only one or a few responses. Look for clues as to why. For example, note if the child incorrectly selected pictures of objects that are similar phonemically or in appearance to the neglected correct answer(s).
- Has incorrect responses that correctly include some of the first or last pictures in the array but omit those in the middle of the array; or if the incorrect responses include mostly incorrect objects.

(Continued)

(Continued)

- Tends to respond incorrectly to the first item of a new span length or new number of response options, then experiences later success on similar items. This is in contrast to a child who responds correctly to sets of similar items then discontinues quickly after reaching his or her maximum span length.

Note any interruptions or distractions that occur during a timed stimulus exposure. Check to see if the resulting change in raw score may have resulted in a higher subtest scaled score. For repeated interruptions, the subtest might be considered spoiled and uninterpretable.

Behind the Scenes

- Picture Span was not originally planned for inclusion in the WISC–V. However, after WPPSI–IV Picture Memory was included in a pilot phase for research purposes, the subtest's clinical utility, psychometric properties, and benefits to expanded construct coverage served to advocate for its inclusion. Most Picture Span items differ from Picture Memory because they involve sequencing, where more credit is awarded for retaining the correct responses in the correct sequence.
- The controlled reuse of stimuli throughout the task and consequent proactive interference distinguishes Picture Span from many other visual working memory measures.
- The early items of Picture Span, as with all items on Picture Memory, draw on the familiarize–recognize paradigm (Reznick, 2009) from infant working memory research to ensure that even children of very low ability can experience some success on the task. In this paradigm, children view a set of stimuli and later recognize them in response to a probe.

- Great care was taken to select objects that would fill reasonably well the dimensions of a square area allocated to each picture. This was done to prevent the child from using stimuli size to facilitate learning.

Letter–Number Sequencing

The examiner reads a sequence of numbers and letters, then the child recalls the numbers in order from lowest to highest and then the letters in alphabetical order. Necessary materials include the *WISC–V Administration and Scoring Manual* and the Record Form.

Letter–Number Sequencing start points differ by age. Children aged 6 to 7 begin with the qualifying items, Sample Item A, then Item 1. However, children aged 8 to 16 start with Sample Item A, then Item 1.

Be sure to administer the demonstration and sample items to all children. The child is first taught to sequence numbers before letters, then administration proceeds to Items 1 and 2. The child is then instructed to sequence within the sets of numbers and letters prior to Item 3.

All test items have three trials. However, as with Digit Span, the trials do not operate as do the multiple-trial items on Block Design. That is, you must administer all three trials of each item regardless of the child's performance on previous trials, because the trials are not of equal difficulty.

For children aged 6 to 7, discontinue only after the child responds incorrectly to either of the Qualifying items *or* obtains a score of 0 on all three trials of an item. For children aged 8 to 16, discontinue only after the child obtains a score of 0 on all three trials of an item. Do not discontinue merely based on the child's sample item performance. Administer Item 1 regardless of sample item performance.

You should practice reading the trials before you administer Letter–Number Sequencing. One of the most common examiner errors is reading the trials too quickly. Read one letter or number per second, and slightly drop your voice inflection on the last letter or number of each trial.

Be very cautious not to read the trial out of the correct response column inadvertently. This is an easy mistake to make, because the correct response column is directly to the right of the actual trials.

The number zero (*0*) and the letter *O* are not included in any trial as they are frequently confused. For a similar reason, the letters I and L are not included in any trial because they are frequently misread as the number 1.

At times, children begin to respond before a trial is completely presented (i.e., while you are still reading more letters or numbers). If this occurs, you should not pause: Continue reading the sequence, let the child respond, assign the proper score to the trial. Then give the prompt to inform the child to wait until you have stopped before responding.

You may repeat item instructions as often as necessary. However, do *not* readminister trials under any circumstances. If the child asks for you to repeat any trial, give the prompt that informs the child that a trial can be read only once.

Items 1 and 2 are teaching items. Corrective feedback is given if the child does not receive a perfect score.

Table 2.17 provides a comparison of Letter–Number Sequencing administration procedures across the WISC–IV and WISC–V. The Remember box lists behavioral observations that the examiner should note during administration.

Table 2.17 Comparison of WISC–IV and WISC–V Letter–Number Sequencing Administration

WISC–IV	WISC–V
Start points:	Start points:
Ages 6–7: Qualifying Items, Demonstration Item A, Sample Item, then Item 1.	Ages 6–7: Qualifying Items, Demonstration Item A, Sample Item A, then Item 1.
Ages 8–16: Demonstration Item A, Sample Item, then Item 1.	Ages 8–16: Demonstration Item A, Sample Item A, then Item 1.
Ages 6–7: After incorrect response to either Qualifying Item, or after scores of 0 on all 3 trials of an item.	Ages 6–7: After incorrect response to either Qualifying Item, or after scores of 0 on all 3 trials of an item.
Ages 8–16: After scores of 0 on all 3 trials of an item.	Ages 8–16: After scores of 0 on all 3 trials of an item.
2 qualifying items, 2 demonstration items with 1 trial apiece, and 1 sample item with 2 trials.	2 qualifying items (both retained), 2 demonstration items with 1 trial apiece (both new), and 2 sample items. Sample Item A has 1 trial, and Sample Item B has 2 trials. Two sample trials are new and 1 is retained.
10 test items with 3 trials apiece, for a total of 30 trials.	10 test items with 3 trials apiece, for a total of 30 trials; 26 trials are new and 4 are retained.

> ## Remember
>
> ### *Behavioral Observations for Letter–Number Sequencing*
>
> #### Note if the child:
>
> - Learns from errors made during the sample items.
> - Attempts to use a problem-solving strategy, such as chunking, rehearsal, or tracking numbers and letters on different hands. Note if these strategies emerge from the beginning of the task, as the child progresses through the task. If the child closes his or her eyes while the items are administered, he or she may be utilizing visualization as a strategy.
> - Responds incorrectly due to transposing numbers and letters or by completely forgetting them.
>
> *(Continued)*

(Continued)

- Responds by providing the letters before the numbers despite attempts to teach the reverse response requirement.
- Shows a pattern of forgetting only numbers or only letters more frequently. Such a pattern could indicate a greater relative comfort with the favored stimuli or stimulus overload. Forgetting letters is more typical because they must be held in memory longer and are repeated last, with more opportunity for the memory trace to decay.
- Shows lapses in attention, concentration, or anxiety that negatively impact performance, or shows any behaviors that may indicate such difficulties.
- Shows any difficulty hearing the stimuli being read aloud, or responds incorrectly by providing a response that sounds similar to a letter or number that is omitted from the final response (e.g., says B instead of D).
- Repeats digits or letters rapidly or before the stimuli has been read completely. Both behaviors may be indicators of impulsivity.
- Shows a pattern of failing the first trial and then correctly responding to the second and/or third trial of a given span length, which may indicate learning or a warm-up effect. If this occurs, consider interpreting the Longest Letter–Number Sequencing score for this subtest.

Behind the Scenes

- The WISC–IV Letter–Number Sequencing instructions attempted to teach the child simultaneously to say the numbers before the letters and to sequence the numbers and the letters. The development team and practitioners using the WISC–IV noted that because the teaching was supplied before

the child completed any trials with multiple numbers or letters children frequently disregarded the sequencing instruction and required multiple corrections on the first few trials. The WISC–V instructions are modified to include staged teaching: The child first learns to repeat numbers before letters. Immediately before test items that contain trials with multiple numbers and multiple letters, the child is instructed to sequence the numbers and the letters. Fewer prompts are required as a result.

- Letter–Number Sequencing has been re-designed so that trials do not include pairs of rhyming letters and numbers and for a more even use of numbers and letters across the subtest. This allows more qualitative observation of the reasons behind errors. A child who merely mishears a number or letter and repeats one that sounds similar demonstrates superior working memory skills relative to a child who completely forgets some or all of the numbers and letters for a given trial.

Processing Speed Subtests

Coding
Using a key, the child copies symbols that are paired with simple shapes or numbers within a time limit of 120 seconds. Necessary materials include the *WISC–V Administration and Scoring Manual*, the Record Form, Response Booklet 1, a #2 pencil without an eraser, and a stopwatch. The Coding Scoring Template is necessary for scoring.

Children aged 6 to 7 start with the Form A demonstration and sample items, then the test items. Children aged 8 to 16 start with the Form B demonstration and sample items, then the test items. Administer all demonstration and sample items as described in the *WISC–V Administration and Scoring Manual*. Practice the verbatim and gestured instructions for the subtest before administering it for the first time. Smooth administration is facilitated by committing the instructions to memory.

Do not permit the child to start early. Watch carefully during administration, because you may need to provide prompts in response to a number of situations. However, do not stop timing to give the prompts. You may need to prompt the child to wait to start until it is time if he or she begins the test items before you have said "Go." If the child attempts to complete a row from right to left rather than left to right or to skip an item, prompt the child to go in order and not to skip any as specified. If the child indicates he

or she has made a mistake and asks what to do, encourage the child to keep working.

Discontinue promptly after 120 seconds. If a child is working on an item when the time limit expires, you may allow him or her to finish that item, but do not score it (i.e., count it as correct or incorrect).

Table 2.18 provides a comparison of Coding administration procedures across the WISC–IV and WISC–V. The Remember box lists behavioral observations that the examiner should note during administration.

Table 2.18 Comparison of WISC–IV and WISC–V Coding Administration

WISC–IV	WISC–V
Start points:	Start points:
Ages 6–7: Form A Sample, then Test Items	Ages 6–7: Form A Demonstration, Sample, then Test Items
Ages 8–16: Form B Sample, then Test Items	Ages 8–16: Form B Demonstration, Sample, then Test Items
Discontinue after 120 seconds.	Discontinue after 120 seconds.
Form A: 2 demonstration (then termed "sample") and 3 sample (then termed "practice") items	Form A: 2 demonstration and 3 sample items
Form B: 2 demonstration (then termed "sample") and 5 sample (then termed "practice") items	Form B: 3 demonstration and 6 sample items
Form A: 59 test items	Form A: 75 test items
Form B: 119 test items	Form B: 117 test items
Form A: 5 shapes and symbols	Form A: 5 shapes and symbols (3 retained shapes and 2 modified; 4 new symbols and 1 retained)
Form B: 9 numbers and symbols	Form B: 9 numbers and symbols (6 new symbols and 3 modified)

Attention
- The time limit for Coding is 120 seconds (2 minutes), not 1 minute and 20 seconds.
- Be sure to watch the child completing the items and correct any skipped items.
- Incorrect timing and failing to correct skipped items are the most commonly encountered Coding administration errors.

Remember
Behavioral Observations for Coding

Note if the child:

- Completes items impulsively, or misses items more frequently as they become more distant from the key at the top of the page.
- Has wandering attention during the task, leading to a lower score due to loss of potential points. If this occurs, administer the other two Processing Speed subtests to obtain more information about performance.
- Has trembling hands, has a tight grip on the pencil, or has sweaty palms causing

(Continued)

(Continued)

his or her hand to slip down or the pencil to slip out of his or her grip.

- Presses down hard, placing undue pressure on the pencil. This could indicate anxiety or fine motor issues.
- Loses time by checking and rechecking answers before moving on.
- Appears to benefit from ongoing experience with items and eventually memorizes one or more of the associated pairs.

After the subtest is complete:

- You may examine the impact of incidental learning on the child's performance by administering Coding Recall from the WISC–V Integrated. It is important to note that Coding Recall must be administered **immediately** after Coding.
- You may examine the impact of graphomotor speed on the child's performance by administering Coding Copy from the WISC–V Integrated.

Behind the Scenes

- The Coding symbols were altered for the WISC–V to ensure they could be written without lifting the pencil, to more readily accommodate digital adaptation of the subtest.
- The items were evenly distributed so that each shape or number occurs twice per row. This ensures more equivalent item difficulty across the subtest, which is a desirable characteristic in tasks designed to primarily measure processing speed.

Symbol Search

For each item, the child views target symbol(s), then marks the symbol in the search group that matches it or indicates that it is not present by marking the NO box. The child works within a time limit of 120 seconds. Necessary materials include the *WISC–V Administration and Scoring Manual*, the Record Form, Response Booklet 1,

a #2 pencil without an eraser, and a stopwatch. The Symbol Search Scoring Key is necessary for scoring.

Children aged 6 to 7 start with the Form A demonstration and sample items, then the test items. Children aged 8 to 16 start with the Form B demonstration and sample items, then the test items. Administer all demonstration and sample items as described in the *WISC–V Administration and Scoring Manual*. Practice the verbatim instructions for the subtest before administering it for the first time. As with Coding, committing the instructions to memory ensures a smoother administration.

Do not permit the child to start completing the test items early. Watch carefully during administration, because you may need to provide prompts in response to a number of situations. However, do not stop timing to give the prompts. You may need to prompt the child to wait to start until it is time if he or she begins the test items before you have said "Go."

At times, children indicate their response by drawing something other than one slash mark. If this occurs, prompt the child to draw only one line to make each mark, as indicated. Some children mark the target symbol instead of the search symbol. If this occurs at any time, provide the necessary prompt.

If the child attempts to skip an item, prompt him or her to go in order and not to skip any. If the child indicates he or she has made a mistake and asks what to do, encourage the child to keep working.

Discontinue promptly after 120 seconds. If a child is working on an item when the time limit expires, you may allow him or her to finish that item, but note to yourself not to award credit (or penalize the score) for the item. If a child aged 6 to 7 completes the subtest before 120 seconds, be sure to note the accurate completion time so that time bonus points may be assigned appropriately when computing the total raw score.

Table 2.19 provides a comparison of Symbol Search administration procedures across the

Table 2.19 Comparison of WISC–IV and WISC–V Symbol Search Administration

WISC–IV	WISC–V
Start points:	Start points:
Ages 6–7: Form A Sample, then Test Items	Ages 6–7: Form A Demonstration, Sample, then Test Items
Ages 8–16: Form B Sample, then Test Items	Ages 8–16: Form B Demonstration, Sample, then Test Items
Discontinue after 120 seconds.	Discontinue after 120 seconds.
Form A: 2 demonstration (then termed "sample") and 2 sample (then termed "practice") items	Form A: 2 demonstration and 3 sample items
	Form B: 2 demonstration and 3 sample items
Form B: 2 demonstration (then termed "sample") and 2 sample (then termed "practice") items	
Form A: 45 test items	Form A: 40 new test items
Form B: 60 test items	Form B: 60 new test items

WISC–IV and WISC–V. The Remember box lists behavioral observations that the examiner should note during administration.

Attention

- The time limit for Symbol Search is 120 seconds (2 minutes), not 1 minute and 20 seconds.
- Be sure to watch the child completing the items. Correct any skipped items, and ensure the child marks each response using only a single slash mark.
- Incorrect timing and failing to correct skipped items or incorrectly constructed marks are the most commonly encountered Symbol Search administration errors.

Remember

Behavioral Observations for Symbol Search

Note if the child:

- Selects responses impulsively based on the general shape, but misses important distinguishing details and therefore chooses incorrect responses. Some distracters (e.g., incorrect only because they are rotated, more readily confused based on aspects of the symbol) are more frequently selected by children with impulsive response styles. Consider deriving the base rates for rotation errors and set errors if the child makes frequent mistakes.
- Has wandering attention during the task, leading to a lower score due to loss of potential points. If this occurs, consider also administering both other Processing Speed subtests to provide additional information about performance.
- Has trembling hands, keeps a tight grip on the pencil, or has sweaty palms causing his or her hand to slip down or the pencil to slip out of his or her grip.
- Is overly concerned with the pencil's variability, marking symbols more than once if a mark is light.
- Loses time by checking and rechecking answers before marking them and moving on.
- Tends to scan the entire search group despite having identified the matching search group symbol close to the target before marking the response. Items with the matching search group symbol close to the target symbol are usually responded to somewhat more quickly. This pattern may indicate the child becomes distracted by irrelevant information or detail at the expense of speed.

(Continued)

(Continued)

- Is able to ignore irrelevant symbols and quickly locate a matching correct symbol, or lingers and examines the irrelevant symbols longer on items with the matching search group symbol placed farther away from the target. The items with the matching symbol placed farther away from the target are usually responded to more slowly.
- On items with no matching symbol, repeatedly checks and rechecks the symbols, obsessively looks for a matching symbol, or marks a similar symbol consistently rather than the NO box.

Behind the Scenes

- The Symbol Search symbols were altered for WISC–V to more readily accommodate observations of errors due to lack of discrimination of a similar symbol (i.e., set errors) or due to marking a rotated symbol (i.e., rotation errors).
- There are a number of different item types on Symbol Search. Each item has either a similar or rotated symbol as a distracter. Half of the items contain a matching symbol in the search group, and half do not. These and other aspects of the items (e.g., correct response location, distracter location) were evenly distributed across each page. This ensures more equivalent item difficulty across the subtest, which is a desirable characteristic in a measure primarily designed to tap speed.

Cancellation

The child views two 17 × 11 arrangements of animals and other items and marks all of the animals within 45 seconds. Materials include the *WISC–V Administration and Scoring Manual*, the Record Form, Response Booklet 2, a red pencil without an eraser, a second pencil for you, and a stopwatch. The Cancellation Scoring Template is necessary for scoring.

Children aged 6 to 16 start with the demonstration item, the sample item, then Item 1.

The demonstration and sample items introduce the child to the structured and random arrangements of objects, respectively, that he or she will see on Items 1 and 2. Be sure to administer the demonstration and sample items as described in the *WISC–V Administration and Scoring Manual*. You should use your own pencil to complete the demonstration item. For the sample item, provide all necessary feedback to teach the child to mark all animals and not to mark anything else.

Small lapses in your concentration can make big differences in scores on this subtest. Do not permit the child to begin either test item early. Watch carefully during administration, because you may need to provide prompts in response to a number of situations. However, do not stop timing to give the prompts. Prompt the child to wait to start until it is time if he or she begins the test items before you have said "Go." If the child indicates a response by drawing something other than one slash mark, prompt him or her to draw only one line to make each mark, as indicated. If the child indicates he or she has made a mistake and asks what to do, encourage the child to keep working.

Be careful to discontinue each test item after 45 seconds. Administer both Items 1 (Random) and 2 (Structured).

Table 2.20 provides a comparison of Cancellation administration procedures across the WISC–IV and WISC–V. The Remember box

Table 2.20   Comparison of WISC–IV and WISC–V Cancellation Administration

WISC–IV	WISC–V
Start point:	Start point:
Demonstration Item (then termed "Sample"), Sample Item (then termed "Practice"), then Item 1	Demonstration Item, Sample Item, then Item 1
Discontinue after 45 seconds for each item.	Discontinue after 45 seconds for each item.
Demonstration Item, Sample Item, and 2 test items	Demonstration Item, Sample Item, and 2 test items; all revised substantively

lists behavioral observations that the examiner should note during administration.

Attention

- Be sure to open the response booklet so that the child can see the entire 17 × 11 spread.
- After 45 seconds, do not allow the child to continue working on a Cancellation test item. It is easy to forget that the time limit for each item is 45 seconds, not 120 seconds.
- Be sure to watch the child completing the items. Ensure the child marks each response using only a single slash mark.

  These are the most commonly encountered Cancellation administration errors.

Remember

Behavioral Observations for Cancellation

Note if the child:

- Selects responses impulsively but misses important features that make the responses incorrect. Distracter pictures were intentionally selected to pull for impulsive responses based on color.
- Displays wandering attention during the task, leading to a lower score due to loss of potential points. If this occurs, consider also administering the other two Processing Speed subtests to provide additional information about processing speed ability.
- Displays trembling hands, has a tight grip on the pencil, or has sweaty palms causing his or her hand to slip down or the pencil to slip out of his or her grip.
- Is overly concerned with the pencil's variability, marking selections more than once if a mark is light.

- Loses time by checking and rechecking answers before marking them and moving on.
- Applies a strategy to the first (random) item. If so, observe the effectiveness of the selected strategy. One common effective strategy is to mark every example of a single target on the page, then do the same for the next target, and so on. Another usually less effective strategy is to attempt to find all targets on a quadrant or quarter of a page or to attempt to impose structure on the random arrangement by marking in "rows" or "columns." Other children may search more haphazardly, quickly marking any animal they see as fast as possible, and making a few errors along the way.
- Modifies his or her Item 1 strategy for Item 2, or employs a strategy for the first time, based on the structured arrangement. Note observed reading behaviors, such as searching the rows from left to right and down the page.
- Completely neglects an entire side of the visual field. Follow up by gaining more information about the child's vision and medical history, including any neurological issues, if this is observed.

After the subtest is complete, you may examine the impact of meaningful stimuli on the child's performance by administering Cancellation Abstract from the WISC–V Integrated. Cancellation Abstract items are composed of abstract shapes rather than meaningful stimuli but are otherwise identical to Cancellation.

Behind the Scenes

- Cancellation was redesigned to provide increased experimental control.
- Each item balances the occurrence of targets and distracters within each quadrant as well as by sheet row and sheet column.

(Continued)

(Continued)

- Each target is balanced with three distracters that use the same colors.
- This ensures more equivalent search difficulty within and across the items, which is a desirable characteristic in a measure primarily designed to tap speed.

Complementary Subtests

Naming Speed Literacy

For each item, the child names as fast as possible various types of elements (e.g., objects of different sizes and colors, numbers and letters). Necessary materials include the *WISC–V Administration and Scoring Manual*, the Record Form, Stimulus Book 3, and a stopwatch.

Children aged 6 start with Demonstration Item A, Sample Item A, then Item 1. Children aged 7 to 8 start with Demonstration Item B, Sample Item B, then Item 2. Children aged 9 to 16 start with Sample Item C, then Item 3.

Administer all demonstration and sample items as described in the *WISC–V Administration and Scoring Manual*. Practice the verbatim instructions for the subtest before administering it for the first time. Smooth administration is facilitated by committing the instructions to memory.

Children aged 6 to 8 must use their finger to track progress along each row as they complete each trial. Prompt the child if he or she neglects to use a finger to track progress. Children aged 9 to 16 need not track progress with a finger, but do not discourage them from doing so.

Do not permit the child to start early. Watch carefully during administration, because you must mark all words that represent misnamed aspects of the elements and/or misnamed letters and numbers, and you may need to provide prompts in response to various situations. However, do not stop timing to give the prompts. You may need to prompt the child to wait to start until it is time if he or she begins the test items before you have said "Go."

Because some children name the stimuli unusually quickly and it is critical that you

are following where the child is on the page, occasionally during administration you may need to clarify which stimulus the child is currently naming. If the child misnames two stimuli (e.g., an object, the size or color of an object, a letter or number) consecutively, point to the second misnamed stimulus and provide the appropriate prompt to keep going from that point. Doing this ensures that you and the child are referencing the same stimulus.

If the child attempts to complete a row from right to left rather than left to right or to skip a row, point to the first stimulus in the row that should be completed and provide the appropriate prompt to keep going from that point.

Encourage the child to keep working quickly. You must monitor and respond to hesitation. Any hesitation, whether at the end of a row or on a single stimulus, requires that you give the prompt to go on to the next row or stimulus.

Synonyms are acceptable for Items 1 and 2. Some commonly used synonyms observed during research phases are listed in the *WISC–V Administration and Scoring Manual*, but others can be acceptable as well.

Typically you should record something for every item so that children cannot detect if an item has been scored correct or incorrect. This subtest's pace, however, requires the child's full attention to the stimulus book, which makes recording less conspicuous. For this reason and because some children respond so quickly that recording everything may be too cumbersome, you should mark ***incorrect responses only*** with a single slash mark.

Because the administration pace is quick, self-corrections occur somewhat frequently on this subtest. A response is not considered complete until the child has said an entire word in an attempt to name the stimulus. Partial words are not considered complete.

If the child self-corrects a response to a stimulus that was already named, record the self-correction. Note "SC" next to the slash mark for any self-corrections that occur after a complete word has been said.

If a child is unable to complete an item trial within 300 seconds (5 minutes), promptly stop timing and proceed to the next trial or item if the discontinue criterion has not been met. Also, if a child aged 6 does not understand Sample Item A and Item 1 is therefore not administered, do not administer Demonstration or Sample Item B or Item 2. However, if a child aged 7 to 8 does not understand Sample Item B and Item 2 is not administered, but the child may be able to name numbers and letters, you may administer Sample Item C and Item 3 to obtain some measure of rapid automatized naming.

Naming Speed Quantity

For each item, the child names quantities of squares within rows of boxes as fast as possible. Necessary materials include the *WISC–V Administration and Scoring Manual*, the Record Form, Stimulus Book 3, and a stopwatch.

Children aged 6 start with Sample Item A, then Item 1. Children aged 7 to 16 start with Sample Item B, then Item 2.

Administer the sample item for the appropriate item, as described in the *WISC–V Administration and Scoring Manual*. Practice the verbatim instructions for the subtest before administering it for the first time. Smooth administration is facilitated by committing the instructions to memory.

Children aged 6 to 8 must use their finger to track progress along each row as they complete each trial. Prompt the child if he or she neglects to use a finger to track progress. Children aged 9 to 16 need not track progress with a finger, but do not discourage them from doing so.

Do not permit the child to start early. Watch carefully during administration, because you must mark all quantities that were misnamed and may need to provide prompts in response to various situations. However, do not stop timing to give the prompts. You may need to prompt the child to wait to start until it is time if he or she begins the test items before you have said "Go."

Because some children name the stimuli unusually quickly and it is critical that you are following where the child is on the page, occasionally during administration you may need to clarify which stimulus the child is currently naming. If the child misnames two quantities consecutively, point to the box containing the second misnamed quantity and provide the appropriate prompt to keep going from that point. This ensures that you and the child are referencing the same box.

If the child attempts to complete a row from right to left rather than left to right, or to skip a row, point to the first box in the row that should be completed and provide the appropriate prompt to keep going from that point.

Encourage the child to keep working quickly. You must monitor and respond to hesitation. Any hesitation, whether at the end of a row or on a single box, requires that you give the prompt to go on to the next row or box.

Typically you should record something for every item so that children cannot detect if an item has been scored correct or incorrect. This subtest's pace, however, requires the child's full attention to the stimulus book, which makes recording less conspicuous. For this reason, and because some children respond so quickly that recording everything may be too cumbersome, you should mark ***incorrect responses only*** with a single slash mark.

Because the administration pace is quick, self-corrections occur somewhat frequently on this subtest. A response is not considered complete until the child has said an entire word in an attempt to name the quantity. Partial words are not considered complete.

If the child self-corrects a response to a quantity that was already named, record the self-correction. Note "SC" next to the slash mark for any self-corrections that occur after a complete word has been said.

The time limit is 300 seconds (5 minutes) for both trials of each item. Stop administration for children aged 6 after Trial 2 of Item 1 has been administered. Stop administration for children aged 7 to 16 after Trial 2 of Item 2 has been administered.

Remember

Behavioral Observations for Naming Speed Literacy and Naming Speed Quantity

Note if the child:

- Misnames stimuli more frequently on Trial 1 than on Trial 2 of an item.
- Displays wandering attention during the task, leading to a lower score due to a longer completion time.
- Loses time by checking and rechecking answers before moving on.
- Appears to benefit from ongoing experience with items, becoming faster as the items progress.

For 9- to 16-year-olds: Tracks progress with his or her finger meticulously. This could indicate anxiety, fine motor issues, or reading fluency issues.

Behind the Scenes

- The objects for the items involving object naming were selected because they are easily recognized by even young children.
- The colors for the object naming tasks were selected to minimize any difficulties due to color blindness. The color green is not used because of the frequent occurrence of red-green color blindness among male children.
- For Naming Speed Literacy, the letters, numbers, and objects begin with similar sounds as others within the subtest because the literature suggests that the use of phonologically (but not visually) similar stimuli in rapid automatized naming tasks predicts unique variance in developing word identification skills (Compton, 2003).

Immediate Symbol Translation

The child learns to associate each symbol viewed on a stimulus page with a meaning. Using the learned associations (i.e., visual-verbal pairs that are introduced periodically throughout the subtest), the child translates groups of symbols viewed on a response page into phrases or sentences. Necessary materials include the *WISC–V Administration and Scoring Manual*, the Record Form, and Stimulus Book 3.

Immediate Symbol Translation has a single start point, Item 1. There is therefore no need to reverse. The discontinue rule involves comparing the cumulative raw score at three decision points A, B, and C (after Items 6, 10, and 14) to a specific value. If the child has not obtained at least as many cumulative raw score points as the specific value for a given decision point, discontinue administration. The values are as follows.

For decision point A, discontinue if the cumulative raw score is less than or equal to 9. For decision point B, discontinue if the cumulative raw score is less than or equal to 20. For decision point C, discontinue if the cumulative raw score is less than or equal to 30.

There are 34 symbols: 29 represent words and 5 are translated only in combination with a word symbol and indicate that the child should modify suffix or tense or should say the plural form of the word while translating.

If while translating the child hesitates for 5 seconds or says he or she doesn't know the meaning of a symbol, prompt the child to go on to the next symbol. Occasionally during administration you may need to clarify which symbol the child is currently translating. Self-corrections may also result in you and the child not referencing the same symbol. In addition, children occasionally may translate symbols from right to left. In any of these situations, point to the first symbol in the sequence and instruct the child to begin again from that point, as instructed in the *WISC–V Administration and Scoring Manual*.

Items 1 to 3 have two trials. These items function like the Block Design dual-trial items: The second trial is administered only if the child does not receive a perfect score on the first trial. However, unlike the dual-trial items on Block Design, the child receives full credit if he or she responds correctly to the second trial.

You may repeat subtest instructions as often as necessary. However, do *not* provide instruction to the child that strays from what is specified in the *WISC–V Administration and Scoring Manual*, as this may unintentionally assist him or her in associating the symbol and meaning.

It is helpful to record the subtest stop time at the end of Immediate Symbol Translation if Delayed Symbol Translation or Recognition Symbol Translation will be administered. Approximately 20 to 30 minutes should elapse after Immediate Symbol Translation before you begin to administer Delayed and/or Recognition Symbol Translation.

Remember

Behavioral Observations for Immediate Symbol Translation

Note if the child:

- Hesitates before responding or immediately answers.
- For responses that are incorrect, uses a form of the correct word or a word that is the same part of speech as the correct response.
- Forms sentences and phrases that represent coherent thoughts even if they are not completely correct.
- Repeats incorrect translations made on earlier items. Doing this may indicate the meaning was initially encoded incorrectly but retention is good.

- Frequently self-corrects on translations that were initially correct. This pattern of responding may indicate nervousness or anxiety.

Delayed Symbol Translation

The child translates symbols viewed on a stimulus page into words, phrases, or sentences using the learned visual-verbal pairs from Immediate Symbol Translation. No new visual-verbal pairs are taught for this subtest. Necessary materials include the *WISC–V Administration and Scoring Manual*, the Record Form, and Stimulus Book 3.

Delayed Symbol Translation has a single start point, Item 1. There is therefore no need to reverse. Discontinue at the same decision point, A, B, or C, as on Immediate Symbol Translation. If the child did not discontinue on Immediate Symbol Translation, administer all items and do not discontinue.

Delayed Symbol Translation cannot be administered if Immediate Symbol Translation was not already administered. Adhere to the 20- to 30-minute interval between the two subtests to ensure a valid score.

If when translating the child hesitates for 5 seconds or says he or she doesn't know the meaning of a symbol, prompt the child to go on to the next symbol. Occasionally during administration you may need to clarify which symbol the child is currently translating. Self-corrections may also result in you and the child not referencing the same symbol. In addition, children occasionally may translate symbols from right to left. In any of these situations, point to the first symbol in the sequence and instruct the child to begin again from that point, as instructed in the *WISC–V Administration and Scoring Manual*.

You may repeat subtest instructions as often as necessary. However, do *not* provide instruction or additional assistance to the child in recalling the meaning of a symbol.

Administer Recognition Symbol Translation immediately after this subtest if it is given.

Remember

Behavioral Observations for Delayed Symbol Translation

Note if the child:

- Hesitates before responding or immediately answers.
- For translations that are incorrect: Uses a form of the correct word or a word that is the same part of speech as the correct translation.
- Forms sentences and phrases that represent coherent thoughts even if they are not completely correctly translated.
- Repeats incorrect translations made on Immediate Symbol Translation. Doing this may indicate the meaning was initially encoded incorrectly but retention is good.
- Frequently self-corrects on translations that were initially correct. This pattern of responding may indicate nervousness or anxiety.

Recognition Symbol Translation

The child views a symbol and listens to response options read aloud by the examiner, then selects the correct translation using the learned visual-verbal pairs from Immediate Symbol Translation. No new visual-verbal pairs are taught for this subtest. Necessary materials include the *WISC–V Administration and Scoring Manual*, the Record Form, and Stimulus Book 3.

Recognition Symbol Translation has a single start point, Item 1. There is therefore no need to reverse. Discontinue at the same decision point, A, B, or C, as on Immediate Symbol Translation. If the child did not discontinue on Immediate

Symbol Translation, administer all items and do not discontinue.

Recognition Symbol Translation cannot be administered if Immediate Symbol Translation was not already administered. However, it can be administered even if Delayed Symbol Translation was administered. In this situation, allow a 20- to 30-minute interval between the end of Immediate Symbol Translation and the beginning of Recognition Symbol Translation to ensure a valid score.

Read each response option aloud to the child. Do not read the letter that precedes the response option.

You may repeat subtest instructions or response options as often as necessary. However, do *not* provide instruction or additional assistance to the child in recalling the meaning of a symbol.

Remember

Behavioral Observations for Recognition Symbol Translation

Note if the child:

- Hesitates before responding or immediately answers.
- Uses process of elimination to narrow the correct translation on sets of items, versus haphazardly guessing the same incorrect translations repeatedly.
- For incorrect translations, selects response options that are from the same part of speech as those of the correct response.
- Repeats errors made on Immediate Symbol Translation and Delayed Symbol Translation.
- Frequently self-corrects on translations that were initially correct. This pattern of responding may indicate nervousness or anxiety.

Behind the Scenes

The Naming Speed and Symbol Translation Subtests

- The Naming Speed and Symbol Translation subtests were not originally planned for the WISC–V. An exhaustive literature review of cognitive processes that are sensitive to specific learning disabilities indicated that rapid automatized naming and visual-verbal associative memory are cognitive processes that are important to specific learning disability assessment. With the addition of these subtests, pairing the WISC–V with one of its linked achievement tests (i.e., the Kaufman Test of Educational Achievement–Third Edition (KTEA–3; Kaufman & Kaufman, 2014) or Wechsler Individual Achievement Test–Third Edition (WIAT–III; Pearson, 2009b) ensures the cognitive processes that have been shown to be sensitive to specific learning disabilities are assessed across the two measures.
- For Naming Speed Literacy, the stimuli vary somewhat from those of classic rapid automatized naming tasks to increase task sensitivity to reading and written expression problems in children who are beyond very early grades.
- Naming Speed Quantity is designed to measure the rapid recognition of quantities. It is similar to tasks in the experimental literature that show more sensitivity to mathematics-related variables than do typical rapid automatized naming tasks that are more traditionally associated with reading- and writing-related skills (Pauly et al., 2011; van der Sluis, de Jong, & van der Leij, 2004; Willburger, Fussenegger, Moll, Wood, & Landerl, 2008).
- For the Symbol Translation subtests, great care was taken to select visual-verbal pairs that varied along a continuum of difficulty with respect to forming an association.

Attention

Common Errors in WISC–V Subtest Administration

The most common errors observed on the WISC–V subtests during research stages are listed next. The subtests are listed by cognitive domain membership.

Verbal Comprehension Subtests {the bullets that follow pertain to all Verbal Comprehension Subtests}

- Where applicable, not administering the items prior to the start point in reverse sequence if the child obtains an imperfect score on either start-point item.
- Neglecting to query sample responses followed by a Q. Query errors were the most frequent error noted in a recent study of Wechsler protocols (Mrazik et al., 2012).
- Not providing the specific query for sample responses noted with an asterisk (*) in the *WISC–V Administration and Scoring Manual*.
- Not providing corrective feedback on teaching items marked with a dagger (†) in response to an imperfect score.
- On Comprehension, failing to query for an additional category sample response on items noted with a section sign (§), indicating there are two or more general concept categories.

Visual Spatial Subtests

- Where applicable, not administering the items prior to the start point in reverse sequence if the child obtains an imperfect score on either start-point item.
- Forgetting to time the child, or forgetting to record completion time.

(Continued)

(*Continued*)
- Improper use of the stopwatch: allowing too little or too much time.

Block Design
- Presenting the wrong blocks for a given item.
- Where applicable, failing to administer Trial 2 of an item if the child did not successfully complete Trial 1.
- Failing to record the correct design for every item using the grid.
- Not penalizing rotation and therefore discontinuing too late. Rotations of 30° or more are scored 0 points.
- Forgetting to correct the first rotation.
- Not following the guidelines about a variety of block faces being presented faceup (Moon, Blakey, Gorsuch, & Fantuzzo, 1991). The extant research does not examine the impact of this common error in clinical populations.

Visual Puzzles
- Failing to administer the demonstration and sample item.
- Allowing additional time beyond the time limit to provide a response.
- Failing to prompt the child to select three response options if he or she selects fewer or more than three.

Fluid Reasoning Subtests
- Failing to administer the sample items.

Matrix Reasoning and Picture Concepts
- Rigidly applying the 30-second guideline as a strict time limit rather than granting more time to respond for a child who is benefiting from the additional time.

Matrix Reasoning and Figure Weights
- Failing to circle the selected response option. This is particularly important for items to which the child does not respond correctly.

Figure Weights
- Allowing additional time beyond the time limit to provide a response.
- Forgetting to provide the verbatim instruction required on the first 3-scale item that the child must now look at all three scales to find the answer.

Picture Concepts
- Failing to prompt the child to select one response option from each row, if needed.
- Failing to circle all selected response options.

Arithmetic
- Failing to record completion times for every item.
- Providing repetition of the item for Items 1 to 19.
- Pausing timing of an item for anything other than a permitted repetition of the item stimulus.
- Allowing additional time beyond the time limit to provide a response.
- Failing to provide repetition of the item for Items 20 to 34.
- Failing to pause timing while providing a repetition of the item for Items 20 to 34.

Working Memory Subtests
- Failing to administer all demonstration and sample items.

Digit Span and Letter–Number Sequencing

- Forgetting to administer the qualifying items to children aged 6 and 7.
- Administering the qualifying items to children aged 8 to 16.
- Failing to read the stimuli at the rate of one per second and/or in a consistent tone and failing to drop your tone of voice only on the last letter or number read.
- Discontinuing after consecutive trials are missed across 2 items rather than only after all trials are missed on a single item.

Digit Span

- Failing to administer all three tasks.

Picture Span

- Neglecting to use the stopwatch to track stimulus exposure time.
- Failing to record all selected response options in the order they were given.
- Neglecting to administer Sample Items A and/or B.
- Administering Sample Item A to a child who does not start with Item 1.
- Forgetting to increase stimulus exposure time beginning with Sample Item B.

Processing Speed Subtests

- Neglecting to watch the child during the tasks so that the appropriate prompt can be provided if the child marks a stimulus with something other than a single slash mark.

Coding and Symbol Search

- Neglecting to watch the child during the tasks so that the appropriate prompts

can be provided if the child is skipping items or stamping multiple stimuli for an item.
- Forgetting to turn the Response Booklet pages for the child.
- Stopping administration after 1 minute and 20 seconds rather than 120 seconds (2 minutes).

Cancellation

- During test items, failing to open the response booklet to expose the entire 17×11 spread.
- Ceasing administration at 120 seconds rather than 45 seconds for each item.

Complementary Subtests

Naming Speed Literacy and Naming Speed Quantity

- Failing to record completion times for every trial administered.
- Recording correct responses. Only incorrect responses are recorded for these subtests.
- Penalizing responses that were self-corrected. If the final response (i.e., named element, aspect of an element, quantity) is correct, credit is awarded accordingly.

Naming Speed Literacy

- Administering unnecessary or wrong tasks to a child, or not administering all of the age-appropriate tasks to a child.
- Penalizing the use of appropriate synonym to name an aspect of an element on Item 1 or Item 2. The use of reasonable synonyms is acceptable.

(Continued)

(*Continued*)

Immediate Symbol Translation and Delayed Symbol Translation

- Recording incorrect responses. Only correct responses are recorded for these subtests.

Immediate Symbol Translation

- Providing additional instruction to assist the child in learning the visual-verbal pairs.
- Discontinuing administration too early or too late. At each decision point, sum the total number of correct responses and discontinue if the sum is less than or equal to the value provided for that decision point.

Delayed Symbol Translation and Recognition Symbol Translation

- Failing to allow approximately 20 to 30 minutes after the end of Immediate Symbol Translation administration before commencing administration of either of these subtests.

- Providing assistance to the child in remembering the visual-verbal pairs. No assistance should be provided.
- Discontinuing administration too early or too late. Discontinue at the same decision point A, B, or C as on Immediate Symbol Translation. If the child did not discontinue on Immediate Symbol Translation, administer all items and do not discontinue.

Recognition Symbol Translation

- Failing to circle the selected response option. This is particularly important for items to which the child does not respond correctly.

FREQUENTLY ASKED QUESTIONS: SUBTEST ADMINISTRATION

Pearson provides responses to frequently asked questions (i.e., FAQs) about the WISC–V on the product website. One portion of the FAQs relates to subtest administration. The questions and responses are reproduced in Quick Reference 2.3.

QUICK REFERENCE 2.3: FREQUENTLY ASKED QUESTIONS: SUBTEST ADMINISTRATION

- Is teaching allowed on the sample items to ensure that children understand the expectations of the subtests?

Yes, many of the subtests have demonstration, sample, and teaching items built in to ensure the child understands the task. These items were added in response to the needs of thousands of children who participated in the development of the scale. Children with special needs were included among these participants.

- How does Block Design work with children with motor deficits such as cerebral palsy? Is there an alternative test?

Whether Block Design is appropriate depends on the severity of the motor impairment. Unless the child has severe motor impairment, they may be able to complete the task. You will need to evaluate the severity and impact of the motor impairment for each case. If Block Design cannot be administered, the Visual Puzzles subtest can be substituted to obtain the FSIQ. The VSI and some ancillary index scores may not be obtained in this situation.

- Are the Comprehension items updated?

As part of any revision, items that may require revision are identified for various reasons (e.g., length of time in use, cultural shifts, wording, vocabulary level, relevance). There have been modifications to the Comprehension items to make them not only culturally relevant but also more child-friendly. For example, more questions related to child-relevant content appear on the WISC–V, and no item contains the word "Advantages" any longer.

- How is color blindness handled in the Naming Speed Literacy subtest?

Individuals with color-perception differences are a group that encompasses greater than 10% of the general population. These issues are much more common in males. We have made every effort to ensure our items, including those on the WAIS–IV, WISC–V, WPPSI–IV, and WASI–II, are free of bias against these individuals. Items are reviewed by color-perception differences experts, as well as individuals with color-perception differences, during the early stages of the test development process. In addition, acetate overlays have been utilized so that the test developers can understand the appearance of the stimuli to individuals with various color-perception differences. Items are also copied in black and white to check appearance to those with monochromatic color perception. All items are also subjected to an electronic "color-blindness" simulator to check item appearance with every type of color-perception difference and ensure that the intensity and saturation of colors are not confused or result in different responses. For the WISC–V, the colors are yellow, blue, and red; green is not included. This means that for the most common color blindness (green/red, which is 7%–10% of boys), the children will be able to take it without a problem. Children with monochromacity (0.00001% of children) should not be administered the WISC–V Naming Speed Literacy items that involve colors; however, they could take Item 3 (Letter-Number) and the Naming Speed Quantity subtest. For children with deuteranopia (1%), the simulation, template, and expert review indicate that they should be able to see the differences between the yellow and blue.

- If a young child is prompted to use finger tracking on a Naming Speed subtest and does not comply, what is the proper course of action?

In this situation, continue providing the prompt until the child complies. The sample items provide ample opportunity for the child to practice until he or she is accustomed to finger tracking.

- On Visual Puzzles, if a child clearly chooses more than 3 pieces, what prompt is provided?

"Which 3 pieces do you mean?" See the sixth bullet on page 170 of the *WISC–V Administration and Scoring Manual*.

Source: from http://www.pearsonclinical.com/psychology/products/100000771/wechsler-intelligence-scale-for-childrensupsupfifth-edition-wisc-v.html#tab-faq. *Wechsler Intelligence Scale for Children, Fifth Edition* (WISC–V). Copyright © 2014 NCS Pearson, Inc. Reproduced with permission. All rights reserved. "*Wechsler Intelligence Scale for Children*" and "*WISC*" are trademarks, in the United States and/or other countries, of Pearson Education, Inc. or its affiliates(s).

CHAPTER 3

WISC–V SCORING: TEST KIT VERSION

This chapter begins with basic subtest scoring instructions and guidelines. A general description of score types and distributions is offered. An overview of the scoring process, from total raw scores to subtest scaled or standard scores to composite scores, is accompanied by a discussion of more complex substitution, proration, and invalidation procedures. A primer on the scoring software is included.

SCORING SUBTESTS

The following sections offer scoring guidelines for the WISC–V subtests. The subtests are organized by cognitive domain. General information about scoring all subtests within the domain is presented first, followed by subtest-specific information in the form of a subtest scoring key. Changes to scoring from the Wechsler Intelligence Scale for Children–Fourth Edition (WISC–IV, Wechsler, 2003) to the WISC–V are highlighted.

In addition to the subtest total raw scores, some subtests permit the calculation of process scores. *Process scores* provide more detailed information relevant to subtest performance. There are various types of process scores: scaled and standard, along with a variety of raw process scores (i.e., longest span and sequence scores, error scores, and process observations). The procedures used to calculate most process scores are listed in the subtest-specific scoring keys. The procedures used to calculate the process observations and contrast scores, a new type of score that examines performance on one score given performance on another, are discussed at the conclusion of each key.

Verbal Comprehension Subtests

In general, items on the Verbal Comprehension subtests require an expressive response (although some items on Information permit responses in the form of gestures). Verbal Comprehension items involve the greatest need to apply judgment in scoring. You should record the child's response word for word, or verbatim. Failure to record the child's response verbatim is one of the most common recording errors seen in studies of Wechsler intelligence scale protocols (Alfonso, Johnson, Patinella, & Rader, 1998; Loe, Kadlubek, & Marks, 2007). Do not fail to record verbatim responses, or scoring will become more difficult and less accurate. Many rich, qualitative observations are impossible without the verbatim responses.

Using Sample Responses, General Scoring Principles, and General Concepts

It is particularly critical to refer to the *WISC–V Administration and Scoring Manual* when scoring verbatim responses. Increased scoring errors occur if you assume you have learned the scoring rules or committed them to memory; and adherence to the scoring rules is strongly related to scoring accuracy (Erdodi, Richard, & Hopwood, 2009).

Matching the child's verbatim response to a sample response is the first and simplest choice when assigning a score. However, the sample responses are not an exhaustive list of every possible answer a child can give to the item. The sample responses are distilled from among approximately 6,000 different responses obtained, read, and scored across various research phases. The most common answers are represented. Other sample responses appear because they illustrate important differences across point values or provide good exemplars of the scoring rules. Nevertheless, it is not an unusual occurrence for at least one of a child's responses not to match any sample response exactly.

If a child's response does not match any sample response for an item, search for a sample response that is similar. The sample responses are organized to facilitate the process of searching for a similar response. Responses that appear together on a single line separated by semicolons typically are related in meaning. More common responses and higher-quality sample responses usually appear in higher positions in the lists for each point value. For responses that are not assigned perfect scores, those with a query also are positioned higher in the lists because of their borderline quality. Responses that are similar in nature but differ in some way that distinguishes their quality often are positioned in analogous areas of the point-value sections. This organization makes scanning and visual comparison easier. For example, a 1-point response and a 0-point response that use the same word may both appear in the upper-right-hand corner within their respective point-value sections.

Compare verbatim responses to all of the sample responses to ascertain if their quality is better than, similar to, or worse than those of a given point value, and score accordingly. Responses should be scored based on their content, not on their eloquence, lengthiness, grammar, pronunciation, or verbosity.

Utilize the general scoring rules for guidance. If the response cannot be matched or easily compared to the sample responses, refer to the general scoring principles and general concepts to score the response. Strong familiarity with the general scoring principles on Similarities and Vocabulary and general concepts on Comprehension improves scoring accuracy and speed.

The general scoring principles for the Similarities and Vocabulary verbal items appear in Quick References 3.1 and 3.2. Scoring keys for

the Verbal Comprehension subtests appear in the Remember box. A comparison of WISC–IV and WISC–V Verbal Comprehension subtest scoring appears in Table 3.1.

Table 3.1 Comparison of WISC–IV and WISC–V Verbal Comprehension Subtest Scoring

WISC–IV	WISC–V
Similarities	
Items 1–2: Score 0–1 point	Items 1–23: Score 0–2 points
Items 3–23: Score 0–2 points	
Maximum Total Raw Score: 44 points	Maximum Total Raw Score: 46 points
	Sample responses for all items revised or new
Vocabulary	
Items 1–4: Score 0–1 point	Items 1–4: Score 0–1 point
Items 5–36: Score 0–2 points	Items 5–29: Score 0–2 points
Maximum Total Raw Score: 68 points	Maximum Total Raw Score: 54 points
	Sample responses for all items revised or new
Information	
Items 1–33: Score 0–1 point	Items 1–31: Score 0–1 point
Maximum Total Raw Score: 33 points	Maximum Total Raw Score: 31 points
	Sample responses for all items revised or new
Comprehension	
Items 1–21: Score 0–2 points	Items 1–19: Score 0–2 points
Maximum Total Raw Score: 42 points	Maximum Total Raw Score: 38 points
	Sample responses for all items revised or new

QUICK REFERENCE 3.1: SIMILARITIES GENERAL SCORING PRINCIPLES

Award 2 points if the response:

- Provides a major classification that is relevant to both of the objects or concepts.

Award 1 point if the response:

- Describes a specific aspect that is common to both of the objects or concepts, describing a minor or less relevant commonality.
- Provides a major classification that is less relevant or more general for both of the objects or concepts.

Award 0 points if the response:

- Describes a property that is not relevant to both of the objects or concepts.
- Is too general.
- Describes differences between the objects or concepts.
- Is otherwise clearly incorrect.

QUICK REFERENCE 3.2: VOCABULARY GENERAL SCORING PRINCIPLES

Award 2 points if the response indicates well-developed conceptualization of the word; for example, if the response:

- Contains a close synonym.
- Describes a major use of a noun.
- Provides a broad classification of the word.
- Offers primary or defining features of a noun.
- Offers a figurative use of the word that is correct.
- Provides several less defining or primary features that are correct and, when taken together, indicate good concept formulation of the word.
- Describes a verb with a defining example of causation or action.

Award 1 point if the response indicates correct but incomplete understanding of the word; for example, if the response:

- Contains a less relevant synonym.
- Describes a minor use of a noun.
- Describes an aspect of the word that is correct but secondary, or not a defining feature.
- Provides an example using the word that is correct but not elaborated upon.
- Provides a common use of the word that is not elaborated upon.
- Correctly defines a closely related form of the word but not the word itself.

Award 0 points if the response does not indicate any clear conceptualization of the word or is just incorrect; for example, if the response:

- Involves a demonstration or gesture(s), not verbally elaborated.
- Does not indicate any clear understanding of the word, even after query.
- Is not completely incorrect but is vague, trivial, or weak, even after query.
- Is a regional use of the word or involves slang usage.
- Is a clearly incorrect definition.

Remember

Verbal Comprehension Subtest Scoring Keys

Subtest	Item Score Range(s)	Scoring Tips
Similarities	0–2 points	• First, use the sample responses that correspond to each item to score the child's response. • If necessary, refer to the General Scoring Principles in the *WISC–V Administration and Scoring Manual* and in Quick Reference 3.1. • When multiple responses are provided score the best response if none of the answers spoils the entire response. • If a 2- or 1-point answer is given along with a spoiled response score the item as 0 points. • If the child makes a remark that is clearly not part of his or her response it should not affect the score. • Award 2, 1, or 0 points for each item.
Vocabulary	Items 1–4: 0–1 point Items 5–29: 0–2 points	Picture Items (1–4): • Use the sample responses that correspond to each item to score the child's response. • When multiple responses are provided, score the best response if none of the answers spoils the entire response. • Score 1 point if the child responds correctly and 0 points if the child responds incorrectly, says he or she doesn't know the answer, or does not respond to the item. • Inappropriate marginal, functional, gestural, or generalized responses are scored 0 points. • Personalized responses are scored 0 points unless accompanied by a correct response. • If a 1-point answer is given along with a spoiled response score the item as 0 points. • If the child makes a remark that is clearly not part of his or her response it should not affect the score. • Award 1 point or 0 points for each item. Verbal Items (5–29): • First, use the sample responses that correspond to each item to score the child's response. • If necessary refer to the General Scoring Principles in the *WISC–V Administration and Scoring Manual* and in Quick Reference 3.2. • Award credit consummate with the definition's quality for word meanings that appear in standard dictionaries.

Subtest	Item Score Range(s)	Scoring Tips
		• Score 0 points for regional or slang word usages that are not improved upon query. • If a 2- or 1-point answer is given along with a spoiled response score the item as 0 points. • If the child makes a remark that is clearly not part of his or her response it should not affect the score. • Award 2, 1, or 0 points for each item.
Information	0–1 point	Verbal Items: • Use the sample responses that correspond to each item to score the child's response. • When multiple responses are provided, score the best response if none of the answers spoils the entire response. • If a 1-point answer is given along with a spoiled response, score the item as 0 points. • If the child makes a remark that is clearly not part of his or her response it should not affect the score. • Award 1 point or 0 points for each item.
Comprehension	0–2 points	• Use the sample responses and general concepts that correspond to each item to score the child's response. • When multiple responses are provided, score the best response if none of the answers spoils the entire response. • If a 2- or 1-point answer is given along with a spoiled response score the item as 0 points. • If the child makes a remark that is clearly not part of his or her response, it should not affect the score. • Award 2, 1, or 0 points for each item.

Visual Spatial Subtests

The Visual Spatial subtests are relatively straightforward to score if performance and completion times are recorded accurately. Scoring keys for the Visual Spatial subtests appear in the Remember box. A comparison of WISC–IV and WISC–V Block Design subtest scoring appears in Table 3.2.

Table 3.2 Comparison of WISC–IV and WISC–V Block Design Subtest Scoring

WISC–IV	WISC–V
Block Design	
Items 1–3: Score 0–2 points	Items 1–3: Score 0–2 points
Items 4–8: Score 0 or 4 points	Items 4–9: Score 0 or 4 points
Items 9–14: Score 0 or 4–7 points	Items 10–13: Score 0 or 4–7 points
Maximum Total Raw Score: 68 points	Maximum Total Raw Score: 58 points

Remember

Visual Spatial Subtest Scoring Keys

Subtest: Score	Item Score Range(s)	Scoring Tips
Block Design: Overall subtest score	Items 1–3: 0–2 Items 4–9: 0 or 4 Items 10–13: 0, 4–7	• For each item, record the completion time in seconds. • In the Constructed Design column, place a checkmark on the grid for correct constructions. For incorrect constructions, shade the grid to indicate the construction that was present at the time limit. • In the Constructed Design column, indicate rotations by drawing in an arrow to indicate the direction of the rotation and the number of degrees rotated. A rotation in a constructed design of 30 degrees or more that remains at the time limit is a rotation error. • A dimension error occurs if the maximum dimension for a square or diamond-shaped design is exceeded during the child's construction **at any time**. • A gaps and/or misalignment error occurs if a gap or misalignment is present in the design that is greater than $1/4$ inch. • For all items, a construction is not awarded any points if it is not complete at the time limit. • For all items, the following errors **that remain uncorrected at the time limit** result in a response being classified as a faulty construction: rotation errors of 30 degrees or more, dimension errors, or gaps or misalignment errors greater than $1/4$ inch between blocks. Note that if an error is corrected before the time limit, no score penalty is levied at the item level for that particular error.

Items 1–3:

• Award 2 points for a correct construction on Trial 1.
• Award 1 point for a correct construction on Trial 2.
• Award 0 points for an incorrect construction on both trials.

Items 4–9:

• Award 4 points for a correct construction.
• Award 0 points for an incorrect construction.

Item 10–13:

• Award 4 points for a correct construction. Award additional time bonus points as appropriate for a correct construction: 71–120 seconds: 0 additional points, total item score of 4 points 51–70 seconds: 1 additional point, total item score of 5 points 31–50 seconds: 2 additional points, total item score of 6 points 1–30 seconds: 3 additional points, total item score of 7 points
• Award 0 points for an incorrect construction.

Subtest: Score	Item Score Range(s)	Scoring Tips
Block Design: No Time Bonus	Items 1–3: 0–2 Items 4–13: 0 or 4 Items 10–13: 0 or 4	• The Block Design No Time Bonus score is a scaled process score. • Apply the same scoring tips used for Block Design overall subtest score, except scoring for Items 10–13 is slightly different: **Items 10–13:** • Award 4 points for a correct construction. • Award 0 points for an incorrect construction. • Do not award any time bonus points.
Block Design: Partial	Item 1: 0 or 1 Items 2–9: 0–4 Items 10–13: 0–12	• The Block Design Partial score is a scaled process score. • In the Optional Partial Score column, record the number of correctly placed blocks for all items. **Items 1–3:** • Award credit for correctly placed blocks on the last trial administered only. **Item 10–13:** • If the child's entire construction is correct, award additional time bonus points as appropriate: 71–120 seconds: 0 additional points, total item score of 9 points 51–70 seconds: 1 additional point, total item score of 10 points 31–50 seconds: 2 additional points, total item score of 11 points 1–30 seconds: 3 additional points, total item score of 12 points
Block Design: Dimension Errors	Maximum of 1 dimension error per item	• The Block Design Dimension Errors score is a raw process score for which base rates are available. • Count the number of dimension errors made at any time during the child's construction (maximum 1 per item). A dimension error occurs if the maximum dimension for a square or diamond-shaped design is exceeded during the child's construction. • Sum the total across the subtest and obtain the base rate for the number of errors.

(Continued)

(Continued)

Subtest: Score	Item Score Range(s)	Scoring Tips
Block Design: Rotation Errors	Maximum of 1 rotation error per item	• The Block Design Rotation Errors score is a raw process score for which base rates are available. • Sum the number of rotation errors made at any time during the child's construction (maximum 1 per item). A rotation in a constructed design of 30 degrees or more that remains at the time limit is a rotation error. • Sum the total across the subtest and obtain the base rate for the number of errors.
Visual Puzzles	0–1 point	• For each item, circle the numbers that correspond to the child's response choices. The correct responses appear in color on the Record Form and are listed in the *WISC–V Administration and Scoring Manual*. • Award 1 point if the child chooses all of the correct responses (i.e., all three responses), and 0 points if the child does not choose all of the correct responses, chooses more than three responses, says he or she doesn't know the answer, or does not respond to the item.

Fluid Reasoning Subtests

The Fluid Reasoning subtests are simple to score if performance and completion times (if applicable) are recorded accurately. Scoring keys for the Fluid Reasoning subtests appear in the Remember box. A comparison of WISC–IV and WISC–V Fluid Reasoning subtest scoring appears in Table 3.3.

Table 3.3 Comparison of WISC–IV and WISC–V Fluid Reasoning Subtest Scoring

WISC–IV	WISC–V
Matrix Reasoning	
Items 1–35: Score 0 or 1 point	Items 1–32: Score 0 or 1 point
Maximum Total Raw Score: 35 points	Maximum Total Raw Score: 32 points
Picture Concepts	
Items 1–28: Score 0 or 1 point	Items 1–27: Score 0 or 1 point
Maximum Total Raw Score: 28 points	Maximum Total Raw Score: 27 points
Arithmetic	
Items 1–34: Score 0 or 1 point	Items 1–34: Score 0 or 1 point (no change)
Maximum Total Raw Score: 34 points	Maximum Total Raw Score: 34 points (no change)

Remember

Fluid Reasoning Subtest Scoring Keys

Subtest	Item Score Range(s)	Scoring Tips
Matrix Reasoning	0–1 point	• For each item, circle the number that corresponds to the child's response choice. The correct responses appear in color on the Record Form and are listed in the *WISC–V Administration and Scoring Manual*. • Award 1 point if the child responds correctly and 0 points if the child responds incorrectly, says he or she doesn't know the answer, or does not respond to the item.
Figure Weights	0–1 point	• For each item, record the completion time and circle the number that corresponds to the child's response choice. The correct responses appear in color on the Record Form and are listed in the *WISC–V Administration and Scoring Manual*. • Award 1 point if the child responds correctly within the time limit and 0 points if the child responds after the time limit or incorrectly, says he or she doesn't know the answer, or does not respond to the item.
Picture Concepts	0–1 point	• For each item, circle the numbers that correspond to the child's response choices. The correct responses appear in color on the Record Form and are listed in the *WISC–V Administration and Scoring Manual*. • Award 1 point if the child chooses all of the correct responses (i.e., the correct response from each row) and 0 points if the child does not choose all of the correct responses, says he or she doesn't know the answer, or does not respond to the item.
Arithmetic	0–1 point	• For each item, record the completion time and the child's response verbatim. The correct responses appear on the Record Form and are listed in the *WISC–V Administration and Scoring Manual*. • Award 1 point if the child responds correctly within the time limit and 0 points if the child responds after the time limit or incorrectly, says he or she doesn't know the answer, or does not respond to the item.

Working Memory Subtests

The Working Memory subtests are relatively straightforward to score if recording is accurate. Correct responses are printed on the Record Form and in the *WISC–V Administration and Scoring Manual*. Remember to award 2 points for all correct Picture Span responses that are also given in the correct sequence but only 1 point for correct responses that are given in an incorrect sequence.

Scoring keys for the Working Memory subtests appear in the Remember box. A comparison of WISC–IV and WISC–V Working Memory subtest scoring appears in Table 3.4.

Table 3.4   Comparison of WISC–IV and WISC–V Working Memory Subtest Scoring

WISC–IV	WISC–V
Digit Span	
All items: Score 0 or 1 point for each trial	All items: Score 0 or 1 point for each trial
Maximum Total Raw Score: 32 points	Maximum Total Raw Score: 54 points
Letter–Number Sequencing	
All items: Score 0 or 1 point for each trial	All items: Score 0 or 1 point for each trial
Maximum Total Raw Score: 30 points	Maximum Total Raw Score: 30 points (no change)

Remember

Working Memory Subtest Scoring Keys

Subtest: Score	Item Score Range(s)	Scoring Tips
Digit Span: Overall subtest score	0–2 points	• For each trial, record the child's response verbatim. The correct responses for each trial appear on the Record Form, and are listed in the *WISC–V Administration and Scoring Manual*. • Award 1 point for each trial if the child responds correctly and 0 points if the child does not respond correctly, says he or she doesn't know the answer, or does not respond to the trial. • Sum the trial scores to obtain the item scores.
Digit Span: Digit Span Forward	0–2 points	• The Digit Span Forward score is a scaled process score. • Range of this score is 0 to 18. • Sum the Forward item scores.
Digit Span: Digit Span Backward	0–2 points	• The Digit Span Backward score is a scaled process score. • Range of this score is 0 to 18. • Sum the Backward item scores.
Digit Span: Digit Span Sequencing	0–2 points	• The Digit Span Sequencing score is a scaled process score. • Range of this score is 0 to 18. • Sum the Sequencing item scores.
Digit Span: Longest Digit Span Forward	n/a	• The Longest Digit Span Forward score is a raw process score for which base rates are available. • Range of this score is 0 to 10. • Equal to the number of digits that were recalled on the last Forward trial that was scored 1 point.

Subtest: Score	Item Score Range(s)	Scoring Tips
Digit Span: Longest Digit Span Backward	n/a	• The Longest Digit Span Backward score is a raw process score for which base rates are available. • Range of this score is 0 to 8. • Equal to the number of digits that were recalled on the last Backward trial that was scored 1 point.
Digit Span: Longest Digit Span Sequence	n/a	• The Longest Digit Span Sequence score is a raw process score for which base rates are available. • Range of this score is 0 to 9. • Equal to the number of digits that were recalled on the last Sequencing trial that was scored 1 point
Picture Span: Overall subtest score	Items 1–3: 0–1 point Items 4–26: 0–2 points	• For each item, record the child's response verbatim. The correct response(s) for each item appear on the Record Form, and are listed in the *WISC–V Administration and Scoring Manual*. **Items 1–3:** • Award 1 point if the child responds correctly and 0 points if the child responds incorrectly, says he or she doesn't know the answer, or does not respond to the item. **Items 4–26:** • Award 2 points if the child chooses all of the correct responses in the correct order. • Award 1 point if the child selects all of the correct responses in an incorrect order. • Award 0 points if the child does not choose all of the correct responses, chooses an incorrect response, says he or she doesn't know the answer, or does not respond to the item.
Picture Span: Longest Picture Span Stimuli	n/a	• The Longest Picture Span Stimuli score is a raw process score for which base rates are available. • Range of this score is 0 to 8. • Equal to the number of pictures on the stimulus page for the last item that received a perfect score.
Picture Span: Longest Picture Span Response	n/a	• The Longest Picture Span Response score is a raw process score for which base rates are available. • Range of this score is 0 to 12. • Equal to the number of pictures on the response page for the last item that received a perfect score.

(Continued)

(Continued)

Subtest: Score	Item Score Range(s)	Scoring Tips
Letter–Number Sequencing: Overall subtest score	0–3 points	• For each trial, record the child's response verbatim. The correct responses for each trial appear on the Record Form, and are listed in the *WISC–V Administration and Scoring Manual*. • Award 1 point for each trial if the child responds correctly and 0 points if the child does not respond correctly, says he or she doesn't know the answer, or does not respond to the trial. • Sum the trial scores to obtain the item scores.
Letter–Number Sequencing: Longest Letter–Number Sequence	n/a	• The Longest Letter–Number Sequence score is a raw process score for which base rates are available. • Range of this score is 0 to 9. • Equal to the number of letters and numbers that were recalled on the last Letter–Number Sequencing trial that was scored 1 point.

Processing Speed Subtests

It may be necessary to exercise some judgment when scoring the Processing Speed subtests. For Coding, as long as the symbol is paired correctly, is distinguishable from other symbols, is not rotated greater than or equal to 90 degrees in either direction relative to the keyed symbol, and resembles the keyed symbol, award credit. Do not penalize the child for slight motor imprecision issues.

Judgment becomes necessary on Symbol Search or Cancellation when the child makes a mark that is not precisely and clearly on a single symbol or object. The child may make inadvertent or stray marks due to motor imprecision or carelessness. Do not penalize the child for such issues as long as the child's intended response is clear. Judge a symbol or object as marked if it is clear that the child meant to mark it. If a mark extends through an adjacent symbol or object, don't judge the symbol or object as

marked unless the child clearly intended to mark it. If a child marks *more* than two responses on a Symbol Search test item, the entire item is scored as incorrect.

If the child marks on an area of white space between symbols or objects, judge the closest object to the mark as the intended selection. If you cannot determine which is closest, do not judge any symbol or object as marked.

Self-corrections are permitted on all Processing Speed subtests. Because self-corrections may result in scoring ambiguity, it is important to attend to the child as he or she responds and note which response was the intended. At times, what appears to be a self-correction actually may be a lapse in the child's attention to instructions.

Scoring keys with tips for the Processing Speed subtests appear in the Remember box. A comparison of WISC–IV and WISC–V Processing Speed subtest scoring appears in Table 3.5.

Table 3.5   Comparison of WISC–IV and WISC–V Processing Speed Subtest Scoring

WISC–IV	WISC–V
Coding	
All items: Score 0 or 1 point	All items: Score 0 or 1 point
Maximum of 6 time-bonus points available for Form A with perfect performance	No time-bonus points available for either Form
Maximum Total Raw Score:	Maximum Total Raw Score:
Form A: 65 points	Form A: 75 points
Form B: 119 points	Form B: 117 points
No process scores available	Rotation errors process score available
Symbol Search	
All items: Score 0 or 1 point	All items: Score 0 or 1 point
No time-bonus points available for either Form	Maximum of 2 time-bonus points available for Form A with perfect performance
Maximum Total Raw Score:	Maximum Total Raw Score:
Form A: 45 points	Form A: 42 points
Form B: 60 points	Form B: 60 points
No process scores available	Set errors process score available
	Rotation errors process score available
Cancellation	
Each item: Score 0–68 points	Each item: Score 0–64 points
Maximum of 4 time-bonus points available for each item with perfect performance	No time-bonus points available for either item
Maximum Total Raw Score: 136 points	Maximum Total Raw Score: 128 points
Cancellation Random process score available	Cancellation Random process score available
Cancellation Structured process score available	Cancellation Structured process score available

Remember

Processing Speed Subtest Scoring Keys

Subtest: Score	Item Score Range(s)	Scoring Tips
Coding: Overall subtest score	0–1 point	• Do **not** score items completed after the time limit expires. • Ensure the correct form of Coding was administered. There are two forms based on the child's age. Do not score the subtest if the wrong form was administered. Norms do not exist for children outside the specified age range for a form. • Do not score items completed after the time limit expires. • The Coding Scoring Template is used to score all responses. • Align the template with the correct responses appearing above the child's responses.

(Continued)

(Continued)

Subtest: Score	Item Score Range(s)	Scoring Tips
		• Note that the number for each test item appears on the scoring template to aid with calculation of total correct responses. • Award 1 point for a response if it is correctly drawn, as long as it is identifiable as the keyed symbol. The symbol does not need to be drawn identical to the keyed symbol, but it must be clear that the drawn symbol is not any other symbol in the key. • Do not award credit for rotated symbols. A symbol is judged as rotated if it is turned 90 degrees or more in either direction in relation to the keyed symbol. • Items the child did not attempt do not count as correct or incorrect. • Do not include demonstration or sample items in the total raw score. • If the child does not understand the task, does not complete any test items, or simply draws a line through the subtest, the total raw score is 0. • The total raw score is equal to the number of correctly drawn symbols within 120 seconds. • Unlike Symbol Search and Cancellation, **do not** subtract the total of incorrect responses from the total of correct responses to obtain the total raw score. • No time-bonus points are available for Coding.
Coding: Rotation Errors	Maximum of 1 rotation error per item	• The Coding Rotation Errors score is a raw process score for which base rates are available. • Sum the number of rotation errors made on the entire subtest. A symbol that is drawn rotated 90 degrees or more relative to the keyed symbol that remains uncorrected at the time limit is a rotation error. • Sum the total across the subtest; this is the raw score for Coding rotation errors.
Symbol Search: Overall subtest score	0–1 point	• Do **not** score items completed after the time limit expires. • The Symbol Search Scoring Key is used to score all responses. The correct responses appear in bold. The pages of the key are double sided. Use Side A to score the responses for pages 8 and 9, Side B to score the responses for pages 10 and 11, and so on. Be careful to use the correct side of the key.

Subtest: Score	Item Score Range(s)	Scoring Tips
		• Place the key over the page in the Response Booklet that is not being scored (e.g., if you are scoring page 10, place Side B over page 11). Ensure the targets in the Response booklet match those on the key. Align the key with the items to be scored on the opposite page. • Count items with the correct symbol and no other symbol marked as correct. • Count items with an incorrect symbol marked as incorrect. • Unless the child self-corrected, only 1 symbol may be marked for an item to count as correct. • Items the child did not attempt do not count as correct or incorrect. • Record the total number of correct and total number of incorrect responses at the bottom of each page attempted, including incomplete pages (e.g., a page with at least 1 of the items completed). • Sum the number of correct responses and incorrect responses across all pages. • Subtract the total of incorrect responses from the total of correct responses. • **For Form A**, this difference of correct minus incorrect responses is equal to the total raw score, but if the child received a perfect score, time-bonus points are available. If the child received a perfect score in 111–119 seconds, the total raw score is 41. If the child received a perfect score in less than or equal to 110 seconds, the total raw score is 42. • **For Form B**, no time bonus is awarded. The difference of correct minus incorrect responses is equal to the total raw score.
Symbol Search: Set Errors	Maximum of 1 set error per item	• The Symbol Search Set Errors score is a raw process score for which base rates are available. • Set errors are designated on the Symbol Search Scoring Key. • Sum the number of set errors made on each page of items. Record the total at the bottom of each page of the Response Booklet. • Sum the totals on each page to obtain the Symbol Search Set Errors raw score. • Maximum raw scores: Form A = 20; Form B = 30.

(Continued)

(Continued)

Subtest: Score	Item Score Range(s)	Scoring Tips
Symbol Search: Rotation Errors	Maximum of 1 set error per item	• The Symbol Search Rotation Errors score is a raw process score for which base rates are available. • Rotation errors are designated on the Symbol Search Scoring Key. • Sum the number of rotation errors made on each page of items. Record the total at the bottom of each page of the Response Booklet. • Sum the totals on each page to obtain the Symbol Search Rotation Errors raw score. • Maximum raw scores: Form A = 20; Form B = 30.
Cancellation: Overall subtest score	0–64 points	• Do not score objects that are marked after the time limit expires. • The Cancellation Scoring Template is used to score all responses on both items. • Place the template over the Response Booklet. Line up the edges of the template and the Response Booklet. The target responses appear in outlined boxes when they are aligned. • Count marks on targets as correct, and count marks on other objects as incorrect even if a single mark passes through more than 1 object. • Record the total correct and total incorrect responses for each item on the Record Form. • For each item, subtract the total of incorrect responses from the total of correct responses to obtain the total raw score for that item. If the number of incorrect responses is greater than the number of correct responses, enter the total raw score for that item as 0. • Sum the total raw scores for Item 1 and 2 to obtain the Cancellation total raw score. • **Do not** sum the numbers of correct and incorrect responses across both items and then subtract those sums to obtain the item score. This results in an inaccurate score if the total incorrect exceeds the total correct on one or both items. Score each item independently, then sum the total raw scores for each item to obtain the Cancellation total raw score.
Cancellation: Random	0–64 points	• Cancellation Random is a scaled process score. • The total raw score for Item 1 is the Cancellation Random total raw score.
Cancellation: Structured	0–64 points	• Cancellation Structured is a scaled process score. • The total raw score for Item 2 is the Cancellation Structured total raw score.

Naming Speed Subtests

The Naming Speed subtests are relatively straightforward to score, but some addition and transferring is involved. The child's responses and completion times must be recorded in the correct boxes carefully during administration.

For Naming Speed Literacy Items 1 and 2, synonyms for an object name or a size are acceptable and are not errors. The *WISC–V Administration and Scoring Manual* provides a list of common synonyms, but the list is not exhaustive. Use your judgment to decide if the child committed an error for synonyms that do not appear in the list.

Do not record correct responses. The typical pace of responding is too quick to allow for this. Only incorrect responses are recorded. A slash mark is placed through each misnamed element, aspect of an element, or quantity. Each slash mark, if not self-corrected, counts as an error. Multiple errors are possible on Naming Speed Literacy Items 1 and 2 for a single pictured object if more than one aspect of the object is misnamed (e.g., color and object misnamed on a single picture is equal to two errors).

Self-corrections are permitted on Naming Speed subtests and are not considered errors as long as they are corrected before the time limit. Self-corrections are not considered errors, although they are tracked for a process score.

Because self-corrections may result in scoring ambiguity, it is important to attend to the child as he or she responds and note the response that was the intended or final response when a self-correction is made.

It is important to attend closely to the addition required across trials for test items on the Naming Speed subtests. For example, for Naming Speed Literacy Item 1, you must sum the completion times of Trial 1 and Trial 2 to obtain the Naming Speed Color–Object total raw score. Also for Item 1, you must sum all errors made across both Trial 1 and Trial 2 to obtain the total number of errors for that item, and enter the total in the NScoe box. The Naming Speed errors should be calculated for all items where even a single error is made, because these process scores are necessary for interpretation.

For children aged 6 to 8, calculating the Naming Speed Literacy subtest total raw score involves transferring item-level performance to the bottom of the page and summing the item-level total raw scores. For children aged 9 to 16, the Naming Speed Literacy subtest total raw score is the same as the Item 3 item-level total raw score, because those children are administered that item only.

Scoring keys with tips for the Naming Speed subtests appear in the Remember box.

Remember
Naming Speed Subset Scoring Keys

Subtest: Score	Item Score Range(s)	Scoring Tips
Naming Speed Literacy: Overall subtest score	All items: 0–600 points (i.e., seconds)	• Record the completion time for each trial. • Do not record correct responses. • Record a misnamed element or aspect with a slash mark. Record a self-correction with an **SC**. • Sum the completion times for the two trials of an item to obtain the item total raw score.

(Continued)

(*Continued*)

Subtest: Score	Item Score Range(s)	Scoring Tips
		• For children aged 6–8, sum the completion times for the administered items to obtain the Naming Speed Literacy total raw score. • For children aged 9–16, the total raw score (the sum of the two trial completion times) for Item 3 is the total raw score. • Transfer all of the item total raw scores to the boxes at the bottom of the Naming Speed Literacy page of the Record Form. • Sum the number of errors across both trials of each administered item. For each item, record the sum as the error score corresponding to that item. Errors do not impact the total raw score but must be used to inform interpretation if any errors were made. • If a child aged 6–8 does not complete **both** of the necessary items, no total raw score for Naming Speed Literacy can be obtained. However, as long as 1 item is complete, the corresponding process score for that item can be obtained. • Both trials of the age-appropriate item(s) must be administered, or no Naming Speed Literacy subtest-level scores can be obtained.
Naming Speed Literacy: Color–Object (NSco) process score	0–600 points (i.e., seconds)	• Naming Speed Color–Object is a standard process score. • This score can be obtained only for children aged 6. • The total raw score for Item 1 is equal to the Naming Speed Literacy Color–Object total raw score.
Naming Speed Literacy: Size–Color–Object (NSsco) process score	0–600 points (i.e., seconds)	• Naming Speed Size–Color–Object is a standard process score. • This score can only be obtained for children aged 6–8. • The total raw score for Item 2 is equal to the Naming Speed Literacy Size–Color–Object total raw score.
Naming Speed Literacy: Letter–Number (NSln) process score	0–600 points (i.e., seconds)	• Naming Speed Letter–Number is a standard process score. • This score can be obtained only for children aged 7–16. • The total raw score for Item 3 is equal to the Naming Speed Literacy Letter–Number total raw score.

Subtest: Score	Item Score Range(s)	Scoring Tips
Naming Speed Literacy: Color–Object Errors (NScoe) process score	0–80	• Naming Speed Color–Object Errors is a raw process score for which base rates are available. • This score can be obtained only for children aged 6. • Self-corrections are not classified as errors. • A response is not considered to be completed until the child has fully named the quantity in question. If a child corrects a word midstream, do not count this as a self-correction or an error if the last portion of what is said reflects a correct name for the element or aspect of the element. • Sum the number of errors across both trials of Item 1. Record the sum as the NScoe score in the box for that item. • Errors do not impact the corresponding total raw score but must be used to inform interpretation if any errors were made.
Naming Speed Literacy: Size–Color–Object Errors (NSscoe) process score	0–120	• Naming Speed Size–Color–Object Errors is a raw process score for which base rates are available. • This score can be obtained only for children aged 6–8. • Self-corrections are not classified as errors. • A response is not considered to be completed until the child has fully named the quantity in question. If a child corrects a word midstream, do not count this as a self-correction or an error if the last portion of what is said reflects a correct name for the element or aspect of the element. • Sum the number of errors across both trials of Item 2. Record the sum as the NSscoe score in the box for that item. • Errors do not impact the corresponding total raw score but must be used to inform interpretation if any errors were made.
Naming Speed Literacy: Letter–Number Errors (NSlne) process score	0–80	• Naming Speed Letter–Number Errors is a raw process score for which base rates are available. • This score can be obtained only for children aged 7–8. • Self-corrections are not classified as errors. • A response is not considered to be completed until the child has fully named the letter or number in question. If a child corrects a name midstream, do not count this as a self-correction or an error if the last portion of what is said reflects a correct name for the letter or number. • Sum the number of errors across both trials of Item 3. Record the sum as the NSlne score in the box for Item 3. • Errors do not impact the corresponding total raw score but must be used to inform interpretation if any errors were made.

(Continued)

(Continued)

Subtest: Score	Item Score Range(s)	Scoring Tips
Naming Speed Literacy: Errors (NSLe) process score	Age 6: 0–200 Age 7–8: 0–200 Age 9–16: 0–80	• Naming Speed Literacy Errors is a raw process score for which base rates are available. • Count the number of errors across the 2 trials for each item that was administered. • Enter the number of errors in the NScoe, NSscoe, and/or NSlne boxes for the administered items. • Transfer the number of errors for each administered item to the Process Analysis page of the Record Form. • For children aged 6–8, sum the errors across the 2 administered items. If both age-appropriate items were not administered, this score cannot be obtained. • Record the sum in the NSLe box in the Raw Score to Base Rate conversion table on the bottom left half of the Process Analysis page of the Record Form. • For children aged 9–16, transfer the number of errors from the NSlne box to the NSLe box in the Raw Score to Base Rate conversion table on the bottom left half of the Process Analysis page of the Record Form.
Naming Speed Quantity: Overall subtest score	All items: 0–600 points (i.e., seconds)	• Record the completion time for each trial. • Do not record correct responses. • Record a misnamed quantity with a slash mark. Record a self-correction with an **SC**. • Sum the completion times for the two trials of an item to obtain the subtest total raw score. • For children aged 6, the Naming Speed Quantity total raw score is equal to the sum of the trial completion times for Item 1. • For children aged 7–16, the Naming Speed Quantity total raw score is equal to the sum of the trial completion times for Item 2. • Both trials of the age-appropriate item must be administered, or no Naming Speed Quantity score can be obtained.
Naming Speed Quantity: Errors (NSQe) process score	0–40	• Naming Speed Quantity Errors is a raw process score for which base rates are available. • Count the number of errors across the two trials for the item that was administered. • Enter the number of errors in the NSQe box. • Transfer the figure in the NSQe box in the Raw Score to Base Rate conversion table on the bottom left half of the Process Analysis page of the Record Form.

Symbol Translation Subtests

The Symbol Translation subtests also are relatively straightforward to score. Responses must be recorded carefully during administration.

For the Immediate and Delayed Symbol Translation subtests, you **must** record performance at the symbol level, and only **correct** responses are recorded. (This is the opposite of what is done on the Naming Speed subtests, where only incorrect responses are recorded). A checkmark is placed in the box above each correctly named symbol for correct responses. The boxes over incorrect translations are left blank. If a box above a symbol is filled with teal, it corresponds to a frequently used conjunction for which credit is not awarded after Item 6. Do not check these boxes.

For Immediate and Delayed Symbol Translation, keep in mind that the translation given for each symbol must be exact to receive credit. Synonyms and incorrect changes in tense, plurality, or sounds at the end of a word are not acceptable. However, errors in word forms aren't incorrect or penalized if they demonstrate retention of the meaning and concept. For example, if "go" is the symbol and the modifier for "past tense" appears above the "go" symbol, if the child says "goed" rather than "went" then credit should be awarded.

Self-corrections are permitted on all Symbol Translation subtests. Award credit for responses that are correct after a self-correction is made. Because self-corrections may result in scoring ambiguity, it is important to attend to the child as he or she responds and note the intended or final response whenever a self-correction is made.

For Immediate Symbol Translation and Delayed Symbol Translation, 1 point is awarded for each checkmark on an item. Sum the number of checkmarks and note it in the Item Score column. The number of points possible for each item is noted in small teal font in the box for each

item score. These cues are especially helpful for Items 14–21 because there are quite a few translations required for these items and there are a number of teal-filled boxes corresponding to frequently used conjunctions that do not receive credit if correctly translated.

For Items 1–3 of Immediate Symbol Translation, score only the last trial that was completed. Score 1 point for each correct translation. Score 0 points for an incorrect translation, if the translation was skipped, or if the child failed to respond after about 5 seconds. Remember to record the number of correct translations for the last completed trial only in the Item Score column.

For Items 4–6 of Immediate Symbol Translation and Items 1–6 of Delayed Symbol Translation, score 1 point for each correct translation. Score 0 points for an incorrect translation, if the translation was skipped, or if the child failed to respond after about 5 seconds. Record the number of correct translations in the Item Score column.

For Items 7–21 of both Immediate Symbol Translation and Delayed Symbol Translation, teal-filled boxes correspond to frequently used conjunctions that do not receive credit if correctly translated. Apart from these conjunctions, score 1 point for each correct translation. Score 0 points for an incorrect translation, or if the translation was skipped, or if the child failed to respond after about 5 seconds. Record the number of correct translations in the Item Score column.

Scoring of Recognition Symbol Translation is very simple. One point is possible per item for a correctly selected translation. Circle 0 or 1 point in the Item Score column for each item.

For all Symbol Translation subtests, record the cumulative raw score at each of the decision points (designated A, B, and C) to determine if the discontinue criterion is met. Scoring keys with tips for the Symbol Translation subtests appear in the Remember box.

Remember

Symbol Translation Subtest Scoring Keys

Subtest	Item Score Range(s)	Scoring Tips
Immediate Symbol Translation	Items 1–2: 0–2 points Item 3: 0–3 points Items 4–6, 12, 13, 15,: 0–5 points Items 7–11: 0–4 points Items 14 & 16: 0–6 points Items 17–18: 0–7 points Items 19 & 21: 0–8 points Item 20: 0–9 points	• Score the translation correct only if it is precise. Remember that errors in word forms aren't penalized. • Award 1 point for each correct translation. • Record a checkmark in the box above each correct translation. • Note incorrect responses for later qualitative observations. • For each decision point, record the cumulative raw score to determine whether the discontinue rule has been met. • For Items 1–3, sum the total number of correct translations for the last trial completed and record the result in the Item Score column. • For Items 4–6, sum the total number of correct translations and record the result in the Item Score column. • For Items 7–21, repeat the process used for Items 4–6 but do not award credit for correct translations of symbols corresponding to the 2 frequently used conjunctions. A teal-filled box appears on the Record Form for these translations.
Delayed Symbol Translation	Items 1–2: 0–1 point Item 3, 8–9: 0–2 points Items 4–6, 11, 15, 16, 18, & 21: 0–5 points Items 7 & 13: 0–3 points Items 10 & 12, 20: 0–4 points Items 14 & 19: 0–6 points	• Score the translation correct only if it is precise. Remember that errors in word forms aren't penalized. • Award 1 point for each correct translation. • Record a checkmark in the box above each correct translation. • Note incorrect responses for later qualitative observations. • For each decision point record the cumulative raw score to determine whether the discontinue rule has been met. • For Items 1–6, sum the total number of correct translations and record the result in the Item Score column. • For Items 7–21, repeat the process used for Items 4–6 but do not award credit for correct translations of symbols corresponding to the 2 frequently used conjunctions. A teal-filled box appears on the Record Form for these translations.
Recognition Symbol Translation	Items 1–34: 0–1 point	• For each item, award 1 point if the child responds correctly. • Award 0 points if the child responds incorrectly, says he or she doesn't know the answer, or does not respond to the item.

WISC–V SCORES

This section offers a general description of WISC–V score types and distributions. Item scores, total raw scores, scaled and standard scores, raw scores, and contrast scores are described and explained.

Item Scores

An item score is equal to the total points that are awarded for aspects of the child's performance on a given item. The range of item scores varies across subtests as well as within some subtests.

Points are awarded for correct responses. For some items, additional points are awarded for correct responses that are higher in quality (e.g., Similarities, Vocabulary, and Comprehension); relative completeness (e.g., Block Design Partial score); and attempts required to produce a correct response (e.g., Block Design items with two trials).

Total Raw Scores

In most cases, the total raw score is merely the sum of the item scores. There are a few exceptions. For Symbol Search and Cancellation, the total raw score is calculated by subtracting total incorrect responses from total correct responses to reflect the contribution of both speed and accuracy to performance. The Naming Speed subtest total raw scores are based on item completion times only, although error scores are calculated and used in interpretation.

Total raw scores are converted to scaled or standard scores. Do not use total raw scores to make inferences about the child's intellectual ability relative to the general population. For this purpose, rely on the scaled and standard scores.

A subtest's total raw score may be invalid occasionally, but **a total raw score of zero does not mean that the score is invalid**. Administration errors, poor effort on behalf of the child, or unexpected interruptions or occurrences during administration may render a subtest score invalid. If a child does not respond correctly to the Digit Span Sequencing qualifying item or to one of the Letter–Number Sequencing qualifying items, the total raw score for the subtest is missing (not zero) and invalid.

For all other primary and secondary subtests that do not have qualifying items and for the Symbol Translation subtests, the child may respond incorrectly to a sample item, thereby ceasing administration prior to administration of the scored test items and resulting in a total raw score of zero. At other times, the child's score on all administered test items may be zero. In these situations, the total raw score is zero. It is not missing or invalid.

If the child is unable to respond correctly to a sample item and administration of a Naming Speed item or subtest does not proceed past the sample item, you should assign the standard score that corresponds to the maximum completion time for the subtest (and for the relevant process score if the child is aged 6 to 8).

Scaled and Standard Scores

The WISC–V has both scaled scores and standard scores. They are scaled to various metrics listed in Quick Reference 3.3.

Scaled Scores

Subtest scaled scores and scaled process scores are scaled to means of 10, standard deviations (*SDs*) of 3, and ranges of 1 to 19.

Standard Scores

Standard scores consist of the published index scores, the FSIQ, the complementary subtest scores and some of the complementary process scores, and the additional index scores in this book. Index scores and the FSIQ are derived from various sums of subtest scaled or standard scores, except for the Storage and Retrieval Index, which is derived from the sum of the two complementary index scores—the Naming Speed Index and the Symbol Translation Index.

QUICK REFERENCE 3.3: WISC–V SCALED AND STANDARD SCORE METRICS

Score Types	Mean	Standard Deviation	Range
Subtest scaled score	10	3	1–19
Scaled process score			
Complementary subtest scores and some complementary process scores	100	15	45–155
Index scores used to describe specific abilities (e.g., primary index scores, Auditory Working Memory Index)			
Composite scores typically used to summarize global performance or that may be compared with Full Scale IQ (FSIQ) performance for clinical purposes (e.g., FSIQ, Nonverbal Index, General Ability Index, & Cognitive Proficiency Index)	100	15	40–160

Standard scores have a mean of 100 and a standard deviation of 15. The range of standard scores varies based on content used to derive that composite score. For standard scores designed to describe specific abilities the range is 45 to 155. For composite scores that are typically used to summarize global performance or that may be compared with the FSIQ for some clinical purposes, the range is 40 to 160.

Intellectual abilities are normally distributed in the general population. For standard scores, about 50% of children score within ±10 points of the mean (90–110), about 68% score within ±15 points (i.e., 1 SD) of the mean (85–115), and approximately 96% score within ±30 points (i.e., 2 SDs) of the mean (70–130). About 2% of children score higher than 130 (more than 2 SDs above the mean), and 2% of children score below 70 (more than 2 SDs below the mean).

Raw Process Scores

The WISC–V features a number of raw process scores that provide information about memory span, errors, and process observations. These do not involve summing item-level scores. They do not result in scaled or standard scores, but base rates (percentile ranks) for performance can be obtained.

Longest Span and Sequence Scores

The longest span and sequence scores provide information about maximum performance on the Working Memory subtests. They are often consistent with the corresponding scaled scores but might be informative if the child has inconsistent performance across trials or items with the same span length. Each subtest-specific scoring key of the Working Memory subtest section of this chapter describes how to calculate the longest span and sequence raw scores.

The Process Analysis page of the Record Form provides space to record the raw score and base rate for each longest span and sequence score. Use Table C.17 of the *WISC–V Administration and Scoring Manual Supplement* to obtain the base rate. Locate the selected reference group in the table and the child's raw score at the far right of the table, and read across the row to the column corresponding to the appropriate process score. Record the value in the Base Rate column of the Raw Score to Base

Rate Conversion table on the Process Analysis page of the Record Form. The longest span and sequence scores are listed in the Remember box.

Remember

Longest Span and Sequence Scores

- Longest Digit Span Forward
- Longest Digit Span Backward
- Longest Digit Span Sequence
- Longest Picture Span Stimulus
- Longest Picture Span Response
- Longest Letter–Number Sequence

Error Scores

The error scores are derived by tallying errors committed across a subtest (e.g., Coding rotation errors) or during an item (e.g., Naming Speed Letter–Number Errors). A total of 10 error scores are available across five subtests. Each subtest-specific scoring section of this chapter describes how to calculate these error scores.

The Process Analysis page of the Record Form provides space to record the raw score and base rate for each error score. Use Table C.18 of the *WISC–V Administration and Scoring Manual Supplement* to obtain the base rate. Locate the selected reference group in the table and the child's raw score at the far right of the table, and read across the row to the column corresponding to the appropriate process score. Record the value in the Base Rate column of the Raw Score to Base Rate Conversion table on the Process Analysis page of the Record Form. The error scores are listed in the Remember box.

Remember

Error Scores

- Block Design Dimension Errors
- Block Design Rotation Errors
- Coding Rotation Errors
- Symbol Search Set Errors
- Symbol Search Rotation Errors
- Naming Speed Literacy Errors
- Naming Speed Color–Object Errors
- Naming Speed Size–Color–Object Errors
- Naming Speed Letter–Number Errors
- Naming Speed Quantity Errors

Process Observations

The process observations are based on your observations of testing behaviors during administration. They are derived by tallying behaviors observed across a subtest (e.g., total "Don't Know" responses given on Similarities). A total of six types of process observations are available across several subtests.

The Record Form does not provide space to count these observations. Simply write the abbreviations introduced in Chapter 2 of this book on the subtest section of the Record Form to record their occurrence. The Record Form also does not provide space to record or calculate the raw score or base rate for process observations.

Use Appendix D of the *WISC–V Technical and Interpretive Manual* to obtain the base rates associated with desired process observations. Locate the selected reference group in the table and the child's raw score at the far right or left of the table, and read across the row to the column corresponding to the appropriate subtest. We suggest you record the raw score and base rate value of any process observations you wish to report on the Behavioral Observations page of the Record Form.

The process observations are listed in the Remember box, along with an indication of which base rates are available. Most will be familiar or are self-explanatory, except perhaps for subvocalization. *Subvocalization* refers to any perceptible self-talk during subtest administration.

Remember

Various Process Observation Base Rates Available by Subtest

Subtest	Don't Know	No Response	Item Repetition	Requested Repetition	Subvocali- zation	Self- Correction
Similarities	Yes	Yes	Yes	No	No	No
Vocabulary	Yes	Yes	Yes	No	No	No
Information	Yes	Yes	Yes	No	No	No
Comprehension	Yes	Yes	Yes	No	No	No
Block Design	No	No	No	No	No	No
Visual Puzzles	Yes	Yes	No	No	Yes	Yes
Matrix Reasoning	Yes	Yes	No	No	Yes	Yes
Figure Weights	Yes	Yes	No	No	Yes	Yes
Picture Concepts	Yes	Yes	No	No	Yes	Yes
Arithmetic	Yes	Yes	Yes	No	Yes	Yes
Digit Span	No	No	No	Yes	No	Yes
Picture Span	Yes	Yes	No	No	Yes	Yes
Letter–Number Sequencing	No	No	No	Yes	No	Yes
Coding	No	No	No	No	No	No
Symbol Search	No	No	No	No	No	No
Cancellation	No	No	No	No	No	No
Naming Speed Literacy	No	No	No	No	No	Yes
Naming Speed Quantity	No	No	No	No	No	Yes
Immediate Symbol Translation	No	No	No	No	No	No
Delayed Symbol Translation	No	No	No	No	No	No
Recognition Symbol Translation	Yes	Yes	No	No	No	No

Contrast Scores

Contrast scores can provide more information about a child's performance on a given task in comparison to other children from the normative sample who scored at the same level on another, related task. They are a different way of looking at discrepancies between scores while taking the child's level of performance into account. A total of six contrast scores are available.

Use Appendix C of the *WISC–V Technical and Interpretive Manual* to derive the contrast scores. Before you can derive a contrast score, you must have already calculated the scaled or standard scores that are involved.

For contrast scores that involve scaled scores (i.e., a range of 1–19), locate the column with the score range that includes the obtained score for the first score in the name of the contrast score. For example, for DSf vs. DSb, find the range in the top row of the table in which the Digit Span Forward scaled score falls.

Then read down the column on the far left or right of the table to find the child's score for the second scaled score in the name of the contrast score. In the previous example, this would be the Digit Span Backward scaled score. Find the cell of the table where the column corresponding to the range of the first score and the row corresponding to the second score meet, and this is the child's contrast scaled score.

For contrast scores that involve standard scores (i.e., those with a mean of 100), locate the range that includes the first standard score in the top row of the table. Then read down the column and find the range including the second standard score, and read across that row to obtain the contrast scaled score.

We suggest you record any contrast scores you wish to report on the Behavioral Observations page of the Record Form. This is easy to do if you detach the Summary and Analysis pages from the remainder of the Record Form, because you can quickly find the scaled and standard scores you will need.

The contrast scores are listed in the Remember box.

Remember

Contrast Scores

- Digit Span Forward vs. Digit Span Backward
- Digit Span Forward vs. Digit Span Sequencing
- Digit Span Sequencing vs. Letter–Number Sequencing
- Cancellation Structured vs. Cancellation Random
- Immediate Symbol Translation vs. Delayed Symbol Translation
- Recognition Symbol Translation vs. Delayed Symbol Translation

---

STEP BY STEP: WISC–V SUBTEST AND COMPOSITE SCORES

This section provides an overview of the scoring process, from total raw scores to subtest scaled scores to index scores. This information is accompanied by a discussion of substitution, proration, and invalidation procedures.

It is important to note that each step should be double checked. A recent study conducted on Wechsler protocols suggests that double checking item-level scoring and each step in the scoring procedure reduces errors by 52.5% and reduces inaccurate FSIQs by 67% (Kuentzel, Hetterscheidt, & Barnett, 2011).

Obtain Total Raw Scores

When calculating the sum of the item scores, remember to include points earned for reversal items and unadministered items prior to the start point, if applicable. After calculating the total raw score for each desired subtest and process score, transfer them to the Total Raw Score to Scaled Score Conversion table on the Summary page of the Record Form. It is a good idea to detach the Summary and Analysis pages before doing this. They are perforated for the purpose of transfer of records in the future if necessary, but it will make your job easier and may prevent errors if you detach them prior to this process. They can be reattached with tape later. Cross-check the two numbers for consistency.

If you intend to calculate any scaled process scores, transfer the associated total raw scores for the relevant process scores to the Total Raw Score to Scaled/Standard Process Score Conversion table on the top of the Process Analysis page at the same time to prevent having to turn back to those pages in the Record Form later. The Process Analysis page is located on the back of the Primary Analysis page.

Follow a similar process for any administered complementary subtests. Transfer the total raw scores to the Total Raw Score to Standard Score Conversion table in the upper right hand corner of the Ancillary and Complementary Analysis page of the Record Form. The Ancillary Analysis page is located on the back side of the Summary page of the Record Form.

Incorrect transfer of raw scores from the subtest-specific Record Form pages to the Summary page where scaled scores are calculated is one of the most common scoring errors on the Summary page (Mrazik, Janzen, Dombrowski, Barford, & Krawchuk, 2012). Simple point-counting errors accounted for more than 60% of scoring errors on Wechsler protocols in a recent study (Kuentzel et al., 2011).

The Attention box lists common errors in obtaining total raw scores.

Attention

Common Errors in Obtaining Total Raw Scores

- Awarding points for sample items, which are not scored.
- Not including points earned from unadministered items (e.g., prior to the start point or prior to the first two items on which the child received full credit if the child reversed) in the total raw score.
- Simple incorrect mental calculation when attempting to sum the item points.
- Not awarding full credit for all items prior to the age-appropriate start point if the child receives full credit on both of the age-appropriate start point items but began with Item 1.
- Neglecting to include points earned from items from the first page of a subtest section on the Record Form, when the subtest spreads across two pages (e.g., Block Design, Information, Similarities, Vocabulary, and Comprehension).
- Awarding credit to items that were mistakenly administered after a discontinue was established.
- On subtests with items for which multiple points are possible (i.e., Block Design, Similarities, Object Assembly, Vocabulary, Comprehension), awarding only 1 point of credit for items on which 2 points or more were earned.
- On subtests with a scoring key or template (i.e., Coding, Symbol Search, and Cancellation), not using the key or template and scoring incorrectly, resulting in an inaccurate total raw score.
- Forgetting to subtract Number Incorrect from Number Correct to obtain the total raw score on subtests scored in this manner (i.e., Symbol Search and Cancellation).
- On Block Design, mistakenly using the instructions for Block Design No Time Bonus or Block Design Partial to obtain the overall subtest total raw score. These should only be used to obtain the total raw scores associated with those respective scaled process scores.
- On Naming Speed Literacy for children aged 6 to 8, neglecting to add both item scores together to obtain the total raw score.

Obtain Scaled or Standard Subtest Scores

Total raw scores are converted to scaled or standard scores. Scaled scores, standard subtest scores, and standard process scores are age-based. The child's age on the date of testing in years, months, and days (i.e., test age; calculated in the upper right-hand corner of the Summary page using the Calculation of Child's Age table) is used to select the proper portion of the appropriate normative table to use.

For primary and secondary subtests, the age span for each page of the normative table is noted at the top of each page of Table A.1 of the *WISC–V Administration and Scoring Manual*. The subtests appear in columns from left to right across Table A.1. Each page contains only one normative age group.

The *WISC–V Administration and Scoring Manual Supplement* is a coil-bound paperback booklet that is easily mistaken for a stimulus book because of its size and because it does not have a hard cover. While it is unnecessary for subtest administration, you must have it available to obtain the process scores or any of the complementary scores. One of these manuals is included in every kit.

Table C.14 of the *WISC–V Administration and Scoring Manual Supplement* contains the analogous information for the process scores associated with primary and secondary subtests. Two normative age groups appear on each page of the table.

For complementary subtests and complementary process scores, the analogous table is C.6 of the *WISC–V Administration and Scoring Manual Supplement*. Each normative age group appears on a two-page spread.

Be very cautious to select the correct portion of the normative tables. Using the incorrect area of the normative table represented 24% of Summary page scoring errors in a recent study of Wechsler protocols (Mrazik et al., 2012). Check the age span label to ensure you are on the page of the table that corresponds to the child's age. For the scaled process scores in Table C.14, check the table header at the top of the panel to ensure you are using the appropriate panel of the page. An area of white space separates the top and bottom panels. The upper panel corresponds to a younger normative age group, and the lower panel corresponds to an older normative age group.

Locate the appropriate column for the subtest or process score in question, and read down the column until you locate the total raw score for that subtest. Read straight across the row to the shaded column that lists the scaled or standard score corresponding to the child's total raw score. For primary and secondary subtests, transfer that value into all the unshaded boxes to the right of the raw score on the Total Raw Score to Scaled Score Conversion Table on the Summary page. Follow a similar process for scaled and standard process scores and the complementary subtests if desired, using the analogous conversion tables on the Ancillary and Complementary Analysis page and the Process Analysis page. If you plan to calculate any of the ancillary index scores, also fill in the appropriate unshaded boxes on the Sum of Scaled Scores table on the Ancillary Analysis page.

If you plan to substitute a subtest when calculating the FSIQ, be sure to also write the scaled score in the unshaded box with parentheses in its row of the Total Raw Score to Scaled Score Conversion Table on the Summary page. These boxes indicate that a subtest scaled score can be used in substitution to calculate the FSIQ (subject to some constraints).

The Attention box lists common errors in using total raw scores to obtain scaled or standard subtest or process scores.

Attention

Common Errors in Obtaining Scaled Scores

- Transferring a total raw score from the subtest page to the wrong row of the Total Raw Score to Scaled/Standard Score Conversion table on the Record Form. For example, the examiner mistakenly transfers the total raw score for Information into the row that corresponds to Block Design.
- Using the wrong page of Table A.1, C.6, or C.14.
- Using the wrong panel of a page from Table C.14.
- Reading down an incorrect column of Table A.1, C.6, or C.14 that corresponds to a different subtest or process score from the one being converted.
- If a total raw score is within the scaled score range (1–19) or standard score range (45–155), mistakenly reading down the Scaled Score or Standard Score column to the number that corresponds to the total raw score, then reading across the row to the column that corresponds to the subtest's total raw score and entering that number as the scaled score or standard score on the Record Form.
- Recording the wrong scaled score in a given row. For example, the examiner mistakenly records the scaled score for Similarities in the row that corresponds to Matrix Reasoning.

Obtain Sums of Scaled and Standard Scores

After obtaining subtest and process scaled scores and standard scores, sums of these scores are calculated to obtain composite scores. On the Record Form Summary page in the Total Raw Score to Scaled Score Conversion table and on the Ancillary and Complementary Analysis page in the Sum of Scaled Scores and the Total Raw Score to Standard Score Conversion tables, the scores of subtests used to derive each composite score (column) have been written in the unshaded boxes with no parentheses. (For the FSIQ, the scaled scores of subtests that may be substituted, subject to constraints, appear in the unshaded boxes with parentheses on the far right column.)

Add the scaled or standard scores for each column. Enter the sums in the boxes at the bottom of the tables in the row labeled Sum of Scaled or Sum of Standard Scores for any desired composite scores.

These instructions work for all composite scores except for the Storage and Retrieval Index. To obtain this index, you will need to complete an additional step. It is a special case because the Naming Speed Index and the Symbol Translation Index are summed to obtain a sum of standard scores to derive the Storage and Retrieval Index.

Substitution

No substitution is permitted for the sums of scaled scores used to calculate the index scores. If you do not have valid scores for all necessary subtests, the corresponding index score cannot be calculated.

Similarly, no substitution is permitted for any additional index score that appears in this book and in the downloadable resources: www.wiley .com/go/itwiscv. The Remember box lists the subtests used to calculate index scores in the published test.

Remember

Subtests Used to Calculate Index Scores (No Substitution Allowed)

Primary Index Scores

Verbal Comprehension Index	Visual Spatial Index	Fluid Reasoning Index	Working Memory Index	Processing Speed Index
Similarities Vocabulary	Block Design Visual Puzzles	Matrix Reasoning Figure Weights	Digit Span Picture Span	Coding Symbol Search

Ancillary Index Scores

Quantitative Reasoning Index	Auditory Working Memory Index	Nonverbal Index	General Ability	Cognitive Proficiency
Figure Weights Arithmetic	Digit Span Letter–Number Sequencing	Block Design Visual Puzzles Matrix Reasoning Figure Weights Picture Span Coding	Similarities Vocabulary Block Design Matrix Reasoning Figure Weights	Digit Span Picture Span Coding Symbol Search

Ancillary Index Scores (Continued)

Quantitative Reasoning Index	Auditory Working Memory Index	Nonverbal Index	General Ability	Cognitive Proficiency
Figure Weights Arithmetic	Digit Span Letter–Number Sequencing	Block Design Visual Puzzles Matrix Reasoning Figure Weights Picture Span Coding	Similarities Vocabulary Block Design Matrix Reasoning Figure Weights	Digit Span Picture Span Coding Symbol Search

The sums of scaled scores used to calculate the FSIQ permit substitution of *only one* subtest if one of the seven "FSIQ subtests" (i.e., the group of seven subtests used to calculate the FSIQ under standard conditions) is missing or invalid. Only one subtest can be substituted, even though multiple subtests are available to choose from.

Substitute the relevant value on the Summary page when you are calculating the sum of scaled scores in the Sum of Scaled Scores to Composite Score Conversion table, in the box corresponding to the Full Scale. Note "SUB" if substitution was used to derive the FSIQ.

The Remember box lists the FSIQ subtests used to calculate the FSIQ with one subtest substitution allowed. The substitutions for these FSIQ subtests are restricted to certain subtests that measure a similar construct as that of the missing FSIQ subtest. These acceptable substitutions are listed in Quick Reference 3.4.

Remember

Seven Subtests Used to Calculate the FSIQ (FSIQ Subtests)

- Similarities
- Vocabulary
- Block Design
- Matrix Reasoning
- Figure Weights
- Digit Span
- Coding

Proration

Subtests can be rendered invalid due to unexpected occurrences during administration. For example, administration errors, low effort on the part of the child, or interruptions during a subtest may render a subtest invalid. In this situation, subtest substitution is the preferred option where available because it provides an additional measure of a similar aspect of the child's cognitive ability (i.e., subtest performance on a subtest from the same scale).

Proration of a sum of scaled scores permits a composite score to be derived if a suitable substitution is unavailable. For the WISC–V, proration is permitted only for deriving the FSIQ. Proration is not permitted when deriving any index score.

When substitution or proration is used, interpret the FSIQ with additional caution and carefully consider the subtests that were used to derive it, particularly if the score will be used to make decisions about diagnosis, services, or placement.

If only one FSIQ subtest is missing, proration may be used to derive the Full Scale sum of scaled scores. Six valid FSIQ subtest scores must be available in order to obtain the prorated Full Scale sum of scaled scores. Table A.8 in the *WISC–V Administration and Scoring Manual* shows the prorated sums of scaled scores for deriving the FSIQ from the sum of six scaled scores rather than seven. Record the value on the Summary page in the Sum of Scaled Scores to

QUICK REFERENCE 3.4: ACCEPTABLE SUBSTITUTIONS FOR FSIQ SUBTESTS (LIMIT OF ONE SUBSTITUTION)

FSIQ Subtest	Acceptable Substitutions
Similarities	Information or Comprehension
Vocabulary	Information or Comprehension
Block Design	Visual Puzzles
Matrix Reasoning	Picture Concepts
Figure Weights	Picture Concepts or Arithmetic
Digit Span	Picture Span or Letter–Number Sequencing
Coding	Symbol Search or Cancellation

Note: Only one substitution is allowed because substitution introduces additional measurement error.

Composite Score Conversion table, in the box corresponding to the Full Scale. Note "PRO" next to that value to indicate the sum of scaled scores was based on proration.

Limits on Substitution and Proration

The use of substitution and proration is limited to reduce the occurrence of measurement error. The limits on substitution and proration are listed in the Attention box.

Attention

Limits on Substitution and Proration

- Substitution cannot be used to derive any index score.
- Proration cannot be used to derive any index score.
- Only one subtest can be substituted for an FSIQ subtest.
- Proration is allowed for the Full Scale sum of scaled scores, but only one FSIQ subtest scaled score can be missing.
- Proration and substitution cannot be combined to obtain the Full Scale sum of scaled scores If a substitution is made, proration cannot be used. If proration is used, a substitution cannot be made.

Substitution, Proration, or Retest: Which Replacement Approach Is Best?

When deriving the FSIQ, the most difficult decisions arise when a subtest's score is missing because the subtest was not administered or was spoiled. For example, a subtest's score may be missing due to task interruption during a subtest with a time limit or due to the child being unable to complete a task such as Block Design due to physical limitations. For whatever reason, when the score of an FSIQ subtest is missing, the published test indicates you must decide if you will substitute another subtest or prorate the Full Scale sum of scaled scores. Additional measurement error is introduced in either case.

Replacement Approach Comparison Studies with the WPPSI–IV Recent investigations conducted on the Wechsler Preschool and Primary Scale of Intelligence–Fourth Edition (WPPSI–IV; Wechsler, 2012) standardization normative sample, the combined special group samples, and the retest sample investigated the impact of three approaches to the problem of missing subtests (Zhu & Cayton, 2013; Zhu, Cayton, & Chen, under review). The three methods were:

1. substitution,
2. proration, and

3. retest (i.e., retesting the child on the same subtest, then using the subtest score from the second testing to calculate the FSIQ).

Results indicated that substitution and proration approaches tend to result in slightly more frequent underestimation of the FSIQ, whereas the retest approach tends to result in slightly more frequent overestimation. Substitution, proration, and retest appear to increase the measurement error in the FSIQ by 20% to 64%, depending on the particular subtest.

Of the three approaches, retest resulted in the least additional measurement error. For retest, only 2.9% to 5.8% of FSIQs in the retest sample changed by at least 6 points, depending on the subtest that was retested.

The substitution and proration approaches introduced amounts of measurement error that were similar to one another, but the specific results (i.e., which method introduced more measurement error) varied according to which subtest was substituted. For substitution, between 6.6% and 15.1% of FSIQs in the normative sample changed by at least 6 points, depending on the subtest that was substituted. For proration, between 9.7% and 14.0% of FSIQs in the normative sample changed by at least 6 points, depending on the subtest that was missing.

Measurement error introduced by the substitution and proration approaches were similar across the nonclinical and clinical samples, with slightly higher percentages of error in the nonclinical sample. Because no retest study was conducted with special groups, the results of the retest approach could not be compared with substitution and proration among clinical samples.

There are important limitations to the aforementioned investigation into the retest approach, despite its apparent reduction in measurement error. These include the testing interval in the retest study, the size of the retest sample, and the child's initial score. With respect to the testing interval, the test-retest interval ranged from 7 to 48 days, with a mean interval of 23 days. The impact of retesting immediately after an interrupted or spoiled subtest, or at the end of the testing session, to obtain a retest score is unknown. One might speculate that immediate retest could result in a larger score increase on some subtests where procedural learning is more likely and a smaller score increase on subtests where children do not have an intervening 23 days to learn additional words and information (e.g., Information). The size of the retest sample was relatively small ($n = 115$). Furthermore, the retest results seem very likely to vary by the child's initial score due to regression to the mean; children with higher scores may have lower scores upon retest, and children with lower scores may have higher scores upon retest.

Replacement Approach Comparison Study with the WISC–V The WISC–V standardization data have been subjected to analyses to compare the substitution and proration approaches. The measurement error of every allowable substitution and every proration scenario was examined. Retest is being examined at the time of this writing (Zhu, Cayton, Raiford, & Chen, in preparation).

Substitution introduced less measurement error than did proration, but the amount of measurement error introduced varied according to which subtest was substituted. After substitution, between 87.8% and 97.6% of FSIQs in the normative sample were within the 95% confidence interval of the original FSIQs, depending on the subtest that was substituted. After proration, between 84.0% and 92.1% of FSIQs in the normative sample were within the 95% confidence interval of the FSIQs, depending on the subtest that was missing. In the normative sample, substitution increased measurement error by 26.9% to 58.5%, whereas proration increased measurement error by 44.2% to 62.7%.

The results for the WISC–V special group samples were also examined. In general, less measurement error was evident in these samples after substitution or proration. After substitution, between 89.8% and 98.4% of FSIQs in the normative sample were within the 95%

confidence interval of the original FSIQs, depending on the subtest that was substituted. After proration, between 83.0% and 94.0% of FSIQs in the normative sample were within the 95% confidence interval of the FSIQs, depending on the subtest that was missing. Hence, for the WISC–V, substitution resulted in slightly more accurate FSIQ scores.

Invalidation of Composite Scores

A composite score is considered invalid if there are too many subtest total raw scores of zero on subtests that contribute to its sum of scaled scores. A score of zero does not indicate that the child does not have the abilities measured by the subtest; it merely indicates that the items on the subtest did not permit the child's ability in that area to be determined.

The limits on the number of total raw scores of zero for each composite score vary based on the number of subtests that contribute to that composite score. For index scores based on only two subtests, one may have a total raw score of zero. For index scores based on three or four subtests (i.e., the Symbol Translation Index and the Cognitive Proficiency Index respectively), a maximum of two scores of zero on the contributing subtests are allowed. For index scores based on five or six subtests (i.e., the General Ability Index and the Nonverbal Index respectively), a maximum of three of the contributing subtests may have total raw scores of zero. For the FSIQ, a maximum of four of the contributing subtests can have total raw scores of zero. Quick Reference 3.5 lists the acceptable number of total raw scores of zero for each composite score.

For the Naming Speed Index, total raw scores of zero are based on completion time so scores of zero are impossible. For the Storage and Retrieval Index, total raw scores of zero are also not possible because it is based on the sum of two standard scores; however, both the Naming

QUICK REFERENCE 3.5: ACCEPTABLE NUMBER OF TOTAL RAW SCORES OF 0 FOR EACH COMPOSITE SCORE

Composite Score	Number of Contributing Subtests	Maximum Number of Subtest Total Raw Scores of 0
Verbal Comprehension Index	2	1
Visual Spatial Index	2	1
Fluid Reasoning Index	2	1
Working Memory Index	2	1
Processing Speed Index	2	1
FSIQ	7	4
Prorated FSIQ	6	3
Quantitative Reasoning Index	2	1
Auditory Working Memory Index	2	1
Nonverbal Index	6	3
General Ability Index	5	3
Cognitive Proficiency Index	4	2
Symbol Translation Index	3	2

Note: If the number of total raw scores of zero for a given composite score exceeds the acceptable number, that composite score is considered invalid.

Speed Index and the Symbol Translation Index must be present in order to calculate the Storage and Retrieval Index.

Obtain Composite Scores

After the sums of scaled and standard scores are calculated, the composite scores are derived. Copy the sum of scaled scores for each desired composite into the Sum of Scaled Scores column in the Sum of Scaled Scores to Composite Score Conversion table on the Summary page and in the Sum of Scaled Scores to Index Score Conversion table on the Ancillary and Complementary Analysis page if ancillary index scores are calculated. Also copy the sum of standard scores for each desired complementary index score into the Sum of Standard Scores column in the Sum of Standard Scores to Index Score Conversion table. Refer to the age-appropriate tables to convert the sums of scaled scores to composite scores. For this step, you will need the Sums of Scaled Scores as well as your selection for the confidence level (90% or 95%).

Use Tables A.2 to A.7 of the *WISC–V Administration and Scoring Manual* to derive the primary index scores (i.e., Verbal Comprehension Index, Visual Spatial Index, Fluid Reasoning Index, Working Memory Index, and Processing Speed Index) and the FSIQ. Use Tables C.1 to C.5 of the *WISC–V Administration and Scoring Manual Supplement* to derive the ancillary index scores (i.e., Quantitative Reasoning Index, Auditory Working Memory Index, Nonverbal Index, General Ability Index, and Cognitive Proficiency Index). Use Tables C.7 and C.8 of the *WISC–V Administration and Scoring Manual Supplement* to derive the first two complementary index scores shown in the table (i.e., Naming Speed Index and Symbol Translation Index).

For each composite score, read down the Sum of Scaled Scores or Sum of Standard Scores column until you locate the appropriate value from your calculated sum of scaled or standard scores.

Read across the row to the composite score, the percentile rank, and the confidence interval. Record these values in the appropriate columns to the right of the Sums of Scaled Scores or Sums of Standard Scores column.

Attention

The FSIQ is not the average of the primary index scores. It is derived from the sum of scaled scores for the seven FSIQ subtests (or all but one of the FSIQ subtests and an acceptable substitution, unless the FSIQ is prorated for six subtests).

You cannot add the primary index scores, sums of scaled scores together and obtain the Full Scale sum of scaled scores.

If you will derive the Storage and Retrieval Index, a final step is necessary. Transfer the Naming Speed Index and Symbol Translation Index values to the boxes labeled 1 and 2 in the row beneath the table labeled Storage & Ret. Sum of Standard Scores. Add them together and enter the sum in the box labeled 3 in the Sum of Standard Scores to Index Score Conversion table above the row. Use Table C.9 in the *WISC–V Administration and Scoring Manual Supplement* to derive the Storage and Retrieval Index using the same procedure outlined above for the Naming Speed Index and Symbol Translation Index.

USING Q–GLOBAL TO OBTAIN THE WISC–V SCORE REPORT

WISC–V score reports are available on Q-global™, Pearson's web-based scoring and reporting platform. This scoring platform can be accessed from any computer with Internet access. You must use a standard browser (e.g., relatively current versions of Microsoft® Internet Explorer®, Firefox®, Chrome®, or Safari®). You must also have a relatively current operating system.

At this time, Q-global does not support data entry access from tablets or handheld devices. However, the reports can be produced in a .pdf format or in a document format, which permits you to read them on a device.

In addition to access to the score report on the Q-global platform, you will need the child's test age and total raw scores. With entry of this information, the scoring assistant outputs every possible score in the published test, as well as the strengths and weaknesses and discrepancy comparisons.

Figure 3.1 depicts the demographics entry pages within the Q-global software. Figure 3.2 depicts the total raw score entry page within the Q-global software.

Substitution is facilitated within the scoring software by accessing a drop-down menu. *If you make a substitution for an FSIQ subtest, all of the index scores that are derived using that subtest are not calculated by the scoring assistant.* As a result, some discrepancy and score comparisons are not available. If you wish to use the FSIQ subtest to obtain the corresponding index score(s) that are based in part on that subtest, the report can be rerun without the substitution at no additional charge.

Ensure you have a good clinical rationale for subtest substitution. Be careful to describe the rationale, the correct results, and any interpretive implications in your report. Figure 3.3 depicts the report configuration page and shows the drop-down menu used to facilitate substitution.

The Full Scale sum of scaled scores is automatically prorated by the scoring software if one FSIQ subtest is missing and a substitution is not selected. No more than one FSIQ subtest may be missing. As outlined in this chapter, proration is not permitted with substitution within the software. Proration is not available for any index score.

Use of the Q-global scoring software is recommended. If you calculate more than the FSIQ and one or two primary index scores, using

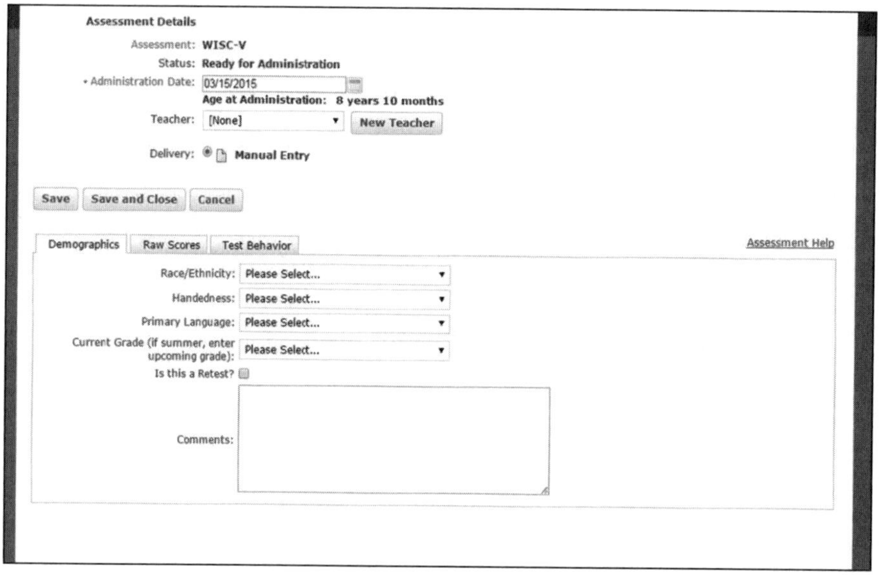

Figure 3.1   Demographics Entry Page   *Wechsler Intelligence Scale for Children, Fifth Edition* (WISC–V). Copyright © 2014 NCS Pearson, Inc. Reproduced with permission. All rights reserved. "*Wechsler Intelligence Scale for Children*" and "*WISC*" are trademarks, in the United States and/or other countries, of Pearson Education, Inc. or its affiliates(s).

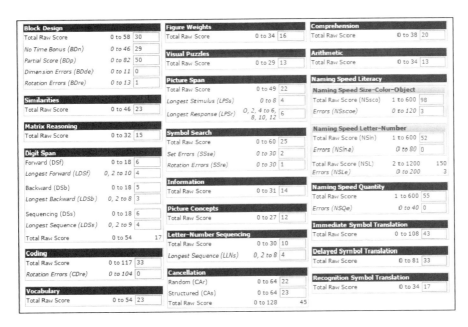

Figure 3.2   Total Raw Score Entry Page   *Wechsler Intelligence Scale for Children, Fifth Edition* (WISC–V). Copyright © 2014 NCS Pearson, Inc. Reproduced with permission. All rights reserved. "*Wechsler Intelligence Scale for Children*" and "*WISC*" are trademarks, in the United States and/or other countries, of Pearson Education, Inc. or its affiliates(s).

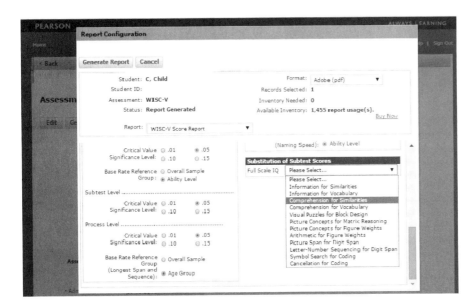

Figure 3.3   Report Configuration Entry Page   *Wechsler Intelligence Scale for Children, Fifth Edition* (WISC–V). Copyright © 2014 NCS Pearson, Inc. Reproduced with permission. All rights reserved. "*Wechsler Intelligence Scale for Children*" and "*WISC*" are trademarks, in the United States and/or other countries, of Pearson Education, Inc. or its affiliates(s).

the score report saves a significant amount of time. With the increased number of index scores relative to the WISC–IV, the consequent greater number of potential discrepancy comparisons, and the inclusion of strengths and weaknesses at the index level, a meticulous examiner easily can spend 60 to 75 minutes double-checking basic arithmetic, transferring total raw scores, looking up and recording standard scores, and performing strengths and weaknesses and discrepancy analyses. Furthermore, using the score report prevents needless computation errors.

Sample outputs from the scoring assistant to illustrate its functionalities appear in Figures 3.4 to 3.8. The figures do not illustrate appearance, but merely typical content.

Q-global can facilitate two types of joint analyses with the Kaufman Test of Educational Achievement–Third Edition (KTEA–3; A. S. Kaufman & Kaufman, 2014) and with the Wechsler Individual Achievement Test–Third Edition

(WIAT–III; Pearson, 2009b) to assist with identification of specific learning disabilities. These include the ability-achievement discrepancy analysis and the pattern of strengths and weaknesses analysis. These methods are described in Chapter 6 of the *WISC–V Technical and Interpretive Manual*. Briefly, the ability-achievement discrepancy analysis involves the use of an ability score to establish an expectation for achievement scores. The pattern of strengths and weaknesses analysis utilizes the primary index scores, two of the ancillary index scores, and the complementary subtests and index scores to establish cognitive strengths and weaknesses. The cognitive strength is compared with the cognitive weakness and the achievement weakness. Sample outputs for each of these analyses appear in Figures 3.9 and 3.10. The KTEA–3 is used to illustrate, but similar outputs are available with the WIAT–III.

Subtest Score Summary

Scale	Subtest Name		Total Raw Score	Scaled Score	Percentile Rank	Age Equivalent	*SEM*
Verbal	**Similarities**	SI	23	10	50	9:2	1.16
Comprehension	**Vocabulary**	VC	23	11	63	9:2	1.24
	(Information)	IN	14	9	37	8:2	1.31
	(Comprehension)	CO	20	13	84	10:6	1.34
Visual Spatial	**Block Design**	BD	30	12	75	11:2	1.04
	Visual Puzzles	VP	13	10	50	8:10	1.08
Fluid Reasoning	**Matrix Reasoning**	MR	15	9	37	7:10	0.99
	Figure Weights	FW	16	9	37	8:2	0.73
	(Picture Concepts)	PC	23	19	99.9	>16:10	1.24
	(Arithmetic)	AR	13	7	16	7:6	1.04
Working Memory	**Digit Span**	DS	17	7	16	6:6	0.95
	Picture Span	PS	22	9	37	7:10	1.08
	(Letter-Number Seq.)	LN	10	6	9	6:6	1.24
Processing Speed	Coding	CD	33	10	50	8:10	1.37
	Symbol Search	SS	25	13	84	10:10	1.34
	(Cancellation)	CA	45	9	37	7:6	1.24

Subtests used to derive the FSIQ are bolded. Secondary subtests are in parentheses.

Figure 3.4 Primary Subtest Summary *Wechsler Intelligence Scale for Children, Fifth Edition* (WISC–V). Copyright © 2014 NCS Pearson, Inc. Reproduced with permission. All rights reserved. "*Wechsler Intelligence Scale for Children*" and "*WISC*" are trademarks, in the United States and/or other countries, of Pearson Education, Inc. or its affiliates(s).

Composite		Sum of Scaled Scores	Composite Score	Percentile Rank	95% Confidence Interval	Qualitative Description	*SEM*
Verbal Comprehension	VCI	21	103	58	95–110	Average	4.74
Visual Spatial	VSI	22	105	63	97–112	Average	4.24
Fluid Reasoning	FRI	18	94	34	87–102	Average	3.67
Working Memory	WMI	16	88	21	81–97	Low Average	4.24
Processing Speed	PSI	23	108	70	98–116	Average	5.61
Full Scale IQ	FSIQ	68	98	45	92–104	Average	3.00

Confidence intervals are calculated using the Standard Error of Estimation.

Figure 3.5   Composite Score Summary *Wechsler Intelligence Scale for Children, Fifth Edition* (WISC–V). Copyright © 2014 NCS Pearson, Inc. Reproduced with permission. All rights reserved. "*Wechsler Intelligence Scale for Children*" and "*WISC*" are trademarks, in the United States and/or other countries, of Pearson Education, Inc. or its affiliates(s).

Index Level Strengths and Weaknesses

Index	Score	Comparison Score	Difference	Critical Value	Strength or Weakness	Base Rate
VCI	103	99.6	3.4	10.79		>25%
VSI	105	99.6	5.4	9.93		>25%
FRI	94	99.6	−5.6	8.98		>25%
WMI	88	99.6	−11.6	9.93	W	<=15%
PSI	108	99.6	8.4	12.33		<=25%

Comparison score mean derived from the five index scores (MIS).
Statistical significance (critical values) at the .05 level.
Base rates are reported by ability level.

Index Level Pairwise Difference Comparisons

Index Comparison	Score 1	Score 2	Difference	Critical Value	Significant Difference	Base Rate
VCI - VSI	103	105	−2	12.46	N	48.8%
VCI - FRI	103	94	9	11.75	N	27.6%
VCI - WMI	103	88	15	12.46	Y	15.6%
VCI - PSI	103	108	−5	14.39	N	42.1%
VSI - FRI	105	94	11	10.99	Y	21.7%
VSI - WMI	105	88	17	11.75	Y	15.1%
VSI - PSI	105	108	−3	13.78	N	47.0%
FRI - WMI	94	88	6	10.99	N	37.4%
FRI - PSI	94	108	−14	13.14	Y	23.3%
WMI - PSI	88	108	−20	13.78	Y	13.5%

Statistical significance (critical values) at the .05 level.
Base rates are reported by ability level.

Figure 3.6   Index Level Strengths and Weaknesses and Pairwise Comparisons *Wechsler Intelligence Scale for Children, Fifth Edition* (WISC–V). Copyright © 2014 NCS Pearson, Inc. Reproduced with permission. All rights reserved. "*Wechsler Intelligence Scale for Children*" and "*WISC*" are trademarks, in the United States and/or other countries, of Pearson Education, Inc. or its affiliates(s).

Subtest Level Strengths and Weaknesses

Subtest	Score	Comparison Score	Difference	Critical Value	Strength or Weakness	Base Rate
SI	10	10.0	0.0	3.07		
VC	11	10.0	1.0	3.26		>25%
BD	12	10.0	2.0	2.78		<=25%
VP	10	10.0	0.0	2.88		
MR	9	10.0	−1.0	2.67		>25%
FW	9	10.0	−1.0	2.08		>25%
DS	7	10.0	−3.0	2.58	W	<=10%
PS	9	10.0	−1.0	2.88		>25%
CD	10	10.0	0.0	3.57		
SS	13	10.0	3.0	3.50		<=15%

Comparison score mean derived from the ten primary subtest scores (MSS-P).
Statistical significance (critical values) at the .05 level.

Subtest Level Pairwise Difference Comparisons

Subtest Comparison	Score 1	Score 2	Difference	Critical Value	Significant Difference	Base Rate
SI – VC	10	11	−1	3.02	N	41.0%
BD – VP	12	10	2	3.04	N	27.0%
MR – FW	9	9	0	2.60	N	
DS – PS	7	9	−2	2.89	N	30.8%
CD – SS	10	13	−3	3.63	N	16.8%

Statistical significance (critical values) at the .05 level.

Figure 3.7 Subtest Level Strengths and Weaknesses and Pairwise Comparisons *Wechsler Intelligence Scale for Children, Fifth Edition* (WISC-V). Copyright © 2014 NCS Pearson, Inc. Reproduced with permission. All rights reserved. "*Wechsler Intelligence Scale for Children*" and "*WISC*" are trademarks, in the United States and/or other countries, of Pearson Education, Inc. or its affiliates(s).

Index Score Summary

Composite		Sum of Scaled/ Standard Scores	Index Score	Percentile Rank	95% Confidence Interval	Qualitative Description	*SEM*
Ancillary							
Quantitative Reasoning	QRI	16	88	21	82–95	Low Average	3.67
Auditory Working Memory	AWMI	13	81	10	75–90	Low Average	4.24
Nonverbal	NVI	59	98	45	92–104	Average	3.35
General Ability	GAI	51	101	53	95–107	Average	3.00
Cognitive Proficiency	CPI	39	98	45	91–105	Average	4.24
Complementary							
Naming Speed	NSI	188	92	30	84–101	Average	5.61
Symbol Translation	STI	249	82	12	76–90	Low Average	3.67
Storage & Retrieval	SRI	174	83	13	77–91	Low Average	4.24

Ancillary index scores are reported using scaled scores and complementary index scores are reported using standard scores.

Figure 3.8 Ancillary and Complementary Summary *Wechsler Intelligence Scale for Children, Fifth Edition* (WISC-V). Copyright © 2014 NCS Pearson, Inc. Reproduced with permission. All rights reserved. "*Wechsler Intelligence Scale for Children*" and "*WISC*" are trademarks, in the United States and/or other countries, of Pearson Education, Inc. or its affiliates(s).

Ability Score Type: WISC-V: FSIQ
Ability Score: 98

Predicted Achievement Method

	Predicted KTEA-3 Score	Actual KTEA-3 Score	Difference	Critical Value (.05)	Significant Difference Y/N	Base Rate
KTEA-3 Subtests						
Phonological Processing	99	67	32	9	Y	<=2%
Math Concepts & Applications	98	70	28	8	Y	<=2%
Letter & Word Recognition	99	97	2	6	N	>25%
Math Computation	99	90	9	7	Y	<=25%
Nonsense Word Decoding	99	85	14	6	Y	<=15%
Silent Reading Fluency	99	80	19	12	Y	<=10%
Math Fluency	99	89	10	10	Y	<=25%
Reading Comprehension	99	68	31	11	Y	<=2%
Written Expression	99	40	59	12	Y	<=2%
Spelling	99	67	32	7	Y	<=2%
Reading Vocabulary	99	85	14	9	Y	<=10%
Listening Comprehension	99	74	25	12	Y	<=2%
Word Recognition Fluency	99	73	26	11	Y	<=2%
Oral Expression	99	68	31	13	Y	<=2%
Decoding Fluency	99	94	5	12	N	>25%
KTEA-3 Composites						
Reading	99	81	18	7	Y	<=5%
Math	98	79	19	7	Y	<=2%
Written Language	99	50	49	8	Y	<=2%
Academic Skills Battery (ASB)	98	70	28	6	Y	<=2%
Sound-Symbol	99	72	27	7	Y	<=2%
Decoding	99	90	9	6	Y	<=25%
Reading Fluency	99	79	20	9	Y	<=5%
Reading Understanding	99	75	24	8	Y	<=2%
Oral Language	99	65	34	12	Y	<=2%
Comprehension	99	69	30	9	Y	<=2%
Expression	99	52	47	11	Y	<=2%
Academic Fluency	99	74	25	9	Y	<=5%

Note: Scores are not reported when the achievement score equals or exceeds the ability scores.

Figure 3.9   Ability-Achievement Discrepancy Analysis   *Wechsler Intelligence Scale for Children, Fifth Edition* (WISC-V). Copyright © 2014 NCS Pearson, Inc. Reproduced with permission. All rights reserved. "*Wechsler Intelligence Scale for Children*" and "*WISC*" are trademarks, in the United States and/or other countries, of Pearson Education, Inc. or its affiliates(s).

Area of Processing Strength: WISC-V Visual Spatial Index: 105
Area of Processing Weakness: WISC-V Working Memory Index: 88
Area of Achievement Weakness: KTEA-3 Reading: 81

Comparison	Relative Strength Score	Relative Weakness Score	Difference	Critical Value (.05)	Significant Difference Y/N	Supports SLD hypothesis? Yes/No
Processing Strength/ Achievement Weakness	105	81	24	10	Y	Yes
Processing Strength Processing Weakness	105	88	17	12	Y	Yes

Note. The PSW model is intended to help practitioners generate hypotheses regarding clinical diagnoses The analysis should only be used as part of a comprehensive evaluation that incorporates multiple sources of information.

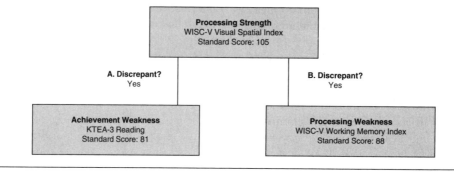

Figure 3.10 Pattern of Strengths and Weaknesses Analysis *Wechsler Intelligence Scale for Children, Fifth Edition* (WISC–V). Copyright © 2014 NCS Pearson, Inc. Reproduced with permission. All rights reserved. "*Wechsler Intelligence Scale for Children*" and "*WISC*" are trademarks, in the United States and/or other countries, of Pearson Education, Inc. or its affiliates(s).

FREQUENTLY ASKED QUESTIONS: SCORING

Pearson provides responses to frequently asked questions (FAQs) about the WISC–V on the product website. Some of the FAQs relate to subtest scoring and use of WISC–V Q-global scoring. The questions and responses are reproduced in Quick Reference 3.6.

QUICK REFERENCE 3.6: FREQUENTLY ASKED QUESTIONS: SUBTEST SCORING

- Does the WISC–V support use of a pattern of strengths and weaknesses approach to learning disability evaluation?

Yes, the WIAT–III and the KTEA–3 scoring reports on the Q-global™ platform can be used to evaluate a specific learning disability, using a pattern of strengths and weaknesses discrepancy analysis approach. The data are too complex to provide in a paper format; the scoring software must be used for this purpose.

- For the BDp score, if a child has to take both trials of an item, do you use the correct placement of blocks on Trial 2 only to get the optional partial score for that item?

Only the last trial administered is counted.

- For the BDp score, if a child has the correct design but rotates it 30 or more degrees, is the optional partial score for that item equal to 0?

Yes.

- For the BDp score, if a child commits a dimension error, which blocks are counted as correct?

Count the blocks that are in the correct position, but not the ones involved in the dimension error.

- For Naming Speed Literacy, the top table on the Process Analysis page of the Record Form provides a space to complete the NSLn raw score and scaled score. However, it indicates that this is for ages 7–8 in light blue ink within the boxes. Is this also where the NSL raw score for ages 9–16 is converted for this age group? If not, where else on the Record Form would you convert the NSL raw score for ages 9–16?

The NSL score is converted on the top right corner of the Ancillary and Complementary Analysis page using the Total Raw Score to Standard Score Conversion table. Refer to Steps 3–4 on pages 70–71 of the *WISC-V Administration and Scoring Manual*.

- On the sheet that was inserted into the WISC-V Administration and Scoring Manual Supplement to display the LPSr scores on Table C.17, are the numbers displayed for the median at age 15 and 16 correct? It seems odd that it would decrease with age.

Yes, the median is correct. The median for age 16 is 9. The 50th percentile is midway between scores of 8 and 10, so the median is correctly calculated by dividing the difference. This slight age-based decrease across some ages occurs because the LPSr is calculated based on the last item with a perfect score. There are some later items that have fewer response options relative to the earlier ones; hence there is a decrease in the measures of central tendency. The LPSr score should be reported alongside LPSs for context.

- In testing a child between the ages of 6:0–7:11, I have obtained an extremely low score on the NSQ score that doesn't make any sense. Is there a problem with this score?

Check to be sure that you are looking at the correct column in Table C.6 of the *WISC-V Administration and Scoring Manual Supplement*. These ages have process scores for NSsco and NSln, and the columns are between the NSL and NSQ columns. Using the incorrect column can result in erroneous, abnormally high scores on NSQ.

- Can I substitute a secondary subtest for a primary subtest when deriving the FSIQ?

A maximum of one substitution may be made when deriving the FSIQ only. No substitutions can be made for any other composite score. The potential FSIQ substitutions are limited in order to

(Continued)

(Continued)

constrain additional measurement error that may be introduced by this practice. Table 2.8 in the *WISC–V Administration and Scoring Manual* indicates allowable substitutions for deriving the FSIQ.

- How was it decided that one subtest score could or could not be substituted for another when deriving the FSIQ?

Because substituted subtests are being used as an estimate of performance on another subtest, only secondary subtests within the same cognitive domain that are highly related to the primary subtest can be substituted.

- Can I administer all of the primary and secondary subtests and choose to use the highest subtest scaled scores when computing the FSIQ?

No. When deriving the FSIQ, you can only substitute a secondary subtest for a primary subtest that is spoiled or invalidated, or for a specific clinical purpose. Secondary subtests can also provide additional information on cognitive functioning. If you need to substitute a secondary subtest in place of a primary subtest for deriving the FSIQ, it is best practice to decide this before you administer the subtest—not after you have derived scaled scores. Secondary subtests are also useful when the primary subtest scores that contribute to a primary index score are widely discrepant. In this situation, additional information from secondary subtests can help to shed light on factors that may contribute to such disparate results.

- Why isn't subtest substitution permitted on any of the index scores?

Because subtest substitution may introduce measurement error into derived composite scores, substitution is limited. The index scores are derived from fewer subtests than the FSIQ, therefore, the risk of such error is greater. If a secondary subtest substitutes for a primary subtest for the FSIQ, the Q-global™ scoring software will not allow calculation of the primary index score that the primary subtest contributes to.

- Is score proration still available?

Prorating is available for the FSIQ only. A maximum of one proration or substitution may be made when deriving the FSIQ. Proration and substitution may not be combined to derive an FSIQ.

- If the Naming Speed Literacy (NSL) standard score is 90, and the Naming Speed Quantity (NSQ) standard score is 92, how is the Naming Speed Index (NSI) 89 and in the Low Average range?

The NSI is not an average of NSL and NSQ, it's a sum of standard scores. Having low scores on both components (i.e., NSL and NSQ) leads to an even lower NSI because in the distribution, having low scores on both is rarer than having a low score on one subtest and an average score on the second subtest. If you are familiar with the statistical phenomenon of regression to the mean, then this will make sense. If not, think about an Olympic gymnast competing in the all-around. It is rare to see someone score a perfect 10 on every event. It is more common to see them score a perfect 10 on one event and 8s on the others. The same applies to low scores. There is a tendency for subsequent observations to be less extreme.

- Why is there a *WISC–V Administration and Scoring Manual Supplement*? What is it for? Do I need to carry it with me?

The supplement contains all tables needed to fill out the Ancillary and Complementary Analysis and Process Analysis pages of the Record Form. You do not need the supplement during administration. You will only need it during scoring and only if you wish to supplement the primary analysis using these other scores.

- Where do I record process observations and contrast scores on the Record Form? Where are the instructions about how to calculate these scores?

The Record Form does not provide designated space to tally or derive process observations or contrast scores because they are not used for every administration or by every practitioner. The Record Form pages associated with each subtest and with summary and analysis were also subject to horizontal and vertical space limitations. These limitations are due to the maximum amount of printed and white space and pages available within a durable, bound paper booklet. There was simply not room to include these optional scores.

Page 50 of the *WISC–V Administration and Scoring Manual* provides the instructions for recording process observations on the Record Form in undesignated space (i.e., the margins of the Record Form). Page 76 of the manual provides instructions on using the tables in Appendix D of the *WISC–V Technical and Interpretive Manual* to obtain the normative information for selected process observations for certain subtests.

The Record Form also does not provide space to derive contrast scores. However, Appendix C of the *WISC–V Technical and Interpretive Manual* contains the necessary directions and tables to derive these scores, as well as the corresponding interpretive information.

- On the Process Analysis page in the Raw Score to Base Rate Conversion table, the number of errors sometimes occurs with multiple base rates. For example, one error for a child aged 9 for BDde corresponds with both < 15 and < 10. What should I do?

Use the smaller of the two numbers because of how cumulative percentages are calculated. Refer to p. 75 of the *WISC–V Administration and Scoring Manual.*

- What is Q-global?

Q-global is a web-based scoring and reporting platform that offers accessibility from any computer connected to the Internet. It allows for quick and automatic organization of examinee information and the ability to generate scores and produce accurate and detailed results. Reports are available in a .pdf or WORD document format. Go to http://www.helloq.com to sign up for a Q-global account.

- When will the WISC–V score report and WISC–V interpretive report writer be available?

The score report is available now on Q-global. The interpretive report generally becomes available approximately 6 months following the publication of a test.

(Continued)

(Continued)

- Can I reprint a scoring report from Q-global at no charge?

Yes. You can reprint a report at no charge if you change any demographic or report options. However, if you alter raw data, a new record is created and a new report usage is required to print the output.

- How do you use subtest substitution and proration for the FSIQ when scoring the WISC–V in Q-global?

A drop-down menu within the WISC–V Q-global scoring software facilitates subtest substitution. Choose your substitution in the drop-down menu.

On rare occasions, an inadequate number of valid subtest scores are obtained to derive the FSIQ, despite the availability of secondary subtests. Q-global automatically prorates the FSIQ if a primary subtest that contributes to it is missing and a secondary subtest is not selected for substitution. If more than one primary subtest is missing, the FSIQ is not calculated. Proration is only available for the FSIQ and only when the prorated sum of scaled scores is based on primary subtests. You cannot combine subtest substitution and proration when deriving the FSIQ.

- Are the allowable substitutions for primary subtests different on Q-global compared to hand scoring?

The rules governing allowable substitutions for core subtests for Q-global and hand scoring (i.e., in the *WISC–V Administration and Scoring Manual*) are the same. Substitution should only be used when the primary subtest is missing or invalid or in certain clinical situations when it is determined that a secondary subtest is a better estimate of the cognitive ability than the primary subtest (e.g., when a child's physical condition interferes with performance). Any substitution selected within Q-global is made on all applicable composites, and any score comparisons that utilize the substituted subtest are affected.

- Why are some score comparisons not available on the Q-global platform if I substitute a secondary subtest for a primary subtest?

The score comparisons are not available because the data they are based on require the missing subtest. For example, pairwise index-level difference comparisons that include the VCI are not provided in Q-global if Information is substituted for Vocabulary when deriving the FSIQ, because the VCI is not calculated.

Some other comparisons may also be unavailable if substitution is used. For example, index-level strengths and weaknesses comparisons require calculation of the mean primary index score or the FSIQ. If the VCI is unavailable, the MIS cannot be calculated. In this situation, the FSIQ becomes the comparison score, and the other available primary index scores are compared with the FSIQ rather than the MIS.

- Are score comparisons with the KTEA-3 and the WIAT–III available on Q-global?

Yes. It is possible to either manually enter the WISC–V scores when creating a KTEA-3 or a WIAT–III score report or import scores from the WISC–V score report on Q-global.

- What is included in the score report with the KTEA–3 and WIAT–III on Q-global?

The report includes two analyses to aid in the identification of specific learning disabilities: the traditional ability-achievement discrepancy analysis and the pattern of strengths and weaknesses discrepancy analysis.

- To use Q-global, do I need to purchase iPads or other tablets?

Q-global is a web-based scoring and reporting system (with some online administration features for rating scales). Q-global can be used with any device you use to access the web; it does not require iPads. Administering the WISC–V on Q-interactive does require the purchase of two iPads. Scoring is included in the Q-interactive test administration using the tablets; no additional purchase is necessary.

- Can you confirm if your Q-global program is compatible with Mac computers?

Yes, you may use Q-global on Macs.

- If one purchases Q-interactive vs. Q-global, would the child's data need to be stored in another location or would it still be uploaded?

With Q-interactive, you are actually administering the test using the tablet devices. The tablets are serving as your stimulus book, and record form for the WISC-V. Data are transferred and stored via best-in-industry standards for security. These precautions help you with HIPPA and FERPA compliance.

When you use Q-global to score the WISC–V, you will still have the paper record form that you will need to store appropriately. Scores would be input into the Q-global system and securely saved there. However, Q-global (for the WISC–V) is only saving raw scores/item score information, not responses as in Q-interactive. Think of Q-global for WISC–V as similar to scoring programs you have used in the past (only this one is web-based with a secure server).

- When you purchase Q-global scoring, can you access it from any computer connected to the Internet or only one computer in the office? Also, what are the pricing options for the reports?

Yes, since Q-global is web-based, you may access it using your username and password from any device that is connected to the Internet. There are two pricing options available. In addition to a per-report price, there is also an unlimited-use subscription option (1-, 3-, and 5-year subscriptions). Please visit PearsonClinical.com/WISCV for pricing.

Source: from http://www.pearsonclinical.com/psychology/products/100000771/wechsler-intelligence-scale-for-childrensupsupfifth-edition---wisc-v.html#tab-faq . *Wechsler Intelligence Scale for Children, Fifth Edition* (WISC–V). Copyright © 2014 NCS Pearson, Inc. Reproduced with permission. All rights reserved. "*Wechsler Intelligence Scale for Children*" and "*WISC*" are trademarks, in the United States and/or other countries, of Pearson Education, Inc. or its affiliates(s).

CHAPTER 4

WISC–V DIGITAL ADMINISTRATION AND SCORING

This chapter describes and illustrates the digital version of the WISC–V on Q-interactive™, a digital assessment platform developed by Pearson. The digital version involves administration of the test using the Q-interactive app, Assess, on two tablet devices that replace the stimulus books and Record Forms. It contains features such as flexible programmed administration guidelines and basic scoring output. This chapter discusses potential clinical applications and digital enhancements relevant to specific clinical groups.

DIGITAL ASSESSMENT ADVANTAGES AND CHALLENGES

There are a number of advantages to digital assessment. The digital medium offers bidirectional feedback, improved visual presentation, and access to constructs impossible to assess in traditional modes (e.g., reaction time). Experimental design can be more readily controlled in the digital format, with tighter standardized presentation and reduced administration errors. Scoring is immediate, clerical errors are eliminated or greatly reduced, and unique types of data (e.g., response time by item) are available (Noyes & Garland, 2008). Other practical advantages include greatly enhanced portability, reduced physical storage space, and potentially reduced costs of assessment (Schroeders & Wilhelm, 2010). With Q-interactive, as long as items were scored as they were administered, postadministration scoring time is completely eliminated, which

offers the practitioner precious minutes back in his or her day.

Despite these advantages, digital assessment also is subject to some challenges. Hardware and software can freeze or crash, sometimes resulting in lost data. Some studies indicate working in a digital format results in relatively greater fatigue, compared with a traditional format. In addition to fatigue, the medium's flexibility can create issues: Progression through items can be more cumbersome. New confidentiality issues must also be considered and worked through when testing in a digital medium (Noyes & Garland, 2008).

EQUIVALENCE OF TRADITIONAL AND DIGITAL MEDIUMS

The equivalence of paper-and-pencil (i.e., traditional) and digital testing mediums has been examined across a variety of ability tests. In general, the impact of testing medium appears to be small in the general population. Mead and Drasgow (1993) found differences across mediums that varied from little to no difference for power tests, to moderate for speeded tests. However, Kim (as cited in Schroeders, 2008) conducted a subsequent meta-analysis with a larger sample of studies that adjusted for within-study dependency of effect-size estimates and found no such differences.

Recent studies of specific ability tasks have found no performance differences across mediums (Schroeders & Wilhelm, 2010; Williams & McCord, 2006). Concerns have been raised about technology proficiency, computer literacy, technological self-efficacy, and computer comfort/anxiety. Recent studies of specific ability tasks that investigated the interaction of technology-related variables such as computer anxiety with format and demographic variables have found no interaction effect on performance (Schroeders & Wilhelm, 2010; Williams & McCord, 2006). With the increased exposure of society to technology, these issues may have even less impact in the future (Williams & McCord, 2006).

Equivalency studies are complete for the WISC–V (Daniel, Wahlstrom, & Zhang, 2014) as well as the Wechsler Adult Intelligence Scale–Fourth Edition (WAIS–IV; Wechsler, 2008), the Wechsler Intelligence Scale for Children–Fourth Edition (WISC–IV; Wechsler, 2003), and a number of other Pearson products (Daniel, 2012a, 2012b, 2012c, 2013). It is important to note that the initial digital adaptations of these tests represent conservative levels of modification. These adaptations do not eliminate all manipulatives and do not require all examinee responses to be digitally captured. Rather, they merely present the stimulus books on a tablet and involve examiner recording, scoring, and item advancement on a second tablet that provides reminders about the basic administration rules.

At present, some materials of the Q-interactive version are not digital. The Block Design blocks are used in the traditional manner. Also, at the time of this writing, paper-and-pencil response booklets are used for administration of the Processing Speed subtests; only administration instructions and scoring of the data are available in Q-interactive. An initial attempt was made to adapt these subtests for digital responses, but the data did not support the inclusion of those first versions. The development effort continues at present, with hopes of publishing fully digital versions of the Processing Speed subtests in 2016. These adaptations will likely show differences from the traditional versions and require equated norms.

TESTING SPECIAL AND CLINICAL POPULATIONS

The WISC–V represented the first effort to collect data for special and clinical group studies in Q-interactive. The *Standards for Educational and Psychological Testing* (American Educational Research Association, American Psychological Association, & National Council on Measurement in Education, 2014) describe the collection and presentation of evidence about how a target construct may be altered (or not altered) by varying administration format. Accordingly, data were collected from a number of special and clinical group populations, and comparison studies were conducted with nonclinical children who took the digital version serving as the matched controls. One report on the results with an intellectually gifted group and with an intellectual disability group is available at the time of this writing, with others forthcoming at www.helloq.com/research.html. The mean scores of these groups as well as the effect sizes of the mean differences relative to nonclinical matched controls indicated that children who are intellectually gifted and children with intellectual disability–mild severity perform consistently regardless of format (Raiford, Holdnack, Drozdick, & Zhang, 2014).

Other questions about testing in a digital format center on examinee behaviors, engagement, and attention, particularly on the part of younger examinees or those from clinical populations. Recent survey research conducted with WISC–IV Q-interactive users (N = 95) indicated that examinees from various clinical populations as well as those who were younger (aged 5–9) most often appeared more engaged, attentive, focused, interested, and willing to respond when tested with the digital version compared to the traditional.

A frequent concern expressed is that children with attention-deficit/hyperactivity disorder (ADHD) may be less attentive to the digital format. For 77 respondents who rated children with ADHD, 57% reported they saw a difference in these children's responses to the digital versus the traditional format. Of those, 82% indicated children with ADHD were more attentive, 9% indicated they were less attentive (i.e., 5% of the original sample), and 9% said the effect was neutral or inconsistent (Daniel, 2013).

For children with autism spectrum disorders, developmental delays, intellectual disability, and learning disability, most frequently practitioners indicated they saw no difference in level of engagement between formats. For those who did report a difference (fewer than half of respondents for every clinical population), a great majority indicated greater levels of engagement or a neutral effect. Across all respondents who rated these special populations, none rated examinees as less engaged with the digital as compared with the traditional format. A small proportion of this sample (7%) reported any difficulties using Q-interactive to test children with specific clinical issues (Daniel, 2013).

Nonetheless, when a test is adapted for a digital format, the two versions should be examined to determine if the scores obtained in the digital format can be interpreted in the same manner (Hambleton, Bartram, & Oakland, 2011; International Test Commission, 2006). Shifts in the scores obtained might occur, resulting in the need to equate the scores across mediums. Therefore, before a test is commercially available on Q-interactive, new types of subtests and

subtests not yet proven equivalent for a particular age group undergo equivalency studies to confirm that the Q-interactive scores are interchangeable with those of the traditional medium.

ADMINISTRATION OF THE WISC–V ON Q-INTERACTIVE

Using the Q-interactive version of WISC–V, this section reviews the web portal and provides samples of administration and scoring features within Assess. Basic scoring output is illustrated. Potential clinical applications and digital enhancements relevant to specific clinical groups are discussed.

The current technical requirements for Q-interactive are listed in Quick Reference 4.1. Information relevant to data security and HIPAA requirements is available on the Q-interactive website (at the present time, http://www.helloq.com).

Q-interactive Web Portal

A secure web portal, Central, serves as the hub of all activities. Central can be used to create examinee profiles (i.e., enter demographics and referral questions), choose subtests to administer from the WISC–V and a variety of other instruments, review scores, and check usage figures. Figures 4.1 and 4.2 illustrate portions of Central

QUICK REFERENCE 4.1: Q-INTERACTIVE TECHNICAL REQUIREMENTS

- Computer with Internet access through a standard browser (e.g., relatively current versions of Microsoft® Internet Explorer®, Firefox®, Chrome®, or Safari®), with iTunes installed
- Two (2) Apple iPads® (iPad 2 or newer) current on iOS, with at least 16 GB of memory, and with iTunes installed
- Wi-fi, 3G, or better/comparable connectivity
- Two antiglare screen covers
- Power cords to recharge iPads
- Examiner stylus for verbatim recording
- Current Assess app installed on each iPad

that facilitate creation of new examinees (i.e., clients) and transfer of cases to and from the Assess app on the tablet device. Support and training is also available via Central on the Support tab. Figure 4.3 illustrates portions of the training options that can be accessed through the Support tab.

Sample Administration and Scoring Features

During WISC–V administration on Assess, two remotely connected tablets replace the stimulus books, Record Form, and stopwatch. At the present time, the *WISC–V Administration and Scoring Manual*, Block Design blocks, and response booklets used for the traditional version are also used for the digital version. The *WISC–V Administration and Scoring Manual*, the *WISC–V Administration and Scoring Manual Supplement*, and the *WISC–V Technical and Interpretive Manual* are available in viewable, but not printable, .pdf format on Central.

Practitioner Tablet Functions

The practitioner tablet permits the examiner to view basic item verbatim instructions (typically only the verbatim instructions and essential prompts) to read aloud. Timing, recording, and most scoring functions are accomplished by touching a series of buttons. Typical buttons that appear on the examiner's (i.e., practitioner's) screen for many subtests are illustrated in Figure 4.4.

Basic administration information is accessed through the use of a few buttons. The information button produces a popover with abbreviated administration directions that are roughly equivalent to the paper Record Form abbreviated

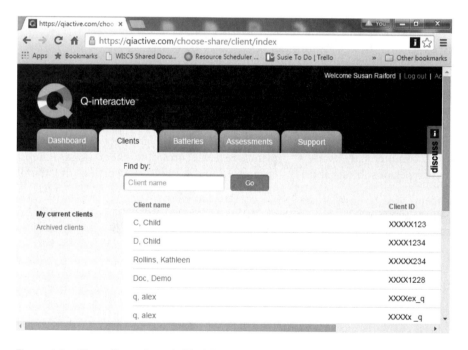

Figure 4.1   Clients List on Central *Wechsler Intelligence Scale for Children, Fifth Edition* (WISC–V). Copyright © 2014 NCS Pearson, Inc. Reproduced with permission. All rights reserved. "*Wechsler Intelligence Scale for Children*" and "*WISC*" are trademarks, in the United States and/or other countries, of Pearson Education, Inc. or its affiliates(s).

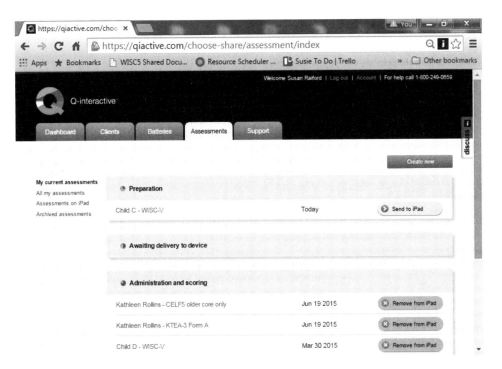

Figure 4.2   List of Assessments (Clients with Batteries Assigned) on Central *Wechsler Intelligence Scale for Children, Fifth Edition* (WISC–V). Copyright © 2014 NCS Pearson, Inc. Reproduced with permission. All rights reserved. "*Wechsler Intelligence Scale for Children*" and "*WISC*" are trademarks, in the United States and/or other countries, of Pearson Education, Inc. or its affiliates(s).

instructions and limited portions of the *WISC–V Administration and Scoring Manual* General Directions sections. The instructions button produces a popover with verbatim prompts and any other important instructions that could be relevant during item administration. The home button can be used to suspend testing and make edits to the battery or view results from other completed subtests. The discontinue button permits a manual discontinue and can be used at most times during administration, even if the discontinue criterion has not been met.

Timing can be started and stopped, and completion times can be adjusted if necessary, using the stopwatch button. For subtests with time limits, the time readout turns to red font to warn the examiner that time has expired or is close to expiring.

There are a number of contextual event buttons that the examiner can use to record various behaviors of interest and to obtain raw process scores based on their occurrence (e.g., rotation errors on Block Design, Don't Know responses on Verbal Comprehension subtests). This is a helpful aspect of the digital version because these observations can be recorded and neatly summarized without additional effort at the end of each subtest. The notes button produces a popover where the examiner also may record other observations or notes about any item or subtest.

Some subtests have features specific to a subtest or subtest type that facilitate recording observations. Block Design provides an example. In the response grid, the blank squares may be touched repeatedly to indicate sides of the block that face up in the examinee's response (red, white, or red and white). The grid may be rotated

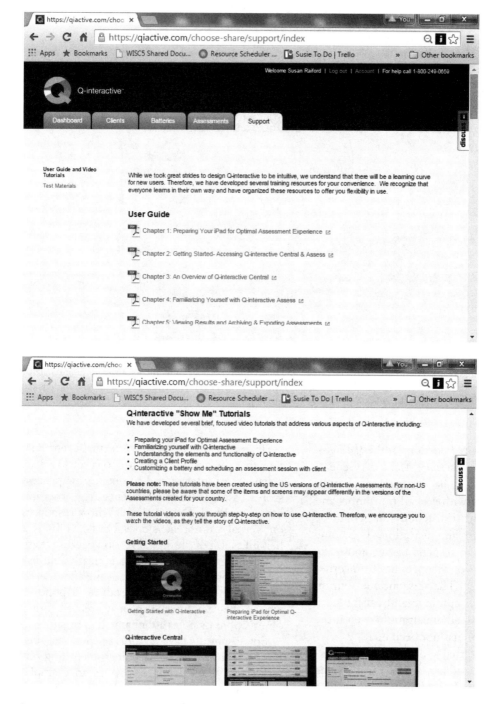

Figure 4.3 Tutorials and Training in Central *Wechsler Intelligence Scale for Children, Fifth Edition* (WISC–V). Copyright © 2014 NCS Pearson, Inc. Reproduced with permission. All rights reserved. "*Wechsler Intelligence Scale for Children*" and "*WISC*" are trademarks, in the United States and/or other countries, of Pearson Education, Inc. or its affiliates(s).

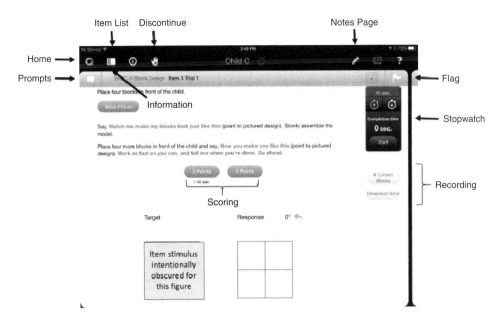

Figure 4.4 Typical Assess Buttons on Practitioner's Screen *Wechsler Intelligence Scale for Children, Fifth Edition* (WISC–V). Copyright © 2014 NCS Pearson, Inc. Reproduced with permission. All rights reserved. *"Wechsler Intelligence Scale for Children"* and *"WISC"* are trademarks, in the United States and/or other countries, of Pearson Education, Inc. or its affiliates(s). *Note:* The item stimulus typically appears on the practitioner's screen but has been intentionally obscured to prevent revealing the item content. The blank grid appears to the right of the item and is not obscured as it does not reveal item content, but only a grid configuration used for recording.

by touching it with two fingers and rotating them in a clockwise or counterclockwise motion, until the desired degree of rotation is visible.

The scoring buttons facilitate assigning the indicated points to a response. The Flag button can be used by the examiner to indicate an open scoring question or some other item-level occurrence. In the rare event where item-level scoring is delayed for additional consideration (e.g., unusual response to a Verbal Comprehension subtest), items can be scored later or a different score can be assigned at a later time. The to-do list permits the examiner to edit scores at any time (even after the battery is complete). An unscored items indicator (i.e., a circled number) appears overlapping the to-do list button to specify the number of administered items awaiting scores (if any).

Some unique features appear on the practitioner's screen for Verbal Comprehension items, and these are illustrated in Figure 4.5. This figure also illustrates a few additional features that appear on Verbal Comprehension items as well as other items and subtests.

Items and subtests are organized within Assess as a series of cards, not unlike many e-reader apps. Similar to those apps, advancement is accomplished by "swiping." In Figure 4.5, a sliver of the next card is visible on the far right, as a reminder to swipe to the next card when the current activity is complete.

When a score is indicated, the Score indicator displays the selected score. The Score indicator is visible on almost every card of every subtest.

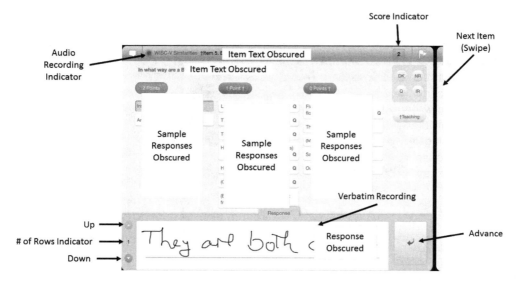

Figure 4.5 Typical Assess Features on Practitioner's Screen for Verbal Items *Wechsler Intelligence Scale for Children, Fifth Edition* (WISC–V). Copyright © 2014 NCS Pearson, Inc. Reproduced with permission. All rights reserved. "*Wechsler Intelligence Scale for Children*" and "*WISC*" are trademarks, in the United States and/or other countries, of Pearson Education, Inc. or its affiliates(s).

For Verbal Comprehension items, Sample Response buttons can be touched to indicate if a response was given that closely matches the examinee's response. In this example, the third button from the top (in the column under 2 Points) is selected. Sample Response buttons do not result in scores automatically being assigned; in this example, the examiner assigned 2 points to the response using the 2 Points button.

Audio recording can be enabled or disabled. When enabled and functioning, the audio recording indicator is alight in red in the upper left of the current card.

A verbatim recording area permits handwriting capture so that responses can be recorded verbatim. An advance button provides clean space within the verbatim recording area and is analogous to the "enter" button on a standard keyboard. Following complete recording, the entire response is still viewable by using the up and down buttons on the left of the verbatim recording area. The rows indicator lists the number of rows used in the verbatim recording area.

The Attention box discusses some issues to be aware of when using the sample response buttons and audio recording.

Attention

Although audio recording is a helpful feature, the examinee's response should not be replayed during administration unless you use headphones, as this is inconsistent with standard administration. Remember that consent should be obtained to record the examinee if audio recording is enabled. At the present time, if the "transfer" feature is used to transfer the case from Assess to Central, all audio files are destroyed. If the "sync" feature is used, however, the audio files are maintained on the tablet.

Employ caution when using the Sample Response buttons without audio recording, because many of the buttons contain multiple responses that do not share identical meanings, and data loss could result if audio recording is not engaged and responses are not recorded verbatim.

We recommend continuing to record verbatim responses in written form so that they may be compared with the sample responses to determine if a query is necessary and the response can be scored, and to avoid inadvertently discontinuing prematurely.

Assess monitors administration automatically, and a series of alert popovers provide reminders of standard administration rules (i.e., start, reversal, discontinue, timing) and are used to confirm that some indicated action was intentional (e.g., swiping backward to the previous item). The examiner can choose to follow the standard administration rules or to override them (e.g., to test the limits, select a different start point from the standard, or extend the administration time for an item or subtest). Samples of typical alert popovers that appear on the practitioner's screen for many subtests are illustrated in Figures 4.6 to 4.8. Note that in the interest of space, not every possible alert popover is included.

Attention

Swiping backward presently only permits administration of the item prior to the one currently being administered. The to-do button permits you to return to previous items to edit scores; however, visual stimuli cannot be exposed through this button. Therefore, for examinees who do not start with Item 1, currently you must immediately assign accurate scores to the start point items for all subtests with visual stimuli that are presented on the client device (i.e., every subtest except for the Processing Speed subtests).

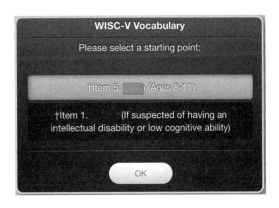

Figure 4.6   Assess Start Popover on Practitioner's Screen

Wechsler Intelligence Scale for Children, Fifth Edition (WISC–V). Copyright © 2014 NCS Pearson, Inc. Reproduced with permission. All rights reserved. "*Wechsler Intelligence Scale for Children*" and "*WISC*" are trademarks, in the United States and/or other countries, of Pearson Education, Inc. or its affiliates(s).

Note: The examiner is asked to select either the age-appropriate start point or Item 1. In this example, the examiner touched the Start Point button for Item 5 on the Start popover. Touching the OK button following this selection advances the app to the sample item, then subtest introductory text, then Item 5.

If you leave these items unscored and swipe forward more than a single item or assign perfect scores then later edit the scores in the Item List popover, Assess does not allow you to expose the visual stimulus for the reversal items. While this should not occur often in a standard administration, it is helpful to remember that you must score these start point items accurately and immediately.

Within Assess, other popovers appear when particular buttons are touched. These popovers operate as storage space for the text of administration directions, prompts, and teaching text. Samples of typical text popovers that appear on the practitioner's screen are illustrated in Figures 4.9 and 4.10. In the interest of space, not all types of text popovers are illustrated.

Figure 4.7   Assess Discontinue Popovers on Practitioner's Screen   *Wechsler Intelligence Scale for Children, Fifth Edition* (WISC–V). Copyright © 2014 NCS Pearson, Inc. Reproduced with permission. All rights reserved. "*Wechsler Intelligence Scale for Children*" and "*WISC*" are trademarks, in the United States and/or other countries, of Pearson Education, Inc. or its affiliates(s).
Note: In the first discontinue popover example on the left, the examiner initiated a manual discontinue using the discontinue button. The popover alerts the examiner that the discontinue criterion has not been met because 2 points were awarded for Item 9 and no score was assigned to Item 10. In the second discontinue popover example on the right, the app detected that the discontinue criterion has been met according to the assigned scores of 0 points on Items 10 and 11. In either case, the examiner may choose to discontinue by touching the discontinue button on the popover, test the limits by touching the test the limits button, or edit the assigned scores using the X button on the upper right of the popover.

Touching the Information button produces the Information text popover. The Information text popover provides basic information relevant to administration and scoring. It is roughly equivalent to the Record Form icon bar for each subtest. The left panel shows the text that is visible when this particular Information popover appears. The left panel also illustrates that scrolling downward (by touching the popover with your finger and dragging it upward) reveals additional text within the popover.

Touching the Instructions button produces the Instructions text popover. This popover contains abbreviated versions of verbatim prompts that apply to the subtest in general and sometimes other abbreviated responses to examinee behaviors.

Practitioner–Client Device Interaction

The practitioner's screen displays various aspects of the examinee's (client's) responses if the subtest is one that permits examinee responses to be indicated using the client's screen. Various actions on the practitioner's screen produce the necessary stimuli on the client's screen. Figures 4.11 and 4.12 illustrate some of these features.

The practitioner's screen permits the examiner to initiate stimulus exposure on the client's screen using a button. Currently this button is labeled Show Picture. In most cases, verbatim instructions to be read aloud as well as other abbreviated instructions relevant to administration appear on the administration card. Beginning with the WISC–V, almost all subtests present the items using a single screen where stimuli

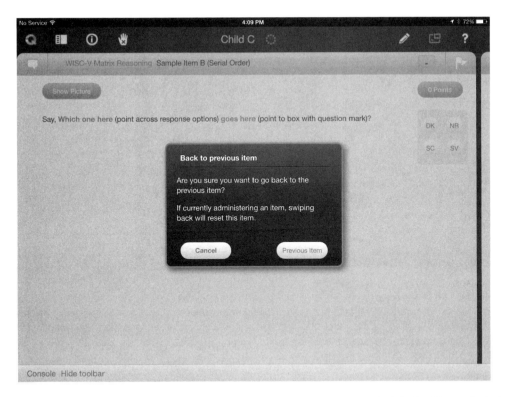

Figure 4.8   Assess "Swiping Backward" Popover on Practitioner's Screen   *Wechsler Intelligence Scale for Children, Fifth Edition* (WISC–V). Copyright © 2014 NCS Pearson, Inc. Reproduced with permission. All rights reserved. "*Wechsler Intelligence Scale for Children*" and "*WISC*" are trademarks, in the United States and/or other countries, of Pearson Education, Inc. or its affiliates(s).
Note: This swiping-backward popover warns the examiner that swiping backward resets all associated values for the current item (e.g., score, timing, recording).

can be exposed, all instructions are available, and performance can be recorded.

The practitioner's screen serves to permit the examiner to indicate similar information to that typically written on the Record Form. Many of these functions were illustrated previously in Figures 4.4 and 4.5, which depict other types of items. In the example illustrated in Figure 4.12, the interaction between the two tablets is evident in the Client View preview. If the examinee selects a response, it is highlighted. Because the examinee may also choose to respond verbally by saying the letter corresponding to the indicated response, the examiner also may touch the Client View preview to indicate the examinee's response. Occasionally sample and teaching items include Show Picture buttons that are used when providing feedback for an incorrect response.

This chapter provides various subtest screen examples, but similar and thorough training videos for each type of subtest are also available on the Q-interactive site's "Support" tab. The

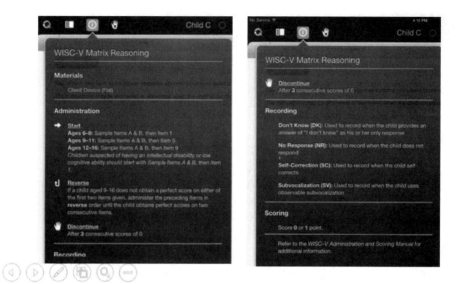

Figure 4.9   Information Text Popover on Practitioner's Screen   *Wechsler Intelligence Scale for Children, Fifth Edition* (WISC–V). Copyright © 2014 NCS Pearson, Inc. Reproduced with permission. All rights reserved. "*Wechsler Intelligence Scale for Children*" and "*WISC*" are trademarks, in the United States and/or other countries, of Pearson Education, Inc. or its affiliates(s).

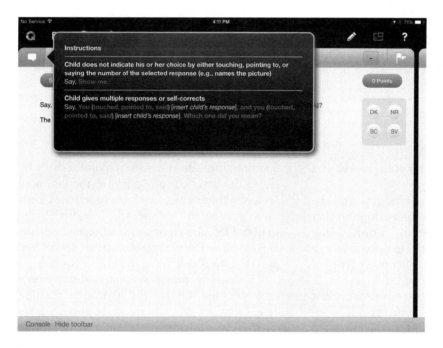

Figure 4.10   Instructions Text Popover on Practitioner's Screen   *Wechsler Intelligence Scale for Children, Fifth Edition* (WISC–V). Copyright © 2014 NCS Pearson, Inc. Reproduced with permission. All rights reserved. "*Wechsler Intelligence Scale for Children*" and "*WISC*" are trademarks, in the United States and/or other countries, of Pearson Education, Inc. or its affiliates(s).

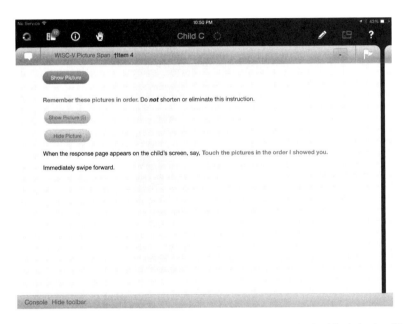

Figure 4.11 Practitioner's Screen View of an Item, Example A *Wechsler Intelligence Scale for Children, Fifth Edition* (WISC–V). Copyright © 2014 NCS Pearson, Inc. Reproduced with permission. All rights reserved. "*Wechsler Intelligence Scale for Children*" and "*WISC*" are trademarks, in the United States and/or other countries, of Pearson Education, Inc. or its affiliates(s).

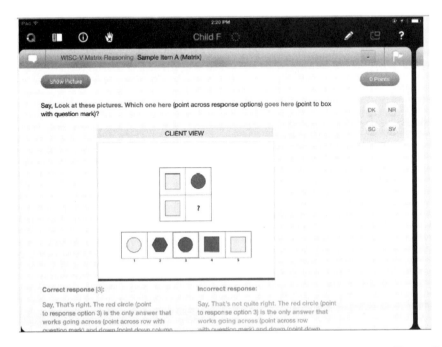

Figure 4.12 Practitioner's Screen View of an Item, Example B *Wechsler Intelligence Scale for Children, Fifth Edition* (WISC–V). Copyright © 2014 NCS Pearson, Inc. Reproduced with permission. All rights reserved. "*Wechsler Intelligence Scale for Children*" and "*WISC*" are trademarks, in the United States and/or other countries, of Pearson Education, Inc. or its affiliates(s).

active link at the time of this writing is: https://qiactive.com/choose-share/support/index.

Basic Scoring Output

When administration of each subtest is completed, an End of Subtest card appears with item-level scores, various other observations that were recorded, and the actual subtest administration time. Touching the Results button on the End of Subtest card produces a Results popover. The Results popover permits immediate access to the subtest scaled score, composite scores, pairwise comparisons, and strengths and weaknesses. Figures 4.13 and 4.14 depict the Results page for subtest scaled and standard scores, in administration order.

Figure 4.15 depicts the Results page for composite scores.

The subtests that were administered are listed in the first column. They currently appear in administration order but can also be ordered by score (high to low or low to high). Touching the triangle-shaped button to the left of a subtest opens a drop-down of additional text that lists the same information from the End of Subtest card.

Advanced Scoring Output

Q-interactive and Q-global (which is described and pictured in Chapter 3) systems are seamlessly connected within Central. Results may be transferred back to Central following administration,

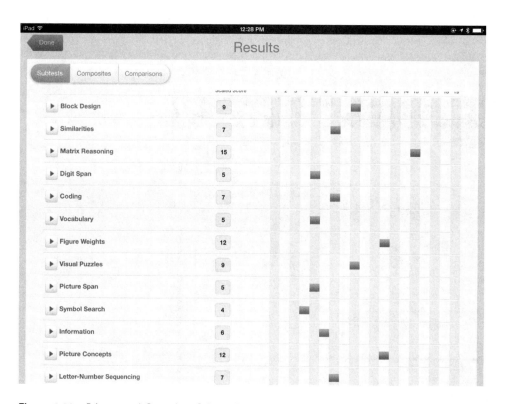

Figure 4.13 Primary and Secondary Subtest Results *Wechsler Intelligence Scale for Children, Fifth Edition* (WISC–V). Copyright © 2014 NCS Pearson, Inc. Reproduced with permission. All rights reserved. "*Wechsler Intelligence Scale for Children*" and "*WISC*" are trademarks, in the United States and/or other countries, of Pearson Education, Inc. or its affiliates(s).

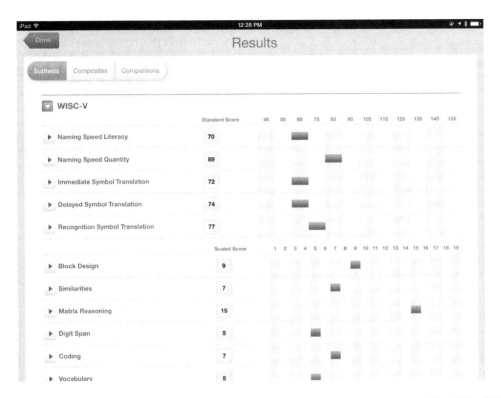

Figure 4.14   Complementary Subtest Results *Wechsler Intelligence Scale for Children, Fifth Edition* (WISC–V). Copyright © 2014 NCS Pearson, Inc. Reproduced with permission. All rights reserved. "*Wechsler Intelligence Scale for Children*" and "*WISC*" are trademarks, in the United States and/or other countries, of Pearson Education, Inc. or its affiliates(s).

where the same interface and selections pictured for Q-global in Chapter 3 are available.

Access to Manuals in Central

As previously noted, the *WISC–V Administration and Scoring Manual*, the *WISC–V Administration and Scoring Manual Supplement*, and the *WISC–V Technical and Interpretive Manual* are all available in digital format on Central. To locate the manuals from the Support tab, select the active link labeled *Test Materials*. Scroll down to the bottom of the webpage because the manuals appear in alphabetical order. See Figure 4.16 for appearance of the links to the manuals.

Potential Clinical Applications and Digital Enhancements

Q-interactive represents a substantial advancement in the clinical assessment field. The adaptation of the WISC–V subtests in a digital environment using tablet devices to replace the stimulus books and Record Form is a welcome change. It is clear that paper response booklets and other manipulatives may also soon be a thing of the past, particularly with the ongoing work to adapt the Processing Speed subtests. Even the Block Design blocks may be subject to digital adaptation. Physical cubes that permit tactile play within an interactive game system and can therefore detect and record movement

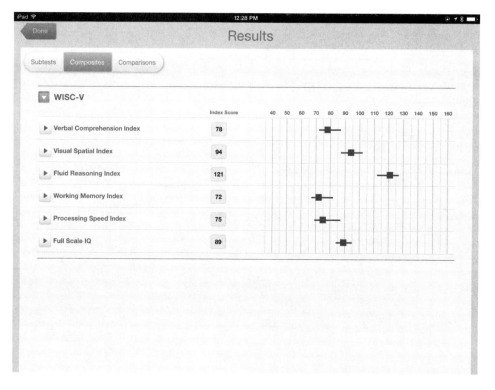

Figure 4.15 Composite Results *Wechsler Intelligence Scale for Children, Fifth Edition* (WISC–V). Copyright © 2014 NCS Pearson, Inc. Reproduced with permission. All rights reserved. "*Wechsler Intelligence Scale for Children*" and "*WISC*" are trademarks, in the United States and/or other countries, of Pearson Education, Inc. or its affiliates(s).

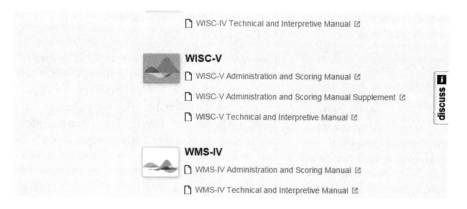

Figure 4.16 Manual Links in Central *Wechsler Intelligence Scale for Children, Fifth Edition* (WISC–V). Copyright © 2014 NCS Pearson, Inc. Reproduced with permission. All rights reserved. "*Wechsler Intelligence Scale for Children*" and "*WISC*" are trademarks, in the United States and/or other countries, of Pearson Education, Inc. or its affiliates(s).

and orientation (e.g., Sifteo Cubes™ by Sifteo, Inc.) are available at this time.

The potential for data, both at the individual level and the group level, is limited only by the imagination. New subtests built purely within the digital realm could make measurement of a number of constructs more feasible. As an example, no currently available battery provides psychometrically rigorous reaction time measures linked with other measures of ability, despite the fact that various types of reaction time have shown sensitivity to dyscalculia (Ashkenazi, Mark-Zigdon, & Henik, 2009),

ADHD (Kuntsi … Asherson, 2010; Lipszyc & Schachar, 2010; Van De Voorde, Roeyers, Verte, & Wiersema, 2010), specific learning disorder in reading (Lipszyc & Schachar, 2010; Van De Voorde et al., 2010), and bipolar disorder (Mattis, Papolos, Luck, Cockerham, & Thode, 2011), to name a few. Increasingly user-friendly visual-spatial working memory and inhibition control measures are also within sight. Scores for latency time, response time, and complex processing speed are also much more feasible given the flexibility and enhanced data capture potential of the digital medium.

PART 3

BASIC WISC–V TEST INTERPRETATION

CHAPTER 5

WISC–V SEX, ETHNIC, AND SOCIOECONOMIC STATUS (SES) DIFFERENCES

INTRODUCTION

Cognitive ability test scores commonly show mean differences across children grouped according to sex, parent education level, and race/ethnicity. For this reason, each age group of the WISC–V normative sample was matched to the 2012 U.S. census proportions for these variables, so that scores derived from performance of the normative sample are representative of performance in the U.S. population. Each age group of the normative sample included half female and half male children, with the exception of the 9-year-old age group, which had 101 female and 99 male children.

Group differences in mean scores do not indicate that a test is biased. Item bias, or differential item functioning based on group membership, is a separate but related validity issue. Item bias indicates that the same item functions differently within two segments of a sample (e.g., White compared with African American) that are matched based on other important characteristics (e.g., age, sex, parent education, geographic region). Item bias was examined statistically during WISC–V development phases. Oversamples of children from different racial/ethnicity categories were tested during development, and results were compared across groups to determine if any items functioned differently based on categorical membership. "Biased" items were then selected for removal from the test before publication (Wechsler, 2014). This chapter examines results at the composite score level *after* that process was completed. Group differences

at this stage are often shown to be related to variation on *other* important characteristics.

For example, children's cognitive ability varies with parent education level, and parent education level in turn differs across racial/ethnic groups, as do a great number of other variables related to socioeconomic status (see Weiss, Chen, Harris, Holdnack, & Saklofske, 2010; Weiss et al., 2006; and Weiss, Locke, Pan, Harris, Saklofske, & Prifitera, 2016, for reviews of these factors). To illustrate, Table 5.1 provides the percentage of adults aged 25 and over from selected racial/ethnic groups in the United States completing various levels of education.

> **Remember**
>
> Racial/ethnic groups vary greatly in the distribution of other important variables related to socioeconomic status and their home environment.

As seen in Table 5.1, the proportion of adults who attain less than a high school diploma or its equivalent varies across racial/ethnic groups. Notably, the percentage of individuals in this category who are Hispanic is approximately triple the analogous percentages of White individuals. The proportion of individuals who are African American and attain less than a high school education is approximately 50% higher that of White individuals. Similar proportions of White, Hispanic, and African American individuals obtain a high school diploma or equivalent. The percentage of White individuals who obtain

Table 5.1 Percentage of Adults from Selected Racial/Ethnic Groups Completing Various Levels of Education

Years of Education	White (Non-Hispanic)	Hispanic (Any Race)	African American	Asian
≤8 Years	4.7	18.5	3.8	6.0
9–11 Years	6.5	15.0	10.4	4.4
High School Diploma or Equivalent	29.8	29.9	33.4	20.5
Some College or Associate's Degree	26.7	21.4	30.1	16.7
Bachelor's Degree or Higher	32.3	15.2	22.2	52.3

Source: U.S. Bureau of the Census (2014).

a bachelor's degree is more than double that of Hispanic individuals who obtain bachelor's degrees and 50% higher than that of African American individuals. Hence, racial/ethnic group means on WISC–V composite scores are expected to show discrepancies that are partially related to group differences in parent education level, or other factors related to socioeconomic status (SES).

Therefore, this chapter compares means and standard deviations (*SD*s) of the composite scores from the published test for children from the normative sample of the WISC–V segmented by sex, parent education level, and race/ethnicity. As parent education level is closely related to the composite scores on measures of intellectual ability, the race/ethnicity means are reported with and without controlling for parent education level and sex.

Remember

U.S. Census Bureau data from 2014 indicate that, relative to White individuals, three times as many Hispanic individuals attain less than a high school diploma. Also, the percentage of White individuals who obtain a bachelor's degree is more than double that of Hispanic individuals.

SEX DIFFERENCES

An array of research supports the general finding that males and females perform differently on measures of cognitive ability. The performance differences between the sexes vary by age. Although the mechanisms of these differences are not known definitively and substantial controversy characterizes theoretical explanations (Keith, Reynolds, Roberts, Winter, & Austin, 2011), research suggests sex-related brain architecture, connectivity, development, and volume may be related to the distinctions in performance (Burgaleta et al., 2012; Rushton & Ankney, 2009; Schmithorst, 2009; Taki et al., 2011).

Sex differences between mean cognitive ability scores vary across the life span. Whereas in many studies the differences across very young males and females are statistically significant, they are slight and may not be practically meaningful. Among young children, females tend to slightly outperform males on formal measures of general intellectual ability (A. S. Kaufman & Kaufman, 1973, 2004; Palejwala & Fine, 2014; Raiford, Coalson, & Engi, 2012) as well as on some specific cognitive abilities (A. S. Kaufman & Kaufman, 1973, 2004; Keith et al., 2011; Palejwala & Fine, 2014; Raiford et al., 2012). *Gc*, which is related to the Wechsler Preschool and Primary Scale of Intelligence–Fourth Edition (WPPSI–IV) Verbal Comprehension Index, is sometimes found to show no sex difference in some young children, however (A. S. Kaufman & Kaufman, 2004; Keith et al., 2011); sometimes, though, young female children show an advantage (Raiford et al., 2012).

The picture appears to change a few years after children enter formal schooling. The pattern of females outscoring males is no longer present around age 7, when male and female children perform roughly the same on composite scores (A. S. Kaufman & Kaufman, 2004). In fact, some results suggest a reversal of the pattern observed in young children: By age 10, the results are mixed. Males on average sometimes outscore females on general intellectual ability measures (Dykiert, Gale, & Deary, 2009; Preiss & Franova, 2006), but in other studies, the reverse is true (Calvin, Fernandes, Smith, Visscher, & Deary, 2010; Shamama-tus-Sabah, Gilani, & Iftikhar, 2012).

There is evidence for sex-related advantages on specific cognitive abilities. Preschool and school-age males have been shown to outscore females on factors related to visual-spatial ability (A. S. Kaufman & Kaufman, 2004; Keith et al., 2011; Jirout & Newcombe, 2015; Palejwala & Fine, 2014), which is analogous to the WISC–V Visual Spatial Index. School-age females appear to show an advantage on the working memory and processing speed factors (Keith et al., 2011), which are analogous to the WISC–V Working Memory and Processing Speed Index. Of these, the processing speed finding is more robust.

For adolescents and adults, results tend to show that males usually outperform females on measures of both overall intellectual ability (Lynn & Irwing, 2008; Nyborg, 2005; Rushton & Ankney, 2009) and of most specific cognitive domains. For example, on the Wechsler Adult Intelligence Scale–Fourth Edition (WAIS–IV; Wechsler, 2008), males score higher on general intellectual ability, represented by the FSIQ, and higher on verbal comprehension, perceptual reasoning, and working memory; but females maintain their school-age advantage on processing speed (Lichtenberger & Kaufman, 2013; Salthouse & Saklofske, 2010).

Each of the 11 age groups in the WISC–V normative sample is equally comprised of males and females, with the exception of the 9-year-old age group, which has 101 female and 99 male children. Table 5.2 presents the mean WISC–V composite scores of female and male children in the normative sample.

The WISC–V Working Memory Index, Processing Speed Index, FSIQ, Nonverbal Index, Cognitive Proficiency Index, and Symbol Translation Index are significantly higher in female than in male children, and the Quantitative Reasoning Index is significantly higher in male than in female children. For all but the Processing Speed Index and the Cognitive Proficiency Index, however, the actual mean differences are very slight (i.e., most differences are less than 1.5 points). The Verbal Comprehension Index, Visual Spatial Index, Auditory Working Memory Index, General Ability Index, Naming Speed Index, and Storage and Retrieval Index show no significant sex differences.

Generally these results are consistent with prior findings that female and male children perform roughly equally on measures of cognitive ability (A. S. Kaufman & Kaufman, 2004) with the exception of processing speed (Keith et al., 2011). Published studies show the female processing speed advantage consistently across all ages, and the Cognitive Proficiency Index includes processing speed subtests. Another set of studies indicates that females outperform males in the academic domain of written communication, a sex difference of moderate effect size that starts young, in first grade, and continues through old age (Camarata & Woodcock, 2006; A. S. Kaufman, Kaufman, Liu, & Johnson, 2009; M. R. Reynolds, Scheiber, Hajovsky, Schwartz, & Kaufman, 2015; Scheiber, Reynolds, Hajovski, & Kaufman, 2015). It is possible that the female advantage in processing speed is related to the female advantage in writing. Although both of these sex differences have been observed in the same large sample (Camarata & Woodcock, 2006), no research has yet determined if they are causally linked or even correlated with each other.

Quick Reference 5.1 summarizes the key results in the WISC–V analysis for differences between female and male children and the developmental trends in sex differences on intellectual ability tests.

Table 5.2   WISC–V Normative Sample Composite Score Means and Standard Deviations, by Sex

Sex	Value	Verbal Comprehension Index	Visual Spatial Index	Fluid Reasoning Index	Working Memory Index	Processing Speed Index	FSIQ
Female	Mean	100.0	99.4	100.1	100.7	103.0	100.7
	SD	14.6	14.5	14.6	14.5	14.8	14.5
	n	1101	1101	1101	1099	1101	1099
Male	Mean	100.0	100.6	99.9	99.4	97.0	99.3
	SD	15.3	15.5	15.5	15.4	14.7	15.4
	n	1099	1099	1099	1099	1099	1099
Mean Difference (Female–Male)		0.0	−1.2	0.2	1.3*	6.0**	1.4*

Sex	Value	Auditory Working Memory Index	Quantitative Reasoning Index	Nonverbal Index	General Ability Index	Cognitive Proficiency Index	Naming Speed Index	Symbol Translation Index	Storage and Retrieval Index
Female	Mean	100.4	99.3	101.0	99.9	102.2	99.7	100.9	100.4
	SD	14.5	14.4	14.5	14.7	14.5	14.5	14.9	14.7
	n	1098	1101	1101	1101	1099	1081	1101	1081
Male	Mean	99.7	100.7	99.0	100.1	97.8	100.4	99.0	99.8
	SD	15.6	15.6*	15.4	15.3	15.2	15.7	15.3	15.4
	n	1099	1099	1099	1099	1099	1078	1099	1078
Mean Difference (Female–Male)		0.7	−1.4*	2.0**	−0.2	4.4**	−0.7	1.9*	0.6

$^*p < .05;$

$^{**}p < .01$

SOCIOECONOMIC STATUS DIFFERENCES

SES is strongly associated with children's intellectual ability test scores from infancy through adolescence (von Stumm & Plomin, 2015). It is often represented in intelligence test research by parent education level. However, a rich body of studies published early in the 20th century until the present day notes the strong relations of various other proxies for SES (e.g., parent occupation level, family income) with intellectual ability. The association of SES with intellectual ability from infancy through preschool, school age, and adolescence has been the subject of substantial investigation.

Infancy and Preschool

In early studies examining the association of parent education and child intellectual ability,

QUICK REFERENCE 5.1: SEX DIFFERENCES ON THE WISC–V AND AS DEVELOPMENTAL TRENDS

- On average, female children scored significantly higher than male children on the Working Memory Index, Processing Speed Index, FSIQ, Nonverbal Index, Cognitive Proficiency Index, and Symbol Translation Index; however, for all but index scores that involve processing speed, the actual mean differences were slight.
- On average, male children scored significantly higher than female children only on the Quantitative Reasoning Index.
- Male children did not score *significantly* higher than female children on the Visual Spatial Index, but they did score *slightly* higher, consistent with prior research.
- Young female children tend to outscore male children on general intellectual ability and many specific cognitive abilities.
- Prior research has indicated that by around ages 7 to 10, the average general intellectual ability scores of females and males are close to equivalent.
- By adolescence and adulthood, the trend begins to reverse, with males outscoring females on general intellectual ability.
- The largest sex difference for the WISC–V was observed on the Processing Speed Index (over a 6-point advantage), followed by the Cognitive Proficiency Index (over a 4-point difference). For both comparisons, females obtained the higher score.
- The processing speed advantage is consistently observed in females across all age ranges, including school-age children, adolescents, and adults.

Goodenough (1927) found significant associations between the Kuhlmann-Binet IQs of preschool children and the number of years of formal schooling for each parent. These associations were greater than other proxies for SES, such as parent occupation. In a study utilizing developmental scales and the Stanford-Binet with children aged 0 to 6, Bayley and Jones (1937) found similar results beginning at age 2. Parent education was noted as superior to other proxy representations for SES in this study. Honzik (1940) obtained similar results with children aged 3 to 8 years. Mother's education was most closely related to child cognitive ability than were a host of other proxy SES variables. Furthermore, results suggested the influence of parent education on children's cognitive ability scores continued to increase throughout the 5-year span.

A. S. Kaufman (1973b) segmented portions of the normative sample for the Wechsler Preschool and Primary Scale of Intelligence (WPPSI; Wechsler, 1967) according to father's occupation, which is closely related to education, and compared the resulting portions of the sample with respect to performance on the three IQ scores. Results indicated a significant relation between father's occupation and mean Verbal IQ, Performance IQ, and FSIQ, and that all IQ scores of children with fathers from professional and technical occupations differed significantly from those of children with fathers from other employment segments. On the extreme ends of the father occupation spectrum, the Verbal IQ differences were 17 points, Performance IQ varied by around 15 points, and the FSIQ differences were 18 points. Hence, the largest difference was noted on the FSIQ, followed by the Verbal IQ, then the Performance IQ. Father's occupation was more predictive of performance than was grouping by rural versus urban domicile or U.S. geographic region.

Among preschool children aged 2:6 to 4:11 on the Kaufman Assessment Battery for Children

(K-ABC; A. S. Kaufman & Kaufman, 1983), the influence of parent education level was strongest on the Simultaneous Processing and Nonverbal scales and the Mental Processing Composite. For these three scales, the approximate differences between extreme levels of parent education were 14 to 15 standard-score points; whereas the difference was least on the Sequential Processing Scale (12).

An investigation conducted on the normative sample of the Wechsler Preschool and Primary Scale of Intelligence–Revised Edition (WPPSI–R; Wechsler, 1989) demonstrated that parent education level was more predictive of Verbal, Performance, and FSIQs than was race/ethnicity, parent occupation, and geographic region (Sellers, Burns, & Guyrke, 1996). The strongest relations with parent education level were noted for the FSIQ and the Verbal IQ, although the correlation with Performance IQ was also significant.

For preschool children aged 3 to 6 on the KABC–II (A. S. Kaufman & Kaufman, 2004), the influence of parent education was most clear on the *Gc* scale, which is conceptually similar to the WPPSI–IV Verbal Comprehension Index, and the Fluid-Crystallized Index, which is analogous to the WPPSI–IV FSIQ. Differences for all composite scores and subtests were statistically significant. The approximate differences between extreme segments of parent education ranged from 15 (*Gsm* and *Glr*) to 22 points (*Gc*). Raiford et al.'s (2014) investigation of the association between parent education level and WPPSI–IV composite scores indicated that verbal and crystallized abilities, as well as general intellectual ability, are more highly correlated with parent education level relative to visual-spatial, fluid reasoning, working memory, and processing speed abilities. A large longitudinal twin study indicated from infancy through age 7 that a number of indicators of SES predicted increasing differences in cognitive ability across that span of development. Measures included parental education, occupation, and income (von Stumm & Plomin, 2015). These results are indicative of the importance of

the home environment in cognitive development among younger children.

School Age

Studies of the association of parent education and child intelligence in school-age children also demonstrate the relationship is powerful for these ages (Buckhalt, El-Sheikh, Keller, & Kelly, 2009; Steinmayr, Dinger, & Spinath, 2010). Among school-age children aged 7 to 18, the mean KABC–II score differences by parent education level were less evident, albeit all were significant. The greatest difference continued to occur on the *Gc* scale, with smaller differences on the remainder of the composite scores. Hence, parent education remained a significant but less important predictor of performance among school-age children.

Weiss et al. (2006) found a similar result for school-age children at the FSIQ level when examining the WISC–IV (Wechsler, 2003) normative sample (aged 6–16), segmented by parent education level. The average FSIQ was more than 20 points lower in children of parents with an eighth-grade education or less relative to children of parents with a bachelor's degree or more. The results for composite scores other than the FSIQ were not reported.

Von Stumm and Plumin (2015) found that parental education, occupation, and income differences resulted in increasingly greater differences in cognitive ability between children with low and high SES backgrounds across the school ages. By age 16, this difference had grown to almost triple that observed at age 2 (von Stumm & Plomin, 2015).

Table 5.3 presents the mean WISC–V composite scores of children in the normative sample segmented into five parent education levels. The sample is matched within each age group to census proportions for parent education level. If the child lives with only one parent or guardian, the education level of that individual is used. If the child lives with two parents or guardians, the education level of those individuals is

Table 5.3   WISC–V Normative Sample Composite Score Means and Standard Deviations, by Parent Education Level

Parent Education Level	Value	Verbal Comprehension Index	Visual Spatial Index	Fluid Reasoning Index	Working Memory Index	Processing Speed Index	FSIQ
8 years or less	Mean	87.8	91.8	90.0	87.0	96.3	87.8
	SD	10.9	12.0	11.2	10.6	14.0	10.2
	n	68	68	68	67	68	67
9–11 years	Mean	88.4	91.5	91.4	91.4	95.7	88.6
	SD	16.3	15.8	16.3	15.5	16.6	16.2
	n	168	168	168	168	168	168
12 years (high school diploma or equivalent)	Mean	94.1	95.4	94.5	95.5	97.8	93.8
	SD	13.3	13.9	14.3	15.0	14.9	13.4
	n	460	460	460	460	460	460
13–15 years (some college)	Mean	100.0	99.5	99.9	100.3	99.4	99.7
	SD	12.5	13.8	13.4	13.5	14.4	12.5
	n	777	777	777	777	777	777
16 years or more (college graduate)	Mean	107.6	106.2	106.6	105.8	103.4	108.0
	SD	14.2	14.6	14.2	14.1	14.8	14.0
	n	727	727	727	726	727	726
% of variance explained*		17.7	10.2	12.3	11.5	2.6	18.7

Parent Education Level	Value	Auditory Working Memory Index	Quantitative Reasoning Index	Nonverbal Index	General Ability Index	Cognitive Proficiency Index	Naming Speed Index	Symbol Translation Index	Storage and Retrieval Index
8 years or less	Mean	86.8	88.7	89.3	87.8	90.1	94.7	92.6	91.8
	SD	11.3	11.8	10.6	10.4	12.4	13.4	12.8	12.0
	n	67	68	68	68	67	68	68	68
9–11 years	Mean	90.0	90.4	90.6	88.6	92.1	95.0	93.0	92.8
	SD	16.5	16.1	16.1	16.1	16.0	14.4	16.0	14.6
	n	168	168	168	168	168	164	168	164
12 years (high school diploma or equivalent)	Mean	96.0	94.9	94.0	93.7	95.9	97.4	96.2	96.1
	SD	14.9	13.9	13.7	13.4	14.3	15.8	15.3	15.1
	n	460	460	460	460	460	450	460	450

(continued)

Table 5.3 *(Continued)*

Parent Education Level	Value	Auditory Working Memory Index	Quantitative Reasoning Index	Nonverbal Index	General Ability Index	Cognitive Proficiency Index	Naming Speed Index	Symbol Translation Index	Storage and Retrieval Index
13–15 years (some college)	Mean	100.1	99.8	99.7	99.7	99.8	100.2	100.1	100.2
	SD	12.7	12.7	13.1	12.7	13.7	14.6	13.9	14.2
	n	777	777	777	777	777	762	777	762
16 years or more (college graduate)	Mean	106.1	106.6	107.3	108.1	105.6	103.3	104.5	105.0
	SD	14.6	14.9	14.3	13.9	14.6	14.8	14.8	14.6
	n	725	727	727	727	726	715	727	715
% of variance explained*		12.5	13.3	14.8	18.8	9.2	3.2	6.4	7.4

*All statistically significant ($p < .001$)

averaged. Partial levels are rounded up to the next level.

The lowermost rows in Table 5.3 present the percentage of score variance accounted for by parent education level. As with other cognitive ability tests, parent education level is strongly related to WISC–V performance. The variance in performance explained by parent education level suggests it has the greatest influence on the General Ability Index, FSIQ, and Verbal Comprehension Index. Relative to the Nonverbal Index, parent education level explains more variability in the FSIQ, the General Ability Index, and the Verbal Comprehension Index. This difference likely reflects their reliance on verbal ability. The influence is least for the Processing Speed Index and the Naming Speed Index.

These results are consistent with those of prior studies—general intellectual ability, as well as verbal and crystallized abilities, are more highly correlated with parent education level relative to other abilities. The strong association between parent education and the verbal skills of school-age children is observed consistently in prior research, including the aforementioned studies.

Quick Reference 5.2 lists the key results in the WISC–V analysis for differences across parent education levels.

RACE/ETHNICITY DIFFERENCES

Comparing the mean score differences of groups of White children to groups of African American children and groups of Hispanic children has been a goal of many investigations. Studies of both preschool and school age children are discussed.

Preschool

An investigation by A. S. Kaufman (1973a) drew groups of White and African American children aged 4 to 6 matched on age, sex, region, father's occupation, and urban-rural residence from the WPPSI normative sample, and compared their performance on the Verbal IQ, Performance IQ, and FSIQ. The mean group difference was greatest on FSIQ (10.8 standard-score points), followed by Verbal IQ (10.5) and Performance

QUICK REFERENCE 5.2: PARENT EDUCATION LEVEL DIFFERENCES ON THE WISC–V

- Parent education level explains more variance in the FSIQ and the General Ability Index than in the Nonverbal Index. This difference likely reflects their reliance on verbal ability.
- Parent education level explains more variance in the composite scores involving verbal ability (e.g., the FSIQ, General Ability Index, and Verbal Comprehension Index) than other abilities.
- The average FSIQ of children with a parent education level of eighth grade or less is about 20 points lower than the average FSIQ of children with a parent education level of a bachelor's degree or higher.
- Of all WISC–V composite scores, the Processing Speed Index and the Naming Speed Index are the least affected by parent education level. Parent education level only explains about 2% to 3% of the variance in these composite scores.

IQ (8.9). When the results were examined by single year increments, the group differences on Performance IQ and on FSIQ decreased for each year the child aged.

A. S. Kaufman and Kaufman (1973) examined 148 pairs of African American and White children matched on age, sex, and father's occupation on the General Cognitive Index (GCI) of the McCarthy Scales of Children's Abilities (McCarthy Scales; McCarthy, 1972). They found no significant racial/ethnic differences on the cognitive scales among children aged 2:6–5:5, but a significant difference for ages 6:5–8:6.

Arinoldo (1981) administered the McCarthy Scales and either the WPPSI or the Wechsler Intelligence Scale for Children–Revised Edition (WISC–R; Wechsler, 1974a) in counterbalanced order to 40 children aged 4:0 to 5:6 and 7:0 to 8:6, then compared the mean McCarthy GCI and WPPSI/WISC–R FSIQ scores across groups of White and African American children. He found smaller group differences for preschool than school-age children, and smaller differences overall on the McCarthy GCI than on the Wechsler FSIQs. In the preschool group, the White group outscored the African American group on the McCarthy GCI by 3.8 points and on the WPPSI FSIQ by 4.2 points. For school-age children, the White group outscored the African American group on the McCarthy GCI by 15.5 points and on the Wechsler FSIQ by 21.3 points. All group differences were

significant ($p < .05$ for preschool, and $p < .001$ for school-age). Hence, the pattern observed by Arinoldo was similar to that observed in the Kaufmans' (1973) investigation: Differences between African American and White groups were relatively larger in the older group.

An investigation with the WPPSI–R normative sample (Sellers et al., 1996) split children by race/ethnicity into Black Hispanic, Black, White Hispanic, Native American, Other Ethnicity, White, and Asian groups; and examined contribution to the three IQ scores of race/ethnicity, parent education level, parent occupation, geographic region, and sex. The strongest predictor was parent education level, followed by race/ethnicity (all $p < .001$), for the three IQ scores. Beyond parent education level, race/ethnicity accounted for 5.9% of the variance for the FSIQ, 4.6% for the Verbal IQ, and 4.9% for the Performance IQ. Unfortunately, group means were not reported, and the results were not reported by age.

For children aged 3 to 6 in the KABC–II normative sample, the percentage of score variance accounted for by race/ethnicity after controlling for sex and mother's education level was greatest for the *Gc* scale (6%). The least variance was accounted for within *Glr* (0.2%) and *Gsm* (1.3%) (A. S. Kaufman & Kaufman, 2004).

The largest adjusted differences between White and African American children occurred on the *Gc* scale (almost 7 standard-score points in favor of Whites) and the Gv scale (4.3 points). The smallest differences were present on the Gsm scale (African Americans outscored White by 0.4 points), analogous to the WPPSI–IV Working Memory Index; and the Glr scale, which showed only a 0.4 point advantage for Whites. For the Fluid-Crystallized Index, analogous to the WPPSI–IV FSIQ, the adjusted mean difference in favor of Whites was 3.6 points (Kaufman & Kaufman, 2004). Between White and Hispanic children, the largest adjusted composite score differences were present on Gc (9.1), the Fluid-Crystallized Index (5.0), and Gsm (4.3). In contrast, Gv (0.6), Glr (0.8), and Nonverbal Index (1.1) showed almost no difference.

The authors noted that adjusting for parent education level among ethnic groups was appropriate because the distribution of parent education differs across racial/ethnic groups (as seen in Table 5.1 of this chapter) but that it does not control thoroughly for the socioeconomic differences across racial/ethnic groups. Parent education level, they indicated, is objectively measured, typically is accurately reported by the parents (which is not the case with many SES variables, such as income), and is plausibly related to child cognitive development. Thus, parent education merely serves as a *proxy variable* for many other aspects of SES that vary by race/ethnicity, and therefore *only provides a **partial** estimate of the impact of SES on racial/ethnic score differences* (A. S. Kaufman & Kaufman, 2004).

Raiford et al. (2014) found that the WPPSI–IV composite scores that involve verbal ability (i.e., the Vocabulary Acquisition Index and the Verbal Comprehension Index) had the greatest residual variance attributable to race/ethnicity, followed by the General Ability Index, and the FSIQ. The Processing Speed Index, Cognitive Proficiency Index, and Working Memory Index showed the smallest residual percentage of variance accounted for by race/ethnicity.

The mean differences between White children compared with African American children and with Hispanic children were greatest. The

unadjusted differences between White and African American children were largest (7–9 standard-score points) on the General Ability Index, FSIQ, Verbal Comprehension Index, Vocabulary Acquisition Index, and Visual Spatial Index. After adjustment for sex and parent education level, the mean group differences shrunk to around 5 to 6 points for each of these composite scores. All differences dropped at least 1.6 standard-score points with the adjustment (Raiford et al., 2014).

The most substantial unadjusted differences (7–10 points) between White and Hispanic children were present on the Vocabulary Acquisition Index, Verbal Comprehension Index, General Ability Index, and FSIQ. Following adjustment, the differences between White and Hispanic children decreased substantially for composite scores that are not derived from Verbal Comprehension subtests. The differences were substantially smaller after adjustment, and none was practically meaningful (Raiford et al., 2014). Weiss et al. (2006) also demonstrated that when additional socioeconomic factors, such as household income, are accounted for among school-age children, the White–Hispanic score differences vanish.

School Age

The differences in cognitive ability scores by racial/ethnic group persist into adolescence and adulthood. For example, among adolescents and adults aged 11 to 24, a White group outscored an African American and a Hispanic group on the Crystallized, Fluid, and Composite IQ scores of the Kaufman Adolescent and Adult Intelligence Test (KAIT; A. S. Kaufman & Kaufman, 1993). The differences between the White and African American groups varied from approximately 10 (Crystallized) to 12 standard-score points (Fluid and Composite). The White and Hispanic group means were discrepant by approximately 9 (Fluid) to 13 points (Crystallized).

For children aged 7–18 in the KABC–II normative sample, the percentage of score variance accounted for by race/ethnicity after controlling for sex and mother's education level was greatest for the *Gc* scale (7%). The least variance was accounted for within *Glr* (0.2%) and *Gsm* (1.3%). About 5% of variance in the Fluid-Crystallized Index was accounted for by race/ethnicity after controlling for sex and mother's education level. These results were consistent with those for children aged 3–6 (A. S. Kaufman & Kaufman, 2004).

Table 5.4 presents the mean WISC–V composite scores of children in the normative sample segmented into five racial/ethnicity groups. The WISC–V normative sample is matched within each age group to census proportions for these five groups. Because the percentages of parents with the five education levels differ across racial/ethnic groups, the scores are reported unadjusted *and* adjusted for parent education level and sex.

The summary rows at the bottom of Table 5.4 present the percentage of score variance accounted for by sex, parent education level, and race/ethnicity combined; sex and parent education level combined; and the residual percentage accounted for by race/ethnicity alone. The Visual Spatial Index, General Ability Index, Verbal Comprehension Index, and FSIQ have the greatest residual variance attributable to race/ethnicity (5.8, 4.4, 3.7, and 3.5% respectively). The Processing Speed Index (0.5%), Naming Speed Index (0.8), and Cognitive Proficiency Index (0.9%), Working Memory Index (1.1%), and Auditory Working Memory Index (1.3%) show the smallest residual percentage of variance accounted for by race/ethnicity.

Because the mean differences between White children compared with African American children and with Hispanic children are greatest, they are discussed in turn.

African American Children

The largest unadjusted and adjusted differences between White and African American children appear on the Visual Spatial Index, General Ability Index, FSIQ, Verbal Comprehension Index, and Nonverbal Index (11–13 points unadjusted and 8–11 points adjusted). For the unadjusted and adjusted means, the smallest differences between White and African American children are present on the Processing Speed Index, Naming Speed Index, Working Memory Index, and Symbol Translation Index (unadjusted 4–7 points; adjusted 3–5 points).

After adjustment for sex and parent education level, the FSIQ difference remains at 8.7 points, or slightly less than two thirds of 1 *SD*. Adjusting for sex and parent education level has the greatest impact on the differences for the General Ability Index (a decrease in the difference of 3 standard-score points), FSIQ (decrease of 2.9), and Verbal Comprehension Index (decrease of 2.8), although all differences drop at least 1 standard-score point with the adjustment.

These results are similar to those previously observed. The White group composite score means remain significantly higher than the African American group means. The differences are noticeably larger on scores that include measures of crystallized ability and acquired knowledge. As noted by A. S. Kaufman and Kaufman (2004), adjustment for parent education alone cannot compensate entirely for the differences in SES across these two population segments. It provides only a crude and incomplete estimate of the impact of socioeconomic differences across the groups. For example, Weiss et al. (2006) demonstrated that living in a home with more than one parent/guardian or with parents who have high expectations of the child's eventual achievement also has an impact on mediating these differences. As these aspects of the home environment also vary by race/ethnicity, they could provide additional explanation of the remaining differences.

Hispanic Children

The most largest unadjusted differences between White and Hispanic children are present on the Verbal Comprehension Index, General Ability Index, and FSIQ (9.5, 9.2, and 9.1 standard-score points, respectively). For the unadjusted means, the smallest differences between White children and Hispanic children are present on the Processing Speed Index (2.6) and the Naming Speed Index (4.9).

Adjustment for sex and parent education level has the largest impact on the General Ability Index and the FSIQ (decreases in the difference of 5.4 points each). After adjustment for sex and parent education level, the FSIQ difference

Table 5.4   WISC–V Normative Sample Composite Score Means and Standard Deviations, by Race/Ethnicity, Adjusted for Sex and Parent Education Level

Race/Ethnicity	Value	Verbal Comprehension Index	Visual Spatial Index	Fluid Reasoning Index	Working Memory Index	Processing Speed Index	FSIQ
Asian	Unadjusted Mean	105.9	109.8	107.0	103.9	106.5	108.6
	Adjusted Mean	103.6	108.2	105.0	101.8	105.0	106.1
	SD	15.0	14.9	13.3	13.1	15.5	14.4
	n	89	89	89	89	89	89
African American	Unadjusted Mean	92.1	90.3	93.7	96.1	96.4	91.9
	Adjusted Mean	93.4	91.2	94.8	97.2	96.9	93.2
	SD	13.7	13.2	14.4	13.9	15.5	13.3
	n	312	312	312	312	312	312
Hispanic	Unadjusted Mean	94.2	96.8	95.6	94.9	98.3	94.4
	Adjusted Mean	97.9	99.5	98.8	97.9	99.9	98.2
	SD	13.5	13.3	13.4	14.5	14.0	12.9
	n	458	458	458	457	458	457
Other	Unadjusted Mean	100.3	99.7	99.8	99.5	101.9	100.4
	Adjusted Mean	100.2	99.8	99.8	99.4	101.6	100.3
	SD	14.6	13.2	16.2	15.7	14.3	14.7
	n	113	113	113	113	113	113
White	Unadjusted Mean	103.7	103.0	102.8	102.7	100.9	103.5
	Adjusted Mean	102.2	101.9	101.4	101.4	100.3	101.9
	SD	14.4	14.8	14.8	14.8	15.1	14.6
	n	1228	1228	1228	1227	1228	1227
[a]% of variance sex, parent education level, and race/ethnicity		21.8	16.8	14.7	12.8	7.5	23.3
% variance sex and parent education level		18.1	11.0	12.8	11.7	7.0	19.8
[b]residual % of variance for race/ethnicity		3.7	5.8	1.9	1.1	0.5	3.5

Table 5.4 (*Continued*)

Race/Ethnicity	Value	Auditory Working Memory Index	Quanti- tative Reasoning Index	Non- verbal Index	General Ability Index	Cognitive Proficiency Index	Naming Speed Index	Symbol Trans- lation Index	Storage and Retrieval Index
Asian	Unadjusted Mean	103.9	107.4	109.3	108.6	106.4	105.2	103.7	105.7
	Adjusted Mean	101.9	105.5	107.0	106.3	104.3	104.3	102.2	104.2
	SD	15.4	15.5	13.3	14.1	14.1	15.6	15.4	15.3
	n	89	89	89	89	89	87	89	87
African American	Unadjusted Mean	95.5	92.7	91.7	91.1	95.4	96.6	95.8	95.5
	Adjusted Mean	96.6	93.9	92.9	92.5	96.4	97.1	96.6	96.3
	SD	13.9	12.9	13.3	13.7	14.2	15.2	15.5	14.8
	n	312	312	312	312	312	302	312	302
Hispanic	Unadjusted Mean	94.5	95.0	95.5	94.5	95.8	96.9	95.3	95.2
	Adjusted Mean	97.7	98.1	99.0	98.3	98.7	98.3	97.4	97.5
	SD	14.1	13.4	13.0	13.1	13.9	15.1	15.5	15.3
	n	457	458	458	458	457	448	458	448
Other	Unadjusted Mean	100.7	99.6	100.0	100.1	100.8	99.1	101.0	100.0
	Adjusted Mean	100.6	99.6	99.9	100.0	100.6	99.1	100.9	99.9
	SD	15.1	15.1	14.6	14.6	14.5	15.0	13.3	13.9
	n	113	113	113	113	113	112	113	112
White	Unadjusted Mean	102.9	103.2	103.1	103.7	102.2	101.8	102.4	102.7
	Adjusted Mean	101.6	101.8	101.7	102.1	101.0	101.2	101.5	101.8
	SD	14.8	14.8	14.9	14.4	15.1	14.7	14.4	14.4
	n	1226	1228	1228	1228	1227	1210	1228	1210
[a] % of variance sex, parent education level, and race/ethnicity		14.0	17.1	19.7	23.9	12.8	4.3	8.4	9.5
% variance sex and parent education level		12.7	13.8	16.1	19.5	11.9	3.5	6.9	7.8
[b] residual % of variance for race/ethnicity		1.3	3.3	3.6	4.4	0.9	0.8	1.5	1.7

[a]Percentage of variance accounted for by sex, parent education level, and race/ethnicity.

[b]Percentage of variance accounted for by race/ethnicity, above that accounted for by parent education level and sex.

QUICK REFERENCE 5.3: RACIAL/ETHNIC DIFFERENCES ON THE WISC–V

- Race/ethnicity, sex, and parent education level together account for 23% of the variance in the FSIQ. After adjustment for sex and parent education level, however, race/ethnicity accounts for only 3.5% of the variance.
- Following adjustment for sex and parent education level, race/ethnicity accounts for about 1% to 6% of the variance in most composite scores.
- For composite scores that do not rely much on acquired knowledge, such as the Working Memory Index, Processing Speed Index, Cognitive Proficiency Index, Naming Speed Index, and Symbol Translation Index, race/ethnicity accounts for almost no variance following adjustment for sex and parent education level.
- Following adjustment for sex and parent education level, the mean FSIQ difference between Hispanic and White children drops from 9.1 points to only 3.7 points. The Nonverbal Index drops to only 2.7 points.
- The unadjusted FSIQ and General Ability Index mean differences between White and African American groups of children are 11–12 points. A similar discrepancy is observed on many intellectual ability measures.
- After adjustment for sex and parent education level, the mean White and African American group differences shrink to around 10 points for the WISC–V FSIQ and the General Ability Index.
- These results are similar to those previously observed. The White group composite score means remain significantly higher than the African American group means. The group mean differences are noticeably larger on scores that include measures of crystallized ability and acquired knowledge.

---

remains at only 3.7 standard-score points (only about a fifth of 1 *SD*) and the Nonverbal Index difference remains at only 2.7. Following adjustment, the differences between White and Hispanic children decrease substantially for composite scores that are not derived from Verbal Comprehension subtests. The Processing Speed Index mean difference is very slight (0.4 points) following adjustment. The Visual Spatial Index (2.4), Fluid Reasoning Index (2.4 points), Cognitive Proficiency Index (2.3), and Naming Speed Index (2.9) group differences decrease to less than 3 points.

In summary, the White and Hispanic group score differences are substantially smaller after adjustment. Similar to the results from the WPPSI–IV (Raiford et al., 2014), even the largest difference is probably not practically meaningful because additional socioeconomic

factors, such as household income, may result in White–Hispanic score differences vanishing entirely (see Weiss et al., 2006).

Quick Reference 5.3 summarizes the average WISC–V racial/ethnic score differences before and after adjustment for sex and parent education level.

Attention

Adjustment for parent education level alone cannot compensate entirely for the mean differences in SES across White and African American groups, because it provides only a crude and incomplete estimate of the SES impact across groups. However, it is one of the few SES variables reported accurately in research.

SUMMARY OF FINDINGS

To summarize, WISC–V mean score differences are evident across sex, parent education level, and race/ethnicity groups. Additional research is needed to more closely examine the impact of other indicators of SES and home environment variables on racial/ethnic differences, particularly for White children compared with African American children. It is critical to examine the results for all composite scores to more fully understand how these differences manifest across specific cognitive abilities. Furthermore, examining patterns of these group mean differences across the infant to adolescent age range may provide insight into their genesis and reveal more about their developmental progression.

It is worth noting that empirical research indicates that intellectual ability test scores predict achievement similarly across genders, parent education levels, and racial/ethnic groups (Konold & Canivez, 2010; Scheiber, 2015; Weiss & Prifitera, 1995). These differences do not hinder a test's predictive validity but merely provide us with an opportunity to learn more about the impact of risk and protective factors in the child's environment throughout childhood.

CLINICAL APPLICATIONS OF SCORE DIFFERENCES

Risk factors and protective factors are likely to exert a great deal of influence on cognitive development during childhood (Bonci, 2011; Brassard & Boehm, 2007). Assessing those factors and utilizing them to design appropriate intervention and treatment plans should be a part of any evaluation.

Although parent education level represented SES and crudely accounts for home environment influences in the analyses for this chapter, it is not malleable in many cases and is merely a proxy for a host of other important variables. It is investigated within this chapter merely because, as noted, it is subjective, easy to obtain, and more readily reported accurately in research settings. Hence, the results of these analyses and of the studies reviewed in this chapter reaffirm the importance of the practitioner's responsibility to consider the role of contextual variables in test interpretation. This is not new information, and is emphasized in many development and intervention models (Avan & Kirkwood, 2010; Bonci, 2011; Brassard & Boehm, 2012; D. Ford, 2012; L. Ford, Kozey, & Negreiros, 2012; Vig & Sanders, 2007).

Most child assessment models emphasize the importance of a number of key influences on child cognitive development related to family and the home environment. Key influences to include poverty, parental substance abuse, parental illiteracy, work constraints and child care, parental expectations, early intervention programs, lack of active involvement in helping the child to learn in the home, developmental risk factors, exposure to maltreatment or violence, developmental protective factors, resilience, community context, and sociocultural considerations (Bonci, 2011; Brassard & Boehm, 2012).

Risk and protective factors are rich areas to discover in the assessment process, and many are amenable to intervention. Some particularly relevant risk and protective factors that can be associated with cognitive development ability and are fertile recommendation targets are listed in Quick Reference 5.4. Refer to Bonci (2011) and to Brassard and Boehm (2007) for a more complete list of protective and risk factors, including those that are relatively static and thus more relevant to conceptualization rather than intervention.

Chapter 6 follows up on the importance of measuring risk factors as part of a comprehensive assessment of children's and adolescents' cognitive functioning. The chapter presents two new questionnaires, one for predicting academic failure and one for predicting behavior problems, that we developed (with Jennie Kaufman Singer) based on home environment data collected during WISC–V standardization.

QUICK REFERENCE 5.4: MALLEABLE RISK AND PROTECTIVE FACTORS FOR CHILD ASSESSMENT AND INTERVENTION

Protective Factors

Child:

- Good nutrition
- Skills to elicit positive attention from others
- Communication behaviors
- Self-help skills
- Independence
- Good peer relationships

Family:

- Time with caring, interested adults
- Affection and strong bonds
- Family support
- Routines and consistency
- Monitored television time
- Reading together
- High parental expectation of child educational attainment
- Parental school involvement and interest
- Parental involvement in teaching the child at home
- Parental interest in reading
- Parental high education attainment

Community:

- Support from friends and religious groups
- Parental involvement in community
- Parent training

Risk Factors

Family:

- Child abuse
- Maternal anxiety or depression
- Extreme poverty
- Unlimited television viewing
- Parental illiteracy or low literacy
- Parental lack of involvement at child's school
- Parental low education attainment

Source: Adapted from Bonci, 2011, and from Brassard and Boehm, 2007.

THE CREATION OF NEW RISK SCALES FOR SCHOOL FAILURE AND JUVENILE DELINQUENCY: THE CHILD AND ADOLESCENT ACADEMIC AND BEHAVIOR QUESTIONNAIRES

Jennie Kaufman Singer, Alan S. Kaufman, Susan Engi Raiford, and Diane L. Coalson

When working with children or adolescents in a school setting, it is appropriate to focus on their cognitive and academic strengths and weaknesses. Giving an intelligence test and an achievement test can provide teachers, parents, and others working with the child a blueprint for how to deal with all manner of learning difficulties and can help provide the most appropriate remediation or school placement. However, there are many other concerns that can impact a child's school performance. In this chapter, we first focus on defining risk and identifying risk factors for school failure and delinquency by reviewing empirical literature. Then we discuss the process of applying the relevant literature to create and validate two new scales: The Child and Adolescent Academic Questionnaire (Academic-Q) and the Child and Adolescent Behavior Questionnaire (Behavior-Q), that identify those at risk for school failure or problematic behaviors leading to a risk of delinquency. All items for these scales were based on a home environment questionnaire administered to the parent or guardian who brought the child or adolescent to be tested as part of the WISC–V standardization. All analyses are derived from data obtained during the standardization and validation of the WISC–V.

REVIEW OF RESEARCH ON RISK FACTORS FOR SCHOOL FAILURE AND DELINQUENCY

Risk was originally determined by clinical judgment or a mental health professional determining, based on relevant case factors, what level of risk would be assigned to particular individuals regarding their likelihood of getting involved (or continuing their involvement) in the criminal justice system. However, this method was not always successful in separating out those individuals who actually would offend. Actuarial scales eventually replaced this clinical model, and forensic psychologists generally depend on standardized risk assessments in order to formulate their ideas regarding whether a person is at low, moderate, or high risk of offense. In the area of school failure, there are known or empirical risk factors; this is an emerging area of research, and currently specific measures are being created and empirically validated for this purpose. Recently several studies have focused on better ways to assess for adolescent risk of dropping out of school and potentially entering the criminal arena (Casillas et al., 2012). The usefulness of such tools is undeniable. Valid risk assessments that enable a teacher or clinician to identify those children of most concern can ameliorate the risk through early intervention.

Static and Dynamic Risk Factors

Two main types of risk are important to assess for negative outcomes. Research on adult recidivism has differentiated between two types of risk factors (Andrews & Bonta, 1994). Static or stable risk, the easiest type of risk factor to measure, focuses on those elements that are not changeable or that change very slowly over time. Age, gender, race, history of abuse or trauma, past substance abuse, having a low IQ, or past criminal behavior all place a student at risk, but as they are historical and demographic, they do not demonstrate a place for an intervention. Actuarial measures that focus on static risk are likely to predict more risk for young males, as these categories are more empirically connected to risk profiles (Slobogin, 2013).

Dynamic risk, or risk factors that can change slowly or more quickly over time, are more difficult to measure. However, dynamic risk factors are the most important areas to assess on an ongoing basis, as these variables are the ones where intervention can change a child's propensity to academically fail or to act out in ways that will get him or her engaged in the criminal justice system (Quist & Matshazi, 2000). Examples of dynamic risk include current substance use, association with delinquent peers, school motivation, and school attendance. It is important to identify which risk factors are dynamic and therefore can be targeted as areas to be worked on to help children and adolescents to reduce their level of risk.

When viewing risk, it is also important to look at intervention needs, as these two areas generally are paired together. For example, if a child has a risk level of current substance abuse, the identified need would include substance abuse treatment. Since treatment intervention and working with identified needs is expensive, it is important to understand which risks are more predictive of poor outcomes, such as failure at school. In the delinquency literature, these needs are known as criminogenic needs, or those areas that contribute to antisocial and criminal behavior. It is generally most important to focus on those risks and needs that will have the greatest likelihood of helping the individual child or adolescent to change his or her at-risk pathway and to become a productive and law-abiding citizen (Andrews et al., 1990). Finally, according to the Risk Needs Responsivity (RNR) model (Andrews & Bonta, 1998), it is also vital to assess intellectual level, mental health, learning ability, and motivation when working to help those children deemed to be at risk so as to adhere to the Responsivity Principle, which requires sensitivity to learning style and ability. The Responsivity Principle is focused on helping all types of learners and individuals to grasp the treatment concepts being taught in an intervention. To adhere to the Risk Principle, (which states that high and moderate risk individuals should be focused on, and that those of like risk should be treated together) risk level should be addressed prior to any treatment. Children at high risk, for example, should never be placed with those at low risk, because to do so would potentially increase the risk level of the lower-risk and need children (Andrews & Bonta, 1990). Risk factors (and the needs they produce) are necessary to assess in juvenile delinquents, and risk assessment instruments can be used to predict further juvenile offending and to help with the best programmatic or placement decisions (Slobogin, 2013). Since school failure is considered a risk of juvenile criminal behavior, both areas are important to understand (Farnworth, Schweinhart, & Berrueta-Clement, 1985). Programs that adhere to the RNR model are more likely to provide change for the individuals in them (Lowenkamp, Latessa, & Smith, 2006).

Holistic View of Risk

There are several domains where a child or adolescent might display either risk or protective factors. Individual-level factors typically have been the main locus for past studies concerning juvenile risk. However, more recent studies also have examined specific family-level and neighborhood-level factors that have been linked to poor outcomes. Neighborhood- or community-level concerns are of particular interest, as many criminal justice theories and policies are focused on neighborhood characteristics and interventions (Grunwald, Lockwood, Harris, & Mennis, 2010). For this reason, it is important to include all of these domains in any review of risk factors for juveniles.

Research in the area of risk assessment has been conducted for decades on adults, but concerns regarding juvenile offending and early intervention techniques have propelled new waves of research regarding various elements of juvenile risk (Slobogin, 2013). Most legal jurisdictions in the United States currently are adopting risk assessments so that juveniles can be routed to the most productive and helpful programs, while making referrals to institutional correctional settings as minimal as possible for troubled youth. A valid risk assessment is seen as part of a comprehensive strategy of evaluating juveniles and helping to avoid delinquent adolescents from reoffending (Schwalbe, 2007).

Risk Factors that Influence School Failure

Elements that put children and adolescents at risk for school failure are critical to measure in a school-based risk assessment. In addition to the negative consequences that arise for juveniles based on their school struggles, failure in school has been noted for years as a risk factor for delinquency as well (Moffit, Caspi, Harrington, & Milne, 2002; Sampson & Laub, 1993). However, those children who are at risk for academic failure need special interventions to help them to get back on track in a school setting. As such, it is important to identify those factors that can alert school personnel prior to failure and dropout.

In the United States, at-risk youth are responsible for mounting costs in the criminal justice system (Lehr, Hansen, Sinclair, & Christenson, 2003). Seventy-five percent of state prison inmates in the United States are high school dropouts; dropping out of school increases the odds of being arrested during a lifetime by over 350% (Harlow, 2003). Studies have found that over 25% of public school students fail to earn a high school diploma (*Education Week*, 2009; Stillwell, 2009). Academic failure has been defined in the literature as a grade point average (GPA) < 2.0 (Lucio, Hunt, & Bornovalova, 2012) and is seen as a major public health issue in the United States. Adolescent girls who score in the bottom 20% in reading and math are five times more likely to become pregnant than are girls in the top 20% (Alliance for Excellent Education, 2003).

Individual risk factors can lead to poor academic achievement, and these risks tend to span areas such as peer rejection, aggression, delinquency, and internalizing problems. Factors from a variety of studies have been shown to put a child or adolescent at risk for academic failure. These risk factors include: poor information processing, specific learning disabilities, low cognitive ability, poor attention span, hypervigilance to threats (perceiving ambiguous stimuli as threatening or hostile), social skills deficits, poor emotion recognition, and poor problem-solving strategies (Howse, Calkins, Anastopoulos, Keane, & Shelton, 2003; Izard et al., 2001; Leech, Day, Richardson, & Goldschmidt, 2003; Sullivan, 2006). Some of these risk factors can be identified as symptoms of common developmental, mood, anxiety, and behavioral disorders, such as autism spectrum disorder, conduct disorder, oppositional defiant disorder, childhood mood dysregulation disorder, posttraumatic stress disorder, specific learning disorders, and attention-deficit/hyperactivity disorder (ADHD).

Family-level risk factors are also very important in predicting a wide range of negative academic outcomes in children and adolescents (Costello, Compton, Keeler, & Angold, 2003;

G. W. Evans, 2004). These risk factors include growing up in single-parent households, as single parents generally have fewer economic, emotional, and psychological resources available for their children (Carlson & Corcoran, 2001), generally have less time and attention to give, and typically show weaker levels of control and lower levels of perceived warmth compared to two-parent families (Astone & McLanahan, 1991). In addition, having parents with low incomes, low levels of education, and few job skills can increase the risk of children having academic problems (National Institute of Child Health and Human Development, Early Childcare Research Network, 2005; Prelow & Loukas, 2003; Rauh, Parker, & Garfinkel, 2003). Marital conflict is closely tied to parental mental health and stress levels and can increase risk of school failure for children living in situations where marital conflict is present (Conger & Ge, 1994). Poor parental mental health, especially having parents who are depressed and have greatly stressful life events, is predictive of poor cognitive and behavioral outcomes in children (K. B. Burt, Hay, Pawlby, Harold, & Sharp, 2004; Gutman, Sameroff, & Cole, 2003; Harland, Reijneveld, Brugman, Verloove-Vanhorick, & Verhulst, 2002; Prelow & Loukas, 2003). Poor parenting—in the form of child maltreatment, harsh discipline, a lack of warmth and sensitivity, having a lack of developed routines, and inconsistency in implementing and enforcing rules—is linked to child maladjustment (Cote, Vaillancourt, LeBlanc, Nagin, & Tremblay, 2006; McCabe, Lucchini, Hough, Yeh, & Hazen, 2005). Higher rates of school absenteeism and school mobility are connected with school dropout (Rumberger & Lim, 2008). Family factors also can be protective. Hill and Tyson (2009) found that when parents provided their children with learning strategies, academic achievement was improved.

Community risk factors are also very important to consider. Concentrated poverty has been linked with lower academic achievement (Gutman, Sameroff, & Eccles, 2002; Prelow &

Loukas, 2003). Neighborhoods characterized as poor and disorganized have been shown to increase the risk that adolescents will have conduct problems and engage in criminal behavior (Sampson & Groves, 1989). Schools that have greater proportions of poor and aggressive students are more likely to result in children who exhibit externalizing problems (Ingoldsby & Shaw, 2002; Kroneman, Loeber, & Hipwell, 2004).

Previous studies have shown that risk factors in multiple domains and specific combinations of risk factors better explain the association between early risk and later problem behavior, including academic struggles (Burchinal, Roberts, Hooper, & Zeisel, 2000; Corapci, 2008). Cumulative risk, or risk factors from several domains, is seen as the best way to account for negative outcomes in youth (Lucio, Hunt, & Bornovalova, 2012). Negative outcomes that are associated with school failure include unwanted pregnancy, poor mental health, alcohol and substance abuse, criminality, incarceration, unemployment, and increased rates of mortality (Richman, Bowen, & Woolley, 2004). Risks tend to be related, and many studies examined educational risks and how they relate to other risky behavior, such as those related to health, poor behavior, and other difficulties. Other studies examined constructs believed to be related to positive academic achievement, such as motivation, school engagement, and self-regulation.

Several studies are longitudinal in nature, as time is an important element of being able to make causal predictions of risk. The risk factor must be present prior to the predicted outcome, which is a weakness of cross-sectional studies (Murray, Farrington, & Eisner, 2009). Another important methodological issue is that prospective studies are much stronger than those that are retrospective in nature. To demonstrate causal risk, a factor has to be significantly correlated to the negative behavior, and the risk variable had to precede the outcome. Causal risk factors can be defined as those risks that, when changed, cause a change in the risk of the outcome (Murray et al., 2009).

Population sampling is an important issue, as those studies with random samples or large cohorts are most robust. Some studies presented here are drawn from the general population of students, while many include only at-risk students. Both types of samples are important for advancing knowledge regarding which risk factors are most important in predicting educational achievement, but the generalizability of each may be limited. Studies, such as meta-analyses, are ideal; they rate the quality of risk assessments by reviewing each study's methodology, including the need to report reliability and validity estimates for the risk instrument. In particular, Murray et al. (2009) noted that cross-sectional data, which measure risk factors and outcomes at one point in time, cannot be used to generate causal risk factors. A prospective longitudinal study is required to identify actual causal risk factors.

Gruber and Machamer (2000) examined the relationship between educational and health risks using a statewide survey that was developed by the Minnesota Department of Education. Their sample consisted of 6,224 students enrolled either in ninth or 12th grade. Risk measures were assessed at one point in time. They found that health risk behaviors, such as substance use, sexual behavior, delinquency, suicidality, and drinking and driving, increased with increases in educational risks. Educational risks measured included being absent or missing school, purchasing drugs or alcohol at school, and using alcohol or marijuana during school hours. Gruber and Machamer performed a log analysis that indicated that educational and health risk factors are linked, because educational risk factors were a significant predictor of having health risk behaviors. Having higher educational risks almost doubled the likelihood of suicidal thoughts or actions, doubled the likelihood of being sexually active or being delinquent (measured in this study as vandalism or assault behaviors), and increased chances of drinking and driving and use of illicit substances by 375% when gender, ethnicity, year in school,

and average grades were statistically controlled. Because educational risks are generally more visible to school personnel, these results were seen as an important way to identify adolescents who were at risk for other negative outcomes.

High levels of depression and anger often are associated with distress, which can affect academic outcomes (Deffenbacher, Lynch, Oetting, & Kemper, 1996). If youth do not feel like they belong or get support from their families, they are more likely to connect with delinquent or gang-affiliated peers (Baumeister & Leary, 1995), but family is a potentially significant source of support and well-being (Helson, Vollebergh, & Meeus, 2000).

Another study examined 310 middle school students in the San Francisco Bay area (Baskin, Quintana, & Slaten, 2014). The researchers found that subjects who felt belongingness within their families were at low risk of psychological distress and thereby had higher levels of academic achievement. However, youth who engaged with delinquent peers and had psychological distress displayed lower levels of academic achievement. In general, the researchers found a significant relationship between psychological distress and academic achievement. There was a direct relationship between friendship with gang members and academic achievement but no such relationship between family belongingness and academic achievement. Psychological distress was found to fully mediate the influence of the relationship between family belongingness and academic achievement, while psychological distress mediated some, but not all, of the effect of friendship with delinquent peers and academic achievement. The authors interpreted their finding to mean that with higher distress, the negative impact of gang friendships is more strongly related to academic outcomes. Lower distress was less related to positive academic outcomes. The authors concluded that counselors working directly with students on their levels of anger and depression can help ameliorate some of the distress that can occur in family or peer relationships, which in turn would decrease the risk of lower academic achievements through these variables.

Foster children are at an increased risk of academic failure, of placement in special education services, and for school dropout (Courtney & Dworksy, 2006; Geenen & Powers, 2006; Smithgall, Gladden, Howard, Goerge, & Courtney, 2004). They are also more at risk of early and continuing substance abuse problems (Leslie et al., 2010; Pilowsky & Wu, 2006) and of displaying higher rates of externalizing behaviors (Leslie, Hurlburt, Landsverk, Barth, & Slyman, 2004). The early school failure and peer rejection often experienced by children in the foster care system predict later association with delinquent peers (Vitaro, Pederson, & Brendgen, 2007). School engagement can lower the odds of children in the foster care system engaging in risky behaviors, including substance use and delinquency (Leslie et al., 2010). Early disengagement from school predicts negative long-term school outcomes (Alexander, Entwisle, & Kabbani, 2001), and school engagement tends to decline with age (Marks, 2000).

Children in foster care showed lower levels of affective and cognitive school engagement than control children and were found to have significantly lower levels of academic competence in comparison with controls (Pears, Kim, Fisher, & Yoerger, 2013). Foster youth also showed higher endorsement of substance use, higher levels of externalizing behavior, and more deviant peer association in comparison with control children. Behavioral school engagement factors were not significantly associated with negative outcomes. Pears et al. surmised that things like early school attendance may be controlled more by parents and therefore may not be a strong measure of school engagement. Interventions that focus on increasing academic skills early in a child's academic career may be very helpful, as previous academic success is linked with greater subsequent school engagement (Marks, 2000; Pears et al., 2013).

Researchers were interested in identifying early warning signs to flag sixth graders who are more likely to drop out in high school (Casillas et al., 2012). Casillas et al. (2012) followed a cohort of approximately 13,000 students from grade 6 through grade 12. Dropout status was examined 1 year beyond their expected graduation date from high school. The researchers identified five warning signs that occurred in sixth grade that predicted dropout: having a final grade of F in math, a final grade of F in English, attending school 80% of school days or fewer per year, having one or more out-of-school suspensions, and having unsatisfactory behavior reports in any subject. Presence of warning flags correctly identified 60% of the students who failed to graduate 1 year past their expected graduation date.

Risky behaviors are often connected, and visible risky behavior can be a strong predictor of more concerning health risks that are generally practiced in private (Irwin, 1989; Irwin & Millstein, 1986). Previous research has found that risk of school failure and dropout has been associated with delinquency (Farnsworth, Schweinhart, & Berrueta-Clement, 1985), substance use (Eggert & Herting, 1993), aggression and later violent convictions (Farrington, 1989), and premature sexual activity (Orr, Beiter, & Ingersoll, 1991).

In both qualitative and quantitative studies, students' self-reported school and neighborhood safety was associated with higher academic performance (Bridgeland, DiIulio, & Burke Morison, 2006; Milam, Furr-Holden, & Leaf, 2010). One study examined the data from 665 students identified as being at risk for school failure by 21 middle and high schools located mainly in disadvantaged neighborhoods in North Carolina and Florida during the 1995–1996 academic school year (Bowen, Richman, Brewster, & Bowen, 1998). Bowen et al. (1998) found that as perceptions of danger or not feeling safe at school increased, students' sense of school coherence, which consisted of statements that focused on school being comprehensible, manageable, and meaningful, significantly decreased. As perceptions of teacher support increased, so did school coherence. Teachers, who have a large role in students' lives, can meaningfully affect students' feelings that they can cope and understand school. Students who are victims of violence at school were more likely to be alienated from their parents and distrustful and critical of their teachers. According to the Bowen et al. study, however, teachers can play a key role in helping students to develop positive coping strategies in response to school bullying. This study also highlighted the way protective factors can ameliorate risk factors in a school setting. An important theme in a lot of the risk literature on youth focuses on promotive or protective factors that have been shown either to decrease or to moderate the effects of risk.

Parenting has been found to moderate school behavior in the areas of school attendance and classroom compliance, either by supervising and regulating child or adolescent behaviors or by providing support and nurturance. Despite the strength of the family in helping focus children on positive school behaviors, most programs for at-risk children and adolescents have focused on either school-based or youth-focused interventions. Some studies have found schools to lack good communication with parents, and strategies that are focused on engaging parents typically have not been well designed (Halsey, 2005; Ouellette, Briscoe, & Tyson, 2004). Parent management training programs, while found to be effective for at-risk adolescents, have several barriers to implementation, including accessibility, child care, distance, sociocultural stigma, and parents' perceptions of the qualifications of the educators and family management trainers (Gross, Julian, & Fogg, 2001). Other barriers to providing parents with appropriate programming include differences in ethnicity and income levels between parents and staff (Lightfoot, 2004). However, when parents from the same school form social networks (generally informal), involvement in parent programs increased (Sheldon, 2002).

Ouellette and Wilkerson (2008) proposed a model program that would utilize video conferencing and interactive discussions via parent phone networks where parents could call other parents in the program with information provided by the program staff. Technical advances since 2008 make their proposal more feasible, especially with the advent of more advanced programs that allow remote participation with program staff that can be located in or out of the district. Programs such as Collaborate (Blackboard Collaborate, 2015) allow individuals to meet and participate in real time through their computers. Parents from schools without an informal social network could increase social contacts via more technological methods.

Several longitudinal studies have found support for using a more holistic or ecological approach to examining multiple risk factors from several domains that are associated with future problems (Gorman-Smith, Tolan, & Henry, 2000; Greenberg, Spelz, DeKlyen, & Jones, 2001; Keller, Spieker, & Gilchrist, 2005). One study looked at risk factors in multiple domains in kindergarteners, which led to poor outcomes in these children by the end of fifth grade (Lanza, Rhoades, Nix, Greenberg, & the Conduct Problems Prevention Research Group, 2010). Lanza et al. (2010) used data from Fast Track, a multisite, multicohort research project that recruited subjects from a wide variety of schools and districts from around the United States. All schools selected came from neighborhoods with high levels of poverty and crime. They looked at 387 subjects (a normative subsample from the group data who were in the control condition) who were generally aggressive and displayed oppositional behavior.

The authors assessed many levels of child, family, parenting, and community risk factors. They found that urban Black children had the highest rates of exposure to the most risk factors, while rural White children tended to have the lowest levels of risk. One exception was that there were higher levels of marital conflict present for rural White children, potentially because most came from two-parent households. Lanza et al. (2010) used a person-centered approach, looking at multiple areas of risk for each child. Each additional risk factor present in kindergarten was associated with significantly higher odds of a negative outcome at grade 5, including externalizing problems, failing grades, and low academic achievement. Students in large, urban areas often perform more poorly compared with suburban students (Belfiore, Auld, & Lee, 2005). This gap is more focused on racial and ethnic minority groups (Ou & Reynolds, 2008).

Another study used a framework of multiple risk factors in order to determine the optimum number of risk factors that are needed to distinguish between students who are and are not at risk for academic failure (Lucio et al., 2012). Lucio et al. (2012) used the statistical methodology of utilizing the receiver operating characteristics (ROC) curve to identify the necessary and sufficient number of risk factors to predict academic failure, defined as GPA < 2.0 from official grade records. Their sample was drawn from the Educational Longitudinal Study (ELS), conducted by the National Center for Educational Statistics using a nationally representative sample of 14,796 students who were surveyed during the spring of 2002. Socioeconomic status (SES) was derived as a composite of five equal variables: father's educational level, mother's educational level, family income, and the father and mother's occupation. Lucio et al. found that girls had significantly higher GPAs than boys and that Asians, then Whites, had the highest GPA. SES was also significantly related to GPA. When the researchers controlled for these variables, they found that nine factors were uniquely related to GPA: academic expectations, academic engagement, academic self-efficacy, attendance, homework completion, school safety, grade retention, school mobility, and school misbehavior. Lucio et al. found that the more risk factors that were involved, the more risk was present for a low GPA or school failure. Utilizing the ROC curve, they found that the presence of at least two of the risk factors put an individual student at risk for academic failure.

Other research studies focused primarily on resilience, or positive factors that promote positive school outcomes. Prior grades and standardized achievement scores have been found to be the strongest predictors of high school GPA (Rumberger & Lim, 2008). Self-regulated learning has been found to provide incremental validity in determining school failure after controlling for standardized achievement and GPA. Prior research has identified motivation, social control, and self-regulation as having a positive effect on academic outcomes (Covington, 2000; Robbins, Oh, Le, & Button, 2009). Martin (2009) examined motivation over the life span. Middle and high school students were found to have less motivation and school engagement than elementary and college students. Students with a high motivation for learning are more likely to have strong academic skills and achievement because they choose more stimulating environments and work harder than students with lower levels of motivation.

Spending time on homework rather than on media was seen as a positive attribute. Xu (2006) found that students spending 3 or more hours on homework per week are more likely to have positive attitudes toward homework than students spending less time on homework. The amount of homework middle school students complete has a positive association with academic achievement, although this was not found to be true for elementary students (Cooper, Lindsay, Nye, & Greathouse, 1998).

Social skills are predictive of positive academic outcomes. Robbins et al. (2009) found that attending extracurricular activities, having a good relationship with school personnel, and involving parents in their school life demonstrate behaviors that are engaging with the social environment. The longitudinal Lleras (2008) study controlled for cognitive skill level in a sample of high school students and found that students with better social skills and more extracurricular activities had higher academic achievement and eventually earned higher salaries.

In a comprehensive risk study, 4,660 middle school students in the seventh and eighth grades were sampled from 24 middle schools from 13 districts in the Midwest and South (Casillas et al., 2012). The most predictive variables for early high school GPA were homework not done, academic discipline, orderly conduct, and family attitudes toward education. These predictors were seen as spanning the domains of motivation, self-regulation, and social control. Thirty-three percent of the explained variation in early high school GPA was attributed to these psychosocial factors and behavioral indicators.

High levels of school engagement predict better academic achievement (M.-T. Wang & Holcombe, 2010), less risky health behaviors (Carter, McGee, Taylor, & Williams, 2007); a lowered risk of substance abuse (Simons-Morton, 2004); and a lowered risk of delinquency (Hirshfield & Gasper, 2011). School engagement is generally divided into behavioral, affective, and cognitive dimensions (Fredricks, Blumenfeld, & Paris, 2004; M.-T. Wang, Willet, & Eccles, 2011). Behavioral factors include student performance at school, attendance at school-related activities, attendance, homework completion, and involvement in extracurricular activities. Affective factors include students' feelings about school, teachers, and peers. Cognitive factors includes the effort students exert on task and skill mastery and their ability to regulate their focus to these tasks (Fredricks et al., 2004; Jimerson, Campos, & Greif, 2003; M.-T. Wang et al., 2011).

Neighborhood influences and children's perceptions of opportunities in their community shape the school functioning among juvenile offenders. Delinquents have a difficult time picturing successful futures, and antisocial adolescents do not expect to have jobs in the future. In a study by Oyserman and Markus (1990), only 14% to 19% of delinquent adolescents expected to be successful in school. Other studies have found that minority youth from low-income neighborhoods develop occupational expectations that mirror the class and race differences in adults employed in their community (Bloom, 2007; Cook et al., 1996; Fogel, 2004; O'Connor, 1997). Neighborhood characteristics, such as the number and visibility of employed role models, are believed to determine youth's beliefs about the opportunities available to them. These beliefs can shape achievement-oriented outcomes such as grades and educational attainment.

A study utilizing data from the Pathways to Desistance Study, a longitudinal investigation of adolescents who were adjudicated of a serious crime in court services in Philadelphia, Pennsylvania, and Phoenix, Arizona, focused on the data of an ethnically diverse subsample of 833 male offenders enrolled between 2000 and 2003 (at ages 14–17) who were found guilty of a serious felony offense (Chung, Mulvey, & Steinberg, 2011). They found that when controlling for parental education, ethnicity, age, prior court petitions, IQ, school orientation, and initial grades, young offenders' expectations to succeed were positively linked to future school functioning. Chung et al. (2011) felt that this relationship was helpful in explaining neighborhood-level effects on grades through the mechanism of future expectations. Offenders who reported higher expectations to succeed in school and work reported better grades 6 months later.

Higher levels of parental education are associated with the perception of more educational and occupational opportunities and increases in expectations to succeed (Chung et al., 2011). After controlling for baseline grades, school orientation, and other individual characteristics, grades were positively linked to the amount of time juveniles spent in residential facilities, where it is assumed that they are schooled regularly and attend classes in more closely supervised and smaller classroom environments. Although court has been seen as a barrier to academic success, Chung et al. found that juveniles' involvement in court proceedings might provide access to important educational and occupational opportunities that are not readily available in their own communities. Finally, Chung and colleagues found that those adolescents who were living in more affluent communities, defined as having higher residential income, and controlling for all individual and demographic factors, reported greater access to educational and occupational opportunities. These perceptions were directly linked to increased grades 6 months later. Optimistic thinking about the future has been connected to how adolescents view their education (Wigfield, Eccles, Schiefele, Roeser, & Davis-Kean, 2006).

Risk Factors that Influence Adolescent Delinquent Behavior

Early behavior problems have classically been the strongest predictors of later antisocial behavior and serious delinquency, school failure, later mental health problems, and eventual unemployment (K. B. Burt et al., 2004; Hanlon, Bateman, Simon, O'Grady, & Garswell, 2004; Moffitt, 1993; Montague, Enders, & Castro, 2005). Desistance from delinquency is thought to be a product of two processes: (1) a higher level of risk factors for offending increase the likelihood of persistence in offending; and (2) having promotive, or protective, factors that affect prosocial behavior might predict a lower probability of offending in the future. Protective or promotive factors have been studied with much less rigor than risk factors (Loeber, Pardini, Stouthamer-Loeber, & Raine, 2007). The resiliency literature in the psychological arena has been slow to transfer to criminological studies of juvenile crime. Prior literature on the juvenile desistence of offending has tried to explain the decrease in delinquent crime as adolescents reach adulthood. Rationales for such decreases include maturation, as physical and mental changes develop; crime naturally declines as adolescents grow up. Another rationale is that decreases in offending behavior are part of social bonding with more prosocial parts of the community. Finally, a reason for desistence focuses on the adolescent's rational choice to stop offending as part of the greater cognitive, social, and physiological change that happens as the adolescent matures (Cusson & Pinsonneault, 1986; Glueck & Glueck, 1940; M. R. Gottfredson &

Hirschi, 1990; Neugarten & Neugarten, 1996; Sampson & Laub, 1993).

Loeber et al. (2007) sampled the risk levels of a group of boys who were a subset of a larger study and who were followed from age 7 to age 20. They checked on the boys yearly, focusing on 250 boys who represented the highest risk to reoffend. Loeber et al. found that those who persisted in crime could be differentiated from the boys who desisted from crime by both risk and promotive factors. The risk factors were from multiple domains and included low resting heart rate (found to be predictive of criminal activity in earlier studies, such as articulated by Raine, 1993). In addition, promotive factors in several domains (cognitive, child, family, and community) were inversely related to delinquent behaviors. The researchers found that overall, the promotive factors, most prominently low peer delinquency and high supervision, did buffer the impact of risk factors but that the risk factors prevailed regarding continued delinquency. The most predictive individual risk factors for continued delinquency included high peer delinquency, high tobacco use, and high interpersonal callousness. Failure to graduate from high school was higher in those adolescents who continued criminal activity but was not significantly different from those who desisted from crime.

Moffitt (1993) distinguished between two types of offenders: those who started offending early in life and persisted throughout a long criminal career (life-course persistent, or LCP), and those who start offending later, in adolescence, and then finish offending as they reach adulthood (adolescent limited, or AL). Piquero and Chung (2001) found that the earlier offending behavior starts, the more likely that these individuals will continue with their delinquent acts. Other researchers have found that approximately 5% of offenders are responsible for 50% to 60% of all crimes and that these offenders are more likely to have early behavior problems. The other 95% of offenders started offending later on and were less violent (Henry, Caspi, Moffitt, & Silva, 1996). Risk factors such as poor parenting, social and family disadvantages, and attention deficits have been associated with long-term offending (Caspi et al., 1997; Fergusson, Lynskey, & Horwood, 1996; Moffitt & Lynam, 1994).

Neuropsychological deficits, most prominently a lack of self-control or impulsivity, have been associated with delinquency (Moffitt, 1993). There have been mixed research findings regarding whether impulsivity is an important empirical risk factor for delinquency. Some research studies have focused on measures of self-regulation constructs covering a wide range of behavior, such as acting without thinking, lack of response inhibition, and speed of processing (quick speed with a willingness to make hasty errors). Poor self-regulation predicts other risky behaviors in youth, such as offending behavior. Some researchers (Farrington et al., 1990; Vitacco & Rogers, 2001; White et al., 1994) have found that impulsivity predicts delinquent behavior. One study found that highly impulsive adolescents who were involved in the court system were more likely to exhibit antisocial behavior at an 18-month follow-up (Vitacco, Neumann, Robertson, & Durrant, 2002). However, a comprehensive study that evaluated many cognitive and neuropsychological constructs of impulsivity found no significant difference between delinquents (both early onset and late onset) and measures of impulsivity that measured speed and accuracy (Carroll et al., 2006). However, Carroll et al. (2006) were able to distinguish offenders from nonoffenders on the Stroop Color and Word Test (Golden, 1978), a measure of response inhibition or selective attention, but were unable to distinguish early-onset from late-onset offenders with this measure.

M. R. Gottfredson and Hirschi's (1990) self-control theory, based on the premise that a lack of self-control is an underlying process that increases risk of criminal behavior, has been a strong topic of empirical study. Self-control theory assumes that crime is a rational choice made by weighing the consequences of criminal actions and that pleasure (defined here as the gains of crime, but not if offenders may get caught) will outweigh pain. The researchers stated that a lack of self-control increases the propensity for criminal activity, as individuals with low self-control do not consider the painful consequences of their actions. Parents' failure to instill this cause-effect lesson is the explanation for why some individuals have lower levels of self-control. Many researchers have found support for this theory (e.g., Brownfield & Sorenson, 1993; C. H. Burt, Simons, & Simons, 2006; M. R. Gottfredson, 2006; Gibbs, Giever, & Higgins, 2003; Higgins, 2002; Hirschi, 2004; Pratt & Cullen, 2000; Winfree & Bernat, 1998).

A more recent study that examines self-control theory and racial disparity in offending used data from the National Longitudinal Survey of Youth, sponsored by the U.S. Bureau of Labor Statistics (Kirchner & Higgins, 2014). Their sample consisted of 1,700 youth who were assessed annually from 1979 to 2006. Kirchner and Higgins's (2014) study found self-control to be linked with parental management and criminal activity, and (Black) race to be linked to poor self-control and offending. Race was a significant predictor of criminal behavior, and the statistical addition of self-control constructs could not reduce that relationship to insignificance. This finding is contrary to M. R. Gottfredson and Hirschi's (1990) contention that self-control constructs should be able to account for racial variation in offending.

As in the school failure literature, children in foster care are considered an at-risk population for participation in the juvenile justice system, partly because of the trauma they may have undergone and partly because of the stress related to being removed from their homes. Some studies have shown that children who were removed from their biological parents exhibit intense difficulties in adaptive behavior and that they have severe behavior problems (Hodges, Doucette-Gates, & Liao, 1999). Child abuse has been associated with many negative outcomes, such as externalizing behaviors as measured by the Child Behavior Checklist (CBCL; Achenbach, 1991).

Several studies have shown support for different types of abuse being linked to a variety of risky behaviors. Physical abuse has been related to antisocial behavior, aggressive behavior, and externalizing behavior problems such as substance abuse (Jaffee, Caspi, Moffitt, & Taylor, 2004; Mahoney, Donnelly, Boxer, & Lewis, 2003; Prino & Peyrot, 1994). Adolescents with a known history of sexual abuse have demonstrated risk factors, such as substance abuse problems, internalizing and externalizing behavior problems, and sexual behavior problems (Letourneau, Schoenwald, & Sheidow, 2004; McCrae, Chapman, & Christ, 2006; Rotheram-Borus, Mahler, Koopman, & Langabeer, 1996). Child neglect has fewer studies that focus on this type of abuse but has been associated with violent behavior and emotional withdrawal (Chapple, Tyler, & Bersani, 2005; Lynch & Cicchetti, 1998). Child maltreatment has also been associated with juvenile court referrals, particularly among low-income and minority youth (Gover, 2002; Malmgren & Meisel, 2004; Mersky & Reynolds, 2007). Other studies show a link between child abuse and adult criminality (Smith, Ireland, & Thornberry, 2005; Widom, 1989).

Yampolskaya, Armstrong, and McNeish (2011) used data on 13,212 children, ages 7 to 17, who were placed in out-of-home care in Florida after first being reported as maltreated between July 2003 and July 2004. They looked at both the severity and chronicity of abuse and found that multiple maltreatment reports (chronic abuse) significantly predicted time to first placement in a detention center and a juvenile justice facility. The severity of abuse did not predict these placements, although prior studies have found that severity of abuse is significantly related to increased behavior problems among low-income young children (Litrownik et al., 2005; Manly, Cicchetti, & Barnett, 1994).

Certain family factors are associated with delinquency, while other family factors are related to lower rates of delinquency. Studies have shown that families that provide emotional and psychological support to their children, provide conventional role models for them, exert social control, and have strong bonds of attachment have children who are less likely to be involved in the juvenile justice system (G. D. Hill & Atkinson, 1988; Laub & Sampson, 1988; Renn, 2002). A longitudinal study of a cohort of juvenile detainees in Tampa, Florida, found that these youth reported that their families had high levels of mental health problems, alcohol or other drug use, and legal problems (Dembo, Williams, Wothke, Schmeidler, & Brown, 1992). These youth also reported a high level of physical and sexual abuse. Dembo, Williams, Wothke, Schmeidler, and Brown (1992) found that family background variables did not explain a significantly higher amount of variance in the youth's substance abuse or delinquent behaviors at a second time period, compared with the amount of variance represented at initial assessment of these variables. Family problems and child abuse influenced the adolescents' initial involvement in delinquent behavior and drug use, but these behaviors were found to continue over time once they were established. Foster children in out-of-home care are also at higher risk for delinquency and violent behavior (Jonson-Reid & Barth, 2000; J. P. Ryan & Testa, 2005).

Another prominent theory that predicts juvenile delinquency is general strain theory (Agnew, 2001), which explains how the impact of stress or strain can increase adolescent antisocial behavior. *Strain* is defined as events or situations that are disliked by most people (Agnew, 2006). Studies have found associations between stress and problematic adolescent behavior (Compas & Wagner, 1991; Hoffmann, Cerbone, & Su, 2000). Lin and Mieczkowski (2011) looked at Eastern versus Western cultural definitions of strain. Western concepts of strain (such as strict parenting, parental rejection, and negative school experiences) can differ for Eastern cultures. Taiwanese or Chinese children, for example, would not view authoritarian parenting as a strain as might children in the United States

(Chun, Moos, & Cronkite, 2006). Using a Taiwanese sample of 1,150 seventh through ninth graders, Lin and Mieczkowski found that male gender, being in a nonintact family, and being an older student were risk factors significantly associated with delinquency. Students experiencing higher teacher strain, being a victim of a crime, and parental strain were more likely to have delinquent involvement. The researchers found that these risk factors predicted delinquency, whether they were measured in an objective or subjective fashion.

Dembo and colleagues (2000) interviewed 164 youth who were part of the Youth Support Project at three different time periods between 1994 and 1997. They found a strong relationship between family problems and self-reported delinquent behavior. The predictor family variables included household family members who had been arrested, held in jail or detention, adjudicated as a delinquent or convicted of a crime, put on community supervision, sent to a training school or prison, alcohol or other drug abuse, and the presence of mental health problems.

Duncan, Brooks-Gunn, and Klebanov (1994) examined duration and timing of child poverty and its relationship to developmental outcomes via a panel study utilizing data from the Infant Health and Development program. The sample included 895 children (measured from infancy to age 6) drawn from large, mostly urban areas with large populations of lower-income families. Duncan et al. found that family income was more powerfully correlated to IQ (as measured by the Wechsler Preschool and Primary Scale of Intelligence [WPPSI; Wechsler, 1967] Full Scale IQ at age 5) than other related measures, such as maternal education, ethnicity, and female head of household status. Regression analyses found that persistent poverty (being in a state of poverty over time) had effects that were roughly twice the size as the effects of transient poverty (living in a state of poverty over a brief time period) in predicting IQ scores. Persistent poverty had effects that were 60% to 80% higher than transient poverty in predicting behavior problems at age 5. The authors suggested that their findings mean that the effects of poverty are cumulative. While female head of household (both briefly and in the long term) had a significant negative association with IQ scores, neither effect remained significant after family income was input into the equation. There was also a negative relationship between both female heads of household factors (transient and long-term exposure to having a female head the family) and behavior problems at age 5, and these relationships remained significant even after family income was added. The authors suggest that being in a one-parent household is stressful for children, as is the transition from a single-parent to a two-parent household. Race was also found to be significant; Black children were more likely to be poor as well as to live in poor neighborhoods than other races.

The most recent area gaining empirical support in the area of assessment of delinquency risk is examining neighborhood context as it influences juvenile offending. Environmental triggers for offending behavior have long been a concern for policy makers and juvenile courts, and some studies have investigated why certain neighborhoods have been unable to control juvenile crime (P. W. Harris, Welsh, & Butler, 2000; Tanenhaus, 2004). Adolescents who are involved in drug-related crimes have been connected to neighborhoods with poor conditions and reduced job opportunities (Grunwald, Lockwood, Harris, & Mennis, 2010; M. Little & Steinberg, 2006; Martinez, Rosenfeld, & Mares, 2008). Studies that have looked at serious adolescent offenders have generally found that all offending was associated with concentrated poverty through its effects on neighborhood disadvantage and association with deviant peers (Chung & Steinberg, 2006). Grunwald, Lockwood, Harris, and Mennis (2010) looked at seriously delinquent youth and the effects of neighborhood disadvantage, which they defined as the percentages of adults living below the poverty line, those unemployed, those on welfare, and yearly income (on a scale). Social capital, or positive and prosocial elements of a neighborhood, was measured by self-reporting answers to statements such as "I feel that I belong and are part of my community" and "Most people in my neighborhood can be trusted." They found that only drug offending was predicted by neighborhood disadvantage and social capital when looking at different types of crimes (including violent and property crime).

Having incarcerated parents has been found to increase the risk of children dropping out of school (Trice & Brewster, 2004), and children with parents in prison or jail were found to be five times more likely to become incarcerated themselves when compared to boys separated from their parents for other reasons (Murray & Farrington, 2005). Aaron and Dallaire (2010) found that a history of parental incarceration predicted family victimization and delinquent behaviors in children in the home. Recent incarceration of a parent predicted family conflict, family victimization, and child delinquency, even after controlling for a previous parental incarceration.

Parental incarceration was also examined by Hannon and DeFina (2012) in light of problems in the United States with mass incarceration. Mass incarceration was predicted to influence rates of juvenile delinquency through many family and individual risk factors. Family risk factors included being raised in a single-parent family, loss of income, and sporadic parental monitoring (DeFina & Hannon, 2010; Western & Beckett, 1999), while individual factors included increased depression, anxiety, and aggression (Geller, Garfinkel, Cooper, & Mincy, 2009; Murray & Farrington, 2008; Wildeman, 2010). Hannon and DeFina found that incarceration appears to be a unique way that social or neighborhood disorganization can harm communities, as higher levels of parental incarceration rates were found to result in higher juvenile arrest rates when holding other neighborhood variables (adult arrest rate, county divorce rate, and child poverty rate) constant.

Many studies have looked at neighborhood effects of juvenile violence (D. Elliott et al., 1996;

Sampson, Raudenbush, & Earls, 1997). Living in highly disadvantaged neighborhoods has been found to be a moderating variable for individual and familial risk factors, disproportionately affecting Black Americans (Attar, Guerra, & Tolan, 1994; Chauhan & Reppucci, 2009; Schuck & Widom, 2005; Turner, Hartman, & Bishop, 2007). Residents living in neighborhoods with large, active social networks can better create social trust and enforce shared community values, which include a desire to live in a crime-free neighborhood (Sampson et al., 1997). Residents living in neighborhoods with active social networks have an easier time supervising adolescents living in the neighborhood, helping these youth to acquire prosocial attitudes, while helping them avoid getting involved with delinquent peers.

Haynie, Silver, and Teasdale (2006) used data from the National Longitudinal Study of Adolescent Health with a sample of 12,747 youth to examine neighborhood-level effects on adolescent violence. They looked at whether having exposure to violent versus academically motivated peers mediated the relationship between neighborhood characteristics (such as economic disadvantage, residential instability, immigrant concentration, and population size) and adolescent violence. They found that neighborhood disadvantage (as measured by a scale that factored in percentages of female heads of households with children under age 18, the unemployment rate, the proportion of families receiving public assistance income, the proportion of nonelderly with income below the poverty line, and the proportion of the population that was African American) was the most significant correlate of adolescent violence across a range of neighborhoods. Peer association (with violent or academically unmotivated peers) partly mediated the association between neighborhood disadvantage and juvenile violence. Path models used found that a small but significant portion of the total effect found for neighborhood disadvantage was mediated through peer networks (Haynie et al., 2006). Exposure to academically motivated peers was associated with a reduction in violence. Bellair and McNulty (2005) found that verbal ability indirectly influenced youth violence through school achievement.

Females have been a growing (although small) proportion of juvenile delinquents over the past 20 years. The office of Juvenile Justice and Delinquency Prevention reports that law enforcement agencies in the United States arrested approximately 2 million people younger than 18 in 2008, and female juveniles accounted for 30% of the arrests. The representation of girls in the juvenile justice system has been rising (Snyder & Sickmund, 2006), but many studies on juvenile offending risks do not include females or do not account for unique risk factors for female juvenile delinquents. However, some empirical studies focus exclusively on young female offenders. Lane (2003) examined both individual and family risk factors for female juvenile offenders, investigating the relationship between the age at which female offenders are first sentenced and individual and family risk factors. The sample included 162 randomly selected adolescent females from the California Youth Authority who took a profile survey in 1996. Lane found that both White and non-White females were sentenced at similar ages, but non-Whites were found to have significantly higher levels of individual risk factors than White juveniles. This finding is in congruence with studies on male juvenile offenders. Female offenders with higher levels of individual risk factors (including physical and sexual abuse, school dropout, alcohol or drug use, gang involvement, poverty, prostitution, pregnancy, and having another person involved in their crime) were more likely to be sentenced at younger ages than those offenders who had fewer individual risk factors. Family risk factors (marital status of parents, family criminal activity, parental educational attainment, and receipt of public assistance) were not found to be significantly related with age of first sentencing.

Another study examined offending patterns of delinquent girls in a prospective study of 501 subjects who were part of a larger study of juveniles released from New York state juvenile facilities in the early nineties. The subjects included those females who were 28 at the start of data collection (they were asked to look back on their past 12 years) Colman, Kim, Mitchell-Herzfeld, & Shady, 2009). The girls were followed for 12 years, beginning at age 16. Coleman et al. (2009) found that 81% recidivated, with 69% being convicted as an adult. Only 19% of the sample was found to completely desist from further offending. This finding is in agreement with previous studies that found most delinquent girls transfer to the adult correctional system (Benda, Corwyn, & Toombs, 2001). However, 32% of the subjects in Colman et al.'s study were classified as rare or nonoffending adults. Colman et al. found that being Black significantly increased the chances of adult arrest, while being Hispanic decreased this risk. Being older at first juvenile arrest marginally decreased the likelihood of adult recidivism.

In regard to family factors, girls who were from homes with a criminally involved family member were at greater risk of reoffending. Girls with histories of sexual abuse were significantly less likely to reoffend, while a history of both physical and sexual abuse significantly increased recidivism risk. Consistent with research on male juvenile delinquents, this study found a select group of female juveniles who were considered to be adolescent-limited offenders and who never or rarely offended after the age of 16. Girls who generally followed the different criminal trajectories described in longitudinal studies on boys were also identified (Ezell & Cohen, 2005; Sampson & Laub, 2003). Colman and colleagues' (2009) finding that 32% of seriously delinquent girls stop reoffending as young women is greater than the 10% of desisters found in longitudinal studies of seriously delinquent boys (Ezell & Cohen, 2005; Sampson & Laub, 2003).

Chauhan and Reppucci (2009) examined 122 girls from a juvenile correctional center who self-identified as either Black or White using a longitudinal design and a variety of risk factors to predict violent and delinquent behavior after release. In particular, they looked at exposure to violence (being personally victimized by parents and peers as well as witnessing violence) as a mediating variable between neighborhood disadvantage and antisocial behavior. Witnessing or experiencing violence has been found to be predictive of antisocial behavior in young people (English, Spatz-Widom, & Brandford, 2001; Molnar, Browne, Cerda, & Buka, 2005). Being a witness or a victim of violence has been found to be very prevalent among high-risk girls (Lipschitz, Rasmusson, Anyan, Cromwell, & Southwick, 2000; Odgers & Repucci, 2002).

Studies with adolescents have found that there is a moderate relationship between witnessing violence and antisocial behavior (Halliday-Boykins & Graham, 2001; Muller, Goebel-Fabbri, Diamond, & Dinklage, 2000). Chauhan and Reppucci found that Black girls were more likely than White girls to live in disadvantaged neighborhoods. No racial differences were found in regard to maternal risk, parental physical abuse, witnessing violence, and antisocial behavior. Reading achievement was assessed by the Woodcock Johnson III Achievement test (Woodcock, McGrew, & Mather, 2001), and White girls were found to have significantly higher reading achievement scores. Parental physical abuse and witnessing violence were significantly related to violent behavior for the whole sample. Witnessing violence was predictive of delinquent behavior for the whole sample. When viewing these results by race, Chauhan and Reppucci found that physical abuse was a stronger correlate for White girls, while witnessing violence was a stronger correlate for Black girls. The researchers interpreted their findings as a suggestion that race moderates the relationship between exposure to violence and antisocial behavior. Weaver, Borkowski, and Whitman (2008) also found that parental physical abuse and witnessing violence was related to criminal behavior in girls.

Another study of girls in the juvenile justice system using official offending records found that there was a direct relationship between neighborhood disadvantage and reoffending behavior (Chauhan, Reppucci, & Turkheimer, 2009). However, a study using self-reported antisocial behavior did not find this relationship to be present in the same sample of high-risk girls (Chauhan & Repucci, 2009).

Since high-risk families may choose to live in high-risk neighborhoods, causal inferences cannot be made about the high levels of risk associated with living in disadvantaged neighborhoods, such as witnessing violence (Attar et al., 1994; Gorman-Smith & Tolan, 1998); experiencing violence (Coulton, Crampton, Irwin, Spilsbury, & Korbin, 2007); forming bonds with deviant peer groups (Brody et al., 2001; Haynie et al., 2006); having academic problems (Bellair & McNulty, 2005; Duncan et al., 1994); and having family risk factors that include substance use and family criminal behavior (Crum, Lillie-Glanton, & Anthony, 1996; McLeod & Nonnemaker, 2000). Kroneman et al. (2004) found that neighborhood-level risk factors have a modest impact for both girls and boys, after accounting for both individual-level and family-level risk factors.

Some studies focused on both the risk and protective factors of juvenile offenders. Gore and Eckenrode (1994) found that self-esteem and willingness to access social support stimulates resiliency in adolescents. In a qualitative study, youth involved in the juvenile justice system were interviewed while they were transitioning back to the community (Todis, Bullis, Waintrup, Schultz, & D'Ambrosio, 2001). Some youth avoided reoffending and successfully integrated back into their communities. These adolescents were determined to have resiliency, which was defined as having an optimistic disposition; better problem-solving skills; better coping skills; and being engaged in school, drug treatment, or work, compared with other group members who were not as successful in community adjustment.

Protective and risk factors interact in ways that can be complex and influence delinquent behavior in ways that are not clear, affecting delinquent behavior to varying degrees (Dishion & Patterson, 2006; Stanovich, 2004). One study conducted an in-depth analysis of interviews with 51 juvenile offenders who were adjudicated for a crime and were either incarcerated or were currently on probation (Unruh, Povenmire-Kirk, & Yamamoto, 2009). The offenders identified their "self" as an important element of risk or protection, as their own choice of actions would influence whether they would be able to go back to the community successfully and avoid reoffending behaviors. Returning to relationships with negative peers was seen as a risk to reoffending, with drug use a specific concern. Youth described a need for a stable home environment as well as support from their family but stated that this type of support was often unavailable (and thus family could be either a protective factor or a risk factor). Having an internal locus of control and high executive functioning skills such as good self-regulation and impulse control were identified by the authors as positive or protective factors in adjudicated youth. Unruh et al. (2009) described interventions that would help juvenile delinquents. One method was identified as cognitive-behavioral therapy (CBT), which has been found to reduce criminogenic behaviors in many populations (Landenburger & Lipsey, 2005; Vaske, Galyean, & Cullen, 2011). Family counseling was also suggested, as youth are dependent on their families for emotional support and a stable living environment. The development of prosocial networks is seen as a vital area to increase, as this area may be a protective factor in reducing reoffending behavior. Prosocial networks are seen as important in reducing offending in adults (Macklin, 2013).

Another study found that resiliency is more related to factors that are behavioral or attitudinal, and under the control of the individual, than to risk factors or environmentally protective factors (L. R. Taylor, Karcher, Kelly, & Valescu, 2003). Family protective factors (such as having both parents living at home with the child) were not found to correlate with resiliency, as measured by the Adolescent Resiliency Attitudes Scale (ARAS; Biscoe & Harris, 1994). Self-esteem has been found to correlate

with the ARAS, while higher depression levels correlated with lower resiliency scores on the ARAS (Biscoe & Vincent, 1998).

Carr and Vandiver (2001) examined risk and protective factors by reviewing the archival profiles of 76 male and female youth offenders ages 11 to 17 at the time of the offense and who were referred to county probation between 1994 and 1998. They looked at five risk constructs, including personal characteristics, familial conditions, drug use, peer selection, school attendance, and school difficulties. Carr and Vandiver reviewed protective factors, which included personal characteristics, familial conditions, positive role models, peer selection, school interests, activities, and hobbies. They found that protective factors, including personal characteristics, family conditions, and social and academic protective influences, could independently differentiate between repeat and nonrepeat offenders. Nonrepeat offenders were characterized as feeling happy about themselves and believed that they got along with others. Nonrecidivating offenders also reported more positive attitudes toward school rules, authority, and police rules and activities. Nonrepeaters also stated that they sought more help with homework and had better academic performance. For family factors, they were characterized as having structure and rules in their household, had family support and guidance, and had few siblings. They also reported having more friends than repeat offenders. Carr and Vandiver found that total amount of stress, total risk factors, and number of prior offenses were not significantly different for repeat versus nonrepeat offenders. However, they did find that certain specific risk factors, including total personal risk factors and total familial conditions, could differentiate between groups. Carr and Vandiver concluded that protective factors could "hold the key to moving youth offenders away from the path of criminality" (p. 424) and that probation officers should coordinate with families, schools, and other agencies to share information regarding the youth's strengths and assets.

In a meta-analysis reviewing what works in young offender treatment, Dowden and Andrews (1999) found that programs for youth that adhered to the RNR principles demonstrated significantly higher effect sizes than those programs that did not adhere to these principles. They concluded that increased adherence to RNR principles is associated with a reduction in juvenile offending behavior.

Risk Assessment Research on Youth

Valid risk assessment instruments can help identify high-risk offenders so that the juvenile court can target them for more intensive treatments to help to avoid their reoffending. Schwalbe (2007) conducted a meta-analysis of risk assessments for juvenile justice and found that, on average, risk assessment instruments used in the field of juvenile justice do predict repeat offending. The average association between risk assessment instruments and repeat offending was $r = .25$, which is the same as those found by Rice and Harris (2005) and lower but comparable with the average effect size of $r = .30$ found by Gendreau, Little, and Goggin (1996) in their reviews of adult risk instruments. Schwalbe found that risk instruments that have higher predictive validity tend to measure key risk factors using multiple items and also measured alternative constructs related to risk, such as personality traits and impairment in functioning. Schwalbe recommended reviewing the methodological qualities of risk assessment when evaluating the utility of the risk instrument. A limitation to determining risk assessment validity was that most risk assessments are not conducted using a variety of samples, as this could influence the level of stable validity for each instrument. He suggested that even cross-validated instruments can be vulnerable to random sampling error when their estimation and validation samples are randomly drawn from the same sample. In general, Schwalbe's study supported the use of risk instruments to help in the decision-making processes for legal jurisdictions in relation to

placement of juvenile offenders. He advised that those who use these assessments demonstrate caution when picking the most valid risk assessments to help guide juvenile placement on the basis of prediction of recidivism risk.

Slobogin (2013) recommended that risk instruments should be used to assess youth at regular intervals rather than be focused only on the front end, that assessments should include both static and dynamic risk factors, and that they be aligned with a risk management program that is flexible and designed to reduce dynamic risk factors. According to Slobogin, risk assessment is very relevant for today's needs, as over 85% of juvenile court jurisdictions in the United States use formal risk assessment at some point in the process of juvenile adjudication. This is a huge jump in usage; prior to 1990, only 33% of jurisdictions in the United States used risk assessment tools (Schwalbe, 2008).

Some of the most popular risk assessment instruments include: the Juvenile Detention Risk Assessment 91 (Steinhart, 2006); the Juvenile Sexual Offense Recidivism Risk Assessment Tool–II (JSORRAT–II; Epperson, Ralston, Fowers, DeWitt, & Gore, 2006); Assessment, Intervention and Moving on (AIM) (Griffin & Beech, 2004); the Estimate of Risk of Adolescent Sexual Offense Recidivism Version 2.0 (ERASOR:Worling & Curwen, 2001) and the Youth Level of Service/Case Management Inventory (YLS/CMI; Viljoen, Elkovitch, Scalora, & Ullman, 2009). The YLS/CMI was created based on the theory of the RNR model (Andrews, Bonta, & Wormith, 2011).

Slobogin (2013) pointed out a few problems with using actuarial tools to predict adolescent risk. These include validity problems if the population being tested is different from the samples that determined the validity of the instrument. Additionally, validity issues might arise if the antisocial problem the adolescent is experiencing is different from the behaviors being predicted by the risk instrument. Finally, the assessment of risk must consider the fast-changing levels of maturity in the realms of emotional, cognitive, and social growth that adolescents generally experience from the ages of 12 to 17. Youth generally develop so fast that is hard to pin down how a behavior found risky at one age might generalize to a new developmental stage later on. In particular, poor parenting and family variables are more important to younger youth, while bad peer influences are more important to assess for older juveniles.

Quist and Matshazi (2000) found the Child and Adolescent Functional Assessment Scale (CAFAS; Hodges & Wong, 1996), a mental health assessment instrument, to be significantly related to juvenile recidivism. The CAFAS is made up of a number of subscales that include measurement of school and/or work roles, home roles, and community roles; behavior toward others; harm to self; moods/emotions; substance use; and thinking. Quist and Matshazi also found that CAFAS scores were able to distinguish whether juveniles were at a higher risk for reoffense, but low scores were less predictive of lack of reoffending behavior.

The research team of Fratello, Salsich, and Mogulescu (2011) described an empirically derived risk assessment developed by New York City's Department of Probation. NYC Probation designed the Risk Assessment Instrument (RAI), which has helped New York City courts to make better decisions about adjudicated youth, including a referral system to either secure detention, release to the community with or without supervision, or release to a variety of community-based, nonresidential programs for youth. The RAI was constructed by examining the characteristics of 1,053 juvenile cases and tracking the sample through sentencing for a 1-year period. Using data from the New York State Office of Court Administration, the Division of Juvenile Justice, and the Criminal Justice Agency, the Center on Youth Justice, a division of the Vera Institute of Justice, empirically derived risk variables that were most related to failure to appear and rearrest. These risk variables included no parent or responsible adult present at probation intake, school attendance of less than 30% in the last full semester, prior arrests or adjudications, and being on probation during a new probation intake. Fratello et al. argued that use of this type of risk assessment can help judges to make better decisions for youth at their arraignments.

DEVELOPMENT AND VALIDATION OF NEW RATING SCALES

We developed two rating scales based on the Home Environment Questionnaire (HEQ) administered to many parents/guardians who brought their child or adolescent to be tested on the WISC–V as part of the standardization data-collection process. Most examiners asked the parent or guardian to fill out the form, usually while the WISC–V testing was in progress; some examiners opted not to administer the form and some parents/guardians opted not to complete it. HEQ data were obtained on 76.2% of the "normal" children and adolescents in the normative sample (i.e., excluding the clinical cases in the sample), although there were some missing data for those who completed the HEQ. At the end of the 51 HEQ items were an additional 50 items that constitute four scales from the Behavioral Assessment Scale for Children–Second Edition (BASC–2; C. R. Reynolds & Kamphaus, 2004): Resilience, Conduct Problems, Executive Functions, and Attention Problems. *Resilience* denotes positive behaviors; the other three scales denote negative behaviors.

The HEQ comprised 51 items that involved socioeconomic indexes (e.g., parent's education, occupation, and income); background information (e.g., number of siblings, marital status of parents); and a variety of other topics, such as the child's habits regarding homework, the nature of family activities, parental awareness of the child's friends and extracurricular activities, types of parental discipline and encouragement, the child's television habits, number of high-tech devices in the home, the child's involvement with these devices and his/her technical competence, and the child's success in school. Most items had multiple parts; for example, the item on how often the child participates in activities was broken into five parts—sports, book/reading clubs, drawing/painting, YMCA/scouts, and youth fellowship.

Each part of an item on the HEQ was counted as a separate item for our analyses, and four additional items were added from the parental consent form (e.g., Was the child in a program for gifted and talented? Has the child been diagnosed with a specific learning disorder?), such that 125 items were analyzed to develop the rating scales. For the analyses to select the rating scales, we used the odd age groups from the normative sample (ages 7, 9, 11, 13, 15) and designated that group the *computation* sample. The even age groups (ages 6, 8, 10, 12, 14, 16) served as the *cross-validation* sample. Sample sizes were 1,200+ for the odd ages and 1,000+ for the even ages.

We decided in advance to develop two rating scales: the Child and Adolescent Academic Questionnaire (Academic-Q), to identify children and adolescents who are at high risk for poor performance in school, and the Child and Adolescent Behavior Questionnaire (Behavior-Q), to identify those who are at high risk for committing delinquent acts. To select items for Academic-Q, we relied primarily on coefficients of correlation with WISC–V FSIQ and secondarily on correlations with the BASC–2 Resilience Scale. To select items for Behavior-Q, we relied on correlations with the BASC–2 Conduct Problems, Executive Functioning, and Attention Problems scales. However, for both scales, the item content was an important criterion for inclusion. Academic-Q items needed to be sensibly related to school failure and to research on that topic; and, likewise, Behavior-Q items had to possess both content validity and support from relevant research on delinquency and criminal behavior. We decided in advance that the two rating scales would have entirely separate content. If an item was eligible for both scales based on data and rational analysis, we opted to include it on the scale that made the most sense conceptually.

The 125 items were initially coded using a multipoint format that ranged from 2 points (yes-no) to 12 points (categories of family income). In order to weight each item equally, we converted each item to a scale where 3 represented the highest risk and 0 represented no risk, with values of 1 and 2 reflecting mild risk and moderate risk, respectively. Yes–No items were scored 3–0. Multipoint items were converted to a 3–2–1–0 system based on frequency distributions. An ideal distribution would have been about 5% to 10% earning ratings of 3; about 15% to 20% earning 2 points; about 25% to 30% earning 1 point; and about half the sample earning 0 points. However, those percentages were just targets; the actual distributions of the multipoint ratings varied from item to item. Therefore, the actual percentages differed from item to item, sometimes widely.

We initially identified 26 items that met the empirical and research-based criteria for inclusion in Academic-Q and 38 for Behavior-Q. We examined item-total correlations, coefficient alpha, and correlations with FSIQ and the four BASC–2 scales for these initial scales. Based on these data and redundancy in item content, we reduced each scale to 20 items. Figure 6.1 shows the final 20-item Academic-Q, and Figure 6.2 shows the final 20-item Behavior-Q. Raw scores for each scale were converted to T-scores (mean = 50, SD = 10), the metric used by the BASC–2. High raw scores and high T-scores denote negative (at risk) behaviors. Raw score to T-score conversion Tables D.1 and D.2 are presented in Appendix D in the downloadable resources: www.wiley.com/go/itwiscv. The two questionnaires and their scoring keys are in Appendix D in the downloadable resources: www.wiley.com/go/itwiscv). Examiners can print out the questionnaires from the downloadable resources. For administration and scoring purposes, we recommend printing copies of the questionnaires in Appendix D from the downloadable resources rather than copying the designed and typeset figures that appear in Figure 6.1 and 6.2 (this chapter). The printable

Child's Name: _____   Date_____

Instructions: In this survey, we hope to gather information related to social and cultural factors that will help us to better understand the child's test results. Your responses are strictly confidential. Try to answer all the questions as best you can. Please circle your answers.

Family Status and Background

1. **What is your marital status?**
   (a) Single
   (b) Divorced, Remarried, or Separated
   (c) Married, Widowed, or Other
2. **How many total siblings does the child have?** (Siblings include the total number of biological brothers and sisters, Stepbrothers and stepsisters, and half-brothers and half-sisters).
   (a) 0–2
   (b) 3
   (c) 4–5
   (d) 6+
3. **What is the highest level of education that the child's *male* parent or guardian completed?**
   (a) Less than high school
   (b) High school/Equivalent
   (c) High school, some college
   (d) Bachelor's degree or more
4. **Which category best describes the child's *male* parent or guardian's line of work?**
   (a) Labor (e.g., food service/hospitality, farming/fishing/forestry, construction)
   (b) Military, industrial, manufacturing, transportation, or semi-skilled (e.g., military, industrial/manufacturing, transportation, homemaker)
   (c) Professional services or sales (e.g., community/social service, art/entertainment media, sales, administrative support)
   (d) Professionals (e.g., management, business/finance, computer/math, architecture/engineering, life/physical sciences, legal, education/library services, healthcare)
5. **What is the highest level of education that the child's *female* parent or guardian completed?**
   (a) Less than high school
   (b) High school/Equivalent
   (c) High school, some college
   (d) Bachelor's degree or more

Continue ⟹

Figure 6.1   The Child and Adolescent Academic Questionnaire (Academic-Q)
Note. For administration and scoring purposes, we recommend printing copies of the questionnaires in Appendix D from the downloadable resources rather than copying the designed and typeset figures that appear in Figure 6.1 and 6.2 (this chapter). The printable questionnaires are the only ones that can be used with the scoring keys that were created to fit over the questionnaires for ease of scoring. The Figures in this chapter merely illustrate the questionnaires and the items.

6. Which category best describes the child's *female* parent or guardian's line of work?
   (a) Labor (e.g., food service/hospitality, farming/fishing/forestry, construction)
   (b) Military, industrial, manufacturing, transportation, or semi-skilled (e.g., military, industrial/manufacturing, transportation, homemaker)
   (c) Professional services or sales (e.g., community/social service, art/entertainment media, sales, administrative support)
   (d) Professionals (e.g., management, business/finance, computer/math, architecture/engineering, life/physical sciences, legal, education/library services, healthcare)
7. What is the child's family's combined annual income before taxes?
   (a) Under $15,000
   (b) $15,000–$39,999
   (c) $40,000–$69,999
   (d) $70,000 or more
8. Does the child's family own or rent the home where the child currently lives?
   (a) Lives with Others
   (b) Rent
   (c) Own
9. How long was the child fed only breastmilk (no formula)?
   (a) Does not apply (child was never fed breastmilk)
   (b) Up to 2 months
   (c) 3–6 months
   (d) 7 months or more

Information and Technology

10. Does the child's family subscribe to a newspaper or magazine?
    (a) Y
    (b) N
11. How many video game devices (e.g., Playstation, iPad, Xbox) does the child's family have in the home?
    (a) 0
    (b) 1
    (c) 2
    (d) 3+
12. How many computers (laptop or desktop) does the child's family own?
    (a) 0
    (b) 1
    (c) 2
    (d) 3+
13. How many touch-screen devices (e.g., iPad, Kindle, Nintendo DS) does the child's family own?
    (a) 0
    (b) 1
    (c) 2
    (d) 3+

Continue

Figure 6.1 (*Continued*)

Family Time, Activities, and Discipline

14. How many hours *per week* does the child use his or her touch-screen phone?
    (a) 0
    (b) 1–2
    (c) 3–4
    (d) 5+
15. How many times *per month* does the child participate in sports (e.g., football, dance, karate, swim)?
    (a) 0
    (b) 1–2
    (c) 3–5
    (d) 6+
16. How many times *per year* does the child's family participate in family activities (e.g., picnics, games) together?
    (a) 0
    (b) 1–2
    (c) 3–5
    (d) 6+
17. How many times *per year* does the child's family participate in educational activities (e.g., museums, zoo, library) together?
    (a) 0
    (b) 1–2
    (c) 3–5
    (d) 6+
18. How often does the child receive grounding as a punishment?
    (a) Never
    (b) Sometimes
    (c) Often
    (d) Frequently

Academic Activities and Expectations

19. How does the child usually do in school?
    (a) Excellent (A's)
    (b) Good (B's)
    (c) Average (C's)
    (d) Needs Improvement (D's)
    (e) Failing (F's)
20. How likely is it that the child will graduate from college?
    (a) Not Likely
    (b) Somewhat Likely
    (c) Likely
    (d) Very Likely

Figure 6.1   (*Continued*)

Child's Name: _____   Date_____

Instructions: In this survey, we hope to gather information related to social and cultural factors that will help us to better understand the child's test results. Your responses are strictly confidential. Try to answer all the questions as best you can. Please circle your answers.

Family Status and Background

1. How many members of the child's immediate family (parents, brothers, sisters) have been diagnosed with learning problems, Attention-Deficit/Hyperactivity Disorder (ADHD), or Mental Health problems?
   - (a) 0
   - (b) 1
   - (c) 2+

Family Time, Activities, and Discipline

2. How well do you know the child's friends?
   - (a) Not at all
   - (b) Very little
   - (c) Somewhat
   - (d) Very well
3. How well do you know the parents/guardians of the child's friends?
   - (a) Not at all
   - (b) Very little
   - (c) Somewhat
   - (d) Very well
4. When the child is with friends, how often do you know where the child is?
   - (a) Never
   - (b) Rarely
   - (c) Sometimes
   - (d) Often
   - (e) Always
5. When the child is with friends, how often do you know who the child is with?
   - (a) Never
   - (b) Rarely
   - (c) Sometimes
   - (d) Often
   - (e) Always

Continue ⟹

Figure 6.2   The Child and Adolescent Behavior Questionnaire (Behavior-Q)

Note. For administration and scoring purposes, we recommend printing copies of the questionnaires in Appendix D from the downloadable resources rather than copying the designed and typeset figures that appear in Figure 6.1 and 6.2 (this chapter). The printable questionnaires are the only ones that can be used with the scoring keys that were created to fit over the questionnaires for ease of scoring. The Figures in this chapter merely illustrate the questionnaires and the items.

6. How many nights per week does the child's family eat dinner together?
   (a) 0–2
   (b) 3–4
   (c) 5
   (d) 6–7
7. How often does the family spend time together?
   (a) Never
   (b) Sometimes
   (c) Often
   (d) Very often
8. How many minutes per day does the child spend reading alone for pleasure?
   (a) 0–15 minutes
   (b) 16–30 minutes
   (c) 31–59 minutes
   (d) 60+ minutes
9. How many times per year does the child's family participate in entertainment activities (e.g., theme parks, movies) together?
   (a) 0
   (b) 1–2
   (c) 3–5
   (d) 6+
10. How many times per year does the child's family participate in out of town vacations together?
    (a) 0
    (b) 1–2
    (c) 3–5
    (d) 6+
11. How often does the child receive verbal encouragement (encouraging words/praise)?
    (a) Never
    (b) Sometimes
    (c) Often
    (d) Frequently
12. How often does the child receive physical encouragement (e.g., hugs, kisses, patting on head/back)?
    (a) Never
    (b) Sometimes
    (c) Often
    (d) Frequently
13. How many hours per week does the child usually watch TV for entertainment (e.g., action, comedy, drama, cartoons)?
    (a) 0
    (b) 1–2
    (c) 3–6
    (d) 7+

Continue ⟶

Figure 6.2   (*Continued*)

Academic Activities and Expectations

14. How likely is it that the child will find better employment than yourself?
    (a) Not Likely
    (b) Somewhat Likely
    (c) Likely
    (d) Very Likely
15. Does the child do his or her homework at the same time every day?
    (a) Y
    (b) N
16. Does the child turn off the television/radio/music/internet when doing homework?
    (a) Y
    (b) N
17. How many days a week does an adult in the child's home check to see if the child's homework has been completed correctly?
    (a) 0–1
    (b) 2–3
    (c) 4
    (d) 5–7
18. How many days a week does an adult in the child's home check the child's backpack for notes and assignments from the teacher?
    (a) 0–1
    (b) 2–3
    (c) 4
    (d) 5–7
19. How likely is it that the child will achieve good grades in school?
    (a) Not Likely
    (b) Somewhat Likely
    (c) Likely
    (d) Very Likely
20. How likely is it that the child will graduate from high school?
    (a) Not Likely
    (b) Somewhat Likely
    (c) Likely
    (d) Very Likely

Figure 6.2 (*Continued*)

questionnaires are the only ones that can be used with the scoring keys that were created to fit over the questionnaires for ease of scoring. The Figures in this chapter merely illustrate the questionnaires and the items.

Reliability of the Rating Scales

Tables 6.1 and 6.2 provide reliability information for the rating scales. Table 6.1 indicates that coefficient alpha for the cross-validation sample was essentially the same as the value for the computation sample for both the Academic-Q (.78, .79) and Behavior-Q (.73, .74). Thus, even though reliability was one of the variables used to select the scales, introducing chance into the procedure, the effects were minimal. The values for the overall sample—.79 for Behavior-Q and .74 for Academic-Q—therefore are good estimates of coefficient alpha for children in general.

Table 6.1 Reliability Coefficients of the Academic-Q and Behavior-Q for the Computation, Cross-Validation, and Overall WISC–V Sample

Risk Scale	Odd Age Groups (7, 9, 11, 13, 15)	Even Age Groups (6, 8, 10, 12, 14, 16)	Overall Sample (Ages 6–16)
Academic-Q	.79	.78	.79
n	1,207	1,018	2,226
Behavior-Q	.74	.73	.74
n	1,272	1,055	2,327

Table 6.2 presents coefficient alpha, standard errors of measurement, and means/SDs for raw scores and T-scores on the Academic-Q and Behavior-Q. Reliability was slightly higher for younger children (.79–.81 for ages 6–11) than older children (.77 for ages 12–16) and for females (.80) than for males (.77). Mean scores on the Academic-Q showed no age or gender differences for the overall sample, and there were no gender differences on Behavior-Q. However, a clear developmental trend was evident for Behavior-Q, with adolescents exhibiting more at risk behaviors than children. The mean T-score for ages 14–16 (55.3) was about 1 SD greater than the mean for ages 6–7 (44.4). This disparity can be explained by looking at the age when most delinquent acts begin. Looking at offending trajectories, youth typically start offending at around age 14 and then desist (or continue to a criminal career) by the time they are about age 24 (Moffitt, 1993). Additionally, peer deviance is a significant risk factor for delinquency, and, developmentally, adolescents are most likely to look to their peers for input regarding their behavior (Fuligni & Eccles, 1993). The intercorrelation between Academic-Q and Behavior-Q was .25 for the computation sample, .30 for the cross-validation sample, and .27 for the overall sample. Thus,

Table 6.2 Means, Standard Deviations (SDs), Reliability Coefficients (Alpha), and Standard Errors of Measurement (SEM) of the Academic-Q and Behavior-Q, by Age and Sex

Risk Scale		Age Group	6–7	8–9	10–11	12–13	14–16	Male	Female	Total Sample
Academic-Q		n	418	408	412	391	597	1,067	1,159	2,226
	Raw Score	Mean	17.6	18.1	17.3	17.6	17.6	17.5	17.8	17.6
		SD	8.9	8.9	8.6	8.3	8.5	8.3	8.8	8.6
	T-Score	Mean	49.5	50.0	49.2	49.5	49.5	49.3	49.7	49.5
		SD	9.8	9.8	9.5	9.2	9.3	9.2	9.8	9.5
		Reliability	.81	.80	.79	.77	.77	.77	.80	.79
		SEM	4.3	4.4	4.3	4.4	4.5	4.4	4.4	4.4
Behavior-Q		n	429	417	430	417	634	1,109	1,218	2,327
	Raw Score	Mean	12.1	12.7	14.4	17.7	21.4	16.4	16.0	16.2
		SD	6.1	7.1	7.8	8.0	8.2	8.6	8.2	8.4
	T-Score	Mean	44.4	45.2	47.2	51.0	55.3	49.4	49.0	49.2
		SD	7.1	8.2	9.1	9.2	9.5	10.0	9.5	9.7
		Reliability	.63	.70	.71	.70	.71	.75	.73	.74
		SEM	4.3	4.5	4.9	5.1	5.1	5.0	4.9	5.0

Academic-Q and Behavior-Q are not only composed of independent items, but they are measuring two aspects of risk that are almost independent of each other.

Note that the sample sizes are 2,226 for the Academic-Q and 2,327 for Behavior-Q, both of which exceed the 2,200 that comprise the WISC–V standardization sample. This excess occurred despite the fact that we had substantial missing data on the HEQ and eliminated all clinical cases (and intellectually gifted) from our analyses—even though clinical cases and gifted children are proportionally included in the WISC–V norms group. That is because our data pool was the 3,500+ children and adolescents tested during the standardization program, not just the final 2,200 who were selected for the normative sample.

Validity of the Rating Scales

Table 6.3 shows the first validity table, correlations with the WISC–V FSIQ. Correlations were .52 for computation sample, a bit lower (.47) for cross-validation sample, and .50 for the total sample, indicating that the Academic-Q significantly predicts low IQ, accounting for about 25% of the variance (moderate effect size). The Behavior-Q correlated significantly (−.12) but trivially (<2% of variance) with FSIQ. Taken together, these results demonstrate both convergent and discriminant validity for the Academic-Q.

The next evidence of validity is presented in Table 6.4, correlations between the two rating scales and the four BASC-2 scales. Correlations are similar for the computational and cross-validation samples, so only the values for the total sample are pertinent. Behavior-Q correlated positively and significantly with the three scales that denote negative behaviors (.23–.30) and negatively (−.24) with the Resilience Scale, all values supporting the convergent validity of the scale (although the values indicate only a small effect size). By contrast, the Academic-Q correlated about .15 with the three negative scales, statistically significant but of trivial effect size. The discriminant validity is given mild support.

Tables 6.5 and 6.6 provide a true test of the validity of the Academic-Q. The scale was intended to predict school failure, so correlations with standardized tests of academic achievement should be negative. Correlations with the KTEA–3 (Table 6.5) and WIAT–III (Table 6.6) reveal significant correlations with reading (.35–.38), math (.38–.40), writing (.38–41), oral

Table 6.3   Validity of the Academic-Q and Behavior-Q: Correlations with WISC–V FSIQ

	Odd Age Groups (7, 9, 11, 13, 15)		Even Age Groups (6, 8, 10, 12, 14, 16)		Overall Sample (6–16)		T-Score Risk Scale	
	Correlation	n	Correlation	n	Correlation	n	Mean	SD
Risk Scale								
Academic-Q	−.52	1,195	−.47	1,018	−.50	2,226	49.5	9.5
Behavior-Q	−.12	1,258	−.12	1,055	−.12	2,327	49.2	9.7
FSIQ								
Mean	101.6		101.4		101.6			
SD	13.5		12.8		13.2			
n	1,603		1,298		2,901			

Note: All correlations are significant at $p < .01$.

Table 6.4 Validity of the Academic-Q and Behavior-Q: Correlations with Four BASC-2 Scales

	Resiliency			Conduct Problems			Executive Function			Attention Problems			Risk Scale		
	Odd Age Groups (7, 9, 11, 13, 15)	Even Age Groups (6, 8, 10, 12, 14, 16)	Overall Sample (Ages 6–16)	Odd Age Groups (7, 9, 11, 13, 15)	Even Age Groups (6, 8, 10, 12, 14, 16)	Overall Sample (Ages 6–16)	Odd Age Groups (7, 9, 11, 13, 15)	Even Age Groups (6, 8, 10, 12, 14, 16)	Overall Sample (Ages 6–16)	Odd Age Groups (7, 9, 11, 13, 15)	Even Age Groups (6, 8, 10, 12, 14, 16)	Overall Sample (Ages 6–16)	Mean	SD	n
Risk Scale															
Academic-Q	−.11	−.09	−.10	.14	.15	.15	.11	.12	.12	.18	.15	.16	49.5	9.5	2,226
Behavior-Q	−.29	−.25	−.27	.24	.21	.23	.30	.31	.30	.28	.29	.29	49.2	9.7	2,327
BASC–2 Scale															
Mean			49.8			48.3			48.8			50.7			
SD			8.3			7.7			8.0			8.3			
n			2,063			2,049			2,060			2,074			

Note: All correlations are significant at $p < .01$.

Table 6.5   Validity of the Academic-Q and Behavior-Q: Correlations with KTEA–3 Composites

| | KTEA–3 Composite | | | | | | | Risk Scale | | |
	Reading	Math	Written Language	Oral Language	Comprehension (Reading and Listening)	Expression (Oral and Written)	Academic Skills Battery	Mean	SD	N
Risk Scale										
Academic-Q	−.38**	−.50**	−.38**	−.47**	−.41**	−.41**	−.49**	52.2	11.3	183
Behavior-Q	−.09	−.11	−.06	−.05	−.10	−.11	−.08	49.0	9.9	197
KTEA–3										
Mean	98.8	98.0	98.59	96.3	98.0	97.1	97.8			
SD	13.7	13.6	12.8	13.8	13.9	13.1	13.5			
n	222	228	226	220	217	226	220			

Note: ** $p < .01$ * $p < .05$.

Table 6.6   Validity of the Academic-Q and Behavior-Q: Correlations with WIAT–III Composites

| | WIAT–III Composite | | | | | | | | Risk Scale | | |
	Oral Language	Total Reading	Basic Reading	Reading Comprehension and Fluency	Written Expression	Mathematics	Math Fluency	Total Achievement	Mean	SD	N
Risk Scale											
Academic	−.43**	−.35**	−.35**	−.30**	−.41**	−.38**	−.35**	−.46**	50.2	9.5	184
Behavior	−.20**	−.16*	−.22**	−.09**	−.26**	−.13	−.16*	−.20**	50.4	9.3	191
WIAT–III											
Mean	102.4	102.2	101.6	103.6	100.5	101.0	100.7	102.4			
SD	13.5	11.7	12.1	11.8	13.6	11.8	13.5	11.6			
n	210	201	204	187	210	211	206	201			

Note: ** $p < .01$ * $p < .05$.

language (.43–.47), and overall achievement (.46–.49). These coefficients are moderate in effect size (accounting for about 15%–25% of the variance). In contrast, Behavior-Q, not expected to predict academic achievement, correlated nonsignificantly (very close to 0) with KTEA–3 composites and only slightly higher (about −.15) with WIAT–III composites. These

data provide good convergent and discriminant validity for Academic-Q.

Table 6.7 presents means and *SD*s for nine clinical samples plus a sample of intellectually gifted children on the two rating scales and comparisons between the means for each validity sample with the mean for normal children and adolescents ($N = 2,226$). Multiple t tests were

Table 6.7   Clinical Validity of the Academic and Behavior Questionnaires: Comparison of Validity Samples with a Large Nonclinical Normal Sample

Group	n	Mean	SD	t of difference	Effect Size (d)[a]	n	Mean	SD	t of difference	Effect Size (d)[a]
Intellectually gifted	93	40.0	4.7	17.94**	−.90	92	47.1	8.2	2.42	−.17
Intellectual disability–mild	55	62.2	10.2	−9.80**	.91	66	56.7	10.0	−6.19**	.54
Intellectual disability–moderate	26	61.6	10.6	−6.42**	.85	32	55.3	10.7	−3.51**	.42
Specific learning disorder (SLD)–reading	25	50.7	8.6	−.62	.09	27	52.5	10.5	−1.74	.23
Specific learning disorder (SLD)–reading and written expression	20	58.5	10.4	−4.20**	.63	21	55.2	11.5	−2.79**	.40
Specific learning disorder (SLD)–math	23	58.2	10.2	−4.35**	.62	26	58.1	9.4	−4.64**	.66
Attention-deficit hyperactivity disorder (ADHD)	45	52.7	9.1	−2.25	.24	46	54.6	10.6	−3.71**	.37
Disruptive behavior	16	60.4	10.9	−4.54**	.75	21	58.1	10.8	−4.15**	.61
Traumatic brain injury (TBI)	15	50.6	9.1	−.43	.08	17	54.1	10.1	−2.05	.35
Autism spectrum disorder (ASD) with language impairment	28	50.7	8.9	−.64	.09	29	56.7	11.1	−4.10**	.51
Autism spectrum disorder (ASD) without language impairment	30	48.3	7.6	.70	−.10	32	53.5	11.6	−2.49	.29
All normal (excluding clinical and gifted cases)	2,226	49.5	9.5	—	—	2,327	49.2	9.7	—	—

** $p < .001$ * $p < .01$.

[a]The effect size (d) is the mean difference divided by the pooled standard deviation. The differences are computed by subtracting the mean for each clinical group from the mean for the large nonclinical normal sample.

Generally, $d = .20$ is considered a small effect; $d = 50$ is medium; and $d = .80$ large (J. Cohen, 1988; Rosenthal, 1996).

conducted; to reduce the results of chance, only the values that were significant at $p < .001$ were interpreted as meaningful, although the one value t $p < .01$ is noted in the table. More important than the statistical significance is the effect size (Cohen's d), which tells the importance of the difference. By convention, values of .20 are considered small, .50 are considered medium, and .80 are large. There are a number of notable findings in this validity table:

Regarding Academic-Q

- The sample of intellectually gifted children performed about 1 *SD below* the mean for the nonclinical normal group on Academic-Q, about the same magnitude as the intellectual disability samples scored *above* the mean for the normal sample. The effect sizes for the intellectually gifted (–.90), intellectual disability–mild (.91), and intellectual disability–moderate (.85) are all large. These data validate the Academic-Q not only as a predictor of school failure but also as a measure of an "enriched home environment" that predicts intellectual giftedness (for children and adolescents who earn low *T*-scores).

- Apart from individuals scoring at the extremes of the IQ distribution, only three other validation samples yielded medium to high effect sizes when compared to normal individuals on Academic-Q: those with disruptive behavior (.75), those with specific learning disorder (SLD)–reading and written expression (.63) and those with SLD–math (.62).
- Effect sizes on Academic-Q for the remaining five validity samples were nonsignificant and basically trivial.

Regarding the Behavior-Q

- None of the effect sizes was large for Behavior-Q, but seven of the 10 validation groups yielded significant differences when compared to the normal sample, and six of these yielded effect sizes in the medium range (.40–.66). Largest effect sizes were for SLD–math (.66) and disruptive behavior (.61), intellectual disability–mild (.54), and autism spectrum disorder (ASD) with language impairment (.51).
- Behavior-Q failed to discriminate for the SLD–reading, traumatic brain injury, and ASD without language impairment.

OVERVIEW OF THE CLINICAL VALIDITY OF THE ACADEMIC AND BEHAVIOR QUESTIONNAIRES

The data in Table 6.7 show mixed evidence of validity for Academic-Q and Behavior-Q. The validity evidence is strongest for (a) Academic-Q with children and adolescents who are intellectually gifted and children and adolescents with intellectual disability; (b) *both* Academic-Q and Behavior-Q for the samples of individuals with disruptive behavior, SLD–math, SLD–reading and written expression, and intellectual disability. From a clinical perspective, both scales should add diagnostic value when assessing children referred for disruptive behavior, SLD, and intellectual disability. Low scores on Academic-Q are associated with intellectual giftedness. However, based on these analyses, the two rating scales did not demonstrate validity with samples of SLD–reading and ASD without language and had only marginal success with ADHD and ASD with language.

CONCLUSION

The two ratings scales we developed, Academic-Q and Behavior-Q, can both provide reliable and valid assessments for those who want quick measures that assess for either academic risk or risk for behavioral problems that can lead to delinquency. These measures can be included in any comprehensive or brief battery for children and adolescents who are referred for assessment. The risk factors in each scale include stable risk factors, such as parental income and level of education that discriminate academic or behavioral risks, as well as dynamic risk factors, such as use and prevalence of technology in the home, parental expectations of school or employment success, and the type of encouragement a child receives in the family setting. Academic-Q and Behavior-Q include items that measure individual-level and family-level variables. Community-level variables were not included in the HEQ and therefore were not available to add for either measure.

Consider the case study of 10-year-old Jaime by Dr. Jennie Kaufman Singer (one of the sample reports at the end of Chapter 11). Jaime's parents took Academic-Q and Behavior-Q as part of his complete assessment. On Academic-Q, Jaime achieved a *T*-score of 44, at the 27th percentile. Jaime does not appear at risk of school failure. His low score on Academic-Q can be expected in light of his high SES, involved parents, and his attendance at a non-public school that focuses on those children with emotional and behavioral disorders. On Behavior-Q, Jaime earned a *T*-score of 71, or a score in the 98th percentile. Jaime would be considered at moderate to high risk for delinquent behaviors according to the Behavior-Q. *T*-scores of 70 are needed to establish a moderate to high risk of delinquent behaviors. Jaime's Behavior-Q *T*-score is between 61 and 81 within a 95% confidence interval. This score is not surprising, given his family's resources, level of education, and the severity of Jaime's behavior. Jaime will require continuing interventions to help prevent him from entering the criminal justice system as he gets older.

Limitations of the present study include a lack of community-level factors included on either Academic-Q or Behavior-Q. Another limitation is that our risk instruments were cross-validated using a random selection of the same large sample (Schwalbe, 2007). Another limitation is our use of a cross-sectional data set, as causal predictions cannot be made when the risk factor and criterion are measured at the same point in time (Murray et al., 2009). Therefore, Academic-Q and Behavior-Q are not able to make causal predictions without further validity studies. However, the risk factors used to create the current risk assessment scales have been identified using data and information from either retrospective or prospective risk studies.

The strengths of this study include having a large sample that is representative of the juvenile population in the United States. Academic-Q and Behavior-Q have good reliability and validity and include both stable and dynamic risk factors. Future studies should focus on validating the risk scales on a variety of samples, including ones drawn from children and adolescents at risk for school failure and those juveniles who have been adjudicated in juvenile court systems. A prospective, longitudinal study would also help enhance the risk scales' validity and have the potential of identifying whether the scales include causal, not only correlational, variables.

CHAPTER 7

DOES WISC–V SCATTER MATTER?

Troy Courville, Diane L. Coalson, Alan S. Kaufman, and Susan Engi Raiford

Evaluating variability across, between, and within the Wechsler composite and subtest scores has been a topic of research for as long as the scales have existed: The inclusion of separate scales for the verbal and performance subtests lent itself to such comparisons from the beginning (Grégoire, Coalson, & Zhu, 2011). Jastak (1949) stated: "The main reason for the psychologist's persistent preoccupation with test scatter is the amount of valuable information it yields as a supplement to quantitative indices of brightness" (p. 177). Almost 70 years after Jastak penned these words, they still hold true, despite his emphasis on evaluating intelligence score differences and qualitative aspects of performance for underlying personality characteristics (rather than patterns of cognitive strengths and weaknesses).

This chapter presents a brief history of scatter research and a preliminary investigation of WISC–V scatter at three levels: index, subtest, and item. At the index level, research that supports the predictive validity of the FSIQ, even when the profile demonstrates significant index-level scatter, will be discussed. Subtest-level scatter and profile analysis have been hotly contested topics for decades, as described in the historical overview of intelligence testing in Chapter 1. Following a brief summary of historical concerns, intelligent evaluation of WISC–V subtest-level variability is described. Evaluations of item-level (intrasubtest) scatter are relatively scarce in comparison, but even at this level the research is long-standing and complex, producing mixed results. Results from item-level (or intrasubtest) scatter on the

WISC–V are presented, as are directions for future research.

In the hands of an intelligent clinician, the WISC–V is a powerful tool for evaluating an individual's pattern of performance and identifying cognitive strengths and weaknesses. It is critical to address the issue of scatter at all levels of interpretation, as each level informs interpretation of higher levels (e.g., item-level variability affects subtest interpretation, subtest variability affects index interpretation, and index variability affects FSIQ interpretation). Although this chapter focuses on quantitative evaluations of scatter, the importance of qualitative analysis of a child's performance cannot be overstated. In fact, the insightful, qualitative observations made by intelligent clinicians often have driven such quantitative analysis, such as those represented in the analyses of item-level scatter.

INDEX–LEVEL SCATTER

Consistent with the scales' structure and age range, early investigations of index-level scatter on the *Wechsler Adult Intelligence Scale* (WAIS; Wechsler, 1939) initially focused on Verbal IQ–Performance IQ discrepancies in adults (Mayman, 1945; Wechsler, 1958). In fact, it was Wechsler's introduction of age-corrected norms that increased the interpretational power of these comparisons (Patterson, 1953). Results from studies of Verbal IQ–Performance IQ discrepancies were mixed, most likely due to the heterogeneity of the scores as well as their application to broadly defined groups of psychiatric and brain-injured patients (Jastak, 1949). Following the publication of the original Wechsler Intelligence Scale for Children (WISC; Wechsler, 1949), studies of Verbal IQ–Performance IQ discrepancies in children ensued and, like those studies with adults (e.g., Loro & Woodward, 1976), produced mixed results. However, the overinterpretation of significant differences between Verbal IQ and Performance IQ became a significant issue, despite Seashore's (1950) publication of normative base rates for WISC Verbal IQ–Performance IQ discrepancies with a strong warning that significant differences between these scores were common:

> The data force upon the interpreters a conclusion of practical, everyday importance. While the theoretical average subject has a Verbal IQ equal to his Performance IQ, all the individual Johns, Marys, and Joes who are real and separate clinical cases can be expected to have relatively large discrepancies between their Verbal and Performance IQ's. In fact, equal IQ's will be rare. (p. 64)

The importance of normative base rates received little empirical attention prior to the release of scatter data for the *Wechsler Intelligence Scale for Children–Revised Edition* (WISC–R; 1974a) by A. S. Kaufman (1976b, 1976c). Descriptive statistics for several scatter measures were provided in these seminal contributions, including the prevalence of Verbal IQ–Performance IQ discrepancies (A. S. Kaufman, 1976c) as well as new methods for evaluating subtest-level scatter. To provide more meaningful comparison scores, Kaufman calculated mean scores for the scaled-score ranges (highest minus lowest scaled score) of the Verbal, Performance, and Full scales (1976b), and established that these ranges were large, even for normal children and adolescents, and did not differ meaningfully by age, sex, race, parent occupation, or overall ability. Further, large amounts of "normal scatter" characterized the profiles of other tests, not just Wechsler's scales (A. S. Kaufman, 1976a).

Based on emerging factor-analytic methodology initiated by Thurstone (1946), A. S. Kaufman's (1975) factor analysis of the WISC–R data revealed a third factor, Freedom from Distractibility, composed of Arithmetic, Digit Span, and Coding. Research on the Freedom from Distractibility factor and Bannatyne's recategorization of the subtests into four categories (spatial, conceptual, sequential, and acquired knowledge) spurred an avalanche of investigations in hopes of more promise for identifying children with learning disabilities and other neurologically related disorders, such as attention-deficit/hyperactivity disorder (ADHD) (Hodges, Horwitz, Kline, & Brandt, 1982). Although the diagnostic utility of these alternate composite scores did not receive consistent support at the individual level, the new scores further demonstrated that evaluation of score differences provided a much richer understanding of an individual's cognitive strengths and weaknesses than the FSIQ, Verbal IQ, and Performance IQ, as well as more direct implications for intervention (A. S. Kaufman, 1981).

The addition of index scores (e.g., the Processing Speed, Working Memory, and Fluid Reasoning indexes) and resulting research on index-level strengths and weaknesses has since proven A. S. Kaufman's (1975) assertion that more discrete measures of cognitive abilities could result in more useful diagnostic information for children with academic and other neurodevelopmental disorders. In fact, the WISC–V is the first version of the WISC to provide the necessary data to complete an evaluation of strengths and weaknesses at the index level, using either the FSIQ or the mean primary index score as the basis for comparison, as suggested by Kaufman for subtest-level interpretation almost 40 years ago. Although this method for index-level analysis and supporting data has been provided in post-publication sources for the WAIS–IV (Grégoire et al., 2011) and the WISC–IV (Longman, 2005; Naglieri & Paolitto, 2005), the inclusion of this information in the *WISC–V Administration and Scoring*

Manual (Wechsler, 2014) represents a substantial improvement over its predecessor. Kaufman's original message has been internalized, as is evident from the fact that it is now accepted that, in order to properly evaluate score differences, it is necessary to consider both the significance and the prevalence of the discrepancy in the normative sample. Manuals for all contemporary intelligence measures include such data, including the WISC–V.

Index-Level Scatter in the WISC–V

In order to shed even more light on index-level scatter, we conducted additional analyses not reported in the WISC–V, including an evaluation of the prevalence of scatter in the normative sample using the index range (i.e., the highest minus the lowest primary index score) and of whether this scatter range varies with demographic variables or special group status. Table 7.1 provides the normative sample means and s (*SD*s) for the index range by age, sex, parent education, race/ethnicity, and ability level (i.e., FSIQ range).

As with previous results of group data, the mean index range and *SD*s reported in Table 7.1 are remarkably consistent across demographic comparison groups and ability level, with mean differences approximating 25 points and *SD*s of approximately 10 points. These findings are consistent with Seashore's (1950) findings related to mean WISC Verbal IQ–Performance IQ discrepancies, in which he astutely reminds us that negligible mean differences in a normative sample should be expected, based on the norming procedure, which results in a normalized distribution around the mean. Thus, for normally distributed measures, one would not expect to see large discrepancies for mean or *SD* differences, because negative and positive differences between scatter indices would offset one another when the mean is calculated. The lack of substantial variability in mean difference scores does suggest that significant index-level

Table 7.1   Mean Index Range (Highest Index minus Lowest Index) for the Five Primary WISC–V Indexes, by Demographic Variables

Demographic Variable	N	Mean	SD
Age			
6–8	598	25.2	10.3
9–12	800	25.3	10.2
13–16	800	24.9	10.3
Sex			
Female	1099	24.9	9.9
Male	1099	25.4	10.6
Parent Education			
0–8	67	24.2	8.6
9–11	168	25.3	11.7
12	460	25.6	10.3
13–15	777	24.9	10
16+	726	25.1	10.2
Race/Ethnicity			
Asian	89	25.7	12.1
African American	312	25.8	10.3
Hispanic	457	24.8	9.9
Caucasian	1227	24.9	10.2
FSIQ Range			
<80	176	23.3	10
80–89	370	24.4	10.2
90–109	1110	25.5	10.2
110–119	342	24.2	9.8
120+	200	27.6	10.9
Normative Sample	2198	25.1	10.2

Note: The WISC–V normative sample includes children ages 6–16 who are matched to the U.S. census data on key background variables with proportional representation of special group cases. *N* = 2,198 instead of 2,200 because of missing data for two cases.

scatter is unlikely attributable to these characteristics, allowing for evaluation of the mean index ranges reported in Table 7.2.

Results in Table 7.2 include two comparison groups: the normative sample and a nonclinical

Table 7.2   Mean Index Range (Highest Index minus Lowest Index) for the Five Primary WISC–V Indexes, by Special Group

Special Group	N	Mean	SD
High IQ			
Intellectually gifted	90	28.4	10.2
Low IQ			
Borderline intellectual functioning	18	26.9	9.5
Intellectual disability–mild	67	20.9	10.8
Intellectual disability–moderate	32	16.5	12
Traumatic brain injury	17	28.2	9.2
Specific Learning Disorder (SLD)			
SLD–mathematics	27	24.9	10.8
SLD–reading	30	23.6	8.5
SLD–reading & writing	22	25.6	8.6
Language-Related Problems			
Autistic spectrum disorder (ASD)			
ASD with language impairment	24	28	14
ASD without language impairment	30	28.1	12.8
Language disorder	22	29.2	14.5
English language learner	15	23	9.9
Behavior-Related Problems			
ADHD	46	25.6	10.2
Disruptive behavior	21	27.1	13.8
Normative Sample	2198	25.1	10.2
Nonclinical Sample	2882	25.3	10.1

Note: The WISC–V normative sample includes children ages 6–16 who are matched to the U.S. census data on key background variables with proportional representation of special group cases. N = 2,198 instead of 2,200 because of missing data for two cases. The WISC–V nonclinical sample includes children ages 6–16 who met criteria for the normative sample but did not meet criteria for any special group. Some of these cases were not included in the normative sample, which was selected specifically to match U.S. census data on key demographic variables, including proportionality of children in special groups.

sample. Creation of the nonclinical sample was designed to enhance sensitivity of special group comparisons by excluding children with any special group status from the normative comparison group; however, means and *SD*s are virtually identical for both samples. Table 7.2 reveals that nearly all special groups have mean index ranges consistent with the "normal" range of about 25. With the exception of the relatively small ranges for the two samples of individuals with intellectual disabilities, mean index ranges for the special groups were 25 + 3. A few special groups revealed more variability than the normal *SD* of 10 (e.g., language disorder group), but small sample sizes preclude interpretation of these differences. Despite the lack of diagnostic utility of the index range as a measure of scatter, the results are notable in view of the suggestion that index ranges of 23 or more points yield FSIQs that are uninterpretable (e.g., Flanagan & Kaufman, 2009). Clearly, FSIQs are interpretable for ranges of 23 as recent evidence indicates from Italy (Orsini, Pezzuti, & Hulbert, 2014) and the U.S. (e.g., Table 7.2) that the *average* person has a range that is even a bit larger than 23. In the forthcoming *Essentials of WISC–V Assessment*, Flanagan and Alfonso (in press) will no longer suggest that 23-point ranges are uninterpretable.

Results reported in Table 7.3 utilize the child's own FSIQ as the comparison score for discrepancies with the five primary index scores, allowing for comparison between the prevalence of three or more index-level strengths in the normative and nonclinical groups with the prevalence in special groups.

The decision to use three or more index score differences as the criterion for rarity was based on normative data indicating that three or more index-level strengths and weaknesses occurred in less than 18.1% of the normative sample, with the prevalence of four or more discrepancies dropping to only 3.5% of the normative sample. Relative to the normative sample (18.1%), 40% of the intellectually gifted, 30% of the autistic spectrum disorder (with language impairment), and 28.6% of children in the disruptive behavior groups obtained the highest percentages of scatter. The results in both Tables 7.2 and 7.3 highlight the need to consider the level of performance when interpreting scatter scores;

Table 7.3 Percentages of Special Groups Obtaining Three or More Significant Differences between Primary Index Scores and Their FSIQ (Index-Level Strengths and Weaknesses)

Special Group	N	% with ≥3 Significant Differences (Strengths + Weaknesses)
High IQ		
Intellectually gifted	90	40.00%
Low IQ		
Borderline intellectual functioning	18	11.10%
Intellectual disability–mild	67	20.90%
Intellectual disability–moderate	32	18.80%
Traumatic brain injury	17	23.50%
Specific Learning Disorder (SLD)		
SLD–mathematics	27	14.80%
SLD–reading	30	20.00%
SLD–reading & writing	22	18.20%
Language-Related Problems		
Autistic spectrum disorder (ASD)		
ASD with language impairment	24	12.50%
ASD without language impairment	30	30.00%
Language disorder	22	13.60%
English language learner	15	13.30%
Behavior-Related Problems		
ADHD	46	8.70%
Disruptive behavior	21	28.60%
Nonclinical Sample	2882	17.50%
Normative Sample	2198	18.10%

Note: The WISC–V normative sample includes children ages 6–16 who are matched to the U.S. census data on key background variables with proportional representation of special group cases. *N* = 2,198 instead of 2,200 because of missing data for two cases. The WISC–V nonclinical sample includes children ages 6–16 who met criteria for the normative sample but did not meet criteria for any special group. Some of these cases were not included in the normative sample, which was selected specifically to match U.S. census data on key demographic variables, including proportionality of children in special groups.

the intellectual disability samples had relatively small index ranges, and the intellectually gifted sample had fairly large index ranges with larger proportions of significant strengths or weaknesses. These findings are consistent with the cautionary advice in findings from McGee, Delis, and Holdnack (2009) in their evaluation of Verbal IQ–Performance IQ discrepancies at the extremes of the distribution.

To summarize the research up to this point, we know that index-level scatter is prevalent within the normative and special group samples; therefore, base rate information is critical for accurate interpretation of discrepancy scores. Table 7.4 provides base-rate information for the prevalence of specified index ranges in the normative sample. A minimum difference of 36 points is required between the highest and lowest index scores to meet the common cutoff of 15% or less to determine whether a difference is clinically meaningful. If the more stringent cutoff of 5% is used, at least a 44-point range between highest and lowest index score is needed to denote unusual index scatter. Index scatter was extreme in the case report for Tom (Chapter 10, Case 6), whose index scores ranged from 72 in Working Memory to 132 in Visual Spatial. Ranges of 60 points or more occurred in less than 1% of children and adolescents in the normative and nonclinical samples, as shown in Table 7.4. Abnormally large index ranges were also seen in

Table 7.4 Index Range (High Score minus Low Score) Required to Be Unusual at Five Different Levels of Abnormality

Normative Frequency	Index Range
<15%	36–38
<10%	39–43
<5%	44–50
<2%	51–55
<1%	56+

Note: Percentages are based on the WISC–V normative sample, ages 6–16 (*N* = 2,198).

the case reports for John (Chapter 12, Case 10) and Jordan (Chapter 14, Case 14).

Strengths, Weaknesses, Assets, and Deficits—Index Level

Recent trends in some patterns of strengths and weaknesses (PSW) approaches to the identification of specific learning disorders suggest that use of an intrapersonal weakness for this purpose is too lenient; rather, it is proposed that the child's intra-individual weakness be accompanied by a normative weakness to control for false positives (Dehn, 2014; Naglieri, 2015). Naglieri used the terms *cognitive strength* and *cognitive weakness* for differences that meet both the intra-individual and normative requirements for significance and the terms *relative strength* or *relative weakness* to describe significant intra-individual score differences that are not normative weakness. Dehn (2014) proposed the terms *asset* and *deficit* to describe significant intra-individual and normative differences to avoid possible confusion with similar terms. We agree with this suggestion and use the terms *asset* and *deficit* to describe mean score differences that are significant at *both* the personal and the normative level.

Tables 7.5 and 7.6 provide base rate information for WISC–V index-level strengths and weaknesses for children as well as for assets and deficits. Values were computed for the normative and nonclinical groups previously described as well as for the special groups. Normative differences were defined as those differences ≥1 SD from the mean standard score of 100 (index score ≤85 or ≥115). Cumulative percentages are also reported for children obtaining 0–5 strengths, assets, weaknesses, and deficits for a preliminary investigation of how the application of more stringent criteria for assets and deficits may impact the identification of specific learning disorder relative to less stringent criteria requiring only an intra-individual weakness. Due to the low sample size in some of the special

groups, only data for special groups with $N \geq 30$ are included in this exploratory analysis.

The most striking feature in Tables 7.5 and 7.6 is the precipitous within-group reductions in the prevalence of assets relative to strengths with the additional requirement of a normative discrepancy. In both the normative and nonclinical samples, the percentage of children obtaining one or more strengths is about 65%; however, that value drops to 7% for assets. Thus, only 7% of strengths in the normative sample qualify as assets. Only 31% of the intellectually gifted group have a relative strength (likely due to elevated scores across subtests), but 24% of these strengths are also assets, suggesting that a much larger proportion of strengths in the intellectually gifted group were of sufficient magnitude to also qualify as assets. Sadly, the drop in percentages between strengths and assets was even more drastic for the remaining special groups, with no strengths qualifying as assets for the SLD–reading and intellectual disability groups. The results for the samples with intellectual disability are intuitive, but not so for the SLD–reading sample. The reductions within the ADHD and ASD (with language impairment) groups were more drastic than those observed in the normative and other clinical groups.

Tables 7.7 and 7.8 feature similar analyses for index-level weaknesses and deficits. Although the drop in prevalence from weaknesses to deficits is not as precipitous as the drop from strengths to assets, the reduced prevalence in some special groups warrants further investigation. Again, the percentages for normative and nonclinical samples are similar, with about 62% obtaining one or more intra-individual index-level weaknesses. These values drop to 23% for deficits when a significant normative difference is also required. The drop for the intellectually gifted group is staggering, with only 2% of the 99% of weaknesses also qualifying as deficits. The percentages for the intellectual disability groups did not change, indicating that the magnitude of

Table 7.5   Percentages of Normative, Nonclinical, and Se ect Special Groups Obtaining 0–5 Index-Level Strengths

| | Normative (n = 2198) | | Nonclinical (n = 2882) | | Special Group | | | | | | | | | | | |
| | | | | | Intellectually gifted (n = 90) | | Intellectual disability–mild (n = 67) | | Intellectual disability–moderate (n = 32) | | Specific learning disorder–reading (n = 30) | | Attention-deficit/hyperactivity disorder (n = 46) | | Autism spectrum disorder with language impairment (n = 30) | |
# Strengths	%	Cum%	%	Cum%	%	Cum%	%	Cum%	%	Cum%	%	Cum%	%	Cum%	%	Cum%
5		0.0		0.0		0.0		0.0		0.0		0.0		0.0		0.0
4	0.2	0.2	0.1	0.1		0.0	4.5	4.5		0.0		0.0		0.0		0.0
3	3.0	3.2	2.3	2.4		0.0	22.4	26.9	25.0	25.0	13.3	13.3		0.0	3.3	3.3
2	17.9	21.1	16.6	19.0	2.2	2.2	37.3	64.2	46.9	71.9	20.0	33.3	28.3	28.3	26.7	30.0
1	**44.4**	65.4	44.7	63.7	28.9	**31.1**	26.9	**91.0**	21.9	**93.8**	46.7	**80.0**	50.0	**78.3**	40.0	**70.0**
0	34.6	100.0	36.3	100.0	68.9	100.0	9.0	100.0	6.3	100.0	20.0	100.0	21.7	100.0	30.0	100.0

215

Table 7.6 Percentages of Normative, Nonclinical, and Select Special Groups Obtaining 0–5 Index-Level Assets

							Special Group							
# Assets	Normative (n = 2,198)		Nonclinical (n = 2,882)		Intellectually gifted (n = 90)		Intellectual disability–mild (n = 67)		Intellectual disability–moderate (n = 32)		Specific learning disorder–reading (n = 30)		Attention-deficit/hyperactivity disorder (n = 46)		Autism spectrum disorder with language impairment (n = 30)	
	%	Cum%	%	Cum%	%	Cum%	%	Cum%	%	Cum%	%	Cum%	%	Cum%	%	Cum%
5		0.0		0.0		0.0		0.0		0.0		0.0		0.0		0.0
4		0.0		0.0		0.0		0.0		0.0		0.0		0.0		0.0
3	0.0	0.0	0.1	0.1		0.0		0.0		0.0		0.0		0.0		0.0
2	1.0	1.0	1.0	1.1	1.1	1.1		0.0		0.0		0.0		0.0		0.0
1	5.9	**6.9**	6.1	**7.2**	23.3	**24.4**		**0.0**		**0.0**		0.0	2.2	**2.2**	10.0	**10.0**
0	93.1	100.0	92.8	100.0	75.6	100.0	100.0	100.0	100.0	100.0	100.0	100.0	97.8	100.0	90.0	100.0

weakness was large enough to also qualify as a deficit. Although the percentages for weaknesses were lower for the SLD–reading and ADHD groups (40% and 52%, respectively) than those for the normative and nonclinical groups, a larger proportion of weaknesses in these special groups also qualified as deficits (27% and 33%, respectively). Results for the ASD (with language impairment) group reveal similar percentages to those of the normative sample for one or more weaknesses (63%), but a larger proportion of these weaknesses also qualify as deficits (40%).

Taken together, these results suggest that caution may be warranted when using the asset/deficit criteria proposed in some PSW approaches to SLD identification. The data indicate that approximately 13% of children with identified SLD–reading may not be identified with stringent application of the deficit criteria. For children identified with ADHD or ASD (with language impairment), approximately 20% would not meet the deficit criteria. The situation for intellectually gifted children with concurrent SLD (i.e., twice exceptional children) would seem to be at the greatest risk of failure to meet the more stringent SLD deficit criteria. Additional research may be warranted prior to utilizing the more stringent requirement, including investigations of children with multiple index-level weaknesses that may cause significant difficulties across several academic areas, with none of the weaknesses also qualifying as a deficit.

Based on the previous analyses, Table 7.9 provides base rate data for children with four or five index scores significantly different from the FSIQ. Remarkably, it is not that unusual to have three or more index scores significantly different from the FSIQ (in either direction) for children in the normative sample (18%). This table was useful for the case reports of John (Chapter 12, Case 10), and Ellie (Chapter 14, Case 13), and Jordan (Chapter 14, Case 14), all of whom had four significant discrepancies—relative strengths + relative weaknesses. As shown, significant discrepancies on four out of five index scores occurs <5% of the time in the normal populations.

Influence of Unusual Index–Level Scatter on FSIQ Predictive Validity

We believe that contemporary research argues against the assertion that marked index-level scatter renders the FSIQ invalid or uninterpretable (e.g., Flanagan & Kaufman, 2009; Sattler, 2008). As indicated by data for the normative sample, substantial index-level variability is normal, not abnormal, with the possible exception of individuals in the extreme tails of the normal distribution. Further, the FSIQ is designed to be a measure of the latent general ability construct, or g (Daniel, 2007). The belief that FSIQs are not interpretable when they are composed of divergent part scores has persisted, despite empirical evidence to the contrary (Daniel, 2007, 2009; Konold & Canivez, 2010; Watkins, Glutting, & Lei, 2007). In situations where there is a significant and unusual amount of index-level scatter, the FSIQ should be reported and interpreted in light of this variability and of variability at lower levels (i.e., the subtest and item levels). However, this does not imply that global scores are the most important outcomes of the evaluation or should overshadow the implications for intervention when a child displays both relatively strong and weak areas of functioning. Intelligent testers know that variability in performance is what drives analysis of PSW and hints that additional testing may be required (Miller, 2013). Case reports in Chapters 6 (Tom), 12 (John), and 14 (Ellie and Jordan) are all marked by significant and unusual index-level scatter and illustrate instances in which the WISC–V global scores are not valuable. These reports demonstrate how these experts addressed issues of extreme index-level variability and used theory-based methods to translate the PSW to meaningful interventions.

Table 7.7 Percentages of Normative, Nonclinical, and Select Special Groups Obtaining 0–5 Index-Level Weaknesses

# Weaknesses	Normative (n=2,198)		Nonclinical (n=2,882)		Special Group											
					Intellectually gifted (n=90)		Intellectual disability–mild (n=67)		Intellectual disability–moderate (n=32)		Specific learning disorder–reading (n=30)		Attention-deficit/hyperactivity disorder (n=46)		Autism spectrum disorder with language impairment (n=30)	
	%	Cum%	%	Cum%	%	Cum%	%	Cum%	%	Cum%	%	Cum%	%	Cum%	%	Cum%
5		0.0		0.0		0.0		0.0		0.0		0.0		0.0		0.0
4	0.3	0.3	0.2	0.2	8.9	8.9		0.0		0.0		0.0		0.0		0.0
3	4.1	4.4	4.0	4.2	26.7	35.6		0.0		0.0		0.0		0.0		0.0
2	20.2	24.5	20.3	24.6	44.4	80.0		0.0		0.0	13.3	13.3	8.7	8.7	23.3	23.3
1	36.0	60.5	38.8	63.4	18.9	98.9	9.0	9.0	9.4	9.4	26.7	40.0	43.5	52.2	40.0	63.3
0	39.5	100.0	36.6	100.0	1.1	100.0	91.0	100.0	90.6	100.0	60.0	100.0	47.8	100.0	36.7	100.0

Table 7.8 Percentages of Normative, Nonclinical, and Select Special Groups Obtaining 0–5 Index-Level Deficits

											Special Group									
# Deficits	Normative (n = 2,198)		Nonclinical (n = 2,882)		Intellectually gifted (n = 90)		Intellectual disability–mild (n = 67)		Intellectual disability–moderate (n = 32)		Specific learning disorder–reading (n = 30)		Attention-deficit/ hyperactivity disorder (n = 46)		Autism spectrum disorder with language impairment (n = 30)	
	%	Cum%	%	Cum%	%	Cum%	%	Cum%	%	Cum%	%	Cum%	%	Cum%	%	Cum%
5	0.0	0.0	0.0	0.0		0.0		0.0		0.0		0.0		0.0		0.0
4	0.0	0.0	0.0	0.0		0.0		0.0		0.0		0.0		0.0		0.0
3	0.0	0.0	0.1	0.1		0.0		0.0		0.0		0.0		0.0		0.0
2	2.4	2.4	2.4	2.4		0.0		0.0		0.0	3.3	3.3	4.3	4.3	6.7	6.7
1	21.0	**23.4**	20.7	**23.1**	2.2	2.2	9.0	9.0	9.4	**9.4**	23.3	**26.7**	28.3	**32.6**	33.3	**40.0**
0	76.6	100.0	76.9	100.0	97.8	100.0	91.0	100.0	90.6	100.0	73.3	100.0	67.4	100.0	60.0	100.0

Table 7.9   Number of Significant Index-Level Discrepancies (Strengths + Weaknesses) Required to Be Unusual at Five Different Levels of Abnormality

Normative Frequency	# Significant Discrepancies
<10%	–
<5%	4
<1%	5

Note: Percentages are based on the WISC-V normative sample, ages 6–16 ($N = 2,198$).

SUBTEST-LEVEL SCATTER

Similar to historical precedents in investigations of index-level scatter, research on subtest-level scatter has been ongoing for decades with a pattern of inconsistent findings and even more controversy (see Chapter 1 for more details). More than two decades before Kaufman's provision of the base-rate information for the WISC–R normative sample, Jastak (1949) noted his growing concerns with scatter analysis:

> In the process of developing a qualitative and quantitative system for scatter analysis certain precautions should be taken to obviate extreme swings of the pendulum from a rigid and faulty statistical base to the loose and vague hypothesizing such as is typical of the projective techniques. (p. 179)

Jastak (1949) went on to note the lack of studies with adequate control groups, heterogeneous clinical samples, lack of a standard scatter score, and the lack of a consistent reference point (e.g., FSIQ, mean subtest score, or a specified subtest, such as Vocabulary). Although we have made progress in all of these areas (e.g., use of control groups, establishing comparison scores, specific inclusion and exclusion criteria for clinical studies), evaluations of subtest scatter continue to yield disappointing results in terms of diagnostic utility. This fact does not imply that evaluation of subtest scatter is a waste of effort. On the contrary, evaluation of subtest scatter is a critical part of any assessment, providing rich information about the child's strengths and weaknesses on more narrow cognitive abilities represented by subtests as compared to the broad abilities represented by the index scores and the FSIQ.

Kaufman (1976a) provided two methods for evaluating subtest scatter within the Verbal, Performance, and Full Scales: (1) the difference between the highest and lowest subtest scaled scores, and (2) the number of subtests that differed from the child's mean scaled scored by 3 or more points. Almost all contemporary measures of intelligence now include the comparison of subtest scores to a mean scaled score for one or more groupings of subtests as the primary means of evaluating subtest-level scatter. In fact, this method was also applied at the index-score level, making the WISC–V the first Wechsler intelligence test to include an evaluation of strengths and weaknesses at both levels as part of the standard scoring procedures. Kaufman (1981) also predicted that the Freedom from Distractibility factor "may hold the key to competent LD assessment" (p. 521). The subtests comprising the Freedom from Distractibility factor would later split into the Working Memory and Processing Speed factors, which are now generally accepted as areas of probable difficulty for many children with specific learning disorders as well as other neurodevelopmental disorders, such as ADHD and autistic spectrum disorders.

Subtest-Level Scatter in the WISC–V

A series of scatter analyses analogous to those at the index level were performed at the subtest level. Table 7.10 provides the normative sample means and *SD*s for the subtest range by age, sex, parent education, race/ethnicity, and ability level (i.e., FSIQ range).

The mean subtest range and *SD*s are consistent across demographic comparison groups and ability level, with mean differences approximating 7 points and *SD*s of about 2 points. Although related to the normalized distribution around the mean (as described at the index level), the finding that the mean subtest range is 7 plus or minus 2 points is

Table 7.10 Mean Subtest Range (Highest Subtest minus Lowest Subtest) for the 10 Primary Subtests, by Demographic Variables

Demographic Variable	N	Mean	SD
Age			
6–8	598	7.3	2.2
9–12	800	7	2.2
13–16	800	6.9	2.2
Sex			
Female	1099	7	2.2
Male	1099	7.1	2.2
Parent Education			
0–8	67	6.7	2
9–11	168	7.1	2.2
12	460	7.1	2.2
13–15	777	7	2.2
16+	726	7	2.1
Race/Ethnicity			
Asian	89	7.5	2.4
African American	312	7.2	2.3
Hispanic	457	6.9	2.2
Caucasian	1227	7	2.1
FSIQ Range			
<80	176	6.6	2.2
80–89	370	6.9	2.2
90–109	1110	7.1	2.2
110–119	342	7	2.1
120+	200	7.5	2.1
Normative Sample	2198	7	2.2

Note: The WISC–V normative sample includes children ages 6–16 who are matched to the U.S. census data on key background variables with proportional representation of special group cases. *N* = 2,198 instead of 2,200 because of missing data for two cases.

Table 7.11 Mean Subtest Range (Highest Subtest minus Lowest Subtest) for the 10 Primary Subtests, by Special Group

Special Group	N	Mean	SD
High IQ			
Intellectually gifted	90	7.6	2
Low IQ			
Borderline intellectual functioning	18	7.5	2.8
Intellectual disability–mild	67	5.7	2.4
Intellectual disability–moderate	32	4	2.6
Traumatic brain injury	17	7	2
Specific Learning Disorder (SLD)			
SLD–Mathematics	27	6.6	2.5
SLD–Reading	30	6.5	1.9
SLD–Reading & writing	22	7	2.2
Language-Related Problems			
Autistic spectrum disorder (ASD)			
ASD with language impairment	24	7.7	3
ASD without language impairment	30	7.6	2.8
Language disorder	22	7.3	3.1
English language learner	15	7.4	2.3
Behavior-Related Problems			
ADHD	46	6.8	2
Disruptive behavior	21	7.3	2.2
Normative Sample	2198	7	2.2
Nonclinical Sample	2882	7.1	2.2

Note: The WISC–V normative sample includes children ages 6–16 who are matched to the U.S. census data on key background variables with proportional representation of special group cases. *N* = 2,198 instead of 2,200 because of missing data for two cases. The WISC–V nonclinical sample includes children ages 6–16 who met criteria for the normative sample but did not meet criteria for any special group. Some of these cases were not included in the normative sample, which was selected specifically to match U.S. census data on key demographic variables, including proportionality of children in special groups.

extraordinarily consistent with the original values reported by A. S. Kaufman (1976a) for the WISC–R, the WAIS–R (McLean, Kaufman, & Reynolds, 1989), and every Wechsler intelligence test revision since that time. The lack of substantial variability in scatter scores by demographic variables does suggest that significant subtest-level scatter is unlikely attributable to these characteristics. Table 7.11 provides subtest ranges for the WISC–V special groups.

With the notable exception of the children with intellectual disability, subtest scatter is in the normal range for most special groups. This pattern is expected based on the lower mean subtest scores obtained by children with intellectual disability, thus reducing their chances of obtaining a larger subtest range. Children in the intellectually gifted group and children with language-related problems obtained slightly higher mean subtest ranges than the normative group, but no mean was even as high as 8.0. In general, results for the normative, nonclinical, and special group samples are similar, with the exception of children in the intellectual disability groups.

Results reported in Table 7.12 show significant subtest strengths and weaknesses on the 10 primary subtests, comparing each scaled score to the child's mean scaled score on the seven subtests that comprise FSIQ.

The decision to use four or more subtest score differences as the criterion for unusualness was based on normative data indicating that four or more subtest-level strengths and weaknesses occurred in less than 17% of the normative sample, with the prevalence of five or more discrepancies occurring in only 6.5% of the normative sample. Results for most groups are not very different from the normal values. Again, scatter is less for the groups with intellectual disability (about 10%) and greater than normal for intellectually gifted (28%). However, the only other notable difference from the two normal samples was for the SLD–Reading group (10%); by contrast, 23% of the SLD group with reading and writing difficulties had four or more significant discrepancies among the 10 subtests. These results are consistent with those of Ryckman (1981), in which children with *severe* learning disabilities obtained higher levels of subtest scatter relative to the WISC–R normative sample. It is possible that the comorbidity of specific learning disorders is related to increased levels of subtest scatter, but additional research is necessary due to the small sample sizes in the WISC–V special groups. In general, results of

Table 7.12 Percentages of Special Groups Obtaining Four or More Significant Differences between Primary Subtest Scores and Their Mean Scaled Score for FSIQ Subtests (Subtest-Level Strengths and Weaknesses)

Special Group	N	% with ≥4 Significant Differences (Strengths + Weaknesses)
High IQ		
Intellectually gifted	90	27.80%
Low IQ		
Borderline intellectual functioning	18	22.20%
Intellectual disability–mild	67	11.90%
Intellectual disability–moderate	32	9.40%
Traumatic brain injury	17	17.60%
Specific Learning Disorder (SLD)		
SLD–Mathematics	27	14.80%
SLD–Reading	30	10.00%
SLD–Reading & writing	22	22.70%
Language-Related Problems		
Autistic spectrum disorder (ASD)		
ASD with language impairment	24	25.00%
ASD without language impairment	30	16.70%
Language disorder	22	22.70%
English language learner	15	20.00%
Behavior-Related Problems		
ADHD	46	15.20%
Disruptive behavior	21	19.00%
Total Nonclinical Sample	2882	17.90%
Total Normative Sample	2198	17.30%

Note: The WISC-V normative sample includes children ages 6–16 who are matched to the U.S. census data on key background variables with proportional representation of special group cases. N = 2,198 instead of 2,200 because of missing data for two cases. The WISC-V nonclinical sample includes children ages 6–16 who met criteria for the normative sample but did not meet criteria for any special group. Some of these cases were not included in the normative sample, which was selected specifically to match U.S. census data on key demographic variables, including proportionality of children in special groups.

the subtest-level scatter analyses suggest that some special groups may be more prone to variable subtest performance than others, but the magnitude of differences and overlapping distributions of scatter scores makes it unlikely that subtest scatter will significantly enhance diagnostic accuracy. Regardless, scatter at the subtest level is a critical step in the assessment process, especially with the two-subtest composition of the primary index scores. Subtest-level scatter analysis informs interpretation at higher levels and provides additional insight into the child's cognitive strengths and weaknesses.

Table 7.13 provides base-rate information for the prevalence of specified subtest ranges in the normative sample. A minimum difference of 10 points is required between the highest and lowest subtest scores to meet the common cutoff of 15% or less to determine whether a difference is clinically meaningful.

Strengths, Weaknesses, Assets, and Deficits—Subtest Level

Although not currently utilized or recommended for the PSW approach to SLD identification, similar methodology to evaluate strengths, assets, weaknesses, and deficits at the subtest level can be applied for a deeper understanding of the magnitude of subtest-level variability. We conducted

Table 7.13   Subtest Range (High Score minus Low Score) Required to Be Unusual at Five Different Levels of Abnormality

Normative Frequency	Subtest Range
<15%	10
<10%	11
<5%	12
<2%	13
<1%	14

Note: Percentages are based on the WISC–V normative sample, ages 6–16 (*N* = 2,198).

Table 7.14   Number of Significant Subtest-Level Discrepancies (Strengths + Weaknesses) Required to Be Unusual at Five Different Levels of Abnormality

Normative Frequency	# Significant Discrepancies
<10%	5
<5%	6
<1%	7+

Note: Percentages are based on the WISC-V normative sample, ages 6–16 (*N* = 2,198).

these analyses, but the results at the subtest level were less meaningful than the comparable analyses at the index level. To read about these analyses, go to Appendix E in the downloadable resources: www.wiley.com/go/itwiscv.

Using the base rate analyses in Appendix E, we developed Table 7.14 to provide base-rate data for children with an unusual number of significant subtest-level discrepancies (i.e., the total number of subtest-level strengths and weaknesses). Like the index-level analyses, these results confirm that variability across scores at the subtest level is common in the WISC–V normative sample. As shown in the table, it is unusual for children to have five or more discrepancies out of the 10 primary WISC–V subtests (≤10% of the time in the normative sample), and even more unusual to have 6 or more (≤5%) or 7+ (≤1%) In Chapter 10, Tom (Case 6) displayed 5 significant discrepancies among the 10 primary WISC–V subtests, evidencing significant scatter (<10%).

ITEM–LEVEL SCATTER

Item-level scatter, or intrasubtest scatter (ISS), provides a measure of inconsistent responses to sequential test items. This type of measure is typically applied to Gaussian scales in which the items are arranged in order of increasing item difficulty, such as those within the WISC–V subtests. For most individuals, it is assumed that easier items will be answered correctly until they reach the ceiling of their performance, followed by incorrect responses (i.e., scores of zero) until the discontinue criterion is met. An atypical response pattern would be characterized by scores of zero on easier items, followed by creditable responses to more difficult items. Theoretically, the degree of item-level scatter has been related to inefficiency of, or damage to, the central nervous system (Hallenbeck, Fink, & Grossman, 1965; Kellerman & Burry, 1981; Rapaport, Gill, & Schafer, 1945) and may tap more qualitative aspects of performance, such as attention and motivation (Godber, Anderson, & Bell, 2000; Kaplan, Fein, Morris, Kramer, & Delis, 1991; Lezak, 2004; Wechsler, 1958).

Juni and Trobliger (2009) suggested three possible reasons for item-level scatter: (1) gaps or idiosyncrasies in knowledge, (2) emotional interference such as anxiety (with particular impact to measures requiring attention and working memory), or (3) emotional interference unique to the examinee for specific items or content. Others have also noted the possible impact of attention, memory loss, or difficulties retrieving information as possible contributors to erratic performance (Groth-Marnat, 2009; Lezak, 2004).

The history of evaluating item-level scatter is long-standing, with the earliest efforts aimed at evaluating its diagnostic utility on the Binet-Simon scales (e.g., Pressey & Cole, 1918). Initial investigations of item-level scatter primarily used samples of adult patients in mental facilities without the inclusion of adequate control groups (J. McV. Hunt, 1936). Based on a review of research on the Stanford-Binet, Harris and Shakow (1937) noted that scatter research with children was less likely to provide clinically useful information than that with adults, based on their findings that only mental age was correlated with ISS in samples of normal, schizophrenic, and delinquent adults.

More recent evaluations of item-level scatter have continued to focus on scatter in adult populations, primarily those with neurological conditions such as traumatic brain injury

(e.g., Mittenberg, Hammeke, & Rao, 1989) and dementia (e.g., Mittenberg, Thompson, Schwartz, Ryan, & Levitt, 1991). Similar to results at the subtest level and early research on ISS, findings have been highly inconsistent. One of the primary issues contributing to this inconsistency is likely the lack of a standard quantitative measure. Numerous indicators of ISS have been developed, but many fail to account for the numerous factors involved in creating such measures, including the number of administered items, how to deal with partial credit, and whether the scatter occurred on easy or more difficult items. Wentworth-Rohr and Macintosh (1972) attempted to address some of these issues by creating a scatter index that included the total raw score, the rank order of items, and where the scatter occurred, but they did not provide enough information for attempts to replicate their method. The complexity of this method highlights another important consideration of scatter scores: user-friendliness.

The need for a user-friendly method was a driving force behind the exploration of WISC–V item-level scatter reported in this chapter, and it continues to be a formidable hurdle for interested researchers. The current method of choice for evaluating item-level scatter is based on the absolute value of the sums of inter-item differences developed by Kaplan et al. (1991). A number of limitations for this method have been noted, with primary concerns related to the lack of control for how far the individual progressed through the item set and where the scatter occurred (Juni & Trobliger, 2009). Advances in item response theory (IRT) have sparked renewed interest by some researchers, including Godber et al. (2000), who found significant differences between healthy children and children with acute lymphoblastic leukemia using a Rasch-based IRT method. However, as noted by the investigators, the clinical application of their method is limited by the fact that entering the item-level responses into a computer program is required—something that time-sensitive clinicians would be unwilling to do for relatively small, but significant, improvements in diagnostic accuracy (Godber et al., 2000).

In addition to providing an excellent review of previous literature and shortcomings of existing methodologies, Juni and Trobliger (2009) developed a method to address some of these shortcomings by coding variable response patterns using an 11-level system. Initial validation efforts appear to be promising. However, this methodology was not attempted for the WISC–V because the coding system was developed using the WAIS–III, which has substantially longer discontinue criteria than the WISC–V, rendering many of the suggested coding levels irrelevant. We are impressed by these investigators' sensitivity to the many confounding variables in previous research on ISS and their obvious understanding of the real-world challenges faced by practicing psychologists.

To explore the occurrence of item-level scatter in the WISC–V, we tested a number of scatter scores, including the current method of choice based on the sum of inter-item differences (Kaplan et al., 1991) and variations of this score using different denominators to appropriately control for the individual's level of performance or progression through the item set (e.g., last credited item, maximum score possible for administered items). Other scatter scores were created based on simple counts of item scores due to their simplicity and the increased likelihood that clinicians would actually use them. In general, results from these exploratory analyses did not provide evidence of clinical utility in terms of distinguishing among normative, nonclinical, and special groups. Correlational analyses indicated that high degrees of scatter on one subtest were unrelated to scatter on other subtests, regardless of whether the subtests were on the same or different scales. It should be noted that the shortened discontinue rules on the WISC–V are likely to reduce opportunities for scatter and could diminish the possibility of obtaining significant group differences. This issue has also been noted by other researchers (Millager, Conture, Walden, & Kelly, 2014).

CONCLUSION

Taken together, it appears that a simple answer to the question posed in the chapter title, Does WISC–V scatter matter?, is "no" for diagnostic utility but "yes" for PSW analyses and for understanding exactly how much variability in an index or subtest profile is required to denote a lot of scatter relative to the normal population. There is ample evidence that index-level and subtest-level variability often have clinically meaningful implications and provide the very foundation for assessment of an individual's intellectual strengths and weaknesses. At the item level, we are currently limited by the need to balance clinical utility with psychometric accuracy, which has proven to be a difficult task. The application of IRT methodology currently holds the most promise for answering this question at the item level. With the increasing availability of digital administration and scoring options, such as the digital version of WISC–V, we remain hopeful that a clinically meaningful index of item-level scatter will soon be introduced to answer this question definitively.

CHAPTER 8

BASIC STEPS FOR WISC–V INTERPRETATION

This chapter offers information relevant to basic WISC–V interpretation. The published composite scores are described. A step-by-step approach to score analysis as it pertains to interpretation is detailed.

UNDERSTANDING THE COMPOSITE SCORES

Between the composite scores that appear on the published test and this book, there are a greater number of such scores available for the WISC–V than any prior Wechsler intelligence scale. The large number of scores provides more flexibility for interpretation and challenges the practitioner to employ careful consideration when selecting the appropriate scores for a particular child. Not all of these scores will necessarily be useful or meaningful when you describe a particular child.

There are two types of composite scores: global composite scores (i.e., useful to describe or summarize overall intellectual ability) and specific composite scores (i.e., useful to provide information about a specific cognitive domain, as opposed to overall intellectual ability). Interpretation requires a clear understanding of the global scores to ensure you select the one(s) that is (or are) most useful for describing overall intellectual ability, given the presenting issues and the purpose of the evaluation.

Interpretation also involves selection of the appropriate specific scores to provide targeted information about the child's cognitive abilities, strengths, and weaknesses, according to your theoretical orientation. As with the global scores, not all specific scores will be useful in every

situation. Subsequent sections of this chapter provide descriptions of the global and specific scores.

Global Composite Scores

Three global composite scores are available within the published test: the FSIQ, the Nonverbal Index, and the General Ability Index. These are described in turn in the next sections.

FSIQ

The FSIQ is the most reliable of the composite scores. It is derived from the sum of seven subtest scaled scores. Of all composite scores, the FSIQ most closely represents general intellectual ability (*g*).

FSIQ interpretation is best approached through understanding the primary index scores, because they represent constructs that contribute vital information to general intellectual ability. Comparing the available primary index scores to an estimate of overall performance (e.g., the mean of all primary index scores [MIS] or the FSIQ) and to one another (e.g., the Verbal Comprehension Index and the Visual Spatial Index) therefore informs FSIQ interpretation.

Some interpretive approaches indicate that composite scores are less valid or less reliable if their component parts are discrepant. In these interpretive approaches, the FSIQ is described as valid, reliable, and interpretable *only* if no significant discrepancy exists between the highest and lowest primary index scores. Similarly, the index scores are described as valid and reliable only if their contributing subtests are not significantly discrepant. Flanagan and

Kaufman (2009), for example, recommended *not* to interpret WISC–IV global scores or index scores whenever there is a range of 1.5 standard deviations (*SD*s) or more between the child's highest and lowest score. For standard scores with mean of 100 and *SD* of 15 (such as FSIQ) a difference of 23 points or more between the child's highest and lowest index score would render the FSIQ "uninterpretable." We do not find sufficient evidence that there is a discrepancy or index score scatter beyond which the FSIQ becomes invalid, unreliable, and uninterpretable. We do believe, however, that when great variability or discrepancy characterizes the primary index scores or the subtest scaled scores, the FSIQ *alone* is insufficient to describe a child's intellectual abilities. However, reliance on *any* single score is never recommended for describing a child's intellectual abilities or identifying his or her strengths and needs.

Recent research indicates that the FSIQ has equal construct validity regardless of primary index score discrepancies. The construct and predictive validity of the FSIQ is independent of the discrepancy (Daniel, 2007). Similarly, the construct and predictive validity of the primary index scores is independent of the amount of discrepancy between subtests (Daniel, 2009). We believe the same to be true of other index scores, such as the Nonverbal Index and the General Ability Index. Furthermore, it is quite typical to have a discrepancy of greater than 1.5 *SD*s (23 points or more) between two primary index scores. Arturo Orsini, who was a leading Wechsler scholar in Italy before his untimely death in 2014, conducted research to indicate that differences of 23 or more points are common within the normal population. Orsini, Pezzuti, and Hulbert (2014) found that 51.6% of the Italian WISC–IV standardization sample had discrepancies of 23 or more points between their highest and lowest index score, and used a respected formula to estimate a similar percentage for the American WISC–IV sample. For the WISC–V, we found that 56.6% of the normative sample (i.e., 1,246 of the 2,200

children) had such a discrepancy. Similarly, 52.5% of special group study cases (261 of the 497 children from these groups) had such a discrepancy. Given the vast evidence in support of the predictive validity of *g* and FSIQ (Daniel, 2007; Deary & Johnson, 2010; Deary, Strand, Smith, & Fernandes, 2007; W. Johnson, Deary, & Iacono, 2009; S. B. Kaufman et al., 2012), it seems counterintuitive to assume that for about 50% of children the FSIQ is not valid. Moreover, because more specific domains of intellectual ability do not show the same *broad* degree of predictive validity as does *g* (L. S. Gottfredson, 2008; Hartmann, Larsen, & Nyborg, 2009; Kotz, Watkins, & McDermott, 2008; Reeve & Charles, 2008), the FSIQ provides essential, clinically rich information when one attempts to understand the expression of intelligent behavior in real-world settings (Jacobson, Delis, Hamilton, Bondi, & Salmon, 2004).

With respect to the FSIQ's reliability in the presence of relatively large discrepancies among primary index scores, we do not find evidence that the FSIQ becomes unreliable in these circumstances. Table 4.3 of the *WISC–V Technical and Interpretive Manual* lists the subtest reliability coefficients for special groups. For the special groups with larger scatter among primary index scores, such as intellectually gifted, specific learning disorder-reading and written expression, and autism spectrum disorder without language impairment, the subtest reliabilities are comparable with those of other special groups with smaller scatter among primary index scores (e.g., intellectual disability–mild, intellectual disability–moderate, borderline intellectual functioning). Because these coefficients are comparable with those of the normative sample, it is more likely that the FSIQ reliability for special samples would be similar to that of the normative sample.

Despite the research and psychometric support for interpreting FSIQ, there are often valid clinical reasons for paying careful attention to variability among the WISC–V primary index scores. Dawn Flanagan articulated some of these reasons cogently (personal communication,

April 23, 2015) in response to the finding that 23-point discrepancies (or even 30-point discrepancies) are common when comparing an individual's lowest and highest index scores:

> While it is certainly important to have actual base rate data when making decisions about whether or not the difference between the lowest and highest scores is unusual in the general population, it is equally important to consider whether or not the FSIQ is actually a good summary score for the individual from a practical standpoint. For example, a 30-point difference between lowest and highest Indexes may not be unusual in the general population; but if the minimum score is deficient, and the maximum score is high average, and the FSIQ is average, then I don't find the descriptor "average" to be an adequate summary of the individual's cognitive capabilities. The implications of interpreting only the average FSIQ may be a lack of understanding of why the individual struggles when performing some "real world" tasks. Hypothetically, if you could remove the attenuating effects of the deficient performance on the FSIQ, the individual's intellectual capacity (as represented by the FSIQ) would be higher and more consistent with the individual's true capabilities, which may be observed when the weaker abilities or processes are minimized through compensatory strategies, accommodations, curricular/instructional modifications, and the like. Yes, our assumption was that a 23-point difference was probably not all that common and we were wrong about that. But when 23 points was used, clinicians were more likely to interpret at the index score level, rather than the FSIQ level, which assists in understanding reason for referral, making diagnoses, and developing educational program plans. I'm not questioning the reliability or validity of the FSIQ (and I'm not questioning the importance of base rate data); I'm simply commenting on the practical utility of a FSIQ (made up of both deficient and average or better performances) in assisting us in understanding an individual's cognitive capabilities. In the forthcoming *Essentials of WISC–V Assessment*, Vinny Alfonso and I will be trying to strike a balance between

the art and the science of test interpretation … which is Alan's "intelligent testing" approach. That means that we will not have strict cut offs for interpret/don't interpret. Rather, we will attempt to assist the reader in exercising clinical judgment based on a number of factors—and base rate data are among those factors.

Behind the Scenes

The subtests that contribute to the FSIQ and the relative contributions of subtests drawn from the primary index scales are carefully selected. The test's developers considered a wide range of factors when determining which subtests would contribute to the FSIQ. The factors included:

- Reliability
- Subtest *g* loadings
- Factor (representing the primary index scales) *g* loadings
- Construct coverage and subtest redundancy
- Other measures and common practice
- Expert input
- Internal stakeholder input
- Administration time
- Relationship with achievement
- Consistency of the FSIQ composition with the WISC–IV FSIQ
- Relationship with the FSIQ of the WISC–IV
- Consistency of the FSIQ composition with related Wechsler intelligence scales (i.e., the Wechsler Preschool and Primary Scale of Intelligence–Fourth Edition (WPPSI–IV; Wechsler, 2012) and the Wechsler Adult Intelligence Scale–Fourth Edition (WAIS–IV; Wechsler, 2008)

Nonverbal Index

The Nonverbal Index offers an estimate of overall ability for children who have expressive issues (e.g., language disorders, autism spectrum disorder with language impairment, English-language learner). The Nonverbal Index provides a more comprehensive choice for estimating overall ability than the Visual Spatial Index or the Fluid

Reasoning Index in these situations, because it includes subtests from every primary domain except for Verbal Comprehension.

Chapter 4 of the *WISC–V Technical and Interpretive Manual* indicates that the Nonverbal Index possesses reliability similar to that of the FSIQ. Evidence in Chapter 5 of the *WISC–V Technical and Interpretive Manual* indicates that the Nonverbal Index demonstrates similar classification accuracy as that of the FSIQ for children with intellectual disabilities and appears promising for use with children identified with conditions (e.g., autism spectrum disorder with language impairment) or situations (e.g., English-language learner) that raise concerns about (English) expressive language.

The Nonverbal Index can be interpreted as an estimate of general intellectual ability that minimizes expressive demands for children with such conditions or who are learning English. It is not a "language free" measure but should be described as "language reduced" (Ortiz, Ochoa, & Dynda, 2012) because it still requires the child to comprehend English subtest instructions.

General Ability Index

Relative to the FSIQ, the General Ability Index offers an estimate of intellectual ability that is less influenced by working memory and processing speed. Chapter 4 of the *WISC–V Technical and Interpretive Manual* indicates that it possesses reliability similar to that of the FSIQ.

The General Ability Index can be interpreted as an estimate of general intellectual ability that minimizes working memory and processing speed demands and is useful for situations in which neurodevelopmental disorders that are associated with difficulties in these areas are present. Children with such issues can obtain relatively lower FSIQ scores than children without these issues, because subtests from the Working Memory and/or Processing Speed domains contribute to the FSIQ. For example, working memory displays sensitivity to specific learning disorders, attention-deficit/hyperactivity disorder

(ADHD), language disorders, and autism spectrum disorder (Archibald & Gathercole, 2006a, 2006b; Belleville, Ménard, Mottron, & Ménard, 2006; Passolunghi, 2006; Pickering, 2006; Roodenrys, 2006; Swanson, 2006); and processing speed is sensitive to specific learning disorders, ADHD, and autism spectrum disorder (Compton, Fuchs, Fuchs, Lambert, & Hamlett, 2012; Mayes & Calhoun, 2007). In these situations, the General Ability Index may reveal meaningful differences between intellectual ability and other cognitive functions (e.g., achievement, memory, or executive functions) that are obscured when the FSIQ is used as a comparison score.

We believe the General Ability Index is most informative when reported with the FSIQ and the Cognitive Proficiency Index as well as the other primary index scores. Working memory and processing speed have proven again and again to be critical components of overall intellectual ability (Blalock & McCabe, 2011; Bunting, 2006; Dodonova & Dodonov, 2012), and excluding them generally results in a less comprehensive score with reduced construct coverage and predictive validity (Rowe, Kingsley, & Thompson, 2010). In most cases, the main utility of the General Ability Index is as a comparison score, not a stand-alone measure of intellectual ability.

Specific Composite Scores

There are a variety of specific composite scores available for the WISC–V within the published test, described and discussed in the sections that follow. New index scores were created for this book for special theoretical and practical situations. These additional index scores are available in this book and in the downloadable resources: www.wiley.com/go/itwiscv. They were developed based on specific theoretical approaches and practical considerations.

WISC–V Published Index Scores

The primary, ancillary, and complementary index scores are included in the published test. A total of five primary index scores, five ancillary index scores, and three complementary index scores appear in the published test.

The primary index scores are derived based on the factor analysis that specifies the latent traits measured by the test. A vast amount of other evidence supports their validity and clinical utility. They permit description of discrete cognitive abilities that cannot be achieved by reporting a global composite score.

The ancillary index scores provide additional information about WISC–V performance for special purposes. Of the five ancillary index scores, three (i.e., the Nonverbal Index, General Ability Index, and Cognitive Proficiency Index) are described in the section of this chapter titled "Global Composite Scores," and two (i.e., the Quantitative Reasoning Index and the Auditory Working Memory Index) are discussed in this section.

The complementary index scores provide further information about additional cognitive abilities that may be assessed if there is a clinical need. There are three complementary index scores.

A basic description of each index score is provided in Table 8.1. The index scores are conceptualized from three different theoretical perspectives, Cattell-Horn-Carroll (CHC), Lurian, and school neuropsychology perspectives, in Chapters 9, 11, and 12 of this volume, respectively. Refer to those chapters depending on your theoretical orientation.

If you are a graduate student or new psychologist, we recommend reading all three chapters—as well as Chapter 10 (interpreting from a cognitive neuroscience perspective) and Chapter 13 (interpreting using George McCloskey's process approach)—to help determine which method of WISC–V interpretation is most conducive to your philosophy and personal orientation regarding assessments and interventions for children and adolescents who are referred for evaluation.

Additional Index and Process Scores in This Book

A number of additional index and process scores are provided in this book and in the

Table 8.1 Basic Descriptions of the WISC–V Index Scores

Index Score	Description
Verbal Comprehension Index (primary)	Best represents acquired knowledge, verbal reasoning, and verbal concept formation.
Visual Spatial Index (primary)	Measures visual-spatial processing, part–whole relationship integration and synthesis, and visual-motor integration
Fluid Reasoning Index (primary)	Best represents inductive and fluid reasoning, broad visual intelligence, conceptual thinking, simultaneous processing, and classification ability
Working Memory Index (primary)	Measures auditory and visual working memory, and ability to withstand proactive interference
Processing Speed Index (primary)	Best represents processing speed, especially quick scanning and discrimination of simple visual information
Quantitative Reasoning Index (ancillary)	Provides an indicator of a child's quantitative reasoning skills
Auditory Working Memory Index (ancillary)	Measures auditory working memory and ability to withstand proactive interference
	Provides a pure measure of auditory working memory, whereas the Working Memory Index provides a measure of working memory from mixed modalities
Naming Speed Index (complementary)	Provides a broad measure of rapid automatized naming drawn from a variety of tasks that require quick and efficient verbal retrieval
Symbol Translation Index (complementary)	Measures visual-verbal associative memory using a variety of conditions (immediate, delayed, and delayed recognition)
Storage and Retrieval Index (complementary)	Provides a broad measure of long-term storage, retrieval accuracy, and fluency

downloadable resources: www.wiley.com/go/ itwiscv. The additional index and process scores were developed based on specific theoretical approaches and practical considerations. The norms for these additional index and process scores are available in the downloadable resources: www.wiley.com/go/itwiscv, which contains appendix matter and the *WISC–V Interpretive Assistant 1.0.*

Table 8.2 provides the subtest composition of the additional index and process scores and the locations of interpretive information for the additional index and process scores based on their theoretical or practical use. Table 8.3 presents the reliability coefficients of the additional index and process scores by age group and overall. The average reliability coefficients were calculated using the same procedures described in Chapter 4 of the *WISC–V Technical and Interpretive Manual.* Similarly, Table 8.4 provides the standard errors of measurement (*SEMs*) of the additional index and process scores by age group and overall.

STEP-BY-STEP SCORE ANALYSIS TO INFORM INTERPRETATION

Our score analysis approach is grounded in five principles.

1. Interpretation relies on both normative-based and intrapersonal-based (ipsative) understanding of intellectual ability.
2. Composite scores (i.e., global composites such as the FSIQ and specific composites such as Fluid Reasoning Index) are the primary level of analysis, because they are the most reliable and comprehensive representatives of the child's performance.
3. Examination of the parts helps to clarify the meaning of the whole. Just as understanding item-level performance clarifies subtest-level results, understanding subtest-level performance clarifies index-level results.
4. Interpretation should be flexible to fit the real constraints and problems in testing situations.

Table 8.2 Subtest Composition and Interpretive Information Location of Additional Index and Process Scores

Additional Index or Process Score	Subtest Composition	Interpretive Information Location
Verbal (Expanded Crystallized) Index (Expanded *Gc*)	Similarities + Vocabulary + Information + Comprehension	Chapter 9
General Verbal Information (*Gc*-K0)	Information + Comprehension + Picture Concepts	Chapter 9
Expanded Fluid Index (Expanded *Gf*)	Matrix Reasoning + Figure Weights + Picture Concepts + Arithmetic	Chapter 9
Induction (*Gf*-I)	Matrix Reasoning + Picture Concepts + Similarities	Chapter 9
Working Memory Capacity (*Gsm*-MW)	Digit Span Backward + Digit Span Sequencing + Letter–Number Sequencing + Picture Span + Arithmetic	Chapter 9
Perceptual Speed (*Gs*-P)	Symbol Search + Cancellation	Chapter 9
Matrix Reasoning Simultaneous	Drawn from the matrix items of Matrix Reasoning	Chapter 11
Matrix Reasoning Successive	Drawn from the series completion items of Matrix Reasoning	Chapter 11
Simultaneous Processing Index	Matrix Reasoning Simultaneous process score + Figure Weights + Picture Concepts	Chapter 11
Successive Processing Index	Digit Span Backward + Digit Span Sequencing + Letter–Number Sequencing + Matrix Reasoning Successive process score	Chapter 11

Table 8.3   Reliability Coefficients of Additional Index and Process Scores

Index Score	6	7	8	9	10	11	12	13	14	15	16	Overall[a]
Verbal (Expanded Crystallized) Index	.93	.95	.94	.95	.95	.94	.96	.95	.96	.95	.96	.95
Gc-K0 (General Verbal Information)	.90	.91	.90	.91	.91	.90	.93	.91	.92	.92	.90	.91
Expanded Fluid Index	.95	.94	.95	.94	.95	.94	.96	.94	.95	.95	.95	.95
Gf-I (Induction)	.94	.91	.92	.91	.92	.90	.93	.92	.91	.91	.91	.92
Gsm-MW (Working Memory Capacity)	.96	.94	.94	.94	.94	.94	.95	.94	.95	.95	.95	.95
Gs-P (Perceptual Speed)	.85	.87	.85	.86	.86	.87	.80	.81	.88	.88	.88	.86
Matrix Reasoning Simultaneous	.82	.83	.83	.73	.76	.68	.77	.75	.75	.74	.81	.77
Matrix Reasoning Successive	.72	.64	.67	.63	.72	.63	.71	.60	.69	.65	.71	.67
Simultaneous Processing Index	.93	.91	.92	.90	.92	.89	.92	.90	.91	.90	.91	.91
Successive Processing Index	.94	.91	.90	.89	.90	.88	.92	.88	.91	.91	.92	.91

[a]Average reliability coefficients were calculated with Fisher's z transformation.

Table 8.4   Standard Errors of Measurement of Additional Index and Process Scores

Index Score	6	7	8	9	10	11	12	13	14	15	16	Overall
Verbal (Expanded Crystallized) Index	3.97	3.35	3.67	3.35	3.35	3.67	3.00	3.35	3.00	3.35	3.00	3.38
Gc-K0 (General Verbal Information)	4.74	4.50	4.74	4.50	4.50	4.74	3.97	4.50	4.24	4.24	4.74	4.50
Expanded Fluid Index	3.35	3.67	3.35	3.67	3.35	3.67	3.00	3.67	3.35	3.35	3.35	3.44
Gf-I (Induction)	3.67	4.50	4.24	4.50	4.24	4.74	3.97	4.24	4.50	4.50	4.50	4.34
Gsm-MW (Working Memory Capacity)	3.00	3.67	3.67	3.67	3.67	3.67	3.35	3.67	3.35	3.35	3.35	3.50
Gs-P (Perceptual Speed)	5.81	5.41	5.81	5.61	5.61	5.41	6.71	6.54	5.20	5.20	5.20	5.70
Matrix Reasoning Simultaneous	1.27	1.24	1.24	1.56	1.47	1.70	1.44	1.50	1.50	1.53	1.31	1.44
Matrix Reasoning Successive	1.59	1.80	1.72	1.82	1.59	1.82	1.62	1.90	1.67	1.77	1.62	1.72
Simultaneous Processing Index	3.67	4.50	4.74	4.97	4.74	5.20	4.24	5.20	4.50	4.50	4.24	4.61
Successive Processing Index	3.97	4.50	4.24	4.74	4.24	4.97	4.24	4.74	4.50	4.74	4.50	4.50

5. A single score should not be used alone to make decisions about a child. Test results should be used to generate hypotheses about the child's intellectual abilities and should be integrated with information obtained from a variety of other sources, including: the referral question; psychosocial, medical, and educational background and history; cultural and linguistic background; testing session behaviors and observations; and other results drawn from an appropriate battery of instruments. It is recommended that other sources of information be used to corroborate test results when making inferences about the child's abilities, strengths, and needs.

The approach facilitates interpretive case formulations from varied theoretical and clinical perspectives. In this book, and in the downloadable resources (www.wiley.com/go/itwiscv), we offer additional scores or data according to the primary theoretical orientation used by the practitioner and according to the referral question.

We agree with Kamphaus, Winsor, Rowe, and Kim's (2011) thesis that test design should occur based on a strong theoretical foundation. However, intellectual theories are in the process of evolving, so they are by definition incomplete and imperfect in their conceptualization. As an example, CHC theory and terminology has evolved considerably over its existence, and its development is projected to continue (Flanagan, Ortiz, & Alfonso, 2013; Schneider & Flanagan, 2015; Schneider & McGrew, 2012).

In addition to theory, clinical and practical utility should guide interpretation. At the genesis of the Wechsler intelligence scales, David Wechsler provided scores for both verbal and nonverbal ability as well as the FSIQ. He observed that both types of scores were clinically and practically useful and essential. This approach was contrary to the predominant thinking of the day, as it went beyond the provision of a single score to describe general intellectual ability. Excluding clinical and practical utility from consideration may lead to missing key information about the child's ability and to measuring aspects that are less relevant to the child's everyday functioning.

We offer these interpretive steps as guidelines for examiners to follow, but not rigidly and not if they have an alternative interpretive system that they prefer. The 17 case reports that appear in Part IV of this book illustrate WISC–V interpretation from eclectic vantage points. Some of the expert clinicians who wrote the reports followed these steps, or at least followed most of them, whereas others did not. These reports exemplify the notion that diversity and eclectic approaches to WISC–V interpretation reflect, at least in our opinion, *intelligent testing* in the 21st century.

Step 1a. Select the Appropriate Global Composite Score to Describe Overall Intellectual Ability

Three global composite scores are available: the FSIQ, the Nonverbal Index, and the General Ability Index. Each may be appropriate to describe overall intellectual ability, depending on the clinical situation and the purpose of the evaluation.

The FSIQ is the most comprehensive and reliable of all of the global scores. A large body of research accrued across 75 years supports its predictive validity and clinical utility. Unless there is a compelling reason to deviate, the FSIQ is the default global score of choice.

The Nonverbal Index is appropriate and informative in a number of situations. If the child is an English-language learner and can comprehend subtest instructions in English, the Nonverbal Index is the global score of choice. It is important to note that the WISC–V Nonverbal Index is not "language free" but should be described as "language reduced" because it still requires the child to comprehend English subtest instructions. A good evaluation also incorporates the methods and models described by Ortiz et al. (2012) rather than relying on the Nonverbal Index alone.

A number of diagnostic scenarios described in the *Diagnostic and Statistical Manual of Mental Disorders, Fifth Edition* (*DSM–5*; American Psychiatric Association, 2013) require use of a score that summarizes nonverbal ability. Become familiar with the diagnostic criteria of all disorders under consideration, and select accordingly.

The *DSM–5* recommends that a nonverbal ability score be compared with language scores to establish that the language impairments are in excess of the child's intellectual limitations to establish a diagnosis of language disorder. So, the Nonverbal Index is the most informative global composite if a diagnosis of language disorder is currently under consideration for a child with an already established intellectual disability.

The Nonverbal Index might also be selected when conducting intellectual ability assessment of a child with language impairment when seeking to establish a diagnosis of intellectual disability or to identify a cognitive developmental delay. In this situation, you might use the Nonverbal Index to determine presence of intellectual disability or cognitive developmental delay. The classification accuracy of the Nonverbal Index is similar to that of the FSIQ, making it a viable option for such purposes. (See Chapter 5 of the *WISC–V Technical and Interpretive Manual.*)

Other situations are less clear cut. Initial evaluations where both intellectual disability and language disorder are possibilities might be best conducted through reporting the FSIQ *and* the Nonverbal Index.

Evaluations of children with autism spectrum disorder present a number of situations where selection of the global composite score may be challenging. Depending on the referral question and degree of language impairment, the FSIQ, the Nonverbal Index, or the General Ability Index may be most descriptive and useful. Several examples follow.

When evaluating for specific learning disorder in a child with an established diagnosis of autism spectrum disorder with significant accompanying language impairment, the language impairment can result in decreased differences between the FSIQ and achievement scores. In this situation, the Nonverbal Index may be useful if an ability–achievement discrepancy is required by the local education agency and the use of the Nonverbal Index is permitted. If significant language impairment is not present, however, and the primary index scores are relatively consistent, perhaps with weaknesses in Fluid Reasoning and Working Memory, the FSIQ is more appropriate because the weaknesses are less characteristic of the disorder in general and more specific to the child. For many of these children, though, the Processing Speed Index is a significant intrapersonal weakness. The General Ability Index may be the most appropriate choice for an ability–achievement discrepancy in this situation.

Some gifted advocates assert that the General Ability Index, an estimate of overall ability with reduced emphasis on working memory and processing speed, is an acceptable score to use in gifted program evaluations (National Association for Gifted Children, 2010; Rimm et al., 2008). There are indications that this is reasonable when using the WISC–V. In particular, recent research suggests that processing speed

can improve when children who are intellectually gifted receive proper gifted education (Duan, Shi, & Zhou, 2010). For this reason, the General Ability Index may better represent intellectual ability in the application process for gifted education programs if processing speed is a weakness. The FSIQ has been found more predictive of achievement than the General Ability Index and could also be reported in this situation if placement in accelerated educational programs is under consideration (Rowe, Kingsley, & Thompson, 2010).

The General Ability Index is also recommended as the global score for comparison with other cognitive functions (e.g., achievement, memory, or executive functions) for children with a variety of other neurodevelopmental disorders characterized by working memory and/or processing speed deficits. The deficits associated with these disorders (e.g., specific learning disorder, ADHD, language disorder, and autism spectrum disorder) could obscure important differences between ability and those other areas. In these situations, the General Ability Index may reveal meaningful differences that are obscured when the FSIQ is used as the global comparison score.

Quick References 8.1 and 8.2 list several examples of appropriate uses of the Nonverbal Index and the General Ability Index.

Also consider using the Visual Spatial Index or the Fluid Reasoning Index if more pervasive intellectual deficits are present across primary index scores other than the Verbal Comprehension Index.

Step 1b. Report and Describe the Global Composite Score

Qualitative descriptors characterize the level of performance relative to the child's same-age peers. Many alternate qualitative descriptor systems have been created by authors of interpretive texts for the Wechsler scales (including us and our colleagues: Flanagan & Kaufman, 2009;

QUICK REFERENCE 8.1: EXAMPLES OF APPROPRIATE USES OF THE NONVERBAL INDEX

- Intellectual ability assessment of a child with low cognitive ability and expressive language issues: In this situation, you might choose to use the Nonverbal Index to determine presence of intellectual disability or cognitive developmental delay
- Differential diagnosis of language disorder that is in excess of intellectual limitations: compare the Nonverbal Index with language scores
- Establishing comorbidity of intellectual disability and language disorder
- Intellectual ability assessment of a child who is an English-language learner and can comprehend spoken instructions in English
- Differential diagnosis between autism spectrum disorder and intellectual disability
- Establishing comorbidity of autism spectrum disorder and intellectual disability
- Establishing diagnosis of a specific learning disorder in a child with autism spectrum disorder and significant accompanying language impairment, if an ability–achievement discrepancy is required by the local education agency

---

QUICK REFERENCE 8.2: EXAMPLES OF APPROPRIATE USES OF THE GENERAL ABILITY INDEX

- Intellectual ability assessment of a child for gifted program admissions evaluations. Report with the FSIQ if admission to accelerated educational programs is also under consideration.
- If an ability–achievement discrepancy is required by a local education agency and working memory and processing speed are lowered due to the likely presence of a specific learning disorder
- If an ability–achievement discrepancy is required by a local education agency to establish specific learning disability classification and working memory and processing speed are lowered due to comorbid ADHD or autism spectrum disorder (without significant accompanying language impairments)

A. S. Kaufman & Kaufman, 2004; Lichtenberger & Kaufman, 2013; Raiford & Coalson, 2014); however, new descriptors are now used that provide parallel structure and eliminate confusing terms such as *borderline*. The new and traditional qualitative descriptions appear in Table 6.3 of the *WISC–V Technical and Interpretive Manual* and are listed in Quick Reference 8.3. The traditional descriptors are listed to allow comparison to past results, if necessary.

Create a table to report the selected measure of overall intellectual ability. This table will also be used to report the selected index scores

at Step 2. Appendix B (in the downloadable resources: www.wiley.com/go/itwiscv) includes a sample table for this purpose. The table should contain columns for the composite score name, standard score, percentile rank, confidence interval, and qualitative descriptive classification.

Transfer the values for the standard score, percentile rank, and confidence interval from the Record Form Summary page, being sure to note below the table the confidence level (i.e., 90 or 95%) upon which the confidence intervals were based. The Q-global scoring software also can be used to generate this information.

QUICK REFERENCE 8.3: NEW AND TRADITIONAL DESCRIPTORS OF COMPOSITE SCORES

Composite Score Range	New Qualitative Descriptor	Traditional Qualitative Descriptor (For Comparison; No Longer Used)
130 and higher	Extremely High	Very Superior
120–129	Very High	Superior
110–119	High Average	High Average
90–119	Average	Average
80–89	Low Average	Low Average
70–79	Very Low	Borderline
69 and lower	Extremely Low	Extremely Low

Source: Adapted from Table 6.3 of Wechsler (2014), *WISC–V Technical and Interpretive Manual.*

If you enter the selected global composite score in the *WISC–V Interpretive Assistant 1.0* on the WISC–V tab, the program provides the percentile rank based on the theoretical normal curve and the qualitative descriptor. All selected composite scores from Steps 2 and 3 may be entered on this tab to generate similar information.

After you have listed the selected score(s) in the table, provide paragraphs that describe the score(s). If you are reporting both the FSIQ and the General Ability Index, provide the descriptions of both scores. The necessary descriptions of each global composite score appear in the first sections of this chapter.

Perform Step 2 only if the General Ability Index was selected as the global score; otherwise, proceed to Step 3.

Step 2a. Report and Describe the Cognitive Proficiency Index

The Cognitive Proficiency Index provides an estimate of cognitive information processing efficiency. Working memory and processing speed subtests contribute to the Cognitive Proficiency Index. These abilities are related because quick processing speed facilitates information processing before decay from working memory occurs (Wechsler, 2014). On the other hand,

slow processing speed ability results in slower information processing and additional opportunity for decay of that information from memory. The Cognitive Proficiency Index is most useful in the context of a pairwise difference comparison with the General Ability Index.

If you are reporting the Cognitive Proficiency Index, transfer the appropriate information from the Record Form Ancillary and Complementary Analysis page into the table you created to report composite scores, using the same procedure as was used for the global composite scores. The Q-global scoring software also can be used to generate this information. If you enter the Cognitive Proficiency Index on the WISC–V tab of the *WISC–V Interpretive Assistant 1.0*, the program provides analogous information to that given for the global composite scores.

Step 2b. Evaluate Pairwise Discrepancy Comparisons with the FSIQ and the Cognitive Proficiency Index

To evaluate the differences between the General Ability Index and the FSIQ, and the General Ability Index and the Cognitive Proficiency Index, use the Ancillary and Complementary Analysis page of the Record Form or the Q-global WISC–V scoring software.

Examine the differences for statistical significance and frequency of occurrence in the normative sample. The critical values and base rates for pairwise difference comparisons are provided in Tables C.10 and C.11 of the *WISC–V Administration and Scoring Manual Supplement*.

Table C.10 provides the relevant critical values for both comparisons at the .01, .05, .10, and .15 significance levels, by age group, and overall. A scan of all values corresponding to .05 indicates that any General Ability Index–FSIQ difference greater than 3 is always significant at the .05 level, so this is an intelligent rule of thumb. Statistically significant differences occur frequently in both normative samples and in clinical populations (Sattler, 2008). Similarly, a General Ability Index–Cognitive Proficiency Index discrepancy of greater than 10 points is always significant at the .05 level. Consider using these intelligent rules of thumb to simplify score analysis and interpretation.

level. Although there are minor fluctuations across ability levels, in general, if the difference is greater than 7 points, the discrepancy between these two scores is unusual.

The discrepancies between the General Ability Index and the Cognitive Proficiency Index vary by ability level and direction of the difference. For those with below-average General Ability Index scores, it is much more common to have a General Ability Index score that is much higher than the Cognitive Proficiency Index than to have the reverse pattern. The opposite is true for those with above-average General Ability Index scores, for whom it is much more common to have a General Ability Index score that is lower than the Cognitive Proficiency Index. There is an easy rule of thumb for this discrepancy when the General Ability Index is average and clear rules of thumb for those with below-average and above-average General Ability Index scores, but those vary by direction of the difference. Consider using these intelligent rules of thumb to simplify score analysis and interpretation.

Intelligent Rules of Thumb

Significant Discrepancies with the General Ability Index at the .05 Level

- A General Ability Index–FSIQ difference greater than 3 points is always significant at the .05 level.
- A General Ability Index–Cognitive Proficiency Index difference greater than 10 points is always significant at the .05 level.

Intelligent Rules of Thumb

Rare Discrepancies with the General Ability Index

- General Ability Index–FSIQ differences are rare at around 7 points, occurring in about 5% to 10% of the sample.
- For an average General Ability Index (90–109), regardless of direction, a difference of 17 or more points is always unusual, occurring in less than 10% of the sample.
- General Ability Index–Cognitive Proficiency Index differences that are rare vary by direction for above- and below-average General Ability Index scores:
  - For a below-average General Ability Index (less than 90), it is very common to have a Cognitive Proficiency Index that

---

Table C.11 of the *WISC–V Administration and Scoring Manual Supplement* provides the base rate information, by overall sample and by General Ability Index ability level, of the General Ability Index discrepancies with the FSIQ and the Cognitive Proficiency Index. Scanning the values across ability levels indicates that any difference greater than 7 points occurs in about 5% to 10% of the sample at every ability is much higher than a General Ability Index. If the difference is in this direction, a difference of 25 or more points is always unusual (<10%).

- In this situation, it is much less common to have a General Ability Index that is higher than a Cognitive Proficiency Index, and a difference of 8 or more points here is always unusual (<10%).
- For an above-average General Ability Index (110 or higher), the reverse pattern is true. It is very common to have a General Ability Index that is much higher than a Cognitive Proficiency Index. If the difference is in this direction, a difference of greater than 28 or more points is always unusual, occurring in less than 5% to 10% of the sample.
- In this situation, it is much less common to have a Cognitive Proficiency Index that is higher than a General Ability Index, and a difference of 8 or more points here is always unusual (<5–10%).

Hypotheses: If the General Ability Index–FSIQ difference is statistically significant and unusual, the influence of working memory and processing speed on intellectual ability may result in a difference in the child's overall performance. If the General Ability Index–Cognitive Proficiency Index difference is statistically significant and unusual, general ability and cognitive proficiency ability may not be commensurate (Wechsler, 2014).

Step 3a. Select the Index Scores (Specific Composite Scores)

We strongly recommend reporting all available primary index scores, because they are derived based on the factor analysis that specifies the latent traits measured by the test. A vast array of other evidence supports their validity and clinical utility. They permit description of discrete cognitive abilities that cannot be achieved by reporting a global composite score.

We also strongly recommend routinely deriving and reporting the Symbol Translation Index. It is a strong measure of learning, which is critical when assessing school-age children. Its correlation with the FSIQ (.55) is actually higher than that of the Processing Speed Index (.54). Its correlation with the Kaufman Test of Educational Achievement–Third Edition (KTEA–3; A. S. Kaufman & Kaufman, 2014) Academic Skills Battery composite (.46) is higher than that of the Processing Speed Index (.35). Similarly, its correlation with the Wechsler Individual Achievement Test–Third Edition (WIAT–III; Pearson, 2009b) Total Achievement composite (.39) is higher than that of the Processing Speed Index (.34) and almost as high as that of the Fluid Reasoning Index (.40). It also shows strong sensitivity to specific learning disorders of every type, but not to ADHD (see the special group studies in chapter 5 of the *WISC–V Technical and Interpretive Manual*).

Index score interpretation is shaped by your theoretical orientation. Conceptualization of the primary index scores depends on your theoretical perspective. Refer to Chapter 9 for CHC, Chapter 11 for Lurian conceptualizations, Chapter 12 for conceptualizations using Dan Miller's school neuropsychology framework, or Chapter 13 for George McCloskey's neuropsychologically oriented process approach.

For example, if your theoretical orientation is CHC theory, you might describe the Visual Spatial Index as a measure of *Gv*, especially Vz (visualization), but if you are using a school neuropsychology approach, you may conceptualize it as measuring neuropsychological constructs including visual-motor construction, problem solving, cognitive flexibility, reasoning, and planning.

Your theoretical orientation may also call for use of some of the additional index scores in this

book and in the downloadable resources: www
.wiley.com/go/itwiscv. For example, if you conceptualize performance using CHC theory, you
may wish to obtain the additional index scores
described in Chapter 9 that provide measures of
the CHC constructs. The *WISC–V Interpretive
Assistant 1.0*, available with the other downloadable resources at the Internet address provided,
calculates all available additional index scores
based upon your entry of subtest scaled scores.

Finally, the referral question and clinical situation may call for use of other index scores from
the published test. For example, if you are using the WISC–V within a battery to identify a
specific learning disorder and inform intervention recommendations, you may notice an average scaled score on Picture Span but a low score
on Digit Span and suspect a cognitive weakness
in auditory working memory. You might then administer Letter–Number Sequencing to obtain
the Auditory Working Memory Index, because
auditory working memory tasks are generally
more related to academic achievement than are
visual working memory tasks, and the two modalities of working memory may be differentially
sensitive to specific learning disorders. All selected index scores are reported and described in
Step 3b.

Step 3b. Report and Describe the Index Scores

Include the selected index scores in the same
table you created to report the global composite
score for overall intellectual ability. List the index
score name, standard score, percentile rank, confidence interval, and qualitative descriptive classification. Transfer the figures for the standard
score, percentile rank, and confidence interval
from the Record Form Summary page.

If you select any of the additional index scores
in this book, use the *WISC–V Interpretive Assistant 1.0* to enter the appropriate subtest scaled
scores on the WISC–V tab. The Step 3 tab automatically calculates each additional index score

for which all of the necessary subtest scaled scores
are present.

After you have listed the selected score(s) in
the table for your report, provide paragraphs that
describe the index score(s) based on your theoretical orientation (see Step 3a). You should
also seek to understand the relations between the
building blocks of the index scores (i.e., the subtest scaled scores; see Step 8).

An extreme discrepancy between the two subtests that contribute to an index score indicates
that the score is a summary of diverse abilities.
It does not indicate that the index score is invalid, unreliable, or should not be interpreted.
Describe the index score as a summary of diverse
abilities, seek to understand the subtest scaled
scores that contribute to that index score, and interpret discrepancies based on that index score
with caution. Recommendations about pairwise
subtest comparisons are provided in Step 8.

Step 4. Report and Describe the Subtest Scaled and Standard Scores

The subtest scaled and standard scores are essential because they are the basic building blocks
that constitute all other scores. Interpretation of
composite score performance is enhanced by understanding those basic building blocks. Furthermore, subtest scaled and standard scores should
be reported because they are adjusted by age and
therefore have the same meaning for any subtest at any age. Most practitioners list the subtest
scaled and standard scores before the index scores
and the FSIQ in their reports for this reason.

Qualitative descriptors for subtest scaled
scores (which are used for primary and secondary subtests) are not included in our score
analysis approach. The range of subtest scaled
scores (1–19) does not allow for fine discrimination between scores when they are converted
to percentile ranks. For those practitioners who
wish to include qualitative descriptors for subtest
scaled scores, examples of subtest qualitative
descriptor systems appear in Sattler (2008).

Qualitative descriptors are applied to the subtest standard scores, because the range is much greater (45–155). The same descriptors are used as those for the composite scores. These appear on the Step 4 tab whenever a complementary subtest standard score is entered.

Create a table to report and describe the subtest scaled and standard scores. Appendix B (in the downloadable resources: www.wiley .com/go/itwiscv) includes a sample table for this purpose. The table should contain columns for the subtest name, subtest scaled score, and percentile rank in a theoretical normal distribution. If you enter a subtest scaled or standard score on the WISC–V tab of the *WISC–V Interpretive Assistant 1.0*, the program provides the percentile rank based on the theoretical normal distribution.

Step 5. Evaluate Index-Level Strengths and Weaknesses

Intra-individual strengths and weaknesses comparisons provide useful information and minimize the likelihood of Type I error relative to several pairwise comparisons (Grégoire, Coalson, & Zhu, 2011; Longman, 2004; Naglieri & Paolitto, 2005). Strengths and weaknesses are identified by comparing the index scores with an indicator of overall performance. If a primary index score is significantly greater than the comparison score it may represent an intrapersonal cognitive strength, and if it is significantly less it may represent an intrapersonal cognitive weakness.

We recommend using the FSIQ as the comparison score. The FSIQ is the best indicator of overall cognitive ability (Wechsler, 2014). It is already available and is a simple option. Another choice is available (i.e., the mean of the five primary index scores in the published test), but this option requires additional calculation and use of relatively complex tables. In addition, validity of the mean of the five primary index scores as an indicator of overall ability is not well established compared with the FSIQ, and reliability

estimates are not available for that score. Finally, since we recommend deriving the Symbol Translation Index routinely, the FSIQ prevents confusion that may be caused by deriving a mean of index scores that is different from that in the published test based only on the five primary index scores.

A review of Table B.1 in the *WISC–V Administration and Scoring Manual*, which contains the critical values for statistically significant differences between each primary index score and the FSIQ, reveals that consulting the table is generally unnecessary. For almost every age group and overall, the Verbal Comprehension Index and the Fluid Reasoning Index differences from FSIQ are significant at the .05 level if the difference is 10 or more. For the Visual Spatial Index compared with the FSIQ, the difference is significant if it is 11 or more for almost every age group as well as overall. For the Working Memory Index, 12 or more is the magic value. There are small fluctuations at the age group level, but those are chance fluctuations as opposed to anything that seems to be a developmental trend.

For the Processing Speed Index, the values are based on retest, and the contributing subtests each have two different forms. For younger children aged 6 to 7, the discrepancy is statistically significant at the .05 level with a difference of 12 or more points. For children aged 8 to 16, the values at which the discrepancy is statistically significant at the .05 level fluctuate between 11 and 14 points, but the overall value is 13. It makes sense to use 12 as the magic number for ages 6 to 7 since these children take different forms of both Coding and Symbol Search. If you use 14 for the other ages, you will always be safe in saying the difference is statistically significant at the .05 level (and sometimes it will be significant at .01).

Table C.1 in Appendix C of this book and the Step 5 tab of the *WISC–V Interpretive Assistant 1.0* (in the downloadable resources: www.wiley .com/go/itwiscv) provide critical values for comparisons of the complementary Symbol Translation Index to the FSIQ. All of the values are equal to 12 when rounded to a whole number, and all comparisons should result in a whole number since both composite scores are whole numbers.

The information in Table C.1 in Appendix C of this book (i.e., critical values for comparing the Symbol Translation Index to the FSIQ) is roughly analogous to the information in Table B.1 of the *WISC–V Administration and Scoring Manual*, but it is simplified in that only the .05 level of significance is provided and values are rounded to the whole number. If you obtain a difference as large as the critical value or larger, the difference is statistically significant.

Consider using the following intelligent rules of thumb to simplify determination of a significant discrepancy between each primary index score and the complementary Symbol Translation Index with the FSIQ.

Intelligent Rules of Thumb

Significant Discrepancies between the FSIQ and Index Scores at the .05 Level

Index Score	Value
Verbal Comprehension Index or Fluid Reasoning Index	10 or more points
Visual Spatial Index	11 or more points
Working Memory Index	12 or more points
Processing Speed Index	Ages 6–7: 12 or more points Ages 8–16: 14 or more points
Symbol Translation Index	12 or more points

Table C.2 in Appendix C of this book and the Step 5 tab of the *WISC–V Interpretive Assistant 1.0* (in the downloadable resources: www.wiley.com/go/itwiscv) provide base rates for comparisons of each primary index score and the complementary Symbol Translation Index to the FSIQ. This table is somewhat comparable to Table B.2 in the *WISC–V Administration*

and Scoring Manual, but it is simplified and expanded. First, the Symbol Translation Index is included. Second, we used only four base rates, excluding 25%. Third, we provided base rates for discrepancies from the FSIQ regardless of the direction of the discrepancy, whereas Table B.2 of the *WISC–V Administration and Scoring Manual* provides base rates separately for strengths and weaknesses.

Consider using the next intelligent rules of thumb to simplify interpretation. If the difference between the FSIQ and any of the higher-order reasoning composites—the Verbal Comprehension Index, the Visual Spatial Index, or the Fluid Reasoning Index—is at least 15, it will always be considered rare and unusual relative to the normative sample. If the difference between the FSIQ and the three remaining index scores—the Working Memory Index, the Processing Speed Index, and the Symbol Translation Index—is at least 21, it will always be considered rare and unusual relative to the normative sample. Consider using the next intelligent rules of thumb to simplify determination of a rare discrepancy between the FSIQ score and these index scores.

Intelligent Rules of Thumb

Rare Discrepancies between the FSIQ and Index Scores

Index Score	Rare Discrepancy Values
Verbal Comprehension Index Visual Spatial Index Fluid Reasoning Index	15 points or more
Working Memory Index Processing Speed Index Symbol Translation Index	21 points or more

---

As described previously, there may be situations in which the Nonverbal Index or the General Ability Index (rather than the FSIQ) serve as the comparison score for the index-level evaluation of cognitive strengths and weaknesses.

If the Nonverbal Index Is Selected as the Global Measure of Performance

Even if you select the Nonverbal Index as the global measure of intellectual ability, you should still use the FSIQ for strengths and weaknesses comparisons. If you selected the Nonverbal Index as the global intellectual ability score and there is no FSIQ, consider simply substituting the Nonverbal Index value for the FSIQ and perform the comparisons anyway. The correlation between the two scores is .93, which is better than the retest stability value for the FSIQ (.92) and only differs slightly from a prorated FSIQ in terms of content.

If the General Ability Index Is Selected as the Global Measure of Performance

If you select the general ability index as the global measure of intellectual ability, you should still use the FSIQ for strengths and weaknesses comparisons. If one is not available, consider simply substituting the General Ability Index for the FSIQ and perform the comparisons anyway, for similar reasons cited for the Nonverbal Index. The correlation between the two scores is .96, which is better than retest stability value for the FSIQ, and the GAI differs only slightly from a prorated FSIQ in terms of content.

It is crucial to ground interpretation of the index-level strengths and weaknesses in the context of Step 3, where the index scores were described in relation to the normative sample as extremely high, very high, high, average, low, very low, and extremely low. At this step, use interpretive statements that refer to both the normative performance and the intrapersonal strengths and weaknesses analysis to avoid confusing those who read your report. For example, if the Verbal Comprehension Index is described as falling in the average range relative to the normative sample at Step 3b but is an intrapersonal strength relative to the comparison score, use a statement such as "Lisa's Verbal

Comprehension ability is average compared to other children her age, but it is one of her personal areas of cognitive strength."

It is typical to have some areas of strength and weakness across intellectual ability domains. A significant strength or weakness relative to an overall indicator of intellectual ability is a normal occurrence and should not be taken as a sign of pathology or abnormality. In fact, according to our calculations, 82.1% of children in the WISC–V normative sample (i.e., $n = 1,806$ of 2,200) have at least one primary index score that is different than the FSIQ at the .05 significance level. The percentage is nearly identical among children in the WISC–V special group study samples: 85.1% (i.e., $n = 423$ of 497).

When the Symbol Translation Index and the primary index scores are considered, according to our calculations, 88.7% of children in the WISC–V normative sample (i.e., $n = 1,951$ of 2,200) have at least one index score that is different from the FSIQ at the .05 significance level. For children in the WISC–V special group samples, 89.3% (i.e., $n = 444$ of 497) have such a discrepancy.

Step 6. Evaluate Subtest-Level Strengths and Weaknesses Comparisons

Subtest-level performance may be examined for intra-individual strengths and weaknesses to clarify interpretation of a composite or of a specific ability. In this procedure, the subtest scaled scores are compared to an indicator of overall subtest-level performance (i.e., comparison score).

As at the index level, these comparisons provide useful information and minimize the likelihood of Type I error relative to several pairwise comparisons. They also can assist with understanding and explaining composite-level performance. It is typical to have some areas of strength and weakness across subtest performance. You should never use a result obtained from a single subtest alone to make clinical decisions.

If all primary subtests are available, you should use the mean of all 10 primary subtests (abbreviated MSS-P in the published test) as the comparison score. If one of these is missing, consider calculating the mean based on the number of subtests you have and perform the strengths and weaknesses comparisons anyway by substituting that value.

The next Intelligent Rules of Thumb box summarizes the critical values and base rates for statistical significance and rarity, respectively. Consider using these intelligent rules of thumb to simplify determination of a significant and rare discrepancy between a primary subtest and the mean of the 10 primary subtests.

Intelligent Rules of Thumb

Significant and Unusual Discrepancies between Primary Subtests and the Mean of the 10 Primary Subtests

- A difference of 4 or more between each primary subtest and the mean of the 10 primary subtests is always significant at the .05 significance level (See Table B.3 of the *WISC–V Administration and Scoring Manual*.)
- A difference of 5 or more between a primary subtest and the mean of the 10 primary subtests is always rare, occurring in <5% to 10% of the normative sample. (See Table B.4 of the *WISC–V Administration and Scoring Manual*.)

Step 7. Evaluate Index–Level Pairwise Comparisons

A pairwise comparison between two index scores may be useful to determine if a given area of intellectual functioning is significantly different from that in another area. As with other comparisons, statistically significant differences occur frequently in both normative samples and in clinical populations (Sattler, 2008).

With rare exceptions, it is unnecessary and inappropriate to conduct every possible pairwise index score comparison that is possible. As the number of score comparisons increases, so does the possibility of finding a significant difference that is due to chance, rather than a true difference in performance (Grégoire et al., 2011). If you conduct pairwise comparisons, having a sound and planned rationale for doing so will ease interpretation and decrease the chances of this family-wise Type I error. For example, if assessing a child suspected of specific learning disorder in reading related to visual-spatial issues, you may wish to compare the Visual Spatial Index and the Working Memory Index with the other primary index scores to understand visual-spatial cognitive ability and working memory in an intra-individual context with other cognitive domains and to facilitate treatment planning.

Comparing Index Scores in the Published Test
For comparisons between two published index scores, examine the differences for statistical significance and frequency of occurrence in the normative sample. Four pairwise comparisons from the published test that may be made more often than others are discussed next.

Visual Spatial Index versus Fluid Reasoning Index
The Visual Spatial Index can be compared with the Fluid Reasoning Index to provide information about the child's visual processing relative to his or her fluid reasoning as assessed using primarily visual stimuli.

Hypothesis: If the Visual Spatial Index is less than the Fluid Reasoning Index, the child may overcome visual-spatial processing limitations on his or her visual problem-solving ability by using verbal mediation and translating the visual information into verbal information (e.g., mentally or verbally rehearsing the changes across rows of a matrix, such as "blue square turns to red square, blue circle turns to red circle") or quantitative strategies (e.g., counting the stimuli). If the Visual Spatial Index is greater than the Fluid Reasoning Index, the child may have good concrete visual processing skills but lower relative ability to utilize the skills to engage in higher-order problem solving (Lichtenberger & Kaufman, 2013; Raiford & Coalson, 2014).

Visual Spatial Index versus Working Memory Index

The Visual Spatial Index can be compared with the Working Memory Index to provide information about the child's visual-spatial processing relative to his or her working memory.

Hypothesis: If the Visual Spatial Index is less than the Working Memory Index, the child may overcome visual-spatial processing limitations when performing working memory tasks by using verbal mediation and translating the visual information into verbal information (e.g., verbally rehearsing an array of objects). If the Visual Spatial Index is greater than the Working Memory Index, the child may have good concrete visual processing skills but lower relative ability to utilize them in situations where the child must maintain distinctions between current and previous information to determine which response is appropriate or relevant at the present time.

Fluid Reasoning Index versus Working Memory Index

The Fluid Reasoning Index can be compared with the Working Memory Index to provide information about the child's fluid reasoning relative to his or her working memory abilities.

Hypothesis: If the Fluid Reasoning Index is less than the Working Memory Index, the child may have relatively weaker visual-spatial problem-solving skills compared with his or her ability to remember distinctions between current and previously presented information. He or she may maintain these distinctions well but be less able to leverage the information to engage in planful higher-order problem solving. If the Fluid Reasoning Index is greater than the Working Memory Index, the child may have good

problem-solving abilities but need greater support maintaining distinctions between current and previously presented information.

Working Memory Index versus Processing Speed Index

The Working Memory Index can be compared with the Processing Speed Index to provide information about the child's working memory relative to his or her processing speed.

Hypothesis: If the Working Memory Index is less than the Processing Speed Index, the child may have relatively weaker ability to remember distinctions between current and previously presented information, and how it is temporally related, compared with his or her perceptual speed where the relevant stimuli remains in the visual field. He or she may process simple information quickly but be less able to capitalize on that speediness to maintain distinctions between relevant and irrelevant stimuli. If the Working Memory Index is greater than the Processing Speed Index, the child may have stronger ability to maintain distinctions between current and previously presented information to determine which response is appropriate or relevant at the present time but may be more concerned with accuracy than with speedy response production.

Comparisons Involving the Additional Index Scores from This Book

Some index-level pairwise comparisons that are of interest from different theoretical perspectives and for practical purposes can be made using the published index scores and the additional index scores in this book. For these comparisons, use the downloadable resources: www.wiley.com/go/itwiscv.

Each pairwise comparison is discussed in the chapters associated with that theoretical orientation. If a comparison involves an index score from this book, it is made using the "Step 7" tab of the *WISC–V Interpretive Assistant 1.0*. The tab indicates which theoretical orientation is associated with each comparison.

Table 8.5   Locations of Pairwise Comparisons with Additional Index Scores

Comparison	Location of Interpretation Discussion, Critical Values, and Base Rates
Gc (Verbal Comprehension Index) vs. Gf (Fluid Reasoning Index)	Chapter 9 (CHC Interpretation)
Verbal (Expanded Crystallized) Index (Expanded Gc) vs. Expanded Fluid Index (Expanded Gf)	Chapter 9 (CHC Interpretation)
Working Memory Index (Gsm) vs. Symbol Translation Index (Glr)	Chapter 9 (CHC Interpretation)
Gc-K0 vs. Verbal Comprehension Index (Lexical Knowledge, or Gc-VL)	Chapter 9 (CHC Interpretation)
Gf-I vs. Quantitative Reasoning Index (Gf-RQ)	Chapter 9 (CHC Interpretation)
Matrix Reasoning Successive vs. Matrix Reasoning Simultaneous	Chapter 11 (Neuropsychological Interpretation)
Successive Processing Index vs. Simultaneous Processing Index	Chapter 11 (Neuropsychological Interpretation)

The pairwise comparisons with additional index scores that appear in this book and on the *WISC–V Interpretive Assistant 1.0*, along with the location of their associated interpretation discussions, critical values, and base rates, are listed in Table 8.5. Refer to Tables 8.3 and 8.4 for the reliability and *SEM* associated with each additional index score.

Step 8. Evaluate Subtest-Level Pairwise Comparisons

Pairwise comparisons between the two subtest scaled scores that contribute to an index score are useful to understand how to interpret that index score. Because only two subtests contribute to most of the index scores, examine the difference

between the subtests to facilitate the index score's interpretation. For example, comparing performance on Block Design and Visual Puzzles can help with interpretation of the Visual Spatial Index and provide useful information relevant to hypotheses about the child's relative analysis and synthesis abilities with uniform, manipulable stimuli and varied, static stimuli.

The next Intelligent Rules of Thumb box summarizes the critical values and base rates for statistical significance and rarity, respectively. Consider using these intelligent rules of thumb to simplify determination of a significant and rare discrepancy between subtests.

Intelligent Rules of Thumb

Significant and Unusual Discrepancies between Subtests

- For each pair of WISC–V subtests, a difference of 4 or more is always significant at the .05 level. (See Table B.7 of the *WISC–V Administration and Scoring Manual*).
- For the primary subtest pairs that make up the five primary index scores:
  - A difference of 4 scaled-score points is rare (<10%) for the Verbal Comprehension, Visual Spatial, and Processing Speed primary subtests. (See Table B.8 of the *WISC–V Administration and Scoring Manual*.)
  - A difference of 5 points or more is rare for the Fluid Reasoning and Working Memory primary subtests. (See Table B.8 of the *WISC–V Administration and Scoring Manual*.)

Base Rates for Subtest-Level Pairwise Comparison for the Gs–P (Perceptual Speed) Index

The base rate for one additional subtest-level pairwise comparison, Symbol Search versus Cancellation, is available because those two subtests compose the *Gs*–P (Perceptual Speed) index. *Gs*–P is the only two-subtest index score created for this book, and a pairwise subtest comparison may be necessary to facilitate interpretation. See the "Step 8" tab of the *WISC–V Interpretive Assistant 1.0* or Table C.3 in Appendix C of this book. Both the program and the table provide the relevant base rates for score differences in the overall normative sample. As with the other base rate table we created, we used only four base rates, excluding 25%, and we provided base rates for discrepancies regardless of the direction.

As shown in the table, any difference of 5 or more is rare in the normative sample. Therefore,

consider using the next intelligent rule of thumb to indicate a rare and unusual difference between Symbol Search and Cancellation.

> ## Intelligent Rules of Thumb
>
> **Unusual Discrepancy between Symbol Search and Cancellation, Relevant to Interpretation of the Gs–P (Perceptual Speed) Index**
>
> - A difference of 5 or more is rare in the normative sample.

PART 4

THEORETICAL FRAMEWORKS FOR WISC–V INTERPRETATION

OVERVIEW OF THE 17 SAMPLE CASE REPORTS INCLUDED IN PART IV

Chapter 9 Interpreting the WISC–V from the Perspective of Cattell-Horn-Carroll Theory

Case 1. Liam, Age 9, by W. Joel Schneider
Caucasian boy with ADHD and reading and writing difficulties

Case 2. Alicia, Age 13, by Jill Hartmann and John Willis
African American girl with low cognitive ability and low achievement

Case 3. Luke, Age 9, by Jennifer T. Mascolo and Dawn P. Flanagan
Caucasian boy with attentional and reading difficulties

Chapter 10 Interpreting the WISC–V from a Cognitive Neuroscience Perspective

Case 4. Josh, Age 8, by Elaine Fletcher-Janzen and Elizabeth Power
Caucasian boy with reading disability and expressive language deficits

Case 5. Tawna, Age 13, Michelle Lurie and Elizabeth Lichtenberger
African American girl with sustained attention and processing speed difficulties

Case 6. Tom, Age 8, by Kristina Breaux
Caucasian boy with high cognitive ability, ADHD, and reading, writing, and math difficulties

Chapter 11 Interpreting the WISC–V from a Neuropsychological Perspective

Case 7. Jaime, Age 10, by Jennie Kaufman Singer
Hispanic Asian boy with low cognitive ability, autistic spectrum disorder, and behavioral difficulties

Case 8. Christopher, Age 11, by Marsha Vasserman
Caucasian boy with phonological dyslexia and visual perceptual disorder

Case 9. Isabella, Age 13, by Michelle Lurie
Hispanic girl with low cognitive ability, ADHD, anxiety, and depression

Chapter 12 Interpreting the WISC–V from Dan Miller's Integrated School Neuropsychological/ Cattell-Horn-Carroll Model

Case 10. John, Age 12, by Daniel C. Miller and Alicia M. Jones
Caucasian boy with writing difficulties, depression, and anxiety

Chapter 13 Interpreting the WISC–V Using George McCloskey's Neuropsychologically Oriented Process Approach to Psychoeducational Evaluations

Case 11. Colin, Age 8, by George McCloskey
Caucasian boy with mild executive function difficulties but no specific learning disability

Case 12. Derek, Age 13, by George McCloskey
Caucasian boy with phonological dyslexia and executive function difficulties

Chapter 14 Interpreting the WISC–V for Children with Reading or Language Problems: Five Illustrative Case Reports

Case 13. Ellie, Age 10, by Michelle Lurie
      Asian American girl with language and reading difficulties
Case 14. Jordan, Age 15, by Marsha Vasserman
      Caucasian boy with hearing and language difficulties
Case 15. Jane, Age 8, by Robert Lichtenstein and Joan Axelrod
      Caucasian girl with reading difficulties
Case 16. Lizzie, Age 8, by Carlea Dries and Ron Dumont
      Caucasian girl with low cognitive ability and memory difficulties
Case 17. Patrick, Age 9, by Nancy Mather and Katie Eklund
      African American boy with reading difficulties

CHAPTER 9

INTERPRETING THE WISC–V FROM THE PERSPECTIVE OF CATTELL-HORN-CARROLL THEORY

A great deal has been written about the Cattell-Horn-Carroll (CHC) constructs and their application to Wechsler interpretation. Dawn Flanagan, Kevin McGrew, and their colleagues have written intelligently on these topics, most notably the cross-battery assessment approach to profile analysis (Flanagan, Alfonso, & Ortiz, 2012; Flanagan, Alfonso, & Reynolds, 2013; Flanagan & McGrew, 1997; McGrew & Flanagan, 1998; Ortiz, Flanagan, & Alfonso, 2015; Schneider & Flanagan, 2015; Schneider & McGrew, 2012). The CHC model has been applied to profile interpretation of the WISC–IV (Flanagan & Kaufman, 2009) and WAIS–IV (Lichtenberger & Kaufman, 2013). A special issue of *Journal of Psychoeducational Assessment* was devoted to the five-factor (CHC) interpretation of the fourth editions of the Wechsler scales (Tobin, 2013), and new resources are becoming available that interpret the WISC–V from the CHC model (Flanagan & Alfonso, in press; Ortiz et al., 2015).

We will be fairly brief in the first part of this chapter, providing a short history of the CHC model; specifying the Broad and Narrow Abilities measured by WISC–V subtests; providing new tables, not offered in the WISC–V manuals, to compute several CHC Narrow Abilities (e.g., the *Gf* ability of Induction and the *Gs* abilities of Perceptual Speed and Rate of Test-taking); offering a table that permits the determination of a child's relative strengths and weaknesses on *six* CHC Broad Abilities (the five primary index scores plus *Glr*, measured by the Symbol Translation Index); and pointing out key contrasts between pairs of WISC–V index scores

or composites that facilitate interpretation from CHC theory. Key research findings describing the relationship between the narrow CHC abilities measured by the WISC–V and academic achievement in reading, math, and writing are summarized. The bulk of the chapter is devoted to clinical case reports, written from a CHC perspective, to illustrate the theoretical model in action.

A BRIEF HISTORY OF CHC THEORY

The CHC approach to intelligence, which forms the theoretical foundation of most of today's intelligence tests, is an amalgam of two related theories of cognitive abilities: Horn and Cattell's (1966) theory of fluid and crystallized intelligence and J. B. Carroll's (1993a) three-stratum theory. The Cattell-Horn's *Gf-Gc* theory had the first, dramatic impact on the interpretation of IQ tests, most notably Wechsler's scales, before J. B. Carroll's (1968, 1993a) exhaustive research entered the realm of IQ testing.

Some years after Spearman (1904, 1927) provided an empirical foundation for his influential and widely accepted *g* theory, Thurstone (1938), Guilford (1956), and other leaders in the field came out strongly in favor of multiple abilities and were anti-*g*. Raymond Cattell, Spearman's doctoral student, following in his mentor's footstep but, taking a step in the direction of multiple abilities, posited two types of *g* abilities:

1. *Fluid intelligence (Gf)*, the ability to solve novel problems via abstract reasoning; and

2. *Crystallized intelligence (Gc)*, a knowledge-based ability dependent on formal education and acculturation.

To Cattell (1941, 1943), *Gf* was mostly a function of biological and neurological factors and was vulnerable to the effects of aging. By contrast, he considered *Gc* to have a strong environmental component and to be largely resistant to the impact of aging. In fact, *Gf* and *Gc* are about equally heritable (Horn, 1985), although Cattell's notions about the different growth curves for *Gf* and *Gc* have been largely supported by a wealth of cross-sectional and longitudinal studies of aging and intelligence (Lichtenberger & Kaufman, 2013; Salthouse, 2010).

John Horn, Cattell's doctoral student, took *Gf-Gc* theory a giant step further. And just as Cattell (1941) built on Spearman's (1904, 1927) *g* theory of intelligence, so, too, did Horn expand his mentor's theory. Horn and Cattell's (1966, 1967) initial research and writing focused on the once-innovative *Gf-Gc* dichotomy. Cattell (1963) remained devoted to *Gf* and *Gc* as the linchpins of the theory, but Horn never really bought into the simple two-factor model. Almost from the beginning—in fact, in Horn's (1965) doctoral dissertation—he advocated multiple abilities. Horn (1965, 1968, 1972) quickly identified four abilities in addition to *Gf* and *Gc*: short-term acquisition and retrieval (*Gsm*), long-term storage and retrieval (*Glr*), visual processing (*Gv*), and speed of processing (*Gs*). That number would grow to nine or 10 *broad abilities* by the mid-1990s as Horn (1989a, 1989b) and colleagues (Horn & Hofer, 1992; Horn & McArdle, 1980; Horn & Noll, 1997; Horn & Stankov, 1982) continued to conduct cutting-edge research. What began as two aspects of *g* had expanded to nine or 10 broad abilities but, despite Cattell's emphasis on *Gf* and *Gc*, Horn did not consider any of the abilities to be more or less important than others. The theory continued to be called the Horn-Cattell *Gf-Gc* theory, but the growing number of broad abilities, such as auditory processing (*Ga*) and quantitative knowledge (*Gq*),

were treated as equals, not as part of any type of hierarchy.

In contrast to Horn's approach, John Carroll (1993a, 1997) developed a hierarchical three-stratum theory:

Stratum III (General), Spearman's *g*, which Carroll (1993a, 1997) considered to be a valid and vital global construct;

Stratum II (Broad), composed of eight broad abilities that correspond closely to Horn's (1989a, 1989b) broad abilities and relate roughly to Gardner's (1983) multiple intelligences; and

Stratum I (Narrow), composed of about 70 fairly specific abilities, often indicating the person's "level of mastery, along a difficulty scale," "speed with which the individual performs tasks," or "rate of learning in learning and memory tasks" (Carroll, 1997, p. 124).

Mark Daniel (1997), who supervised the development of numerous Kaufman tests over the years, said about Carroll's theory, "Never before has a psychometric-ability model been so firmly grounded in data" (p. 1043).

Horn's (1989a) theory always focused on the broad abilities (Carroll's Stratum II) but respected the value of the narrow abilities as well. Neither Horn the man nor Horn the theorist ever had any use for Spearman's *g* or Carroll's Stratum III. Otherwise, the Carroll and Cattell-Horn models were similar enough to warrant being merged into a single theory.

Ultimately, both the Cattell-Horn and Carroll models started from the same point—Spearman's (1904) *g-factor* theory—and ended up with remarkably consistent conclusions about the structure of intelligence. The CHC model, the blend of the Cattell-Horn expanded *Gf-Gc* theory and Carroll's three-stratum model, is a psychometric theory that rests on a large body of research accumulated over generations in a plethora of empirical investigations. CHC also owes a debt to Thurstone's (1938) pioneering primary mental abilities theory: "to a considerable extent, modern hierarchical theories derive from this theory" (Horn & Noll, 1997, p. 62).

Without fanfare, Horn and Carroll agreed to merge their models into a single theory in a personal communication to Richard Woodcock in July 1999. But about a dozen years before that, in a 1986 Dallas meeting, Horn, Carroll, and Woodcock sat around a table as the intimate link between the Cattell-Horn *Gf-Gc* theory and Carroll's compendium of factor-analytic research was discovered. Kevin McGrew (2005) recalled, "A collective 'Ah Ha!' engulfed the room as Carroll's WJ [Woodcock-Johnson] factor interpretation provided a meaningful link between the theoretical terminology of Horn and the concrete world of WJ tests" (p. 144). Although CHC theory was still not yet conceived, that 1986 meeting was the flash point that ultimately bridged the gap from theory to practice (McGrew, 2005). In Chapter 1 (in the section titled "The WISC–V Is Optimally Useful When It Is Interpreted from a Theoretical Basis"), two milestone meetings were discussed involving test authors and theorists—the one in 1986 and a later one in 1999. Both meetings were instrumental in the birth of CHC theory. In a very real way, theory development and test construction were intertwined with no real method for discerning cause and effect. The development of the Woodcock Johnson Third Edition (WJ III; Woodcock, McGrew, & Mather, 2001) and the Stanford-Binet Intelligence Scales, Fifth Edition (SB5; Roid, 2003) led to the creation of CHC theory. Or was it the other way around?

CONTEMPORARY CHC THEORY

As the evidence base for the CHC model of cognitive abilities grew, so did its influence on the structure of intelligence as it is operationalized in published tests. The model has formed the basis for most contemporary IQ tests, namely the Woodcock-Johnson IV (WJ IV; Schrank, McGrew, & Mather, 2014), the Differential Ability Scales–Second Edition (DAS–II; Elliott, 2007), the Reynolds Intellectual Assessment Scales (RIAS; C. R. Reynolds & Kamphaus, 2003), the Kaufman Assessment Battery for Children–Second Edition (KABC–II, A. S. Kaufman & Kaufman, 2004), and the SB5. The WISC–V also fits nicely into that group of CHC-based tests, even if the publishers are more inclined to list neurodevelopmental, neurocognitive, working memory, and other cognitive research as additional bases for test development.

As with development of the WJ III, revisions to CHC theory and the WJ IV content were reciprocal in nature, with changes in one driving changes in the other. However, the WJ IV represents the first revision in which none of the original CHC theorists was alive at the time of publication, producing an imbalance in this reciprocal relationship, with the WJ IV manuals now serving as the official source for the latest CHC theory and model of cognitive abilities (J. Schneider, personal communication, March 15, 2015). As predicted by Schneider and Flanagan (2015), an increasing number of scholars have developed their own interpretive models based on CHC theory (e.g., Dawn Flanagan's cross-battery approach and Dan Miller's integrated school neuropsychology/CHC assessment model described in Chapter 12), resulting in "unnecessary confusion and fragmentation," (p. 327) as well as a need to distinguish "official" and "unofficial" sources of CHC theory, taxonomy, and nomenclature. This confusion typically peaks shortly after the release of a test revision, as practitioners gradually adopt the newer test (hopefully, within a year of publication).

According to the latest "official" version of the CHC model of cognitive abilities, the comprehensive WJ IV battery (including the Cognitive, Oral Language, and Achievement batteries) measures 10 broad abilities, including Domain-Specific Knowledge (*Gkn*), Quantitative Knowledge (*Gq*), Reading and Writing (*Grw*), Comprehension-Knowledge (*Gc*),

Fluid Reasoning (*Gf*), Short-term Working Memory (*Gwm*), Long-term Retrieval (*Glr*), Visual Processing (*Gv*), Auditory Processing (*Ga*), and Processing Speed (*Gs*). Measures of 35 narrow abilities are dispersed among these broad domains, with anywhere between one (for *Gq*) to eight (for *Grw*) narrow-ability measures for each broad domain (LaForte, McGrew, & Schrank, 2014).

It is important to note that even the comprehensive WJ IV battery does not attempt to completely cover the ever-increasing taxonomy of cognitive abilities represented in CHC theory. Prior to the 2014 release of the WJ IV, Schneider and McGrew (2012) listed 16 broad abilities to reflect the range of the major human intellectual skills and 80 to 90 specific narrow abilities, as determined by the body of research conducted by John Horn (1989a, 1989b) and his colleagues; by John Carroll's (1993a) overview of the relevant factor-analytic literature; and by subsequent research investigations (Flanagan et al., 2013). The taxonomy and nomenclature changes to CHC theory are clearly explained in the WJ IV manuals, and most will have a relatively minor impact on other CHC-based approaches to interpretation: The reader is referred to those manuals for a complete description of contemporary CHC theory, including descriptions of changes to the CHC model since the WJ III (see McGrew, LaForte, & Schrank, 2014).

The renaming of the former broad Short-term Memory ability (*Gsm*) as Short-term Working Memory (*Gwm*) represents a terminology change with more direct implications for CHC-oriented clinicians using the WISC–V. At this time, the authors are choosing *not* to adopt the terminology change suggested in the WJ IV manuals and instead retain the former *Gsm* term. All of the authors, including the WJ IV authors, seem to be in agreement that additional research is necessary to clarify the nature of short-term and working memory as well as their interrelationship and their relations to other, related constructs, such as fluid reasoning, executive

functions, and processing speed. At the time of this writing, cognitive research suggests that short-term memory and working memory are highly related abilities that share common neural networks; however, working memory measures place greater demands on those neural networks, indicated in executive function measures, than simpler short-term memory measures, and the activated brain regions vary with content (e.g., verbal or visual; Dang, Braeken, Colom, Ferrer, & Liu, 2014; Unsworth, Fukuda, Awh, & Vogel, 2014). Thus, the complex structure and interdependencies of short-term and working memory (as well as their subcomponents and relations with other types of memory, such as implicit, explicit, declarative, semantic, narrative, and procedural memory) remain an open question. Perhaps *Gsm* and *Gwm* should both be broad abilities that differ in terms of their underlying processing and attentional demands. Or, even more likely, perhaps *Gsm* should be reclassified and subsumed as a narrow *Gwm* ability. In the authors' view, the most likely hope for rapidly advancing our understanding of the complex nature of memory and learning (both key aspects of intelligence) will arise from the collaborative, multidisciplinary research efforts that are being used with increasing frequency. It is beyond the scope and purpose of any intelligence test to accurately describe and measure the complex, interwoven cognitive abilities contributing to memory and learning.

The authors also agree with Flanagan's concern that the confusion among clinicians may be unintentionally exacerbated by simultaneous terminology changes to the narrow abilities comprising the former *Gsm* broad ability. As she explained in an email (D. P. Flanagan, personal communication, February 13, 2015):

> I do agree that the broad ability should be Short-term Working Memory. I've always thought that working memory was too important to be considered a narrow ability construct. What I found confusing was the WJ IV's use of the terms "Short-term Working Memory (*Gwm*)," "Working Memory

Capacity (WM)," and "Attentional Control." I am not sure how you measure Attentional Control separate from Working Memory. Also, I thought practitioners would be confused by the constructs *Gwm* and WM and perhaps find them somewhat redundant.

Regardless of the choice to use the previous *Gsm* or newly introduced *Gwm* terminology, it is the clinician's responsibility to understand the nature of the cognitive ability (or abilities) being measured by *any* subtest or composite score. Without this understanding, it is impossible to accurately and effectively interpret and describe test performance to other clinicians, researchers, educators, and, most important, to the parents and children. For CHC-oriented clinicians who may be concerned about the use of two different terms with different acronyms, it is helpful to remember that the *definition* of this broad ability remains unchanged in the WJ IV, despite the renaming and introduction of a new acronym.

CHC-BASED INTERPRETATION OF THE WISC-V

Not only the instruments but the most prominent, research-based approach to the interpretation of nearly all cognitive tests stems from the CHC model: the cross-battery assessment (XBA) approach, developed by Dawn Flanagan and her colleagues (e.g., Flanagan & McGrew, 1997; Flanagan et al., 2007, 2013), which is rooted in Woodcock's (1990) seminal work. The cross-battery approach, now in its third edition (Flanagan et al., 2013), urges clinicians to select tasks from a variety of cognitive, achievement, and neuropsychological tests rather than relying on a single instrument. That flexible, theory-driven approach enables the assessment of a more complete array of broad and narrow abilities than is found in a single battery (such as the WISC-V) alone. XBA's huge popularity is evident by even a cursory glance at many

of the excellent listservs, such as Kevin McGrew's amazing CHC listserv. An update to the XBA software (i.e., the X-BASS Cross-Battery Assessment System) extends coverage to the WJ IV, KTEA-3, and WISC-V, along with other recent publications, resulting in coverage of approximately 800 subtests from over 100 psychological tests (Ortiz et al., 2015).

For interpretation from the perspective of XBA and CHC, both broad and narrow abilities are crucial. Regarding CHC and *g*, Alan wrote the following (A. S. Kaufman, 2009):

It has never been clear whether Carroll's Stratum III (*g* or general ability) is part of CHC theory or not. The topic was rarely talked about while Horn and Carroll were alive because it was their one main bone of contention. To Carroll, *g* was a crucial and fundamental concept; to Horn it was anathema. So Stratum III has usually been ignored, and its role in CHC theory remains ambiguous (McGrew, 2005) ...

Regardless, broad abilities rule the roost, both from a theoretical perspective and for determining which scales constitute most of today's IQ tests. (pp. 84, 86)

CHC Broad Abilities Measured by the WISC-V

Each of the five WISC-V primary index scores corresponds to a single broad ability, and the complementary Symbol Translation Index corresponds to a sixth (*Glr*—Long-Term Storage & Retrieval). Each of these six index scores is listed next along with the CHC broad ability it measures and the definition of each ability (Flanagan et al., 2013, Rapid Reference 1.1, p. 17).

1. Verbal Comprehension Index (Similarities, Vocabulary) ≈ Crystallized Intelligence (*Gc*)—The breadth and depth of knowledge and skills that are valued by one's culture.
2. Visual Spatial Index (Block Design, Visual Puzzles) ≈ Visual Processing (*Gv*)—The

ability to make use of simulated mental imagery (often in conjunction with currently perceived images) to solve problems. Further, *Gv* is a person's "ability to generate, perceive, analyze, synthesize, store, retrieve, manipulate, transform, and think with visual patterns and stimuli (Lohman, 1994)" (Flanagan et al., 2007, p. 286).

3. Fluid Reasoning Index (Matrix Reasoning, Figure Weights) ≈ Fluid Reasoning (*Gf*)—The deliberate but flexible control of attention to solve novel, on-the-spot problems that cannot be performed by relying exclusively on previously learned habits, schemas, and scripts.

4. Working Memory Index (Digit Span, Picture Span) ≈ Short-Term Memory (*Gsm*)—The ability to encode, maintain, and manipulate information in one's immediate awareness. "An example of *Gsm* is the ability to remember a telephone number long enough to dial it or the ability to retain a sequence of spoken directions long enough to complete the tasks specified in the directions" (Flanagan et al., 2007, p. 284).

5. Processing Speed Index (Coding, Symbol Search) ≈ Processing Speed (*Gs*)—The ability to perform simple, repetitive cognitive tasks quickly and fluently.

6. Symbol Translation Index (Immediate Symbol Translation, Delayed Symbol Translation, Recognition Symbol Translation) ≈ Long-Term Storage & Retrieval (*Glr*)—The ability to store, consolidate, and retrieve information over periods of time measured in minutes, hours, days, and years. "*Gc*, *Gq* [Quantitative Knowledge], and *Grw* [Reading & Writing] represent what is stored in long-term memory, whereas *Glr* is the efficiency with which this information is initially stored in and later retrieved from long-term memory" (Flanagan et al., 2007, p. 289). *Gsm* measures immediate recall after a few seconds, while *Glr* begins "within a few minutes or hours of performing a task" (p. 289).

CHC Narrow Abilities Measured by the WISC–V

Different CHC-based approaches to interpretation may classify the same subtest in different ways. For example, some CHC-oriented clinicians may classify WISC–V Similarities and Picture Concepts as verbal measures of inductive reasoning (I; a narrow ability within the broad *Gf* domain), despite assertions by other CHC-oriented clinicians that inductive and deductive fluid reasoning tasks should be classified as measures of crystallized intelligence if they "rely primarily on past experience and prior knowledge" (Schneider, 2013a, p. 296). From our perspective, however, we believe that the processes involved in successful inductive reasoning (e.g., categorization and the ability to identify a common rule or theme among related objects) are indeed utilized during task completion on Similarities and Picture Concepts, especially as item difficulty increases. As Alan emphasized years ago: A test is only novel once (A. S. Kaufman, 1979, 1994a), and that novelty translates to any problem-solving situation, whether the stimuli are familiar or abstract.

Overall, the WISC–V measures 13 CHC narrow abilities. Some are measured only by a single subtest (Picture Span) or part-subtest (Digit Span Forward), but most permit systematic analysis of a child's narrow abilities.

Narrow Gc (Crystallized Intelligence or Comprehension-Knowledge) Abilities

Within the broad domain of *Gc*, the WISC–V measures two narrow abilities, K0 (General Verbal Information) and VL (Lexical Knowledge). The two-subtest Verbal Comprehension Index primarily measures Lexical Knowledge so, in that sense, the Verbal Comprehension Index is really a "narrow" broad ability. However, the two secondary VC subtests (as well as the secondary Picture Concepts subtest from the *Gf* domain) measure Lexical Knowledge. Examiners who administer secondary subtests, most notably Information and Comprehension—longtime regulars on old versions of WISC—are able to add breadth to the measurement of the child's *Gc* and to compare the child's ability on each narrow aspect of Crystallized Intelligence.

| KO (General Verbal Information) | Information + Comprehension + Picture Concepts |
| VL (Lexical Knowledge) | Verbal Comprehension Index, composed of Vocabulary + Similarities |

General Verbal Information According to Flanagan et al. (2013), General Verbal Information refers to "the breadth and depth of knowledge that one's culture deems essential, practical, or otherwise worthwhile for everyone to know" (p. 389).

Lexical Knowledge According to Flanagan et al. (2013), Lexical Knowledge pertains to the "extent of vocabulary that can be understood in terms of correct word meanings" (p. 389).

Narrow Gv *(Visual Processing) Abilities*
Within the *Gv* domain, the two primary Visual Spatial Index subtests each measure the same narrow ability, Vz—Visualization. Like the Verbal Comprehension Index, the Visual Spatial Index is a fairly narrow broad ability. However, the Working Memory Index subtest Picture Span measures *Gv* as well as *Gsm*, so the WISC–V provides measurement of two *Gv* narrow abilities:

| Vz (Visualization) | Visual Spatial Index, composed of Block Design + Visual Puzzles |
| MV (Visual Memory) | Picture Span |

Visualization Flanagan et al. (2013) say that Visualization is "the ability to perceive complex patterns and mentally simulate how they might look when transformed (e.g., rotated, changed in size, partially obscured)" (p. 393).

Visual Memory According to Flanagan et al. (2013), Visual Memory is "the ability to remember complex visual images over short periods of time (less than 30 seconds)" (p. 394).

Narrow Gf *(Fluid Reasoning) Abilities*
Each of the two Fluid Reasoning Index subtests measures a different aspect of *Gf*. Taken together, the two primary and two secondary Fluid Reasoning subtests measure the narrow abilities of I—Induction—and RQ—Quantitative Reasoning. The Verbal Comprehension Index subtest Similarities measures both *Gc* and *Gf* and is also included in the mix. The two *Gf* narrow abilities are Induction and Quantitative Reasoning.

| I (Induction) | Matrix Reasoning + Picture Concepts + Similarities |
| RQ (Quantitative Reasoning) | Quantitative Reasoning Index, composed of Figure Weights + Arithmetic |

Induction According to Flanagan et al. (2013), induction is "the ability to observe a phenomenon and discover the underlying principles or rules that determine its behavior" (p. 389).

Quantitative Reasoning Flanagan et al. (2013) state that quantitative reasoning is "the ability to reason, either with induction or deduction, with numbers, mathematical relations, and operations" (p. 394). This CHC narrow ability corresponds to the ancillary Quantitative Reasoning Index.

Narrow Gsm *(Short-Term Memory or Short-Term Working Memory) Abilities*
The Working Memory subtests measure two *Gsm* narrow abilities: MW—Working Memory Capacity—and MS—Memory Span. It measures MW extensively and MS barely. Arithmetic is also noted as a measure of MW, which is supported by secondary factor loadings on the Working Memory factor.

MS (Memory Span)	Digit Span Forward
MW (Working Memory Capacity)	Digit Span Backward + Digit Span Sequencing + Letter–Number Sequencing + Picture Span + Arithmetic

Memory Span Flanagan et al. (2013) define memory span as "the ability to maintain information, maintain it in primary memory, and immediately reproduce the information in the same sequence in which it was represented" (p. 392).

Working Memory Capacity According to Flanagan et al. (2013), working memory capacity is "the ability to direct the focus of attention to perform relatively simple manipulations, combinations, and transformations of information within primary memory while avoiding distracting stimuli and engaging in strategic/controlled searches for information in secondary memory" (p. 392).

Narrow Gs (Processing Speed) Abilities

The Processing Speed Index measures two narrow abilities, R9 (Rate of Test-Taking) and P (Perceptual Speed). The index itself is a blend of both narrow abilities (Coding = R9 and Symbol Search = P), but the measurement of these Gs narrow abilities is more extensive than that because of the secondary Cancellation subtest and the complementary Naming Speed Index.

R9 (Rate of Test-Taking)	Coding
P (Perceptual Speed)	Symbol Search + Cancellation
N (Number Facility)	Naming Speed Quantity

Rate of Test-Taking Flanagan et al. (2013) describe the rate of test-taking as "the speed and fluency with which simple cognitive tests are completed" (p. 397).

Perceptual Speed To Flanagan et al. (2013), perceptual speed is "the ability with which visual stimuli can be compared for similarity or difference" (p. 397).

Number Facility Flanagan et al. (2013) define number facility as "the speed at which basic arithmetic operations are performed accurately" (p. 397).

Narrow Glr (Long-Term Storage and Retrieval or Long-Term Retrieval) Abilities

The inclusion of two WISC–V complementary index scores, the Naming Speed Index and the Symbol Translation Index, expands the number of broad abilities measured from five to six. Symbol Translation is pure *Glr* whereas Naming Speed is an amalgam of *Gs* and *Glr*. The WISC–V measures these two narrow abilities.

MA (Associative Memory)	Symbol Translation Index = Immediate Symbol Translation + Delayed Symbol Translation + Recognition Symbol Translation
NA (Naming Facility)	Naming Speed Literacy

Associative Memory According to Flanagan et al. (2013), associative memory is "the ability to remember previously unrelated information as having been paired" (p. 392).

Naming Facility Flanagan et al. (2013) describe naming facility as "the ability to rapidly call objects by their names" (p. 392). Naming Speed Quantity is not categorized as measuring Naming Facility; because this subtest requires handling numbers, Flanagan and Alfonso categorize it as *Gs*-N (Number Facility) but not as *Glr*-NA (Mascolo, personal communication, January 11, 2015)

Making Pairwise Comparisons Involving the Six Broad Abilities

Chapter 8 (Step 3a) provides guidelines and tables for determining a child's relative strengths and weaknesses on the six CHC abilities measured by the WISC–V and for determining whether these significant discrepancies are unusual within the normal population. In general, identifying significant and unusual strengths and weaknesses among the six CHC broad abilities is enough profile interpretation for most examiners in typical circumstances. However, some examiners may also prefer to make specific pairwise comparisons based on their theoretical orientation or the specific referral questions. The following pairwise comparisons may be of particular interest: *Gc* versus *Gf* and *Gsm* versus *Glr*. We also thought it would be of interest to CHC-oriented examiners to compare expanded versions of *Gc* versus *Gf*, so we constructed normative tables to permit computation of standard scores on two new indexes: Expanded *Gc* (also interpretable as "Verbal") versus Expanded *Gf*:

coefficients and Table 8.3 provides standard errors of measurement (*SEMs*) for Expanded *Gc* and Expanded *Gf*. Table 9.1 provides critical values at the .05 level of significance for Expanded *Gc* versus Expanded *Gf* and *Gsm* versus *Glr*, and Table 9.2 provides base rates of 15%, 10%, 5%, and 2% for all comparisons (regardless of the direction of the difference). The critical values for the comparisons between *Gc* and *Gf* appear in Table B.5 of the *WISC–V Administration and Scoring Manual* with the label Verbal Comprehension Index—Fluid Reasoning Index.

We integrated data from Table B.5 in the *WISC–V Administration and Scoring Manual* and our own Tables 9.1 and 9.2 and derived two intelligent rules of thumb to consider using when testing for statistical significance at the .05 level and for determining rarity of the discrepancies.

Expanded *Gc* [Also referred to in this book as Verbal (Expanded Crystallized) Index]	Similarities + Vocabulary + Information + Comprehension
Expanded *Gf* [Also referred to in this book as Expanded Fluid Index]	Matrix Reasoning + Figure Weights + Picture Concepts + Arithmetic

Examiners can compute these new indexes, and make comparisons involving them, in the downloadable resources: www.wiley.com/go/itwiscv. Also, Table 8.2 provides reliability

Intelligent Rules of Thumb

Significant Discrepancies between Broad Abilities at the .05 Level

Comparison	Value
Gc vs. *Gf*	12 or more points
Expanded *Gc* vs. Expanded *Gf*	12 or more points
Gsm vs. *Glr*	14 or more points

Table 9.1   Critical Values for Statistically Significant Differences at the .05 Level of Significance between Broad Abilities, by Age Group and Overall Normative Sample

Comparison	Age Group											Overall
	6	7	8	9	10	11	12	13	14	15	16	
Expanded *Gc* vs. Expanded *Gf*	13	12	12	12	12	13	11	12	11	12	11	12
Gsm vs. *Glr*	13	14	14	14	14	13	13	14	14	14	14	14

Table 9.2   Differences between Broad Abilities Obtained by Various Base Rates of the Normative Sample

	Gc–Gf	Expanded Gc vs. Expanded Gf	Gsm vs. Glr
≤15	19	17	22
≤10	22	19	26
≤5	26	23	30
≤2	32	27	36
Mean	10.8	9.3	12.2
SD	8.3	7.0	9.5

Intelligent Rules of Thumb

Rare Discrepancies between Broad Abilities

Comparison	Rare Discrepancy Value
Gc vs. Gf Expanded Gc vs. Expanded Gf Gsm vs. Glr	22 or more points is always rare, occurring in ≤15% of the sample

Interpreting Narrow Abilities

The WISC–V assesses 13 narrow abilities, three for Gs and two for each of the other broad abilities. Of this group of narrow abilities, the *WISC–V Administration and Scoring Manual* provides index scores for five:

Lexical Knowledge (VL) = Verbal Comprehension Index

Visualization (Vz) = Visual Spatial Index

Quantitative Reasoning (RQ) = Quantitative Reasoning Index

Associative Memory (MA) = Symbol Translation Index

Naming Facility (NA) = Naming Speed Index

Of the remaining eight narrow abilities, four are composed of two or more subtests and merit interpretation. We have constructed new norms tables for these four narrow abilities: (Appendix A in the downloadable resources: www.wiley.com/go/itwiscv):

General Verbal Information (K0): Information + Comprehension + Picture Concepts

Induction (I): Matrix Reasoning + Picture Concepts + Similarities

Working Memory Capacity (WM): Digit Span Backward + Digit Span + Letter–Number Sequencing + Picture Span + Arithmetic

Perceptual Speed (P): Symbol Search + Cancellation

Table 8.2 provides reliability coefficients, and Table 8.3 provides *SEM*s for each of the four new narrow ability index scores. Tables 9.3 and 9.4 provide data on statistical significance and base rates to enable examiners to compare the child's index scores on these pairs of narrow abilities:

Gc—General Verbal Information versus Lexical Knowledge

Gf—Induction versus Quantitative Reasoning

These comparisons can be completed using the *WISC–V Interpretive Assistant 1.0* in the downloadable resources: www.wiley.com/go/itwiscv (see the Step 7 tab), or they can be hand-completed as follows:

1. Obtain standard scores for the four narrow abilities either from Appendix A in the downloadable resources: www.wiley.com/go/itwiscv (Induction, General Verbal

Table 9.3 Critical Values for Statistically Significant Differences at the .05 Level of Significance between Narrow Abilities, by Age Group and Overall Normative Sample

Comparison	Age Group											Overall
	6	7	8	9	10	11	12	13	14	15	16	
Gc-KO vs. Gc-VL	16	15	17	15	15	17	13	15	15	15	15	15
Gf-I vs. Gf-RQ	14	14	14	14	13	14	12	13	13	14	14	14

Table 9.4 Differences between Narrow Abilities Obtained by Various Base Rates of the Normative Sample

	Gc-KO vs. Gc-VL	Gf-I vs. Gf-RQ
≤15	14	18
≤10	17	21
≤5	20	25
≤2	24	29
Mean	7.8	10.0
SD	6.4	7.5

Information) or from the *WISC–V Administration and Scoring Manual* (Lexical Knowledge, Quantitative Reasoning).

2. Subtract the lower *Gc* index from the higher *Gc* index.
3. Subtract the lower *Gf* index from the higher *Gf* index.
4. Locate the differences in Tables 9.3 and 9.4 to determine its statistical significance and its base rate in the normal population.
5. Consult Flanagan et al. (2013) to interpret the clinical and educational implications of any noteworthy discrepancies *within* the *Gf* or *Gc* broad abilities and to determine which additional tasks from other test batteries might be best to administer as part of the XBA.

The next intelligent rules of thumb could be helpful when comparing these narrow abilities.

Intelligent Rules of Thumb

Significant Discrepancies between Narrow Abilities at the .05 Level

Comparison	Value
Gc-KO vs. Gc-VL Gf-I vs. Gf-RQ	15 or more points

Intelligent Rules of Thumb

Rare Discrepancies between Narrow Abilities

Comparison	Rare Discrepancy Value
Gc-KO vs. Gc-VL Gf-I vs. Gf-RQ	18 or more points is always rare, occurring in ≤15% of the sample

Examiners who wish to engage in thorough CHC analysis of the WISC–V—even if they opt not to administer tasks from other assessment batteries—need to allow sufficient time for the WISC–V evaluation. In addition to the 10 primary subtests that are needed to obtain the five primary index scores, examiners should consider administering the Symbol Translation subtests to derive the sixth broad ability of *Glr*. The secondary Information, Comprehension, Picture Concepts, and Arithmetic subtests should be administered if comparison between the child's performance on the two *Gf* and the two *Gc* narrow abilities is desired.

Narrow Abilities and Academic Achievement

A growing body of research has identified which specific narrow abilities are most related to different aspects of reading, math, and writing (Flanagan et al., 2013; Schneider & McGrew, 2012). The 13 WISC–V narrow abilities show notable relationships to specific aspects of achievement, based on Flanagan et al.'s (2013, pp. 46–63) summary and overview of research results (text in quotes is from Flanagan et al.):

Reading

Gc

Lexical Knowledge (VL) is important and becomes "increasingly important with age" (p. 48).

Gsm

"Memory Span (MS) is important especially when evaluated within the context of working memory capacity" (p. 49).

Glr

"Naming Facility (NA) or rapid automatic naming is very important during the elementary school years. Associative Memory (MA) was also found to be related to reading at young ages (e.g., elementary school)" (p. 51).

Gs

"Perceptual Speed (P) is important during all school years, particularly the elementary school years" (p. 51).

Math

Gf

Induction (I) is "consistently related to math achievement at all ages" (p. 55).

Gc

Lexical Knowledge (VL) is important and becomes "increasingly important with age" (p. 55).

Gsm

"Memory Span (MS) is important especially when evaluated within the context of working memory" (p. 56).

Gv (the broad ability)

"*Gv* may be important primarily for higher-level or advanced mathematics (e.g., geometry, calculus" (p. 56).

Gs

"Perceptual Speed (P) is important during all school years, particularly during elementary school" (p. 57).

Writing

Gf

Induction (I) is "related to basic writing skills primarily during the elementary school years (e.g., 6–13) and consistently related to written expression at all ages" (p. 60).

Gc

"Lexical Knowledge (VL) and General Verbal Information (K0) are important primarily after age 7. These abilities become increasingly more important with age" (p. 60).

Gsm

"Memory Span (MS) is important to writing, especially spelling skills, whereas Working Memory Capacity (MW) has shown relations with advanced writing skills (e.g., written expression)" (p. 60).

Glr

"Naming Facility (NA) or 'rapid automatic naming' has demonstrated relations with written expression, primarily the fluency aspect of writing" (p. 60).

Gs

"Perceptual Speed (P) is important during all school years for basic writing and related to all ages for written expression" (p. 60).

The WISC–V narrow abilities share close relationships with various aspects of academic achievement, especially Lexical Knowledge, Working Memory Capacity, Induction, and Perceptual Speed. However, three other abilities, not measured by the WISC–V, are also exceptional predictors of reading, math, and writing: Language Development (narrow *Gc* ability), General Sequential Reasoning (narrow *Gf* ability), and Phonetic Coding (narrow *Ga* ability). Overall, the results of the extensive literature on the relation of CHC narrow abilities to academic achievement supports (a) the essential role of supplementing the WISC–V with other tasks via a theory-based model such as XBA (Flanagan & Alfonso, in press; Flanagan et al., 2013) and (b) the validity of using CHC theory as a foundation for the development of educational interventions.

From a practical, clinical perspective, John Willis (personal communication, December 7, 2014) made the following interesting comment:

An all-too-common purpose for testing is prediction of achievement. I have always thought that it was easier simply to test achievement. However, if future or "expected" achievement must be predicted, it is necessary but not sufficient to apply our thorough understanding of research data on correlations between various aspects of academic achievement and various cognitive abilities (e.g., Flanagan et al., 2013; Ortiz et al., 2015). We must consider not only the probable level of achievement if the examinee's instructional program remains unchanged, but also the

possible level of achievement if an appropriate instructional program can be implemented with fidelity.

INTRODUCTION TO CASE REPORTS

Three case reports are presented to illustrate application of CHC-based interpretive approaches using the WISC–V. The first report on Liam, age 9, was contributed by Joel Schneider. Similar to his other authored works, the report is beautifully written, reading more like a high-quality short story than a typical evaluation. The vivid descriptions of the subtle interplay between characteristics of Liam's personality and his test performance leave the reader feeling as if they know Liam personally, an intention of the author that is revealed only in his post-hoc comments. Dr. Schneider also graciously provided some introductory and concluding statements about intelligent assessment and report writing that are useful for all clinicians, regardless of theoretical orientation.

Jill Hartmann and John Willis coauthored the second case report on Alicia, age 13. As with Liam, the reader gains a sense of "knowing" Alicia after reading the report, based on numerous references to observed behaviors and interactive exchanges during the evaluation. The report provides an excellent example of report writing that fosters a collaborative team spirit in addressing Alicia's academic needs, beginning with the testing-purpose explanation provided to Alicia prior to testing and culminating with the description of recommendations and diagnostic possibilities as *options* for discussion with the larger treatment team.

The third and final report selected for this chapter was coauthored by Jennifer Mascolo and Dawn Flanagan, providing an outstanding example of CHC-based interpretation using the Cross-Battery Assessment (XBA) method. Luke, age 9, continues to have serious difficulties reading, despite a rather exhaustive history of psychological and physical evaluations to determine the contributing factors. Impressive detailed descriptions of Luke's classroom environment underscore the importance of considering these factors for all children through direct observation. Expert use of testing the limits while maintaining a standard administration provides insights into Luke's response processes as well as interventions that may prove effective in addressing his needs. Recommendations are plentiful, providing enough detail about available resources to make them readily available, wasting no time in meeting Luke's academic needs.

CASE 1—LIAM, AGE 9: EMOTIONALLY INTELLIGENT TESTING WITH THE WISC–V AND CHC THEORY

W. Joel Schneider

With every new assessment case, there is an opportunity to accomplish something of great value: to help a person understand the world and to help the world understand a person. The experience of being assessed by an empathic professional is not merely informative but can itself be therapeutic (Finn, 2007). At the end of this experience, an evaluation report is written to inform appropriate decision makers (e.g., parents, teachers, administrators, physicians, etc.). A truly excellent report is designed to facilitate in the mind of the reader a useful and accurate sense of empathy for the evaluee so that better decisions can be made on the evaluee's behalf. I believe that all other goals of report writing should be subordinate to this purpose, and that this implies a need to rethink many traditional report-writing practices.

I am hardly the first person to suggest that too often psychological reports are confusing, alienating, and/or irrelevant (Donders, 1999; Fischer, 1994; Harvey, 1997; Hass & Carriere, 2014; Mastoras, Climie, McCrimmon, & Schwean, 2011). Calls for better reports and advice on how to write them have been with us for a long time (Lodge, 1953; Tallent & Reiss, 1959; J. L. Taylor & Teicher, 1946). My first reports were filled with excruciatingly detailed explanations of the quirky particulars of test construction, the inscrutable mechanics of statistical inference, and that charming dialect of professional patois psychologists use to confuse themselves and others. It took an embarrassingly long time for me to realize that writing this way was a bad idea. It took an even longer time for me to stop doing it. In fact, I still slip up.

It was surprisingly difficult to make my reports easy to read and understand, in part because of the *curse of knowledge* (the expert's inability to see things from a nonexpert's perspective; Camerer, Loewenstein, & Weber, 1989) but also for petty reasons. Steven Pinker (2014) hypothesized that one reason academic writing is often unpleasant to read is that the goal of many writers is not so much to be understood but to protect themselves from the charge of philosophical naïveté by their peers. I cannot speak for all academics, but it was definitely true in my case (and sometimes still is). Furthermore, I have worked very hard to incorporate mathematical sophistication into my interpretive process. It was painful to write a report in which all that hard work was not evident to the next professional who read the report. I was a surly ballerina continuously announcing to the audience that these seemingly simple moves are definitely *not* easy.

Fortunately for me (and the people I later assessed), our profession has a few traditions and features that induce self-reflection and self-correction. Being supervised by experienced and level-headed clinicians helped eliminate some of my worst habits, but supervising graduate students really drove the lesson home. Observing how tone-deaf the reports were when students attempted to mimic my report-writing style was humbling. Yikes! I did an about-face and dramatically simplified my writing style (and probably overcorrected a little).

My primary approach to report writing is to begin with a thorough interview, trying to understand a person's life story. Once I have a sense of who the person is and what the person (or the person's parents) would like to know, I attempt to supplement my narrative understanding with quantitative tests and rating scales. After I believe that I understand what the tests are telling me, I attempt to translate this information back into a narrative.

In terms of cognitive assessment, I primarily use the Cattell-Horn-Carroll (CHC) Theory of Cognitive Abilities (McGrew, 2009; Schneider & McGrew, 2012) as my guiding framework. However, as articulated eloquently by Cathy Fiorello (2014), CHC theory is only a good starting point when trying to figure out what a test score means. A population-level taxonomy of abilities could not begin to cover all the possible twists and turns an assessment can take with an individual. Furthermore, in some ways it is less important how high or low an ability is but what is done with it that counts. For this reason, I try to mix my report of ability levels with examples of how each ability is manifest in the person's life.

It would be difficult to infer what went into making a film just by watching it. Likewise, a good evaluation report does not include a blow-by-blow account of how it came to be. First, I present the evaluation report. Afterward, I present an account of a few critical decision points in the report-writing process.

Following the report is a brief review of the WISC–V and a figure showing the four-factor structure that emerges when exploratory factor analysis (EFA) is conducted rather than confirmatory factor analysis (CFA). For an in-depth look at a variety of alternate approaches to CFA (different from the methodology used in the *WISC–V Technical and Interpretive Manual*) and a detailed report of the four-factor solutions (not five-factor) that emerge when EFA is applied, consult the rigorous study conducted by Canivez and Watkins, especially for this book, that appears in Appendix I in the downloadable resources: www.wiley.com/go/itwiscv. Canivez and Watkins conducted these analyses as part of their review of the WISC–V (Chapter 20).

Psychological Evaluation Report

Disclaimer: Although this report was based on a real individual, the name and several other details of the report have been altered to protect the anonymity of the family who generously allowed me to have this report published.

Reason for Referral
Liam's parents are worried that their son is beginning to fall behind in school and hope to understand his strengths and weaknesses better so that they can be more effective when they assist him with his schoolwork. They strongly suspect that their son has attention problems that were downplayed in a previous evaluation.

Relevant Background Information
Liam is a 9-year-old boy just shy of his 10th birthday. He is of mostly English and Scottish heritage and lives in a midsize city in the midwestern region of the United States. He is the youngest of five boys in the family. His parents are both college-educated with careers involving high levels of responsibility.

Birth and Early Development
Liam was delivered 3 weeks early because there was a true knot in the umbilical cord, raising the risk of asphyxia. During Liam's delivery, both mother and child lost consciousness for a short but terrifying period of a few minutes. The doctors were relieved that there were no obvious consequences after consciousness was regained. In his first week Liam was severely jaundiced, requiring several days of phototherapy to reduce toxic levels of bilirubin. It is impossible to know with any certainty whether any of these problems before, during, and after Liam was born have anything to do with his current difficulties, but all of them are associated with increased risk of attention and learning problems. On the other hand, it is quite possible, and even likely, that his attention problems would have occurred even if his delivery had been without incident.

Because one of Liam's siblings has a pervasive developmental disorder, any signs of similar symptoms in Liam as a baby and then as a young child were especially noticeable to his parents. In truth, there were and are some similarities between Liam and this brother. Liam is extremely sensitive to particular textures and is often uncomfortable in his clothes. He has very particular food preferences. When he plays alone, he primarily experiments with objects rather than engaging in imaginative play. When stressed or excited, he used to flap his hands in a manner that is common among children with autism. (His mother suspects that this was simply learned by observing his brother.) In addition, Liam was starting to show problems with attention and impulsivity.

2011 Evaluation

Because of the concerns listed above, Liam was evaluated by a clinical psychologist in 2011 when Liam was 6 years old. Liam and his mother were interviewed for about 1 hour, and Liam was given an IQ test and an academic achievement test. Other than the fact that Liam rushed through his work and made careless errors, the evaluator did not see attention problems severe enough to warrant a diagnosis of attention-deficit/hyperactivity disorder (ADHD). The evaluator concluded that his problems were primarily behavioral in nature. No mention of any symptoms of autism was made in the report. Liam's cognitive ability scores on the IQ test were mostly average, as were his academic ability scores. His reading decoding skills were low average and his spelling ability was high average.

Current Academic Difficulties

Liam is currently in the fourth grade. His moderate attention deficits are partially reduced with stimulant mediation prescribed by his physician. These deficits are beginning to interfere with his performance in school, causing his grades to drop. His teacher noted that when motivated, Liam is capable of doing everything she asks him to do and that he excels in math and science-related areas, but lately his efforts have been flagging in most domains. Although never defiant at school, Liam finds diverse and creative ways to avoid doing his schoolwork in its intended spirit. That is, he often takes shortcuts so that it appears that he has completed the work, but upon inspection, he has not shown that he has mastered the skills the assignment was intended to foster.

Procedures for Evaluation

- Interviews with Liam, his parents, and his teacher

- Wechsler Intelligence Scale for Children–Fifth Edition (WISC–V)
- Woodcock-Johnson Tests of Cognitive Ability, Fourth Edition (WJ IV, Selected Tests)
- Kaufman Test of Educational Achievement–Third Edition (KTEA–3)
- Behavioral Assessment Scales for Children (BASC–2, Parent Forms)

Relevant Behavioral Observations

Liam was initially excited about the evaluation process and we quickly developed a natural rapport. He was eager to talk about a wide variety of topics, both light and serious. He answered all my questions directly and thoughtfully, often with self-awareness and humor. I found him to be a gentle soul: sensitive, warm, and kind.

Liam's attentional deficits were not at all apparent at first, but they were unmistakably obvious as time went on. Over the course of five testing sessions, as the novelty of the situation wore off, the time that he was able to stay engaged without distraction became progressively shorter. Although Liam clearly wanted to perform to the best of his ability on all tests, he needed frequent prompts to do so.

To a degree that is unusual even among other children with ADHD, Liam's mental energy is quickly drained by any task requiring sustained mental focus. He often whined and expressed his dismay at how difficult the tests were. At first this was confusing to me because his complaints were most intense, not when the tasks were well beyond his ability, but when they were well within it. That is, he would repeatedly protest (e.g., "I don't like this." "Do I have to do this?" "This is physically impossible!") as he *successfully* completed item after item. Even when he was not complaining, it was obvious that many of the tests were wearing him out. To illustrate, he let out quiet grunts, as if heaving medium-size stones, each time he (correctly) solved simple math problems (e.g., $6 + 7 = ?$, $9 - 2 = ?$, $2 \times 3 = ?$).

Interestingly, his discomfort was less intense on tests normally considered to demand attention (e.g., short-term memory tests). That is, he was more tolerant of tests in which he needed to focus in short bursts and he could see the end in sight. Tests that were untimed, open-ended, and of indeterminate length (e.g., defining vocabulary words, solving logic problems, and answering questions about reading passages) were especially unpleasant to him because he knew that he needed to concentrate but did not know when the task would end.

In the course of testing, sometimes many test items would be revealed at once and he could see that he had, what was to him, a long way to go before finishing. This was often greeted with a whimper. If I gave sympathy and encouragement, he would take a deep breath, steel himself to the approaching unpleasantness, and then attempt to complete the task to the best of his ability. Thus, his tendency to be overwhelmed by task length did not appear to lower his scores but did influence how long it took to complete each test, including many short breaks between items.

Between tasks, there was no sense of resentment toward me for asking him to work hard. As soon as the pressure was off, he went back to being his cheerful, delightful self.

Liam often used his self-awareness to advocate for himself. He knew when he was nearing his limits and would suggest solutions so that he could work longer. For example, he suggested that "running laps" would make him feel better after sitting for a long time. (We had been sitting for 30 minutes.) He ran up and down the hall several times and then was able to work for about 20 minutes without interruption or visible discomfort. Because he was genuinely trying to figure out how to get through the evaluation instead of merely avoiding doing work, I came to trust Liam's judgment about what he needed.

In the sessions in which he had recently taken his prescribed stimulant medication, Liam was better able to focus on the task at hand. However, even when medicated, he still found sustained mental effort extremely taxing.

Cognitive Abilities

General Ability
When Liam is alert, motivated, relaxed, and under close supervision, Liam's performance on most cognitive tests is in the average range, if not slightly better. However, when these optimal conditions are not present, his performance tends to worsen considerably.

Language Ability and General Knowledge
Liam understands speech and communicates effectively. He enjoys engaging in verbal wordplay and witty banter, which is one of the ways in which his family expresses affection. His informal verbal communication style feels more sophisticated than his average test scores would suggest. Sometimes he uses his sensitivity to the subtle meanings of words to his advantage (e.g., selectively interpreting adult commands in a literal sense so as to give the appearance of compliance without having to exert unwanted effort). Had Liam been able to maintain consistent enthusiasm for testing, it is likely that his language ability scores would likely have been somewhat higher, perhaps in the high-average range.

Overall, Liam's scores on general knowledge tests are on the lower half of the average range. However, as is true with most people, Liam's knowledge is more developed in some areas than in others. Liam is unusually motivated to perform scientific experiments. This is an interest shared by his mother, who often helps Liam replicate demonstration projects they have seen on the television show *Mythbusters*. He was quite proud of his mastery of scientific subjects and spontaneously offered to explain to me various scientific ideas (e.g., why earthquakes happen). His knowledge of the humanities and the social sciences is less well developed, mostly because his interests lie elsewhere.

Logical Reasoning and Novel Problem Solving
On formal tests of reasoning, which measure the ability to solve unfamiliar logic problems, Liam's performance is average. However, Liam's average

score is average in an interesting way because his performance varies quite a bit from test to test and from situation to situation.

One of the logical reasoning test scores at the end of this report is misleadingly high. On the WISC–V Figure Weights subtest, he earned a score that is higher than 99.6% of his same-age peers, but his true ability level is probably in the high-average range. Figure Weights is a multiple-choice test, and when he encountered difficult items, he announced that he would guess because he knew that he had a 20% chance of getting it right. (Upon further querying, I found that he had an advanced understanding of probability and could calculate odds correctly in a variety of situations.) For the last seven (and most difficult) items on this test, he looked at the problem for about 10 seconds and then pointed to an answer, saying "I'm guessing." Luck was with him and he guessed right four out of seven times. With purely random guesses, getting four or more questions right out of seven would occur only 3% of the time. It is possible that some unconscious and intuitive aspect of intelligence was at work, slightly increasing the odds of guessing correctly. However, such intuition cannot be relied upon consistently. If he were to retake a similar test, it is unlikely that he would obtain such a high score again. Indeed, on similar measures, his performance was average.

Liam is the kind of child who delights in giving adults a gentle ribbing when they contradict themselves or demonstrate a minor lapse in logic. More generally, he is attentive and sensitive to logical consistency in all things. He firmly wishes for ideas to be logically tidy—so much so that when something does not fit within his logical framework, he has a tendency to dismiss it out of hand, refusing to consider the matter any further. Several times during testing he announced that some of my questions made no sense—and that was that—on to the next question! For example, on a vocabulary test in which he needed to find pairs of synonyms, some of the correct answers were only approximately the same (e.g., *thick* and *wide*). The near but inexact similarities between

the correct word pairs upset him, and he announced that the test was unfair: "I *really* don't like this. None of them are right." No amount of prompting to try to think of an answer (or even guess) helped. This did not appear to be merely avoidance of effort. After the testing was complete, I revisited these items and suggested that he find the words that were the most similar to each other, even though they were not exactly the same. Still, he refused to make an attempt, not out of defiance but on principle.

I believe that he knew the correct answers in these situations but that the small differences between the words loomed large in his mind and to say that they were in any way similar was somehow offensive to him. In further discussions, he explained (and his teacher confirmed) that this happened often in the classroom and that it upset him greatly when test questions violated his expectations or were, in his opinion, illogical. To some degree, thinking concretely is typical for children Liam's age. However, it is expressed with more than typical emotional fervor in Liam's case and occasionally interferes with optimal performance.

Visual–Spatial Reasoning

Much of human intelligence is devoted to solving problems nonverbally, *in the mind's eye*. Artists, engineers, architects, and designers often visualize solutions to problems in their heads before committing resources to a particular approach. In everyday life, visualizing can dramatically increase the probability of successfully solving particular problems. For example, imagining how to fit a large couch through a doorway reduces the time and effort it would otherwise take with a purely trial-and-error approach.

The first test I gave to Liam was a measure of visual-spatial ability. Liam was dismayed that it required concentrated effort to solve the puzzles and was quickly discouraged despite my best efforts to buoy his spirits. It was especially disappointing to him that the evaluation was not going to be as fun as he initially believed it would be. Giving up quickly on difficult test items brought him a temporary sense of relief but resulted in a test score that was an underestimate of his ability.

Liam was under the impression that he was being graded on the test and believed that it was unfair that he was given no opportunity to study for it. After a short discussion, Liam accepted that these tests served a different kind of purpose. He felt better about the matter when he learned that no one else was given the opportunity to study for the tests and that, in part, the tests measured the ability to figure things out for the first time. Follow-up testing (and test scores from the 2011 evaluation) revealed that, under optimal conditions, Liam's visual-spatial ability is at least average and probably high average.

Auditory Processing

In the same way that we can manipulate visual images in our heads, we can also play with sounds in our thoughts. For example, even after he lost his hearing, Beethoven was able to compose music by "hearing" in his mind how certain sounds would blend.

One ability that is particularly important for beginning readers is the ability to pull apart and blend units of sounds that make up words. For example, the word "cat" has three sounds: /k/, /a/, and /t/. Beginning readers need to be able to distinguish these sounds from each other so that they can see the correspondence between individual sounds and specific letters: /k/ = C, /a/ = A, and /t/ = T. In this way, unfamiliar words can be "decoded" one letter-sound at a time.

Children who have poor auditory processing abilities often have difficulty learning to read and spell. As will be seen later, Liam has weak spelling skills. It was therefore reasonable to assume that his poor spelling ability would be accounted for by low auditory processing ability. However, across several auditory processing tests in various formats, Liam's auditory processing ability is average. Therefore, auditory processing deficits do not explain his spelling problems.

Furthermore, Liam's difficulty articulating the /r/ sound is a production problem, not a result of an inability to perceive the sound correctly. Liam can hear the /r/ sound accurately but cannot produce it consistently.

Memory

Working Memory

Working memory refers to the ability to hold onto information in one's head just long enough to use it, usually just for a few seconds. For example, working memory is used to remember two-digit numbers just long enough to add them together in one's head. Working memory is used in almost every task that involves more than a few steps. Deficits in working memory can limit performance in the areas of mathematical reasoning, reading comprehension, and writing composition. Fortunately, no such deficits were observed in Liam. His performance on working memory tests is average to high average.

Because the use of working memory requires the effortful direction of attention, working memory tests are thought by some people to act as markers of ADHD. Although it is true that people with ADHD tend to score a little lower on working memory tests on average, about half of people with ADHD score in the average range or better. (The *average range* is usually defined as scores between the 25th and 75th percentile.) Therefore, good performance on working memory tests does not rule out an ADHD diagnosis.

Learning Efficiency

Some people are able to learn new information quickly and effortlessly whereas others need to be exposed to new knowledge many times before it is finally learned. Liam's learning rate is average, but only when he is able to devote his attention to the material.

Memory Retrieval Fluency

Memories are not retrieved instantaneously, and some memories are easier to retrieve than others. Everyone has experienced the tip-of-the-tongue phenomenon when a particular fact is temporarily inaccessible to memory. For example, I often have to strain to remember what the capital of Canada is, even though I know that I know it (… Ottawa!).

For some people, memory retrieval is particularly effortful and causes many short delays in speech and thought (accompanied by frequent *ah*s and *um*s). Problems with memory retrieval can manifest in disfluent reading, writing, and calculation. People with especially fluent memory retrieval ability are known to have an advantage in creative problem solving because they can generate and evaluate many ideas quickly. Fortunately, Liam's memory retrieval fluency is at least average and likely in the high-average range when he is fully alert and motivated. His fluent memory retrieval is manifest in his quick wit and in his creative and spontaneous ideas for experiments.

Information-Processing Speed

On very simple and repetitive tasks (e.g., verifying whether pairs of numbers are the same), some people can process familiar information quickly, smoothly, and efficiently. Others process information slowly, often in fits and starts. One of the primary causes of slow information-processing speed is impaired attentional control. That is, they are unable to direct the focus of attention smoothly as they process each bit of information. Under optimal conditions, Liam's information-processing speed appears to be average.

Academic Skills

Reading Skills

The ability to read is not just a single skill but a collection of many related subskills. Not all reading subskills are necessarily equally well developed.

Reading Decoding The ability to read single words, often presented without context, is *reading decoding*. If a word is unfamiliar, it must be sounded out. Liam's ability to sound out words according to standard pronunciation rules is average.

Skilled readers rarely need to sound out familiar words because the words are recognized immediately on sight. Liam's performance on a sight-word reading task slightly underestimated his decoding ability because of impulsive responding. At the beginning of the test, when all the words were easy to read, he got into a particular rhythm of reading. When the words became a little harder to read, he failed to adjust his reading speed and got several words in a row wrong—words that later testing revealed that he actually did know how to read. When focused, Liam's ability to recognize words is average.

Reading Fluency In order for a person to become a skilled reader, reading decoding must become fluent and automatic so that attention can be devoted to the meaning of the text rather than to the pronunciation of the words. On tests of reading fluency, Liam was able to read single words and simple sentences at an average rate.

Reading Comprehension Liam's ability to understand text is average, as would be expected from his language abilities, reading decoding, and reading fluency skills. Liam's interest was piqued several times by the content of the reading comprehension test items. He wanted to engage in extended conversations about what he read. For this reason, it was particularly interesting to note how easily and quickly answering these reading comprehension items fatigued him. It would be understandable if he were bored by the text, but this was clearly not the case. It was not so much that reading per se fatigued him. It was reading and then having to return to the text in order to answer detailed questions that was particularly taxing. Having to answer "main idea" questions was particularly aversive because, in his opinion, these were "opinions, not facts." Nevertheless, he was usually able to answer these questions correctly when given encouragement.

Writing Skills

Handwriting   Writing neatly is not a priority for Liam. Although it is possible to read his writing, it often requires effort to do so. Even his best writing is fairly messy.

Spelling   Liam knows that he is not a good speller; it is already a part of his emerging identity, even to the extent that it is a point of pride. His performance on a spelling test was low, although with a little more effort I suspect that he could have gotten at least a low-average score.

It is particularly puzzling as to why his spelling skills are low because his reading decoding skills are average. Many people are poor spellers because they cannot hear the individual sounds in words that correspond to each letter. As mentioned before, Liam has no such deficits.

I was not able to arrive at a definitive explanation for his spelling deficits. One clue as to why his spelling skills are poor is that most of his spelling errors had to do with spelling words in a phonologically regular manner (i.e., spelled just as they sound). He did this even when those letter combinations never occur in standard written English (e.g., *draw* = "jra"). I believe that incorrect spelling does not bother him and thus he is not motivated to learn from his mistakes. Learning to spell words with irregular spelling is probably unappealing to him because it requires learning endless particulars and exceptions. His preference for logical tidiness may also extend to English spelling. He would prefer (as many of us do) that English spelling were more regular, following the pronunciation of words more closely.

It is possible that Liam's spelling (and written grammar) deficits result from a subtle language processing problem that was not detected in this evaluation. Liam's mother also struggles with spelling, even though she has excellent reading skills and is highly motivated to spell correctly. She suspects that Liam's struggles with spelling are similar to hers. When focused on writing correctly, she can usually recall the correct spelling of words because she has memorized them by brute force. However, when performing a cognitively demanding task while writing, she frequently makes inexplicable letter substitutions. Other family members have more pronounced spelling and reading deficits, with some members having dyslexia or dyslexic tendencies.

Written Grammar   Liam's spoken grammar is excellent, but his ability to find and correct written grammar errors and punctuation problems is low. It seems doubtful to me that there is a strictly cognitive reason that he does not capitalize the first words in sentences, put quotation marks in appropriate places, insert commas between clauses, and end sentences with periods or question marks. As with spelling, not bothering with proper punctuation is now part of his identity. In his own words, delivered with a wry smile, "Oh no. I don't *do* commas."

Writing Fluency   Surprisingly, Liam is able to write very quickly. On a writing speed test, he was able to compose short simple sentences at a rate faster than 97% of children his age. However, on this test, he was so devoted to writing quickly that his hand cramped up severely. Although he pushed through the pain until the end of the test, he was unable to use a pencil for the rest of the testing session that day.

Written Expression   Although his knowledge of the mechanics of writing is low, his ability to express his ideas in writing is at least average. On a task in which he had to recall and write down a story that had been told to him, he whined and complained throughout the task but retold the story quite thoroughly. At the end, he asked if he could extend the story. Curious, I allowed him to do so. Immediately, all fatigue was gone as he gleefully wrote down a silly alternate ending to the story. He then drew a detailed picture of one of the story's characters. Thus, it is not writing per se that tires him, but writing on a narrowly defined topic not of his own choosing.

Mathematics Skills

Liam is proud of his math skills. While taking the math tests he did not complain or show signs of fatigue.

Computation Skills   Liam knows his basic math facts (e.g., 4 + 5 =9). Although he made several impulsive calculation errors, he self-corrected almost all of them after he noticed that his answers did not make sense. His knowledge of basic math calculation procedures involving whole numbers, decimals, and fractions is average for his age.

Math Fact Recall Fluency   Being able to recall math facts automatically and without effort is an essential task for anyone who hopes to master algebra and higher forms of mathematics. If attention is devoted to recalling math facts, it is difficult to remember where one is in solving a multistep problem. For this reason it bodes well that Liam's ability to recall math facts fluently is high average.

Math Problem Solving   Liam has an intuitive sense about solving mathematics problems and appears to enjoy solving problems of moderate difficulty. His performance in this area was high average. This strength fits well with his long-standing ambition to have a career in a science-related field.

Behavioral and Emotional Functioning

Attentional Deficits

A common misunderstanding about ADHD is that people with the disorder simply cannot direct their attention at all, even when they want to. When children with ADHD arc observed to control their attention, people with this misunderstanding assume that the children therefore do not really have ADHD. Furthermore, if they *can* control their attention, then it is assumed that any attentional lapses are willful, and therefore blameworthy. Actually, the total inability to control attention is very rare and is more consistent with a severe brain injury than with garden-variety ADHD.

To make a comparison, it is not that people with severe headaches are *unable* to smile pleasantly, and it is not that they *refuse* to smile pleasantly; it *simply does not occur to them* to do so most of the time. Given the right incentives, people with severe headaches can smile pleasantly but possibly only with great effort.

Likewise, it is not that people with ADHD *can't* pay attention, nor is it that they *won't* pay attention. Rather, much of the time they simply *don't* pay attention. Often they are willing and able to do so when prompted, but they *do* require the prompt.

Liam is usually quite willing and able to control his impulses and direct the focus of his attention when prompted by situational demands. However, doing so is not his natural inclination, in part because engaging in activities requiring sustained mental focus is more tiring and unpleasant for him than it is for most people. When fatigued, his ability to control his attention and his impulses is reduced considerably.

Social Adjustment

Liam is fortunate to come from a loving home with parents who are tolerant of his special needs but still insist on good behavior and encourage academic success. Liam's relationship with his older brothers is generally positive. In the rough-and-tumble economy of brotherly love, Liam both dishes out and receives a bit of teasing and light torment, but it is never terribly serious.

Liam makes friends easily. Although Liam believes that his friends find him to be "a little wild" and his mother believes that he might be "a little bossy," Liam has been able to sustain these friendships over time.

One of the reasons that he is liked by his friends is that he has a natural generosity and enjoys sharing what he has (e.g., food and toys). On one occasion, he helped a friend become close with a girl even though he too liked the girl. He recognized that his friend liked the girl more than he did and so he thought it was the right thing to do.

Emotional Regulation

Liam is mostly a very cheerful person. However, he frequently has fairly intense nighttime anxiety, which on occasion has resulted in insomnia and daytime fatigue. Often it is difficult for him to articulate exactly what he is afraid of. Although there is no history of trauma, he fears intruders coming into the house. His mother describes his nighttime anxiety as similar to a panic attack.

His anxiety is often made more intense by his extreme sensitivity to particular textures in his clothes. He prefers to go shirtless at home whenever possible, and this seems to help him to focus when completing his homework.

When stressed, Liam calms himself by taking warm baths. Immersing himself so that all but his face is underwater seems to block out unpleasant sensory stimulation. If allowed, Liam would take frequent short baths, but on average he is restricted to bathing only twice per day.

Summary

Liam is a 9-year-old boy of European heritage who is beginning to fall behind academically despite average cognitive ability and academic skills. He often fails to complete classwork due primarily to moderate attention deficits and mild problems of impulsivity. These symptoms are only partially remediated by stimulant mediation. Although he is socially and emotionally well adjusted in general, Liam has significant nighttime anxiety, which at times interferes with his ability to sleep, which, in turn, worsens his attention problems.

DSM–5 Diagnosis

> 314.01 Attention-deficit/hyperactivity disorder, combined presentation
>
> V62.21 Academic or educational problem

Recommendations for Liam's Parents

- As parents, you are admirably attuned to Liam's needs and limits. With loving understanding, you have been able to create an environment in which Liam is developing into a kind, generous, and thoughtful human being. There is little advice I can give to improve upon what you are already doing so well. There is every reason to believe that with continued support, Liam will continue to develop in a positive direction. Even so, your worries about his future are legitimate, and I share them. It is hard for any child to learn how to see things through when they are difficult, unpleasant, or tedious. With Liam's particular sensitivities and attention deficits, it is even harder. I see it as an especially hopeful sign that he was aware of his own limits and could advocate for himself in the testing environment. In my conversations with Liam's teacher, it appears that this skill has not yet generalized to the school environment. He may need explicit guidance in how to communicate his needs appropriately to school personnel and other authority figures.

- Consider teaching Liam relaxation skills such as meditation so that when he is frustrated or overwhelmed, he can quietly take a brief break and calm himself. I am happy to recommend books on this topic. If teaching these skills proves difficult, I am happy to recommend a behavioral specialist who could work with Liam to master these skills. A behavioral specialist is also likely to be helpful in working with Liam to master his nighttime anxiety.

- To a remarkable degree, you have balanced tolerating Liam's special needs and maintaining high expectations for good conduct and academic achievement. This has required a deftly agile and flexible approach to parenting. Because Liam's academic performance has recently dropped, it is probably time, at least in the near future, to err on the side of maintaining high expectations. Even so, in the long term, no academic achievement is worth losing the warm relationship that you and he currently enjoy. In my short experience with Liam, I found that Liam could tolerate quite a bit of frustration if he understood the overall reason for the hard work he was doing. Before attempting homework assignments likely to be unpleasant for him, it might be helpful to quickly review why completing the assignment thoroughly is important. For example, "This assignment is about how to use commas to help readers understand what you mean when you write. I know that commas are not your favorite topic, but I've seen some hilarious misunderstandings when people forget to use a comma properly. Look at this sentence: *Let's eat, Joe.* Now look at what it means when the comma is missing. See? That's pretty funny! So in this case, putting the comma in the right place is a life-and-death matter … at least for Joe. I know this assignment might not be terribly exciting, but let's get through it for Joe's sake. Also, I think most people really appreciate it when your writing has commas in the right places. It communicates your thoughts clearly, and it shows that you take your work seriously. That is something that employers really like to see. If I didn't use commas in my writing, there is no way I would have been hired for the job I have."

- Consistent routines in the household have been very helpful to Liam. Without them, it is likely that there would be considerable conflict about when, how, and why homework and household chores are to be done. As he gets older, he is likely to experiment with asserting his independence about homework completion. Because it is easier to maintain a standard than it is to reestablish it, I recommend maintaining these routines as long as possible but judiciously adapting them as Liam matures.

- Liam's preference for logical tidiness does not mean that he is an inflexible person or even that he is a "rigid thinker" in every domain. To the contrary, he is quite flexible on most matters and values compromise when there are disagreements. It is likely that he will come to value ambiguity as he matures but that also he

will retain a greater than average preference for orderly thought. As this personality trait can be leveraged for success in many careers, it should be encouraged when appropriate and gently redirected when it gets in the way of his success.

Test Scores

Warning: Psychological test data are easily misinterpreted by people unfamiliar with psychological tests and psychological testing principles. Please consult a licensed psychologist before acting on any interpretation of these scores. Note that the labels used in the *Range* columns of the tables correspond to Figure 9.1, not necessarily to the range labels suggested in each test's manual. Table 9.5 presents Liam's WISC–V scores.

Table 9.5 Liam's Wechsler Intelligence Scale for Children, Fifth Edition (WISC–V) Scores

Scale	Score	Percentile	Range
Full Scale IQ	109	73	Average
Verbal Comprehension Index	106	66	Average
Similarities	10	50	Average
Vocabulary	12	75	High Average
Information	7	16	Low Average
Comprehension	9	37	Average
Visual Spatial Index	100	50	Average
Visual Puzzles	13	84	High Average
Block Design	7–W	16	Low Average
Fluid Reasoning Index	126–S	96	High
Matrix Reasoning	11	63	Average
Figure Weights	18–S	99.6	Extremely High
Picture Concepts	8	25	Low Average
Arithmetic	11	63	Average

(continued)

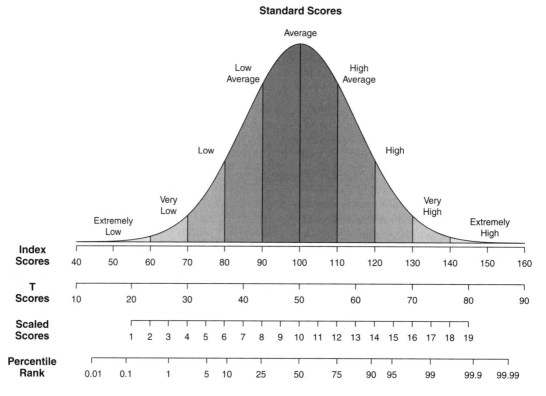

Figure 9.1   Standard Scores, Percentile Ranks, and the Normal Curve

Table 9.5   (*Continued*)

Scale	Score	Percentile	Range
Working Memory Index	**107**	**68**	**Average**
Picture Span	12	75	High Average
Digit Span	10	50	Average
Letter–Number Sequencing	12	75	High Average
Processing Speed Index	**100**	**50**	**Average**
Coding	11	63	Average
Symbol Search	9	37	Average
Cancellation	10	50	Average
Naming Speed Index	**112**	**79**	**High Average**
Naming Speed Literacy	102	55	Average

Table 9.5   (*Continued*)

Scale	Score	Percentile	Range
Naming Speed Quantity	118	88	High Average
Symbol Translation Index	**104**	**61**	**Average**
Immediate Symbol Translation	101	53	Average
Delayed Symbol Translation	104	61	Average
Recognition Symbol Translation	108	70	Average

Note: Scaled scores have a mean of 10 and a standard deviation of 3. Index scores have a mean of 100 and a standard deviation of 15.

Table 9.6 Liam's Kaufman Test of Educational Achievement, Third Edition (KTEA–3) Scores

Scale	Score	Percentile	Range
Reading	91	27	Average
Letter & Word Recognition	84	14	Low Average
Reading Comprehension	101	53	Average
Math	108	70	Average
Math Concepts	114	82	High Average
Math Computation	101	53	Average
Written Expression	81	10	Low Average
Written Expression	84	14	Low Average
Spelling	79	8	Low
Sound-Symbol	104	61	Average
Phonological Processing	114	82	High Average
Nonsense Word Decoding	93	32	Average
Decoding	88	21	Low Average
Letter & Word Recognition	84	14	Low Average
Nonsense Word Decoding	93	32	Average
Reading Fluency	103	58	Average
Word Recognition Fluency	106	66	Average
Decoding Fluency	91	27	Average
Silent Reading Fluency	112	79	High Average
Reading Understanding	97	42	Average
Reading Comprehension	101	53	Average
Reading Vocabulary	93	32	Average

Table 9.6   (Continued)

Scale	Score	Percentile	Range
Comprehension	101	53	Average
Reading Comprehension	101	53	Average
Listening Comprehension	100	50	Average
Expression	85	16	Low Average
Written Expression	84	14	Low Average
Oral Expression	90	25	Low Average
Orthographic Processing	101	53	Average
Word Recognition Fluency	106	66	Average
Spelling	79	8	Low
Letter Naming Facility	117	87	High Average
Academic Fluency	112	79	High Average
Decoding Fluency	91	27	Average
Math Fluency	110	75	High Average
Writing Fluency	129	97	High
Oral Language	98	45	Average
Oral Expression	90	25	Low Average
Listening Comprehension	100	50	Average
Associational Fluency	107	68	Average
Oral Fluency	107	68	Average
Associational Fluency	107	68	Average
Object Naming Fluency	104	61	Average

Note: Index scores have a mean of 100 and a standard deviation of 15.

Table 9.7   Liam's Woodcock–Johnson IV Scores

Scale	Score	Percentile	Range
Auditory Processing (Ga)	105	63	Average
Phonological Processing	102	55	Average
Nonword Repetition	105	63	Average

Note: Scaled scores have a mean of 10 and a standard deviation of 3. Index scores have a mean of 100 and a standard deviation of 15.

Critical Decision Points in the Report–Writing Process

How Much Detail to Include?

Except in special circumstances, I do not include sensitive details about the family's history in my reports. Although the report expresses admiration for the parents, it actually downplays the level of respect I felt as I listened to their story and observed them interact with Liam. Because it was relevant to Liam's story, I mentioned that an older brother had a pervasive developmental disorder. I omitted the fact that another brother has a serious neurological disorder with progressive symptoms. I omitted the fact that with all these difficulties, his parents found room in their home and in their hearts for foster children, each of whom had their own challenges. I omitted how active they are in their community, advocating for children with special needs. I omitted the story of how Liam's mother overcame considerable hardship in her own family of origin. I omitted how empathic she was for everyone involved in her family's struggles. I omitted details about how respected Liam's father is in his profession. I did not write about my conversation with him about the deep connection he felt toward his own father and how this influences his parenting style. I omitted the story of the fascinating way in which the family's mutual passion for competitive bowling strengthens the family bonds.

It would not necessarily have been a mistake to include these kinds of details in the report. However, the report is already quite long and

I believed that Liam's story could be understood without these added details, interesting as they are to me.

Disparity between Conclusions in Current and Previous Evaluations

Although Liam's physician had prescribed stimulant mediation, an ADHD diagnosis was never formalized, in part because of the conclusions in the 2011 evaluation. One of the reasons that the current evaluation was conducted was to verify that ADHD was indeed the correct diagnosis.

I am extremely reluctant to criticize another professional's work (and do so here with trepidation). In the report I omitted how angry Liam's mother still was about how she perceived she was treated by the psychologist who evaluated Liam in 2011.

In the course of obtaining services for two of Liam's older brothers, Liam's mother has had contact with many mental health professionals and has largely been very satisfied with their services. However, the 2011 evaluation experience was extremely upsetting to her. According to Liam's mother, the evaluator seemed to discount her observations and made several remarks she found to be deeply insulting. For example, the evaluator directed her to not read the report because the evaluator believed that she would not understand it and could not understand it, even if it were explained to her. In fact, because Liam's mother has educated herself about the evaluation reports completed for her older son, this particular report was fairly easy for her to understand, even without the help of the psychologist. In frustration, Liam's mother ripped up the report shortly after receiving it. However, she allowed me to request that the report be sent again so that I could see the previous scores. Obviously, I cannot know for certain what exactly happened between Liam's mother and this psychologist, but my sympathies were with Liam's mother.

In addition, I omitted the fact that I disagreed with the reasoning in the previous report but I countered indirectly a line of reasoning used in the report. The report mentions that Liam's scores were about equal on "ADHD subscales" and "non-ADHD subscales" on the WISC–IV. I do not believe that a WISC profile has much bearing on whether or not a person has ADHD. There is no WISC profile that for me would either rule in or rule out an ADHD diagnosis. At best, certain profiles might add a little more credibility to a diagnostic decision but not much. I believe that a person's observed behavior is much more important than cognitive ability scores when considering a diagnosis of ADHD. Furthermore, after a single testing session, I do not believe that the evaluator had enough data to discount Liam's mother's years of direct observation of her son. To be fair, it is harder to diagnose ADHD in a 6-year-old than in a child about to turn 10. Most 6-year-olds are naturally a little scattered, and perhaps the evaluator did not wish to overpathologize what appeared at the time to be ordinary rambunctiousness.

Level versus Process

My reports rarely include much detail about how I go about interpreting test data. In this report I included much more detail than usual because Liam's scores, once the highs and lows were understood in context, were not particularly informative; they were mostly average. What was interesting to me was the story of how those scores were obtained. I wanted a potential reader to get a feel for what it was like to be with Liam, to get a sense of his considerable strengths and also his significant weaknesses. Given the conclusions of the previous report from 2011, I wanted to make it extremely clear that although Liam could at times focus quite well, ADHD was indeed the correct diagnosis.

Follow-up Testing

If the WISC–V scores were taken at face value, his profile might seem much more interesting. The high Figure Weights score and the low Block Design score certainly draw the eye. However, only the most obtuse clinician would have applied a by-the-book interpretation to these scores in Liam's case—he announced

repeatedly that he had no idea what the right answers were and that he was guessing on the last Figure Weights items. He all but announced that he had stopped trying on Block Design quite early on and deliberately failed some items so that the task would end. Because Liam's WISC–IV Block Design score from 2011 was 10 and because his Visual Puzzles score was 13 in the current evaluation, it did not seem to be worthwhile to administer a follow-up test. It was reasonably certain that his visual-spatial ability was at least average. Of course, if visual-spatial deficits were a referral concern, I would have needed a higher level of certainty and additional follow-up tests would have been administered.

Assessing Profile Unusualness

What would I have done if Liam had earned the same WISC–V scores but had not been vocal about what he was doing? Although it would be obvious that the profile was strange, it would have been nice to know exactly how strange. I use the Mahalanobis distance index of subtest scatter to measure how unusual a profile is, but I condition the Mahalanobis distance on the overall score or on the factor scores. The ordinary Mahalanobis distance tells us how unusual a profile is in the general population (Crawford & Allan, 1994). It is also possible to ask how unusual a profile of subtest scores is among people with a particular set of factor scores. This tells us if the within-factor subtest scatter is unusual.

The WISC–V Verbal Comprehension Index has two subtests, but I prefer to use all the information that I have. Therefore, using the correlation matrix from the WISC–V manual, I make a Gc composite score (Schneider, 2013a) from all four Gc subtests (Similarities, Vocabulary, Information, and Comprehension). I do likewise with the four Gf subtests (Matrix Reasoning, Figure Weights, Picture Concepts, and Arithmetic), three Gwm subtests (Picture Span, Digit Span, and Letter–Number Sequencing), and three Gs subtests (Coding, Symbol Search, and Cancellation). For Gv, Gl (Learning Efficiency), and Gr (Retrieval Fluency), the official composite scores are sufficient (Visual Spatial Index, Naming Speed Index, and Symbol Translation Index, respectively).

Custom Composite Scores	
Gc	97
Gv	100
Gf	113
Gwm	108
Gs	100
Gr	111
Gl	105
G	106

From here the calculation details are not important, but I can use the composite scores to

predict what the likely range is for the subtest scores (Schneider, 2013b). As seen in Figure 9.2, Figure Weights is far from expectations. Less extreme but also far from expectations are Block Design, Visual Puzzles, and Picture Concepts. Given this set of composite scores, only about 5% of WISC–V subtest profiles are this unusual. Thus, even if Liam had not revealed that he was giving up on Block Design or that he was guessing on Figure Weights, it would have been clear that something was strange with those scores and would likely have triggered me to conduct follow-up tests.

My best guess is that Liam's true Block Design score is around 10 and his Figure Weights score is around 14 or 15.

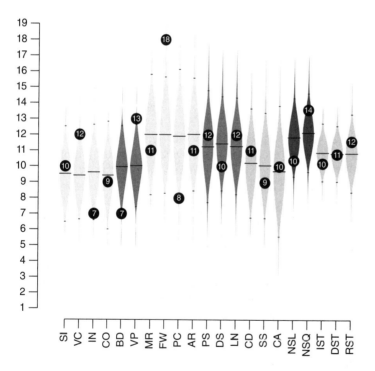

Figure 9.2 Liam's Profile Compared to Expectations, Given Custom Composite Scores
Abbreviations are: SI = Similarities, VC = Vocabulary, IN = Information, CO = Comprehension, BD = Block Design, VP = Visual Puzzles, MR = Matrix Reasoning, FW = Figure Weights, PC = Picture Concepts, AR = Arithmetic, PS = Picture Span, DS = Digit Span, LN = Letter–Number Sequencing, CD = Coding, SS = Symbol Search, CA = Cancellation, NSL = Naming Speed Literacy, NSQ = Naming Speed Quantity, IST = Immediate Symbol Translation, DST = Symbol Translation, RST = Recognition Symbol Translation.

Prediction Models

Normally I use the correlation matrices in the test battery manuals to create prediction models with the free structural equation modeling package lavaan (Rosseel, 2012). With these models I can see which academic abilities are in line with expectations and which cognitive weaknesses are the most likely explanations for any observed academic weaknesses (Schneider, 2010, 2013a). However, with Liam's relatively simple profile, this would be mathematical overkill.

A Few Thoughts about the New WISC–V

There is a secret but widely shared pleasure in rooting for the underdog. A young and scrappy David Wechsler, armed with his namesake tests, may once have faced off against that erstwhile Goliath, the Stanford-Binet, but that was a long time ago. Underdog enthusiasts now have other tests to root for and often have a long list of gripes about King David's tests. I certainly have mine. If I am being honest, though, I must admit that, on balance, the Wechsler tests have been good stewards of the realm.

Although to my impatient nature, progress has been slow, it is clear that each successor in the Davidic line has been noticeably better than its predecessor. To be fair, there is considerable risk in innovating too quickly. It is easy to forget that "creative destruction" involves actual destruction and that in the wreckage there are things that were once cherished and beautiful. It is therefore prudent for leaders to give ground gradually to overeager radicals and at the same time patiently prod the hidebound forces of orthodoxy out of complacency. The worst thing to happen to the Wechsler tests would be for them to lose sight of David Wechsler's vision (see Kaufman, 2009, pp. 29–54). The second worst thing would be for them to remain as they are. The new WISC–V would never be mistaken for the cutting edge of cognitive assessment, but it is keeping up with the times without sacrificing the qualities that made it great in the first place. This is no easy feat,

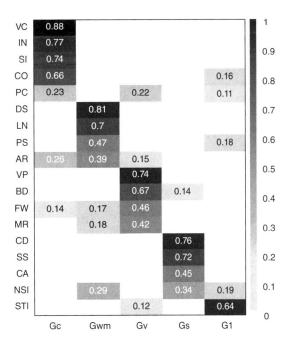

Figure 9.3 Five-Factor Exploratory Factor Analysis of the WISC–V

and the authors are to be commended for their accomplishment.

This was my first experience with the WISC–V, and I was quite happy with it overall. The inclusion of Visual Puzzles corrects the great injustice done to Block Design in the transition from the WISC–III to the WISC–IV; it was stripped of its friend Object Assembly and pretty much was the only good measure of *Gv* on the WISC–IV. Now Block Design has a *Gv* friend again! The factor analyses of the WISC–IV suggested that Picture Concepts just did not have much in common with Matrix Reasoning, other than *g* (Schneider, 2013b; Weiss, Keith, Zhu, & Chen, 2013b). Figure Weights is a much better *Gf* mate to Matrix Reasoning than Picture Concepts was on the WISC–IV.

I am happy that there is a learning subtest on the WISC–V. However, I wish that a more creative choice had been made as to the format. We now have rebus learning tests on several major batteries that are quite similar to each other. I wish that Symbol Translation had a "friend" such as a story memory test so that a broad Gl (Learning efficiency) composite could be calculated.

Likewise, the Naming Speed tests are a welcome addition to the WISC–V. but they are unaccompanied by another Gr (Retrieval Fluency) test. Of course, in CHC theory, $Gl + Gr = Glr$. The Storage and Retrieval composite is a measure of Glr. Unfortunately, the Glr idea always made more theoretical sense than its empirical support would suggest. Carroll (1993a) and Cattell (1987) both thought of the learning aspects of long-term memory and the retrieval fluency aspects as distinct enough to belong in separate broad factors of ability. An informal factor analysis in Figure 9.3 using the WISC–V correlation matrix supports this idea.

CASE 2—ALICIA, AGE 13: LOOKING UNDER THE HOOD

Jill Hartmann and John Willis

Fordham Middle School
  SPECIAL EDUCATION SERVICES
  25 Post Road, Fordham, NA 555–1212

Educational Evaluation

Name: Alicia Portman

Dates of Evaluation: 11/30/2014, 1/5/2015, 1/8/2015, and 1/11/2015

Parent: Sally Portman

Birth Date: 3/13/2001

Address: 26 N. Stone Highway, Fordham, NA

Age: 13 years, 8 months

School: Fordham Middle School

Examiners: Jill A. Hartmann, M.Ed., SAIF; John O. Willis, Ed.D., SAIF

Grade: 7

Report Date: 01/13/2015

Summary

Alicia was cheerful, friendly, cooperative, and diligent throughout the evaluation. It was a pleasure to work with her. Alicia demonstrated significant weaknesses in reading, writing, math, oral language, cognitive abilities, and adaptive behavior. Within those weaknesses, she did best with fluid reasoning (using logic to solve problems), processing speed and academic fluency, and writing. We recommend intensive, direct instruction in basic reading skills, reading comprehension, oral language, and math, and assistance with organizational skills.

Background

Reason for Referral

Alicia was referred by the Fordham Middle School special education team for assessment as part of a reevaluation process to determine if she meets the criteria for special education services. Referral questions included Alicia's reading, writing, math, oral language, and cognitive abilities.

History

Alicia lives at home with her mother and her older sister, Corinne, a high school freshman. Alicia said that she sees her father, who lives about an hour away, about once a month. Alicia, Corinne, and their parents are African American. Alicia's mother is a paralegal and her father, an Air Force veteran, is a salesman in an automobile dealership.

Alicia is currently in the seventh grade at Fordham Middle School. Because of language delays, she attended a special education preschool program before entering kindergarten. She attended a transition year class between kindergarten and first grade because she had been struggling to master basic reading, writing, and math skills. Alicia was initially identified with a developmental delay and a speech and language impairment in the spring of 2004, when she was 3 years old. She has carried a special education identification throughout the subsequent years, and she is currently identified with disabilities of Speech or Language Impairment and Other Health Impairment. Her difficulties with language make it very difficult for Alicia to keep up with the academic pace in the classroom. Teachers report concerns with organizational skills. Alicia is a very hard-working student and maintains many friendships with her peers in the seventh grade.

Alicia's reported difficulties include reading comprehension, math problem solving, answering higher-order thinking questions, organizing and structuring written assignments, and understanding abstract concepts. She is given daily, direct, pull-out instruction. Please see Alicia's Individualized Education Program (IEP). She also has the support of a paraprofessional daily. Alicia has difficulty accessing the grade-level curriculum.

Alicia passed the hearing screening and near and far vision screening administered by the school nurse, Martha Kleppman, R.N., a month before the evaluation. Her school medical record and cumulative file do not mention any health issues, and neither Alicia nor her mother reported any medical concerns.

Previous Testing

Alicia's last evaluation was completed in January of 2012, when she was in the fourth grade. At that time, she was administered the Comprehensive Test of Nonverbal Intelligence—Second Edition (CTONI–2), Wechsler Intelligence Scale for Children–Fourth Edition (WISC–IV), Wide Range Assessment of Memory and Learning—Second Edition (WRAML2), Kaufman Test of Educational Achievement –Second Edition (KTEA–II), and Vineland Adaptive Behavior Scales–2nd Ed. (Vineland–II). Please see the report in Alicia's file.

Current Evaluation

Tests Administered

Wechsler Intelligence Scale for Children–Fifth Edition (WISC–V)

Wechsler Individual Achievement Test–Third Edition (WIAT–III)

Vineland Adaptive Behavior Scales–Second Edition (Vineland–II)

Test Findings

At the end of this report is an explanation of the scoring system used with Alicia's tests and a list of the names and brief descriptions of the tests that Alicia took. Please note that, throughout the report, we are reporting test scores as *percentile ranks* as described in the section of this report titled "Scores Used with the Tests in This Report." Percentile ranks tell the percentage of students her age whose scores Alicia matched or exceeded. For example, a percentile rank of 14 would mean that she scored as high as or higher than 14% of students her age and lower than the other 86%.

Assessment Observations

During the assessment, Alicia was cheerful, friendly, and very cooperative. We met on several different occasions and, most of the time, she was focused and attentive. As we walked down the hall, she saw some of her friends and she gave them a warm, friendly greeting. They responded with an equally warm greeting. She explained how much she liked the friends she has in school. On one of the last times we met, she said how excited she was that the Patriots won the playoff game over the weekend and she was wearing her Patriots shirt in support of the team. It was a real pleasure to work with Alicia.

There were no outside distractions during our testing sessions. The room temperature was comfortable and the room was well lit. The table and chair were appropriate for Alicia.

When asked, Alicia said that her parents and case manager had told her about the evaluation, but she did not remember what the reason was for it. We explained that the purpose of the evaluation was to help Alicia's teachers learn more about the best ways to teach Alicia. Everyone is better at some things than at others, and the tests could help determine which were which for Alicia. Alicia's teachers do not want to waste Alicia's time teaching things she already knows, and they do want to be sure to teach things Alicia does not know yet. Therefore, both right and wrong answers on the tests are valuable. We also explained that there would be some items that would be too easy, designed primarily for younger students, and some that would be much too difficult, designed primarily for older students. Those items are included to make sure we do not miss any extreme strengths or weaknesses.[1] We also warned Alicia that we were not allowed to indicate whether specific responses were right or wrong, although we would discuss the results at the end of the evaluation.

Alicia worked hard throughout the evaluation. She appeared to be pleased when she believed she had answered a question correctly or solved a nonverbal problem. When she was unable to solve a problem or answer a question or when she thought her response was wrong, she was obviously disappointed. Alicia was reluctant to give up on even the most difficult items and usually offered a reasonable guess when she did not know an answer. Alicia occasionally commented that some of the test items were very hard. She appeared to take appropriate care with easy items, avoiding careless mistakes. Alicia's attention was generally good, and it was easy to redirect her on the few occasions when her attention did wander.

Her attitude and good effort suggest that Alicia's scores are reasonably valid indications of her current educational functional levels.

Verbal Comprehension/Knowledge

Verbal Comprehension/Knowledge includes a person's fund of general verbal information, vocabulary, understanding, thinking, and communication skills. Verbal comprehension/knowledge abilities are important for reading, writing, math "story problems," and oral communication.

The WISC–V Verbal Comprehension Index consists of oral questions requiring oral responses. On these subtests the examinee is asked to explain how two different words (such as *moose* and *deer* or *hope* and *fear*) are alike and to define vocabulary words. When asked how two words were similar, Alicia either could not think of how they were the same and reluctantly responded, "I don't know," or she would give different functions or uses of the items but could not provide the fundamental connection between the two. When asked to define words, she would either answer "I don't know" or offer a sentence that used the word. When prompted to explain more, she could not. On this Index, Alicia earned a standard score of 65, which is in the lowest 1% of scores for children her age (percentile 1).[2]

Alicia's scores on vocabulary tests were varied. She had the most difficulty with the WISC–V Vocabulary subtest of defining words (lower part of the lowest 1% of scores for her age). She scored a little higher (percentile 2) for naming pictures on the WIAT–III Expressive Vocabulary. Her highest vocabulary score was on the

Table 9.8   Alicia's WISC–V Verbal Comprehension and WIAT–III Oral Language Scores by Norms for Her Age

Subtest or Composite	Scaled or Standard Score[a]	95% Confidence Interval[b]	Percentile Rank[c]
WISC-V			
Similarities	5		5
Vocabulary	2		0.4
Verbal Comprehension Index	65	60–75	1
Information	*2*		*0.4*
Comprehension	*6*		*9*
WIAT-III			
Receptive Vocabulary	88	70–106	21
Oral Discourse Comprehension	64	51–77	1
Listening Comprehension	71	59–83	3
Expressive Vocabulary	70	51–89	2
Oral Word Fluency	85	71–99	16
Sentence Repetition	49	34–64	0.1
Oral Expression	61	48–74	0.5
Oral Language Composite	66	55–77	1

[a]These are scaled scores and standard scores. Please see the section of this report titled "Scores Used with the Tests in This Report" for an explanation of these statistics. The middle half of scaled scores includes scores from 8 through 12. The middle half of standard scores ranges from 90 to 110.

[b]Even the best tests can never be perfectly consistent. This range shows how much scores are likely to vary 95% of the time just by random variation.

[c]Percentile ranks tell the percentage of same-age children who scored the same as Alicia or lower. For example, a percentile rank of 21 would mean that Alicia scored as high as or higher than 21% of children her age and lower than the other 79%.

WIAT–III Receptive Vocabulary, on which the examiner said a word and Alicia simply had to select the named picture (e.g., "beagle" or "running") from several pictures on a multiple-choice test (percentile 21). The more oral language Alicia had to use, the more difficulty she had with the vocabulary test. (All of her scores are compared to other children her age performing the same tasks.)

Alicia's difficulties with both receptive (understanding) and expressive (speaking) oral language were evident in her other WIAT–III scores. She was able to name words in a given category (such as "vegetables") as fast as or faster than 16% of children her age (but not as fast as the other 84%: percentile 16). Alicia listened to short passages played from a CD and tried to answer questions about the passages. She had difficulty recalling facts from the passages and scored in percentile 1 for her age. The most challenging task for Alicia was repeating dictated sentences word for word. She usually captured the general idea of the sentence, but made many errors on the precise words and word order, so her score was in the lowest part of percentile 1.

The WISC–V includes two additional verbal subtests, Information and Comprehension, that are not included in the Verbal Comprehension Index. Information incudes factual questions of general knowledge, such as "Who was the first President of the United States?" Alicia did not know or could not recall much of the tested information. Her score was in the lowest 1% of scores for children her age (percentile 1). The Comprehension questions involve social and practical understanding, such as "Tell me two reasons we have traffic lights." The relatively long and complex language of the Comprehension questions challenged Alicia. She asked to have most questions repeated, and her responses included false starts and spontaneous corrections. Alicia often thought aloud as she constructed responses to the questions and managed to earn at least partial credit for her final responses. Through this process, Alicia scored a little higher on Comprehension: percentile 9 for her age.

Alicia scored higher on the WISC–V subtests that allowed her to use her verbal reasoning abilities (Similarities [percentile 5] and Comprehension [percentile 9]) than on the WISC–V subtests

that directly tapped acquired knowledge (Vocabulary and Information, both in the lower part of percentile 1).

The Vineland Adaptive Behavior Scales is not a test but a questionnaire on which a parent, caregiver, or teacher rates the frequency and independence of specific behaviors (such as tying shoes, counting change, or taking telephone messages). Those ratings are then converted to scores based on comparisons to the ratings of other children the same age.

Scores based on ratings of Alicia's communication skills by her mother and her teacher were generally low, mostly in the lowest 9% to 25% of ratings for children her age. The one score below that range was low in percentile 1 for receptive communication according to ratings by Alicia's mother, which also lowered the total domain score. The specific items given low ratings by Alicia's mother appeared to reflect inconsistent following of instructions and requests in the home. On the whole, Alicia's functional use of language was rated higher than her performance on formal tests but not unexpectedly so.

Table 9.9 Alicia's Vineland Adaptive Behavior Scales Communication Scores by Norms for Her Age

Domain	v-Scale or Standard Score[a]		Percentile Rank	
	Mother	Teacher	Mother	Teacher
Receptive Communication	5	11	0.1	9
Expressive Communication	12	13	16	25
Written Communication	12	11	16	9
Communication Domain	70	80	2	9

[a]The v-scale scores are similar to the WISC–V scaled scores, but the middle half of v-scale scores includes scores from 13 through 17. Please see the section of this report titled "Scores Used with the Tests in This Report" for an explanation of these statistics.

Visual-Spatial Ability

Visual-spatial abilities involve perceiving, understanding, and mentally manipulating shapes, diagrams, and visual arrays. Visual-spatial abilities are important for early learning of visual information, such as letters and numbers, and for sorting out charts and diagrams, and for some visual aspects of math. Mental visualization might sometimes support some aspects of listening and reading comprehension.

The WISC–V Visual Spatial Index consists of items presented visually and they require the examinee to respond nonverbally. On these subtests, the examinee is asked to arrange patterned blocks to match the pictured designs and to identify on a multiple-choice test the three pieces that would fit together to make up a given puzzle shape. When Alicia was asked to use the patterned blocks to replicate the pictured design, she had a lot of difficulty right away. We spent a lot of time going over the explanation and demonstration that are given when the sample item is incorrect. She was able to copy two of the initial items, and she replicated a third item but it was over the time limit. When asked to identify the three pieces that made up the puzzle, she did identify three pieces, however, they were not the correct pieces. Sometimes she would identify two pieces that fit, but the third was incorrect. On both subtests, Alicia struggled to see how the parts could fit together to make the whole. On this index, Alicia's score for visual-spatial ability was in percentile 1 compared to children her age.

Table 9.10 Alicia's WISC–V Visual Spatial Scores

Subtest or Composite	Scaled or Standard Score	Confidence Interval	Percentile Rank
Block Design	3		1
Visual Puzzles	4		2
Visual Spatial Index	64	59–75	1

Fluid Reasoning Ability

Fluid reasoning is solving new, unfamiliar problems by inductive, deductive, or quantitative logical reasoning. Fluid reasoning is needed, obviously, for solving logical problems, mathematics reasoning, inferential reading comprehension, making predictions, and higher-level written expression skills.

The Fluid Reasoning Index of the WISC–V consists of nonverbal tasks. On one subtest, the examinee must choose one of several pictures or designs to logically complete a pattern of pictures or designs. On the other subtest, the examinee is first shown a balanced scale with various numbers of different shapes on each side of the scale and is then shown another scale with a collection of shapes on one side and nothing on the other side. The child is asked to choose the picture of shapes that would balance the scale. Alicia seemed to enjoy the two logical reasoning tasks and was quick to answer. She had more success on these tasks than on most of the other WISC–V tasks. On the Fluid Reasoning Index, Alicia's score of 79 was a percentile of 8, as high as or higher than the scores of 8% of children her age. Although in the lowest 8% of scores, Alicia's Fluid Reasoning Index was significantly higher[3] than her Verbal Comprehension, Visual-Spatial, and Working Memory Index scores.

Table 9.11 Alicia's WISC–V Fluid Reasoning Scores

Subtest or Composite	Scaled or Standard Score	Confidence Interval	Percentile Rank
Matrix Reasoning	6		9
Figure Weights	7		16
Fluid Reasoning Index	79	73–88	8

Working Memory Ability

Short-term or working memory includes both simple memory span (e.g., remembering a telephone number long enough to type it into the keypad) and working memory with mental rearrangement (such as for some reason, repeating the telephone number in reversed order). Working memory provides a mental note pad that supports many aspects of mental activity.

The WISC–V Working Memory Index consists of subtests that require remembering data (e.g., repeating dictated digits) or remembering visual data and recalling them in the order they were shown. Alicia had a lot of difficulty recalling the numbers I dictated and asked her to repeat back to me. When I asked her to repeat them back in reverse order (e.g., 3 9 7 would be 7 9 3), she was unable to do so. She had to give up on the items and did not give me any numbers at all. When asked to repeat them in number order sequence (3 9 7 would become 3 7 9), she did provide some answers but was unable to give them to me in number order. On the visual memory task (looking at a row of pictures and then, on a page of several pictures, pointing to the same pictures in the same order), she also had great difficulty. On some of the initial tasks, she was successful. When the pictures increased to three pictures, she could identify the pictures but not in the order in which I showed them. Alicia was able to point to the pictures correctly and in the right order on the first item with four pictures; however, after that, she was unable to identify the correct pictures. During both of these subtests, she appeared frustrated on items that were difficult for her. On the Working Memory Index, Alicia earned a percentile of 1, indicating a weakness in working memory that would be likely to interfere with many tasks that would require short-term mental storage and manipulation of data.

Table 9.12   Alicia's WISC–V Working Memory Scores

Subtest or Composite	Scaled or Standard Score	Confidence Interval	Percentile Rank
Digit Span	2		0.4
Picture Span	4		2
Working Memory Index	62	57–73	1

Processing Speed Ability

Processing speed is the ability to perform simple tasks rapidly. Slow processing would not only limit the speed of carrying out simple tasks, such as very easy arithmetic, but also speed with more complex operations, such as more difficult mathematics, writing, and reading.

The WISC–V Processing Speed Index (PSI) consists of subtests that measure speed on simple paper-and-pencil tasks. Alicia was asked to transcribe a digit-symbol code as quickly as possible. Alicia was also asked to decide if a target symbol appeared again in a row of symbols and mark the symbol or "NO" accordingly. On both subtests, the score is the number of items completed correctly within a time limit. Like most examinees, Alicia did not make any mistakes on either of these simple subtests, but she worked slowly: percentile 9, faster than 9% of children her age and slower than the other 91%. Her Processing Speed Index was, however, significantly higher than her Verbal Comprehension, Visual-Spatial, and Working Memory Index scores.

Table 9.13   Alicia's WISC–V Processing Speed Scores

Subtest or Composite	Scaled or Standard Score	Confidence Interval	Percentile Rank
Coding	7		5
Symbol Search	6		16
Processing Speed Index	80	73–91	9

Reading Ability

Reading ability includes reading comprehension, word reading, phonics, and reading fluency (speed and accuracy). Reading is, of course, a very important skill for almost all areas of school work.

Word Reading   The WIAT–III Word Reading and Pseudoword Decoding subtests ask the student to read aloud "real" words and phonetically regular nonsense words (such as *tunket*). Alicia was able to recognize some familiar words on the Word Reading list and tried to apply phonics skills to read other real words and the nonsense words on the Pseudoword Decoding subtest. Her mispronunciations of some of the real words (errors similar to reading *deny* as "denny") suggested that the limitations of Alicia's oral vocabulary impaired her reading of words. However, on both the nonsense words and obviously unfamiliar real words, Alicia also had difficulty holding all the pieces together as she sounded out words of more than one syllable. Even when she correctly identified all of the sounds represented by the letters, she lost some sounds or remembered some incorrectly when she tried to blend all of the sounds into the whole word. For the most part, Alicia correctly read sounds represented by single consonants or vowels and by digraphs such as *th* or *ck*. She was inconsistent with *gh*. Alicia usually read consonant blends (such as *bl* and *nd*) correctly. Sounds spelled with two vowels (such as the *ai* in *trail* or the *ea* in *clean*) were difficult for Alicia unless it was the same vowel repeated (as in *feet*). After the test was completed, we read aloud to Alicia some nonsense words similar to ones she had missed and she had no difficulty pronouncing the sounds when she imitated us. Her difficulty was with knowing the spellings of the sounds, not with recognizing and being able to pronounce the spoken sounds.

Reading Comprehension The WIAT–III Reading Comprehension subtest measures literal and inferential reading comprehension skills using a variety of passage and question types that resemble those used in a school setting. Alicia was asked to read a passage, either silently or out loud, and answer a comprehension question presented orally by the examiner. She read the passages silently and was able to answer some of the concrete questions correctly. She had difficulty with many of the questions, especially on those questions requiring abstract answers, but—if she understood the passage—Alicia was able to make inferences and predictions.

Alicia's Reading Comprehension score was in percentile 5 for her age, not much different from her score for Oral Discourse Comprehension (percentile 1).

Oral Reading Fluency The WIAT-III Oral Reading Fluency subtest required Alicia to orally read both expository and narrative passages. Alicia made many errors in her reading (percentile 5) but read relatively quickly (percentile 18), so her total oral reading fluency score was percentile 10 for her age (higher than or equal to 10% of students her age and lower than the other 90%). Most of her errors were omissions and substitutions.

Table 9.14 Alicia's WIAT–III Reading Scores

Subtest or Composite	Standard Score	95% Confidence	Percentile Rank
Word Reading	79	73–85	8
Pseudoword Decoding	83	78–88	13
Basic Reading	**81**	**77–85**	**10**
Oral Reading Accuracy	76	63–89	5
Oral Reading Rate	86	79–93	18
Oral Reading Fluency	**81**	**74–88**	**10**
Reading Comprehension	75	64–86	5
Reading Comp. and Fluency	**74**	**66–82**	**4**
Total Reading	**77**	**72–82**	**6**

Writing Ability

Writing ability includes spelling, punctuation, grammar, and the many aspects of written expression, including planning, organization, vocabulary, style, and writing fluency. Writing skills are necessary for most parts of the school curriculum.

Sentence Composition The WIAT–III Sentence Composition subtest consists of two components: Sentence Combining and Sentence Building, which measure sentence formulation skills. Alicia was asked to combine two or three sentences into one sentence that kept the meaning of the original sentences. Alicia was able to combine some of the sentences successfully. As the sentences increased in length and complexity, Alicia quickly experienced more difficulty. She had difficulty including all the information required to receive credit and finding a way to combine the sentences. Each item on the Sentence Building component supplied Alicia with a target word and asked her to write one meaningful sentence using that word. Alicia had difficulty thinking of a sentence for one of the words, and she did not use the correct meaning of the target word for some other items. Alicia's Sentence Building score was in the 9th percentile for age.

Essay Composition Alicia was given a topic and specific instructions and was asked to write about the topic within a time limit. The subtest considers written expression productivity, theme development, text organization, grammar, and mechanics in its measure. Alicia wrote about half a page, writing as many or more words as 25% of students her age. The Theme Development and Text Organization score is based on the essay introduction, the conclusion, the paragraphs, the transitions, the reasons given for opinions, and elaborations on basic ideas. Alicia did have an introduction sentence and a conclusion sentence. Her essay was one paragraph and did not contain any transitions. She did provide two reasons for her opinion but did not elaborate on either of those reasons, so her score was in percentile 12.

Spelling Alicia wrote words that were dictated and used in a sentence, just like a school spelling test. Her correct spellings and her errors were very similar to those on her word-reading subtest. After the WIAT–III was completed, we read

the spelling words to Alicia again and asked her to repeat each one. She was able to pronounce all of the words correctly, including those she had misspelled.

Table 9.15 Alicia's WIAT–III Written Expression Scores

Subtest or Composite	Standard Score	95% Confidence	Percentile Rank
Sentence Building	80	67–93	9
Sentence Combining	83	71–95	13
Sentence Composition	80	70–90	9
Word Count in essay	90	77–103	25
Theme Development and Text Organization	82	68–96	12
Essay Composition	85	75–95	16
Spelling	79	72–86	8
Written Expression Composite	79	72–86	8

Mathematics Achievement

Mathematics achievement includes math computation, math problem solving (which may overlap with reading comprehension or listening comprehension and with fluid reasoning), and math fluency (speed and accuracy of computation). Carrying out math computation and going through the steps of solving problems both place demands on working memory.

Math Problem Solving This WIAT–III subtest measures untimed math problem-solving skills in the following domains: basic concepts, everyday applications, geometry, and algebra. Alicia had difficulty understanding what the verbally framed problems were asking and keeping track of all the details. When she did attack a problem correctly, she sometimes made computational errors.

Math Computation The WIAT–III Numerical Operations subtest measures untimed written math calculation skills in the following domains: basic skills, basic operations with integers, geometry, and algebra. Alicia was able to add more than two single-digit numbers, complete some basic multiplication facts, and complete some basic, one-digit subtraction problems. She did have trouble subtracting when borrowing ("regrouping" or "renaming") was involved, completing some basic two-digit addition problems, and completing some one- and two-digit multiplication examples. Alicia's problem-solving, numerical operations, and total math scores on the WIAT–III were all in the lowest 1% of scores for her age.

Math Computation Fluency The WIAT–III includes three math fluency subtests: adding pairs of numbers ranging from 0 to 10, subtracting numbers ranging from 0 to 10, and multiplying pairs of numbers ranging from 0 to 9. On each subtest, the score is based on the number of correct examples completed within the short time limit. Alicia worked relatively quickly on the addition (percentile 14) and subtraction

(percentile 6) subtests without making errors. She was slower and less accurate with the multiplication (percentile 1). Her total math fluency score was in percentile 4 for her age.

Adaptive Behavior

As noted above, the Vineland Adaptive Behavior Scales is not a test but a questionnaire on which a parent, caregiver, or teacher rates the frequency and independence of specific behaviors. Those ratings are then converted to scores based on comparisons to the ratings of other children the same age. Three domains are assessed: Communication, Daily Living Skills, and Socialization. Alicia's usual adaptive behaviors were rated by her mother for the home environment and by her special education teacher for the school environment. Some differences between adaptive behavior in the home environment and in the school environment are to be expected. The Vineland–II uses the following classification names for its scores: Low, Moderately Low, Adequate, Moderately High, and High. Please see the section of this report titled "Scores Used with the Tests in This Report" for more information on the scoring systems for the tests Alicia took.

The Communication Domain measures how a student listens and pays attention and how he or she uses language to speak and write. Based on the Parent/Caregiver Rating Form for home, Alicia's Communication Domain score was Low for her age. Based on the Teacher Rating Form, Alicia's Communication Domain score was Moderately Low for her age. Alicia's scores for communication skills were mostly in the lowest 9% to 25% of ratings for children her age. As noted above, the one score below that range was low in percentile 1 for receptive communication according to ratings by Alicia's mother, which also lowered the total domain score. The specific items given low ratings by Alicia's mother appeared to reflect inconsistent following of instructions and requests in the home. Alicia's total Communication score was Low at home and Moderately Low in school.

Table 9.16   Alicia's WIAT–III Math Scores

Subtest or Composite	Standard Score	95% Confidence	Percentile Rank
Math Problem Solving	61	53–69	0.5
Numerical Operations	67	58–76	1
Mathematics Composite	64	57–71	1
Math Fluency– Addition	84	73–95	14
Math Fluency– Subtraction	77	67–87	6
Math Fluency– Multiplication	64	54–74	1
Mathematics Fluency Composite	73	66–80	4

Table 9.17   Alicia's Vineland Adaptive Behavior Scales by Norms for Her Age

Domain	v-Scale or Standard Score[a]		Percentile Rank		Descriptions	
	Mother	Teacher	Mother	Teacher	Mother	Teacher
Receptive Communication	5	11	0.1	9	Low	Mod Low
Expressive Communication	12	13	16	25	Mod Low	Adequate
Written Communication	12	11	16	9	Mod Low	Mod Low
Communication Domain	70	80	2	9	**Low**	**Mod Low**
Personal Daily Living Skills	10	15	5	50	Mod Low	Adequate
Academic/Domestic Daily Living	13	9	25	2	Adequate	Low
School/Community Daily Living	15	14	50	37	Adequate	Adequate
Daily Living Skills Domain	85	84	16	14	**Mod Low**	**Mod Low**
Interpersonal Relationships	11	14	9	37	Mod Low	Adequate
Play and Leisure Time	7	15	0.4	50	Low	Adequate
Coping Skills	11	13	9	25	Mod Low	Adequate
Socialization Domain	71	91	3	27	**Mod Low**	**Adequate**
Adaptive Behavior Composite	73	84	4	14	**Mod Low**	**Mod Low**

[a]The v-scale scores are similar to the WISC–V scaled scores, but the middle half of v-scale scores includes scores from 13 through 17. Please see the section of this report titled "Scores Used with the Tests in This Report" for an explanation of these statistics.

The Daily Living Skills Domain measures Alicia's daily habits and hygiene. It also measures Alicia's understanding about time, money, and math and her ability to follow directions. It represents the practical skills and behaviors that are needed to take care of oneself in a school or community environment. Alicia's score was Moderately Low for independent Personal Daily Living Skills at home, apparently because she performed many routines with reminders rather than fully independently. Academic Daily Living skills (understanding about the concepts of time, money, and math) were Low in school because of the academic skill demands. Alicia was rated Moderately Low (percentiles 14 to 16) for overall Daily Living skills at home and in school.

At home, Alicia's Socialization skills (how Alicia interacts with others, uses play and leisure time, and how she demonstrates responsibility

and sensitivity to others—the skills and behaviors needed to get along with others and for use in leisure activities) were Moderately Low, but in the school environment they were Adequate.

Overall, Alicia's independent adaptive behavior was rated Moderately Low at home (percentile 4) and at school (percentile 14).

Conclusions

As discussed, Alicia was extremely cooperative and motivated during the assessment. Her scores appear to be reasonably accurate measures of her current educational functioning levels and are consistent with her previous evaluation.

1. Oral language skills are a challenge for Alicia. For example, compared to other children her age, she had difficulty selecting the correct

picture to match a named vocabulary word, and obtained increasingly lower scores on a test of naming pictures and on a test of defining vocabulary words. Thus, the more complex the language involved, the more difficulty Alicia experienced. The limits of Alicia's oral vocabulary impede her progress in all academic work. Alicia did a little better on verbal language tests that allowed her to use her reasoning abilities than on tests that primarily required language skills and language recall.

2. Although her overall cognitive abilities on the WISC–V were in the lowest 1% of scores for students her age, Alicia did better on tasks that required fluid reasoning (percentile 8) than on tests of verbal comprehension and knowledge and tests of visual-spatial ability and working memory (all percentile 1). She was capable of solving some logical puzzles and figuring out the answers to some questions that she did not automatically know. This fluid reasoning ability was still only in the lowest 8% of scores for her age, but it was an ability that she could put to practical use.

3. Alicia also scored significantly higher for processing speed (percentile 9) than for verbal comprehension and knowledge, visual-spatial ability, and working memory. In general, if Alicia can do a task, she can do it quickly and efficiently. Alicia's relatively fast processing speed could be seen in her higher scores on oral word fluency (percentile 16), oral reading rate (percentile 18), word count on a timed writing task (percentile 25), and math computation fluency (percentiles 1 to 14).

4. Alicia's reading skills were low (percentile 6 overall). She demonstrated slightly higher foundation decoding skills than comprehension skills. She did not appear to have particular difficulty with the sounds in spoken words, but her phonics skills were only partially developed. Alicia's limited oral vocabulary and lack of background knowledge impaired her reading skills. Alicia was sometimes able to figure out answers to questions by using logical reasoning.

5. Alicia also struggled with spelling and writing. She was able to compose coherent sentences and an essay, and she wrote relatively quickly, which raised her composite score for written expression, but her overall writing score was only in percentile 8. Her writing reflected the weaknesses seen in oral vocabulary and oral language.

6. Alicia's math skills were very low (percentile 1) with slightly stronger math fluency (addition percentile 14, subtraction percentile 6, and multiplication percentile 1). Language comprehension was an issue with math problem solving. Alicia's math skills appeared to follow a typical academic development trend but were far below age and grade expectations.

7. Alicia's adaptive behavior skills were rated as "moderately low" overall (percentile 4 at home and 14 in school), with specific areas of adaptive behavior ranging from low in percentile 1 to average in percentile 50. We observed positive social interactions in the hallway and enjoyed our own interactions with Alicia.

Recommendations

The following recommendations should be discussed, amended, added to, developed, or rejected by all of the participants in the postevaluation conference. The selection and presentation of these preliminary recommendations are ours, so nothing here would be binding on anyone unless and until it was approved by Alicia's parents and by the Fordham Middle School Evaluation/Placement Team or were otherwise legally ordered. *The recommendations are, of course, only our personal opinions.* Also, our recommending something here does not imply that it is not already being done, just that, prior to the conference, we thought it was a good idea, based on what we had learned about Alicia so far.

1. Probably the single most helpful thing the school could do for Alicia would be to help her build her oral vocabulary skills.

Oral vocabulary is the foundation for oral communication, reading, and writing. We have a teachable moment every time Alicia fails to understand a word that she hears or reads and every time she misuses a word. It would be helpful to assign someone to help Alicia build a notebook of new words. She should be encouraged to discover and report new words to add to the personal notebook or computer file, and the assigned staff member should use a variety of exercises to help Alicia learn the meaning and usage of each new word. The words should be reviewed with her regularly, and the assigned vocabulary guru should circulate new words to Alicia's parents and teachers to help them (including her father when they visit) work with Alicia on the new words. It takes many repetitions of a word in meaningful contexts to get the word to sink in and stick. (We all encounter new words, learn their meanings, and promise ourselves to permanently add them to our vocabularies, but we seldom follow through successfully.) Writing on the computer is an ideal time to work on vocabulary, since it is so easy to substitute a clearer, more precise word with the aid of word processing software.

2. In general, although Alicia writes relatively quickly, word processing would allow teachers to work with her on written expression. The ease of editing, revision, reorganization, and expansion allows each piece of writing to be a lesson in various writing skills without the need to recopy the parts that are already correct. (We are not talking about automatic spelling and grammar check utilities but about a teacher working with Alicia on her story or essay.)

3. Another implication of Alicia's limited oral vocabulary is that teachers cannot assume that she is familiar with the new technical vocabulary or even common words in their lessons. Preteaching of vocabulary, prudent with all students, would be especially helpful for Alicia.

4. The speech and language pathologist should be consulted regarding additional work on oral language skills. This is an essential, core area for academic progress.

5. Although Alicia's cognitive abilities were low on the WISC–V and previous WISC–IV, one of her stronger areas was reasoning abilities. Given sufficient time and the needed resources, Alicia was able to figure out answers to questions that initially baffled her. Alicia should be given the time and encouragement as well as directed questions to use logical reasoning to solve problems and figure out answers.

6. Alicia's reading skills are very weak for her age. She needs intensive, direct, daily instruction in basic reading skills. As described, her skills are developing in a typical sequence, so instruction can continue from Alicia's current skill level. She needs instruction in phonetic word attack, syllabication, and word recognition. The direct instruction in basic reading skills needs to be integrated with oral vocabulary development. Alicia should also be taught to spell the same sounds, syllables, and words that she is learning to read so the reading decoding and spelling encoding skills can reinforce each other.

7. Reading comprehension also requires direct instruction. We do not recommend simply teaching Alicia gimmicks, such as reading questions before beginning to read the passage, but focusing on the meaning of each sentence and building an understanding of the passage. This instruction needs to be coordinated with oral language instruction.

8. Alicia should be taught using a multisensory approach. The more avenues that are used to teach the skill, the more opportunity Alicia will have to learn the skill. This would include verbal, visual, auditory, and kinesthetic.

9. Alicia also needs intensive, direct instruction in math. It would help if she were taught the multiplication tables so she did not have to stop and figure out simple products in the middle of a problem (a heavy load on Alicia's working memory). One way to learn multiplication facts is to complete a blank 10×10 grid of products *every* day and then be allowed and encouraged to use the completed (and dated) grid as a crib sheet for that *one* day. The student may use any method to complete the sheet, including counting on and off from adjacent products, identifying and applying patterns, or even using two straight-edges down from the top margin and across from the left and counting the enclosed squares. The shortcuts developed by the student actually help with the learning. Even if some products are never memorized, the student at least has a tool for deriving them when they are needed.

10. Alicia should be taught additional basic computational skills in the regular sequence. A math "mastery notebook" might be helpful. Each page would cover one process or piece of information, such as the steps in long division or the formula for the volume of a cylinder. The page would have a title, a definition or verbal explanation, an illustration (very important for visual learners), and an example worked out step by step. The book should also contain glossaries of symbols and terminology, with illustrations when appropriate. Once Alicia has completed a page, it should be laminated and placed in her notebook. A separate photocopy should be updated frequently and placed in a very safe location, since this notebook should be of lifelong value.

11. A balance needs to be created between the necessary direct instructional services and Alicia's need for the social and academic benefits of participation in regular classes.

12. When Alicia is trying to remember information, it is important that she associates it with something meaningful. Teachers can help by adding meaningful verbal labels to the information they are trying to get across. Cueing prior knowledge is also going to help Alicia with making meaningful associations and using her reasoning ability.

13. Alicia should be encouraged to continue working on her organizational skills. It is recommended that she be helped to organize her papers in her binders, her backpack, and her locker at least once, if not twice, a week. The long-term goal of the support would be independent organization.

14. In order to better sort and file her papers, it would be helpful if Alicia established the habit of putting the date on the papers she receives. When she is filing and sorting her papers, a date would make it much easier to put them in order.

15. Teachers can help by breaking down directions, projects, and other tasks into step-by-step instructions. Alicia should master one step before moving on to the next step. Visual aids may take some of the load off Alicia's working memory.

16. The team will be considering possible disability identifications for Alicia. Three of the possible categories include the following.

    Speech or language impairment means a communication disorder, such as stuttering, impaired articulation, a language impairment, or a voice impairment, that adversely affects a child's educational performance.

    Other health impairment means having limited strength, vitality, or alertness, including a heightened alertness to environmental stimuli, that results in limited alertness with respect to the educational environment, that (i) is due to chronic or acute health problems such as asthma, attention deficit disorder or attention-deficit/hyperactivity disorder, diabetes, epilepsy, a heart condition, hemophilia, lead poisoning, leukemia, nephritis, rheumatic fever, sickle cell anemia, and Tourette syndrome; and (ii) adversely affects a child's educational performance.

Intellectual disability means significantly subaverage general intellectual functioning, existing concurrently with deficits in adaptive behavior and manifested during the developmental period, that adversely affects a child's educational performance.

Thank you to Alicia for participating in this reevaluation process! We hope that anyone involved in this process will feel free to contact us with any questions regarding this evaluation. Thank you for the opportunity to work with Alicia.

Endnotes

[1] Most tests increase in difficulty from the lowest-numbered to the highest-numbered items and require that the student be given specified numbers of passed, easier items and more difficult, failed items to ensure the student's full range of abilities is assessed.

[2] Percentile ranks tell the percentage of same-age children who scored the same as Alicia or lower. For example, a percentile rank of 9 would mean that Alicia scored as high as or higher than 9% of children her age and lower than the other 91%.

[3] On even the best-constructed tests, there is some random variation in scores. In this report, a "significant difference" is a difference between scores too great to have occurred just by random variation more than 5 times in 100.

Scores Used with the Tests in This Report

When a new test is developed, it is *normed* on a *sample* of hundreds or thousands of people. The sample should be like that for a good opinion poll: female and male, urban and rural, different parts of the country, different income levels, and so on. The scores from that norming sample are used as a yardstick for measuring the performance of people who then take the test. This human yardstick allows for the difficulty levels of different tests. The student is being compared to other students on both difficult and easy tasks. You can see from Table 9.18 (a variant of Figure 9.1) that there are more scores in the middle than at the very high and low ends. Many different scoring systems are used, just as you can measure the same distance as 1 yard, 3 feet, 36 inches, 91.4 centimeters, 0.91 meter, or 1/1760 mile.

Percentile Ranks (PR) simply state the percentage of persons in the norming sample who scored the same as or lower than the student. A percentile rank of 50 would be Average—as high as or higher than 50% and lower than the other 50% of the norming sample. The middle half of scores falls between percentile ranks of 25 and 75.

Standard Scores ("quotients" on some tests) have an average (*mean*) of 100 and a *standard deviation* of 15. A standard score of 100 would also be at the 50th percentile rank. The middle half of these standard scores falls between 90 and 110.

Scaled Scores ("standard scores" on some tests) are standard scores with an average (*mean*) of 10 and a *standard deviation* of 3. A scaled score of 10 would also be at the 50th percentile rank. The middle half of these standard scores falls between 8 and 12.

v-**Scale Scores** have a *mean* of 15 and *standard deviation* of 3. A *v*-scale score of 15 would also be at the 50th percentile rank and in stanine 5. The middle half of *v*-scale scores falls between 13 and 17.

Table 9.18 A Depiction of the Normal Curve as It Relates to Performance on Clinical Tests of Intelligence, Achievement, and Adaptive Behavior

There Are 200 &s.
Each & =1%.

Percentage in each	2.2%	6.7%	16.1%	50%	16.1%	6.7%	2.2%
Standard Scores	-69	70–79	80–89	90–109	110–119	120–129	130
Scaled Scores	1 2 3	4 5	6 7	8 9 10 11	12 13	14 15	16 17 18 19
v-Scale Scores	1–8	9 10	11 12	13 14 15 16	17 18	19 20	21–24
Percentile Ranks	-02	03–08	09–24	25–74	75–90	91–97	98–
WISC-V Classification	Extremely Low	Very Low	Low Average	Average	High Average	Very High	Extremely High
WIAT-III Classification	Very Low <55	Low 55–69	Below Average 70–84	Average 85–115	Above Average 116–130	Superior 131–145	Very Superior 146–
Vineland Adaptive Levels	Low -70	Moderately Low 71–85		Adequate or Average 86–114	Moderately High 115–129	High 130–	

Adapted from J. O. Willis and R. P. Dumont, *Guide to identification of learning disabilities* (Acton, MA: Copley Custom Publishing, 1998, p. 27). Also available at http://alpha.fdu .edu/psychology/test_score_descriptions.htm.

Alicia's Test Scores

Table 9.19   Alicia's Achievement Test Scores in Standard Scores and Percentile Ranks for Her Age

WIAT–III Composites and Tests	Test Score[1]	95% Confidence[2]	Percentile[3]	WIAT–III Classification[4]
Reading Decoding				
reading <u>words</u> aloud from a list	79	73–85	8	Below Average
reading <u>nonsense words</u> aloud (to test phonics)	83	78–88	13	Below Average
Basic Reading Composite	**81**	**77–85**	**10**	**Below Average**
Reading Fluency				
oral reading accuracy for short passages	76	63–89	5	Below Average
oral reading rate for short passages	86	79–93	18	Average
Oral Reading Fluency Composite	**81**	**74–88**	**10**	**Below Average**
Reading Comprehension				
reading comprehension: answering questions about stories	75	64–86	5	Below Average
Reading Comprehension and Fluency Composite	**74**	**66–82**	**4**	**Below Average**
Total Reading Composite	**77**	**72–82**	**6**	**Below Average**
Rapid Automatized Naming and Retrieval Speed				
speed of naming things in specific categories	85	71–99	16	Below Average
Writing				
Sentence Building	*80*	*67–93*	*9*	*Below Average*
Sentence Combining	*83*	*71–95*	*13*	*Below Average*
Sentence Composition	80	70–90	9	Below Average
Word Count	*90*	*77–103*	*25*	*Average*
Theme Development and Organization	*82*	*68–96*	*12*	*Below Average*
Essay Composition	85	75–95	16	Average
Written Spelling of dictated words	79	72–86	8	Below Average
Written Expression Composite	**79**	**72–86**	**8**	**Below Average**
Math				
math problem solving ("story" or "word" problems)	61	53–69	0.5	Low
math numerical operations with paper and pencil	67	58–76	1	Low
Mathematics Composite	**64**	**57–71**	**1**	**Low**

Table 9.19   *(Continued)*

WIAT–III Composites and Tests	Test Score[1]	95% Confidence[2]	Percentile[3]	WIAT–III Classification[4]
math fluency—addition	84	73–95	14	Below Average
math fluency—subtraction	77	67–87	6	Below Average
math fluency—multiplication	64	54–74	1	Low
Math Fluency Composite	73	66–80	4	Below Average
Oral Language				
Receptive Vocabulary	*88*	*70–106*	*21*	*Average*
Oral Discourse Comprehension	*64*	*51–77*	*1*	*Below Average*
Listening Comprehension	71	59–83	3	Below Average
Expressive Vocabulary	*70*	*51–89*	*2*	*Below Average*
Oral Word Fluency	*85*	*71–99*	*16*	*Average*
Sentence Repetition	*49*	*34–64*	*0.1*	*Very Low*
Oral Expression	61	48–74	0.5	*Low*
Oral Language Composite	66	55–77	1	Low

[1]These are the standard scores used by the test publisher.

[2]Test scores can never be perfectly reliable, even on the very best tests. Lucky and unlucky guesses, barely beating or missing time limits, and other random influences inevitably alter scores. This score interval shows how much scores are likely to vary 95% of the time just by pure chance.

[3]Percentile ranks tell the percentage of students of the same age or grade whose scores Alicia tied or exceeded. For example, a percentile rank of 36 would mean that Alicia scored as high as or higher than 36% of peers and lower than the other 64%.

[4]These are the classification categories recommended for the WIAT–III.

Table 9.20   Alicia's Scores for Her Age on the Wechsler Intelligence Scale for Children–Fifth Edition (WISC–V)

Test scores in *italics* are <u>not</u> included in the composite and full scale scores.

Subtest/Composite	Test Score[1]	95% Confidence[2]	Percentile[3]	WISC–V Qualitative Descriptor[4]
Verbal Comprehension Subtests		999–999		
Explaining how two different things could be similar (SI)	5	2–7	5	Very Low
Defining vocabulary words (VC)	2	1–4	0.4	Extremely Low
Answering questions of social and practical comprehension (CO)	2	1–4	0.4	Extremely Low
Answering questions of general information (IN)	6	4–8	9	Low Average
Verbal Comprehension Index (SI VC)	65	60–75	1	Extremely Low

(continued)

Table 9.20 (*Continued*)

Subtest/Composite	TestScore[1]	95% Confidence[2]	Percentile[3]	WISC–V Qualitative Descriptor[4]
Visual–Spatial Subtests				
Copying geometric designs with patterned cubes (BD)**	3	1–5	1	Extremely Low
Visually selecting puzzle pieces to match a whole puzzle (VP)*	4	2–6	2	Very Low
Visual–Spatial Index (BD VP)	64	59–75	1	Extremely Low
Fluid Reasoning Subtests				
Completing multiple-choice, logical matrix puzzles (MR)	6	4–8	9	Low Average
Solving mental equations using pictures of weights (FW)*	7	5–9	16	Low Average
Fluid Reasoning Index (MR FW)	79	73–88	8	Very Low
Working Memory Subtests				
Repeating series of dictated digits forward and backward (DS)	2	1–4	0.4	Extremely Low
Recalling previously seen pictures in the same sequence (PS)	4	2–6	2	Very Low
Working Memory Index (DS PS)	62	57–73	1	Extremely Low
Processing Speed Subtests				
Speed of transcribing a digit-symbol code on paper (CD)**	7	5–9	16	Low Average
Speed of finding matching symbols in rows of symbols (SS)**	6	4–8	9	Low Average
Processing Speed Index (CD SS)	80	73–91	9	Low Average
Full Scale Total (SI VC BD MR FW DS CD)	64	60–71	1	Extremely Low

Note: Abbreviations are: SI = Similarities, VC = Vocabulary, IN = Information, CO = Comprehension, BD = Block Design, VP = Visual Puzzles, MR = Matrix Reasoning, FW = Figure Weights, DS = Digit Span, PS = Picture Span, CD = Coding, SS = Symbol Search.

[1] These are scaled scores for subtests and standard scores for composites. Please see the explanation of test scores presented earlier in this report in the section titled "Scores Used with the Tests in This Report."

[2] Test scores can never be perfectly reliable, even on the very best tests. Lucky and unlucky guesses, barely beating or missing time limits, and other random influences inevitably alter scores. This score interval shows how much scores are likely to vary 95% of the time just by pure chance.

[3] Percentile ranks tell the percentage of students of the same age or grade whose scores Alicia tied or exceeded. For example, a percentile rank of 36 would mean that Alicia scored as high as or higher than 36% of peers and lower than the other 64%.

[4] Different tests use different descriptors for test scores. The *WISC–V Technical and Interpretive Manual* (p. 152) states, "Qualitative descriptors are only suggestions and are not evidence-based; alternate terms may be used as appropriate." These descriptors are *not* applied to subtest scaled scores in the *WISC–V Technical and Interpretive Manual*.

*time limits

**time limits and bonus points for speed

Table 9.21   Alicia's Vineland–II Adaptive Behavior Scale Scores in Standard Scores, Percentile Ranks, and Adaptive Levels for Her Age

Parent/Caregiver Rating Form, completed by Sally Portman

Area	Score[1]	95% Confidence[2]	Percentile[3]	Adaptive Level [These are not the score classifications used elsewhere.]
Receptive communication	5	3–7	0.1	Low
Expressive communication	12	10–14	16	Moderately Low
Written communication	12	10–14	16	Moderately Low
Total Communication Domain Score	70	61–79	2	Low
Personal daily living skills	10	7–13	5	Moderately Low
Domestic daily living skills	13	11–15	25	Adequate
Community daily living skills	15	13–17	50	Adequate
Total Daily Living Skills Domain Score	85	75–95	16	Adequate
Interpersonal relationships	11	9–13	9	Moderately Low
Play and leisure time	7	4–10	0.4	Low
Coping skills	11	8–14	9	Moderately Low
Total Socialization Domain Score	71	62–80	3	Moderately Low
Adaptive Behavior Composite	73	67–79	4	Moderately Low

These are v-scaled scores for subtests and standard scores for composites, as described the section of this report titled "Scores Used with the Tests in This Report"."

[2]Test scores can never be perfectly reliable, even on the very best tests. Lucky and unlucky guesses, barely beating or missing time limits, and other random influences inevitably alter scores. This score interval shows how much scores are likely to vary 95% of the time just by pure chance.

[3]Percentile ranks tell the percentage of students of the same age or grade whose scores Alicia tied or exceeded. For example, a percentile rank of 36 would mean that Alicia scored as high as or higher than 36% of peers and lower than the other 64%.

Table 9.22   Alicia's Vineland–II Adaptive Behavior Scales Scores in Standard Scores, Percentile Ranks, and Adaptive Levels for Her Age

Teacher Rating Form, completed by Kathryn Potter

Area	Score	95% Confidence	Percentile	Vineland Adaptive Level [These are not the score classifications used elsewhere.]
Receptive communication	11	9–13	9	Moderately Low
Expressive communication	13	11–15	25	Adequate
Written communication	11	9–13	9	Moderately Low
Total Communication Domain Score	80	73–87	9	Moderately Low

(continued)

Table 9.22 *(Continued)*

Teacher Rating Form, completed by Kathryn Potter

Area	Score	95% Confidence	Percentile	Vineland Adaptive Level [These are <u>not</u> the score classifications used elsewhere.]
Personal daily living skills	15	14–16	50	Adequate
Domestic daily living skills	9	8–10	2	Low
Community daily living skills	14	13–15	37	Adequate
Total Daily Living Skills Domain Score	84	77–81	14	Moderately Low
Interpersonal relationships	14	13–15	37	Adequate
Play and leisure time	15	14–16	50	Adequate
Coping skills	13	12–14	25	Adequate
Total Socialization Domain Score	91	86–96	27	Adequate
Adaptive Behavior Composite	84	79–89	14	Moderately Low

Tests Taken by Alicia

Wechsler Intelligence Scale for Children–Fifth Edition (WISC–V) (David Wechsler, Pearson, 2014)

The WISC–V is an individual test that does not require reading or writing. Verbal Comprehension subtests are oral questions requiring oral answers. Fluid Reasoning subtests are nonverbally presented, unfamiliar problems that require logical reasoning. Visual-Spatial subtests are visual puzzles. Working Memory subtests require remembering data (e.g., repeating dictated digits) or remembering and mentally manipulating data (e.g., repeating dictated digits in reversed order). Processing Speed subtests measure speed on fairly simple paper-and-pencil tasks. Each composite includes two subtests. Seven of these subtests are included in the Full Scale IQ (FSIQ). One additional subtest of the same ability can be substituted for one primary subtest in the FSIQ if absolutely necessary. Subtest scores and composite scores are based on the scores of the 2,200 children originally tested in a very carefully designed, nationwide sample, but still must be interpreted very cautiously for any individual,

especially one who may have somewhat unusual patterns of strengths and weaknesses. As with any test, influences such as anxiety, motivation, fatigue, rapport, and experience may invalidate test scores.

Wechsler Individual Achievement Test–Third Edition (WIAT–III) (Pearson, 2009b)

The WIAT–III offers standard scores, percentile ranks, stanines, and other scores, based either on the student's age or the grade (fall, winter, and spring norms for grades Pre-K through 8, full-year norms for grades 9 through 12, and separate college norms). The standardization sample consisted of 2,775 students in 14 grade groups: PK–12 and 1,826 students in 14 age groups, ranging in age from 4 to 19. The sample was stratified for age, grade, gender, race/ethnicity, geographic region, and parents' education level, based on 2005 U.S. Census data. Students, including children in special education, were drawn from public and private schools in 32 states. To link the WIAT–III with a Wechsler intelligence test, a subset of 1,284 students were also given the test appropriate for their age.

Vineland Adaptive Behavior Scales–Second Edition (VABS–II) (Sara S. Sparrow, Domenic V. Cicchetti, & David A. Balla, Pearson, 2005)

The Vineland Adaptive Behavior Scales are *not* "tests" but questionnaires completed by teachers or parents or by an evaluator working with a parent or other care-taker (Survey Interview Form). They include domains of Communication, Daily Living Skills, Socialization, and, for younger students, Motor Skills, with subdomains within each domain. There is also a Maladaptive Behavior scale for the Interview forms. The Interview forms were normed on a representative, national sample of 1,085 children ages 0 through 4 years, 2,290 children ages 5 through 21 years, and 320 persons ages 22 to 90 years.

CASE 3—LUKE, AGE 9: A CHC-BASED CROSS-BATTERY ASSESSMENT CASE REPORT

Jennifer T. Mascolo and Dawn P. Flanagan

This case report includes the results of a psychoeducational evaluation that was conducted following Cross-Battery assessment (XBA) principles and procedures and interpreted within the context of the Cattell-Horn-Carroll (CHC) theory of cognitive abilities. The evaluation is of a student who was suspected of having a specific learning disability (SLD) in the area of reading. The WISC–V and KTEA–3 were the core batteries used in this evaluation. Determination of SLD was guided by the Dual-Discrepancy/Consistency (DD/C) operational definition of SLD (Flanagan, Ortiz, & Alfonso, 2013) and the Pattern of Strengths and Weaknesses Analyzer within the Cross-Battery Assessment Software System (X-BASS; Ortiz, Flanagan, & Alfonso, 2015).

Confidential Psychoeducational Evaluation Report

Name: Luke Harris

Gender: Male

Evaluation Date(s): 2/5, 2/18, 2/19

Grade: 4

Age: 9 years, 11 months

Date of Report: 3/1/15

Reason for Referral

Luke is a fourth-grade student who was referred to the Committee on Special Education for eligibility consideration in the spring of 2014, following pervasive academic weaknesses and an inability to read independently. Private speech-language, neurodevelopmental, and psychoeducational evaluations revealed generally average

language ability and average or better cognitive functioning, with the exception of working memory and processing speed. Academic performance was well below average, and significant attention difficulties were noted. Based on a consideration of all documentation, including a diagnosis of attention-deficit/hyperactivity disorder (ADHD Inattentive Type) and related learning difficulties, the multidisciplinary team classified Luke as other health impaired (OHI).

An Individual Education Program (IEP) was implemented in March of 2014. Luke's IEP provides supplemental instructional support in reading, writing, and math, along with instructional modifications and test accommodations in the general education setting. Luke also receives reading tutoring from an Orton-Gillingham–trained tutor, using traditional methods that focus primarily on decoding. Nevertheless, Luke is reluctant to read aloud in class and avoids reading in general. According to his mother, Mrs. Harris, Luke does not appear to be benefitting from current educational supports.

Recently, Luke began taking 18 mg of Concerta. Although Mrs. Harris reported immediate and positive medication effects (e.g., improved handwriting, increased focus of attention), she questions the ADHD diagnosis and believes that Luke may be dyslexic. Therefore, she is seeking the current evaluation to improve diagnostic clarity and obtain additional information about Luke's learning needs that may better inform instruction and intervention.

Background Information

Luke is a 9-year, 11-month-old student in the fourth grade at Maybach Elementary School. He is an only child who lives with his mother and father in a single-family home. His mother is a supervisor at a local day care center and his father is a machine operator, who was placed on temporary disability this past summer following a job-related accident. Mr. Harris is recovering and has returned to work part time. Luke participates in several activities with his family, including watching movies and television, sharing meals and conversation, taking trips, visiting with relatives, and attending church. Luke also maintains independent interests such as ice hockey, bike riding, rock climbing, camping, and playing Xbox games. Luke also reportedly likes archery, Legos®, and building with wood.

Mr. and Mrs. Harris report that Luke is the product of a healthy pregnancy. He reached all developmental milestones within or ahead of time. Luke was noted to be colicky up until 10 months of age. Medical history is unremarkable, with the exception of asthma, seasonal allergies, and scarlet fever in 2008.

Educationally, despite seemingly adequate listening comprehension, Luke experienced early difficulties with literacy-based tasks (e.g., phonetic coding, reading, and copying from the board). Math and science skills were noted to be stronger than English language arts skills. Luke's behavior is reported to be generally well modulated in school and at home. Nevertheless, Luke's parents report that Luke has always had difficulty with focusing and concentrating, especially during homework. In addition, Luke's parents report that he displays some behaviors that are consistent with his diagnosis of ADHD, including processing information more slowly and with more mistakes than peers; missing details; difficulty following instructions; and problems with motor skills (e.g., poor handwriting). Social relationships are described as "good." Current interventions include home-based tutoring, medication, and in-school academic support.

School-based hearing and vision tests have been historically good, though Luke's reading difficulties prompted a developmental vision evaluation in 2013, which revealed that Luke is hyperopic (farsighted) and has convergence insufficiency, which can result in difficulty reading near-point print. Luke wears glasses for these conditions. Although hearing is within normal limits and the results of a speech-language evaluation were within normal limits and did not suggest auditory processing deficits, an audiological evaluation was sought by Mr. and Mrs. Harris due to persistent reading concerns and to rule out auditory processing deficits. The audiological evaluation revealed weaknesses with "temporal sequencing and binaural integration." Temporal sequencing influences all aspects of speech and general listening and includes the ability to perceive the order of sounds as well as discriminate between similar words and consonants. *Binaural integration* refers to the ability to bring together differing stimuli presented simultaneously to each ear. As such, Luke may have difficulty hearing when there is background noise or difficulty understanding when information is being presented in both ears, such as when more than one person is talking at a time. Weaknesses in temporal sequencing and binaural integration represent abnormalities of the auditory system and often coexist with ADHD. Some auditory processing difficulties include: confusing syllable sequences or leaving off word endings; trouble paying attention to and remembering information presented orally; and low academic performance, especially in the areas of reading, comprehension, and spelling.

In addition to vision and hearing evaluations, an occupational therapy evaluation, pursued due to "concerns regarding his ocular motor and visual motor integration skills for reading and writing tasks," revealed decreased motor dexterity and a pencil grip that limited control and efficiency during writing tasks. Subsequently, Luke received occupational therapy to address these observed difficulties in March of 2013. Upon attainment of the goals that were set for him, services were discontinued in November of 2014.

Paternal family history is significant for "learning struggles" and attention disorders.

Evaluation Procedures and Tests Administered

Behavior and Classroom Observation

Parent Interview

Student Interview

Teacher Interview

Work Sample Review

Wechsler Intelligence Scale for Children®– Fifth Edition (WISC®–V)

Woodcock-Johnson® IV Tests of Cognitive Abilities (WJ IV), selected subtests

Kaufman Test of Educational Achievement, Third Edition (KTEA™–3), Form A

Test of Orthographic Competence (TOC)

Behavior Assessment System for Children, Second Edition (BASC–2): Teacher, Parent, and Self-Report Scales

Behavior and Classroom Observations

Luke was seen on three separate occasions for testing. He was compliant at each session and readily conversed with this evaluator, offering his opinions regarding his level of interest in a task and/or its perceived difficulty. Although he was less inclined to read aloud to this evaluator, he complied during reading tasks and appeared to put forth consistent effort throughout the evaluation.

To provide further information about Luke's academic performance, he was observed in his fourth-grade classroom. Luke spends the majority of instructional periods in a general education classroom learning English Language Arts (ELA), math, social studies, science, and religion. Luke, along with his classmates, switches classrooms for specials including, media, art, music, and gym. A foreign language teacher, Mrs. Carty, provides Spanish instruction once weekly in the classroom. In addition to his teacher, Mrs. Moore, a full-time classroom aide, Ms. Dryden, provides instructional support. Nineteen students were present during the observation (9 boys, 10 girls).

The physical classroom contained six seating groups, each comprised of four student desks facing one another. There was a smart board and bulletin board along one wall and a whiteboard along another wall. Four computer stations were to the left of the smart board. Computers are reportedly used for independent writing work. One student was observed sitting at a computer during smart board instruction to "follow along" with the teacher, as the computer displayed the near-point projection from the smart board. Student work was displayed on the walls in various locations across the classroom. Further, there was a classroom behavior chart, multiplication chart, word wall, writing tips poster, and science poster in the classroom. A word wall was also hanging up in the classroom with parts of words highlighted in various colors. Finally, there was a large U-shaped desk in the classroom that is designated for small-group instruction. However, it did not appear that it was used for small-group instruction because it was crowded with stacks of books and papers.

A Daily Schedule, written in script on the board, outlined the sequence of instructional and recreational activities for the day. Specific subjects were abbreviated (e.g., Vocab. for Vocabulary, SS for Social Studies). Additionally, a numbered list containing two assignments appeared to the right of the daily schedule, which included a grammar assignment and a classroom craft. Instructional materials include *My Math*, Volume I (McGraw-Hill), *Science: A Closer Look* (Macmillan/McGraw-Hill), *Storytown* (Harcourt), *Social Studies* (Scott Foresman), and *Simple Solutions: Grammar* (Bright Ideas Press, LLC).

Following morning routine, Mrs. Moore taught a math lesson on mixed numbers and improper fractions. She used the whiteboard to review the difference between a whole number and a fraction. She used the smart board to review vocabulary (e.g., numerator/denominator) and to provide examples of each fraction type. During instruction, Luke was oriented to Mrs. Moore and appeared to follow along in his book. Luke appeared responsive to teacher directives (e.g., "turn to page 543") and appeared to transition easily between activities (e.g., teacher-led instruction to seatwork). Luke did not volunteer to participate but complied when asked to answer a question. When asked to explain the difference between a mixed fraction and an improper fraction, Luke provided an answer that had already been given by another student. When prompted further, Luke was able to provide a correct response. Luke appeared to look down and remain quiet as other students answered questions. During independent seatwork, the classroom aide checked in with Luke to ask if he understood what he was supposed to do. Luke appeared engaged in math seatwork and did not request support.

Luke was again observed during a social studies lesson. During this lesson, students were arranged in groups, with 10 students in Luke's group. Luke appeared to listen as others read. When he was called upon to read, he held his head down and read quietly. His reading was markedly dysfluent. He made several errors (e.g., read "to" as "for"). Mrs. Moore provided immediate correction for each of his errors. Luke often paused in anticipation of support rather than attempting to decode a word he did not know. Although Luke listened as others read or spoke, he appeared mildly distracted by another group that was working in a separate part of the classroom, especially as the group began an open-ended discussion.

Evaluation Results

The results presented in this report were compiled from tests of which some do not share a common norm group; however, test results have been interpreted following the cross-battery assessment approach and integrated with data from other sources including educational records, parent/teacher interviews, behavioral observations, work samples, and other test findings *to ensure ecological validity*. Standardized procedures were followed for all test administrations. No single test or procedure was used as the sole criterion for classification, eligibility, or educational

planning. Unless otherwise noted, the results of this evaluation are considered a reliable and valid estimate of Luke's demonstrated skills and abilities at this time.

Cognitive

To obtain information regarding Luke's level of cognitive functioning, the WISC–V was used as the core battery and supplemented with selected tests from the Woodcock-Johnson® Tests of Cognitive Abilities, Fourth Edition (WJ IV). Collectively, selected subtests from the WISC®–V/WJ IV batteries allowed for a comprehensive assessment of seven CHC cognitive ability domains considered important for overall learning as well as the acquisition and development of specific academic skills. These domains are: Crystallized Intelligence (Gc), Fluid Reasoning (Gf), Visual Processing (Gv), Short-Term Memory (Gsm), Processing Speed (Gs), Long-Term Retrieval (Glr), and Auditory Processing (Ga).

The WISC–V yields a Verbal Comprehension Index, Fluid Reasoning Index, Visual Spatial Index, Working Memory Index, Processing Speed Index, and Storage and Retrieval Index. These indexes provide estimates of Gc, Gf, Gv, Gsm, Gs, and Glr, respectively. Selected subtests from the WJ IV were used to obtain an estimate of Ga as well as to test hypotheses about Luke's performance in certain cognitive domains. A description of Luke's performance in each of the seven CHC domains is described below. Individual composites and subtest scores are referred to throughout this report and appear in separate tables at the end of this report.

The mean standard score for all indexes (and certain subtests) on the WISC–V and all composites and subtests on the WJ IV is 100, with a standard deviation of 15. WISC–V subtest scaled scores are based on a mean of 10 and a standard deviation of 3. Standard Scores between 85 and 115 (and scaled scores between 7 and 13) are considered to be within normal limits because nearly 70% of the general population performs within this range. Table 9.23 provides

Table 9.23 Classification System for Interpreting Luke's Test Scores

Standard Score Range for Composites	Scaled Score Range for Subtests	Classification
<70	1–3	Lower Extreme
70–84	4–6	Well Below Average/ Normative Weakness
85–89	7–8	Low Average*
90–110	9–11	Average*
111–115	12–13	High Average*
116–129	14–16	Well Above Average/ Normative Strength
>130	17–19	Upper Extreme

*Within Normal Limits (Low Average, Average, or High Average classification) represents a very large range (in which most people perform) along the ability continuum

information about how scores were interpreted in this evaluation.

Crystallized Intelligence (Gc) *Crystallized intelligence* refers to the breadth and depth of a person's acquired knowledge of a culture and the effective application of that knowledge. This store of primarily verbal or language-based knowledge typically develops largely as a function of educational and general life experiences. The WISC–V measures crystallized intelligence via the subtests that make up the Verbal Comprehension Index—Vocabulary and Similarities. The Vocabulary task required Luke to define words presented orally by the examiner. The Similarities task required Luke to draw conceptual similarities between two words presented orally by the examiner. Luke's verbal responses were generally clear and complete on both tasks. When queried to extend upon an initial response, Luke typically improved his initial response, adding depth and clarity. Luke obtained a scaled score of 10 on both subtests, indicating that his performance ranked

at the 50th percentile and fell in the Average range relative to same-age peers from the general population.

Overall, Luke's Verbal Comprehension Index of 100 [94–106] is Average and reflects mainly his knowledge of word meanings. In addition, his vocabulary knowledge is consistent with other language abilities that were assessed previously, such as listening comprehension and oral expression. Luke also spoke fluently and evidenced normal syntax, morphology, and pragmatics throughout the evaluation, which again is consistent with his observed *Gc* ability on the WISC–V. In general, Luke's *Gc* ability ought to facilitate his learning and academic performance.

Nevertheless, deficits in basic foundational skills, including reading decoding and spelling, continue to constrain Luke's ability to use his *Gc* effectively on literacy-based tasks. As such, specific recommendations designed to harness his *Gc* capabilities to enhance his performance on literacy-based tasks are offered at the end of this report. Also offered are recommendations designed to remediate foundational skill deficits.

It is also noteworthy that Luke's listening comprehension skills were measured in a quiet, one-to-one setting. As such, his reported auditory processing difficulties did not appear to interfere significantly with his ability to perform tasks that relied on listening comprehension.

Fluid Reasoning (Gf) *Fluid reasoning* is the ability to reason, form concepts, and solve problems that often include novel information or procedures. In addition, these types of tasks tend to involve basic reasoning processes that depend minimally on learning and acculturation. The WISC–V measures fluid reasoning via the subtests that make up the Fluid Reasoning Index—Matrix Reasoning and Figure Weights.

The Matrix Reasoning task primarily measures inductive reasoning and required Luke to view an incomplete visual matrix or series and select the response option that best completed the matrix or series. Luke obtained a scaled score of 9 on this task, which ranked at the 37th percentile and fell in the Average range. The Figure Weights task required Luke to view two scales, one with missing weights, and choose one from a set of options that balanced the scale. This subtest assesses both deductive reasoning and quantitative reasoning. Luke obtained a scaled score of 11 on this task, which ranked at the 65th percentile and fell in the Average range.

Overall, Luke's Fluid Reasoning Index of 100 [94–106] is Average and is consistent with past evaluation results, which also showed average reasoning ability relative to same-age peers. Luke indicated that the WISC–V reasoning tasks were typically "easy" for him and reported that he used strategies, such as verbalizing a pattern, when trying to solve a particular item. On certain items Luke reported that he was able to identify the correct response by focusing on the "whole" item rather than parts of an item. These comments imply that Luke was focused and thoughtful throughout the administration of the reasoning subtests. In general, Luke's *Gf* performance reflects the level of reasoning ability necessary to support learning and, therefore, ought to facilitate his learning and academic performance, particularly on higher level application-type tasks (e.g., math problem solving).

Similar to his language abilities, however, deficits in basic academic foundational skills, coupled with specific cognitive processing weaknesses (including working memory and processing speed), obstruct his ability to reason effectively and consistently in the classroom. Specific recommendations designed to minimize the effects of limited foundational skills as well as memory and processing speed weaknesses on Luke's ability to use reasoning more effectively in the classroom are offered at the end of this report.

Visual Processing (Gv) *Visual processing* is the ability to analyze and synthesize visual information including the ability to perceive, store and recall, manipulate, and think with visual images and patterns. The WISC–V measures visual processing via the subtests that make up the Visual Spatial Index—Block Design and Visual Puzzles. These subtests primarily measure the ability to mentally analyze and synthesize visual images to construct more complex images. The Block Design task required Luke to quickly re-create a pictured or modeled design, using two-color blocks. Luke obtained a scaled score of 16 on this task, which ranked at the 98th percentile and fell in the Well Above Average range relative to same-age peers. The Visual Puzzles task required him to view a completed puzzle and select the three response options that would effectively reconstruct the puzzle. Luke obtained a scaled score of 14 on this task, which ranked at the 91st percentile and fell in the Well Above Average range.

Overall, Luke's Visual Spatial Index of 129 [120–133] is in the Well Above Average range and is considered both a relative and normative strength for him. Specifically, he performed as well as or better than 97% of his peers in the area of visual processing. Luke commented that both *Gv* tasks were "easy." Interestingly, Luke attributes his excellent performance in this domain to "always doing puzzles" when he was younger. Although Luke no longer completes puzzles, he enjoys visual activities, including building with Legos. Given his strength in this domain and confidence in performing visual-spatial tasks, an attempt was made to capitalize on this strength in intervention planning, as may be seen in some of the recommendations offered at the end of this report.

Short-Term Memory (Gsm) *Short-term memory (Gsm)* refers to the ability to encode, maintain, and manipulate information in one's immediate awareness. The WISC–V measures short-term memory via the subtests that make up the Working Memory Index—Digit Span and Picture Span. Working memory assists an individual in controlling attention and resisting distractions. The Digit Span task required Luke to listen to a number sequence read by the examiner and recall the numbers in the same order (Forward task), reverse order (Backward task), and ascending order (Sequencing task). Luke obtained a scaled score of 6 on this task, which ranked at the 9th percentile and fell in the Well Below Average range. Luke's performances across conditions were not significantly different from one another. However, the sequencing task was more challenging than the other conditions due to increased demands on mental manipulations, which places additional constraints on working memory and attention. When asked about his use of strategies, Luke stated, "I was just saying them in my head first" for the Forward and Backward condition, but he noted, "It was hard remembering the numbers then putting them in order" for the sequencing condition and noted that he did not have a particular strategy for approaching the task.

The Picture Span task required Luke to view a page of pictured objects for a specified time and then select the pictures in sequential order from a series of response options. Luke obtained a scaled score of 10 on this task, which ranked at the 50th percentile and fell in the Average range. Despite average performance, Luke noted that it was "hard remembering things." It was observed that Luke verbally rehearsed and shortened the names of the objects shown (e.g., if shown a picture of a small dog, a triangular hat, and a black car, he might say dog, hat, car in his mind rather than focus on minor visual details), which aided his recall.

Given the variability in Luke's performance on working memory tasks, his Working Memory Index of 88 is not considered to be the best estimate or a good summary of his working memory ability. In an attempt to obtain more information about Luke's working memory, the WISC–V Letter–Number Sequencing subtest was administered. Letter–Number Sequencing required Luke to listen to a sequence of numbers and letters and recall the numbers in ascending order followed by the letters in alphabetical order. Luke obtained a scaled score of 7 on this

task, which ranked at the 16th percentile and fell in the Low Average range. Luke reported that this task was difficult and that it was not only hard remembering the numbers, but, similar to WISC–V Digit Span Sequencing, it was particularly hard to put them in order. When asked if he had a strategy to facilitate his performance, he indicated, "I just said them again in my mind." Luke's performance on the Digit Span and Letter–Number Sequencing subtests combined to yield an Auditory Working Memory Index of 81 (76–88), which is ranked at the 10th percentile and falls in the Well Below Average range relative to same-age peers.

Overall, it appears that when Luke is required to hold a typical amount of information in mind while working on a task, he likely experiences cognitive overload (i.e., too much information to be processed simultaneously), which leads to making mistakes or an inability to complete a task successfully. It was observed that Luke can best employ working memory in problem solving when a visual recognition paradigm is used, as in Picture Span. However, as language demands increase and task parameters place a higher demand for mental manipulation (e.g., reversing or sequencing numbers), Luke's working memory performance declines. That is, when task demands extend beyond Luke's processing limits, academic performance is adversely affected. Overall, Luke's working memory difficulties are consistent with his diagnosis of ADHD. These difficulties with working memory are very likely contributing to his academic difficulties as well as his ability to consistently demonstrate critical thinking and reasoning ability during academic lessons and classroom activities, particularly in the presence of background noise.

It is noteworthy that Luke reported that he feels the impact of his working memory weakness (likely coupled with his auditory processing weaknesses) in class. For example, he stated, "I'm confused with a lot of directions in class." He defined "*a lot*" as multistep or lengthy directions. Further, Luke appeared particularly upset that he is unable to access extra credit points on in-class tests because the extra credit question is typically read "one time only," and, given his inability to remember it, he is unable to attempt an answer. Specific recommendations regarding how Luke may circumvent the limits of his working memory capacity and reduce cognitive load on learning during instruction are offered at the end of this report.

*Processing Speed (*Gs*)*   *Processing speed* (*Gs*) refers to an individual's ability to quickly and efficiently perform relatively simple cognitive tasks, especially when under pressure to maintain attention and concentration. The WISC–V measures processing speed via the subtests that make up the Processing Speed Index—Coding and Symbol Search. The Coding task required Luke to copy symbols that corresponded to specific numbers as quickly as possible within a 2-minute time limit. Luke experienced difficulty with this task. He obtained a scaled score of 7 on Coding, which ranked at the 16th percentile and fell in the Low Average range. On the Symbol Search task, Luke was required to quickly scan a set of symbols and identify whether the target shape was repeated in the stimulus shapes. He obtained a scaled score of 10 on Symbol Search, which ranked at the 50th percentile and fell in the Average range. There was a statistically significant difference between the Coding and Symbol Search scaled scores, meaning that Luke's obtained PSI of 92 may not be the most accurate estimate or summary of his processing speed.

Specific task characteristics and task demands may explain the significant difference in performance on the Coding and Symbol Search subtests. For example, on the Coding task, Luke was required to identify a number, scan the key to find the number, and draw the symbol associated with that number in a small box. Performance on this task is facilitated by memory and motor dexterity, both of which are problematic for Luke. As such, Luke needed to reference the key frequently to identify the correct symbol and appeared to draw the symbols more slowly than is typical.

Conversely, the Symbol Search task required visual scanning, which is a strength for Luke. In addition, the motor demands for Symbol Search are much simpler as compared to Coding. That is, on the Symbol Search task, Luke identified his response with a single hash mark as opposed to drawing an abstract form.

Luke's performance on additional measures of processing speed was also variable. For example, on a measure of number facility in which Luke was required to quickly solve a series of simple math computations using paper and pencil (KTEA–3 Math Fluency), he obtained a standard score of 79, which is ranked at the 8th percentile and falls in the Well Below Average range. Conversely, on a task in which Luke was required to quickly identify matching number pairs in a row of numbers (WJ IV COG Number Pattern Matching), he obtained a standard score of 93, which is ranked at the 32nd percentile and falls in the Average range. Likewise, on a task that required Luke to name the quantity of squares inside boxes as quickly as possible, he earned a standard score of 90, which is ranked at the 25th percentile and falls in the Average range. Using cross-battery software, two processing speed composites were generated—one that included the processing speed tasks on which Luke performed average (i.e., Symbol Search, Number Pattern Matching, and Naming Speed Quantity; XBA *Gs* Composite 1 = 93 [88–98], 31st percentile, Average) and one that included the processing speed tasks on which Luke demonstrated weaknesses (i.e., Coding and Math Fluency; XBA *Gs* Composite 2 = 78 [73–83], 8th percentile, Well Below Average).

Like his performance on working memory tasks, Luke's variability in performance on measures of processing speed, as seen in the substantial difference between his XBA *Gs* composites, appears to be consistent with his diagnosis of ADHD as well as his reported auditory processing weaknesses. Overall, Luke is often slow to complete tasks, especially demanding ones. In addition, he may not "catch" all instructions necessary for completing a task;

he may be slow to copy information from the board at school; and he may be slow to retrieve information from long-term stores. As a result of his variable processing speed, Luke may need extra support at home and at school, even though he is taking medication for ADHD.

It is also noteworthy that Luke's ability to quickly process information is mediated by the nature of the stimuli and the degree to which demands are placed on memory. As noted by his teacher, Mrs. Moore, Luke often complains that information is presented too quickly and that he cannot keep up. Further, regarding academic impact, Luke's teacher indicated that Luke's processing speed weaknesses affect his reading and computational speed as well as his ability to retrieve verbal information and communicate his thoughts in a timely manner. Luke's issues with speed are particularly relevant to his motivation as, according to Mrs. Moore, the intensive effort that Luke must expend to get through tasks results in a reduced motivation to produce. This is consistent with Luke's self-report wherein he noted that he is "always behind" and cannot "keep up" with his class. Specific recommendations designed to circumvent the impact of slow processing speed on Luke's ability to learn, complete classwork, and access the curriculum in a manner consistent with his peers are offered at the end of this report.

Long-Term Storage and Retrieval (Glr) Long-term storage and retrieval (Glr) refers to the ability to take in and store a variety of information (e.g., ideas, names, concepts) in one's mind and then retrieve it quickly and easily at a later time by using association. This ability does not represent *what* is stored in long-term memory or what you know. Rather, it represents the *process* of storing information, which is related to learning efficiency as well as the speed at which information is retrieved from long-term stores, which is often called *speed of lexical access* (LA). Both learning efficiency and speed of lexical access are important for learning and overall academic success. The WISC–V measures long-term storage and retrieval via the associative memory

subtests that make up the Symbol Translation Index (Immediate Symbol Translation, Delayed Symbol Translation, and Recognition Symbol Translation) and the speed of lexical access subtests that make up the Naming Speed Index (Naming Speed Literacy and Naming Speed Quantity).

The Immediate Symbol Translation subtest required Luke to pair new symbols with a word and then to "read" sentences comprised only of those symbols. Delayed Symbol Translation required Luke to recall the meanings of the symbols learned on Immediate Symbol Translation after a 20 to 30 minute delay. Recognition Symbol Translation required Luke to recognize the meaning of each symbol when provided four options by the examiner. Luke's performances on these tasks ranged from Average to High Average. Overall, based on these performances, Luke obtained a Symbol Translation Index of 104 (98–109), which ranks at the 61st percentile and is classified as Average, suggesting that Luke's learning efficiency via associative memory is typical with respect to same-age peers. Overall, Luke's performances on these tasks suggest that once he adequately encodes information, he can retrieve it for later use.

The Naming Speed Literacy subtest required Luke to quickly name letters and numbers on a page and assesses speed of lexical access, while Naming Speed Quantity required the examinee to quickly name the quantity of blue squares inside boxes and assesses number facility (a Gs task). While Luke performed in the Average range on Naming Speed Quantity (standard score = 90; 25th percentile), he performed in the Well Below Average Range on Naming Speed Literacy (standard score = 72; 3rd percentile), suggesting that his ability to make automatic visual-verbal associations is extremely limited. Rapid naming of letters and numbers is an important skill, as it is related to the acquisition and development of early reading and writing skills. Rapid naming (of letters and numbers) is a skill that is typically practiced in the very early grades and, therefore, is typically well developed in children of Luke's age. Because of the statistically significant variability between these two naming speed subtests, the Naming Speed Index of 79 is not considered a good estimate or summary of this ability. It is likely that Luke performed in the Average range of the Naming Speed Quantity task because it shows greater sensitivity to math skills, which is not an area of concern for Luke. Conversely, Naming Speed Literacy is sensitive to reading difficulties.

There is a need to determine whether Luke's speed of lexical access is deficient, as suggested by his Naming Speed Literacy score of 72, or whether he may instead have difficulty performing speeded tasks that use orthography (letters, numbers), as opposed to shapes and pictures, since his performance on Naming Speed Quantity (involving shapes) was average.

Luke was administered two additional speed of lexical access tasks that did not involve orthography (i.e., KTEA–3 Associational Fluency and Object Naming Facility). The Associational Fluency task required Luke to rapidly produce words related to a specific condition or object (e.g., name as many colors as you can as quickly as you can). On this task Luke obtained a standard score of 84, which ranked at the 14th percentile and falls in the Well Below Average range. The Object Naming Facility task required Luke to rapidly name known objects. He obtained a standard score of 76 on this task, which ranked at the 5th percentile and is classified as Well Below Average. Based on these two subtest performances, Luke earned a KTEA–3 Oral Fluency Composite of 77 (72–82), which ranked at the 5th percentile and fell in the Well Below Average range relative to same-age peers.

Luke was also administered several subtests that required rapidly working with orthographic units, namely WJ IV Letter Pattern Matching, WISC–V Naming Speed Literacy, and KTEA–3 Letter Naming Facility. On the Letter-Pattern Matching test, Luke was required to draw lines through the letters or sets of letters that were alike in each row. On this test he obtained a score of 81, which ranked at the 10th percentile and is classified as Well Below Average. As discussed,

Luke earned a score of 72 on Naming Speed Literacy. On a task very similar to Naming Speed Literacy, Luke was required to name letters on a page as quickly as possible (KTEA–3 Letter Naming Facility). His score on this test was a 73 (4th percentile; Well Below Average). Cross-Battery software was used to create an orthographic processing (OP) composite based on these three tasks. Luke's XBA OP Composite of 68 ranks at the 2nd percentile and is classified as Lower Extreme.

Similarly, on a separate measure of orthographic processing called the Test of Orthographic Competence (TOC), Luke obtained an Orthographic Ability score of 66 (61–71), which is ranked at the 1st percentile and is classified as Lower Extreme. Interestingly, Luke's highest score on the TOC was on a punctuation task, wherein he demonstrated Average performance (TOC Punctuation SS = 90). This is noteworthy because Luke committed several punctuation errors throughout testing. As such, Luke's intact performance may relate to the fact that he was specifically directed to consider punctuation, thereby increasing his awareness and focus on properly punctuating written statements. Further, the writing demands of this task were lessened in that Luke was neither required to generate any of the statements nor required to spell any words; rather, he simply had to capitalize and/or add end punctuation. It is significant to note that as the number of corrections within a sentence increased to beyond 2, Luke was unable to identify all necessary corrections. Consistent with Luke's Orthographic Ability score on the TOC was his Orthographic Processing Composite of 66 (1st percentile; Lower Extreme) on the KTEA–3.

Overall, Luke performed in the Well Below Average to Lower Extreme ranges of ability in two critical areas that are strongly related to reading: speed of lexical access and orthographic processing, respectively. Most reading intervention programs focus more on the phonological processing component of reading. Recommendations for programs and techniques that assist with the orthographic processing component of reading are offered at the end of this report.

In addition, Luke's processing speed was variable, which also interferes with reading. A consideration of Luke's difficulties in speed of lexical access, working memory, and processing speed suggests that the efficiency with which Luke processes and uses information is low. In other words, the capacity of Luke's cognitive system to process information automatically is quite limited at times. Specific accommodations, modifications, and compensatory strategies will likely be necessary to minimize the effects of this limitation on Luke's overall learning.

Auditory Processing (Ga) *Auditory processing (Ga)* refers to the ability to perceive, analyze, and synthesize a variety of auditory information (e.g., sounds). Many tests of auditory processing measure phonetic coding, which is the ability to hear phonemes distinctly. Phonetic coding (also called phonemic awareness) is very important for developing reading and spelling skills, especially during the elementary school years. The KTEA–3 measures auditory processing via the Phonological Processing subtest.

KTEA–3 Phonological Processing assesses phonological awareness skills, auditory perception and discrimination, and higher-level processing via phonetic analysis and synthesis in the context of sequencing, assembling, and segmenting sounds. Luke demonstrated proficiency in blending orally presented speech sounds to form whole words as well as in rhyming and matching sounds. Luke obtained a Phonological Processing score of 93, which ranked at the 32nd percentile and fell in the Average range. Despite average phonological processing in the current and prior evaluations, Luke's ability to decode nonsense words was generally weak and is described later in this report.

Notwithstanding Luke's average blending and rhyming skills, phoneme segmentation and deletion tasks wherein Luke was required to isolate sounds in words or delete a specific sound

from a given word (e.g., say "store" without the *s* to make "tore") proved more difficult. This is likely due to the increased memory demands inherent in these tasks. In fact, Luke had specific difficulty with increasingly lengthy words and, in such cases, would tend to blend, as opposed to segment, final sounds (e.g., if given the word "father," he might say, "f-a-*ther*").

In addition to specific auditory processing skill weaknesses, Luke's prior audiology and central auditory processing evaluations revealed "poor pitch discrimination skills and poor auditory sequencing ability." Further, weaknesses in binaural separation and integration were noted, which can result in "difficulty hearing in background noise or listening when more than one person is talking at the same time." Additionally, temporal processing weaknesses were noted that impact the degree to which Luke fully processes auditory information that "is influenced by time in some way" (e.g., keeping pace with a teacher's instruction or noting rapid changes in tone or prosody, such as when a teacher is attempting to emphasize a key word or phrase).

Academic Functioning

To document Luke's current level of academic functioning, selected tests from the Kaufman Tests of Educational Achievement, Third Edition (KTEA–3) were administered. The administration of these measures allowed for an assessment of foundational skills, fluency with those skills, and higher-level application of basic skills in the areas of reading, writing, and math. Given that Luke demonstrated generally average functioning on a prior speech and language evaluation as well as past academic measures of listening comprehension and oral expression, these domains were not assessed directly in the current evaluation.

Basic Reading Skills Regarding Basic Reading Skills (BRS), Luke demonstrated consistent weaknesses on measures that required him to recognize real words (KTEA–3 Letter

Word Recognition SS = 67; 1st percentile; Lower Extreme) and decode nonsense words (KTEA–3 Nonsense Word Decoding SS = 73; 4th percentile; Well Below Average) in untimed conditions. Based on these two subtests, Luke obtained an overall KTEA–3 Decoding Test Composite of 69 (66–72), which ranked at the 2nd percentile and is classified as Lower Extreme.

Luke had a tendency to read letter by letter but would sometimes attempt to "chunk" parts of words, although he was typically incorrect in his responses. At times, Luke would evidence letter reversals, reading a "*b*" as a "*d*." Error analysis revealed several normative weaknesses across error categories. Specifically, when asked to decode real words, Luke had difficulty with vowel sounds, unpredictable word patterns, dipthongs, and silent letters. Further, he evidenced syllable insertions, misordered sounds, and whole word errors (e.g., reading "understood" as "undressed"). When asked to read a list of nonsense words, Luke also evidenced vowel confusion with short and long vowel sounds and evidenced difficulty with blends and with inserting and omitting syllables.

Testing of limits revealed that Luke's ability to decode a word improved greatly with semantic cues. For instance, he was unable to decode the word "ocean" and read it as "okeen," but when told "this is the place where fish live," he quickly responded with "ocean." Similarly, he read "shoes" as "shows" until told that it has something to do with "dressing in clothes," to which he responded, "shoes."

Overall, the present findings are consistent with past evaluations, which showed that Luke omitted medial and ending sounds in words and often made up words after identifying an initial letter sound. Past evaluations found Luke's reading decoding skills to be "*limited* to *very limited.*" His current teacher noted that he cannot read independently, and his mother noted an avoidance of reading. Luke's deficit in reading decoding, coupled with his poor sight-word vocabulary (i.e., he recognizes very few words automatically), precludes reading fluency.

It appears that Luke is at the partially alphabetic phase of word reading. That is, Luke understands that there is a relationship between letters and sounds. However, he relies on beginning and ending sounds and, therefore, continues to make errors in reading words, particularly in isolation. It is important for reading interventions to assist in moving Luke's word reading from the partially alphabetic phase to the fully alphabetic phase. These types of interventions are offered at the end of this report. Any remedial reading intervention suggested for Luke will need to be one that minimizes the effects of working memory demands, in particular. For example, Luke cannot decode multisyllabic words in part because he cannot keep the complete phonemic string in mind long enough to say the word.

Reading Fluency Luke's reading fluency skills were assessed via three measures. The first two measures required Luke to read isolated real words (KTEA–3 Word Recognition Fluency SS = 68; 2nd percentile; Lower Extreme) and nonsense words (KTEA–3 Decoding Fluency SS = 67; 1st percentile; Lower Extreme) aloud as quickly as possible during two 15-second trials. The third measure required Luke to silently read simple sentences, with a 2-minute time limit, and mark a "yes" or "no" in a response booklet to indicate whether the statement was true or false (KTEA–3 Silent Reading Fluency SS = 70; 2nd percentile; Well Below Average). Based on these three measures, Luke earned a Reading Fluency Composite of 65 (59–71), which ranked at the 1st percentile and falls at the Lower Extreme of the ability continuum compared to same-age peers.

It is noteworthy that the timed nature of the tasks that comprised the Reading Fluency Composite were particularly challenging for Luke, who began committing several whole-word errors when reading words in isolation (e.g., reading "very" as "they," reading "did" as "it"). Continued difficulty with vowel sounds, consonant omissions, and consonant blends were evident during real-word reading.

Despite consistent subtest score performances, the nonsense-ord decoding task appeared most challenging for Luke. Specifically, he made frequent errors with initial and ending sounds (e.g., reading "jull" as "pull" and "frop" as "golp") and also indicated that he needed to "skip" an item. Furthermore, Luke demonstrated letter reversals, reading "*d*" and "*p*" as "*b*." It may have been that Luke's awareness of the timed nature of the task and his perceived difficulty on the initial real-world task created a heightened sense of urgency, which resulted in seemingly more errors. In fact, on the second trial of the nonsense-word reading task, Luke correctly decoded only one of nine words. Luke's ability to fluently (automatically) decode at the word and sentence level is deficient and, therefore, precludes meaningful comprehension of text. His reading fluency deficiency is related not only to his decoding deficit but also to his deficit in orthographic processing.

Reading Comprehension Luke's reading comprehension skills were assessed via the KTEA–3 Reading Comprehension subtest. On this untimed test of silent reading comprehension, Luke was asked to read narrative and expository passages and answer literal and inferential comprehension questions. Given his substantial decoding and fluency weaknesses, Luke read from a second- (rather than fourth-) grade item set. Early items in this set required Luke to read simple directions and respond by performing an action (e.g., "touch your toes"). Luke earned a Reading Comprehension score of 73, which ranked at the 4th percentile and was classified as Well Below Average.

Error analysis revealed normative weaknesses in both literal and narrative passage comprehension. These findings are consistent with district evaluation reports that indicated "very limited" passage comprehension (e.g., WJ III Reading Comprehension Composite SS = 74) as well as teacher reports, which indicate that Luke's severe decoding and fluency weaknesses interfere with his ability to demonstrate text comprehension. Although weaknesses in working memory, processing speed, and speed of lexical access may also interfere with reading comprehension, it will be difficult to determine the extent of these influences until significant improvements have been made in reading.

Written Expression Luke's written language skills were assessed via the KTEA–3 Spelling and Written Expression subtests. Luke was asked to spell target words that were dictated in the context of a sentence (KTEA–3 Spelling SS = 71; 3rd percentile; Well Below Average). Luke committed several errors including, inserting or omitting syllables and/or vowels (e.g., spelling "dry" as "driy"), omitting silent word endings and consonant digraphs (e.g., spelling "phone" as "fon"), and committing whole-word errors (e.g., spelling "do" as "bow"). Additionally, Luke demonstrated difficulty with unpredictable letter patterns (e.g., spelling "said" as "sed"). Finally, he evidenced *b* and *d* reversals, (e.g., spelling "better" as "deter") and committed errors when asked to form contractions (e.g., spelled "don't" as "downt"). Luke's spelling difficulties preclude him from participating in class spelling tests. As such, he receives a modified spelling list that is provided by his private reading tutor. In addition to impacting his participation in class-wide assessments, his spelling difficulties significantly detract from the readability of his work.

For example, on the KTEA–3 Written Expression subtest, Luke was asked to write sentences from dictation, add capitalization and punctuation, complete or combine sentences, and write an essay. Although Luke's responses were semantically appropriate, they were syntactically incorrect and contained several punctuation and capitalization errors. For instance, when asked to write a short essay, Luke wrote:

> The Dragin is herming. The tounan and Kyra
> is ssent to resu the toun from the Drager and
> She asks two people to helpe Her She finily fins
> it and savs the Day.

The corrected version (below) demonstrates the intended meaning:

> The dragon is harming the town. Kyra is sent to rescue the town from the dragon. She asks two people to help her. She finally finds it and saves the day.

Luke obtained a Written Expression score of 89, which ranked at the 23rd percentile and falls in the Low Average range. This performance shows that although Luke is able to plan and generate ideas for writing, his difficulties with writing mechanics, which appear to stem from both phonological and orthographic processing weaknesses, substantially detract from the quality and readability of his work. His spelling and written expression performances combined to yield a KTEA–3 Written Language Composite of 80 (76–84), which ranked at the 9th percentile and is classified as Well Below Average.

Given that untimed writing tasks were difficult for Luke (Spelling and Written Expression tasks), it was not surprising that a timed writing task (Writing Fluency) also proved difficult. On this task, Luke was required to write one sentence about each picture presented in a response booklet and was tasked with completing as many items as possible within 5 minutes. Luke earned a Writing Fluency score of 75, which ranked at the 5th percentile and is classified as Well Below Average. Luke's sentences on this task reflected multiple spelling errors, article omissions, letter reversals, and several punctuation and capitalization errors. For instance, in attempting to write the sentence "the girl kicks the ball," Luke wrote, "Gers kiks the dall." He also wrote "The bab crals" to communicate "The baby crawls."

Luke's printing was legible, with inconsistently sized and spaced letters. Mrs. Moore noted similar difficulties in the classroom and stated that, despite instruction, Luke cannot write in, or read, script. Further, he reportedly does not attend to margins or other spatial aspects of writing (e.g., words that overhang a line).

Luke's generally Well Below Average to Lower Extreme performance in all aspects of reading and writing severely compromise his ability to learn and achieve in the classroom at a rate and level typical of same-age peers. Similarly, his substantial reading and writing difficulties severely compromise his ability to do seatwork and homework independently and to access the general education curriculum in a manner consistent with typically achieving peers.

Math Calculation and Math Problem Solving
Luke's math skills were assessed via the KTEA–3 Math Computation and Math Concepts and Applications subtests. The math computation subtest required Luke to write answers to a series of printed problems involving basic operations with whole numbers and fractions as well as problems involving algebra, square roots, and exponents (KTEA–3 Math Computation SS = 97; 42nd percentile; Average range). The math concepts and applications subtest required Luke to respond orally to items that required him to apply mathematical principles to everyday situations. Skill categories assessed included number concepts, operations, time and money, measurement, geometry, fractions, decimals, data investigation, and other higher-level math concepts (KTEA–3 Math Concepts & Applications SS = 89; 23rd percentile, Low Average range). These two subtests combine to yield a KTEA–3 Math Composite of 92 (88–96), which is ranked at the 30th percentile and is classified as Average. Luke's math knowledge and math achievement skills are significantly above his reading and writing skills and are generally consistent with the math skills of typically achieving same-age peers.

Notwithstanding generally average computation and problem-solving skills, Luke struggled on a timed math task that required him to write as many answers to addition, subtraction, multiplication, and division problems as possible, in 1 minute (KTEA–3 Math Fluency SS = 79; 8th percentile, Well Below Average). Luke did not make any errors on this subtest, indicating that his poor performance is related to slow processing speed and lack of automaticity, not accuracy.

While math has historically been described as Luke's stronger subject and there is not a suspected disability in this domain, specific recommendations to strengthen automaticity with math facts and support access to the general education math curriculum are provided at the end of this report. It is noteworthy that word problems were read to Luke in this evaluation, thereby circumventing the impact of Luke's decoding weaknesses on his math performance. Although Luke receives specific reading supports, his math lessons are taught partially via smart board technology, and the students are presumed to be reading along with text shown on the screen. This means that Luke is required to rely primarily on listening skills to acquire information relating to new math concepts. Further, while descriptions of math concepts and written steps are provided in Luke's textbook, his inability to decode such information limits his in-class performance and his ability to demonstrate his knowledge fully.

Functional Manifestations of Cognitive Weaknesses

Information from classroom observation, teacher, parent, and student interviews as well as a records review suggests that Luke's identified cognitive weaknesses manifest in real-world settings (e.g., school) in the following ways.

Regarding long-term retrieval, Luke's difficulty with rapid automatic naming/speed of lexical access, specifically when it involves orthography (e.g., letters and numbers), impacts his ability to quickly access phonological representations during decoding. That is, while he can isolate single letters and identify an associated sound, he does so slowly and he has particular difficulty with larger orthographic units (e.g., common letter blends such as "sh" and entire words). Further, his difficulty with orthographic processing results in a limited sight-word vocabulary and persistent spelling difficulties. His weakness in orthographic processing is evident in his writing samples. For example, he often spells the same word inconsistently within the same paragraph, reverses letters, omits punctuation, and capitalizes letters within words.

Luke's weakness in short-term memory, specifically working memory, impacts his ability to decode and spell multisyllabic words, draw meaning from text, and take notes. With regard to the latter, for example, Luke is unable to hold a typical amount of information in working memory long enough to summarize it succinctly and in a manner that would facilitate efficient note taking. As a result, Luke tries to record information verbatim and often finds that he loses pace with the rest of his class, ends up with an incomplete set of notes, and has little understanding of the lesson. His slow processing speed also contributes to his difficulties with note taking. In short, Luke's weakness in working memory constrains his ability to manipulate or transform information effectively to achieve success in a variety of important school-related tasks.

Finally, Luke's processing speed weakness manifests as slowed reading speed, difficulty with automatic math computations, and limited written output due to time parameters. Luke reported that he is often behind the rest of the class in his written work and is rarely able to complete copying tasks. Presently Mrs. Moore accommodates Luke by taking his notebook and completing the writing for him and/or having the classroom aide complete writing. Luke's processing speed weakness is particularly noteworthy because it places continued demands on his working memory, which can result in information overload, loss of meaning, and difficulty applying higher-level thinking and reasoning skills without supports to aid memory.

Consideration of Exclusionary Factors as Primary Cause of Luke's Weaknesses

Luke's specific cognitive and academic weaknesses identified in the present evaluation do not appear to result *primarily* from a perceptual disturbance, social emotional difficulty, or pervasive cognitive weakness. Further, there do not appear to be any primary physical health conditions, environmental/economic, cultural/linguistic, or instructional factors that are *primarily* related to Luke's identified difficulties.

Notwithstanding, based on the available data, there are specific factors that appear to contribute to Luke's observed learning difficulties. These include his hyperopic (farsighted) status along with a "significant accommodative (focusing) infacility" described in a 2013 optometric evaluation. Specifically, Luke hyperfocuses on near-point objects, which results in "visual fatigue, blurring and jumping of print, and small-word confusion." Further, reading comprehension is negatively correlated with time. That is, lengthier reading tasks can result in eye fatigue and difficulty with sustained convergence, both of which can render reading effortful beyond Luke's decoding deficits. The end result can be waning attention, disengagement, and overall reduced comprehension.

Additionally, though hearing is within normal limits, Luke's documented weaknesses with "temporal sequencing and binaural integration" can impact his ability to keep pace with teacher-led instruction and focus on instructional material in the context of environmental noise (e.g., low-level talking in the classroom and/or during small-group work)

Finally, motivational factors appear to be contributing to Luke's academic weaknesses in that Luke feels that he is "not normal" and is frustrated with his inability to read grade-level text independently and to keep pace with his classmates. As he described to this evaluator, "I can't keep up. I'm on number one and the rest of my class is like already passed number three." Further, to address this slower pacing, Luke reportedly must place his work aside and complete it at a later time, which is typically during recess or homework. He reported that "no matter what" he does, he can "never catch up." Collectively, these feelings can result in reduced effort during in-class tasks as Luke experiences little success in regard to completion. Further, this evaluator observed that Luke tends to wait for adult assistance when he encounters difficulty rather than

make an independent effort to attempt the task or item.

Processing Strengths and Weaknesses Analysis

To more objectively evaluate the interaction between Luke's cognitive and academic performances, data from this evaluation were entered into the *Cross-Battery Assessment Software System (X-BASS), Dual Discrepancy/Consistency Model: PSW Analyses for SLD* program (Ortiz, Flanagan, & Alfonso, 2015). The data support that, despite specific cognitive weaknesses, Luke displays generally average overall cognitive ability, particularly in domains considered important for acquiring grade-appropriate academic skills, such as fluid reasoning and crystallized intelligence. His pattern of performance is marked by domain-specific cognitive weaknesses in working memory, processing speed, orthographic processing, and speed of lexical access and unexpected underachievement in basic reading skills, reading fluency, and written language, particularly spelling. It is very likely that Luke's domain-specific cognitive weaknesses explain, in part, his weaknesses in reading and writing, and there is empirical evidence as well as ecological validity to support these cognitive-achievement relationships. The results of Luke's pattern of strengths and weaknesses analysis are found at the end of this report. In short, the results of this analysis, coupled with the exclusionary factors analysis, support the presence of a specific learning disability in the areas of basic reading skills, reading fluency, and written expression.

Summary and Diagnostic Impressions

Luke is a fourth-grade student who was referred to the Committee on Special Education for eligibility consideration in the spring of 2014, following pervasive academic weaknesses and an inability to read independently. Luke was diagnosed with ADHD (inattentive type) and classified as other health impaired. His IEP provides for supplemental instructional support and accommodations in the general education setting. Additionally, he receives private reading tutoring and home-based support, and is receiving pharmacological intervention. Despite the recent evaluation findings, Luke's mother, Mrs. Harris, questioned the ADHD diagnosis and was interested in improving diagnostic clarity, as Luke appeared to be benefiting minimally from the current instructional supports.

To address the current referral concerns, Luke was administered cognitive and academic measures from the WISC–V, WJ IV, KTEA–3, and TOC. Additionally, other procedures including interviews, observations, record reviews, and rating scales were used in this evaluation. Standardized test results were interpreted primarily within the context of CHC theory, cross-battery assessment and the Dual-Discrepancy/Consistency Model of specific learning disability identification.

Luke performed in the Average to Well Above Average range across several cognitive domains. Findings suggest that Luke has adequate verbal ability (*Gc*) and is able to apply reasoning skills to solve problems involving figural forms and patterns (*Gf*). He also has Average phonemic awareness skills (*Ga*), including blending and rhyming. Additionally, Luke's associative memory (MA), an important part of Long-Term Storage and Retrieval (*Glr*), is within the Average range of functioning. Further, his visual processing skills (*Gv*), as estimated primarily by measures of visualization, are Well Above Average. Conversely, Luke has limitations in higher-level phonological processing skills (e.g., deleting and segmenting) and difficulty attending in the presence of background noise when processing speech in time-sensitive conditions (e.g., following a fast-paced lecture). Further, his ability to hold, transform, and manipulate information in working memory (*Gsm*) as well as his ability to quickly process information (*Gs*) is weak. Luke has a weakness in Speed of Lexical Access (LA), or quickly retrieving letters,

words, and objects (e.g., pictures) from memory. Relatedly, Luke has a significant weakness in Orthographic Processing (OP), which limits his ability to automatically recognize letters and words.

Academically, Luke demonstrated a relative strength in mathematics (computation and applied problems) but performed in the Well Below Average range in the area of math fluency. Literacy-based domains, including reading decoding, reading fluency, reading comprehension, and written expression (including spelling) were Well Below Average or lower.

In addition to these findings, interviews, observations, records reviews, and rating scales each supported the presence of specific functional manifestations that were consistent with the standardized test findings, thereby establishing the ecological validity of such results. Further, processing strengths and weaknesses analyses suggested the presence of specific cognitive weaknesses, especially in the areas of working memory, processing speed, and orthographic processing, that are moderately to strongly related to Luke's specific academic weaknesses in reading decoding, reading fluency, and spelling. These areas are further impacted by noted weaknesses in speed of lexical access and cognitive efficiency.

Based on these facts and a consideration of exclusionary criteria, Luke's pattern of results support the presence of a specific learning disability, primarily in the areas of basic reading skills, reading fluency, and written expression. While reading comprehension is weak, difficulties with text comprehension appear primarily related to decoding and fluency deficits. It is also clear that while Luke's ADHD (inattentive type) and weaknesses in the auditory system are contributing to his difficulties in reading and writing, they are not the primary cause of these difficulties.

Overall, it seems likely that Luke's pattern of cognitive strengths ought to enable learning and achievement, especially when specific cognitive weaknesses are minimized through compensatory strategies, accommodations, and curricular modifications. These supports need to be accompanied by evidence-based interventions that provide explicit instruction in Luke's main areas of academic weakness and cognitive processing weakness (i.e., orthographic processing). These types of recommendations follow.

Recommendations

The following recommendations aim to (1) remediate Luke's specific academic weaknesses; (2) enable Luke to more fully access the general education curriculum; and (3) circumvent or minimize the impact of documented cognitive weaknesses via the provision of accommodations and compensatory techniques. Interventions attempt to capitalize on Luke's visual processing strengths where possible.

Reading

1. To circumvent or minimize the impact of Luke's reading difficulties, it is suggested that a ***virtual backpack of Luke's classroom texts be provided via an audio book service***, such as Learning Ally™. Learning Ally™ provides accessible downloadable, human-narrated audio books. Additional features, such as word highlighting, tailored adjustments (e.g., text size, reading rate), and bookmarking (to hold one's place), should be explored with Luke prior to implementing. Luke should have access to these books during independent in-class reading and home-based reading.

2. Provide ***targeted instruction in sound segmentation and phoneme deletion***. Such instruction can occur in the context of Luke's private reading tutoring or via home-based programs. Consider using Elkonin boxes to make segmentation more concrete and to reduce memory demands during training. A description of Elkonin boxes and their use is available on www.readingrockets.org/strategies/elkonin_boxes.

3. To build confidence during small-group read-alouds, provide Luke with an ***opportunity to preview and practice small sections of text*** prior to the read-aloud (e.g., a chapter title, a figure caption, or question stem) and contribute throughout, as such sections appear (e.g., "Luke, can you read our chapter's title," "Luke, what is Figure 1 telling us about?").

4. Continue to capitalize on Luke's intact language skills (e.g., Listening Comprehension), and allow Luke to engage in reading activities by ***encouraging him to answer questions or offer insights following other's reading***.

5. Encourage Luke to ***visually follow along with text readings*** by using a finger, index card, ruler, or other reading guide.

6. Given Luke's substantial weaknesses in reading, intensive, consistent remediation is warranted. To address the intensity of remediation that Luke requires, ***Mindplay Virtual Reading Coach (MVRC)*** is suggested. This program, which can be implemented at home or school, provides interactive instruction that is delivered via a virtual reading coach. The program begins with phonological awareness and phonics skills training. When Luke demonstrates accurate decoding skills, vocabulary and grammar and meaning instruction begin. Finally, fluency training is delivered to improve silent reading rate. The recommended parameters for implementation are 4 times a week for 30 minutes. A minimum of 40 hours of use is recommended (i.e., 20 weeks).

Orthographic Processing

1. Consider integrating a program that focuses on teaching Luke orthographic processes. One such program is Lindamood-Bell Seeing Starts ® Program for Reading Fluency and Spelling.

2. Explicitly teach Luke specific orthographic structures (e.g., spelling conventions for specific syllable types)

3. Engage Luke in repeated readings to improve the speed with which he can process print.

4. Increase print exposure via daily reading practice. Luke can select texts of interest and play

them via the Learning Ally audio, while ensuring that he is visually following the printed text. This can be accomplished through using text highlighting features available in the Learning Ally program.

5. Incorporate the "spelling deck" drills into Luke's Orton-Gillingham sessions to ensure a balance between encoding and decoding activities.

Writing

1. To address difficulties with writing mechanics, consider providing Luke with a *writing checklist* for tasks such that he is able to proofread his work. It may be necessary to pair a proofreading checklist with *common rules for capitalization and punctuation*.

2. Provide Luke with a *guided notes system*, where possible, so as to reduce the writing demands and allow Luke to keep pace with teacher-led instruction. There is a guided notes maker available online (https://www.interventioncentral.org/rti2/guided_notes). If guided notes cannot be created, consider providing a *blank outline template* and teaching Luke how to use it to record pertinent information.

3. Continue to use the modified spelling list provided by Luke's tutor but have him *practice and preview class spelling words* in a *cover-copy-compare* format. A worksheet and instructions are available at https://www.interventioncentral.org/academic-interventions/writing/how-master-spelling-or-sight-words-cover-copy-compare. Additionally, an online version that allows Luke to type in his responses is available at http://www.amblesideprimary.com/ambleweb/lookcover/lookcover.html. Alternatively, words with specific spelling patterns can be created, so that Luke can practice patterns that posed difficulty for him in the current evaluation. For increased motivation, the class word list can form the basis for bonus points that can be added to Luke's weekly spelling grade.

Processing Speed

1. To address Luke's difficulty with time parameters of tasks, consider specific instructional modifications, such as *reducing the quantity of work* required during seatwork and homework sessions.

2. Encourage Luke to *access his textbooks online* so that he can *preview* chapter content (e.g., end of chapter questions, titles, subtitles) and pertinent vocabulary prior to their presentation in class. Chapter and vocabulary previews can be incorporated as a specific, weekly homework assignment. To provide motivation, completed previews can be awarded a point and a biweekly reward offered (e.g., extra computer time).

3. Begin to *increase Luke's awareness of time* by referencing the clock and providing him with interim counts of time and qualitative markers of expected performance (e.g., "10 minutes left, you should be finished with planning your writing and moving on to your illustration").

4. Help Luke *plan for long-term projects* by using a *written schedule* that incorporates smaller tasks while allowing for consistent movement toward completion. Consider using the following templates available online (e.g., a printable calendar page, a numbered "to do" list with a "date completed" column for check-off). To allow for greater flexibility and choice, consider also using a project planner graphic organizer that contains space for various smaller tasks without identifying a specific order of completion.

5. To allow Luke to more efficiently navigate specific reading tasks (e.g., answering end-of-chapter questions), *teach Luke specific reading strategies*, such as *skimming* or *scanning*. It is important to note that given Luke's reading decoding weaknesses, such a strategy would need to be monitored and/or Luke would need to be taught how to navigate to specific text selections if using an audio book reader.

6. To circumvent the full impact that Luke's processing speed weakness can have on

specific academic tasks, consider engaging him in *online activities or games that aim to increase fluency*. One such resource that is presented in a visually engaging arcade-like format, thereby capitalizing on Luke's visual processing strength, is www .arcademicskillbuilders.com/games/.

Short-Term Memory

1. To address Luke's difficulty with short-term memory, *deliver instructional information in manageable parts*. One way to break down instructions for Luke is to use explicit numerical and/or temporal markers, with pauses, where possible (e.g., "*first*, you are going to take out your math book; *now*, turn to page *11*, and *finally*, complete items *1 through 5*") rather than a more implicit directive (e.g., "take out your book and complete the first five items on your 'check my understanding' page"). Alternatively, have the classroom aide ask Luke to paraphrase Mrs. Moore's instruction and provide support, as needed.

2. Consider *providing written instructions*, where possible, for Luke to reference when completing tasks. It is important to note that such instructions may need to be read to Luke, but a written record can lessen his anxiety in regard to "missing" important information.

3. Use *elaborative rehearsal*, where possible, to connect new information with prior knowledge (e.g., "Today, we are learning about the life cycle of a butterfly, which is *just like last week* when we talked about the life cycle of a frog … there are *stages of change* that *each of these living things go through*"). In this way, the stage is set for new learning while pointing out how what is about to be learned relates (or is similar to) some previously learned information.

4. Ensure that Luke's *attention is secured and maintained* (i.e., through body language and eye contact) during the provision of oral instructions.

5. It is recommended that Luke be *encouraged to ask for repetition* or help while in class if he has missed or forgotten important information. When he asks for help, it is recommended that his teacher first ask him to identify what he does and does not know. This will discourage him from using a teacher's assistance as a strategy for automatically getting the answer. However, as he may not always attempt to access help, it is important that his teachers *look for nonverbal cues* (e.g., a confused facial expression) and "check in" with him. Further, teachers should reinforce Luke's help-seeking behaviors.

6. To build Luke's confidence as a learner, *praise him where possible, by highlighting what he has done correctly*. For instance, if he requires help on a math problem, his teacher can say, "You have started this problem correctly, and it looks like you just need help with reducing your answer to its simplest form."

Long-Term Retrieval

1. Based on Luke's reported difficulty with memorizing and recalling math facts or procedures, he should be encouraged to use *mnemonics* where possible (MDAS, "My Dear Aunt Sally," for order of operations) as well as use *resources in his academic environment* (e.g., refer to the multiplication chart on the classroom wall) or *instructional resource aids* (e.g., My Math series flashcards that contain specific procedures, concepts, and vocabulary).

2. To address word-retrieval difficulties that can arise from long-term retrieval weaknesses, consider providing Luke with *word banks*, where possible during writing tasks. Word banks based on chapter vocabulary in science and social studies texts can be generated online with e-learning tools. Further, use of such tools should be incorporated into Luke's homework plan (e.g., assign a preview of chapter terms for vocabulary and require him to create his own word bank).

3. To circumvent the impact of word-retrieval difficulties, *provide opportunities to build Luke's vocabulary*. This can be accomplished through naturalistically extending upon his words (e.g., if he asks to "start" a task, the teacher can say, "Yes, you can 'begin,'" thereby providing an alternate word). A word-a-day application, online word games, and board games that focus on word usage are other ideas to consider. Additionally, to capitalize on his visual processing strength, consider having Luke use Vocabutoons®, which are visual cartoons that teach vocabulary.

Miscellaneous Recommendations

1. To address reported difficulties with binaural integration and temporal sequencing of auditory information, Luke may benefit from the *generous use of examples and demonstration* in the classroom. Further, the use of *multimodality learning* that is presented sequentially (e.g., orienting Luke to a visual diagram first, prior to speaking about the diagram, pointing to each relevant section of the diagram before providing information regarding the section) may prove beneficial.

2. To minimize the impact of background noise when the class is split into smaller learning groups, the implementation and use of an *FM system* may be particularly beneficial for Luke. The demands of the listening task and the level of environmental noise should dictate the need for such technology, with increases in either resulting in consideration of its use. Alternatively, *using the current small-group U-shaped learning desk* for instruction can prove beneficial, as the desk arrangement allows for the students to face the teacher with backs toward the second group, thereby localizing voices and minimizing distractions.

3. Luke should be *encouraged to practice self-advocacy* and ask for repetition or explanation of directions or information that he finds difficult to understand.

4. *Optimize listening conditions* where possible by providing Luke with *preferential seating* or ensuring that the *teacher maintains physical proximity* during the provision of important instructions or auditory information.

5. To *capitalize on Luke's visual processing strengths*, it is recommended that Luke be provided with *visual organizers* to arrange information in visual format. Graphic organizers can be used to keep track of Luke's assignments, his ideas when generating written work, or after reading a story. Graphic organizers can be downloaded for free from numerous websites, including http://www.teachervision.fen.com/graphicorganizers/printable/6293.html?detoured=1 and http://www.educationoasis.com/curriculum/graphic_organizers.htm

6. Given that Luke cannot read script and also struggled with other orthographic forms (e.g., abbreviations), *consider writing the weekly schedule in print format* for Luke and/or familiarize him with common abbreviations that are used by providing him with an abbreviations key that can be affixed to the inside cover of his workbook or placed on his desk.

Homework

1. Consider *modifying Luke's homework* to include home-based assignments that are purposefully designed to support his access to the curriculum and that offer opportunities for repeated practice (e.g., text preview with web-based audio glossaries, previewing of visual chapter summaries, web-based fluency drills).

2. Familiarize Luke with the several *e-learning tools available in his school textbooks* and incorporate these, where possible, as added supports to be incorporated into weekly homework assignments. Examples of tools to consider include:

   (a) the *tutor* function in Luke's online math text (*My Math*) that provides a video-recorded, teacher-led example highlighting concepts to be taught;

   (b) the *e-glossary* in Luke's science textbook that provides an audio-recorded definition of pertinent terms, which can be used as part of a text preview assignment. *Vocabulary games* can reinforce terms and are also available for each lesson. Finally, *animated lesson summaries* and online *quizzes* can be used to reinforce and assess what Luke has learned; and

(c) *content-based learning resources*, such as the American Museum of Natural History link that supplements content material in Macmillan/McGraw Hill Science textbooks. These additional resources can be used during small-group work or provided to Luke to use to reinforce challenging concepts (http://www.amnh.org/explore/resource-collections/macmillan-mcgraw-hill-science-2008); and

(d) Harcourt Storytown's online resources available at (http://www.harcourtschool.com/storytown/), which include

i. a *multimedia grammar glossary* that can be used to teach and/or strengthen Luke's knowledge of grammar concepts (e.g., abbreviations); and

ii. *Ideas for Writers* writing prompts, which can be used to offer Luke ideas in the planning/idea stage of writing tasks.

3. To facilitate the **continued development of orthographic awareness**, engage Luke in a variety of **letter games**. These brief games can be played using Luke's modified spelling list and can include the following:

(a) *Matching*—have Luke match visually similar words (e.g., words with similar beginning consonants or medial vowel combinations).

(b) *Whole Word*—have Luke look at a word, letter by letter, as he reads each letter aloud. Cover the word and have Luke attempt to spell the word orally. Reveal the letter to determine if there is a match. Alternatively, uncover each letter at a time and start again when a revealed letter does not match the dictated spelling.

(c) *Letter in a Word*—Have Luke carefully review his spelling words, paying attention to the position of specific letters (e.g., first letter of the word, last letter), then cover the words and ask him questions (e.g., what was the first letter? Which letter was third? Last?). If the response is incorrect, reveal the word and allow Luke to study again until the response is correct.

Home

1. Continued reinforcement of skills and opportunities for practice, specifically in regard to literacy (i.e., reading and writing), are important. Some simple ways to provide such opportunities include:

(a) Consider purchasing **paper-and-pencil activities** that engage Luke in reading and writing for fun (e.g., MadLibs, word searches, crosswords).

(b) Allow Luke access to an **iPhone** or other device capable of **texting** or instant messaging in an effort to encourage written production (e.g., asking Luke to text his father or mother with a short message).

(c) Encourage Luke to **write** (or cross off) items from a **shopping list**, write **thank-you** notes, or write in **important dates** on a family calendar (birthdays, upcoming trips).

2. Allow Luke to select a **preferred space** at home to complete writing tasks. Ensure that the space is properly lit, inviting, with a large enough desk or tabletop space for all materials to be kept close at hand.

3. Have Luke select preferred writing instruments and tools (e.g., **novelty pencils**, **highlighters**, **date stamps**, **correction tape**), and consider storing them in a portable writing carrel for easy access and transportability.

4. Consider purchasing **magnetic writing words** and a **magnetic whiteboard** that can be used by Luke as a fun tool to generate ideas for writing. Two such resources are Educational Insights Magnetic Sight Words and Sentence Builders, containing words and punctuation (available at Amazon.com for $11.02) or Magnetic Poetry Kid's Kit, containing 350 words (available at Amazon.com for $15.59).

5. Provide a means for Luke to **display his written work in a fun way** (e.g., a document frame, on the refrigerator with his own clip magnet, hung by clothespin on a colored string along his bedroom wall). Involve Luke in the display of such work and take the opportunity to offer concrete praise.
6. Consider purchasing **personalized stationary** (Post-its, writing pad, pencils) for Luke's personal use.

7. Model **writing for fun**. Consider placing a family blackboard or whiteboard in a central area and write short messages to one another. Alternatively, write notes to Luke and place in his lunchbox, write Luke a message with window markers on a car window, or leave him a message on a mirror in the home. Encourage Luke to participate in similar activities where he writes or draws for fun.

Psychometric Data Summary

*** Please note that these scores are provided for professional reference. For interpretation of implications, refer to the Confidential Evaluation Report***

Table 9.24   Luke's Cognitive Test Scores

Composite/Subtest (For composites, indexes, some subtests, and WISC–V Naming Speed and Symbol Translation subtests: $\bar{x} = 100$, SD = 15 For other WISC–V subtests: $\bar{x} = 10$, SD = 3)	Standard Score	Confidence Interval	Percentile Rank	Qualitative Classification
CRYSTALLIZED INTELLIGENCE (Gc)				
WISC–V Verbal Comprehension Index	100	94–106	50	Average
WISC–V Similarities	10	–	50	Average
WISC–V Vocabulary	10	–	50	Average
FLUID REASONING (Gf)				
WISC–V Fluid Reasoning Index	100	94–106	50	Average
WISC–V Matrix Reasoning	9	–	37	Average
WISC–V Figure Weights	11	–	63	Average
VISUAL PROCESSING (Gv)				
WISC–V Visual Spatial Index	129–S	120–133	97	Well Above Average
WISC–V Block Design	16–S	–	98	Well Above Average
WISC–V Visual Puzzles	14–S	–	91	Well Above Average
SHORT–TERM MEMORY (Gsm)				
WISC–V Working Memory Index	88–W	83–95	21	Low Average
WISC–V Auditory Working Memory Index	81–W	76–88	10	Well Below Average
WISC–V Digit Span	6–W	–	9	Well Below Average
WISC–V Letter Number Sequencing	7	–	16	Low Average
WISC–V Picture Span	10	–	50	Average

Table 9.24   *(Continued)*

Composite/Subtest (For composites, indexes, some subtests, and WISC–V Naming Speed and Symbol Translation subtests: $\bar{x} = 100$, SD = 15 For other WISC–V subtests: $\bar{x} = 10$, SD = 3)	Standard Score	Confidence Interval	Percentile Rank	Qualitative Classification
PROCESSING SPEED (*Gs*)				
WISC–V Processing Speed Index	92	85–100	30	Average
WISC–V Coding	7	–	16	Low Average
WISC–V Symbol Search	10	–	50	Average
XBA Processing Speed Composite (XBA *Gs* Comp 1)	93	88–98	31	Average
WISC–V Symbol Search	10	–	50	Average
WJ IV COG Number-Pattern Matching	93	87–100	32	Average
XBA Processing Speed Composite (XBA *Gs* Comp 2)	78—W	73–83	8	Well Below Average
WISC–V Coding	7	–	16	Low Average
KTEA–3 Math Fluency	79	71–87	8	Well Below Average
WJ IV COG Letter-Pattern Matching	81	74–88	10	Well Below Average
LONG-TERM RETRIEVAL				
WISC–V Naming Speed (NS)	79—W	74–88	8	Well Below Average
WISC–V Naming Speed Literacy	72	66–78	3	Well Below Average
WISC–V Naming Speed Quantity	90	84–96	25	Average
WISC–V Symbol Translation Index	104	98–109	61	Average
WISC V Immediate Symbol Translation	96	91–101	39	Average
WISC–V Delayed Symbol Translation	115	110–120	84	High Average
WISC–V Recognition Symbol Translation	101	95–107	53	Average
AUDITORY PROCESSING (Ga)				
KTEA–3 Phonological Processing (BRS; *Ga*: PC)	93	87–99	32	Average

Table 9.25   Luke's Performance in a Variety of Ability, Processing, and Achievement Domains

Composite/Subtest ($\bar{x}=100$, *SD* = 15)	Standard Score	Confidence Interval	Percentile Rank	Qualitative Classification
ORTHOGRAPHIC PROCESSING (OP)				
Orthographic Processing (XBA OP Comp)	68	63–73	2	Lower Extreme
WJ IV COG Letter-Pattern Matching	81		10	Well Below Average
WISC–V Naming Speed Literacy	72	66–78	3	Well Below Average
KTEA–3 Letter Naming Facility	73	58–88	4	Well Below Average

(continued)

Table 9.25   (*Continued*)

Composite/Subtest ($\bar{x}$=100, *SD* = 15)	Standard Score	Confidence Interval	Percentile Rank	Qualitative Classification
COGNITIVE EFFICIENCY (CE)				
WJ IV Cognitive Efficiency Cluster	78	72–84	7	Well Below Average
WJ IV COG Letter-Pattern Matching	81	74–88	10	Well Below Average
WJ IV COG Numbers Reversed	81	74–87	10	Well Below Average
SPEED OF LEXICAL ACCESS (LA)				
KTEA–3 Oral Fluency Composite	77	72–82	6	Well Below Average
KTEA–3 Associational Fluency	84	71–97	14	Well Below Average
KTEA–3 Object Naming Facility	76	66–86	5	Well Below Average
Grw-R BASIC READING SKILLS				
KTEA–3 Decoding Test Composite	69	66–72	2	Lower Extreme
KTEA–3 Letter and Word Recognition	67	64–70	1	Lower Extreme
KTEA–3 Nonsense Word Decoding	73	69–77	4	Well Below Average
***Grw*-R READING FLUENCY**				
KTEA–3 Reading Fluency Test Composite	65	59–71	1	Lower Extreme
KTEA–3 Word Recognition Fluency	68	58–78	2	Lower Extreme
KTEA–3 Decoding Fluency	67	58–76	1	Lower Extreme
KTEA–3 Silent Reading Fluency	70	62–78	2	Well Below Average
Grw-R READING COMPREHENSION				
KTEA–3 Reading Comprehension	73	67–79	4	Well Below Average
Grw-R WRITTEN EXPRESSION				
KTEA–3 Written Language Composite	80	76–84	9	Well Below Average
KTEA–3 Spelling	71	68–74	3	Lower Extreme
KTEA–3 Written Expression	89	81–97	23	Low Average
Gq MATH CALCULATION				
KTEA–3 Math Composite	92	88–96	30	Average
KTEA–3 Math Computation	97	91–103	42	Average
KTEA–3 Math Concepts & Applications	89	85–93	23	Low Average
OTHER COMPOSITES				
KTEA–3 Orthographic Processing	66	59–73	1	Lower Extreme
Spelling	71			
Letter-Naming Facility	73			
Word Recognition Fluency	68			
KTEA–3 Academic Fluency	69	63–75	2	Lower Extreme
Decoding Fluency	67			
Writing Fluency	75			
Math Fluency	79			

Table 9.26 Luke's Performance on the Test of Orthographic Competence

Composite/Subtest ($\bar{x}$= 100, *SD* = 15)	Standard Score	Confidence Interval	Percentile Rank	Qualitative Classification
Conventions Composite	77	72–82	6	Well Below Average
Punctuation	90	83–97	25	Average
Abbreviations	75	68–82	5	Well Below Average
Spelling Speed Composite	80	75–85	9	Well Below Average
Letter Choice	85	78–92	16	Below Average
Word Scramble	85	78–92	16	Below Average
Spelling Accuracy	63	58–68	<1	Lower Extreme
Sight Spelling	75	68–82	5	Well Below Average
Homophone Choice	70	63–77	2	Well Below Average
Orthographic Ability	66	61–71	1	Lower Extreme

CHAPTER 10

INTERPRETING THE WISC–V FROM A COGNITIVE NEUROSCIENCE PERSPECTIVE

This chapter is the first of four devoted to neuropsychological approaches to interpretation. The unifying theme behind these chapters is an emphasis on brain-behavior relations in the expression of cognitive abilities. This chapter describes those aspects of cognitive neuroscience research that are most relevant to neuropsychologically oriented interpretation of a child's intellectual or cognitive test results. The three subsequent chapters describe various neuropsychologically oriented approaches to cognitive assessment. Chapter 11 provides a general overview of neuropsychological interpretive approaches, with an emphasis on Lurian- and process-based approaches, such as those stemming from the work of Edith Kaplan and her colleagues. Chapters 12 and 13 represent contributions from outstanding neuropsychologically oriented clinicians, with each chapter presenting a unique approach to assessment and interpretation. Chapter 12 describes Dan Miller's integrated school neuropsychological/Cattell-Horn-Carroll interpretive approach, and Chapter 13 describes George McCloskey's process-oriented approach to interpretation.

The division of content matter and case reports between Chapters 10 and 11 is perhaps arbitrary and artificial. Cognitive neuroscience is not currently recognized as an applied, clinical approach to psychological test interpretation; however, the research from this vast, multidisciplinary field has served (and continues to serve) as a guiding force in the practice of clinical neuropsychology and throughout WISC–V

development. Although the case reports selected for inclusion in this chapter could have been included as exemplars in other chapters, each case in this chapter was specifically chosen for inclusion because it illustrates an interpretive consideration (e.g., stage of brain development, attentional difficulties, brain training as an intervention) related to the cognitive neuroscience research that is summarized in this chapter.

INTRODUCTION

Cognitive neuroscience is broadly defined as "the scientific investigation of the nervous system" (Bear, Conners, & Paradiso, 2016, p. 3). Based on this broad definition of cognitive neuroscience, it is very likely that most readers could easily be classified as cognitive neuroscientists, with this vast field including specialists in neurology, neuroanatomy, psychiatry, neuropsychology, cognitive psychology, developmental psychology, biopsychology, molecular biochemistry, biology, psychopharmacology, brain imaging, biotechnology, and a host of other specialties with interests in brain-behavior relations. "Some neuroscientists are zooming in on the fine structure of the individual nerve cells, or neurons. Others are charting the biochemistry of the brain, surveying how our billions of neurons produce and employ thousands of different kinds of proteins" (Zimmer, 2014, p. 36). Likewise, this chapter spans a broad range of topics, including genetic and environmental influences on intelligence; prenatal, postnatal, and childhood brain development; neural plasticity (including the somewhat controversial topic of brain training); advances in brain imaging; and neuroanatomical correlates of cognitive functions (e.g., fluid reasoning, working memory, and executive functions).

An even greater appreciation for the scope and immensity of this body of research materializes when one considers the levels of analysis (in order of increasing complexity): molecular neuroscience (e.g., effects of neurotransmitters), cellular neuroscience (e.g., types of neurons), systems neuroscience (e.g., mapping neural circuitry of the visual system), behavioral neuroscience (e.g., which systems underlie different types of attention), and cognitive neuroscience (e.g., which systems underlie intelligence, language, or self-awareness) (Bear et al., 2016). The two highest and most complex levels of neuroscience research (i.e., behavioral and cognitive) have the most direct relevance to the measurement of intelligence and are the primary focus of this chapter. Intelligent interpretation can and should be influenced by relevant research at lower levels, due to the hierarchical, reciprocal relationship among levels of cognitive neuroscience research; however, a thorough synopsis of research at these additional levels is well beyond the scope of this chapter as well as the expertise of the authors.

GENETIC AND ENVIRONMENTAL INFLUENCES ON INTELLIGENCE

Historically, research related to the genetics or heritability of intelligence has been highly controversial, primarily due to instances of misguided and discriminatory research efforts in the past, combined with unwarranted and unethical claims about resulting implications for group differences. Thankfully, research in the field of behavioral genetics persisted throughout these controversial time periods, yielding important insights into the heritability of intelligence through extensive research

using twin, sibling, adoptive, and other familial studies. Early twin and family studies correctly predicted polygenic influences on intelligence but overestimated the average heritability of intelligence, producing heritability estimates of around 70% (Wadsworth, Corley, & DeFries, 2014). Improvements in psychometric methodology allowed for more accurate measurement, eventually yielding heritability estimates of approximately 50% (A. S. Kaufman, 2009), with effects due to shared family environment accounting for approximately 20% of the variance in intelligence (Plomin & DeFries, 1980). Replications of this general finding ensued, with more recent researchers noting that additional research is unnecessary to establish that the heritability of intelligence in developed countries ranges from 40–60% (E. Hunt & Jaeggi, 2013).

As in most areas of research, early stages are more exploratory in nature, tending toward more limited research designs with methodological issues. Early research in behavioral genetics is no exception, with subsequent research revealing a more complex relationship between genetic and environmental influences on intelligence. Evidence of complex interactions began to emerge, indicating that genetic and environmental influences varied with such factors as age, socioeconomic status (SES), and gender. It soon became clear that establishing the genetic determinants of intelligence would be extremely challenging, due to the complexity of interactions among genetic and environmental factors (Finkel & Reynolds, 2014).

As insights into the human genome were discovered, researchers began to target specific genes related to intelligence. Early efforts using single nucleotide polymorphisms (SNPs) have been a bit disappointing, with each identified gene accounting for only 1% to 2% of the genetic variance in intelligence (Finkel & Reynolds, 2014). Genome-wide association studies (GWAS) offer more promise than targeted gene studies because of their capability to scan millions of genetic markers for associations with intelligence. GWAS is currently the preferred method for identifying specific genes with small effects, such as intelligence. Using this more powerful methodology, Davis and colleagues (2010) evaluated genetic markers at the extreme ranges of ability, finding 28 SNPs associated with general cognitive ability. Additional SNPs have since been identified but still fall short of expectations based on heritability estimates from previous twin and familial research in terms of predicting variance in intelligence (Finkel & Reynolds, 2014).

Results from more recent genetic studies continue to tackle the complex issue of genetic influences on intelligence, providing intriguing results and offering new directions for future research. In general, heritability appears to increase with age, with estimates ranging from 30% to 40% in childhood to 80% in middle adulthood (Chavarría-Siles, Fernández, & Posthuma, 2014). Although genetic influences tend to increase with age, the influence of shared environmental factors decreases. Thus, shared environment appears to have more influence relative to genetic factors in younger children than in older children and adults. This finding underscores the importance of early childhood experiences in cognitive development.

Results for sex differences are somewhat mixed, most likely due to differences in the age of participants or measures used, but generally indicate that females have faster processing speed than males, and males have stronger visual-spatial abilities than females (Wadsworth et al., 2014). Other research suggests that the relative influence of genetic and environmental forces varies with SES: (a) higher genetic and lower environmental influences occur in high-SES individuals, and (b) lower genetic and higher environmental influences occur in low-SES individuals (Chiang et al., 2011; Turkheimer & Horn, 2014). To further complicate the matter, genetic influences also appear to vary with overall cognitive ability level (Chiang et al., 2011). Clearly, there are still many unanswered questions about gene–environment interactions and the factors with which they

vary; yet advances in the field of neuroscience offer new hopes for finding answers.

Regarding this gene–environment discussion, consult Chapter 5 for demographic differences in the WISC–V normative sample, including group differences related to age, parent education (a proxy variable for SES), and sex as well as race/ethnicity. This chapter also summarizes pertinent demographic differences on other measures of intelligence across the life span.

Heritability appears to have a greater influence on overall intelligence than on specific cognitive abilities (Wadsworth et al., 2014) and is also indicated as a predictor of cognitive change or decline in older age (Deary et al., 2012). Genetic influences in other areas of cognitive function yield heritability estimates for academic achievement that are similar to those for general intelligence (~60%), with variability across more specific domains (e.g., reading and math) (Wadsworth et al., 2014). For language acquisition, environmental influences explain more variance than genetic factors in children ages 2 to 4 years, but this pattern reverses between the ages of 7 and 10 (Hayiou-Thomas, Dale, & Plomin, 2012); again, these findings underscore the importance of considering developmental level and age in behavioral genetics research.

In the authors' opinion, investigations related to the genetic determinants associated with specific psychological disorders and brain development, at all levels, are likely to hold the most promise for understanding (and possibly treating) childhood developmental disorders such as specific reading disability and autism spectrum disorders. Continued research on genetic abnormalities associated with intellectual disability (e.g., phenylketonuria [PKU], Down syndrome, fragile-X syndrome) offers promise for targeting genes in future investigations (Carlier & Roubertoux, 2014). Distinct sets of genes appear to be implicated in the development of specific neuron types (e.g., light-sensitive neurons in the eye versus dopamine-producing neurons in the substantia nigra) (Zimmer, 2014). Development of the superior longitudinal fasciculus, a major frontoparietal connection, has unique genetic influences; these research findings suggest that at least some different genes differentially influence the development of brain structure (e.g., lobes) and function (e.g., major connective pathways) (Chavarría-Siles et al., 2014; Horton & Reynolds, 2015). Thus, recent findings from research on gene-brain relations suggest that the multiple, interacting genes direct aspects of developing brain structure and its underlying functional circuitry and are critically important to intelligence, including individual differences in cognitive abilities.

Since the mapping of the human genome was completed in 2003, interest in genetic research has quickly risen to a level that few could have foreseen. The pace of publications is staggering, making it especially challenging to stay abreast of recent findings. Fortunately, the simultaneous increase in cross-disciplinary research and data-sharing efforts is beginning to address this issue. For example, researchers at the Allen Institute for Brain Science in Seattle are actively assembling a map of the molecular machinery of active genes within human neurons and have successfully charted over 20,000 protein-coding genes from approximately 700 brain locations. At each studied site, neurons switch on a specific combination of genes to perform tasks in different brain locations. Based on initial efforts, it is estimated that almost 84% of genes in human DNA become active at some time in the brain, a much higher percentage than that of other studied organs (Zimmer, 2014). This continuously updated "brain atlas" is posted online (at http://human.brain-map.org/) for other researchers studying genetic influences on cognitive disorders or related fields (Zimmer, 2014).

Although the chemical properties of DNA are well understood, its structure and function remain largely a mystery. Approximately half of the human genome is believed to contain the regulatory information necessary for controlling the expression of about 30,000 protein-coding genes as well as non-protein-coding genes that may serve functional purposes (e.g., gene

sequencing). Even less is known about the function of the noncoding or highly repetitive sequences that comprise the other half of the genome (Collins, Green, Guttmacher, & Guyer, 2003). One of the primary goals of genetic research is to discover how variations in DNA sequence relate to individual phenotypic differences, such as common diseases and developmental disorders. And although the etiology of most phenotypes is extraordinarily complex, the pace of advances at all levels of neuroscience research is bringing us closer to that goal.

Prior to concluding this section on genetic and environmental influence on intelligence, it is important to note that the relative lack of detailed information on environmental influences does not in any way reflect a reduced emphasis on these factors in the development of intelligence. On the contrary, environmental influences are much more amenable to effective intervention at the present time, and they are of critical importance during the formative childhood years. The cry for more and better measures of environmental factors has long been made by researchers hoping to better address these research questions (Wadsworth et al., 2014), providing an obvious opportunity for collaboration with experts in test development to achieve this goal. Although the questionnaire was designed for different purposes, the parents or guardians of almost all children participating in the WISC–V standardization completed a home-environment questionnaire, resulting in the development of two new risk questionnaires described in Chapter 6, one to predict academic failure and one to predict delinquency. Additional research regarding environmental risk factors for academic failure and delinquency is also provided in that chapter.

Given the historical misuse and misunderstanding of results from genetic research, it is more important than ever for researchers from all relevant disciplines to avoid the mistakes of the past, in which premature and exaggerated claims led to greater difficulties for upcoming researchers interested in the role of genes and the environment in predicting intelligence. More recent surveys confirm that the public is interested in the possible benefits of genetic research but remains concerned about the possible misuse of such information (Collins et al., 2003). This history makes it even more critical that today's researchers thoroughly consider the social implications of research on the influences and interactions between genes and the environment on intelligence. There is still much to learn about the interactive roles of genes and the environment on intelligence: Intelligent research is necessary to accomplish this lofty goal.

CHILDHOOD BRAIN DEVELOPMENT

A detailed description of brain development is well beyond the scope of this chapter, but a basic understanding of brain development is critical for interpretation from a neuropsychological perspective, especially when working with children. Generally speaking, brain development can be temporally divided into that occurring before birth (prenatal) and that occurring after birth (postnatal). The main stages of prenatal brain development in children closely resemble those of other mammals; however, the postnatal period of human brain development is relatively protracted, leaving more time for the influence of external forces outside the womb (e.g., environmental and cultural influences). Within a week of conception, the rapidly proliferating cell cluster (i.e., blastocyst) differentiates into three layers, with the outermost layer (the ectoderm) subsequently folding over itself to form the neural tube, the progenitor of the brain and spinal cord. The bulges that form at the top end of the neural tube develop into the brain, and the bottom end develops into the spinal cord (M. H. Johnson, 2011).

Development continues through the proliferation and differentiation of neurons and their migration to particular locations through passive or active means. Passive migration occurs when new neurons simply displace older neurons, pushing them away from the point of origin. Passive migration is the primary means of neuronal travel in prenatal development, contributing to the formation of such brain structures as the brain stem, hippocampus, and thalamus. The active migration of neurons that give rise to the cerebral cortex and other similarly layered brain regions follows a different path, literally, using glial fibers as guides to lead new neurons past older neurons toward their ultimate location. By the time an infant draws his or her first breath, the majority of brain cells have migrated to their adult locations and the distinctive folds of major cerebral divisions are present; however, brain development is far from complete (M. H. Johnson, 2011).

The postnatal period of brain development is much more prolonged, with development of the prefrontal cortex (PFC) extending through early adulthood (Dumontheil, 2014). Development within the first few years of life is the most dramatic, with gray matter volume more than doubling in the first year and overall brain volume quadrupling between birth and adulthood (M. H. Johnson, 2011; Walhovd, Tamnes, & Fjell, 2014). These volumetric increases are almost entirely accounted for by the development and bundling of nerve fibers as well as by their myelination to improve efficiency of electrical conduction (M. H. Johnson, 2011). Most notable is the extreme dendritic branching, axonal growth, and synaptogenesis that occurs between birth and approximately 2 years of age, resulting in a number of functional synapses that far surpasses that in the adult brain. Not surprisingly, this sprawling neuronal structure seems especially well suited to receiving the barrage of environmental stimuli during early brain development, especially when followed by the synaptic pruning and myclination of subcortical white matter that ultimately results in more efficient neural circuitry. Importantly, these processes occur at different rates in different parts of the brain, with those areas related to sensory functions developing first, followed by development of the temporal and parietal cortices, and culminating in development of the PFC.

This synopsis of brain development dramatically oversimplifies the process (see M. H. Johnson, 2011, for additional details), but it does highlight some important implications for neuropsychological consideration:

- Brain development occurs at an extremely rapid pace prenatally through the first few years of life, with slower yet substantial changes continuing through early adulthood. Some change in cognitive function should be expected with brain maturation.
- Development of the brain and associated cognitive functions involves an ongoing interplay between genetic and environmental (both prenatal and postnatal) influences.
- The nature of childhood brain development involves increased plasticity relative to adults. Identification and intervention may be especially beneficial during the preschool early childhood years.

As noted previously, the vast majority of volumetric increase in the postnatal brain is due to white matter development associated with the growth of the neural network circuitry, also referred to as the connectome. Recent research suggests that the connectome plays a key functional role in cognition and that abnormalities or disturbances in this network may be related to specific neurodevelopmental disorders.

The accumulated research findings on neurodevelopment have been internalized by Elaine Fletcher-Janzen and Elizabeth Power in their case report of 8-year-old Josh, who was referred for difficulties in reading and expressive language. Josh's neurodevelopmental process-oriented report appears at the end of this chapter, along with two additional case reports that involve referral issues directly relevant to summaries of recent cognitive neuroscience research: Michelle Lurie and Elizabeth Lichtenberger's report of Tawna, age 13, referred for problems with sustained attention and processing speed; and Kristina Breaux's report of Tom, age 8, a boy with gifted intelligence who has ADHD and experiences academic difficulties.

Additional details regarding the neurodevelopmental process are provided in the next sections.

Development of the Neural Network

Comparisons of the human brain to that of lower mammals suggest that maximizing efficiency is a major driving force in brain development. For example, cortical folding decreases distances between critical areas of the brain and is much more pronounced in primates and humans than in lower mammals (Hofman, 2015). The mature human brain contains approximately 85 billion neurons, with each neuron connected to approximately 10,000 other neurons (Piore, 2014). At first glance, the "topology of the brain's long-range communication network looks like a 3-D chessboard with a number of highly connected neocortical and subcortical hub regions" (Hofman, 2015, p. 70). However, when improved technology recently allowed scientists to zoom in on the neural circuitry, the tangled mass revealed a highly organized structure, with circuits intersecting at right angles to form a gridlike pattern (Hofman, 2015; Zimmer, 2014). Using a minuscule portion of mouse tissue, these researchers noted that each neuron made nearly all of its connections with one other neuron, seeming to avoid connections to the tightly packed neurons around it. Although it is not known yet if this is a rule for all brain areas, it is consistent with other research emphasizing the importance of efficient neural networks to intelligence (Zimmer, 2014).

Jung and Haier (2007) reviewed 37 studies that looked at neural networks, finding that variations in network distribution were predictive of individual differences in intelligence and reasoning. This meta-analysis culminated in Parieto-Frontal Integration Theory (P-FIT; Jung & Haier, 2007; Chavarría-Siles et al., 2014).

The P-FIT model of intelligence identifies the widely distributed components of this critical neural network as including the dorsolateral PFC, the inferior and superior parietal lobule, the anterior cingulate gyrus, and regions within the temporal and occipital lobes. In particular, the structural integrity of the arcuate fasciculus was found to be related to general intelligence. Attentional control, working memory, and processing speed serve as the required feed-forward and feedback resources for proper P-FIT function (Duggan & Garcia-Barrera, 2015). The P-FIT model was subsequently tested and supported using an adult sample (Colom et al., 2009), providing additional evidence of the now-established fact that performance on general intelligence measures involves the combined and coordinated activation of multiple cortical areas. Not surprisingly, the P-FIT network has also been found to be important to higher-order cognitive abilities, such as fluid reasoning, working memory, and executive function (Duggan & Garcia-Barrera, 2015).

In general, current research indicates the presence of at least three core neural networks related to higher levels of cognitive functioning in the mature brain, including:

1. a central-executive frontoparietal network that includes the dorsolateral PFC and posterior parietal cortex; this network is reportedly related to working memory and executive function;
2. a default-mode network that includes the ventromedial PFC and posterior cingulate cortex; this network is reportedly related to metacognition and social cognition; and
3. a salience network that includes nodes in the right frontoinsular cortex and anterior cingulate gyrus, reportedly a network that is related to attention, perception, and emotional processes (Chavarría-Siles et al., 2014).

Additional research with children and adolescents is necessary to evaluate the interactive relationship between the ongoing development of neural circuitry (i.e., the connectome) and associated cognitive abilities. Because these efforts may hold the key to understanding and treating a variety of developmental disorders, results from recent longitudinal studies that addressed this complex issue are described in the subsequent section describing neuroanatomical correlates of cognitive abilities.

NEURAL PLASTICITY

Neural plasticity can be defined as any structural brain change due to experience, behavior, emotion, cognition, or physical injury (Pascual-Leone et al., 2011). According to Hunt and Jaeggi (2013), neural plasticity is an intrinsic property of the brain "to escape the restrictions of the genome, and adapt to environmental pressures, physiologic changes, and experiences" (p. 44). For this reason, plasticity could be viewed as the most important characteristic of the brain, allowing for memory and learning as well as recovery from damage or injury. In fact, development of the neural network is entirely dependent on neural plasticity, further emphasizing the importance of this characteristic during childhood brain development.

Long-term potentiation (LTP) is a form of neural plasticity important to memory and learning that results in structural brain changes due to repetitive high levels of activation in the synaptic cleft. Other forms of plasticity involve the creation of new neurons, development of connections between neurons, and the selective elimination of synapses (Gale, O'Callaghan, Godfrey, Law, & Martyn, 2004). As previously discussed, early childhood brain development is marked by a dramatic increase in synaptic growth, followed by a period of selective pruning to increase efficiency of the neural circuit. This critical time period in development provides an excellent example of plasticity due to normal developmental processes.

As with other aspects of the nervous system, neural plasticity is influenced by genetic factors, which lead to individual differences in the brain's ability to adapt to environmental stimuli, learn from experience, and adapt to injury or abnormality (Garlick, 2002). In years past, neural plasticity was believed to be almost exclusive to infancy and childhood, but years of research have revealed a surprising amount of plasticity in adult neurons (Johnson, 2011; Jolles & Crone, 2012). Like intelligence, plasticity generally follows a ∩-shaped trajectory, with increasing plasticity throughout the developmental childhood period and decreasing plasticity in the declining years of older adulthood. Despite the emphasis on positive aspects of plasticity in this chapter, the downward trajectory in older adulthood serves as a reminder that plasticity is not always a good thing. Other examples may include the persistence of posttraumatic stress disorder symptoms despite treatment or the phantom pains that some amputees feel when the brain rewires to adjacent locations in the absence of activation (Blackwell, Rodriguez, & Guerra-Carrillo, 2015).

Plasticity and Cognitive Training

Any discussion of neural plasticity would be incomplete without addressing the current controversies around brain training. These controversies culminated on October 15, 2014, when *A Consensus on the Brain Training Industry from the Scientific Community* was jointly released by the Stanford Center on Longevity and the Max Planck Institute for Human Development in Berlin, bearing the signatures of almost 70 experts in neuroscience, psychology, and gerontology (See statement at: http://longevity3 .stanford.edu/blog/2014/10/15/the-consensus-on-the-brain-training-industry-from-the-scientific-community/). The statement was released in response to growing concerns with exaggerated and misleading claims of effectiveness, especially those reported by trusted news sources and appearing with increasing frequency in public media (e.g., a prime-time

commercial spot during the 2013 Super Bowl). Although the statement is directed primarily at adult brain-training programs (with specific admonition to those claiming to prevent or cure dementia), the concerns it raises also apply to brain training with children. In addition to unfounded claims of effectiveness, the statement notes aggressive advertising practices; preferential reporting of positive results; possible conflicts of interest for investigators; and a lack of sound methodology in published studies as points of concern. The authors of the joint release emphasized that there is inadequate evidence to support that brain training significantly improves cognitive performance beyond the trained skill, based on the contradictory and questionable evidence available at the time of the statement's release.

Without doubt, the inconsistent results of outcome studies related to brain-training programs are somewhat troubling, but the extent of the issue is difficult to determine due to numerous possible confounds and limitations in much of the brain-training research (Jolles & Crone, 2012). The most obvious limitation is the relative lack of studies including children as compared to adults. In fact, many studies have used samples of healthy young adults, who may represent the worst sample to use in intervention studies due to the likelihood they are operating at near-peak performance levels in most areas, cognitively speaking. If brain training capitalizes on neural plasticity, it should be most effective in young children, who are at their peak in terms of neural network development (Dehn, 2014; E. Hunt & Jaeggi, 2013). Other limitations in previous brain-training research include the lack of adequate control groups, the use of a limited number of cognitive measures, lack of long-term follow-up, neuroimaging limitations, as well as a lack of independent replication (Jolles & Crone, 2012; Thompson et al., 2013). Clearly, additional research on the effectiveness of brain training is necessary in both adult and child populations.

Importantly, more promising results generally have been noted for childhood training interventions that are specifically targeted to the identified cognitive processes underlying a known disability, such as reading (Shaywitz & Shaywitz, 2013) or math (Kucian et al., 2011); or for those interventions targeting core neural networks, such as the executive attention network (Diamond, Barnett, Thomas, & Munro, 2007; Rothbart & Posner, 2015). These findings suggest that the question may not be whether cognitive training works but what types of training appear to work for which populations. Additionally, these results may shed light on the contradictory results of previous investigations on working memory training effectiveness, in which healthy young adults were used as subjects and the training was not targeted at improving an established deficit in a basic cognitive process.

The fact that cognitive abilities develop over time and change throughout the course of a life clearly demonstrates that neural plasticity is a lifelong process (Otero, 2015). Childhood offers the unique advantage of intervening during brain development, when the neural circuitry is primed for maximum intervention effectiveness. The choice of intervention should be based on the needs of the individual child, and intelligent testing requires knowing the tools being used. Prior to using or recommending cognitive training or any other intervention, intelligent testers will ask themselves such relevant questions as: Is there adequate evidence of reliability and validity to support claims of effectiveness? Have I considered other interventions with proven effectiveness? Do the results generalize to broader contexts? For whom does the intervention work best? How long do the results last? And most important, is this the most appropriate intervention for *this* child?

The more consistent finding of positive results in children does not negate the need for additional empirical evidence of validity or for research that evaluates child and program characteristics associated with improved results. Future research on the use of combined training approaches has been suggested by several experts. Training on multiple core cognitive processes (e.g., attention, working memory, inhibition) has been proposed on the basis that these processes serve as the building blocks for more complex processes, such as fluid reasoning (E. Hunt & Jaeggi, 2013; Jolles & Crone, 2012). This research would also allow for evaluation of whether children and adults respond differently to such combined trainings. Another suggestion combines process-focused training with strategic training, in which children are also provided explicit instructions on relevant strategies, such as chunking information on working memory tasks (Jolles & Crone, 2012). Results from a study on the combined effects of medication and working memory training suggest that these interventions may be more effective when used together than when used independently (Holmes et al., 2010). Any one of these methods could be combined with interventions that show more general benefits for cognition, such as exercise (Jolles & Crone, 2012) or meditation (Rothbart & Posner, 2015). When combined with the recent advances in neuroimaging, the possibilities for cognitive training leave the authors optimistic about future progress in this area.

BRAIN IMAGING

Prior to describing the neuroanatomical correlates of cognitive ability, intelligent testers should have a basic understanding of brain imaging techniques that are utilized to investigate the neural underpinnings of cognitive function. This section briefly describes common imaging techniques, including their applications and some of the pros and cons of each method. The section concludes with a description of recent advances that offer intriguing possibilities for future research of normal and abnormal brain function associated with neurodevelopmental, psychiatric, and other brain-related disorders.

Electroencephalography (EEG) has been used for many years to record electrical activity for brain waves and states of awareness using electrodes placed on the scalp. Although the advent of high-resolution imaging techniques has largely displaced EEG as a diagnostic tool, it is still commonly used to identify epilepsy, depth of coma, and sleep disorders. EEG has poor spatial resolution but excellent temporal resolution (milliseconds), so it continues to be used in conjunction with other imaging methods with superior spatial resolution (e.g., magnetic resonance imaging [MRI]). The alpha and theta wavelengths measured by EEG have been associated with task difficulty and cognitive demand (Howard-Jones, Ott, van Leeuwen, & De Smedt, 2014). Relative to methods with better spatial resolution, EEG is inexpensive and noninvasive, and recent advances in portability make it even more appropriate for use with children (Howard-Jones et al., 2014; Tzeng et al., 2013).

MRI uses magnetic fields and radio waves to produce detailed images of many brain slices, allowing for localization of specific brain structures (within a few millimeters) as well as measures of brain-matter density. As noted above, MRI has poor temporal resolution relative to EEG, and it is more expensive. Especially problematic for children is the need to stay completely motionless during the scanning procedure. Despite its outstanding production of detailed structural brain images, MRI does not provide valuable information about brain function during active information processing. The advent of positron emission tomography (PET) addressed this shortcoming by using radioactive tracers to provide useful information about the working brain, enabling researchers to identify brain regions associated with simple tasks. Unfortunately, its spatial resolution falls short of MRI, and the need to inject short-lived radioactive isotopes makes PET a much less attractive option for children.

Functional MRI (fMRI) combines positive attributes of MRI and PET, producing detailed images of the brain during task performance. The development of fMRI led to rapid advancements in our understanding of cognitive function, aided by ongoing improvements in resolution and methods for statistical analysis (Shaywitz & Shaywitz, 2013). It has become commonplace to utilize fMRI in studies of cognitive ability, leading to further advances in mapping the brain's function. Use of fMRI does not require the injection of radioactive tracers (making it safe for repeated use), instead relying on blood-oxygen-level-dependent (BOLD) signals to measure activity levels. Although considered less invasive than other methods, the scanning environment is noisy and restricts the child's movement, thus limiting the types of tasks administered.

An important limitation of all the aforementioned methods is the relative lack of information obtained about the brain's underlying neural network, without which the various brain regions could not process information. More recent studies have paired fMRI with magnetoencephalography (MEG) or diffusion tensor imaging (DTI) to allow for closer examination of the neural networks that comprise the connectome. MEG measures the brain's magnetic fields through the use of a helmet and tasks are performed in a shielded room. Child-size helmets are available; however, current helmet design limits visibility of parts of the frontal cortex, which is critical for cognitive function. MEG research has already produced charts of functional connections for such cognitive functions as attention, memory, and language processing (Tzeng et al., 2013). DTI is a variation of MRI that uses radio frequency and magnetic fields to track the movement of water molecules through the brain, producing images of the critically important networks of nerve fibers that interconnect brain regions. DTI provides important information about the integrity of neural networks without the use of a helmet.

The pairing of fMRI and DTI is the current method of choice for evaluating ongoing cognitive function, allowing for detailed images of both structural and functional aspects of the working brain during task performance—and there is already promise that diffusion-weighted imaging, will be superior to previous methods for viewing white matter, including MEG and DTI (Chavarría-Siles et al., 2014).

Without doubt, the advances in neuroimaging techniques, neuroengineering, and methodology for statistical analysis over the last 30 years have spawned a dramatic increase in our knowledge of the brain and its function. Yet there are some general limitations and considerations that deserve special note. For now, the data obtained from functional imaging are reliable only at the group level, and evaluation of results may be complicated by the subtraction-based methodology to isolate cognitive functions. A simple brain image yields 40,000 to 50,000 data points. As in other areas of research with large variable numbers, there is error associated with multiple comparisons as well as error associated with multiple testings. Furthermore, interpretation of results is not straightforward and can be counterintuitive, with increased activation related to lower ability and decreased activation related to higher ability: These counterintuitive results may be due to lower processing demands after information is consolidated (Shaywitz & Shaywitz, 2013).

The "perfect data storm" created by the enormous amount of data obtained from collaborative neuroimaging research efforts creates another challenge for the future (Zimmer, 2014). Although the degree of resolution provided by fMRI is described as excellent, it is grossly inadequate to evaluate active cognitive function at the molecular and cellular levels. Although we are now capable of producing three-dimensional (3-D) images of a single neuron, doing so for a piece of mouse brain no bigger than a grain of salt produces about as much data as 25,000 high-definition movies (Zimmer, 2014). As noted in a recent position paper regarding the Brain Research through Advancing Innovative Neurotechnologies (BRAIN) initiative, the primary obstacle at this time is "data analysis rather than data acquisition" (Jorgenson et al., 2015, p. 4).

Despite all of these issues, the authors believe our understanding of cognitive function

and dysfunction will soon make enormous strides with the recent advances in imaging of the neural network. The integrity of this network (or lack thereof) has already been implicated as a potential source of cognitive dysfunction in numerous conditions (Chavarría-Siles et al., 2014), and we believe it is likely to be indicated as a contributing causal factor in many psychological and cognitive disorders, especially those that are developmental in nature. Although not yet applicable for use in a living brain, the use of trans-synaptic tracers is emerging as a method to study neural connections at the cellular level. Amazing methods of rendering the brain transparent while leaving the connectome intact (e.g., CLARITY) should provide an additional boost to our understanding of neural circuitry (Zimmer, 2014). These are exciting times in the field of neuroimaging: The rapid rate of advances in this field will continue to drive progress in our common neuroscientific interest in the brain and how it functions.

NEUROANATOMICAL CORRELATES OF COGNITIVE ABILITIES

The preceding sections provide necessary foundational information for a deeper understanding of the neuroanatomical correlates of cognitive abilities and how these relate to WISC–V interpretation from a neuropsychologically oriented perspective. In particular, the complexity of the relationships between the developing brain and emerging cognitive abilities make the acquisition of a sound, neuropsychological knowledge base an especially daunting challenge for clinicians working with children. Regardless, we have acquired a wealth of information regarding the brain regions associated with various cognitive abilities, and the recent emphasis on the underlying neural circuitry that allows these brain regions to work in coordination is likely to reveal much more in the near future. This section briefly summarizes the neuroanatomical correlates of cognitive abilities and functions directly measured by the WISC–V (e.g., visual-spatial ability, fluid reasoning, working memory) as well as contributory cognitive functions (i.e., attention and executive functions) that typically are included as part of a neuropsychological evaluation. The section concludes with descriptions of a recent research related to the emergence of cognitive abilities, offering promise for understanding the complexities of this phenomenon from a developmental perspective.

Neuroanatomical Correlates of General Cognitive Ability

Performance on measures of general intelligence involves the coordinated efforts of multiple brain regions, including regions in the prefrontal, parietal, temporal, and occipital lobes. An organized network of neural connections allows these regions to communicate during cognitive task performance (Jung & Haier, 2007). Not surprisingly, neuroimaging research generally indicates positive correlations between development of these brain areas and general cognitive ability (e.g., FSIQ), with development of the frontal lobes suggested as the most critical brain area related to general cognitive ability (Shaw et al., 2006; Wechsler, 2014). The connectivity between these structural regions is critical to their coordinated functioning during cognitive processing, including important connections between the frontal and parietal lobes (Colom et al., 2009) and between cortical and subcortical structures in the basal ganglia (Koziol & Budding, 2011). Thus, general cognitive ability as measured by the FSIQ can be thought of as an indicator of how well these brain regions and their connective networks function as a coordinated unit during higher-order cognitive processing.

Neuroanatomical Correlates of Specific Cognitive Abilities

The inclusion of a section on neuroanatomical correlates of specific cognitive abilities may lead some readers to the false conclusion that these abilities are somehow localized in specific brain regions; however, that is not the case. Results from functional neuroimaging studies have confirmed the involvement of multiple brain regions for all broad cognitive abilities as well as for some narrow abilities as defined by Cattell-Horn-Carroll (CHC) theory (e.g., working memory).

Consistent with Wechsler's original distinction between the verbal and performance scales, there does appear to be some lateralization of cognitive function, with areas of the left hemisphere more strongly associated with processing auditory-verbal-crystallized measures (e.g., the Verbal Comprehension Index), and areas of the right hemisphere more strongly associated with processing of visual-spatial measures (e.g., the Visual Spatial Index) (Dehn, 2014; Gläscher et al., 2009). Contemporary views are generally consistent but place less emphasis on the division, noting that both hemispheres are involved in processing verbal and visual information, with the left hemisphere being more involved with processing of detailed and crystallized information and the right hemisphere being more involved with processing of holistic and novel information (Dehn, 2014; Hale & Fiorello, 2004).

The Verbal Comprehension Index represents "an interaction of basic language skills and complex problem solving and reasoning" (Wechsler, 2014, p. 25). The development of language skills varies with the development of associated brain areas, especially within the frontal and temporal regions (Dehaene-Lambertz, Hertz-Pannier, Dubois, & Dehaene, 2008). For most children, basic language skills are adequately developed by the time they reach school, and the acquisition of reading skills links language to the brain's visual system, resulting in changes to brain regions associated with oral language (Monzalvo & Dehaene-Lambertz, 2013). Listening comprehension typically is developed by age 4, and ongoing development of the frontal lobes allows for higher-order processing of verbal information, such as that involved in reasoning (Colom et al., 2013). Results from the Gläscher et al. (2009) lesion-mapping study are consistent with the role of the frontal lobes in higher-order verbal abilities, finding a strong relation between damage to the left inferior frontal cortex and deficits in verbal comprehension ability.

Visual-spatial abilities are measured by the Visual Spatial Index and involve the coordinated action of several brain regions, with areas in the right hemisphere playing an important role: These include right-sided areas of the basal ganglia, thalamus, and the inferior and superior parietal cortex, among others (Barbey, Colom, Solomon, Krueger, Forbes, & Grafman, 2012; Burgaleta et al., 2012). Similar to measures in other cognitive domains (e.g., fluid reasoning and working memory), increasing cognitive complexity of visual-spatial tasks is associated with increased involvement of the frontal lobes.

The Fluid Reasoning Index provides a measure of fluid reasoning. With its high correlation to general intelligence, it is not surprising that neuroimaging studies of fluid reasoning indicate a similar activation pattern involving several brain regions. In general, fluid reasoning tasks activate the frontal lobes and their associated networks to areas of the prefrontal, temporal, parietal, and occipital cortices. Importantly, variations in regional activation appear to be more related to the type of reasoning required (e.g., inductive versus deductive) and the meaningfulness of stimuli (e.g., familiar versus unfamiliar objects) than the modality (e.g., verbal/auditory versus visual) (Goel, 2007; Wechsler, 2014).

Measures of working memory, such as those comprising the Working Memory Index, involve the maintenance and manipulation of information during active processing and are consistently shown to activate brain regions in the PFC (particularly the dorsolateral PFC) as well as areas of the premotor, parietal, and cingulate cortex (Dumontheil & Klingberg, 2012; Fried, Rushmore, Moss, Valero-Cabré, & Pascual-Leone, 2014). Like general intelligence and fluid reasoning, the neural connections

between the frontal and parietal lobes are critical for working memory performance and likely are reflected in the high intercorrelations among these measures. Unlike fluid reasoning, stimulus modality (i.e., verbal versus visual-spatial) appears to activate somewhat different brain areas, with verbal tasks showing increased activation in the left dorsolateral PFC and visual-spatial tasks showing increased activation in the right dorsolateral PFC (Nee et al., 2013; Owen et al., 2005). Results from a recent study using repetitive transcranial magnetic stimulation to disrupt function of the right dorsolateral PFC provide strong support for this dissociation, finding transient impairment in visual-spatial working memory performance and transient improvement in verbal working memory performance (Fried et al., 2014).

The Processing Speed Index provides a measure of processing speed. The neuroanatomical correlates of processing speed are dispersed throughout the entire brain and are strongly related to measures of white matter volume (Betjemann et al., 2010) and white matter integrity in the corpus callosum and frontal, parietal, and temporal lobes (Aukema et al., 2009; Turken, Whitfield-Gabrieli, Bammer, Baldo, Dronkers, & Gabrieli, 2008). Processing speed is viewed by some to be a foundational process related to the development of other cognitive abilities (Duggan & Garcia-Barrera, 2015). Adults with high cognitive ability have faster reaction times and require fewer resources for cognitive processing (Deary, Penke, & Johnson, 2010): Additional research is needed to how the rapid development of white matter relates to processing speed and the emergence of cognitive abilities during childhood.

Although not directly measured by the WISC–V, attention and its underlying neural systems are required for effective cognitive processing, and descriptions of attentional abilities are standard sections in most neuropsychological reports. In light of brain-imaging advances over the last 20 years, Rothbart and Posner's (2015) description of the human attention system poses three anatomically and neurochemically separable networks for alerting, orienting, and executive attention. The alerting network includes the locus coeruleus and areas of the right frontal and right parietal cortices. The primary neurochemical modulator for this system is norepinephrine, and the system supports maintenance of arousal and sustained vigilance. The orienting network is responsible for aligning attention to incoming stimuli, regardless of modality. It involves the frontal eye fields and superior parietal lobe for intentional orienting of attention and the temporal parietal junction and superior colliculus for the automatic orienting of attention after a cue. The primary neurochemical modulator for this system is acetylcholine. The executive system is responsible for monitoring thoughts and for regulating conflict among thoughts, feelings, and behaviors. This system's primary neurochemical modulators include dopamine and serotonin, and the related brain regions include the anterior cingulate cortex (ACC), anterior insula cortex, frontal cortex, and striatum (Petersen & Posner, 2012; Rothbart & Posner, 2015). Stated more generally:

- subcortical regions are more associated with the arousal aspects of *sustained attention*, whereas
- the PFC and ACC are more associated with *selective and focal attention*, including inhibition of irrelevant stimuli and the allocation of attentional resources (Dehn, 2014).

Executive function has been referred to as "top of the list of the most elusive constructs in neuropsychology" (Duggan & Garcia-Barrera, 2015, p. 438). Most contemporary definitions of executive function include a variety of processes, including inhibition, shifting, planning, and decision making. All of these executive functions activate the frontal lobe, with most occurring in the lateral PFC and some (e.g., motivation and decision making) involving the ACC (Dehn, 2014). Neuroanatomical research suggests that executive functions and general intelligence both

involve prefrontal and parietal connections, but executive functions may activate unique brain areas, including ventral and anterior frontal cortex areas (Duggan & Garcia-Barrera, 2015). These findings suggest that general intelligence may be more related *to complexity*, whereas executive functions may be more related to *novelty*.

As noted throughout this chapter, our understanding of brain structure and function has grown exponentially over the last few decades on the heels of advances in functional neuroimaging. Our knowledge of the functional connections that link the areas of the brain is sparse relative to that of brain structures, but ongoing and future research efforts will undoubtedly shed new light on the neuroanatomical correlates of cognitive abilities.

IT IS COMPLICATED: THE EMERGENCE OF COGNITIVE ABILITIES

Astute readers will have noted that the preceding section on neuroanatomical correlates of cognitive function was based on research from mature brains, which fail to consider the additional complexities of neural development on emerging cognitive abilities in childhood. This complexity was anticipated by many experts in childhood development and related fields and was eloquently expressed by Chavarría-Siles et al. (2014):

> Results from cumulative research indicate a strong relationship between genes, brain structure, and behavior, suggesting that highly heritable aspects of intelligence may be fundamental to individual differences in cognitive abilities; however, links between specific brain regions and cognitive ability are likely to vary according to developmental stage (e.g., early and late childhood, adolescence, young adulthood, and older adulthood). (p. 245)

Fortunately, results from recent cross-sectional and longitudinal research on the development of cognitive abilities are beginning to reveal some of the complex interrelationships between emerging cognitive abilities (e.g., attention, working memory, fluid reasoning) and offer possible explanations for some of the contradictory results of previous research with adult populations. Building on results from cross-sectional studies, Demetriou and colleagues (2014) evaluated the relations among processing speed, attention, working memory, and fluid reasoning using structural equation modeling with results from 14 studies. Based on this meta-analysis, the authors propose that development of fluid reasoning arises in four developmental cycles with two phases each, early and late. Within each cycle, the early phase is marked by the acquisition of new mental representations, and the later phase aligns or relates these representations to other representations. Insight into these newly aligned representations occurs at the transition between cycles, activating transition to the next cycle (Žebec, Demetriou, & Kotrla-Topić, 2015).

The first cycle of fluid reasoning development occurs between birth and 2 years, a time in which episodic representations dominate. Ages 2 to 6 mark the second cycle of fluid reasoning development, in which episodic representations are elevated into symbolic, mental representations. Rule-based representations emerge between the ages of 6 and 10, followed by principle-based concepts between the ages of 11 and 18. Transitional periods between each cycle of fluid reasoning development occur at ages 4, 8, and 14, respectively (Demetriou et al., 2014; Žebec et al., 2015). It is notable that the age ranges identified by this study are remarkably consistent with those noted by other developmental researchers interested in emerging cognitive abilities (e.g., Pascual-Leone, 1970; Piaget, 1970).

The most notable finding from this line of research indicates that processing speed is more predictive of fluid reasoning in the early phase of each cycle, whereas working memory is more predictive of fluid reasoning in the late phase of each cycle (Demetriou et al., 2014). A follow-up study confirms this cyclical pattern of fluid reasoning development and also suggests that awareness of mental processes (i.e., cognizance) mediates relations between basic cognitive processes (i.e., processing speed, attentional control, working memory) and fluid reasoning during childhood development (Spanoudis, Demetriou, Zazi, Giorgala, & Zenonos, 2015). For example, toddlers may understand that perception provides a source of knowledge, but the awareness of their own or others' mental representations does not occur until 4 to 5 years, aligning with the transition period between the first and second cycles of fluid reasoning development. Replication and brain-imaging studies will be necessary to determine if these findings are related to structural or functional aspects of brain development and if they occur at older ages. The importance of cognizance during the transition to higher levels of reasoning supports the inclusion of such measures (e.g., theory of mind, self-awareness, metacognition) as part of a comprehensive childhood neuropsychological evaluation.

CONCLUSION

The privilege of employing clinical judgment carries with it the obligation of acquiring and maintaining expertise. (Dehn, 2014, p. 235)

The rapid growth and pace of advancements in this field posed a substantial challenge for the authors, portending similar challenges for the intelligent clinician. Research emanating from this multidisciplinary field has exploded over the last 10 to 30 years, making it highly likely that the authors inadvertently missed something of relevance. Furthermore, the nitrous-fueled pace of published investigations may support, clarify, or contradict our findings by the time this text appears in print.

Regardless, intelligent testing from *any* perspective is enhanced by consideration of recent cognitive neuroscience research. Periodic reviews of the literature are necessary, aided substantially by the use of cross-disciplinary research databases and the availability of online articles prior to their appearance in print. Note that an unfiltered search of the term *cognitive neuroscience* will yield an overwhelming number of articles. For the most relevant literature to interpretation of a *child's* test results, it is helpful to narrow the search to the subspecialty of *developmental* cognitive neuroscience and combine this search term with the specific topic of interest, such as intelligence, cognitive ability, information processing, memory, learning, reasoning, metacognition, neural plasticity, brain training, brain imaging, brain development, molecular genetics, or environmental risk. The website for the Cognitive Neuroscience Society (www.cogneurosociety.org), founded in 1994, highlights recent publications in the field and holds an annual, 3-day conference for researchers investigating the biological foundations of mental processes from multiple perspectives.

Spurred by advances in neuroimaging technology and the successful completion of the genome project, The United States launched the BRAIN Initiative with the goal of developing new technology to revolutionize our understanding of the brain (Jorgenson et al., 2015; Zimmer, 2014). This initiative has already crossed international boundaries, with similar efforts evolving in Europe under the EU Human Brain Project (Piore, 2014). Speculation about the future role of cognitive neuroscience is promising, with eagerly anticipated advances in molecular genetics and longitudinal studies involving children. Neural implants have been successfully placed in mouse brains, with future hopes for use in restoring memory or physical function in some forms of paralysis (Piore, 2014; Zimmer, 2014). Other researchers are planning to use nanoparticles to serve as a mind–machine interface for areas in which an implant would be difficult or impossible (Piore, 2014). Despite these exciting hopes for future advances in cognitive neuroscience, it is wise to remember that overoptimism regarding early genetic and brain-training research efforts did not pan out. As noted by intelligent researchers,

"neuroscience is not a prescriptive panacea" (Howard-Jones et al., 2015, p. 146).

INTRODUCTION TO CASE REPORTS

The case reports selected for inclusion in this chapter were chosen based on their relevance to constructs important to cognitive neuroscience, as reviewed and summarized in the previous sections.

Elaine Fletcher-Janzen and Elizabeth Power wrote the first illustrative report in this chapter (on Josh, age 8). In each section of the report, the authors refer to developmental expectations for children of Josh's age prior to describing his performance, evidencing a thorough understanding of emerging cognitive behaviors during childhood brain development. Elaine made the following cogent remarks about the importance of considering neurodevelopment in selecting appropriate measures of cognitive ability (E. Fletcher-Jansen, personal communication, December 9, 2014).

> The organization of the assessment is based on principles of neurodevelopment—in that we closely and carefully follow those processes that can be localized in the brain from the basic input/output to the more complex associative cortices. Also, that the constructs inherent in each subtest/measure are tapping into different areas of the brain at different ages (a good example is why the Planning/*Gf* Scale on the KABC–II really only plays out factorially at ages 7 and above—and that executive functioning is more visually dependent up to that age). I thought at one time that only neuropsychologists could understand this, but now that I have talked to hundreds of school psychology students and school psychologists around the country, I see that the practicality of neurodevelopment (and the model) is easily understood by those who know children well. A neuropsychologist will use the model in a much more complex way, but the basic principles of neurodevelopment are there and functional even at the student level.

Michelle Lurie and Elizabeth Lichtenberger coauthored the second case report on Tawna, age 13. Based on a complex history of emotional and increasing attentional difficulties, the authors zeroed in on these issues. In particular, this comprehensive neuropsychological evaluation includes a thorough evaluation of selective, sustained, and executive attention as well as related executive functions (inhibition and switching). Recommendations included working memory training combined with strategy training, a combination proposed by researchers for improved effectiveness.

The final report selected for this chapter was written by Kristina Breaux, an expert in reading disabilities, on Tom, age 8. Based on reports of his difficulties with sustained attention and his love of video games, Tom was administered the WISC–V using Pearson's Q-interactive platform and paired tablets. Background information revealed a history of attentional problems and persistent reading difficulties despite previous interventions. Tom's parents report strong maternal and paternal familial histories of language and reading difficulties, despite their success at obtaining high levels of education and occupation, suggesting a possible genetic predisposition for Tom to have similar difficulties. Of particular relevance was the inclusion of useful information regarding Tom's awareness, or cognizance, of his cognitive difficulties, noted as an important aspect of developing executive functions in the previously described research.

CASE 4—JOSH, AGE 8: A NEURODEVELOPMENTAL PROCESSING "NO NUMBERS" APPROACH TO CASE REPORT WRITING

Elaine Fletcher-Janzen and Elizabeth Power

Psychoeducational Evaluation

~CONFIDENTIAL~

Student: Josh Brown

Examiner: Dr. Fletcher-Janzen and Ms. Power

Date of birth: 05/29/2006

Testing Date(s): 12/18/14, 01/20, 01/23/15

Age: 8 years, 7 months

Date of Report: 02/01/2015

Grade: 3

Teacher: Mrs. Grey

Program: ED-Self-Contained

Resident School District: South Chicago

Reason for Referral

Josh is an 8-year-old Caucasian male in third grade at Little Chicago Elementary School in South Chicago, Illinois. He has received special education services under the eligibility criteria of emotional disability, with secondary eligibility for speech/language impairment since kindergarten. Josh's Individualized Education Program (IEP) team have referred him for a comprehensive evaluation to determine if he has a learning disability and also to further clarify the nature of his emotional difficulties so that programming may be more effective.

Background Information

Background information was obtained through a structured developmental questionnaire, parent interview, and record review.

Family History

Josh lives with his mother, mother's fiancé, grandparents, half brother (14), and half sisters (4 and 5) in Chicago, IL. Ms. Brown and her fiancé, Mr. Green, are biological parents to Josh's younger half sisters. Josh's mother and biological father separated when he was 2 1/2 years old. Josh's mother completed 2 years of college, attended dental school, and currently works as a homemaker. Mr. Brown, Josh's biological father, completed some college, heating and air conditioning school, and works locally. Ms. Brown has primary custody of Josh, and he visits his father every other weekend, on holidays, and for 2 weeks during the summer. Ms. Brown's fiancé has lived in the home for 5 years. The family has lived in their current home for 8 years, and family life is reported to be stable. The family speaks English only.

Medical/Developmental History

Ms. Brown received prenatal care and had abnormal weight gain during pregnancy. She took 100 mg of Zoloft daily for anxiety. Josh was born at term after 5 hours of labor, and anesthesia was used. He weighed 7 lbs. 7 oz. at birth and was jaundiced and placed under bilirubin lights for a few hours postbirth. Josh and his mother left the hospital after 2 days.

Ms. Brown reports that all developmental milestones were reached at appropriate ages, with the exception of toilet training, which occurred later at age 4. Bed-wetting occurred after toilet training, but only when Josh was ill. Ms. Brown reported that Josh had unclear speech and had some difficulty learning to ride a bicycle. Currently Josh experiences chronic coughs, constipation, stomach pain (related to constipation), and ear infections. Josh bruises easily and bites his nails at home and at school.

Josh passed his vision screening in 2014 but failed his hearing screenings twice in the fall of 2014. He passed a follow-up audiogram in January of 2015.

Josh is not currently on any medications.

Family history is positive for anxiety (mother, maternal grandmother), substance abuse (father), learning disability (father, maternal grandfather), speech delay (father, uncle), autism (sister), Type 2 diabetes, stroke (maternal and paternal grandfathers), and high blood pressure (sister, uncle, maternal grandparents). Ms. Brown reports that her health is "great" and Josh's father's health is "okay."

Social/Emotional History

Ms. Brown reported that Josh has a history of temper tantrums and excessive crying. When he was younger, he would cry because others could not understand him. According to an eligibility report from April 2012, Josh's behavior significantly changed after his parents separated, as he "whined and wanted more attention."

Ms. Brown reports that Josh currently gets along well with his siblings. Although he is closer to his mother, he also has good relationships with his father and mother's fiancé. Josh engages in many activities with his family, including watching movies, playing games, and eating meals together. Ms. Brown reported that she enjoys her son's curiosity as he is always asking her questions and "he wants to know everything." At home, Josh becomes upset easily and may cry over "silly things." Ms. Brown reports that she is mainly in charge of discipline within the home, and behavior management techniques may include time-outs in his bedroom or removal of television/games.

Educational History

Prior to his initial evaluation for special education services at age 3, Josh was not enrolled in any formal early intervention programs. He was found eligible for special education services in May 2009 for developmental delays in communication and social/emotional development. He received special education during prekindergarten at Hepburn School and kindergarten in a developmental kindergarten classroom at Truman River Elementary School. At the start of first grade, Josh began attending a self-contained classroom for children with emotional disabilities back at Hepburn School. Josh continues to receive special education services within the same program.

Previous Test Results

In general, the evaluation results from Josh's last evaluation in 2012 indicate average overall cognitive functioning with delays in expressive language, receptive language, visual-motor integration, written expression, emotional regulation, and coping skills.

Evaluation Procedures

Record review

Parent interview

Classroom observation

Student interview

Wechsler Intelligence Scale for Children–Fifth Edition (WISC–V)

Beery-Buktenica Developmental Test of Visual-Motor Integration, Sixth Edition

Test of Memory and Learning, Second Edition

Delis-Kaplan Executive Function System, Trail Making Test

Comprehensive Executive Function Inventory (parent and teacher)

Behavior Assessment Scale for Children–Second Edition (parent and teacher)

Adaptive Behavior Assessment System, Second Edition (parent and teacher)

Kaufman Test of Educational Achievement–Third Edition (KTEA–3)

Conners Comprehensive Behavior Rating Scale (CBRS)

Testing Observations

Josh is an 8-year, 7-month-old Anglo male of average weight and height. He came to the testing session in a calm and cooperative manner. Josh was dressed appropriately and appeared clean and well groomed. At the beginning of the session, Josh was hesitant to speak and minimally responded to questions with a quick "yes" or "no." However, after discussing his personal interests, he began to take part in the conversation and then initiated new subjects. Overall, it was difficult to understand and follow Josh's ideas because his stories were disorganized and he often misused temporal and spatial concepts. On the other hand, he appeared to easily understand the examiner's test directions, responded to test prompts without repetition, and tried his best to answer questions that required oral expression. It therefore appears that his receptive language was age-appropriate and his pragmatic need for language and conversation were evident even though his oral articulation of ideas was compromised.

Notwithstanding good rapport, Josh found it very difficult to maintain his attention and effort throughout the testing session. When Josh perceived a task as being too difficult, tears would form in his eyes and he would claim that he "couldn't do it" because it was "too hard." Whenever a test item approached frustrational level, Josh would become distracted and disengaged from the task. Positive reinforcement helped a little with reorienting him to the task, but, overall, his attention fatigued after 15 to 20 minutes. In addition, he would stand up during some of the subtests because movement appeared to help him stay focused and self-regulate. Josh also was able to maintain good rapport with the examiner, and he enjoyed praise and success.

Given that the evaluation was accommodated to Josh's emotional and attentional deficits, it appears that the results of this evaluation are representative of his best efforts with guidance. Therefore, the results are deemed to be an accurate representation of his current cognitive and emotional functioning in the classroom setting with implications for other areas such as home and community.

Evaluation Results

Intellectual Functioning

Overall intellectual ability is estimated from a profile obtained from many test scores and refers to an individual's overall capacity to reason, solve problems, and learn useful information in an efficient and timely fashion. The WISC–V was used to obtain an overall picture of Josh's cognitive functioning and as a routing test to indicate where further investigation should be directed. Usually, a single score obtained from the WISC–V can represent a child's overall cognitive ability; however, in Josh's case, the profile of scores is quite variable and therefore should be viewed as a picture of processing strengths and weaknesses.

Josh's profile on the WISC–V shows that he has problem-solving abilities in the average range and low-average abilities in visual-spatial problem-solving and verbal reasoning areas. Josh's lowest performance was in the area of working memory, which should be investigated further. On the other hand, Josh's performance on processing speed measures was in the high-average range not only compared to his own performance but to that of other students his age. These scores indicate that he does very well in activities that require visual matching, basic visual scanning, visual short-term memory, and psychomotor speed.

The following results provide an in-depth follow-up evaluation of Josh's cognitive profile found on the WISC–V and with other measures designed to look further into specific strengths and weaknesses and the potential impact on academic and social/emotional functioning. These results are determined from a neurodevelopmental perspective where tasks are viewed comprehensively from basic to more complex skills as a child develops and grows.

Cognitive Processes

Auditory Processing Auditory processes range from basic functioning such as hearing and auditory perception to more integrated skills such as being able to understand directions. These processes provide the basis of the mature ability to fully comprehend and problem-solve information that is presented in an auditory format. At this stage in development, we would expect a typically developing 8-year-old student to be able to follow simple directions without visual cues, be able to rhyme and manipulate sounds in words, and answer concrete and simple inferential comprehension questions (without visual cues).

While Josh has a history of ear infections, and failed hearing screenings, he did pass a recent audiological examination. Therefore, we can assume at the most basic level that Josh can currently hear and perceive sounds. His receptive language ability scores indicate that he hears and understands what is said to him. He is also able to follow multi-step directions without visual cues. Josh's listening comprehension is somewhat low for his age, but is he able to recall stories immediately and, after 25 minutes, he is also able to answer simple concrete and inferential questions about the stories. Therefore, we can assume that Josh's auditory processing abilities are on track and that any observed differences in his auditory skills may be more due to other factors that are more about language and reading such as phonological awareness. In the classroom we see that Josh is able to follow along when he receives auditory information and that he understands and remembers what is being said to him by teachers and peers in most situations.

Visual Processing

Visual processes range from visual acuity, basic visual perception, and visual-spatial recognition to more mature skills in integrating visual with auditory information. The most complex visual abilities involve visual problem solving of novel tasks. Typically developing 8-year-olds should be able to immediately recall designs, identify and match images, and store and retrieve visual information from long-term memory. They should also be able to sustain efforts and invent strategies for solving difficult visual problems.

Josh passed his vision screening at school and is able to see his teacher's white board from his seat in the middle of the classroom. He can perceive, copy, and match basic shapes through drawing activities and can identify basic colors. Josh's visual working memory and problem-solving appear to be age appropriate because he is able to hold abstract images in his mind, mentally manipulate the images, and then produce new information or solve problems. Visual cues and prompts work well for Josh. It should be noted that Josh attends better to activities when he is provided with visual and motor cues. For example, Josh enjoys and accepts using a visual schedule in the classroom to help him predict upcoming events and keep on track.

Sensory Motor Functioning

Motor skills and abilities range from gross motor such as balance, gait, and understanding where the body is in space, to fine motor skills such as handwriting. At this stage, we'd expect someone Josh's age to be able to imitate hand movements, have good hand-eye coordination, and have smooth motor control during sports activities. In addition, we would also expect the student to avoid becoming too distracted or over-sensitized by other sensory stimuli within his classroom.

Josh receives occupational therapy services for delays in adaptive functions, such as shoe tying and writing. According to his occupational therapist, Josh has slightly below average hand strength and dexterity. When writing, he does not consistently put spaces between words and he often reverses letters, such as *b* and *d*. When Josh is confident of his visual-motor activity, he enjoys it and displays good fine motor control. However, when using fine motor movements to write letters or copy, he is quick to experience frustration. It appears that Josh does have mild fine motor problems, but they quickly exacerbate to moderate problems when he is stressed or addressing orthographic aspects letters and words.

In regard to sensory stimulation, Josh appears to be overly sensitive to busy or nonstructured classes. He will frequently cover his ears to protect from sounds and is easily distracted when there are a lot of noises or multiple activities around him. This appears to be more of a function of being overwhelmed with the environmental demands as opposed to a hearing sensitivity issue. For example, staff members report that music class is consistently difficult for Josh because the structure is less organized and so he frequently becomes off task, avoidant, and disruptive.

Language

Language processes range from basic speech and understanding the speech of others, to the ability to orally express abstract thoughts, engage in conversation, and problem-solve aloud. The mechanics of language, such as producing basic speech, provide the basis for being able to express one's thoughts fluently at a later age. Apart from the mechanics of language, it is important to be able to use language to communicate wants and needs. In addition, the ability to understand the intent of others and respond back within the context of the situation as in pragmatic speech is very important. A typically developing 8-year-old expresses intelligible speech, follows directions, articulates wants/needs, uses appropriate prosody when reading, and understands nonverbal language/communication.

Josh receives speech/language services on a weekly basis for deficits in speech intelligibility and for receptive and expressive language. Josh's receptive language ability is in the average to low-average range, and he exhibits age-appropriate pragmatic understanding of communication and social relationships via speech. However, expressive and oral language is significantly difficult for him. Josh has articulation errors with the following sounds: /l/, /r/, /th/, and /l/ blends. Most of Josh's language deficits are within the expressive language area.

He has difficulty identifying associations between words and using sequential, spatial, and temporal concepts. He also struggles with answering "wh" (e.g., what, where, etc.) questions. Josh struggles with organizing his thoughts, formulating sentences, and using correct subject-verb agreement. Delays in Josh's expressive language impact his everyday academic and emotional functioning as he struggles to communicate his wants/needs and only uses minimal necessary language skills for academic tasks. We see Josh having great difficulty in expressing himself with peers and staff. This sustained inability to fully communicate has significantly affected his ability to create meaningful and fluent discourse in relationships. The frustration of not being able to express himself takes a toll on his self-concept and self-efficacy, and therefore communication with teachers is an emotionally sensitive experience. Like many children with phonological issues, he is acutely aware of the tone of voice of others and is hypersensitive to perceived criticism or negative tone.

Executive/Attention

Attention and executive functions are abilities essential for orienting to a task, staying on task, problem solving, good judgment, and adapting to changes and stressors in the environment. As a child grows, he/she organizes the world via basic attention skills, such as the ability to attend to important things in the moment, sustaining attention, and shifting attention from one task to another. As the child develops, attention skills become more complex and begin to include organization skills and, later, in early adulthood, in independent decision making, planning, strategizing, and self-regulation. At this stage in development of attention/executive functions, we would expect Josh to be able to hold attention for 30 to 45 minutes and use basic executive functions, such as inhibition and organization with assistance from parents and teachers. We would also expect him to enjoy challenges and be patient when tasks become a little difficult. We would want him to stay with the task until he could figure out new ways to complete it or to get assistance when he needs it.

Josh is able to orient and react to basic auditory and visual stimuli. He responds when his name is called and directs his attention appropriately. While Josh is alert to stimuli in his environment, he struggles to maintain this alertness for extended periods of time. When Josh does not appear to be paying attention to instruction, he is often seen biting his nails while looking around the room. This general anxious state or hypervigilance means that his attention is divided, and he may miss out on material presented during class. He has difficulty with tasks that require working memory and sequencing, which would normally allow him to put events into perspective and react accordingly. Therefore, emotional regulation is also difficult for Josh. When faced with conflict, he often cries easily, and it can be difficult to redirect him when he is upset.

In general, we can assume that Josh is consistently in a state of hyperarousal where he spends a great deal of time attending to possible threats as opposed to what is really going on around him in the classroom. He is hypervigilant and always on the lookout for stressors and things that he views as frightening and/or negative. This constant state of arousal disallows the development and maturation of executive functions and so his ability to self-soothe, problem-solve, and accurately read a situation in front of him is compromised and similar to that of a much younger child. We see Josh decompensating when he thinks he has failed, become nervous and agitated when there is a lot of activity in the environment, and preoccupied with his failures rather than successes. On the surface, these types of behaviors can be misconstrued as simple attention deficits; however, in this case, the attentional and executive function deficits are more due to anxiety and depression and therefore require specialized interventions in the classroom and home.

Memory

Memory processes begin with short-term memory, working memory, and procedural memory and eventually bridge to semantic memory and long-term storage and retrieval. In order to successfully navigate the basics of schoolwork, adequate short-term and working memory systems are needed. At this stage in development, we would expect Josh to have appropriately developed immediate and working memory leading to storage and retrieval from long-term memory.

Josh does not seem to have significant deficits in his delayed memory abilities. He is able to recall concrete and abstract visual stimuli as well as verbal information immediately and after longer periods of time. Josh can remember much better when information is presented in familiar context, such as in stories. For the latter, he can recall lengthy sentences with multiple concepts. He also appears calm and confident in these types of activities, and therefore his memory works well.

Josh's memory seems most impacted by deficits in simple short-term auditory memory. He struggles to retain simple auditory information, such as a strand of five digits, and this may be due to a combination of expressive language fluency, phonological sequencing, and probably anxiety. In the classroom, Josh benefits from having information presented in a visually explicit manner. Staff members mention that it is best to break down tasks into small steps, rephrase questions, and provide him with additional time to process information. Visual cues in the environment also help him remember the moment-to-moment tasks that he has to keep in mind, or directions from the teacher.

Social/Emotional Functioning

Social skills and emotional regulation skills range from being able to identify basic human emotions and facial recognition to perspective-taking/theory of mind, humor, and conflict resolution abilities. It should again be noted that Josh receives special education services within a classroom for children with emotional disabilities. At this point in social development, we would expect an 8-year-old student to recognize views of others in classroom interactions, value friendships, notice his/her impact of behavior on others, and show basic skills of conflict resolution.

Josh's social functioning appears to be typically developing in that he wants to relate to peers and enjoys playing with friends who are his age, as well as older and younger students. One area of concern regarding his social interactions can be attributed to Josh's expressive language delays. Josh has difficulty communicating feelings to others and using words to negotiate conflict resolution. Delays in language may cause problems with his emotional growth in that it is hard to keep up with friends and express a range of ideas and responses. Josh has experienced long-term frustration and sadness about his inability to communicate freely with others. The toll of not being able to express himself, complete basic academic activities, and relate the way he wants to the world is heavy indeed, and his depressive feelings may well be expressed as anger and frustration in the classroom.

Ms. Brown reports that Josh does not exhibit any social or emotional delays within the home. She perceives him as a child who responds appropriately to stressors. According to past reports, Ms. Brown has not observed the same behaviors at home as Josh's education team. This is understandable, considering the demands of the two environments are very different.

Academic Achievement: Reading

Basic reading skills start with understanding of phonics and phonemic awareness followed by the polishing and fluency of word reading and reading fluency. These basic skills evolve into reading comprehension and the complex ability to think about what is read and apply it to other events. At this stage in development, we'd expect an 8-year-old student to have well-developed phonemic and phonological awareness, read third-grade words fluently and accurately in narratives, and answer concrete and simple inferential comprehension questions.

The results of the assessment indicate that Josh has severe difficulties with phonological awareness activities. For example, rhyming and

deleting sounds in words are difficult tasks for him. He can identify individual letter sounds, but he struggles to connect and blend two-letter sounds together. Significant delays in phonological awareness such as this are also evident when we ask him to try and read phonologically predictable nonsense words—he simply cannot phonologically decode basic words. The ability to take apart and analyze letter sounds in words and then blend requires an individual to have strong working memory, which is also difficult for children, like Josh, who have attention and emotional problems.

In terms of reading fluency, it appears that Josh has the cognitive ability to access information rapidly, but his problems with letters and sounds impede his ability to read without effort. These delays also impact his abilities to identify sight words and decode words at second- and third-grade levels. His basic reading deficits also impact his reading comprehension, as he is not able to accurately decode and make sense of words and get to a rapid pace of reading where he is reading to learn, not reading to read. In the classroom we see that reading is a slow and laborious activity for Josh. He tries to read quickly but has to slow down to read harder words and then the meaning for the sentence is lost. This is an exhausting way to read, the constant slowing to decode and then re-upload of the meaning is a stop-start process that requires a great deal of sustained attention and intrinsic reward at the end of the activity. Josh does not receive implicit or explicit rewards for reading, and consequently his motivation and self-efficacy is very low in this area, and it is easy to understand why he cries with frustration.

Math

Foundational math skills involve number concepts and fact recognition. This evolves into math facts fluency and fluidity with math operations (+ − x ÷) culminating in mathematical problem solving of word problems, multistep processes, and abstract math theory such as algebra and geometry. Eight-year-old

CASE 4—JOSH, AGE 8: A NEURODEVELOPMENTAL PROCESSING "NO NUMBERS" APPROACH TO CASE REPORT WRITING   **355**

students are typically able to add and subtract up to four-digit numbers, use times tables (up to 10×10), understand estimation, and are beginning to work with decimals and fractions.

Josh is able to identify numbers up to 100, add one-digit numbers, and subtract one-digit numbers but begins to struggle with math computation when multiple digits are presented. When solving equations with multiple digits, Josh does not appear to understand regrouping or other math strategies, with the exception of counting on his fingers. Josh also appears to give up easily when he perceives math problems as too challenging. Based on strengths in visual-spatial functioning and quantitative reasoning, it is possible that Josh has the ability to solve third-grade math equations, but at this time, Josh's delay in math facts appears to be impacting his math problem solving. Josh needs to be fluent in math facts so that he can pay attention to the problem at hand, not the mechanics of basic multiplication, etc. In addition, math problem solving is negatively impacted by attention and executive function problems because Josh needs those skills to organize his way through math problems.

Writing

Writing development is a cognitively demanding process that begins with the mastering of the mechanics of basic spelling and handwriting. It evolves into spelling multisyllabic words and employing grammar rules into written texts in a fluent manner. Writing culminates into written expression of abstract thoughts, such as creative writing or persuasive writing. At this point, 8-year-old students are expected to use basic mechanics and conventions of writing (e.g., handwriting, spelling, capitalization, punctuation, etc.) and content aspects of writing that involve conveying meaning. Eight-year-olds are also expected to start using planning and revision during written expression activities.

Josh struggles with basic handwriting, spacing, and spelling due to deficits in fine motor and phonological functioning. According to Josh's occupational therapist, he does not write

independently. Writing is not a preferred task, and it can be difficult to engage Josh within this process because he becomes emotional and defensive during this difficult activity. In addition, his phonological deficits translate into orthographic deficits, as spelling is dependent on phonological knowledge. Delays in writing mechanics contribute to deficits in his ability to achieve fluency in writing mechanics and then convey meaning in his writing. Deficits in executive functioning also significantly impact writing, as it requires planning, organization, and working memory. So, again, we see that his mechanical deficits and anxious and depressive feelings get in the way of the organizational skills necessary to be successful.

Summary

Josh is an 8-year, 7-month-old Caucasian male in the third grade referred for a comprehensive evaluation to determine if a learning disability is present and to gain further insight into his current emotional functioning. Josh currently receives special education services under the primary criteria of emotional disability and the secondary criteria of speech/language impairment.

The results of this evaluation suggest that Josh's overall cognitive abilities are in the low-average range with a specific profile of processing strengths and weakness. Josh has individual strengths in fluency of ideas, receptive language, visual perception, and memory for verbal and visual stimuli. He is a pleasant and friendly young boy who enjoys relating to others, has social interests, and is curious about the world.

In terms of a learning disability, there appears to be a distinct pattern of phonological deficits that are significantly impeding his ability to gain the basic sound-blending skills necessary to decode words, achieve fluency in word calling, and then gain meaning from text. This is a common form of reading disability that has profound impact on reading acquisition skills and most academics. Josh also appears to have associated expressive language deficits that relate to phonological awareness and decoding fluency. These same processing deficits may also impede his ability to command the automatic recall of math facts. Although numbers are not letters, math facts are usually recalled in an oral/linguistic format and while Josh has age-appropriate fluency of ideas, he cannot achieve fluency of reading sounds and math facts to a level that allows him to progress academically.

The sustained and long-term failure to progress in academics has also affected Josh's emotional life and created a hypersensitivity to criticism or failure, which, in turn, prevents him from establishing a good self-concept and sustained motivation. This negative self-perspective also has affected his attention and executive functioning, so he pays attention to failure and struggle as opposed to the learning content at hand. Although Josh demonstrates age-appropriate social skills in many ways, he lacks self-confidence and experiences depression. He feels deeply about his academic and linguistic deficits and becomes emotionally overwhelmed when experiencing failure or frustration. Josh is very anxious at school and is hypervigilant about perceived threats in the environment because he is constantly reminded of his own lack of academic success.

Josh receives special education services under the primary criteria of emotional disability and speech/language impairment. He initially met the emotional disability criteria in 2012 because he had trouble developing and maintaining relationships with others and exhibited inappropriate types of behaviors/feelings under normal circumstances. This appears to still be the case, and current assessment results indicate that there is a subtle interplay with Josh's emotional reactions to the demands of school and a distinct and significant phonological reading/learning disability. It is recommended that the special education eligibility criteria be extended to include specific learning disability as well.

Recommendations

Classroom

- Reading
  - Josh will benefit from a multisensory approach when learning to read. All modalities (touch, sight, and sound) should be exploited during Josh's reading interventions. Some established reading programs that might suit Josh's learning style are:
    - *Phono-Graphix:* a systematic and multisensory reading program designed to teach the underlying principles of the alphabetic code. It teaches students to segment, blend, and manipulate phonemes, and also emphasizes that sounds are represented by letters or pictures, rather than stressing that letters are represented by sounds.
    - *Read 180:* this intervention program takes a balanced literacy approach in order to meet the needs of students who are struggling in one or more areas of the five components of reading. Within this program, children learn about phonics, fluency, vocabulary, decoding and word recognition, spelling, and comprehension. Depending on the child's reading level, the software included with the program can be adjusted.
    - *Wilson Reading System:* this reading intervention program is sequenced into 12 steps, based on six syllable types: closed syllables with short vowels, syllables with long vowels and a silent *e*, open syllables ending with the consonant "le," "R" controlled syllables, and vowel digraph/diphthong syllables. Throughout the program, students are taught to use a unique finger-tapping system to analyze spoken words into phonemes to assist with spelling. The student is taught to say each sound while tapping a different finger to his/her thumb.
  - Emphasize Dolch sight words with Josh. Begin by reviewing preprimer words and work up to a grade 3 level.

- When possible, focus on reading accuracy instead of timing. Josh is sensitive and nervous about being timed, and this interferes with production.
- Math
  - Encourage Josh to use TouchMath to ensure for better math computation. TouchMath is a multisensory approach that uses hands-on activities, pictures, and symbols such as letters and numerals to build better math literacy. He will be able to assign real value (dots) to numerals for easy counting.
  - When Josh appears confused about math assignments, provide him with open-ended prompts, such as "What do we do next?" When working on math, Josh may give up easily because the task seems overwhelming to him. Breaking up the assignment into smaller chunks or prompting him to complete one step at a time may help him to be more confident in his approach.
  - Provide Josh with real-world math applications. If Josh knows the importance of learning different math strategies, the information may have more meaning and be better stored in his long-term memory.

Social/Emotional

- At all times staff and family will need to use a positive or neutral tone of voice with Josh. He is very sensitive to prosody, and once he perceives negative tone, he resorts to feelings that do not support a good outcome. Therefore, a sustained campaign of soft, respectful, and supportive speech on the part of staff and family will help reduce his anxiety and defensiveness. On the other hand, when he is compliant and helpful, the tone should not be effusive but supportive and reflective of his effort, for example, "That's nice, Josh, I saw you worked really hard on that and it paid off—good for you."
- Psychoeducation with Josh and his family on the physiological nature of anxiety and depression (hyperarousal, etc.) and evidence-based coping strategies for reduction (e.g., relaxation breathing, cognitive behavioral controls, etc.).
- Psychoeducation for Josh and his family concerning family coping with disabilities and ways to support Josh in years to come.
- Counseling (individual and small group) that allows Josh to use figures or pictures to express his feelings. Josh may respond well to drawing pictures first and then communicating his thoughts about the picture. In addition, play therapy techniques may allow him to communicate his concerns during sessions.
- Allow Josh to have a "safe space" in his classroom or in a designated area outside of the classroom. Within the safe space, Josh can keep objects that make him feel secure, such as a picture of a loved one or pet. Josh may also choose to keep fidgets or a sensory bottle to help him calm down when he is upset. This would be a designated and acceptable area designed for him to self-soothe and think about ways to handle stressful situations. If successful, the safe space can be localized to his desk or a box within his desk, etc.
- Provide Josh with an individualized visual schedule on a daily basis. While Josh proves to have flexible thinking, he will feel more secure seeing the structure of upcoming classes, activities, etc.

Home

- Josh's family is encouraged to attend psychoeducation and counseling in order to strengthen the bonds between family members and learn how to best support one another during times of frustration.
- When disciplining Josh, always provide him with a reason for why his behavior was inappropriate. For example, if Josh gets into trouble for jumping on the bed, his mother might say, "Josh, you are getting a time out for 10 minutes because you were jumping on the bed. When you jump on the bed without someone watching you, you can fall and hit your head and get hurt."

- Reinforce positive behavior in the home setting. Josh does not always need to be given tangible rewards, such as money, for doing chores; he can be given verbal praise (e.g., "good job!") when performing such tasks. When positively praising Josh, always specifically state why you are providing him with praise. For example, "Josh, I am so proud of how you took out the garbage without me having to ask you. Thank you so much for helping me!"
- Encourage Josh to talk about his day at school when he arrives home. Josh enjoys telling stories and being asked for insight. These conversations will foster bonds between family members and will allow him more practice using expressive language.

Psychometric Results

Test Scores

Warning: Psychological test data are easily misinterpreted by individuals unfamiliar with psychological tests and the evaluation process. Please consult a licensed psychologist or school psychologist to assist with interpretation of the numerical scores below. Josh's scores appear in Table 10.1 to 10.10.

Table 10.1   Josh's WISC–V Scores

Scale/Index	Scaled Score	Standard Score	Qualitative Descriptor
Block Design	9		Average
Visual Puzzles	4–W		Below Average
Visual Spatial		81	Low Average
Similarities	6		Low Average
Vocabulary	7		Low Average
Verbal Comprehension		81	Low Average
Matrix Reasoning	6		Low Average
Figure Weights	9		Average

Table 10.1   (Continued)

Scale/Index	Scaled Score	Standard Score	Qualitative Descriptor
Fluid Reasoning		85	Low Average
Digit Span	4–W		Below Average
Picture Span	7		Low Average
Working Memory		74	Below Average
Coding	12–S		Average
Symbol Search	13–S		High Average
Processing Speed		114–S	High Average
Full Scale IQ		82	Low Average

Table 10.2   Josh's Kaufman Test of Educational Achievement–Third Edition (KTEA–3) Scores

Core Subtests and Composites	Standard Score	Qualitative Descriptor
Letter & Word Recognition	70	Below Average
Reading Comprehension	63	Well Below Average
Reading	65	Well Below Average
Math Concepts & Applications	74	Below Average
Math Computation	76	Below Average
Math	74	Below Average
Written Expression	N/A	N/A
Spelling	62	Well Below Average
Written Language	N/A	N/A
Academic Skills Battery Composite	N/A	N/A

Oral Subtests and Composites	Standard Score	Qualitative Descriptor
Associational Fluency	93	Average
Listening Comprehension	85	Low Average

Table 10.2   (*Continued*)

Oral Subtests and Composites	Standard Score	Qualitative Descriptor
Oral Expression	61	Well Below Average
Oral Language	**74**	**Below Average**
Associational Fluency	93	Average
Object Naming Facility	94	Average
Oral Fluency	**92**	**Average**

Reading-Related Subtests and Composites	Standard Score	Qualitative Descriptor
Phonological Processing	77	Below Average
Nonsense Word Decoding	64	Well Below Average
Sound–Symbol	**67**	**Well Below Average**
Letter & Word Recognition	70	Below Average
Nonsense Word Decoding	64	Well Below Average
Decoding	**66**	**Well Below Average**
Silent Reading Fluency	69	Well Below Average
Word Recognition Fluency	55	Well Below Average
Decoding Fluency	62	Well Below Average
Reading Fluency	**59**	**Well Below Average**
Reading Comprehension	63	Well Below Average
Reading Vocabulary	72	Below Average
Reading Understanding	**66**	**Well Below Average**

Cross-Domain Subtests and Composites	Standard Score	Qualitative Descriptor
Reading Comprehension	65	Well Below Average
Listening Comprehension	87	Low Average
Comprehension	**74**	**Below Average**
Written Expression	N/A	N/A
Oral Expression	61	Well Below Average
Spelling	62	Well Below Average

Table 10.2   (*Continued*)

Cross-Domain Subtests and Composites	Standard Score	Qualitative Descriptor
Letter Naming Facility	90	Average
Word Recognition Fluency	55	Well Below Average
Orthographic Processing	**64**	**Well Below Average**
Writing Fluency	65	Well Below Average
Math Fluency	78	Below Average
Decoding Fluency	62	Well Below Average
Academic Fluency	**64**	**Well Below Average**

Table 10.3   Josh's Beery-Buktenica Developmental Test of Visual-Motor Integration, Sixth Edition (VMI) Scores

Assessment	Standard Score	Qualitative Descriptor
Visual Perception	98	Average
Motor Coordination	53	Well Below Average

Table 10.4   Josh's Test of Memory and Learning, Second Edition (TOMAL–2) Scores

Subtest	Scaled Score	Qualitative Descriptor
Memory for Stories	12	Average
Memory for Stories Delayed	8	Average
Facial Memory	7	Average
Word Selective Reminding	11	Average
Word Selective Reminding Delayed	10	Average
Abstract Visual Memory	11	Average
Memory for Location	8	Average

Table 10.5   Josh's Delis–Kaplan Executive Function System (D-KEFS) Scores

Trail Making Test	Scaled Score	Qualitative Descriptor
Visual Scanning	11	Average
Number Sequencing	13	High Average
Letter Sequencing*	N/A	N/A
Number/Letter Switching*	N/A	N/A
Motor Speed	14	High Average

*Student did not complete subtest

Table 10.6   Josh's Comprehensive Executive Function Inventory (CEFI) Scores

Scale	Teacher Standard Score	Quali- tative Descriptor	Parent Standard Score	Quali- tative Descriptor
Attention	77	Below Average	114	High Average
Emotion Regulation	79	Below Average	104	Average
Flexibility	96	Average	106	Average
Inhibitory Control	84	Low Average	114	High Average
Initiation	74	Below Average	110	High Average
Organization	88	Low Average	121	High Average
Planning	86	Low Average	115	High Average
Self- Monitoring	79	Below Average	121	High Average
Working Memory	76	Below Average	119	High Average

Table 10.7   Josh's Behavior Assessment Scale for Children, Second Edition (BASC-2) Scores

Scale / Index	Teacher T-Score	Quali- tative Descriptor	Parent T-Score	Quali- tative Descriptor
Hyperactivity	67	At Risk	43	Average
Aggression	54	Average	42	Average
Conduct Problems	47	Average	43	Average
Externalizing Problems	56	**Average**	42	**Average**
Anxiety	52	Average	43	Average
Depression	71	Clinically Significant	59	Average
Somatization	43	Average	50	Average
Internalizing Problems	57	**Average**	51	**Average**
Attention Problems	62	At Risk	48	Average
Learning Problems	62	At Risk	N/A	N/A
School Problems	63	**At Risk**	N/A	**N/A**
Atypicality	63	At Risk	46	Average
Withdrawal	49	Average	53	Average
Behavioral Symptom Index	64	**At Risk**	48	**Average**
Adaptability	41	Average	55	Average
Social Skills	49	Average	59	Average
Leadership	47	Average	51	Average
Study Skills	45	Average	N/A	N/A
Functional Communi- cation	26	Clinically Significant	37	At Risk
Activities of Daily Living	N/A	N/A	49	Average
Adaptive Skills	40	**Average**	50	**Average**

Table 10.8   Josh's Conners Comprehensive Behavior Rating Scale (CBRS) Scores

Scale	Teacher T-Score	Quali-tative Descriptor	Parent T-Score	Quali-tative Descriptor
Emotional Distress	44	Average	48	Average
Upsetting Thoughts	44	Average	45	Average
Worrying	N/A	N/A	52	Average
Social Problems	59	Average	54	Average
Defiant/ Aggressive Behaviors	56	Average	46	Average
Academic Difficulties	73	Clinically Significant	62	At Risk
Language	86	Clinically Significant	66	At Risk
Math	50	Average	56	Average
Hyperactivity/ Impulsivity	41	Average	46	Average
Separation Fears	53	Average	53	Average
Perfectionistic and Compulsive Behaviors	45	Average	43	Average
Violence Potential Indicator	50	Average	50	Average
Physical Symptoms	45	Average	48	Average
Social Anxiety	43	Average	N/A	N/A

Table 10.9   Josh's Adaptive Behavior Assessment System, Second Edition (ABAS–2) Teacher Scores

Skill Area	Scaled Score	Standard Score	Qualitative Descriptor
Communication	2		Well Below Average
Functional Academics	4		Below Average
Self-Direction	9		Average
Conceptual		78	Below Average
Social	9		Average
Leisure	10		Average
Social		94	Average
Community Use	6		Below Average
School Living	6		Below Average
Health and Safety	6		Below Average
Self-Care	9		Average
Practical		84	Below Average
General Adaptive Composite		84	Below Average

Table 10.10   Josh's Adaptive Behavior Assessment System, Second Edition (ABAS–2) Parent Scores

Skill Area	Scaled Score	Standard Score	Qualitative Descriptor
Communication	11		Average
Functional Academics	7		Low Average
Self-Direction	9		Average
Conceptual		**95**	**Average**
Social	10		Average
Leisure	7		Low Average
Social		**94**	**Average**
Community Use	9		Average
Home Living	10		Average
Health and Safety	11		Average
Self-Care	11		Average
Practical		**102**	**Average**
General Adaptive Composite		**96**	**Average**

CASE 5—TAWNA, AGE 13: EIGHTH-GRADE GIRL WITH ADHD STRUGGLING WITH PROCESSING SPEED, SUSTAINED ATTENTION, AND EMOTIONAL FUNCTIONING

Michelle Lurie and Elizabeth Lichtenberger

Neuropsychologial Assessment

Name: Tawna Simpson

Age: 13 years, 5 months

Education: 8th grade

Reason for Evaluation

Tawna Simpson is a 13-year-old African American girl who lives with her biological parents, her 9-year-old brother and 7-year-old sister. Tawna is an eighth grader at a public middle school in Oklahoma. This evaluation was initiated by her parents due to difficulties Tawna is having at school. In particular, they are concerned because Tawna appears unmotivated and disorganized, and her grades are poor. She also has had ongoing social difficulties and recently diagnosed anxiety and depressive disorders. Therefore, the purpose of this evaluation is to better understand Tawna's neurocognitive and emotional functioning. Based on the test results, various academic and treatment recommendations will be made.

Background Information

Developmental History and Health

Tawna is the product of a normal pregnancy and an uneventful labor and delivery, weighing 8 lb. 2 oz. at birth. Tawna's parents described her as an easygoing baby who evidenced no delays in reaching her developmental milestones. In general, Tawna is a healthy young woman with no significant medical history. Her parents stated that Tawna has had no surgeries, hospitalizations, concussions, or head injuries.

Tawna's vision and hearing are described as intact. She has a healthy appetite for a range of foods. Tawna reported initial insomnia and indicated that she is "distracted by many things," so she can't easily fall asleep. Tawna's parents reported that she has some somatic complaints that she uses to avoid school.

The family history is notable for depression, autism spectrum disorder, and attention-deficit/hyperactivity disorder (ADHD). At the time of testing, Tawna was on no medication.

Academic History

Tawna evidenced no delays in acquiring basic preacademic skills in preschool although some social difficulties were noted. However, at the end of third grade, Tawna's teacher reported some "focus issues." These were also identified by Tawna's fourth-grade teacher, so Tawna was tested for ADHD in fourth grade. This brief partial assessment did not support a diagnosis of ADHD; however, some anxiety and depression were identified.

Since sixth grade, Tawna has had ongoing struggles completing assignments and paying attention. Tawna's parents and middle school teachers reported that she lacks motivation at school and is not interested in her grades. She does not finish classwork and fails to complete this work at home. Therefore, her grades are impacted by missing assignments. She struggles particularly in science and math but does somewhat better in social studies and language arts. Her parents rate Tawna as performing below grade level in all areas (grades of C and D). Tawna complained of problems with distractibility in the classroom and said that she struggles "to pay attention in class when the teacher is talking to everyone." She has no particular organizational system and does not use a planner to write down her assignments. Rather, she attempts to record assignment due dates on sticky notes and to stick them to a mirror in her room.

Homework has been an ongoing struggle for Tawna and her parents since elementary school, according to her mother. Tawna appears unfocused when her parents assist her with homework; she frequently tells her parents that she has no homework even when assignments are due; she fails to attend to the written directions on assignments; and she does not appear to put forward effort on homework. In fact, her parents indicated that Tawna will manipulate the situation to try to get her parents to complete tasks for her, but when they refuse to do so, she completes the task incorrectly, which they see as possibly deliberate.

Emotional and Social Development

Tawna's parents described her as an intelligent, caring, and strong-willed young woman who is musically talented. Her math teacher described her as "well nice and well behaved." At the same time, her parents recognized that Tawna has struggled with interpersonal difficulties from a young age. She can be very socially engaging but can also be rude, obnoxious, controlling, and jealous with her peers. Her parents have observed that Tawna tends to "create social drama," and she does not appear to recognize the impact of her actions on others. Her mother described Tawna as "missing social cues."

Tawna has an intact relationship with her parents and siblings. However, she generally does not choose to interact with her family, and she prefers to spend her afternoons alone in her room on her phone or computer, or drawing. Tawna does not participate in any structured after-school activities.

According to her parents, Tawna tends to be "hyper in general" at home but mostly happy. At the same time, she tends to be controlling, and she complains and sulks when she does not get her way. However, she is never rageful or argumentative. Rather, she tends to avoid conflictual conversations with her parents and ignores their requests.

In a recent comprehensive psychological evaluation, the assessing clinical psychologist diagnosed Tawna with Unspecified Anxiety Disorder and Persistent Depressive Disorder.

These findings were the result of an evaluation that included: the Beck Youth Inventory–Second Edition (BYI–II; Beck, Beck, & Jolly, 2005), Millon Adolescent Clinical Inventory (MACI; Millon, Millon, Davis, & Grossman, 1993), Sentence Completion, and comprehensive interviews with Tawna, her parents, and her teachers. The results of the psychological evaluation concluded: "Tawna struggles with a high level of anxiety and depression, along with some anger control problems. Her personality profile is comprised of dependent personality traits with schizoid features. Over an extended period of time, Tawna has developed a dysthymic symptom pattern of dejection and discouragement. Lacking in self-esteem and fearful of provoking the anger of others, she has become increasingly pessimistic about her future." The assessing psychologist recommended that a neuropsychological assessment be completed to further evaluate her attentional and academic difficulties that coexist with her psychological problems.

Behavioral Observations

Tawna presented as an amicable young woman who approached the testing with a good attitude. She was cooperative and willing to put forward adequate effort at all times. Tawna tended to be somewhat quiet and reserved. Nonetheless, she responded honestly and openly to all verbal questions, and she freely shared her concerns. Tawna's mood was somewhat depressed and her affect was flat.

The most notable observation of Tawna's performance was her extremely slow task completion. Not only did Tawna appear to take a great deal of time to formulate verbal responses, but she also worked exceptionally slowly on written tasks. She had problems paying attention to details, both visually and verbally, and at times she was careless. Her stamina was normal. No problems with expressive or receptive language were observed. On the basis of these behavior observations, this assessment appears to be a valid measure of Tawna's functioning.

Tests Administered

Clinical interviews with Mr. Simpson, Mrs. Simpson, and Tawna Simpson

Wechsler Intelligence Scale for Children–Fifth Edition (WISC–V)

California Verbal Learning Test–Children Version (CVLT–C)

Rey Complex Figure Test and Recognition Trial (RCFT)

A Developmental Neuropsychological Assessment—Second Edition (NEPSY–II): Selected Subtests

Delis-Kaplan Executive Functioning System (D-KEFS): Selected Subtests

IVA+Plus Continuous Performance Test (IVA+Plus)

Wisconsin Card Sort Test–64: Computer Version 2 (WCST–64)

School Motivation and Learning Strategies Inventory (SMALSI)

Wechsler Individual Achievement Test–Third Edition (WIAT–III): Selected Subtests

Gray Oral Reading Test–Fifth Edition (GORT–5)

Clinical Evaluation of Language Fundamentals–Fifth Edition (CELF5): Structured Writing

Conners 3 Parent Rating Scale

Achenbach: Child Behavior Checklist, Teacher Report Form, & Youth Self Report

Behavior Rating Inventory of Executive Function (BRIEF): Parent and Teacher Forms

Test Results

Intellectual Abilities

In order to assess Tawna's intellectual ability, she was administered the WISC–V, which is an individually administered test of a child's intellectual ability and cognitive strengths and weaknesses. This test has six composite scores: Verbal Comprehension Index, Visual Spatial Index, Fluid Reasoning Index, Working Memory Index, Processing Speed Index, and Full Scale IQ. The Full Scale IQ (FSIQ) is derived from a combination of the subtest scores and is considered the most representative estimate of global intellectual functioning. Tawna's general cognitive ability is within the Average range of intellectual functioning, as measured by the FSIQ. Her overall thinking and reasoning abilities exceed those of approximately 37% of children her age (FSIQ = 95). Similarly, when Tawna's overall abilities are examined with the General Ability Index, which is a measure less impacted by working memory and processing speed factors, her intellectual ability remains in the Average range (100; 50th percentile).

Tawna's verbal reasoning abilities as measured by the Verbal Comprehension Index are in the Average range and above those of approximately 58% of her peers (103). Her ability to access and apply acquired word knowledge in terms of verbal reasoning and concept formation were equally well developed. Tawna's knowledge of vocabulary words and her verbal abstract reasoning were both Average.

Similar to her verbal reasoning and concept formation, Tawna's visual-spatial reasoning abilities were intact, as evidenced by her Average overall functioning on the Visual Spatial Index (94; 34th percentile). Her visuoconstructional and visuomotor skills on a task of recreating block designs were Average, as were her visual-perceptual and spatial reasoning abilities on a nonmotor visual task.

Consistent with her other intellectual abilities, Tawna's ability to detect the underlying conceptual relationship among visual stimuli and use reasoning to identify and apply rules were in the Average range. Specifically, Tawna performed in the Average range on the Fluid Reasoning Index (97; 42nd percentile). Her performances were evenly developed on subtests of her nonverbal reasoning. Although her attention and focus challenged her on a measure of mental arithmetic, she still performed in the Average range (25th percentile) on that reasoning task.

Unlike her consistently Average abilities in the domains of verbal knowledge and reasoning, visual-spatial reasoning, and nonverbal reasoning, Tawna showed an inconsistent ability to register, hold, and manipulate visual and auditory information in conscious awareness. Overall, she performed better than approximately 21% of her age-mates on the Working Memory Index (88). However, on these tasks, Tawna's performances were inconsistent and unreliable, which reflects an impaired ability to hold visual and auditory information in temporary storage and to manipulate it.

Tawna's speed and accuracy of visual scanning and visuomotor coordination was a significant weakness compared to her other abilities. She evidenced Very Low functioning on the Processing Speed Index (72; 3rd percentile). Both on a measure of visual scanning and discrimination and on a measure of paired associate learning and graphomotor speed, Tawna generally worked accurately but extremely slowly. Her visual scanning speed and speed of sequencing information was also impaired on measures of executive functioning discussed below.

Attention and Executive Functions
Executive Functioning   On a battery of executive functioning subtests, Tawna demonstrated Average cognitive flexibility on verbal tasks but extremely impaired cognitive flexibility on visual tasks requiring her to sequence two sets of data simultaneously (D-KEFS Color-Word Interference Subtests: 20th–50th percentiles versus D-KEFS Trail Making Subtests: 1st–5th percentiles). She worked exceptionally slowly on these tasks. Mild problems with inhibition were noted on tasks designed to assess the ability to inhibit automatic responses in favor of novel responses and the ability to switch between response types. In contrast, Tawna evidenced intact performance on a computerized measure of her ability to form abstract concepts and

to resist perseveration (WCST–64: 63rd–86th percentile). Adequate problem-solving skills were noted on this task, and Tawna appeared to benefit from the immediate feedback provided. Similarly, no deficits with problem solving and planning were noted on another problem-solving task on which no feedback was provided (D-KEFS Tower Test: 75th percentile).

Sustained Attention and Response Control
Tawna consistently showed impaired performance on measures of sustained attention and response control. She had moderate to severe difficulties on a subtest that uses an auditory continuous performance paradigm to measure selective and sustained attention, response inhibition, and executive functioning. The first part of this subtest is designed to assess selective auditory attention and the ability to sustain it (i.e., vigilance). The second part of this subtest is designed to assess the ability to shift and maintain a new and complex set involving both inhibition of previously learned responses and correctly responding to matching or contrasting stimuli. Tawna struggled particularly on this second part of the subtest that requires more executive control than the first part due to the cognitive load and working memory requirements of the task (NEPSY–II Auditory Attention: 9th percentile; and NEPSY–II Response Set: 1st percentile).

In order to further assess her sustained attention and response control, Tawna was administered the IVA+Plus. This task is intended to be mildly boring and demanding of sustained attention over a 13-minute period of time. On this task Tawna was required to self-regulate and respond to target stimuli (the number 1 presented in either an auditory or visual format on the computer) and refrain from responding to nontarget stimuli (the number 2 presented in the same formats). In terms of her sustained attention, deficits were noted on the IVA+Plus. Tawna struggled to remain vigilant to visual targets although her auditory vigilance was intact. Likewise, problems in her visual focus and response speed were noted. In addition, impairment was noted in her response control, and Tawna was extremely impulsive when presented with both visual and auditory nontargets. This indicates serious difficulties with response inhibition. In addition, her stamina was weak in the auditory domain, which is consistent with her complaints of difficulties remaining attentive during lectures. A high level of distractibility was apparent. It is likely that Tawna tends to struggle to remain on task for extended periods of time, and her performances will likely decrease in quality as she works on a task.

Rating Scales Further measures of Tawna's attentional functioning were obtained by having Tawna, her teacher, and her mother complete various rating scales. Tawna was rated by her mother as evidencing serious problems with inattention but no hyperactivity/impulsivity. Significant executive functioning problems were noted by Mrs. Simpson in terms of impaired behavior regulation (cognitive shifting, inhibition, and emotional control) as well as impaired metacognition (initiating tasks, working memory, planning tasks, organizing materials, and self-monitoring). Tawna also rated herself as struggling with extreme problems of inattention as well as impulsivity. Her math teacher also identified executive functioning problems in terms of global deficits in metacognition, but no problems with attention or impulsivity were noted.

Language Tawna evidenced High Average performances on measures of phonemic verbal fluency, but her semantic verbal fluency was weaker than expected and in the Low Average range (84th percentile on D-KEFS Letter Fluency versus 25th percentile on D-KEFS Category Fluency). Tawna's ability to respond to complex auditory directions was Average (NEPSY–II Comprehension of Instruction: 63rd percentile). Similarly, her listening comprehension was Average on a task of oral discourse comprehension and High Average on a measure

of receptive vocabulary (63rd percentile on WIAT–III Listening Comprehension).

Memory

Tawna was administered tests of memory assessing how well she takes in, stores, and remembers information presented both visually and verbally.

Visual Memory Tawna evidenced significant impairment on a test of spatial memory for novel visual material. This test assesses spatial recall, visual content recognition, and overall visuospatial memory. Both her initial recall and her delayed recall were impaired on this measure (<1st percentile on NEPSY–II Memory for Designs). Significant difficulties were also noted on a complex test of spatial memory requiring Tawna to reproduce a detailed design from memory. On both the immediate recall trial and the delayed recall trial, Tawna struggled to recall the details from the figure, and she produced the spatial outline with few particulars included (1st percentile on RCFT Immediate Recall). Although her recognition memory was stronger on this task, she was unable to recognize several important details from the figure (5th percentile on RCFT Recognition Total).

Verbal Memory Tawna's performances were in the Low Average to Average range on a complex measure of contextual verbal memory (NEPSY–II Narrative Memory: 25th–37th percentile). Some impairment was also noted on a measure of the strategies and processes involved in learning and recalling verbal material. On this task, Tawna's ability to repeat a list of words the first time she heard it indicates a Low Average initial attention span for auditory-verbal information (i.e., CVLT–C). Similarly, on her fifth learning attempt, her performance was also Low Average. Overall, her total recall of the word list across the five learning trials was Low Average compared to others her age. Tawna's use of semantic clustering was Average compared to others her age. She did not overly use serial clustering (which is usually an ineffective learning strategy). In addition, she evidenced an active learning style, in that she recalled an expected percentage of words from different regions of the list. However, Tawna's consistency index was Low Average. Children with problems in consistency may know information one time and not the next; their thoughts may be described as "scattered." After a short delay, Tawna's recall of the list was Low Average. Following a delay of about 20 minutes, Tawna's recall of the first list was Extremely Low for her age. Category cueing after both the short delay and the long delay improved subsequent performance. On a delayed recognition test for the words, Tawna's ability to discriminate between words that were on the list and those that were not was Low Average for her age. Tawna's ability to recognize information was better than her ability to recall it.

Taken together, these findings suggest that Tawna experienced difficulty in encoding and retrieving both visual and verbal information from memory.

Academic Skills and Learning Strategies

On a self-report of her learning strategies and motivation for academic success, Tawna reported having intact study strategies, note-taking and listening skills, reading comprehension skills, writing skills, and test taking strategies. However, she reported impaired organizational skills and time management skills. In terms of her motivation to succeed academically, no impairment was noted. However, Tawna did report significant test anxiety as well as severe attention deficits.

In order to assess her academic achievement, Tawna was administered the GORT–5 as well as subtests from the WIAT–III and the CELF5.

Reading

Tawna's reading rate was Average and her reading accuracy was Superior on measures of reading fluency (GORT–5 Rate: 37th percentile and GORT–5 Accuracy 91st percentile). Overall her reading fluency was intact (63rd percentile on GORT–5 Fluency). However, Tawna struggled on a task of reading comprehension (25th percentile on GORT–5

Comprehension). Therefore, although Tawna might read fairly quickly and very accurately, she does not always understand the content of what she is reading, and she is rarely able to make predictions or inferences from what she reads.

Mathematics

Tawna evidenced Average performances on a measure of math calculation as well as on a measure of her math problem-solving skills (55th percentile on WIAT–III Math Problem Solving and 37th percentile on Numerical Operations). In contrast, Tawna struggled on measures of her timed math fact retrieval, and her performances were far below grade level on these timed tasks of math fluency (5th–13th percentile on WIAT–III Math Fluency subtests).

Written Language

Tawna performed within the High Average range on tasks that required her to correctly spell verbally presented words (WIAT–III Spelling: 79th percentile). Her performances were Average on a measure assessing her ability to use situational information (i.e., a story title, an introductory sentence, and an incomplete sentence) to create a short narrative. Tawna's writing mechanics and organization were strong, but she failed to carefully follow task directions and this impacted her overall performance (CELF5 Structured Writing: 50th percentile).

Neuropsychological Implications and Diagnostic Impression

Tawna Simpson is a pleasant young woman who is struggling with multiple difficulties in her psychological and neurocognitive functioning. Her processing speed, sustained attention, and response control are areas of particular impairment. Her pattern of neurocognitive deficits, in combination with her reported persistent pattern of inattention and impulsivity that interferes with academic and social functioning, is consistent with ADHD. In addition, Tawna works exceptionally slowly on both verbal and nonverbal tasks. Although Tawna clearly wants to be successful academically, these deficits interfere with her ability to achieve this goal, and this is tremendously distressing for her. Complicating these neurocognitive deficits are her difficulties in emotional functioning, which were detailed in her recent comprehensive psychological evaluation by a clinical psychologist. Tawna's symptoms of anxiety and depression, anger control problems, and symptoms of ADHD will be considered in recommendations for treating her present emotional and neurocognitive difficulties.

Based on these findings, the following diagnoses are made:

300.00 Unspecified anxiety disorder

300.4 Persistent depressive disorder

314.01 ADHD; Combined Type

V62.3 Academic problem

Recommendations

1. It is critical that Tawna participate in **psychotherapy** to address her anxiety and depression as well as her interpersonal difficulties. A focus of therapy should also be her poor body image and low self-esteem.

2. Likewise, **psychopharmacological interventions** for both neurocognitive and psychological struggles are strongly recommended.

3. Should Tawna continue to struggle even with this additional support, the possibility of a **less demanding academic environment** might be considered. A recommendation will be made.

4. Due to her diagnosis of ADHD, Tawna should receive interventions in the school under the other health impaired category.

5. **Preferential seating** is recommended.

6. Clearly testing indicates the functional implications of Tawna's psychological and neurocognitive struggles on her academic fluency. Therefore, **extended time** on class tests and standardized testing (50%)

is essential. This includes extended time on college entrance exams.

7. Tawna's teachers should **communicate weekly with her parents via email** to alert them to upcoming assignments and due dates. They should recognize that at present Tawna does not have the executive functioning skills needed to do this independently.

8. Tawna's **grades should be updated regularly online** when she turns in assignments so that her parents are able to monitor her progress and to check for any missing assignments.

9. Tawna's parents are willing to meet with the teachers regularly to **review Tawna's tests and quizzes** so that they are able to work with her on areas of difficulty. Her teachers are encouraged to schedule these meetings.

10. **Visual aids on reading comprehension tasks** should be encouraged. For example, Tawna's teachers should allow and encourage her to highlight text as needed, to make annotations on the side, etc.

11. **Oral testing** is preferable when possible.

12. Due to impaired visual-motor coordination speed, Tawna should not be required to rely on her note-taking skills. Tawna's teachers might provide her with an **outline of the lesson,** and she could fill in the main ideas on the lesson outline. The Livescribe SmartPen will be very helpful for note taking. It is likely that she will benefit from having **instructor handouts** and **lecture outlines** available prior to the lecture for her to review. Similarly, provide Tawna with **study questions** before reading, not after. This will also allow her to focus her attention on the relevant information and aid comprehension.

13. The use of a **notebook computer** in the classroom as needed is recommended.

14. Tawna is encouraged to **check her work** to improve self-monitoring.

15. Tawna should be trained to be an **active listener and an active reader**. She should establish a purpose for reading/listening,

scan the pages of the text before reading, relate the events in the text or lecture to her current knowledge, predict future events based upon the text or lecture, summarize the main ideas, generate questions when reading, make inferences from the text or lecture, and organize ideas (perhaps graphically on paper).

16. Tawna has serious difficulty learning new information. Compared to other students her age, she may need **more repetition of material** to learn it. Care should be taken not to frustrate her by presenting too much information too quickly. She may benefit from **shorter periods of learning** and **longer breaks between periods of learning**. Tawna may benefit from having **lessons repeated** to her on different days, perhaps in condensed form, in order to ensure that this information is encoded into her memory. Tawna should be encouraged to associate new material with previously learned material and to elaborate new concepts. Her **learning assignments should be shorter** than those of her peers and she will need **more repetition** to learn the material. In addition, Tawna would likely benefit from memory training exercises designed to enhance her encoding skills. Therefore, strategies to improve her memory and learning would be helpful.

17. **Sessions** with a learning specialist are essential to improve organizational and time-management skills and to teach memory strategies.

18. **Regular exercise** is strongly recommended, and Tawna has expressed a desire to participate in cheerleading.

It has been our utmost pleasure to work with Tawna. We hope that this assessment has been helpful in terms of shedding light on her difficulties and we trust that with appropriate interventions, Tawna's difficulties will diminish. Please feel free to contact us should you have questions about this assessment. Tawna's scores appear in Tables 10.11 to 10.19.

Psychometric Summary

Table 10.11   Tawna's Wechsler Intelligence Scale for Children–Fifth Edition (WISC–V) Scores

Composite	Composite Score	Percentile Rank	Qualitative Description
Verbal Comprehension (VCI)	103	58	Average
Visual Spatial (VSI)	94	34	Average
Fluid Reasoning (FRI)	97	42	Average
Working Memory (WMI)	88	21	Low Average
Processing Speed (PSI)	72—W	3	Very Low
Full Scale (FSIQ)	95	37	Average

Ancillary Composite	Index Score	Percentile Rank	Qualitative Description
Quantitative Reasoning (QRI)	94	34	Average
Auditory Working Memory (AWMI)	84	14	Low Average
Nonverbal (NVI)	85	16	Low Average
General Ability (GAI)	100	50	Average
Cognitive Proficiency (CPI)	76—W	5	Very Low

Verbal Comprehension Subtests	Scaled Score	Percentile Rank
Similarities	10	50
Vocabulary	11	63

Visual Spatial Subtests	Scaled Score	Percentile Rank
Block Design	10	50
Visual Puzzles	8	25

(continued)

Table 10.11   (Continued)

Fluid Reasoning Subtests	Scaled Score	Percentile Rank
Matrix Reasoning	9	37
Figure Weights	10	50
(Arithmetic)	8	25

Working Memory Subtests	Scaled Score	Percentile Rank
Digit Span	10	50
Picture Span	6	9
(Letter-Number Sequencing)	4–W	2

Processing Speed Subtests	Scaled Score	Percentile Rank
Coding	5	5
Symbol Search	5	5

Table 10.12   Tawna's California Verbal Learning Test (CVLT–C) Scores

Level of Recall	Standard Score
Trial 1	−1.0
Trial 5	−1.0
Short Delay Free Recall	−2.0
Short Delay Cued Recall	−.5
Long Delay Free Recall	−2.5
Long Delay Cued Recall	−1.0

Table 10.13   Tawna's Rey Complex Figure Test and Recognition Trial (RCFT) Scores

	T Score	Percentile Rank
Immediate Recall	27	1
Delayed Recall	<20	<1
Recognition Total Correct	34	5
Copy	–	2–5
Time to Copy	–	>16

Table 10.14   Tawna's Wisconsin Card Sort Test–64: Computer Version 2 (WCST–64) Scores

WCST Scores	Standard Scores	Percentile Rank
Perseverative Errors	116	86
Nonperseverative Errors	105	63

Table 10.15   Tawna's Delis-Kaplan Executive Function System (D-KEFS) Scores

Trail Making Test	Scaled Score	Percentile Rank
Visual Scanning	5	5
Number Sequencing	5	5
Letter Sequencing	1	<1
Number-Letter Switching	4	2

Verbal Fluency Test	Scaled Score	Percentile Rank
Letter Fluency	13	84
Category Fluency	8	25
Category Switching	9	37

Color-Word Interference Test	Scaled Score	Percentile Rank
Color Naming	8	25
Word Reading	10	50
Inhibition	8	25
Inhibition/Switching	8	25

Tower Test	Scaled Score	Percentile Rank
Total Achievement Score	12	75

Table 10.16   Tawna's A Developmental Neuropsychological Assessment–Second Edition (NEPSY–II) Scores

Attention and Executive Functioning	Scaled Score	Percentile Rank
Auditory Attention	6	9
Response Set	3	1

Table 10.16   *(Continued)*

Language	Scaled Score	Percentile Rank
Comprehension of Instruction	11	63

Memory	Scaled Score	Percentile Rank
Narrative Memory Free Recall	8	25
Narrative Memory Free/Cued	9	37
Memory for Designs	2	<1
Memory for Designs-Delayed	4	2

Table 10.17   Tawna's Wechsler Individual Achievement Test–Third Edition (WIAT–III) Scores

Subtests	Standard Score	Percentile Rank
Listening Comprehension	107	68
Math Problem Solving	102	55
Numerical Operations	95	37
Spelling	112	79
Math Fluency—Addition	83	13
Math Fluency—Subtraction	81	10
Math Fluency—Multiplication	75	5

Table 10.18   Tawna's Gray Oral Reading Test–Fifth Edition (GORT–5) Scores

	Scaled Score	Percentile Rank
Rate	9	37
Accuracy	14	91
Fluency	11	63
Comprehension	8	25

Table 10.19   Tawna's Clinical Evaluation of Language Fundamentals–Fifth Edition (CELF5) Scores

Supplementary Scores	Scaled Score	Percentile Rank
Structured Writing	10	50

CASE 6—TOM, AGE 8 (DIGITAL ADMINISTRATION): EVALUATION OF A TWICE EXCEPTIONAL CHILD: GIFTED WITH DYSLEXIA AND SYMPTOMS OF INATTENTION AND SOCIAL-BEHAVIORAL ISSUES

Kristina Breaux

Psychoeducational Report

Student's Name: Tom Rice

Date of Birth: 12/9/06

Grade level: 2

Age at Testing: 8 years 0 months

Dates of Testing: 12/31/14, 1/1/15, 1/5/15

Evaluated by: Kristina Breaux, PhD

Reason for Referral

Mr. and Mrs. Rice requested this evaluation to determine if a learning disability may be contributing to Tom's difficulties with reading and to obtain specific suggestions for helping him learn. Tom's teacher, Mrs. Sanchez, reported that Tom has difficulty sustaining attention in class and getting along with peers. Thus, a secondary purpose of this evaluation was to rule in/out the possibility of attention/deficit-hyperactivity disorder (ADHD) or a related condition and to provide suggestions for improving attention and social-behavioral skills.

History and Background Information

Mr. and Mrs. Rice provided information about family life, family history, birth and developmental history, and educational history. Tom's teacher, Mrs. Sanchez, provided information about Tom's current performance at school.

Family Life

Tom is an 8-year-old boy who lives with his younger brother, Charles (age 5), and his parents.

His father, Gordon Rice, is an accomplished artist with a master's degree who works as a college professor. His mother, Pamela Rice, has a master's degree and works in a research position at a university. Charles has not experienced any learning difficulties, although he has had some behavioral issues at school. Charles and Tom enjoy a close relationship. Tom typically sleeps from 8:30 p.m. to 6:30 a.m.; no sleeping difficulties were reported.

Tom enjoys drawing, storytelling, and playing video games. He's interested in mythical creatures such as dragons. Tom's parents describe him as creative, intensely curious, and excitable as well as emotionally and physically sensitive. At home, Tom is typically focused for long periods of time on an activity of his choosing, such as drawing. Tom has a strong desire to be in control of activities and social situations. For example, Tom frequently refuses to allow Charles to insert an idea into a game they are playing. He acts out when that control is challenged, sometimes becoming physically aggressive with his brother or playmates. During difficult homework tasks, Tom occasionally acts out by screaming and crying. Tom cries more than most kids his age, according to his parents. Mr. and Mrs. Rice use logical consequences and time away to discipline their children.

Academically, Mr. and Mrs. Rice reported that Tom has made progress in reading, but it's still not clicking for him. He has completed summer and weekend reading workshops with a reading specialist, and Tom's parents read with him for 20 minutes every night. He reads well some nights, but other nights he can barely read at all. Tom's parents worry that his self-concept has begun to be affected by his academic struggles. Tom has made comments about girls being smarter than boys and about his younger brother thinking he is smarter than Tom. Tom often refuses to attempt something unless he knows he can succeed at it. Socially, he is struggling to develop friendships and interact with peers. As a toddler and preschooler, Tom had many friends, but he has not made any new friends since kindergarten. In the long term, Tom's parents hope he'll go to college one day, find a career that he's passionate about, and become a well-rounded, interesting adult.

Family History

Mr. and Mrs. Rice come from academically oriented and accomplished families, although some family members experienced speech and learning difficulties. Tom's mother reported having difficulty learning to read as a child, and she has always struggled with spelling. Her brother was a late talker. Tom's father reported that he had difficulty articulating the /r/ sound until eighth grade and may also have had some attention difficulties. Mr. Rice's sister also had difficulty articulating the /r/ sound, and his uncle was a late talker. Additionally, Mrs. Rice reported a history of depression and anxiety within her immediate family.

Birth and Developmental History

Mrs. Rice's pregnancy with Tom was full term with no complications. She labored in the hospital for roughly 20 hours. She was given Pitosin and an epidural. Tom was delivered naturally with the aid of vacuum extraction. He was born in good condition. Tom had few ear infections, but he was a challenging baby with a sensitive tummy. While breastfeeding, Mrs. Rice had to eliminate many foods from her diet, yet Tom's digestive issues and night waking continued until he weaned. This family follows "attachment parenting" practices. The entire family coslept in the same bed until just recently. Mom breastfed both kids until they were almost 3 years old.

Tom demonstrated some atypical behavior as an infant, such as avoiding eye contact; Mrs. Rice's mother commented at the time that "he looks at things, but not people." This behavior has persisted; Tom continues to be uncomfortable sustaining eye contact with people. As an infant, Tom didn't mimic behaviors or interact with toys the way most children do. He wasn't interested in sounds as expected. Concerns eventually led to a hearing test at 19 months, which returned normal results.

Tom's speech and language skills were slow to develop. Tom preferred using baby sign language to communicate. At 17 months, his speech was difficult to understand. He was using 4 words and 21 signs. At 19 months, he was evaluated by a speech and language pathologist who reported that Tom's comprehension and vocabulary skills were good. Around the age of 3 or 4, Tom began stuttering. He would get stuck on a word and become very frustrated. The stuttering lasted a month or so and then went away. It has recurred for brief periods.

Early gross motor milestones were met as expected; however, Tom's gross motor coordination was reported as an area of concern by Tom's parents and teacher. Tom has not learned to jump rope or ride a bike. Balancing is difficult and uncomfortable for him, and his movements are often uncoordinated.

Tom displayed tactile and oral sensitivities until the age of 5. Tactile irritants included certain fabrics, seams and tags in his clothing, and the feeling of walking barefoot in the grass. He was also a picky eater, avoiding foods based on color or texture. Tom has always been very sensitive to pain.

Tom is in good physical health; he's had no serious injuries or surgeries. He takes Zyrtec most days for seasonal allergies but takes no other medications.

Education

Prior to age 3, Tom stayed home with his father while his mother worked. At ages 3 and 4, Tom attended preschool 2 to 3 days a week. During this time, he began protesting and having tantrums when he was dropped off each morning. His parents used a sticker chart with rewards to modify this behavior. For kindergarten, Tom had a good experience attending public school. He got along well with his teacher, and his best friend was in his class. He learned all his letters and sounds by the end of the year, including about 30 sight words, and displayed no behavior issues at school.

For first grade, Tom transitioned to a different teacher and was no longer in class with his best friend. He didn't get along well with his new teacher. The teacher reported that Tom was not paying attention. He sometimes rolled around on the floor under his desk. His grades were good (As and Bs), but he wasn't making progress in reading. Tom tested into Tier 1 reading instruction. He had difficulty blending sounds. Spelling was also difficult. Even though he could spell some words in isolation, he misspelled them when writing in context. At this time, Tom's parents began seeing social problems. He said he didn't know how to make friends. He began chewing on his shirt sleeves at school. In January of first grade, Tom's parents moved him to a private school to take advantage of smaller class sizes and more attention from teachers. His teacher tutored him three times a week for a month in reading. Tom also began seeing a reading specialist one Sunday per month for 3 hours of phonics instruction using an Orton-Gillingham approach that was explicit, systematic, and multisensory. He continued this program for 2 weeks in the summer and made good progress.

Tom currently attends second grade in a class of nine students. His teacher, Mrs. Sanchez, expressed deep concern for him because of severe attentional and behavioral issues at school. She said Tom has roughly two to four good days a month where he gets his work done in class and does not have a behavioral incident with his peers. Most days he has difficulty paying attention and staying on task. For much of the day, he "zones out" and seems to be in his own world. Mrs. Sanchez expects Tom to complete several tasks each morning when he arrives, which takes most students between 10 to 20 minutes. Afterward, the students are rewarded with a computer game or reading activity on the iPad, which Tom enjoys. Tom often takes 40 minutes or more (with prompting) to complete his work because he's off task.

Mrs. Sanchez explained that Tom has difficulty with peer interactions during transition times or on the playground. Tom does not respect the personal space of others and tends to annoy his peers. Tom insists on being in control and playing on his terms. If his peers challenge him or he feels misunderstood, he sometimes responds with physical aggression. For example, on one occasion, Tom spit in a boy's face; on another occasion, he held a boy down on the playground. During an aggressive incident, Tom typically smiles and acts like it's funny. Afterward, he is remorseful, though he sometimes lies about what happened. A parent of one of Tom's classmates has labeled Tom a bully and does not want his son interacting with Tom.

Academically, Mrs. Sanchez reported that Tom is about half a grade level behind in reading and spelling. Learning phonics rules has been challenging for him. Tom can often sound out words if he stays with it, but he's quick to give up on a task that he perceives to be difficult. When asked about Tom's strengths, Mrs. Sanchez listed reasoning skills, receptive and expressive language abilities, creative storytelling, and mathematics.

Vision and Hearing Screenings

Tom's mother reported normal results from annual vision and hearing screenings. No visual or hearing problems were observed during testing.

Test Behaviors and Observations

Tom was tested over three 2.5-hour testing sessions. He arrived for each session comfortably dressed and in a talkative mood. His vivid imagination was immediately apparent. When he arrived the first day, he said he was pretending that he was coming to a prison. When he arrived the second day, he said he was pretending to be a dog, and he was wearing a soccer medal as his leash. When asked what kind of dog he was, he described a small mixed breed in great detail. When he arrived for the third session, he was eager to talk about a movie he had watched earlier that day. He talked about the movie several times during our time together. Tom made eye contact intermittently and demonstrated an appropriate range of affect during conversation. His speech was sometimes difficult to understand. When asked about his strengths, Tom said he's good at drawing, telling stories, and creating things. When asked about the things that are hard for him, he mentioned reading.

Most tests were administered with two iPads, one for Tom and one for the examiner. Tom was excited about using an iPad for testing and seeing the visual feedback from his touch responses, although he commented that testing with an iPad didn't allow him to see how much of the test he had completed and how much was remaining.

Tom was cooperative for short periods of time (approximately 10 to 15 minutes). He had difficulty sustaining effort and focus, requesting frequent breaks for snacks, water, and the restroom. Tom was given prompts to redirect him to the task at hand and encouragement to persevere on difficult tasks. Tom was motivated to put forth his best effort because his parents promised him a cash reward for his cooperation during the testing. Tom followed verbal instructions without difficulty when he listened to them, but he usually tried to begin the tasks before the instructions were finished. On some tasks, he needed correction on the teaching items because he hadn't followed the instructions. When he was unsure of an answer, he typically did not want to take a guess. Although Tom had difficulty sustaining motivation and attention during testing, he exhibited an appropriate level of effort and was given a number of supports to encourage his best effort. Thus, the results reported here are believed to be a good estimate of Tom's current skill and ability levels.

Assessment Instruments

Behavior Assessment System for Children, Second Edition (BASC–2)

Kaufman Test of Educational Achievement, Third Edition (KTEA–3)

Wechsler Intelligence Scale for Children, Fifth Edition (WISC–V)

Wechsler Individual Achievement Test, Third Edition (WIAT–III)

The KTEA–3, WISC–V, and WIAT–III were administered on Q-interactive with touch tablets (iPads).

Test Results and Clinical Impressions

A summary of scores and test descriptions are provided in the Score Summary at the end of this report.

Intellectual Functioning

Tom's overall cognitive functioning is very high. Tom's scores on the FSIQ and General Ability Index are at the 91st and 97th percentiles, respectively. The General Ability Index does not include the working memory or processing speed subtests, so it provides a measure of cognitive ability that minimizes the impact of working memory and processing speed. Tom's General Ability Index is 8 points higher than his FSIQ, which is a statistically significantly and unusual difference, occurring in less than or equal to 5% of the normative sample. This suggests that reducing the influence of working memory and processing speed results in a significant improvement in his overall performance.

The scatter in Tom's WISC–V profile was dramatic. The range of 60 points in his five indexes (from 72 in Working Memory to 132 in Visual Spatial) is huge; discrepancies that large occurred less than 1% of the time among normal children and adolescents. Similarly, he displayed a huge amount of scatter on the subtests. He had 5 significant discrepancies (relative strengths + relative weaknesses among the 10 primary WISC–V subtests; less than 10% of the WISC–V normative sample had 5 or more significant discrepancies). His range of scaled scores from a low of 4 on Picture Span to a high of 19 on Similarities (15 points) occurs less than 1% of the time in normal children. (See Chapter 7 for a discussion of

WISC–V scatter at the index level and the subtest level).

Tom showed significant strengths in the areas of verbal comprehension and visual spatial skills. To assess Tom's verbal comprehension, he was asked to describe how two concepts are similar (Similarities) and to provide oral definitions of concepts (Vocabulary). Tom's extremely high score on Similarities was equal to or higher than 99.9% of children his age. A high score on Similarities also suggests a strength in abstract reasoning, cognitive flexibility, and associative and categorical thinking. Tom's score on Vocabulary was high average (75th percentile). Tom has a strong oral vocabulary, but some of his definitions did not conform to traditional definitions or include the most pertinent characteristics. Tom's score on Similarities was 7 points higher than his score on Vocabulary, which is a statistically significant and unusual difference, occurring in less than or equal to 0.5% of the normative sample. This pattern of performance suggests a strength in abstract reasoning and cognitive flexibility relative to lexical knowledge.

Tom demonstrated extremely high performance on measures of visual-spatial skills, performing as well as or better than 98% of children his age. Tom loved the Block Design subtest because he said he enjoys building and creating things. Tom did not work particularly fast or slow. He did not receive any time bonuses, but he successfully constructed all but one design (the most difficult one) within the allotted time. He scored slightly higher on Block Design (99th percentile) than Visual Puzzles (91st percentile). His performance suggests very advanced visuospatial processing skills with relatively greater preference and skill on tasks involving concrete visual feedback, trial-and-error problem solving, and visual-motor integration.

In the area of fluid reasoning, Tom's performance was mixed. Tom scored in the average range (63rd percentile) on Matrix Reasoning. His highest score (84th percentile) in this area was on Figure Weights, which measures quantitative fluid reasoning and inductive logic with relatively

low working memory demands. His lowest score (5th percentile) was Arithmetic, which requires mentally solving arithmetic problems within a time limit. The first half of the Arithmetic problems can be read only one time, whereas the second half may be repeated once. Sometimes Tom would repeat back the problem he heard and solve that problem correctly, but he had misremembered the problem. On some items, he appeared to be daydreaming while the problem was read to him, so he didn't remember any of it. His score on Arithmetic was 8 points lower than his score on Figure Weights, which is a statistically significant and unusual difference, occurring in less than or equal to 0.2% of the normative sample. This pattern of performance suggests that Tom can best express quantitative reasoning ability when a visual rather than verbal stimulus and response format is used and when auditory working memory demands are reduced.

Significant normative weaknesses were identified in the area of working memory, including measures of auditory working memory and visual working memory. On measures of auditory working memory, he scored somewhat higher on simpler tasks that required no manipulation of information (Digit Span Forward, 25th percentile) compared to tasks with increased complexity (Digit Span Backward, Digit Span Sequencing, Letter–Number Sequencing, scores ranging from 2nd to 16th percentiles). Tom's lowest subtest score (2nd percentile) on the WISC–V was on Picture Span, a measure of visual working memory. Picture Span requires memory for objects in a sequence and uses proactive interference by presenting the target objects in a random array with other objects. During this task, Tom did not subvocalize or appear to use a verbal mediation strategy. These results suggest significant weaknesses in both auditory and visual working memory.

Tom's overall processing speed ability was estimated in the average range (45th percentile). To assess processing speed, Tom was asked to use a key to copy symbols that correspond to numbers (Coding) and to scan search groups and indicate whether target symbols are present in each group (Symbol Search). His score on Coding (63rd percentile) was somewhat higher than his score on Symbol Search (25th percentile), but this difference was not statistically significant. These results suggest an age-appropriate ability to rapidly identify visual information, make quick and accurate decisions, and rapidly implement those decisions.

Tom's scores on the Verbal Comprehension, Visual Spatial, and Fluid Reasoning Indexes were significantly higher than his scores on the Working Memory and Processing Speed Indexes. This pattern of performance suggests a high capacity for complex problem solving despite relatively lower working memory and processing speed abilities.

Tom's General Ability Index score is 47 points higher than his Cognitive Proficiency Index score, which is a statistically significant and unusual difference, occurring in less than or equal to 2.4% of the normative sample. This discrepancy suggests that higher-order cognitive abilities, such as verbal comprehension, visual-spatial processing, and fluid reasoning, are strengths compared to abilities that support cognitive processing efficiency, such as working memory and processing speed. A large Cognitive Proficiency Index < General Ability Index discrepancy is a significant predictor of a specific learning disability in reading and has also been reported among children with ADHD–inattentive type.

Tom scored in the average range (37th percentile) on the Symbol Translation Index and each of the Symbol Translation subtests. These scores indicate an age-appropriate ability to encode and retrieve newly learned visual-verbal associations after short and long delays. Hence, visual-verbal associative memory does not seem to be a primary weakness that is contributing to Tom's learning difficulties.

Tom's Storage and Retrieval Index score (as well as his scores on the Naming Speed Index and Symbol Translation Index) is in the average range, suggesting an age-appropriate capacity for new learning and rapid access to existing verbal knowledge stores. Hence, long-term storage and retrieval does not seem to be a primary weakness that is contributing to Tom's learning difficulties.

The Naming Speed Index is discussed in the "Rapid Automatic Naming" section of this report.

Implications

Tom is an intellectually gifted child. He exhibited particular strengths with abstract verbal reasoning problems (making connections between concepts) and hands-on visual-spatial problem solving. He has strong fluid reasoning skills and age-appropriate processing speed abilities.

Tom exhibits significant working memory impairment, which can be difficult to differentiate from attention problems on the basis on informal interactions. Children with poor working memory tend to have atypically high ratings of attention problems, including short attention span, high distractibility, problems in self-monitoring the quality of their work, forgetting things previously learned, lacking interest in school, and paying attention only to things that are of interest. Children with poor working memory often appear to be lacking motivation, spacing out, or daydreaming.

Socioemotional Functioning

Tom's socioemotional functioning was assessed using the BASC–2. Tom's mother, father, and teacher completed a survey by responding to True/False statements and rating the frequency of Tom's behavior and feelings. Tom also completed a self-report questionnaire with assistance. All items were read aloud to him and clarified or reworded as needed.

Tom's self-report suggested strong self-esteem. He endorsed statements indicating that he feels good about himself, likes who he is, and doesn't want to be different. He provided At Risk ratings for *School-Related Problems*, including

Attitude toward Teacher and *Attitude toward School*. He acknowledged interpersonal difficulties by endorsing statements such as "Other children hate to be with me" (sometimes), "My classmates make fun of me" (sometimes), and "I feel that nobody likes me" (sometimes). Regarding school, he endorsed statements such as "I hate school" (sometimes), "I can't wait for school to be over" (true), and "School is boring" (almost always). However, not all statements were negative; he endorsed "My school feels good to me" (sometimes). Regarding his teacher, he endorsed statements such as "Teachers are unfair" (sometimes), "My teacher understands me" (false), and "My teachers make me feel stupid" (sometimes). He also endorsed positive statements about his teacher, such as "My teacher trusts me" (sometimes) and "My teacher is proud of me" (sometimes). When asked directly, Tom reported liking his teacher, but he expressed frustration with the work and the demands placed on him.

Tom's mother, father, and teacher provided consistent At Risk ratings for the following domains: *Behavioral Symptoms*, *Adaptive Skills*, and *Functional Impairment*. On the Clinical Scales, consistent At Risk ratings were reported for *Aggression*, *Atypicality*, *Withdrawal*, and two out of three raters provided At Risk ratings for *Conduct Problems* as well as Clinically Significant ratings for *Depression*. On the Adaptive Scales, consistent At Risk ratings were reported for *Social Skills*, and two out of three raters provided At Risk ratings for *Adaptability* and *Functional Communication*. Both parents reported At Risk ratings for *Activities of Daily Living*. On the Content Scales, ratings for *Developmental Social Disorders* were At Risk according to both parents and Clinically Significant according to the teacher, consistent At Risk ratings were provided for *Executive Functions*, and two out of three raters provided At Risk ratings for *Bullying*, *Negative Emotionality*, and *Resiliency*.

Implications

Tom is at risk for impaired functioning and maladjustment due to his difficulties with emotional expression and control and with social, communication, and daily living skills. Tom does not report symptoms of depression, although he has made comments at school and home that are indicative of depression and suggest that he has begun questioning his intelligence and academic aptitude.

Tom exhibits poor working memory on the WISC–V, which can cause symptoms of inattention that closely resemble, but do not preclude a diagnosis of, ADHD. Children with poor working memory without ADHD differ from children with ADHD in the following ways. Children with poor working memory (1) do not typically have the social problems that are more characteristic of ADHD, and (2) usually score in the normal range on systematic assessments for attentional deficits or show problems only related to inattention (not hyperactivity or impulsivity). Tom's BASC–2 results indicated difficulties with social skills as well as some impulsive symptoms at home and at school. A moderately high number of disruptive, impulsive, and uncontrolled behaviors were reported, including interrupting others during conversation, disrupting others, aggression toward peers, and difficulty with self-control.

The Teacher, Parent, and Self-Report profiles for Tom appear most similar to that of children with ADHD. Mr. and Mrs. Rice reported that inattention does not typically interfere with his functioning at home unless he is doing homework. At home, Tom focuses on activities of his choosing for long periods of time, such as creating a storybook or drawing. However, signs of ADHD may be minimal or absent when the individual is involved in activities of interest. As shown on the BASC–2, Tom exhibits some behaviors that are characteristic of emotional-behavioral disturbance (EBD), such as easily losing his temper and becoming upset and acting aggressively toward his peers. These behaviors have been described for children with ADHD, particularly children who are intellectually gifted with ADHD. Tom also exhibits some behaviors that are characteristic of autism spectrum disorder (ASD), such as avoiding eye contact, difficulty with social skills, and odd behaviors, such as seeming out of touch with reality, acting strangely, and saying things that don't make sense. Social difficulties and atypicality have also been described for some children with ADHD.

Gross Motor Skills

Tom meets diagnostic criteria for developmental coordination disorder, or motor dyspraxia. Based on the information reported by Tom's parents and teacher, Tom's gross motor skills are substantially below what is expected for his age. Specifically, Tom has not learned to jump rope or ride a bike, he has trouble balancing, and his movements are uncoordinated when he runs or tries to do jumping jacks. Tom's parents reported that he tends to lean his body on walls or tables and seems weak in his upper body. In addition, Tom exhibits poor visuo-spatial memory (see WISC–V results), which is the trademark memory deficit of children with developmental coordination disorder. Half of all children with ADHD also have developmental coordination disorder.

Rapid Automatic Naming

Rapid automatic naming (RAN) tends to correlate with reading ability. RAN performance also relies on continuous responding and sustained attention to stimuli in order to perform well. To assess Tom's rapid automatic naming ability, he was given three tests that involve rapidly naming stimuli, including objects, letters, numbers, and quantities (WISC–V Naming Speed Literacy and Naming Speed Quantity; KTEA–3 Letter Naming Facility). Tom performed in the lower half of the average range (27th to 47th percentiles) on these measures. On the WISC–V letter-number naming task, Tom made two errors because he said *yellow* for Y, suggesting some interference of the color stimuli from the prior task. Two errors is considered unusual, occurring

in less than or equal to 10% of the normative sample.

Tom's naming speed ability is adequate for his age, but he exhibited some difficulty with tasks that involve switching between categories of elements (such as letters and digits) as opposed to naming only letters, and he exhibited some cross-task interference, both of which suggest difficulties with executive control of attention and working memory.

Phonological Processing

Phonological processing ability, the ability to recognize and manipulate the phonological components of spoken language, is the most powerful predictor of reading performance. Tom's performance on a measure of phonological processing was at the low end of the average range (25th percentile). His performance across the subtest was mixed. He demonstrated a strength in blending, listening to words spoken one syllable or phoneme at a time and then saying the word altogether. His performance was average in the areas of rhyming, sound matching, and segmenting. Tom's weakest performance was on a task that required him to delete a phoneme from a word (e.g., say plane, but don't say /l/ − pane).

Implications
Tom's blending skills are strong, suggesting that when individual phonemes are provided to him, he's able to blend phonemes together to form a word. He also showed age-appropriate segmentation skills. Thus, Tom's ability to analyze and synthesize the sounds within words is adequate. However, he has difficulty with the more complex phonological processing tasks, which place heavy demands on phonological processing and auditory working memory. A weakness in complex phonological processing may contribute to his difficulties in reading and spelling.

Oral Language

Tom's oral receptive language skills were assessed with a Listening Comprehension subtest, which includes measures of Receptive Vocabulary and Oral Discourse Comprehension. Tom's performance suggested high average (82nd percentile) receptive language skills. Tom scored in the high average range on Receptive Vocabulary and in the average range on Oral Discourse Comprehension. On the Oral Discourse Comprehension subtest, Tom was asked to listen to recordings of stories and passages of increasing length, and then answer open-ended questions about them. This subtest was individually administered in a quiet room, with prompts before each item to make sure Tom was attentive and ready to listen. Thus, Tom's performance reflects his listening skills under optimal circumstances.

Tom's oral expression skills were not formally assessed as part of this evaluation due to time limitations and reports of strong expressive language skills from his parents and teacher. However, an informal oral language sample was recorded and analyzed. He demonstrated age-appropriate grammar and vocabulary, but his speech was sometimes difficult to understand. Some difficulty with articulation was observed. Specifically, Tom tends to confuse /v/ and /th/ when speaking, reading, and spelling. For example, he said "each uver" for *each other*, he spelled *of* "uth" and *very* "thare." According to Tom's mother, Tom used to confuse /y/ and /l/ when speaking, and sometimes he has difficulty perceiving the difference between /f/, /v/, and /th/.

Implications

Tom's vocabulary is well developed for his age, and his listening comprehension skills are age-appropriate when he is focused and attentive to the information. Given Tom's difficulty sustaining attention in academic settings, listening comprehension is expected to be challenging under less ideal circumstances. Tom's listening difficulties are primarily attributed to inattention and poor working memory rather than a language comprehension deficit. Tom also exhibits difficulty with articulation and phonemic discrimination that is affecting his reading and spelling development.

Reading

Tom's basic reading skills were estimated to be in the low-average range. On a measure of single word reading, Tom scored at the 9th percentile. The number of words he read correctly was the same as the average number of words read correctly in early grade 1. On a measure of pseudoword decoding, Tom scored at the 14th percentile. On both the word reading and pseudoword reading tests, Tom painstakingly sounded out words letter by letter. On most words, he needed to be prompted to "say it all together." With prompting, Tom correctly blended together many of the words that were phonetically regular. Tom had particular difficulty decoding words with irregular, or unpredictable, patterns, which rely more heavily on orthographic memory. In addition, his errors indicated a normative weakness in reading vowel teams/diphthongs, silent letters, and prefixes and suffixes. On one such item, Tom said, "I can't remember the sound *oa* makes." He read VCE (silent-e) words correctly some of the time but was inconsistent in applying his knowledge of this rule.

On a measure of Reading Comprehension, Tom scored at the 9th percentile. He missed both literal and inferential comprehension questions. Given that Tom's demonstrated listening comprehension skills are in the average range (68th percentile), his weakness in reading comprehension is primarily attributed to poor basic reading skills.

To assess reading fluency, Tom was given a test of timed single word reading, silent reading fluency, and oral reading fluency. His performance on Word Recognition Fluency was at the 9th percentile, consistent with his performance on a test of untimed word reading. Tom's performance on measures of Silent Reading Fluency and Oral Reading Fluency were similarly low (8th and 9th percentiles, respectively). Tom's Oral Reading Fluency score was based on grade 1 passages because the grade 2 passages were too difficult for him (although his performance on grade 1 passages was still compared to that of same-age peers). Tom read word by word. He did not chunk words or phrases together, nor did he read with appropriate prosody.

Implications

Tom's reading skills are in the very low to low-average range. These results are consistent with Mrs. Sanchez's report that he is reading at about a first-grade level. Weaknesses in word recognition, decoding, and fluency are interfering with Tom's comprehension of text. Tom attempts to sound out words and apply the phonics rules he's been taught, but he does not always remember or apply those rules consistently. Tom has particular difficulty reading words with irregular letter-sound correspondence and recognizing morphemes (root words, prefixes, suffixes).

Visual–Motor Integration and Graphomotor Skills

On a measure of Writing Fluency, Tom wrote 33 words in 5 minutes and scored in the low-average range (12th percentile). On a measure of Alphabet Writing Fluency, Tom wrote 11 letters in 30 seconds and scored in the average range (32nd percentile).

Tom wrote with his right hand using an adaptive tripod pencil grasp. Tom used his finger at times to ensure adequate spacing between words. He used incorrect letter formation for certain letters, including lowercase d, b, p, and q; however, his handwriting was legible. Tom's visual-motor integration skills were within the average range when he was assessed at age 4 with the Beery-Buktenica Developmental Test of Visual-Motor Integration. Tom's drawing skills are similar to those of his peers.

These test results and observations suggest adequate visual-motor integration skills; however, his writing speed is slow when spelling and sentence formulation is required.

Spelling and Written Expression

On a measure of Spelling, Tom scored in the low-average range (10th percentile). Tom's spelling errors included some letter reversal errors (b/d, p/q). Errors due to phonemic discrimination included "uth" for *of* and "thare" for *very*. Tom's misspellings are mostly phonetically acceptable ("wut" for *what*; "hom" for *home*). He did not know when he had spelled a word incorrectly. Tom was given an informal assessment requiring him to circle the correct spelling of a word among three choices, using his misspellings as distractors. He could not identify the correct spelling of the words he missed.

Tom scored in the average range on a measure of written expression that involved (a) writing a sentence using a target word, and (b) combining two to three sentences into one complete sentence. On most items, he wrote complete sentences and showed appropriate use of capitalization and punctuation. He sometimes omitted a word from his sentence, or omitted a letter from a word when copying (wo for *won*; fas for *fast*), suggesting difficulties with attention, working memory, and/or self-monitoring for errors.

Implications

Tom's spelling errors indicate a reliance on a phonologically based strategy for spelling. He has difficulty recognizing correct and incorrect spellings, suggesting poor orthographic memory. His spelling includes frequent letter reversals. Tom's written expression skills are about average compared to his peers; his errors include letter and word omissions, which are likely due to weaknesses in executive control of attention and working memory.

Mathematics

Tom's overall mathematics skills are in the low-average range. Tom's math computation skills are bordering between the low-average to average range (19th and 25th percentiles compared to age-matched and grade-matched peers, respectively). Tom's procedural skills for addition and subtraction are adequate; however, his mistakes involve failing to attend to the operation sign or self-monitor for simple errors. On a test of math problem solving, Tom scored in the low-average range (12th and 18th percentile as compared to age-matched and grade-matched peers, respectively). Tom had difficulty interpreting graphs, number lines, calendars, and analog clocks and attending to/remembering the details of word problems (which were printed and read aloud to him).

Implications

Tom's knowledge of math facts and computation procedures are about average compared to his peers; however, he has difficulty self-monitoring for errors. Tom's practical math problem-solving skills are an area of weakness, yet Tom's demonstrated above-average quantitative reasoning abilities on the WISC–V when auditory working memory is not required. These results suggest that working memory and executive control of attention are interfering with his performance in math.

Summary of Findings and Analyses for the Identification of a Specific Learning Disorder

Tom has extremely high general cognitive ability, and he has received high-quality literacy instruction, yet he experiences significant reading and spelling difficulties. His visual-spatial abilities are extremely high, yet he exhibits a significant processing weakness in auditory and visual working memory. Tom has difficulty with more complex phonological processing tasks, yet his blending, rhyming, and segmentation skills are average or above. Despite his weaknesses in auditory working memory, Tom exhibited strong phonological blending skills and strong listening comprehension skills. These results suggest that Tom's strengths in vocabulary and verbal comprehension and reasoning may strengthen his performance on auditory verbal tasks.

Tom tends to rely on a phonological strategy for reading and spelling. His orthographic memory is poor. His primary academic weakness in basic reading/decoding is consistent with his working memory weakness and significantly discrepant from his processing strength. Tom's reading speed and accuracy is similar when reading words in isolation and in the context of a passage. Thus, he does not rely on contextual language comprehension to facilitate word recognition.

Tom demonstrates weaknesses in mathematics, despite average to above-average quantitative reasoning skills. Difficulties with attention and self-monitoring are likely contributing to errors in math computation and applications including word problems. Specific skill deficits were observed in visual-spatial aspects of math problem solving, including interpreting graphs, number lines, and clocks. Tom has exceptional visual-spatial reasoning skills but may require more explicit, systematic instruction in these areas.

Based on Tom's strengths and weaknesses across socioemotional, cognitive, language, and achievement domains and the information from his history and background, a diagnosis of specific learning disorder in reading, spelling, and mathematics is well supported. Tom's reading and spelling difficulties most closely resemble a mixed phonological-orthographic dyslexia, with particular deficits in orthographic and morphological awareness. Diagnoses of ADHD and developmental coordination disorder are also well supported.

Diagnoses

- Specific learning disorder with impairments in reading (word reading accuracy, reading fluency, and comprehension), written expression (spelling accuracy), and mathematics (accurate calculation, accurate math reasoning). *DSM–5* 315.00, 315.2, 315.1
- Attention/deficit-hyperactivity disorder (ADHD), Combined presentation, Severe. *DSM–5* 314.01

- Developmental coordination disorder. *DSM-5* 315.4

Treatment options for ADHD may be discussed in greater detail with a developmental-behavioral pediatrician or a child psychologist or psychiatrist.

Consultation with an occupational therapist to provide recommendations for motor skills therapy is recommended.

Recommendations

Tom has many helpful supports in place already. He has parents who are supportive, nurturing, and highly involved in his education, and he receives high-quality instruction both at school and through a reading enrichment program. Consider the following recommendations as part of a collaborative discussion with those who are involved in Tom's education.

Social/Emotional/Behavioral

- Increase praise, approval, and appreciation of good behavior. Deliver short praises throughout the day. Aim to keep the reward to punishment ratio at 2:1 or greater.
- Positives before negatives. Consider establishing a reward program before implementing a discipline program. Deliver rewards and punishments as swiftly as possible after a target behavior.
- Think aloud, think ahead. Before beginning an activity or situation where Tom tends to exhibit undesirable behavior, ask Tom to recite the rules as well as any consequences or rewards, relevant to the upcoming activity. This level of preparation is especially important before transition periods.
- Provide external/visible reminders of rules and instructions.
- Consider a response-cost system whereby all reinforcements (points/tokens) are given at the beginning of the day, for example, with the goal of ending the day with a minimum

number to earn a reward. Inappropriate behavior results in the loss of a point/token. To maintain effectiveness, the specific reward must continually change or rotate to avoid habituation. Keep a daily record of points/tokens with a tally of each negative behavior that is targeted for modification.

- Small group training, with additional support at home and school, is recommended to help Tom learn and practice social skills with his peers. Incorporating the steps of problem solving (identification of problem, thinking of solutions, foreseeing consequences, action/resolution) may help reduce aggression and impulsivity. Another important skill for Tom to practice is incorporating more social graces, or niceties, with peers, including greetings, compliments, offering to help, recognizing the feelings of others, and apologies.

Attention and Working Memory

Tom has difficulty clearing working memory of information that is no longer relevant to the task at hand. At times, he may not have sufficient working memory capacity because he continues to think about other things without redirecting his attention. Clearing working memory and redirecting attention takes time before beginning a new activity. The goal, of course, is not to stifle his creative thought life but to encourage it at more appropriate times.

- Tom has a consistent bedtime and wake time throughout the week, which is important for establishing appropriate sleep-wake cycles. Maintaining this routine is very important.
- Physical activity can be helpful for fueling the brain and promoting a more alert state of mind by oxygenating the body. Consider encouraging Tom to walk before school or during recess, for example. Encourage proper breathing techniques and good posture at school and during homework times.
- Tom has difficulty intentionally suppressing intrusive thoughts, which contributes to poor

working memory but also fosters exceptional creativity and problem-solving abilities. Tom will need help developing strategies that help him focus in the classroom; however, providing him with many opportunities to exploit and celebrate his creative mind will be equally important for his intellectual development and self-esteem. Incorporate hands-on projects, especially constructing things in a three-dimensional space. Encourage opportunities to solve a problem creatively, applying the concepts he's learned in class.

- While doing homework, experiment with music or white noise to see if Tom's attention improves with auditory stimulation.
- To avoid distractibility or habituation to a task ("tuning out"), vary the nature and length of instructional activities to continually redirect Tom to new tasks. Require active participation and interaction with others during learning activities whenever possible.
- Telling Tom to pay attention or stay on task is probably not helpful for improving his attention, and it also promotes a dependence on others. Providing cues to signal off-task behavior is preferable for improving his self-awareness. Place a reminder card on his desk with a cue to pay attention (Tom may help choose an appropriate word/phrase or picture). Try using nonverbal cues, such as tapping a finger on the reminder card on his desk. If Tom does not notice or respond well to a nonverbal cue, consider simply asking him, "What are you supposed to be doing right now?" Praise a correct response.
- Divide work into smaller components that increase the likelihood of successful completion and help Tom establish a productive pace.
- Record the strategies being used at home and at school, and track progress daily. Tom's teacher might rate his level of attention each day using her own rating system and document which strategies are being implemented at school. Consider also asking Tom to use a rating system that allows him to reflect on his own state of mind and provide daily ratings.

With practice and feedback from his teacher (giving him cues for when he seems well focused or off task), his ratings may become more consistent with his teacher's ratings. One goal is to understand what contributes to Tom's good attention/behavior days and how much progress is being made. A second goal is to improve Tom's self-awareness and control over his own attention. (Digital applications such as Review360 are available to foster collaboration between parents and teachers with the goal of improving behavior and tracking progress.)

- On a regular basis, ask Tom to repeat back instructions in order to ensure that he has understood or has not forgotten crucial information. Attempting to remember information boosts memory performance on subsequent retrieval attempts. Asking Tom to repeat instructions also provides an opportunity for him to recognize when he forgets or becomes distracted, bringing his own level of attention and task comprehension into conscious awareness, and it provides an opportunity for him to redirect his attention or resolve any comprehension problems. Ideally, Tom would ask for help when he is unsure about a task or needs instructions to be repeated. Much of the time, however, Tom won't realize what he has missed.
- Keep instructions as brief and linguistically simple as possible. Use simple sentences with pauses between sentences. Avoid giving multistep instructions all at once.
- Improve memory for task instructions with repetition. For tasks that take place over an extended time period, repeating just the crucial information rather than the original instruction is likely to be most useful.
- Memory aids (e.g., pictorial graphic organizers) are recommended as a reminder of the instructions or information or to guide the completion of a specific activity.
- Preteaching is recommended for increasing the meaningfulness of any new or complex information by providing a context for it.

Context facilitates learning and helps prevent overburdening of working memory capacity. Use preparatory sets, which build background knowledge about a particular topic, focus attention on particular themes or words, and provide an expectation of what to look for or listen to in any new material.

- Encourage Tom to generate some of his own strategies for learning. Doing so may give him a greater sense of ownership in his education. Tom has insight into his own strengths and weaknesses and will likely generate some creative solutions. Expect some trial and error in finding what works best, allowing him to try things and experience the results.

Phonological Processing and Articulation

- Tom has had difficulty with phonemic discrimination, which can make reading and spelling more difficult. Errors were observed in his pronunciation, reading, and spelling of words with the /th/ and /v/ sounds. Supplemental instruction is recommended to improve his ability to discriminate between these sounds, both receptively (listening, reading) and expressively (speaking, spelling).
- Ensure that Tom pronounces words correctly while reading, and ask him to read his spelling words to ensure that his pronunciation is acceptable. If he pronounces a word incorrectly, assess whether the problem is receptive, expressive, or both. To assess phonemic discrimination, ask him to detect differences between minimally paired words that differ in sound only by their first phoneme [e.g., Teacher asks, "Do these two sound the same?" *wait–late* (different), *wait–wait* (same)]. Use the printed word as a visual cue to help support auditory perception.

Reading

Tom has been receiving explicit, systematic, synthetic phonics instruction over the last year, which has reportedly been helpful in improving his reading and spelling performance. Incorporating elements of analytic phonics instruction and strategies for improving orthographic processing is recommended. To improve Tom's orthographic processing and visual inspection of words, consider the following:

- Ask Tom to find a target word among orthographically similar words (e.g., *memory*: *mamory, menory, memory, momory*). Select words that are in Tom's spoken vocabulary and also at an appropriate reading level. Create distractors that resemble the kinds of reading errors Tom tends to make. Ask Tom to read each target word aloud before beginning, and then allow him to work independently. As a part of instruction, this task may be untimed initially, and then timed to track speed of orthographic processing.
- Present Tom with read and spell groups of visually similar words (e.g., *though, thought, through, tough*) in isolation and in context. [e.g., The train drove ___ (*thought, though, through*) a tunnel.]
- To improve attention to vowel patterns that have been taught, present pairs of words that differ only by their vowel type. Word pairs can be presented simultaneously (stacked or side by side) or using flip strips or letter cards to change the vowel of the word. If teaching short and long vowel patterns, for example, present pairs such as *bit/bite, cub/cube* (VCE pattern) or *sit/seat, met/meat* (*ea* vowel team), or *ran/rain, pan/pain* (*ai* vowel team).
- Give Tom word sorting tasks with orthographically similar words.
- Improve Tom's ability to recognize meaningful units of words when reading, including compound words, syllables (pre-tend), rimes (-an, -og), roots (aqua, gen), and affixes (-ed, pre-).
- Teach or reinforce instruction in the six syllable types. Teach syllable division of written words by "scooping" (drawing curved lines underneath the letters to indicate syllables) or reconstructing words using syllable cards.

- Ask Tom to read words that are visually separated by syllable. Present similar words together such as compound words (*cow boy*, *sun shine*) or words with affixes (un- *lock*, pre- *view*).
- Teach Tom to visually chunk words into morphemes. Activities might include the following: (a) Cut up word cards to physically separate prefixes or suffixes from the root word or to separate compound words; after cutting up the cards, mix them up and ask him to find the right cards to spell a specific word. (b) Ask him to read from flip booklets that expose the prefix or suffix, and change the root of the word to form new words. (c) Have Tom study groups of inflected or derived words together or words that share a common structural feature (e.g., *librarian*, *politician*, *musician*) by reading and spelling them in isolation and in sentences.

Tom relies almost exclusively on sounding out to decode. In particular, he exhibited difficulty reading vowel teams/diphthongs, silent letters, and prefixes and suffixes. Teach Tom to use various strategies for decoding words, including the following:

- Encourage Tom to find the part(s) of the word that he knows and then segment the word into recognizable chunks, reading the word one part at a time.
- Teach Tom to identify words by analogy, using his knowledge of word families/onset-rime patterns. Ask Tom to divide multisyllabic words into syllables and read one syllable at a time.
- Have Tom use morphological analysis to identify word parts (e.g., prefixes, suffixes).
- Teach Tom strategies to develop his reading fluency at the level of the word, phrase, sentence, and passage.
- Having Tom practice identifying words in isolation prior to reading them in text, which may improve automatic word recognition while reading in context.
- Ask Tom to orally read "phrase cards" with the goal of using these cards to improve

how quickly he can read them all accurately. Start with prepositional phrases, and begin to vary those phrases (preposition, article, and/or morphological ending) to ensure that he attends to the orthography. For example, if the initial phrase was "on the chair," the phrase cards might include "on the chair," "on a chair," "on the chairs," "off the chair," "off a chair," "off the chairs," and so on. Each of these phrases is visually similar, so careful visual attention is necessary for accuracy. Once he becomes more proficient in quickly reading the phrases, move onto longer phrases, such as "jumped on the chair" and "sitting on the chair," and then move onto sentences that contain those phrases (e.g., "The dogs jumped on the chair") and vary the sentences (e.g., "The dogs are jumping on the chair" and "The dog jumps on a chair").

- Teach Tom to read aloud the same passage repeatedly to improve the rate and accuracy of his reading. Other variations might include reading a passage aloud to Tom and then asking him to read it, or alternating the reading of sentences.
- Practice echo reading by having a parent/teacher read aloud and then ask Tom to read the same sentence(s) aloud, imitating the intonation and phrasing used.
- Teach Tom to use fix-up comprehension strategies and self-monitoring. Fix-up strategies may include rereading (perhaps reading it aloud or more slowly), reading on, or seeking help. Self-monitoring strategies may include summarizing or paraphrasing what was read, identifying main ideas and details, predicting/confirming or asking/answering questions about the text, and teaching/explaining what was read to someone else.

Spelling

Spelling is typically the most persistent area of difficulty for students and adults with dyslexia. Accommodations for spelling weaknesses are seldom sufficient and are not recommended as a substitute for instruction. Tom relies primarily on sounding out words to spell. Tom needs instruction to improve his memory for orthographic patterns and promote other strategies for spelling, including the following.

- Before beginning spelling instruction, ask Tom to read his spelling words. Listen for pronunciation errors that could impact his spelling performance. If Tom cannot read a word, focus instruction on reading before spelling.
- Practice generating alternatives, spelling the same word (or pseudoword) different ways. This task requires Tom to apply what he knows about the different orthographic patterns that are used for representing sounds.
- Spell by analogy. Provide practice generating possible spellings of the same sound or rime and then identifying the correct one (e.g., lait versus late).
- Syllabication. Teach the six syllable types and how to spell multisyllabic words one syllable at a time, remembering that every syllable needs a vowel (with a few exceptions). Color-code different word parts to assist with awareness of patterns. Building upon her study of morphological analysis, encourage Teach syllabication as a strategy. Teach Tom to self-check that every word has a vowel, and every syllable has a vowel (with very few exceptions). Teach Tom to spell multisyllabic words one syllable at a time. For example, how many syllables are in the word *party*? Two: ___ ___. Spell the word one syllable at a time: *par-ty*. Check that each syllable has a vowel (*y* is considered a vowel in this example). If the spelling isn't correct, encourage Tom to generate a second or third spelling using the same strategy.
- Teach strategies for spelling exception words and homophones, such as using mnemonics (e.g., build: *u* and *i* will build a house; separate: there's *a rat* in separate), saying the word as it sounds (e.g., Wed-nes-day), and spelling the word in parts (e.g., spell the root first, and then add affixes: *take … mis- take*).

Recommendations for Spelling Instruction and Homework

- Weave together reading, spelling, and vocabulary instruction to strengthen the multilayered representations of words in memory. Incorporate phonological, orthographic, morphological, syntactic, semantic, and pragmatic layers of word knowledge. For example, teach Tom that past tense is formed by adding -ed to words even though the -ed ending may have three different sounds (/t/, /d/, /ed/). Similarly, plurals are formed by adding –s or –es to words even though the –s ending may have different sounds (/ez/, /s/, /z/). Ask him to sort words using suffixes to mark tense or number. For example, includes words with plural pronounced /ez/ (*horses*), plural pronounced /s/ (*bats*), plural pronounced /z/ (*knees*), or with no suffix (*geese*).
- Use carefully controlled materials that explicitly highlight the rule or pattern that Tom needs to learn (e.g., vary words by one feature and hold other things constant, such as changing the initial phoneme or the morpheme being taught).
- Teach explicit spelling rules and patterns and the exceptions to those rules, but still allow for discovery. Allow Tom to discover patterns and rules through word sorting and carefully controlled materials. Examples of patterns to teach via discovery include when to use different spellings of the same sound: ou or ow to spell the /ow/ sound, tch or ch to spell the final /ch/ sound, dge or ge to spell the final /j/ sound.
- Use visual imagery. Instruct Tom to look at the word and say it aloud. Then have him close his eyes and imagine the word in his mind, naming the letters.
- Consider using the "Look-say-cover-write-check" technique: Tom looks carefully at the word he is trying to spell and notices the parts of the word that are tricky. He says the word as he's looking at it. Next, he covers it up, and writes the word as he says it. Finally, he uncovers the word and checks his spelling

while saying the word again. Repeat until the word is committed to memory.

- Spell new or challenging words by working from *recognition* to *partial recall* to *full recall*. Begin with a recognition task where Tom must circle/point to the correct spelling among distractors. Once he can do that reliably, ask him to spell words by filling in the missing letters (e.g., b _ nd). Begin with only one or two missing letters, working up to filling in all the blanks. Full recall involves writing the word from dictation (no blanks provided) or in a sentence.

- Ensure that Tom's spelling homework consists of assignments that are effective for helping him learn. Incorporate the strategies and tasks that work best for him into class and homework assignments.

Handwriting

- Reinforce the goal of writing as effective communication, emphasizing legibility and good form, not necessarily perfect penmanship.

- Tom uses improper letter formation for certain letters (d, b, p, q). Teach Tom proper letter formation using large movements (e.g., writing large on a white board) or multisensory techniques (e.g., writing in sand or shaving cream). Model the process of letter formation rather than only asking Tom to copy letters that are already finished or printed on a worksheet.

- Teach strategies to reduce letter reversals of b/d/p/q. Correct letter formation is critical to distinguish these letters. Use visual imagery and verbal mediation strategies. For example, when forming the letter b, start with the stick first, followed by the circle. It may be helpful to refer to them as a bat and a ball, always in that order (first you grab the bat, then you hit the ball). When reading, teach Tom that if he sees the bat first, then it's a b (say to yourself "bat-ball, b"). Once he can recognize and write b without confusion, then teach d. When forming the letter d, do the reverse; start with the circle first, then the stick (first you grab the doorknob, then you open the door). When reading, teach Tom that if he sees the doorknob first, then it's a d (say to yourself "doorknob, door, d"). Provide pictures of the letters formed using these images.

Written Expression

- Tom may need more time and support on writing assignments as compared to his typically achieving peers due to weaknesses in the subskills involved in writing as well as impairments in working memory. As Tom is working to formulate his ideas, he must devote extra effort to letter formation, spacing between words, and written mechanics. The writing process places heavy demands on his limited working memory capacity.

- Address low-level skills during the revision stage, emphasizing writing for purposes of communication, creativity, and expression (e.g., the goal of writing is not to spell words correctly; spelling is important for effective communication).

- Encourage Tom to read his own writing aloud and listen for types of errors systematically. For example, first listen for omitted words; on the next reading, attend to subject-verb agreement. Teach Tom to look specifically for the types of errors that he tends to make and that relate to skills he has been taught. Provide a checklist, mnemonic, or other reminder of what to look for.

Mathematics

- Tom tends to begin solving math problems before taking the time to understand the problem thoroughly. As a result, he often solves the wrong problem or makes simple errors. Teach strategies for improving Tom's math vigilance, including attention to operation sign, and self-monitoring for errors. Teach "understanding the problem" as a necessary first step that takes time. For example, before Tom begins solving an arithmetic problem, teach him to first say the problem, aloud or silently, pointing to the sign as he says the operation. Similarly, "checking the answer" is a necessary final step that takes time.

- Tom needs instructional support learning to interpret graphs, number lines, calendars, and analog clocks, and attending to/remembering the details of word problems.
- Ensure that printed word problems are read aloud to Tom as many times as he needs. Encourage him to draw pictorial representations of math problems to aid working memory.

Score Summary

Age-based norms are reported for all scores.

Socioemotional Functioning
The BASC–2 has both Clinical and Adaptive scales. Clinical scales serve as indicators for atypical or potentially problematic areas, whereas the Adaptive scales serve as indicators

of typical or positive social and emotional functioning. Results are reported as T scores, which indicate distance of scores from the norm group mean. They are standard scores with a mean of 50 and a standard deviation of 10. For the Clinical and Adaptive scales, scores that fall within 41–59 are considered to be in the average range. Alternately, Clinical scales designate scores between 60–69 as "at risk" while Adaptive scales consider scores falling within 31–40 as "at risk." Scores below these ranges are considered "clinically significant."

Figures 10.1 through 10.5 present Tom's BASC–2 results.

● Gen.-Sep. Sex

◆ Gen.-Comb. Sex

○ Clin.-Comb. Sex

◇ ADHD-Comb. Sex

Figure 10.1   Tom's Report Key

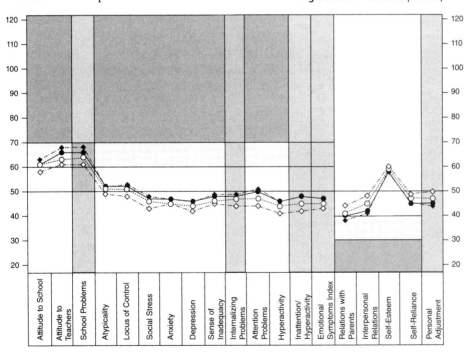

Figure 10.2   Tom's Self-Report

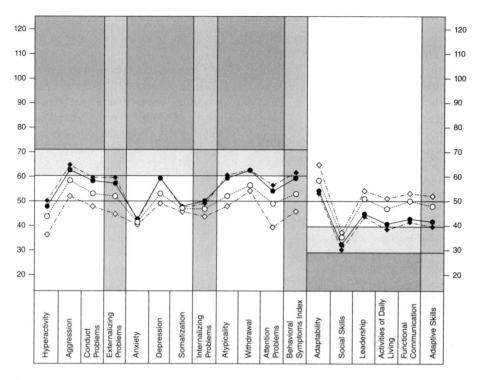

Figure 10.3 Tom's Mother Report

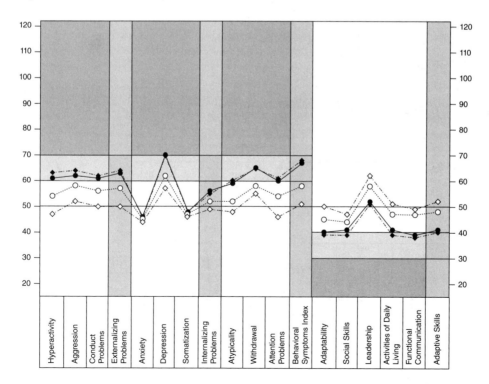

Figure 10.4 Tom's Father Report

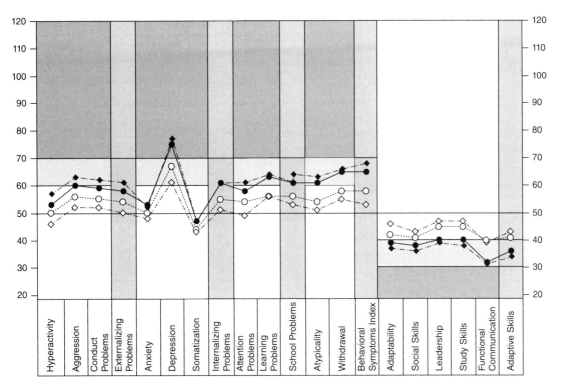

Figure 10.5   Tom's Teacher Report

Normative Groups

General population boys

General population combined sex

Clinical combined sex

ADHD combined sex

BASC–2 Summary of Results and Description of Scales   Table 10.20 presents Tom's BASC–2 self-report results, and Table 10.21 presents Tom's BASC–2 parent and teacher results.

Table 10.20   Tom's Self-Report

Clinical Scales (Level of Distress)	Scale Definitions	Tom's Results
Attitude to School	The tendency to feel alienated, hostile, or dissatisfied toward school	At risk
Attitude to Teachers	The tendency to resent or dislike teachers or think they are unfair	At risk
School Problems		At risk
Atypicality	Excessive thoughts and behaviors that are considered odd or unusual	
Locus of Control	The belief that rewards and punishments are controlled by external events or other people	

(continued)

Table 10.20 *(Continued)*

Clinical Scales (Level of Distress)	Scale Definitions	Tom's Results
Social Stress	Feeling lonely, isolated, or picked on in social situations	
Anxiety	The tendency to be nervous, fearful, or worried about real or imagined problems	
Depression	Excessive feelings of unhappiness, sadness, or stress	
Sense of inadequacy	The tendency to feel unsuccessful or generally inadequate	
Internalizing Problems		
Attention Problems	The tendency to be easily distracted and unable to concentrate for an extended period of time	
Hyperactivity	The tendency to be overly active, rush through work or activities, and act without thinking	
Inattention/Hyperactivity		
Emotional Symptoms Index		

Adaptive Scales (Positive Adjustment)	Scale Definitions	Tom's Results
Relations with Parents	The tendency to feel valued and supported by parents	
Interpersonal Relations	Feeling liked and respected by peers	
Self-Esteem	Feelings of self-respect and self-worth	
Self-Reliance	Thinking that one is dependable and being confident of one's abilities	
Personal Adjustment		

Table 10.21 Tom's Reports by Parents and Teacher

Clinical Scales (Disruptive Behaviors/ Internal Problems)	Scale Definitions	Mother Results	Father Results	Teacher Results
Hyperactivity	Tendency to be overly active, rush through work or activities, and act without thinking		At risk	
Aggression	Tendency to act in a hostile manner, verbal or physical, that is threatening to others	At risk	At risk	At risk
Conduct Problems	Tendency to engage in antisocial and rule-breaking behavior, including destroying property		At risk	At risk
Externalizing Problems			At risk	At risk
Anxiety	Tendency to be nervous, fearful, or worried about real or imagined problems			
Depression	Feelings of unhappiness, sadness, and stress that may result in an inability to carry out everyday activities or may bring on thoughts of suicide		Clinically significant	Clinically significant

Table 10.21   (*Continued*)

Clinical Scales (Disruptive Behaviors/ Internal Problems)	Scale Definitions	Mother Results	Father Results	Teacher Results
Somatization	Tendency to be overly sensitive to and complain about relatively minor physical problems and discomforts			
Internalizing Problems				At risk
Atypicality	Tendency to behave in ways that are considered odd	At risk	At risk	At risk
Withdrawal	Tendency to evade others to avoid social contact	At risk	At risk	At risk
Attention Problems	Tendency to be easily distracted and unable to concentrate more than momentarily		At risk	
Learning Problems	Presence of academic difficulties, particularly understanding or completing homework			At risk
School Problems	Includes Learning Problems and Attention Problems			At risk
Behavioral Symptoms Index	Includes Hyperactivity, Aggression, Depression, Attention Problems, Atypicality, Withdrawal	At risk	At risk	At risk

Adaptive Scales (Positive Features/Skills)	Scale Definitions	Mother Results	Father Results	Teacher Results
Adaptability	Ability to adapt readily to changes in the environment		At risk	At risk
Social Skills	Skills necessary for interacting successfully with peers and adults in home, school, and community settings	At risk	At risk	At risk
Leadership	Skills associated with accomplishing academic, social, or community goals, including the ability to work with others			At risk
Activities of Daily Living	Skills associated with performing basic, everyday tasks in an acceptable and safe manner	At risk	At risk	
Functional Communication	Ability to express ideas and communicate in a way others can easily understand		At risk	At risk
Adaptive Skills		At risk	At risk	At risk

Table 10.21   (*Continued*)

Content Scales	Scale Definitions	Mother Results	Father Results	Teacher Results
Anger Control	Tendency to become irritated and/or anger quickly and impulsively; inability to regulate affect and self-control		At risk	
Bullying	Tendency to be intrusive, cruel, threatening, or forceful to get what is wanted through manipulation or coercion		At risk	At risk
Developmental Social Disorders	Tendency to display behaviors characterized by deficits in social skills, communication, interests, and activities	At risk	At risk	Clinically significant
Emotional Self-Control	Ability to regulate one's affect and emotions in response to environmental changes			Clinically significant
Executive Functioning	Ability to control behavior by planning, anticipating, inhibiting, or maintaining goal-directed activity and by reacting appropriately to environmental feedback in a purposeful, meaningful way	At risk	At risk	At risk
Negative Emotionality	Tendency to react in an overly negative way to changes in everyday activities or routines	At risk		At risk
Resiliency	Ability to access both internal and external support systems to alleviate stress and overcome adversity		At risk	At risk

Clinical Indexes	Scale Definitions	Mother	Father	Teacher
ADHD Probability				At risk
Emotional-Behavioral Disturbance (EBD) Probability		At risk		Clinically significant
Functional Impairment		At risk	At risk	At risk

Intellectual Functioning

Table 10.22 presents Tom's WISC–V subtest level scaled score results, and Figure 10.6 presents Tom's subtest scaled score profile.

Table 10.23 presents Tom's WISC–V composite score summary, and Figure 10.7 presents Tom's WISC–V composite score profile.

Table 10.24 presents Tom's WISC–V ancillary and complementary index score summary, and Table 10.25 presents Tom's WISC–V ancillary and complementary subtest score summary.

Table 10.26 presents the WISC–V subtest descriptions.

Language Processing and Academic Achievement

Composite and subtest standard scores reported in this section from the KTEA–3 and the WIAT–III range from 40 to 160 with a mean of 100 and a standard deviation of 15.

Table 10.22   Tom's WISC–V Subtest Score Summary

Scale	Subtest Name	Subtest Abbreviation	Scaled Score	Percentile Rank	Age Equivalent	*SEM*
Verbal Comprehension	**Similarities**	SI	19–S	99.9	>16:10	1.16
	Vocabulary	VC	12	75	8:10	1.24
	(Information)	IN	—	—	—	—
	(Comprehension)	CO	—	—	—	—
Visual Spatial	**Block Design**	BD	17–S	99	>16:10	1.04
	Visual Puzzles	VP	14	91	13:6	1.08
Fluid Reasoning	**Matrix Reasoning**	MR	11	63	8:10	0.99
	Figure Weights	FW	13	84	9:10	0.73
	(Picture Concepts)	PC	—	—	—	—
	(Arithmetic)	AR	5–W	5	6:2	1.04
Working Memory	**Digit Span**	DS	6–W	9	<6:2	0.95
	Picture Span	PS	4–W	2	<6:2	1.08
	(Letter–Number Sequencing)	LN	6–W	9	<6:2	1.24
Processing Speed	**Coding**	CD	11	63	8:6	1.37
	Symbol Search	SS	8–W	25	<8:2	1.34
	(Cancellation)	CA	—	—	—	—

Subtests used to derive the FSIQ are bolded. Secondary subtests are in parentheses.

Subtest Scaled Score Profile

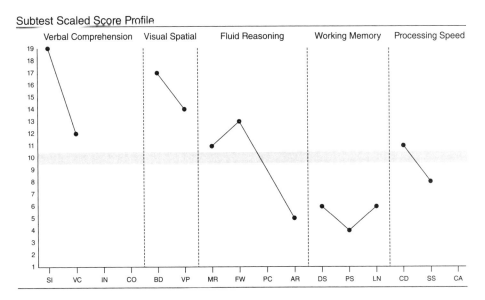

Figure 10.6   Tom's WISC–V Subtest Scaled Score Profile

Table 10.23   Tom's WISC-V Composite Score Summary

Composite	Abbreviation	Standard Score	Percentile Rank	95% Confidence Interval	Descriptor	SEM
Verbal Comprehension Index	VCI	130	98	120–135	Extremely High	4.74
Visual Spatial Index	VSI	132—S	98	122–137	Extremely High	4.24
Fluid Reasoning Index	FRI	112	79	104–118	High Average	3.67
Working Memory Index	WMI	72—W	3	67–82	Very Low	4.24
Processing Speed Index	PSI	98—W	45	89–107	Average	5.61
Full Scale IQ	FSIQ	120	91	114–125	Very High	3.00

Composite Score Profile

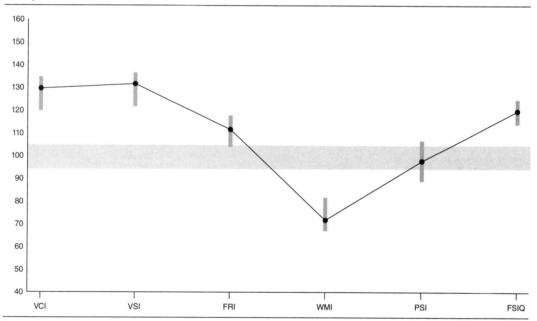

Note. Vertical bars represent the Confidence Intervals.

Figure 10.7   Tom's WISC-V Composite Score Profile

Table 10.24   Tom's WISC–V Ancillary and Complementary Index Score Summary

Index Score	Abbreviation	Standard Score–S or W	Percentile Rank	95% Confidence Interval	Descriptor	*SEM*
Ancillary						
Quantitative Reasoning Index	QRI	94—W	34	88–101	Average	3.67
Auditory Working Memory Index	AWMI	78—W	7	72–87	Very Low	4.24
Nonverbal Index	NVI	113	81	106–119	High Average	3.35
General Ability Index	GAI	128	97	121–133	Very High	3.00
Cognitive Proficiency Index	CPI	81—W	10	75–90	Low Average	4.24
Complementary						
Naming Speed Index	NSI	93—W	32	85–102	Average	5.61
Symbol Translation Index	STI	95—W	37	89–102	Average	3.67
Storage & Retrieval Index	SRI	92—W	30	86–99	Average	4.24

Table 10.25   Tom's WISC–V Ancillary and Complementary Subtest Score Summary

Scale	Subtest/Process Score	Abbreviation	Standard Score	Percentile Rank	Age Equivalent	*SEM*
Naming Speed	Naming Speed Literacy	NSL	91	27	7:2	6.87
	Naming Speed Quantity	NSQ	99	47	7:10	6.54
Symbol Translation	Immediate Symbol Translation	IST	97	42	7:2	5.81
	Delayed Symbol Translation	DST	100	50	8:2	5.81
	Recognition Symbol Translation	RST	91	27	<6:2	6.71

Table 10.26   WISC–V Subtest Descriptions

Block Design	Working within a specified time limit, the child views a model and/or a picture and uses two-color blocks to re-create the design.
Similarities	The child is read two words that represent common objects or concepts and describes how they are similar.
Matrix Reasoning	The child views an incomplete matrix or series and selects the response option that completes the matrix or series.
Digit Span	The child is read a sequence of numbers and recalls the numbers in the same order (Forward task), reverse order (Backward task), and ascending order (Sequencing task).
Coding	Working within a specified time limit, the child uses a key to copy symbols that correspond with simple geometric shapes or numbers.
Vocabulary	For picture items, the child names the depicted object. For verbal items, the child defines the word that is read aloud.

(continued)

Table 10.26 *(Continued)*

Figure Weights	Within a specified time limit, the child views a scale with missing weight(s) and selects the response option that keeps the scale balanced.
Visual Puzzles	Within a specified time limit, the child views a completed puzzle and selects three response options that, when combined, reconstruct the puzzle.
Picture Span	The child views a stimulus page with one or more pictures for a specified time and then selects the picture(s) (in sequential order, if possible) from options on a response page.
Symbol Search	Working within a specified time limit, the child scans search groups and indicates whether target symbols are present.
Letter–Number Sequencing	The child is read a sequence of numbers and letters and recalls the numbers in ascending order and then the letters in alphabetical order.
Naming Speed Literacy	The child names elements (e.g., objects of various size and color, letters and numbers) as quickly as possible.
Naming Speed Quantity	The child names the quantity of squares inside a series of boxes as quickly as possible.
Immediate Symbol Translation	The child learns visual-verbal pairs and then translates symbol strings into phrases or sentences.
Arithmetic	For both the picture and verbal items, the child mentally solves arithmetic problems within a specified time limit.
Delayed Symbol Translation	The child translates symbols into words, phrases, or sentences using recalled visual-verbal pairs from Immediate Symbol Translation.
Recognition Symbol Translation	The child views a symbol and selects the correct translation, from response options the examiner reads aloud, using recalled visual-verbal pairs from Immediate Symbol Translation.

For consistency with the WISC–V, the same standard score ranges and descriptors are used to describe these results. Example of how to interpret results: If Tom scored at the 12th percentile, he scored as well or better than 12% of children his age. If the standard score is 82 with a confidence interval of 68 to 96, we can be 95% confident that Tom's true standard score falls between 68 and 96. His score range is 82 ± 14.

Table 10.27 presents Tom's rapid automatic naming subtest score summary, along with descriptions of the subtests.

Table 10.28 presents Tom's phonological processing subtest score summary, along with the subtest description.

Table 10.29 presents Tom's language subtest score summary, along with the subtest description.

Table 10.30 presents Tom's reading subtest score summary, along with the subtest descriptions.

Table 10.31 presents Tom's reading-related composite score summary, along with the composite score descriptions.

Table 10.32 presents Tom's graphomotor (writing fluency) subtest score summary, along with the subtest descriptions.

Table 10.33 presents Tom's spelling/written expression subtest score summary, along with the subtest descriptions.

Table 10.27   Tom's Rapid Automatic Naming Subtest Score Summary

Subtest	Standard Score	95% Confidence Interval	Percentile Rank	Descriptor
KTEA–3 Letter Naming Facility	99	79–119	47	Average
WISC–V Naming Speed Index	93	85–102	32	Average

Subtest/Index	Description
Letter Naming Facility	The student names upper- and lowercase letters as quickly as possible.
Naming Speed Index	[See WISC–V subtest descriptions for Naming Speed Literacy, Naming Speed Quantity.]

Table 10.28   Tom's Phonological Processing Subtest Score Summary

Subtest	Standard Score	95% Confidence Interval	Percentile Rank	Descriptor
KTEA–3 Phonological Processing	90	83–97	25	Average

Subtest	Description
Phonological Processing	The student responds orally to items that require manipulation of the sounds within words.

Table 10.29   Tom's Oral Language Subtest Score Summary

Subtest	Standard Score	95% Confidence Interval	Percentile Rank	Descriptor
WIAT–III Listening Comprehension	114	101–127	82	High average
Receptive Vocabulary	115		84	High average
Oral Discourse Comprehension	107		68	Average

Subtest	Description
Listening Comprehension	The student listens to vocabulary words and points to a picture that illustrates each word (Receptive Vocabulary), and then listens to passages and orally responds to open-ended questions (Oral Discourse Comprehension).

Table 10.30   Tom's Reading Subtest Score Summary

Subtest	Standard Score	95% Confidence Interval	Percentile Rank	Descriptor
KTEA–3 Letter & Word Recognition	80	75–85	9	Low average
KTEA–3 Nonsense Word Decoding	84	79–89	14	Low average
KTEA–3 Reading Comprehension	82	72–92	12	Low average
KTEA–3 Word Recognition Fluency	80	67–93	9	Low average
KTEA–3 Silent Reading Fluency	79	68–90	8	Very low

(continued)

Table 10.30   *(Continued)*

Subtest	Standard Score	95% Confidence Interval	Percentile Rank	Descriptor
WIAT–III Oral Reading Fluency	80[a]	72–88	9	Low average
Accuracy	75	63–87	5	Very low
Rate	82	72–92	12	Low average

Subtest	Description
Letter & Word Recognition	The student identifies letters and reads grade-appropriate words.
Word Recognition Fluency	The student reads as many words as possible within a time limit.
Nonsense Word Decoding	The student pronounces made-up words.
Reading Comprehension	The student reads symbols, words, sentences, and passages appropriate to his or her grade level, and then responds to comprehension questions.
Silent Reading Fluency	The student has 2 minutes to silently read simple questions and circle yes or no to each one.
Oral Reading Fluency	The student reads passages aloud under timed conditions.

[a]Score is based on the grade 1 item set.

Table 10.31   **Tom's Reading-Related Composite Score Summary**

Composite	Standard Score	95% Confidence Interval	Percentile Rank	Descriptor
KTEA–3 Reading	80	74–86	9	Low average
KTEA–3 Sound-Symbol	85	80–90	16	Low average
KTEA–3 Decoding	80	76–84	9	Low average
KTEA–3 Orthographic Processing	82	72–92	12	Low average

Composite	Description
Reading	Letter & Word Recognition + Reading Comprehension subtests
Sound-Symbol	Phonological Processing + Nonsense Word Decoding subtests
Decoding	Letter & Word Recognition + Nonsense Word Decoding subtests
Orthographic Processing	Spelling + Letter Naming Facility + Word Recognition Facility

Table 10.32   **Tom's Graphomotor (Writing Fluency) Subtest Score Summary**

Subtest	Standard Score	95% Confidence Interval	Percentile Rank	Descriptor
KTEA–3 Writing Fluency	82	68–96	12	Low average
WIAT–III Alphabet Writing Fluency	93	77–109	32	Average

Subtest	Description
Writing Fluency	The student writes simple sentences, each one describing a different picture, within a time limit. Score is based on word count.
Alphabet Writing Fluency	The student writes letters of the alphabet within a 30-second time limit.

Table 10.33   Tom's Spelling/Written Expression Subtest Score Summary

Subtest	Standard Score	95% Confidence Interval	Percentile Rank	Descriptor
KTEA–3 Spelling	81	76–86	10	Low average
WIAT–III Sentence Composition	101	90–112	53	Average
Sentence Combining	94		34	Average
Sentence Building	109		73	Average

Subtest	Description
Spelling	The student writes single letters and spells words dictated by the examiner.
Sentence Composition	The student combines the information from two or three sentences into single sentences that mean the same thing, and then the student writes sentences that use specific words.

Table 10.34 presents Tom's mathematics subtest score summary, along with the subtest descriptions.

Table 10.35 presents Tom's mathematics composite score summary, along with the subtest descriptions.

Analysis for the Identification of a Specific Learning Disability

Pattern of Strengths and Weaknesses (PSW) Analysis Table 10.36 presents Tom's PSW analysis output with decoding as the achievement weakness, and Figure 10.8 presents the corresponding figure.

- Area of Processing Strength: WISC–V Visual Spatial Index: 132
- Area of Processing Weakness: WISC–V Working Memory Index: 72
- Area of Achievement Weakness: KTEA–3 Decoding: 80

Table 10.37 presents Tom's PSW analysis output with spelling as the achievement weakness, and Figure 10.9 presents the corresponding figure.

- Area of Processing Strength: WISC–V Visual Spatial Index: 132

Table 10.34   Tom's Mathematics Subtest Score Summary

Subtest	Standard Score	95% Confidence Interval	Percentile Rank	Descriptor
WIAT–III Math Problem Solving	82	73–91	12	Low average
WIAT–III Numerical Operations	87	79–95	19	Low average

Subtest	Description
Math Problem Solving	The student solves untimed math problems related to basic skills (counting, identifying shapes, etc.) and everyday applications (time, money, word problems, etc.). Word problems are read aloud; independent reading is not required.
Numerical Operations	The student solves untimed written math problems in basic skills and basic operations with integers.

Table 10.35 Tom's Mathematics Composite Score Summary

Composite	Standard Score	95% Confidence Interval	Percentile Rank	Descriptor
WIAT-III Mathematics	83	76–90	13	Low average

Composite	Description
Mathematics	Math Problem Solving + Numerical Operations subtests

Table 10.36 Tom's PSW Analysis: Decoding

Comparison	Relative Strength Score	Relative Weakness Score	Difference	Critical Value (.01)	Significant Difference Y/N	Supports SLD hypothesis? Yes/No
Processing Strength/Achievement Weakness	132	80	52	12	Y	Yes
Processing Strength/Processing Weakness	132	72	60	15	Y	Yes

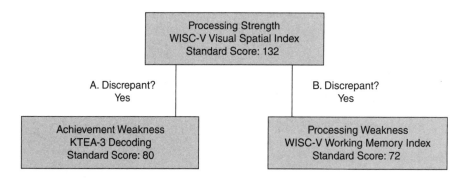

Figure 10.8 Tom's PSW Analysis: Decoding

Table 10.37 Tom's PSW Analysis: Spelling

Comparison	Relative Strength Score	Relative Weakness Score	Difference	Critical Value (.01)	Significant Difference Y/N	Supports SLD hypothesis? Yes/No
Processing Strength/Achievement Weakness	132	81	51	13	Y	Yes
Processing Strength/Processing Weakness	132	72	60	15	Y	Yes

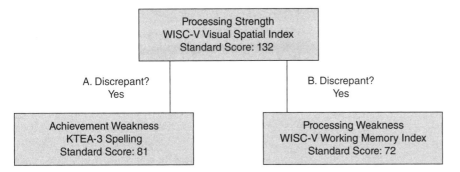

Figure 10.9   Tom's PSW Analysis: Spelling

- Area of Processing Weakness: WISC–V Working Memory Index: 72
- Area of Achievement Weakness: KTEA–3 Spelling: 81

Table 10.38 presents Tom's PSW analysis output with mathematics as the achievement weakness, and Figure 10.10 presents the corresponding figure.

- Area of Processing Strength: WISC–V Visual Spatial Index: 132
- Area of Processing Weakness: WISC–V Working Memory Index: 72
- Area of Achievement Weakness: WIAT–III Mathematics: 83

Table 10.38   Tom's PSW Analysis: Mathematics

Comparison	Relative Strength Score	Relative Weakness Score	Difference	Critical Value (.01)	Significant Difference Y/N	Supports SLD hypothesis? Yes/No
Processing Strength/Achievement Weakness	132	83	49	14	Y	Yes
Processing Strength/Processing Weakness	132	72	60	15	Y	Yes

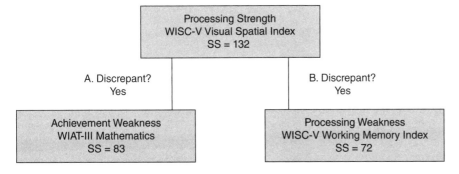

Figure 10.10   Tom's PSW Analysis: Mathematics

CHAPTER 11

INTERPRETING THE WISC–V FROM A NEUROPSYCHOLOGICAL PERSPECTIVE

As noted previously, the division of content matter and case reports between this chapter and the previous chapter is a bit arbitrary. Growth within each of the fields has benefited the other due to shared emphases on exploring the relations between the brain and mental functioning. Common origins in neurology and psychology make these complementary and intertwined fields of study. The topics presented in Chapter 10 (e.g., childhood brain development, neuroimaging, neuroanatomical correlates of cognitive abilities) provided basic foundational knowledge to more fully appreciate the focus of this chapter, the clinical application of neuropsychologically oriented approaches to interpreting the WISC–V: where research meets practice, so to speak. The next two chapters—Chapter 12 on Dan Miller's Integrated School Neuropsychological/Cattell-Horn Carroll Model and Chapter 13 on George McCloskey's neuropsychologically oriented process approach—provide more specific examples of neuropsychological applications to test interpretation, including illustrative case reports.

This chapter provides a general overview of neuropsychologically oriented approaches, focusing on Lurian- and process-oriented approaches that stem from the work of Edith Kaplan and her colleagues. Interpretation of WISC–V performance from these perspectives is described, and four new Lurian-based scores are introduced that may be of special interest to those interpreting the WISC–V from a neuropsychological perspective (i.e., the Successive and Simultaneous Processing Indexes and scaled scores for each Matrix Reasoning item type). The three case reports selected for inclusion at the end of this chapter include a Lurian-based interpretation and two reports from a more general neuropsychological perspective. Taken together, the case reports included in Chapters 10 to 13 represent a broad range of approaches to interpreting the WISC–V scores within the context of a comprehensive neuropsychological evaluation.

HISTORY OF CLINICAL NEUROPSYCHOLOGY

Specialization in clinical neuropsychology is recognized by the American Psychological Association (APA) and the Canadian Psychological Association. Definitions of clinical neuropsychology can be accessed easily via several organizational websites (e.g., APA, National Academy of Neuropsychology), and all of them are similar. According to the National Academy of Neuropsychology Policy and Planning Committee (2001), a clinical neuropsychologist is defined as:

a professional within the field of psychology with special expertise in the applied science of brain-behavior relationships. Clinical neuropsychologists use this knowledge in the assessment, diagnosis, treatment, and/or rehabilitation of patients across the lifespan with neurological, medical, neurodevelopmental and psychiatric conditions, as well as other cognitive and learning disorders. The clinical neuropsychologist uses psychological, neurological, cognitive, behavioral, and physiological principles, techniques and tests to evaluate patients' neurocognitive, behavioral, and emotional strengths and weaknesses and their relationship to normal and abnormal central nervous system functioning. The clinical neuropsychologist uses this information and information provided by other medical/healthcare providers to identify and diagnose neurobehavioral disorders, and plan and implement intervention strategies. (p. 1)

The practice of clinical neuropsychology "can be depicted as having a long history and a short past" (Hartlage & Long, 2009, p. 3). Although the concept of brain–behavior relations was noted by Pythagoras as early as 550 BC, the term *neuropsychology* was not introduced until the early 1960s (Klove, 1963), and the field of study was not formalized until the formation of the International Neuropsychological Society (INS) in 1967 (Bilder, 2011). The National Academy of Neuropsychologists (NAN; later renamed the National Academy of Neuropsychology) first met in 1981(Hartlage & Long, 2009). Of course, progress in the study of brain–behavior relations did not stagnate during this unnamed time period. Early practitioners provided an amazing wealth of information despite the lack of any in vivo brain imaging during those early years, and the field of neuropsychology made notable and consistent progress.

Rourke (1982) described three stages in the history of clinical neuropsychology: the single-test approach phase, the test battery/lesion specification stage, and the functional profile stage. Based on substantial advances in the field since the time of Rourke's writing, Miller (2013) introduced a new historical phase, the *integrative and predictive stage*, beginning with the declaration of the 1990s as the "decade of the brain" (p. 23) and extending beyond that decade into the present time. During the single-test approach stage spanning the first half of the 20th century, the primary focus was distinguishing between patients with and without brain damage, often with the use of a single measure. For example, Wechsler and others attempted to identify subtest configurations indicative of "organic" brain dysfunction (Hartlage & Long, 2009). The increasing availability of

psychological tests led neuropsychologists to discover that multiple measures provided a much better understanding of patients' cognitive functioning, including visual-spatial abilities, attention, and memory. The development of test batteries commenced, and the return of wounded soldiers after World War II provided an unfortunate but needful sample on which to test these batteries as well as an impetus for innovators to arise in this new field, including Ward Halstead, Ralph Reitan, Alexander Luria, and Edith Kaplan (Miller, 2013).

With the goal of creating a measure of the biological underpinnings of cognitive function, Halstead began development of a neuropsychological test battery based on his work with hundreds of brain-injured patients. Following his premature death, his student, Reitan, refined and expanded the scale, eventually resulting in the Halstead-Reitan Neuropsychological Test Battery (Reitan, 1955). Unlike Halstead and Reitan's quantitative approach to assessment, Luria, a Russian contemporary of the duo, emphasized the qualitative aspects of an individual's performance, writing two influential texts, *The Working Brain* (1966b, 1973b) and *Higher Cortical Functions in Man* (1973a). One of Luria's students, Anne-Lise Christensen, "manualized" a portion of Luria's clinical method in the 1970s (Christensen, 1975), and Charles Golden (to the consternation of many exclusively qualitative Lurians) standardized a complete battery in the 1980s (Golden, 1981) to produce what became known as the Luria-Nebraska Neuropsychological Test Battery (Adams & Spencer, 2011; Hartlage & Long, 2009).

Spurred by Luria's emphasis on qualitative aspects of performance, the 1960s and 1970s served as the stage for a meeting of like-minded clinicians and researchers in Boston, who used a flexible test battery that varied with the specific referral question rather than the structured Halstead-Reitan or Luria-Nebraska batteries. This approach was subsequently referred to as "the Boston Process Approach" (Milberg, Hebben, & Kaplan, 1996), with a basic tenet that the way an individual arrives at an answer is as important, if not more important, than the score. Astute observation of how individuals approach a task and testing of limits are hallmarks of the process-assessment approach. Although similar to Luria's clinical method in qualitative emphasis, the process approach to neuropsychological assessment and interpretation often utilizes quantitative information obtained from standardized tests (Miller, 2013).

Despite an increasing awareness that the developmental trajectory of cognitive abilities in childhood was strikingly different from that in adults, the development of neuropsychological measures for children lagged substantially behind that for adults. Early efforts to simply modify existing adult measures, such as the Halstead-Reitan and Luria-Nebraska, downward for children were disappointing, providing limited information about the localization of brain dysfunction or how to remediate dysfunction through intervention. The introduction of brain imaging techniques in the 1970s reduced the need for localization of brain lesions, ushering in the functional profile stage of clinical neuropsychology in which the identification of an individual's profile of cognitive strengths and weaknesses took on primary importance. Unfortunately, the availability of neuropsychological measures for children was still woefully lacking relative to that for adults.

With the publication of the Kaufman Assessment Battery for Children (K-ABC) in 1983, Alan and Nadeen Kaufman were the first to offer a neuropsychological theory-based measure of intelligence that emphasized children's cognitive processing rather than general cognitive ability (Naglieri, Das, & Goldstein, 2012). Their emphasis on cognitive processes marked a prescient shift in the field that we are witnessing today, with a move beyond identification of the structural components of intelligence toward a greater understanding of how these structural components function together during cognitive processing. The current integrative and predictive stage of clinical neuropsychology

arrived shortly thereafter in 1990 and, with it, the increasing availability of cognitive and neuropsychological measures designed specifically for children, including the *Test of Memory and Learning* (Reynolds & Bigler, 1994), the *Cognitive Assessment System* (CAS; Naglieri & Das, 1997), and the *NEPSY: A Developmental Neuropsychological Assessment* (NEPSY; Korkman, Kirk, & Kemp, 1998).

For neuropsychologists today, there are many available instruments to use as part of a comprehensive neuropsychological evaluation with children or adults. When combined with recent and reciprocal advances in neuroscience, we are at an exciting time in our understanding of brain–behavior relations, seemingly on the verge of major discoveries. This flood of knowledge comes at a cost, making it a constant challenge for the intelligent tester from any theoretical orientation to stay abreast of current relevant research. With neuropsychology's close relation to cognitive neuroscience and increasing multidisciplinary research efforts, the need for adequate preparation and ongoing training is especially relevant for clinical neuropsychologists.

TRAINING REQUIREMENTS FOR NEUROPSYCHOLOGISTS

Unlike the term *psychologist*, which is almost always regulated by acts of state licensing boards, the term *neuropsychologist* is not always state-regulated, allowing some practitioners to claim expertise without meeting the necessary training requirements. According to the APA website, specialized training for clinical neuropsychology includes knowledge of neuroanatomy, neuroscience, brain development, neurological disorders, neurodiagnostic techniques, and normal and abnormal brain function (APA, 2010). Participants in a joint task force with members from APA's Division 40 and the INS first established training and credentialing guidelines for neuropsychologists in 1987, with the most recent revision occurring at a 1997 meeting held in Houston, informally referred to as the Houston conference (Hannay et al., 1998). Training requirements supported by NAN are consistent with those of APA Division 40 and the INS, and can be generally summarized as follows:

- doctorate in psychology from an accredited program with didactic and experiential training in neuroscience and neuropsychology;
- 2 or more years of supervised experience providing neuropsychological services in a clinical setting, at least 1 of which occurs at the postdoctoral level;
- licensing and certification obtained according to state or district laws regarding the provision of psychological services to the public; and
- peer-reviewed tests of competency to practice neuropsychology.

Thus, the completion of a doctoral degree in psychology at an APA-accredited institution is viewed as the entry level for the practice of clinical neuropsychology. After completing the doctoral coursework, dissertation, and APA-accredited 1-year internship required for the doctoral degree, aspiring clinical neuropsychologists are required to obtain an additional 2 years of supervised residency at an APA-accredited program and state licensure as a practicing psychologist.

At present, board certification is not required for professional practice in clinical neuropsychology; however, such certification is viewed by APA, NAN, and INS as the clearest evidence of obtaining the advanced training, supervision, and practice for the competent, independent practice of clinical neuropsychology. Certification as a clinical neuropsychologist can currently be obtained through two credentialing boards, the American Board of Professional Neuropsychology (ABPN) and the American Board of Clinical Neuropsychology (ABCN). Both boards require 3 years of supervised neuropsychological experience, passage of written and oral exams, as well as the submission of work samples for

meticulous peer review. The American Board of Professional Psychology formally recognized the ABCN in 1984, whereas the ABPN continues to award certification in clinical neuropsychology independently.

Specialization in pediatric neuropsychology had a rockier start, with the creation of the American Board of Pediatric Neuropsychology in 1996, followed by two reorganizations and a rejected application for membership in the American Board of Professional Psychology. The ABCN began awarding added qualifications certificates based on peer review and additional examination for child and adolescent neuropsychology in 2007, only to drop the certificate in 2010 (Miller, 2013). Fortunately, the ABCN recently performed an about-face, announcing its first subspecialty credential in pediatric clinical neuropsychology. Initially only ABCN-certified neuropsychologists were eligible for this subspecialty, but acceptance of applications from psychologists in the midst of ABCN certification commenced in January 2015. Even in these situations, however, the subspecialty certificate is not awarded until the candidate obtains ABCN certification. Detailed requirements for subspecialization in pediatric clinical neuropsychology can be found at the ABCN website but generally involve: (1) a thorough credential review for adequate education, training, and practice in pediatric neuropsychology; (2) passage of a written exam; and (3) submission of a practice sample case for peer review.

Certification in school neuropsychology through the American Board of School Neuropsychology (ABSNP) recognizes, but does not require, a doctorate in psychology, licensure as a psychologist, or completion of an APA-accredited internship, instead requiring relevant training, experience, and certification as a school psychologist. As with certification in clinical neuropsychology, certification in school neuropsychology requires 3 years of supervised experience, the passage of written and oral exams, and the evaluation of submitted work samples.

Contemporary Approaches to Neuropsychological Evaluation

Using their advanced training, clinical neuropsychologists assess, diagnose, and treat or rehabilitate individuals with a wide range of problems related to disorders of the nervous system, including dementia, psychiatric disorders, neurodegenerative disorders (e.g., Parkinson's disease and multiple sclerosis), epilepsy, traumatic brain injury, attention-deficit/ hyperactivity disorder [ADHD], learning disabilities, and other neurodevelopmental disorders. Based on its broad definition as the study of brain–behavior relations, it might be expected that neuropsychology would focus on all aspects of behavior, including social, emotional, sensory, and motor behavior; however, the primary focus of neuropsychology has been on cognitive behavior (Koziol & Budding, 2011; Lezak, 2004). Cognitive functions are typically easier to measure than emotional, motivational, and social behaviors, leading to a more readily available supply of child-appropriate cognitive tests. This emphasis on cognition in no way implies that these behaviors are not important aspects of a neuropsychological evaluation. Some tests, such as the NEPSY–II (Korkman, Kirk, & Kemp, 2007), have begun to incorporate such measures, but their numbers and evidence of clinical utility are still lacking relative to that of cognitive measures. Because the WISC–V is a measure of intellectual ability, this chapter likewise emphasizes cognitive aspects of neuropsychological function.

For any neuropsychologist, the choice of using a fixed or flexible battery (or some combination of the two) should be made prior to the evaluation. Both strategies have pros and cons, and neither protects the clinican from making diagnostic errors: The test (or test battery in this case) is just a tool (Koziol & Budding, 2011). The emphasis on flexible neuropsychological test batteries in this chapter is based on the obvious fact that the WISC–V alone (or any other single measure) does not cover all of the domains in a comprehensive neuropsychological evaluation; any test must be supplemented with other measures to accomplish this feat, resulting in the need for a flexible-battery approach. Although this approach has numerous advantages (e.g., the ability to streamline a test battery based on the referral question), intelligent testers should remain aware of its limitations, including differences in the tests' normative groups or "missing" an unknown area of concern due to a customized battery based solely on the referral question (Koziol & Budding, 2011).

One of the primary issues facing a neuropsychologist employing the flexible-battery approach is test selection. This is especially important when working with children, as the choice of measure should be made based on the child's neurodevelopmental level. Measures also should be selected based on the goals of the evaluation, taking care to note that a poorly defined referral question makes this task unnecessarily difficult. Most important, the selection of measures should be based on a thorough evaluation of the test and what it measures. This is best accomplished through an objective evaluation of the task (i.e., task analysis) rather than by relying on the test name or what the publisher says it measures (Koziol & Budding, 2011; Miller, 2013). Because task analysis is critical to test selection in a flexible-battery approach and to the accurate identification of underlying cognitive processes, additional details of task analysis appear in appropriate subsequent chapter sections.

Processing–Based Approaches to Neuropsychological Evaluation

The recent switch to emphasizing function over structure in cognitive assessment is not surprising, given the advances in our understanding of the neuroanatomical and neurophysiological correlates of cognitive abilities during in vivo task performance. Difficulties in cognitive processing have been implicated in a number of neuro-developmental disorders, including learning disabilities, reading disabilities, dyscalculia, autistic spectrum disorder, and ADHD. Importantly, more recent definitions of such disorders (e.g., specific learning disabilities) reference difficulties with psychological processes, leading to various models of identification based on processing strengths and weaknesses in use today.

Simply stated, the completion of any cognitive task, no matter how simple, involves multiple mental processes, ranging from the more basic processes associated with sensation, perception, and motor functioning to the higher-order processing associated with reasoning and intentional executive control involved in complex decision making. Dysfunction at any level in this processing system can have detrimental effect on cognitive performance. Measures of intelligence or cognitive ability, such as the WISC–V, traditionally have emphasized higher-order processing, such as fluid reasoning or working memory (Dehn, 2014).

In addition to providing measures of higher-order processing, many intelligence and cognitive ability tests include measures of acquired knowledge or crystallized ability, such as that represented by the WISC–V Verbal Comprehension Index. Although measures of acquired or crystallized knowledge such as the Verbal Comprehension Index might be viewed primarily as the *products* of cognitive processing (Dehn, 2014), these abilities continue to supply an expanding base of knowledge to support the effective processing of new information, such as that measured by tests of fluid reasoning. In other words, the crystallized knowledge that has been acquired was, at one time, novel information. This encoded information includes more than semantic or declarative content; it also includes information related to contextual aspects of knowledge acquisition, such as effective (or ineffective) learning strategies or approaches to problem solving, which can subsequently be

retrieved and applied in novel situations. The Verbal Comprehension Index and similar measures of acquired knowledge are, not surprisingly, the best broad-ability measures for predicting academic achievement: yet another example of past performance serving as a good predictor of future performance. The Verbal Comprehension Index is often an area of relative weakness in children with language and reading difficulties, prompting further evaluation of associated processes (e.g., auditory processing, expressive language, encoding, long-term retrieval) to more accurately pinpoint the source of the problem and to help identify the most appropriate intervention. Measures of crystallized intelligence are also more impervious to the effects of aging and brain injury, making them important measures in neuropsychological evaluations as estimates of premorbid functioning or decline associated with neurodegenerative disorders. That being said, the focus of this chapter is on process-oriented neuropsychological approaches to interpretation of the WISC–V. As such, the chapter emphasizes cognitive processes such as fluid reasoning, working memory, and executive functions.

Interpretation of the WISC–V from a Lurian Perspective

Perhaps the two most important and enduring aspects of Alexander Luria's legacy in neuropsychology are the concepts of complex functional systems and syndrome analysis (Das, 2010). Consistent with results from functional imaging studies, Luria posited that cognitive functions are multifaceted activities involving interactive subcomponents that are mediated by interactive networks (Otero, 2015). Because of the highly interactive nature of this complex functional system, disturbance in any one of these components would have primary and secondary effects on mental function, resulting in more widespread disturbance (Princiotta & Goldstein, 2015). In Luria's own words: "As I have said already, any human mental activity is a complex functional system effected through a combination of concertedly working brain structures, each of which makes its own contribution to the functional system as a whole" (1973b, p. 38). Luria also noted that localization of dysfunction appeared to vary with the level of complexity, with basic sensory and motor functions being more localized to specific brain regions than higher-level functions that require the coordinated effort of more numerous brain areas (Horton & Reynolds, 2015). In order to understand the nature of underlying neural processes contributing to higher-level cognition, Luria (1966b) utilized qualitative *syndrome analysis* as "an essential step in the clinical analysis of disturbances of higher cortical functions from local brain lesions" (p. 84), as well as error analysis to investigate why an individual was unable to perform a specific task. Entirely consistent with the intelligent testing philosophy, Luria was keenly focused on gaining a thorough understanding of the individual's unique pattern of cognitive functioning across a variety of mental tasks.

Luria's association with Vygotsky undoubtedly influenced his beliefs about the important influence of the unique environmental and historical factors affecting an individual's mental functioning, considerations that are now routinely included in any intelligent evaluation of cognitive ability. Luria noted the relevance of neural plasticity in rehabilitation, noting that successful rehabilitation following brain injury involved the successful recruitment of alternate brain areas to perform old tasks in new ways (Horton & Reynolds, 2015). Luria's belief that information gleaned from studies of neural stimulation and destruction would be most informative was eerily prescient of recent neuroscientific advances in transcranial stimulation in attempts to move the field beyond correlational studies into an era in which such causal research is possible (Princiotta & Goldstein, 2015). With all of these insights and contributions to the field of neuropsychology, it is not surprising that Lurian-based approaches to neuropsychological assessment are still alive and well in contemporary practice (McCrea, 2009).

According to Luria, human cognitive abilities exist in a framework of three separate but interrelated functional units (Horton & Reynolds, 2015; Otero, 2015). The first functional unit regulates cortical arousal and attention (including selective or focused attention and sustained attention) and is located primarily in the brain stem, diencephalon, and medial regions of the cortex (Naglieri et al., 2012). Note that inhibition of irrelevant or distracting stimuli is viewed as a component of focused attention rather than an executive function. The second functional unit encodes incoming information, applies simultaneous and/or successive processing as necessary, and associates this information with previously acquired information (Dehn, 2014). Simultaneous processing requires the integration of information for holistic processing, whereas successive processing requires linear processing in sequential steps. Simultaneous and successive processing often are utilized concurrently, sharing common brain regions in the occipital, parietal, and temporal lobes posterior to the central sulcus of the brain (Naglieri et al., 2012). The third functional unit supports higher-level cortical functions, such as strategy development and application, self-monitoring and awareness, and the directed, conscious control of mental activities. The third unit is associated with the frontal and prefrontal cortex (Naglieri et al., 2012; Princiotta & Goldstein, 2015).

The KABC–II (A. S. Kaufman & Kaufman, 2004) extended its coverage of Lurian-based processes with the addition of planning and learning scales to the retained simultaneous and sequential (i.e., successive) processing scales of the original K-ABC. Measures of simultaneous processing on the KABC–II are represented by visual processing tasks and sequential processing is represented by short-term memory tasks. Planning is measured by fluid reasoning tasks, and learning is measured using long-term retrieval. Similar measures often are categorized in the same way according to Luria's functional units and associated processes, including those on the WISC–V.

The planning, attention, simultaneous, and successive (PASS) theory emerged from the influences of Luria as well as from the fields of cognitive psychology and neuropsychology (Dehn, 2014). According to the PASS model, planning processes involve executive control; attention involves arousal and maintenance of mental focus; and simultaneous and successive processing are used to perceive, encode, or transform information (Floyd & Kranzler, 2012). Naglieri and Das operationalized the PASS model in the CAS (1997) and in the CAS–II (Naglieri et al., 2014), including four composite scores to represent the level of functioning in each of the PASS processes. The CAS–II does not include measures of verbal ability or crystallized intelligence; however, a teacher rating form is available to obtain information about the PASS processes observed in the classroom.

It is important to remember that many tasks involve the coordinated use of one or more of the PASS processes, including concurrent simultaneous and successive processing. Although shared brain regions have been identified in both types of processing, neuroimaging suggests that simultaneous processing relies more heavily on interhemispheric activation than does successive processing (McCrea, 2009). More specifically, lesions to the occipitoparietal lobe have been related to difficulties in tasks requiring the organization of information into a gestalt, whereas lesions to the left temporal region are more associated with sequencing difficulties (McCrea, 2009). The first and third functional units share a particularly strong reciprocal relationship, in which attention is required for planning, and planning regulates attention. The ascending and descending reticular formation serves as a direct link between these functional units, transmitting neural impulses back and forth from the lower parts of the brain to the frontal cortex (Naglieri et al., 2012).

Although development of the WISC–V was not based on Lurian or PASS theory, the scores it provides can be interpreted easily from a Lurian processing perspective, as evidenced in the case report on Jaime, age 10, by Dr. Jennie Kaufman Singer (Case 7 later in this chapter). Jaime's performance was extremely low on measures of processing speed, a basic cognitive process associated with Luria's first functional unit. Evaluation of the second functional unit revealed problems with both successive and simultaneous processing, as evidenced by Jaime's poor performance on sequencing and visual-spatial subtests. Dr. Singer astutely noted the increased difficulties with tasks having motor demands, another indication of possible problems with processing associated with the first functional unit. As might be expected with deficiencies at the first and second units, Jaime also evidenced impaired ability on measures of fluid reasoning and complex working memory, which represent functioning in the third functional unit. Jaime seems to have more difficulty with simultaneous processing than sequential processing, but both types of processing improved with meaningful stimuli as opposed to abstract geometric shapes or patterns.

In order to facilitate interpretation of the WISC–V from a Lurian or other process-oriented neuropsychological perspective, each of the primary index scores is described in terms of the Lurian functional unit or units involved as well as in terms of the required processes according to PASS processing theory. Traditional descriptions of contributory cognitive functions for each primary index score are also provided for neuropsychologists operating from other theoretical orientations.

Verbal Comprehension Index
The Verbal Comprehension Index is derived from performance on the Similarities and Vocabulary subtests, and is the index score that best represents acquired knowledge, verbal reasoning, and verbal concept formation. From a Lurian perspective, the Verbal Comprehension

Index involves coordinated processing of the second and third functional units, especially simultaneous processing and reasoning. Responses to items on the supplemental Comprehension subtest also involve metacognition and an awareness of self and others, which are also relevant to functioning of the third functional unit. From a more general neuropsychological perspective, the Verbal Comprehension Index taps long-term retrieval, learning, receptive and expressive language, and executive functions (e.g., concept recognition and generation; Flanagan et al., 2010; Miller, 2010, 2013; Miller & Maricle, 2012; see Chapter 12). Relative to the other index scores, the Verbal Comprehension Index places lower demands on processing in children with normal cognitive functions; in fact, some experts suggest that the Verbal Comprehension Index (or other measures of crystallized intelligence) should not be interpreted as a process at all but rather be viewed as the product of previous processing (Dehn, 2014). The authors disagree for two reasons. First, the scoring of verbal responses often reflects the level of abstraction used by the child, with more concrete responses earning less credit than those responses reflecting abstract thought or conceptualization. Second, poor performance on the Verbal Comprehension Index may be indicative of difficulties with auditory processing, encoding, expressive language, or concept formation, all of which involve active processing.

Visual Spatial Index
The Visual Spatial Index is derived from performance on the Block Design and Visual Puzzles subtests, and measures visual-spatial processing, part-whole relationships, integration and synthesis, and visual-motor integration. From a Lurian perspective, the Visual Spatial Index involves coordinated processing of the second and third functional units, especially planning, simultaneous processing, and reasoning. In more traditional neuropsychological terms, the Visual Spatial Index taps visual-perceptual and visual-motor abilities as well as a number of executive

functions (planning, problem solving, cognitive flexibility, and reasoning; Flanagan et al., 2010; Miller, 2010, 2013; Miller & Maricle, 2012).

Fluid Reasoning Index
The Fluid Reasoning Index is derived from performance on the Matrix Reasoning and Figure Weights and is the score that best represents inductive and fluid reasoning, broad visual intelligence, conceptual thinking, and classification ability. From a Lurian perspective, the Fluid Reasoning Index involves coordinated processing of the second and third functional units, with an emphasis on the higher-level cortical functions associated with the third unit. Thus, the Fluid Reasoning Index involves planning and reasoning as well as simultaneous and successive processing. More specifically, the Fluid Reasoning Index measures neuropsychological constructs within or serving the executive function domain, including planning, executive attention, problem solving, and cognitive flexibility (Flanagan et al., 2010; Miller, 2010, 2013; Miller & Maricle, 2012).

Working Memory Index
The Working Memory Index is derived from performance on the Digit Span and Picture Span subtests, thus providing a mixed measure of both auditory and visual working memory. From a Lurian perspective, the Working Memory Index involves coordinated processing of all three functional units, including attention, sequential reasoning, planning, and executive functions. From a more general neuropsychological perspective, successful Working Memory Index performance requires selective and executive attention, visual-spatial ability (for Picture Span), and response inhibition (Flanagan et al., 2010; Miller, 2010, 2013; Miller & Maricle, 2012).

Processing Speed Index
The Processing Speed Index is derived from performance on the Coding and Symbol Search subtests and provides a measure of speed in performing mental operations or, more specifically,

the quick scanning and discrimination of simple visual information. From a Lurian perspective, successful performance on the Processing Speed Index requires the coordinated efforts of all three functional units, including attention, simultaneous and successive processing, as well as planning and self-monitoring. In more general neuropsychological terms, the Processing Speed Index measures mental speed and efficiency, selective and sustained attention, visual scanning, immediate visual memory for objects, and response inhibition (Flanagan et al., 2010; Miller, 2010, 2013; Miller & Maricle, 2012).

We have developed four additional scores to allow for further evaluation of possible differences in simultaneous and successive processing that may be of particular interest to those applying a Lurian or other process-oriented approach to WISC–V interpretation. Two scores are derived from Matrix Reasoning—one from the 2×2 matrix items, which probably emphasize simultaneous processing, and the other from the series completion items, which seem more dependent on successive processing. In addition, we provide a Simultaneous Processing Index (Figure Weights, Picture Concepts, and the 2×2 Matrix Reasoning items) and a Successive Processing Index (Digit Span Backward, Digit Span Sequencing, Letter–Number Sequencing, and the series completion Matrix Reasoning items). To learn more about these four scores and to make comparisons that involve them, see Appendix F in the downloadable resources: www.wiley.com/go/itwiscv.

Interpretation of the WISC–V from Other Process-Oriented Approaches

In regard to the influence of brain imaging advances on neuropsychology, Otero (2015) noted:

> Although these technologies are favored for investigation the structural and functional dynamics of the brain, it is these authors' opinion that the understanding and assessment of neurocognitive processes by studying patterns of neurocognitive strengths and weaknesses in developmental, psychiatric, psychosocial, and learning disorders are best

> achieved through formal assessment procedures. (p. 194)

Although we may eventually reach a time when we are able to measure cognitive processes directly, for now, these mental activities must be inferred from test performance. As noted by Floyd and Kranzler (2012), "it seems prudent to conclude that during complex cognitive tasks, an examinee's performance is far too multifaceted to deconstruct to the process level" (p. 518). Undaunted by this challenge, there are several interpretive approaches that emphasize cognitive processing in addition to Lurian- and PASS-based approaches, including the process approach advocated by Edith Kaplan and the Processing Assessment method used by Milton Dehn (2014). Other process approaches emphasize task analysis (or a similar analysis of task content by another name), such as Silver's (1993) information processing model and the cognitive hypothesis testing (CHT) model by Hale and Fiorello (2004). Brief descriptions of these approaches are provided, with the reader referred to the original sources for more information. Dan Miller's Integrated School Neuropsychological/Cattell-Horn-Carroll (SNP/CHC) model and George McCloskey's process approach to interpretation are described in their respective chapters (12 and 13).

Consistent with the intelligent testing philosophy, contemporary practice in neuropsychology utilizes both quantitative and qualitative approaches to interpretation. Following in the steps of Luria, Edith Kaplan was one of the strongest advocates of the Boston process approach, developing tests and methods for testing the limits, including the *WISC–III as a Processing Instrument* (WISC–III PI; Kaplan, et al., 1999) and the *WISC–IV Integrated* (Wechsler, Kaplan, Fein, Morris, Kramer, & Delis, 2004). Although Edith is no longer with us, her influence lives on in the WISC–V Integrated, a measure specifically designed to investigate the reasons underlying poor WISC–V performance. Aspects of Kaplan's approach permeate other process-oriented approaches and measures, such as those with error scores and base rates for observed behaviors (e.g., WISC–V Integrated and NEPSY–II): a fitting tribute to her lasting impact on neuropsychology.

Dehn (2014) described the difference between his approach to processing assessment and more typical neuropsychological approaches as the level of process analysis, with his approach focusing more on interpretation of higher-level processing than lower-level processing. Dehn's theory of psychological processing and learning emphasizes the increased difficulty of assessing processes in children: "For each academic skill there is an optimal set of psychological processes that function as aptitudes. For successful learning of an academic skill, the combined set of aptitudes must attain a sufficient threshold of development" (p. 20). Academic skills that should be assessed correspond to the eight areas described in specific learning disability criteria, including basic reading skills, reading fluency, reading comprehension, mathematics calculation and problem solving, written and oral expression, and listening comprehension. Psychological processes are defined as neuropsychological operations involved in perceiving, manipulating, storing, retrieving, and expressing information, including those processes that facilitate and regulate other processes (what some refer to as executive functions). Aptitudes are described as specific cognitive abilities that enable skill acquisition, and many of these abilities are actually psychological processes (e.g., working memory). Key features of Dehn's theory note the neurological basis of psychological processes and the central, core importance of memory processes to academic learning. Also key to Dehn's approach is the need for thorough task analysis when selecting measures for processing assessment.

Task-Analysis Approaches in Contemporary Neuropsychological Assessment
In any flexible-battery approach to neuropsychological assessment, knowledge of what a subtest or task measures is of critical importance. Overreliance on published descriptions or, worse yet,

the task name can lead to faulty assumptions and errors in interpretation. The need for task analysis has long been acknowledged (Silver, 1993). Hale and Fiorello's (2004) CHT model provides a contemporary approach that emphasizes the importance of task analysis (referred to as *demands analysis*) to interpretation.

SILVER'S (1993) INFORMATION-PROCESSING MODEL

In addition to CHC theoretical foundations, Luria's neuropsychological processing model, and the theories that form the core of cognitive development and function, alternate models may be applied to interpret the profile of test scores. Silver's (1993) information-processing model, for example, has historically been a foundation of Kaufman's intelligent testing approach (A. S. Kaufman, 1994a; A. S. Kaufman & Lichtenberger, 1999, 2006). Floyd and Kranzler (2012) pointed out that Silver's information-processing model, which analyzes tasks in terms of their input, integration, storage, and output,

> is somewhat dated and does not reflect the complexity of processing in more contemporary models. As a result, it does not include an array of processing steps (e.g., memory retrieval).... It also tends to focus on general categories of processing (related to cognitive abilities) rather than specific processes. (p. 515)

In its defense, however, Floyd and Kranzler (2012) noted that it "may sensitize those interpreting intelligence tests ... to the construct-irrelevant influences related to input (e.g., visual acuity problems) and output (e.g., motor deficits)" (p. 515). Furthermore,

> it seems to make practical sense to examine the influences associated with input of information into the cognitive system and the output via responses when clinicians are evaluating item-level performances; these influences are observable for the most part. Labeling of these

steps is modeled well by the interpretive [approach] of Kaufman and Lichtenberger. (p. 520)

The well-known theories of intelligence and neuropsychological processing are concerned with the *integration* (interpreting and processing information) and *storage* (storing the information for later retrieval) aspects of Silver's information-processing model. But to be an effective detective in identifying a child's strengths and weaknesses, clinicians also need to consider the nature of the *input* (how information from the sense organs enters the brain) and *output* (expressing information via language or muscle activity). Some tasks are auditory-vocal, like Vocabulary and Similarities (excluding the early picture items) and others, like Block Design and Symbol Search, are visual-motor. Visual Puzzles, Matrix Reasoning, Picture Concepts, and Figure Weights require the ability to process visual information, but the response can be either motor (pointing to the correct response) or vocal (naming the letter). It would be wise not only to think carefully about the sensory modalities that each WISC–V task requires but to *observe* whether the child consistently responded by pointing or naming. This approach is entirely consistent with Hale and Fiorello's popular and well-articulated cognitive hypothesis testing approach to interpretation (Fiorello, Hale, & Wycoff, 2012; Hale & Fiorello, 2004).

Regarding input, the WISC–V Verbal Comprehension subtests tend to be auditory, whereas Visual-Spatial, Fluid Reasoning, and Processing Speed subtests all require the processing of visual stimuli. However, the understanding-of-directions component of most of the subtests with visual stimuli (e.g., Coding, Figure Weights) can present difficulty for children with weak auditory reception skills. The input aspect of WISC–V tasks is more subtle than a simple auditory-visual dichotomy, however. Verbal Comprehension subtests present different auditory challenges for children. Some tasks, such as Information and Comprehension, demand understanding of long questions, whereas Vocabulary and Similarities require the ability to interpret single words in isolation. The former types of tests are difficult for children who cannot make sense of long strings of words (perhaps because of a memory, sequential, or auditory processing deficit); the latter can become trouble spots for children who need context clues, maybe because of an auditory discrimination problem or hearing impairment. Performance subtests, too, present different types of input challenges.

WISC–V tasks differ in terms of the amount of output required. The tasks like Matrix Reasoning and Picture Concepts that can be solved by pointing barely tax children's motor abilities, quite a contrast to the psychomotor speed that is needed to score well on Processing Speed subtests and the construction abilities required for Block Design. Likewise, children with verbal expression problems often can handle the one-word responses required for most Information items or a task like Letter–Number Sequencing but crumble when they have to use their own words to answer Comprehension or Vocabulary items or to rapidly name objects or numbers on the Naming Speed subtests.

Even the five primary index scales and the complementary subtests correspond primarily to different aspects of the information-processing model. Verbal Comprehension, Fluid Reasoning, and Visual Spatial refer to cognitive abilities akin to *Gc*, *Gf*, and *Gv*, respectively, and are best interpreted as measures of integration. Working Memory (*Gsm*), Symbol Translation (*Glr*), and Naming Speed are measures of storage, whereas Processing Speed factor is primarily an output factor. The century-old Block Design and Comprehension subtests place heavy demands on all four components of Silver's information-processing model, making an examiner's ability to be a good detective essential for identifying a child's deficit areas.

For some children, such as those with auditory processing disorders, sensory impairments, or physical disabilities, the key to profile interpretation may reside within a simple information-processing model. Clinicians need to be prepared to evaluate problems with input or output as the child's problem area, not necessarily the integrative aspects of Fluid Reasoning or Visual Spatial subtests or the storage component of Working Memory or Symbol Translation tasks. There is no question that CHC theory, neuropsychological processing models, and theories related to cognitive development and function are the straws that stir the drink of WISC–V interpretation. But keep Silver's simple information-processing model, sometimes referred to as the "learning disabilities model," in the back of your mind.

HALE AND FIORELLO'S DEMANDS ANALYSIS

The *demands analysis* is a key feature of Hale and Fiorello's (2004) CHT approach to interpretation. Their method of task analysis combines Kaplanesque qualitative observation with aspects of the shared-abilities method in search of the reasons behind poor performance. Aspects of task input and output are analyzed, and inferences about the underlying cognitive processes are inferred from the demands analysis and iterative hypothesis testing. Worksheets are provided to guide the clinician through the demands analysis, with input and output requirements gleaned from a review of the task materials and the examinee's responses. For example, subtest instructions are thoroughly reviewed prior to task administration on characteristics such as length, verbiage, and use of demonstration, sample, or practice items. Output analysis includes a description of response type (e.g., verbal versus motor response) and format (e.g., free recall or recognition). General classes of processes are described (as well as their many component subprocesses) according to the brain regions involved, including attention and executive frontal lobe processes, concordant/convergent left-hemisphere processes, and discordant/divergent right-hemisphere

processes (Floyd & Kranzler, 2012). Materials for the demands analysis provide a wealth of information about the possible cognitive processes contributing to performance but also underscore the complexities associated with teasing out the more basic processes from those involved in higher-order thinking.

NEUROPSYCHOLOGICAL CASE REPORT CONTENT

Although there is much variety in neuropsychological report writing, there are also commonalities. At a minimum, the case report should include:

> background to the referral, relevant history, reasons for assessment, neuropsychologists observations of patient's behavior, test administered and results for cognitive domains tested, any additional findings (e.g. questionnaires for mood) and finish the report with a summary and recommendations. (Clare, 2010, p. 139)

Note that the order of sections is not fixed, as evidenced by the variability across the neuropsychologically oriented case reports in Part IV of this book. Hebben and Milberg's (2009) text, *Essentials of Neuropsychological Assessment*, served as the primary resource for these sections.

Identifying Information

This section should include the child's name, age, grade, date of birth, date of testing, and date of the report. If the examiner is someone other than the report writer, his or her name should be listed.

Reason for Referral

Referral questions are critical to assessment, providing a goal or aim for the evaluation and limiting its scope. Unfortunately, referral questions are often vague, referring to general academic difficulties (e.g., reading problems). Intelligent testers try to gain as much possible information about the specifics of the referral question prior to the evaluation. In addition to providing the reasons for the evaluation, the source of the referral should be provided as well as his or her relationship to the child. Typically, a summary of the child's difficulties is included. If the evaluation is being requested by a third party, such as a court, this should be noted as well as the child's knowledge about the purpose of testing.

Records Reviewed

This is where the clinician lists all sources of information for the background and history section, including dates for the obtained information, where the information came from, and any possible bias in the informant.

History and Background Information

> It is only within the context of a patient's history that an accurate interpretation of their test data and thus a diagnosis can be made. (Hebben & Milberg, 2009, p. 44)

A summary of relevant historical and background information is written based on information from review of records, interviews (with the child, parent/guardian, caretaker, teacher, therapist, or other involved parties), and previous evaluations. For children, it is especially important to note pre-, peri-, and postnatal factors that may be relevant to the evaluation (e.g., risk factors) as well as other medical, educational, social, or familial factors.

Behavioral Observations

Although most intelligent clinicians sprinkle behavioral observations throughout the report, this section is important for describing such things as the child's appearance and demeanor,

hygiene, level of engagement or motivation, affect or mood, interpersonal behavior (e.g., observed interactions with parents, teachers, and classmates), and the clinician's perceptions of the child's language production and comprehension obtained before and during the evaluation.

Cognizance—A New Area for Reports?

Based on recent research discussed in Chapter 10 describing the possible mediating role of cognizance (awareness of mental processes and states) in cognitive development (Spanoudis et al., 2015), we suggest that this domain be considered as an addition to neuropsychological reports. Although the number of standardized measures of this domain may be relatively limited at this time, intelligent clinicians can use other techniques to supplement the information provided by those that are available (e.g., the Theory of Mind test on the NEPSY–II). More informal methods for obtaining this type of information may include direct questioning of the child about how he or she solved the problem, behavioral observations of employed strategies, or posing hypothetical situations that require the child to demonstrate these abilities (i.e., "How would it feel if… ?"). Simply asking children about how they believed they performed on a task could provide some insight into their level of self-awareness.

Tests Administered

All procedures and administered tests should be noted here. The full names of measures should be included with their acronyms, as well as which version. The date of publication can provide useful information about the relative age of the test norms.

Test Results

This is where the results of the evaluation are presented, typically organized according to cognitive domain or function. Examples of headers within this section include: Intellectual Functions; Attention and Executive Functions;

Memory and Learning; and Language and Motor Abilities. Elaine Fletcher-Janzen (personal communication, December 8, 2014) described her approach to organizing this section, which beautifully incorporates developmental expectations for child:

> In a case report, each processing area has 4 sections: (1) a description of the process and its developmental trajectory, (2) how we could expect someone the child's age to perform in this area, (3) the assessment results (summary, no numbers) of where the subject child is in terms of strength or weakness in this area, and (4) how this hooks into the classroom or home. The latter is very important because it translates into the summary and recommendations. The report is written with as little jargon as possible and is intended for student, parent, and teacher level. (On the surface, it sounds like a quick eval—but if I was taken to court on it—I can deconstruct it and lay it out as show them a full neuropsychological assessment—it just doesn't look like one.
>
> So in general I see the whole process as: (1) knowing neurodevelopment, (2) knowing how to assess and analyze results, and (3) knowing how to translate all of these data into an understandable format and interventions. These are distinct areas of expertise—and they are synergetic and the whole process fails if one fails. Sort of like Musketeers really!

Summary and Impressions

This section should provide a snapshot of the child as well as interpretation of test results. The summary should, if possible, clearly respond to the referral question, a much easier task if the question was well defined. Results should be presented with as little jargon as possible in this section and throughout the report. Summaries of the child's strengths and weaknesses across the various domains of functioning should be made in the context of the child's unique personal history and circumstances. In general, this section should convey the reason for referral, obtained results, and interpretive conclusions.

Recommendations

Recommendations might be viewed as the most important aspect of the case report. Recommendations are especially helpful when organized by the intended target, whether it is the child, parent/guardian, teacher, or some other person involved in the intervention plan. Recommendations must be clear and written at a level appropriate for the audience. Recommendations are particularly important for comprehensive neuropsychological reports based on the view that some of these reports are more concerned with playing pin the tail on the lesion and making diagnostic conclusions without providing useful recommendations or interventions (Miller, 2013; Pelletier, Hiemenz, & Shapiro, 2004).

MULTIPLE ASSESSMENTS OF THE SAME CHILD OR ADOLESCENT: TAKING INTO ACCOUNT PRACTICE EFFECTS ON WECHSLER'S SCALES

Neuropsychologists and other clinicians are often faced with the need to reevaluate a child, or are evaluating a child who has been evaluated on several previous occasions. Too often, examiners ignore the impact of practice effects and the Flynn effect (Flynn, 1984, 2009) on the child's profile of scores. These effects are also important considerations when a flexible-battery approach is used. The norms from different tests vary in age; examiners should select tests, at least in part, based on when the test was standardized and what tests have previously been administered to the child or adolescent.

WISC–V Practice Effects

Historically, practice effects on Wechsler's FSIQ have been about 6 to 7 points with differences substantially larger on nonverbal and fluid tasks (8–10 points) than verbal ones (2–3 points). These findings have been found, in general, on all Wechsler scales, including the more recent versions that have replaced Verbal and Performance IQs with Factor Indexes (Flanagan & Kaufman, 2009; Lichtenberger & Kaufman, 2013). Intervals are typically about 1 month (A. S. Kaufman, 1994b; A. S. Kaufman & Lichtenberger, 2006), but similar results have been identified for longer intervals as well (Matarazzo, Carmody, & Jacobs, 1980).

WISC–V stability was assessed for 218 children and adolescents, ages 6–16 years (mean age = 11.4, standard deviation [SD] = 3.1), tested twice with an interval of about 1 month. Intervals ranged from 9–82 days with a mean interval of 26 days; the test-retest sample was roughly stratified on U.S. Census data (Wechsler, 2014, pp. 63–66). WISC–V practice effects are summarized in Table 11.1 for FSIQ, the primary indexes, and selected other indexes for the total sample of 218 (Wechsler, 2014, Table 4.7).

Table 11.1 Practice Effects on the WISC–V over a 1-Month Interval for Primary, Symbol Translation, and Global Indexes

Primary Index + Symbol Translation Index		
Symbol Translation Index	+8.8	.58
Processing Speed Index	+7.9	.52
Visual-Spatial Index	+6.7	.45
Fluid Reasoning Index	+4.9	.37
Verbal Comprehension Index	+3.1	.24
Working Memory Index	+2.4	.17
Global Index		
Nonverbal Index	+7.0	.50
Full Scale IQ (FSIQ)	+6.0	.44
General Ability	+5.6	.41
FSIQ by Age Group		
6–7 (n = 35)	+7.5	.61
8–9 (n = 42)	+4.7	.35
10–11 (n = 38)	+5.2	.35
12–13 (n = 42)	+5.8	.44
14–16 (n = 55)	+6.6	.46

Note: Data are from Wechsler (2014, Tables 4.7 and 4.8). Standard difference is the difference between the two test means divided by the square root of the pooled variance, computed using Cohen's (1996) formula. The Symbol Translation Index is included because it measures *Glr*, an important ability in CHC theory.

Practice effects for WISC–V are entirely consistent with gain scores on previous versions of WISC as well as WAIS. Practice effects are about 6 points on the FSIQ and General Ability Index and 7 points on the Nonverbal Index. Differences are larger (5–8 points) on the Processing Speed Index, Visual Spatial Index, and Fluid Reasoning Index than on the Verbal Comprehension Index and Working Memory Index (2–3 points). The largest practice effects—gains of almost 9 points—were on the Symbol Translation Index (STI), a measure of learning ability and long-term retrieval. This finding is consistent with the large practice effects on the KABC–II Learning/*Glr* scale (A. S. Kaufman & Kaufman, 2004), suggesting that incidental learning has taken place and that some of the associations learned during the administration of the Symbol Translation Index tasks have been retained in long-term storage. In general, the finding that the largest gains are on nonverbal, fluid, processing speed, and learning tasks is sensible in that none of these tasks resembles the kinds of tests or tasks given by teachers in school. In that sense, the tasks with the largest practice effects are novel the first time they are administered, but that novelty wears off when they are administered the second time. The largest practice effects in the Wechsler literature are the gains of 9 to 11 points on WISC–R Performance IQ, probably because that scale included three subtests that each gave multiple bonus points for quick, perfect performance; subtests with bonus points, as well as processing speed subtests like Coding, have been shown to yield the largest practice effects (A. S. Kaufman, 1979).

The fact that an array of WISC–V subtests lose their novelty the second time they are administered (and the third, fourth, etc.) means that children and adults who are tested on a Wechsler Scale should, ideally, be retested on a different intelligence test when they are retested. That does not often happen because the WAIS and WISC remain the gold standards for neuropsychological evaluations. When someone has been assessed within the last 6 months or 1 year on a Wechsler scale, then administer a different test, such as the WJ IV or CAS2. But if examiners opt to give the WISC–V for a second time, it is incumbent on them to take into account the impact of practice effects when interpreting the validity of IQs for an individual, especially on nonverbal, speed, fluid, and learning tasks—the very tasks that are the *least* dependent on cultural experiences and environmental influences. The well-known IQ gain of 6–7 points must be internalized by anyone who writes or reads case reports on individuals tested multiple times on a Wechsler scale. When a person has been tested multiple times on Wechsler's scales, the first Wechsler scale administered should ordinarily be considered the best estimate of that person's intelligence—so long as the scores are deemed valid by the examiner and there are no new circumstances (e.g., head injury or successful pharmaceutical intervention to control anxiety, depression, or ADHD symptoms) that cloud the clinical picture.

How Long Do Practice Effects Last?

Research, though mostly with adults, suggests that these practice effects continue well past 1 month. Catron and Thompson (1979) showed that the gain in Performance IQ was still going strong after 4 months (8 points), although the gain on Verbal IQ had dwindled to 1 point. Further, in their review of the stability of intelligence and the resilience of practice effects, Calamia, Markon, and Tranel (2012) stated: "Retest scores are assumed to be highest at short intervals and then decrease with time (Theisen, Rapport, Axelrod, & Brines, 1998). However, several studies have found practice effects to persist years after testing, e.g., 3 years (Van der Elst, Van Boxtel, Van Breukelen, & Jolles, 2008), 5 years (Ronnlund, Nyberg, Backman, & Nilsson, 2005), or even 7 or more years (Salthouse, Schroeder, & Ferrer, 2004)" (p. 547).

In a comprehensive review of 11 WAIS test-retest studies, Matarazzo et al. (1980) found gains of about 2 points on Verbal IQ and 7 to 8 points on Performance IQ with intervals ranging from 1 week to 13 years. A. S. Kaufman (1994b) concluded the following based on the results of a plethora of data on test-retest studies for Wechsler scales at all ages of childhood, adolescence, and adulthood:

> The expected increase of about 5 to 8 points in global IQ renders any score obtained on a retest as a likely overestimate of the person's true level of functioning—especially if the retest is given within about six months of the original test, or if the person has been administered a Wechsler scale (*any* Wechsler scale) several times in the course of a few years. (p. 832, italics in original)

A. S. Kaufman and Lichtenberger (2006) cautioned clinicians and researchers about the importance of taking Wechsler practice effects fully into consideration when conducting neuropsychological assessment or neuropsychological research:

> Gains in intelligence that are sometimes attributed to recovery from an illness or operation or to any intervention designed to improve cognitive abilities may be nothing more than a demonstration of the Wechsler practice effect. The most notable instance of such an occurrence concerns patients who had undergone carotid endarterectomy, surgery for the removal of arteriosclerotic deposits that partially block blood flow in the artery leading from the heart to the brain. Several investigators (e.g., Juolasmaa, [Outakoski, Hirvenoja, Tienari, Sotaniemi, & Takkunen], 1981) interpreted pre- to post-surgery gains on the WAIS as clear-cut evidence of cognitive improvement following the surgery. As optimistic as such a finding would be, Matarazzo, Matarazzo, Gallo, and Wiens, (1979) argued that the gains demonstrated by the surgical patients on the retest were not appreciably different from the gains shown by nonpatients. Although Shatz (1981) called the conclusion of no discernible intellectual gains following surgery premature because of uncontrolled variables in the available test-retest studies, a subsequent well-controlled investigation by Parker, Granberg, Nichols, Jones, and Hewett (1983) concluded that gains in test scores of surgical patients after a 6-month interval were not significantly greater than gains displayed by the control groups. (p. 206)

Although a bulk of the neuropsychological literature involves adult subjects, these cautions are equally applicable for children and adolescents tested on the WISC–V, whether as part of a research project or when a child with neurological impairment is tested multiple times on a Wechsler scale—whether the same scale or any combination of the WPPSI–IV, WISC–V, and WAIS–IV—to evaluate response to intervention, including surgery.

How to Deal with Practice Effects as Clinicians

How should clinicians interpret whether a WISC–V retest shows a true gain in a child's or adolescent's intellectual function rather than displaying nothing more than the practice effect? Matarazzo's opinions based on WAIS and WAIS–R data provide a good starting point for the WISC–V, in view of the fact that FSIQ, General Ability Index, and Nonverbal Index gains are all in the same 6- to 7-point ballpark as previous editions of WISC and WAIS. Matarazzo and colleagues emphasized that the overall practice effect of about 7 points on Wechsler's FSIQ is merely the average gain. In fact, even gains *twice* that large are common in the normal population (Matarazzo & Herman, 1984). Matarazzo et al. (1980) suggested using the rule of thumb that a gain of at least 15 points is needed in a person's FSIQ from one administration to the next to denote a "significant" improvement (i.e., a gain that cannot be simply attributed to the known practice effect). Note, however, that "a 20- to 25-point gain is needed for Performance IQ" (A. S. Kaufman & Lichtenberger, 2006, p. 207), and similar magnitudes of gain would be needed to denote "significant" improvement on the PSI, VRI, FRI, and STI.

Multiple Assessments and Progressive Error

But what about individuals who have been tested three, four, or five times between early childhood

and early adulthood, usually on the most recent version of Wechsler's scales? The practice effects caused by repeated testing on the same IQ test have a special name—*progressive error* (Kausler, 1991). That type of practice effect has been observed in numerous longitudinal investigations of the aging process. Performance IQ is well known to decline dramatically with increasing age (Horn & Hofer, 1992). However, in some longitudinal studies in which adults are tested many times on Wechsler's adult tests, the researchers have discovered that there is no age-related decline in Performance IQ. For example, Schmitz-Scherzer and Thomae (1983) tested adults on the German WAIS as many as five times across the life span and reported no decline in nonverbal ability through old age. The well-known decreases with age on visual-spatial ability, fluid reasoning, and processing speed were masked in this study by the powerful opposite influence of progressive error. "When individuals are tested repeatedly on Wechsler's Performance tasks, they no longer measure the kind of intelligence that thrives on novel problem-solving tasks with visual-spatial stimuli, and it becomes questionable whether they measure intelligence" (A. S. Kaufman & Lichtenberger, 2006, p. 165).

Progressive error is often referred to in the aging-IQ literature as "test experience effects" (Salthouse, in press). These effects—when contrasted to true "age effects"—have been systematically modeled and studied in a variety of longitudinal investigations in which more than two assessments have been conducted (e.g., Ferrer, Salthouse, McArdle, Stewart, & Schwartz, 2005; Ferrer, Salthouse, Stewart, & Schwartz, 2004; Rabbitt, Diggle, Smith, Holland, & McInnes, 2001; Tucker-Drob, Johnson, & Jones, 2009; Wilson, Li, Bienas, & Bennett, 2006). Much data have been accumulated to support the scientific, empirical basis of progressive error. Consider, for example, the findings of Rabbitt, Lunn, Wong, and Cobain (2008): "During a 20-year longitudinal study, 5,842 participants aged 49 to 93 years significantly improved over two to four successive experiences of the Heim AH4–1 intelligence test (first published in 1970), even with between-test intervals of 4 years and longer" (p. 235). Rabbitt et al. (2008) concluded: (a) "significant practice improvements are found even when intervals between successive presentations of the task are as long as 4 years"; (b) "that even the oldest participants show gains … over periods of 8 and of 12 years"; and (c) "that younger participants gain more from practice than do relatively older participants" (p. P239).

Even more important for WISC–V interpretation is the study conducted by Sirois et al. (2002) that was *not* based on adult data. They tested male children and adolescents five times on Wechsler's scales, with intervals of about 1 year between assessments. Verbal IQ decreased slightly (about 2 points) over time, but the progressive error was quite evident in the mean Performance IQs earned over five administrations: 108.5 at the baseline test, increasing steadily to 116.1 on the fifth test. Although Sirois et al. only provided data on the separate Verbal and Performance IQs, we estimated mean FSIQs from Wechsler's norms tables. Using Sirois et al.'s data, we compared the change in IQ earned by the male children and adolescents from the first annual reevaluation to the fourth annual reevaluation. The IQ on the first reevaluation (administered about 1 year after the baseline test) was 106.5; by the fourth reevaluation, that IQ had risen to 109.7. The gain in Wechsler FSIQ due to progressive error was 3.2 points. That result is consistent with estimates of progressive error ("test experience") from Salthouse's (2014a, 2014b, in press) series of studies on adults tested multiple times to better understand cognitive decline.

The Bottom Line about Practice Effects

The question is: What should neuropsychologists internalize from present and past data on Wechsler practice effects? The gain of 6 to 7 points found on WISC–V global scores, consistent with FSIQ gains on all versions of WISC

and WAIS, tells us the average gain to expect in global ability, just due to the experience of taking a Wechsler scale a few months earlier. Matarazzo et al. (1980) found gains of 5 points on Full Scale IQ based on studies with a wide variation in test intervals, some as long as 13 years. Investigations of test experience based on children (Sirois et al., 2002) or adults (Rabbitt et al., 2008; Salthouse, 2014a, 2014b, in press) tested multiple times on a Wechsler scale suggests a 3-point effect. Therefore, the practice effect of 6 to 7 IQ points that predominate the Wechsler literature for individuals tested twice over brief intervals provides the best estimate of short-term improvements on Wechsler's scales. In contrast, the 3 to 5 IQ points found in studies that utilized longer intervals are the best estimates of practice effects for individuals retested after a long interval (e.g., 4 years) or tested three or more times over the course of a decade.

Clinicians need to internalize these practice effects and progressive errors. It is common to read case reports on individuals tested multiple times on Wechsler's scales, but it is uncommon to read about the possible impact of yesterday's test scores on today's profile. FSIQ and other global estimates will be affected to a known degree. Nonverbal, fluid, processing speed, and learning ability will be affected far more than verbal and working memory abilities. Understanding these well-researched practice effects will affect our understanding of an individual's strengths and weaknesses, assets and deficits, and overall level of functioning. Suggested interventions are likely to be impacted as well.

Neuropsychologists routinely apply standard errors of measurement and confidence intervals to facilitate profile interpretation. It has become standard practice for clinicians to adjust IQs by the Flynn effect (Flynn, 1984, 1987, 2009), now that it is widely accepted that the norms for IQ tests become outdated at the rate of 3 points per decade in the United States. As a result of the Flynn effect, obtained IQs become spuriously inflated by the degree to which the norms are outdated. It is common for clinicians to subtract

3 points for each decade that norms are outdated, especially when important decisions rest on the exact magnitude of a person's IQ (A. S. Kaufman & Weiss, 2010). In a recent meta-analysis of the Flynn effect that spanned 285 studies ($N = 14,031$), the authors concluded that their results "supported previous estimates of the Flynn effect and its robustness across different age groups, measures, samples, and levels of performance" (Trahan, Steubing, Hiscock, & Fletcher, 2014, p. 1332). It is now time for neuropsychologists to attribute the same importance to practice effects that they give to errors of measurement and norms obsolescence.

INTRODUCTION TO CASE REPORTS

The illustrative case reports selected for this chapter all provide examples of neuropsychologically oriented approaches to interpretation. Jennie Kaufman Singer applied a Lurian-based approach in her evaluation of Jaime, age 10. Despite the identification of Jaime's atypical development during infancy and identification of an unspecified learning disability by age 5, interventions resulting from previous evaluations focused almost exclusively on Jaime's problematic, sometimes aggressive behavior, which is admittedly a growing source of concern as he matures physically. Dr. Singer astutely presents a chronological history of test results to reveal the widening academic gap between Jaime and his peers, emphasizing the need for prompt academically focused interventions in addition to current services. Process analysis of reading-related measures is deftly employed to target very specific interventions for use at home and at school. Jaime is fortunate that Dr. Singer saw past his obvious behavioral problems to clarify the existence of severe specific learning disabilities.

As clinicians we do not always know the outcome of our recommendations. However, Dr. Singer informed us that Jaime's report played a large role in his qualification for receipt of

special services at a California state agency. This agency provides exceptional care and treatment for qualified children and adults who have intellectual and developmental disabilities—just what the Dr. ordered.

Next, Marsha Vasserman introduces us to Christopher, age 11, whose struggles with reading and writing seem more arduous than expected based on his long-standing history of vision problems. Results from this thorough neuropsychological evaluation are highly variable, requiring detective-like inspection to tease out the web of interacting forces contributing to Christopher's academic difficulties. The wealth of information provided by this detailed process analysis is perfectly complemented by a process-like description of Christopher's performance over the course of the testing session. Although each and every child is unique, Christopher's performance was especially variable. He is much more likely to receive the targeted interventions he needs thanks to the sleuthing of Dr. Vasserman, perhaps avoiding some of the social and psychological problems associated with unidentified learning disabilities as children go untreated.

The last case report in this chapter was generously supplied by esteemed pediatric neuropsychologist Dr. Michelle Lurie. Isabella, age 13, was referred for evaluation by her psychiatrist in hopes of gaining a better understanding of Isabella's emotional and cognitive functioning. Dr. Lurie delivers on this by interweaving the impact of Isabella's emotional struggles with her cognitive difficulties throughout the report. The reader feels the pain resulting from Isabella's conflicting needs for acceptance and her fear of rejection as she becomes more aware of her cognitive limitations. The exhaustive assessment of Isabella's attentional difficulties is especially noteworthy, using multiple modalities and measures both with and without medication. As is done throughout the report, interventions for emotional and cognitive difficulties are presented with a lovely description of their reciprocal interactions.

CASE 7—JAIME, AGE 10: A FOURTH-GRADE BOY ON THE AUTISM SPECTRUM STRUGGLING WITH BEHAVIORAL AND LEARNING PROBLEMS

Jennie Kaufman Singer

Report of Psychoeducational Evaluation

Name: Jaime

Date of Birth & Age: 11/10/2004

Age: 10 years, 2 months

Grade and School: Fourth Grade, Sandia School

Evaluation Dates: December 31, 2014, January 3, 10, and 11, 2015

Examiner: Jennie K. Singer, Ph.D.

Report Date: January 15, 2015

Reason for Referral

Jaime was referred for evaluation by his mother. Jaime has had difficulty with learning to read and with some other subjects at school. Jaime is of both Hispanic and Asian ethnicity. His father is a physician from Ecuador (he serves as a hospital administrator in the United States), and his mother is Korean American, a former elementary school teacher. His behavior has been the focus of most other evaluations, and although prior reports addressed Jaime's academic strengths and weaknesses, no formal specific learning disabilities have been identified. This report is intended to give specific information that will focus on helping Jaime advance his reading and academic performance. This evaluation will aim to give recommendations that will aid educators working with Jaime in helping him learn in the ways most beneficial to him and to diagnose his learning disabilities.

Evaluation Procedures

Wechsler Intelligence Scales for Children–5th Edition (WISC–V)

Kaufman Test of Educational Achievement– Third Edition Comprehensive Form (KTEA–3)

Interview with Jaime's mother

Review of records

Summary of Background Information

Jaime is a 10-year and 2-month-old boy who is currently living with both of his biological parents and his 11-year-old sister in Davis. He is in fourth grade at Sandia School, a nonpublic school for students with autism spectrum disorders and behavioral difficulties. He currently gets a variety of services, such as speech therapy, occupational therapy, social skills groups, and individual therapy.

Jaime's mother reports that when she was 7 months pregnant with Jaime she was hospitalized with a very high fever caused by viral meningitis. She lost weight and was very weak for the remainder of her pregnancy. Jaime was born at term with no complications, and he had a strong Apgar rating. Jaime did not meet early developmental milestones and was first able to hold his head up at 9 months of age. He was accepted to Alta Regional Center as an infant, as he was still unable to crawl, sit up, or roll over at 13 months old. He was enrolled in speech, occupational, and physical therapy at the Children's Therapy Center (CTC) in Woodland, and with practice he was able to walk at 19 months. By age $2\frac{1}{2}$ he appeared to be "caught up," and he was released from the Sacramento City Unified School District by age 3 with no testing because he "looked normal." When Jaime was close to age 4 he began having behavioral issues, such as hair pulling. He was brought back to the CTC for therapy that he had discontinued 9 months earlier. He was enrolled via private pay for occupational therapy (OT), speech therapy, and social groups. By the time he was almost 5 years old, he was assessed by the school district and was given services that included a special education preschool with a qualifier of specific learning disability.

Jaime's behavioral issues increased, and he was suspended from kindergarten. He had difficulties that manifested in his fleeing the school campus and hitting his para-educator when he was triggered. He was given a main qualifier of severely emotionally disturbed in first grade, and his behavior again worsened. Jaime began to attack people at this time, and he was not allowed to partake of the Children's Development Center (CDC) after-school program or the other after-school program, Access. He was removed from his social groups and was deemed "too violent" to participate in OT. Jaime's mother notes that even though Jaime's academic skills were falling more and more short of grade level, Individualized Education Programs (IEPs) continued to focus mainly on Jaime's behavior.

In the fall of his second-grade year, the school district recommended Sandia School, as Jaime's behavior was becoming more agitated and violent both at home and at school. Jaime transitioned very well to the nonpublic school, and was able to take the van to and from school each day. In third grade, he brought a serrated bread knife into the school van and he attempted to hurt a peer before a teacher was able to remove the knife from him. He was first hospitalized for behavioral issues and stated depression in the late fall of that year and then hospitalized again in January of 2014.

This past August Jaime displayed his displeasure by putting 40 pushpins into his skin. He has been noted to have a "hyposensitivity to pain" in a report (dated 10/28/14) by the MIND Institute. At this time he is able to cope at school and perform well behaviorally because of the numerous behavioral incentives used. At home, Jaime is still physically and verbally aggressive. His mother and sister are the main targets of his aggression. Jaime's mother stated that things such as losing a chess piece during a chess game or being asked to brush his teeth are potential triggers for his rage. She recalls incidents where Jaime has slapped her in the face or has thrown things, and pulled his hair and screamed when very upset. Other triggers include being asked to put the dishes away, do his homework, or take a bath. He has hit his sister and has brought a rake into the house using it in a threatening manner.

Jaime generally wakes up early, around 4:15 a.m. His mother said that she will not get up with him until 5 a.m. This can cause stress for the family, as Jaime may get furious if denied the television clicker at 4 a.m. He has started hitting his mother in the morning if not given the clicker, stating "I won't kill you if you give me the clicker" and "I'm going to kill you in your sleep with an anchor." Jaime is generally on better behavior with his father, who works outside of the home. Jaime's mother is the main caregiver and only recently has started to work at 60% time after quitting her job about 2 years ago. A recent intake report for Applied Behavioral Analysis (ABA) dated 8/10/13 stated that Jaime uses behaviors such as elopement, aggression, and property destruction in order to both gain attention and escape unpleasant demands. Jaime's mother has worked hard the past year with an ABA therapist in order to work on Jaime's behavior and her own responses to managing it. Jaime currently wears a GPS anklet that was obtained from the police department after Jaime ran away from his house on many occasions.

Currently, Jaime is in the fourth grade. According to his most recent IEP, dated 3/4/14, he receives OT for fine motor issues, speech therapy consultation, as well as individual and group therapy at school. Goals focus on Jaime's behaviors such as aggression, cursing, and property destruction (such as throwing a chair) as well as academic concerns such as learning sight words. Jaime was recently moved to a higher academic level group; however, when this move proved taxing to him, he was moved back down to a lower-level reading group (but he maintained the higher group for math). He remarked to his mother that it was "too much pressure." Watching other students finish assignments quickly can trigger Jaime to feel low self-esteem and humiliated. Jaime is also noted to have a good sense of humor and to love singing and dancing when there is music on.

No current medical problems were reported, although Jaime still sleeps with pull-ups and has been given a diagnosis of enuresis in the past. Jaime has been taking medications for his behavior since he was $4^1/_2$. His current medications include: lamotrigine, Seroquel, Intuniv ER, risperidone, Zoloft, and metformin. Note that Jaime currently takes metformin to reduce his risk of secondary diabetes due to side effects of his other medications. Jaime is not currently diagnosed with diabetes.

Jaime's mother reported that the Davis school psychologist has opened up the topic of residential care in the future. She is concerned that she may not be able to handle Jaime when he becomes even bigger and stronger. In early reports starting in 2009, Jaime was diagnosed with pervasive developmental disorder NOS and a mood disorder. His behaviors, although not classical autism, were found to meet criteria for autism spectrum disorder by Dr. N., MD, of the MIND Institute on 10/28/14. He was found to meet all *DSM-5* diagnostic criteria at level 3, "Requiring substantial support." He was found to have no accompanying intellectual impairment, no language impairment, and an association with mood disorder NOS. Jamie's prior scores appear in Tables 11.2 to 11.13.

Prior Cognitive Assessments

Table 11.2 Jaime's Wechsler Preschool and Primary Test of Intelligence–III (WPPSI–III) Scores, September 2009

Scale	Standard Score	Percentile Rank	Description
Verbal	102	55	Average
Performance	96	39	Average
Processing Speed	91	27	Average
Full Scale	97	42	Average

Table 11.3 Jaime's WPPSI–III Scores, 2010

Scale	Standard Score	Description
Verbal	98	Average
Performance	103	Average
Full Scale	99	Average

Table 11.4 Jaime's Wechsler Intelligence Scales for Children–Fourth Edition (WISC–IV) Scores, December 2011

Index	Standard Score	Description
Verbal Comprehension	91	Average
Perceptual Reasoning	73 (sig. scatter)	Very Low
Working Memory	77	Very Low
Processing Speed	85	Low Average

Table 11.5 Jaime's Wechsler Intelligence Scales for Children–Fourth Edition (WISC–IV) Scores, March 2014

Index	Standard Score	Percentile Rank	Range Classification
Verbal Comprehension	87	19	Low Average
Perceptual Reasoning	86	18	Low Average
Working Memory	80	9	Low Average
Processing Speed	70	2	Low

Prior Academic Testing

Table 11.6 Jaime's Woodcock Johnson–III Scores, December 2011

Cluster	Description
Broad Math	Average
Broad Written Language	Low Average
Broad Reading	Very Low

Table 11.7 Jaime's Comprehensive Test of Phonological Processing (CTOPP) Scores, November 2012

Scale	Standard Score	Percentile Rank
Phonological Awareness	74	3
Phonological Memory	64	<1
Rapid Naming	66	1
Alternate Phonological Awareness	74	4

Table 11.8   Jaime's Wechsler Achievement Test–Third Edition (WIAT–III) Scores, November 2013

Subtest	Standard Score	Subtest	Standard Score
Reading Comprehension	88	Early Reading Skills	77
Numerical Operations	89	Word Reading	62
Math Reasoning	94	Pseudoword Decoding	62
Spelling	74	Oral Reading Fluency	40
Math Fluency-Addition	82		
Math Fluency-Multiplication	81		
Math Fluency-Subtraction	71		

Note: These scores were determined to be potential underestimates of Jaime's ability

Table 11.9   Jaime's Comprehensive Test of Phonological Processing (CTOPP) Scores, April 2014

Composite	Standard Score	Percentile rank	Classification
Phonological Awareness	73	3	Low
Rapid Naming	73	3	Low

Table 11.10   Jaime's Wide Range Assessment of Memory and Learning (WRAML) Scores, April 2014

Index	Standard Score	Percentile rank
Visual Memory	60	.4

Table 11.11   Jaime's Peabody Picture Vocabulary Test–4 (PPVT–4) Scores, April 2014

Word Classification	Accuracy in Word Classification	Percentage of Accuracy
Noun	29 out of 38	76%
Verb	8 out of 12	67%
Attribute	6 out of 10	60%

Table 11.12   Jaime's Expressive Vocabulary Test–2 (EVT–2) Scores, April 2014

Word Classification	Accuracy in Word Classification	Percentage of Accuracy
Noun	30 out of 46	65%
Verb	5 out of 5	100%
Attribute	8 out of 10	80%

Table 11.13   Jaime's Beery Test of Visual Motor Integration–6th Edition (VMI–6) Scores, April 2014

Test/Subtest	Standard Score	Performance Level
VMI	86	Below Average
Visual Perception	85	Below Average
Motor Coordination	63	Very Low

Behavioral Observations

Jaime is a 10-year-old fourth-grade boy who was tested over 4 days. He presented as well dressed and groomed and as slightly tall for his age. He is a good-looking boy with short black hair. Jaime has been assessed several times, and he was not excited to be tested again. On the first day, he was also sleepy at first, having just woken up from a nap. However, he approached the testing in a serious and motivated fashion, requiring very few prompts to stay on task. He took only one break, and then he was ready to go back and finish the first day of tasks. He was disappointed that the examiner would have to come back, as he clearly did not enjoy most of the tasks. On the first testing day, he became tearful after the first task when it became too difficult to put colored blocks into the pictured pattern. On consequent tasks he reacted calmly when the items became too difficult. He used subvocalization at times, talking in low tones to himself during challenging items. He sat still and focused for the entire 2-hour session.

On the second and subsequent sessions, Jaime was awake, alert, and motivated to do well on the tasks presented to him. He displayed a cautious style of response, hesitating and sometimes failing to answer more challenging items. He was able to use his words well to tell the examiner when he had "enough" of testing for a specific subtest and when he was done for the day. He used his fingers and whisper-counting during math items. He was fully cooperative during all of the testing and worked happily for a prize at the end of the testing session. During the sessions he also demonstrated a great attachment to his mother, who sat next to him during the assessment sessions. He also was happy to share a prize with his sister after the testing. It is the opinion of this examiner that the scores obtained reflect Jaime's true ability levels at this time. Jamie's test scores appear in Tables 11.14 and 11.15.

Test Results

Cognitive Functioning:

Table 11.14   Jaime's Wechsler Intelligence Scale for Children–Fifth Edition (WISC–V) Scores

Index/IQ	Index	%ile	Category
Verbal Comprehension	89–S	23	Low Average
Visual Spatial	84–S	14	Very Low
Fluid Reasoning	69	2	Extremely Low
Working Memory	91–S	27	Average
Processing Speed	60	.4	Extremely Low
FSIQ	73	4	Very Low

Subtest	Scaled Score	Percentile
Block Design	6	9
Similarities	8	25
Matrix Reasoning	3	1
Digit Span	8	25
Coding	4	2
Vocabulary	8	25
Figure Weights	6	9
Visual Puzzles	8	25
Picture Span	9	37
Symbol Search	2–W	0.4

Table 11.14   (Continued)

Subtest	Scaled Score	Percentile
Information	7	16
Picture Concepts	9	37
Letter-Number Sequencing	7	16
Cancellation	3	1
Comprehension	7	16
Arithmetic	9	37
Naming Speed Literacy	82	12
Immediate Symbol Translation	77	6
Delayed Symbol Translation	80	9
Composites		
Quantitative Reasoning	85	16
Auditory Working Memory	87	19
Nonverbal	71	3
General Ability	75	5
Cognitive Proficiency	73	4

Academic Achievement

Table 11.15   Jaime's Kaufman Test of Educational Achievement–Third Edition Comprehensive Form (KTEA–3) Scores

Index/Subtests	Standard Score	%ile	Grade Level or Profile Level
Reading	60	.4	Low
Letter/Word Recognition	56	.2	K.8
Reading Comprehension	69	2	1.4
Math	79	8	Below Average
Math Concepts/ Application	88	21	3.2
Math Computation	74	4	2.1
Written Language	55	.1	Low

(continued)

Table 11.15   (*Continued*)

Index/Subtests	Standard Score	%ile	Grade Level or Profile Level
Written Expression	43	<.1	K.5
Spelling	73	4	1.9
Academic Skills Battery Composite	65	1	Low
Sound-Symbol	84	14	Below Average
Phonological Processing	98	45	3.8
Nonsense Word Decoding	75	5	<1.0
Decoding	65	1	Low
Letter/Word Recognition	56	.2	K.8
Nonsense Word Decoding	75	5	<1.0
Reading Fluency			
Word Recognition Fluency	57	.2	<1.0
Reading Under-standing	69	2	Low
Reading Comprehension	69	2	1.4
Reading Vocabulary	77	6	1.9
Oral Language	90	25	Average
Oral Expression	92	30	2.7
Listening Comprehension	87	19	2.2
Associational Fluency	97	42	3.8
Oral Fluency	95	37	Average
Associational Fluency	97	42	3.8
Object Naming Facility	96	39	3.6

Table 11.15   (*Continued*)

Index/Subtests	Standard Score	%ile	Grade Level or Profile Level
Comprehension	76	5	Below Average
Reading Comprehension	69	2	1.4
Listening Comprehension	87	19	2.2
Expression	65	4	Low
Written Expression	43	<.1	K.5
Oral Expression	92	30	2.7
Orthographic Processing	70	2	Below Average
Word Recognition Fluency	57	.2	<1.0
Spelling	73	4	1.9
Letter Naming Facility	93	32	2.11

Profile of Cognitive and Academic Strengths and Weaknesses

Jaime's FSIQ of 73 on the WISC–V places him at the fourth percentile for children his age and in the "Very Low" category. The chances are 95 out of 100 that his true FSIQ is somewhere in the range 68–80. Overall there are significant differences between many of his abilities. His indexes range from standard scores of 60 (extremely low) on processing speed to 91 (average) in the area of working memory. Because of the large differences in Jaime's ability levels across different tasks, his FSIQ is not the best score to use when describing Jaime. However, it should be noted that overall, Jamie's level of cognitive functioning is quite low, and that when looking at previous Wechsler tests' FSIQ of 97, it is apparent that the gap between Jaime and his peers is widening over the years. With the band of error considered, Jaime does potentially meet criteria for an intellectual disability. When his lack of daily living skills is added to this low score, it seems likely that Jaime will meet criteria for an intellectual disability in the future, possibly when he is a teenager. Since he does not currently meet these criteria, he is still eligible to be diagnosed with specific learning disabilities.

Jamie's profile can best be understood using Luria's neuropsychological theory governing brain processes in three main functional units. The first unit is responsible for arousal and attention, recognizing incoming stimuli and the receiving and processing of information. Speed and efficiency of effort is included in this unit. Jaime displayed difficulty with speeded tasks. He performed extremely low on tasks that required any type of speeded component including those tasks (such as on Coding, Symbol Search, and Cancellation subtests of the WISC–V). Jaime was very efficient at these paper-and-pencil tasks, not missing any items, but was extremely slow in comparison with others his age. Processing speed is a significant weakness for Jamie.

The second unit is responsible for analyzing, coding, and storing information that is taken in via the senses either holistically or sequentially. The second unit is involved with visual-spatial skills, auditory verbal skills, and learning and memory. Jaime displayed visual-spatial skills in the low-average range. He struggled more on those tasks that had a motor component (he performed in the very low range on Block Design where he put together colored blocks to copy a design) than those tasks where these skills were utilized without any motor requirements. He performed in the low-average range on tasks where he solved visual puzzles and put pictures in order to tell a story that makes sense. Jaime is stronger on tasks where there is meaningful information.

Jaime performed in the low-average to average range on tasks that required verbal comprehension. This is an area of strength for Jamie. He was able to describe how two objects were alike, define vocabulary words, and answer arithmetic questions orally similar to same-age peers. Jaime

has good oral and listening skills, and he can work best when able to voice his answers aloud and respond to an auditory task. Jaime performed in the low-average range on tasks where he recited digits aloud forward and backward from memory and on a task where he orally sequenced letters and numbers. He again displayed his relative strength on the auditory channel with sequential information. Jaime also displayed a relative strength in working memory, or the ability to hold information in his head long enough to manipulate that information and to get what was learned into his long-term memory. He is able to use his working memory in the average range, or similar to same-age peers.

The third functional unit is responsible for utilizing executive functions to organize and formulate plans and make decisions and for self-monitoring. It is important for mental efficiency and speed of learning as well as the efficient use of working memory. Jaime had difficulty on some tasks that required fluid reasoning. He performed in the very low range on tasks that required him to use a motor component to complete a visual reasoning task and where he needed to manipulate pictures of figures in his head. He performed in the below-average range on a task where he demonstrated his level of knowledge orally.

Jamie's performance on the KTEA–3 also displayed a wide variety of skill levels. He earned scores that ranged from very low to average achievement. Jaime earned a standard score of 65 on the Academic Skills Battery (ASB), which encompasses Reading, Math, and Written Language scores. Jaime performed in the very low range for reading and written language and in the low range in math. Jamie's scores are consistent enough that the ASB can be used as a measure of his overall skills in these areas. However, looking at math tasks across both the WISC–V and the KTEA–3, it appears that Jaime has a relative strength (or the low to low-average range) in understanding mathematics concepts. He has much more difficulty when asked to compute math problems. The reasons for this include the writing component involved with math computation as well as the need to view and manipulate numbers. Although Jaime is able to name and phonologically process his letters, he displays a clear weakness in orthographic processing, or understanding the symbols used in language. This difficulty manifests in his math work in obscuring things like plus and minus signs. Jaime also displays difficulty on word problems in math.

Jaime has a weakness and a specific learning disability in reading. He has difficulty in decoding words (including nonsense words) and in spelling, and in comprehending or understanding what he has read. Combined with his difficulties in orthographic processing, he displays signs of severe dyslexia (now called specific learning disorder, reading). His previous test results show that Jaime has made progress over the years in his phonological processing (he scores in the average range on the K-TEA–3 on this task), although this area should also be taught when remediating his reading. Error analysis on reading and spelling tasks revealed that Jaime has a weakness in reading long vowels, and unpredictable patterns of letters in a word. He also has difficulty with single or double consonants, consonant blends, and long-vowel diphthongs. He is also likely to make whole-word errors.

Jaime has a specific learning disorder in written language. He has difficulty forming letters and words, with the spacing in between words, and with the differences between capital and lower case letters. He performed in the very low range on the written expression subtest and in the low range on a spelling task.

Jaime again demonstrated a strength on tasks that rely on the auditory-verbal channel. He performed in the average range on a task where he listened to stories and answered questions pertaining to his comprehension. He also performed in the average range when asked to quickly name letters and objects.

Jaime's responses on several subtests were further examined to identify specific skill strengths and/or weaknesses, using the KTEA–3's Error Analysis procedure. First, his errors on each subtest were totaled according to error categories. Then the number of errors Jaime made in each error category was compared with the average number of errors made by students in the norm sample who were at the same grade level and who attempted the same items. As a result, Jaime's performance in each error category could be rated as strong, average, or weak. On Phonological Processing, all of Jaime's errors were considered average for his age. On Letter and Word Decoding, Nonsense Word Decoding, and Spelling, Jaime showed a weakness in the areas of long vowels. On Letter and Word Decoding, he showed additional weaknesses reading unpredictable patterns and on whole words. On Nonsense Word Decoding, Jaime displayed weaknesses on single and double consonants, prefix and suffix inflection, and whole-word errors. On the Spelling subtest, Jaime showed areas of weakness spelling single and double consonants, initial and final consonant blends, dipthongs, silent letters, suffix inflection, and unpredictable patterns. On Math Applications and Concepts, Jaime showed weakness in solving word problems but did well on most other areas. On Oral Expression, Jaime showed weakness on understanding the task but otherwise was average on other areas of this task. On a written expression task, Jaime displayed strengths on sentence structure, capitalization, and punctuation. These findings can help guide specific areas of instruction when planning interventions.

Diagnostic Impressions

299.00 autism spectrum disorder associated with a mood disorder, severe, without associated communication or language disorder, without intellectual impairment, and associated with a known medical or genetic condition (in utero infection)

315.00 specific learning disorder with impairment in reading, severe

315.2 specific learning disorder with impairment in written expression, severe

307.6 enuresis, nocturnal only

Summary

Jaime is a 10-year-old boy who is currently in the fourth grade at Sandia School, a nonpublic school for children with autism and behavioral difficulties. He is doing very well behaviorally at school, while at home he appears to have difficulty with the tasks of daily living, regulating his mood and behavior, and aggressive and elopement behaviors. Jamie's mother has been working with an ABA clinician in her home many days per week. She is currently seeking assistance with the Alta Regional Center with Jamie's current diagnosis of autism spectrum disorder. Overall, Jamie's cognitive functioning ranges from extremely low to average. Jaime has strengths in the areas of math conceptualization, oral fluency, oral expression, and auditory comprehension. Jaime has weaknesses and requires remediation in the areas of reading decoding, reading comprehension, spelling, orthographic processing and writing. Jaime has several areas of processing difficulties, and his speed, especially when completing a written task, is a weakness for Jamie. Although Jaime qualifies at this time for diagnosis of specific learning disorders in the areas of reading and writing, it is important to note that Jamie's overall level of cognitive functioning is very close to having an intellectual disability. When viewing Jamie's cognitive functioning over time, and taking into consideration his very low levels of functioning in the cognitive domain, the social domain, and the practical domain of self-management, he should be assessed again in a few years for an intellectual developmental disorder. It is important that Jaime receives the remediation and help he needs at this time so as to potentially start helping him to read and write and to increase his social and self-care skills. It is also important to recognize Jamie's limitations so as to help prepare for his future as an adult.

Recommendations

Based on the results of this evaluation, the following are my recommendations:

1. Jaime would benefit from working with a tutor regarding his reading and writing. Given his learning disorders in this area, he will need more practice in learning how to read and to write. A tutor who is familiar with either the Orton-Gillingham or Wilson methods of reading instruction (a multisensory phonics model) or who is familiar with Lindamood-Bell techniques would be ideal. Lindamood-Bell programs include the LiPs program for phonemic awareness, and Visualization and Verbalization designed to improve reading comprehension and critical thinking skills. When Jaime is ready for more daily instruction in this area, it is recommended that he have tutoring (if possible) 3 or 4 days per week. This could be at a time when he is taking time off from his daily ABA work. Rewards and games should be utilized in his instruction. It is very important that Jaime focus on learning more sight words, using his strength in long-term memory and retrieval when reading rather than his weaker decoding skills. He also needs to focus on learning sound pairs of vowels and consonant blends so that he can read unfamiliar words with more ease.

2. Currently Jaime is working on a computer program for reading, *Ticket to Read*. This program features instruction in decoding, fluency, and increasing sight-word recognition while providing prizes and other features of a computer game. It is recommended that Jaime work on this

program each day he agrees, possibly with the help of his ABA therapist. Other computer programs include *RAVE-O* (Retrieval, Automaticity, Vocabulary, Engagement, and Orthography), a comprehensive fluency program that was developed by Maryanne Wolf at Tufts University.

3. Occupational therapy should focus on helping Jaime to form words and to write with more ease.

4. Since the areas of reading and writing are difficult for Jamie, it is also important for him to start implementing technology to help him in these areas. Recommended are the programs *Dragon Naturally Speaking* to aid him in being able to voice his ideas when writing. This program takes some time to really learn an individual's voice, and practice in using this program will aid Jaime in his schoolwork. He will require accommodations of this type as he goes into more advanced work in higher grades.

5. Other technologies, such as e-book readers and audio books, can assist Jaime in being able to listen to his books with or without following along with text. Since Jaime learns strongest through the audio channel, this method can assist him in learning material utilizing his strengths. As book material continues to get harder with advanced grades, this accommodation will be increasingly important for Jaime.

6. As Jaime approaches more advanced classwork, he should be allowed to digitally tape lectures or lessons so that he can listen to them again later. He will also need a note taker to help him with organizing material that is important for him to learn for tests and projects.

7. If taking any type of test or exam, Jaime will need at least double the time given to other students. He should be allowed to take his test or exam utilizing his technology so that he can answer questions via *Dragon Naturally Speaking* or orally, and such that the test questions are read to him (with or without technology).

8. A specific math intervention for Jamie: Provide him with a series of pictures depicting groups of animals, people, objects, and other things. Have him use the pictures to formulate word problems in which addition or subtraction are used to find the solution. If this is too difficult, he can find the sum of all of the pictures in each category.

9. Jaime needs auditory and pictured prompts for tasks that he needs to complete in the home. If there is a sequence of items he must complete for a task (such as getting dressed), these sequences may need to be posted in the home, if needed. Jamie's reticence in brushing his teeth and getting dressed are likely due to difficulties in his executive functioning (planning and organizing) as well as the more physical concerns he may have about finding the tasks too difficult. It is also recommended that a therapist (ABA or occupational) help Jaime to break down his physical demands into small movements that he can master more easily. Rewards and praise will hopefully help this process to be less painful for Jaime and have the effect of reducing his anger or rage at being asked to leave a preferred activity in order to do something he finds very difficult to accomplish. Jaime should also have a warning (possibly with a timer) so that he can "get ready" mentally for his next task.

10. Due to Jaime's double deficit in phonological processing and naming speed, which generally leads to significant reading difficulty with both the phonological and orthographic, he needs exposure to new words before he will be able to read them automatically. Some children respond well to a multisensory or VAKT (verbal-auditory-kinesthetic-tactile) approach because they need input from more than one modality to help them perceive or retain information. Other children are overloaded by

multisensory inputs and become confused by having to assimilate information through multiple systems at the same time. For example, Jaime might be able to listen better if he closes his eyes, in order to reduce multisensory stimulation. Thus, it is important not to rely on the multisensory aspect of instruction alone to provide the primary strategy for reading. Learning letters through various sensory modalities may improve storage, but it may not help with retrieval because letters are only accessed visually for reading.

11. Use materials that explicitly highlight the rule or pattern that Jaime needs to learn (e.g., vary words by one feature and hold other things constant, such as changing the initial phoneme or the morpheme being taught). Provide repeated opportunities for Jaime to apply the rule or pattern. Allow Jaime to discover patterns and rules through word sorting and carefully controlled materials. Instruction that follows frequent test-teach-retest cycles is responsive, customized to Jaime's needs, and allows continuous evaluation and modification of the instruction based on his performance.

12. Before teaching a particular skill, assess what Jaime already knows and needs to be taught; plan targeted instruction that begins with what he knows and works toward the unknown; assess whether the instruction was effective; and modify accordingly.

13. Provide visuals: Use visual materials (e.g., illustrations, graphic organizers, symbolic reminders) to support instruction whenever possible. Simplify the language of instruction, as Jaime may benefit most from instruction that is delivered using simple, precise, and transparent language. Avoid excessive elaboration or wordy instructions.

14. Teach visual (orthographic) processing strategies: Accurate reading depends first and foremost on visual (orthographic) processing. An illustrative intervention recommendation to improve Jaime's visual inspection of words while reading follows: Ask Jaime to find a target word among orthographically similar words (e.g., find *memory: mamory, menory, memory, momory*). Select words that are in Jaime's spoken vocabulary and also at an appropriate reading level. Create distractors that resemble the kinds of reading errors Jaime tends to make (i.e., long vowels, reading unpredictable patterns, whole-word errors, single and double consonants, prefix and suffix inflection). Ask him to read each target word aloud before beginning, and then allow him to work independently. As a part of instruction, this task may be done untimed initially and then under timed conditions to track speed of orthographic processing. Present Jaime with visually similar words (e.g., *though, thought, through, tough*) and ask him to highlight or indicate the differences between the two words. Then put the words into context to associate the meaning with each visual representation. Improving the recognition of differences between orthographically similar words will likely improve automatic word recall. Word sorts are a way of organizing words based on a particular category. Ask Jaime to complete word sorting based on various visually based patterns. Morphological patterns can be used (*-ing, -ed, -tion*). Focus can be placed on the initial, medial, and final letter patterns.

15. Expect that more time and repetition for practice may be needed. Research suggests that students with double deficits benefit from phonologically based interventions, and similar treatment approaches are appropriate. However, students with a double deficit may require more repetition to acquire skills such as identifying onset-rime patterns and phoneme segmentation than students with a phonological-only weakness.

16. It is recommended that Jaime's mother continue to pursue help from Alta Regional Center. While Jaime does not necessarily display classical autism, his clear difficulties in the areas of social skills, communicating his needs, lack of ability to regulate his mood or behavior, his sensory issues, and his focus in specific and fixed interests demonstrate that he is clearly on the autism spectrum. Thus, Jaime and his family would benefit from in-home help with safety and care for him such that his mother is able to go to work without worrying about how Jaime can cope without her in the home.

17. It is further recommended that Jaime be re-assessed by age 13 to rule out an intellectual developmental disorder.

Note: As a direct result of this case report, Jaime was accepted at a state agency in California that provides qualified children and adults who have intellectual and developmental disabilities with services for their care and treatment.

CASE 8—CHRISTOPHER, AGE 11: PHONOLOGICAL DYSLEXIA IN CHILD WITH VISUAL PERCEPTUAL DISORDER

Marsha Vasserman

Name: Christopher

Age: 11 years 4 months

Grade: 6

Examiner: Dr. Vasserman

Reason for Referral

Christopher is an 11-year-old Caucasian boy who was referred for neuropsychological evaluation in the context of refractive strabismic amblyopia as well as reading, spelling, and writing difficulties. Christopher has a long-standing history of visual difficulties, which have been treated with vision therapy and eye patching. His reading weaknesses have been mainly attributed to these visual concerns but have not improved over time with treatment. His parents requested this evaluation to determine if Christopher has a reading disability and to identify what supports and services he requires.

Relevant Background Information

Birth and Developmental History

Christopher was born full term following an uncomplicated pregnancy, labor, and delivery. His infancy period was typical, with all milestones achieved on time. At the age of 15 months, an eye turn was identified and Christopher avoided visual activities. Glasses were prescribed at 19 months of age, and Christopher was diagnosed with refractive strabismic amblyopia, which required surgery to at age 3. His vision is poor but is close to normal with corrective lenses. Christopher has participated in vision therapy since approximately 18 months old. Eye drops and patching have also been utilized to improve visual skills. Aside from the visual concerns, Christopher has been a relatively healthy child with no chronic illnesses, hospitalizations, or significant injuries. He is an active boy who enjoys sports and participates in several leagues. Hearing is within normal limits. He has a good appetite, and there are no concerns about sleep. Christopher was evaluated by a local neurologist, due to difficulties in school, and a neuropsychological evaluation was recommended at that time.

Family History

Christopher is the second of four children born. He gets along well with his siblings and parents. Family history is significant for undiagnosed learning struggles, difficulties with attention, anxiety, cancer, and diabetes.

School History

Christopher attended a local preschool program, which noted difficulties with drawing and coloring skills. He has been in regular education, and no concerns regarding academic development were observed in kindergarten, although his pace of work was reportedly slow. A similar pattern was described through first and second grade whereby Christopher was somewhat slower than other children in picking up academic skills. He had increased difficulty as the material became harder and began making self-deprecating comments during homework (e.g., "I'm dumb." "I don't get it"). Currently, Christopher is a sixth grader. He reportedly struggles with decoding of words and has great difficulty with fluent and accurate reading, frequently guessing at or making up words. Reading comprehension is also an issue in part because Christopher struggles greatly to read the text. In contrast, listening comprehension skills are reported to be well developed. Christopher's knowledge of mathematics is noted to be age appropriate although he continues to at times use his fingers to complete problems. Word problems are difficult due to reading demands. Last, spelling is also problematic, and while he enjoys creative writing, Christopher at times struggles with organization of his thoughts and ideas.

Social and Emotional History

Christopher is a friendly, social, and well-liked boy who is generally quite happy and has multiple friends. He is described as a leader with good ability to resolve conflicts. He enjoys physical activities, such as riding his bike and scooter, and participates in soccer and martial arts. His mood is described as happy overall.

Behavioral Observations

Christopher was a friendly and cooperative boy who easily separated from his parents and quickly established a good working rapport with the examiner. He was talkative and discussed a variety of topics, including his interests, friends, family, and school difficulties. His effort and motivation were judged to be appropriate based on observation and performance on symptom validity measures. Christopher did not demonstrate any difficulties with focus or concentration during the two lengthy assessment sessions. Several observations are notable. Christopher often used self-talk to help him with problem solving. Anxiety was also evident when he made a mistake, which often resulted in him freezing and having difficulty quickly reengaging after such moments. Christopher worked very slowly, particularly on writing tasks and his handwriting was noted to be messy. Although clearly a very verbal child, Christopher made multiple phonological errors when speaking. For example, he said "thermometer" for *thermometer*, "transpitate" for *transport*, "farmin" for *vermin*, and "permiter" for *perimeter*. In addition, when reading, he struggled greatly with decoding even simple words for a sixth grader, such as athletic, flown, or Korea. He frequently used his fingers to complete simple math problems and at times transposed numbers when rewriting problems. Notably, Christopher was generally able to identify and self-correct such errors. Overall, Christopher's attention, motivation, and effort were adequate on this assessment. As such, the results are believed to be an accurate reflection of his current functioning.

Instruments Used

Auditory Consonant Trigrams (ACT)

Beery Visuomotor Integration Test (VMI); Behavior Assessment System for Children–Second Edition, parent reports (BASC–2)

Behavior Rating Inventory of Executive Functioning, parent reports (BRIEF)

Biber Cognitive Estimations Test

California Verbal Learning Test–Children's Edition (CVLT–C)

Child Behavior Checklist (CBCL)

Clinical Evaluation of Language Fundamentals–Fourth Edition (CELF4)

Delis-Kaplan Executive Functioning System (D-KEFS)

Dot Counting Test

Grooved Pegboard

NEPSY–II

Oral and Written Language Scales—2nd Edition (OWLS–II)

Rey Complex Figure Test (RCFT)

SNAP–IV

Stroop Color Word Interference Test

Teacher Rating Form (TRF)

Tower of London (TOL)

Trail Making Test (TMT)

TOMM

Wechsler Individual Achievement Test–Third Edition (WIAT–III)

Wechsler Intelligence Scale for Children–Fifth Edition (WISC–V)

Evaluation Results

Please note: Standard scores (Sts) have a mean of 100 with a standard deviation of 15. Scaled scores (Scs) have a mean of 10 with a standard deviation of 3. T-scores have a mean of 50, with a standard deviation of 10. Last, Z-scores have a mean of 0, with a standard deviation of 1. Scores within 1 standard deviation of the mean are considered average.

Intellectual Functioning

To assess his overall intellectual functioning, Christopher was administered the WISC–V. The WISC–V is a multifaceted test of intelligence that evaluates an individual's ability to reason with verbal and nonverbal information as well as his or her visual-spatial understanding, and ability to use working memory and processing speed. Christopher's overall performance on this administration of the WISC–V was low average with significant discrepancies between domains (FSIQ Sts = 87). Christopher's solidly average verbal reasoning skills contrasted with his relative weaknesses in visual perception, nonverbal reasoning, and speed of visual information processing. When looking at his more general reasoning skills, while parsing out the contribution of working memory and processing speed, Christopher's performance was average. His performance across these domains is described in greater detail in the relevant sections below.

Language Functioning

Christopher appeared to understand questions and task instructions and rarely required repetition. Conversational skills were well developed, and he discussed various topics and interests. Multiple phonological errors were evident in Christopher's speech and at times interfered with his ability to express his ideas. For example, he said "thermometer" for *thermometer*, "transpitate" for *transport*, and "farmint" for *vermin*, as mentioned in Behavioral Observations.

Christopher's performance across language tasks was variable. Regarding receptive language, he showed adequate skill in identifying, isolating and manipulating phonemes, the smallest units of language (CTOPP–2 Phonological Awareness Sts = 86), and his overall phonological awareness skills were largely age appropriate. Comprehension of lengthier stories was also average, while relatively more difficulty was observed in sound blending and sentence repetition. Expressive skills were more variably developed, with a strong vocabulary, and age-appropriate verbal fluency and initiation. There was no evidence of word-finding difficulty on assessment. In contrast, Christopher had great difficulty in speeded label retrieval, working slowly across tasks of naming speed (WISC–V Naming Speed Sts = 76; Stroop Color Naming T-score = 36).

Visual–Spatial Functioning

Christopher's visual perceptual skills were inconsistent. Perception of angular and line relationships in space was impaired. However, Christopher identified visual similarities and solved visual puzzles with average skill. Furthermore, his ability to reason and problem-solve using visual material was within normal limits (WISC–V Fluid Reasoning Index Sts = 88).

Motor Functioning and Visual–Motor Integration

Christopher exhibited right-hand dominance for all drawing and writing tasks, alternating between a tripod and a thumb-over grip. His motor imitation skills were average with both hands. Fine motor speed and dexterity was average with his dominant hand and low average with his non-dominant hand. His graphomotor control and precision were low average and while he worked carefully, he had some difficulty with accuracy and in controlling his pencil. When required to integrate visual input with a motor output, such as is required in copying tasks, Christopher's performance was very inconsistent. Although he copied simple designs with low-average skill, he had marked difficulties copying a complex figure. His approach was poorly organized, and his reproduction was distorted, with many misplaced details. Last, Christopher's handwriting was poor. It consisted of inconsistently formed letters, with poor spacing between words as well as inconsistent vertical spacing.

Attention/Concentration and Executive Functions

The role of executive functions can be thought of as organizing, directing, managing, and integrating a variety of important cognitive abilities in order to reach a goal or produce a more complex level of cognitive functioning. Executive control encompasses a variety of important high-level skills, such as sustaining attention over a period of time or in spite of distraction, organizing one's thoughts and behavior before acting, utilizing feedback in order to succeed in a given task, juggling multiple pieces of information at once (mental flexibility), and using planning and organizational skills when approaching a task.

Christopher's attention and focus were strong within this one-on-one assessment setting. He did not require repetition, redirection, or additional breaks. His parents and teachers described him as a focused and hardworking student. No attention difficulties were reported either at home or at school, although Christopher at times makes careless errors. Similarly, no concerns were noted about his executive functioning skills in his daily activities.

Christopher's simple auditory attention and visual scanning skills were average, as were his verbal fluency, verbal initiation, and shifting of attention. In contrast, tasks placing greater demands on working memory and divided attention reflected this to be an area of difficulty. For example, his performance was borderline impaired when required to divide his auditory attention. Similarly, as he had to hold greater amounts of information and more complex rules in mind, his accuracy decreased significantly, resulting in increased errors. Other areas within the executive functioning domain also proved challenging for him. Response inhibition was impaired across tasks, as was his ability to use inhibition and judgment to make cognitive estimations. Tasks requiring planning and organization proved particularly difficult for Christopher.

He greatly struggled to organize visual information and keep track of steps taken. Further, when required to plan his actions in order to solve problems efficiently, Christopher's performance was impaired. Although he took his time to think and work problems out, he often utilized trial and error and showed poor planning. His pace was slow and he made multiple errors.

Learning and Memory

Verbal Memory Although Christopher's learning of verbally presented information was average overall, he showed minimal benefit from repetition, and his learning curve was shallow over the course of multiple repetitions. Nonetheless, he learned an average number of words and remembered what he learned after short and lengthy delay periods. Christopher seemed to benefit from time to consolidate information, as he recalled more information after 20 minutes than he originally learned.

Visual Memory Christopher's memory for visual information was variable, depending on the level of organization demanded and visual-motor integration skills involved. For example, he had no difficulty identifying differences in visual scenes and recognized scene details after a delay. However, he had greater difficulty in recalling a complex figure, with borderline performance. He also had difficulty differentiating figure details. Notably, Christopher's approach to copying the figure was poorly organized and his reproduction was highly distorted, likely impacting his later recall.

Academic Functioning

Reading Christopher's reading skills were unevenly developed. His sight word vocabulary was average. Although Christopher achieved an average score when required to apply rules of phonics to decode nonsense words, his performance was highly inconsistent and dysfluent, and he made multiple self-corrections in the process. This was also observed when he read passages aloud, reflecting poor reading accuracy and fluency.

His weaknesses in fluency and accuracy, as well as working memory, impacted his understanding of the text. However, when allowed to refer back to text, Christopher's comprehension was much improved, with age-appropriate performance.

Math Christopher's knowledge of mathematics was average across tasks. He showed good understanding of basic calculations, such as addition, subtraction, and multiplication. He has not yet mastered division or fractions. He adequately applied his knowledge to word problems that were read to him, and his automaticity with basic math facts was mostly average. He struggled on a subtraction fluency task, but this appeared to be somewhat due to anxiety and his becoming stuck after making an error.

Written Expression Christopher's spelling skills were slightly below age expectations when spelling words in isolation. His ability to generate ideas and to write sentences and short paragraphs was within the average range, but his mechanics of writing were underdeveloped. His spelling was poor when writing in context. In addition, he at times omitted word endings and small words.

Social and Emotional Functioning

Christopher's is a well-liked, friendly, and kind boy who easily makes friends. He is described as a leader and is able to navigate difficult social situations and conflicts with grace and maturity. His parents and teachers do not report any concerns about Christopher's mood, anxiety, or social development; however, they both noted that he is prone to somatic complaints, such as headaches and stomachaches. Christopher also denied general worry or sadness, although he reported some worry about his grades.

Summary

Christopher is an 11-year-old boy who was referred for neuropsychological evaluation in the context of refractive strabismic amblyopia as well as reading, spelling, and writing difficulties. Christopher has a long-standing history of visual difficulties, which have been treated with vision therapy and eye patching. His reading weaknesses have been mainly attributed to these visual concerns but have not improved over time with treatment. His parents requested this evaluation to determine if Christopher has a reading disability and to identify what supports and services he requires.

Christopher is a child with largely average intellectual skills, with stronger verbal abilities in the context of relative weaknesses in visual spatial, nonverbal reasoning, and processing speed domains. Christopher demonstrated multiple strengths with well-developed verbal learning and memory skills, contextual nonverbal memory, adequate verbal fluency and mental flexibility, as well as well-developed mathematics and written expression skills. Notably, while language was generally an area of adequate functioning for Christopher and standardized assessment did not reflect significant phonological awareness problems, qualitative observation reflected multiple phonological errors in speech as well as in reading and spelling. In addition, significant rapid naming difficulties were identified. Difficulties were also seen in the domains of visual perception, visual motor integration, and relative weaknesses in graphomotor precision. Further, the attention and executive functioning domain was one that proved particularly difficult for Christopher, with specific weaknesses noted in complex working memory, divided attention, cognitive estimation, selective attention, as well as planning and organization. Last, reading accuracy and fluency were significantly underdeveloped, while comprehension and written expression were areas of strength.

Diagnostically speaking, Christopher's combination of phonological awareness difficulties, significant impairments in rapid naming, weaker spelling, as well as poor reading fluency and accuracy are consistent with the pattern of cognitive weaknesses observed in children with phonological dyslexia. It should be noted that while

Christopher clearly has visual perceptual weaknesses, his rapid naming difficulties were isolated to tasks requiring rapid retrieval rather than visual scanning. Thus, Christopher's reading difficulties are related to the underlying cognitive linguistic processes associated with phonological dyslexia rather than his visual perceptual weaknesses. At this time, Christopher meets criteria for the diagnosis of *Specific Learning Disorder, with impairment in reading, and with impairment in reading fluency and accuracy*, also known as phonological dyslexia. Christopher also demonstrates weaknesses in visual perception, graphomotor precision, and handwriting, consistent with the diagnosis of *Development Coordination Disorder*, sometimes referred to as dysgraphia. Christopher demonstrated rather significant difficulties on executive functioning tasks, particularly in planning, organizing information, complex working memory, divided attention, and cognitive estimation. He does not demonstrate any behavioral correlates, such as problems with focus, sustained attention, distractibility, or daily executive functioning skills. These weaknesses in complex working memory, divided attention, cognitive estimation, and planning, can be said to reflect an *Unspecified Neurodevelopmental Disorder*.

Last, Christopher is a sweet, friendly, and well-adjusted child who is insightful into his learning weaknesses and who shows developing self-advocacy skills. Although he experiences some sadness and worry related to his learning difficulties, at this time he does not display significant social or emotional concerns. However, as children with learning disabilities are at greater risk for depressive and anxiety disorder, his functioning in this domain should be monitored.

Recommendations

- Christopher's parents are encouraged to share the results of this evaluation with his school in order to determine if he is eligible for special education services and the development of an Individualized Education Program (IEP), under the classification of specific learning disability.

- Christopher will require intensive and multi-sensory reading remediation 3 times per week with a learning specialist to target his inconsistent phonological awareness, poor fluency, and accuracy. Programs such as Orton Gillingham, Wilson Reading Method, and RAVE-O have been shown to have a positive effect on children with reading disabilities.

- Christopher requires access to audio books to ensure continued language development as well as access to age appropriate content. Programs such as Bookshare (www.bookshare .org) and LearningAlly (www.learningally .org) are recommended as they provide various literary titles as well as classroom texts in audio format.

- Additionally, many popular titles are available through iTunes, Amazon. and the New York Public Library (http://www.nypl.org/ebooks)

- Christopher requires the following classroom and standardized testing accommodations:
  - 100% extended time on assessments
  - Large-print reading materials
    - Alternatively, use of iPad or Kindle can allow customization of print size and words per page across many titles.
  - Christopher should be allowed to write his answers directly on exam booklets rather than transfer them to scantrons.
  - Due to poor visual motor integration skills and low-average processing speed, note taking is likely to be particularly difficult. Christopher should be provided with access to teacher notes or to the notes of a classmate to ensure he does not miss essential information.
  - Christopher should be taught to type. Once proficient at typing, he should be given the opportunity to use a computer for writing assignments.
    - Type 2 Learn is a program that teaches children to touch type (ttl4.sunburst .com)

- Christopher should be provided with a reader for exams assessing nonreading skills, such as mathematics, social studies, and science.
- As Christopher's reading difficulties are addressed through intervention, he should not be penalized for spelling errors in his work.
- Christopher demonstrates many weaknesses in complex working memory and executive functioning. Although these do not appear to translate into behavioral concerns, it is not uncommon for children with reading and executive functioning weaknesses to struggle with reading comprehension and academic writing as the academic demands increase. If this is something that becomes an issue for Christopher in the future, the following is recommended:
  - http://www.eblcoaching.com is a specialized tutoring service that provides support in reading comprehension and writing as well as organizational and study skills.

Resources

- *Overcoming Dyslexia: A New and Complete Science-Based Program for Reading Problems at Any Level* by Sally Shaywitz
- Yale Center for Dyslexia and Creativity— http://dyslexia.yale.edu/index.html
- www.ldonline.org—website with information and resources about various learning disabilities.
- www.wrightslaw.com—website with information about special education law and process

Note: The next scores are provided for professional use only, by persons trained in psychological test theory, development, administration, scoring, and interpretation. A significant risk of misinterpretation of these scores exists. Please refer to the body of the report for interpretive information. If you have any questions about these scores, please speak with your psychologist. Christopher's test scores appear in Tables 11.16 to 11.24.

Test Scores

Table 11.16   Christopher's Intellectual Functioning Scores

Wechsler Intelligence Scale for Children–Fifth Edition (WISC–V)

Composite	Standard Score
Verbal Comprehension	100–S
Visual Spatial	89
Fluid Reasoning	88
Working Memory	91
Processing Speed	86
FSIQ	87
General Ability Index	91
Cognitive Proficiency Index	85

Subtests	Scaled Score
Verbal Comprehension	
Similarities	10
Vocabulary	10
Visual Spatial	
Block Design	8
Visual Puzzles	8
Fluid Reasoning	
Matrix Reasoning	9
Figure Weights	7
Working Memory	
Digit Span	8
Picture Span	9
Processing Speed	
Coding	7
Symbol Search	8

Process Analysis	Scaled Score
Digit Span Forward	8
Digit Span Backward	9
Digit Span Sequencing	9

Table 11.17 Christopher's Language Functioning Scores

Wechsler Intelligence Scale for Children–5th Ed (WISC–IV)

Naming Speed	76
Naming Literacy	77
Naming Quantity	78

Comprehensive Test of Phonological Processing–2nd Ed (CTOPP-2)

Composite	Standard Score
Phonological Awareness	86
Alternate Phonological Awareness	88

Subtest	Scaled Score
Elision	8
Blending Words	7
Phoneme Isolation	8
Blending Nonwords	8
Segmenting Nonwords	8

Boston Naming Test–2nd Ed (BNT-2)

	Z-Score
Total Correct	−.2

Subtest	Scaled Score
Recalling Sentences	7
Understanding Spoken Paragraphs	11

Delis–Kaplan Executive Function System (D-KEFS)

Measure	Scaled Score
Verbal Fluency	
Letter Fluency	9
Category Fluency	10
Category Switching	8
Switching Accuracy	8

Table 11.18 Christopher's Memory and Learning Scores

California Verbal Learning Test–Children's Edition (CVLT-C)

Measure	T/Z-Scores
List A Total Trials 1-5	44
List A Trial 1 Free Recall	1
List A Trial 5 Free Recall	−1
List B Free Recall	−1
Short Delay Free Recall	−0.5
Short Delay Cued Recall	0.5
Long Delay Free Recall	0.5
Long Delay Cued Recall	1
Semantic Cluster Ratio	0.5
Serial Cluster Ratio	−0.5
Learning Slope	−2.5
Perseverations	0
Intrusions (Free and Cued Total)	NA
Correct Recognition Hits	0
Discriminability	−1.5

Rey Complex Figure Test (RCFT)

Measure	Z-Score
Immediate Recall	−1.2
Delayed Recall (30-minute)	−1.4
Recognition: True Positives	−0.8
Recognition: Total Correct	−2
Picture Memory	10
Picture Memory Recognition	12

Table 11.19   Christopher's Attention and Executive Functioning Scores

Test of Executive Control	T-score
Sustained Accuracy	45
Selective Attention	61
Response Speed	52
Response Variability	47
Target Correct	60
Standard Correct	46
Incorrect	54
Commissions	61
Target RT	45
Standard RT	50
Standard RTSD	52
Standard ICV	55

Delis-Kaplan Executive Function System (D-KEFS)

Verbal Fluency

Letter Fluency	9
Category Fluency	10
Category Switching	8
Switching Accuracy	8
Percent Set-Loss Errors	
Percent Switching Accuracy	

Auditory Consonant Trigrams Test (ACT)

Measure	T-score
0 Second Delay	50
3 Second Delay	35
9 Second Delay	40
18 Second Delay	34
Total Correct	32

Trail Making Test (TMT)

	Z-Score
Trails A	0.5
Trails A Errors	

Table 11.19   (*Continued*)

	Z-Score
Trails B	0.5
Trails B Errors	

Tower of London–2nd Ed (TOL-2)

Measure	Standard Score
Total Correct	88
Total Move Score	<60
Total Initiation Time	104
Total Execution Time	<60
Total Time	<60
Total Time Violations	<60
Total Rule Violations	<60

Stroop Color and Word Test (Stroop)

Measure	T-score
Word Score	48
Color Score	36
Color-Word Score	31
Interference Score	43

BIDER Cognitive Estimations Test

Measure	Z-score
Quantity	0.2
Time	−3
Weight	−2.8
Distance	−2.5
Composite	−4.2

Digit Span

Digit Span	Scaled Score
Total	8
Digit Span Forward	9
Digit Span Backward	9

SNAP-IV Rating Scale

Scale	Parent	Teacher
Inattention	1.00	0.56
Hyperactivity/Impulsivity	0.11	0.00
ODD	0.50	0.00

Table 11.19 *(Continued)*

Behavior Rating Inventory of Executive Function (BRIEF)

Index/Scale	Parent T-Score
Inhibit	44
Shift	43
Emotional Control	48
Initiate	44
Working Memory	46
Plan/Organize	50
Organization of Materials	52
Monitor	60
Task Completion	NA
Behavioral Regulation Index (BRI)	45
Metacognition Index (MI)	55
Global Executive Composite (GEC)	49

Table 11.20   **Christopher's Fine Motor Functioning Scores**

Grooved Pegboard

Measure	Z-Score
Pegboard-Dominant Hand	-0.4
Pegboard-Nondominant Hand	-0.5

NEPSY – 2nd Edition (NEPSY-II)

Sensorimotor Subtests	Scaled Score
Visuomotor Precision	
Combined	7
Time	
Errors	
Imitating Hand Positions	
Total	8
Dominant	
Nondominant	

Table 11.21   **Christopher's Visual Perception and Visual-Motor Integration Scores**

Beery–Buktenica Developmental Test of Visual-Motor Integration–6th Ed (Beery VMI)

Measure	Standard Score
Beery VMI	87
Visual Perception	98
Motor Coordination	86

Rey Complex Figure Test (RCFT)

Measure	Z-Score
Copy	−5

Benton Judgment of Line Orientation - Form H (JOLO)

	Z-Score
Total Correct	−2.5

Table 11.22   **Christopher's Academic Functioning Scores**

Wechsler Individual Achievement Test–3rd Ed (WIAT-III)

Subtests/COMPOSITES	Standard Score
BASIC READING	93
Word Reading	95
Pseudoword Decoding	92
Reading Comprehension	99
Spelling	87
MATHEMATICS	103
Math Problem Solving	102
Numerical Operations	105
MATH FLUENCY	98
Math Fluency - Addition	108
Math Fluency - Subtraction	85
Math Fluency - Multiplication	105

Table 11.22   (Continued)

Gray Oral Reading Tests–Fifth Edition, Form A (GORT-5)

Measure	Scaled Score
Reading Rate	5
Reading Accuracy	4
Reading Fluency	4
Reading Comprehension	7
Composite	Standard Score
Oral Reading Index	76

Oral and Written Language Scales–2nd Edition

	Standard Score
Written Expression	103

Table 11.23   Christopher's Symptom Validity Scores

TOMM	Raw
Trial 1	49
	Raw
Reliable Digit Span	7
Dot Counting Test E-score	12.5

Table 11.24   Christopher's Social-Emotional Functioning Scores

Behavioral Assessment System for Children–2nd Ed (BASC-2) >65 = Clinically Significant

Clinical Scales	Parent T-score	Teacher
Externalizing Problems:	40	42
Hyperactivity	41	45
Aggression	48	44
Conduct Problems	44	40
Internalizing Problems:	43	52
Anxiety	56	58
Depression	42	50
Somatization	48	41

Table 11.24   (Continued)

Clinical Scales	Parent T-score	Teacher
Behavioral Symptoms Index:	42	44
Atypicality	47	50
Withdrawal	42	42
Attention Problems	44	44
School Problems	NA	58
Learning Problems	NA	66
Adaptive Skills:	55	55
Adaptability	41	57
Social Skills	59	59
Study Skills	NA	55
Leadership	60	52
Activities of Daily Living	43	0
Functional Communication	54	44

Behavioral Assessment System for Children–2nd Ed (BASC-2) Self

Clinical Scales	T-Score
School Problems	47
Attitude to School	51
Attitude to Teachers	47
Internalizing Problems:	58
Atypicality	55
Locus of Control	57
Social Stress	49
Anxiety	59
Depression	52
Sense of Inadequacy	62
Inattention/Hyperactivity	45
Attention Problems	53
Hyperactivity	45
Emotional Symptoms Index	58
Relations with Parents	60
Interpersonal Relations	52
Self-Esteem	54
Self-Reliance	51

CASE 9—ISABELLA, AGE 13: TEENAGE GIRL WITH LOW COGNITIVE ABILITY, ADHD, AND EMOTIONAL ISSUES

Michelle Lurie

Neuropsychological Assessment

Name: Isabella Sanchez

Age: 13 years, 2 months

Grade: 7th grade

Referred by: Lucy Martinez, M.D.

Parent: Maria Sanchez

Reason for Evaluation

Isabella Sanchez is a 13-year-old Hispanic girl who lives in Dallas with her mother and her 11-year-old brother. Isabella is in the seventh grade at Arapaho Elementary. This testing was initiated by her parents upon referral from psychiatrist Dr. Lucy Martinez due to Isabella's academic and memory difficulties, her poor self-esteem, her hyperactivity, and her anxiety. Therefore, the purpose of this evaluation is to better understand Isabella's neurocognitive and emotional functioning. Academic and treatment recommendations will also be made when necessary.

Background Information

Developmental History and Health

Isabella is the product of a teenage pregnancy complicated with hypertension. Isabella's mother was 16 years old when she became pregnant with Isabella, and she reports that she knows few details about Isabella's father. She was hospitalized from 5 months with preeclampsia and therefore delivery was induced at 27 1/2 weeks gestation. Isabella weighed only 3 lbs. 0 oz. at birth. She remained in the neonatal intensive care

unit and was discharged from the hospital at 2 months. Ms. Sanchez and Isabella lived with Isabella's grandmother while her mother finished high school. Medical problems after discharge consisted of digestive problems, sucking problems, and immature lungs. She underwent breathing treatments and was on a heart monitor. Nonetheless, Isabella was described as an easygoing baby who was doted on by relatives.

As might be expected for a premature baby, Isabella evidenced delays in reaching some developmental milestones. For example, Isabella did not crawl until age 14 months or stand alone until age 16 months. Isabella's speech was also delayed, and she was slow to learn the alphabet, name colors, and count. She said her first word at age 18 months and was talking in full sentences by age 3 1/2. She continues to have some difficulty with verbal and written expression. Isabella speaks primarily Spanish at home. Isabella began toilet training at age 2. However, she continues to evidence nocturnal enuresis.

In general, Isabella is a healthy child. No surgeries, hospitalizations, or head injuries were reported. She was diagnosed with ADHD in kindergarten by psychiatrist Dr. Martinez and has tried various stimulant medications. At the time of testing, Isabella was on Vyvanse. No hearing or vision concerns were noted. Likewise, no problems with Isabella's sleep habits were reported. Isabella has a healthy appetite for a range of foods.

No notable maternal family history was reported. Isabella's mother completed high school and works in an office. Her paternal family history is unknown, and Ms. Sanchez has had no contact with Isabella's father since her pregnancy.

Academic History

Isabella attended day care beginning at age 6 months where she remained until grade school. During this time serious difficulties with her pre-academic skills were noted. Isabella transitioned to Arapaho Elementary in kindergarten. Isabella has always needed ongoing academic support. Her teachers have consistently reported problems with retention of material, concentration, spelling, written expression, and difficulties with math comprehension as well as story comprehension. At present Isabella is rated as performing far below grade level in all areas. She is described by her teachers as a pleasant student who has serious focus difficulties and severe problems mastering new concepts.

Emotional and Social Development

Isabella was described by her mother as a very loving and sympathetic young woman. Her language arts teacher described her as a kind and good-humored young woman who is obedient to her teachers and kind to her classmates. Isabella was described by her science teacher as wanting to learn and do better.

Despite these strengths, Isabella has some struggles. Her mother is concerned about Isabella's self-esteem and her belief that she is inferior at times. Isabella reports that she does not like school because "her teachers are mean and the girls hate her." Ms. Sanchez reports that Isabella worries and is nervous. She also indicated that Isabella is impulsive and will have occasional temper tantrums. She is described as "having so much energy" and she cannot stay seated at mealtime.

From a social perspective, Isabella is described as only sometimes getting along with her peers, and she is socially immature. Isabella is bullied by other students regarding her capacity to learn, and she often comes home crying and frustrated.

Behavioral Observations

Isabella presented as an amicable, soft-spoken young woman who approached the testing with a good attitude. She was appropriately groomed and dressed and well oriented. Isabella tended to be somewhat quiet and reserved. Nonetheless, she responded honestly and openly to all verbal questions. Some mild problems with expressive and receptive language were observed. Isabella's mood was somewhat depressed, and her affect was constricted.

Isabella took her stimulant medication on the first day of testing. She was alert and her stamina was intact, despite indicating that her medication tends to sedate her. In contrast, Isabella did not take her stimulant medication on the second day of testing at the request of this examiner, and she was much less alert on this testing session. Isabella's fatigue was attributed to her difficulty sleeping the night prior to testing. Clearly, Isabella was extremely lethargic and heavy-eyed during this testing session, and on two occasions she went to the restroom to put cold water on her face. Her endurance was severely impaired, particularly when contrasted to her intact stamina on the first day of testing.

In the structured one-on-one testing environment, Isabella did not evidence any distractibility. She had no overt difficulties with impulsivity or restlessness. However, on both days of testing, Isabella evidenced extremely slow task completion on verbal and nonverbal tasks. On the basis of these behavior observations, along with symptom validity measures, this assessment appears to be a valid measure of Isabella's functioning.

Tests Administered

- Clinical interview with Ms. Sanchez
- Clinical interview with Isabella Sanchez
- Review of medical and educational records
- Exchange of information with Dr. Martinez
- Wechsler Intelligence Scale for Children–Fifth Edition (WISC–V)
- California Verbal Learning Test–Children Version (CVLT–C)
- Rey Complex Figure Test and Recognition Trial (RCFT)
- A Developmental Neuropsychological Assessment–Second Edition (NEPSY–II): Selected subtests
- Delis-Kaplan Executive Functioning System (D-KEFS): Selected subtests
- IVA+Plus Continuous Performance Test (IVA+Plus)
- Wisconsin Card Sort Test–64: Computer Version 2 (WCST–64)

- Wechsler Individual Achievement Test–Third Edition (WIAT–III): Selected Subtests
- Gray Oral Reading Test–Fifth Edition (GORT–5)
- Clinical Evaluation of Language Fundamentals–Fifth Edition (CELF5): Structured Writing
- Beck Youth Inventory–Second Edition (BYI–II)
- Millon Adolescent Clinical Inventory (MACI)
- Sentence Completion
- Conners 3 Parent Rating Scale
- Achenbach Child Behavior Checklist
- Achenbach Teacher Report Form
- Achenbach Youth Self Report
- Behavior Rating Inventory of Executive Function (BRIEF): Parent and teacher forms
- Adaptive Behavior Assessment System–Second Edition (ABAS–II)

Test Results

Psychological Functioning

Expressed Concerns   Isabella described herself as a young woman who is struggling with low self-esteem. She only "sometimes" feels as if she can do things without help and only "sometimes" feels smart. She also indicated that she is "never" good at remembering things. Isabella reported that she is struggling with internalizing behaviors in terms of moderate to extreme affective problems. In fact, Isabella has struggled with some prior suicidal ideation, which was most notable when she was bullied last year, but she notes that her depression is less severe recently. Isabella indicated that she does not know why she feels sad but that "people bring me down for no reason … I don't know if they are playing around … I feel sad." She also indicated that "it is easier to be alone because you will feel less hurt" and that "you are supposed to only count on yourself." A high level of anxiety was also reported, which is primarily related to school performance. Isabella worries about not passing seventh grade and she tends to worry about the future.

In terms of her family life, Isabella described the environment at home as calm and "okay" and her family as "funny and awesome." She indicated that she is close to her mother, and she described her mother as "kind." She is close to her brother.

Personality Profile   Isabella identifies "lonely/depressed" as the problem that is troubling her the most. Her personality profile is characterized by her apprehensive and fearful mistrust of others, her strong need for attachment and nurturance, a marked deprecation of her self-worth, a shyness with peers, and a social awkwardness and hesitation in most relationships. Isabella very much desires closeness and affection with others but self-protectively denies or restrains this need for emotional support. Fearing rejection, she experiences sadness about her loneliness and anxiety about her isolation and low sense of self-worth. Her self-image of being weak and fragile makes the ordinary responsibilities of her life often seem excessively demanding.

Isabella's lack of self-assertiveness is notable, as is a tendency to deprecate her own aptitudes and an unwillingness to assume increasingly mature and responsible roles. Despite her strong desire to feel close and warm with others, she has felt it best to deny these needs and maintain a safe measure of distance, at least when social relationships are concerned. Isabella is likely to have withdrawn into increasingly isolated activities, such as daydreaming or watching TV excessively. Not surprisingly, she only rarely will act out or be provocative or overtly resentful. It is possible that Isabella's sluggish exterior and flat affect overlies restrained feelings of anger, anxiety, and depression.

Isabella is clearly struggling with her social relationships. She views her classmates as "unkind." In fact, although problems with peers are common during adolescence, Isabella finds these relationships to be more painful than most, experiencing rejection and a sense of isolation from peers. As a consequence, she may retreat to her family, thereby delaying movement toward autonomy.

Rating Scales On rating scales, Ms. Sanchez reported that Isabella is struggling with some internalizing behaviors. She identified Isabella as having moderate anxiety problems, somatic problems, and depressed behaviors. Isabella's mother also noted mild peer relations problems. No externalizing concerns were rated by Ms. Sanchez. Isabella's teacher did not describe any concerns in this regard.

Adaptive Behavior Isabella's mother was asked to complete a rating of Isabella's adaptive behavior. Adaptive skills are practical everyday skills required to function and meet environment demands, including effectively taking care of oneself and interacting with others. The categories of adaptive behaviors assessed include Conceptual (communication and academic skills), Social (interpersonal and social competence), and Practical (independent living and daily living skills). Isabella was rated by her mother as evidencing adaptive living skills in the Extremely Low range (Standard Score = 69). Isabella's Conceptual Skills were Extremely Low, with a relative weakness in her self-direction. Similarly, Isabella's Practical Skills were Extremely Low, and relative weaknesses were noted in community use and home living. In contrast, Isabella's Social Functioning was Average, and a relative strength.

Intellectual Abilities

In order to assess Isabella's intellectual ability, she was administered the WISC–V, which is an individually administered test of a child's intellectual ability and cognitive strengths and weaknesses. This test has six composite scores: Verbal Comprehension Index, Visual Spatial Index, Fluid Reasoning Index, Working Memory Index, Processing Speed Index, and FSIQ. The FSIQ is derived from a combination of the subtest scores and is considered the most representative estimate of global intellectual

functioning. Isabella's general cognitive ability is within the Very Low range of intellectual functioning, as measured by the FSIQ. Her overall thinking and reasoning abilities exceed those of approximately only 6% of children her age (FSIQ = 77). Likewise, if one calculates a General Ability Index (GAI), a measure less impacted by working memory and processing speed factors, Isabella's intellectual ability is similarly impaired (General Ability Index = 76; 5th percentile).

Isabella's verbal reasoning abilities as measured by the Verbal Comprehension Index are in the Very Low range and above those of approximately 5% of her peers (Verbal Comprehension Index = 75). These subtests are designed to measure a child's ability to access and apply acquired word knowledge in terms of verbal reasoning and concept formation. Isabella's knowledge of vocabulary words was only mildly impaired, but she struggled particularly on a task assessing her verbal abstract reasoning, scoring at only the 2nd percentile.

Isabella also evidenced Very Low overall functioning on the Visual Spatial Index (VSI = 76; 5th percentile) indicating impaired visual-spatial reasoning abilities. Her visuoconstructional and visuomotor skills were weak, and Isabella also evidenced serious difficulty on a measure of visual-perceptual and spatial reasoning ability.

Isabella performed in the Low Average range on the Fluid Reasoning Index (FRI = 85; 16th percentile). A relative strength was noted on a task assessing her ability to detect the underlying conceptual relationship among visual stimuli. In contrast, Isabella evidenced mild to moderate difficulty on measures of nonverbal reasoning and mental arithmetic.

Consistently Low Average to Average performances were noted in Isabella's ability to register, hold, and manipulate visual and auditory information in conscious awareness. She performed better than approximately 21% of her age-mates on the Working Memory Index (WMI = 88), and a relative strength was evident in Isabella's ability to repeat, reverse, and sequence series of digits.

Isabella's speed and accuracy of visual scanning and visuomotor coordination was Very Low on the Processing Speed Index (PSI = 77; 6th percentile). On these tasks Isabella generally worked accurately but extremely slowly both on a measure of visual scanning and discrimination and on a measure of paired associate learning and graphomotor speed. Her visual scanning speed and speed of sequencing information was also impaired on measures of executive functioning discussed below.

Attention and Executive Functions
Executive Functioning On a battery of executive functioning subtests, Isabella demonstrated Average cognitive flexibility on verbal tasks but extremely impaired cognitive flexibility on visual tasks requiring her to sequence two sets of data simultaneously. She worked exceptionally slowly on these tasks. This was to a large extent due to Isabella's great difficulty sequencing the information (numbers and letters), and Isabella frequently had to go back to the beginning of the sequence (a, b, c …) to determine her next response.

Serious problems with inhibition were noted on tasks designed to assess the ability to inhibit automatic responses in favor of novel responses and the ability to switch between response types. Isabella's speed and her accuracy were consistently impaired on these tasks. Isabella evidenced mild impairment on a computerized measure of her ability to form abstract concepts and to resist perseveration. Some difficulties were noted initially understanding the task, and when faced with feedback indicating that her problem-solving strategy was ineffective, Isabella appeared to stumble and struggled to generate an alternative problem-solving approach. Nonetheless, as the task progressed, Isabella appeared to develop a better understanding of how to master it.

Sustained Attention and Response Control Variable performances were noted on measures of sustained attention and response control.

Without stimulant medication, Isabella was administered a subtest that uses an auditory continuous performance paradigm to measure selective and sustained attention, response inhibition, and executive functioning. The first part of this subtest is designed to assess selective auditory attention and the ability to sustain it (i.e. vigilance). Surprisingly, even without stimulant medication, Isabella's performance was very strong on this component of the task. The second part of this subtest is designed to assess the ability to shift and maintain a new and complex cognitive set involving both inhibition of previously learned responses and correctly responding to matching or contrasting stimuli. Isabella struggled on this second part of the subtest that requires more executive control than the first part due to the cognitive load and working memory requirements of the task. A high level of impulsivity was noted on this component of the subtest.

In order to further assess her sustained attention and response control *with stimulant medication*, Isabella was administered the IVA+Plus. This task is intended to be mildly boring and demanding of sustained attention over a 13-minute period of time. On this task Isabella was required to self-regulate and respond to target stimuli (the number 1 presented in either an auditory or visual format on the computer) and refrain from responding to nontarget stimuli (the number 2 presented in the same formats). In terms of her sustained attention, deficits were noted on the IVA+Plus. Isabella struggled to remain vigilant to visual targets, although her auditory vigilance was intact. Mild problems in her visual and auditory focus were noted, but Isabella's response speed was intact. In terms of her response control, impairment was noted in both the visual and the auditory domains, with serious distractibility evident. Nonetheless, Isabella's stamina was intact in both domains reflecting a good attitude towards the test. Overall the results on the IVA+Plus were consistent with ADHD; Combined Type (even with stimulant medication).

Rating Scales Further measures of Isabella's attentional functioning were obtained by having Isabella's mother and teachers complete various rating scales. Isabella was rated by her mother as evidencing severe problems with inattention, hyperactivity/impulsivity, and executive functioning. Moderate learning problems were also noted by Ms. Sanchez. Similarly, Isabella's language arts teacher also indicated serious concerns in this regard, as did her science teacher. Her keyboarding teacher rated Isabella as struggling with both behavior regulation problems (in the form of disinhibition and impaired emotional control) and metacognition problems (in the form of impaired working memory and poor self-monitoring).

Language

Isabella evidenced moderate impairment on measures of both phonemic verbal fluency and semantic verbal fluency. Similarly, her listening comprehension was moderately impaired on a task of oral discourse comprehension and mildly impaired on a measure of receptive vocabulary.

In order to further assess her language skills, Isabella was administered the Clinical Evaluation of Language Fundamentals–Fifth Edition (CELF5). The Core Language Score of the CELF5 is a measure of general language ability and provides an easy and reliable way to quantify Isabella's overall language performance. Isabella received a Core Language Score of 75 (5th percentile), which places Isabella in the Low/Moderate range of language functioning. Isabella struggled on measures of receptive language skills (Receptive Language Index score = 75; 5th percentile) as well as on measures of expressive language skills (Expressive Language Index score = 80; 9th percentile). Deficits were noted on subtests of Isabella's ability to understand relationships between words, Isabella's ability to formulate sentences when given grammatical constraints, and when required to imitate sentences presented by the examiner. Isabella also had difficulty when listening to oral narratives and answering questions about the content of the information given, when assembling grammatically correct sentences from visually and auditorily presented words or phrases, and when interpreting various sentences.

Memory

Isabella was administered tests of memory assessing how well she takes in, stores, and remembers information presented both visually and verbally.

Visual Memory Isabella evidenced significant impairment on a test of spatial memory for novel visual material. This test assesses spatial recall, visual content recognition, and overall visuospatial memory. Both her initial recall and her delayed recall were impaired on this measure. Significant difficulties were also noted on a complex test of spatial memory requiring Isabella to reproduce a detailed design from memory. On both the immediate recall trial and the delayed recall trial, Isabella struggled to recall the figure and the particular details within the figure. Despite these notable struggles, Isabella's recognition memory was significantly stronger on this task and in the Average range.

Verbal Memory Isabella's performances were in the impaired range on a complex measure of contextual verbal memory. She was able to spontaneously recall only two details from the text, and she did not benefit from cueing. Some impairment was also noted on a measure of the strategies and processes involved in learning and recalling verbal material. On this task, Isabella's ability to repeat a list of words the first time she heard it indicates a Low Average initial attention span for auditory-verbal information. Similarly, on her fifth learning attempt, her performance was Low Average. Within the first five trials, Isabella reached a learning plateau somewhat faster than others her age did, limiting the number of new words she recalled. Isabella's use of semantic clustering was Low Average compared to others her age. This tendency not to recall words with similar meanings together led to some inefficiency in her learning strategies. After both a short delay and a longer delay, Isabella's recall of the list was mildly to moderately impaired. Category cueing was not particularly helpful. In terms of learning errors, Isabella's tendency to report intrusions was mildly elevated for her age indicating mild difficulties in discriminating relevant from irrelevant responses. Similarly, on a delayed recognition test for the words, Isabella's ability to discriminate between words that were on the list and those that were not was impaired for her age, suggesting that Isabella has some difficulties in discriminating relevant from irrelevant responses when trying to recognize verbal information. Isabella's ability to recognize information was about the same as her ability to recall it. Taken together, these findings suggest that Isabella experienced mild difficulty in encoding verbal information and significant difficulty in retrieving information from memory.

Academic Skills

In order to assess her academic achievement, Isabella was administered the Gray Oral Reading Test–Fifth Edition (GORT–5) as well as subtests from the WIAT–III and the CELF5.

Reading Isabella's reading rate was Average on a measure of reading fluency. However, deficits were noted in Isabella's reading accuracy and she tended to skip words, insert words, and substitute words. Similarly, Isabella struggled on a task of reading comprehension. Therefore, although Isabella might read at an adequate speed, she does not appear to clearly understand the content of what she is reading, and she is rarely able to make predictions or inferences from what she reads.

Mathematics Isabella evidenced Low Average performance on a measure of math calculation and on measures of her timed math fact retrieval. Isabella's math problem-solving skills were particularly weak and in the Borderline range. Overall Isabella's performances were far below grade level on these mathematics tasks.

Written Language Isabella performed within the Average range on tasks that required her

to correctly spell verbally presented words. Her performances were mildly impaired and in the Low Average range on a measure assessing her ability to use situational information (i.e., a story title, an introductory sentence, and an incomplete sentence) to create a short narrative.

Neuropsychological Implications and Diagnostic Impression

Isabella Sanchez is a pleasant young woman who is evidencing some neurocognitive and psychosocial struggles. A moderate degree of intellectual impairment is noted, and this combined with severe adaptive behavior deficits likely leads to challenges in a range of areas. Isabella struggles to keep up both in the classroom and in social environments, and she is not always able to correctly assess others' motives and to make deductions. As a result, Isabella has been taken by surprise by social rejection, and she has come to the conclusion that it is safer to depend only upon herself and to isolate herself from her peers. Isabella feels inferior to her peers, both intellectually and physically. This causes sadness and increases her social withdrawal. Likewise, a high level of anxiety is evident, and Isabella is extremely concerned about her academic struggles.

From a neurocognitive perspective, deficits are evident in the areas of attention and response control, memory, executive functioning, and language skills. It does not appear that Isabella's history of bilingualism would account for the severity of her struggles. Her academic functioning is below grade expectancy, particularly in mathematics problem solving and reading/listening comprehension. Although Isabella clearly wants to be successful academically, her intellectual and neurocognitive deficits interfere with her ability to achieve this goal, and this is tremendously distressing for her. Complicating these neurocognitive deficits are challenges in emotional functioning. Isabella struggles with anxiety and depression, along with low self-esteem. Some avoidant personality traits are evident, along with dependent personality features.

Based on these findings, the following diagnoses are made:

F41.9 unspecified anxiety disorder

F34.1 persistent depressive disorder

F90.2 ADHD; combined Type

V62.3 academic problem

F70 intellectual disability, mild severity

Recommendations

1. It is critical that Isabella participate in **psychotherapy** to address her anxiety and depression as well as her interpersonal difficulties. A focus of therapy should also be her poor body image and low self-esteem.
2. Likewise, ongoing **psychopharmacological interventions** for ADHD are necessary. However, it is recommended that Isabella's psychological struggles also be addressed with medication.
3. A "**lunch bunch**" group at school might be useful to help facilitate social relationships.
4. The possibility of a **less demanding academic environment** might be considered. In particular, a school for students with learning challenges would likely improve Isabella's self-concept while simultaneously reducing her anxiety and depression.
5. Due to her diagnosis of ADHD, along with her intellectual and academic impairments, Isabella should receive **special education support** in the school.
6. **Preferential seating** is essential.
7. **Extended time** on class tests and standardized testing (50%) is essential.
8. Isabella's teachers should **communicate weekly with her mother via email** to alert her to upcoming assignments and due dates. They should recognize that at present Isabella does not have the executive functioning skills needed to do this independently.
9. **Visual aids on reading comprehension tasks** should be encouraged. For example, Isabella's teachers should encourage her to highlight text as needed, to make annotations on the side, etc.
10. Isabella should not be required to rely on her note-taking skills. Isabella's teachers might provide her with an **outline of the lesson,** and she could fill in the main ideas on the lesson outline. It is likely that she will benefit from having **instructor handouts** and **lecture outlines** available prior to the lecture for her to review. Similarly, provide Isabella with **study questions** before reading, not after. This will also allow her to focus her attention on the relevant information and aid comprehension.
11. The use of a **notebook computer** in the classroom as needed is recommended. Isabella should learn to keyboard quickly and accurately.
12. Isabella is encouraged to **check her work** to improve self-monitoring.
13. Compared to other students her age, Isabella will need **more repetition of material** to learn it. Care should be taken not to frustrate her by presenting too much information too quickly. She may benefit from **shorter periods of learning** and **longer breaks between periods of learning**. Isabella may benefit from having **lessons repeated** to her on different days, perhaps in condensed form, in order to ensure that this information is well encoded into her memory. Isabella should be encouraged to associate new material with previously learned material and to elaborate new concepts. When trying to remember information, as when studying for a test, Isabella should **practice over a number of days** rather than trying to cram everything into a short time period. Her **learning assignments should be shorter** than those of her peers, and she will need **more repetition** to learn the material.

In addition, Isabella would likely benefit from memory training exercises designed to enhance her encoding skills. Therefore, strategies to improve her memory and learning would be helpful.

14. Ms. Sanchez is encouraged to seek out services for Isabella through **DARS** (Texas **Department of Assistive and Rehabilitative Services**).

It has been my utmost pleasure to work with Isabella. I hope that this assessment has been helpful in terms of shedding light on her difficulties and I trust that with appropriate interventions, Isabella's difficulties are diminished. Please feel free to contact me should you have questions about this assessment. Isabella's test scores appear in Tables 11.25 to 11.35.

Psychometric Summary

Table 11.25 Isabella's Green's Medical Symptom Validity Test Scores

Paired Associates	Free Recall
Good Effort; Poor memory	Good Effort; Normal range memory

Table 11.26 Isabella's Wechsler Intelligence Scale for Children–Fifth Edition (WISC–V) Scores

Composite	Standard Score	Percentile Rank	Qualitative Description
Verbal Comprehension (VCI)	76	5	Very Low
Visual Spatial (VSI)	75	5	Very Low
Fluid Reasoning (FRI)	85	16	Low Average
Working Memory (WMI)	88	21	Low Average
Processing Speed (PSI)	77	6	Very Low
Full Scale (FSIQ)	77	6	Very Low

Table 11.26 (Continued)

Ancillary Index	Standard Score	Percentile Rank	Qualitative Description
Quantitative Reasoning (QRI)	77	6	Very Low
Auditory Working Memory (AWMI)	92–S	30	Average
Nonverbal (NVI)	76	5	Very Low
General Ability (GAI)	76	5	Very Low
Cognitive Proficiency (CPI)	79	8	Very Low

Verbal Comprehension Subtests	Scaled Score	Percentile Rank
Similarities	4	2
Vocabulary	7	16

Visual Spatial Subtests	Scaled Score	Percentile Rank
Block Design	6	9
Visual Puzzles	5	5

Fluid Reasoning Subtests	Scaled Score	Percentile Rank
Matrix Reasoning	10–S	50
Figure Weights	5	5
(Arithmetic)	7	16

Working Memory Subtests	Scaled Score	Percentile Rank
Digit Span	9	37
Picture Span	7	16
(Letter–Number Sequencing)	8	25

Processing Speed Subtests	Scaled Score	Percentile Rank
Coding	7	16
Symbol Search	5	5

Table 11.27 Isabella's California Verbal Learning Test (CVLT–C) Scores

Level of Recall	Standard Score
Trial 1	−1.0
Trial 5	−1.5
Short Delay Free Recall	−1.5
Short Delay Cued Recall	−2
Long Delay Free Recall	−2.0
Long Delay Cued Recall	−1.5

Table 11.28 Isabella's Rey Complex Figure Test and Recognition Trial (RCFT) Scores

Condition	T Score	Percentile Rank
Immediate Recall	<20	<1
Delayed Recall	<20	<1
Recognition Total Correct	52	58
Copy	−	≤1
Time to Copy	−	>16

Table 11.29 Isabella's Wisconsin Card Sort Test—64: Computer Version 2 (WCST-64) Scores

WCST Error Score	Standard Score	Percentile Rank
Perseverative Errors	89	23
Nonperseverative Errors	88	21

Table 11.30 Isabella's Delis-Kaplan Executive Function System (D-KEFS) Scores

Trail Making	Scaled Score	Percentile Rank
Visual Scanning	5	5
Number Sequencing	4	2
Letter Sequencing	4	2
Number-Letter Switching	1	<1

Table 11.30 (Continued)

Verbal Fluency	Scaled Score	Percentile Rank
Letter Fluency	6	9
Category Fluency	5	5
Category Switching	9	37

Table 11.31 Isabella's A Developmental Neuropsychological Assessment–Second Edition (NEPSY–II) Scores

Attention and Executive Functioning	Scaled Score	PercentileRank
Auditory Attention	12	75
Response Set	5	5
Inhibition—Naming	6	9
Inhibition—Inhibition	3	1
Inhibition—Switching	3	1

Memory	Scaled Score	Percentile Rank
Narrative Memory Free Recall	5	5
Narrative Memory Free/Cued	5	5
Memory for Designs	3	1
Memory for Designs—Delayed	6	9

Table 11.32 Isabella's Wechsler Individual Achievement Test–Third Edition (WIAT-III) Scores

Subtest	Standard Score	Percentile Rank
Listening Comprehension	78	7
Math Problem Solving	71	3
Numerical Operations	82	12
Spelling	101	53
Math Fluency–Addition	85	16
Math Fluency–Subtraction	87	19
Math Fluency–Multiplication	86	18

Table 11.33   Isabella's Gray Oral Reading Test—Fifth Edition (GORT-5) Scores

GORT-5 Score	Scaled Score	Percentile Rank
Rate	9	37
Accuracy	7	16
Fluency	8	25
Comprehension	5	5

Table 11.34   Isabella's Clinical Evaluation of Language Fundamentals—Fifth Edition (CELF5) Scores

Core/Index Score	Standard Score	Percentile Rank
Core Language Score	75	5
Receptive Language Index	75	5
Expressive Language Index	80	9
Language Content Index	78	7

Subtest	Scaled Score	Percentile Rank
Word Classes	6	9
Formulated Sentences	5	5
Recalling Sentences	7	16
Understanding Spoken Paragraph	5	5
Sentence Assembly	8	25
Semantic Relationships	6	9

Supplementary Score	Scaled Score	Percentile Rank
Structured Writing	7	16

Table 11.35   Isabella's Adaptive Behavior Assessment System—Second Edition (ABAS–II): Parent Rating Summary Scores

Composite	Standard Score	Percentile Rank
GAC	69	2
Conceptual	65	1
Social	95	37
Practical	65	1

Skills Area	Scaled Score	Percentile Rank
Communication	4	2
Community Use	2	<1
Functional Acad.	5	5
Home Living	2	<1
Health/Safety	7	16
Leisure	7	16
Self-Care	5	5
Self-Direction	2	<1
Social	11	63

INTERPRETING THE WISC–V FROM DAN MILLER'S INTEGRATED SCHOOL NEUROPSYCHOLOGICAL/CATTELL-HORN-CARROLL MODEL

Daniel C. Miller and Alicia M. Jones

The purpose of this chapter is to discuss how results from the WISC–V (Wechsler, 2014) can be interpreted from a neuropsychological perspective. Neuropsychological evaluations usually include more than just a measure of cognitive abilities, so this chapter starts with a review of the Wechsler family of products that are often used together. The next section of the chapter reviews which neurocognitive constructs are addressed by these Wechsler products. The chapter ends with a case study example that illustrates how the WISC–V and related products can be used in a pediatric/school neuropsychological assessment.

THE WECHSLER FAMILY OF PRODUCTS

"Standardized intellectual measures are psychometrically some of the best tools available to practitioners, and often serve as a foundation for interpreting pediatric and school neuropsychological test results" (Miller & Hale, 2008, p. 445). The WISC–V is a compilation of tests designed to measure various aspects of cognitive or intellectual functioning. Administration of the WISC–V often serves as baseline assessment for a broader test battery. Hypotheses are generated about an examinee's strengths and weaknesses from the initial WISC–V results, and then additional measures are administered to verify or clarify those hypotheses. If clinicians want to use the WISC–V as part of a comprehensive neuropsychological assessment, they should be equally familiar with the *Wechsler Intelligence Scale for Children–Fifth Edition Integrated* (WISC–V Integrated; Wechsler & Kaplan, 2015). The WISC–V Integrated is designed to systematically test the limits for various tests from the WISC–V and provide clinicians with more clinically relevant qualitative information about the examinee's performance.

When conducting a comprehensive neuropsychological assessment, the WISC–V and the WISC–V Integrated should be used together in order to more fully understand an examinee's neurocognitive strengths and weaknesses. In addition to these two tests, the clinician should be equally competent to administer, at a minimum, a standardized test of achievement, such as the Wechsler Individual Achievement Test–Third Edition (WIAT–III: Pearson, 2009b), and a test of learning and memory (e.g., the Wide Range Assessment of Memory and Learning—Second Edition [WRAML–2; Sheslow & Adams, 2003]; the Test of Memory and Learning—Second Edition [TOMAL–2; C. R. Reynolds & Voress, 1997]; or the Wechsler Memory Scale–Fourth Edition [WMS–IV; Wechsler, 2009]).

COVERAGE OF BASIC NEUROCOGNITIVE CONSTRUCTS BY THE WISC–V, THE WISC–V INTEGRATED, AND THE WIAT–III

In this chapter, the tests from the WISC–V, WISC–V Integrated, and WIAT–III are classified according to the Integrated School Neuropsychological/Cattell-Horn-Carroll (SNP/CHC) Model developed by Miller (2013) (see Table 12.1). See Miller (2013) for how other common neuropsychological tests are classified into the Integrated SNP/CHC Model. The purposes of the Integrated SNP/CHC Model are to: (1) facilitate clinical interpretation by providing an organizational framework for the assessment data; (2) strengthen the linkage between assessment and evidence-based interventions; and (3) provide a common frame of reference for evaluating the effects of neurodevelopmental disorders on neurocognitive processes (Miller, 2013). The complete SNP Model includes the integration of academic achievement and social-emotional functioning with the major neuropsychological assessment components (see Miller, 2013; Miller & Maricle, 2012, 2014, for comprehensive reviews).

The Integrated SNP/CHC Model is based on current psychometric theory and research (Flanagan, Alfonso, & Ortiz, 2012; Horn & Blankson, 2012; Keith & Reynolds, 2012; Schneider & McGrew, 2012; Schrank & Wendling, 2012) and ongoing discussions with the CHC theorists and cross-battery researchers. The Integrated SNP/CHC Model encompasses four major classifications: (1) basic sensorimotor functions, (2) facilitators and inhibitors for cognitive processes and acquired knowledge skills, (3) basic cognitive processes, and (4) acquired knowledge. Within each of these major classifications, the neuropsychological constructs are further classified into broad areas and even further classified into second-order classifications and then third-order classifications, as appropriate. As an example, tests within the broad classification of sensorimotor functions can be further classified into the second-order classifications of: lateral preference, sensory functions, fine motor functions, visual-motor integration skills, visual scanning, gross motor functions, and qualitative behaviors. Some of these second-order classifications can be further subdivided into third-order classification. For example, the sensory functions can be subdivided into auditory and visual acuity, tactile sensation and perception, kinesthetic sensation and perception, and olfactory sensation and perception. For the sake of simplifying the Integrated SNP/CHC Model for this chapter, Table 12.1 presents only the broad and second-order classifications of the model.

Basic Sensorimotor Functions

The WISC–V or the WISC–V Integrated tests do not provide direct measures of basic sensorimotor functions. However, qualitative observational data and known historical medical information can provide a clinician with explanations for poor performance on several of the WISC–V/WISC–V Integrated tests. It is important to note that any impairment of the examinee's sensory functions (e.g., ability to see, hear, or feel) can adversely affect higher-order cognitive functioning. Similarly, poor fine motor and/or visual-motor integration skills can adversely affect successful performance on the WISC–V Block Design test or the WISC–V Integrated Block Design Multiple Choice test. Additionally, the WISC–V Coding, Symbol Search, and Cancellation and the WISC–V Integrated Cancellation Abstract tests all require visual scanning or tracking, so problems with these sensory abilities could be the underlying causes of poor performance on one or more of these tests.

A training clinician should note suspected or known sensorimotor deficits or neuropathological behaviors (e.g., hand tremors or motor awkwardness) during the WISC–V visual-spatial test administration and follow up with a referral to an occupational or physical therapist or other

Table 12.1 Coverage of the Basic Neurocognitive Constructs by the WISC–V, WISC–V Integrated, and WIAT–III

Integrated SNP/CHC Broad Classifications	Integrated SNP/CHC Second-Order Classifications	WISC–V	WISC–V Integrated	WIAT–III
Basic sensorimotor functions	Lateral preference			
	Sensory functions			
	Fine motor functions			
	Visual-motor integration skills			
	Visual scanning/tracking (indirect measures)	Coding Symbol Search Cancellation	Cancellation Abstract Qualitative Behaviors	
	Gross motor functions			
	Quantitative behaviors			
Cognitive processes: Visuospatial	Visuospatial perception	Block Design Block Design No Time Bonus Block Design Partial	Block Design Multiple Choice Qualitative Behaviors	
	Visuospatial reasoning	Visual Puzzles		
Cognitive Processes: Auditory/ Phonological	Sound discrimination and Auditory/phonological processing			
Cognitive Processes: Learning and Memory	Rate of learning			
	Immediate verbal memory	Digit Span Forward		Sentence Repetition
	Visual immediate memory		Coding RecallSpatial Span Forward Qualitative Behaviors	
	Delayed verbal memory			
	Delayed visual memory		Qualitative Behaviors	
	Verbal-visual associative learning and recall	Immediate Symbol Translation Delayed Symbol Translation Recognition Symbol Translation		
Cognitive Processes: Executive Functions	Cognitive flexibility			
	Concept recognition and generation	Similarities	Similarities Multiple Choice	
	Problem solving, fluid reasoning, and planning	Comprehension Matrix Reasoning Picture Concepts Figure Weights	Comprehension Multiple Choice Figure Weights Process Approach	
	Response inhibition			

(continued)

Table 12.1 (*Continued*)

Integrated SNP/CHC Broad Classifications	Integrated SNP/CHC Second-Order Classifications	WISC–V	WISC–V Integrated	WIAT–III
Facilitators/ Inhibitors: Allocating and Maintaining Attention	Selective/focused and sustained attention			
	Attentional capacity	Digit Span Forward	Spatial Span Forward	
Facilitators/ Inhibitors: Working Memory	Working memory	Arithmetic Digit Span Backward Digit Span Sequencing Letter–Number Sequencing Picture Span	Arithmetic Process Approach Part A Arithmetic Process Approach Part B Written Arithmetic Spatial Span Backward Sentence Recall Qualitative Behaviors	
Facilitators/ Inhibitors: Speed, Fluency, and Efficiency of Processing	Performance fluency	Cancellation Cancellation Random Cancellation Structured Coding Symbol Search Naming Speed Literacy Naming Speed Quantity	Coding Copy Cancellation Abstract Cancellation Abstract Random Cancellation Abstract Structured Qualitative Behaviors	Oral Word Fluency
	Acquired knowledge fluency			Oral Reading Fluency Oral Reading Accuracy Oral Reading Rate Alphabet Writing Fluency Math Fluency- Addition Math Fluency- Subtraction Math Fluency- Multiplication
Acquired Knowledge: Acculturation Knowledge	Semantic memory (General information)	Information	Information Multiple Choice	

Table 12.1 (*Continued*)

Integrated SNP/CHC Broad Classifications	Integrated SNP/CHC Second-Order Classifications	WISC–V	WISC–V Integrated	WIAT–III
Acquired Knowledge: Language Abilities	Oral expression	Vocabulary	Vocabulary Multiple Choice Picture Vocabulary Multiple Choice	Oral Expression Expressive Vocabulary
	Receptive language (Listening Comprehension)			Listening Comprehension Oral Discourse Comprehension Receptive Vocabulary
Acquired Knowledge: Reading Achievement	Basic reading skills: Phonological decoding			Early Reading Skills Pseudoword Decoding Word Reading
	Reading comprehension skills			Reading Comprehension
Acquired Knowledge: Written Language Achievement	Written expression Expository composition			Written Expression Sentence Composition Sentence Combining Sentence Building Essay Composition Word Count Theme Development and Text Organization Grammar and Mechanics
	Orthographic spelling			Spelling
Acquired Knowledge: Mathematics	Mathematical calculations		Written Arithmetic	Numerical Operations
	Mathematical reasoning	Arithmetic	Arithmetic Process Approach Part A Arithmetic Process Approach Part B	Math Problem Solving

specialist if warranted (Miller & Hale, 2008). If sensorimotor deficits are suspected within a neuropsychological evaluation, it is recommended that additional tests be administered, such as the sensorimotor subtests from the NEPSY–II (Korkman, Kirk, & Kemp, 2007) or the sensorimotor portion of the *Dean-Woodcock Neuropsychological Battery* (Dean & Woodcock, 2003).

Cognitive Processes: Visuospatial

The WISC–V, used in combination with the WISC–V Integrated, has a good representation of visuospatial measures (see Table 12.1). In the Integrated SNP/CHC Model (Miller, 2013), visuospatial processes are further classified into two narrower abilities: visuospatial perception and visuospatial reasoning. Miller (2013) classified the WISC–V Block Design test as a visuospatial perception type of task. The Block Design test requires many neurocognitive processes, and any number of these isolated processes or several processes working in tandem can cause poor performance on the task. The WISC–V Block Design test has several process scores. The Block Design No Time Bonus process score minimizes, but does not completely eliminate, the processing speed requirements of the task. The Block Design Partial score is based on the number of blocks correctly placed at the time limit, providing some credit for the work completed and thus reduction of the emphasis on speed. Base rates for the number of breaks in configuration and rotation errors made during the performance of the task are also available. Base rates represent the proportion of the sample that demonstrated those relevant behaviors.

The WISC–V Integrated Block Design Multiple Choice test requires the examinee to visually match the correct constructed design from four possible pictured alternatives. This reduces the motor planning and motor output requirements of the task.

The Visual Puzzles test is new to the WISC–V and strengthens the overall assessment of visuospatial skills. In the Integrated SNP/CHC Model (Miller, 2013), Visual Puzzles is classified as a visuospatial reasoning type of task. The test requires the examinee to look at a completed puzzle and then select three response options, which can be visually combined to reconstruct the completed puzzle. Visual Puzzles requires a whole-to-part analysis and synthesis and, when contrasted with Block Design, does not require any motor output.

Cognitive Processes: Auditory/ Phonological

In the Integrated SNP/CHC Model, Miller (2013) views the cognitive processes of auditory/phonological processing very narrowly. This broad classification is thought to include the two second-order classifications of sound discrimination and auditory/phonological processing. None of the WISC–V, WISC–V Integrated, or WIAT–III tests is specifically designed to measure these cognitive processes (see Table 12.1). Basic auditory processes certainly do influence higher-order language skills and acquired knowledge skills, such as academic achievement. If a referral question is specifically related to a suspected phonological processing deficit, the examiner should supplement the assessment battery with a direct measure of phonological processing, such as the Phonological Processing test from the NEPSY–II (Korkman et al., 2007) or the *Comprehensive Test of Phonological Processing–Second Edition* (Wagner, Torgeson, Rashotte, & Pearson, 2013).

Cognitive Processes: Learning and Memory

A thorough assessment of learning and memory processes is very complex. Some tests focus on only one aspect of learning and memory, such as immediate memory or working memory. Miller (2013) classified the broad area of learning and memory into six second-order classifications:

rate of learning, verbal immediate memory, visual immediate memory, delayed verbal memory, delayed visual memory, and verbal-visual associative learning and recall. When a clinician uses the WISC–V, WISC–V Integrated, and the WIAT–III together, there is good coverage of most aspects of learning and memory (see Table 12.1). More comprehensive coverage of learning and memory can be obtained by supplementing an assessment battery with one of the stand-alone learning and memory tests, such as the WRAML–2, the TOMAL–2, or the WMS–IV.

The WISC–V has added new tests (the Symbol Translation tests) that are designed to measure verbal-visual associative learning and recall. On these tasks, the examinee is asked to learn visual-verbal pairs and then translate various symbol strings into phrases. The Immediate Symbol Translation portion of the test measures immediate verbal-visual associative learning. After a 20- to 30-minute delay, the Delayed Symbol Translation portion of the test is administered, which measures delayed recall of verbal-visual associative learning. A third portion of the test, called Recognition Symbol Translation, can be administered. On this portion of the test, the examinee is shown a symbol and selects the correct translation from a set of response options that the examiner reads aloud. This portion of the test measures recognition recall, as opposed to free recall as required in the Delayed Symbol Translation portion of the test. These three scores do not contribute to any of the primary Index scores on the WISC–V, although they do contribute to a complementary Index score. They add considerable depth to the test from a neuropsychological perspective. Verbal-visual associative learning is an important cognitive process required to be an efficient reader (Litt & Nation, 2014).

The WISC–V includes the Digit Span Forward test, which is a measure of immediate verbal memory; the WISC–V Integrated Coding Recall and the Spatial Span Forward tests are designed to measure aspects of immediate visual memory. The WISC–V Integrated also includes qualitative scores for the Coding test designed to measure visual immediate memory. When the WIAT–III is included in an assessment battery, its Sentence Repetition test adds an additional measure of immediate verbal memory.

Performance on the Sentence Repetition test can be compared to performance on the Digit Span test to determine if the increase in contextual cues helps or hinders performance. As previously mentioned, if the assessment battery were to include a broader stand-alone learning and memory test, those tests typically include memory for stories subtests that have the highest contextual or semantic loading, and performance on these measures can be compared to memory for sentences, words, or numbers and letters. Measuring how well a child learns verbal material with different levels of contextual cues or semantic loading has implications for direct instruction.

The only learning and memory areas not covered by the combined WISC–V, WISC–V Integrated, and WIAT–III battery are rate of learning and delayed verbal and visual memory. Rate of learning tasks are very important from a neuropsychological perspective, and they typically require an examinee to learn a list of repeated words over multiple trials. The instructional implications are quite different for a child who can learn a list of words after repeated exposure compared to a child who has difficulty learning the words despite repeated exposure. There are many examples of list learning tests, such as tests appearing on the NEPSY–II or on the *California Verbal Learning Test—Children's Version* (Delis, Kramer, Kaplan, & Ober, 1994). Delayed verbal and visual memory, including both aspects of free recall and recognition, can be assessed using more comprehensive learning and memory batteries (e.g., WRAML–2, TOMAL–2).

Cognitive Processes: Executive Functions

The assessment of executive functions has taken on more importance in recent years (Maricle,

Johnson, & Avirett, 2010). However, historical conceptualization of executive functions within conventional intelligence tests has been poor, despite advances in executive function research and modeling. In the Integrated SNP/CHC Model, Miller (2013) identified four second-order classifications of executive functions: (1) cognitive flexibility (set shifting); (2) concept recognition/generation; (3) problem solving, fluid reasoning, and planning; and (4) response inhibition. The WISC–V used with the WISC–V Integrated has good coverage of two of the four executive function areas: (1) concept recognition/generation and (2) problem solving, fluid reasoning, and planning areas (see Table 12.1). Specifically, the WISC–V Similarities test is a good measure of verbal reasoning and concept recognition. The test requires an examinee to read two words and describe how they are similar. When an examinee achieves a low score on the WISC–V Similarities test, the Similarities Multiple Choice test from the WISC–V Integrated should be administered. The Similarities Multiple Choice version of the test lessens the language processing and memory retrieval demands by providing the examinee with multiple-choice answers to the test items.

The WISC–V Comprehension, Matrix Reasoning, Picture Concepts, and the Figure Weights tests measure the problem solving, fluid reasoning, and planning second-order classification of executive functions. The Comprehension test is designed to measure verbal reasoning, receptive and expressive language skills, prior experience and learning, and commonsense problem solving. The Matrix Reasoning test measures fluid reasoning or nonverbal problem-solving skills. The Picture Concepts test is designed to measure abstract, categorical reasoning ability. The Figure Weights is new to the WISC–V and is an adaptation from the WAIS–IV. On the Figure Weights test, the examinee views a scale with missing weight(s) and selects a weight from a set of options that will balance the scale. This is a measure of quantitative fluid and inductive reasoning. On

the WISC–V Integrated, a test called Figure Weights Process Approach allows examinees additional time to task completion and allows for a second-choice answer for items that were missed.

When an examinee achieves a low score on the WISC–V Comprehension test, the examiner should administer the WISC–V Integrated Comprehension Multiple Choice test. The value of administering this modified version of the Comprehension test is to test the limits (Milberg, Hebben, & Kaplan, 1996) and determine if lowering the oral expressive and memory retrieval demands of the task changes task performance. If the referral question for a child relates to suspected problems with cognitive flexibility or response inhibition, the examiner is encouraged to add to the assessment battery tests such as the Inhibition test from the NEPSY–II or the Color-Word Interference test from the *Delis-Kaplan Executive Function System* (D-KEFS; Delis, Kaplan, & Kramer, 2001).

Facilitators/Inhibitors: Allocating and Maintaining Attention

In the Integrated SNP/CHC Model (Miller, 2013), the broad area of attention is further sub-classified into the second-order classifications of selective/focused and sustained attention and attentional capacity. Miller (2013) suggested that attentional processes act as *facilitators* to enhance the performance of other cognitive functions, or they may act in the opposite way as *inhibitors* to degrade the performance of other cognitive functions. Although presented as a broad domain, this ability is necessary for successful performance on all cognitive measures.

The WISC–V, WISC–V Integrated, and WIAT–III combined test battery does not have any tests that are specifically designed to measure selective/focused and sustained attention (see Table 12.1). The WISC–V Coding, Symbol Search, and Cancellation tests and the WISC–V Integrated Cancellation Abstract test all require the examinee to use elements of selective and sustained attention, and these processes should be considered as potential causal factors related to poor performance on these tasks.

The second-order classification of Attentional Capacity refers to one's ability to pay attention to test content that increases in complexity from single digits or letters, to word, sentences, then stories. The tests categorized in this area are the same ones classified in the verbal and visual immediate memory categories, but these are re-classified here to emphasize the potential contribution of attention as opposed to memory on the task performance. The clinician needs to look for two patterns to aid in interpretation. The first pattern of performance is when an examinee performs well on small chunks of information (e.g., memory for numbers or letters) but performance suffers as the content to be learned increases in complexity. This pattern of performance is frequently observed in children with attention deficit hyperactivity disorder (Miller, 2013). The second pattern of performance is when an examinee performs increasingly better on tasks having higher levels of contextual cues, such as memory for stories, compared to learning isolated chunks of information, such as strings of digits. This pattern of performance is often observed in examinees who are not challenged enough by the simpler tasks and need the challenge of the more difficult tasks to be motivated to perform. In order to observe these patterns of performance, a clinician would need to supplement the assessment battery with memory for stories tests from other test batteries, such as those from the NEPSY–II, WRAML–2, TOMAL–2, or WMS–IV.

Facilitators/Inhibitors: Working Memory

Working memory is "a memory system that underpins our capacity to 'keep things in mind' when performing complex tasks" (Baddeley, Eysenck, & Anderson, 2008, p. 9). The key component of a working memory task is the requirement for active manipulation of information held in immediate awareness. Working memory has been shown to facilitate or inhibit cognitive processes associated with reading, mathematics, and writing achievement in children (Dehn, 2008; J. J. Evans, Floyd, McGrew, & LeForgee, 2002).

The WISC–V contains five tests designed to measure aspects of working memory: Arithmetic, Digit Span Backward, Digit Span Sequencing, Letter–Number Sequencing, and Picture Span (see Table 12.1). On previous versions of the WISC, the Arithmetic test was a supplemental subtest for the Working Memory Index score, although now it is in the Fluid Reasoning domain and contributes only to a Quantitative Reasoning Index or as a substitute for the Full Scale IQ (FSIQ). The Arithmetic test requires multiple cognitive processes including: verbal working memory, attention/concentration, selective/sustained attention, immediate memory, long-term retrieval, fluid reasoning skills, and mathematical reasoning skills (Miller & Hale, 2008). When an examinee achieves a low score on the Arithmetic test relative to other test scores, the clinician is encouraged to administer the WISC–V Integrated Arithmetic subtests. The WISC–V Integrated Arithmetic subtests are all variations of the WISC–V Arithmetic test designed to tease out the underlying reasons for poor performance. The input requirements of the task are modified as well as the processing speed demands to determine their influence on the overall performance of the task.

The WISC–V Digit Span test is a core test for the Working Memory Index score and measures verbal working memory. Spatial Span is a WISC–V Integrated test and measures visual working memory (Smyth & Sholey, 1992), selective and sustained attention (Lezak, Howieson, Bigler, & Tranel, 2012), and attentional capacity (Miller, 2013). The WISC–V and the WISC–V Integrated also provide several useful base rates for qualitative behaviors, such as the Longest Digit Span Backward, Longest Digit Span Sequence, Longest Letter–Number Sequence, and the Longest Spatial Span Backward scores.

The WISC–V Letter–Number Sequencing test is a supplemental test of verbal, and possibly visual, working memory (Miller & Hale, 2008). On this task, the examiner reads a sequence of letters and numbers and then asks the examinee to recall the numbers first in ascending order and then the letters in alphabetical order. The WISC–V has a new test called Picture Span, which is a measure of visual working memory and working memory capacity (Wechsler, 2014). On this test, the examinee views a stimulus page with one or more objects for a designed time period and then selects the pictures(s) in sequential order from options on a response page. The WISC–V Integrated has a new test called Sentence Recall, which is a measure of verbal working memory. The Sentence Recall test is a complex task that requires the examinee to answer "yes" or "no" to two questions that the examiner reads aloud, then repeat the last word in each of the sentences. In summary, the WISC–V used in combination with the WISC–V Integrated gives fairly extensive coverage of working memory.

Facilitators/Inhibitors: Speed, Fluency, and Efficiency of Processing

In the Integrated SNP/CHC Model (Miller, 2013), the theoretical classification of processing speed was significantly expanded from the previous school neuropsychological conceptual model (Miller, 2007). The construct of processing speed has been poorly defined and operationalized in past tests of intelligence. Schneider and McGrew (2012) broadened the conceptualization of processing speed, which influenced changes in Miller's school neuropsychological model. Within Miller's (2013) Integrated SNP/CHC Model, the broad classification of speed, fluency, and efficiency of processing facilitators/inhibitors is further sub-classified into the second-order classifications: (a) performance fluency, (b) retrieval fluency, and (c) acquired knowledge fluency. Measures of

performance fluency do not require any memory retrieval and principally are designed to measure automaticity of processing. Performance fluency has five third-order classifications: (1) psychomotor fluency, (2) perceptual fluency, (3) figural fluency, (4) naming fluency, and (5) oral motor fluency. Retrieval fluency is defined as how quickly information can be retrieved from long-term memory; acquired knowledge fluency relates to the automaticity of academic achievement including reading fluency, writing fluency, and mathematics fluency (Miller, 2013).

The WISC–V Coding, Symbol Search, and Cancellation tests are measures of perceptual fluency, which is a type of a broader performance fluency measure (see Table 12.1). The Cancellation test also has process scores for the Random and Structured portions of the test to aid in clinical interpretation. The WISC–V Integrated has a Cancellation Abstract test that uses different stimuli with lower semantic and categorization loads and examines the impact of those changes on performance. It too has process scores for the Random and Structured portions of the test.

The WISC–V Integrated has the Coding Copy test which can be administered when the WISC–V Coding test score is low relative to other scores. The Coding Copy version of the test reduces the memory demands of the task and can, therefore, provide additional information about the potential reasons for poor performance on the WISC–V version of the test.

The Naming Speed Literacy and Naming Speed Quantity tests are new to the WISC–V. The Naming Speed Literacy test requires the examinee to name objects of various size and color or letters and numbers as quickly as possible. Naming fluency is a type of broader performance fluency measure. Naming fluency, or rapid automatized naming (RAN), tests are frequently used for diagnosing reading disabilities in children (Korkman et al., 2007). The Naming Speed Quantity test requires the examinee to name the quantity of squares inside a series of boxes within a designed time period. This type of naming fluency task has been shown to be a predictor of mathematics skills (Willburger, Fussenegger, Moll, Wood, & Landerl, 2008). These two tests are welcome additions to the WISC–V from a neuropsychological perspective.

For more complete coverage of the Speed, Fluency, and Efficiency of Processing Facilitators/Inhibitors domain, clinicians are encouraged to supplement the WISC–V with the WIAT–III. Within this broad classification, retrieval fluency is one of the second-order classifications. The WIAT–III Oral Word Fluency test is an example of a retrieval fluency task, where an examinee is asked to name as many items that fit into a particular category (e.g., items of food) as quickly as possible.

Within the Integrated SNP/CHC Model (Miller, 2013), acquired knowledge fluency is also designed as a second-order classification within the broad classification of speed, fluency, and efficiency of processing facilitators/inhibitors. Academic fluency measures represent the automaticity of processing for rapid reading, writing, and solving math problems. Clinicians will need to add the WIAT–III tests of Oral Reading Fluency (Accuracy and Rate), Alphabet Writing Fluency, Math Fluency–Addition, Math Fluency–Subtraction, and Math Fluency–Multiplication into their assessment battery if they want to measure acquired knowledge fluency.

Acquired Knowledge: Acculturation Knowledge

Acquired knowledge is a broad construct that encompasses the wealth of information learning through formal instruction or life experiences (Miller, 2013). Horn and Blankson (2012) used the term *acculturation knowledge* as an example of acquired knowledge, and it is synonymous with the CHC term *comprehension-knowledge*. *Semantic memory* is the term Miller (2013) used to describe encyclopedic information retrieved from long-term memory and is considered

a second-order classification of acculturation knowledge within the Integrated CHC/SNP Model. The WISC–V Information test is an example of a semantic memory type of test that can be supplemented with the WISC–V Integrated Information Multiple Choice test (see Table 12.1). The multiple-choice version of the test minimizes the oral expressive and memory retrieval demands of the task.

Acquired Knowledge: Language Abilities

In the Integrated SNP/CHC model, language abilities are classified under the broad construct of acquired knowledge (Miller, 2013). According to the model, language abilities can be further subdivided into the second-order classifications of oral expression or receptive language (listening comprehension). The WISC–V Vocabulary test is classified as a test of oral expression. When an examinee achieves a low score relative to other scores on the WISC–V, the clinician is encouraged to administer the Vocabulary Multiple Choice and the Picture Vocabulary Multiple Choice tests from the WISC–V Integrated. These modified versions of the standard WISC–V Vocabulary test lessen the demands of oral expression and memory retrieval, which can aid in the clinical interpretation of the poor performance on the standard version of the test. An additional measure of oral expression may be obtained by administering the Expressive Vocabulary portion of the Oral Expression test from the WIAT–III.

The other second-order classification of language abilities in the Integrated SNP/CHC Model is receptive language or listening comprehension skills. Receptive language skills are required for any of the verbally administered tests from the WISC–V and WISC–V Integrated, but no tests from these batteries were specifically designed to measure receptive language skills. If a clinician wants to measure receptive language skills as part of a comprehensive test battery, it is recommended that the

Listening Comprehension test with the Oral Discourse Comprehension portion and the Receptive Vocabulary test from the WIAT–III be included.

Acquired Knowledge: Reading, Writing, and Math Achievement

In neuropsychological assessments for school-age populations, a measure of cognitive functioning, such as the WISC–V, is typically administered together with an achievement test, such as the WIAT–III. The WIAT–III provides excellent coverage of the basic acquired knowledge areas of reading, writing, and mathematics (see Table 12.1). The next section of the chapter provides a case study example of how the WISC–V, WISC–V Integrated, and WIAT–III can be used in a school/pediatric neuropsychological evaluation.

CASE 10—JOHN, AGE 12: A NEUROPSYCHOLOGICAL CASE STUDY USING THE WISC-V WITH A 10-YEAR-OLD BOY WITH A SUSPECTED SPECIFIC LEARNING DISABILITY IN WRITTEN EXPRESSION

Daniel C. Miller and Alicia M. Jones

The following is a case study example of a 12-year-old male who is being home schooled. He is experiencing significant difficulties with writing activities. This case study example used the WISC–V and the WIAT–III in addition to a thorough clinical interview and behavioral observations. The utility of the WISC–V and WIAT–III are highlighted in this case study for the purposes of this chapter. At the end of this report, there is a review of the case study with suggestions for additional testing that would normally be completed for a more comprehensive evaluation.

School Neuropsychological Evaluation

This report is to be interpreted and used only by individuals properly trained and certified by state agencies, and/or by parents or legal guardians of the stated child. This report is confidential and must not be released to persons who do not have a legitimate professional interest in the child.

IDENTIFYING INFORMATION

Student's Name: John Doe

Student's Date of Birth: 11/18/2002

Student's Age: 12 years, 1 month

Student's Gender: Male

Student's Ethnicity: Caucasian

Student's School: Home schooled Student's Grade: 7th

Names of Student's Parents/Guardians: Jane Doe & John Doe, Sr.

Primary Language Spoken at Home: English

Examiner's Name: Seymore Children, Ph.D.

Date of Report: January 17, 2015

Reason for Referral

John is a 12-year-old male referred for a school neuropsychological evaluation by his parents. He displays writing difficulties below grade level and characteristics of depression and anxiety. He has also been screened for characteristics associated with Asperger's disorder, but additional evaluation was recommended to confirm this diagnosis. His writing difficulties initially presented 3–4 years ago and include: rushing through reports or essays, refusing to brainstorm and organize ideas, difficulty forming appropriate and capitalized letters, slowly drafting simple sentences, and not following lines on paper appropriately. Due to his difficulties with writing and composition, his mother speculated that he may have dysgraphia or a specific learning disability in written expression, which is negatively impacting his academic performance. During writing tasks, John often experiences emotional stress prior to initiating a writing assignment, which frequently interrupts his writing process and completion of the assignment. John is often hard on himself and has a difficult time persevering through tasks. He had a psychological evaluation at age 8 for his emotional dysregulation. He is currently receiving psychological counseling as well as pharmacological intervention to manage his emotional disturbances, particularly his anxiety and depression. John has primarily received his education through home schooling, but he has also attended co-op classes, private school, and Technology School.

Referral questions from John's parents are as follows:

- What are the current diagnostic impressions that are applicable to his academic and social-emotional challenges?
  - Given that his mother suspects dysgraphia, this learning disability will be ruled in or out based on diagnostic criteria and assessment results.

- What are effective interventions for the home and academic settings to help develop John's academic and social-emotional skills, particularly for his writing challenges and perseverance?

Background Information

Family History

John currently lives with his biological parents, Mr. and Mrs. Doe, his older sister, Janie (age 16), and the family's two dogs. Mrs. Doe home schools both John and Janie, and Mr. Doe works as an IT/database developer. John has a typical relationship with his sister and sees his paternal grandparents once every few years. The family has moved twice in the last couple of years, but Mrs. Doe reported that John and his sister have adjusted well to the changes. English is the primary language spoken in the home.

Mrs. Doe is the primary disciplinarian at home with support of Mr. Doe when necessary. Mrs. Doe reported that loss of privileges (e.g., computer time), discussion of behavior, ignoring behavior, and verbal reprimands are effective discipline techniques for John; rewards and acquiescence are less effective. However, during testing, the examiner noted that John seemed to respond more cooperatively and in a motivated manner when Mrs. Doe reminded him of a reward he would obtain afterward (e.g., Slurpee) if he performed with his best effort. Mrs. Doe noted that the family spends an adequate amount of time together, particularly on the weekends if they go out to dinner or participate in knight fighting as an extracurricular activity. Although John is less interested in knight fighting, he typically spends the time engaging with same-age peers (i.e., playing at the nearby playground).

Mrs. Doe reported a family history of mood and anxiety disorders on both sides of the family. John's parents, sister, and maternal grandparents have suffered from mental illness (e.g., depression) and nervousness. Both Mr. Doe and his mother have diabetes, and John's maternal grandmother has a history of migraine headaches. Mrs. Doe also noted a history of cancer with her great-uncle and aunt.

Birth and Developmental History

Mrs. Doe received appropriate prenatal care during her pregnancy with John. She did experience high blood pressure during the 40-week pregnancy, but no other complications were reported. Mrs. Doe underwent a scheduled caesarean delivery, and she reported that spinal anesthesia was used. John was born at 9 pounds and 8 ounces. Both he and his mother were reported to be in excellent condition after birth.

John reached all of his developmental milestones. He is predominantly right-handed, and Mrs. Doe reported a mild concern with pencil grip. During the first 4 years, John displayed temper tantrums and had some difficulty separating from his parents.

Health History

John was diagnosed with asthma at age 10 and has endured seasonal allergies since age 8. He also wears glasses to correct his vision. Mrs. Doe reported that at age 1 he was sensitive to and fascinated by lights of any kind. He is still sensitive to loud sounds. In 2007 John did undergo surgery after breaking his right arm. Consequently, he engaged in occupational therapy shortly after the surgery. Mrs. Doe reported that he participated in arm exercises for mobility, but he has had no residual difficulties using that arm.

Mrs. Doe also noted that John has always been a picky eater and in the past has experienced nightmares and cosleeping with his parents. John currently refuses to go to bed at times, but often his medication will act as a sedative. He typically goes to bed at 11 p.m. and receives enough rest. Mrs. Doe reported that John has engaged in biting his hands and feet, and as a toddler, he would bang his head when angry.

John is currently taking Prozac (40 mg once per day in the evening). He took Ziprasidone (20 mg once per day in the evening in the past, but recently this medication was increased to 40 mg) to manage his mood and anxiety difficulties. He also takes Zyrtec as needed for his allergies. John currently attends cognitive-behavioral therapy primarily to manage his anxiety. Mrs. Doe noted that he requested to return to counseling last year. He was recently diagnosed with depression in addition to his anxiety. Mrs. Doe reported that John tends to engage in perfectionist behavior and thinking. If John feels like he has failed a task, he often shut downs and gives up trying to complete the task. The examiner noted this behavior during testing when John became overwhelmed with a task, particularly during the writing tasks, or when he thought he performed poorly on a task.

Social History
Mrs. Doe described John as calm, happy, affectionate, active, and alert at age 2; however, she noted that it was often difficult for strangers to evoke a smile from John. Although he was sociable, active, and happy between the age of 2 and 5, he also displayed fearful feelings. Mrs. Doe reported that John currently is self-conscious, hides his feelings, overreacts to problems, gets mad very easily, worries, and displays sadness. He responds angrily to teasing, even to mild, gentle comments from his family. His biggest fear is failing at what he tries to do.

John prefers to play alone and has only a few close friends. Mrs. Doe reported that he performs or plays better in a one-on-one setting; for instance, during a recent trip to the mall with two same-age peers, John was only able to spend time with them for about an hour before he stated that he was ready to go home because "he had better things to do with his time." When he does play games with friends or same-age peers, he may not participate fully if it is not an online game, or he will try to negotiate which game they play according to his preferences. However, Mrs. Doe reported that during his technology class, he often helps another younger classmate with their gaming projects. John enjoys reading nonfiction books, playing video and computer games, and spending time with his family, especially when they go to the park.

Mrs. Doe reported that John has a keen sense of humor and is very intelligent; she also noted that he is very caring and considered the "peacemaker of the family." She finds it difficult to counter his logic during discussion when he attempts to avoid a task that she has asked him to complete. Mrs. Doe also stated that John is very

hard on himself, particularly if he feels he has failed.

Educational History
John has been home-schooled for the majority of his academic career. During the kindergarten and first-grade years, he enjoyed school and worked well with Mrs. Doe. Since those early years, Mrs. Doe reported that he has excelled academically, performs well on most assignments, and has received accelerated learning materials. Mrs. Doe noted that John is very bright and possibly gifted, but his capabilities are at times overshadowed by his writing difficulties. His current academic strengths include: math, history, spelling, social studies, reading, and science. His current academic areas of improvement include: English, writing, and athletics/physical education. Mrs. Doe indicated that he does not enjoy art or expressing his feelings in written form. He would rather explain how to do something or verbalize facts. Mrs. Doe noted that John's strong skills include: memorization, reading fluency, overall intelligence, vocabulary/expression, reading comprehension, conceptualization, and spelling; however, his areas of improvement include the following skills: paper/report-writing, handwriting, organizing his ideas during writing tasks, and working hard without giving up.

Mrs. Doe reported that John knew all of his letters and corresponding sounds by 18 months. He began reading and writing by age 3. Mrs. Doe noted that he taught himself how to write, but he formed some bad habits in letter formation that teachers have been unable to remediate. During writing tasks, he often appears anxious, uptight, or nervous. He often tries to avoid writing tasks and shows no interest in writing activities. The examiner noted that when John was presented with a writing task, he stated that he "did not want to do it" and became very upset and overwhelmed. Breaks during testing seemed to help him calm down, but the examiner noticed that he seemed to want to quickly work through the writing tasks. Mrs. Doe noted that his frustration and overwhelming feelings during testing were typical responses to academic tasks during home school lessons, particularly for writing tasks or tasks he generally finds uninteresting.

Mrs. Doe reported that if John attended regular public school, he would probably be placed in gifted classes, particularly in accelerated math classes. Although he would be classified as a sixth grader in general education, Mrs. Doe reported that they are currently working through pre-algebra using *The Art of Problem-Solving*, which is an advanced curriculum. His history curriculum also includes seventh- to eighth-grade material. During fifth grade, he attended private school part-time and was enrolled in engineering and communications classes for sixth to eighth graders. John also attends outside co-op classes with other home-schooled students three–four times a year for an extended period of time. Parents of the home schoolers teach the classes, but it provides an opportunity for him to engage with same-age peers in a pseudoacademic setting. John is currently attending Technology School and excelling in a game design class. He previously completed a 3D modeling course at this school.

Educational Interventions (Response to Interventions)
To support his writing difficulties, particularly with letter formation and spacing concerns, Mrs. Doe reported that they have used *Handwriting Without Tears* curriculum and have tried occupational therapy. She has also allowed John to complete writing assignments on the computer or to dictate his responses instead of writing them, which seemed to help him provide more content in his final product. He often has to be coerced or rewarded in order to complete writing tasks.

Previous Testing Results
At age 5, John received IQ and achievement testing (WPPSI–III and WIAT–II), which revealed above-expected and superior strengths in verbal (127) and performance (133) domains and in mathematics (160) and oral language (142). However, John's processing speed (107) was a relative weakness. Interestingly, John's

writing skills (i.e., printing letters, writing his name, and spelling) were found to be intact and in the superior range. John was screened for Asperger's Disorder at age 7. Both his parents rated his behavior in the highly probable range for characteristics associated with the disorder.

John was evaluated again at age 8, but the results from the IQ and achievement administrations (WISC–IV and WIAT–II) were not considered valid since he was unable to persevere through difficult tasks and did not give his best effort. He became very overwhelmed during this previous testing. Consequently, he was screened for anxiety and Asperger's Disorder again using his parents' ratings of several characteristics and behaviors (Conners Comprehensive Behavior Rating Scales—Parent). John's parents reported very elevated concerns in the following areas: emotional distress, upsetting thoughts, worrying, social problems, defiant/aggressive behaviors, separation fears, and perfectionistic and compulsive behavior, which corresponded to Generalized Anxiety Disorder, Major Depression, Social Phobia, and Autism Spectrum Disorder. His parents decided to have him begin counseling to manage his anxiety and social-emotional difficulties. During the IQ and achievement testing, it is worth noting that John performed in the superior range on tasks that involved perceptual reasoning (139). His academic strengths included: reading, mathematics, oral language and spelling. In contrast, John performed at expected levels on tasks measuring processing speed (100), working memory (99), and written expression (110).

Mrs. Doe reported that John also received an evaluation through Learning Rx (an academic program that focuses on improving math proficiency skills) at age 8. He demonstrated above-average performance in mathematics. Although John's baseline performance was lower than expected for his age in tasks that involved long-term memory, retrieval fluency, short-term memory, visual processing, and executive processing speed, he improved in all areas of cognitive functioning measured. John also received occupational therapy at age 10 in large part due to his fine motor difficulties (i.e., poor handwriting skills).

Current Assessment Instruments and Procedures

Record Review, Parent Interview, Teacher Reports, Student Interview, and Classroom Observations

Wechsler Intelligence Scale for Children–Fifth Edition (The WISC–V is an individually administered clinical instrument designed to assess the cognitive ability and problem-solving processes of children aged 6–0 through 16–11.)

Wechsler Individual Achievement Test–Third Edition (WIAT–III) (The WIAT–III is an individually administered test that evaluates academic achievement in reading, math, and writing, and oral language [expressive and receptive.])

Test Observations and Related Assessment Validity

John was dressed and groomed appropriately during each testing session. He displayed age-appropriate conversational proficiency and appeared at ease during testing sessions. Although John generally persisted during tasks, he became uncooperative and shut down when presented with tasks that he found difficult, overwhelming, or boring. His motivation waned during tasks that he found less interesting (i.e., Digit Span, Symbol Search). Breaks during the testing sessions, including drawing time, seemed to help John calm down in order to return to testing. His activity level was typical for his age, but he often asked how much of the test we had remaining during each session and at times appeared fidgety or restless in his chair. He was unable to test beyond an hour and a half per session. At times he was prompt and careful when responding to items, but he also had to frequently be reminded to listen to directions, sample items, and read questions in their entirety before impulsively responding. Rapport was established between the student and examiner. He seemed to respond favorably to praise and feedback on his performance during testing.

The reader is reminded that these results are compiled from tests that were not normed from the same sample; however, test results have been integrated with data from other sources including review of records, interview, observations, other test results, and work samples to ensure ecological validity. Standardization was followed for all administrations. No single test or procedure was used as the sole determining criteria for eligibility or educational planning. Unless otherwise noted, these results are considered a valid estimate of John's demonstrated skills and abilities at this point in time.

Evaluation Results

Performance levels for all tests administered will be reported according to the scale shown in Table 12.2.

The test results section is organized into the following areas:

   I. Classroom Observations

  II. Cognitive Processes: Visuospatial

 III. Cognitive Processes: Learning and Memory

 IV. Cognitive Processes: Executive

  V. Facilitators/Inhibitors: Allocating and Maintaining Attention

 VI. Facilitators/Inhibitors: Working Memory

VII. Facilitators/Inhibitors: Speed, Fluency, and Efficiency of Processing

VIII. General Intellectual Functioning

 IX. Acquired Knowledge: Acculturation Knowledge

  X. Acquired Knowledge: Language Abilities

 XI. Acquired Knowledge: Reading Achievement

XII. Acquired Knowledge: Written Language Achievement

XIII. Acquired Knowledge: Mathematics Achievement

Table 12.2 Performance Scale

Standard Score	Scaled Score	Percentile Rank	Normative Classification	Proficiency Classification
>129	>15	>98%	Superior	Markedly Advanced
121–129	15	92–98	Well Above Expected	Advanced
111–120	13–14	76–91	Above Expected	Very Proficient
90–110	8–12	25–75	At Expected	Proficient
80–89	6–7	9–24	Slightly Below Expected	Inefficient
70–79	4–5	2–8	Below Expected	Deficient
<70	1–3	<2	Well Below Expected	Markedly Deficient

I. Classroom Observations

John participates in a game design class once a week at the Technology School as an extracurricular activity. There were three students in the class, including John, and one instructor. During the observation, each student worked independently at his own computer station while designing individual games. The examiner noted that John seemed to be very engaged as he worked on his game design project. The instructor rotated among the three students to provide feedback and troubleshoot any issues with their games. When he offered John suggestions pertaining to his gaming figures (i.e., label the function or purpose for each figure) and time periods/ages for the game (i.e., Stone Age, Medieval Times, Modern Day), John explained that labeling the figures and including different time periods were not necessary. However, he typed the label descriptions for the instructor, and they talked about including a "Future" time period in the game. The examiner noticed that when the instructor went to help the other two students, John stopped working and attended to the discussions between the other students and the instructor. John also interjected and provided his own insight or opinions regarding their discussion. At one point during the class, John left from his seat to go over to another student's workstation while the student was talking with the instructor about a specific aspect of his game. When John did focus on his own work, he repeatedly tapped his foot and hummed. John appeared to enjoy the class and participated fully. He also seemed to want to help or be involved with the other students' projects.

During the structured setting for testing, the examiner noted that John seemed to find certain tasks engaging and appeared motivated to perform well (i.e., Figure Weights, Block Design, Matrix Reasoning, Visual Puzzles, Spelling). He seemed to become fidgety during parts of the testing session, often sliding in his chair, laying his head down on the table, or sitting up on his knees in the chair. The examiner also noticed that John appeared inattentive during parts of testing even with multiple breaks. He seemed anxious during timed tasks and at times jerked his head back and forth or tried to write/draw quickly during such tasks.

II. Cognitive Processes: Visuospatial

For the purposes of this report, visual-spatial processes include *visual-spatial perception* and *visual-spatial reasoning*. Visuospatial perception measures a student's ability to make visual discriminations, locate objects in space, and construct objects. Visuospatial reasoning measures the student's ability to recognize spatial configurations, identify objects with missing parts, and match similar visual patterns.

Current Levels of Functioning

1. *Visuospatial Perception:* John performed in the well-above-expected to superior range during a task that involved re-creating designs with blocks. He was able to build models of pictured designs quickly and accurately.

The examiner tested the limits with the most difficult item on the task since John noted that he really wanted to return to this design to solve it. He was able to partially build the correct design with additional time. The examiner noted how engaged and motivated he appeared during the task. However, after the task was completed, the examiner noticed that John seemed to shut down and become unmotivated to complete any additional tasks. He may have given up in part due to a perceived "failure." Although he was unable to solve the last block design item in its entirety within the time limit, he still performed in the above-expected range. His behavior after the task corresponds with some of Mrs. Doe's concerns regarding his being too hard on himself and displaying signs of perfectionism and fear of failure, even though his performance compared to his same-age peers was exceptional. This suggests that John may need additional feedback and support with identifying his strengths as opposed to focusing on his mistakes during academic lessons.

2. *Visuospatial Reasoning:* John performed in the above-expected range during a task that involved mentally manipulating shapes and fitting them together to match a solid design. He performed this task accurately and quickly and seemed to be very engaged during the task. Although Mrs. Doe noted that he dislikes puzzles, he may find academic tasks that involve models or puzzles easy to manage and engaging.

Instructional Implications: John was able to accurately and quickly process visual information and manipulate it mentally or physically with the use of manipulatives. He may benefit from tasks that involve logical reasoning (e.g., brain teasers), visual stimuli (e.g., pictures or designs), and kinesthetic/tactile skills (i.e., when he is allowed to build or finish a complete product) that are incorporated into his home school lessons, particularly for writing tasks, where he could initially build or model components of the assignment before completing the full assignment.

He will have little difficulty understanding concepts conveyed in a graphical format (i.e., math or science questions). Although John's performance was above expected, he may benefit from additional praise and discussion regarding which skills he performed well during a task in order for him not to simply focus on what he did not do well; this may prevent his shutting down.

III. Cognitive Processes: Learning and Memory

Memory is a significant contributor to the learning process. Memory is comprised of multiple interactive systems: immediate memory and long-term retrieval. Each of the types of memory may be tested using different modalities; for example, visual immediate memory or verbal immediate memory. Verbal–Visual Associative Learning and Recall measures the student's ability to learn and recall later information that requires verbal and visual associations.

Current Levels of Functioning: John performed at expected levels during tasks that involved learning and associating visual symbols with words. Although he displayed intact immediate memory for newly presented symbol-word pairings, he exhibited greater retention and recall after a 30-minute delay. He performed equally well when he simply had to recognize the word associated with the symbol from four response choices.

Instructional Implications: John may find tasks that associate verbal and visual information easier to recall after receiving time to process newly presented information. He seemed to also recognize newly presented information after hearing verbal cues in multiple-choice format. John will have little to no difficulty with reading fluency tasks.

IV. Cognitive Processes: Executive Functions

Executive functioning can be conceptualized into two broad areas: cognitive and behavioral/emotional control. Each of these broad areas has some relationship to the frontal lobes of the brain. The **cognitive** aspects of executive functioning include concept generation and problem solving. Concept recognition and generation measures the student's abilities to recognize or generate multiple ways of classifying or categorizing objects, pictures, or words. Problem solving, fluid reasoning, and planning measures the student's ability to solve problems, apply reasoning skills, and use planning strategies. The **behavioral/emotional** aspects of executive functioning relate to the inhibitory controls of behavior (e.g., impulsivity, regulation of emotional tone, etc.).

Current Levels of Functioning

1. *Concept Recognition and Generation:* John performed at expected levels during a task where he had to verbally describe and conceptualize specific similarities between two objects, ideas, or emotions. He seemed to have intact expressive and receptive language skills, which suggests that he will be able to complete oral tasks with little to no difficulty and understand directions or questions with ease.

2. *Problem Solving, Fluid Reasoning, and Planning:* John displayed expected to superior levels of fluid reasoning or problem-solving skills. During a task where he had to verbalize underlying concepts and principles in response to questions, John seemed to provide terse answers. He needed prompting to provide additional explanation. He also appeared less engaged during this task, which may suggest that his performance was more indicative of his motivation than his actual ability since he appeared to have strong expressive and receptive language skills throughout testing sessions. In contrast to his verbal reasoning skills, his visual and quantitative reasoning skills ranged from expected to superior levels. During these tasks, he seemed to be very engaged and often responded impulsively and excitedly claiming that he "knew what to do for the

task" before the directions could be read. He was able to determine the underlying rules or relationships among pictures, objects, and shapes and apply those rules to determine missing components in matrices and balancing scales or links among pictured objects in rows. These results suggest that John may find puzzle-like tasks manageable.

Instructional Implications: Mrs. Doe reported mild concerns with John's ability to transition from one activity to another (i.e., leaving the computer to finish schoolwork) and his ability with figuring out where to start in a task. John may benefit from alternating between engaging and less engaging tasks as well as from tasks presented in manageable chunks or time frames (i.e., instead of giving him five tasks from his home school lesson schedule for the day, provide him the first task with a general time frame and a computer break before the next task). He also might benefit from using sample written assignments and graphic organizers (e.g., brainstorm or topic maps/webs) to help him identify appropriate writing structure and to generate ideas for where he could start in his own writing.

Mrs. Doe also noted that he feels overwhelmed and melts down when presented with writing assignments, often saying that "it's too much!" John may benefit from breaking writing tasks down into puzzle-like components in order to teach style, organization, and revision. For instance, providing John with a paragraph with sentences arranged out of order may allow him to practice reorganizing ideas in a logical manner and may help him organize his own writing. He may need writing tasks broken down into steps (e.g., topic/thesis statement; body paragraph examples) instead of writing a complete paragraph or report in one sitting. Additionally, since John has such strong expressive language skills, he may also need to verbalize and audio record his responses to prepare for a written assignment before transferring his thoughts and ideas to written format.

V. Facilitators/Inhibitors: Allocating and Maintaining Attention

Attention is a complex and multifaceted construct used when an individual must focus on certain stimuli for information processing. In order to regulate thinking and to complete tasks of daily living such as schoolwork, it is necessary to be able to attend to both auditory and visual stimuli in the environment. Attention can be viewed as the foundation of all other higher-order processing. In other words, if attention is compromised, it can adversely affect other cognitive processes of language, memory, visuospatial skills, and so on. Attention can be divided into four subareas: selective/focused attention, sustained attention, and attentional capacity. Only attentional capacity was measured in this evaluation.

Current Levels of Functioning: John displayed adequate attentional capacity during a task where he had to simply repeat number sequences. However, the examiner noted that he did not find this task interesting, and each question required some coaxing in order for him to respond. The task required him to pay attention, and he may have been bored. John was able to maintain up to 5 numbers in his short-term memory and accurately repeat them back.

Instructional Implications: These results suggest that John can focus and retain information (e.g., directions) for immediate use during schoolwork. However, he may need to be prompted or reminded to pay attention to important information prior to completing a task.

VI. Facilitators/Inhibitors: Working Memory

Working memory is a memory system that underpins our capacity to keep things in mind when performing complex tasks. Information placed in working memory may come from sensory memory, short-term memory, or long-term memory. The key component of a working memory task is the requirement for active manipulation of the information. Working memory has been shown to be a required cognitive process for

components of reading, mathematics, and writing achievement in children.

Current Levels of Functioning: Mrs. Doe reported mild concerns with John's ability to follow multistep directions. He performed in the below-expected to above-expected range on tasks that involved actively manipulating information. He seemed to be able to accurately and quickly solve verbally presented math problems with ease, but the examiner had to repeat a couple of the items in part because John did not seem to be attending fully. He was also able to repeat verbally presented number strings in backward order; the examiner noted that he quietly repeated some of the number strings to himself before responding. Additionally, John was able to accurately recall visual stimuli (e.g., pictured objects), in the order that they were presented; he performed better on this task than when he was just presented with numerical or verbal information.

In contrast, during a task that required John to manipulate sequences with numbers and letters, he performed below expected. More specifically, he was able to recall the numbers first in ascending order, but he was unable to recall the letters alphabetically in order. He retained less stimuli (i.e., he could only recall up to four units of information) during the working memory task compared to a previous immediate memory task. Compared to his same-age peers, he performed in a similar manner on immediate memory and working memory tasks, but he recalled fewer pieces of information from working memory. These results suggest that John was unable to simultaneously manipulate two different forms of information.

Instructional Implications: Verbal repetition may be a compensatory strategy for John to enhance his immediate verbal working memory. John may be able to retain and manipulate information at a higher rate when the information has some context or meaning attached to it. He may also benefit from focusing on one type of stimuli or content area during schoolwork or having directions broken down into smaller, manageable steps.

VII. Facilitators/Inhibitors: Speed, Fluency, and Efficiency of Processing

The facilitators/inhibitors of speed, fluency, and efficiency of processing are conceptualized to be composed of four second subclassifications: performance fluency, retrieval fluency, acquired knowledge fluency, and fluency and accuracy. Only performance fluency and acquired knowledge fluency measures were administered in John's case study. Performance fluency is defined as the ability to quickly perform simple, repetitive tasks. Acquired knowledge fluency relates to the automaticity of academic achievement including: reading fluency, writing fluency, and mathematics fluency.

Current Levels of Functioning

1. *Performance Fluency:* John performed at expected levels on tasks that measured how quickly he could perform simple tasks. Mrs. Doe reported that he does not like being timed, and the examiner noted that he appeared anxious or nervous during such timed tasks, which may have influenced his performance. He performed better when provided stimuli in a structured manner (as opposed to random order) and when he simply had to mark target stimuli (as opposed to drawing full symbols). During naming tasks, he seemed to perform better when the cognitive load was less (i.e., simply reading letters as opposed to pictured objects representing numbers).

2. *Acquired Knowledge Fluency:* John displayed above-expected reading fluency, which Mrs. Doe noted as a strength. He performed at expected levels for math fluency, although the written component on these tasks may have slowed down his ability to process information quickly. In other words, his answers were correct, but he worked through the task at a slower pace. He seemed to respond more quickly on math tasks where he was able to verbalize problem-solving process and answers.

Instructional Implications: Mrs. Doe reported that John often takes a long time to write simple sentences and does not write in an organized sequence that is easy to follow. She also noted that he does not perform well on timed tasks. John's performance was negatively impacted when a task involved extensive writing or a higher cognitive load. In addition, Mrs. Doe reported that John experiences emotional stress before a writing task and often refuses to break it into smaller chunks in an effort to "just get it done." John may benefit from additional time on schoolwork or tests, particularly those that involve writing or complex content. In order for him to accurately complete timed tasks, he needs the material to be presented in an organized manner with little writing required. Since John has intact expressive language skills, he may find it helpful to verbalize his answers during timed tasks in order to increase his processing speed.

VIII. General Intellectual Functioning

The WISC–V was administered to provide measures of John's overall cognitive functioning, as well as his functioning across different cognitive domains (e.g., verbal comprehension and visual-spatial abilities).

John exhibited cognitive strengths across all domains, particularly for fluid reasoning and visual-spatial skills. He has intact expressive and receptive language skills, working memory, and processing speed. However, his working memory and processing speed are negatively impacted when the cognitive load is increased or there is an extensive writing component involved. His overall abilities correspond with Mrs. Doe's reports of his having advanced or gifted skills. John's index profile truly reflects extreme scatter, as discussed in Chapter 7 in this volume. His WISC–V indexes ranged from 98 to 140; ranges of 42 or more points occurred less than 10% of the time in the standardization sample (see Table 7.4). Even more notable are the two relative strengths and two relative weaknesses that John displayed on his Index

Table 12.3   John's Wechsler Intelligence Scale for Children–Fifth Edition (WISC–V) Results

WISC–V	Standard Score	Confidence Interval (95%ile)	Percentile Rank	Classification
Verbal Comprehension	103—W	95–110	58	At Expected
Visual Spatial	129—S	119–134	97	Well Above Expected
Fluid Reasoning	140—S	130–144	99.6	Superior
Working Memory	107	99–114	68	At Expected
Processing Speed	98—W	89–107	45	At Expected
Full Scale	117	111–122	87	Above Expected

profile. Less than 5% of the normative sample had significant discrepancies on four of the five indexes (see Table 7.9).

IX. Acquired Knowledge: Acculturation Knowledge

Semantic memory is factual information stored in long-term memory.

Current Levels of Functioning: John performed in the well-above-expected range in tasks that involved retrieving information from semantic memory. He was able to recall general information in response to questions about various topics and concepts and clearly verbalize his answers. John's long-term memory retrieval seems to be intact.

Instructional Implications: John may have little to no difficulty retaining information and recalling it later for application across different subject areas.

X. Acquired Knowledge: Language Abilities

We all live in a highly verbal society; therefore, language skills are necessary for successful academic and behavioral functioning in school-age children. The language domain is categorized into *oral expression* and *listening comprehension (receptive language)*.

Current Levels of Functioning
1. *Oral Expression—Vocabulary Knowledge:* John exhibited vocabulary knowledge and ex-

pressive language skills at expected to superior levels, which suggests that he will find tasks that involve verbalization or speaking (e.g., discussions or public speeches) manageable, particularly when he is motivated to expound on his responses.
2. *Receptive Language (Listening Comprehension):* John displayed well-above-expected to superior receptive language skills, which suggests that his ability to comprehend information to answer questions is a relative strength. However, Mrs. Doe noted that at times he might lose track of what he has been told to do, particularly if he is distracted. John may benefit from gentle reminders to attend to directions or concepts presented. He may also need encouragement to repeat back directions or concepts to ensure that he knows what he needs to accomplish.

Instructional Implications: Since John has strong expressive and receptive language skills, he may need to use these as compensatory strategies during schoolwork, particularly for writing assignments, timed tasks, or application of more complex information.

XI. Acquired Knowledge: Reading Achievement

Reading achievement includes basic reading decoding skills, reading comprehension skills, and reading fluency skills.

Current Levels of Functioning: John performed in the above-expected to well-above-expected levels on reading tasks. He was able to decode familiar and nonsense words and read them accurately. Any errors he made were typically mispronunciations of one phoneme in advanced vocabulary or multisyllabic nonsense words. Reading comprehension is a relative strength for John. He was able to comprehend full reading passages and answer general content questions afterward.

Instructional Implications: John may find reading and comprehending text across different subject areas easy to manage.

XII. Acquired Knowledge: Written Language Achievement

Written language achievement includes written expression, expository composition, and orthographic spelling.

Current Levels of Functioning: John displayed a scattered performance across various writing tasks. He was able to combine simple sentences and use targeted words correctly in sentences, but he made errors in letter formation and capitalization (i.e., writing legibly and using capital letters instead of lowercase). Despite being exposed to appropriate capitalization and punctuation rules, John often uses capital letters in the middle of words, and his letter formation is often unusual, overly large, or illegible. Mrs. Doe reported that he does not always use lined paper appropriately or evenly space his words and letters, and he prefers to print instead of writing in cursive. The examiner noted some illegibility, uneven spacing, and unusual letter formation in his writing samples on specific tasks. John also commented a few times that his "hands hurt" after writing tasks, but he engaged in drawing activities during breaks from testing.

Mrs. Doe reported that one of John's weaker areas is paper/report-writing; John's performance and reaction to the task of writing an essay aligned with Mrs. Doe's concerns as he performed well below expected on this task. John became very overwhelmed and initially shut down before each writing task, including the essay composition. When he was ready for the task, he wrote for less than the time limit even

with prompting to try to write a full page, and he used very few words in bullet points for the topic. He was not able to organize his thoughts and write in complete sentences. When the examiner tested the limits with this task by allowing the student to type his essay as opposed to writing it, he was able to write some additional words and provide an introductory sentence, concluding sentence, and one sentence describing each bulleted reason/point. The sentences were also grammatically correct with appropriate word choice. Mrs. Doe reported that he often will write more if allowed to type or dictate his responses, and his prior writing samples from home school lessons indicate that he knows how to write grammatically correct sentences with appropriate punctuation and capitalization. Mrs. Doe noted that if the prompt from the task during testing had been more factual (i.e., how to design a game) instead of explaining one's feelings regarding a game, John may have been able to type more. Interestingly, John performed in the superior range on a spelling task, which suggests that his vocabulary knowledge and decoding skills are relative strengths.

Instructional Implications: John may benefit from breaking writing tasks into more manageable steps, using a computer to type writing assignments, and verbalizing his thoughts as a part of a brainstorming process before completing the assignment in written form.

XIII. Acquired Knowledge: Mathematics Achievement

Mathematics achievement includes mathematical calculations and mathematical reasoning.

Current Levels of Functioning: John performed in the slightly below-expected to well-above-expected range during math tasks. When John was able to simply verbalize his thought process and answers to verbally presented word problems (some with accompanying visual stimuli), he performed accurately and engaged in mental math as he talked through steps to a solution. However, during a math computation task, John had to write his answers, which may have overwhelmed him and affected his performance on the task.

Instructional Implications: John may benefit from simply verbalizing his answers during math tasks, including his steps (i.e., to show his work), instead of having to extensively write out his work for problems.

Summary

From a neuropsychological perspective, John displayed strong fluid reasoning or problem-solving skills, oral language skills, and visual-spatial skills. He was able to apply rules and concepts to new information as well as generate his own rules from given information. He was also able to express himself clearly and understand and respond to orally presented information. He was able to mentally scan/track and spatially manipulate shapes, objects, and designs to create new figures. His attentional capacity was at expected levels; however, his behavior during parts of the testing session seemed characteristic of restlessness or lack of motivation. John exhibited intact math skills, particularly for problem solving, and reading skills, including decoding, fluency, and comprehension. He was able to retrieve stored information from long-term retrieval and apply it during various tasks. His delayed and recognition verbal and visual recall seemed to be stronger than his immediate memory. John's mathematical, performance, and naming fluency are intact; however, increased cognitive load (i.e., complex content) and writing components may have impeded his processing speed, but not his accuracy. John's verbal and visual working memory appeared adequate, but increased semantic load for a task, particularly for different forms of content (i.e., letters versus numbers), seemed to affect his verbal working memory.

John has significant writing difficulties, in part related to his anxiety toward writing tasks and distorted perception of his abilities. His writing displayed unusual letter formation, capitalization use, and uneven spacing. He became very overwhelmed, unmotivated, and uncooperative prior to writing tasks in particular, and seemed to have trouble expanding on his ideas and writing in an organized, cohesive manner. His writing fluency also seemed to impact his performance in other tasks that required a writing component.

Diagnostic Impressions

Based on the current school neuropsychological assessment, the most appropriate *DSM–5* diagnosis for John is specific learning disorder (SLD) with impairment in written expression. There is evidence to support a diagnosis of SLD with mild impairment in clarity or organization of written expression. John does display writing difficulties in spite of intact executive functioning and visual-spatial perception/reasoning skills, which is characteristic of individuals with dysgraphia. He may be able to use compensatory strategies to better support his written expression. The examiner recommends that John receive accommodations to better support his writing difficulties. In addition, continued treatment for his anxiety may also help with his writing demands.

The specific *Diagnostic and Statistical Manual* (*DSM–5*; American Psychiatric Association, 2013) criteria for specific learning disorder with impairment in written expression (315.2 [F81.81]) is as follows:

A. Difficulties learning and using academic skills, as indicated by the presence of at least one of the following symptoms that have persisted for at least 6 months, despite the provision of interventions that target those difficulties: …
   4. Difficulties with written expression (e.g., makes multiple grammatical or punctuation errors within sentences; employs poor paragraph organization; written expression of ideas lacks clarity).

John demonstrated severe difficulties composing an essay. Even when the examiner tested the limits by allowing him to complete the task with a computer, his performance was relatively the same, and he was unable to write a significant amount of additional content in paragraph form. Additionally, John was able to compose simple sentences that were coherent and meaningful, but he used capitalization inappropriately, formed unusual or illegible letters, and wrote with uneven spacing at times.

B. The affected academic skills are substantially and quantifiably below those expected for the student's chronological age, and cause significant interference with academic or occupational performance, or with activities of daily living, as confirmed by individually administered standardized achievement measures and comprehensive clinical assessment. For individuals age 17 years and older, a documented history of impairing learning difficulties may be substituted for standardized assessment.

John became very overwhelmed prior to writing tasks. He shut down and displayed anxious feelings when presented with these tasks specifically. Compared to his cognitive abilities (e.g., executive functioning, visual-spatial perception/reasoning), his academic performance on writing tasks was significantly lower than expected. Mrs. Doe reported that John avoids writing tasks or rushes through them during homeschool lessons. She also noted that he has to be coerced to complete his writing assignments and refuses to plan out his ideas before writing the final product.

C. The learning difficulties begin during school-age years, but may not become fully manifest until the demands for those affected academic skills exceed the individual's limited capacities (e.g., as in timed tests, reading or writing lengthy complex reports for a tight deadline, excessively heavy academic loads).

Mrs. Doe reported that John's writing difficulties presented 3 to 4 years ago. He often becomes very anxious and uptight during writing tasks and typically gives up without finishing the assignment.

D. The learning difficulties are not better accounted for by intellectual disabilities, uncorrected visual or auditory acuity, other mental or neurological disorders, psychosocial adversity, lack of proficiency in the language of academic instruction, or inadequate educational instruction.

In spite of interventions and accommodations during home school lessons, John's performance on writing tasks was below his expected age/grade level. Although he began writing early and on his own, Mrs. Doe has attempted to remediate some of his "bad habits" (e.g., letter formation and spacing). There is no indication of intellectual disability, uncorrected visual/auditory acuity, or psychosocial adversity. Although John is currently being treated for anxiety and depression, Mrs. Doe reported that he generally is hard on himself and often has difficulty persisting through tasks he finds challenging or uninteresting (i.e., even beyond writing tasks).

Specify current severity:
Mild: John displays difficulty in one academic domain (e.g., written expression), but his difficulty is mild enough that he may be able to use compensatory strategies (e.g., audio recording or typing) or function well when provided with appropriate accommodations and support services, especially during the school years.

Intervention Strategies and Recommendations

Recommendations for Instruction in Academic Settings

1. In order to improve John's written expression, the following interventions should be considered.
   - John may benefit from the use of a computer or laptop for writing assignments in order to be able to fully express his thoughts and ideas.
   - It may be helpful to allow John to verbalize or audio record his brainstorm ideas or outline for a writing assignment before he has to actually write or type it. This may facilitate organization and clarity of his thoughts and ideas.
   - John should be encouraged to practice identifying style, organization, and

clarity errors in samples of writing (e.g., paragraphs or essays) in order for him to learn how to sequence ideas in a logical order.

- It may be helpful to break writing tasks into manageable chunks (i.e., prewriting, introduction, thesis statement/topic sentences, examples, etc.) instead of John rushing through a writing assignment.
- Graphic organizers (e.g., topic maps or brainstorm webs) may help John organize his thoughts and ideas before completing a writing assignment. These can be paired with verbalizing or audio recording as suggested above.

2. In order to improve John's processing speed, the following interventions should be considered.
- During timed tasks, John may benefit from a more structured presentation of the task with limited writing in order to improve his speed. The semantic or cognitive load for the task should also be limited; in other words, the task should be simple and straightforward if he has to be timed.
- For any assignments that require a writing component, John may benefit from extended time in order to accurately process the information. It might also help to break the activity or the assignment into manageable steps to aid his processing speed.
- It might also be beneficial to not inform John of timing since this seems to make him anxious. The instructor can simply note what time he started and ended a task for future reference.

3. In order to improve John's verbal working memory, the following recommendations should be considered.
- John may benefit from verbally repeating information that needs to be manipulated in order to retain the information in his immediate memory.
- He may also need contextual cues (e.g., pictures; response options) provided for newly

learned information in order to recognize or manipulate the information and provide it in a new format.
- John may need to be reminded to attend to newly presented information and multistep directions in order to help his retention.
- It might be helpful to limit the forms of content that need to be manipulated and recalled (i.e., focus on one subject area or part of a task), so John can accurately use the information.

Recommendations for Instruction at Home

1. In order to improve John's anxious and social-emotional behavior, the following interventions should be considered.
- John displays characteristics associated with an anxiety disorder that manifests as a specific phobia to written expression tasks. The examiner recommends that John's parents seek additional evaluation of his anxiety levels.
- John also displays characteristics associated with Autism Spectrum Disorder (ASD). The examiner recommends that John's parents seek additional evaluation of his atypical social-emotional behavior.
- John may benefit from knowing the daily schedule, including home and academic activities, in order for him to not feel overwhelmed with transitioning to a new activity or task.
- He may need additional praise and discussion of the tasks he does well in order for him to not focus on his mistakes and label them as failures.
- It may help to discuss John's current medication regimen and counseling sessions with his primary physician and counselor to ensure that he is improving in regulating his anxiety and expressing his emotions in a healthy manner.

2. In order to improve John's motivation during home or academic activities, the following interventions should be considered.

- John's parents might consider implementing a token economy to encourage appropriate behavior and work ethic. For instance, if John wants to earn computer time, he has to complete a portion of his writing assignment in order to earn tokens (e.g., marbles; stars; Slurpee cups) to "purchase" a reward or privilege. It might help for John and his parents to create the reward/privilege board together and discuss appropriate token amounts so he can feel a sense of ownership over his behavior and academic work.
- For specific assignments that John finds less interesting, it might be helpful for his parents to discuss the relevance or importance of the skill or material in order for John to feel motivated to complete the task. He may not understand why exposure to various topics is important for his future career decisions.
- Linking schoolwork or home activities to video/computer games, real-world scenarios, or challenge/brain buster problems or puzzles might also motivate John by enabling him to use his strong reasoning skills.

Recommendations for John

1. In order to improve John's anxious and moody behavior, the following interventions should be considered.
   - John may need to maintain an art journal where he can express how he feels throughout the day, particularly if he begins to feel overwhelmed or starts to shut down in response to a task.
   - John may need to verbalize three things he does well every day in order to begin recognizing his strengths instead of focusing on his mistakes. He may benefit from having this discussion with his parents and his counselor.
   - It is important for John to be able to recognize triggers for his anxiety and understand his options for how he can best respond when he feels overwhelmed. He should continue to discuss or practice these options during counseling.

John's Test Scores

Table 12.5 Cognitive Processes: John's Visuospatial Scores

	Visuospatial Perception						
Instrument: Subtest	Well Below Expected Level	Below Expected Level	Slightly Below Expected Level	At Expected Level	Above Expected Level	Well Above Expected Level	Superior
	Visual-Motor Constructions						
WISC–V: Block Design							(16)
• WISC–V: Block Design No Time Bonus						(15)	
	Recognizing Spatial Configurations						
WISC–V: Visual Puzzles					(14)		

Table 12.6   Cognitive Processes: John's Learning and Memory Scores

Verbal-Visual Associative Learning and Recall							
Instrument: Subtest	Well Below Expected Level	Below Expected Level	Slightly Below Expected Level	At Expected Level	Above Expected Level	Well Above Expected Level	Superior
Verbal-Visual Associative Learning							
WISC–V: Immediate Symbol Translation				93			
Verbal-Visual Associative Delayed Recall							
WISC–V: Delayed Symbol Translation				99			
Verbal-Visual Associative Recognition							
WISC–V: Recognition Symbol Translation				99			

Table 12.7   Cognitive Processes: John's Executive Functions Scores

Concept Recognition and Generation							
Instrument: Subtest	Well Below Expected Level	Below Expected Level	Slightly Below Expected Level	At Expected Level	Above Expected Level	Well Above Expected Level	Superior
Concept Recognition							
WISC–V: Similarities				(9)			
Problem Solving, Fluid Reasoning, and Planning							
Verbal Deductive and Inductive Reasoning							
WISC–V: Comprehension				(8)			
Visual Deductive and Inductive Reasoning							
WISC–V: Matrix Reasoning						(16)	
WISC–V: Picture Concepts				(12)			
Quantitative Reasoning							
WISC–V: Figure Weights						(18)	

Note: Standard scores appear in normal font. Scaled scores appear in (parentheses).

Table 12.8   Facilitators/Inhibitors: Allocating and Maintaining Attention (John's Scores)

Instrument: Subtest	Well Below Expected Level	Below Expected Level	Slightly Below Expected Level	At Expected Level	Above Expected Level	Well Above Expected Level	Superior
Attentional Capacity							
Attentional Capacity for Numbers or Letters with Verbal Response							
WISC–V: Digit Span Forward				(9)			

Table 12.9   Facilitators/Inhibitors: Working Memory (John's Scores)

Instrument: Subtest	Well Below Expected Level	Below Expected Level	Slightly Below Expected Level	At Expected Level	Above Expected Level	Well Above Expected Level	Superior
Working Memory							
Verbal Working Memory							
WISC–V: Arithmetic				(12)			
WISC–V: Digit Span Backward				(11)			
WISC–V: Letter–Number Sequencing			(5)				
Visual Working Memory							
WISC–V: Picture Span					(14)		

Qualitative Behaviors from the WISC–V	
Test/Qualitative Behavior	Total Age Sample Base Rate
Longest Digit Span Forward vs. Backward: Percentage of same-age peers with a better verbal immediate memory (Digit Span Forward) compared to verbal working memory (Digit Span Backward).	83
– Longest Digit Span Forward: Percentage of same-age peers who achieved this number of the longest digit span forward (verbal immediate memory).	93
– Longest Digit Span Backward: Percentage of same-age peers who achieved this number of the longest digit span backward (verbal working memory).	70.5

Table 12.10   Facilitators/Inhibitors: Speed, Fluency, and Efficiency of Processing (John's Scores)

	Performance Fluency						
Instrument: Subtest	Well Below Expected Level	Below Expected Level	Slightly Below Expected Level	At Expected Level	Above Expected Level	Well Above Expected Level	Superior
	Perceptual Fluency						
WISC–V: Cancellation				(10)			
• Cancellation Random				(9)			
• Cancellation Structured				(11)			
WISC–V: Coding			(7)				
WISC–V: Symbol Search				(12)			
	Naming Fluency						
WISC–V: Naming Speed Literacy				98			
WISC–V: Naming Speed Quantity				90			
	Acquired Knowledge Fluency						
	Reading Fluency: Rapid Phonological Decoding						
WIAT–III: Oral Reading Fluency					114		
• Oral Reading Accuracy					112		
• Oral Reading Rate					111		
	Mathematical Fluency						
WIAT–III: Math Fluency-Addition				98			
WIAT–III: Math Fluency—Subtraction				96			
WIAT–III: Math Fluency—Multiplication				99			

Table 12.11   Acquired Knowledge: Acculturation Knowledge (John's Scores)

	Semantic Memory						
Instrument: Subtest	Well Below Expected Level	Below Expected Level	Slightly Below Expected Level	At Expected Level	Above Expected Level	Well Above Expected Level	Superior
	General Information						
WISC–V: Information						(15)	

Table 12.12 Acquired Knowledge: Language Abilities (John's Scores)

Oral Expression							
Instrument: Subtest	Well Below Expected Level	Below Expected Level	Slightly Below Expected Level	At Expected Level	Above Expected Level	Well Above Expected Level	Superior
Vocabulary Knowledge							
WIAT–III: Oral Expression (Expressive Vocabulary)					117		
• WIAT–III: Expressive Vocabulary							146
WISC–V : Vocabulary				(12)			
Receptive Language (Listening Comprehension)							
Receptive Language With Verbal Response							
WIAT–III – Listening Comprehension							138
• Oral Discourse Comprehension						125	
Receptive Language With Nonverbal Motor Response							
WIAT–III: Receptive Vocabulary							137

Table 12.13 Acquired Knowledge: Reading Achievement (John's Scores)

Reading Achievement Scores							
Instrument: Subtest	Well Below Expected Level	Below Expected Level	Slightly Below Expected Level	At Expected Level	Above Expected Level	Well Above Expected Level	Superior
Basic Reading Skills: Phonological Decoding							
WIAT–III: Pseudoword Decoding					112		
WIAT–III: Word Reading					115		
Reading Comprehension Skills							
WIAT–III: Reading Comprehension						124	

Note: Standard scores appear in normal font. Scaled scores appear in (parentheses).

Table 12.14   Acquired Knowledge: Written Language Achievement (John's Scores)

Written Language Achievement Scores							
Instrument: Subtest	Well Below Expected Level	Below Expected Level	Slightly Below Expected Level	At Expected Level	Above Expected Level	Well Above Expected Level	Superior
Written Expression							
WIAT–III: Written Expression				97			
Expository Composition							
WIAT–III: Sentence Composition				107			
• Sentence Combining					114		
• Sentence Building				100			
WIAT–III: Essay Composition	48						
• Word Count	57						
• Theme Development and Text Organization	57						
• Grammar and Mechanics		77					
Orthographic Spelling							
WIAT–III: Spelling							141

Table 12.15   Acquired Knowledge: Mathematics Achievement (John's Scores)

Mathematics Achievement Scores							
Instrument: Subtest	Well Below Expected Level	Below Expected Level	Slightly Below Expected Level	At Expected Level	Above Expected Level	Well Above Expected Level	Superior
Mathematical Calculations							
WIAT–III: Numerical Operations			80				
Mathematical Reasoning							
WIAT–III: Math Problem Solving						121	

Note: Standard scores appear in normal font. Scaled scores appear in (parentheses).

Comments on the Case Study

To further clarify the reasons for John's current difficulties, the testing battery typically would be expanded in a comprehensive school neuropsychological evaluation. John achieved a scaled score of 7 on the WISC–V Coding test. Due to this low score compared to his other scores, the Coding Copy test from the WISC–V Integrated normally would be administered to test the limits and provide additional diagnostic information about his performance. Note: The WISC–V Integrated was not yet available when this chapter was written. Only John's verbal-visual associative learning and recall aspects of learning and memory were assessed. Typically, a more thorough learning and memory assessment would be conducted specifically to examine the role that increased or decreased contextual cues plays in John's ability to learn and recall new materials. For example, John's performance would be examined for his ability to learn groups of digits, words, sentences, and then stories.

John appears to be suffering from an anxiety disorder that has become a specific phobia related to written expression. John is under a physician's care and treatment for anxiety. Typically, this evaluation would include a more in-depth assessment of John's anxiety levels using behavioral rating scales such as the *Behavior Assessment Scale for Children–Second Edition* (BASC–2; Reynolds & Kamphaus, 2004) and the *Multidimensional Anxiety Scale for Children–2nd Edition* (March, 2012).

SUMMARY

The WISC–V, used in combination with the WISC–V Integrated and the WIAT–III, can provide a good starting point for a school/pediatric neuropsychological assessment. The new Visual Puzzles, Immediate Symbol Translation, Delayed Symbol Translation, Recognition Symbol Translation, Figure Weights, Picture Span, and Naming Speed tests on the WISC–V all add a greater depth to the neuropsychological utility of the test. Other test batteries and selective assessments can be added to the WISC–V, WISC–V Integrated, WIAT–III battery to cover neurocognitive processes not measured by these tests (e.g., sensorimotor functions or auditory processing) based on the specific referral question(s).

One of the benefits of a school/pediatric neuropsychological type of evaluation is the assessment of more discrete neurocognitive constructs, which allows clinicians to generate targeted interventions that potentially have more ecological validity (Miller, 2013). Too often clinicians in traditional practice just superficially examine their data and make general boilerplate recommendations and interventions that vary little from case to case. It is important that the neurocognitive strengths and weaknesses derived from a test of cognitive functions, such as the WISC–V, be used to develop targeted evidence-based interventions.

INTERPRETING THE WISC–V USING GEORGE McCLOSKEY'S NEUROPSYCHOLOGICALLY ORIENTED PROCESS APPROACH TO PSYCHOEDUCATIONAL EVALUATIONS

GEORGE McCLOSKEY, EMILY HARTZ, AND JAIME SLONIM

INTRODUCTION TO THE INTERPRETIVE APPROACH

The neuropsychologically oriented process approach (NOPA) that was applied in the assessments reported in this chapter has evolved out of years of research and practice that started with reading Alan Kaufman's (1979) book, *Intelligent Testing with the WISC–R*, and Ulric Neisser's (1966) book, *Cognitive Psychology*, during my school psychology doctoral internship year in 1979 and the subsequent readings of Reuven Feuerstein's (1980) concepts of dynamic assessment, cognitive modifiability, and instrumental enrichment while I was a practicing psychologist in Pinellas County, Florida, in the early 1980s. (In this chapter, the "I" refers to George McCloskey, first author of this chapter.)

The basic assessment techniques used in the reports in this chapter began to take shape with my work on error analysis conducted for developing new item-level interpretive techniques while a research associate at American Guidance Service in the mid-1980s for the first edition of the Kaufman Test of Educational Achievement (A. S. Kaufman & Kaufman, 1985). The error analysis and assessment approaches that I was developing were greatly enhanced by a reading of the work of A. R. Luria (1973b, 1980) and

exposure to the ideas of Edith Kaplan (Kaplan, 1988; Kaplan, Fein, Morris, Kramer, & Delis, 1999) and Marit Korkman, Ursula Kirk, and Sally Kemp (Korkman, Kirk, & Kemp, 1998), the authors of neuropsychological assessments being developed in the 1990s while I was serving as the northeast region clinical measurement consultant for the Psychological Corporation.

Additional influences from cognitive neuroscience, neurology, and neuropsychology that extend through the first decade of the new millennium and beyond included the work of Arnsten and Robbins (2002); Berninger (1994; Berninger & Richards, 2002); Cytowic (1996); Dehaene (1997, 2009, 2011, 2014); Ivry and Robertson (1998); Kosslyn and Koenig (1992); Levine (1994; Levine, Gordon, & Reed, 1998); Posner (Posner & Raichle, 1994; Posner & Rothbart, 2007); Sporns (2011); Stuss and Knight (2002, 2013); and Temple (1997). The neuropsychological aspects of the process approach developed to that point were further refined after moving back into test development and working closely with Edith Kaplan while serving as a project director for the WISC-IV Integrated (Wechsler, Kaplan, Fein, Kramer, Delis, & Morris, 2004). From the mid-2000s to the present day, the NOPA used with the students described in this chapter has been articulated more fully in chapters on the WISC–IV Integrated (McCloskey, 2009b; McCloskey & Maerlender, 2005) and the *Wechsler Adult Intelligence Scale–Fourth Edition* (WAIS–IV; McCloskey, 2009b) and expanded on in other sources (McCloskey & Perkins, 2012; McCloskey, Perkins, & Van Diviner, 2008; McCloskey, Whitaker, Murphy, & Rogers, 2012).

The NOPA applied in this chapter recognizes that brain function can be defined and assessed using a set of psychological constructs collectively referred to here as cognitive capacities. These cognitive capacities represent patterns of neural activation within various cortical and subcortical regions of the brain that are involved in the production of perception, thought, action and the cognitive aspects of emotion (Berninger, 1994; Berninger & Richards, 2002; Kosslyn & Koenig, 1992; Levine, 1998; Mapou & Spector, 1995; McCloskey, 2009a; Posner & Rothbart, 2007; Sporns, 2011).

The NOPA applied in this chapter embodies six basic conceptions (McCloskey & Maerlender, 2005):

1. WISC-V subtests (and the subtests of all other tests of cognition and achievement) are complex tasks, with each one requiring the use of multiple cognitive capacities for successful performance.
2. Variations in input, processing, and/or output demands can greatly affect performance on tasks involving identical or similar content.
3. The specific cognitive capacities that children use to perform a task depend on the children's perceptions about what cognitive capacities they believe they need to use in order to perform the task.
4. Careful, systematic observation of task performance greatly enhances the understanding of task outcomes.
5. What the child does wrong is as important as what the child does right when attempting to more completely understand what cognitive capacities were applied by the child during task performance.

6. Specific observations can lead to enhanced hypothesis generation and subsequent hypothesis confirmation or refutation.

The NOPA model applied in the cases reported in this chapter also reflects a more careful use of many terms that are frequently associated with intellectual assessment. Intellectual capacities have often been described in terms of abilities, processes, and skills, but these terms typically are used interchangeably in discussions of intelligence and in psychological reports describing the results of an intellectual assessment. In the model described in this chapter, the terms *ability*, *process*, and *skill* have distinct, noninterchangeable definitions, and each represents a critical component of cognition. In addition to these three core terms, the role of the more recently introduced concept of executive functions is defined, and the more traditional but highly ambiguous terms *memory*, *achievement*, *learning*, and *strategy* and the more generalized meaning of the term *ability* are clarified as well as other terms, such as *sensory processing*, *motor functioning*, and *processing speed* (McCloskey et al., 2012). Effective application of tests of cognition requires not just an understanding of the distinctions between the various categories of cognitive capacities but also an understanding of how the components of cognition interrelate during the occurrence of learning and production (Floyd, 2005; McCloskey et al., 2012; Saklofske, Prifitera, Weiss, Rolfhus, & Zhu, 2005).

Interpretation of the WISC–V can occur on multiple levels. Each of these levels represents a particular degree of aggregation, or disaggregation, of the information gathered during administration and assembled after administration. Each successive level, from bottom to top, represents an aggregation of information that obscures the details revealed by the levels below it. The Full Scale IQ (FSIQ) obscures variability that may be present at the index level. Each Index score obscures the contribution of individual subtest scores to the index. Each subtest score obscures the contribution of individual item scores to the subtest. Each item score obscures the variability in the application of specific cognitive constructs that may be occurring and that may be observed during individual item administration. Although interpretation at each level can be viewed from a neuropsychological perspective, some levels are more suited to the application of a wide range of neuropsychological capacities than others. While there may be merit in the interpretation of FSIQ and of primary, ancillary, and complementary Indexes in specific instances, the approach to assessment demonstrated in the cases described in this chapter reflects the basic tenet of NOPA wherein the most effective neuropsychological interpretation of WISC–V performance will be found at the subtest, item, and task-specific cognitive capacities levels (McCloskey, 2009a, 2009b; McCloskey & Maerlender, 2005).

The focus of the NOPA is on how examinees perform the items of each WISC–V subtest as well as the scores they earn on each of those subtests. Therefore, the key to effective interpretation of test performance after administration is careful observation of test performance during administration. Integration of what was observed during administration with what is scored after administration enables the clinician to characterize more accurately the specific cognitive strengths and weaknesses of the child. This critical perspective of the NOPA applied here essentially means that the categorization of subtests based on a priori factor-analysis results does not represent a stable structure that can be used in all cases to construct indexes and to offer interpretations of task performance after test administration. From the NOPA perspective, prior to administration of a subtest, the only answer to the question "What does this specific subtest measure?" is "It depends." That is to say, it depends on what the child thinks the subtest requires in the way of cognitive capacities for successful performance, and it depends on the way the child engages these cognitive capacities during task performance. When interpreting individual case performance, a task can be assigned to a specific cognitive capacity category only after testing

has occurred, not before. It is interesting to note that this perspective has been voiced in publications discussing factor-analytic results such as J. B. Carroll's (1993a) *Human Cognitive Abilities*:

> [C]onsiderable confusion exists about the identification of factors in the domain of visual perception . . . . Some sources of confusion are very real, and difficult to deal with. This is particularly true of confusion arising from the fact that test takers apparently can arrive at answers and solutions—either correct or incorrect ones—by a variety of different strategies. French (1965) demonstrated that different "cognitive styles" can cause wide variation in factor loadings; some of his most dramatic cases had to do with spatial tests, as where a sample of subjects who reported "systematizing" their approach to the Cubes test yielded a large decrease of the loading of this test on a Visualization factor (that is, decreased correlations of Cubes with other spatial tests), as compared to a sample where subjects did not report systematizing. It has been shown (Kyllonen, Lohman, & Woltz, 1984) that subjects can employ different strategies even for different items within the same test. Lohman et al. (1987) have discussed this problem of solution strategies, even rendering the judgment that factor-analytic methodology is hardly up to the task of dealing with it because a basic assumption of factor analysis is that factorial equations are consistent over subjects. (p. 309)

For this reason, while all WISC–V composite and subtest scores are reported in the tables at the end of each report, the narrative body of the report is organized according to the specific cognitive capacities that are being assessed, and WISC–V subtest- and item-level interpretations appear within these various cognitive capacity sections based on how the child performed the task rather than by the WISC–V Index structure or by a specific structural interpretive approach, such as the Cattell-Horn-Carroll (CHC) and neuropsychological approaches described in earlier chapters of this book.

INTRODUCTION TO THE REPORTS

Readers will quickly realize that the reports provided in this chapter are quite voluminous. There are good reasons for this. The most important one is that school districts and parents who request evaluations have come to expect this type of report from me, and it is one of the main reasons why they requested my services in the first place. Second, I consider my reports to be a means of teaching about the NOPA; I try to record in as much detail as possible the assessment methods used, my observations of how the child performs each task—especially the errors they made, and the connections between the behaviors observed and the cognitive capacities that likely were engaged to produce the behaviors so that others can follow my clinical thinking as closely as possible.

Although reports typically are 30 to 50 pages in length, the format of the report—frontloading the three to eight pages of summary material—enables the much shorter summary to be the focal point of the sharing of results with parents, school-based teams, and other professionals in a session that lasts an hour or less. What may not be readily apparent from reading these reports is my practice of not providing recommendations in the report until after meeting with the school-based team when such a meeting is possible. The first draft of the report that is shared with parents and others has a blank recommendations section. Although I enter team or parent meetings with a very specific list of recommendations that I think to be appropriate for the situation, my intention is to have a similar list evolve naturally out of the discussion with the team. If all of the points on my list do not emerge from the group discussion, I will introduce the remaining points for discussion with the group near the end of the meeting.

During the meeting, I help the team maintain a solution-focused mindset by discussing (1) what the child can do, (2) what the child has difficulty doing, (3) what most likely could be done to affect positive change, and (4) who can do what needs to be done to help the child achieve the positive outcomes that are possible. Note that I always provide statements in the Conclusion section that reflect a positive growth mindset (Dweck, 2006) indicating what may result if time, energy, and effort are invested in the application of appropriate strategies. Also note that the recommendations that are recorded after the team meeting address the three parties most critical to the attainment of positive outcomes by stating (1) what the child can do to help himself or herself, (2) what the parent(s) or guardian can do to help the child, and (3) what school staff can do to help the child. Stating recommendations in this way emphasizes the point that all parties must be involved to maximize the likelihood of realizing the desired positive outcomes.

If I were a clinician tasked with assessing many more students in a short period of time, I would be writing shorter reports that likely would look more like the summary only, but the clinical thinking applied prior to the writing of the summary would mirror what is recorded in the detailed individual sections of the reports provided in this chapter. Some clinicians may wish to adopt an intermediate strategy, such as providing the content of the detailed sections in bullet point lists instead of narrative format—a strategy that can save a great deal of time. Whatever the report format used, applying the NOPA techniques and getting the picture right is the critical aspect of the clinical work. Deriving sound conclusions and offering sound recommendations are much more important than the format in which they are documented.

CASE 11—COLIN, AGE 8: AN EIGHT-YEAR-OLD BOY WITH MILD EXECUTIVE FUNCTION DIFFICULTIES BUT NO SPECIFIC LEARNING DISABILITIES

George McCloskey

Colin's parents first contacted me in mid-October at the recommendation of a psychiatrist whom I have collaborated with on several cases in recent years. Colin's parents were requesting an evaluation because they had been contacted by Colin's teacher. She expressed concerns about Colin's academic progress, indicating that he was lagging behind his peers in all academic areas. She also noted that Colin was having a lot of difficulty sustaining attention and regulating his activity level. Colin's parents were wondering if Colin may have a learning disability and/or if his attention difficulties were interfering with his learning (although they did not specifically mention attention-deficit/hyperactivity disorder [ADHD]).

I was not able to schedule an evaluation with Colin until December. Fortunately for Colin, his parents had talked with his teacher in late October about her concerns. During that meeting, Colin's teacher offered to make some adjustments in her classroom routines and agreed to provide some accommodations for Colin, such as allowing him to take movement breaks throughout the day, consistently praising him for his work efforts, and encouraging him to sustain attention and increase the quality of his production through positive statements.

The teacher's implementation of these adjustments was very effective; by the time of the first evaluation session in December, Colin's teacher was reporting that Colin's daily production and subject area grades were improving. At the time of the classroom observation, I was able to see how Colin's teacher was implementing her strategies and the positive effect that they were having on Colin.

Although specific dates of testing and other possible identifying information have been omitted from the case report for privacy purposes, all observational and testing sessions were conducted within a 3-month time period. The evaluation conducted with Colin reflected mostly cognitive and academic areas of strength. Colin did not demonstrate any cognitive processing deficits or severe skill deficits that might be indicative of a learning disability. The few weaknesses that were identified were associated with some specific executive function difficulties. The extreme contrast between Colin's behavior during the assessment and his behavior in the classroom during the observation and as reported by his teacher strongly suggested that Colin's executive function difficulties could be addressed through teacher-implemented strategies similar to those that his teacher already had begun to use. It was for these reasons that the recommendations in the report are worded in the form of "Colin's teacher can continue to … " Over time and with proper consultation, it is likely that Colin's teachers will be able to move away from strategies that emphasize external control and into bridging strategies that will move him further along the continuum toward internally guided self-regulation.

Psychoeducational Evaluation Report

NAME: Colin

REPORT DATE: XX/XX/XXXX

SCHOOL DISTRICT: XX

SCHOOL: XX Elementary School

BIRTH DATE: XX/XX/XXXX

GRADE: 3 (Fall 2014)

DATES OF EVALUATION: XX/XX, XX/XX, XX/XX/XXXX

C.A. AT EVALUATION: 8–3, 8–4

CURRENT EDUCATIONAL PROGRAM: General elementary school education program.

Reason for Referral/Purpose of Report

Based on the recommendation of Dr. YY, Colin's parents requested that a neuropsychologically oriented psychoeducational evaluation be completed to assist in determining Colin's current profile of strengths and needs with regard to his cognitive, academic, and social/emotional functioning. The resultant findings will be utilized to help clarify educational goals and to inform educational intervention and programming.

Information from the Parent

At the time of the initial contact with the psychologist, Colin's parents expressed concerns with reports from the school that Colin's rate of acquisition of reading, writing, and math skills was lagging somewhat behind his peers, with the greatest concern expressed in the area of math. Colin's teacher also indicated that Colin was having difficulty focusing and sustaining attention during academic instruction. Colin's parents expressed a desire to know if Colin's academic struggles were related to an underlying learning disability.

At the time of the first evaluation session, Colin's parents indicated that, in recent weeks, Colin's teacher had been making some adjustments in her approach to working with Colin that have resulted in enhanced focus during instructional time as well as increased proficiency across curricular domains. Despite noticeable improvement in sustained focus during academic instruction, Colin's parents indicated that there are times when Colin becomes easily distracted and finds it difficult to focus his attention on homework.

At the time of the second evaluation session on XX/XX/XXXX, Colin's parents related that they had been receiving favorable reports from Colin's teacher; Colin had made considerable progress in math and in reading comprehension. At the time of the third session on XX/XX/XXXX, the positive progress reports were continuing.

Assessment Procedures

Colin was seen for an evaluation by Dr. George McCloskey, a consulting school psychologist, at the request of Colin's parents. At the time of the assessment, Colin was not taking any medication that would be likely to affect his performance.

On XX/XX/XX, Colin was administered the following in a morning evaluation session. The testing session lasted approximately 2 1/2 hours with a 20-minute snack break and 2–3 additional short breaks.

Student Interview

Wechsler Intelligence Scale for Children–Fifth Edition (WISC–V) (Core and selected supplemental and complementary subtests)

On XX/XX/XXXX, Colin was administered the following in an afternoon evaluation session. The testing session lasted approximately 2 1/2 hours with 2 short rest and snack breaks:

Wisconsin Card Sorting Test (WCST)

Children's Memory Scale (CMS) (selected subtests)

Delis-Kaplan Executive Function System (D-KEFS) (selected subtests)

Kaufman Test of Educational Achievement–Third Edition (KTEA–3) (selected subtests)

On XX/XX/XXXX, Colin was administered the following in a morning evaluation session. The testing session lasted approximately 1 hour with no rest break:

Process Assessment of the Learner–Second Edition (PAL–II) (selected subtests)

NEPSY-II Developmental Neuropsychological Assessment (selected subtests)

Kaufman Test of Educational Achievement–Third Edition (KTEA–3) (selected subtests)

On XX/XX/XXXX, Colin was observed for 2 1/2 hours in the general education program during Spanish class and Language Arts class.

In addition to interviews, direct assessment, and classroom observations, Colin's parents and classroom teacher completed the Behavior Rating Inventory of Executive Function (BRIEF), the ADHD–IV Rating Scale, and the McCloskey Executive Functions Scales (MEFS).

Summary of Colin's Assessment Performance

Based on the assessment work completed and the information gathered and interpreted, the following summary, conclusions, and recommendations are offered:

Table 13.1   Summary of Colin's Assessment Performance

Strengths	Challenges
Reasoning Abilities	
Colin was most effective when he was required to reason with orally presented verbal information and offer verbal responses, earning scores in the above average to very superior range with such tasks. When presented with information that required reasoning with quantity, Colin earned scores in the above average range. When he was asked to reason with visually presented nonverbal materials, Colin earned scores in the upper end of the average range and in the above average range.	When engaged with visuospatial and quantitative reasoning tasks, Colin often was not able to sustain adequate executive control over task performance, thus resulting in inconsistent patterns of performance where relatively easier items were answered incorrectly but much more difficult items were answered correctly. It is very possible that Colin's scores on these tasks would have been even higher had he been able to use executive functions to sustain consistent effort.
Language Abilities	
The overall impression gleaned from conversation, observation of and interaction with Colin is that he was very adept at understanding conversational speech, test directions, and expressing his thoughts effectively in conversation. Colin also performed very effectively with tasks that assessed his receptive language ability and his basic phonological processing capacities.	On basic measures of expressive fluency and speed, however, Colin earned scores that ranged from the extremely low range to the superior range. When responding to each of these tasks, Colin exhibited a great deal of difficulty with controlling the tone and volume of his voice.
Visual Processing	
Colin's performance with tasks requiring visual processing varied from the middle of the average range to the above average range.	
Memory Capacities Applied with Auditorily Presented Verbal Information	
Colin's performance on tasks requiring the use of immediate and working memory capacities produced scores in the average and above average ranges. Tasks involving retrieval from long-term storage resulted in scores in the average to very superior range.	
Memory Capacities Applied with Visually Presented Nonverbal Images	
	Colin's performance on a task requiring the use of immediate visual memory for objects produced a score in the low range.

(*continued*)

Table 13.1 (*Continued*)

Strengths	Challenges
Processing Speed with Non-Academic Tasks	
Colin earned scores in the average range on tasks that required speeded performance, visual processing, and motor production.	
Reading Skills	
Colin earned scores that varied from the average range to the superior range on measures of reading skills, reading knowledge bases, and cognitive processes that support reading skill development.	
Handwriting (Graphomotor) Production	
Colin earned scores in the average to superior ranges on formal measures of handwriting production and speed.	Although Colin was able to print letters and words very quickly, the letters he produced were poorly formed and difficult to decipher at times.
Written Expression Skills	
Colin earned a score in the average range when spelling words from dictation.	Colin earned scores in the below average range on measures of writing skills as well as on a measure of recognition of correct word spellings.
Math Skills	
Colin earned a score in the superior range when required to solve applied math problems that were presented both auditorily and visually; he earned a score in the average range when required to recall and record basic math facts.	Colin earned a score in the below average range when required to perform calculations involving addition, subtraction, and multiplication with many procedural errors noted.
Executive Functions – Control of Attention and Effort during Assessment Sessions	
In the one-to-one context of the assessment session, Colin was able to focus and sustain attention on most of the tasks that were presented.	Colin very often chose to engage in a very high level of motor activity while maintaining his concentration and focus on a task. At times, Colin required a great deal of prompting and negotiating in order to sustain effort for the minimum amount of time possible for task completion. This was especially the case for all tasks that required Colin to use a pencil and paper. Even with prompting and cueing, Colin sometimes disengaged with tasks to take a break; at other times, Colin would stop working and comment on a task.

Table 13.1   *(Continued)*

Strengths	Challenges
	Transitions from one task to another were accomplished only with much prompting or redirecting. The amount of prompting, negotiating, and discussion that occurred during the assessment sessions extended the amount of time required to complete the evaluation.

Executive Functions – Direction of Reasoning Abilities during Assessment Sessions

Colin earned scores in the upper end of average to above average ranges when the task objective was ambiguous, but the need for strategy generation and refinement was minimal.	Colin earned scores in the below average to extremely low ranges when the task objective was unambiguous, but the need for strategy generation and refinement was much greater.

Executive Control of Verbal Fluency during Assessment Sessions

	Colin's difficulties with specific language fluency tasks suggest that when executive function demands are increased, his capacity for effective processing of printed material may be adversely affected, resulting in decreased efficiency of the reading process.

Executive Control of Visuospatial Processing and Visual–Motor Production

Colin demonstrated the ability to direct visual processing when performing many complex visual tasks.	Colin often was not able to sustain adequate executive control over task performance, thus resulting in inconsistent patterns of performance where relatively easier items were answered incorrectly but much more difficult items were answered correctly. It is very possible that Colin's scores on these tasks would have been even higher had he been able to use executive functions to sustain a consistent effort.

Executive Control of Working Memory during Assessment Sessions

	Although Colin performed in the average and above range on all of the tasks that required him to hold and manipulate auditorily presented verbal information, his performance varied depending on the nature of the material presented. When required to hold and repeat random series of numbers, Colin was much less effective than when he was required to hold and manipulate contextually meaningful verbal information (such as a story narrative or a math word problem) or when he was provided with direct cues as to how to organize

(continued)

Table 13.1   *(Continued)*

Strengths	Challenges
	decontextualized, relatively meaningless information (say the numbers first from lowest to highest and then the letters in alphabetical order). Colin's relatively less efficient performance with decontextualized information appears to be related more to a lack of effective strategy generation and use as opposed to any specific limitation of auditory working memory capacity.
Executive Control of Processing Speed during Assessment Sessions	
	Although Colin earned scores in the average range on tasks that assessed processing speed, his rate of production often varied significantly. At times, Colin would interrupt his work to make comments or react to the materials; at other times, he would just stop working for short periods even though he was aware that he was being timed and speed of performance was important. Colin's work pace varied considerably within and across many tasks; at times he would work very quickly and make errors due to the loss of balance between speed and accuracy; at other times, he would work very slowly and overemphasize accuracy of performance, stopping to erase and redo minor imperfections.
Executive Control of Reading during Assessment Sessions and Classroom Observation	
Colin did not exhibit executive function difficulties when reading in the classroom during observation; he maintained good focus during the reading process, refrained from talking to peers, and resisted distraction from extraneous activity occurring in the classroom.	Colin exhibited a number of executive function difficulties when reading text passages and individual word lists during the assessment sessions; he called out words in a very loud and animated voice, missed important details when reading for meaning, and interrupted performance during a timed silent reading task.
Executive Control of Writing during Assessment Sessions	
As was the case with reading, Colin did not exhibit executive control difficulties when engaged with writing tasks during classroom observations. He immediately complied with all requests to complete worksheets that required written responses and his work pace was consistent with that of most of the students in the class. Colin was extremely slow when entering the contents of a written research paper into a computer file, but he was distracted by the group reading lesson that was occurring nearby that involved all of the students in the class except Colin.	Colin often was unable to sustain attention and effort with writing tasks and the legibility of his handwriting varied greatly as he had difficulty maintaining a balance between speed of production and accuracy of letter formation and letter/word spacing.

Table 13.1 *(Continued)*

Strengths	Challenges
Executive Control of the Use of Mathematics during Assessment Sessions	
Colin sustained attention and effort when performing math calculations with pencil and paper and when listening to orally presented math problems.	Despite a high level of focused concentration, Colin made several calculation errors on paper-and-pencil type problems similar to the orally presented math word problems that he was able to complete without the use of pencil and paper.
Parent and Teacher Ratings of Executive Functions	
Parent and teacher ratings gathered utilizing the BRIEF and the ADHD-IV Rating Scales yielded scores in the typical ranges.	Ratings gathered with the MEFS identified executive function weaknesses within the School Arena for a majority of the self-regulation executive capacities within 6 of the 7 clusters: Attention, Engagement, Optimization, Efficiency, Inquiry and Solution. Colin's parents identified somewhat fewer weaknesses in 5 of the 7 clusters (all but Memory and Solution) when compared to Colin's teacher.
Within both the MEFS Self and Social Arenas, parent and teacher ratings were highly consistent, with executive function strengths far outnumbering weaknesses.	Within both the MEFS Self and Social Arenas, parent and teacher ratings reflected a few concerns within the Efficiency and Inquiry Clusters.
Parent and teacher MEFS ratings of Colin's Self-Realization, Self-Determination, and Self-Generation were indicative of a child who is engaged with many aspects of these executive function capacities at an advanced level.	
Social/Emotional Functioning	
Although this area was not formally assessed with rating scales, interviews of Colin's parents and teacher did not reveal any concerns that might be indicative of difficulties with social or emotional functioning.	

Conclusions

Colin is an outgoing, physically active, and inquisitive 8-year-old boy with varied interests, a good sense of humor, and exemplary social skills when engaged with friends. At the beginning of the current school year, teacher reports indicated that Colin evidenced difficulty with reading, writing, and math skill acquisition, demonstrated erratic performance in the classroom, and struggled to focus and sustain attention during instructional time. Following discussion with Colin's parents, Colin's teacher made some adjustments in her teaching approach that have resulted in notable improvements in Colin's classroom production and academic skill development over the course of the past few months. Although improvements have been noted, questions remained about the nature of Colin's inconsistent performance and slower rate of skill acquisition at the start of the school year.

During the current assessment, Colin demonstrated many cognitive strengths with tasks that assessed reasoning, language, memory, and visuospatial abilities. Colin's performance did not reflect any process deficits that would be indicative of learning disabilities. In fact, he performed very well on most measures of basic cognitive processes (phonological processing; orthographic processing; graphomotor functioning; rapid automatic letter and word naming; and rapid quantity labeling) that underlie the acquisition and development of academic skills. Consistent with his cognitive abilities and cognitive processing strengths, Colin performed in the average range or better on most measures of reading, writing, and math skills with only a few exceptions as noted below. Parent and teacher reports along with test performance indicate that Colin exhibits a number of executive function strengths that he uses to regulate his perceptions, feelings, thoughts, and actions in social interactions and for the purposes of exerting self-control at home and in school.

In contrast to his many cognitive, academic, social-emotional, and executive function strengths, parent and teacher ratings coupled with Colin's performance on specific assessment tasks indicated a number of executive function self-regulation challenges primarily when dealing with academic tasks. Within the academic arena, parent and teacher ratings reflected executive function challenges with self-regulation executive functions involving Attention, Engagement, Optimization, Efficiency, Memory, Inquiry, and Solution. Most notable within these general areas were difficulties with monitoring work output and correcting errors and difficulties with generating and using routines and strategies for problem solving or for completing routine work. During the assessment sessions, the most notable executive function challenges were difficulties with modulating activity level, difficulties with maintaining focus during task

performance and transitions, and difficulties with generating and using strategies for efficient and effective task performance, especially in the absence of specific cues for how to engage with a task. These difficulties were most evident when Colin was required to write in a thoughtful manner or to use pencil and paper to perform math calculations.

Although some of the executive function difficulties that Colin exhibited during assessment sessions and that Colin's parents and teacher identified in their MEFS ratings —difficulties with focusing and sustaining attention—are those most often associated with a diagnosis of ADHD, these were identified as problematic only in relation to work on academic assignments and only at certain times. Additionally, although Colin's behavior during individual assessment sessions did reflect other executive function difficulties that are also associated with ADHD, namely lack of adequate inhibition and difficulty with modulating perceptions, feelings, thoughts, and actions, parent and teacher ratings did not identify these executive functions as problematic at this time. Colin's teacher even noted that her ratings reflecting executive function difficulties were based on the first 5 months of the school year and, thus, did not take into account the significant improvement that Colin has demonstrated over the course of the past 4 to 6 weeks.

It is important to note that during classroom observations, Colin was able to inhibit impulsive responding effectively, modulate his activity level, and sustain attention and focus during tasks and periods of transition, except in the most difficult of circumstances.

The executive function difficulties identified in parent and teacher ratings and exhibited during the assessment sessions sometimes result in inconsistent or inadequate academic production. The results of the current evaluation do not indicate the presence of any specific learning disabilities that might act to impede learning in specific areas involving speaking, listening, reading, writing, or mathematics. Colin is more accurately characterized as having mild producing difficulties rather than learning difficulties or ADHD. When learning does not occur as well as might be expected, it is likely due to a lack of effective, efficient strategy generation and use rather than to a lack of capacity to learn new material. When demonstrating what has been learned through tests or assignments, Colin's executive function difficulties are likely to result in inconsistent performance; he may work too slowly or too quickly, manage his time inefficiently, and make errors that he does not correct, and he may not generate or apply efficient strategies for problem solving.

Colin's executive function challenges reflect a lack of maturation of specific neural networks rather than hard-wired deficits that are not amenable to change. In fact, in regard to maturation of neural networks, it is important to keep in mind that Colin is young for his grade; from now through 12th grade, nearly all of the other students in his classes are likely to be older than Colin, and this age difference will contribute greatly to maturational differences that may be noted between Colin and his same-grade peers in terms of executive function development and use.

It is important to recognize that in addition to the lag created by the age difference, Colin's executive function difficulties are reflecting maturational delays in the development of specific frontal lobe neural circuits rather than the result of any type of neural damage or deficit. Although he is experiencing growth in his capacity for accessing and using executive functions, his rate of growth is likely to be somewhat slower than same-age peers, resulting in a relative level of immaturity in the use of these capacities when compared with his same-grade peers. Fortunately, it is likely that Colin will gain greater access to the executive functions that are most problematic for him simply with the passage of time, but his development will likely continue to lag behind that of same-grade peers.

Activating and using self-regulation capacities when he perceives a task to be uninteresting and/or unrelated to those things that hold great intrinsic motivational value are likely to prove very challenging for Colin. Conversely, when he perceives a task to be interesting, Colin will likely be able to activate and utilize even those executive functions that are less well developed to achieve his desired outcomes with relative ease. The situations most likely to highlight Colin's executive function challenges are those where progress toward his personal goals is impeded or when Colin is required to shift from his internally motivated functioning to respond to external demands for production. In these situations, Colin may expend a great deal of energy resisting engagement with tasks or performing poorly, not because he does not want to engage or to be successful but rather because he is not able to generate a strategy that would enable him to engage the executive functions needed to immediately produce efficiently and effectively.

Colin's teacher has modified her approach to dealing with Colin in ways that have enabled him to demonstrate improvements in his ability to focus, to sustain attention and effort, and to produce academically. At this point in time, parents and teachers can continue to provide structured situations in order to help Colin maintain his internal motivation and use it to help him to self-regulate in ways that will enable him to produce at a level that is consistent with his cognitive abilities and academic skills.

Given Colin's difficulties with generating his own efficient and effective strategies for task completion and his difficulties with monitoring his work and correcting his errors, educational transition periods, such as the move from elementary to middle school, middle school to high school, and high school to college, are likely to be very challenging. It is very likely that Colin will need explicit instruction in study skill and test-taking strategies that he can then apply to his academic classes to produce and achieve at a level commensurate with his abilities and skills. If such assistance is provided at these critical times, Colin is likely to develop the requisite tools needed to produce and succeed academically.

Recommendations

The results of this evaluation were discussed with Colin, his parents, and school staff in order to develop appropriate recommendations to facilitate successful learning, and academic performance. The recommendations that resulted from these discussions are recorded in the sections below.

What Colin Can Do for Himself to Ensure that He Does Well in School

1. Colin can continue to read for pleasure and engage in the wide variety of activities that interest him.
2. Colin can continue to maintain a positive attitude toward school and learning.
3. Colin can listen to and act on his parents' advice about the best time to do his homework and the best strategies for approaching his homework.
4. Colin can make use of taught strategies for improving problem-solving efficiency and accuracy of work completion.

What Colin's Parents Can Do to Help Colin Gain Academic Success

1. Continue to be supportive of Colin's efforts in school and continue to help Colin see school as a positive and important influence in his life.
2. Continue to communicate directly with school staff to monitor Colin's academic progress and to ensure that Colin's educational needs are being addressed properly.
3. Continue to encourage Colin to do his best in school and continue to praise him when it is apparent that he is putting forth his best efforts to succeed.
4. Continue to impose structure for homework time and completion, but acknowledge and act on the need to be flexible about the structure as situations dictate.
5. Maintain a growth mindset regarding Colin's executive function challenges; recognize that change is possible when enough time, energy,

and effort are focused on what needs to be accomplished.
6. Continue to support Colin in a patient, caring, and loving manner.
7. Continue to consult with Dr. YY in an effort to determine if, and when, pharmacological interventions might be needed to help Colin overcome specific executive function difficulties. If pharmacological intervention is tried at any point in the future, Colin should be monitored closely to determine if desired effects are being achieved and/or if undesired side effects are occurring. If Colin were to exhibit any unusual behaviors while taking medication, these should be reported to Dr. YY immediately.

What School Staff Can Do to Help Colin Improve Cognitive, Social/Emotional, and Adaptive Functioning and Achieve Academic Success
Given Colin's specific profile of cognitive, academic, and social-emotional strengths and his profile of executive function strengths and challenges, school staff can help Colin in the following ways:

1. Colin is benefiting from the explicit statements that are being provided by his teacher that clarify the expectations for classroom behavior, routines, and academic production. The clearer and more explicit these statements, the greater the likelihood that Colin will grasp what is required for success and engage the executive functions needed to meet expectations.
2. Colin's teacher can continue to help him maintain a positive motivation for succeeding in school by praising him when he engages with good effort and when he meets expectations; whenever possible, Colin is being provided with specific feedback about the adequacy of his performance and suggestions for how to improve his performance.
3. Colin's teacher can continue to help Colin identify strategies to improve efficiency and efficacy with projects and assignments and to

monitor production, locate errors, and revise mistakes.

4. To help Colin improve his ability to find and fix mistakes that he makes, he could be allowed to revise his work after being provided with feedback from his teacher and prior to the grading of his products.

5. Colin's teacher can continue to prompt Colin for attention when necessary and ensuring that Colin knows what he should be attending to and how long he should be attending to it. Colin is benefiting from a gradual transition from teacher-directed to self-directed cueing of the focusing and sustaining of attention. This is being effected by asking Colin self-reflective questions such as "Colin, what should you be doing (listening to, thinking about, focusing on, etc.) now?" and discussions that enable Colin to keep in mind the goal of self-directing attention without the need of teacher assistance.

6. Colin's teacher can continue to allow Colin to take activity breaks during the day. These are intended to help Colin increase his ability to focus and sustain attention during instruction. Ideally, the number of breaks allowed should be decreased gradually over time with the goal being that, by the end of the school year, Colin is able to focus and sustain attention without the need for activity breaks.

7. Colin would benefit from instruction emphasizing the use of self-regulated strategy development approaches to writing such as those described in the text *Best Practices in Writing Instruction* (2nd ed., Graham & MacArthur, 2013).

8. Colin's progress should be monitored during the remainder of the academic year to ensure that his academic skill acquisition and executive function development and use continues in a manner consistent with the past few months. If difficulties are encountered, the pupil services team should meet with the psychologist and Colin's parents to discuss modifications to the current recommendations.

Detailed Description of Findings and Interpretation of Assessment Results

Assessment Session Observations Prior to the first evaluation session, Colin greeted the psychologist at the front door with a smile. In an interview prior to the start of testing, Colin appeared to be very comfortable in the presence of the psychologist and readily conversed about his interests and school. Colin conversed in a very natural manner, was able to clearly articulate his thoughts and feelings, and occasionally posed a question of his own to the psychologist.

When asked about his favorite school subject, Colin responded playfully with "recess." More seriously, Colin responded that he likes science because he likes to build things. When asked about reading, Colin noted that he is "a good reader" and that he likes to read for pleasure; he offered the names of some books that he has read lately. When asked about math and writing, Colin simply noted that he was doing okay in these subjects but did offer that he was keeping a sketch book for writing—an activity he appeared to like. When asked if he was having any difficulties with any school subject or if he found any schoolwork to be challenging, Colin answered "not really."

When asked about personal interests, Colin stated that he likes to draw and play the video game Minecraft with his friends from school. When the weather is good, Colin reported that he likes to ride his bike. Colin also mentioned that he likes to go to summer camp.

Regarding use of technology, Colin indicated that he does not have a cell phone; he uses the home computer to watch videos and work on math at the IXL website.

When asked about friends and social activities, Colin indicated that he is friends with several of his classmates but did not comment about his social activities with his peers.

During the evaluation sessions, Colin quickly became very comfortable in the presence of the psychologist, so much so that at times he found it difficult to stay focused on the tasks presented and would stop working and initiate conversation about a topic of interest. When redirected back to the task at hand, however, Colin was effectively able to refocus his effort and attention to the material presented.

As the first session progressed, Colin's activity level gradually escalated. After working with the psychologist for about an hour, Colin left the room and returned with a large rubber ball that he sat on subsequent to placing it on top of a dining room chair. Throughout the remainder of the session, Colin was usually bouncing on his rubber ball on the chair while performing tasks. Occasionally he would dismount and walk around the corner of the table while performing tasks. Colin's voice level also rose, and, at times, he became very silly and giggled or called out. Often while working on some tasks, especially those that required the use of pencil and paper, Colin would hum loudly or make loud noises while working productively.

It is important to note that although Colin's level of physical activity and vocalizations appeared to be affecting his ability to give his best effort in his work on some tasks, for other tasks Colin appeared to perform better when he was in motion and making noises. It is also important to note that during the first two assessment sessions, the psychologist allowed Colin to self-regulate his approach to the testing situation rather than attempting to impose a specific structure or level of control on his activity level or vocalizations. By doing so, the psychologist was able to observe the kind of self-restraint that Colin did or did not exert in a situation where there were no specific cues for how to regulate, and to observe the amount and quality of his production under such circumstances.

Despite his high activity level, Colin readily engaged with each task that was presented and appeared to offer his best efforts in his attempts to complete these tasks. The only exception to this was Colin's resistance to performing specific writing tasks during the afternoon session on XX/XX/XXXX. When Colin resisted engaging with these tasks, the psychologist engaged in more active prompting in an effort to improve Colin's effort, but, even with the greater structure

and clearer demands for specific behaviors, Colin was not able to fully engage with these tasks.

Prior to the start of the third evaluation session, Colin was notified by his parents and by the psychologist that it was important for him to try to approach all tasks as if he were doing them in his classroom at school by remaining in his chair, not moving around the room, and not bouncing on a ball. Although Colin was acquiescent and it was evident that he was trying to follow the imposed guidelines, he was not able to fully comply with the directives. He frequently left his seat to look out the window.

Additional observations regarding Colin's performance of specific tasks are integrated throughout the detailed interpretation sections of this report.

Classroom Observations On XX/XX/XXXX, Colin was observed during Spanish and language arts classes at Westwood Elementary School.

Spanish During this class period, all of the students were very active and tended to talk among themselves while engaging in the completion of teacher-assigned activities. Although the teacher frequently prompted for quiet, the noise level in the classroom quickly rose again after each prompt. Colin was seated at a table with five other students at the front of the classroom directly in front of the board where lessons were delivered. Despite the high level of activity and noise in the classroom, many students remained engaged with their assigned tasks and were very productive. Colin was among the students who were able to focus on completing assignments. Although he occasionally made comments to other students at his table, he was not disruptive of the learning process, worked diligently on his assignments, and completed assigned tasks well within the allotted time frame. When the class was cued to put away materials to prepare for class change, Colin and his tablemates responded immediately and efficiently and were the first table to be ready to leave class, which meant that they were first to be called to line up to leave.

Language Arts This class was started by having two teacher-appointed "learning ambassadors" read the day's lesson goals to the entire class. Colin was one of the two ambassadors on this day. On cue, Colin orally read some of the lesson goals in an audible and articulate voice.

After the introduction, Colin returned to his desk located in a pod with three other desks. Colin's desk was cluttered with many different objects, such as pencils, crayons, notepads, paste sticks, a pencil sharpener, Post-it notes, and scissors. Colin and two other students in the room were the only students to have this much material out on their desks; the other students' desks were uncluttered.

During the first part of the class, the teacher provided a group lesson on strategies for reading informational texts. Lecture was interspersed with short video clips demonstrating points in the lecture. Colin attended to the lesson without distraction. He frequently volunteered to answer questions posed by the teacher and, when called upon, he was able to deliver well-stated, accurate responses. After the lecture, the students were provided with a short snack break. At the end of the snack break, the teacher guided the class in a reading of an informational article and asked students questions about what was being read. Again, Colin focused and sustained attention throughout the discussion and volunteered to respond to questions.

After the group reading, the teacher instructed the students to continue reading silently and underline specific words in the passage that represented key points in the reading. On this particular day, the classroom teacher's own parents, both of whom are retired teachers, were serving as classroom aides. They circulated throughout the classroom, answering students' questions and helping students to stay focused on the assignment. At the end of the silent reading period, the teacher asked Colin for the words he underlined and the reasoning for his selections. Colin provided a good list of words in addition to well-thought-out reasons why he selected those words.

After the group lesson, the teacher provided instructions for what each group of students would be doing next. Colin's group joined the teacher for a guided reading lesson. When called upon, Colin read orally with good fluency and without hesitation. When asked comprehension questions, Colin provided well-articulated responses.

After the small-group reading lesson, Colin and his group were told that they could return to their desks or go out into the hall to continue reading their books independently. Colin and two other students opted to go out in the hall where they sat against the wall and read quietly. Occasionally one of the other students engaged Colin in conversation, but both returned to their reading very quickly.

Colin returned to his seat after approximately 10 minutes of silent reading and began to work on a teacher-assigned worksheet that he had started the previous day. Colin's progress with the worksheet was consistent with that of the other students in the room.

Colin left the classroom for about 5 minutes to frequent the restroom. When he returned, the teacher prompted him to transition to another activity. Colin required more time to complete the transition than was typical for most children in the class.

Colin worked on a worksheet for a different assignment as directed by the teacher. Despite the fact that several different tasks were being worked on during this class, Colin did not exhibit any difficulty shifting between activities, and his work pace remained consistent with the majority of the students in the class.

The teacher checked Colin's progress with his latest assignment and told him to obtain a laptop computer from the hall to work on another assignment. Unfortunately, Colin tried three different computers but none of them was functional. This process required more than 5 minutes, and the class began to transition to a group lesson while Colin was still trying to login to a computer. The teacher had to log Colin on to the class computer so he could complete an assignment that he had not finished. (The teacher noted that Colin was the only student in the class that had not yet competed this assignment.) Colin remained at the computer transferring material that he had written into a Word file for a report he was completing. Colin's rate of copying was extremely slow, typing only 37 words into the file in 10 minutes. It is important to note that Colin was very distracted while typing as he was trying to listen to the story that the teacher was reading to the rest of the class. After 10 minutes of copying,

Colin stopped typing and went to join the group even though he did not finish copying all of his written text into the file. When he left the computer station, he did not take his worksheet and folder back to his desk.

For a detailed description and interpretation of assessment results for Colin, go to Appendix G in the downloadable resources: www.wiley.com/go/itwiscvwww.wiley.com/go/itwiscv

Test Results

Cognitive Abilities

Table 13.2   Colin's Wechsler Intelligence Scale for Children–Fifth Edition (WISC–V) Scores

	Standard Score	Percentile	Standard Scores within Descriptive Category Ranges						
			Extremely Low	Low	Below Average	Average	Above Average	Superior	Very Superior
Global Composites									
FSIQ–Full Scale IQ	122	93						122	
GAI–General Ability Index	126	96						126	
Indexes									
VCI–Verbal Comprehension	133–S	99							133
FRI–Fluid Reasoning	118	88					118		
VSI–Visual Spatial	122	93						122	
QRI–Quantitative Reasoning	117	87					117		
WMI–Working Memory	91–W	27				91			
AWMI–Auditory Working Memory	113	81					113		
PSI–Processing Speed	108–W	70				108			
Verbal Comprehension Subtests									
Similarities (VCI)*	16	98							16
Comprehension	13	84					13		
Vocabulary (VCI)*	16	98							16
Information	11	63				11			

Table 13.2 (*Continued*)

	Standard Score	Percentile	Standard Scores within Descriptive Category Ranges						
			Extremely Low	Low	Below Average	Average	Above Average	Superior	Very Superior
Fluid Reasoning Subtests									
Figure Weights (FRI)*	13	84					13		
Matrix Reasoning (FRI)*	13	84					13		
Arithmetic	13	84					13		
Picture Concepts	12	75				12			
Visual Spatial Subtests									
Block Design (VSI)*	12	75				12			
Visual Puzzles (VSI)	16	98							16
Quantitative Reasoning Subtests									
Figure Weights (QRI)	13	84					13		
Arithmetic (QRI)	13	84					13		
Working Memory Subtests									
Picture Span (WMI)	6—W	9		6					
Digit Span (WMI)*	11	63				11			
Letter–Number Sequencing	14	91						14	
Processing Speed Subtests									
Coding (PSI)*	10	50				10			
Symbol Search (PSI)	13	84					13		
Cancellation	10	50				10			

Note: Standard scores range from a low of 40 to a high of 160, with 100 as the average score.

The Full Scale IQ is derived from seven subtests from all five Primary Index scales. The General Ability Index (GAI) is derived from the six subtests from the six subtests contributing to the Verbal Comprehension, Fluid Reasoning, and Visual Spatial Indexes.

Note: Scaled scores range from a low of 1 to a high of 19, with 10 as the average score.

*denotes subtest scores used to derive the FSIQ. ( ) indicate the Index to which the subtest scores contribute. Abbreviations are:
VCI = Verbal Comprehension Index, FRI = Fluid Reasoning Index, VSI = Visual Spatial Index, QRI = Quantitative Reasoning Index, WMI = Working Memory Index, PSI = Processing Speed Index.

Executive Functions

Table 13.3   Colin's Delis–Kaplan Executive Function System (D–KEFS) Scores

| | Standard Score | Percentile | Standard Scores within Descriptive Category Ranges | | | | | | |
			Extremely Low	Low	Below Average	Average	Above Average	Superior	Very Superior
Verbal Fluency Test									
Letter Fluency	11	63				11			
Category Fluency	13	84					13		
Color Word Interference Test									
Color Naming Speed	9	37				9			
Color Naming Errors	–	30				30			
Word Reading Speed	10	50				10			
Word Reading Errors	–	100				Ave			
Inhibition Speed	4	2	4						
Inhibition Errors	7	16			7				
Inhibition/Switching Speed	6	9		6					
Inhibition/Switching Errors	7	16			7				
20 Questions									
Initial Abstraction	7	16			7				
Total Questions	3	1	3						
Weighted Achievement	2	<1	2						

Note: Scaled scores range from a low of 1 to a high of 19, with 10 as the average score.

Table 13.4   Colin's Wisconsin Card Sorting Test (WCST) Scores

| Indexes | Standard Score | Percentile | Standard Scores within Descriptive Category Ranges | | | | | | |
			Extremely Low	Low	Below Average	Average	Above Average	Superior	Very Superior
% Total Errors	112	79					112		
% Perseverative Frrors	109	73				109			
% Nonperseverative Errors	107	68				107			
Percentage of Conceptual-Level Responses	113	81					113		

Table 13.4   (Continued)

Performance Characteristics	Raw Score	Level	Standard Scores within Descriptive Category Ranges						
			Extremely Low	Low	Below Ave	Average	Above Average	Superior	Very Superior
Categories (Sets) Completed	6	Ave				Ave			
Trials to Complete 1st Category	11	Ave				Ave			
Failure to Maintain Set	0	Ave				Ave			

Trials to Completion for Categories 1–6: 11, 12, 26, 12, 13, 19

Note: Standard scores range from a low of 55 to a high of 145, with 100 as the average score. WCST scores are positively weighted; the higher the score, the better the level of performance; for example, the higher the score for Perseverative Errors, the lower the percentage of errors made relative to the standardization sample of same-age peers.

Memory for Auditorily Presented Verbal Information

Table 13.5   Colin's Children's Memory Scale (CMS) Scores

	Standard Score	Percentile	Standard Scores within Descriptive Category Ranges						
			Extremely Low	Low	Below Average	Average	Above Average	Superior	Very Superior
Immediate Recall of Story Details	11	63				11			
Immediate Recall of Story Themes	13	84					13		
Delayed Recall of Story Details	13	84					13		
Delayed Recall of Story Themes	14	91						14	
Delayed Recognition of Story Details	14	91						14	
Sequences (Verbal Fluency)	13	84					3		

Note: Scaled scores range from a low of 1 to a high of 19, with 10 as the average score.

Table 13.6   Colin's NEPSY–II Scores

	Standard Score	Percentile	Standard Scores within Descriptive Category Ranges						
			Extremely Low	Low	Below Average	Average	Above Average	Superior	Very Superior
Language									
Comprehension of Instructions	14	91						14	

Note: Scaled scores range from a low of 1 to a high of 19, with 10 as the average score.

Table 13.7   Colin's Process Assessment of the Learner–Second Edition: Diagnostic Assessment of Reading and Writing (PAL–II) Scores

	Standard Score	Percentile	Standard Scores within Descriptive Category Ranges						
			Extremely Low	Low	Below Average	Average	Above Average	Superior	Very Superior
Orthographic Processing									
Receptive Coding	7	16			7				
Word Choice Total Time	8	25				8			
Word Choice Total Correct	7	16			7				
Graphomotor Functioning (Handwriting)									
Alphabet Writing Legible Letter Writing	14	91						14	
Alphabet Writing Legible Letter Writing (Total)	9	37				9			
Alphabet Writing Total Time	13	84					13		
Copying Task A Legible Letters (15″)	10	50				10			
Copying Task A Total Legible Letters	9	37				9			
Copying Task A Total Time	14	91						14	
Copy Task B Legible Letters 30″	13	84					13		
Copy Task B Legible Letters 60″	14	91						14	
Copy Task B Legible Letters 90″	14	91						14	
Oral-Motor Functioning									
Rapid Automatic Switching— Words & Digits	13	84					13		

Note: Scaled scores range from a low of 1 to a high of 19, with 10 as the average score. Scaled scores and percentile ranks are based on grade-based (3rd grade) norms.

Table 13.8 Colin's WISC–V and KTEA–3 Basic Cognitive Processes and Abilities Scores

	Standard Score	Percentile	Standard Scores within Descriptive Category Ranges						
			Extremely Low	Low	Below Average	Average	Above Average	Superior	Very Superior
KTEA–3 Subtests									
Phonological Processing	118 (121)	88 (93)					118	(121)	
Object Naming Facility	92 (94)	30 (34)				92 (94)			
Letter Naming Facility	102 (104)	55 (61)				102 (104)			
WISC–V Subtests									
Naming Speed Literacy	111	77					111		
Naming Speed Quantity	106	66				106			

Note: Standard scores range from a low of 40 to a high of 160, with 100 as the average score. KTEA–3 standard scores and percentile ranks in the first row are based on grade-based (Winter 3rd grade) norms. Scores in the second row in parentheses ( ) are based on age-based norms for the age group 8–0 to 8–3. WISC–V standard scores and percentile ranks are based on age-based norms for the age group 8–0 to 8–3.

Academic Skills

Table 13.9 Colin's Kaufman Test of Educational Achievement–Third Edition (KTEA–3) Scores

	Standard Score	Percentile	Standard Scores within Descriptive Category Ranges						
			Extremely Low	Low	Below Average	Average	Above Average	Superior	Very Superior
Reading Subtests									
Letter-Word Recognition	115 (121)	84 (92)					115	(121)	
Nonsense Word Decoding	118 (123)	88 (94)					118	(123)	
Silent Reading Fluency	103 (111)	58 (77)				103	(111)	
Word Recognition Fluency	99 (104)	47 (61)				99 (104)			
Decoding Fluency	119 (120)	90 (91)						119 (120)	
Reading Vocabulary	107 (112)	68 (79)				107	(112)	
Reading Comprehension	107 (116)	68 (86)				107	(116)	

(*continued*)

Table 13.9 *(Continued)*

	Standard Score	Percentile	Extremely Low	Low	Below Average	Average	Above Average	Superior	Very Superior
Written Expression Subtests									
Spelling	98 (105)	45 (63)				98 (105)			
Written Expression	88 (94)	21 (34)			88	(94)			
Writing Fluency	78–97	7–42		78	(82)	99 (100)			
	(82)–(100)	(12)–(50)							
Mathematics Subtests									
Math Fluency	96 (102)	40 (55)				96 (102)			
Math Computation	87 (95)	19 (37)			87	(95)			
Math Concepts & Applications	122 (134)	93 (99)						122	(134)

Note: *See narrative text discussion of Written Expression assessment for an explanation of the multiple Writing Fluency scores. Standard scores range from a low of 40 to a high of 160, with 100 as the average score. Standard scores and percentile ranks in the first row are based on grade-based (Winter 3rd grade) norms. Scores in parentheses ( ) are based on age-based norms for the age group 8–0 to 8–3.

Executive Functions by Report

Table 13.10 Colin's Behavior Rating Inventory of Executive Functions (BRIEF) Scores

Scales	T-Scores and (Percentile Ranks)	
	Parents	Teacher
Inhibit	46 (46)	55 (75)
Shift	36 (9)	44 (45)
Emotional Control	36 (6)	45 (50)
Initiate	63 (88)	57 (70)
Working Memory	54 (69)	52 (65)
Plan/Organize	56 (76)	59 (83)
Organize Materials	61 (83)	61 (84)
Monitor	53 (69)	52 (68)

Note: T-scores range from a low of 10 to a high of 120 with 50 as the average score. The BRIEF ratings are negative indicators, that is, high scores indicate a lack of functioning in a category. For example, for the Item "Makes Careless Errors," a rating of "Often" earns 3 points, while a rating of "Never" earns only 1 point. Since high ratings reflect a lack of functioning, the higher a percentile rank for a Scale or Index, the greater the deficiency of behavior perceived by the rater.

Color Code Level Descriptors for Scores:

Typical Range	Mildly Elevated	Moderately Elevated	Highly Elevated

Table 13.11 Colin's ADHD Rating Scale–IV Scores

Scales	Percentile Ranks/Ranges	
	Parents	Teacher
Inattention	86	50–75
Hyperactivity/Impulsivity	80	50–75
Total Scale	84	50–75

Note: The ADHD IV ratings are negative indicators; that is, high scores indicate a lack of functioning in a category. For example, for the Item "Is easily distracted" a rating of "Very Often" earns 3 points, while a rating of "Never or Rarely" earns 0 points. Since high ratings reflect a lack of functioning, the higher a percentile rank for a Scale, the greater the deficiency of behavior perceived by the rater.

Color Code Level Descriptors for Scores:

Typical Range	Mildly Elevated	Moderately Elevated	Highly Elevated

Table 13.12   Colin's McCloskey Executive Functions Scales (MEFS) Results

Parent & Teacher Ratings		Self Rating	
AA	Always or almost always does on own without prompting	AA	I always or almost always do this on my own. I don't need to be prompted or reminded to do it.
F	Frequently does on own without prompting	F	I frequently do this on my own without prompting.
S	Seldom does it on own without being prompted or reminded to do it	S	I seldom do this on my own without being prompted or reminded to do it.
AP	Does this only after being prompted, reminded or cued to do it	AP	I do this only after being prompted or reminded to do it.
H	Only does it with direct assistance	DA	I can only do it with help.
UA	Cannot do even with direct assistance	UA	I can't do this, even when I get help with it.

Table 13.13   Colin's School Arena Results

Cluster	ExecutiveFunction	Parents	Teacher	Item
Attn	Aware	F	S	Knows what he or she should be doing for school tasks and knows when to do it.
Attn	Focus	S	S	Focuses attention on school tasks.
Attn	Sustain	S	AP	Sustains attention for school tasks until a task is completed.
Engage	Initiate	AP	S	Starts schoolwork.
Engage	Effort	AP	S	Puts adequate energy into school tasks.
Engage	Inhibit	F	F	Maintains emotional control when doing challenging schoolwork.
Engage	Pause	S	S	Returns to a school task after a brief pause.
Engage	Flexible	S	AP	Willing to try a different way to do school tasks when he or she gets stuck.
Engage	Flexible	AA	F	Accepts changes in schoolwork or school routines without getting upset about it.
Engage	Shift	F	S	Moves from one school task to another without difficulty.
Optimize	Modulate	F	S	Physical activity level fits the situation when doing school tasks.
Optimize	Modulate	AA	F	Emotional response fits the situation when working on school tasks.
Optimize	Monitor	AP	AP	Checks schoolwork to avoid careless errors on tests and other schoolwork.
Optimize	Monitor	S	AP	Checks to make sure that he or she has everything they need before leaving.
Optimize	Correct	S	AP	Corrects errors that are made in schoolwork.
Optimize	Balance	S	S	Balances the elements of a school assignment.
Efficiency	Sense Time	S	S	Keeps track of time when doing school tasks.
Efficiency	Pace	S	S	Changes pace when taking tests or doing school assignments.

(continued)

Table 13.13 (*Continued*)

Cluster	Executive Function	Parents	Teacher	Item
Efficiency	Routines	S	S	Uses well-rehearsed or practiced routines for school tasks.
Efficiency	Routines	S	S	Generate good ideas and gets them down on paper quickly and efficiently.
Efficiency	Routines	S	S	Uses routines and strategies to do well on tests.
Efficiency	Routines	S	S	Uses routines and strategies to get assignments and projects done.
Efficiency	Routines	AA	S	Participates in discussions about topics that he or she knows a lot about.
Efficiency	Routines	F	S	Brings home all the materials needed to complete homework and other school tasks.
Efficiency	Routines	AA	F	Hands in homework, assignments or important papers when they are completed.
Efficiency	Sequence	F	AA	Gets the steps in the right order when working on school tasks.
Memory	Working Memory	F	F	Can keep information in mind for short periods of time when doing school tasks.
Memory	Store/ Retrieve	S	S	Stores and recalls specific information about school subjects
Memory	Store/ Retrieve	F	F	Does well on tests that require recall of stored facts no matter what the format.
Inquiry	Gauge	S	S	Accurately estimates the difficulty of and what it takes to complete school tasks.
Inquiry	Anticipate	S	S	Anticipates events at school.
Inquiry	Estimate Time	S	AP	Accurately estimates how long it will take to do school tasks
Inquiry	Analyze	S	AP	Examines and analyzes things in more detail when doing school tasks.
Inquiry	Compare	F	AP	Evaluates the quality and/or adequacy of his or her work on school tasks.
Solution	Generate	S	S	Comes up with new ways to solve problems with school tasks.
Solution	Associate	S	S	Sees or understands how two or more things or ideas are similar in school.
Solution	Organize	AP	S	Organizes school tasks.
Solution	Plan	AP	S	Makes plans for school tasks.
Solution	Prioritize	AP	S	Orders school tasks according to their relevance, importance, or urgency.
Solution	Decide	AP	AP	Makes own decisions about what to do for school and/or when to do it.
SRealize	Self Analysis	O	S	Realistically analyzes and comments about his or her school performance.
SDeterm	Goal Setting	S	S	States realistic goals for schooling based on personal interests.
SDeterm	Goal Setting	O	S	States realistic goals for work beyond school based on personal interests.
SDeterm	Long-Term Planning	S	S	States realistic plans for accomplishing long-term schooling goals.
SDeterm	Long-Term Planning	S	N/R	States realistic plans for accomplishing long-term work goals.

Table 13.14   Colin's Self Arena Results

Cluster	Executive Function	Parents	Teacher	Item
Attn	Aware	AA	F	Is aware of own feelings, thoughts, and actions.
Attn	Focus	F	F	Focuses attention on own actions.
Attn	Sustain	F	F	Sustains attention to own actions.
Engage	Initiate	S	F	Does self-care tasks.
Engage	Effort	F	F	Puts adequate energy into taking care of self.
Engage	Inhibit	F	F	Considers the consequences before saying or doing things he or she may regret.
Engage	Inhibit	F	F	Controls emotional reactions well in frustrating situations.
Engage	Stop	F	F	Knows when to stop talking about a single topic.
Engage	Stop	S	F	Stops playing a game or stops doing something that is fun when asked to do so.
Engage	Stop	F	AA	Stops doing harmful or bothersome things to self when asked to do so.
Engage	Stop	AA	AA	Stops negatively feeling or thinking the same way about himself or herself.
Engage	Pause	F	F	Returns to what they were thinking about or doing after a brief pause.
Engage	Flexible	F	F	Accepts the need to think about or feel differently about himself or herself.
Engage	Flexible	AA	F	Accepts when it is necessary to change personal habits that cause problems.
Engage	Shift	F	S	Changes personal habits when they are causing problems.
Optimize	Modulate	F	S	Adjusts physical activity level when working alone.
Optimize	Modulate	F	F	Avoids being overstimulated or understimulated by sights, sounds, or touches.
Optimize	Monitor	F	F	Checks on his or her appearance, cleanliness, and personal hygiene.
Optimize	Correct	F	AA	Changes his or her opinions about self or others that were caused by misperception.
Optimize	Balance	AA	F	Maintains a balance in his or her own activities.
Efficiency	Sense Time	S	S	Keeps track of time when working independently.
Efficiency	Pace	F	S	Changes pace when working independently.
Efficiency	Routines	S	AA	Uses well-rehearsed or practiced routines for hygiene and self-care.
Efficiency	Sequence	F	S	Gets the steps in the right order when performing personal care tasks.
Memory	Working Memory	F	F	Can keep information in mind when doing things alone.

(*continued*)

Table 13.14   (*Continued*)

Cluster	Executive Function	Parents	Teacher	Item
Memory	Store/ Retrieve	F	F	Stores and recalls specific information about himself or herself.
Memory	Store/ Retrieve	F	AA	Does well in situations that require recall of facts about himself or herself.
Inquiry	Gauge	F	F	Figures out what it takes to maintain self-control in difficult situations.
Inquiry	Anticipate	S	F	Anticipates the consequences of his or her own thoughts, feeling, and actions.
Inquiry	Estimate Time	S	AP	Accurately estimates how long it will take to do things when alone.
Inquiry	Analyze	F	F	Examines and analyzes in more detail own thoughts and feelings about self.
Inquiry	Compare	AA	S	Evaluates the quality and/or adequacy of his or her thoughts and feelings.
Solution	Generate	S	F	Comes up with new ways of thinking or feeling about self.
Solution	Associate	F	F	Sees or understands how things he or she has done or thought are alike.
Solution	Organize	AA	F	Organizes his or her own thoughts and feelings.
Solution	Plan	AA	F	Makes plans for the use of his or her own time.
Solution	Prioritize	F	F	Orders own thoughts and feelings or personal activities according to urgency.
Solution	Decide	AA	F	Makes own decisions about what to do and when to do it when alone.
SRealize	Self Aware	S	VO	Makes realistic comments about own mental and emotional strengths and weaknesses.
SRealize	Self Aware	O	O	Makes realistic comments about his or her own physical abilities.
SRealize	Self Aware	O	O	Makes realistic comments about what he or she feels or thinks about himself or herself.
SRealize	Self Analysis	O	S	Realistically analyzes and comments about his or her ability to manage self.
SDeterm	Goal Setting	VO	N/R	Expresses strong desires to make his or her own decisions about what to do.
SDeterm	Long-Term Planning	O	S	States realistic plans for accomplishing social and/or personal goals.
SGenerate	Self Gener	S	N/R	Asks questions about the meaning or purpose of life.
SGenerate	Self Gener	N/R	S	Asks questions about the purpose or meaning of school.
SGenerate	Self Gener	S	N/R	Asks questions about why we exist.
SGenerate	Self Gener	N/R	N/R	Asks questions about what happens to us when we die.
SGenerate	Self Gener	S	S	Wants to know why things are considered right or wrong.
SGenerate	Self Gener	O	S	Asks questions about the right way to treat other people.

Table 13.15   Colin's Social Arena Results

Cluster	Executive Function	Parents	Teacher	Item
Attn	Aware	AA	F	Makes eye contact with, listens to, and touches others in an appropriate way in social situations.
Attn	Focus	F	F	Focuses attention on others in social situations.
Attn	Sustain	F	F	Sustains attention to others in social situations.
Engage	Initiate	AA	F	Initiates socially appropriate interactions with other students.
Engage	Effort	AA	F	Puts adequate energy into interacting with others.
Engage	Inhibit	F	F	Waits for turn.
Engage	Inhibit	AA	AA	Refrains from acts of physical aggression.
Engage	Inhibit	AA	F	Does not make inappropriate or thoughtless comments.
Engage	Inhibit	F	F	Maintains emotional control when disagreeing with others.
Engage	Stop	S	F	Stops doing things that annoy others when asked to do so.
Engage	Pause	F	F	Pauses to listen to what another person has to say during conversations.
Engage	Flexible	F	F	Accepts a good idea when it is what most others in a group want to do.
Engage	Flexible	AA	F	Accepts changes in a person he or she knows or to accept unfamiliar persons.
Engage	Shift	AA	F	Changes from one activity to another in social situations without difficulty.
Optimize	Modulate	F	F	Physical activity level fits the situation when working in a group.
Optimize	Modulate	F	F	Emotional response fits the situation when interacting with others.
Optimize	Monitor	F	F	Recognizes situations in which his or her behavior bothers or upsets others.
Optimize	Correct	F	AA	Apologizes when aware of offending others.
Optimize	Balance	AA	F	Maintains a balance in social situations.
Efficiency	Sense Time	S	S	Keeps track of time when talking to or doing things with others.
Efficiency	Pace	F	F	Changes pace in social situations.
Efficiency	Routines	F	AA	Uses well-rehearsed or practiced social greetings or conversation starters.
Efficiency	Sequence	F	S	Gets the order of events right when telling stories or explaining things to others.
Memory	Working Memory	F	AP	Can keep information in mind for short periods of time when talking with others.
Memory	Store/ Retrieve	F	S	Stores and recalls specific information about others or about social situations.

(continued)

Table 13.15 (*Continued*)

Cluster	Executive Function	Parents	Teacher	Item
Memory	Store/ Retrieve	F	S	Does well in social situations that require recall of facts about others.
Inquiry	Gauge	AA	F	Figures out how to interact appropriately in various social situations.
Inquiry	Anticipate	F	F	Anticipates how what he or she says or does will affect others.
Inquiry	Est. Time	S	S	Accurately estimates how long it will take to do things with others.
Inquiry	Analyze	F	F	Examines and analyzes in more detail what others are saying or doing in social situations.
Inquiry	Compare	AA	S	Evaluates the quality and/or adequacy of his or her social interactions.
Solution	Generate	F	F	Come up with new ideas about things to say to, or do with, others.
Solution	Associate	F	F	Sees or understands how one social situation can be similar to another.
Solution	Organize	F	F	Organizes age appropriate social activities.
Solution	Plan	AA	F	Makes plans for age appropriate social activities.
Solution	Prioritize	F	F	Handles social activities according to their relevance, importance or urgency.
Solution	Decide	F	F	Makes own decisions about what to do with others and/or when to do it.
SRealize	Other Aware	O	O	Makes realistic comments about other's mental and emotional strengths and weaknesses.
SRealize	Other Aware	O	S	Makes realistic comments about the physical abilities of others.
SRealize	Other Aware	O	S	Makes realistic comments about what other people feel or think about others.
SRealize	Other Aware	O	S	Makes realistic comments about what others feel or think about him or her.
SRealize	Other Aware	O	S	Makes realistic comments about what other people feel or think about themselves.
SRealize	Self Analysis	O	S	Realistically analyze his or her ability to know what others think or feel about them.

Note: SRealize = Self-Realization; SDeter = Self-Determination; SGenerate and Self Gener = Self Generation.

CASE 12—DEREK, AGE 13: A TEENAGE BOY EXHIBITING PHONOLOGICAL DYSLEXIA AND EXECUTIVE FUNCTION DIFFICULTIES

George McCloskey

Introduction

Derek was very reluctant to admit that he was experiencing significant difficulties with processing information during classes and when studying and taking tests. During the assessment, it was clear that both a phonological dyslexia and executive function and executive skills difficulties (including many typically associated with a diagnosis of ADHD) were negatively impacting his performance of many tasks.

Derek's case exemplifies the need to look beyond the FSIQ and primary Index scores to obtain a clear picture of his cognitive functioning. Note the pattern of scores earned on the reading subtests that were administered despite years of high-quality tutoring using direct multisensory instruction of alphabet principle and synthetic phonics:

WISC–V Similarities 12, Comprehension 10, Vocabulary 11, Information 11

KTEA–3 Silent Reading Fluency 103

WIAT–III Reading Comprehension 101 but KTEA–3 *Reading Comprehension 88

KTEA–3 Word Recognition Fluency 92 but KTEA–3 *Letter-Word Recognition 75

KTEA–3 Reading Vocabulary 90

KTEA–3 Phonological Processing 83

KTEA–3 Decoding Fluency 74 and KTEA–3 Nonsense Word Decoding 64

This is an overarching pattern that I frequently see in the performance of phonologic dyslexics—average or better reasoning combined with average listening and reading comprehension that is better than word list reading, which is better than nonsense word decoding. This pattern has been discussed and documented in other work (Pennington, 1991, 2008).

When executive capacity difficulties also are present, dissociations such as those noted with asterisks above often occur along with variations in performance of tasks involving speeded performance. Typically, fluency measures are poorer than untimed skills measures (Word Recognition Fluency is lower than Letter–Word Recognition; Decoding Fluency is lower than Nonsense Word Decoding). For Derek, these dissociations were reversed; when speed was combined with high-frequency words or simpler decoding patterns, Derek was able to offer enough correct responses to earn scores that were higher than when he was struggling with attempting to read more difficult words or decode more challenging patterns within nonsense words; when these latter tasks were attempted, Derek was unable to balance speed and accuracy, which resulted in many word reading and decoding errors on words and nonsense words that he was able to pronounce correctly when cued to slow down and look carefully at all the letters.

Many specific assessment techniques were used with Derek to assess his use or disuse of executive functions. Of particular note was the cascading production decrements that reflected executive function difficulties. One such cascade involved control of the orthography-phonology connection (KTEA–3 Letter–Naming Facility 100 but WISC–V Naming Speed Literacy [rapid automatic switching task involving executive functions] only 78, and D-KEFS Color–Word Interference Inhibition scaled score only 1 and Inhibition Switching scaled score only 4). Another cascade involved control of the writing process (KTEA–3 Writing Fluency 101 but WJ–III Writing Fluency only 81). Two other cascades reflected the interaction of Derek's phonological dyslexia with his executive function difficulties and their impact on verbal fluency (D-KEFS Category Fluency scaled score 9 but [Initial] Letter Fluency scaled score only 6) and on reading comprehension (WIAT–III Reading Comprehension 101 [the directions allow for cueing to improve questionable responses, a factor that greatly improved Derek's ability to eventually produce a 2-point response] but KTEA–3 Reading Comprehension only 88 [Derek had to read and answer the comprehension questions without any assistance or cues for clarification]).

Derek's case is an excellent example of the important distinction between executive functions and executive skills (see McCloskey, Gilmartin, & Stanco, 2014, for an explanation of the difference between executive skills and executive functions). Derek was keenly aware of the need to focus and sustain attention (the executive functions of Perceive, Focus and Sustain were being used effectively), but he nevertheless struggled greatly with his actual efforts to focus and sustain attention due to deficient attention skills. While the commands to attend were being delivered through executive function cueing, the activation and use of the neural networks involved in the acts of focusing and sustaining attention were not developed enough to enable their consistent application of the skill of attending for long periods of time.

The assessment revealed that a major difficulty for Derek was a lack of knowledge of and/or use of strategies that he could consciously identify and apply in situations where his cognitive capacities were not getting the job done. Derek's parents initially were not willing to have Derek evaluated by a psychiatrist regarding the ADHD-like symptoms reported by parents and observed during the assessment. By the end of an hour discussion, however, it appeared that there had been some movement toward keeping an open mind to a psychiatric evaluation.

Derek's case also highlights the distinction between learning difficulties and producing difficulties as well as the interplay between the two when they co-occur. Derek's phonological dyslexia has impeded, but not stopped, the development of reading skills. Derek's strong motivation and self-determination (an

upper-level executive function) have enabled him to persevere in his efforts to improve his reading. Derek's struggles with learning to read and write are compounded by his executive skill and executive function difficulties. These executive capacity difficulties reduce Derek's reading and writing production by making it difficult for him to focus and sustain attention for reading and writing tasks. They also make it difficult for him to effectively coordinate all the processes, abilities, skills, and knowledge bases needed to read and write, thereby compromising his comprehension of what he reads and interfering with his ability to express his thoughts effectively when writing. Derek's problems with math are not the result of any specific process deficits that interfere with processing quantitative information and creating quantitative mental representations, any lack of quantitative reasoning ability, or any lack of knowledge or skill regarding how to perform calculations. Derek's problems with math are due to producing difficulties associated with his executive function and executive skill deficits including problems with focusing and sustaining attention, impulsive responding, lack of monitoring and correcting performance, and poor direction of retrieval of the information needed to successfully complete specific math problems.

Given the nature of Derek's executive skill difficulties, a diagnosis of ADHD could be warranted, thereby providing a clear link between his producing difficulties and a familiar clinical diagnosis. It is important to keep in mind, however, that many students with producing difficulties exhibit specific executive skill and/or executive function difficulties that may be very different from those associated with ADHD (McCloskey, Hewitt, Henzel & Eusebio, 2009; McCloskey & Perkins, 2012). In these cases, the specific profile of executive function weaknesses may not match any specific diagnosis other than executive dysfunction, which in actuality is a classification offered by the World Health Organization (*ICD*-9-CM code *799.55 Frontal lobe and executive function deficit*; World Health Organization, 1980, 2004), but not offered in *DSM-5* (American Psychiatric Association, 2013).

Psychoeducational Evaluation Report

NAME: Derek

REPORT DATE: XX/XX/XXXX

SCHOOL DISTRICT: X

SCHOOL: X Middle School

BIRTH DATE: XX/XX/XXXX

GRADE: 8 (Fall XXXX)

DATES OF EVALUATION: XX/XX, XX/XX/XXXX

C.A. AT EVALUATION: 13–5

CURRENT EDUCATIONAL PROGRAM: General education curriculum with in-class support and supplemental reading instruction

Reason for Referral/Purpose of Report

Derek's mother requested that a neuropsychologically oriented psychoeducational evaluation be completed to assist in determining Derek's current profile of cognitive and academic functioning strengths and weaknesses and to help with clarifying educational goals and specifying an appropriate educational program and/or methods of instruction for meeting educational goals.

Information from the Parent

Derek's mother expressed concerns about Derek's ability to handle his academic coursework during the current school year. Mrs. M noted that Derek struggled with his courses in seventh grade and that the struggle has continued through the first half of eighth grade. She stated that Derek was diagnosed with dyslexia at an early age and received tutoring at YY for several years to improve his reading skills.

Although Derek has been classified as a student with a learning disability and has received resource room assistance in previous years, Derek's involvement with the resource room was limited in seventh grade due to his strong desire to be included in as many general education classes as possible and remains limited in eighth grade despite his struggles in seventh grade.

Although Derek feels better about being in general education classes, Mrs. M thinks that the pace of instruction is a bit too fast for Derek; he struggles to keep up with homework assignments and with studying for tests. She noted that she spends a great deal of time assisting Derek with organizing his belongings, keeping track of and completing assignments, and preparing for tests. Some accommodations, such as leaving the classroom to take tests on a computer-based system, do not seem particularly helpful. In addition, some of the assessment procedures used by teachers, such as needing to copy math test problems from the test sheet to a worksheet and then transferring answers back to the test sheet to complete multiple-choice test questions, also seem to be problematic for Derek. The additional steps required in this process often result in errors.

According to Mrs. M, some of the specific difficulties that Derek is encountering with coursework included trouble with focusing and organizing his thoughts for writing assignments; she indicated that Derek can talk about the ideas he has and what he wants to write, but he has a great deal of trouble getting his ideas onto paper in an organized, coherent manner. She also noted that Derek has a great deal of difficulty with recalling the procedures for completing math calculations. His recall for math seems to vary from one day to the next; at times, Derek is able to remember what he was studying for math, but, at other times, he seems unable to recall what he had been studying and practicing. Science presents as a challenge for Derek as well; the curriculum is not textbook-based, and study notes often are not available for use by Derek.

Mrs. M is hoping that the current assessment will provide a clearer picture of Derek's cognitive and academic strengths and weaknesses so that specific accommodations or strategies can be utilized in order to help Derek improve his academic performance. She also is wondering if the public school program is able to address Derek's educational needs in an appropriate manner.

Assessment Procedures

Derek was seen for an evaluation by Dr. George McCloskey, a consulting school psychologist, at the request of Derek's mother.

On XX/XX/XXXX, Derek was administered the following in a morning evaluation session that lasted approximately 3 hours with no formal rest breaks:

Student Interview

Wechsler Intelligence Scale for Children–Fifth Edition (WISC–V) (primary and other selected subtests)

Wisconsin Card Sorting Test (WCST)

On XX/XX/XXXX, Derek was administered the following in a morning evaluation session that lasted approximately 3 hours with no formal rest breaks:

Children's Memory Scale (CMS) (selected subtests)

Delis-Kaplan Executive Function System (D-KEFS) (selected subtests)

NEPSY–II Developmental Neuropsychological Assessment (selected subtest)

Wechsler Individual Achievement Test–Third Edition (WIAT–III) (selected subtests)

Kaufman Test of Educational Achievement–Third Edition (KTEA–3) (selected subtests)

Rey Complex Figure Test (RCFT)

In addition to the evaluation sessions involving interviews and direct assessment, Derek's mother completed the McCloskey Executive Functions Scales (MEFS) Parent Form and Derek completed the MEFS Self-Report Form.

Because the family may be moving to a different school district in the very near future, Derek's mother requested that school staff not be involved in the assessment process, that a school-based observation of Derek not be conducted by the psychologist, and that recommendations be provided in a general manner so that they could be applied at a new school should the need arise.

Summary of Derek's Assessment Performance

Based on the assessment work completed and the information gathered and interpreted, the following summary, conclusions, and recommendations are offered.

Conclusions

Derek is a physically active 13-year-old boy who enjoys the challenges of individual sports and is socially engaged with friends. He has been able to earn passing grades in all school subjects but often has difficulty performing consistently on tests and assignments. He enjoys reading despite the challenges he has faced with learning to read. He is very determined to be successful in school and is willing to work hard to achieve good grades, but the difficulties he is experiencing with school have been a source of frustration for him and his mother.

Derek was diagnosed with dyslexia in early elementary school and has received tutoring and special education services to help him improve his reading skills. Derek has a strong desire to participate only in general education courses, but he struggled in seventh grade with the pace of instruction, assignments, and tests; these difficulties have continued into the eighth grade.

During the current assessment, Derek demonstrated good problem-solving, language, and visuospatial abilities. He also demonstrated effective use of memory systems when the information involved had a meaningful context such as retelling stories or retrieving word definitions.

Table 13.16   Summary of Derek's Assessment Performance

Strengths	Challenges
Reasoning Abilities	
Derek demonstrated average to above-average ability to reason with language.	Derek frequently responded to test items in a very impulsive manner; he seemed compelled to provide an answer very quickly, but frequently would monitor his initial response and make changes to it almost immediately after providing it.
Derek demonstrated at least average ability to reason with nonverbal information such as pictures and geometric designs; process-oriented assessment procedures indicted that Derek's ability to reason with nonverbal information is much better developed than what he was able to demonstrate during the standardized administration of each task.	Derek's ability to reason with quantity was compromised by a lack of effective strategies to ensure efficient use of working memory and brief lapses of attention.
Derek demonstrated average ability to reason with quantities.	Derek demonstrated the ability to direct reasoning applied with nonverbal visual materials when specific direction was not provided by the psychologist, but he applied this ability inconsistently.
Language Abilities	
Derek experienced no difficulties with comprehending instructions for tasks or with following the examiner in conversation. Derek demonstrated an effective command of grammar, syntax, and morphology and used these skills to provide well-articulated responses during the assessment and to express his thoughts effectively in conversation.	Although Derek demonstrated effective receptive language abilities, he performed poorly on some standardized measures of receptive language. Derek's poor performance with these tasks appeared to be due to an inability to sustain attention and the inconsistent application of working memory capacities rather than variability in receptive language capacities.
Derek demonstrated average basic language fluency ability when tasks did not involve the use of executive functions to direct and integrate retrieval and production.	Derek struggled with tasks of basic language fluency and speed when these tasks required the use of executive functions to direct and integrate task performance. He was not able to exercise the executive control needed to balance speed and accuracy while inhibiting responses or when inhibiting and shifting responses.
Visual Processing	
Derek demonstrated at least average visual perception and discrimination abilities, but these were applied inconsistently, often resulting in below-average scores on specific tasks requiring the use of these abilities.	Although Derek demonstrated effective use of visuospatial processing capacities with some tasks, these capacities often were applied in a very slow, inefficient, or disorganized manner; as a result, he often earned scores that were much lower than would have been the case had Derek been able to engage executive functions to effectively engage his abilities in a consistent manner.

(*continued*)

Table 13.16 *(Continued)*

Strengths	Challenges
Memory Capacities Applied with Auditorily Presented Verbal Information	
Derek demonstrated at least average capacity for initially registering information in immediate memory, holding and manipulating information in working memory, and storing and retrieving information from recent and remote long-term storage when the information being presented was highly contextual and meaningful.	Derek earned scores in the below-average range and lower on many tasks that required the holding and manipulating of information before providing an answer. These tasks were most difficult for Derek when they involved information that was lacking in a broader context or meaning beyond the assessment situation (e.g., repeating a randomly ordered series of numbers in reverse).
	The specific difficulties that Derek encountered only with some tasks involving memory capacities suggests that the difficulties were more likely to be due to inefficient use of executive functions to recognize the need for generating and applying effective strategies for initially registering, holding, manipulating, storing, and retrieving information rather than any specific deficits in memory capacity.
Memory Capacities Applied with Visually Presented Nonverbal Images	
	Derek's performance on a task requiring the use of immediate visual memory for objects produced a score in the below-average range.
Processing Speed with Nonacademic Tasks	
When tasks did not require much in the way of executive control of production, Derek earned scores mostly in the average range for nonacademic and academic speeded tasks.	When tasks required increased executive control of production, Derek earned scores in the below-average to extremely low ranges for nonacademic and academic speeded tasks.
Reading Skills	
Derek earned reading comprehension scores in the average range when required to read sight words quickly, when required to read sentences and make judgments about the accuracy of each sentence, and when required to read paragraphs and answer questions about the content of each paragraph.	Derek only earned a score in the below-average range when he was required to read passages and read and answer the comprehension questions.
	Derek earned scores in the extremely low range when required to read lists of words and decode lists of nonsense words; when reading word lists, Derek demonstrated a lack of inhibition, frequently misreading words by substituting a familiar word that started with the same letter or letter cluster as the word on the page. Derek also had difficulty balancing speed and accuracy in his word reading; the faster Derek tried to read, the more frequent the word reading errors occurred.

Table 13.16   (*Continued*)

Strengths	Challenges
Written Expression Skills	
Derek earned a score in the average range when writing sentences that matched pictures.	When the demand for executive control of writing increased, Derek only earned a score in the below-average range when required to write sentences that matched pictures and to use specific words in each sentence.
Math Skills	
	Derek earned scores in the below-average to extremely low ranges on tasks that assessed the accuracy of math computation and mental math skills.
	Derek also exhibited executive function difficulties when attempting to complete math calculations. He sometimes confused operation signs, adding instead of subtracting, or vice versa. He often got confused about the order of the steps in the calculation process for tasks such as long division and multiplication of multidigit numbers.
Attention and Effort during Assessment Sessions	
Despite the fact that each evaluation session lasted almost 3 hours, Derek was able to sustain a good level of effort throughout the assessment sessions without showing signs of fatigue.	Although Derek was outwardly extremely compliant and readily engaged with every task administered, Derek struggled greatly in his attempts to focus and sustain his attention for each task.
Parent and Self Ratings of Executive Functions	
	Derek's mother identified multiple self-regulation executive function and executive skill deficits within the school arena across the 7 clusters of Attention, Engagement, Optimization, Efficiency, Memory, Inquiry, and Solution.
Within both the MEFS Self and Social Arenas, ratings provided by Derek and his mother were more consistent, with executive function strengths outnumbering weaknesses.	Derek's mother's ratings did indicate some executive function difficulties within the Self and Social arenas within the Engagement, Optimization, Efficiency, and Inquiry clusters.
Both Derek and his mother rated Derek as being very self-determined and usually aware of himself and of others.	Derek's self-ratings did not acknowledge any difficulties with the use of executive functions or executive skills to complete school tasks, reflecting a lack of adequate self-analysis.
Social/Emotional Functioning	
Although this area was not formally assessed with rating scales, interviews of Derek and his mother did not reveal any concerns that might be indicative of difficulties with social or emotional functioning.	

Derek's cognitive strengths were countered by very slow processing speed for many tasks and a number of executive function deficits. These included difficulties with focusing and sustaining attention despite willingness to engage with and exert effort for tasks; difficulties with inhibiting impulsive responding; difficulties with consistently directing the use of reasoning, language, visuospatial, and memory capacities, and difficulties with monitoring his performance for accuracy.

The difficulties that Derek encountered when earning below-average or lower scores reflected a lack of use of executive functions to generate and apply strategies that focus on ensuring efficient performance. Specific strategies that were lacking included:

- a strategy for focusing and sustaining attention during longer tasks;
- a strategy for conducting efficient hypothesis testing of problem-solving solutions;
- a strategy for efficient use of immediate and working memory capacities; and
- a strategy for efficient retrieval of information from long-term storage.

Derek's inability to consistently direct the use of his cognitive abilities often resulted in scores in the below-average range and lower. Had Derek been able to more effectively direct consistent production using the abilities that he does possess, he would have been able to earn scores in the above-average to superior ranges for many tasks.

Derek demonstrated average reading comprehension skills; however, he exhibited difficulties with word reading and word decoding skills as well as a very slow reading rate. These difficulties are consistent with his diagnosis of dyslexia and are likely to impact his ability to complete assignments that require a great deal of reading, especially if the reading material is more complex in nature. He also struggled with a basic writing fluency task that required increased executive function control to handle constraints placed on the writing process (use of specific words in sentences) and performed poorly with basic math fact and math calculation tasks. Derek's executive function difficulties were apparent when performing academic tasks; he frequently misread words on impulse and was unable to balance speed and accuracy when completing math fact items; he made many errors with math calculations that involved lack of attention to operation signs, and he confused the steps in the order of operations of multistep calculations.

Although some students use their executive functions to identify the need for generating and applying strategies and for directing the generation of their own strategies, many students need to be taught strategies that they can use and then be cued to use these strategies in the situations where they are needed. Based on the data collected during this assessment, it is clear that Derek is a student who requires direct instruction in the development and use of cognitive strategies that would address the difficulties listed above.

In addition to Derek's lack of use of effective cognitive strategies during direct assessment, Derek's mother completed rating forms and identified several areas of difficulty with the use of self-regulation executive capacities. These difficulties encompassed both executive function deficits wherein Derek needed to be reminded or prompted to perform and executive skill deficits wherein Derek was judged unable to perform unless direct assistance was provided and, at times, he was not able to perform even when such direct assistance was provided. Derek's mother identified self-regulation executive function and executive skill deficits within the 7 clusters of Attention, Engagement, Optimization, Efficiency, Memory, Inquiry, and Solution. These difficulties were most pervasive when dealing with school tasks, although some difficulties were identified in the Self arena and, to a much lesser degree, in the Social arena.

Derek's mother indicated that Derek often demonstrates awareness of self and others but does not always engage in realistic self-analysis. In contrast to the input from Derek's mother,

Derek rated himself as not having any executive function or executive skill deficits and as usually demonstrating realistic self-analysis.

Derek and his mother both rated Derek as often or very often demonstrating a high degree of self-determination. Derek's high level of self-determination also is evident in his strong desire to be placed in general education for all his courses. Although Derek is a very self-determined individual and wants to be viewed by others as very competent and self-sufficient, the executive function difficulties that he demonstrates combined with his reading disability make it difficult for him to demonstrate the level of self-competency and self-sufficiency that he desires.

The executive function and executive skill difficulties identified by Derek's mother and observed directly during the current assessment have resulted in inconsistent or inadequate academic production that has led to a great deal of frustration on the part of Derek and his mother.

The results of the current evaluation indicate that while Derek does have a specific learning disability in the form of dyslexia, he also exhibits producing difficulties that are related to his executive function difficulties. When learning does not occur as well as might be expected, it is likely to be a lack of effective, efficient generation and use of strategies that is at fault rather than a lack of capacity to learn new material. When demonstrating what has been learned through tests or assignments, Derek's executive function and executive skill difficulties are likely to result in inconsistent performance; he often works slowly but responds impulsively, loses his focus and does not sustain attention, manages his time inefficiently, makes errors that he does not correct, and does not generate or apply efficient strategies for problem solving.

It is important to note that many of the specific executive functions that were identified as most problematic for Derek by his mother involved focusing and sustaining attention, responding impulsively, maintaining an inflexible stance, and an inability to stop ongoing perceiving, feeling,

thinking, and acting. All of these are hallmarks of the executive function difficulties most common among individuals diagnosed with ADHD.

It is important to recognize that Derek's executive function difficulties are likely to be reflecting maturational delays in the development of specific frontal lobe neural circuits rather than the result of any type of neural damage or deficit. Although Derek is experiencing growth in his capacity for accessing and using executive functions and executive skills, his rate of growth is likely to be somewhat slower than same-age peers, resulting in a relative level of immaturity in the use of some of these capacities when compared with his same-age peers. Fortunately, it is likely that Derek will gain greater access to the executive functions that are most problematic for him simply with the passage of time, but his development will likely continue to lag behind that of same-age peers. Interventions aimed at improving Derek's capacity for accessing and using executive functions for self-regulation may eventually help to reduce the gap between Derek and his same-age peers.

At this point in time, Derek would benefit from a greater understanding of the nature of his difficulties and instruction in strategies that he can learn and use to begin to improve his self-regulation capacities. It is important for Derek to understand that these strategies can be effective, but they will only be effective if he is committed to learning and applying them on a regular basis. Additionally, it is very possible that the success of instructional interventions may hinge on effective pharmacological treatment designed to enable Derek to gain greater access to the cognitive strategies that he can learn to use.

Recommendations

The results of this evaluation have been shared with Derek's mother and will be shared with school staff on XX/XX/XXXX. A set of general recommendations is provided here as a starting point for discussion with Derek, his mother, and school staff regarding an appropriate educational program for Derek. Additional and/or more specific recommendations for Derek's educational program will be discussed at the meeting with Derek, his mother, and school staff, and these will be used to revise the recommendations provided here. The results of this assessment also should be shared with a physician who can further assess issues related to ADHD.

What Derek Can Do for Himself to Improve Mental Functions and Manage His Reactions to Frustrating Situations

1. Derek can try to accept the fact that he demonstrates many executive function difficulties that are making it difficult for him to consistently produce at a high level with his school courses.
2. Derek can recognize the need to learn strategies that could help him to improve his performance on school assignments and tests.
3. Derek can continue to maintain a positive attitude toward school and learning and devote more time and effort to exploring college majors and career options that might interest him.
4. Derek can continue to strive to be highly self-sufficient and self-competent but also acknowledge that he will need some assistance in order to learn how to compensate for his executive function difficulties.

What Derek's Mother Can Do to Help Derek Gain Academic Success

1. Continue to be supportive of Derek's efforts in school and continue to help Derek see school as a positive and important influence in his life.
2. Continue to communicate directly with school staff to monitor Derek's academic progress and to ensure that Derek's educational needs are being addressed properly.
3. Consult with a physician to determine if pharmacological interventions would help Derek improve his ability to focus and sustain attention and inhibit impulsive responding.

4. If pharmacological interventions are tried, Derek should be monitored closely to determine if desired effects are being achieved and/or if undesired side effects are occurring. If Derek exhibits any unusual behaviors while taking medication, these should be reported to his physician as soon as possible.
5. During discussions with Derek, use brain-based language to remind him that the difficulties that he is encountering are a result of the state of his brain functioning rather than a conscious choice on his part. When specific neural networks in Derek's frontal lobes are depleted, he is much less able to focus and sustain his attention and effort for school-related tasks. This is the case with all children but, for Derek, the depletion of this frontal lobe neural network occurs more often than it does for other children of similar age. With conscious efforts to change, application of learned strategies, and maturation over time, Derek is likely to show an increase in the frequency and duration of his ability to focus and sustain attention and inhibit impulsive responding as a result of the strengthening of this frontal lobe neural network. Patience will be required as this developmental process unfolds.

What Educators Can Do to Help Derek Improve Cognitive, Social/Emotional, and Adaptive Functioning and Achieve Academic Success

Based on Derek's specific profile of cognitive and academic strengths and weaknesses, he would benefit greatly from the following:

1. Placement in general education courses whenever possible with assistive technology supports.
2. An assistive technology assessment to help identify those technology supports that would be most effective; for example, the use of an iPad and headphones during classes.
3. A set of books to keep at home or access to online versions of course textbooks or course materials.

During classroom instruction, the following accommodations and instructional approaches should be used:

1. Given Derek's slow speed when reading and writing and his difficulties with sustaining attention, he should be afforded extra time to complete tests and assignments and should be allowed to use a word processor instead of handwriting in situations where keyboarding would enable him to increase his written production. Additionally, Derek could be provided with a skeletal outline of class notes or a copy of teacher-provided notes.
2. A reduction in the amount of assigned homework is warranted.
3. Cueing and prompting for attention during class will help Derek to focus his efforts on his schoolwork.
4. Use of testing formats that enable Derek to demonstrate his knowledge rather than require him to overcome his executive function difficulties; for example, allowing Derek to record his answers directly on test forms instead of using separate answer sheets.
5. Allow for retakes of tests after Derek reviews his mistakes; use the retake score as the actual grade.

Additionally, Derek would benefit from direct instruction designed to teach:

1. Study skills strategies that specifically address note taking, storing and retrieving information, and organizing newly learned information.
2. Strategies for test taking.
3. Strategies to improve writing skills. The most effective approach here would be the self-regulated strategy development approach described by Graham, MacArthur, and Fitzgerald (2007).
4. Strategies to improve comprehension of material read for classes.
5. Strategies for improving the effective application of the decoding skills that have been taught in order to improve word level reading skills.
6. Strategies for checking his work for errors and correcting errors that he finds.

The evidence-based literature sources for instructional techniques that would help Derek to develop and then self-regulate strategies can be found in the professional literature using the search term "Cognitive Strategy Instruction." An excellent open-source reference for these strategies is the website maintained by the University of Nebraska–Lincoln located at cehs.unl.edu/csi.

Detailed Description of Findings and Interpretation of Assessment Results

Assessment Session Observations and Student Interview   In an interview prior to the start of testing, Derek appeared to be comfortable in the presence of the psychologist and readily conversed about his interests and school. Derek conversed in a very natural manner, clearly articulated his thoughts and feelings, and appeared to be expressing himself in a very forthright manner. His affect was appropriate for the situation, and he demonstrated an appropriate range of emotional reactions when expressing his views. Derek appeared to be in a good mood during both assessment sessions, and he did not present as depressed or anxious in a manner that would affect the outcome of the assessment. In all his interactions with the psychologist during both evaluation sessions, Derek acted in a very mature manner that gave an impression of a high degree of personal competence and control. He used formal greetings and was very respectful when addressing the psychologist and others. He also demonstrated a strong need to know the parameters within which he was expected to function; he asked how long the assessment would take and what he would be doing; he asked what time we would be finished and self-initiated making calls to his mother to make arrangements for being picked up at the right time.

Regarding school, Derek stated that his current math course is very challenging. In addition to difficulties with recall of math facts and procedures, Derek has trouble demonstrating his knowledge on math tests as they require him to copy the math problem from the test form to his work paper, work out the answer, and then transfer his answer to the test paper and locate and then select a multiple-choice answer. The back-and-forth transfer of information is very difficult for him, and he frequently makes errors with this process. Science also is a difficult subject; the course is being taught from resource material, and there are no textbooks or notes that can be shared with him. Derek acknowledged that he has dyslexia and that reading is a challenge for him, but he also indicated that he likes to read and does so often but he did not share any specifics about the kinds of reading material that interests him the most.

When asked about personal interests, Derek stated that he has been participating in mixed martial arts for about $2\frac{1}{2}$ years, takes classes, and participates in 60- to 90-minute practice sessions three times per week. He was excited about the fact that his uncle has taken up the sport as well and started classes at the same gym about 2 months ago. Derek stated that he prefers to be involved more in physical activities than sitting and using the computer. His preference is to be out playing basketball with his friends rather than playing video games; however, he will occasionally engage in the latter activity with his peers. Derek has an Xbox and when asked what games he likes to play, he specifically mentioned Halo, Grand Theft Auto, and Call of Duty. He indicated that he does not spend that much time on the computer; Derek reported that he does not access social media sites such as Facebook and noted that he deleted his Instagram account a few months ago. He uses an iPad and an iMac

Pro and mostly accesses websites and does work for school on these devices. Derek uses his cell phone to talk to and text with friends; he indicated that he talks with friends more than he texts with them.

When asked about friends and social activities, Derek indicated that he has several friends that he knows from school and others that he knows from the neighborhood where he lives. He also mentioned that he takes CCD (religious studies) classes and will be continuing them until his confirmation in the Catholic church.

During the two evaluation sessions, Derek readily engaged with each task that was presented and appeared to be offering his best efforts in his attempts to complete these tasks. Despite the fact that each evaluation session lasted almost 3 hours, Derek was able to sustain a good level of effort throughout the assessment sessions without showing signs of fatigue. Derek worked diligently throughout each session, never asking for a rest break. Although he always attempted to provide a good effort, Derek did have a great deal of difficulty with keeping his attention focused on the tasks that he was performing. At times, he would just stare off into space and then realize that he was supposed to be responding to a question or starting to work on a task. He frequently responded to test items in a very impulsive manner; he seemed compelled to provide an answer very quickly, but frequently would monitor his initial response and make changes to it almost immediately after providing it. Specific observations related to these difficulties and other observations about Derek's performance of specific tasks are integrated throughout the detailed interpretation sections of this report.

For a detailed description and interpretation of assessment results for Derek, go to Appendix G in the downloadable resources: www.wiley.com/go/itwiscvwww.wiley.com/go/itwiscv.

Test Results

Cognitive Ability

Table 13.17   Derek's Wechsler Intelligence Scale for Children–Fifth Edition (WISC–V) Scores

Scales	Standard Score	Percentile	Extremely Low	Low	Below Average	Average	Above Average	Superior	Very Superior
			Standard Scores within Descriptive Category Ranges						
FSIQ – Full Scale IQ	89 (98)	23 (45)			89				
GAI – General Ability Index	99 (109)	47 (73)				99			
Indexes									
VCI–Verbal Comprehension	108–S	70					108		
FRI–Fluid Reasoning	100–S (118)	50 (88)				100			
QRI–Quantitative Reasoning	88	21			88				
VSI – Visual Spatial	81 (100)	10 (50)			81				
WMI–Working Memory	82	12			82				
AWMI–Auditory Working Memory	87	19			87				
PSI–Processing Speed	75–W	5		75					

Note: Standard scores range from a low of 40 to a high of 160, with 100 as the average score.

The Full Scale IQ is derived from seven subtests from all five Primary Index scales. The General Ability Index (GAI) is derived from the six subtests from the six subtests contributing to the Verbal Comprehension, Fluid Reasoning, and Visual Spatial Indexes. Scores within ( ) indicate the score Derek could have earned had he been able to inhibit impulsive responding and carefully check his work for errors on specific subtests.

	Standard Score	Percentile	Extremely Low	Low	Below Average	Average	Above Average	Superior	Very Superior
			Scaled Scores within Descriptive Category Ranges						
Verbal Comprehension Subtests									
Similarities (VCI)*	12–S	75				12			
Comprehension	10	50				10			
Vocabulary (VCI)*	11	63				11			
Information	11	63				11			

(*continued*)

Table 13.17   (*Continued*)

	Standard Score	Percentile	Standard Scores within Descriptive Category Ranges						
			Extremely Low	Low	Below Average	Average	Above Average	Superior	Very Superior
Fluid Reasoning Subtests									
Matrix Reasoning (FRI)*	10 [16]	50 [98]				10			
Figure Weights (FRI)*	10	50				10			
Arithmetic	6 [9]	9 [37]		6					
Picture Concepts	8 [13]	25 [84]				8			
Visual Spatial Subtests									
Block Design (VSI)*	6 [8]	9 [25]		6					
Visual Puzzles (VSI)	9 [12]	37 [75]				9			
Working Memory Subtests									
Digit Span (WMI)*	7	16			7				
Picture Span (WMI)	7	16			7				
Letter-Number Sequencing	8	25				8			
Processing Speed Subtests									
Coding (PSI)*	4–W	2	4						
Symbol Search (PSI)	7	16			7				

Note: Scaled scores range from a low of 1 to a high of 19, with 10 as the average score.

*denotes subtest scores used to derive the FSIQ. ( ) indicate the Index to which the subtest scores contribute. Scores within [ ] indicate the score Derek could have earned had he been able to inhibit impulsive responding and carefully check his work for errors. When prompted to inhibit, monitor and correct after standardized assessment, Derek was able to perform at the level indicated within the [ ]. Abbreviations are: VCI = Verbal Comprehension Index, FRI = Fluid Reasoning Index, VSI = Visual Spatial Index, WMI = Working Memory Index, PSI = Processing Speed Index.

Executive Functions

Table 13.18   Derek's Delis–Kaplan Executive Function System (D–KEFS) Scores

	Standard Score	Percentile	Standard Scores within Descriptive Category Ranges						
			Extremely Low	Low	Below Average	Average	Above Average	Superior	Very Superior
Verbal Fluency Test									
Letter Fluency	6	9		6					
Category Fluency	9	37				9			

Table 13.18 (*Continued*)

	Standard Score	Percentile	Standard Scores within Descriptive Category Ranges						
			Extremely Low	Low	Below Average	Average	Above Average	Superior	Very Superior
Color Word Interference Test									
Color Naming Speed	7	16			7				
Color Naming Errors	—	1	1st						
Word Reading Speed	5	5		5					
Word Reading Errors	—	1	1st						
Inhibition Speed	1	<1^t	1						
Inhibition Errors	1	1	1						
Inhibition/Switching Speed	4	2	4						
Inhibition/Switching Errors	1	<1	1						
20 Questions									
Initial Abstraction	13	84					13		
Total Questions	9	37				9			
Weighted Achievement	10	50				10			

Note: Scaled scores range from a low of 1 to a high of 19, with 10 as the average score.

Table 13.19 Derek's Wisconsin Card Sorting Test (WCST) Scores

Indexes	Standard Score	Percentile	Standard Scores within Descriptive Category Ranges						
			Extremely Low	Low	Below Average	Average	Above Average	Superior	Very Superior
% Total Errors	97	42				97			
% Perseverative Errors	95	37				95			
% Non-perseverative Errors	97	42				97			
Percentage of Conceptual-Level Responses	99	47				99			

Performance Characteristics	Raw Score	Level	Extremely Low	Low	Below Ave	Average	Above Average	Superior	Very Superior
Categories (Sets) Completed	6	Ave				Ave			
Trials to Complete 1st Category	10	Ave				Ave			
Failure to Maintain Set	0	Ave				Ave			

Trials to Completion for Categories 1–6: 10, 15, 33, 16, 11, 14

Note: Standard scores range from a low of 55 to a high of 145, with 100 as the average score. WCST scores are positively weighted; the higher the score, the better the level of performance; for example, the higher the score for Perseverative Errors, the lower the percentage of errors made relative to the standardization sample of same-age peers.

Memory for Auditorily Presented Verbal Information

Table 13.20   Derek's Children's Memory Scale (CMS) Scores

Subtests	Standard Score	Percentile	Standard Scores within Descriptive Category Ranges						
			Extremely Low	Low	Below Average	Average	Above Average	Superior	Very Superior
Immediate Recall of Story Details	13	84					13		
Immediate Recall of Story Themes	13	84					13		
Delayed Recall of Story Details	12	75				12			
Delayed Recall of Story Themes	12	75				12			
Delayed Recognition of Story Details	7	16			7				
Sequences (Verbal Fluency)	3	1	3						

Note: Scaled scores range from a low of 1 to a high of 19, with 10 as the average score.

Basic Cognitive Processes and Abilities

Table 13.21   Derek's WISC–V and KTEA–3 Basic Cognitive Processes and Abilities Scores

	Standard Score	Percentile	Scaled Scores within Descriptive Category Ranges						
			Extremely Low	Low	Below Average	Average	Above Average	Superior	Very Superior
KTEA–3 Subtests									
Phonological Processing	83	13			83				
Object Naming Facility	96	39				96			
Letter Naming Facility	100	50				100			
WISC–V Subtests									
Naming Speed Literacy	78	7		78					
Naming Speed Quantity	72	3		73					

Note: Standard scores range from a low of 40 to a high of 160, with 100 as the average score. WISC–V standard scores and percentile ranks are based on age-based norms.

Academic Skills

Table 13.22   Derek's Kaufman Test of Educational Achievement–Third Edition (KTEA–3) Scores

	Standard Score	Percentile	Scaled Scores within Descriptive Category Ranges						
			Extremely Low	Low	Below Average	Average	Above Average	Superior	Very Superior
Reading Subtests									
Letter-Word Recognition	75	5		75					
Nonsense Word Decoding	66	1	66						
Silent Reading Fluency	103	58				103			
Word Recognition Fluency	92	30				92			
Decoding Fluency	74	4		74					
Reading Vocabulary	90	25				90			
Reading Comprehension	88	21			88				
Written Expression Subtests									
Writing Fluency	101	53				101			
Mathematics Subtests									
Math Fluency	68	2	68						
Math Computation	80	9			80				

Note: Standard scores range from a low of 40 to a high of 160, with 100 as the average score. Standard scores and percentile ranks are based on age-based norms.

Table 13.23   Derek's Wechsler Individual Achievement Test–Third Edition (WIAT–III) Scores

	Standard Score	Percentile	Scaled Scores within Descriptive Category Ranges						
			Extremely Low	Low	Below Average	Average	Above Average	Superior	Very Superior
Reading Subtests									
Reading Comprehension	101	53				101			

Note: Standard scores range from a low of 40 to a high of 160, with 100 as the average score. Standard scores and percentile ranks are based on age-based norms.

Table 13.24   Derek's Woodcock–Johnson Tests of Achievement–Third Edition (WJ III) Scores

			Scaled Scores within Descriptive Category Ranges						
	Standard Score	Percentile	Extremely Low	Low	Below Average	Average	Above Average	Superior	Very Superior
Written Expression Subtests									
Writing Fluency	81	10	81						

Note: Standard scores range from a low of 40 to a high of 160, with 100 as the average score. Standard scores and percentile ranks are based on age-based norms.

Executive Functions by Report

Table 13.25   Derek's McCloskey Executive Functions Scales (MEFS) Scores

Parent & Teacher Ratings		Self Ratings	
AA	Always or almost always does on own without prompting	AA	I always or almost always do this on my own. I don't need to be prompted or reminded to do it.
F	Frequently does on own without prompting	F	I frequently do this on my own without prompting.
S	Seldom does it on own without being prompted or reminded to do it	S	I seldom do this on my own without being prompted or reminded to do it.
AP	Does this only after being prompted, reminded or cued to do it	AP	I do this only after being prompted or reminded to do it.
DA	Only does it with direct assistance	DA	I can only do it with help.
UA	Cannot do even with direct assistance	UA	I can't do this, even when I get help with it.

	Mother	Derek
BECOMING AWARE		
Knows what he should be doing for school tasks and knows when to do it.	AP	AA
Makes eye contact with, listens to, and touches others in an appropriate way in social situations.	AA	F
Is aware of own feelings thoughts and actions. (Says things that reflect awareness of feelings, thoughts and actions).	F	AA
FOCUSING ATTENTION		
Focuses attention on school tasks.	AP	AA
Focuses attention on others in social situations.	F	AA
Focuses attention on own actions.	F	AA

Table 13.25 (*Continued*)

	Mother	Derek
SUSTAINING ATTENTION		
Sustains attention for school tasks until a task is completed.	DA	S
Sustains attention to others in social situations.	F	AA
Sustains attention to own actions.	F	F
INITIATING		
Starts schoolwork.	DA	AA
Initiates socially appropriate interactions with other students.	F	AA
Does self-care tasks.	S	AA
GETTING ENERGIZED FOR / PUTTING EFFORT INTO		
Puts adequate energy into, school tasks.	S	F
Puts adequate energy into, interacting with others.	F	AA
Puts adequate energy into, taking care of self.	S	AA
INHIBITING		
Waits for turn.	AA	AA
Considers the consequences before saying or doing things he may regret.	S	AA
Refrains from acts of physical aggression.	AA	AA
Does not make inappropriate or thoughtless comments (e.g., name-calling, insulting, inappropriately tattling on others).	F	AA
Controls emotional reactions well in frustrating situations.	S	AA
Maintains emotional control when doing challenging schoolwork.	S	AA
Maintains emotional control when disagreeing with others.	S	AA
STOPPING		
Knows when to stop talking about a single topic.	AP	AA
Stops playing a game or stops doing something that is fun when asked to do so.	F	F
Stops doing things that annoy others when asked to do so.	F	AA
Stops doing harmful or bothersome things to self (picking at skin, biting nails, etc) when asked to do so.	AA	AA
Stops negatively feeling or thinking the same way about himself.	F	AA
PAUSE & CONTINUE		
Returns to a school task after a brief pause.	DA	F
Pauses to listen to what another person has to say during conversations.	S	AA
Returns to what they were thinking about or doing after a brief pause.	S	AA

(*continued*)

Table 13.25 (*Continued*)

	Mother	Derek
FLEXIBLY ENGAGING		
Willing to try a different way to do school tasks when he gets stuck.	DA	AA
Accepts a good idea when it is what most others in a group want to do.	F	AA
Accepts the need to think about or feel differently about himself when the way he is thinking or feeling is not working out well.	S	F
Accepts changes in schoolwork or school routines without getting upset about it.	F	AA
Accepts changes in a person he knows or to accept unfamiliar persons without getting upset.	AA	AA
Accepts when it is necessary to change personal habits because they are causing difficulties.	AA	F
SHIFTING		
Moves from one school task to another without difficulty.	DA	F
Changes from one activity to another in social situations without difficulty.	AA	AA
Changes personal habits when they are causing problems.	AA	F
MODULATING or ADJUSTING		
Physical activity level fits the situation when doing school tasks (not hyperactive or inactive).	S	AA
Physical activity level fits the situation when working in a group (not hyperactive or inactive).	S	AA
Adjusts physical activity level when working alone so as not to be hyperactive or inactive.	S	F
Emotional response fits the situation when working on school tasks (doesn't overreact or underact).	F	F
Emotional response fits the situation when interacting with others (doesn't overreact or underreact).	S	AA
Avoids being overstimulated or understimulated by sights, sounds, or touches.	AP	AA
MONITORING		
Checks schoolwork to avoid careless errors on tests and other schoolwork.	DA	S
Recognizes situations in which his behavior bothers or upsets others.	S	AA
Checks to make sure that he has everything he needs before leaving class or school.	DA	F
Checks on his appearance, cleanliness, and personal hygiene.	F	AA
CORRECTING		
Corrects errors that are made in schoolwork.	DA	AA
Apologizes when aware of offending others.	AA	AA
Changes his opinions about self or others that were caused by misperceptions about himself or another person.	F	AA

Table 13.25 (*Continued*)

	Mother	Derek
BALANCING		
Balances the elements of a school assignment (speed vs. accuracy, quality vs. quantity; general vs. specific statements; depth vs. breadth, etc.).	DA	F
Maintains a balance in social situations (talking vs. listening, sharing too much vs. sharing too little; being humorous vs. being serious).	F	AA
Maintains a balance in his own activities (play vs. work; time alone vs. time with others; sleep vs. awake).	AP	F
GAUGING or "SIZING UP"		
Accurately estimates the difficulty of school tasks and/or tests and what it takes to complete them and/or do well with them.	DA	AA
Figures out how to interact appropriately in various social situations.	F	AA
Figures out what it takes to maintain self-control in difficult situations.	F	AA
ANTICIPATING		
Anticipates events at school (e.g., recognizes the need to prepare for tests or assignments; connects homework with grades, etc.).	DA	F
Anticipates how what he says or does will affect how others feel, think, or act.	AA	AA
Anticipates the consequences of his own thoughts, feelings, and actions (e.g., recognizes that if he doesn't do a chore, he won't be able to play with a friend and will feel disappointed about it).	AA	AA
ESTIMATING TIME		
Accurately estimates how long it will take to do something when involved with one or more school tasks.	DA	AA
Accurately estimates how long it will take to do something when talking to others or doing things with others.	S	AA
Accurately estimates how long it will take to do something when doing things alone.	S	AA
ANALYZING SITUATIONS		
Examines and analyzes things in more detail when doing school tasks.	DA	AA
Examines and analyzes in more detail what others are saying or doing in social situations.	F	AA
Examines and analyzes in more detail thoughts and feelings he has about himself or things he does alone.	F	AA
EVALUATING/COMPARING		
Evaluates the quality and/or adequacy of his work on school tasks.	AP	F
Evaluates the quality and/or adequacy of his social interactions.	S	F
Evaluates the quality and/or adequacy of his thoughts and feelings about himself or about the things done when alone.	F	AA

(*continued*)

Table 13.25 (*Continued*)

	Mother	Derek
GENERATING SOLUTIONS		
Comes up with new ways to solve problems with school tasks.	DA	AA
Come up with new ideas about things to say to, or do with, others.	F	F
Comes up with new ways of thinking or feeling about himself or new ways of doing things for himself.	F	AA
MAKING ASSOCIATIONS		
Sees or understands how two or more things or ideas are similar and can use that knowledge to solve a problem with schoolwork.	S	AA
Sees or understands how one social situation can be similar to another and can use that knowledge to solve a social relationship problem.	F	AA
Sees or understands how two or more things he has done, or ideas he has had, are similar and can use that knowledge to solve a personal problem.	F	AA
ORGANIZING		
Organizes school tasks.	DA	AA
Organizes age appropriate social activities.	F	AA
Organizes his own thoughts and feelings.	F	AA
PLANNING		
Makes plans for school tasks.	DA	AA
Makes plans for age-appropriate social activities.	F	AA
Makes plans for the use of his own time.	F	AA
PRIORITIZING		
Orders school tasks according to their relevance, importance, or urgency.	DA	AA
Handles social activities according to their relevance, importance, or urgency.	F	AA
Orders own thoughts and feelings or personal activities according to their relevance, importance, or urgency.	F	AA
DECISION MAKING		
Makes own decisions about what to do for school and/or when to do it.	DA	AA
Makes own decisions about what to do with others and/or when to do it.	F	AA
Makes own decisions about what to do and when to do it when alone.	F	F

Table 13.25 *(Continued)*

	Mother	Derek
SENSING TIME		
Keeps track of time (e.g., realizes how much time has passed) when doing school tasks.	DA	AA
Keeps track of time (e.g., realizes how much time has passed) when talking to or doing things with others.	S	AA
Keeps track of time (e.g., realizes how much time has passed) when working independently.	AP	AA
PACING		
Changes pace (works slower or works faster) when taking tests or doing school assignments.	AP	AA
Changes pace in social situations (e.g., talks slower or talks faster to maintain the pace of the conversation).	F	AA
Changes pace (goes slower or faster) when working independently.	S	AA
USING ROUTINES/COMPLETING ASSIGNMENTS (EXECUTING)		
Uses well-rehearsed or practiced routines for school tasks (e.g., recognizing words by sight, printing or writing letters and words, reciting basic math facts).	S	AA
Uses well-rehearsed or practiced social greetings or conversation starters.	AA	AA
Uses well-rehearsed or practiced routines for hygiene and self-care.	F	AA
Generate good ideas and gets them down on paper quickly and efficiently.	DA	AA
Uses routines and strategies to do well on tests.	DA	AA
Uses routines and strategies to get assignments and projects done.	DA	AA
Participates in discussions about topics that he knows a lot about.	AA	AA
Brings home all the materials need to complete homework and other school tasks.	DA	AA
Hands in homework, assignments, or important papers when they are completed.	AP	AA
SEQUENCING		
Gets the steps in the right order when working on school tasks.	AP	AA
Gets the order of events right when telling stories or explaining things to others.	F	AA
Gets the steps in the right order when performing personal care tasks.	F	AA
HOLDING and WORKING WITH INFORMATION IN MIND		
Can keep information in mind when doing school tasks (for example, can add three or more numbers without pencil and paper; can remember directions that were just given by the teacher).	S	AA
Can keep information in mind for short periods of time when talking with others (for example, can follow and participate in a longer conversation).	F	AA
Can keep information in mind when doing things alone (for example can write an essay or remember a story that was just read).	F	F

(continued)

Table 13.25 (*Continued*)

	Mother	Derek
STORING and RETRIEVING		
Stores and recalls specific information about school subjects no matter how questions are worded.	S	AA
Stores and recalls specific information about others or about social situations.	F	AA
Stores and recalls specific information about himself.	AA	AA
Does well on tests that require recall of stored facts no matter what test format is used.	AP	AA
Does well in social situations that require recall of facts about others.	F	AA
Does well in situations that require recall of facts about himself.	AA	AA
SELF-REALIZATION: SELF-AWARENESS		
Makes realistic comments about his own mental and emotional strengths and weaknesses.	S	VO
Makes realistic comments about his own physical abilities.	O	VO
Makes realistic comments about what he feels or thinks about himself.	O	VO
SELF-REALIZATION: AWARENESS OF OTHERS		
Makes realistic comments about the mental and emotional strengths and weaknesses of others.	O	VO
Makes realistic comments about the physical abilities of others.	O	VO
Makes realistic comments about what he thinks other people feel or think about others.	O	VO
Makes realistic comments about what he thinks others feel or think about his.	O	VO
Makes realistic comments about what he thinks other people feel or think about themselves.	O	VO
SELF-REALIZATION: SELF-ANALYSIS		
Realistically analyzes and comments about his school performance.	S	O
Realistically analyzes and comments about his ability to know what others appear to think or feel about his.	S	VO
Realistically analyzes and comments about his ability to manage himself.	S	O
SELF-DETERMINATION: GOAL-SETTING		
States realistic goals for schooling based on personal interests.	O	VO
States realistic goals for work beyond school based on personal interests.	O	VO
Expresses strong desires to make his own decisions about what to do rather than be told what to do by parents or others.	VO	VO

Table 13.25   (*Continued*)

	Mother	Derek
SELF-DETERMINATION: LONG-TERM PLANNING		
States realistic plans for accomplishing long-term schooling goals.	S	VO
States realistic plans for accomplishing long-term work goals.	O	VO
States realistic plans for accomplishing social and/or personal goals.	O	VO
SELF-GENERATION		
Asks questions about the meaning of life.	N/R	N/R
Asks questions about the purpose or meaning of school.	N/R	N/R
Asks questions about why we exist.	N/R	N/R
Asks questions about what happens to us when we die.	N/R	N/R
Wants to know why things are considered right or wrong.	N/R	N/R
Asks questions about the right way to treat other people.	N/R	N/R

INTERPRETING THE WISC–V FOR CHILDREN WITH READING OR LANGUAGE PROBLEMS: FIVE ILLUSTRATIVE CASE REPORTS

This chapter presents case reports on five children, ages 8 to 15 years, with academic problems, primarily in reading or language. Certainly these children are not unique in their presenting symptoms—most, if not all, of the 17 children assessed for the case studies spread throughout Part IV of this book were referred, at least in part, because of similar academic difficulties. However, most of the other children had emotional problems or low intellectual functioning, or an array of behavioral and cognitive symptoms that complicated the diagnostic process. Or they were included in the first five chapters of Part IV because the report writer's interpretive model was closely aligned with a specific theory-based approach, such as those described in the chapter on the Cattell-Horn-Carroll model (Chapter 9) and neuropsychologically oriented chapters (Chapters 10–13). The report writers in this chapter vary in assessment orientation, but all skillfully employ strategies for understanding, identifying, and providing interventions for children who have not yet met with much success in the school environment.

The chapter begins with an introduction to each of the five case reports that appear in this chapter. The chapter continues with a conceptual integration of all 17 illustrative case reports presented in Part IV, based on a number of common, recurring themes across reports despite the wide range of children and intelligent testers involved. The chapter concludes with the five case reports of children whose primary reason for referral was a reading or language problem.

INTRODUCTION TO THE FIVE CASE REPORTS ON CHILDREN WITH READING OR LANGUAGE PROBLEMS

Diane L. Coalson and Nadeen L. Kaufman

The first two cases are described in two very different reports about two very different children; yet both children share common strengths and weaknesses in their daily academic functioning. The first report, by Michelle Lurie (Nadeen's first doctoral student, 20 years ago), portrays Ellie, age 10½, a fourth-grade girl who was adopted from China when she was approximately 6 years old. The second, by Marsha Vasserman, describes Jordan, age 15, who suffered from profound hearing loss unbeknownst to anyone until he was 1½ years old. Both of these reports provide exceptional examples of the cognitive-developmental sequelae of unidentified problems and how faulty, yet understandable, assumptions can be made based solely on appearances or historical background (or any other single indicator, for that matter). Ellie and Jordan both struggle with serious social communication difficulties, but the authors address these issues differently based on a sensitive understanding of disparities between each child's peer group and an astute anticipation of how these peer-group interactions will change over time. Both case report writers demonstrate how a comprehensive battery of well-selected tests can help uncover variability within an individual's overall functioning and how expert examiners can unravel the profile by conducting the detective work necessary to go beyond first appearances to discover hidden causes of difficulties. Both evaluators are neuropsychologists who found similar patterns of neurodevelopmental speech and language disorders present in children so apparently different.

The third report in this chapter was coauthored by Robert Lichtenstein and Joan Axelrod, providing an insightful look into Jane, age 8, who, unlike Ellie and Josh, had no significant risk factors or signs of cognitive difficulties until she faced increasing demands on her reading abilities at school. Excellent observations can supply a great deal of information, and the authors' use of this technique during various classroom activities led directly to insightful and carefully-worded recommendations for Jane. Consistent with Response to Intervention (RTI) philosophy, Lichtenstein and Axelrod describe Jane's performance without the inclusion of a specific diagnosis; however, the "Clinical Impressions" section reflects an incisive knowledge of Jane's strengths and weaknesses. The introductory paragraphs to Jane's report succinctly summarize Lichtenstein and Axelrod's philosophy that many reports are often an exercise in obscurity and technical detail. Their consumer-responsive approach to report writing is well articulated (see Lichtenstein's 2013a, 2013b, 2014, trio of *NASP Communiqué* articles) and has gained a following among practitioners. Joel Schneider echoes similar sentiments in the several heartfelt pages he wrote that precede his case report of Liam (age 9) in Chapter 9 on CHC theory and in the articulate debriefing that followed his report.

In the fourth report, Carlea Dries and Ron Dumont introduce us to Lizzie, age 8, who, without their expertise, might not be receiving the help she so desperately needs to maximize her potential. Despite being in special education her whole school career, Lizzie has never received Individualized Education Program (IEP) services, an unfortunate oversight that should be remediated by this evaluation's ever-important diagnostic label. To support this type of intervention, the authors skillfully present how Lizzie qualifies for services regardless of whether her results are viewed from an RTI school philosophical environment or some type of discrepancy model. Active progress monitoring is a current, but not always utilized, source of continual information; here it is specifically recommended.

The fifth and final report in this chapter, by Nancy Mather and Katie Eklund, describes Patrick, age 9, who continues to struggle with reading despite a slew of evaluations from various experts (i.e., occupational therapist, speech and language pathologist, ophthalmologist, and a clinical psychologist) and subsequent intervention application with little improvement. A wonderful "plan of attack" is described at the beginning of the report to justify the initial selection of measures, followed by a dogged pursuit of basic language and reading-related processes to pinpoint the unique features of Patrick's specific learning disability for more targeted interventions.

CONCEPTUAL AND CLINICAL INTEGRATION OF ALL 17 CASE REPORTS IN THE BOOK

Nadeen L. Kaufman and Diane L. Coalson

As one might expect, the variety seen across 17 case reports is substantial, including children of various ages, ethnicities, and socioeconomic statuses, as well as inestimable variety in their accumulated life experiences. Similarly, the experts who graciously agreed to contribute these reports are equally varied in life experiences, with different training backgrounds, areas of specialty, theoretical orientations, and report-writing styles. Consider, for example, two boys with serious visual difficulties, who both exhibit reading disorders, in the case reports by Nancy Mather and Katie Eklund (Patrick, 9) and by Marsha Vasserman (Christopher, age 11). Both boys share poor reading and writing skills, yet they differ in their visual-spatial abilities. Note the difference in a neuropsychological approach to an assessment (Vasserman) versus a special education context (Mather and Eklund).

Thus, it may be surprising (and somewhat comforting) that common themes across the reports were fairly easy to spot, confirming that intelligent testing crosses the invisible boundaries that sometimes seem to separate practitioners like an impenetrable forest. The following sections note these commonalities as well as some key differences among reports. A list of the case reports and their authors is provided to cue the reader's memory and to serve as a convenient reference.

Case No.	Child Name and Age	Case Author	Chapter
1	Liam, Age 9	W. Joel Schneider	9
2	Alicia, Age 13	Jill Hartmann and John Willis	9
3	Luke, Age 9	Jennifer Mascolo and Dawn Flanagan	9
4	Josh, Age 8	Elaine Fletcher-Janzen and Elizabeth Power	10
5	Tawna, Age 13	Michelle Lurie and Elizabeth Lichtenberger	10
6	Tom, Age 8	Kristina Breaux	10
7	Jaime, Age 10	Jennie K. Singer	11
8	Christopher, Age 11	Marsha Vasserman	11
9	Isabella, Age 13	Michelle Lurie	11
10	John, Age 12	Dan Miller and Alicia Jones	12
11	Colin, Age 8	George McCloskey	13
12	Derek, Age 13	George McCloskey	13
13	Ellie, Age 10	Michelle Lurie	14
14	Jordan, Age 15	Marsha Vasserman	14

Case No.	Child Name and Age	Case Author	Chapter
15	Jane, Age 8	Robert Lichtenstein and Joan Axelrod	14
16	Lizzie, Age 8	Carlea Dries and Ron Dumont	14
17	Patrick, Age 9	Nancy Mather and Katie Eklund	14

Integrating Observational Data into Reports

All of the authors included numerous behavioral observations in their reports, including those made during the testing session and those collected during classroom or informal interactions. This type of observational information can bring the child to life in the mind of the reader. For example, Kristina Breaux's insightful case report of Tom might be termed dense and complex, but note how her descriptive language helps the reader to see the child being evaluated. He virtually pops into life both at home and at school. Joel Schneider also produces a lifelike image through his vivid descriptions of Liam, who is easily imagined wearing a wry smile as he engaged in word play with his esteemed tester. Michelle Lurie's description of Isabella's simultaneous need for affection and fear of rejection pulls on the heartstrings of the reader.

Many of the authors incorporated descriptive and relevant behavioral observations to inform or support interpretation of test results. The interaction between a child's level of motivation across tasks can be especially informative, as noted by several authors, including Dan Miller and Alicia Jones in their description of John. The role of motivation is very evident in John's testing behavior, which was very influenced by what challenged and delighted him versus what was boring. The authors also noted such relevant behaviors as perfectionism and atypical social interactions and even described John observing other students. Similar observations were noted by Schneider in his report on Liam, who sighed in exasperation on those tests in which he could see how many more items remained, going so far as to openly admit guessing on the last Figure Weights items while simultaneously providing an explanation of the probabilities involved in guess rates. The possible impact of eye fatigue was noted by Mather and Eklund after astutely noting Patrick rubbing his eyes, but only after tasks requiring reading. Other contributors noted observations of anxiety during the testing, making note of its possible impact on performance as well as differences observed across tasks. Michelle Lurie and Elizabeth Lichtenberger noted anxiety during testing for Tawna, who, at 13, had reached an age where even she was aware of her need for better coping skills. Vasserman also noted these signs in 11-year-old Christopher, as well as his self-initiated use of self-talk as a coping strategy during the reading tasks he dreaded.

In fact, behavioral observations were often used to inform intervention as well as interpretation. Jane was busted using sly tactics to avoid reading tasks through creative classroom observations made by Robert Lichtenstein and Joan Axelrod. In Vasserman's report for Jordan, who is hard of hearing, she used her successes with reinforcement, demonstrations, and practice to offer similar recommendations for others. The simple, positive impact of a little praise going a long way was noted by Jill Hartmann and John Willis in their report on Alicia.

We would be remiss if we did not mention the *CSI*-like description of physical aspects of the classroom environment contained within Jennifer Mascolo and Dawn Flanagan's report on Luke. We could almost imagine the authors sneaking in to clear a space on the table that was supposed to be used for break-out groups so Luke had a better workspace. In all seriousness, this description was quite impressive and highlighted the importance of noting this type of information about the classroom environment, including the student to teacher ratio, which was also provided in the Mascolo and Flanagan report.

Consideration of Complicating Factors and False Assumptions

One of the more striking features shared across several of the contributed reports involved the masking effects of children's unique physical or personal histories that resulted in especially complex assessment situations or, more unfortunately, the realization that there had been missed opportunities for the children to receive the help they needed at a much earlier time during development. Several of the children presented had extremely rough starts in life, placing them at greater risk of academic and emotional problems. Schneider's report on Liam notes premature birth due to a knot in the umbilical cord, followed by an unexplainable period of lost consciousness for both mother and child. An even more dramatic entry into the world is described in the report by Carlea Dries and Ron Dumont for Lizzie, who was born via emergency C-section with a critically low Apgar rating, followed by successful resuscitation efforts. If that wasn't enough of a challenge, Lizzie has since suffered from severe obstructive apnea and was awaiting results for cystic fibrosis testing at the time of the report's writing. When combined with her strong desire to remain in a mainstream classroom with her new friends, it is likely that all of the readers are pulling for Lizzie to experience increased health and academic success despite all of her challenges.

The discovery that there might have been missed opportunities for helping a child can be especially discouraging, as noted by several report writers. The first example comes from the report on Jordan, age 15, submitted by Vasserman. Jordan's profound deafness was missed during his infancy hearing screening and went unnoticed until he was 17 months of age. Despite receiving cochlear implants in both ears by the age of 3, Jordan has experienced ongoing difficulties with language and reading that were, sadly, attributed to his history of hearing difficulties. In reality, test results revealed a language disorder as well as an other specified neurodevelopmental disorder, based on the extent and breadth of resulting academic difficulties. While it is fortunate that Vasserman identified a source for some of his difficulties, the delayed identification of Jordan's comorbid diagnoses underscores the importance of continuing to question our own assumptions when things just don't seem right.

Lurie's report on Ellie, age 10, describes a particularly rough start, with Ellie being abandoned at 2 weeks of age in China due to her suffering from congenital syphilis, followed by transfers between orphanages and foster homes until her adoption at around the age of 6 (her birthdate is not known for sure). In addition to her attachment difficulties, Ellie's problems in language and reading were mistakenly (and understandably) attributed to her ongoing acquisition of English; however, when her difficulties persisted, her teachers and parents became suspicious that something more was going on, eventually leading to the fortunate consultation with Dr. Lurie.

Mascolo and Flanagan's report for Luke includes a "rule-out" section for these types of physical limitations, in addition to other factors that may limit or clarify a diagnosis, such as environmental, cultural, language, or instructional factors. The inclusion of a section to explicitly note the ineffectiveness of previous interventions may be especially useful for those children attending schools that are using the RTI method for identification of specific learning disabilities.

Going Beyond the Standard Administration

Not surprisingly, the experienced, intelligent testers who were asked to provide the illustrative case reports for Part IV of this book often go beyond the call of duty while performing their role. Many of the authors utilized testing of limits or process-oriented approaches to dig deeper into the meaning behind a child's performance. Joel Schneider went back to question Liam on some items he had missed when seeming to lose

interest, and, voilà, he was able to pass more of the items. Mascolo and Flanagan include a report on Luke's self-reported response processes in each section of their report, a habit to which many of us should aspire. Breaux's report was complicated by many interacting factors affecting Tom's performance and provides an excellent example of an evaluator considering all possibilities for a complex test interpretation and diagnosis. Of special interest, this is the only case report that used an iPad administration of the WISC–V, as well as for the Wechsler Individual Achievement Test–Third Edition (WIAT–III; Wechsler, 2009) and the Kaufman Test of Educational Achievement–Third Edition (KTEA–3; Kaufman & Kaufman, 2014). Tom, age 8, took this digital format style in stride.

Other case reports also provide excellent examples of supersleuthing to uncover the underlying processes of a child's academic difficulties. Vasserman's report on Christopher was marked by extreme variability in responding, requiring an increasingly focused evaluation characteristic of the process-analysis approach popularized by Edith Kaplan. Similarly, Lurie and Lichtenberger's report required detective-like skills to get at the heart of Tawna's attentional and executive function difficulties. And no discussion of process analysis would be complete without mentioning George McCloskey's thorough and exhaustive process-oriented approach in his reports on Colin, age 8, and Derek, age 13. McCloskey makes no apologies for the length of his reports, noting that it is one of the primary reasons behind his referrals (i.e., a thorough, detailed evaluation is desired) and that it in no way implies that those who follow his interpretive approach will need to produce reports of that length. The length of the report is the primary reason that McCloskey "frontloads" his summary sections, as do Dries and Dumont in their report for Lizzie. Here, the writers start off with the referral questions but then leap to the summary before starting in with the "Case Formulation." All the information is there, but in a different presentation sequence.

A final note: When asked to provide a title for his first case report on Colin, McCloskey offered the title "The Case of an Elementary Age Student with Mild Executive Function Difficulties." He rejected (but enjoyed) Nadeen's original suggestion of a title: "A Normal Child with the Unbelievable Luck of Having His Functional Processes Dissected." Basically, every potential diagnosis was rejected for Colin. His ultimate diagnosis was "Normal." But how lucky was Colin to have George McCloskey analyze every aspect of his cognitive processing and translate each aspect into meaningful intervention suggestions? How lucky would all of us have been to have that happen to us as schoolchildren?

Handling Sensitive Topics with Compassion and Professionalism

We were highly impressed with how many of our case contributors dealt with such sensitive topics as:

- addressing discrepant or unanticipated results,
- dealing with frustrated parents and or resistant school administrators,
- describing the impact of emotional and behavioral factors on test performance, and
- wording used in descriptions of cognitive weaknesses or other problems.

All intelligent testers will eventually have to deal with the need to explain why their results appear to be discrepant from those of previous or other evaluations. When information gathered underscores discrepancy, rather than agreement, it is often easy to ignore these differences and eliminate them from the report. It is not unusual to uncover unexplainable or seemingly contradictory results within your own evaluation, as noted by Schneider regarding his confessed inability to explain Liam's spelling difficulties. Elaine Fletcher-Janzen and Elizabeth Power's report on Josh, age 8, provides another good example of dealing with contradictory information, with the writers providing reasonable hypotheses about the discrepancy rather than

leaving the reader hanging. Without directly pointing out the poor quality of a previous evaluation, Lurie and Lichtenberger described the previous assessment as "brief and partial," noting the need to delve deeper into the issue as part of their own evaluation. Schneider included some especially insightful comments about the hesitance of professionals to judge other professionals' work.

A unique example of dealing with sensitive topics faced Miller and Jones in their evaluation of John, who is homeschooled by his mother, thus making her both the informing interviewee and the teacher. Great tact is utilized in communicating here, as well as far greater documentation of interpretation, implications, and recommendations than would be seen in a different report. Note the specific referral questions in the Miller and Jones report, making it easier to return later to specifically address them. Perhaps this is why John was not also diagnosed as gifted, since it was not part of the referral questions. John might have merited this diagnosis based on his WISC–V Fluid Reasoning Index of 140 and his Visual Spatial Index of 129.

Several of the children were nervous about the testing or suffered from anxiety, depression, or low self-esteem. Softly worded recommendations were frequently used in these situations, as evidenced in two reports, one on Alicia, by Hartmann and Willis, and one on Lizzie, by Dries and Dumont. Special sensitivity to the awkwardness of adolescence and the need for children this age to fit in and be like everyone else is evident in the report on Jordan, by Vasserman, as well as the report for Jane, by Lichtenstein and Axelrod.

The Hartman and Willis report on Alicia includes excellent examples of wording that might be used just prior to testing an especially anxious or nervous child, providing a sort of inoculation effect against expected failure on more difficult tasks. These authors also provide a great example of how one might foster team spirit simply through the wording used in a report, offering their recommendations as options and opinions for discussion as part of the next team meeting. Other examples of sensitive wording in reports were used to soften descriptions of characteristics that may be viewed negatively by the reader or the child. Some of our favorites include the use of the phrases "strong need to feel competent" and "well able to manage social situations" by Lichtenstein and Axelrod when describing Jane's tendency to exaggerate her abilities or get things her way. Dries and Dumont present Lizzie's low scores with the phrase "which is higher than 25% of children her age" rather than the converse. However, Diane's personal favorite came from Joel Schneider, in his report on Liam, who demonstrates perfectionistic tendencies and a somewhat rigid thinking style. Schneider refers to these characteristics as Liam's preference for "logical tidiness," a term Diane plans to use from here on out to describe her own similar tendencies.

Just Plain Good Report Writing

The case reports received were chock full of examples of good report writing, as one might expect. For example, many reports included excellent summaries of test results from multiple sources—integrating results taken from teachers, parents, test observations, and testing performance—to lead the reader toward an understanding of how each informational source interacted with other sources. This type of complex integration prepares those who are going to provide recommendations with a gestalt of what and why requests for help are being suggested. The complex task of providing a comprehensive summary of test results from different sources highlights one of the writer's difficult choices: how much to explain in a report. The report on Josh, by Fletcher-Janzen and Power, provides a superb example of a concise yet thorough summary for a child with difficulties in multiple interrelated areas, who has been in special education since age 3. Also notable is Vasserman's summary of Christopher, as she integrates several test results to confirm a hypothesis, thereby providing extra validity for her conclusions. This efficiency in documenting past sources of information needn't exclude

interesting or highly descriptive bits of information. For example, in Jennie Kaufman Singer's report for Jaime, age 10, the "Summary of Background Information" includes a noteworthy incident when Jaime, who is relative insensitivity to pain, put 40 pushpins into his skin. Schneider provides additional insightful comments, in the material immediately following his case report on Liam, on how some sensitive information can be "too much information."

The Use of Numbers in Case Reports

Related to the issue of how much information to include in a report is the issue of how to report scores in an accurate yet clearly meaningful way for the various readers. Many of the case reports include the traditional score summaries at the end, limiting the text of the report to percentages, which are more easily understood than scaled or standard scores. Others report few or no numbers at all, relying on word-speak rather than number-speak. Examples of this type of approach include the consumer-friendly approach advocated by Lichtenstein and Axelrod and the report by the duo of Fletcher-Janzen and Power. Lichtenstein and Axelrod's section on Memory and Learning interpretation for Jane represents a good justification for discounting a test score, as does the report on Liam by Schneider. Mather and Eklund demonstrate interesting integration of test behaviors and numerical scores in their report of Patrick.

Singer's report on Jaime contains several good examples of smart number use in report writing. A sentence in the first paragraph of Jaime's report highlights the importance of using bands of error, especially when facing borderline results for some sort of criterion: "With standard error of measurement, Jaime does potentially meet criteria for an intellectual disability." Also commendable is the way in which Singer presents the tremendous amount of previous test and background information in a succinct way for the reader. Having the numbers from similar, recently administered tests helps the reader to see decline or progress much more readily.

First and Foremost, Make Recommendations and Interventions that Count

Many highlights noted in contributed reports focused on recommendations and interventions: a hallmark of the intelligent testing philosophy. Many of the authors based recommendations on their own observations or actions during the assessment or found recommendations waiting to be found with historical and collateral information in the report. A close review of previous interventions can reveal what has worked and not worked in the past. Mather and Eklund explain how it helps to know what interventions were applied in the past and how they worked. Miller and Jones performed a cautious review of interventions past before making their own recommendations to address John's handwriting—his greatest academic difficulty. Mascolo and Flanagan utilized an extensive history of ineffective interventions to provide the necessary evidence to show that current educational supports were insufficient to meet Luke's needs while simultaneously noting the immediate positive effect of medication reported by Luke's mother. An empathetic understanding of the hardships faced by parents of children with special needs pervades the recommendations for Liam made by Schneider.

Certain recommendations for effective reading programs popped up in case reports for children with reading difficulties, including the Wilson Reading System, Phono-Graphix, and Lindamood methods. Many authors included web links to training programs or other supportive material. The location of recommendations varies somewhat across reports: Miller and Jones note instructional implications in each section of their report on John; by contrast, Mascolo and Flanagan prioritize and categorize their recommendations for Luke at the end of the report, in separate sections for general and targeted interventions. Miller and Jones declared John's test results to be valid, but it is easy to understand that whoever works academically with John must include his interest needs, as well as his emotional issues, such as anxiety. Also, Miller and Rice prescribe recommendations directly for the child to utilize himself. Referring suggestions to an appropriately aged child is frequently a source of success for interventions. McCloskey's recommendations actually include a heading that reads "What Can "X" Do for Himself/Herself?"

Good Case Report Writers Are Good Teachers

Whenever possible, intelligent report writers should take the opportunity to teach the reader in order to clarify understanding. The teaching can be subtle, such as when Fletcher-Janzen and Power note that the WISC–V is referred to as a "routing test to indicate where further investigation should be directed." In subsequent test interpretation subsections, one smooth, well-explained topic (e.g., auditory processing; sensory-motor processing) uses the report to teach the reader, define exactly what and why these interpretive results are being reported, and what daily life activities they translate to at school and at home. A common difficulty well handled in one recommendation is how to help the child discriminate between the letters *b* and *d*, as described by Mather and Eklund in their report on Patrick. Once internalized, the evaluator can use this technique for most *b* and *d* visual discrimination problems.

Other examples of teaching permeate the reports. Vasserman provides a concise and simple definition of executive functions that any parent (and many children) could understand. Mascolo and Flanagan teach the reader about the links between processing speed deficits, increased effort, and reduced motivation in their report on Luke and let the teacher know what behaviors they might see in class. Schneider describes the tip-of-the-tongue phenomenon to describe retrieval difficulties in his report on Liam.

CASE 13—ELLIE, AGE 10: COMPLEXITY IN DIAGNOSIS: NEUROPSYCHOLOGICAL ASSESSMENT OF A CHINESE ADOPTEE

Michelle Lurie

Neuropsychological Assessment

Name: Ellie Brown
Age: 10 years, 10 months
Education: 4th grade

Date of Birth: XX/XX/XXXX
Dates of Eval: XX/XX/XXXX
Parents: Tom & Jenny Brown

Reason for Evaluation

Ellie Brown is a 10-year-old girl who lives in Oklahoma with her parents and her younger sister. Ellie was adopted from China shortly before what was estimated to be her sixth birthday. Ellie is currently in the fourth grade at Pepper Elementary. This testing was initiated by her parents upon referral from neurologist John Smith, M.D., due to Ellie's difficulties with memory, reading, spelling, and writing. Therefore, the purpose of this evaluation is to better understand Ellie's neurocognitive and emotional functioning and to make academic and treatment recommendations.

Background Information

Developmental History and Health

Ellie was abandoned at a hospital in China at age 3 weeks and very few details are available regarding her early history. According to her records, Ellie had congenital syphilis and she remained at the hospital for 2 months. Ellie was sent to an orphanage at age 2 months. She was sent to a foster home at age 3, only to be sent back to the orphanage after a year to await adoption. Although no evidence of physical abuse was reported during these early years, Ellie was clearly neglected and evidenced developmental delays.

Ellie has generally been a healthy young girl. She has a very good appetite for a range of foods and she sleeps well. Ellie has had no surgeries or head injuries. However, she apparently evidenced two febrile seizures in China. MRI, CT, and EEG test results in the United States were normal. Ellie has had no further seizures.

Academic History

Ellie returned with Mr. and Mrs. Brown to the United States at age 4 years. Some attachment issues are reported, and Ellie has always resisted physical affection. She has been more likely to connect with her teachers than with her parents. Ellie spoke very little as a young child and evidenced language delays when moving to the United States. She refused to use any Chinese words. At age 4, Ellie began a mother's-day-out program a few days a week. She did well in this program and her English-language skills began to develop. At age 6, Ellie began kindergarten in public school. Although some delays were noted during these early years, they were attributed to her ongoing language struggles. In second grade her teacher identified more notable learning issues, and these were even more extreme in third grade. This year in fourth grade, her parents have requested special education services for Ellie, but since Ellie evidenced adequate overall functioning and excellent behavior in the classroom, the school has refused to provide a comprehensive assessment or special education resources. At present, Ellie is apparently working at a third-grade level in language arts, and she struggles in English, reading, spelling, writing, history, and science. She excels in mathematics and is working easily at a fourth-grade level in this area. Deficits in memory were reported. Ellie is also described as extremely literal and as struggling with abstract thinking and reasoning. She continues to evidence struggles with verbal expression and word usage, and she will use words such as "fumbs" for "thumbs" and "thingers" for "fingers" as well as "pineapple" for "pine needle." A serious difficulty with phonics is described, and she struggles to articulate many words. She struggles with plural words and tenses. As a result, difficulties understanding her speech and language are reported. Ellie repeats stories over and over again. Despite her struggles, Ellie works hard and does not give up easily when faced with challenging tasks. She does particularly well in a multisensory learning environment but struggles with purely auditory instruction.

Emotional and Social Development

Ellie was described by her parents as a pleasant child who is full of joy and rarely gets upset. She always looks at the positive, has a good attitude, is very honest, and is easy to be around. Ellie is a rule follower, and she is obedient and cooperative. She generally gets along well with her sister and parents, although some ongoing attachment issues are reported.

Ellie has never had any real friends. Although she is well liked by her peers and generally responds appropriately, she cannot sustain a conversation with them. She can be socially awkward, particularly around adults. Although Ellie is uncoordinated, she plays basketball and she swims. Although she enjoys these activities, she does not seek out social interaction with her teammates. Ellie also participates in Sunday school, choir, and a youth group at church. She enjoys baking and crafts.

Behavioral Observations

Ellie presented as a shy and quiet young girl who was well groomed and well oriented. Ellie was pleasant and agreeable, and rapport was established. However, she did not volunteer information and she responded very briefly to all questions. Her eye contact was good, although Ellie tended to have a somewhat vacant look on her face and a vague smile. In fact, Ellie tended to giggle and laugh at odd times during the testing, and her affect was not always appropriate to the context. Her behavior was observed to be more socially appropriate with her parents and sister, and she was less awkward when interacting with them in the waiting room.

Ellie appeared to put forward her best effort, and she worked diligently with no complaints. Ellie was not easily distracted and her level of focus was strong. She evidenced intact frustration tolerance during the testing, and she persevered even with challenging tasks.

In terms of her language skills, overt problems with expressive language were evident, and Ellie's language was at times confusing and difficult to understand. She mumbled at times and articulation errors were noted. In contrast, few receptive language difficulties were noted and she had minimal difficulty understanding instructions. On the basis of these behavioral observations, along with symptom validity testing, this assessment appears to be a valid measure of Ellie's functioning.

Tests Administered

- Clinical interview with Mr. and Mrs. Brown
- Clinical interview with Ellie Brown
- Medical Symptom Validity Test (MSVT)
- Wechsler Intelligence Scale for Children–Fifth Edition (WISC–V)
- California Verbal Learning Test–Children Version (CVLT–C)
- Rey Complex Figure Test and Recognition Trial (RCFT)
- A Developmental Neuropsychological Assessment–Second Edition (NEPSY–II): Selected Subtests
- IVA+Plus Continuous Performance Test (IVA+Plus)
- Wisconsin Card Sort Test-64: Computer Version 2 (WCST-64)
- Wechsler Individual Achievement Test–Third Edition (WIAT–III): Selected Subtests
- Comprehensive Test of Phonological Processing–Second Edition (CTOPP–2): Selected Subtests
- Clinical Evaluation of Language Fundamentals–Fifth Edition (CELF5)
- Gray Oral Reading Test–Fifth Edition (GORT–5)
- Beck Youth Inventory–Second Edition (BYI–II)
- Sentence Completion
- Kinctic Family Drawing
- Conners 3 Parent Rating Scales
- Achenbach Child Behavior Checklist
- Short Sensory Profile
- Behavior Rating Inventory of Executive Function (BRIEF)

- Adaptive Behavior Assessment System–Second Edition (ABAS–II)
- Childhood Autism Rating Scale—Second Edition (CARS2)
- Gilliam Asperger's Rating Scale (GADS)

Test Results

Intellectual Abilities

In order to assess Ellie's intellectual ability, she was administered the WISC–V, which is an individually administered test of a child's intellectual ability and cognitive strengths and weaknesses. This test has six composite scores: Verbal Comprehension Index, Visual Spatial Index, Fluid Reasoning Index, Working Memory Index, Processing Speed Index, and Full Scale IQ. The Full Scale IQ (FSIQ) is derived from a combination of the subtest scores and is considered the most representative estimate of global intellectual functioning. However, in Ellie's case, the FSIQ is likely not the best measure of her intellectual functioning, due to the significant variability within the index scores. She displayed three significant strengths and one significant weakness in her index profile, reflecting an unusual degree of scatter (four significant discrepancies out of five indexes occurs less than 5% of the time among normal children; see Chapter 7, Table 7.9). Therefore, it is more meaningful to consider Ellie's unique cognitive strengths and weaknesses.

Ellie demonstrated a significant weakness in her verbal reasoning abilities as measured by the Verbal Comprehension Index (65; 1st percentile). Her performance was in the Extremely Low range on this index reflecting serious weaknesses in her ability to access and apply acquired word knowledge. Her verbal abstract reasoning is particularly deficient, and Ellie responded in a very rigid, black-and-white manner on this task. In fact, Ellie clearly has an impaired ability to think abstractly in a flexible manner, and she was consistently very literal. Deficits were also noted in Ellie's knowledge of vocabulary words and her general fund of information. On the other hand, Ellie's commonsense reasoning was relatively stronger and only mildly impaired on a measure less impacted by expressive language deficits.

In sharp contrast to her deficits in verbal reasoning, Ellie demonstrated a relative strength on the Visual Spatial Index (100; 50th percentile). Her performances were consistently Average on these measures of her ability to understand visual-spatial relationships to construct geometric designs from a model.

Ellie's performances on measures of fluid reasoning were extremely variable. Although she evidenced Low Average performance on the Fluid Reasoning Index (85; 16th percentile), significant variability between the subtests comprising this index was noted. Ellie struggled on a measure requiring her to apply the quantitative concept of equality to understand the relationship among objects. In contrast, intact performance was noted on a task requiring Ellie to identify the underlying conceptual rule that links stimuli and then to apply that concept appropriately. Ellie's performance was also Average on a timed measure of mental arithmetic, consistent with the school's report of her math achievement.

No deficits were noted in Ellie's ability to register, hold, and manipulate visual and auditory information in conscious awareness. She performed in the Average range on the Working Memory Index (94; 34th percentile). Ellie's ability to identify visual and auditory information, to hold it in temporary storage, and to manipulate it was consistently intact.

Similarly, no areas of weakness were evident in Ellie's speed and accuracy of visual scanning and visuomotor coordination on the Processing Speed Index (100; 50th percentile). Ellie performed in the Average range both on a measure of paired associate learning and graphomotor speed, and on a measure of visual scanning and discrimination.

Attention and Executive Functions

Deficits in higher-level reasoning were noted. Ellie evidenced an impaired ability to formulate basic concepts, to sort objects into categories, and to shift cognitive set from one concept to another on a measure of executive functioning assessing initiation, cognitive flexibility, and self-monitoring. Similarly, deficits were noted on a computerized measure of her ability to form abstract concepts, although she evidenced a strong ability to resist perseveration on this task.

In contrast, no deficits in sustained attention and response control were evident. Ellie had no difficulty on a subtest that uses an auditory continuous performance paradigm to measure selective and sustained attention, response inhibition, and executive functioning. The first part of this subtest is designed to assess selective auditory attention and the ability to sustain it (i.e., vigilance). The second part of this subtest is designed to assess the ability to shift and maintain a new and complex set involving both inhibition of previously learned responses and correctly responding to matching or contrasting stimuli. Ellie evidenced High Average performance on both components of this task.

In order to further assess her sustained attention, Ellie was administered the IVA+Plus. This task is intended to be mildly boring and demanding of sustained attention over a 13-minute period of time. On this task Ellie was required to self-regulate and respond to target stimuli (the number "1" presented in either an auditory or visual format on the computer) and refrain from responding to nontarget stimuli (the number "2" presented in the same formats). No areas of concern were noted on this task, and Ellie was able to remain alert to both visual and auditory targets. She was not distractible and her response control was intact in both domains.

Further measures of Ellie's attentional functioning were obtained by having Ellie's mother complete various rating scales. Ellie was rated by her mother as evidencing moderate problems with inattention but no hyperactivity/impulsivity. No significant executive functioning problems were noted.

Language and Phonological Processing
Ellie was administered measures to assess how well she understands and uses words and sentences to communicate with others. Ellie's listening comprehension skills were Average on tasks assessing her receptive vocabulary as well as on measures of her oral discourse comprehension. However, variability in verbal fluency was noted. Ellie evidenced High Average semantic verbal fluency but very weak phonemic verbal fluency. This deficit in phonemic verbal fluency is consistent with deficits in reading, spelling, and phonological awareness discussed later in this report.

On more complex language assessment with the CELF5, Ellie received a Core Language score of 82 (12th percentile), which is in the Low Average range. Although Ellie's Receptive Language Index of 95 was in the Average range, significant impairment was noted in her expressive language skills, as evidenced by her Expressive Language Index of 78. In fact, Ellie's expressive language skills are significantly weaker than her receptive language skills. Her overall Language Memory Index was only at the 9th percentile, indicating that Ellie is at risk in the language areas. On the CELF5, Ellie performed in the Average range on measures of her ability to interpret spoken directions of increasing length and complexity, her ability to interpret sentences that make comparisons and specify relationships, and her ability to assemble syntactic structures by producing grammatically correct sentences from visually and auditorily presented phrases. In contrast, mild deficits were noted in Ellie's ability to understand relationships between words, and more serious impairments were noted on measures of Ellie's ability to formulate sentences when given grammatical constraints, as well as her ability to recall and reproduce sentences of varying length and syntactic complexity. When formulating sentences, Ellie made numerous errors, such as "The boy and the girl is playing," and her sentences were at times nonsensical, such as "Before they were buying groceries before they were checking out."

In order to assess her phonological processing, Ellie was administered measures of phonological awareness and rapid naming. *Phonological awareness* refers to the ability to understand the sound structure of oral language. For example, it includes a child's ability to understand that letters represent sounds, how sounds are blended, and how those sounds can build words. Phonological memory is the ability to hold a sound in one's short-term or working memory. Rapid naming measures one's ability to retrieve language information from long-term or permanent memory. Research indicates that these three kinds of phonological processing appear to be especially relevant for mastery of written language.

In the area of phonological awareness, Ellie's overall score falls within the moderately impaired range. Within this skill area, Ellie evidenced impaired performance on a measure requiring her to combine sounds to form words, as in blending the sounds "c-oh-n" together to form the word "cone." Her performances were also weak when required to remove sounds from spoken words to form other words, such as removing the *b* from "bold" to say "old" as well as on a subtest assessing Ellie's ability to identify target sounds in words (such as the second sound in the word "dog").

In contrast, Average performances were noted in the area of phonological memory when required to recall a series of numbers of varying length as well as on a measure of her ability to repeat nonwords, such as "mistruf."

Similarly, Ellie displayed Average overall ability in her efficient retrieval of phonological information from long-term memory. Her speed of naming numbers was intact, but she was a little slow when required to rapidly name letters. This mild deficit in efficiency and fluency impacts the automaticity of the reading process, and this drains resources in mental energy which might otherwise be directed to the higher-level skill of comprehension.

Memory

Symptom validity testing indicated good effort and intact memory. Ellie was administered further tests of memory assessing how well she takes in, stores, and remembers information presented both visually and verbally.

Visual Memory Ellie evidenced High Average performances on both initial and delayed recall trials of a test of spatial memory for novel visual material. This test assesses spatial recall, visual content recognition, and overall visuospatial memory. In contrast, difficulties were noted on a complex test of spatial memory requiring Ellie to reproduce a detailed design from memory. In particular, some organizational deficits were noted on this task. Mild to moderate impairment was noted in her initial recall and in her delayed recall. Her recognition memory was mildly impaired.

Verbal Memory Ellie's performances were intact on a complex measure of contextual verbal memory, and she was able to recall an expected number of details from this detailed auditory task. More difficulty was evident on a measure of the strategies and processes involved in learning and recalling verbal material. On this task, Ellie's ability to repeat a list of words the first time she heard it indicates an Average initial attention span for auditory-verbal information. On her fifth learning attempt, however, her performance was Low Average. Her responses reflected a somewhat atypical pattern of recall from different regions of the test. After a short delay, Ellie's recall of the list was Low Average, but she did better after a longer delay, performing in the Average range. Category cueing was consistently beneficial. On a delayed recognition test for the words, Ellie's ability to discriminate between words that were on the list and those that were not was Average for her age. Ellie's ability to recognize information was about the same as her ability to recall it. Taken together, these findings suggest that Ellie exhibited Low Average to Average encoding and retrieval skills in learning verbal information.

Sensorimotor Functioning

Sensorimotor tests were administered to assess how well Ellie could control her hand movements. Ellie is right-handed. Ellie had no difficulty bilaterally on measures of finger dexterity and motor speed. In contrast, Ellie's motor programming was impaired on a task assessing her ability to learn and automatize a series of rhythmic movements. Variability was noted in Ellie's graphomotor skills. Although she worked very slowly on these tasks, her accuracy was strong. That is, she worked carefully and deliberately.

On a short sensory profile, Ellie was rated by her parents as evidencing typical performance in all areas and no sensory concerns were noted.

Visual–Spatial

Ellie's ability to reproduce simple visual-spatial designs was intact. However, her ability to reproduce a much more complex design was weak.

Academic Skills

In order to assess her academic achievement, Ellie was administered the GORT–5 as well as subtests from the WIAT–III.

Reading   Ellie's performances were consistently impaired on reading measures. Her word attack was extremely weak when required to read nonsense words. When required to decode isolated words, Ellie's performances were mildly impaired. Similar impairment was noted on measures of reading fluency, and both her reading rate and her reading accuracy were below grade level. Her reading was stilted, she skipped words, inserted words, mispronounced words, and confused words (such as "least" for "last," "server" for "severe," and "protect" for "predict"). More notable difficulties were evident in Ellie's reading comprehension skills, and her responses did not always relate to the question in a meaningful way.

Mathematics   Ellie's math skills are an area of relative strength. She evidenced Average performance on a measure of math problem-solving skills. Similarly, Ellie performed within normal limits on measures of her timed math fact retrieval. Mild deficits were noted in Ellie's untimed math calculation skills due to inability to divide numbers or to understand basic fractional concepts.

Written Language   Ellie had serious difficulty on tasks that required her to correctly spell verbally presented words. She made some unusual errors, such as "bag" for "page," as well as some less concerning errors, such as "campt" for "camped." Her performances were variable on a measure of sentence writing. She had no difficulty when required to combine sentences, but she struggled to generate sentences using a target word. Ellie's sentences were often meaningless and contained numerous spelling errors, such as "An football tean are go the chapen-ship."

Psychological Functioning

Ellie rated herself as evidencing intact self-esteem and no problems with anger, depression, or anxiety. She described her father as "nice" and her mother as "loving." Her family was described as "kind." Ellie indicated that her family treats her "kind and nice." She was unable to successfully complete most of the items on a sentence completion task due to her impaired expressive language skills.

Variability was noted on measures of social perception. Ellie evidenced strong performance on a task assessing her ability to understand mental functions such as belief, intention, deception, emotion, imagination, and pretending. This test also assesses the ability to recognize that others have their own thoughts, ideas, and feelings that may be different from one's own, the ability to recognize how emotion relates to social context and to recognize the appropriate affect given various social contexts. In contrast, serious deficits were noted on a task assessing Ellie's ability to discriminate among common facial expressions. It is uncertain whether this impairment was due to a true struggle with facial affect discrimination or if this impairment reflected difficulty understanding the instructions.

On rating scales, Mrs. Brown did not report that Ellie is struggling with internalizing or externalizing behaviors. At the same time, serious problems with Ellie's peer relations were noted. Nonetheless, Ellie was not rated as meeting diagnostic criteria for an autistic spectrum disorder on the CARS2 or the GADS.

Mrs. Brown was also asked to complete an adaptive behavior rating scale. Adaptive skills are practical everyday skills required to function and meet environmental demands, including effectively taking care of oneself and interacting with other people. The categories of adaptive behaviors assessed include Conceptual (communication and academic skills), Social (interpersonal and social competence skills), and Practical (independent living and daily living skills). Mrs. Brown rated Ellie as evidencing Average Conceptual skills, although variability in this domain was noted with a *strength in self-direction* and a *weakness in communication*. Ellie's Social functioning was rated as Borderline and a significant *weakness in her interpersonal skills* was identified. No deficits in Ellie's Practical skills were noted, and a *strength in health and safety* was identified. Overall Ellie's adaptive functioning was rated at the 34th percentile in the Average range.

Neuropsychological Implications and Diagnostic Impression

Ellie Brown is a young girl whose neurocognitive profile reflects some developmental unevenness in her functioning. Ellie's visual-spatial skills are intact, reflecting strong constructional abilities. She also evidences intact ability to register, maintain, and manipulate information in conscious awareness as well as adequate cognitive efficiency when problem solving, learning, and reasoning. Her sustained attention and response control are areas of strength. However, Ellie struggles in other areas. Specifically, significant deficits are consistently noted in her storage, retrieval, and application of word knowledge. Her expressive language skills are an area of significant impairment, and this deficit is apparent on both verbal and written tasks. In addition, Ellie tends to be extremely concrete and she struggles with abstractions. Ellie's novel problem solving is variable and deficits in higher-level thinking are evident. Some notable academic deficits are

apparent in areas of reading and spelling. No concerns about Ellie's emotional functioning are noted, but serious social difficulties are evident.

Based on these findings, the following diagnoses are made:

315.0 developmental reading disorder

315.39 language disorder

Recommendations

Educational Interventions

- Clearly Ellie qualifies for special education services as both learning disabled and speech and language impaired. Therefore, in any academic environment, specific academic interventions and intensive language-based support are necessary. A multisensory and phonetically based approach to reading is strongly recommended.
- Work with a certified academic language therapist (CALT) would likely be extremely beneficial.
- Frequent sessions with a speech and language therapist are critical due to Ellie's language disorder. These could be provided through the school district.
- In any classroom environment, various modifications would be critical. For example, **preferential seating** in the front of the classroom would be necessary. In addition, Ellie should not be required to rely on her note-taking skills. Ellie's teachers might provide her with an **outline of the lesson,** and she could fill in the main ideas on the lesson outline. **50% extended time on testing** is recommended on academic tasks. This will also eventually be relevant for college entrance exams. Rather than essay-type tests, Ellie will better be able to demonstrate her knowledge through **multiple-choice and fill-in-the-blank tests**.
- Due to deficits in fluid reasoning abilities, Ellie will likely have difficulty making deductions,

inductions, and predictions; drawing inferences; answering critical thinking questions; interpreting graphs or charts (although her good visual-spatial strengths might help her deal with these types of visual stimuli); and applying problem-solving skills. She may evidence ineffective strategies for task completion, a struggle perceiving relationships, difficulties deriving solutions to new or novel problems, and a struggle to extend her knowledge through critical thinking. These deficits likely impact Ellie's reading comprehension and math reasoning skills as well as her ability to organize her written expression in a manner that clearly illustrates the relationships between ideas.

- When learning new information, Ellie should have material presented in smaller segments than others her age, especially due to lack of automaticity reported in test results. Basic skills should be practiced until they are overlearned. When trying to remember information, as when studying for a test, Ellie should practice over a number of days rather than trying to "cram" everything into a short time period.

- To improve her reading comprehension strategies, Ellie is encouraged to try to restate difficult material in her own words when reading, write down the page numbers for things she does not understand so that she can ask about them later, make a list of words she doesn't understand when reading so she can ask about them later, and try to relate what she reads to what she already knows. Ellie's parents are encouraged to read *7 Keys to Comprehension: How to Help Your Kids Read It and Get It!* by Susan Zimmerman and Chryse Hutchins in order to help Ellie develop strategies to read for meaning and comprehend text.

- Due to Ellie's reading and language difficulties, a special education environment might be appropriate.

- Ellie might benefit from a social skills group, and a referral will be made.

It has been my utmost pleasure to work with Ellie and her lovely parents. I hope that this assessment has been helpful in terms of shedding light on her difficulties and I trust that with appropriate interventions, Ellie's difficulties will be diminished. Please feel free to contact me should you have questions about this assessment.

Psychometric Summary

Table 14.1 Ellie's Wechsler Intelligence Scale for Children–Fifth Edition (WISC–V) Results

Composite	Composite Score	Percentile Rank	95% Confidence Interval	Qualitative Description
Verbal Comprehension (VCI)	65–W	1	60–75	Extremely Low
Visual Spatial (VSI)	100–S	50	92–108	Average
Fluid Reasoning (FRI)	85	16	79–93	Low Average
Working Memory (WMI)	94–S	34	87–102	Average
Processing Speed (PSI)	100–S	50	91–109	Average
Full Scale (FSIQ)	80	9	75–86	Low Average

Ancillary Composite	Index Score	Percentile Rank	90% Confidence Interval	Qualitative Description
Quantitative Reasoning (QRI)	82	12	78–88	Low Average
Auditory Working Memory (AWMI)	103–S	58	97–109	Average
Nonverbal (NVI)	92	30	87–98	Average
General Ability (GAI)	76	5	72–82	Very Low
Cognitive Proficiency (CPI)	96	39	90–102	Average

Table 14.1   (*Continued*)

Verbal Comprehension Subtests	Scaled Score	Percentile Rank
Similarities	2–W	0.4
Vocabulary	5	5
(Information)	5	5
(Comprehension)	7	16

Visual Spatial Subtests	Scaled Score	Percentile Rank
Block Design	10	50
Visual Puzzles	10	50

Fluid Reasoning Subtests	Scaled Score	Percentile Rank
Matrix Reasoning	10	50
Figure Weights	5	5
(Arithmetic)	9	37

Working Memory Subtests	Scaled Score	Percentile Rank
Digit Span	9	37
Picture Span	9	37
(Letter-Number Seq.)	12	75

Processing Speed Subtests	Scaled Score	Percentile Rank
Coding	10	50
Symbol Search	10	50

Secondary subtests are in parentheses.

Table 14.2   Ellie's Green's Medical Symptom Validity Test Results

Paired Associates	Free Recall
Good Effort; Normal range memory	Good Effort; Normal range memory

Table 14.3   Ellie's A Developmental Neuropsychological Assessment–Second Edition (NEPSY–II) Results

Attention and Executive Functioning	Scaled Score	Percentile Rank
Animal Sorting	7	16
Auditory Attention	13	84
Response Set	13	84

Language	Scaled Score	Percentile Rank
Word Generation—Semantic Fluency	12	75
Word Generation—Initial Letter Fluency	6	9

Memory	Scaled Score	Percentile Rank
Memory for Designs	12	75
Memory for Designs Delayed	12	75
Narrative Memory Free & Cued Recall	10	50
Narrative Memory Recognition	—	26–50

Sensorimotor	Scaled Score	Percentile Rank
Fingertip Tapping—Dominant Hand	11	63
Fingertip Tapping—Nondominant Hand	12	75
Manual Motor Sequences	—	3–10
Visuomotor Precision—Time	6	9
Visuomotor Precision—Accuracy	—	>75

Visuospatial	Scaled Score	Percentile Rank
Design Copying	—	26–50

Social Perception	Scaled Score	Percentile Rank
Affect Recognition	3	1
Theory of Mind	—	>75

Table 14.4 Ellie's Wisconsin Card Sort Test–64: Computer Version 2 (WCST–64) Results

WCST Scores	Standard Scores	Percentile
Perseverative Errors	>145	>99
Nonperseverative Errors	61	<1
Conceptual Level Responses	82	12

Table 14.5 Ellie's California Verbal Learning Test–Children's Version (CVLT–C) Results

Level of Recall	Standard Score
Trial 1	0
Trial 5	–1.5
Total Trial 1–5	T=47
Short Delay Free Recall	–1.5
Short Delay Cued Recall	0.5
Long Delay Free Recall	–0.5
Long Delay Cued Recall	0

Table 14.6 Ellie's Rey Complex Figure Test and Recognition Trial (RCFT) Results

	T Score	Percentile Rank
Immediate Recall	36	8
Delayed Recall	32	4
Recognition Total Correct	41	18
Copy	–	≤1
Time to Copy	–	>16

Table 14.7 Ellie's Gray Oral Reading Test–Fifth Edition (GORT–5) Results

	Scaled Score	Percentile Rank
Rate	8	25
Accuracy	7	16
Fluency	7	16
Comprehension	6	9

Table 14.8 Ellie's Wechsler Individual Achievement Test–Third Edition (WIAT–III) Results

Subtest	Standard Score	Percentile Rank	Grade Equiv.	Age Equiv.
Listening Comprehension	98	45	5.4	10:6
Math Problem Solving	96	39	5.3	10:4
Sentence Composition	91	27	5.0	10:4
Word Reading	81	10	2.5	8:0
Pseudoword Decoding	64	1	<1.0	6:0
Numerical Operations	87	19	4.2	9:4
Spelling	75	5	2.1	7:4
Math Fluency–Addition	98	45	5.1	10:4
Math Fluency–Subtraction	100	50	5.2	10:8
Math Fluency–Multiplication	90	25	4.3	9:8

Table 14.9 Ellie's Clinical Evaluation of Language Fundamentals–Fifth Edition (CELF5) Results

Core/Index Scores	Standard Score	Percentile Rank
Core Language Score	82	12
Receptive Language Index	95	37
Expressive Language Index	78	7
Language Memory Index	80	9

Subtests	Scaled Score	Percentile Rank
Word Classes	8	25
Following Directions	10	50
Formulated Sentences	5	5
Recalling Sentences	5	5
Sentence Assembly	9	37
Semantic Relationships	10	50

Table 14.10   Ellie's Comprehensive Test of Phonological Processing—Second Edition (CTOPP–2) Results

Composite Scores	Standard Score	Percentile Rank
Phonological Awareness	73	3
Phonological Memory	95	37
Rapid Symbolic Naming	98	45

Subtests	Scaled Score	Percentile Rank
Elision	6	9
Blending Words	5	5
Phoneme Isolation	6	9
Memory for Digits	9	37
Nonword Repetition	9	37
Rapid Digit Naming	11	63
Rapid Letter Naming	8	25

Table 14.11   Ellie's Adaptive Behavior Assessment System—Second Edition (ABAS–II) Results

Parent Rating Summary		
Composite	Composite Score	Percentile Rank
GAC	94	34
Conceptual	95	37
Social	75	5
Practical	105	63

Skills Areas	Scaled Score	Percentile Rank
Communication	6	9
Community Use	11	63
Functional Academics	8	25
Home Living	10	50
Health/Safety	12	75
Leisure	7	16
Self-Care	11	63
Self-Direction	14	91
Social	3	1

CASE 14—JORDAN, AGE 15: COGNITIVE DEVELOPMENT IN A CHILD WHO IS HARD OF HEARING: IS IT MORE THAN JUST HEARING?

Marsha Vasserman

Name: Jordan

Age: 15 years 2 months

Grade: 10

Examiner: Dr. Vasserman

Reason for Referral

Jordan is a 15-year-old Caucasian boy attending eighth grade at a parochial school. He has bilateral sensorineural hearing loss with subsequent, sequential bilateral cochlear implants. Jordan has a history of difficulty with language acquisition despite cochlear implants and intensive language services. He was referred by his audiology treatment team in order to clarify the diagnostic picture, better understand his slow language development, and aid with educational and treatment planning.

Relevant Background Information

Developmental, Medical, and Family History

Jordan is the product of a normal pregnancy and delivery, which was followed by an uncomplicated neonatal period. Gross motor development was somewhat delayed, with Jordan not walking independently until 17 months, although no other gross motor concerns were noted, and he is well coordinated. Fine motor skills developed appropriately. Language milestones were significantly delayed. Jordan passed his newborn hearing screen, which was determined to have been a false negative. His parents expressed concern when Jordan was around 12 months due to limited babbling. Bilateral profound hearing loss was diagnosed at 17 months. Jordan received his first implant in the right ear at 20 months, with a second left implant at age 3. Shortly after the first implantation, Jordan spoke his first words, but

vocabulary acquisition was slow and his grammar continues to be weak. Storytelling and conversational skills continue to be poor.

Overall, Jordan is a healthy and athletic child. Medical history is not significant for seizures, chronic illnesses, or infections. Jordan sustained a concussion at age 10 when a peer ran into him during a game. He recovered quickly with no lasting effects. His vision is within normal limits. His hearing with implants is in the mild hearing loss level, with discrimination of speech sounds occurring at 15dB. He does not currently take any medication and has no allergies. There are no concerns regarding sleep or appetite.

Jordan lives with his parents and three younger siblings. Parents are employed as teachers and both completed bachelor degrees. Family history is significant for autism spectrum disorder, anxiety, reading disability, and ADHD.

Educational and Social History

Jordan has attended his current school since prekindergarten. He has been evaluated multiple times through the Board of Education (BOE), with evaluations reflecting poor language development, with stronger receptive language skills in the context of poor expressive vocabulary and sentence formulations. Recommendations included intensive auditory, speech and language therapy, and continued use of a Frequency Modulation (FM) unit in school.

Jordan currently attends 10th grade, in a general education classroom with 30 students. He has Teacher of the Deaf (TOD) services as well as private speech and language therapy. Academically, Jordan's writing is better than his speech, but even in writing, his sentence structure and grammar is poor. Weaknesses in reading were also reported, particularly guessing at words and exhibiting weaknesses in comprehension. Jordan enjoys math but has struggled with the introduction of the Common Core curriculum due to the increased language demands. Teachers reported that Jordan struggles to learn material and does not acquire knowledge at the same rate as his peers. Individual support to reinforce the material at the end of the day has been helpful, and Jordan receives 30 minutes of daily individual support through the Learning Center at school.

Socially, teachers describe Jordan as a respectful, well-mannered student, whose behavior is never problematic. He has friends in school and is well liked, but he is not able to communicate at the same level as other children. He enjoys sports and plays basketball.

Behavioral Observations

Jordan was seen for one testing session. Overall, he presented as a polite, cooperative, earnest boy. Receptively, Jordan utilized visual cues and lip reading to support his understanding. Nonetheless, he required repetition and re-explanation of instructions and often sought to clarify directions. He benefited significantly from demonstration and practice. Expressive language was poor, and he struggled significantly to express his ideas. Articulation weaknesses moderately impacted his intelligibility, particularly as lengthier output was required. Jordan was somewhat shy but appropriately related and engaged with the examiners.

Jordan willingly engaged in all tasks presented to him, and he demonstrated strong attention and persistence across tasks, throughout the day. Overall, he strived to do well and required few breaks and minimal prompting. Given adequate effort and motivation, this evaluation is considered a valid estimate of his current cognitive abilities (Reliable Digit Span = 10; Test of Memory Malingering [TOMM] Trial 1 = 49).

Instruments Used

Wechsler Intelligence Scale for Children–Fifth Edition (WISC–V); Oral and Written Language Scales–Second Edition (OWLS–II); Delis-Kaplan Executive Function System (D-KEFS) Verbal Fluency; Rey Complex Figure Test (RCFT); Wide Range Assessment of Memory and Learning–Second Edition (WRAML–2); Tests of Everyday Attention for Children (TEA-Ch); Tower of London–Second Edition (TOL–2); Stroop Color and Word Test (Stroop); Trail Making Test (TMT); Auditory Consonant Trigrams Test (ACT); Grooved Pegboard; Beery-Buktenica Developmental Test of Visual-Motor Integration–Sixth Edition (Beery VMI); Wechsler Individual Achievement Test–Third Edition (WIAT–III); TOMM.

Test Results

Please note: Standard Scores (Sts) have a mean of 100 with a standard deviation of 15. Scaled Scores (Scs) have a mean of 10 with a standard deviation of 3. T-scores have a mean of 50, with a standard deviation of 10. Last, Z-scores have a mean of 0, with a standard deviation of 1. Scores within 1 standard deviation of the mean are considered average.

Intellectual Functioning

Jordan was administered the Wechsler Intelligence Scale for Children–Fifth Edition (WISC–V), an individually administered, norm-referenced test that is used to assess general intellectual performance. Jordan's overall intellectual ability was average compared to others his age (FSIQ = 92). Jordan's average to above-average skill on nonverbal tasks, as well as tasks assessing visual processing speed and working memory, contrasted with his poor verbal abilities and verbal knowledge. Jordan's Index profile reflects an enormous amount of scatter (see Chapter 7). His WISC–V Indexes ranged from 76 to 123; ranges of 47 or more points occurred less than 5% of the time in the standardization sample (see Table 7.4). Similarly, fewer than 5% of normal individuals had significant discrepancies (relative strengths or weaknesses) on four of the five WISC–V Indexes (see Table 7.9). Again, Jordan's three relative strengths and one weakness highlight the unusual variability in his cognitive profile. Even more notable are the two relative strengths and two relative weaknesses that John displayed on his Index profile. Given the significant discrepancy in his performances among different domains, his overall IQ is not an accurate reflection of his functioning. His performance is described in greater detail in the relevant sections below.

Language Functioning

During casual conversation, Jordan willingly answered questions posed to him, but his responses tended to be short and limited in content. While Jordan ultimately understood directions, he required frequent repetition and clarification and sometimes appeared to guess at what was being asked of him. Jordan's articulation was poor, and intelligibility decreased as the length of utterance increased. This was compounded by difficulties with syntax and grammar which made it difficult to understand him, particularly when content was not familiar to the examiner.

Jordan recently underwent a full communication evaluation, which found significant weaknesses in vocabulary development, expressive language, and sentence repetition, with relatively stronger receptive language. Nonetheless, overall language skills were found to be well below expectations. Accordingly, the current evaluation supplemented those results with several other tasks.

Consistent with previous evaluations, Jordan exhibited low-average listening comprehension (OWLS–II Listening Comprehension Sts = 80). Expressively, at the single word level, basic rapid naming skills were age appropriate. His ability to quickly generate and retrieve words was largely within the average range, with improved performance once structure was provided. In contrast, consistent with previous assessment, significant weaknesses were evident in word knowledge and expressive vocabulary (WISC–V Vocabulary Scs = 5). He was likewise weak in verbal reasoning skills and his fund of acquired knowledge (Similarities Scs = 6; Information Scs = 6).

Memory and Learning

Jordan's *verbal memory* was generally age appropriate (WRAML–2 Verbal Memory Sts = 95; Verbal Recognition Sts = 96). Jordan benefited from repetition and acquired information at a rate similar to peers, effectively retaining it over time, and demonstrating adequate recall and recognition of learned information. His contextual learning was also average. However, while he recalled a number of details from the stories, he was unable to adequately sequence the story after a delay, thus lacking cohesiveness and recalling details in random order.

To assess his ability to learn, store, and recall visually presented information, Jordan was administered a complex figure-copying task. Although when copying Jordan worked slowly and carefully and his approach was reasonably organized, he had some difficulty perceiving the gestalt of the figure and synthesizing the pieces. Notably, Jordan's independent recall both immediately and after a delay was impoverished. However, his ability to discriminate details from extraneous information was average, suggesting that he adequately encoded the information but had difficulty with independent retrieval.

Attention, Speed, and Executive Functioning

Executive functions are skills that help individuals develop and carry out their plans so that a goal can be achieved. The effectiveness of these executive functions can influence how well individuals respond to situations and complete assignments. Executive functions include the use of attention, the speed and accuracy of generating ideas and actions, the ability to control actions so that the best action is used in a situation, the ability to use thinking flexibly and keep thinking on track, and the ability to come up with a strategy or plan of action.

Parents and teachers described Jordan as highly organized and neat with his belongings and in accomplishing independent tasks. He prefers to do his homework independently, but requires individual support due to the complexity of the curriculum.

Notably, Jordan was highly focused throughout the assessment. He exhibited good attention and worked diligently. His mental efficiency and ability to quickly process simple, visual information was superior (Processing Speed Sts = 123). He worked accurately and quickly, particularly when making visual comparisons. Transcription skills and associated learning were average (Coding Scs = 11) to high (Symbol Search Scs = 17).

Jordan's performance on short tasks of simple attention was age appropriate across auditory and visual modalities (WISC–V Digits Forward Scs = 10; Picture Span Scs = 13; TEA-Ch Sky

Search Attention Score Scs = 8). Similarly, sustained auditory attention was also within normal limits. In contrast, when asked to divide attention between both visual and auditory modalities, Jordan struggled significantly. Similar difficulties were observed when required to divide auditory attention.

Jordan's cognitive flexibility and ability to shift his attention was average, as was his response inhibition for overlearned responses. However, Jordan exhibited relative difficulty planning his actions on a novel problem-solving task. He worked slowly and thoughtfully, but inefficiently, resulting in utilization of more moves and more time than expected.

Fine Motor, Visual–Spatial, and Visual–Motor Integration

Jordan displayed right-hand dominance for all writing and drawing tasks and utilized a thumb-over pencil grasp. Fine motor speed and dexterity were average for the dominant (right) hand but significantly below expectations for the nondominant hand. Graphomotor control and precision were age appropriate.

Jordan's visual-spatial perception and processing were strong (Visual Spatial Sts = 114). He demonstrated effective analysis and synthesis of abstract visual information (Block Design Scs = 14; Visual Puzzles Scs = 11). His nonverbal reasoning skills were low average (Fluid Reasoning Sts = 88), with typically developed pattern recognition and low-average quantitative reasoning abilities (Matrix Reasoning Scs = 8; Figure Weights Scs = 8).

When required to integrate visual input with a motor response, such as on copy tasks, Jordan's performance was consistently below age expectations, despite taking his time. Qualitatively, while he worked slowly and carefully, difficulties were noted in his approach to planning and visual organization.

Academic Functioning

Reading At the single-word level, Jordan's sight word vocabulary was poor, and while he was able to apply rules of phonics for decoding, this process lacked automaticity. Comprehension of text was below age expectations, with borderline impaired performance. Jordan showed greater difficulty in verbally expressing his answers but performed better when able to respond using a visual multiple choice format (OWLS–II Reading Comprehension Sts = 88).

Written Expression Jordan's handwriting consisted of well-formed, printed letters. Spelling skills were commensurate with decoding and word-reading abilities and were characterized by multiple phonologically-based errors, which appear to be also related to his mishearing of certain sounds. For example, Jordan spelled *enormous* "enlormis" and *invitation* was spelled as "intertation" and "intation"). In terms of longer written composition, Jordan's performance was low average and impacted by his overall language difficulties (OWLS–II Written Expression Sts = 84). Notably, Jordan was able to generate ideas, particularly when provided with visual cues and structure. However, sentence structure, word usage, as well as use of prepositions and pronouns were quite underdeveloped.

Mathematics Jordan's computational skills were at the lower limit of the low-average range (WIAT–III Numerical Operations Sts = 80). Notably, his approach to certain types of problems, such as long division, was well executed, suggesting he had good understanding of the process of solving such problems. But misunderstanding of certain questions due to impaired language impacted his performance across calculation and math application tasks.

Social-Emotional Functioning

Jordan is a sweet, hard-working, compliant boy. He was quiet but socially appropriate throughout the assessment. His presentation during the current evaluation reflected a generally euthymic mood, an appropriate range of affect, and good frustration tolerance. Teachers and parents described Jordan as being socially engaged and well liked by his peers but struggling significantly with communication. This is likely to become particularly salient at this stage, as he is entering adolescence and peer relationships become more based on conversation and shared information than shared activities. Further, while Jordan was described as a generally happy adolescent, his parents noted some frustration with homework.

Summary and Clinical Impressions

Jordan is a 15-year-old boy attending eighth grade at a parochial school. He has bilateral sensorineural hearing loss with subsequent, sequential bilateral cochlear implants. Jordan has a history of difficulty with language acquisition despite cochlear implants and intensive language services. He was referred by his audiology treatment team in order to clarify the diagnostic picture, better understand his slow language development, and aid with educational and treatment planning.

Intellectually, Jordan exhibited overall average cognitive skills, with strengths in visual-spatial abilities and weaknesses in verbal reasoning and comprehension. Visual processing speed was also an area of significant strength. While simple working memory skills were intact, he struggled with divided attention, particularly when dividing attention between auditory and visual tasks. Because he is hard of hearing, Jordan uses much more effort and cognitive resources for listening tasks, which leaves fewer available resources to devote to other cognitive tasks. This finding is particularly salient as divided attention is required to function effectively in the classroom (for example, listening to a lecture and taking notes). It will be particularly important to ensure appropriate accommodations to minimize the impact these divided attention weaknesses have on Jordan's performance. Otherwise, Jordan's attention and focus were strong. Additionally, in terms of executive functions, Jordan exhibited good cognitive flexibility and inhibition but had more difficulties with planning. Learning and memory were also within normal limits, but Jordan had difficulties with cohesively recalling narrative information and sequencing it appropriately. Language continues to be an area of significant struggle, with specific weaknesses in vocabulary development, grammar, and syntax

as well as articulation. Although graphomotor control was generally adequate, visual-motor integration and visual planning were below expectations. Finally, Jordan's academics, across the areas of reading, writing, and math, were consistently below age expectations.

Diagnostically speaking, Jordan's poor language skills are beyond what would be expected based on his chronic history of hearing difficulties. Thus, these deficits in language skills across the areas of vocabulary, grammar and syntax, and discourse are consistent with a diagnosis of a *language disorder (315.39, F80.9)*. Notably, language deficits significantly impact Jordan's functioning across other domains, including academics, social interactions, and social-emotional experiences. In Jordan's case, his language deficits are so significant that they are impacting not only language-based skills, such as reading and writing, but also his math skills. Further, due to language difficulties, Jordan utilizes far more cognitive energy than peers just to understand what is being asked of him. During the one-on-one evaluation, he was able to ask questions and he benefited from demonstration and practice, while in the classroom opportunities to do so are likely more limited. Finally, although Jordan does not qualify for specific learning disorder, his hearing difficulties and language impairment have so significantly impacted his development and academic achievement that this, in conjunction with weaknesses in visual-motor integration and planning, is consistent with a diagnosis of *other specified neurodevelopmental disorder associated with hearing impairment (315.8, F88)*.

Jordan is a hard-working, compliant adolescent who demonstrates many social strengths, despite language deficits. He is generally happy, although some frustrations have been noted as he is aware of his limitations, and his social experiences are negatively impacted by his language weaknesses. It is important to consider that because Jordan's language weaknesses limit his ability to express himself efficiently to peers and to adults, anxiety or mood symptoms could go unrecognized. Consequently, it will be important to closely monitor Jordan's emotional functioning.

Recommendations

Academic Placement and Services

- Jordan's parents are urged to request a meeting to amend his Individual Educational Service Program based on the results of this evaluation.
- Based on Jordan's cognitive profile, he requires placement in a small-sized classroom within a small school. At minimum, Jordan's school setting should include:
  - structured classrooms with lower student to teacher ratios;
  - teachers with experience working with students with language and learning weaknesses as well those who are deaf or hard of hearing;
  - consultation with Teacher of the Deaf on a weekly basis;
  - presentation of information in smaller units and clarification of information;
  - presentation of auditory material with visual cues and supports;
  - a reduced workload;
  - review of previously learned skills;
  - a classroom comprised of socially appropriate peers without significant behavioral difficulties
  - age-appropriate computer software to develop vocabulary in video-game format.
- Jordan should receive daily individual speech and language therapy focusing on his language and reading comprehension, vocabulary, communication skills, and written expression skills.
- Additionally, given Jordan's articulation weaknesses, and in light of his hearing loss, Jordan will benefit from a more kinesthetic approach to speech therapy. Programs such as Speech Buddy can be helpful as they teach appropriate tongue placement and mouth positioning. This physical method is likely to be more effective for improving Jordan's articulation. Speech Buddy tools can also be used at home for 10 minutes a day to improve articulation (http://www.speechbuddy.com)

- Jordan may benefit from the introduction of sign language to support his communication. Additionally, cued speech can also be incorporated as it is easily learned by those who interact with him frequently.
- Jordan is currently behind academically. He requires daily individualized work with a learning specialist, such as can be provided through Special Education Teacher Supports Services (SETSS), to target reading comprehension, written expression (spelling, grammar, and content), and math concepts.
  - The person who works with Jordan should be familiar with working with children with language disorders and hearing difficulties, and focus should be on developing skills for reading comprehension and on understanding math processes conceptually. Multisensory methods are likely to be most effective for Jordan.
  - Jordan will also benefit from practice and strategies for organizing his ideas, making outlines, and adding details to his writing, particularly with the support of graphic cues. He will likely benefit from using graphic organizers to help structure and complete his writing assignments. Draft Builder and Solo by the Don Johnston Company (www.donjohnston.com) are recommended, as is Inspiration (www.inspiration.com) These newer programs come with text-to-speak capabilities. This suite of programs contains a talking word processing program (Write:Outloud), a word prediction program (Co:Write), and a writing organization program (Draft: Builder). Another resource is Read and Write Gold by Text Help (www.readwritegold).
  - Jordan may benefit from programs such as Lindamood Bell Visualizing and Verbalizing to help develop listening and reading

comprehension, as this program teaches children to pair verbal information with visualization strategies to improve understanding and retention. When assessing his comprehension, support him by breaking down passages into smaller, more manageable chunks; provide visual supports; and minimize the need for expressive language to explain what he understood. These modifications will all be beneficial for Jordan.

- Jordan requires multisensory, multimodal math programs to help him grasp math instruction on a conceptual level. Options for multimodal math programs include *Making Math Real*, *Math-U-See*, and *Touch Math*.

- Given Jordan's struggles with divided attention and poor visual-motor integration:
  - He requires a note-taker during academic classes to allow him to focus on the lesson without worrying about missing content. When required to listen to information, particularly new content, Jordan should not be expected to do anything else at the same time.
  - Wherever possible, Jordan should be provided with copies of class notes prior to lessons; Jordan may also benefit from a note-taking "buddy system" where he exchanges notes with a responsible peer.

- Transition planning should focus on appropriate vocational goals for Jordan. A vocational assessment is also recommended to assess Jordan's interests and how they line up with his strengths.

Academic Accommodations

- Given Jordan's visual-motor integration and divided attention weaknesses, as well as difficulty formulating language, he should receive the following in-class and standardized assessment recommendations:
  - Jordan requires *100%* extended time for examinations.
  - Jordan needs a reader for exams.
  - He will benefit from testing in a separate location with minimal distractions.

- Directions and questions should be clarified as needed.
- Short breaks will allow him to recoup his energy and focus.
- Given Jordan's hearing difficulties, preferential seating is required, with him being seated in close proximity to the teacher and away from noisy areas.
- Teachers and parents should provide directions and instruction in simple, short chunks. Additionally, repetition of directions and instruction, visual supports, as well as checks for understanding, should be utilized.
- Jordan will benefit from frequent breaks to help him recoup his cognitive energy and refocus. Breaks typically need only be 1 or 2 minutes in duration and are best taken with a motor activity or a relaxing activity. He might get a drink of water, pick up papers, or simply bring his work to show the teacher.
- Given Jordan's hearing difficulties, he should continue to use an FM unit. Electrically coupled personal FM units (those that plug directly into the cochlear implant) have shown greater improvement in speech recognition in noise and should be considered, if not already in use.
- In light of Jordan's hearing difficulties, to aid with effective communication, Jordan's teachers should consider the following:
  - Speak directly facing Jordan, with face fully visible and in adequate lighting.
  - Ensure his attention.
  - Provide directions in a variety of formats (e.g. written and spoken).
  - Check for comprehension.
- The following modifications to the classroom environment are recommended:
  - Close doors to reduce hallway noise.
  - Put felt or rubber feet on chairs and desks to reduce extraneous noise.
  - In discussion-based classes, utilize circular seating and a "one person speaks at a time" rule.

All of these accommodations need to be implemented with sensitivity in view of Jordan being at the socially difficult age of 15. The accommodations call attention to him as being slow and different and may affect his emotional growth and experiences. Attention must also be focused on transitioning him to adult demands of the real world when all of these accommodations may no longer be feasible.

Table 14.12   Jordan's Intellectual Functioning Results

Wechsler Intelligence Scale for Children–Fifth Edition (WISC-V)

Index	Standard Score
Verbal Comprehension	76–W
Visual Spatial	114–S
Fluid Reasoning	88
Working Memory	107–S
Processing Speed	123–S
FSIQ	92

Subtests	Scaled Score
Verbal Comprehension	
Similarities	6–W
Vocabulary	5–W
Information	6
Visual Spatial	
Block Design	14–S
Visual Puzzles	11
Fluid Reasoning	
Matrix Reasoning	8
Figure Weights	8
Working Memory	
Digit Span	9
Picture Span	13
Processing Speed	
Coding	11
Symbol Search	17–S

Table 14.13   Jordan's Language Functioning Results

Peabody Picture Vocabulary Test–Fourth Edition (PPVT–4)*

Total	Standard Score
*Results from 1/30/14	70

Clinical Evaluation of Language Fundamentals—Fourth Edition (CELF–4)

Measure	Standard Score
Core Language Index	74

Subtest	Scaled Score		
Concepts and Following Directions	8		
Formulated Sentences	5		
Recalling Sentences	3		
Word Classes—Receptive	5		
Word Classes—Expressive	5	5*	Borderline
Word Classes—Total	5	5*	Borderline

*Results from 1/30/14

Oral and Written Language Scales—Second Edition (OWLS–II)

	Standard Score
Listening Comprehension	80

Delis-Kaplan Executive Function System (D-KEFS)

Measure	Standard Score
Verbal Fluency	
Letter Fluency	8
Category Fluency	10
Category Switching	9
Switching Accuracy	8
Percent Set-Loss Errors	7
Percent Switching Accuracy	6

Table 14.14 Jordan's Memory and Learning Results

Rey Complex Figure Test (RCFT)

Measure	Z-Score
Immediate Recall	−1.8
Delayed Recall (30-minute)	−1.7
Recognition: True Positives	−0.4
Recognition: Total Correct	−0.2

Wide Range Assessment of Memory and Learning—
Second Edition (WRAML–2)

Measure	Standard Score
Verbal Memory	95
Verbal Recognition	96

Measure	Scaled Score
Story Memory	9
Story Memory Delay Recall	8
Story Recognition	9
Verbal Learning	9
Verbal Learning Delay Recall	8
Verbal Learning Recognition	9

	Z-Score
Verbal Learning Slope	0.12
Verbal Learning Retention	0.29

**Table 14.15 Jordan's Attention and Executive
Functioning Results**

Tests of Everyday Attention for Children (TEA-Ch)

Measure	Scaled Score
Sky Search	
Total Targets	9
Time per Target	8
Attention Score	8
Score!	11
Sky Search DT	6
Score DT	2

Delis–Kaplan Executive Function System (D-KEFS)
Verbal Fluency

Letter Fluency	7
Category Fluency	10
Category Switching	9
Switching Accuracy	8
Percent Set-Loss Errors	7
Percent Switching Accuracy	6

Auditory Consonant Trigrams Test (ACT)

Measure	Z-Score
0-Second Delay	0.1
3-Second Delay	0.5
9-Second Delay	−1
18-Second Delay	−1.3
Total Correct	−0.9

Trail Making Test (TMT)	Z-Score
Trails A	0.7
Trails B	0.4

Tower of London—Second Ed. (TOL–2)

Measure	Standard Score
Total Correct	88
Total Move Score	86
Total Initiation Time	100
Total Execution Time	70
Total Time	80
Total Time Violations	94
Total Rule Violations	104

Table 14.15 *(Continued)*

Stroop Color and Word Test (Stroop)

Measure	T-score
Word Score	52
Color Score	50
Color-Word Score	54
Interference Score	46
Digit Span	**Scaled Score**
Total	9
Digit Span Forward	10
Digit Span Backward	8
Digit Span Sequencing	9

Table 14.16 Jordan's Visual Perception and Visual-Motor Integration Results

Beery-Buktenica Developmental Test of Visual-Motor Integration—Sixth Ed. (Beery VMI)

Measure	Standard Score
Beery VMI	73
Motor Coordination	100

Rey Complex Figure Test (RCFT)

Measure	*Z-Score*
Copy	−1.2
Time to Copy	1.1

Table 14.17 Jordan's Fine Motor Functioning Results

	Grooved Pegboard
Measure	*Z-Score*
Pegboard—Dominant Hand	0.2
Pegboard—Nondominant Hand	−1.8

Table 14.18 Jordan's Academic Functioning Results

Wechsler Individual Achievement Test–Third Edition (WIAT–III)

Subtests/COMPOSITES	Standard Score
BASIC READING	76
Word Reading	72
Pseudoword Decoding	82
READING COMP and FLUENCY	
Reading Comprehension	77
WRITTEN EXPRESSION	
Spelling	78
MATHEMATICS	80
Math Problem Solving	82
Numerical Operations	80
MATH FLUENCY	85
Math Fluency—Addition	93
Math Fluency—Subtraction	79
Math Fluency—Multiplication	88

Oral and Written Language Scales—Second Edition (OWLS-II)

	Standard Score
Written Expression	84
Reading Comprehension	88

Note. All scores derived from age-based norms.

Table 14.19 Jordan's Symptom Validity Results

TOMM	Raw Score
Trial 1	49
Reliable Digit Span	10

CASE 15—JANE, AGE 8: CONSUMER-RESPONSIVE APPROACH TO ASSESSMENT REPORTS

Robert Lichtenstein and Joan Axelrod

Psychological and psychoeducational assessment reports have long been criticized for being inaccessible to most readers—weighed down by jargon, test scores, excessive length, and overly difficult reading level (Brenner, 2003; Groth-Marnat, 2009; Harvey, 2013; Hass & Carriere, 2014). As an alternative, Lichtenstein (2013a, 2013b, 2014) proposed that school psychologists adopt a "consumer-responsive" approach. The core assumption of this approach is that reports should be readily understood by, and useful to, those individuals who are in the best position to use the information in the interests of the child: parents, teachers, and other school personnel. Key characteristics of consumer-responsive reports are briefly summarized here and illustrated in the sample report below.

The structure and content of a consumer-responsive report are guided by purpose rather than by convention. Consequently, consumer-responsive reports are child-focused rather than test-focused. Of paramount importance is to answer the referral question and to highlight those findings that help the reader understand the child's situation, functioning, and needs. Thus, the evaluator organizes findings by themes rather than discussing the results of each test administered in turn. These themes might be areas of functioning (e.g., language, memory, written language) or referral questions (e.g., suspected learning disability, impact of emotional factors, ill-suited learning environment). Consumer-responsive reports are relevant and economical. The evaluator reports findings selectively rather than exhaustively, dispensing with information that is of little relevance and serves only to obscure the main findings. A helpful strategy is to compose the Summary and Recommendations section first, which then provides guidance as to what to include and emphasize in the body of the report.

To be useful, reports must be understood by the primary consumers. Meaningful information, including psychological constructs, can and should be conveyed at reading levels accessible to the general population. Readability statistics, such as those generated by the Flesch-Kincaid tests (which are included as a feature of Microsoft Word), can provide useful feedback for report writers. As a rough guide, evaluators should aim for a Flesch-Kincaid grade level score below 12.0. Consumer-responsive reports further enhance readability, with little loss of meaning, by favoring verbal descriptors of performance levels (e.g., "above average" or "extremely low") over reliance on standard scores and confidence intervals. This can be accomplished without compromising the value of quantitative findings for measurement-savvy readers by including a full account of scores and psychometric data in a "Data Summary" as an appendix to the report.

Psychoeducational Assessment

Name: Jane Smith

Date of birth: 7/19/2007

Testing dates: 11/4/2015; 11/6/2015

Age: 8-3

Grade: 2

Reason for Referral

Jane was referred for psychoeducational evaluation because her parents are concerned that she is unhappy about going to school and seems to be having difficulty learning to read.

Assessment Procedures

Parent interview

Teacher interview

Classroom observation

Bender Visual-Motor Gestalt Test (Bender-Gestalt 2)

Wechsler Intelligence Scale for Children– Fifth Edition (WISC–V)

Comprehensive Test of Phonological Processing (CTOPP–2)— phonological awareness subtests

Wechsler Individual Achievement Test–Third Edition (WIAT–III)—reading and writing subtests

Assessment Findings

Background Information

Jane is currently in the second grade at Standard Elementary school, which she has attended since school entry in kindergarten. School records indicate that her attendance had been excellent through the first grade, but she has been absent five times over the first two months of second grade. When Jane was in first grade, her mother requested a speech and language evaluation because of the family history of reading difficulty and because Jane was expressing some reluctance about school. That evaluation indicated that Jane's language skills fell in the average to above-average range on all subtests of the CELF–5.

Interviews

Jane's mother was interviewed by phone. She reported that the family has lived in Everytown since before Jane was born. Her mother works as a bookkeeper for a local business. Her father is a high school science teacher. Jane has been in good general health with no known medical problems other than typical childhood illnesses. She reached early developmental landmarks such as walking and talking at the expected times. Her mother recalls that Jane spoke relatively early. There is a family history of reading delays and difficulties.

Jane's mother describes her as a sweet, lively, and creative girl. She loves to do arts and crafts projects, often making interesting greeting cards and objects from scrap materials she finds around the house. She generally has a positive, upbeat disposition. However, Jane often complains that she doesn't want to go to school, saying that school is "boring." She sometimes balks at doing homework but, with a little urging, will typically complete any assigned work.

Jane's teacher, Ms. Marple, reported that Jane is usually involved and cooperative with classroom activities. She is very social and has many friends in her class. She will often take a leadership role during play or cooperative learning activities. She tends to volunteer more during math activities than during reading or language arts. Her teacher also reported that Jane is making slow, but steady, progress in reading. Her skills lag behind those of some of her closer friends, and she seems self-conscious about reading in front of them.

Behavioral Observations

Classroom

Jane was observed in her second-grade classroom on two occasions. On the first occasion, the entire class was gathered on the rug as the teacher led a discussion about a folktale they had read. Jane sat in the middle of the group among several other girls. When the teacher asked students to explain the moral of the folktale, many children volunteered. Jane hesitated, looked around at her peers, and then raised her hand. The teacher called on another student who explained the moral. When the teacher then asked for evidence of the moral, Jane raised her hand quickly and offered a supporting event from the story.

During the second observation, the class was working in small groups in learning centers, while one group at a time read with the teacher. When Jane's group was called to read, Jane wandered to her cubby, explaining she had to find her book. After Jane joined the group, the teacher asked who wanted to read first. Most students volunteered, but Jane did not. When it was her turn, she read more hesitantly than the others in her group, even though the text appeared to be fairly simple and repetitive. Whenever Jane encountered a word she did not know, she would look toward the teacher, wait for the teacher or another student to supply the word, then say, "Oh yeah" and continue reading. After about 20 minutes, the group was directed to work independently at a learning center. Jane asked if she could get a drink of water. When she found her seat, she opened her book and slowly began turning pages, looking at the pictures and periodically gazing at peers at her table.

Testing Sessions

Jane was evaluated in two sessions, each approximately 90 minutes long. She was cooperative and talkative throughout both sessions. She adapted quickly to the testing situation and willingly answered any questions presented to her, often with rather extensive commentary. She attempted each task presented and pursued most of them with apparent determination. However, her determination flagged somewhat around the 1-hour mark, as she became less animated and cheery in her responses to test questions. She did not hesitate to ask questions or make suggestions. For example, after completing several tasks, she asked if we could play a game that she had noticed on the office shelf.

Jane was strategic in her approach to tasks and would sometimes mention the little "tricks" she used to make a task easier. For example, when she was copying block constructions, she asked if she could build her design right next to the model. She was very sensitive to task difficulty; when she perceived that an item or a task might be challenging, she would quickly comment, "This is hard!" If encouraged to try, she would usually persist, which often resulted in successful performance. However, when she sensed she was not doing well or was making errors, she seemed to withdraw effort and would try to change the subject or activity.

Test Results

Jane is currently functioning in the average range of overall cognitive ability. Her overall (FSIQ) score on the Wechsler Intelligence Scale for Children–Fifth Edition (WISC–V) fell just above the mean for her age, at approximately

the 65th percentile. Her performance on most scales of the WISC–V fell solidly in the average range, but with some variation in performance. She displayed mild weakness in language and word use, obtaining a Verbal Comprehension scale score at approximately the 25th percentile. She demonstrated above-average ability on the Visual Spatial scale, performing at approximately the 85th percentile. She also exhibited strengths in verbal memory (scoring at approximately the 90th percentile on the Auditory Working Memory scale); and in numerical reasoning (scoring at approximately the 80th percentile on the Quantitative Reasoning scale).

Verbal Comprehension

Jane exhibited a solid foundation of verbal knowledge for her age and an ability to use the information she knows to solve problems and explain her thinking. She was able to provide basic information about the world around her (WISC–V Information), and she could apply the information she has learned to make connections and solve problems. For example, she was able to explain the rationale behind various social conventions, such as offering apologies (WISC–V Comprehension), and to describe how seemingly different words or objects (e.g., "shirt" and "hat") were alike in some way (WISC–V Similarities). She had more difficulty, however, when she had to define words (WISC–V Vocabulary), sometimes because a word was unfamiliar and sometimes because she couldn't find the words to express herself well.

Nonverbal Reasoning and Problem Solving

Jane was also able to recognize logical patterns and rules in visual information. When she was shown a pattern or sequence of objects/designs, she could identify the rule and apply it to parallel examples (WISC–V Matrix Reasoning; Figure Weights).

Visual Perception and Spatial Abilities

Jane's ability to work with visually presented material—to see how visual details or parts are organized into a picture or image—is a personal strength. This was reflected in her above-average performance on tasks in which she arranged blocks to match a pattern (WISC–V Block

Design) or where she visually recognized how puzzle pieces could be arranged to form a design (WISC–V Visual Puzzles). She was also able to accurately copy and recall complex figures (Bender-Gestalt 2).

Memory and Learning

Jane exhibited solid verbal memory skills for her age. Her verbal *memory span* (i.e., how many items she can hold in memory) was solidly average for her age. Moreover, she was able to remember information and then mentally reorganize it. For example, she could remember random numbers and reorganize them in order from smallest to largest (WISC–V Digit Span, Letter–Number Sequencing).

Jane performed reasonably well on a task in which, through repeated exposures, she learned to associate words with symbols and then "read sentences" consisting of several symbols (WISC–V Symbol Translation). She made good use of sentence syntax—knowing what type of word belongs where in a sentence—to help her recall each word, but she had some difficulty retaining symbols that were not easily linked to their associated words.

Despite her otherwise strong visual problem-solving skills, Jane was less successful when she had to remember a sequence of pictures (WISC–V Picture Memory). This was one of the later tasks administered, and she seemed fatigued when it was presented, so the score may not be a reliable assessment of her ability to remember visually presented information.

Processing Efficiency

In addition to reasoning and memory skills, school performance also depends on the ability to focus attention efficiently and to produce learned information quickly and accurately. On memory tasks that required focused attention (WISC–V Digit Span, Letter–Number Sequencing), Jane's recall was very consistent, suggesting a good ability to maintain focus and to mentally organize information. She also performed well on the Processing Speed subtests (WISC–V Coding, Symbol Search, Cancellation), which are sensitive to attentional control

and regulation. On these tasks, Jane had to scan an array of symbols or images and quickly locate and respond to details in the array. Both her speed and accuracy on these tasks were solidly average for her age. (Cognitive Processing Index approximately 65th percentile.).

Although Jane showed good attentional control, her scores on tasks where she had to quickly retrieve the names of letters or numbers were slightly below average for her age. That is, her naming speed was a little slow (WISC–V Naming Speed). However, on another rapid naming task (WIAT–III Alphabet Writing Fluency), she quickly wrote the alphabet, never losing her place in the sequence. She also showed good spacing and placement of letters on the page.

Phonological Processing

One of the important skills necessary for reading development is the ability to isolate and manipulate the individual sounds in spoken words, sometimes described as phonological awareness. Jane's scores on tasks requiring phonological awareness (CTOPP–2 Elision, Sound Blending, Phoneme Isolation; WIAT–III Early Reading) were in the below-average to low end of average range for her age. While she could identify the first or last sounds of words, she had difficulty discerning the middle sound of a word or detecting the two sounds in a blend.

Academic Functioning

Many of the reading and writing tasks of the Wechsler Individual Achievement Test–Third Edition (WIAT–III) were challenging for Jane. She was able to read some high-frequency words but often confused words with words of similar letter configuration, even if they were phonologically quite different (e.g., "then" and "this"). She was able to sound out many consonant-vowel-consonant words, both actual and nonsense words. She seemed to know the short vowel sounds /ă/, /i/, /u/, and /o/, but had difficulty with /ě/. She could not sound out other, more difficult syllable patterns, and she sometimes confused consonants or consonant combinations (e.g., reading "th" as "ch"). Similarly, when spelling, she could encode the sounds of simple one-syllable words but did not know spelling conventions such as silent e.

Jane struggled when asked to read second-grade-level passages (WIAT–III Oral Reading Fluency). She recognized some common words and made use of context clues to guess at other words. However, she would sometimes guess based on the beginning of a word rather than decode it accurately (e.g., "bald" as "bark"). She read very slowly and, because she missed so many words in a passage, she had difficulty answering comprehension questions about what she had read (WIAT–III Reading Comprehension).

On a writing task (WIAT–III Sentence Composition), Jane was able to compose very simple sentences made up of high-frequency words but had difficulty generating more complex sentence structures.

Clinical Impressions

Jane is an observant girl who takes in a lot of information from her surroundings. Her keen observational skills also contribute to her good social awareness and understanding of social conventions. Classroom observations and behavioral reports suggest that she is well able to manage social situations with peers and adults.

Jane is currently functioning in the average range of cognitive ability, with some noteworthy strengths and weaknesses. Her overall reasoning and problem-solving skills are typical for her age, and she shows above-average ability to recognize visual patterns and copy designs. She also shows solid memory numerical reasoning. These abilities help her to perform capably in academic areas such as math.

Jane displays weaknesses in some important language-based skills that are the building blocks of early reading development (naming speed and phonemic awareness). Her struggles in this area are significant, especially when compared to her other cognitive abilities. She has great difficulty remembering the sounds of each letter in a word and then quickly blending the sounds into a recognizable word. Consequently, her reading is slow and effortful, and she needs a lot of practice and feedback to learn unfamiliar words. She tries

to rely on how words look rather than sounding them out phonetically. Although she understands that letter sounds can be combined to decode or spell a word, this process is very effortful for her. However, because her language comprehension skills are solid, she can often use the meaning of a sentence to make good guesses about unrecognized words.

Another factor that may be interfering with Jane's reading progress is that she has a strong need to feel competent. When faced with a task on which she does not expect to succeed, she tends to avoid it. She made valiant efforts to tackle challenging tasks during testing when encouraged to persist. Even then, she would give up as doubt and self-consciousness set in. It is understandable that she gets discouraged and tends to avoid reading tasks in the general education classroom, where she is concerned about what her classmates think. Her tendency to avoid reading deprives her of the very practice she needs to overcome weakness in this area.

Summary and Recommendations

Jane is an intellectually capable and interpersonally engaging 8-year-old who is highly attuned to her social environment. She has pronounced weakness in phonological processing that causes her difficulty with rapid, accurate word decoding and with spelling. She is self-conscious of her weakness in these academic areas, leading to frustration and avoidance. However, her strengths in other cognitive areas—visual-spatial ability, memory, reasoning—can be used to help her to overcome some of her reading problems. These strengths also offer opportunities for her to experience success in other classroom activities and to feel competent. Given these findings, recommendations are as follows:

1. Jane should have direct, systematic instruction in phonetic decoding and should practice syllable patterns until they are automatic.
2. To increase reading fluency, Jane should have extensive opportunities to read and reread text aloud, beginning with phonetically controlled texts but gradually introducing more generic

texts that are within her current level of reading ability. Because she is self-conscious about her reading, it may be useful to provide these opportunities individually or in very small groups out of the earshot of her more able peers.

3. To determine the effectiveness of these recommendations and other remedial supports, Jane's progress in word decoding and oral fluency should be monitored using brief curriculum-based measures at least once every 2 weeks. If progress is less than satisfactory, more intensive supports should be considered.

4. It will be important to find opportunities for Jane to use and display her strengths in social skills as well as math and nonverbal reasoning skills. For example, she might be asked to teach a math game to a group of peers or to make a poster illustrating a book or story the class has shared.

5. Teachers should be aware of Jane's tendency to avoid tasks where she feels less competent and should try to find opportunities to engage her and offer positive support if she seems to be avoiding a particular task.

Score Summaries

Wechsler Intelligence Scale for Children–Fifth Edition (WISC–V)

Full Scale and Primary Index Scales These composite scores are based on a mean of 100 and standard deviation of 15. Scores of 90 to 109 are considered to be within the Average range. (See descriptors below.)

Ancillary Index and Complementary Index Scale Scores These composite scores are based on a mean of 100 and standard deviation of 15. Scores of 90 to 109 are considered to be within the Average range. (See descriptors below.)

Ancillary and Complementary Index Subtest Scores, by Index Scale Subtest scaled scores are based on a scale of 1 to 19, with a mean of 10 and standard deviation of 3. Scores of 8 to 12

Table 14.20 Jane's WISC–V Full Scale and Primary Index Scale Results

Composite Scale	Composite Score	Confidence Interval (95%)	Percentile Rank	Range
Full Scale IQ	106	100–111	66th	Average
Verbal Comprehension Index	89–W	82–98	23rd	Low Average
Visual Spatial Index	117–S	108–123	87th	High Average
Fluid Reasoning Index	109	101–116	73rd	Average
Working Memory Index	103	95–110	58th	Average
Processing Speed Index	105	95–113	63rd	Average

are considered to be within Average range. (See descriptors below.)

These are standard scores, based on a mean of 100 and standard deviation of 15. Scores of 90 to 109 are considered to be within the Average range. (See composite score descriptors above.)

Wechsler Individual Achievement Test–Third Edition (WIAT–III)

WIAT–III composite and subtest scores are based on a mean of 100 and a standard deviation of 15. Scores of 90 to 110 are considered to be within the Average range. (See descriptors below.)

Comprehensive Test of Phonological Process (CTOPP–2)

CTOPP–2 composite scores are based on a mean of 100 and a standard deviation of 15. Scores of 90 to 110 are considered to be within the Average range.

Bender Visual-Motor Gestalt Test–Second Edition

Bender-Gestalt standard scores are based on a mean of 100 and a standard deviation of 15. Scores of 90 to 109 are considered to be within the Average range.

Table 14.21   Jane's WISC–V Ancillary Index and Complementary Index Scale Results

Composite Scale	Composite Score	Con- fidence Interval (95%)	Per- centile Rank	Range
Ancillary Index Scales				
Quantitative Reasoning Index	114	107–120	82nd	Average
Auditory Working Memory Index	119	110–125	90th	High Average
Nonverbal Index	109	102–115	73rd	Average
General Ability Index	104	98–109	61st	Average
Cognitive Proficiency Index	106	98–113	66th	Average
Complementary Index Scales				
Naming Speed Index	88	81–98	21st	Low Average
Symbol Translation Index	98	91–105	45th	Average
Storage and Retrieval Index	91	85–98	27th	Average

Note. Composite Score Range Descriptors are:

130 and above	Extremely High
120–129	Very High
110–119	High Average
90–109	Average
80–89	Low Average
70–79	Very Low
69 and below	Extremely Low

Table 14.22   Jane's WISC–V Primary and Secondary Subtest Results, by Primary or Ancillary Scale

Verbal Comprehension	
Subtest	Scaled Score
Similarities	9
Vocabulary	7–W
Information	(9)
Comprehension	(11)

Visual Spatial	
Subtest	Scaled Score
Block Design	14
Visual Puzzles	12

Fluid Reasoning	
Subtest	Scaled Score
Matrix Reasoning	10
Figure Weights	13
Picture Concepts	(11)
Arithmetic	(12)

Working Memory	
Subtest	Scaled Score
Digit Span	13
Picture Span	8
Letter–Number Sequencing	(14)

Processing Speed	
Subtest	Scaled Score
Coding	10
Symbol Search	12
Cancellation	(10)

Quantitative Reasoning	
Subtest	Scaled Score
Figure Weights	13
Arithmetic	12

Auditory Working Memory	
Subtest	Scaled Score
Digit Span	13
Letter–Number Sequencing	14

Table 14.22   (*Continued*)

Nonverbal

Subtest	Scaled Score
Block Design	14
Visual Puzzles	12
Matrix Reasoning	10
Figure Weights	13
Picture Span	8
Coding	10

General Ability Index Subtests

Subtest	Scaled Score
Similarities	9
Vocabulary	7—W
Block Design	14
Matrix Reasoning	10
Figure Weights	13

Cognitive Proficiency

Subtest	Scaled Score
Digit Span	13
Picture Span	8
Coding	10
Symbol Search	12

Note: Subtest Score Range Descriptors are:

16 and above: Far above average

13–15: Above average

8–12: Average

5–7: Below average

4 and below: Far below average

Table 14.23   Jane's WISC–V Complementary Scale Subtest Scores Naming Speed

Subtest	Standard Score
Naming Speed Literacy	92
Naming Speed Quantity	89

Symbol Translation	
Subtest	Standard Score
Immediate Symbol Translation	95
Delayed Symbol Translation	102
Recognition Symbol Translation	99

Table 14.24   Jane's Wechsler Individual Achievement Test–Third Edition (WIAT–III) Results

Composite Scale	Composite Score	Confidence Interval (95%)	Percentile Rank	Range
A. Total Reading	79	75–83	8th	Below Average
B. Basic Reading	84	81–87	14th	Below Average
C. Reading Comprehension and Fluency	74	66–82	4th	Below Average
D. Written Expression	89	81–97	23rd	Average

Subtest*	Standard Score	Confidence Interval (95%)	Percentile Rank	Range
Early Reading Skills	91	78–104	27th	Average
Word Reading (A, B)	81	77–85	10th	Below Average
Pseudoword Decoding (A, B)	87	82–92	19th	Average
Reading Comprehension (A, C)	82	73–91	12th	Below Average
Oral Reading Fluency (A, C)	74	66–82	4th	Below Average
Alphabet Writing Fluency (D)	101	85–117	53rd	Average
Sentence Composition (D)	77	68–86	6th	Below Average
Spelling (D)	98	91–105	45th	Average

*Letters indicate composite scales to which subtests contribute.

Note. Composite Score Range Descriptors are:

Above 145	Very Superior
131–145	Superior
116–130	Above Average
85–115	Average
70–84	Below Average
55–69	Low
Below 55	Very Low

Table 14.25   Jane's Comprehensive Test of Phonological Process (CTOPP–2) Results

Composite Scale	Composite Score	Confidence Interval (95%)	Percentile Rank	Range
Phonological Awareness	82	74–90	12th	Below Average

Table 14.26   Jane's Phonological Awareness Subtest Results

Subtest	Scaled Score
Elision	6
Blending Words	8
Phoneme Isolation	7

Note. Subtest Score Range Descriptors are:

17–20	Very Superior
15–16	Superior
13–14	Above Average
8–12	Average
6–7	Below Average
4–5	Poor
1–3	Very Poor

Table 14.27   Jane's Bender Visual-Motor Gestalt Test—Second Edition Results

Phase	Standard Score	Confidence Interval (95%)	Percentile Rank	Range
Copy	119	109–125	90th	High Average
Recall	112	103–119	79th	High Average

Note: Standard Score Range Descriptors are:

145 and above	Extremely High
130 –144	Very High
120–129	High
110–119	High Average
90–109	Average
80–89	Low Average
70–79	Low
55–69	Very Low
54 and below	Extremely Low

CASE 16—LIZZIE, AGE 8: LOW COGNITION, LOW ACHIEVEMENT—STILL WITH A LEARNING DISABILITY

Carlea Dries and Ron Dumont

Name: Elizabeth (Lizzie) Reid

Grade: 2nd

Date of birth: 8/5/2006

Age: 8-3

Examiner: Carlea Dries, M.A., M.Ed., N.C.C. **Informant**: Mother

Dates of testing: 11/15/2014 & 11/22/2014

Reason for Referral

Lizzie is an 8-year-old girl of Caucasian descent, presently in the second grade, who was referred for an evaluation by her mother, Mrs. Reid. She is seeking an evaluation to determine whether Lizzie has a specific learning disability and/or memory deficits or is, as described by her school, "functioning about where we might expect, given her abilities." Mrs. Reid reported that she firmly believes Lizzie is falling behind academically and is functioning at about a first-grade level. Lizzie's teachers suspect that she has memory deficits as she has difficulty with retention and immediately forgets topics that are taught in class. Mrs. Reid stated that Lizzie requires "extensive repetition and clarification" of material that is presented to her and that her attention often has to be redirected. This assessment was conducted in order to explore Lizzie's cognitive and academic profile, to highlight any factors that appear to impact her scholastic performance, and to provide recommendations that may help alleviate the effects of such factors.

This evaluation format begins with a summary and recommendations and then is followed by the rationale and formulation for the summary and recommendations. Score summaries and explanations of the assessments given are provided at the end of the report.

Summary

Results of this evaluation suggest that although Lizzie's overall cognitive abilities are low, they do not, by themselves, explain her lack of progress in the basic academic skills expected of someone her age and given the current interventions and specialized teaching techniques she has received. Despite documented low cognitive functioning, she appears to be a child who also has significant deficits in short-term memory (particularly in the area of auditory memory) and a relative strength in storage and retrieval. These issues, validated by result of both the WISC–V and the WRAML2 and the relevant subtests of the WJ IV Cog and WJ IV OL, and implicated in her lower academic achievement, seem consistent with the concerns raised by Lizzie's parents and teachers.

Lizzie's cognitive abilities ranged from Very Low to Low Average, indicating that she is performing below the level of her same-age or grade peers. Lizzie's scores indicated a limited acquired knowledge base (i.e., Verbal Comprehension), difficulty reasoning and solving problems using unfamiliar information (i.e., Fluid Reasoning), difficulty holding and manipulating information in immediate awareness (i.e., Working Memory), and difficulty with speed and accuracy of visual identification and decision making. Lizzie did relatively better on tasks that involved analyzing and thinking about visual shapes (i.e., Visual Spatial). There was also a relevant, meaningful difference in favor of her performance on the Symbol Translation Index when compared with her performance on the Naming Speed Index. This difference supports the finding of improvements in her working memory performance when auditory information was paired with a visual component. Therefore, Lizzie's visual processing is more efficient than her auditory processing.

Lizzie's performance on the WRAML2 indicated that her overall memory functioning is in the Very Low range (General Memory). Although there were no significant differences among her verbal memory, visual memory, and attention/concentration, analyses of her scores suggest that Lizzie may benefit from repetition of information and time to process the information. Additionally, Lizzie's learning and memory may be enhanced by visual, as opposed to verbal, stimuli. This finding was also supported by her performance on the subtests involving visual stimuli on the WJ Ach and her performance on aspects of the WISC–V.

Lizzie's performance on measures of academic achievement was significantly lower than expected for a child her age as well as significantly lower than expected given her measured abilities on the WISC–V. With a WISC–V Full Scale Composite in the Very Low range, a majority of Lizzie's achievement scores are predicted to fall in the Low Average range. (Although measures of IQ and Achievement are not perfectly related, an IQ score can be used as a broad predictor of expected achievement.) Instead, Lizzie's overall academic achievement fell in the Extremely Low range. She scored in the Very Low range on two major indexes of academic achievement (i.e., Reading, and Writing) and in the Low range for Mathematics. Lizzie's overall scores on the WJ IV Achievement indicated that her academic functioning is at a kindergarten level. Lizzie's current WJ IV achievement standard scores were compared to scores from her most recent prior evaluation (done in 2013). That comparison suggests that Lizzie is not progressing as one might expect, given the length of time between testing sessions (i.e., one year) and the special education services she is receiving. It is possible that her insufficient progress is due, at least in part, to deficits in memory indicated by the current evaluation.

Overall, Lizzie's profile is consistent with a learning disorder in memory. This evaluation demonstrated that Lizzie has deficits in auditory short-term working memory and relative assets in long-term storage and retrieval. Her performance indicated that her learning and processing is strengthened by repetition, additional time to process information, and reinforcement from visual stimuli.

Recommendations

The results of testing indicated that Lizzie appears to have a learning disorder in memory and an auditory processing deficit that result in significant learning problems across most academic areas. Comparisons between Lizzie's current (2014) and past (2013) performance on individually administered tests of achievement suggest that she is not progressing academically as would be expected given the interventions the school has used. Additional recommendations should be developed collaboratively between Lizzie's school and Mr. and Mrs. Reid.

1. Given the discrepancies between Lizzie's cognitive and academic testing, it is recommended that Lizzie's school consider her for eligibility as a student with a specific learning disability. If the school utilizes a Response to Intervention model, Lizzie appears to be eligible because of the apparent lack of academic progress being made, despite documented interventions. If the school utilizes a discrepancy model, Lizzie also appears to qualify since her academic achievement in several areas is well below what one would predict given her cognitive abilities.

2. Given that Lizzie is now in a mainstream environment, it is important that her academic progress be monitored on a regular basis.

3. Plan complementary reading and spelling instruction. Lizzie's spelling level may not be commensurate with her reading level. Avoid using graded spelling lists that may include words that Lizzie cannot yet read. Before asking Lizzie to spell new words, assess whether she can read the words. Provide an opportunity for Lizzie to spell words after learning to read them, and teach spelling rules and patterns that relate to the words she is learning to read.

4. Use materials that explicitly highlight the rule or pattern that Lizzie needs to learn. Provide repeated opportunities for Lizzie to

apply the rule or pattern. Use explicit instruction and teach strategies step by step. Make sure Lizzie masters each step in the process and provide immediate feedback on her errors.

5. Explicitly teach Lizzie reading and spelling strategies and when to apply them. Provide repeated opportunities for Lizzie to apply learned rules or strategies using a variety of materials and examples.

6. Prepare Lizzie to listen or read. Provide Lizzie with an overview of the content, text structure, and unfamiliar vocabulary words that will be introduced in a reading passage or lesson. Prime background knowledge of the subject area, and encourage Lizzie to connect the topic to previously learned information. When giving sequential information, tell Lizzie how many steps or events to listen or look for. Start with a few steps or events in order. Move on to more steps or events only after Lizzie is able to recall all requested information related to the most recent set of steps or events.

7. Provide comprehension instruction that incorporates both listening and reading tasks. Explicitly teach strategies and model their use. Demonstrate using a think-aloud approach, and then provide opportunities for Lizzie to demonstrate those strategies.

8. Emphasize vocabulary as a part of reading and spelling instruction. Teach word meaning, word structure, and grammatical usage in context using both reading and listening tasks. Tasks might also include sorting words into different semantic categories (e.g., positive, negative, neutral) and linguistic categories (e.g., adjectives, nouns).

9. To support Lizzie's memory deficits, Lizzie may benefit from extensive repetition, practice, and review in learning activities. Lizzie will need repeated exposure to new words before she will be able to read or spell them automatically.

10. When giving instructions, pause at regular intervals to allow Lizzie to process the information. Allow sufficient time for her process information and respond. For example, wait at least 5 seconds to give Lizzie time to process the question and formulate an answer.

11. Simplify the language of instruction. Lizzie may benefit most from instruction that is delivered using simple, precise, and transparent language. Avoid excessive elaboration or wordy instructions, and avoid covert meaning or coded imperatives. Rather than saying "Would you like to bring your pencil?" or "We are going to write a story," it would be more precise to say "Please bring your pencil" and "I'd like you to write a story." Repeat key instruction words. When switching topics or tasks, use overt language to indicate the transition. Avoid providing multiple verbal directions all at once. Give one direction at a time, and provide the next one after Lizzie has finished the previous step.

12. To take advantage of Lizzie's visual processing abilities, Lizzie may benefit from the use of visual stimuli during instruction and learning activities.

   (a) Consider using graphic organizers and story maps to arrange information, using pictures and imagery to support learning activities, and tracking academic progress on simple line graphs or charts.

   (b) When giving explanations or examples, provide Lizzie with visual cues to use as a reference.

   (c) Mental imagery may also be used to support text comprehension. For example, create a drawing to represent the main ideas or storyline of a text (such as cartoon sequences or pictures to capture the main idea), and then ask Lizzie create images of key details from the text.

   (d) Provide visual cues to aid reading and spelling. For example, to support spelling instruction, teach Lizzie to look at the word and say it aloud. Then have Lizzie close her eyes and imagine the word in her mind, naming the letters.

Next, have Lizzie open her eyes and write the word. Finally, have Lizzie check her spelling and repeat steps to correct errors.

Case Formulation

Background Information

Lizzie lives with her biological mother and father and a younger brother (age 6). Mr. Reid works as an Internet computer programmer and Mrs. Reid is an attorney. Mrs. Reid reported that Lizzie gets along with the members of the family as well as friends from school and her neighborhood.

Developmental and Medical History

Lizzie was born via emergency C-section at 37 weeks. She weighed 8 lbs 4 oz. At birth, Lizzie had a critically low Apgar score, and there was difficulty resuscitating her. She was placed on an oscillating ventilator for 2 weeks. Lizzie was in the neonatal intensive care unit (NICU) for 2 months.

Lizzie's medical history is significant for central and obstructive apnea. Mrs. Reid reported that 4 days after coming home from the hospital Lizzie turned blue, stopped breathing, had no pulse, and CPR was initiated. Approximately 1 year later, Lizzie was admitted to the hospital due to an acute, life-threatening episode of apnea. During this time Lizzie had a seizure, but it was believed to be secondary to her apnea. Lizzie continued to have episodes of central and obstructive apnea up until 24 months of age. Due to this she was taking oxygen on an as-needed basis until she was 2 years old.

Mrs. Reid reported that Lizzie has difficulty sleeping and wakes up every night at least once between 1:00 a.m. and 4:00 a.m., but she is able to fall back asleep. She also snores very loudly, which Mrs. Reid suspects may be due to obstructive apnea. Lizzie takes 1 mg melatonin every night. Lizzie was recently genetically tested to determine whether or not she has cystic fibrosis. Results were not available at the time of this report.

Mrs. Reid reported that Lizzie's developmental milestones were 1 to 3 months delayed.

She qualified for early intervention at around 4 months old and received speech, physical therapy, and occupational therapy (amount and frequency unknown) until she placed out at 3 years of age. At that time she qualified for a preschool disabled program in her local school district, and currently she receives special education services at her elementary school.

In 2013 Lizzie had been identified as having a central auditory processing disorder (CAPD). Additionally, Dr. Rey, a neurologist, diagnosed Lizzie with dyslexia in 2014. However, because the assessments done by the outside evaluators and the school consistently found low cognitive ability, the school's multidisciplinary team would not identify Lizzie as a child with a specific learning disability, arguing that there was no discrepancy between Lizzie's cognitive abilities and her academic performance and that, in fact, given the RTI strategies the school was using, she was "performing very well given her identified low cognitive abilities."

Academic Functioning

At age 3 Lizzie qualified for a preschool disabled program in the Alfieri Public Schools. She was held back from starting kindergarten for 1 year because it was believed that she was not yet ready.

Lizzie attended Jones Elementary School for kindergarten and first grade. Lizzie was initially evaluated by the Child Study Team in 2010 and found to be eligible for special education services under the classification of other health impaired due to the disabling impact of her medical history.

Lizzie was reevaluated in 2013. At that time, Mrs. Reid requested that the school's multidisciplinary team consider putting Lizzie in the mainstream classroom. Lizzie's IEP was modified for second grade, and Mrs. Reid stated that Lizzie is now in the mainstream classroom. She receives replacement instruction in the resource setting for language arts and math. She also receives multisensory reading sessions once a day for 30 minutes. Her program is further supported through the provision of speech/language and occupational therapies twice per week for 25 minutes per session for each related service.

Mrs. Reid reported that she feels Lizzie is functioning academically at an early first-grade level "at most" and receiving grades in the 70% to 80% range. Lizzie reportedly has difficulty in all subjects.

Social Functioning

Mrs. Reid reported that Lizzie does not have difficulty initiating or maintaining friendships. She has friends at school and gets along with her classmates. Lizzie has two friends that Mrs. Reid reports she is very close to, and, upon Mrs. Reid's request to the school, Lizzie is now in the same class with them. Lizzie also has one or two friends on her swimming team.

Behavioral Observations

Lizzie was evaluated over 3 days utilizing testing sessions that each took approximately 2 hours. During each session, Lizzie was offered and took several short (5- to 10-minute) breaks. During the first day, the entire WISC–V was administered. During the second and third days, the WRAML2, core tests of the WJ IV Achievement, and the selected tests of the WJ IV Cog and WJ IV OL were administered.

For the majority of testing, Lizzie exhibited effort and appeared motivated. However, Lizzie had difficulty sustaining attention, and on multiple occasions throughout the testing sessions, the examiner had to prompt Lizzie and redirect her focus. For example, when presenting the cards on the picture memory subtest of the WRAML2, the examiner would direct Lizzie's gaze toward the cards because they were removed after 10 seconds. Throughout the testing sessions, directions often had to be repeated slowly to ensure Lizzie comprehended them. However, at times, Lizzie would look at the examiner on a later item of a subtest and would be unable to recall what she was supposed to do. For example, on the Understanding Directions subtest of the WJ IV OL, after completing 16 items, she asked "What?" on the following two items and was encouraged to provide her best guess. Although it is likely that some of Lizzie's scores are deflated due to her difficulty sustaining attention

and difficulty recalling information, these behaviors appear to be consistent with the behaviors reported by Mrs. Reid. For this reason, the results of this assessment appear to be valid and reliable indicators of Lizzie's current functioning.

Tests Administered

Wechsler Intelligence Scale for Children–Fifth Edition (WISC–V)

Wide Range Assessment of Memory and Learning Second Edition (WRAML2)

Woodcock Johnson IV Tests of Achievement, Form A (WJ IV ACH)

Selected test of the Woodcock Johnson IV Tests of Cognitive Abilities (WJ IV COG)

Selected test of the Woodcock Johnson IV Tests of Oral Language (WJ IV OL)

Assessment Results

Please note that various test publishers may use different qualitative descriptors to describe the same standard or scaled score. For consistency and ease of interpretation, the following descriptors are used to describe Lizzie's scores on the WISC–V, WJ IV (Achievement, Cognitive and Oral Language), and WRAML2:

Extremely High: 98% and above

Very High: 92–97%

High Average: 76–91%

Average: 25–75%

Low Average: 9–24%

Very Low: 3–8%

Extremely Low: 2% and below

A summary of Lizzie's scores from this evaluation is provided in the Score Summary section at the end of the report.

Cognitive Functioning Lizzie's cognitive functioning was assessed using the Wechsler Intelligence Scale for Children–Fifth Edition (WISC–V). Lizzie's performance on the WISC–V revealed significant differences between her Working Memory and her Auditory Working Memory as well as differences between her short-term memory and her storage and retrieval abilities. Additionally, there seemed to be a pronounced difference in favor of her visual memory skills when compared to her auditory memory skills. A more detailed analysis of her scores in individual domains is provided below.

The Full Scale IQ (FSIQ) is usually considered the score most representative of general intellectual functioning. It is derived from seven subtests: Block Design, Similarities, Matrix Reasoning, Digit Span, Coding, Vocabulary, and Figure Weights. Lizzie's performance on these tasks yielded an overall FSIQ in the Very Low range.

The Similarities and Vocabulary subtests were used to assess the Verbal Comprehension Index. These subtests measured Lizzie's ability to access and apply acquired word knowledge. The WISC–V evaluates verbal skills in the context of reasoning, retrieving semantic knowledge, verbal expression, and abstraction, reflecting proficiency in language and culture. All items were presented orally and required a verbal response. In this assessment of her verbal knowledge and comprehension, Lizzie performed in the Very Low to Low Average range. Lizzie's low Verbal Comprehension Index scores seem to reflect her poorly developed word knowledge, problems with verbal expression, and general difficulties with reasoning and problem solving. Lizzie typically provided responses that were lacking specific details. Even when she was prompted for more information or clarification regarding a response, she seldom was able to improve the answer.

The Block Design and Visual Puzzles subtests were used to assess the Visual Spatial Index. The Visual Spatial Index provides a measure of visual-spatial processing, integration and synthesis of part-whole relationships, attentiveness to visual detail, nonverbal concept formation, and visual-motor integration. The stimuli are nonverbal (aside from the directions), and items were presented to Lizzie visually. Lizzie's solutions require motor responses and, to a lesser extent, verbal responses. Lizzie performed best in this area, obtaining an overall score that was in the Low Average to Average range. Lizzie's Visual Spatial Index scores suggest a relative strength with tasks that required spatial processing, visual discrimination, visual attention, and general visual reasoning ability.

The Matrix Reasoning and Figure Weights subtests were used to assess the Fluid Reasoning Index. The Fluid Reasoning Index is a measure of fluid and inductive reasoning, broad visual intelligence, conceptual thinking, and classification ability. In this area, Lizzie performed in the Extremely Low to Low Average range. Lizzie's low Fluid Reasoning Index scores may suggest that she has difficulties identifying and linking visual information to abstract or quantitative concepts.

The Digit Span and Picture Span subtests were used to assess the Working Memory Index. The Working Memory Index is a measure of Lizzie's ability to register, maintain, and manipulate visual and auditory information in conscious awareness. Lizzie performed in the Very Low to Low Average range, suggesting difficulties in maintaining and manipulating information in working memory. As there is significant variation based on the requirements of the activities, it is important to examine Lizzie's memory skills in more depth.

The Digit Span subtest assessed Lizzie's short-term working memory using three separate, though related, memory tasks. Lizzie was first read a sequence of numbers and asked to recall the numbers in the same order (Forward task); next she was read a sequence of numbers and asked to recall them in reverse order (Backward task); finally, she was read a sequence of numbers and asked to repeat them back in ascending order (Sequencing task). At no time did she see the numbers, and the examiner is not permitted to repeat any of the trials. While both the Backward and Sequencing components require the resequencing of information, the primary difference between these two components is how that sequence is determined. In the Backward task, the numbers in the sequence must be maintained and then reordered backward in order to repeat them successfully. In the Sequencing task, not only must the numbers be retained, but the relative value of the numbers must also be maintained so that they can be repeated back in numerical order—lowest to highest. All tasks require registration of information, brief focused attention, auditory discrimination, and auditory rehearsal. There were no differences between her performances on the three component tasks, resulting in overall performance in the Very Low range. For the items on which she had difficulty, it was apparent from her responses that she had not been able to adequately register all of the numbers she had heard, thus impacting her ability to recall the complete set of numbers either forward, backward, or in sequential order. Aside from requesting the trials be repeated, Lizzie did not employ any observable strategy to improve her performance. She did not attempt to self-correct any errors when she noted making them.

On the Picture Span subtest, Lizzie viewed a stimulus page with one or more pictures of nameable objects for a short, specified time and then selected the picture(s) (in sequential order, if possible) from options on a response page. This task is a measure of visual working memory and working memory capacity. The use of semantically meaningful, concrete stimuli (nameable pictures) may have assisted Lizzie in her ability to recall the information. In contrast to her difficulties on the Digit Span subtest, she was able to identify the accurate objects and sequence on par with individuals her own age, earning a result in the Average range.

The Letter–Number Sequencing subtest was also administered to Lizzie in an effort to determine if the variation in Lizzie's working memory performance may have been due to the format in which the information was presented (i.e., auditory or visual). On this task, Lizzie needed to simultaneously track letters and numbers, arrange the numbers in ascending order, then arrange the letters in alphabetical order following the numbers, and perform both mental operations without forgetting any part of the series. Similar to the Digit Span subtest, this

activity involves attention, short-term auditory memory, and information processing. After hearing the directions, Lizzie asked if she would be able to use "scrap paper"; she did not appear frustrated when the request was denied. Similar to her difficulties on the Digit Span subtest, on most Letter–Number Sequencing items for which she did not receive credit, she had stored only small pieces of the information correctly but not the entire prompt. Her performance on this task was in the Very Low range.

The Digit Span—Picture Span—Letter–Number Sequencing comparison provides information about Lizzie's performance across various working memory tasks that differ according to stimulus and response modality. Lizzie's performance on Picture Span is superior to that on Digit Span and Letter–Number Sequencing, indicating that she can best utilize working memory in problem solving when visual, rather than verbal, stimuli are used or when a recognition rather than recall approach is required. Given the variation in her performance within the working memory domain, it appears that Lizzie has measurable difficulty in auditory working memory when compared with visual working memory.

The Auditory Working Memory Index, derived from the Digit Span and Letter–Number Sequencing subtests, is an indicator of Lizzie's auditory working memory skills. Whereas the previously described Working Memory Index provides a composite measure of working memory across mixed modalities (i.e., auditory and visual), the Auditory Working Memory Index gives a purer measure of auditory working memory. Lizzie's low Auditory Working Memory Index scores further supports the presence of auditory processing difficulties, including inattention, distractibility, and low auditory working memory storage and manipulation. The discrepancy in favor of Lizzie's performance on the traditional Working Memory Index when compared with her Auditory Working Memory Index score again supports the idea that presenting information visually helps to improve working memory functioning as opposed to tasks that are reliant on verbal presentations alone.

The Coding and Symbol Search subtests were used to assess the Processing Speed Index, a measure of Lizzie's speed and accuracy for visual identification, decision making, and implementation. The subtests contributing to the Processing Speed Index are not measures of simple reaction time or visual discrimination since a cognitive decision-making or learning component is inherent in the tasks. Lizzie's performance in this domain ranged from Very Low to Average.

The Naming Speed Index, composed of Naming Speed Literacy and Naming Speed Quantity, provides a broad estimate of automaticity of basic naming ability drawn from a variety of tasks. Lizzie scored Very Low in this area.

The Symbol Translation Index, composed of Immediate Symbol Translation, Delayed Symbol Translation, and Recognition Symbol Translation, provides a broad estimate of visual-verbal associative memory drawn from a variety of conditions. Lizzie's Low Average performance suggests adequate encoding ability as well as the capability to retrieve newly learned visual-verbal associations after short and long delays. It is worthy to note that Lizzie's performance on the Recognition Symbol Translation task resulted in her highest score on the entire test and further supports the hypothesis that Lizzie's verbal-visual associative memory is best demonstrated when recognition rather than simply recall is required.

There was a relevant, meaningful difference in favor of her performance on the Symbol Translation Index when compared with her performance on the Naming Speed Index. This difference again supports the finding of improvements in her working memory performance when auditory information was paired with a visual component.

Cognitive Summary The WISC–V results demonstrate that Lizzie's cognitive skills are lower than those of her same-age peers. Although her scores across the domains were in the Very

Low to Low Average range, aspects of her performance on the Visual Spatial, Working Memory, and Symbol Translation Indexes provide strong evidence for both strength and difficulty, depending on the specific requirements of the tasks. These results suggest that Lizzie has an especially difficult time holding and manipulating auditory information in immediate awareness and maintaining attentional control. However, she does much better on tasks that require her to perceive, analyze, and think about visual shapes and patterns.

Achievement Lizzie's academic achievement in Reading, Writing, and Mathematics was measured using the Woodcock Johnson Tests of Achievement, Fourth Edition (WJ IV Ach): Standard Battery. All results were calculated using grade-based norms so that Lizzie could be compared to others in the same grade. Lizzie's total achievement standard score fell in the Extremely Low range.

Reading Abilities Lizzie's ability to decode, read quickly, and comprehend what she is reading was assessed using three tasks. On a test that assessed her capability to identify letters and words presented in isolation (i.e., Letter-Word Identification), Lizzie demonstrated an ability to read two- to three-letter words (e.g., *at*, *car*) but an inability to read words with four or more letters (e.g., *have*, *going*). When Lizzie attempted to sound out the longer words, it was notable that she was able to correctly sound out the beginning portion of the word but seemed to guess, with low accuracy, on the remainder of the word. For example, when sounding out the word *them*, she said "thowl." Lizzie was unable to complete the Sentence Reading Fluency test, which assessed comprehension by requiring her to read simple sentences as quickly as possible and then indicate whether each sentence was true or false. Lizzie was asked to read the first sample sentence and was only able to read *an* and *is*. Due to her inability to read sentences, the test was discontinued and not scored. On a test that required Lizzie to demonstrate her reading comprehension, vocabulary, and reasoning (i.e., Passage Comprehension), Lizzie's performance on this test was impacted by her inability to read even very simple sentences. Overall, Lizzie's Reading Ability score was in the Extremely Low range.

Mathematics Abilities Lizzie's mathematical achievement, including problem solving, understanding numbers, automaticity, and reasoning, was assessed using three tasks. On a test that required Lizzie to solve simple math problems using a pencil and paper (i.e., Calculation), Lizzie presented difficulty in correctly computing even simple single-digit addition or subtraction problems. On a test that required Lizzie to solve as many basic math problems as possible within a specific amount of time (i.e., Math Facts Fluency), thereby testing her automaticity with mathematical facts, Lizzie made 20 errors on the 40 mathematical problems she computed. Four of her errors were made on addition problems while 16 of her errors were on subtraction problems. Most of her errors on the subtraction problems indicated that she added the numbers instead of subtracted them. For example, when given the math problem *2–1=*, she responded "3." The Applied Problems assessed Lizzie's reasoning abilities by requiring her to listen to math word problems, recognize the procedure to be followed, and then perform relatively simple calculations. She presented with difficulty in retaining the information and completing the necessary steps to complete the problems. Overall, Lizzie earned a Broad Math Ability score in the Very Low range.

Writing Abilities Lizzie's written language achievement, including spelling single-word responses, fluency in writing, and the quality of written responses, was assessed using three tasks. On a test that required her to write single-letter and/or single-word responses (i.e., Spelling), Lizzie demonstrated an overall ability to write single letters; however, she did confuse *w* and *m*. She was able to spell two-letter words, but

she was unable to meet with success when the task demands increased to words containing three or more letters. Lizzie was able to properly identify the first letter of words; however, she seemed to lack the phonological awareness skills to sound out and spell words. For example, she spelled *camp* as "cup" and *from* as "frumm." Lizzie was unable to complete the Sentence Writing Fluency test that required her to quickly write complete sentences using the three target words provided in the Response Booklet. Lizzie was typically unable to read the three provided words, which was necessary to write the sentences correctly. On the sample items the examiner read her the three words she needed to use; however, Lizzie had difficulty writing a complete sentence. For example, when given the words *pig*, *fat*, and *is*, she wrote the sentence "the is pig fat." Her score on a test that required her to complete sentences or write original sentences using provided visual cues (i.e., Writing Samples) reflects her tendency to write one-word answers when asked to write complete sentences. For example, when asked to write a sentence describing a picture of baby birds being fed a worm, she wrote, "burt." Overall, Lizzie received a Broad Written Language score in the Extremely Low range.

It should be noted Lizzie was assessed using the WJ III Ach (Form B) in 2013. In 2013, her Brief Achievement Score was in the Low Average range. Her mathematics abilities were in the Low Average range. Her reading and writing abilities fell into the Very Low range. When Lizzie's scores from 2013 are compared to 2014, it appears that she is maintaining a similar relative standing. However, as she gets older and the school's curriculum builds on foundational skills, she will need to show greater progress to not fall further behind.

Memory and Learning Lizzie's memory was assessed using the Wide Range Assessment of Memory and Learning, Second Edition (WRAML2). All results were calculated using age-based norms so that Lizzie could be compared to same aged peers. The WRAML2 includes a measure of general memory ability, the General Memory Index, which is a distillation of verbal memory, visual memory, and attention and concentration. Lizzie's General Memory Index fell in the Very Low range. As seen in other test results, Lizzie's memory abilities differ depending upon the task demands.

Verbal Memory The Verbal Memory Index is an estimate of how well Lizzie can learn and recall verbal information. It is derived from the Story Memory and Verbal Learning subtests. When she was read two short stories and asked to recall as many parts of the story that she could (i.e., Story Memory), Lizzie was able to remember parts of the first, simplest story; however, she was unable to recall any parts of the second story, which was much more complex. After Lizzie was read the second story, and she was asked to recall any parts that she could remember, she said, "I forgot." When encouraged to remember anything, she said, "he caught three fish," despite the story being about a girl who went fishing and did not catch any fish. On the first story, Lizzie performed better with recalling information verbatim compared to recalling information in her own words. After approximately 20 minutes, Lizzie was asked to retell the stories again (i.e., Story Memory Delay Recall). She was able to provide more details on this portion of the task than she had on the initial presentation. After completing the Story Memory Delay Recall subtest, Lizzie was asked multiple-choice questions about details of the stories (i.e., Story Memory Recognition). The visual clues improved her performance. On a subtest that required her to listen to a list of 13 simple words four times and immediately recite back as many words as possible each time (i.e., Verbal Learning), Lizzie remembered more words then the prior trial. For example, she recalled seven words on her fourth trial compared to only one word on her first trial. For this reason it is possible that Lizzie's learning is enhanced by multiple exposure and repetitions. After approximately 20 minutes, Lizzie was asked

to again recall as many words as possible. This time the examiner does not read the list of words beforehand (i.e., Verbal Learning Delay Recall). Lizzie was able to recall six words. Approximately 10 minutes later, the examiner read a list of 34 words to Lizzie, some of which were on the list of original words from the Verbal Learning subtest and some of which were not. After each word was read Lizzie was asked to identify whether or not it was on the original list of 13 words. Lizzie made more phonological errors (six errors) compared to semantic errors (one error). Lizzie's semantic error was that she incorrectly identified *eye* as being one of the words on the original list, which was semantically similar to the word *ear* from the original list. One of Lizzie's phonological errors was that she incorrectly identified *pail* as being one of the words on the original list, which was phonologically similar to the word *nail* from the original list. Overall, Lizzie produced a Verbal Memory Index in the Extremely Low range.

Visual Memory The Visual Memory Index is an estimate of how well Lizzie can learn and recall visual information. It is derived from the Picture Memory subtest and the Design Memory subtest. On the Picture Memory subtest, Lizzie was shown four common but visually complex scenes for 10 seconds each. After each one, a comparable scene was presented and she was asked to identify the elements that had been moved, changed, or added. On this task, Lizzie made four commission errors on this subtest, which was similar to the commission errors for children her age. Commission errors occur when Lizzie erroneously marked elements that had not been moved, changed, or added. After approximately 20 minutes, Lizzie was asked to look at 44 picture elements, some of which were previously seen on the Picture Memory subtest and some of which were not. Lizzie was asked to mark *yes* or *no* next to each picture based on whether she believed the pictured element was previously seen. On this subtest (i.e., Picture Memory Recognition), Lizzie's performance appeared to be supported by the provision of visual clues. On the

Design Memory subtest, Lizzie was shown five cards with different abstract geometric forms for 5 seconds each, followed by a 10-second delay. After each exposure, Lizzie was asked to draw what she remembered of the card that was just exposed. After about 20 minutes, Lizzie was asked to look at 46 geometric shapes or groups of shapes, half of which she had seen during the Design Memory subtest. Lizzie was asked to mark *yes* or *no* next to each shape or grouping of shapes based on whether she thought she saw the shape on any of the five stimulus cards previously presented. Lizzie's performance on the Design Memory Recognition task increased significantly. Overall, Lizzie produced a Visual Memory Index score in the Very Low range.

Attention/Concentration The Attention/Concentration Index is an estimate of how well Lizzie can learn and recall relatively nonmeaningful rote, sequential information. It is formed from two subtests, Finger Windows and Number Letter. On the Finger Windows subtest, Lizzie is shown a vertically resting card containing asymmetrically located holes. The examiner demonstrates increasingly longer series of pencil pokes through different windows on the board and Lizzie was asked to immediately replicate these patterns. During the administration of this task, Lizzie required redirection to focus and attend to the visual prompt. This inattention appeared to directly impact her score. On the Number Letter subtest, Lizzie was asked to repeat a sequence of single digits and letters that were presented orally by the examiner. In an apparent effort to improve her performance, Lizzie requested repetition of the data set; she continued to put forth effort even after being informed repetition was not permitted. Overall, Lizzie produced an Attention/Concentration Index in the Very Low range.

Lizzie's ability to listen and understand the English language was assessed using the Woodcock Johnson IV Cognitive (WJ IV Cog) and Woodcock Johnson IV Oral Language (OL), selecting specific tests that relate to her memory skills. On a test that required her to listen to a story and immediately recite back as much as possible (i.e., Story Recall from the WJ IV Cog), she was able to recall some of the targeted details, earning a Low Average result. On a test measuring her ability to listen and follow increasingly complex directions (i.e., Understanding Directions from the WJ IV OL), Lizzie demonstrated an ability to follow directions when they were listed simply and in order (e.g., point to the sun then the butterfly). However, she was unable to follow directions when they became more complex and she had to identify what item to point to by deciphering provided clues (e.g., point to the cloud nearest to the tallest tree, then the other two clouds). Her performance yielded a Very Low score.

Memory and Learning Summary Lizzie's overall general memory score was in the Extremely Low range. Although there were no significant differences between her verbal memory, visual memory, and attention/concentration, Lizzie's scores on these memory tasks indicated that her performance on the verbal learning delay recall subtests was higher than her immediate verbal recall. Moreover, on the Verbal Learning subtest, her performance was highest on the fourth trial, after hearing the word list four times. She recalled one word on the first trial and seven words on the fourth trial. These scores provide some indication that repetition and additional time to process information can positively impact her performance. It was also notable that Lizzie's recognition ability was higher on visual stimuli (i.e., Visual Recognition Index) as opposed to verbal stimuli (i.e., Verbal Recognition Index). These scores suggest that Lizzie may benefit from being provided visual stimuli, as opposed to verbal stimuli, to reinforce and support her ability to learn and remember material.

Table 14.28   Lizzie's Score Summaries

WISC-V Composites	Standard Score	Percentile Rank	Classification
Full Scale IQ	72	3	Very Low
Verbal Comprehension	76	5	Very Low
Visual Spatial	89–S	23	Low Average
Fluid Reasoning	74	4	Very Low
Working Memory	79	12	Very Low
Processing Speed	83	13	Low Average
Quantitative Reasoning	66	1	Extremely Low
Auditory Working Memory	67	1	Extremely Low
Nonverbal	80	9	Low Average
General Ability	73	4	Very Low
Cognitive Proficiency	78	7	Very Low
Naming Speed	**74**	**4**	**Very Low**
Naming Speed Literacy	80	9	Low Average
Naming Speed Quantity	69	2	Extremely Low
Symbol Translation	**89–S**	**23**	**Low Average**
Immediate Symbol Translation	90	25	Average
Delayed Symbol Translation	85	16	Low Average
Recognition Symbol Translation	97	42	Average
Storage & Retrieval	**77**	**6**	**Very Low**

WISC-V Subtest	Scaled Score	Percentile Rank	Classification
Block Design	7	16	Low Average
Similarities	5	5	Very Low
Matrix Reasoning	6	9	Very Low
Digit Span	4	2	Extremely Low
Coding	8	25	Average
Vocabulary	6	9	Low Average

Table 14.28   (Continued)

WISC-V Subtest	Scaled Score	Percentile Rank	Classification
Figure Weights	5	5	Very Low
Visual Puzzles	9	37	Average
Picture Span	9	37	Average
Symbol Search	6	9	Low Average
Information	5	5	Very Low
Picture Concepts	5	5	Very Low
Letter–Number Sequencing	4	2	Extremely Low
Cancellation	6	9	Very Low
Comprehension	5	5	Very Low
Arithmetic	3	1	Extremely Low

WJ IV Ach Composite/Test	Standard Score	Percentile Rank	Classification
Reading	**64**	**1**	**Extremely Low**
Letter–Word Identification	83	13	Low Average
Sentence Reading Fluency			
Passage Comprehension	45	<0.1	Extremely Low
Mathematics	**78**	**7**	**Very Low**
Calculation	67	1	Extremely Low
Math Facts Fluency	89	23	Low Average
Applied Problems	78	7	Very Low
Writing	**65**	**1**	**Extremely Low**
Spelling	72	3	Very Low
Sentence Writing Fluency	70	2	Extremely Low
Writing Samples	63	1	Extremely Low

WRAML2 Index	Standard Score	PR	Classification
General Memory	**64**	**1**	**Extremely Low**
Verbal Memory	72	3	Very Low
Visual Memory	73	4	Very Low
Attention/ Concentration	70	2	Very Low

Table 14.28 (*Continued*)

WRAML2 Index	Standard Score	PR	Classification
General Recognition	75	5	Very Low
Verbal Recognition	65	1	Extremely Low
Visual Recognition	93	32	Average
Core Subtests			
Story Memory	70	2	Very Low
Design Memory	70	2	Very Low
Verbal Learning	80	9	Low Average
Picture Memory	85	16	Low Average
Finger Windows	75	5	Very Low
Number Letter	75	5	Very Low
Delay Recall Subtests			
Story Memory Recall	85	16	Low Average
Verbal Learning Recall	90	25	Average
Sound Symbol Recall	70	4	Very Low

Table 14.28 (*Continued*)

WRAML2 Index	Standard Score	PR	Classification
Recognition Subtests			
Story Recognition	75	5	Very Low
Design Recognition	105	63	Average
Picture Memory Recognition	85	16	Low Average
Verbal Learning Recognition	65	1	Extremely Low

WJ IV Cognitive Test	Standard Score	PR	Classification
Story Recall	92	29	Average

WJ IV Oral Language Test	Standard Score	PR	Classification
Understanding Directions	60	0.4	Very Low

CASE 17—PATRICK, AGE 9: DOES MY SON HAVE A READING DISABILITY?: APPLICATION OF THE WISC–V AND WJ IV

Nancy Mather and Katie Eklund

Name: Patrick Jackson

Birth Date: 01/16/2006

Age: 9 Years, 1 Month

Grade: 3.6

Ethnicity: African American

School: Randall Academy

Evaluation Dates: 2/16/2015; 02/17/2015

Evaluators: Nancy Mather, Ph.D., Katie Eklund, Ph.D.

Reason for Referral

Ms. Holly Jackson referred her son, Patrick, for a reevaluation. Although results from a previous evaluation 1 year prior suggested that Patrick did not have a reading disability, Ms. Jackson continues to have concerns about her son and believes he really does have a reading disability. Patrick, who is currently in third grade, has a history of speech and language delays as well as slow development of reading and spelling skills. Ms. Jackson requested an updated evaluation that would provide additional recommendations to meet his current educational needs and address his continued reading challenges. Ms. Jackson is also concerned that Patrick is placed in the lowest math group, as she believes he has excellent math aptitude and should be doing better than he is doing.

Background Information

Patrick lives with his biological parents and one younger sister who is 6 years old. His father is a financial advisor and his mother is a kindergarten teacher at a neighboring school. Although there is no known established history of reading and

writing difficulties, Mr. Jackson suspects that his father had difficulty with reading.

Patrick has attended Randall Academy in Chandler, Arizona, since kindergarten and generally earns passing grades in all of his school subjects. He began speech and language therapy at age 3 but was dismissed from services at the age of 6 in first grade. With the exception of speech and language development, his developmental milestones were reached within normal limits.

Although generally healthy, Patrick has a history of ear infections, allergies (nuts, watermelon, strawberry, and dog saliva), and asthma. He has taken the medications Proventil for his asthma as well as Benadryl and EpiPen as needed. In 2013, concerns were noted about his vision and he was seen by Parker Thompson, O.D., who prescribed a bifocal correction to address mild myopic and accommodative refractive concerns. In addition to glasses, Dr. Thompson recommended an occupational therapy evaluation to address concerns regarding his fine motor coordination. After the occupational therapy evaluation, Patrick was provided services to improve his strength and motor skills and was assigned home exercises to improve his hand strength, manual dexterity, and visual tracking.

Throughout his school years, Patrick has required extra assistance in learning to read. He has received instruction in the Spalding method, a systematic phonics approach, since kindergarten, including additional tutoring in this method during the summer months. Patrick has also received a great deal of support from his parents at home to assist with his challenges in learning to read and write. He has had difficulty with letter orientation (*p-q*, *b-d*) since the first grade and often uses an index card when reading, to keep his place in the text. Although the *p-q* confusion is now resolved, Patrick still has a tendency to reverse the letters *b* and *d*.

Patrick has had a 504 plan in school since the age of 6. This plan addresses his visual challenges for reading going from distance to near (board to desk reading), eye tracking for reading (staying on the lines when reading text), as well as his health needs for asthma and food allergies. He is currently placed in the lowest groups in his classroom for both reading and mathematics. Teacher reports indicate that Patrick has difficulty remaining in his seat during class and trouble sustaining attention during seatwork. He is often observed talking with his peers, fiddling with pencils or objects on his desk, or walking across the classroom instead of completing his work. While his teacher reports he is very social and gets along well with his peers, she believes his inattention and distractibility impact his classroom work production.

Patrick reported that he enjoys sports like swimming and soccer and likes doing projects at school. He is an avid chess player and competes regularly in tournaments. He noted that he finds it more difficult when the teacher "just talks" and he has to "just listen." He also commented that his math class is "way too easy" and "it's stuff I already learned in second grade." Because his math class is "boring," he stated that he wishes he could spend more time in classes like P.E. and Art. He mentioned that even though he is in the third grade, his teacher sometimes gives them tasks to do that are "really for students in fifth grade."

Prior Evaluations

In October of 2013, Ms. Jackson requested a speech/language evaluation. The speech/language pathologist conducted an informal observation of Patrick (10/24 and 10/29/2013) and concluded: "Patrick's speech-language skills do not impede his ability to progress in the general education classroom, socialize/interact with peers, or express himself clearly." Any observed errors were considered to be unremarkable due to the fact that they were isolated instances.

In January of 2014, Patrick was evaluated by Dr. Regina Hall, a psychologist from Pediatric Psychologists in Chandler, AZ. He was administered the following tests:

Beery-Buktenica Developmental Test of Visual-Motor Integration–Sixth Edition (VMI)

Gray Oral Reading Test–Fifth Edition (GORT–5)

Woodcock-Johnson III Normative Update Tests Cognitive Ability (WJ III COG)

Woodcock-Johnson III Normative Update Tests of Achievement, Form B (WJ III ACH)

Review of Records

Dr. Hall provided the following summary and conclusions: "Patrick exhibited strengths in nonverbal conceptual thinking, auditory processing, and verbal comprehension. He had weaknesses in processing speed, long-term retrieval, and basic reading skills, but they are not severe enough to be considered a learning disorder. These may, however, be maximized (i.e., his strengths) and minimized (i.e., his weaknesses) with interventions and accommodations designed to support his learning." Patrick also had above-average performance on tasks involving visual-spatial thinking and on tasks involving mathematical calculations. In fact, his score on the Calculation test was the same as or exceeded 87% of his age peers. A variety of recommendations were made to address his strengths and weaknesses.

Results from the Current Evaluation

Tests Administered

Wechsler Intelligence Test for Children–Fifth Edition (WISC–V) by Dr. Katie Eklund (Scores are at the end of report in a section called Score Summaries.)

Woodcock-Johnson IV by Dr. Nancy Mather (Scores are in **Appendix H** in the downloadable resources: www.wiley.com/go/itwiscv).

Tests of Cognitive Abilities (WJ IV COG)

Tests of Oral Language (WJ IV OL)

Tests of Achievement (WJ IV ACH) Standard & Extended

(All WJ IV tests were scored by age norms.)

Mindplay Universal Screening Procedure (RAPS 360)

Test Behaviors

Patrick was cooperative during four 1½-hour-long testing sessions. Although he maintained attention overall, on several occasions he would lose his focus, start talking about some other topic, and then have to be redirected to the task at hand. For example, when asked how two animals were alike, Patrick started talking about how rabbits come out in the winter and summer and how rabbits like to hide in bushes. Patrick also had difficulty sitting still during the assessment. He tended to squirm in his seat and then stand up and then sit back down again. In general, his attention and interest increased on tasks that involved visual stimuli (such as pictures, blocks, and designs) and decreased on tasks that involved language and lengthy verbal instructions. During one testing session, Patrick forgot to bring his glasses, so only oral tests that did not involve visual stimuli were administered. The present test results are considered to be a valid and reliable assessment of Patrick's current levels of cognitive and academic functioning.

Description of Tests and Score Interpretation

Tests of intellectual ability generally measure the thinking skills that underlie school tasks and therefore help us to determine how well a child might be expected to perform in school. Patrick was administered the Wechsler Intelligence Scale for Children–Fifth Edition (WISC–V; Wechsler, 2014). This test measures several aspects of a child's cognitive functioning and is often used to provide an estimate of a child's cognitive potential. In addition to the Full Scale IQ, which is a measure of general intellectual ability, five primary index scores that measure specific cognitive abilities are provided: Verbal

Comprehension, Visual Spatial, Fluid Reasoning, Working Memory, and Processing Speed. Ten primary subtests were administered to obtain these five primary index scores and the Full Scale IQ. In addition, the General Ability Index and the Cognitive Proficiency Index were obtained from these 10 primary subtests to provide a contrast of higher-order reasoning and cognitive processing; a discrepancy between these abilities is commonly observed in children with learning disabilities, and this type of discrepancy can inform recommendations for the classroom.

Two other WISC–V ancillary index scores were relevant to the purpose of this evaluation. For this reason, two of the secondary subtests, Letter–Number Sequencing and Arithmetic, were also administered to obtain the Quantitative Reasoning Index and the Auditory Working Memory Index. Five complementary subtests, the Naming Speed subtests (i.e., Naming Speed Literacy and Naming Speed Quantity) and the Symbol Translation subtests (i.e., Immediate, Delayed, and Recognition Symbol Translation) were administered because they assess abilities that are known to be related to reading disabilities. Three complementary index scores, Naming Speed, Symbol Translation, and Storage and Retrieval, were also obtained from the complementary subtests to allow examination of rapid automatized naming, visual-verbal associative learning, and general long-term storage and retrieval, respectively.

Various tests from the Woodcock Johnson IV (WJ IV) were also administered to assess Patrick's abilities (Schrank, McGrew, & Mather, 2014). The WJ IV is composed of three assessment instruments: the WJ IV Tests of Cognitive Abilities (WJ IV COG), the WJ IV Tests of Oral Language (WJ IV OL), and the WJ IV Tests of Achievement (WJ IV ACH). These tests measure a broad range of intellectual and oral language abilities, as well as academic achievement.

Throughout this report, the WISC–V and WJ IV results are mostly described using the labels for ranges based upon the standard scores (i.e., "High Average", "Average", "Low Average", etc.). Percentile ranks are also used to describe some of the WISC–V and WJ IV results. A percentile rank specifies the percentage of individuals of the same age that scored the same as or below the subject's obtained score. On the WJ IV, the proficiency labels (i.e., "limited," "average," "advanced," etc.) and the instructional implications ("impossible" to "very easy") are based on the Relative Proficiency Index (RPI). The RPI is an index of the student's predicted quality of performance on tasks similar to the ones tested. For example, an RPI of 71/90 means that the student would be predicted to demonstrate 71% proficiency with similar tasks that average individuals in the comparison group (age) would perform with 90% proficiency. Tasks at this age level would be "difficult." In contrast, someone with an RPI of 96/90 would have "average to advanced proficiency" and would find similar tasks to be "easy." The next table depicts the proficiency and instructional implications labels for the RPI.

Patrick was also administered the Mindplay Universal Reading Screener (RAPS 360), an online assessment that identifies specific gaps in reading (phonological awareness, phonics, fluency, vocabulary, and reading comprehension) as well as a measure of listening vocabulary.

Cognitive and Oral Language Results

Overall Intellectual Ability

- Wechsler Intelligence Scale for Children–Fifth Edition (WISC–V)
- WJ IV Cognitive Battery (WJ IV COG) and WJ IV Oral Language (WJ IV OL)

Both scores of overall intellectual ability indicate that Patrick is currently functioning in the Average range compared to his age peers (WISC–V FSIQ = 103, 58th percentile; WJ IV COG General Intellectual Ability (GIA) (SS = 99, 46th percentile). Both the WISC–V and WJ IV have alternate estimates of intelligence that remove lower-level processing subtests. The General Ability Index provides an

estimate of general intellectual ability, specifically verbal problem solving, abstract conceptual reasoning, and visual-perceptual reasoning, that is less reliant on working memory and processing speed compared with the Full Scale IQ.

Patrick's WISC–V General Ability Index (standard score of 115, 84th percentile) was higher than his FSIQ. Similarly, on the WJ IV COG his *Gf-Gc* Composite, a combination of reasoning and language abilities, was a standard score of 121, 87th percentile. Based on the results of the WISC–V and WJ IV COG, the majority of Patrick's abilities fell within the Average to High Average range. Significant strengths and weaknesses, however, existed among his cognitive and linguistic test scores.

Verbal Comprehension/Oral Language In general, Patrick's proficiency in language use and comprehension, as well as his general knowledge and vocabulary, were a relative strength. His performance on the WISC–V Verbal Comprehension Index was in the High Average range (86th percentile). Patrick was able to describe how two words are similar and provide definitions for words. While it occasionally took him some time to arrive at the correct answer, talking out loud about how two objects were alike (Similarities) or defining a word (Vocabulary) appeared to be a useful strategy for Patrick. His Verbal Comprehension Index was a strength relative to the average of all five WISC–V primary index scores. His stronger scores in these areas suggest good development of verbal concepts and reasoning, and effective communication of knowledge.

On the WJ IV COG and WJ IV OL, Patrick demonstrated advanced proficiency on tasks involving vocabulary knowledge and general information. His abilities to engage in conversation, follow directions, and relate and retell stories were typical for his age. On the Mindplay Universal Reading Screener (RAPS 360), Patrick's listening vocabulary, the grade level at which a student recognizes spoken words and understands their meanings, was at the 8th-grade level.

Table 14.29 Instructional Implications for Relative Proficiency Index (RPI)

RPI Score	0/90 to 3/90	3/90 to 24/90	24/90 to 67/90	67/90 to 82/90	82/90 to 95/90	95/90 to 98/90	98/90 to 100/90
Proficiency Range	Negligible	Very Limited	Limited	Limited to Average	Average	Average to Advanced	Advanced
Instructional Implications	Impossible	Extremely Difficult	Very Difficult	Difficult	Manageable/ Appropriate	Easy	Very Easy

Phonological Processing and Phonetic Coding
Phonological processing tasks involve accessing words through sounds, whereas phonetic coding tasks involve the oral abilities to blend and break apart word parts and speech sounds. Patrick exhibited weaknesses on phonological processing tasks that also involved working memory and speed (RPI = 74/90). He had difficulty thinking of words that contained certain sounds, rapidly retrieving words that started with a certain sound, and substituting one sound for another within a word. In contrast, Patrick had advanced proficiency on two phonetic coding tasks. His RPI of 98/90 on the WJ IV OL Phonetic Coding cluster suggests that when average age mates have 90% proficiency blending and segmenting sounds, Patrick will have 98% success; these types of tasks will be easy for him. Thus, his difficulties with speech sounds appear to be more related to memory and speed of retrieval rather than to his abilities to blend and segment speech sounds.

Patrick's facility with both blending and segmenting speech sounds was readily apparent. For example, when asked to identify the number of syllables in a word, Patrick put his hand on his chin and counted the number of times his chin dropped. (The chin drops because each syllable contains a vowel sound which makes a speaker open the mouth.) His high score on the Phonetic Coding cluster can most likely be attributed to his experience with the Spalding method, which provides systematic instruction in both blending and segmenting. His advanced abilities to blend together and segment speech sounds suggest that weaknesses in phonological awareness are not

contributing factors to his reading and spelling difficulties.

Visual-Spatial Skills Patrick demonstrated above-average abilities on the Visual Spatial Index on the WISC-V (77th percentile; High Average range). He was able to solve visual-spatial problems by assembling colored block to duplicate pictures of abstract designs (Block Design) and selecting pieces of a puzzle and mentally assembling them to reconstruct a puzzle (Visual Puzzles). His Visual Spatial Index was a strength relative to the average of all five WISC-V primary index scores. His performance on the WJ IV COG Visual Processing factor was similar (83rd percentile). Patrick became more engaged during these types of tasks, and remarked about how much fun they were.

Fluid and Quantitative Reasoning Patrick obtained scores in the above average range on measures of fluid reasoning. His WISC-V Fluid Reasoning Index was in the High Average range (79th percentile), and was a strength relative to the average of all five WISC-V primary index scores. Stronger scores in this area indicate a well-developed ability to abstract conceptual information from visual details and to effectively apply that knowledge. Specifically, he demonstrated high average ability to complete designs by picking out the "missing piece" from several possible choices and showed good attention to detail in picking out pairs of pictures that went together from rows of different choices. He obtained a similar score on the WJ IV COG, Fluid Reasoning cluster (85th percentile). His

WISC–V Quantitative Reasoning Index (QRI) was in the Average range (73rd percentile), and his WJ IV COG Quantitative Reasoning cluster was in the High Average range (85th percentile). These scores suggest Patrick has a good aptitude for mathematics. During one of the tests, Patrick commented that he liked the task because "it was kind of like playing chess."

Working Memory In contrast to Patrick's strong verbal, visual-spatial, and reasoning abilities, his performance on working memory tasks was a relative weakness. Working memory measures Patrick's ability to register, maintain, and manipulate visual and auditory information in conscious awareness. His WISC–V Working Memory Index was in the low average range (13th percentile) and was a weakness relative to the average of all five WISC–V primary index scores. His WISC–V Auditory Working Memory Index was even lower, falling in the very low range (7th percentile). Lowered auditory working memory performance is commonly seen among children with specific reading disabilities.

Similar scores were obtained on the WJ IV COG Short-Term Working Memory cluster (8th percentile). His scores were in the Average range, however, on tests that involved only memory span or the ability to repeat back information verbatim (Auditory Memory Span, 36th percentile). On several occasions during testing, Patrick asked for information to be repeated (i.e., "Can you say that again?") and appeared to become discouraged when he couldn't remember the sequence of numbers or words. Observation of Patrick's behavior suggested that the inconsistency in these results may have been more related to fluctuations in his attention rather than to weaknesses in memory per se. In support of this observation, his longest span results (corresponding to the three parts of WISC–V Digit Span and WISC–V Letter–Number Sequencing) were somewhat stronger than his actual scores, which indicates he intermittently missed some trials due to lapses in attention.

Processing Speed Patrick also demonstrated a significant weakness in processing speed as his performance was in the Very Low range (7th percentile, WISC–V; 7th percentile, WJ IV COG). His WISC–V Processing Speed Index was a weakness relative to the average of all five WISC–V primary index scores. The subtests in this area assess Patrick's ability to quickly and correctly scan, sequence, or discriminate simple visual information. They also measure short-term visual memory, attention, and visual-motor coordination. His RPI of 17/90 on the WJ IV COG Cognitive Processing Speed cluster suggests that when typical age peers have 90% proficiency, Patrick will only have 17% or very limited proficiency. Processing speed underlies many academic tasks in school, including basic reading, spelling, and math skills. These types of tasks are difficult for Patrick. Even though he was wearing glasses, Patrick rubbed his eyes several times after completing these tests. While he remained focused during these tests, he mentioned several times that he needed more time to finish the task.

Rapid Automatized Naming and Visual-Verbal Associative Memory As with other timed measures, Patrick's WISC–V Naming Speed Index was in the Low Average range (16th percentile). The Naming Speed Index includes two timed tests and provides a broad estimate of naming automaticity and verbal retrieval abilities. Low scores can occur due to visual-processing deficits or information retrieval difficulties. His performance on the Naming Speed Literacy subtest, which required naming objects, letters, and numbers, was somewhat lower than his score on the Naming Speed Quantity subtest, which required identifying the number of squares within a series of boxes. Such a pattern is common in children with specific reading disabilities.

Patrick's Symbol Translation Index was in the Average range (27th percentile). The Symbol Translation Index is a measure of visual-verbal associative memory drawn from a variety of conditions: immediate memory of taught symbol-meaning pairs, a delayed condition when he was required to recall the pairs from 20 minutes prior, and a delayed recognition condition that required him to recognize the meaning when the symbol was shown. Patrick showed relatively consistent performance across these conditions. Because these subtests are given near the end of the WISC–V, Patrick's inattention may have interfered with his performance to some extent. While his scores on immediate, delayed, and delayed recognition tasks were all in the Average range, his performances on the two delayed conditions were unusually lower than his performance on the immediate condition. This suggests that after a delay, Patrick retains relatively less of the information he learns than do his same-age peers.

Academic Functioning Results

- Woodcock-Johnson Tests of Achievement (WJ IV ACH)
- Mindplay Universal Reading Screener (RAPS 360)

Reading   In contrast to his average to advanced proficiency on many other cognitive and academic areas, Patrick's reading proficiency was limited. His RPI on the Broad Reading cluster was 11/90, suggesting that when typical age peers have 90% success on reading tasks, Patrick would have only 11% success. This suggests that classroom reading tasks will be very difficult. His proficiency in word reading (Letter-Word Identification test) was very limited, and his ability to apply phonics (Word Attack test) was limited. The prescriptive plan developed from RAPS 360 indicated Patrick needs to complete 87 specific objectives to achieve grade-level reading scores. Weaknesses were noted in long vowel sounds, vowel teams, and spelling rules.

Patrick's greatest area of weaknesses, however, was his reading fluency and rate. His RPI on the Reading Rate cluster was only 2/90. He had extremely limited proficiency on the Sentence Reading Fluency test, where he was asked to read a series of sentences as quickly as he could. His

RPI was only 1/90, indicating that when average age peers have 90% success reading sentences quickly, Patrick would have only 1% success. His performance was similar on the Word Reading Fluency test, which required the rapid reading of words (RPI = 4/90). He will find classroom reading tasks that involve timed or rapid reading to be extremely difficult. On the RAPS 360, Patrick's reading rate was measured at 35 words per minute (wpm) on third-grade level material, whereas a typical silent reading rate for this grade would be 115 wpm.

On several occasions, Patrick misread common words that share a similar appearance, such as "these" for *those*, "farm" for *frame*, and "part" for *pair*. He did not attempt to self-correct any of these errors. Patrick lacked confidence in his ability to pronounce less familiar words as well as applying phonic skills to pronounce phonically regular nonsense words. These low reading scores are surprising in light of the fact that he has been receiving instruction in a structured phonics intervention since kindergarten as well as receiving help at home.

Written Language   Patrick's RPI of 79/90 on the Written Language cluster indicates his proficiency in written language was limited to average. Although Patrick was able to express his ideas in writing (Writing Samples RPI = 94/90), he had difficulty with spelling and tended to spell words the way they sound rather than the way they look (Spelling RPI = 42/90). As examples, he spelled the words *some* as "sum," *paying* as "paing," and *digging* as "digin." He reversed the letters *b* and *d*, spelling *baby* as "bady." These types of difficulties suggest problems with memory for spelling patterns, related to orthography (the writing system of a language), rather than difficulty sequencing sounds in order, which would be more related to the phonological awareness ability of segmentation.

Mathematics   Overall, Patrick's proficiency on math calculation and math problem-solving tasks was average. His RPI of 92/90 on the Broad

Mathematics cluster suggests that when typical age mates have 90% success, Patrick will have 92% success. On the Applied Problems test, Patrick was able to solve some difficult problems, but then missed some easier problems, such as items involving counting money. He had average proficiency on a task involving solving math facts quickly (Math Facts Fluency RPI = 95/90). In contrast, on the Calculation test, his RPI 64/90 was limited (percentile rank of 24). Patrick made several careless errors on problems. Even so, this score was somewhat surprising as his Basic Math Skills score in 2013 exceeded 86% of his age peers. This seeming decline in scores may be more of a reflection of what he has been taught rather than what he is capable of learning as well as an artifact of different norms (WJ III versus WJ IV). Either way, his interest in and aptitude for mathematical computations seem much higher than his present performance levels. In general, Patrick was more engaged in questions that involved mathematical calculations and problem solving than he was with tasks involving reading and spelling.

Analysis of Strengths and Weaknesses

Patrick demonstrated meaningful score differences indicating a pattern of consistent strengths and weaknesses on both the WISC–V and WJ IV COG. On the WISC–V, Patrick's primary index scores were compared to the mean of his primary index scores. On the WJ IV COG his *Gf-Gc* composite score was compared to his other abilities, as were several other abilities (GIA, Scholastic Aptitudes, Oral Language, and Academic Knowledge). These comparisons are designed to show discrepancies between the predictor (e.g., the *Gf-Gc* Composite) and other abilities (e.g., Reading).

In addition, on the WJ IV, three types of variation procedures were analyzed: intra-cognitive, intra-oral language, and intra-achievement. These procedures are used to document a pattern of strengths and weaknesses across the various clusters and tests. Patrick had significant strengths in vocabulary, reasoning, visual

processing, and phonetic coding. He had significant weaknesses in processing speed, working memory, basic reading skills, and reading rate.

Patrick's WISC–V General Ability Index (84th percentile) and Cognitive Proficiency Index (4th percentile) were examined to gain a broader perspective on his higher-order reasoning abilities relative to his cognitive proficiency. The Cognitive Proficiency Index provides an estimate of the efficiency of information processing in service of higher-order reasoning and problem solving. The subtests that contribute to the General Ability Index are drawn from the Verbal Comprehension, Visual Spatial, and Fluid Reasoning scales, and the subtests that contribute to the Cognitive Proficiency Index are drawn from the Working Memory and Processing Speed scales, all of which have been previously described.

Patrick's Cognitive Proficiency Index is significantly lower than his General Ability Index, and a difference such as seen in Patrick's performance is very rarely seen (<0.3% of children with a similar general ability level show a difference this large). Patrick's cognitive proficiency is therefore a significant and very unusual weakness. While such a difference is uncommonly observed, it is more frequently seen among children with learning problems and neurodevelopmental disorders. Patrick's cognitive processing limitations may have affected his acquisition of basic reading skills and have also reduced his scores on overall measures of cognitive ability, such as the FSIQ score on the WISC-V and the GIA on the WJ IV COG.

Similar results were obtained for conceptually similar cluster scores from the WJ IV COG: the *Gf-Gc* Composite (92nd percentile) and the Cognitive Efficiency cluster (4th percentile). When Patrick's WJ IV COG *Gf-Gc* composite score (based on higher-level measures of reasoning and knowledge) and his WISC–V Verbal Comprehension, Visual Spatial, and Fluid Reasoning Index scores are compared to his other cognitive abilities, he has significant weaknesses in both processing speed and working memory. When these composites are compared to his academic achievement, he has significant weaknesses in reading and spelling. For example, when his WJ IV COG *Gf-Gc* composite score is compared to his WJ IV Broad Reading cluster, only 2 out of 1,000 students would have a reading score as low. This discrepancy suggests that Patrick's aptitude for learning is much higher than his current levels of reading performance. When other WJ IV COG ability scores (General Intellectual Ability, Scholastic Aptitude, Oral Language, and Academic Knowledge clusters) are compared to his academic performance, weaknesses are found in reading, particularly his reading rate.

Conclusion

Although many of Patrick's cognitive test scores were within the Average and High Average ranges, he demonstrated significant weaknesses on measures of working memory and processing speed, both correlates of reading disability. In addition, he had very limited to limited proficiency on all reading tests. What is of greatest concern is the fact that Patrick has made insufficient academic progress in reading even with substantial additional assistance from both home and school. Although he has received targeted reading instruction with the Spalding method since kindergarten, he continues to struggle using phonics, pronouncing multisyllabic words, and reading at an adequate rate. The persistence and relative severity of his reading difficulties, his slow processing speed and word perception, his limited response to systematic interventions, and the types of reading and spelling errors he makes all support the conclusion that Patrick has a severe reading disability. In addition, his mild difficulties regulating attention also interfere with his listening and learning. The answer to the referral question is: "Yes, Ms. Jackson. Your son does have a reading disability."

Recommendations

School programming considerations and instructional goals and strategies are provided below to address Patrick's weaknesses while building upon many of his well-developed skills.

School Programming

1. Patrick will require specific accommodations in the classroom, such as extended time on reading assignments and shortened homework assignments. Until his reading performance improves, Patrick will need adjustments in the difficulty level in both school and homework assignments. Although he is earning good grades, because of accommodating teachers and a substantial amount of home support, his reading level and speed at which he is able to complete tasks are well below that of his same age peers.

2. Patrick would benefit from sitting at the front of the classroom so as to maximize his attention. He would also benefit from frequent breaks when in-seat classroom assignments are given, such as having him deliver notes to the office or an opportunity to work with a peer on an assignment. Consider seating him away from auditory distractions, such as doors opening and closing or air conditioning or heating units.

3. When possible, break Patrick's in-class assignments into smaller, more manageable chunks. Give him one part at a time with instructions to hand each in as it is completed and pick up the next. Each time he hands in a portion of the work, provide reinforcement for completed work. Using this technique, he will be more likely to stay on task and complete assignments.

4. Because Patrick completes visually based tasks that require spatial manipulation with relative ease, provide him with hands-on activities, such as completing science projects, so that he can demonstrate his strengths in visual-spatial thinking and reasoning.

5. Because of mild issues with attention, Patrick will have difficulty listening to instruction that is delivered primarily in a lecture style. To maximize his attention, incorporate hands-on activities into the instruction as much as possible.

6. Visual organizers, like a daily planner or assignment list, are recommended as a way to help Patrick structure his classroom assignments and homework. As Patrick appears to respond well to visual stimuli, using visual cues may help him attend to homework and/or classroom assignments. Encourage his teacher to check his planner at the beginning and/or end of each school day.

7. Because of age-appropriate language and math skills, Patrick should not be retained in third grade regardless of his performance on high-stakes state standardized tests, such as AZMerit. If needed, provide Patrick with a reader when he takes this test so that all of his attention can be focused upon answering questions rather than on decoding words.

8. Due to his low working memory, he may benefit most from instructions delivered simply, precisely, and clearly. Avoid elaborate wording and emphasize key words. Keep spoken information short and provide reminders. Give one direction at a time. Do not provide the next step until he has finished with the previous step.

9. Patrick's low working memory and processing speed taken together could sometimes look in the classroom as though he is inattentive and noncompliant. Without quick processing speed, it is easy for information held and being processed in working memory to decay before it can be acted upon and fully understood. Due to his lower cognitive proficiency/efficiency, it is important to give adequate time to process information, repeat it when needed, and provide ample cues and support; the combination of low working memory, slow processing speed, and challenges with attention can be misinterpreted as noncompliance.

Reading and Spelling

1. To make progress, Patrick requires specialized reading instruction. Patrick would benefit from participation in an online reading program, Mindplay Virtual Reading Coach (MVRC). The program begins with an initial reading assessment (RAPS 360—already completed) that determines exactly which skills Patrick needs to develop and then plans a prescriptive program based upon his assessment results. Patrick should spend 30 minutes a day, 4 to 5 days a week with this program, ideally for the next 6 months. A home version is available at www.myreadingteam.com, and a school version is available at www.mindplay.com. Patrick will need to understand that this program is like working one on one with a reading tutor and is not based on games. It may be necessary to create some type of reinforcement program to reward Patrick for daily completion of the activity. For example, he could earn points that could then be traded in for a pizza or movie tickets. So that Patrick will not become overwhelmed with homework demands, allow him to substitute 30 minutes daily of MVRC for homework in the Accelerated Reader.

2. Determine a strategy that will help Patrick remember the orientation of the letters *b* and *d*. Two examples include:

   (a) Teach Patrick how to form the letters *b* and *d* using uniquely different stroke sequences. To form a *b*, have the student start at the top line, write a vertical line down to the baseline and then, starting at the midline, make a forward half-circle (clockwise). In D'Nealian handwriting, the student is taught to make a vertical line down and then come up from the base with a half-circle counterclockwise). For the letter *d*, he should start at the midline and form a backward circle (counterclockwise), like the movement for starting the letter c, then continue the upward stroke to the top line and back down again.

   (b) Have Patrick make a b with the left hand and a d with the right (forefinger straight up, circle with thumb and other fingers) to form a "bed." Tell him that the b comes first in the alphabet so check the left hand for b; the d comes after it, so look at the right hand.

3. Provide Patrick with instruction that increases his recognition of common letters patterns, builds his understanding of spelling rules, and shows him how to use structural analysis (breaking words apart into syllables) to make them easier to pronounce. Reading and spelling instruction will be most effective if the patterns taught for reading are taught for spelling at the same time. Teach Patrick how to find prefixes and suffixes. An easy strategy to use is based on the REWARDS program. When presented with a multisyllabic word, ask Patrick to: (a) circle the prefix, (b) circle the suffix, (c) underline the vowel in the root word, and (d) draw scoops under each part saying: What part? What part? What part? What word?

4. Use a systematic spelling program, such as Scholastic Spelling or Spellography, that will provide Patrick with a solid foundation in common orthographic spelling patterns and in how to spell common high-frequency words.

5. To build speed and accuracy in pronunciation of sight words and phonetically irregular words, use 1-minute speed drills. Time Patrick daily on reading lists of common, irregular words as quickly as he can. Record and display his daily performance on some type of graph. Also have him practice spelling these words.

6. To help increase reading speed, provide daily practice with repeated reading. Have Patrick read out loud the same passage three to four times to improve the rate and accuracy of reading. Select high-interest passages that are at the high end of his instructional reading level. Record the number of words read per minute as well as the number of errors. Practice rereading until an acceptable rate and accuracy are achieved. Chart his progress and performance on each rereading.

7. Use Patrick's knowledge, curiosity, and intellect to build interest in reading by selecting books that cover various subject areas. Encourage him to read for entertainment and communication as well as for fun. Draw on his strengths in the areas of verbal comprehension and reasoning by engaging him in the study of words, for example, pronunciation, meaning, usage, and from what language they were derived. Encourage him to recognize patterns that govern spelling or pronunciation.

8. Provide Patrick with previews of content, text structure, and new or difficult vocabulary words that will be introduced in lessons or passages. Priming background knowledge of the subject area concerned will help Patrick connect new topics and information to previously learned information.

Mathematics

1. Move Patrick into a higher math group. Teach any missing skills, as needed.

2. Review with Patrick basic math skills including multiplication of two-digit numbers and simple division. Introduce fractions and decimals.

3. Review counting coins up to five dollars.

4. Consider use of an online math program, such as ALEKS (http://www.aleks.com), to supplement math instruction. This program will design a math curriculum to accelerate Patrick's mathematical abilities.

5. Provide practice in math facts and math using fun video games. Many of these can be found on www.coolmath.com.

6. Provide review of different types of math problems. A good book to use would be *Math4Today*, which provides daily 10-minute worksheets with a variety of math problems geared at a fourth-grade level (his instructional level).

7. To maximize attention, alternate instruction in math skills with games to reinforce and develop those skills.

Score Summaries

Table 14.30   Patrick's WISC–V Composite Scores

WISC–V Composite Scores	Standard Score* (95% Confidence Interval)**	PR***	Qualitative Range
Verbal Comprehension Index	116 (108–122)	86th	High Average
Visual Spatial Index	111 (102–118)	77th	High Average
Fluid Reasoning Index	112 (104–118)	79th	High Average
Working Memory Index	83 (75–95)	13th	Low Average
Processing Speed Index	78 (68–86)	7th	Very Low
Mean Primary Index Score (MIS)	100		
Full Scale IQ	103 (97–09)	58th	Average
Quantitative Reasoning Index	109 (102–115)	73rd	Average
Auditory Working Memory Index	78 (72–87)	7th	Very Low
General Ability Index	115 (109–120)	84th	High Average
Cognitive Proficiency Index	74 (69–83)	4th	Very Low
Naming Speed Index	85 (78–95)	16th	Low Average
Symbol Translation Index	91 (85–98)	27th	Average
Storage and Retrieval Index	84 (78–92)	14th	Low Average

Table 14.31   Patrick's WISC–V Index-Level Strengths and Weaknesses Analysis

Primary Index Score	Significant Strength or Weakness Relative to Mean Primary Index Score?	Base Rate of Difference[a]
Verbal Comprehension Index	S	≤5%
Visual Spatial Index	S	≤15%
Fluid Reasoning Index	S	≤15%
Working Memory Index	W	≤5%
Processing Speed Index	W	≤5%

[a]The base rate of the difference is the frequency with which the difference is observed in the normative sample.

Table 14.32   Patrick's WISC–V Index-Level Pairwise Comparison

Index Scores	Significant Difference?	Base Rate of Difference[a]
General Ability Index– Cognitive Proficiency Index	Y	0.3%

[a]The base rate of the difference is the frequency with which the difference is observed in the normative sample.

Table 14.33   Patrick's WISC–V Primary and Secondary Subtest Score Summary

Cognitive Domain	Scaled Score* (95% Confidence Interval)**	PR**	Qualitative Range
Verbal Comprehension			
Similarities	13	84th	Above Average
Vocabulary	13	84th	Above Average
Visual Spatial			
Block Design	11	63rd	Average
Visual Puzzles	13	84th	Above Average
Fluid Reasoning			
Matrix Reasoning	11	63rd	Average
Figure Weights	13	84th	Above Average
Arithmetic	10	63rd	Average

(continued)

Table 14.33 *(Continued)*

Cognitive Domain	Scaled Score* (95% Confidence Interval)**	PR**	Qualitative Range
Working Memory			
Digit Span	6	9th	Below Average
Picture Span	7	16th	Below Average
Letter-Number Sequencing	6	9th	Below Average
Processing Speed			
Coding	6	9th	Below Average
Symbol Search	5	5th	Very Low
Mean Primary Subtest Scaled Score (MSS-P)	9.8		

Table 14.34 Patrick's WISC–V Subtest-Level Strengths and Weaknesses Analysis

Subtest	Significant Strength (S) or Weakness (W) Relative to Mean Primary Index Score	Base Rate of Difference[a]
Similarities	S	≤10%
Vocabulary	S	≤10%
Block Design		
Visual Puzzles	S	≤10%
Matrix Reasoning		
Figure Weights	S	≤10%
Digit Span	W	≤10%
Picture Span		
Coding	W	≤10%
Symbol Search	W	≤5%

[a]The base rate of the difference is the frequency with which the difference is observed in the normative sample.

Table 14.35 Patrick's WISC–V Complementary Subtest Score Summary

Subtest	Standard Score*	PR**	Qualitative Range
Naming Speed Literacy	85	16th	Low Average
Naming Speed Quantity	89	23rd	Low Average
Immediate Symbol Translation	100	50th	Average
Delayed Symbol Translation	90	25th	Low Average
Recognition Symbol Translation	91	27th	Average

Table 14.36 Patrick's WISC–V Process Score Summary

Process Scores	Scaled Score	PR**	Qualitative Range
Digit Span Forward	7	16th	Low Average
Digit Span Backward	5	5th	Very Low
Digit Span Sequencing	6	9th	Low Average
Longest Digit Span Forward	–	61st	Average
Longest Digit Span Backward	–	41st	Average
Longest Digit Span Sequencing	–	49th	Average
Longest Letter–Number Sequencing	–	65th	Average

*Standard score: Calculated value of Patrick's scores that can be compared to scores for a group of individuals of similar age; the average (mean) of the age group's score is 100, and the majority of the group's scores fall between 85 and 115. For composite standard scores, the score can be compared to scores of other children aged 6 to 16.

**Confidence Intervals (CI): Compares the subject's score to same age scores with 100, indicating the average score of the standardization sample. The 95% confidence band indicates the range in which the subject's true score would lie with 95% certainty; given unexpected and unintended testing error or variations, we cannot be 100% confident of the subject's true score. (e.g., Verbal Comprehension SS of 115 (108–122) means that Patrick's score falls in the average range when compared to other individuals his same age. Also, if tested again, Patrick's score in this index would fall within the range of 108 to 122, with a 95% certainty).

***Percentile rank (PR): Specifies the percentage of individuals of the same age that score the same or below the subject's achieved score (e.g., Block Design PR of 75: 75% of individuals score the same or lower than Patrick).

+Scaled score: Calculated value of Patrick's scores that can be compared to scores for a group of individuals of similar age; the average (mean) of the age group's score is 10, and the majority of the group's scores fall between 7 and 13.

For a complete score report on the WJ IV for Patrick, go to Appendix H in the downloadable resources: www.wiley.com/go/itwiscv

PART 5

INDEPENDENT WISC–V TEST REVIEWS

CHAPTER 15

OUR WISC–V REVIEW

Matthew R. Reynolds and Megan B. Hadorn

In the intelligence testing world, David Wechsler is still considered the king (A. S. Kaufman, 1993, 2009). His influence on intelligence testing is likely unparalleled. And despite his passing more than three decades ago and the arrival of a number of theory-based intelligence tests, the Wechsler tests are still the most widely used. The Wechsler Intelligence Scale for Children (WISC) is one of those widely used tests.

The newest WISC, the Wechsler Intelligence Scale for Children–Fifth Edition (WISC–V; Wechsler, 2014), was recently released. Because of the popularity of the WISC, updating the test is a tricky endeavor. Among other things, it requires incorporating new theory and research without eliminating what makes the test so popular thereby alienating its users. The WISC–V predecessor, the Wechsler Intelligence Scale for Children–Fourth Edition (WISC–IV; Wechsler, 2003), contained significant changes that were described as "radical" (Burns & O'Leary, 2004) and even risky (Baron, 2005). Many of the changes, however, were generally lauded by reviewers (e.g., Baron, 2005; Burns & O'Leary, 2004; Flanagan & Kaufman, 2004; A. S. Kaufman, Flanagan, Alfonso, & Mascolo, 2006). In fact, despite some critiques, A. S. Kaufman and colleagues (2006) called the WISC–IV the "best WISC ever" (p. 293). Is the WISC–V the best WISC ever? Or was the WISC–IV the pinnacle of all WISCs? Time, along with many other well-informed reviews and research, will tell. Here is our overview and initial impression of the WISC–V.

WISC–IV

To provide some context to our description of changes made for the WISC–V, it is first worthwhile for us to discuss some of the changes that were made on the WISC–IV.

Eliminated Composites and Subtests

Some of the most radical changes made to the WISC–IV involved what was eliminated, not what was added. The elimination of the Verbal IQ and Performance IQ scores was one of the most notable changes. The move was generally hailed by reviewers, and, not surprisingly, we have yet to encounter any large movements calling for their reinstatement. Although the composite was not eliminated, another popular move was changing the name of the Freedom from Distractibility Index to the Working Memory Index, a term that seemed to more accurately describe the index. (Freedom from Distractibility had a long and controversial past, and it was time for the name to go so researchers could ultimately free themselves from being distracted by this index.) Last, some long-standing subtests were eliminated; others were assigned the dreadful supplemental status. Despite the lighter test kits, and beyond the sentimental loss, the elimination of some of these subtests, particularly those that required more interaction between the examiner and examinee, concerned some (Burns & O'Leary, 2004). Nevertheless, in the end it also resulted in a test that had less emphasis on motor abilities and speed (A. S. Kaufman et al., 2006). Were any composites or subtests kicked off Wechsler Island during the development of the WISC–V?

Factor Indexes

Although several indexes and subtests were eliminated from the WISC–IV, five new subtests were included, representing an increased focus on the measurement of fluid reasoning, working memory, and processing speed. This focus, along with the elimination of the Verbal IQ and the Performance IQ, resulted in greater emphasis on four more well-defined and empirically supported factor indexes: the Verbal Comprehension Index, the Perceptual Reasoning Index, the Working Memory Index, and the Processing Speed Index.

The move was generally lauded. The factor indexes were not only more defensible empirically but also aligned more closely with the Cattell-Horn-Carroll (CHC) theory of intelligence (Carroll, 1993a; Schneider & McGrew, 2012). Nevertheless, some reviewers and researchers thought that the Perceptual Reasoning Index would be better interpreted as separate Fluid Reasoning and Visual Spatial Indexes (e.g., Flanagan & Kaufman, 2004; A. S. Kaufman et al., 2006; Keith, Fine, Taub, Reynolds, & Kranzler, 2006; Weiss, Keith, Zhu, & Chen, 2013b). Both interpretations appeared plausible based on within-battery factory analysis (cf. Keith et al., 2006; Watkins, 2006; Weiss et al., 2013b), but CHC theory and subsequent factor analysis of the WISC–IV subtests with other IQ tests seemed to favor a two-factor interpretation of the Perceptual Reasoning Index (e.g., M. R. Reynolds, Keith, Flanagan, & Alfonso, 2013).[1] The treatment of the Perceptual Reasoning Index was one of the big questions for the WISC–V. Would Perceptual Reasoning stay unified or would it split?

Full Scale IQ

Another major change on the WISC–IV was that the FSIQ was composed of some different subtests. Ten subtests, described as "death-and-taxes" constants, composed the FSIQ across the first three WISCs (A. S. Kaufman et al., 2006, p. 281). But on the WISC–IV, only five of those death-and-taxes subtests were included in the FSIQ. Five newcomers, including three subtests that were brand new to the WISC–IV, were included in the WISC–IV FSIQ.

Further, the WISC–IV FSIQ included a more equal proportion of subtests across cognitive domains. It included three subtests from the Verbal Comprehension domain, three from the Perceptual Reasoning domain, and two subtests from each of the Working Memory and Processing Speed domains. The Wechsler Intelligence Scale for Children–Third Edition (WISC–III; Wechsler, 1991), in contrast, included four subtests from the Verbal Comprehension domain, four subtests from the Perceptual Reasoning domain, and one each from the Working Memory and Processing Speed domains. (It is also notable that Arithmetic was the representative from the Working Memory domain, and this subtest has traditionally been one of the highest g-loaded tests). Thus, the WISC–IV FSIQ included four subtests (i.e., 40% of the IQ) from domains that have subtests that typically do not have as high g loadings (Processing Speed in particular). Further, Arithmetic was no longer included in the FSIQ. Although the new FSIQ was praised for being more descriptive of constructs measured by the test, A. S. Kaufman and colleagues (2006) wondered about potential effects related to including subtests with lower g loadings and eliminating some of those subtests with higher g loadings (e.g., Arithmetic). Others were disappointed that although the composition of the FSIQ changed, the administration time for the test was not reduced (Baron, 2005). Hence a big question for the WISC–V was: What recipe of subtests would compose the FSIQ?

WISC–V

The WISC–V (Wechsler, 2014) is an individually administered measure of intelligence published by PsychCorp. The test battery is designed for use among children aged 6 years to 16 years and 11 months (6:0–6:11). The WISC–V provides estimates of general intellectual functioning (FSIQ), broad cognitive abilities (e.g., working memory, processing speed), so-called ancillary abilities (e.g., auditory working memory, nonverbal intelligence), and other cognitive abilities purportedly associated with academic abilities (e.g., Naming Speed and Symbol Translation). The WISC–V, like its predecessor, certainly contains some big changes, some of which may relieve or concern examiners.

Subtests

The WISC–V includes 21 subtests. The subtests are categorized as primary, secondary, or complementary.

Retained and Modified Subtests

Of the 21 WISC–V subtests, 13 have been retained and altered to varying degrees from the WISC–IV (i.e., Block Design, Similarities, Matrix Reasoning, Digit Span, Coding, Vocabulary, Symbol Search, Information, Picture Concepts, Letter–Number Sequencing, Cancellation, Comprehension, and Arithmetic). These

13 subtests are either primary or secondary subtests. The most salient subtest changes are listed in Table 15.1, but see pages 7–12 in the *WISC–V Technical and Interpretive Manual* (Wechsler, 2014) for more details.[2]

Significant Modifications to the 13 Retained WISC–V Subtests
- Block Design (primary)
  - Addition of a new process score: Block Design Partial.
- Arithmetic (secondary)
  - Examinees are now told that items may be repeated.
  - Timing is paused during repetitions of longer items (to control for reading rate variability).
  - Items were altered to be more developmentally and culturally appropriate.
  - Items were added to create adequate floors and ceilings.

Table 15.1 Changes to 13 Retained Subtests

Subtest	Revised Scoring Criteria	New or Modified Sample Items	Total Items	Retained Items	Modified Items	New Items
Similarities	✓	✓	23	7	8	8
Vocabulary	✓		29	15	-	14
Information	✓		31	8	4	19
Comprehension	✓		19	4	2	13
Block Design			13	5	-	8
Matrix Reasoning		✓	32	12	-	20
Picture Concepts		✓	27	-	20	7
Arithmetic			34	6	18	10
Digit Span			54	3	-	51
Letter–Number Sequencing		✓	30	4	-	26
Coding	✓		A: 75 B: 117	-	-	-
Symbol Search			A: 40 B: 60	-	-	A: 40 B: 60
Cancellation			2	-	2	-

- Now listed as a Fluid Reasoning subtest and not a Working Memory subtest.
- Digit Span (primary)
  - Addition of a new task: Digit Span Sequencing (examinees rearrange numbers in ascending order; adapted from the WAIS–IV).
  - Retention of Digit Span Forward for instructional value and adequate floors.
  - Total raw score now derived from three tasks: Digit Span Forward, Digit Span Backward, and Digit Span Sequencing.
- Letter–Number Sequencing (secondary)
  - Revised for more even distribution of letters and numbers.
  - Similar-sounding letters and numbers (e.g., *3* and *b*) are no longer included in same trial.
  - Addition of "stepwise" instructions, in which examinees are told to (a) repeat numbers before letters, then (b) sequence repeated numbers and letters.
- Coding (primary)
  - Simplified instructions.
  - Revised to balance shapes and numbers.
  - Symbols revised for easier differentiation during scoring.
  - Symbols that are rotated iterations of one another have been removed.
  - Revised scoring criteria delineates acceptable degrees of symbol rotation.
  - Of the five shapes on Form A, three are retained and two are modified.
  - Of the nine symbols on Form B, three are modified and six are new.
- Symbol Search (secondary)
  - Simplified instructions.
  - Two new error types:
    - Set errors: Incorrect but similar symbols are selected.
    - Rotation errors: Symbols are rotated to any degree.
  - Balanced target symbols for more even difficulty and reduced influence of guessing.
  - Fewer items per page and larger symbol size.
- Cancellation (secondary)
  - Simplified instructions.

- Pictured objects and animals are more internationally recognizable.
- Target and distractor pictures are more consistent in color and form.

New Subtests Adapted from Other Wechsler Tests

Three subtests have been adapted from other Wechsler tests: Figure Weights and Visual Puzzles from the *Wechsler Adult Intelligence Scale–Fourth Edition* (WAIS–IV; Wechsler, 2008) and Picture Span from the Picture Memory subtest of the *Wechsler Preschool and Primary Scale of Intelligence–Fourth Edition* (WPPSI–IV; Wechsler, 2012). These three subtests are all considered primary subtests.

- Figure Weights (primary)
  - Examinees review a scale with missing weight(s) and then choose an option to balance the scale.
  - Supposed to measure fluid reasoning.
  - Consists of 34 items and includes a time limit.
- Visual Puzzles (primary)
  - Provides a picture of a complete puzzle, then examinees must select three pictured "pieces" that, when placed together, would complete the pictured puzzle.
  - Supposed to measure visual-spatial ability.
  - Consists of 29 items and includes a time limit.
- Picture Span (primary)
  - Displays a page with pictures, and after the examinee has had a certain amount of time to view the pictures, he or she is asked to choose those pictures (preferably in order) from a response page.
  - Supposed to measure (visual) working memory.
  - Consists of 26 items.

Eliminated Subtests

- Two subtests have been entirely thrown off Wechsler Island: Word Reasoning and Picture Completion.

- Word Reasoning eliminated due to construct redundancy with Vocabulary.
- Picture Completion eliminated to make room for new subtests.

Complementary Subtests

Five subtests have been created specifically for the WISC–V to assess new introduced constructs: Naming Speed Literacy, Naming Speed Quantity, Immediate Symbol Translation, Delayed Symbol Translation, and Recognition Symbol Translation. These subtests do not contribute to the FSIQ or to primary or ancillary indexes and are referred to as complementary subtests. These subtests are available for clinical use because the constructs they measure (i.e., naming speed and visual-verbal associative memory) are supposed to be associated with achievement skills.

- Naming Speed Literacy
  - Examinees quickly name pictured objects using simple and common constructions.
- Naming Speed Quantity
  - Examinees quickly name the number of squares in individual boxes.
- Immediate Symbol Translation
  - Examinees are taught visual-verbal pairs (simple symbols associated with a particular word) that they then use to read phrases and sentences.
- Delayed Symbol Translation
  - Examinees again translate the visual-verbal pairs into phrases and symbols.
- Recognition Symbol Translation
  - Using the visual-verbal pairs from Immediate Symbol Translation, the examinee views a symbol and chooses its meaning from words read aloud by the examiner.

Composites

WISC–V Composite Overview

Seven primary subtests contribute toward the FSIQ, and 10 are needed to calculate the five primary indexes. Standard administration of the 10 primary subtests is recommended to provide a broad understanding of student abilities. Secondary and complementary subtests may provide more thorough and more specific information about an individual's abilities and are available for administration when needed. Combinations of primary and secondary subtests may be used to form ancillary indexes: Quantitative Reasoning, Auditory Working Memory, Nonverbal, General Ability, and Cognitive Proficiency. Complementary subtests contribute to the complementary indexes; these indexes are intended to provide supplemental information linked to academic achievement: the Naming Speed Index, the Symbol Translation Index, and the Storage and Retrieval Index.

The alterations in subtest classification and terminology represent a significant change from the WISC–IV. The WISC–IV categorized subtests as either "core" or "supplemental" to distinguish which subtests typically contributed to the FSIQ and index scores ("core" subtests) and which could be substituted if the need arose ("supplemental" subtests). Because the WISC–V only allows one subtest to be substituted for the FSIQ and none for the indexes, the subtests are referred to as the "primary" subtests needed for comprehensive evaluations (or substituted in FISQ), "secondary" subtests that provide additional information or may be substituted in the FSIQ, and "complementary" subtests that are available when needed. The changes are useful in delineating the subtests, but they may be confusing at first for examiners used to WISC–IV terminology. If subtests had feelings, the supplemental subtests probably always felt secondary, so maybe the change better suits them.

Composite Descriptions and Commentary

As the reader may have noticed, several WISC–V composites are new, some have been retained, and several others have been retained but modified from the WISC–IV. As these composites are likely to be interpreted the most, they deserve more attention.

Full Scale (Global Intelligence)
- Full Scale IQ (FSIQ)
  - Subtests included:
    - *Same:* Similarities, Vocabulary, Block Design, Matrix Reasoning, Digit Span, and Coding
    - *New:* Figure Weights
  - *Subtests eliminated:* Comprehension, Picture Concepts, Letter–Number Sequencing, Symbol Search

FSIQ Comments
- The FSIQ has been reduced to seven subtests from 10 subtests.
  - Big changes to the FSIQ!
  - How does it affect administration time for the FSIQ?
  - How does it affect g measurement?
- Administration time for the seven FSIQ tests is on average about 48 minutes.
  - On the WISC–IV, about half of the normative sample took about 67 minutes to complete the 10 subtests needed for the FSIQ.
- Two subtests with weaker g loadings were eliminated, two subtests with moderately strong g loadings were eliminated, and one subtest with a moderately strong g loading was added.
  - g loading for Figure Weights (.68), which was added to the FSIQ, is medium to strong.
  - g loading for Picture Concepts (.54), which was eliminated from the FSIQ, is medium and relatively lower than other Fluid Reasoning subtest g loadings.
  - g loading for Symbol Search (.41), which was eliminated from the FSIQ, is the third weakest subtest g loading out of all the primary and secondary subtests.
  - g loadings for Letter–Number Sequencing (.64) and Comprehension (.60), which were eliminated from the FSIQ, are medium to strong but in the lower half of g loadings compared to all of the primary and secondary subtests.
- Processing Speed subtests and Working Memory subtests are less represented (29%) in the FSIQ than on the WISC–IV (40%)

but slightly more represented than on the WISC–III (20%).
- One of the other primary or secondary subtests may be used to substitute for calculation of the FSIQ.
  - Subtest must be from the same domain as the one being substituted for.
  - Only one substitution is allowed.
  - Additional substitution rules are listed on page 34 of the *WISC–V Administration and Scoring Manual* (Wechsler, 2014).
- Averaged internal consistency reliability estimate was .96 (Wechsler, 2014); the estimate for the WISC–IV was .97 (Wechsler, 2003).
- Based on our analysis with WISC–V data, the g factor saturation in the FSIQ is .82 using the total sample.
  - Previous research found the g factor saturation in the WISC–IV FSIQ to be .83 using the total sample (M. R. Reynolds, Floyd, & Niileksela, 2013).
  - Similar findings across WISC versions, but with three fewer tests.
- Based on the g saturation estimate, we estimated the implied correlation between the g factor and WISC–V FSIQ to be .91.
- The General Ability Index overlaps more with the FSIQ on the WISC–V than on the WISC–IV (only Digit Span and Coding are not included on the General Ability Index).

Five Primary Index Scales (i.e., Broad Cognitive Abilities)
There are five primary indexes on the WISC–V compared to four on the WISC–IV. These five broad cognitive abilities that have been empirically supported with factor analysis are similar to five broad cognitive abilities from CHC theory. The associated CHC term is listed next to each index in parentheses.

Primary Indexes Retained
- Verbal Comprehension Index (*Gc*)
  - Core subtests included:
    - Same: Similarities and Vocabulary
    - New: None

- Core subtests eliminated from the Verbal Comprehension Index:
  - Comprehension
- Additional Verbal Comprehension subtests not included in the Verbal Comprehension Index:
  - Comprehension
  - Information
- Comments:
  - The Verbal Comprehension Index has changed from three to two subtests.
  - Despite one fewer subtest, the internal reliability estimates are similar.
  - Correlation of the Verbal Comprehension factor with the second-order *g* factor (.85) is almost identical to that found with the WISC–IV (Weiss et al., 2013b).
- Working Memory Index (*Gsm*)
  - Core subtests included:
    - *Same:* Digit Span
    - *New:* Picture Span
  - Core subtest eliminated from the Working Memory Index:
    - Letter–Number Sequencing
  - Additional Working Memory subtests not included in the Working Memory Index:
    - Letter–Number Sequencing was eliminated from the composite but included on the test. It may be combined with Digit Span for an Auditory Working Memory Index.
  - Comments:
    - More of a balance between visual and auditory memory, intended to expand the breath of coverage.
    - Arithmetic had previously been associated with working memory but is now associated with fluid reasoning.
    - Working Memory factor correlation with *g* factor (.81) is not much different from the WISC–IV Working Memory factor with the *g* factor (.85) in the five-factor model (e.g., Weiss et al., 2013b).
    - Working Memory correlated .94 with the *g* factor in the WISC–IV four-factor model, in which Arithmetic was

included—the strongest correlation with *g* in that model (Keith et al., 2006).
- Processing Speed Index (*Gs*)
  - Core subtests included:
    - *Same:* Coding and Symbol Search
    - *New:* None
  - Core subtests eliminated from Processing Speed Index:
    - None
  - Additional Processing Speed subtest not included in the Processing Speed Index:
    - Cancellation
- Comments:
  - Little has changed with the Processing Speed Index.
  - The Processing Speed factor has the weakest correlation with *g* (.51); the correlation found with Processing Speed and *g* on the WISC–IV was .55 (e.g., Weiss et al., 2013b).
  - Cancellation has a relatively lower loading on the Processing Speed factor (.41) and on the *g* factor (.21).

New Primary Indexes Another major change on the WISC–V is that the Perceptual Reasoning Index from the WISC–IV was split into two separate indexes.

- Visual Spatial Index (*Gv*)
  - Core subtests included:
    - Retained from WISC–IV: Block Design
    - New subtest: Visual Puzzles
  - Additional Visual Spatial subtests not included in Visual Spatial Index:
    - None
  - Comments:
    - The *WISC–V Technical and Interpretive Manual* reports that Figure Weights also loaded on a Visual Spatial factor but was not retained on the factor.
    - The Visual Spatial factor correlation with second-order *g* factor was .88, which is stronger than the Visual Spatial factor correlation with *g* on the WISC–IV (.78) (e.g., Weiss et al., 2013b).

- Subtests had similar *g* factor loadings: Block Design = .67 and Visual Puzzles = .69.
- Fluid Reasoning Index (*Gf*)
  - Core subtests included:
    - Retained from WISC–IV: Matrix Reasoning
    - New subtest: Figure Weights
  - Additional Fluid Reasoning subtests not included in Fluid Reasoning Index:
    - Retained from WISC–IV: Picture Concepts
    - Moved: Arithmetic is associated with Fluid Reasoning, not Working Memory
  - Comments:
    - The Fluid Reasoning factor has a perfect correlation with the second-order *g* factor, similar to that of the WISC–IV (Keith et al., 2006; Weiss et al., 2013b) and to other measures (e.g., M. R. Reynolds & Keith, 2013).
    - Arithmetic appears to measure multiple abilities beyond fluid reasoning.
    - Arithmetic may not fit with any broad cognitive ability.

Five Ancillary Index Scales

The ancillary indexes are indexes that may be calculated, but they are not derived from factor-analytic findings.

Indexes Retained

- General Ability Index
  - Subtests: Similarities, Vocabulary, Block Design, Matrix Reasoning, Figure Weights
  - Comments:
    - Useful index of general intelligence that does not include Working Memory or Processing Speed subtests.
    - Practitioners may be confused when to use the General Ability Index instead of the FSIQ for placement purposes (e.g., gifted evaluations).
    - Interpretation of both the FSIQ and the General Ability Index together may be confusing, especially when they do not differ by much but are statistically significantly different.
- Cognitive Proficiency Index
  - Subtests: Digit Span, Picture Span, Coding, and Symbol Search
  - Comments:
    - Combination of primary Working Memory Index subtests and primary Processing Speed Index subtests.
    - Mostly used to compare with General Ability Index.

New Indexes

- Quantitative Reasoning Index
  - Subtests: Figure Weights and Arithmetic
  - Comments:
    - Quantitative Reasoning is supposed to be closely related to general intelligence.
    - Needs some validity evidence to determine whether it is a subfactor of Fluid Reasoning and its relation to general intelligence.
- Auditory Working Memory Index
  - Subtests: Digit Span and Letter–Number Sequencing
  - Comments:
    - Measure of auditory working memory.
    - It was the Working Memory Index on the WISC–IV, but differs due to the added Sequencing task for Digit Span.
- Nonverbal Index
  - Subtests: Block Design, Visual Puzzles, Matrix Reasoning, Figure Weights, Picture Span, and Coding
  - Comments:
    - Included on the WPPSI–IV.
    - Measure of intelligence from subtests that do not require verbal responses.
    - Subtests do require verbal instructions.
    - The *WISC–V Technical and Interpretive Manual* provides suggestions for when it may be used (e.g., autism evaluation for an estimate of general intelligence).
    - More research likely needed with this index.

Complementary Index Scales

- Naming Speed Index (*Glr?*)
  - Subtests: Naming Speed Literacy and Naming Speed Quantity
  - Comment:
    - Measure of basic naming automaticity.
- Symbol Translation Index (*Glr*)
  - Subtests: Immediate Symbol Translation, Delayed Symbol Translation, and Recognition Symbol Translation
  - Comment:
    - Measure of visual-verbal associative memory.
- Storage and Retrieval Index (*Glr)*
  - Indexes: Naming Speed Index and Symbol Translation Index
    - Combination of the Symbol Translation Index and the Naming Speed Index
- Comment:
  - Measure of long-term storage and retrieval accuracy and fluency.

WISC–V Test Materials

The WISC–V test kit includes three stimulus books, the *WISC–V Administration and Scoring Manual*, the *WISC–V Technical and Interpretive Manual*, scoring templates, a scoring key, Block Design blocks, a #2 pencil without an eraser, a red pencil without an eraser, and the *WISC–V Administration and Scoring Manual Supplement*. Protocols include the Record Form and two response booklets. The first stimulus book includes materials needed for subtests that contribute toward the FSIQ and one additional primary subtest. The second stimulus book contains material needed for additional primary subtests and the secondary subtests. The third stimulus book contains the complementary subtests, which are less likely to take part in regular administration.

Administrative instructions, prompts, and directions are still in the separate *WISC–V Administration and Scoring Manual*. This manual is more stable than its predecessors, thanks to the addition of extra spine support. Keeping administration manuals and stimulus books separate (e.g.,

rather than in an easel) requires more horizontal space for test administration and more testing materials to maneuver simultaneously. The addition of tabs to locate subtests would make the *WISC–V Administration and Scoring Manual* more user-friendly, although perhaps they are not included to encourage examiners to administer the subtests in the prescribed order. Although the instructions included in the *WISC–V Administration and Scoring Manual* are unquestionably essential for skilled administration, at times the sheer amount of verbiage makes it difficult to discriminate desired information when under administrative constraints, especially when instructions for samples or demonstration carry over onto another page. No audio CD was included in the WISC–V, and an opportunity to ease examiner burden and maintain standardization during subtests such as Letter–Number Sequencing and Digit Span seems lost.

On a more positive note, the test developers explicitly attempted to improve some practical aspects of test administration when evaluating and revising test materials. Test materials were reconsidered to ensure greater durability, subtests were redistributed across stimulus books to reduce weight and increase stability, and scoring templates are now more substantial.

WISC–V Administration Modifications

Testing Experience

The WISC–V developers reported that time constraints were carefully incorporated into test construction and that efforts were made to create a more efficient testing experience. It is hoped that fewer total items and condensed discontinue rules should move examiners and examinees more quickly through subtests, and now that fewer subtests contribute to the FSIQ, the overall testing experience may require less endurance for examinees and examiners alike if the goal is to obtain the FSIQ (on average 48 minutes). Nevertheless, although direct comparisons cannot be made because of how the information is reported in the manuals, it seems as if the administration of the 10 primary subtests (on average 65 minutes) does not differ much from the average 67 minutes it took most children to take the WISC–IV core subtests.

For those who are intimidated by new tests (and Wechsler tests in particular), developers have condensed administrative procedures. Simpler test instructions and scoring directions and guidelines have been provided in the most recent edition, and subtest instructions have been shortened.

Instructions and Teaching

The WISC–V has increased opportunities for examinees to learn and understand tasks prior to testing, which will undoubtedly improve practical use. Subtest instructions have been revised for greater simplicity and clarity. Added demonstration items, sample items, and teaching items provide students with more hands-on experience before their responses will count (for or against them). The WISC–V includes extra instructions to supplement regular instructions when examinees appear confused. These modifications should significantly benefit students who have difficulty with executive skills or language comprehension, and such changes may provide a more accurate understanding of examinee's actual abilities.

The scoring criteria for verbal responses have received more attention from the developers, which should please examiners. Less emphasis has been placed on specific vocabulary and terminology, and more weight has been given for general meaning. This change is good news for (young) examinees, who may lack a sophisticated vocabulary yet understand the conceptual basis of an item. Similarly, the word *advantages* has been eliminated from the Comprehension subtest; previous reviews noted that some students may not understand the word (e.g., Burns et al., 2004). Finally, specific-use prompts are included to help examiners handle relatively uncommon questions or behaviors from examinees. These prompts will come as a relief to any new graduate student or examiner who has been stumped by an examinee's creative question.

Scoring

Standard scores (mean [M] = 100 and standard deviation [SD] = 15) and scaled scores ($M = 10$ and $SD = 3$) are available for the indexes and subtests respectively. (Complementary subtests are the exception and use standard scores.) These scores allow examiners to compare examinees' performances to their peers from the normative sample. To better understand and represent an examinee's performance, test interpretation may also incorporate percentile ranks, confidence intervals, descriptive classifications, and age equivalents. (The misleading nature of age equivalents should render their use to be extremely limited.)

Serious attention was paid to the descriptive ranges provided by the WISC–V. Revisions made good effort to be more comprehensible to parents or lay-people unfamiliar with standardized testing. The more accessible and less value-laden WISC–V descriptive ranges are as follows: Extremely High, Very High, High Average, Average, Low Average, Very Low, and Extremely Low. This change should make it simpler for practitioners to communicate results with family and teachers and avoid the use of *borderline* and *superior* to describe performance. Why this same consideration was not paid to scaled scores is uncertain, as we could argue that scaled scores likewise offer another confusing element to unfamiliar audiences. Consistent use of standard scores might provide somewhat more nuanced and more cohesive results. Although there may be good reasons for the continued use of scaled scores that go beyond tradition (e.g., to make it easier to compare scores from previous versions of the WISC or so that too much interpretive attention is not afforded to subtest scores), it is not immediately clear to us.

TECHNICAL INFORMATION

The *WISC–V Technical and Interpretive Manual* is 268 pages (Wechsler, 2014), 100 pages longer and more comprehensive than the analogous WISC–IV manual. There is also a *WISC–V*

Technical and Interpretive Manual Supplement. According to the *WISC–V Technical and Interpretive Manual*, the *Standards for Educational and Psychological Testing* (American Educational Research Association, American Psychological Association, & National Council on Measurement in Education, 1999) were followed throughout test development. The information laid out in the *WISC–V Technical and Interpretive Manual* basically supports that statement.

Although users should expect nothing less out of such a revered and widely used test, it is encouraging that the developers firmly thought that the test could and should be improved. The revision goals were thoroughly discussed in the *WISC–V Technical and Interpretive Manual.* The goals for the revision were to update the theoretical foundation, improve the psychometric properties, enhance the clinical utility, and increase the developmental appropriateness and user-friendliness of the test. A comprehensive research program that took 5 years in five stages was used to meet these goals and develop the WISC–V. The research stages included a conceptual stage, pilot stage, national tryout stage, standardization stage, and final assembly and evaluation stage. Here is a summary of some of the technical information provided in the manual.

Norming Sample

A sample stratified on age, sex, race/ethnicity, parent education level, and geographic region was consistent with the U.S. English-speaking population of children and adolescents based on the 2012 census. Tables are included that break down the proportions in each stratification variable. There were 11 age groups across the ages 6 to 16 years with 200 participants (100 boys and 100 girls) in each age group and a total sample size of 2,200. These numbers are in accordance with what is considered a "good" sample size, with *good* being the highest standard (Alfonso & Flanagan, 2008). Overall, the WISC–V norming sample is solid.

Item Bias

The *WISC–V Technical and Interpretive Manual* mentions two approaches to item bias. The first was to use experts to identify problematic items. We are not sure if the experts examined items that were potentially biased or those that were culturally insensitive. Experts generally are not adept at identifying items that are biased in the statistical sense. The other step was to perform differential item functioning using samples of 54 African American and Hispanic children. Not much detail is presented about the analysis other than that the samples were used to identify and flag items that potentially had problems so they could be reviewed. It is not clear if such analysis was performed with gender either. Unless we are missing something, details seem to be lacking. We are not suggesting a nefarious agenda, but more information would be useful.

Reliability Evidence

Internal Consistency

Split-half reliability estimates were reported for subtests, where possible, to estimate internal consistency. (Because split-half reliability estimates are not appropriate for Processing Speed subtests, test-retest correlations were reported.) Composite reliability formulas were used to estimate the reliability of composites.

Internal consistency estimates for the primary and secondary subtests, averaged across the ages, ranged from .81 (Symbol Search) to .94 (Figure Weights). Estimates within each age group ranged from .67 (Symbol Search for 12- and 13-year-olds) to .96 (Figure Weights for 10-year-olds). The average internal reliability estimates for the five primary indexes ranged from .88 (Processing Speed Index) to .93 (Fluid Reasoning Index); the other three indexes all had averaged estimates of .92. Estimates within each age group ranged from .84 for the Processing Speed Index (12- and 13-year-olds) to .95 for the Fluid Reasoning Index (12-year-olds). The estimates are very similar to the WISC–IV.

The average internal consistency for the Verbal Comprehension Index on the WISC–IV was .94, whereas it was .92 on the WISC–V, but the WISC–V Verbal Comprehension Index contains one fewer subtest.

The average internal consistency estimate for the FSIQ was .96 (minimum .96 and maximum .97 across the ages). The average on the WISC–IV was .97, but the WISC–V FSIQ has three fewer subtests than the WISC–IV FSIQ. The internal consistency coefficient for the General Ability Index was .96 and for the Cognitive Proficiency Index was .93. Internal consistency coefficients for the other ancillary indexes were also very high: Quantitative Reasoning Index (.95), Auditory Working Memory Index (.93), and Nonverbal Index (.95).

Test-Retest Stability

Stability coefficients were reported for all of the scores. A total of 218 participants across the ages were administered the WISC–V on two occasions. There was, on average, a 26-day interval between the first and second test administration. Correlations were corrected for variability. Subtest stability correlations for primary and secondary subtests ranged from .71 (Picture Concepts) to .90 (Vocabulary). These were similar to those found with the WISC–IV, where they ranged from .71 (Picture Concepts) to .92 (Vocabulary). All of the remaining subtest stability correlations were in the .80s, except for Matrix Reasoning (.78).

The stability coefficient for the FSIQ was .92. The highest stability coefficient was found for the Verbal Comprehension Index (.94), with the remaining corrected stability coefficients for the primary indexes in the .80s (Visual Spatial Index = .84; Processing Speed Index = .83; Working Memory Index = .82; Fluid Reasoning Index = .75). The *WISC–V Technical and Interpretive Manual* suggested the relatively lower stability coefficient for the Fluid Reasoning Index may be due to guessing. The stability coefficients for the ancillary and complementary composites were in the .80 range, with the exception of the General

Ability Index (.91). WISC–V scores are generally stable.

Comparing performance across the administrations, on average, the participants scored higher on the second administration for all subtests and composites (other than one portion of a complementary subtest that included only 17 participants). Standardized differences were presented in the *WISC–V Technical and Interpretive Manual*. The Processing Speed Index (.52 or 7.9 IQ points) and Nonverbal Index (.50 or 7 IQ points) were susceptible to the largest test-retest gains, followed by the Visual Spatial Index (.45 or 6.7 IQ points) and FSIQ (.44 or 6 IQ points). The smallest gains were for the Auditory Working Memory Index (.16 or 2.2 IQ points), the Working Memory Index (.17 or 2.4 IQ points), the Quantitative Reasoning Index (.24 or 3.2 IQ points), and the Verbal Comprehension Index (.24 or 3.1 IQ points). The Symbol Search subtest had the largest gains (.51) with Comprehension showing the smallest (.07).

The *WISC–V Technical and Interpretive Manual Supplement* included the stability scores across the age groups. One general trend across the different age groups was that gains in memory scores were higher, or showed more practice effects, for 12- to 13- and 14- to 16-year-olds compared to the younger ages. The gains in Vocabulary were highest in the youngest (6–7) age group and negligible in the older groups. Comprehension scores increased in the 6–7 and 8–9 age groups but not in the older age groups. Matrix Reasoning was particularly susceptible to practice effects in the youngest age group (.75), but less so in the older age groups, the next highest gain was in the oldest age group (.48). Similarly, practice effects for Symbol Search were more prominent in the 6–7 age group (.70) compared to the older age groups. (The next highest gain was for 12- to 13-year-olds [.57].) The FSIQ showed the largest practice effects for the 6–7 age group (.61 or 7.5 FSIQ points); they were slightly less in the older age groups (ranging from .35 to .46 or 4.7 to 6.6 FSIQ points). There was no strong discernible trend, though.

The 6.6 FSIQ point gain was in the oldest age group.

Interscorer Agreement

Scorers tended to score the WISC–V similarly, with interscorer agreement of the norm sample protocols ranging from .98 to .99. Further evidence of interscorer agreement was obtained by nine doctoral-level graduate students raters who scored the Verbal Comprehension subtests that require more subjective scoring than the other subtests. Despite unfamiliarity with WISC–IV scoring criteria, they showed high interscorer reliabilities with intraclass coefficients ranging from .97 to .99.

Validity Evidence

Test Content

According to the *WISC–V Technical and Interpretive Manual*, the goal was to sample from domains of intelligence that the test was designed to measure. Several sources were used to guide improvement in content validity. In all, there is not much presented in the test content section; rather, the reader is referred to Chapter 2 in the manual. Some more explicit links may have been helpful.

Response Processes

The *WISC–V Technical and Interpretive Manual* indicates that evidence of response processes may be informed by theory and psychometric analysis. Not much was provided in terms of psychometric analysis, but descriptions of how the developers obtained information about how participants understood instructions and directions and applied their problem-solving processes were provided. On some subtests, children were questioned about the strategies that they used to solve the problems. This questioning assisted in making adjustments to item content or instructions. It is laudable that some of these details were reported, as others have noted that such information is often lacking in technical manuals (Kranzler & Floyd, 2013).

As is recommended in the *WISC–V Technical and Interpretive Manual*, future research will provide a better understanding of the response processes. Nevertheless, it would have been nice to break down the hypothesized processes by each subtest, for example, by using task analysis, or even by including what subtests required motor or verbal responses. A simple breakdown in a table could provide researchers or practitioners some hypotheses to test about the processes.

On another note, research about problem-solving styles and relations to tests or factors is interesting but not very common (e.g., French, 1965). The research could be illuminating. Specifically, it would be interesting to get more detailed information about what strategies are used for Arithmetic. Some have hypothesized that the use of different strategies is why Arithmetic may have such a strong g loading (e.g., Keith & Reynolds, 2010).

Internal Structure

The *WISC–V Technical and Interpretive Manual* provides a brief yet informative outline of how the internal structure of the Wechsler tests has evolved over the years, including results of factor-analytic research. Intercorrelation and confirmatory factor analysis studies were reported as evidence of the internal structure.

Intercorrelations of Scores Ultimately factor analysis provides the most rigorous information about relations among subtest scores, but the *WISC–V Technical and Interpretive Manual* includes an intercorrelation table with the correlations between subtests, process scores, and all of the composites averaged across the age ranges. These correlation matrices by age are included in a supplement (http://downloads.pearsonclinical.com/images/Assets/WISC-V/WISC-V-Tech-Manual-Supplement.pdf). Hypotheses about what correlations should be expected were presented (e.g., all scores are positively correlated; subtests within domains are more highly correlated than between domains). Most of the predictions were upheld. But the sheer number of correlations makes it difficult to glean too much information from them.

Confirmatory Factor Analysis The *WISC–V Technical and Interpretive Manual* provides a rationale for and results from confirmatory factor analysis of the WISC–V subtests. Much more detail about the confirmatory factor analysis (CFA) models was presented in the *WISC–V Technical and Interpretive Manual* compared to the WISC–IV. It was laudable that all subtests were used in the CFAs rather than only the primary subtests. (Analysis with only the primary subtests were also reported, however.) Moreover, it is laudable that higher-order models were used.

A number of CFA models were tested, including a one-factor model and a two-factor Verbal-Performance model. The structure, however, was predicted to be hierarchical and multidimensional in nature, thus, a number of second-order CFA models were tested, along with alternatives. Many of the models were nested, but information criteria (both the Akaike information criterion, or AIC, and the Bayesian information criterion, or BIC) were included for comparing nested and nonnested models. The CFA results showed that, as expected, the test is multidimensional and hierarchical in nature. Overall, a higher-order model with five factors (Verbal Comprehension, Visual Spatial, Fluid Reasoning, Working Memory, and Processing Speed) provided the best fit. Some other models also fit well and were plausible. Further, additional analyses were performed on a few subtests that were suspected to be factorially complex.

CFA Highlights

- A one-factor model was implausible. A single general factor is inadequate in describing the structure of the test.
- A Verbal–Performance factor structure was implausible. No reason to bring those back!
- Correlations between the first-order factor loadings and a second-order factor were consistent with prior research.

- Fluid Reasoning and *g* were correlated perfectly.
  - A fairly common finding (Gustaffsson, 1984; M. R. Reynolds et al., 2013; Weiss et al., 2013).
  - Is *g* redundant with Fluid Reasoning, or is Fluid Reasoning redundant with *g*? That question is likely one of the most fascinating questions in intelligence assessment (M. R. Reynolds, 2014).
- Three first-order factors correlated strongly with *g*: Visual Spatial (.88), Verbal Comprehension (.85), and Working Memory (.81).
- The Processing Speed factor correlation with *g* was substantially lower (.51).
- Subtest factor loadings on *g* were mostly similar to the WISC–IV.
  - Although the Fluid Reasoning factor had a perfect correlation with *g*, the Verbal Comprehension subtests generally had the highest *g* loadings.
  - Similar to the WISC–IV, the three highest *g* loadings were found on the Vocabulary, Arithmetic, and Information subtests. (The latter two are not primary subtests.)
  - Similar to the WISC–IV, the three lowest *g* loadings were found for Symbol Search, Coding, and Cancellation.
- Arithmetic loaded on Fluid Reasoning, Working Memory, and Verbal Comprehension.
  - The Arithmetic loading on Verbal Comprehension was not substantial (.16).
- Although distinct, in a first-order CFA model, the Fluid Reasoning and Visual Spatial factors were correlated very strongly (.91) when the entire sample was used, as shown in the second-order model; however, the Fluid Reasoning factor correlated more strongly with a second-order *g* factor (i.e., perfect correlation) than did the Visual Spatial factor.

Relations with External Variables

Validity studies were performed with eight other measures. WISC–V scores were correlated with four intelligence measures (i.e., WISC–IV, WPPSI–IV, WAIS–IV, and KABC–II, *n*s ranging from 89 to 242), with two standardized achievement tests (the Kaufman Test of Educational Achievement–Third Edition; A. S. Kaufman & Kaufman, 2014 [KTEA–3] and the Wechsler Individual Achievement Test–Third Edition; Pearson, 2009b [WIAT–III], *n*s ranging from 207 to 211), with an adaptive behavior measure (i.e., Vineland Adaptive Behavior Scales–Second Edition, Sparrow, Cicchetti, & Balla, 2005, [Vineland–II], *n* = 61), and with a measure of behavior functioning (Behavior Assessment System for Children–Second Edition, M. R. Reynolds & Kamphaus, 2004 [BASC–2], *n* = 2,302). Such validity studies result in an overwhelming number of correlations. We certainly cannot summarize all of them in this review, but the *WISC–V Technical and Interpretive Manual* does a suitable job in describing them.

WISC–V with Other Intelligence Measures

Most of the correlations reported are with the WISC–V and other Wechsler intelligence tests, but there are also correlations with the Kaufman Assessment Battery for Children–Second Edition (KABC–II; A. S. Kaufman & Kaufman, 2004). As expected, the correlations between the WISC–V FSIQ and other Wechsler FSIQs, as well as a comparable index from the KABC–II (i.e., Fluid-Crystallized Index), were all very strong (i.e., >.80). Similarly strong correlations were reported for the WISC–V General Ability Index and General Ability Index from the other Wechsler tests.

The Verbal Comprehension Index from the WISC–V also demonstrated strong correlations with comparable indexes on the other tests (>.80 on the WISC–IV and WAIS–IV and >.70 for the WPPSI–IV and KABC–II). The Visual Spatial Index and Fluid Reasoning Index did not have directly comparable indexes on the WISC–IV or WAIS–IV but had moderately strong correlations with the Perceptual Reasoning Indexes on those tests. (A very strong correlation was found for the Visual Spatial Index and the PRI from the WAIS–IV.) The Visual Spatial Index and Fluid Reasoning Index both correlated with the *Gc* index from the KABC–II (.55 and .52, respectively) and similarly correlated with corresponding indexes on the KABC–II (Visual Spatial Index with *Gv* = .53; Fluid Reasoning Index with *Gf* = .50). Those correlations may be lower than expected, but it is not clear if that finding is due to the WISC–V or the KABC–II. Additional research with other *Gv* and *Gf* indexes would be useful. The Working Memory Index and Processing Speed Index correlations are generally what would have been expected and tended to correlate strongest with their corresponding indexes on the WAIS–IV (i.e., > .75). One confusing finding was the relatively weaker correlation between the Processing Speed Index on the WISC–V and WPPSI–IV (.39). The Working Memory Index had the strongest correlation with the *Gsm* index (.63) from the KABC–II. The KABC–II does not have a processing speed index; the strongest correlation between the Processing Speed Index and KABC–II indexes was .25 (with *Gv*); the remaining correlations were negligible. Cross-battery factor analysis with the KABC–II and WISC–V could shed some more light on the structure of the scores across those measures (Keith & Reynolds, 2010; Woodcock, 1990).

WISC–V with Achievement and Behavior

The correlations with the standardized achievement measures are too much to report. But all of the correlations are reported in multiple tables in the *WISC–V Technical and Interpretive Manual.* The WISC–V FSIQ and WIAT–III Total Achievement composite correlated (.81) almost as strongly as the FSIQ correlated with the FSIQs from other Wechsler tests.

Last, the correlations between the WISC–V composites and indexes from the Vineland and BASC–2 were generally weak or nonexistent. Hence, in nonclinical populations, there are relatively weak or nonexistent relations between WISC–V scores and scores from behavior scales. The correlation between the FSIQ and adaptive composite from the Vineland was .01. What does that mean? We are not aware of a standard for expected correlations between adaptive behavior and intelligence. Harrison (1987) reviewed several studies and concluded that there is a moderate relationship between adaptive behavior and intelligence, but there was a great degree of variability across studies. The raters in the WISC–V validity study were all parents; perhaps the correlation would differ if teachers rated the students. Perhaps cognitive ability and adaptive behavior correlations are moderated by ability level so that the measures are more strongly related at lower ends of ability.

Test Criteria

Special Groups

Several studies were performed with a number of special groups (e.g., gifted, intellectual disability, traumatic brain injury). A comprehensive description of these studies is beyond this review, and only a few are described. Students who were identified as intellectually gifted scored, on average, close to 2 standard deviations above the mean on the FSIQ. (The average for the General Ability Index was similar to that of the FSIQ.) The mean FSIQ for those who were previously identified with a mild intellectual disability was more than 2 standard deviations below the mean. Other studies that compared special groups to matched controls showed those previously identified with specific learning disorders (SLDs) in reading or in reading and writing had the largest effect size differences on the Working Memory Index and Verbal Comprehension Index. (The reading and writing SLD group difference on Fluid Reasoning Index was also the same as the Verbal Comprehension Index.) The ancillary indexes also showed large standardized differences in these two learning disability groups (ranging from .80 to 1.31) with the SLD groups scoring substantially lower.

The largest effect size differences for the primary indexes for students diagnosed with

SLD in math were on the Visual Spatial Index and the Fluid Reasoning Index respectively. The students diagnosed with SLD also scored quite a bit lower on the Quantitative Reasoning Index, Nonverbal Index, and General Ability Index ancillary indexes. The largest effect size differences were for the Quantitative Reasoning Index and the Nonverbal Index. The standardized differences on the ancillary indexes (ranging from .23 to .63) were not as large as those found in the reading and reading and writing SLD groups.

SCORES DIFFERENCES AND TEST INTERPRETATION

The *WISC–V Technical and Interpretive Manual* outlines potential interpretations for WISC–V scores. It recommends collecting as much evidence to corroborate interpretations as possible. Although it is stated that the outline provides basic information, it is actually quite lengthy and can get rather complicated, especially if users believe reading it is necessary to interpret all of the possibilities with each test administration.

Information is reported about score differences that can be used to guide interpretation of within-individual differences between the various WISC–IV scores. This information includes statistical significance (with varying levels of alpha by age group and by overall sample), score differences between composites that share subtests (e.g., FSIQ and Verbal Comprehension Index difference), score differences between indexes that do not share subtests (e.g., Visual Spatial Index and Processing Speed Index), base rates for score differences, and frequency of subtest scatter (e.g., frequency of difference between highest and lowest subtest scores). The test record includes three pages for analysis; each page is used for a different type of analysis (i.e., Primary, Ancillary and Complementary, and Process).

Primary Analysis

The 10 primary subtests are recommended for standard administration so that the FSIQ and five primary indexes are interpreted in each administration. Briefly, it is generally recommended to interpret the broadest scores first and work down. For example, first, in Steps 1 to 6, the FSIQ is interpreted, followed by the five primary indexes. These steps are similar to the WISC–IV, although with the additional step due to another primary index to interpret. Second, in Step 7, the primary indexes are evaluated for strengths and weaknesses by comparing them to overall performance. Third, in Step 8, "interpretive hypotheses" are used to compare the primary indexes to each other (e.g., Verbal Comprehension Index versus Visual Spatial Index, Verbal Comprehension Index versus Fluid Reasoning Index, etc.). All in all, there are a lot of comparisons to be made in these steps. There is a lot to think about here too. Although one sentence in the *WISC–V Technical and Interpretive Manual* indicates that pairwise primary index comparisons should be used to evaluate specific hypotheses in Step 8, nothing else is really discussed with regard to that statement; rather, descriptions about how to calculate those score differences and what they mean follow. We think the test publisher is generally recommending examiners to compare the primary indexes to the average of the other abilities (Step 7) and use the pairwise comparisons in some situations to test hypotheses (Step 8). We are not entirely clear, however. Users will likely have to make some choices in deciding the best approach to interpreting the test. Having choices is not a bad thing, as long as it is recognized that those choices are available.

Next, there is interpretation of subtests. The subtests are evaluated for differences from the average of all of the subtest scores (Step 9) and whether pairs of subtests within an index differ from each other (Step 10; e.g., Digit Span versus Picture Span). Again, there are a lot of possible interpretations. We imagine that most examiners will use more streamlined interpretations. Step 9 and Step 10, for example, in our view, may not be used all that often, unless for example a subtest score is ridiculously different from the average (in which case the examiner may want to check for a scoring or administration error first). There are also some scenarios where the subtests would be evaluated against each other, but comparing all of them routinely may be too much.

Ancillary and Complementary Analysis

Interpretive options are also provided for the other composites and subtests. Subtests that comprise these composites should not be part of routine administration of the WISC–V. The *WISC–V Technical and Interpretive Manual* (Wechsler, 2014) is very clear that interpretation of those scores is optional, and any one analysis can be used if needed.

There are a total of eight ancillary and complementary composites that can be reported and described. In addition, there are pairwise comparisons that can be made with these composites (i.e., General Ability Index versus FSIQ and Cognitive Proficiency Index; Working Memory Index versus Auditory Working Memory Index, and Naming Speed Index versus Symbol Translation Index). Next, some pairwise comparisons may be made between subtests for the indexes that include two or three subtests.

General Ability Index versus FSIQ

Perhaps the most interesting and widely used interpretation that will be used beyond the FSIQ and primary indexes is the comparison of the General Ability Index with the FSIQ (and the Cognitive Proficiency Index). Some more research is needed on when to choose one over the other. One consequence of the WISC–V FSIQ using fewer subtests is that there is more overlap between the General Ability Index and the FSIQ. Although the *WISC–V Technical and Interpretive Manual* states that practical differences might be important, we wonder how important some of those differences might be. That is, for example, if there is a significant difference of 5 points and it occurs infrequently, is the practical difference enough to warrant interpretation of both the FSIQ and the General Ability Index? Doing so may induce unnecessary confusion in some situations—for example, when discussing the difference between a score of 105 and 100. That is, reporting and describing both the FSIQ and the General Ability Index (as recommended) might unnecessarily obfuscate the test results. Yet doing so might be important, for example, for a gifted evaluation, where cutoffs are used. (We are not advocating that strict cutoffs should be used, only attempting an example.) If a cutoff of 130 is used, what happens when the General Ability Index is 133 but the FSIQ is 127? Or perhaps more interestingly, what happens when there is a difference between the FSIQ and the General Ability Index, the FSIQ score is above the cutoff, and the General Ability Index is not above the cutoff? Do you use the General Ability Index? We have encountered these questions by those in the field when using the WISC–IV. We anticipate similar questions with the WISC–V.

Process Analysis

A number of process-type scores may also be interpreted to better understand the types of errors committed on subtests. Various comparisons can be made (e.g., Block Design with and without time bonus), and base rates are also provided for observations found in the norming sample for some subtests.

We think it is important for examiners to pay close attention to examinee errors and behaviors that may influence performance during testing. If any information helps with providing some awareness that may help an individual, then it is certainly worth reporting and describing the errors and observations. How useful the process scores themselves are, however, is not necessarily known. The scores may add a layer to an assessment so long as broad, sweeping generalizations or important diagnostic decisions are not derived from process scores.

Intelligence and Achievement

The WISC–V was linked with achievement scores from the KTEA–3 and the WIAT–III. Linking the test with these measures of achievement allows for the calculations of ability and achievement discrepancies and what is referred to as a pattern of strengths and weaknesses analysis of cognitive processing and academic skills. Information from these analyses may help practitioners in evaluations for students with possible SLDs. It is our opinion that intelligence tests remain an important component of a comprehensive evaluation of students with SLDs. The WISC–V is certainly one of the tests that can be used. Because they are linked, WISC–V data are likely more informative for these purposes if they are used with the KTEA–3 or WIAT–III scores.

COMMENTARY

Everyone is likely to have an opinion about the WISC–V. We have yet to spend the amount of time with the WISC–V that we have had with the WISC–IV. But our initial thoughts are that the test is likely an upgrade, and it is even better than the WISC–IV. Yes, the WISC–V is likely the best WISC ever. Although we have made critiques throughout this review, we want to make it clear that we hold the WISC–V in high regard in terms of measuring intelligence. We have no reservations about using the measure to estimate a child's intellectual functioning and hope that our critiques are not removed from the context of our general evaluation of the instrument. Intelligence tests, including the WISC–V, continue to set the standard for other psychoeducational measures.

Six Final Thoughts

First, test developers obviously cannot, and should not, cater to the wish and critique of every published review of their test. Nevertheless, one thing that we noticed while performing this review was the influence of previous reviews of the WISC–IV on the current WISC–V (e.g., Baron, 2003; Burns & O'Leary, 2004; Flanagan & Kaufman, 2004; A. S. Kaufman et al., 2006). Previous reviewers mentioned, for example, the time to obtain a FSIQ should be decreased, that the WISC–IV did not include measures of long-term retrieval or visual working memory, and that there may be a possible split in the Perceptual Reasoning Factor; some even described some flimsy test materials. The publishers of the WISC–V addressed all those listed weaknesses, along with a number of others. The process in addressing those weaknesses was particularly impressive and well thought out and researched. Trying to attend to every comment ever made by a reviewer would result in a disaster; reviewers themselves have nowhere near the intimate knowledge of the test that the publisher has. But genuinely listening to those who often have experience actually using the test, along with a number of other psychological instruments, is a useful step in improving measures. Kudos to the WISC–V developers.

Second, sometimes the Wechsler tests have been criticized for lacking a theoretical foundation. The WISC–IV, in contrast, was lauded for incorporating more theory but also criticized for not going all the way and basing it explicitly on theory (viz., CHC theory; e.g., Keith et al., 2006; A. S. Kaufman et al., 2006). The updated theoretical foundation section in the *WISC–V Technical and Interpretive Manual* was rather forceful in its rebuttal of the assertion that the Wechsler tests lack a theoretical foundation. The description of current research in intelligence and neuropsychology in the *WISC–V Technical and Administration Manual* is worth reading.

Nevertheless, the WISC–V is even more closely aligned with CHC theory than the WISC–IV was. Perhaps the developers should have emphasized CHC theory more in the *WISC–V Technical and Interpretive Manual*. But, in general, what they wrote was correct: Structural models have generally converged on some consensus with regard to cognitive ability factors. CHC is a general descriptive system that has helped clarify the nature and classification of those factors. But factor-analytic results have long converged on certain factors. For example, Wolfle (1940) summarized factor-analytic findings up until 1940 and highlighted generally agreed on factors at that time, namely verbal, number, space, memory, speed, and reasoning factors. The WISC–V basically aligns with those factors (minus the number factor, which was mostly numbers and not reasoning with numbers), although the memory factor at that time was mostly described by measures of associative memory and recognition, making it more closely related to new Symbol Transition Index than to the Working Memory Index. Those descriptions were around for 50 years before CHC theory but are fairly consistent with the most important CHC broad ability factors. Granted, it did take a long time for the WISC to include those factors.

The bottom line is that the Wechsler tests have been pivotal to intelligence testing over the years, and we do not see a lack of strict allegiance and homage to CHC theory as a monumental weakness of the WISC–V. CHC theory, along with other structural intelligence theories, has obviously informed the recent revisions of the Wechsler tests. Those who understand CHC theory will easily understand the constructs measured by the WISC–V using CHC theory. Those who study CHC theory also know that it is not the be-all and end-all of intelligence theories but generally a working guide that incorporates important research from many of the most influential intelligence researchers over the last one hundred years. We think the theoretical background of the test is adequately addressed in the *WISC–V Technical and Interpretive Manual*. The scoring structure of the test with regard to the FSIQ and the primary indexes reflects the factor structure. Yes, that structure aligns with CHC theory. Like CHC theory, the WISC too has evolved from years of psychometric research.

Third, the interpretation of the WISC–V at times seems overly complicated, and some interpretations likely are not well supported. New terms for describing scores (e.g., primary, secondary) and the sheer number of scores and possible score differences are likely to overwhelm some users. Although the *WISC–V Technical and Interpretive Manual* seems to suggest that all of the steps for primary analysis are not always necessary, it is not entirely clear, as it is with the ancillary and complementary analysis. New users would probably do well by focusing on the basics first. For example, sticking with the primary analysis, and probably an abbreviated version most of the time (e.g., excluding Steps 9 and 10), with the exception of consideration of the General Ability Index. But we look forward to reading what experts in intelligence test interpretations suggest.

Fourth, although perhaps a subtle change, it is worth a comment. The new descriptive classification system may eliminate the words *superior* and *borderline* from intelligence testing forever! What a welcome change. Madonna's song "Borderline" came out in 1984. Coincidentally, that was probably the last time the word was relevant for IQ testing (though perhaps that is an exaggeration).

Fifth, we have some obvious omissions in this review; namely, we avoided discussion of Q-interactive (i.e., the WISC going digital) and computer scoring. Consider this an old-school review. Users should take advantage of computer scoring, however. Quite frankly, hand-scoring is cumbersome and sometimes difficult and confusing.

Our sixth and final comment is related to the FSIQ. The biggest change to the WISC has to be related to the FSIQ. The FSIQ has three fewer subtests, but the representativeness of Processing Speed and Working Memory subtests has been reduced again, closer to WISC–III levels. Being able to obtain a FSIQ in seven subtests is going to make some folks happy due to the reduced testing time. Perhaps it will scare some others. We look forward to future discussions and opinions.

Here are some issues that we see. If psychometric *g* is the intended construct that is represented by the FSIQ, then perhaps the change is not a big difference (e.g., the *g* saturations in the FSIQ appear similar). Some may wonder why not just use the General Ability Index, and fully rid the global composite of Processing Speed and Working Memory subtests (or use a similar composite with only the highest *g*-loaded subtests). That question leads to another more basic question: Is the best measure of *g* a composite that samples widely from a large domain of human cognitive abilities, or is it one that samples only from cognitively complex tasks (and perhaps fewer tests)? (Technically, it might be possible to do both.) The question is one that dates back to the origin of IQ testing and the study of intelligence. But, to flesh it out some, the General Ability Index comes closer to the argument for using more cognitively complex tasks (and ultimately fewer subtests; are five subtests enough?). The FSIQ is in between the "sampling broadly" and "weighting some abilities more than others" viewpoints; more abilities are represented (processing speed and working memory represented in the FSIQ), but some abilities (e.g., the more cognitively complex *Gc* and *Gf*) are represented more than others.[3] Both test developers and theorists may debate the question about the best *g* indicator. (Some might argue that a *g* factor might not be interpreted because it lacks psychological meaning.)[4] From a practical standpoint, however, the simple selection and interpretation of the General Ability Index versus the FSIQ is likely one of the most pressing concerns (especially in the context of high-stakes evaluations for giftedness eligibility or for intellectual disabilities). Perhaps more research will clarify what the best recipe is for global composites. Right now, more guidance is needed on when to use the General Ability Index versus FSIQ. We imagine that it will not be an issue in the majority of cases, but in the cases in which it is an issue, it will be an important one.

Final Wrap-up

It is easier to be critical about specifics of a measure. Many times specific and picky critiques actually may indicate that the test itself is of high quality. That is certainly the case with the WISC–V.

The WISC–V is an intelligence test steeped in tradition. The WISC set an early standard for intelligence measurement in children. The standard has been continually raised over the years with the development of other more theory-based measures; some may even have wondered whether the WISC deserved such a high status in intellectual assessment due to its lack of responsiveness to what was happening around it in the IQ testing world. Well, make no mistake about it: The WISC–V is modernized to be consistent with contemporary theory and research. The WISC–V is undeniably an excellent measure of intelligence. That is really not up for debate.

NOTES

[1] Splitting the factor into two factors was one of the subjects of a special issue in the *Journal of Psychoeducational Assessment* (Tobin, 2013). Some authors did not favor splitting the factor, some seemed to favor it, and yet others were rather ambivalent. Rather than pick a side, we encourage the readers to read that special issue.

[2] Note that all items published in the first three editions of the WISC have been removed because copyright laws now leave them available in the public domain and vulnerable to test insecurity (Wechsler, 2014).

[3] After so many subtests (e.g., 10). the representativeness of complex tasks may not matter at all as long as the tasks vary somewhat.

[4] And what to make of the perfect correlation between *g* and Fluid Reasoning?

CHAPTER 16

REVIEW OF THE WISC–V

RON DUMONT AND JOHN O. WILLIS

A psychologist teleported 75 years from 1939 into the future would still recognize the WISC–V as a direct descendant of the Wechsler-Bellevue (Wechsler, 1939; see also A. S. Kaufman, 2009; Willis, Dumont, & Kaufman, 2013), but the evolution through the four previous editions of the WISC (Wechsler, 1949) to the WISC–V has certainly wrought a series of significant changes. Having used all five editions of the WISC, we find almost all of the changes from the WISC–IV (Wechsler, 2003) to the new edition to be improvements.

GENERAL DESCRIPTION OF THE WISC–V

The Wechsler Intelligence Scale for Children–Fifth Edition (WISC–V; Wechsler, 2014) is a comprehensive clinical tool, intended for assessing cognitive functioning of children aged 6 years 0 months through 16 years 11 months. Published by Pearson, the WISC–V is an individually administered tool to be used by trained examiners. It includes 21 subtests: 13 retained (with changes) from the Wechsler Intelligence Scale for Children–Fourth Edition (WISC–IV; Wechsler, 2003) and eight new to the WISC. Two of the new subtests were adapted from the Wechsler Adult Intelligence Scale–Fourth Edition (WAIS–IV; Wechsler, 2008) and one from the Wechsler Preschool and Primary Scale of Intelligence–Fourth Edition (WPPSI–IV; Wechsler, 2012). The test provides a composite score (Full Scale IQ [FSIQ]) that represents general intellectual ability and five primary index scores (Verbal Comprehension, Visual Spatial, Fluid Reasoning, Working Memory, and Processing Speed). Along with the FSIQ and five primary composites, the WISC–V provides examiners the opportunity to compute five ancillary index scores (Quantitative Reasoning, Auditory Working Memory, Nonverbal, General Ability, and Cognitive Proficiency) and an additional three complementary index scores (Naming Speed, Symbol Translation, Storage and Retrieval). The FSIQ and the primary and ancillary index scores are standard scores with a mean of 100 and a standard deviation (*SD*) of 15 for 33 age bands. The primary and secondary subtests on the WISC–V use scaled scores with a mean of 10 and an *SD* of 3. The five complementary subtests yield standard scores with a mean of 100 and an *SD* of 15. There are also 10 process scores (such as Digit Span Forward, Backward, and Sequencing) that can be converted to scaled scores (or for Naming Speed Color-Object, Size-Color-Object, and Letter–Number, standard scores). Base rates can be derived for 16 additional Process scores (e.g., Longest Digit Span Forward).

According to the test developers, the revision goals of the WISC–V can be grouped into five categories:

1. Update the theoretical foundations of intellectual assessment (e.g., revisions based on structural intelligence models as well as neurodevelopmental and neurocognitive models).
2. Increase developmental appropriateness (e.g., revisions to instructions, scoring criteria, and time bonuses).
3. Increase user-friendliness of the scale (e.g., revisions to materials, administration, and scoring directions).

4. Improve psychometric properties (e.g., updated norms and norming methods).
5. Increase clinical utility of the scale (e.g., revised test structure to provide a five-factor solution, addition of ancillary scales and process scores). Additionally, the separation of perceptual reasoning into the visual-spatial and fluid reasoning composites and the inclusion of both the ancillary and complementary scales reflect consideration and integration of Cattell-Horn-Carroll (CHC) factors.

Two primary subtests compose the Verbal Comprehension Index: Similarities and Vocabulary. Two secondary Verbal Comprehension subtests, Information and Comprehension, are also available, and either one may substitute for one of the primary Verbal Comprehension subtests if needed in the computation of the FSIQ (the only composite for which a substitution is permitted). The four Verbal Comprehension subtests assess verbal knowledge, reasoning, comprehension, and conceptualization. (Because the two Verbal Comprehension Index subtests both rely heavily on vocabulary knowledge, we wonder if Information and Comprehension, which involve more general knowledge and which use longer, more complex language in the questions, might have formed a useful Ancillary composite.)

Two primary subtests compose the Visual Spatial Index: Block Design and Visual Puzzles. These subtests measure visual-perceptual and visual-spatial perception, analysis, and reasoning. Visual Puzzles, which is not normally included in the FSIQ, can be substituted for Block Design if needed in the computation of the FSIQ (but only one substitution is allowed in computing the FSIQ).

Two primary subtests compose the Fluid Reasoning Index: Matrix Reasoning and Figure Weights. In addition, two secondary fluid reasoning subtests, Picture Concepts and Arithmetic, are also available. For computation of the FSIQ, Picture Concepts can be substituted for either Matrix Reasoning or Figure Weights,

or Arithmetic can be substituted for Figure Weights, if needed. These subtests measure abstract conceptual reasoning.

Two primary subtests compose the Working Memory Index: Digit Span and Picture Span. Picture Span, which is not normally included in the FSIQ, can be substituted for Digit Span in computing the FSIQ. There is also one secondary subtest, Letter–Number Sequencing, which can also be used to replace Digit Span in computing the FSIQ. These subtests measure attention, concentration, memory span, and working memory.

Two primary subtests compose the Processing Speed Index: Coding and Symbol Search. Symbol Search, which is not normally part of the FSIQ, can be substituted for Coding in computing the FSIQ, as can Cancellation, a secondary subtest. These subtests measure the speed of mental and graphomotor processing.

Accompanying the WISC–V test kit (Wechsler, 2014) are three manuals: *WISC–V Administration and Scoring Manual*, *WISC–V Administration and Scoring Manual Supplement*, and the *WISC–V Technical and Interpretive Manual*. An additional *WISC–V Technical and Interpretive Manual Supplement* is available from the publisher's website (Pearson, 2014). The *WISC–V Administration and Scoring Manual* contains the information needed to administer subtests, score responses, and complete the majority of the Record Form. The *WISC–V Technical and Interpretive Manual* contains psychometric, technical, and basic interpretive information. The *WISC–V Administration and Scoring Manual Supplement*, although not needed during the administration of the test, does contain tables needed to fill out the ancillary, complementary, and process analysis pages of the Record Form.

During revision from the WISC–IV to the WISC–V, the Stimulus Book artwork was updated to be more attractive and engaging for children. Outdated items were revised or removed, and new items were incorporated to reflect more contemporary ideas and situations.

To ensure copyright protection, all items from the WISC–IV that had originally appeared on the WISC, WISC–R, or WISC–III were replaced. Administration and scoring procedures were simplified to improve the user-friendliness of the scale. Instructions to examiners are more succinct and understandable. Along with the shortening of instructions, the total number of items has been reduced, and the discontinue rules have been modified to shorten testing time.

SPECIFIC DESCRIPTION

The age range of the WISC–V is 6:0 to 16:11. For all ages, the subtest scores can be combined and interpreted at various levels, including the Full Scale IQ (FSIQ), five primary index scales, five ancillary index scales, and three Complementary scales. The FSIQ provides a general overview of the child's intelligence and the factor-based primary index scales give a more comprehensive description of a child's cognitive functioning. The ancillary index scales (e.g., Quantitative Reasoning Index, Nonverbal Index) are relevant in settings where more domain- or process-specific evaluations are required (e.g., assessing a child with language delays). The complementary index scales (e.g., Storage and Retrieval Index) provide further information regarding cognitive processes that may be assessed if a clinical need exists. It is estimated that, across all ages, the average administration time is 48 minutes to obtain the FSIQ (seven subtests) and 65 minutes to obtain the FSIQ and the primary indexes (10 subtests). To administer all subtests, including those needed for ancillary and complementary scales, the total time would be approximately 120 minutes.

The FSIQ and the primary index scales are derived from five cognitive domains: Verbal Comprehension, Visual Spatial, Fluid Reasoning, Working Memory, and Processing Speed. Notably, the Perceptual Reasoning Index from the Wechsler Intelligence Scale for Children–Fourth Edition (WISC–IV; Wechsler, 2003) has been replaced by the Visual Spatial Index and the Fluid Reasoning Index. These revisions were intended to more accurately reflect the configuration of subtests and contributing cognitive abilities assessed by the composites and to increase its consistency with the other Wechsler intelligence scales (e.g., WPPSI–IV; Wechsler, 2012).

During the revision process, two WISC–IV subtests were removed (Word Reasoning and Picture Completion), while 13 subtests were retained with revision of item content, administration, and/or scoring procedures.

The WISC–V is different from previous editions in various ways. Specifically, significant efforts were made to decrease the testing time (e.g., shortening subtest instructions, modifying discontinue rules). The addition of the Fluid Reasoning Index and Visual Spatial Index and the availability of several new ancillary and complementary indices (e.g., Quantitative Reasoning, Nonverbal Index) enhance the scale's clinical utility in comparison with its earlier versions. Finally, the WISC–V administration and scoring directions and repetition rules have been simplified and made more explicit for examiners.

SCORING SYSTEM

The scoring for the WISC–V can be done by hand with the two scoring manuals or through the scoring software. Total raw scores from the subtests and 10 process scores (e.g., Block Design No Time Bonus) can be converted into two types of age-corrected standard scores: scaled and composite scores. Scaled scores (mean [M] = 10, SD = 3) are derived from total raw scores for each subtest. Sums of various subtest scaled scores are then used to derive specific composite scores (M = 100, SD = 15) such as FSIQ. The five complementary subtests and three composites use standard scores (M = 100, SD = 15). Age-based percentile ranks are also available for all scores.

Practitioners may conduct discrepancy analysis by comparing different composite indices and may analyze examinees' cognitive strengths and weaknesses by comparing a primary index score with an indicator of overall performance (FSIQ or mean primary index score). Subtest scores for the 10 primary subtests can be compared to the mean scaled score for either the seven FSIQ subtests or the 10 primary subtests. Each of the primary index scores can be compared to each of the others, and space is also provided to compare the two subtests in each of the primary composites. Critical values (.01, .05, .10, and .15) and base rates (based on either the overall norming sample or a specific level of ability) are provided for all comparisons.

Base rates are provided for 16 process scores, such as Longest Digit Span Forward, Block Design Dimension Errors, and Coding Rotation Errors. Critical values and base rates are also provided for certain comparisons of regular and Process subtest scores, such as Block Design versus Block Design No Time Bonus . Age equivalents (the use of which we do not recommend) are also provided for subtest and process scores.

Test Materials and Stimuli

Accompanying the WISC–V test kit are the three manuals mentioned earlier. Note that early printings of the *WISC–V Administration and Scoring Manual Supplement* contains an errata sheet for Table C.17 (corrected Longest Picture Span Response scores). The *WISC–V Administration and Scoring Manual* (Wechsler, 2014) is organized with appropriate tabs (i.e., general guidelines, subtest administration, appendixes) but not with tabs for the 21 subtests and presents the verbal administration instructions in a different color font. The manual provides explanations for scoring items as well as sufficient sample responses to aid examiners in differentiating 0-, 1-, and 2-point responses. For each subtest, the Record Form provides notations for the appropriate start points for different age groups and reversal and discontinue rules; for some subtests, the

Record Form provides correct responses. The test kit includes three stimulus books (one each for the primary, secondary, and complementary subtests); the three manuals; nine blocks for Block Design; and scoring keys and templates for subtests that require them. The organization of the three Stimulus Books is handy, but we fear this organization may encourage examiners to habitually travel light, abandoning the materials for the secondary and complementary subtests. The materials are attractive and appear to be sturdy.

TECHNICAL ADEQUACY

The next sections address the quality of the psychometric properties of the WISC-V.

Standardization

The standardization sample for the WISC–V included 2,200 children divided into 11 age groups ranging from 6 to 16, with 200 participants in each age group. The sample was representative of the 2012 U.S. census with respect to age, sex, race, parent education level, and geographic region. Approximately 8% to 10% of the standardization sample included children from six special groups, including individuals with developmental delays, intellectual disability, attention-deficit/hyperactivity disorder, specific learning disorder, speech and language impairment; and individuals who are gifted and talented.

Reliability

The test authors present in the *WISC–V Technical and Interpretive Manual* a comprehensive analysis of the scale's reliability and validity and provide tables with appropriate statistics.

Internal Consistency
Internal consistency of the WISC–V was measured through the split-half method, and the

coefficients were obtained through the formula recommended by Guilford (1954) and Nunnally and Bernstein (1994) for most subtests and composites. Test-retest coefficients were calculated for Coding, Symbol Search, Cancellation, Naming Speed Literacy, Naming Speed Quantity, Immediate Symbol Translation, and Delayed Symbol Translation. The average coefficient values for internal consistency for subtest-level performance were reported separately for each of the 11 age bands along with 13 separate special populations (e.g., intellectually gifted, specific learning disorder—mathematics). For both the composite- and subtest-level performance, the overall average coefficient values, incorporating all ages and groups, generally ranged from good (>.80) to excellent (>.90). Overall, the WISC–V reliability measures for the subtests maintain or improve on the WISC–IV subtest reliabilities.

The reliabilities for the 16 primary and secondary subtests across all ages ranged from .67 to .96 with averages (using Fisher's z transformation) from .81 to .94. Reliabilities for the FSIQ were .96 and .97 (average .96). For the five primary index scores, reliabilities ranged from .84 to .91 with average reliabilities of .92 and .93. The five ancillary index scores showed reliabilities from .91 to .97 with average reliabilities from .93 to .96. The five complementary subtests had reliabilities ranging from .78 to .93 and averages from .83 to .88. The three complementary index scores had reliabilities from .86 to .95 across all ages and averages from .90 to .94.

Test–Retest Stability

The test-retest stability of the test scores was examined by administering the WISC–V twice, with test-retest intervals ranging from 9 to 82 days, and a mean interval of 26 days. Test-retest reliabilities were computed using Pearson's product-moment correlation. At the subtest level, test-retest reliabilities ranged from acceptable (.71) to excellent (.90). In addition, the test-rest reliabilities for the composites were reported to be acceptable to excellent (.75–.94),

with an excellent correlation (.92) reported for the FSIQ stability.

Interrater Reliability

During standardization, most of the objective subtests of the WISC–V (e.g., Block Design, Picture Memory, and Matrix Reasoning) were scored by two independent scorers. After comparisons, the interrater agreement was found to range from .98 to .99. Further interrater reliability was assessed by a group of nine doctoral students, none of whom had prior experience with the WISC–V. Each was assigned to score the four Verbal Comprehension subtests requiring subjective judgment in scoring. The correlations for these subtests ranged from .97 to .99.

Validity

The examination of the WISC–V's validity was based on evidence that supported the scale's use as a measure of cognitive ability in respect to content, response processes, internal structure, and relation to external variables. Research on the Wechsler scales has provided strong evidence of validity based on the scales' internal structure.

Content Validity

Significant efforts were made to ensure that the items and the subtests of the WISC–V adequately sampled the cognitive domains they are intended to measure. Comprehensive literature reviews were conducted at each research stage of the test construction to examine the test content and analyze the new items and subtests. Expert and advisory panels were formed, and members were selected based on their expertise in areas of child and clinical psychology, neuropsychology, and learning disabilities. The *WISC–V Technical and Interpretive Manual* of the WISC–V also provides detailed rationales for each subtest's content and structure.

Response Processes

During the test development stage, the test authors examined both empirical and quantitative data regarding the response processes. Response frequencies for multiple-choice items were examined to identify responses that were commonly given in error. Where appropriate, the authors asked examinees for the rationales behind their responses (e.g., Picture Concepts) and also interviewed examinees about the problem-solving strategies that they used to solve some of the subtests (e.g., Matrix Reasoning). Direct questioning was also used for several subtests (e.g., Visual Puzzles and Figure Weights) to better illuminate children's understanding of the puzzles and the directions. The authors used the findings to make appropriate changes to the item content or directions.

Internal Structure

The internal structure of the instrument was examined by analyzing the interrelations among test items, subtests, and composite scores to provide support for its validity. Intercorrelations among subtests provided initial evidence of both the convergent and discriminant validity of the WISC-IV. Additionally, confirmatory factor analysis indicated a five-factor model for all age bands.

Correlations with Other Tests

Test scores of WISC-V were examined in relation to previous editions of the instrument and related measures to provide further support for the test's concurrent, convergent, and divergent validities. Notably, correlation coefficients between the WISC-V and WISC-IV subtest and composite scores were found to be adequate, ranging from .59 to .82 and .63 to .86, respectively. Evidence of criterion validity was also shown by moderate to high correlations between the WISC-V and the WISC-IV, WPPSI-IV, WAIS-IV, Kaufman Assessment Battery for Children–Second Edition (KABC-II; A. S. Kaufman & Kaufman, 2004), and Wechsler Individual Achievement Test–Third Edition (WIAT-III; Pearson, 2009b). Also, as expected, low correlations were found between the Vineland Adaptive Behavior Scales–Second Edition (Vineland-II; Sparrow, Cicchetti,

& Balla, 2005) (a scale assessing four broad domains of adaptive behavior) and the Behavior Assessment System for Children (BASC-2 Parent Rating Scales; C. R. Reynolds & Kamphaus, 2004) (a multidimensional rating scale of behaviors). Overall, the comparison analysis illustrated that the WISC-V correlated favorably with other tests measuring similar constructs but did not correlate highly with instruments measuring different constructs.

COMMENTARY AND RECOMMENDATIONS

The next sections address the strengths and limitations of the WISC-V.

Strengths of the WISC-V

The WISC-V has a number of positive features that make it an attractive tool for assessing cognitive functioning in children and adolescents. Overall, each of the revision goals has been met, including improved psychometric properties, modifications and changes to the composites and subtests that better incorporate contemporary theories of intelligence, and the addition of several complementary scales that further extend the breadth of the test. The test also has excellent psychometric properties and technical adequacy.

Separation of Fluid Reasoning and Visual Spatial Composites

The Performance IQ of the WISC, WISC-R, and WISC-III was gradually divided, first into Perceptual Organization and Processing Speed on the WISC-III (where they and the Verbal Comprehension and Freedom from Distractibility factors coexisted with the Performance and Verbal IQs) and then into Perceptual Reasoning and Processing Speed on the WISC-IV (where Freedom from Distractibility was renamed Working Memory and the four factors completely replaced the Verbal and Performance

IQs). This division greatly enhanced interpretation of the WISC–III and WISC–IV and more closely aligned the WISC with CHC theory (see, e.g., Flanagan & Kaufman, 2009; Flanagan, Ortiz, & Alfonso, 2013) with the WISC-IV Verbal Comprehension, Working Memory, and Processing Speed aligning with the CHC broad abilities of Verbal Comprehension–Knowledge (*Gc*), Short-Term Memory (*Gsm*), and Processing Speed (*Gs*). However, Perceptual Reasoning remained a mixture of measures of Visual-Spatial ability (*Gv*), Fluid Reasoning (*Gf*), and a secondary *Gc* loading on at least one subtest. Following the precedent of the 2012 WPPSI–IV and borrowing and revising subtests from the WPPSI–IV and WAIS–IV, the WISC–V offers Fluid Reasoning and Visual Spatial composites along with the familiar Verbal Comprehension, Working Memory, and Processing Speed composites. The division of Perceptual Reasoning into Fluid Reasoning and Visual Spatial composites brings the WISC–V into closer alignment with CHC theory (not an explicit goal of the revision process) and is, in our opinion, a significant enhancement of the test interpretation process.

Working Memory

The addition of a visual memory task (Picture Span) to the Working Memory composite conforms to much of current neuropsychological research but complicates interpretation for examiners applying CHC theory (see, e.g., Flanagan et al., 2013) and muddles comparison of WISC–V Working Memory scores with scores from the WISC–IV. Happily, the WISC–V includes an ancillary Auditory Working Memory composite consisting of the Digit Span and Letter–Number Sequencing subtests that composed the WISC–IV Working Memory Index. We hope that examiners attempting to compare current and previous test scores will administer Letter–Number Sequencing and make an apples-to-apples comparison between WISC–IV and WISC–V measures of working memory.

General Ability Index and Cognitive Proficiency Index

Theorists studying the Wechsler scales have long pondered the difference between subtests requiring higher-level intellectual processes and those tapping more automatic aspects of cognitive processing efficiency. See, for example, Bannatyne (1974), J. Cohen (1959), Dumont and Willis (2001), A. S. Kaufman (1975, 1979, 1994a), Prifitera and Dersh (1993), Prifitera and Saklofske (1998), and Rugel (1974). This research eventually led to publication of WISC–IV norms for a General Ability Index, derived from scores on the six Verbal Comprehension and Perceptual Reasoning subtests, and a Cognitive Proficiency Index, derived from the four Working Memory and Processing Speed subtests, with both composite scores based on the WISC–IV normative sample. However, Pearson made the General Ability Index norms available only through its website (Raiford, Weiss, Rolfhus, & Coalson, 2005/2008) and Cognitive Proficiency Index norms required access to separate publications, such as Flanagan and Kaufman (2009); Prifitera, Saklofske, and Weiss (2008); and Weiss, Saklofske, Prifitera, and Holdnack (2006). The WISC–V provides norms for both the General Ability Index and Cognitive Proficiency Index scores in Tables C.4 and C.5 and critical values and base rates for differences between General Ability Index and Cognitive Proficiency Index in Tables C.10 and C.11 of the *WISC–V Administration and Scoring Manual Supplement* (Wechsler, 2014). The inclusion of the norms in the WISC–V kit reduces inconvenience and costs for evaluators and may add legitimacy to these important scores.

Five subtests compose the General Ability Index (both of the Verbal Comprehension primary subtests, only one of the two Visual Spatial primary subtests, and both of the Fluid Reasoning Index primary subtests), while four subtests compose the Cognitive Proficiency Index (both of the Working Memory Index primary subtests and both of the Processing Speed Index primary subtests). Conspicuously missing from the General Ability Index is the second Visual Spatial Index primary subtest (Visual Puzzles). We could not find an explanation for the elimination of this one subtest. Presumably, Visual Puzzles is not included because, although it is a primary subtest, it is not used in the calculation of the FSIQ. Although the Cognitive Proficiency Index is a reflection of complete abilities (all four primary subtests needed for the two composite index scores), the General Ability Index, like the FSIQ, appears to undervalue the contribution of visual-spatial abilities in the computation of the overall General Ability Index. (The Nonverbal Index has a similar issue. It does not include Symbol Search, even though it too is totally nonverbal.)

Complementary Scales

The addition of the new Naming Speed, Symbol Translation, and Storage and Retrieval scales greatly increases the potential utility of the WISC–V for both neuropsychological and educational assessment. No past Wechsler scale included any explicit measure of naming speed or of storage and retrieval. The *WISC–V Technical and Interpretive Manual* (Wechsler, 2014) notes that these tasks were not designed as measures of intelligence but as measures of cognitive processes. Despite this disclaimer, Naming Speed appears to closely match the criteria for being a measure of Processing Speed (*Gs*) (Flanagan et al., 2013) or Long-Term Storage and Retrieval (*Glr* Naming Facility) (Schneider & McGrew, 2012), and the Storage and Retrieval Index appears to be an unequivocal measure of Long-Term Storage and Retrieval (*Glr*).

Limitations

The WISC–V also has some limitations that should be noted. Although the *WISC–V Technical and Interpretive Manual* (Wechsler, 2014) provides some basic step-by-step instructions and examples to assist examiners in how to conduct both primary and ancillary profile analysis when evaluating an examinee's cognitive strengths and weaknesses, the manual does not elaborate further on score interpretation. The five ancillary and three complementary index scores appear, on face value, to be important and relevant aspects of

a child's cognitive functioning; however, research is needed to demonstrate how best to use these new scales. Given all the new subtests and scales, time will tell if practitioners will use the entire test or simply administer enough to obtain an FSIQ (seven subtests) or the five primary composites (10 subtests). Ideally, in selecting the subtests and composites to be used in each evaluation, examiners would thoughtfully consider referral questions and data, and an examiner's selections would range from seven to 21 subtests across a range of referrals.

Experienced examiners will need to be careful in adjusting to the changes from the WISC–IV to the WISC–V. There is new terminology to learn, such as primary, secondary, complementary, and ancillary. Examiners will have to exercise impulse control to avoid summing the 10 primary subtest scaled scores to find the FSIQ instead of using only the seven primary (FSIQ) subtests. We have already observed instances of deficient impulse control. The temptation is powerful simply to add the sums of scaled scores for the five primary composites to calculate the sum of scaled scores for the FSIQ in the "Sum of Scaled Scores to Composite Score Conversion" box on the front page of the Record Form.

We applaud the decision to limit subtest substitutions to the FSIQ and to permit only a single substitution in that calculation. We hope that examiners will follow that rule. One issue with the use of substitution is the fact that the manual does not explain what to do with the index score calculation if a substitution is made for the FSIQ. Presumably, if a substitution is necessary, then the index for which the substitution is made must not be calculated. We fear that those using substitution may ignore or disregard this fact and calculate FSIQ *and* indexes.

Given the vast amount of data entry that must be done to complete the four scoring pages (Summary, Primary Analysis, Ancillary and Complementary Analysis, and Process Analysis), we fear errors will be made. By our count, there are more than 550 entries to make on those pages. Clearly, Pearson's computer scoring software is likely to enjoy widespread use.

CHAPTER 17

REVIEW OF THE WISC–V

Daniel C. Miller and Ryan J. McGill

One of the major goals of the Wechsler Intelligence Scale for Children–Fifth Edition (Wechsler, 2014) was to incorporate contemporary intellectual assessment research into the revision. Advances in intellectual theory along with advances in theories of cognitive development, neurodevelopment, and cognitive neuroscience all influence this current version of the Wechsler scales. The purpose of this chapter is to provide an objective review of the strengths and weaknesses of the WISC–V. Table 17.1 provides an overview of these identified strengths and weaknesses of the scale and the subsequent sections of this chapter will expound more of the details.

ORGANIZATION OF THE WISC–V

The organizational structure of the WISC V is a significant departure from the previous version and now includes additional scales, batteries, and reference terminology; although many of these changes are consistent with those that have been made in recent revisions of instruments within the Wechsler family of products (e.g., WAIS–IV, WPPSI–IV). An outline of the subtest, scale, and composites scores contained within the WISC–V is provided in Tables 17.2 and 17.3. The WISC–V provides users with a multitude of scores including: subtest scores, index scores, composite scores, process scores, contrast scores, and base rate scores. In this chapter we focus primarily on the allocation and integrity of the traditional WISC–V standard scores (subtest, index, and composites), although some discussion regarding the process and base rate measures is provided.

The WISC–IV is composed of a total of 21 subtests, and, each subtest is grouped into three separate categories: primary, secondary, or complementary (for primary and secondary subtests mean [M] = 10, standard deviation [SD] = 3, range = 1 to 19). The primary subtests (n = 10) combine to form the Full Scale IQ Composite (FSIQ; M = 100, SD = 15) and the primary indexes. It should be noted that FSIQ is linearly derived from a combination of seven of the primary subtests; the remaining primary measures combine to form the primary index-level scores. Users have the option of limiting administration to the seven primary FSIQ subtests if their only concern is obtaining an overall estimate of an examinee's general cognitive ability; however, the *WISC–V Technical and Interpretive Manual* (Wechsler, 2014) encourages users to administer all 10 of the primary subtests to provide a broader sampling of cognitive functioning. Although users may substitute one secondary subtest to calculate the FSIQ, no substitutions are permitted at the index level. The five primary index scales include: Verbal Comprehension; Visual Spatial; Fluid Reasoning; Working Memory; and Processing Speed.

Ancillary index scales are composed of various combinations of the primary and secondary subtests (n = 6). Ancillary index scores include: Quantitative Reasoning, Auditory Working Memory, Nonverbal, General Ability, and Cognitive Proficiency. The remaining five complementary subtests combine to form additional complementary index scales. These scales include: Naming Speed, Symbol Translation, and Storage and Retrieval. All WISC–V index scores contain two or more subtest measures

Table 17.1   **Strengths and Weakness of the WISC–V**

Strengths	Weaknesses
Theoretical Foundation	
• Integration of additional neuropsychological constructs (e.g., enhanced working memory, associative learning and recall, rapid automatized naming, etc.) is a welcome addition.	• A unified theory of intellectual ability for the entire test is lacking.
Family of Related Products	
• The WISC–V fits in the middle of a full range of cognitive assessment products designed for all ages, including the WPPSI–IV and the WAIS–IV. • The WIAT–III is a measure of academic achievement often used in conjunction with the WISC–V. • A digital version (Q–interactive) of the full menu of the WISC–V subtests is available.	• Data are lacking on the relationship between the WISC–V and a comprehensive test of learning and memory. • Data are lacking on the relationship between the WISC–V and a comprehensive test of neuropsychological functioning (e.g., NEPSY–II).
Psychometric Properties	
• The test has a representative standardization sample. • In general, relevant psychometrics for the instrument is strong. • The manual contains a wealth of information related to the development of the measure. • There is an adequate representation of relevant subpopulations (e.g., special education) within the normative sample. • There are strong internal consistency reliability estimates. • There is good convergent and divergent validity. • Floors and ceilings for individual subtests have been improved. • Item biases based on race or ethnicity do not appear to be present.	• Confidence intervals are based on true scores, which may not be ecologically valid. • Exploratory factor analysis (EFA) results are lacking. • The Arithmetic subtest still remains cognitively complex, which makes this subtest hard to classify using factor analysis. • Coefficient alpha is used to estimate the reliability of multidimensional measures. • Further research needs to be conducted on the validity of using the WISC–V for determining cognitive strengths and weaknesses for diagnosing specific learning disorders • Decomposition procedures were not reported so that users can appropriately apportion higher-order and lower-order variances in the WISC–V subtests. • Complementary measures are not specified in the structural model.

Table 17.1 (*Continued*)

Strengths	Weaknesses
Quality of Testing Materials and Administration Issues	

Strengths	Weaknesses
• A significant number of test items were replaced or revised from the prior version for security reasons. • Subtests are arranged in stimulus books in a logical order. • Testing time was minimized by reducing the number of test items and modifying discontinuation rules. • Eight new subtests were added to the test. • Instructions were simplified for better ease in understanding. • Instructions are succinct. • The number of practice items increased. • The number of items with time bonuses was reduced.	• The plastic coil bindings tend to twist off and require adjustments. • The WISC–V no longer uses substitutes for invalid or contaminated subtests.

Interpretative Options	

Strengths	Weaknesses
• Multiple psychometric comparisons between indices are provided. • Significance-level options for critical values have been expanded. • Base rates for several qualitative behaviors have been included. • An attempt has been made to adhere to a more Cattell-Horn-Carroll – based structure. It is not perfect, but it will help users with interpretation (e.g., splitting the Perceptual Reasoning Index). • *Gf* Composite significantly improved with the inclusion of the Figure Weights subtest.	• Little information is provided on supplementary measures and process scores. How do they aid in diagnostic decision making? • Little information is provided on interpreting profiles of neurocognitive strengths and weaknesses.

with the exception of the Storage and Retrieval Index, which is a combination of the Naming Speed and Symbol Translation standard scores. Taken as a whole, we believe the structural and design features of the WISC–V result in a more clinically useful instrument with broad applications for assessment psychologists as compared to its predecessor.

We now provide a more in-depth discussion in regard to the conceptual and technical properties of the measurement instrument.

THEORETICAL FOUNDATION OF THE TEST

Incorporating contemporary intellectual assessment research into the WISC–V was one of the goals of the most recent revision to the test. This goal was partially met by significantly enhancing the assessment of these neuropsychological constructs: fluid reasoning, visual-spatial processing, working memory, naming fluency, and verbal-visual associative learning and recall.

Table 17.2 WISC–V Subtests and Subtest Categories

Subtest	Subtest Categories			
	Primary FSIQ	Primary	Secondary	Complementary
Similarities	✓	✓		
Vocabulary	✓	✓		
Information			✓	
Comprehension			✓	
Block Design	✓	✓		
Visual Puzzles		✓		
Matrix Reasoning	✓	✓		
Figure Weights	✓	✓		
Picture Concepts			✓	
Arithmetic			✓	
Digit Span	✓	✓		
Picture Span		✓		
Letter-Number Sequencing			✓	
Coding	✓	✓		
Symbol Search		✓		
Cancellation			✓	
Naming Speed Literacy				✓
Naming Speed Quantity				✓
Immediate Symbol Translation				✓
Delayed Symbol Translation				✓
Recognition Symbol Translations				✓
Total	7	10	6	5

However, there are two dominant contemporary intellectual theories, one based on the work of Cattell-Horn-Carroll (CHC) (Schneider & McGrew, 2012) and the other based on Lurian theory (Luria, 1966a, 1973a, 1973b, 1980); yet the WISC–V did not adopt either one of those theoretical approaches. Rather the WISC–V is simply a collection of subtests, all designed to measure difference aspects of intellectual functioning. The test authors acknowledge that some researchers have asserted that the Wechsler intelligence tests lack a unified theoretical foundation (Coalson, Raiford, Saklofske, & Weiss, 2010; A. S. Kaufman, 2010; Raiford & Coalson, 2014). The authors contend that the WISC–V is consistent with Wechsler's view of intelligence, which is thought to encompass a variety of qualitatively different abilities (Wechsler, 2014).

Table 17.3 Organizational Framework for the WISC–V

Subtest	Full Scale Level FSIQ	Primary Index Level					Ancillary Index Level				
		Verbal Comprehension Index	Visual Spatial Index	Fluid Reasoning Index	Working Memory Index	Processing Speed Index	Quantitative Reasoning Index	Auditory Working Memory Index	Nonverbal Index	General Ability Index	Cognitive Proficiency Index
Similarities	✓	✓								✓	
Vocabulary	✓	✓								✓	
Information	*										
Comprehension	*										
Block Design	✓		✓						✓	✓	
Visual Puzzles	*		✓						✓		
Matrix Reasoning	✓			✓					✓	✓	
Figure Weights	✓			✓			✓		✓	✓	
Picture Concepts	*										
Arithmetic	*						✓	✓			
Digit Span	✓				✓			✓			✓
Picture Span	*				✓				✓		✓
Letter–Number Sequencing	*							✓			
Coding	✓					✓			✓	✓	✓
Symbol Search	*					✓				✓	✓
Cancellation	*										

(continued)

Table 17.3 *(Continued)*

Complementary Subtests	Complementary Index Scale Level		
	Naming Speed Index	Symbol Translation Index	Storage and Retrieval Index
Naming Speed Literacy	✓		✓
Naming Speed Quantity	✓		✓
Immediate Symbol Translation		✓	✓
Delayed Symbcl Translation		✓	✓
Recognition Symbol Translation		✓	✓

*Denotes allowable FSIQ subtest substitution.

†The Storage and Retrieval Index is a combination of the Naming Speed Index and the Symbol Translation Index standard scores and thus is a linear combination of the constituent subtest measures within these indexes.

650

It is important to recognize that even though the WISC–V may not be guided by an overall theory, the FSIQ does highly correlate with other full-scale intelligence test scores for tests such as the Kaufman Assessment Battery for Children–Second Edition (KABC–II: A. S. Kaufman & Kaufman, 2004) and the Woodcock-Johnson–Fourth Edition (WJ IV; Schrank, McGrew, & Mather, 2014). The WISC–V subtests can easily be interpreted within a cross-battery assessment perspective (Flanagan, Ortiz, & Alfonso, 2013) or Miller's (2013) Integrated School Neuropsychological/CHC (SNP) model.

FAMILY OF RELATED PRODUCTS

One of the major advantages of the WISC–V is the integration of this particular test into an entire family of intellectual functioning measures that span early childhood through older adult age ranges. The WISC–V is designed to assess intellectual functioning in school-age children, ages 6:0 through 16:11 years. The Wechsler Preschool and Primary Scale of Intelligence–Fourth Edition (WPPSI–IV; Wechsler, 2012) is designed to measure intellectual functioning in young children aged 2:6 to 7:7 years, and the Wechsler Adult Intelligence Scale–Fourth Edition (WAIS–IV; Wechsler, 2008) is designed to measure intellectual functioning in individuals aged 16:0 to 90:11 years. In the recent revisions of these three Wechsler products, the test developers have strived to measure comparable cognitive constructs across the developmental spectrum and have been largely successful in doing so.

The WISC–V is a comprehensive intelligence test, but no one battery of tests is designed to measure all aspects of a person's cognitive, academic, and social emotional capabilities. The WISC–V often will be used in combination with a comprehensive test of achievement, such as the Wechsler Individual Achievement Test–Third Edition (WIAT–III; Pearson, 2009b), and a behavioral

rating scale, such as the Behavior Assessment Scale for Children–Second Edition (BASC–2; C. R. Reynolds & Kamphaus, 2009). The *Technical and Interpretative Manual* (Wechsler, 2014) provides psychometric concurrent validity data for the WISC–V, WIAT–III, and the BASC–2 Parent Rating Scale comparisons.

In neuropsychological assessments, the WISC–V is often used in conjunction with other instruments, such as the NEPSY–II: A Developmental Neuropsychological Assessment (Korkman, Kirk, & Kemp, 2007), or a comprehensive test of learning and memory, such as the Children's Memory Scale (CMS; M. J. Cohen, 1997). It is recognized that publishers cannot provide all possible test comparisons with the WISC–V as part of the initial validation, but with the inclusion of several new neuropsychologically based tests on the WISC–V, the comparison of these tests to similar ones on the NEPSY–II would have been helpful. When the CMS is revised, it is hoped that a WISC–V concurrent validity study will be provided. Finally, the addition of the WISC–V Integrated test (Wechsler & Kaplan, 2015) will strengthen the clinical utility of the WISC–V from a neuropsychological perspective.

One of the most innovative features of the WISC–V is the inclusion of the full battery of tests in Pearson's digital platform, Q-interactive. The Q-interactive software requires the clinician to have two Apple iPads, one for the examiner and one for the examinee, linked electronically. Q-interactive allows the clinician to choose custom tests from a full array of Pearson assessment products, administer digital versions of the tests on the iPad, score the results electronically, and manage individual client records. In this day and age of tablets and smart phones and other advances in technology, digital versions of tests are welcome additions to the profession. The Q-interactive platform is relatively new to the field so practitioners and researchers are just starting to evaluate the digital versions of the products, compared to the paper-and-pencil versions (Dumont, Viezel, Kohlhagen, & Tabib, 2014).

QUALITY OF TESTING MATERIALS

The overall production quality of the materials is very good. The WISC–V test kit includes: *Administration and Scoring Manual, Administration and Scoring Manual Supplement, Technical and Interpretative Manual*, three stimulus books, Symbol Search scoring key, Cancellation scoring template, Coding scoring template, set of nine red and white blocks, a red pencil and a #2 pencil (without erasers), a set of Record Forms, a set of Response Booklet 1 forms, and a set of Response Booklet 2 forms. The only minor criticism of the production quality of the test is the use of plastic coils to bind the stimulus books and manuals. The publisher does acknowledge that after repeated uses of the bound booklets, the plastic coils will twist off and require the user to adjust them accordingly. This is a minor annoyance but one that could be fixed through better engineering of the bindings. Of course, this would be a moot point if the digital version of the test was administered.

The subtests are arranged in the stimulus books in a logical order to make administration easier. The test authors did a good job in reducing the total test time required by reducing the number of test items and modifying discontinuation rules. These changes were made in recognition of the increased time constraints on practitioners and to minimize the sustained attention requirements for children who are being assessed.

Due to copyright laws and because prior test items have become more widely known to the public, many of the test items on the WISC–V are new or were revised in some fashion. These changes were made to increase the security of the test. Another major goal of the test revision was to increase the developmental appropriateness of the instrument. The test developers seem to have accomplished this by simplifying the subtest instructions for easier understanding and making the instructions more succinct. To ensure that children understand the task requirements, more practice items were added to the subtests,

as appropriate. Finally, the idea that quick task completion is always essential was deemphasized somewhat in the WISC–V by reducing the number of subtests with time bonus points.

NEW WISC–V SUBTESTS

The WISC–V includes eight new subtests: Figure Weights, Visual Puzzles, Picture Span, Naming Speed Literacy, Naming Speed Quantity, Immediate Symbol Translation, Delayed Symbol Translation, and Recognition Symbol Translation. Figure Weights was originally introduced on the WAIS–IV (Wechsler, 2008) and is designed to measure aspects of fluid and quantitative reasoning. Figure Weights and the Matrix Reasoning subtests now form the Fluid Reasoning Index, which significantly improves the quality of that index.

Visual Puzzles is another subtest adapted from the WAIS–IV version (Wechsler, 2008). The subtest is designed to measure visual-spatial reasoning during a non-motor construction task. The subtest also requires some mental rotations, visual working memory, understanding of part-to-whole relationships, and visual analysis and synthesis. Visual Puzzles and Block Design now form the Visual Spatial Index. Splitting the WISC–IV Perceptual Reasoning Index (PRI) into the Visual-Spatial and Fluid Reasoning Indices strengthens the WISC–V considerably. In an effort to improve the quality of the Working Memory Index, the Picture Span subtest was added. Picture Span is designed to measure visual working memory and visual working memory capacity.

The Naming Speed Literacy, Naming Speed Quantity, Immediate Symbol Translation, Delayed Symbol Translation, and Recognition Symbol Translation subtests are referred to by the test authors as complementary subtests. These subtests were specifically included in the WISC–V for use with special clinical populations, such as during the assessment of specific learning disorders. Speeded naming tasks require a child to name colors, words, or letters as quickly as possible. These tasks are often referred to in the neuropsychology literature as rapid automatized naming (Miller, 2013). These types of speeded naming tasks have been shown to predict or be associated with disorders of reading and spelling (Crews & D'Amato, 2009) and disorders of mathematics (McGrew & Wendling, 2010). The Naming Speed Literacy and the Naming Speed Quantity subtests are not intended to be measures of intelligence and, as a result, are not included in any of the indices; however, they should prove to be useful additions to the test for assessing children with suspected processing disorders.

The Immediate Symbol Translation, Delayed Symbol Translation, and Recognition Symbol Translation subtests measure different aspects of visual-visual associative learning and recall. These subtests are also not intended to be measures of intelligence but rather used as supplemental measures for evaluating potential learning disorders in children. These types of tasks often predict performance on reading decoding, reading accuracy, reading fluency, and reading comprehension tests (Litt, de Jong, van Bergen, & Nation, 2013).

SUBTEST MODIFICATIONS

Word Reasoning and Picture Completion from the WISC–IV were dropped in this revision. The following subtests had modifications made to their recording and scoring of items: Similarities, Vocabulary, Information, Comprehension, Block Design, Digit Span, Letter–Number Sequencing, Coding, and Symbol Search. In another revision, test items were added to Similarities, Vocabulary, Information, Comprehension, Block Design, Matrix Reasoning, Picture Concepts, Arithmetic, Digit Span, Letter–Number Sequencing, Coding, Symbol Search, and Cancellation. In total, these subtest modifications in combination with the addition of the new subtests reflect a major revision to the scale.

INTERPRETATIVE OPTIONS

The *WISC–V Technical and Interpretive Manual* encourages examiners to interpret the WISC–V in a top-down fashion, beginning with the FSIQ, using a series of iterative steps designed to provide users with multiple levels of information about an individual's performance. The FSIQ is the most reliable score on the WISC–V and is considered to be the score that is most representative of *g*. The FSIQ is best interpreted after considering the degree of variability in the profile of primary index scores. Comparisons can be made between the FSIQ and each primary index score using a priori critical values to determine if the observed differences are statistically significant. WISC–V critical value options have been expanded compared to those in the WISC–IV with the number of options increasing from two to four (now includes .01, .05, .10, and .15). Additionally, examiners can then determine the relative clinical significance of the difference value using base rates provided in the *Administration and Scoring Manual*.

The *WISC–V Technical and Interpretive Manual* suggests that primary interpretation of the WISC–V should focus on the profile of obtained primary index scores in order to determine the presence of individual cognitive strengths and weaknesses. Profile variability can be examined both within an index (e.g., subtest differences) and across Indexes using procedures similar to those previously described with the FSIQ. It is suggested that examiners begin by describing the overall index score profile and then proceed to evaluating the level of performance and the degree of variability for each measure individually. Although the implication is that profile variability and scatter are potentially clinically relevant, limited evidence is provided within the *WISC–V Technical and Interpretive Manual* to support these claims.

Similar evaluation procedures can be used to examine cognitive strengths and weaknesses at the subtest level. However, due to the fact that subtest variability is common within the population (see Watkins, Glutting, & Youngstrom, 2005, for a review), inferences at this level of interpretation should be made cautiously. Accordingly, the *WISC–V Technical and Interpretive Manual* warns that subtest-level profile analysis should be conducted only when the examiner has a clear rationale for doing so.

Although administration of the primary battery yields a comprehensive evaluation of intellectual ability, supplementing the 10 primary subtests with the five complementary subtests may be warranted depending on the clinical needs of the client. The *WISC–V Technical and Interpretive Manual* states that profile analysis with the ancillary and complementary scales is optional. That is, examiners should administer these measures only when there is a specific clinical purpose to do so (e.g., suspected memory or other related neurocognitive impairment). If these measures are administered, examiners may employ the procedures described earlier for examining individual cognitive strengths and weaknesses. As would be expected, the empirical literature regarding the technical properties and potential clinical applications of the test is in its infancy. We encourage users of the WISC–V to keep abreast of subsequent developments in that regard and to modify or supplement their interpretations of the measurement instrument accordingly.

PSYCHOMETRIC ADEQUACY OF THE WISC–V

The sections that follow address the quality of the WISC–V's psychometric properties.

Standardization Sample

The *WISC–V Technical and Interpretive Manual* presents extensive and detailed information on the standardization procedures for the instrument and the development of the normative

sample. The normative sample included 2,200 children and adolescents divided into 11 age groups. The normative sample was obtained through proportional sampling and stratified across key demographic variables, such as age, sex, ethnicity, geographic region, and parent educational level.

Inspection of the normative tables provided in the *WISC–V Technical and Interpretive Manual* revealed a close match between obtained proportions and parameter estimates from the 2012 U.S. census. Additionally, an effort was made to include participants with relevant special education classifications in the normative sample. As a result, the normative sample closely matches U.S. population estimates for several relevant special education classifications (e.g., specific learning disorder, intellectual disability, and attention-deficit/hyperactivity disorder). A list of exclusionary criteria is also provided. Some of the factors that were exclusionary include: language and primary method of communication limitations, disruptive behavior or inability to test, motor difficulties that would impact test performance, taking medications that would impact cognitive performance, and diagnoses of a neurological or psychological condition that would impact test performance (e.g., epilepsy, mood disorder).

Subtest scaled scores were developed using the inferential norming method (Zhu & Chen, 2011). This procedure examines obtained means, *SD*s, and skewness estimates using linear to fourth-degree polynomials to determine the best-fitting curve for each age group based on theoretical conjecture and the pattern of growth curves observed in the WISC–V. The selected curves were then used to estimate population parameters and generate theoretical distributions for each age group. The percentages for each raw score were then converted to scaled or standard scores using the midinterval percentile method.

Composite scores (e.g., FSIQ) are based on the respective sums of age-based scaled or standard scores. As previously mentioned, the lone exception is the Storage and Retrieval Index, which is derived from summing the Naming Speed Index plus the Symbol Translation Index. Tables provided within the *Technical and Interpretative Manual* indicate that the means, *SD*s, and sum of scaled or standard scores for each composite were relatively consistent across age groups. More important, evidence was provided that suggests that the distributions of the scaled score sums approximate the normal distribution. For each scale, the distribution of scaled scores was used to convert obtained percentiles to standard scores. The *Technical and Interpretative Manual* indicated that standard score distributions were smoothed visually to ensure consistency with the normal distribution. Because nonnormal distributions were obtained for several scores on the WISC–V (e.g., span and sequence, error, and process scores), standard scores could not be developed; therefore, these measures are reported as base rates or cumulative percentages. The cumulative percentages reflect the base rate of an occurrence of a behavior that was observed in the normative sample.

Item Gradients, Floors, and Ceilings

All WISC–V index and composite score ranges are adequate, generally reflecting a range of values that is sufficient for estimating the broad spectrum of cognitive performance. Index-level scores (e.g., Verbal Comprehension Index, Visual Spatial Index, Fluid Reasoning Index, Working Memory Index, Processing Speed Index) ranged from 45 to 155 whereas composite-level scores involving multiple cognitive domains (i.e., FSIQ, Nonverbal Index, General Ability Index, and Cognitive Proficiency Index) ranged from 40 to 160. Additional items were added to several subtests (e.g., Digit Span, Vocabulary, Information) to expand the range of ability sampled by these measures. Inspection of the conversion tables for subtest, index, and composite scores provided in the *Administration and Scoring Manual* revealed that each of the WISC–V measures generally met the guidelines suggested by Bracken (2007)

for floors, ceilings, and item gradients. These results suggest that WISC–V measures contain a sufficient number of items for ensuring adequate construct variation.

Reliability Evidence

The *Technical and Interpretative Manual* reports three methods of estimating reliability: internal consistency, test-retest stability, and interscorer agreement. Internal consistency estimates were obtained using the split-half method, using the Spearman-Brown correction formula for all subtests except Coding, Symbol Search, Cancellation, Naming Speed Literacy, Naming Speed Quantity, Immediate Symbol Translation, and Delayed Symbol Translation. Due to the speeded nature of the aforementioned measures, test-retest coefficients were used as reliability estimates for these measures. A table in the *WISC–V Technical and Interpretive Manual* presents subtest, process, and composite score reliability coefficients for each of the 11 age groups as well as the average coefficients across the age groups. Internal consistency estimates across the age groups ranged were .96 to .97 for the FSIQ and ranged from .88 to .95 for Index scores and .81 to .94 for subtest scores. Coefficients for all of the indexes, with the exception of the Processing Speed Index, exceeded .90 at all age levels. As would be expected, the range of subtest-level coefficients (.76 to .95) was slightly more expansive across age groups. It should be noted that the coefficients for the Verbal Comprehension Index are lower than those that were reported for that same index in the WISC–IV (Wechsler, 2008). It is suggested that this is the result of the fact that the WISC–V Verbal Comprehension Index contains only two subtest measures whereas the WISC–IV Verbal Comprehension Index contained three.

The *Technical and Interpretative Manual* also reports standard errors of measurement (*SEM*), based on the reliability coefficients. Overall average *SEM*s for the composite- and index-level scores ranged from 2.90 (FSIQ) to

5.24 (Processing Speed Index), and subtest-level values ranged from .73 (Figure Weights) to 1.34 (Symbol Search). Hanna, Bradley, and Holen (1981) noted that these estimates should be considered optimistic given that they do not account for potential sources of error such as administration or scoring errors.

The WISC–V *Administration and Scoring Manual* provides estimated true score confidence intervals (90% and 95%) that correspond to the observed standard score obtained for indexes and composites. In contrast to estimation methods that utilize the observed score and *SEM*, the true score estimation method utilizes an estimated true score (transformation of observed standard score) and the standard error of the estimate (*SEE*), resulting in an asymmetrical confidence interval (McDonald, 1999). This asymmetry occurs because the estimated true score is closer to the mean than the observed score. The estimation method using the *SEE* serves as a correction for regression to the mean. However, the bands reported in the *Administration and Scoring Manual* utilized the average reliability coefficient across ages rather than age-based coefficients in the estimation equations. Thus, if users wish to report more precise confidence bands that correspond more closely to the examinee's age, they will have to use observed level estimation methods to hand-calculate them on a case-by-case basis. According to Glutting, McDermott, and Stanley (1987), these procedures are appropriate for individual decision making.

Test-retest stability was estimated by administering the WISC–V twice to a stratified subsample of 218 participants comprising five age bands from the normative sample. Retest intervals ranged from 9 to 82 days with a mean interval of 26 days. Uncorrected stability coefficients for all ages were .91 for the FSIQ, .68 to .91 for index scores, and .63 to .89 for subtest scores. Corrected coefficients were slightly higher.

In order to examine interscorer agreement, all WISC–V standardization record forms were double scored by two independent examiners,

and bivariate correlations were used as an index of agreement between the two forms. While the *Technical and Interpretative Manual* indicates that not all subtests were examined, it does not specify the subtests that were selected for inclusion. Overall, coefficients ranged from .98 to .99. Given the fact that the Verbal Comprehension subtests require more judgment in scoring, these measures were selected for additional examination. A sample of 60 record forms was randomly selected from the standardization sample and independently scored by nine raters who were in the process of completing clinical assessment training. None of the raters had any previous experience with the WISC–V measurement instrument. Coefficients were .98 for Similarities, .97 for Vocabulary, .99 for Information, and .97 for Comprehension.

Evidence of Validity

Consistent with the most current version of the Standards for Educational and Psychological Testing (American Educational Research Association, American Psychological Association, & National Council on Measurement in Education, 2014), validity evidence was provided in the areas of test content, response processes, internal structure, relations with other variables, special group studies, and the potential consequences of testing.

Content Validity
Content validity was estimated by surveying the relevant technical literature to substantiate the use of the WISC–V subtests for each latent trait estimated by each measure. An expert advisory panel was also formed to evaluate new items as well as to ensure improved subtest content coverage and theoretical relevance. Individual members of the advisory panel are listed in the *WISC–V Technical and Interpretive Manual*.

Construct Validity
As expected, subtest intercorrelations were all positive across age groups, reflecting Spearman's

(1904) positive manifold and measurement of the general ability factor (g). Consistent with current and previous iterations of the Wechsler scales (e.g., Canivez, 2014a; Watkins, 2006), moderate to high correlations between the WISC–V index scores were also observed. Despite the significant content and structural modifications specified in the WISC–V revision plan, results from exploratory factor analysis (EFA) were not reported in the *WISC–V Technical and Interpretive Manual*, a departure from previous versions of this instrument. The structural validity of the WISC–V was largely estimated using confirmatory factor analytic (CFA) procedures. CFA is generally preferred to EFA when the theory underlying the structure of a measurement instrument such as the WISC–V is known or has been well established in the technical literature (Schmitt, 2011). It should be noted that many researchers (e.g., Gorsuch, 1983; Haig, 2005) highlight the complementary nature of EFA as it relates to CFA and advocate the use of multiple factor-analytic procedures to obtain a clear picture of the most optimal measurement model that can explain cognitive test data.

Due to recent investigations suggesting that a five-factor measurement model provided a better fit to other versions of the Wechsler scales (e.g., Weiss, Keith, Zhu, & Chen, 2013a, 2013b), the WISC–V was developed under the theoretical assumption that the scale provides an estimate of general ability (g) along with five additional second-order cognitive factors (e.g., Verbal Comprehension, Visual-Spatial Processing, Fluid Reasoning, Working Memory, and Processing Speed). CFA procedures were utilized to examine the tenability of the five-factor model for all 16 of the WISC–V primary and secondary subtests when compared to competing one-, two-, three-, and four-factor hierarchical models. The results of the CFA examinations indicated that a five-factor model adequately fit the WISC–V data set and provided for statistically significant improvements to model fit when compared to several competing four-factor measurement models. However, additional clarification with respect to determining how to appropriately constrain the Arithmetic subtest was needed.

As a result of the multidimensional nature of the Arithmetic measure, conflicting results have been obtained in previous CFA examinations of the WISC–IV. Specifically, Keith, Fine, Taub, and Kranzler (2006) found that Arithmetic best loaded on a hypothetical Fluid Reasoning factor; Weiss et al. (2013b), however, found that Arithmetic cross-loaded on both the Perceptual Reasoning and the Working Memory Index within a four-factor model and loaded solely on a Fluid Reasoning factor in a five-factor model. Interestingly, in a CFA analysis of the WAIS–IV, Weiss and colleagues (2013a) found that Arithmetic cross-loaded on the Verbal Comprehension Index and Working Memory Index in a four-factor model and cross-loaded on the Working Memory Index and Fluid Reasoning Index (indirectly through an intermediate Quantitative Reasoning factor) in a five-factor measurement model.

Accordingly, contrasting five-factor models were examined in which (a) Arithmetic was constrained to load only on the Working Memory Index; (b) Arithmetic was constrained to load only on the Fluid Reasoning Index; (c) Arithmetic was freed to cross-load on the Fluid Reasoning Index and Working Memory Index; (d) Arithmetic was freed to cross-load on the Verbal Comprehension Index and Working Memory Index; and (e) Arithmetic was freed to cross-load on the Verbal Comprehension Index, Working Memory Index, and Fluid Reasoning Index. Results indicated that a constrained loading on the Fluid Reasoning Index alone was not tenable due to a g loading for Fluid Reasoning (1.03) that was greater than 1.0, suggesting an improper solution (Brown, 2015). Ultimately, it was determined that the model in which Arithmetic was specified to cross-load on the Verbal Comprehension Index, Working Memory Index, and Fluid Reasoning Index best fit the WISC–V across five age groups and thus served as the final validation model (see Figure 17.1). Subsequent analysis indicated that the validation

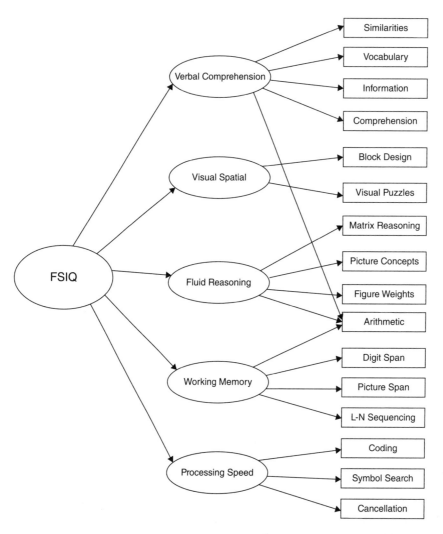

Figure 17.1   Final Five-Factor WISC–IV Validation Model for Primary and Secondary Subtests

model also provided excellent fit for the primary battery composed of the 10 primary subtests (see Figure 17.2). Additional commentary in the *WISC–V Technical and Interpretive Manual* revealed that incremental improvement in fit was obtained with a slight modification to the final validation model in which Figure Weights was unconstrained to cross-load on both the Fluid Reasoning Index and Visual Spatial Index. However, it was argued that this cross-loading

made little sense theoretically and ultimately was not retained. Interestingly, inspection of the standardized coefficients in the final validation model again reveals isomorphism between *g* and Fluid Reasoning (1.00). Golay, Reverte, Rossier, Favez, and Lecerf (2013) argue that this common observation in CFA research with the Wechsler scales is potentially an artifact of constraining nontrivial cross-loadings to zero, which has been shown to distort the underlying structure

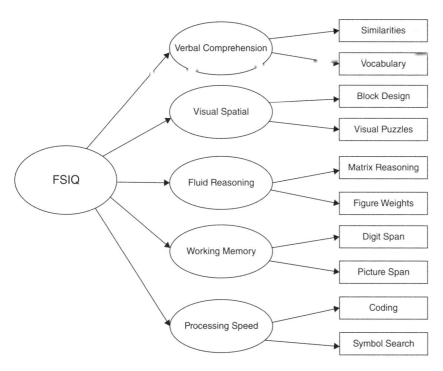

Figure 17.2   Five-Factor Validation Model for the Primary Subtests

of measurement models (see Asparouhov & Muthen, 2009). Unfortunately, ancillary and complementary measures on the WISC–V were not specified in any of the validation models; thus, the relationship of these measures within the WISC–V structural/interpretive model is not known.

Additionally, the aforementioned cross-loadings (both specified and implied) also create a potential confound in regard to estimating model-based reliability of some of the WISC–V subtest measures. As discussed previously, coefficient alpha was the primary metric utilized to estimate the internal consistency of the nonspeeded WISC–V measures. According to Nunnally and Bernstein (1994), coefficient alpha can broadly be defined as a measure of the interclass correlation between all the items contained within a measure and is commonly (albeit incorrectly; see Yang & Green, 2011) interpreted as an index for estimating the

degree to which a set of items measures a single unidimensional latent construct. The assumption that all true score variance is attributable to a single latent dimension is critically important when determining whether the use of coefficient alpha is appropriate, as the coefficient cannot account for multiple sources of influence on the observed interclass correlation in psychological measures that are inherently multidimensional (Reise, Bonifay, & Haviland, 2013). Although most of the research examining the effects of multidimensionality on the usefulness of coefficient alpha has been concerned with extricating higher-order variance (g) from lower-order variance (group factors), a Monte Carlo simulation conducted by Zinbarg, Revelle, and Yovel (2007) revealed that coefficient alpha may overestimate the reliability of a measure even more when items within a measure are influenced by multiple common or group factors (e.g., WISC–V index-level abilities). In such circumstances, the use of alternative omega coefficients has been advised (Dunn, Baguley, & Brunsden, 2013; Yang & Green, 2011). Until such coefficients are calculated for WISC–V measures that are suspected of being influenced by multiple group factors (e.g., Arithmetic, Figure Weights), users have no way of appropriately determining the mechanism(s) underlying the reliable variance that is observed within these measures.

Subtest g loadings ranged from .21 (Cancellation) to .72 (Vocabulary). With the exception of Arithmetic (.70), measures from the Verbal Comprehension Index loaded highest on the general factor. The results are consistent with previous research (e.g., Keith et al., 2006). However, decomposition procedures (e.g., Schmid-Leiman, 1957) whereby subtest variance is appropriately apportioned to higher-order and lower-order dimensions were not reported. Given the hierarchical model nature of the structural model, such analyses are crucial for guiding the interpretative focus of users of this measurement instrument in clinical settings (Canivez, 2013b).

Despite the ambitious structural validation procedures that were employed, the absence of several plausible measurement models (e.g., correlated factors, bifactor) from the CFA analyses is noteworthy. The *WISC–V Technical and Interpretive Manual* notes that validation studies were constrained to facilitate the examination of various hierarchical iterations. As it relates to measures of cognitive ability, the hierarchical or indirect hierarchical model implies that a higher-order construct (e.g., g) has indirect effects on subtest measures whereas lower-order broad abilities have direct effects. Thus, in the WISC–V, g-factor effects on the subtests are hypothesized to channel through the latent abilities estimated by the index scores. Alternatively, the bifactor or direct hierarchical model (Holzinger & Swineford, 1937) suggests that both the higher-order g-factor and the broad second-order abilities have direct effects simultaneously on the subtests. Recently rediscovered (see Reise, 2012), the bifactor model has been found to provide better fit to data from multiple

versions of the Wechsler scales (Canivez, 2014b; Gignac, 2006; Gignac & Watkins, 2013; Golay et al., 2013; Nelson, Canivez, & Watkins, 2013; Watkins & Beaujean, 2014) when compared to rival measurement models, such as the correlated factors model and the indirect hierarchical model.

Ideally in CFA, a hypothesized measurement model is examined to determine how well it fits the data in relationship to all relevant competing models. Failing to specify a model that has been found to fit the data in previous researches is akin to using a convenience sample to make inferences regarding population parameters. This is not to suggest that the final validation presented in the *WISC–V Technical and Interpretive Manual* is wrong; however, the absence of relevant measurement models from the WISC–V structural analyses points to the need for additional research to be conducted so that users can be confident in the factor structure implied by the configuration of the measurement instrument.

Relationships with Other Measures and Variables

Convergent and divergent validity was estimated by examining correlations between the WISC–V and a number of other measures, including commonly used measures of intellectual functioning and achievement. Overall conclusions indicate that the WISC–V correlated highly with instruments purported to measure similar cognitive and intellectual constructs. Of particular importance, scores on the WISC–V demonstrated high consistency with those from the previous edition, with correlations (corrected) ranging from .63 to .86 for composites and indexes and .57 to .82 for subtests. Of particular note, given the bifurcation of the WISC–IV's PRI into separate Visual Spatial and Fluid Reasoning indices in the current edition, correlations between the Perceptual Reasoning Index and Visual Spatial Index (.66) and the Perceptual Reasoning Index and Fluid Reasoning Index (.63) were similar. Correlations between the WISC–V indexes and theoretically consistent scores on the KABC–II were generally moderate to strong, with a strong correlation observed between the Verbal Comprehension Index and Crystallized Ability Composite (.74) and moderate correlations observed between the Working Memory Index and Short-Term Memory Composite (.63), Visual Spatial Index and Visual Processing Composite (.53), and Fluid Reasoning Index and Fluid Reasoning Composite (.50). Predictive relationships of the WISC–V with the WIAT–III and with the Kaufman Test of Educational Achievement–Third Edition(KTEA–3, A. S. Kaufman & Kaufman, 2014) batteries were commensurate with estimates obtained from other measures of intellectual functioning. Consistent with previous research (e.g., Keith, Fehrmann, Harrison, & Pottebaum, 1987), preliminary evidence for divergent validity was established as a result of trivial or negative correlations between WISC–V scores and measures from behavior rating scales, such as the BASC–2 and the Vineland Adaptive Behavior Scales–Second Edition (Vineland–2; Sparrow, Cicchetti, & Balla, 2005).

Small-Group Studies

Small special subsamples (20–95 participants) and matched controls were compared to test for clinically significant group differences. Groups included individuals identified with giftedness, various levels of intellectual disability, specific learning disorder, attention-deficit/hyperactivity disorder, traumatic brain injury, and autism spectrum disorder. Observed mean differences were consistent with theoretical expectations. Although the *Technical and Interpretative Manual* suggests that the WISC–V is useful for determining individual cognitive strengths and weaknesses that may be relevant for diagnosing specific learning disorders, the evidence provided in the specific learning disorder tables suggests that this conclusion may be optimistic. Generally, the most discernible discrepancy between learning disability subgroups was consistently lower scores across indexes when compared to matched controls. Limited evidence

of breakout scores was observed. For instance, in the specific learning disorder–reading group, WISC–V index score means fluctuated only by four standard score points with all scores falling within the low-average to average range. The lone exception was the Quantitative Reasoning Index ($M = 79.9$) in the specific learning disorder–math group, which is theoretically consistent given the traits purported to be sampled by that measure. Overall the WISC–V appears to be an adequate instrument for discriminating between individuals suspected of giftedness and intellectual disability, although additional evidence is needed for establishing the potential diagnostic utility of the instrument (Canivez & Gaboury, 2013; Styck & Watkins, 2013).

Consequences of Testing

According to Braden and Niebling (2012), evidence based on the consequences that result from testing should include evaluations of diagnostic utility at the individual level. Accordingly, differential item functioning analysis was used to examine potential item bias and content fairness. Although the item characteristic curves were not provided in the *WISC–V Technical and Interpretive Manual*, the test authors indicate that inspection of the curves suggest that WISC–V items do not appear to discriminate between individual examinees on the basis of race or ethnicity. However, examiners must remain vigilant with respect to the intended and unintended consequences that may result from clinical use of the WISC–V (Hubley & Zumbo, 2011).

CONTRIBUTIONS THE WISC–V WILL MAKE TO THE FIELD

The WISC–V is a significant and positive revision from its predecessor. The integration of additional neuropsychological constructs, which have been shown to predict various aspects of academic achievement, is a welcome addition to the test. The move from a four-factor model of interpretation to a five-factor model of interpretation better reflects current conceptualizations of intelligence. The test offers multiple psychometric comparisons between indices and subtests, which should enhance the test's clinical utility. The digital version of the test is a significant advancement for the assessment field. Like any new major test that is published, assessment specialists are encouraged to read future research studies that continue to validate the psychometric properties and clinical applications of the WISC–V.

CHAPTER 18

INDEPENDENT WISC–V TEST REVIEW: THEORETICAL AND PRACTICAL CONSIDERATIONS

JACK A. NAGLIERI

I still have my copy of the original *Wechsler Intelligence Scale for Children* (WISC; Wechsler, 1949) which I was required to purchase (for about $60) in 1973 for the first graduate course I took on assessment. I also still use my 1972 edition of *Wechsler's Measurement and Appraisal of Adult Intelligence* (Matarazzo, 1972), which Joe Matarazzo signed for me when I received an award from the Italian American Psychological Assembly for "outstanding achievements and contributions to psychology" during the APA convention in Washington, DC. These tools formed the foundation of my learning about intelligence and its measurement, and they guided my assessment of so many children I evaluated in schools and my clinical practice over the years that followed. But it wasn't until 1977 when my understanding of the Wechsler was greatly enhanced when I took assessment for a second time as part of my PhD program. By chance or fate, the professor who taught me how to interpret the *Wechsler Intelligence Scale for Children–Revised* (WISC–R; Wechsler, 1974a) was also assigned to be my advisor and later became my dear friend. I also still have my signed copy of *Intelligent Testing with the WISC–R* (A. S. Kaufman, 1979) and all the subsequent editions of that book that have been published. It is an honor to have the opportunity to contribute to this edition of such an important tool for practitioners.

I have always been a firm believer that the concept of general intelligence which the Wechsler scales represent remains, as noted by Anastasi and Urbina (1997), one of the most valuable contributions that psychology has made to society. It is with great confidence as well as research support (see Brunnert, Naglieri, & Hardy-Braz, 2009; Naglieri & Otero, 2012b) that I have recommended the use of nonverbal measures of general ability such as the *Wechsler Nonverbal Scale of Ability* (Wechsler & Naglieri, 2006) and the *Naglieri Nonverbal Ability Test* (Naglieri, 2008a). These tools meet the need to evaluate general ability using nonverbal content just as this method was originally intended by those who developed it—the U.S. Military. It is amply documented (Naglieri, 2008b, 2015) and clearly stated by Yoakum and Yerkes (1920) that the Army Beta (so-called nonverbal) test was intended for those who had difficulty reading or spoke English poorly as well as those who were illiterate or not able to understand English (p. 51). The Army Alpha contained verbal and quantitative tests and was appropriate only for men who could read and write English sufficiently. The testing procedures were intended to be fair for diverse populations, perhaps best illustrated when Yoakum and Yerkes stated: "men who fail in alpha are sent to beta in order that injustice by reason of relative unfamiliarity with English may be avoided" (p. 19). These two tests were not developed to measure different types of intelligence. Importantly, it was the Army Alpha and Beta that Wechsler used when he assembled the Wechsler-Bellevue in 1939.

Wechsler, like Yoakum and Yerkes, did not believe that his Verbal and Performance scales measured two different abilities. This point was emphasized by A. S. Kaufman in the foreword of the *Wechsler Nonverbal Scale of Ability* (WNV) *Administration Manual* (Wechsler & Naglieri, 2006) when he wrote:

> The emphasis in the WNV Manual that the Full Scale measures general ability nonverbally—and not nonverbal ability—is an important distinction that further ties the WNV to Dr. Wechsler. Although his intelligence tests in the 1930s and 1940s departed from the one-score Stanford-Binet by offering separate Verbal and Performance IQs as well as a profile of scaled scores, Dr. Wechsler remained a firm believer in Spearman's g theory throughout his lifetime. He believed that his Verbal and Performance Scales represented different ways to access g, but he never believed in nonverbal intelligence as being separate from g. Rather, he saw the Performance Scale as the most sensible way to measure the general intelligence of people with hearing impairments, language disorders, or limited proficiency in English. (p. iii)

The use and number of nonverbal tests of general ability has increased in recent years as the percentage of people in the United States with limited English language skills has increased. (For a review of nonverbal tests, see Naglieri and Goldstein, 2009.) As noted by Yoakum and Yerkes nearly 100 years ago, it is clear that verbal tests are not appropriate for those with limited English-language skills. This point raises another critically important question relating to Wechsler's tests, as well as all ability tests that have verbal and quantitative content: "Is it really a good idea to measure intelligence using subtests that also require knowledge?"

The idea that verbal tests of intelligence can perhaps be better thought of as tests of achievement, or at least tests of general ability that are confounded by knowledge, was first presented by Alan and Nadeen Kaufman when they began development of the Kaufman Assessment Battery for Children (K–ABC; A. S. Kaufman &

Kaufman, 1983). When Alan Kaufman described the WISC–R Verbal scale as achievement (he associated it with what would be the achievement portion of the K–ABC), I remember thinking "That makes a lot of sense." His comment reminded me of my experiences giving the WISC and the *Peabody Individual Achievement Test* (Dunn & Markwardt, 1970), which both had an Information subtest: I noted that the questions were essentially the same, but the interpretation was very different: intelligence or achievement! The second point made by the Kaufmans was equally true and even more important: They wanted to build their test of intelligence on a theory of intelligence. Additionally, the test should be fair for diverse populations and inform instruction. These were revolutionary ideas in the late 1970s. It was clear to me that this was the way to advance the field of intelligence testing. I owe much of my understanding of how best to build a modern measure of ability to my experiences helping develop the K-ABC.

My own efforts on the *Cognitive Assessment System* (CAS; Naglieri & Das, 1997) and the CAS2 (Naglieri, Das, & Goldstein, 2014) have focused on building a test grounded in neurocognitive theory, with the goal that the test content should be as free of acquired knowledge as possible so that the items would be accessible for diverse populations. Equally important, the test should be consistent with the theory (e.g., Planning, Attention, Simultaneous, and Successive scales match the brain-based theory). Evidence that the scales a test yields are predictive of achievement would be critical to understand the basic validity of the approach. Evidence must be found that the theoretically derived scales are sensitive to the cognitive problems experienced by those who have, for example, attention deficits and specific learning disabilities (SLDs). Research must show that the scales are nondiscriminatory as emphasized by the Individuals with Disabilities Education Act (IDEA). And finally, there should be a strong connection between test results and instruction. I have shown that all these criteria can be met with a brain-based neurocognitive theory that includes only four dimensions: Planning, Attention, Simultaneous, and Successive neurocognitive processes (Naglieri, 2015; Naglieri & Conway, 2009; Naglieri & Otero, 2012a). These standards, which I have held my own test to, form the basis of my review of the WISC–V.

WISC–V AND THEORY

It was encouraging to see that the authors of the *WISC–V Technical and Interpretive Manual* (Wechsler, 2015) included a section titled "Update Theoretical Foundations." I wondered if the development of the fifth edition was actually guided by a theory. That hope was quickly dashed by the very first sentence: "Various theories and models relevant to intellectual assessment influenced the WISC–V." Next was a section about structural intelligence models, which begins with a discussion to clarify whether Wechsler believed in general ability (as Kaufman has asserted) or if his tests measure specific abilities. There was no real resolution of that topic. Next the discussion continued with the position that because factor-analytically derived models are widely accepted, the "verbal comprehension, visual spatial, fluid reasoning, working memory and processing speed abilities are important" (p. 23). It seems clear that the factor-analytic results obtained for this version of the Wechsler were used to define the "structural theory." That is the method that has been used by Pearson and the previous publisher, the Psychological Corporation, for many years.

Next the manual states: "Theory is not the only consideration that drives development of the … WISC–V" (p. 23). This is followed by a long section titled "Neurodevelopmental and Neurocognitive Research." Reading this interesting summary of research leads one to wonder what relevance it has for the theory behind the WISC–V, but the answer becomes clear on page 25. The authors argue that because children use their brains to solve the subtests of this test, this somehow supports the as yet not clearly defined neuropsychological theory behind the WISC–V. One can only conclude that no clearly defined theory was used to develop the fifth edition of this test and that users are, unfortunately, encouraged to find a model, hypothesis, or conceptualization that best fits the WISC–V scores a child or adolescent may earn.

The need for a theory is among the most practical of issues because it has tremendous implications for eligibility determination/diagnosis and intervention. The first chapter of the *WISC–V Technical and Interpretive Manual* contains a section on subtest content, where the authors provide considerable discussion about the "constructs [each] subtest is designed to measure" (p. 7). If there was a specific theory, each subtest should represent the construct corresponding to the scale upon which the subtest is placed. For example, the Similarities, Vocabulary, Information, and Comprehension subtests could have been deemed measures of Verbal Comprehension. (My preference would be to state, for example, that general ability is measured using subtests that require verbal comprehension and expression.) Instead, the WISC–V authors give a list of as many as a dozen abilities or other factors that may be involved in answering the items on the various WISC–V subtests. The list includes everything from verbal concept formation to cognitive flexibility, to auditory comprehension, and many more—which are justified because they appeared in a few books. This is the clearest evidence that the theoretical construct underlying each subtest is undefined; there is no unifying theory upon which the WISC–V was built. Instead, a few new subtests were added based on a rationale that is not well articulated, and the factor structure was used to identify the concepts the scales represent. Without a clear theory to guide the interpretation of the WISC–V, the responsibility for understanding learning success and failure, connecting the test results to legal definition of an SLD in IDEA, and determining what type of instructional intervention to use will become much more difficult.

WISC–V AND ACHIEVEMENT

One of the most important types of validity evidence for an ability test is its correlation with achievement. This kind of validity is important because we use tests like the WISC–V to help explain why a student referred for an evaluation is having trouble in school. The answer to this question helps us understand how well the intelligence test we use is related to current academic performance, and we hope it also provides good prediction of future performance. The *WISC–V Technical and Interpretive Manual* includes an important section on the relationships with the Wechsler Individual Achievement Test—Third Edition (WIAT–III; Pearson, 2009b). The results are most informative, especially when the correlation between the WISC–V and WIAT–III is understood in relation to the results previously reported for the WISC–IV and WIAT–II (Wechsler, 2003).

Before the correlations between the WISC–V and WIAT–III can be evaluated, we first have to consider the similarity in content between these two seemingly different tests. We assume that because the WISC–V is a measure of intelligence and the WIAT–III is a measure of ability, the content of these tests is different. That assumption has been questioned (Naglieri & Bornstein, 2003). Both tests have items requiring math facts (Arithmetic on the WISC–V and Mathematics and Math Fluency on the WIAT–III) and questions requiring knowledge of words (Vocabulary and Similarities on the WISC–V and Oral Language, Basic Reading, and Reading Comprehension on the WIAT–III). The similarity in content across these two tests, which are intended to measure two distinct constructs (intelligence versus achievement), ensures that they will be correlated simply because of the similarity of the knowledge both demand. This is a significant conceptual and methodological issue that should be addressed in the WISC–V (or any of the traditional IQ test) manual.

The similarity in content between Wechsler's intelligence and achievement tests has an effect on any study of WISC–V validity; the obtained correlation should be considered an overestimate of the relationship between general ability and achievement. Some indication of how much of an overestimate the shared content creates can be gleaned from the correlations of the several WISC–V scales with the WIAT–III. Examination of Table 5.13 of the *WISC–V Technical and Interpretive Manual* provides these correlations. The WISC–V Full Scale IQ correlation is .81 with the Total Achievement score from the WIAT–III. The Verbal Comprehension Index correlated the highest (.74) with the WIAT–III Total Achievement scale; the remaining scales correlated substantially lower (Visual Spatial = .46; Fluid Reasoning = .40; Working Memory = .63; and Processing Speed = .34). As expected, the Verbal Comprehension scale correlated the highest with the WIAT–III; the best explanation for that finding is the similarity in content across the two tests. The correlation between the four remaining scales yields a good estimate of the relationship between the WISC–V and achievement without the overlap in test question content. The average of those values is .47, which gives a very different view of validity.

A similar pattern involving correlations with the WIAT–II (Wechsler, 2001) is found in the WISC–IV manual (Table 5.15). The highest correlation between the WIAT–II Total Achievement and WISC–IV was found for the Verbal Comprehension scale; all other correlations were lower. Most interesting is the difference between the Total Achievement and Full Scale score correlations for the WISC–IV (.87) and WISC–V (.81). These findings beg the questions: Why isn't the WISC–V correlation with the WIAT–III higher than the WISC–IV/WIAT–II correlation, given that the new version now has five scales rather than four? Is this a sampling issue, or have the structure and new items on the WISC–V rendered the new test less effective than the previous edition?

WISC–V PROFILES AND ELIGIBILITY DETERMINATION

The authors of the *WISC–V Technical and Interpretive Manual* rightfully remind the reader "Intelligence tests were not originally designed to serve as neuropsychological measures," but they also suggest that "the WISC–V primary index scores represent cognitive processes of interest in neuropsychological assessment ... and [they can be used] to generate hypotheses about neuropsychological processing deficits" (p. 34). This statement suggests that the scales measure cognitive processes that could be used for eligibility determination. There are at least two important prerequisites for recommending that scores on a test of ability be used to measure cognitive processes. First, the test should be built on a theory of brain-based cognition, which was addressed earlier in this review; and second, there should be evidence of distinct profiles for students with SLDs. Examination of the profiles for students with SLDs in reading (Table 5.28) and reading and written expression (Table 5.30) does not suggest that practitioners should anticipate specific primary or ancillary scale profiles. Equally important is the implication that the WISC–V can be used to measure processing strengths and weaknesses to meet criteria in IDEA 2004.

In 1999, I suggested that evidence for an SLD could be found if a pattern of strengths and weaknesses in basic psychological processes that corresponded to similar variability in achievement test scores was obtained during a comprehensive evaluation (Naglieri, 1999). This approach unites the definitional criteria found in IDEA 2004 for SLD with the method for making the eligibility determination (Hale, Kaufman, Naglieri, & Kavale, 2006). The authors of the *WISC–V Technical and Interpretive Manual* describe this approach as a "legally acceptable and clinically sound approach for helping practitioners identify SLDs and develop intervention plans based on a child's strengths and weaknesses" (p. 183), but the evidence

that this method applies to the scores from the WISC–V is lacking. What would be needed are: (a) a theory-based definition of the basic psychological processes, preferably defined according to a neuropsychological framework (e.g., Otero, 2015); (b) distinct profiles for students with SLDs; and (c) research evidence that profiles have relevance for instructional decision making. Much research is needed to demonstrate the utility of WISC–V profiles for eligibility determination and instructional relevance.

Determining eligibility for educational services as well as diagnosis of childhood disorders certainly involves thoughtful integration of information from a variety of sources and a wide variety of tools. I agree completely with this statement from the *WISC–V Technical and Interpretive Manual*: "The practitioner, using tests as part of the assessment activity, is responsible for interpreting results and making diagnostic, treatment, or intervention decisions" (p. 186). The critical issue is, however, how the profile of scores and interpretations offered in the WISC–V manual help or hinder the practitioner making accurate decisions that can have a profound influence on a young person's life.

WISC–V AND RACE/ETHNICITY

The WISC–V Technical and Interpretive Manual has a section titled "Consequences of Testing" (p. 147) that discusses, for example, the importance of the clinical diagnostic utility at the individual level and the item bias procedures used during test development. The manual also reports (see Chapter 2) that "problematic items were deleted on the basis of formal expert review of the items and empirical data from statistical analyses of differential item function (p. 32). This is good test development. Some argue (Braden & Niebling, 2012) that it is also important to look at test score differences between groups (as noted in the WISC–V manual), but WISC–V mean score differences for diverse populations was given little attention. The one study that is reported involves a group of Asian and Hispanic English Language Learners (ELL); and that study only has 16 participants. The results of this study are consistent with expectations discussed earlier in this review—these children earned low scores on the verbal (i.e., achievement-based) subtests Similarities, Vocabulary, and Information and the scale that they comprise, Verbal Comprehension Index. The Verbal Comprehension Index mean (85.6) is 1 standard deviation below the normative mean and substantially lower than that of the matched control group. It is certainly expected that children learning English would earn low scores on tests that require comprehension and expression of their second language. What is concerning about the description of these findings is the manner in which the findings are interpreted. My concern is with the statement: "subtests requiring minimal expressive language and reduced receptive language *abilities*" (emphasis added) (p. 141), which implies that the verbal tests on which these children did poorly are measures of verbal ability. This can lead consumers to conclude that a child learning English has low verbal ability when he or she may not have. It would be in the best interest of students who are learning English that all subtests that demand knowledge and use of words not be interpreted as a measure of *ability* (Fagan, 2000; Suzuki & Valencia, 1997). The authors of the WISC–V should have made it clear that when this test is given to those with limited knowledge of English, the Verbal Comprehension Index should be considered spoiled (or more a measure of verbal expression and comprehension of English) and not used to create a Full Scale IQ.

CONCLUSIONS

Any review of the fifth edition of the Wechsler scales has to begin by recognizing the enormous impact this tool has had on the field of psychology and education. The test's use is unsurpassed by any measure of intellectual ability and the test name has come to represent the very definition of intelligence. As the description and number of abilities in Wechsler's test measures has changed, there has been a growing awareness that the essential ingredients initially developed in 1917 (Naglieri, 2015) by the U.S. Army do not sufficiently meet the needs of the field today. The publisher's efforts to sustain the Wechsler brand reflect the recognition that more information is needed from the test. The solution to the dilemma—make the WISC better but do not change it too much—apparently has led to reliance on factor analysis and diverse interpretive solutions. The authors of the WISC–V have made a valiant attempt to strengthen the integrity of this time-honored test. Even given all the efforts to inform users of the various ways to interpret the scores the WISC–V yields, these ideas are constrained by the historically determined content. All this raises the question: How can the field move forward and achieve a more effective way to measure intelligence? I believe we can add to what the WISC–V measures and meet the demands of our current educational and psychological professions by including additional measures in our comprehensive assessments.

In my recent book chapter titled "Hundred Years of Intelligence Testing: Moving from Traditional IQ to Second-Generation Intelligence Tests" (Naglieri, 2015), I have provided both the rationale and research evidence of the advantages to new approaches to understanding human functioning. The two tools I describe as second generation are the K–ABC, first and second editions (A. S. Kaufman & Kaufman, 1983, 2004) and the *CAS*, first and second editions (Naglieri & Das, 1997; Naglieri, Das, & Goldstein, 2014). The advantages these modern approaches to measuring ability have led me to the conclusion that objective analysis of the Wechsler (and other traditional IQ tests) gives a better appreciation of the advantages new approaches to understand learning and learning difficulties can provide. We can augment our understanding of intelligence defined within a neurocognitive theory with these new tools, and, for the sake of the children and adolescents we work so diligently to help, we should.

CHAPTER 19

SOME IMPRESSIONS OF, AND QUESTIONS ABOUT, THE WISC–V

George McCloskey

Recognizing the need to provide a test that would appeal to a broad range of practitioners who hold widely varying opinions and beliefs about the nature of intelligence and the best way to interpret test results, the test developers have assembled an impressive array of 21 subtests for the fifth edition of the WISC. Each of these subtests is well developed; great attention has been paid to the drafting (or revising) of subtest directions, the development of new items or the revision of old ones, and the need for psychometric integrity. The 21 subtests are multifaceted tasks, most of which have great clinical utility from a neuropsychological perspective.

Various combinations of these 21 subtests can produce as many as 14 composites, as shown in Figure 19.1.

Although the exercise of organizing and interpreting the information obtained from the WISC–V can seem as daunting as visually making sense of Figure 19.1, the *WISC–V Technical and Interpretive Manual* offers a stage approach for the interpretation of test results. This stage approach starts with the Full Scale IQ (FSIQ). This is followed by interpretation of the primary index scores. Note that the primary index level has been expanded to encompass five specific indexes: Verbal Comprehension, Visual Spatial ("Perceptual" from the Perceptual Reasoning Index), Fluid Reasoning ("Reasoning" from the now-defunct Perceptual Reasoning Index), Working Memory, and Processing Speed. Interpretive techniques applied at the primary index stage involve the profiling

of primary index strengths and weaknesses and primary index pairwise comparisons. Primary index interpretation is followed by primary index subtest score interpretation involving the profiling of subtest strengths and weaknesses and within-index subtest pairwise comparisons.

The *WISC–V Technical and Interpretive Manual* then addresses the ancillary and complementary index scores, noting that interpretation of these scores is based on clinical need. Interpretation at this stage involves comparisons and contrasts among specific pairs of ancillary and/or complementary index scores (e.g., General Ability Index versus Cognitive Proficiency Index). This stage is followed by subtest score pairwise comparisons within the ancillary and complementary indexes. Index and subtest interpretive stages are followed by subtest-level process score analyses, consideration of process observations, and process score and complementary subtest contrast score interpretations. The interpretive stages conclude with a discussion of different types of analyses for the identification of specific learning disorders (SLDs).

The interpretive approach outlined in the *WISC–V Technical and Interpretive Manual* provides much food for thought in that it raises many more questions about interpretation of test scores than it answers. These questions include:

- What does the term *Full Scale IQ* mean, and what should a general estimate of intelligence encompass?

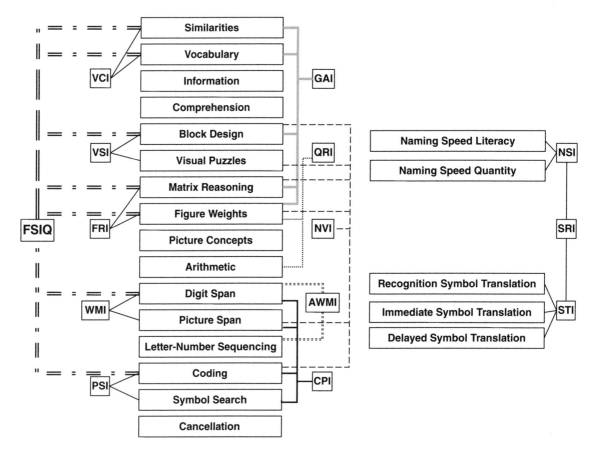

Figure 19.1   WISC–V subtests and composites

Note: Composite score abbreviations are: VCI = Verbal Comprehension Index; VSI = Visual Spatial Index; FRI = Fluid Reasoning Index; WMI = Working Memory Index; PSI = Processing Speed Index; GAI = General Ability Index; QRI = Quantitative Reasoning Index; NVI = Nonverbal Index; AWMI = Auditory Working Memory Index; CPI = Cognitive Proficiency Index; NSI = Naming Speed Index; SRI = Storage and Retrieval Index; STI = Symbol Translation Index.

- Why are some indexes primary, some ancillary, some complementary, and some nonexistent?
- Why does the test include subtests that do not contribute to any index?
- What is the difference between an ability and a process?
- Is cognition the same thing as intelligence, and if they are not the same, which one is the WISC–V measuring?

In this chapter I offer a few thoughts, from a strictly clinical perspective, on each of these points.

WHAT DOES THE TERM *FULL SCALE IQ* MEAN, AND WHAT SHOULD A GENERAL ESTIMATE OF INTELLIGENCE ENCOMPASS?

Despite all the data analyses, discussions, and debates, the concept of general intelligence has defied a singular definition for more than a century. Decades of research and contentious debates caused an exasperated Arthur Jensen (1998) to offer the following gloomy proclamation:

My study of these two symposia and of many other equally serious attempts to define "intelligence" in purely verbal terms has convinced me that psychologists are incapable of reaching a consensus on its definition. It has proved to be a hopeless quest. Therefore, the term "intelligence" should be discarded altogether in scientific psychology, just as it discarded "animal magnetism" and as the science of chemistry discarded "phlogiston." "Intelligence" will continue, of course, in popular parlance and in literary usage, where it may serve a purpose only because it can mean anything the user intends, and where a precise and operational definition is not important.

Largely because of its popular and literary usage, the word "intelligence" has come to mean too many different things to many people (including psychologists). It has also become so fraught with value judgments, emotions, and prejudices as to render it useless in scientific discussion. (p. 48)

Although statements such as this may reflect the views of some psychologists today, there remains a large contingent of true believers who espouse the virtues of general estimates of intelligence (e.g., L. S. Gottfredson, 1997, 1998, 2008).

Wechsler himself believed that there was a benefit to obtaining an estimate of general intelligence. He believed that such estimates were reflective of "the capacity of the individual to act purposefully, to think rationally, and to deal effectively with his environment" (1944, p. 3), and noted that "[w]hat intelligence tests measure is something much more important: the capacity of an individual to understand the world about him and his resourcefulness to cope with its challenges" (1975, p. 139). But Wechsler acknowledged that such estimates could not fully describe a person's capabilities or predict their success in life. Fully acknowledging its limitations, Wechsler endorsed the pooling of all subtests to produce a single, global Full Scale IQ (FSIQ).

Wechsler (1958) expressed his perspective on the advantages of the FSIQ with the following analogy:

> If the different tests were taken to represent generically different entities, one could no more add the values assigned to them in order to obtain an [IQ] than one could add 2 dogs, 3 cats and 4 elephants, and expect the unqualified answer of 9. That, of course, does not mean that their addition is impossible. If instead of being concerned with the characteristics of the dog, the cat and the elephant, which differentiate them from one another, we restrict our interest to those which they all have in common, we can say that 2 dogs, 3 cats and 4 elephants make 9 animals. The reason we can get an answer of 9 here is because dogs, cats and elephants are in fact all animals. The addition would no longer be possible if for cats we were to substitute turnips. (p. 7)

This analogy seems to me quite ironic. It certainly supports the idea that subtests can be combined to offer a numerical value for the overarching construct of intelligence. But more important, the analogy can be extended to reveal the disastrous results of using the overarching construct to attempt to make practical decisions that will affect the child. Surely Wechsler would not suggest that it is just fine to state that there are nine animals if one is ordering food for these nine animals or attempting to transport them from one location to another. In the clinical assessment of intelligence, we must be mindful of the elements that are being combined to produce the overarching construct and their real impact on overall functioning. Otherwise we may end up trying to feed an elephant with a cup of dog chow or ordering an 18-wheeler to transport a cat to the veterinarian's office. In my mind, *not* concerning ourselves with "the characteristics of the dog, the cat and the elephant that differentiate them from one another" is perhaps the worst thing we can do when assessing a child. Without a clear picture of the child's intellectual strengths and weaknesses, we are unable to make meaningful, practical recommendations about educational options.

Whether one agrees with Wechsler about the relevance of global estimates of intelligence or not, it seems fitting that the test that bears his name would include a Full Scale IQ score in keeping with his original conceptions about general intelligence. Unfortunately, the current version of the WISC represents a significant departure from the concept of Full Scale IQ even though it offers an index with that name. In the tradition of Wechsler, the term *Full Scale* should be reserved for a score that represents the sum of all of the tasks in the battery—each of which is believed to assess a different facet of intelligence and worthy of acknowledgment in the full scale. As Wechsler himself asserted, such a score would represent the general quality of an individual's ability, summing over the variations represented in individual task performance.

The WISC–V FSIQ does not in fact represent a full scale IQ. It is not based on the summing of all 21 of the subtests included in the test; nor the 16 subtests excluding the five complementary tasks that are identified in the test manual as "not measures of intelligence"; nor even the 10 subtests that compose the five primary indexes. Rather, the FSIQ is a truncated estimate based on seven equally weighted subtests: two from each of the Verbal Comprehension Index and the Fluid Reasoning Index and one each from the Visual Spatial Index, Working Memory Index, and Processing Speed Index.

There can be little doubt that decades of large-group research will be summoned to defend the idea of a less-than-full FSIQ. These analyses will be used to show that a seven-subtest FSIQ is just as good as a 21 subtest FSIQ in that they "correlate highly" and "predict in a similar manner and to the same degree." But as all clinicians know, there is a great deal of difference between the view when staring at printouts from very large data sets and the view when sitting across the desk from an individual child. Both Spearman and Wechsler recognized this fact and warned against the over-interpretation of any general estimate of intelligence, even one obtained from a summation of all tasks of a test.

Table 19.1   Comparison of WISC–V FSIQ with WJ IV GIA

WISC–V FSIQ Subtests	WJ IV GIA Subtests
Similarities	Oral Vocabulary
Vocabulary	Number Series
Matrix Reasoning	Verbal Attention
Figure Weights	Letter-Pattern Matching
Block Design	Phonological Processing
Digit Span	Story Recall
Coding	Visualization

As intelligence tests have evolved over multiple generations of revisions, it seems even more difficult than ever to understand exactly what it is that theoreticians, researchers, and test developers believe they are measuring with a Full Scale IQ. Comparing the WISC–V with one of its competitors provides a most baffling illustration of this dilemma. Table 19.1 shows the composition of the WISC–V FSIQ with the Woodcock-Johnson IV (WJ IV General Intellectual Ability composite [GIA]; WJ IV equivalent of the FSIQ).

Looking at these two sets of tasks, it is hard to see how the FSIQ and the WJ IV GIA could ever be considered as even roughly equivalent measures of the same construct, whatever that construct might be. The WJ IV purports to be based on a version of J. B. Carroll's (1993a) expansion of the original concept of Fluid and Crystallized intelligence proposed by Cattell (1963) and further elaborated on by Horn and Cattell (1966). The WISC–V claims to be theoretical in that its contents reflect current research in multiple fields that impact the concept of intelligence. It seems that Jensen was correct in that after more than 100 years of researching and theorizing, we still are no closer to a consensus view on the nature of intelligence.

For some theoreticians, researchers, and clinicians, the answer to what is measured, or what should be measured, with the FSIQ harkens back to the work of one of the pioneers in intelligence research—Charles Spearman. From the perspective of this group, general intelligence is about the measurement of *g*. Spearman's statistical studies showed that "*g* has a much greater relative influence or 'weight' in some of the abilities tested than in others. Means were even found of measuring this relative weight" (1927, p. 75). From a *g* perspective, the FSIQ should be comprised of those tasks that are the best possible measures of *g*—those that are most *g* saturated. In his classic *Bias in Mental Testing*, Jensen (1980) expounded on the nature of *g* and on modern studies that examined the nature of *g*. Jensen's work had a great influence on many psychologists who now believe that "*g* is key" and that intelligence tests should be thought of exclusively as measures of *g*.

There is a great irony in all of this in the sense that Spearman himself eschewed the idea of general intelligence. In *The Abilities of Man: Their Nature and Measurement*, Spearman (1927) gave this analogy to point out what he believed to be the absurdity of constructing tests of general intelligence:

> Let us compare a person's mental measurement (his "intelligence quotient" or "IQ") as based on averaging or sampling with his record in any other sphere of activity, say that of sports. Suppose some lad to be the champion of his school in the 100 yards race, the 1/4 mile, the 1/2 mile, and also in the high and broad jumps. Could all this be taken as a representative sample of his sporting ability in general? So far as here indicated, he might perform very badly indeed in countless other branches of sport, such as cricket, lawn tennis, shooting, baseball, rowing, putting the weight, riding, mountaineering or flying. And even if he were to be measured in every one of these also, how could the result be pooled into any sort of average? Shall all sports mainly dependent on the "eye" as cricket, tennis, billiards, etc. be reckoned as one ability? Or as a myriad? … In a rough way, no doubt, a person can be said to have had much success at such sports as he has attempted. But there appears no serious

prospect of calculating his "S.Q." to several places of decimals, and then piling upon this result a mass of higher "mathematics." (p. 69).

If some doubt exists as to Spearman's (1927) perspective on mental measurement and the absurdity of the concept of FSIQ, consider his further statement:

> As for the prevalent procedure of throwing a miscellaneous collection of tests indiscriminately into a single pool this—whether or not justifiable by the theory which gave birth to it—certainly cannot be justified simply by claiming that the results give a "general level," and "average," or even a "sample." No genuine averaging, or sampling, of anybody's abilities is made, can be made, or even has really been attempted. When Binet borrowed the idea of such promiscuous pooling, he carried it into execution with a brilliancy that perhaps no other living man could have matched. But on the theoretical side, he tried to get away too cheaply. And this is the main cause of all the present trouble. (pp. 70–71)

Spearman (1927) also was very adamant on the matter of *g*; it represented a relative quality inherent in any test of mental ability, but its nature remained unknown and unexplained:

> But notice must be taken that this general factor *g*, like all measurements anywhere, is primarily not any concrete thing but only a value or magnitude. Further, that which this magnitude measures has not been defined by declaring what it is like, but only by pointing out where it can be found. It consists in just that constituent—whatever it may be—which is common to all the abilities inter-connected by the tetrad equation . . . . Eventually, we may or may not find reason to conclude that *g* measures something that can appropriately be called "intelligence." Such a conclusion however, would still never be the definition of *g*, but only a "statement about" it. (pp. 75–76)

Modern-day proponents of *g*, such as L. S. Gottfredson (1997, 1998, 2008), would say that in fact we have found reason to conclude that *g* measures something that can be called intelligence. They would argue therefore that a highly *g*-saturated FSIQ would be preferred to an FSIQ that offers "broad coverage" of multiple domains. Wechsler himself, however, did not believe that the concept of *g* was synonymous with general intelligence and therefore argued against the idea of creating an intelligence test based on a collection of highly *g*-saturated tasks. He believed that intelligence was best represented as an amalgam of multiple abilities and that a test of general intelligence should sample as many different domains as possible. Exactly how many different domains of ability exist and which of those should be included in a test of intelligence, however, were never really clearly articulated by Wechsler (1944). He did believe that his test included a sufficient number of tasks assessing multiple domains. Most important, he believed that the incorporation of the performance subtests was a unique feature that enabled the Wechsler scales to offer a broader sampling of general intelligence and therefore an FSIQ based on all subtests that would represent the best measure of a person's intelligence.

Perhaps out of respect for Wechsler's original ideas, the stewards of his test initially resisted, and then only grudgingly accepted, the need to consider offering clinicians an alternative to the FSIQ that is based on the idea that a measure highly saturated in *g* may be the best representation of general intelligence. Starting with the WISC–IV, the test publisher acquiesced to requests for a General Ability Index that was comprised only of the subtests of the Verbal Comprehension Index and the Perceptual Reasoning Index. I made the argument for this index while a senior research associate and clinical advisor to the Wechsler test development group during the development of the WISC–IV. The argument was based on the fact that gifted children typically performed much better on the Verbal Comprehension Index and the Perceptual Reasoning Index than they did on the Working Memory Index and Processing Speed Index and, conversely, that intellectually disabled children

typically performed better on the Working Memory Index and Processing Speed Index than on the Verbal Comprehension Index and the Perceptual Reasoning Index. A technical report was issued enabling clinicians to derive the General Ability Index (Raiford, Weiss, Rolfhus, & Coalson, 2005), but this technical report remained a well-hidden secret to many in the field. When the WAIS–IV was published, a General Ability Index was provided but mentioned only in the *WAIS–IV Technical and Interpretive Manual* (Wechsler, 2008). Moreover, the General Ability Index norm tables were buried in the middle of the *WAIS–IV Technical and Interpretive Manual* rather than included with the other index score norm tables in the *WAIS–IV Administration and Scoring Manual* (Wechsler, 2008).

The WISC–V also includes a General Ability Index based on the subtests of the Verbal Comprehension Index and the Fluid Reasoning Index and one subtest from the Visual Spatial Index, but the developers seem hardly able to hide their disdain for the existence of this measure, again burying it in the *WISC–V Administration and Scoring Manual Supplement* rather than featuring it prominently in the norm tables of the *WISC–V Administration and Scoring Manual* (Wechsler, 2014).

It would seem that there is a very real distinction between the globalist interpreters who side with Wechsler and view the FSIQ as representing at least a sampling of a wide variety of abilities and the globalists who follow Spearman's original ideas about *g* and Jensen's update of these ideas and believe that a highly *g* saturated measure, such as the General Ability Index, is a better indicator of general intelligence.

By offering an FSIQ that draws from at least five different subdomains of ability, it would appear that the WISC–V development team chose to honor Wechsler's original ideas about FSIQ; but the fact that the WISC–V FSIQ is based on only seven subtests seems out of step with Wechsler's original conception of what should comprise the FSIQ. Perhaps a compromise was needed here, but why seven subtests? Why not at least 10? Even better, why not 16? I fear that this decision was based on clinicians' demands for shorter tests rather than on any sound theoretical premise. The FSIQ emphasis in interpretation does in fact defer to Wechsler's original ideas. While perhaps it is laudable, in one sense, to reflect Wechsler's original notions, it would seem that the development team missed a chance to address in a more coherent manner the issue of what really constitutes a global estimate of intelligence. The need for a broader perspective is hinted at but not really articulated clearly. For example, as noted previously, a General Ability Index is provided, and the manual describes some situations in which the General Ability Index might be a useful measure. Additionally, another global measure—the Nonverbal Index—is provided with statements about situations in which it may be a useful estimate of general intelligence.

Given the split in the globalist perspective on FSIQ interpretation, the developers may have better served the needs of a greater number of clinicians by viewing the traditional Wechsler FSIQ as just one of several options for providing a global estimate of general intelligence. Instead of addressing only the FSIQ as the first tier of interpretation, they could have suggested choosing the best global estimate that would fit the needs of the clinical context. Doing this would not have been that much of a stretch, given that the manual discusses using other index scores to represent general intelligence at various points.

Choosing a global estimate of intelligence would mean selecting from among the FSIQ, the General Ability Index, and the Nonverbal Index. Some *g* theorists may even argue that the General Ability Index would have been a stronger measure of *g* if it did not include the Block Design subtest of the Visual Spatial Index. Likewise, from a *g* theory perspective, the Nonverbal Index could have been constructed without Picture Span or Visual Puzzles and could have included Picture Concepts instead. This at least would have provided some clear justification for inclusion of the Picture Concepts subtest in the battery. Table 19.2 presents the global interpretation options.

Table 19.2   Global Interpretation Options

Traditional Wechsler Model	*g* Model
FSIQ	General Ability Index
Similarities, Vocabulary, Matrix Reasoning, Figure Weights, Block Design, Digit Span, and Coding	Similarities, Vocabulary, Matrix Reasoning, and Figure Weights
	Cognitive Proficiency Index (General Ability Index Contrast)
	Digit Span, Picture Span, Coding, and Symbol Search
Nonverbal Index	*g* Nonverbal Index
Matrix Reasoning, Figure Weights, Block Design, Visual Puzzles, Picture Span, and Coding	Matrix Reasoning, Figure Weights, Picture Concepts, and Block Design

WHY ARE SOME INDEXES PRIMARY, SOME ANCILLARY, SOME COMPLEMENTARY, AND SOME NONEXISTENT?

The WISC–V represents a significant advance in thinking at the index level. The four primary indexes of the WISC–IV have been expanded to five, and other clinically relevant indexes have been added. After consideration of the global FSIQ, emphasis is placed only on the interpretation of the five primary indexes. At the ancillary level of interpretation, clinicians find a hodgepodge of indexes; some are dyads, similar to the primary indexes but containing one subtest used in the five primary indexes; others are the global contenders that could be applied in specific situations when the clinician thinks that the FSIQ needs to be qualified in order to effectively describe general intellectual functioning. As noted earlier, three of these indexes, the Nonverbal Index, the General Ability Index, and the Cognitive Proficiency Index (*g* contrast) could have been included at the global interpretation level as viable alternatives to the FSIQ; that is, valid representations of a general level of intellectual functioning.

One puzzling aspect of the construction of the primary indexes is why Similarities and Vocabulary were combined to produce an index that lacks the kind of homogeneity represented in the other four indexes. Additionally, why not make use of the excellent subtests that are available to create other empirically sound indexes? There certainly is substantial evidence from both the neuropsychological literature (Banich, 2004; Dehaene, 2014; Frakowiak, Friston, Frith, Dolan, & Mazziotta, 1997; Gazzaniga, 2000; Luria, 1980; Rapp, 2001; Temple, 1997) and the factor-analytic literature (especially Carroll's (1993a) work) to justify an index structure such as the one proposed in Table 19.3.

This index structure uses all of the subtests except the five complementary subtests and offers

Table 19.3 Possible Index Structure Based on the 16 Subtests

Index	Subtest Composition
RVI: Reasoning with Verbal Information	Similarities, Comprehension
RLTI: Retrieval from Long-Term Storage	Vocabulary, Information
RNVI: Reasoning with Nonverbal Visual Information	Matrix Reasoning, Picture Concepts
RQI: Reasoning with Quantitative Information	Figure Weights, Arithmetic
VSI: Visual Spatial	Block Design, Visual Puzzles
WMI: Working Memory	Digit Span, Picture Span
PSI: Processing Speed	Coding, Symbol Search
AWMI: Auditory Working Memory	Digit Span, Letter–Number Sequencing
IVM: Immediate Visual Memory	Picture Span, Cancellation

a broad view of intellectual functioning across a maximum number of ability domains.

WHY DOES THE TEST INCLUDE SUBTESTS THAT DO NOT CONTRIBUTE TO ANY INDEX?

The interpretive structure outlined in the *WISC–V Technical and Interpretive Manual* makes no mention of what to do with the subtests that are not used in construction of any of the indexes. These include the Information, Comprehension, Picture Concepts, and Cancellation subtests. In the modified index model presented earlier, this problem would be solved. As it stands in the manual, clinicians are left wondering why these subtests are part of the test battery but seem to have no specific purpose. Obviously great care was put into revising these subtests and ensuring that they are solid measures. Surely the time and cost expended in the development of these four subtests was not done merely to ensure that "alternate" subtests are available in case administration of an FSIQ subtest is spoiled in some way. That would be an unconscionable extravagance. Ignoring the potential contributions of these subtests to a comprehensive assessment battery and to index-level interpretive options is truly baffling.

WHAT'S THE DIFFERENCE BETWEEN AN ABILITY AND A PROCESS?

During my first reading of *Carroll's Human Cognitive Abilities* in 1994, I was intrigued by Carroll's (1993a) efforts to define the words *ability* and *process* in an introductory chapter but disappointed to find that the definitions were simply circular in nature. This disappointment launched me on a 10-year research project to define these terms meaningfully in a more neuropsychologically oriented manner. The fruits of this project (though not necessarily the explanation of the neuropsychological basis of the definitions) are offered in Chapter 36 of the third edition of *Contemporary Intellectual Assessment* (McCloskey, Whitaker, Murphy, & Rogers, 2012).

In short, a *process* is a narrowly focused capacity produced by a small set of neural networks responsible for some aspect of creating a meaningful mental representation of stimuli that can be further acted upon in mind. When a process network is not functioning properly, the resulting process deficit impedes, but does not prevent, specific types of new learning. The best example of a process described in the neuropsychological literature would be the neural networks that are responsible for sub–word sound unit phonological processing. When these networks are disrupted, the resulting process deficit leads to difficulties with learning how to decode words, a condition most often referred to as dyslexia.

In contrast, an *ability* involves a much larger number of neural networks functioning in concert to act on the mental representations that result from the use of processes. Examples of abilities are our language, reasoning, and visuospatial capacities. Ability deficits are more pervasive in their effect on cognition and more difficult to alter because they involve such a wide variety of neural networks in their activity. An example of this would be a severe deficit in the ability to reason with language, which is typically classified as a form of intellectual disability, and one that affects in a very broad manner the development of both listening and reading comprehension and the ability to write in a manner that reflects the use of reasoning with language.

Although specific noncircular definitions such as those offered here may not be widely accepted within psychology and education, there seems to be some type of distinction between them that is implied in the names of some tests. For example, a test of basic processes related to reading and writing has been titled *Process Assessment of the Learner–Second Edition*

(PAL–II; Berninger, 2007) whereas a measure of intelligence intended to compete with the WISC series was titled *Differential Ability Scales* (Elliott, 1990, 2007). More important, some kind of distinction between an ability and a process, though still not explicitly defined, became the basis for several distinguishing statements in the *WISC–V Technical and Interpretive Manual* and was used to explain the somewhat mystifying inclusion of the five WISC–V complementary subtests. Throughout the manual, the subtests included in primary and ancillary indexes are referred to as measures of ability. In descriptions of each of the five complementary subtests, the *WISC–V Technical and Interpretive Manual* offers the following statement: "This subtest was not designed as a measure of intelligence but as a measure of cognitive processes" (Wechsler, 2014, pp. 13–14). It seems that, at least in the minds of the developers of the WISC–V, there certainly is a difference between an ability and a process, and that distinction is critical enough to deem only one of them a component of intelligence. Given the statements made that qualify the nature of the complementary subtests, one wonders why they are even there. A group of surprise offerings for your enjoyment, compliments of the chef! There is no question that Naming Speed Literacy and Naming Speed Quantity are excellent measures that can be critical components in the assessment of children suspected of having specific learning disabilities in reading, writing, or math; but why are they part of the WISC–V instead of the WPPSI–IV or a version of the PAL–II that would start at age 4?

Declaring cognitive processes to be beneath consideration for inclusion in measures of intelligence seems out of step with Wechsler's original position that as many different mental capacities as possible be represented in a global estimate of intelligence. It also seems inconsistent with the inclusion of Digit Span and Coding in the FSIQ and of Digit Span, Picture Span, Coding, and Symbol Search in the primary indexes. And what are we to make of the pattern of strengths and weaknesses discrepancy analysis procedure used to help with the identification of specific learning disabilities that requires the identification of processing strengths and weaknesses as represented in the form of WISC–V index scores? Is there a difference between a process and an ability? And what is the definition of processing? It seems that it is time for the field of mental measurement to come to grips with defining these basic constructs. Unfortunately, the WISC–V nomenclature obscures rather than clarifies our understanding of them.

IS COGNITION THE SAME THING AS INTELLIGENCE, AND IF THEY ARE NOT THE SAME, WHICH ONE IS THE WISC–V MEASURING?

The sheer number of options for interpretation can pose many interpretive puzzles that must be solved in order to ensure that test results accurately characterize something important about a child's mental functioning. One of these puzzles is to decide whether the scores derived from the WISC–V represent measures of intellectual functioning based on a factor-analytic perspective or measures of cognition from a neuropsychological perspective.

It would seem that the WISC–V has opted for the measurement of intelligence rather than the measurement of cognition. Although the *WISC–V Technical and Interpretive Manual* states that the WISC–V interpretive structure reflects a neuropsychological as well as a factor-analytic perspective, it is very clear that the factor-analytic perspective drives the majority of ideas about interpretation. Emphasis is placed on the order of interpretation, moving from the Full scale to the primary index level and then on to the ancillary and complementary index levels. At the subtest level, clinicians are provided with yardsticks for indicating significant differences and base rates for differences between subtests within indexes or simply noting subtest strengths and weaknesses in relation to an arithmetic mean based on the average

of certain subtest combinations. Additional subtest-level information is provided in the form of process scores and some process observations are quantified, but the interpretive emphasis is clearly in line with current structural theories of intelligence, such as the Cattell-Horn-Carroll (CHC) theory based on Carroll's factor-analytic studies. The interpretive approach espoused in the manual locks subtests into a rigid framework that may fail to accurately characterize the mental capacities of many children whose performance does not fit the preconceived mold.

Unlike the measurement of intelligence that emphasizes a global score and index scores thought to represent factor-analytically derived broad ability domains, the measurement of cognition from a neuropsychological perspective emphasizes how mental activity emerges from the use of multiple neural networks. Mental constructs are based on observable variation in the performance of neural networks and the occurrence of double dissociations that indicate that while specific mental activities often may occur in tandem, they in fact are separate mental capacities because cases can be found wherein a child can perform well with one activity and poorly with another, and vice versa. As a result, subtest-level interpretation becomes critical in understanding a child's performance and necessitates a clearly articulated model of what each subtest measures, how subtests may be combined to form clinically meaningful clusters, and how observations of performance can inform interpretation regarding what a subtest is or is not measuring in a specific case. Major differences in the factor-analytic intelligence and neuropsychological approaches to assessment can be seen in the structural diagrams provided in Figures 19.2 and 19.3.

As shown in Figure 19.2, the domains assessed by the factor-analytic model are much narrower than those assessed by the cognitive neuropsychological model. The cognitive neuropsychological model has the benefit of addressing domains based not only on the norm-referenced scores but also on the process-oriented observations

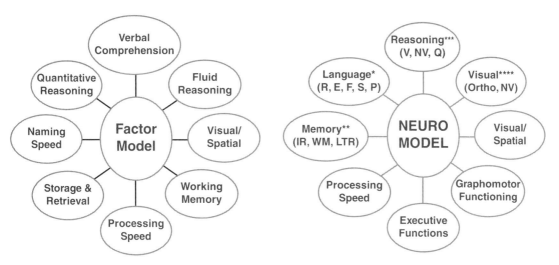

*R = Receptive, E = Expressive, F = Fluency, S = Speed, P = Phonological
**IR = Initial Registration, WM = Working Memory, LTR = Retrieval from Long Term Storage
***V = Verbal; NV = Nonverbal; Q = Quantitative
****Ortho = Orthography; NV = Nonverbal

Figure 19.2   Domains in the factor-analytic model of intelligence

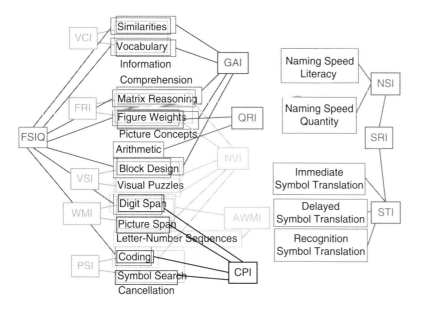

Figure 19.3   Domains in the neuropsychological approach to assessment

made by the clinician. This strength allows the model to incorporate information beyond the test scores, enabling assessment of the elusive factors that Wechsler believed to be beyond description with only numbers, yet so critical in getting the right picture of a client's mental capacities and functioning.

Many of the critical constructs within the cognitive neuropsychological model have been of great interest to researchers and clinicians since the early years of mental testing. Spearman (1927) offered this observation about factors that emerged in his studies of mental abilities:

> Still another great functional unity has revealed its existence; this, although not in itself of cognitive nature, yet has a dominating influence upon all exercise or even estimation of cognitive ability. On trying to express it by any current name, perhaps the least unsatisfactory—though still seriously misleading—would be "self-control." It has shown itself to be chiefly responsible for the fact of one person's ability seeming to be more "profound" or more inclined to "common sense" than that of persons otherwise equally capable. (p. 413)

As early as 1927, Spearman was grappling with the influence of frontal lobe executive functions on the performance of standardized intelligence tests. It appears that Walter Mischel's (2014) work with the marshmallow test in the 1960s could have helped Spearman gain greater insight into this elusive concept he called self-control. A neurocognitive model enables clinicians to factor into the picture the effects of mental constructs such as executive functions (self-control) on the performance of cognitive tasks.

Additionally, although Spearman (1927) believed strongly in the unitary nature of g, he was able to see that the possibility existed that the statistical analyses that revealed g to be a unitary trait may be hiding a deeper reality:

> The foregoing physiological considerations forcibly bring up the question as to whether the universal factor g can, or cannot ... be composed of *two or more* sub-factors (universal or otherwise). . . .
>
> There are, however, certain cases where the g does admit of resolution into a plurality of sub-factors.
>
> One such case is where these are fixedly inter-linked, as occurs when one of them acts through the medium of the other. (p. 93, emphasis in original)

Hmm. Say, perhaps as in the case of mental capacities that may travel together through specific parts of neural networks but then travel their own separate paths beyond a specific point? Such musings seem to suggest that the neuropsychological nature of cognitive functioning needs to be given prominence over the mathematical calculations based on the products of these neural networks in action. It would seem that to really understand the cognitive functioning of a child, it is critical to observe carefully while conducting the assessment the behavior of the child and use that information to understand scores derived from the norm-referenced administration and scoring procedures in a manner akin to that used by A. R. Luria, the results of which were summarized in his phenomenal opus, *Higher Cortical Functions in Man* (1966a, 1980). Through careful observation, Luria was able to single-handedly match the neuropsychological research output of the entire Western scientific community, as acknowledged by Hans-Lukas Teuber in his preface to Luria's masterpiece:

> Quantification is a major strength of the British and American traditions in psychology. If a book like Professor Luria's had been written here, it would teem with means and standard deviations, not to speak of analyses of variance and covariance. Yet the sobering fact is that most of Professor Luria's conclusions would not be changed if he had chosen to use these refinements. His own enormous clinical experience and his intuitive sense for what are reasonable interpretations are playing for him the role of large sample statistics. (Luria, 1966a, p. xiii)

The good news here is that the WISC–V provides an exceptionally well-developed set of 21 subtests that can be used by experienced clinicians who are competent in the use of a cognitive neuropsychological approach to interpretation. Clinicians cannot just rely on the *WISC–V Technical and Interpretive Manual* for much in the way of guidance when applying this interpretive perspective.

I know that the cognitive neuropsychological approach to interpretation often is maligned because statistical analyses seem unable to support it in the way that they can support the factor-analytic approach. This may be true at this point in time, but statistical analyses are not the only way to confirm or validate an interpretive approach. Results are the most critical method.

The following analogy may help skeptics to appreciate what can be accomplished with a cognitive neuropsychological approach. One of our cars was making a very strange noise so we took it to a recommended repair shop. The mechanics drove the car into the bay and attached it to a computer that provided a readout of the codes indicating what was wrong with the car. Based on the computer printout, the mechanics replaced certain parts and drove the car out of the bay. When driving home, the car began to make the same noise. We returned to the shop and told the mechanics about our problem. They were steadfast in their belief that they had fixed the car because they had followed every one of the recommendations on the computer analysis printout. But when I asked them, "Did you drive the car?" they looked perplexed and replied that they had not. I implored them to please drive the car, and then we would talk. The chief mechanic grudgingly complied with my request. Ten minutes later as he pulled back into the parking area, he confidently stated, "Yes, I heard the noise and I know exactly what I need to do to fix it!"

As factor-analytic models become more prominent as the scientifically backed methods for interpretation of assessment results, as computer scoring and interpretation programs become the norm, and as pressure increases to reduce time spent in assessment activities, I fear clinicians will become more like the mechanics who only drive the car into the bay and hook it up to the computer to find out what is wrong when what they really need to do in some situations is give it a test drive and trust their experience and clinical acumen to guide them in the diagnosis and remediation of problems. In psychological assessment, careful observation and understanding of the child, the teacher, and the parents very often is critical in getting the picture right. Hopefully as we transition into the future of iPad administrations and immediate access to computer-generated interpretive printouts, we will not lose touch with the ability to see what we need to see and to connect with the children we assess with clarity and compassion.

CHAPTER 20

REVIEW OF THE WECHSLER INTELLIGENCE SCALE FOR CHILDREN–FIFTH EDITION: CRITIQUE, COMMENTARY, AND INDEPENDENT ANALYSES

Gary L. Canivez and Marley W. Watkins

WISC–V REVIEW

Description

The Wechsler Intelligence Scale for Children–Fifth Edition (WISC–V; Wechsler, 2014) is the latest edition of Wechsler's test of child intelligence with its origin dating back to the first Wechsler Intelligence Scale for Children (WISC; Wechsler, 1949). The WISC–V is a major revision of the Wechsler Intelligence Scale for Children–Fourth Edition (WISC–IV; Wechsler, 2003) with national standardization for youth ages 6 to 16 years. The WISC–V includes an *Administration and Scoring Manual*, an *Administration and Scoring Manual Supplement*; a *Technical and Interpretive Manual*; three stimulus books; a Record Form; two response booklets (Coding and Symbol Search [Response Booklet 1], Cancellation [Response Booklet 2]); a scoring key for Symbol Search, scoring templates for Coding and for Cancellation; and the standard Block Design set. While the *WISC–V Administration and Scoring Manual* includes norms and analyses tables for the Summary and Primary Analysis pages, norms and analysis tables for the Ancillary and Complementary Analysis and Process Analysis pages are included in the *WISC–V Administration and Scoring Manual Supplement*.

Pearson also makes available a *WISC–V Technical and Interpretive Manual Supplement: Special Group Validity Studies with Other Measures and Additional Tables* (Pearson, 2014), which is available as a free download at http://downloads.pearsonclinical.com/images/Assets/WISC-V/WISC-V-Tech-Manual-Supplement.pdf. Within this supplement are full correlation matrices and descriptive statistics by age. This is a welcome addition and a positive contrast to the WISC–IV[UK]; there the publisher did not provide a technical manual disclosing psychometric characteristics of the UK standardization sample; the publisher also refused to make available standardization sample correlation matrices and descriptive statistics necessary for fully understanding the psychometric characteristics of WISC–IV[UK] scores (Canivez, Watkins, James, James, & Good, 2014).

As with earlier editions, the WISC–V includes numerous subtests that provide estimates of general intelligence consistent with Wechsler's "global capacity" definition of intelligence (Wechsler, 1939, p. 229) but also are combined to measure various group factors. The WISC–V, like the WISC–IV, overlaps in age with the *Wechsler Preschool and Primary Scale of Intelligence–Fourth Edition* (WPPSI–IV; Wechsler, 2012) (age 6 years through 7 years 7 months) and the *Wechsler Adult Intelligence*

Scale–Fourth Edition (WAIS–IV; Wechsler, 2008) (age 16 years) to allow clinicians the opportunity to select the more appropriate instrument depending on referral question and child characteristics.

Development

The *WISC–V Technical and Interpretive Manual* notes that revision goals included updating theoretical foundations, increasing developmental appropriateness, increasing user-friendliness, improving psychometric properties, and enhancing clinical utility and that these goals were based on considerations of structural models of intelligence, neurodevelopmental and neurocognitive research, psychometric results, clinical utility, and clinicians' practical needs. Subsequently, around 15 pages of text were devoted to an explication of evidence to justify each goal. Although not explicitly mentioned, this revision's recent normative sample removes the threat of normative obsolescence (Wasserman & Bracken, 2013).

Evolution of the Wechsler scales based on references to intelligence structure suggested by J. B. Carroll (1993a, 2003, 2012), Cattell and Horn (1978), Horn (1991), and Horn and Blankson (2012) denote a hierarchical structure with general intelligence and group factors of verbal comprehension (VC), visual spatial (VS), fluid reasoning (FR), working memory (WM), and processing speed (PS) that is consistent with what has come to be known as Cattell-Horn-Carroll (CHC; McGrew, 1997, 2005) theory. Thus, measurement of intelligence by the WISC–V continues to include narrow ability subtests (16), group factors (5), and general intelligence (Spearman, 1927).

Modifications and simplification of instructions and item phrasing were reportedly studied in children ages 4:6 to 5:11 and incorporated in the WISC–V. The number of demonstration, sample, and teaching items were increased. The number of items with time bonuses was reduced. Discontinue rules within subtests were reduced,

and for most primary and secondary subtests it is now three consecutive zero-point responses. Test stimuli included in the stimulus books are attractive, in full color, and visually engaging. Materials also appear to be of high quality and likely to withstand the demands of frequent use without significant deterioration. The *WISC–V Administration and Scoring Manual*, like other recent editions, includes the crack-back binding to allow the manual to stand during administration.

Word Reasoning and Picture Completion subtests from the WISC–IV were eliminated, and Visual Puzzles and Figure Weights (present in the WAIS–IV) and Picture Span (adapted from Picture Memory in the WPPSI–IV) were added. Five "complementary scale" subtests (Naming Speed Literacy, Naming Speed Quantity, Immediate Symbol Translation, Delayed Symbol Translation, and Recognition Symbol Translation) were added but are not measures of intelligence. Subtests retained from the WISC–IV had administration, item content, and scoring changes. It was reported that all retained subtests had both low-difficulty and high-difficulty items added to achieve adequate floor and ceiling levels.

Organization and subtest administration order of the WISC–V reflects a new four-level organization. At the Full scale level, the FSIQ is composed of seven primary subtests across the five domains: Verbal Comprehension, Visual Spatial, Fluid Reasoning, Working Memory, and Processing Speed; if one of the FSIQ subtests is invalid or missing, a secondary subtest from within the same domain may be substituted. Only one substitution is allowed. Administration of these seven subtests should take around 50 minutes. The primary index scale level is composed of 10 WISC–V subtests (primary subtests), which are used to estimate the five WISC–V factor index scores: Verbal Comprehension Index, Visual Spatial Index, Fluid Reasoning Index, Working Memory Index, and Processing Speed Index . No substitutions are allowed for the primary index scales. Administering the 10 primary subtests should take around 65 minutes. The ancillary index level is composed of five scales that are not factorially derived—Quantitative Reasoning, Auditory Working Memory, Nonverbal, General Ability, and Cognitive Proficiency—and reflect various combinations of primary and secondary subtests. The Complementary Index level is composed of three scales—Naming Speed, Symbol Translation, and Storage and Retrieval—derived from the newly created complementary subtests: Naming Speed Literacy, Naming Speed Quantity, Immediate Symbol Translation, Delayed Symbol Translation, and Recognition Symbol Translation. Complementary subtests are not intelligence subtests and may not be substituted for primary or secondary subtests.

In prior versions of the WISC, the FSIQ was based on 10 subtests; the WISC–V FSIQ is based on seven subtests. Additionally, the subtests that comprise the FSIQ differ between the WISC–IV and WISC–V: Only six of the WISC–V FSIQ subtests were used to compute the WISC–IV FSIQ. Similar changes in the underlying composition of the WISC–III and WISC–IV were noted and generated the caution that "research findings with previous WISCs are now less generalizable to the WISC–IV" (A. S. Kaufman, Flanagan, Alfonso, & Mascolo, 2006, p. 281). That caution can now be extended to the WISC–V. Although the general intelligence construct appears to be robust to changes in subtest composition (Johnson, te Nijenhuis, & Bouchard, 2008), the resulting measured FSIQ scores may differ (Floyd, Clark, & Shadish, 2008). This difference may be especially important when FSIQ scores are applied in high-stakes situations, such as Atkins cases (Taub, 2014).

Interpretation

The *WISC–V Administration and Scoring Manual* provides detailed and annotated descriptions of the sequential procedures (with examples) of transformation of raw scores to scaled scores and scaled scores to standard scores. It also explains the methods for calculating deviations (with

examples) and use of tables for statistical significance and base rates (where available). Such detail should allow clinicians ample instruction for such critical derivations.

WISC–V interpretation considerations and methods presented in the manual begin with reporting and describing performance of the individual using the standard scores that indicate how the child performed relative to same-age peers. Percentile ranks, confidence intervals based on standard errors of measurement, and qualitative descriptors of performance further describe the child's performance. These are normative (nomothetic) interpretations. The qualitative descriptors in the WISC–V have changed from the traditional Wechsler qualitative descriptors and likely will be favorably received. The new descriptors are now symmetrical in terminology ranging from extremely high to extremely low. Terms of borderline, superior, and very superior have been abandoned.

The remaining analyses and interpretations are intra-individual comparisons (comparing the child's performance on different scales) and dependent on statistical significance of score differences (alpha levels now provided for .01, .05, .10, and .15), by age group or the overall sample. Primary index score strengths and weaknesses are ipsative comparisons, and the scores can be either compared to the mean primary index score or to the FSIQ. Users select the alpha level for the comparisons, which ranges from .01 to .15. Base rates for differences in the population can be based either on the overall sample or by ability level. Subtest score strengths and weaknesses are also ipsative comparisons, and subtest scores can be compared to the mean of all 10 primary subtest scores or the mean of the seven FSIQ subtests. Users also select the alpha level for comparisons, which ranges from .01 to .15. Pairwise difference scores can be calculated for all possible combinations of the five primary index scores (10 comparisons) with statistical significance of the difference based on the user-selected alpha level (.01–.15). Pairwise differences also have population base rates based on either the overall sample or ability level. There are also five specific subtest-level pairwise comparisons examining the difference between each of the two subtest indicators of the primary index scores; statistical significance is dependent on the user-selected alpha level (.01–.15).

Ancillary index scores may also be derived and reported as standard scores and include percentile rank, confidence intervals based on standard errors of measurement, and qualitative descriptors. Like the primary index scores, ancillary index scores are normative (nomothetic) interpretations. Four ancillary index score pairwise comparisons are provided with statistical significance based on user-selected alpha (.01–.15) and also include population base rates. Six ancillary index subtest pairwise comparisons may be calculated and also utilize user-selected alpha (.01–.15) and population base rates.

Complementary index scales may also be derived as subtest standard scores, and their combinations provide for three complementary index composite scores, which include percentile rank and confidence intervals. Last, there are a host of process scores and analyses including pairwise comparisons and base rates.

Analyses for specific learning disability identification include description of ability-achievement discrepancy (AAD) analysis with a preference for using regression-based discrepancy rather than the simple difference method. Learning disability identification using the pattern of strengths and weaknesses (PSW) is also described.

Technical Qualities

Standardization
The *WISC–V Technical and Interpretive Manual* includes detailed and extensive information regarding standardization procedures and the normative sample of 2,200 children between the ages of 6 and 16 years with 100 boys and 100 girls at each age level. Raw score to scaled score conversions are reported by 3-month blocks in the *WISC–V Administration and Scoring*

Manual so that approximately 67 children are included in each 3-month block, well above the minimum number of 30 to 50 suggested by researchers (Kranzler & Floyd, 2013; Zhu & Chen, 2011). Normative data were collected between April 2013 and March 2014 and stratified according to the October 2012 U.S. census data to achieve proportional representation across key demographic variables of age, sex, race/ethnicity, parent education level (a proxy for socioeconomic status), and geographic region. Additionally, a representative proportion of children with special education diagnoses (developmental delay = 0.6%; intellectual disability = 1.6%; specific learning disability = 1.7%; speech/language impairment = 1.5%; attention-deficit/hyperactivity disorder = 1.1%; gifted/talented = 1.7%) were included and accounted for around 8% to 10% of the children in each age group. Table 3.1 of the *WISC–V Technical and Interpretive Manual* presents exclusionary criteria that prevented individuals from being included in the normative sample. Tables 3.2 through 3.5 illustrate close approximation to population percentages supporting generalizability to the United States as a whole.

Primary and secondary subtest scaled scores (mean $[M] = 10$, standard deviation $[SD] = 3$, Range = 1 to 19) for each of the age groups were derived from an inferential norming procedure using raw score means, *SDs*, and skewness estimates that were examined from linear through fourth-order polynomial regressions with comparison to theoretical distributions and growth curve patterns that produced percentiles for each raw score. Smoothing (method not disclosed) eliminated minor irregularities of scaled score progression. Item gradients (e.g., the change in scaled score created by a 1-point increase in raw scores) for the primary subtests were adequate per the standards provided by Wasserman and Bracken (2013).

Standard scores ($M = 100$, $SD = 15$) are used for all composite scores (FSIQ, primary index scores, ancillary index scores, complementary index scores) and complementary subtests.

Composite scores for the five primary index scales, ancillary index scales (except Nonverbal, General Ability, and Cognitive Proficiency), and complementary index scales range from 45 to 155, and the FSIQ, Nonverbal, General Ability, and Cognitive Proficiency composite scores range from 40 to 160. Thus, the floors and ceilings for composite scores are 3.7 to 4.0 *SDs*. Given these floors, index scores should be adequate for identification of children with mild to moderate intellectual disabilities but may be inadequate for children with severe to profound intellectual disabilities (Wasserman & Bracken, 2013). These ceilings should allow identification of most candidates for gifted programs but may not be adequate for identification of exceptionally gifted children (Wasserman & Bracken, 2013). Item gradients for the primary index scales were generally within acceptable limits except at the floors of the Fluid Reasoning and Working Memory index scores.

Age-equivalent scores are also provided despite the caution in the *WISC–V Technical and Interpretive Manual* of "common misinterpretation and psychometric limitations" (p. 53) and the long-standing admonitions against using them. Given the many weaknesses of age-equivalent scores and the potential for misuse, it might be advantageous to no longer provide them to examiners.

Reliability

Reliability estimates of WISC–V scores reported in the *WISC–V Technical and Interpretive Manual* were derived using three methods: internal consistency, test-retest (stability), and inter-scorer agreement. Internal consistency estimates were produced by Spearman-Brown corrected split-half correlations for all subtests except Coding, Symbol search, Cancellation, Naming Speed Literacy, Naming Speed Quantity, Immediate Symbol Translation, and Delayed Symbol Translation, as these are speeded tests. For these subtests, the short-term test-retest (stability) method was used to estimate reliability. Table 4.1 in the *WISC–V Technical and Interpretive Manual*

presents internal consistency reliability estimates for the WISC–V primary and secondary subtests, process scores, and composite scores by age. Average coefficients across the 11 age groups for the composite scores ranged from .88 (Processing Speed Index) to .96 (FSIQ and General Ability Index) and were higher than those obtained for subtests and process scores; a typical and expected result.

WISC–V primary and secondary subtest internal consistency estimates ranged from .81 (Symbol Search) to .94 (Figure Weights) while process scores ranged from .80 (Digit Span Backward) to .88 (Block Design Partial). Internal consistency estimates across the 11 age groups ranged from .96 to .97 for the FSIQ, from .84 to 94 for primary index scores, from .91 to .96 for ancillary index scores, and from .75 to .93 for process scores. Reliability estimates for the complementary subtests, process, and composite scores are provided in Table 4.2 of the *WISC–V Technical and Interpretive Manual*. Average coefficients across the 11 age groups ranged from .90 to .94 for composite scores and from .82 to .89 for subtests and process scores. Internal consistency reliability coefficients ≥ .90 have been recommended for high-stakes decisions (Kranzler & Floyd, 2013), which arguably include decisions about diagnosis as well as decisions about remedial or tailored instructional interventions for individual children (Stone, Ye, Zhu, & Lane, 2010). The Figure Weights, Arithmetic, and Digit Span subtests met that standard. Among the primary index scores, only the Processing Speed Index failed to meet the .90 standard.

Standard errors of measurement based on reliability coefficients from Table 4.1 are presented in Table 4.4 of the *WISC–V Technical and Interpretive Manual* and are the basis for estimated true score confidence intervals reported in the *WISC–V Administration and Scoring Manual* Tables A.2 through A.7 and in the *WISC–V Administration and Scoring Manual Supplement* Tables C.1 to C.5 and C.7 to C.9. Formulae for the estimated true score confidence interval *and* the obtained score confidence interval are provided in the *WISC–V Technical and Interpretive Manual*. Those clinicians preferring to use the obtained score confidence interval (when interest is in estimating the true score *at the time of the evaluation* and not the long-term/future estimate [Glutting, McDermott, & Stanley, 1987]) should be able to produce them from the provided formula and the detailed example (p. 62). Due to the generally high reliability estimates in Table 4.1, estimated true score and obtained score confidence intervals will likely be quite close.

Reliability estimates in Table 4.1 and standard errors of measurement in Table 4.4 should be considered best-case estimates because they do not consider other major sources of error, such as transient error, administration error, or scoring error (Hanna, Bradley, & Holen, 1981), which influence test scores in clinical assessments. Another factor that must be considered is the extent to which subtest scores reflect portions of true score variance due to a hierarchical general intelligence factor *and* variance due to specific group factors because these sources of true score variance are conflated. Later in this chapter, model-based reliability estimates will be provided to illustrate the contrast with important consequences for interpretation.

Short-term test-retest stability estimates were provided for WISC–V scores where the WISC–V was twice administered to a sample of 218 children (demographic descriptive statistics are provided in the *WISC–V Technical and Interpretive Manual* Table 4.6) with retest intervals ranging 9 to 82 days ($M = 26$ days). Uncorrected stability coefficients were .91 for the FSIQ, .68 (Fluid Reasoning Index) to .91 (Verbal Comprehension Index) for primary index scores; .76 (Quantitative Reasoning Index) to .89 (General Ability Index) for ancillary index scores; and .63 (Picture Concepts) to .89 (Vocabulary) for primary and secondary subtests. Corrected (for variability) stability coefficients were slightly higher. Kranzler and Floyd (2013) also recommended that short-term

test-retest stability coefficients should be $\geq$ .90 for high-stakes decisions. Only the Vocabulary subtest along with the Verbal Comprehension Index, FSIQ, and General Ability Index met that standard. Mean differences across the retest interval were mostly small but reflected some practice effects, particularly for Processing Speed subtests (and the Processing Speed Index). Long-term stability (retest interval exceeding 1 year) estimates of the WISC–V were not expected to be included in the *WISC–V Technical and Interpretive Manual* but should be examined in the coming years. Not included in stability examinations were ipsative-based strengths and weaknesses or pairwise difference scores that are significant components of WISC–V interpretation.

Interscorer agreement was estimated by double-scoring most WISC–V subtests for all standardization sample record forms by two independent scorers. Because most WISC–V subtests have simple and objective criteria, interscorer agreement ranged from .97 to .99, which is extremely high. What is unknown is the degree to which clinicians not trained or employed by the test publisher achieve such impressive agreement when they administer and score the WISC–V because "there are innumerable sources of error in giving and scoring mental tests" (Terman, 1918, p. 33). Changes in standardized administration of cognitive tests, even something as minor as voice inflection, have been shown to influence test scores (D. Lee, Reynolds, & Willson, 2003). Likewise, examiner familiarity and examinee characteristics may impact test scores (Fuchs & Fuchs, 1986; Szarko, Brown, & Watkins, 2013). In fact, considerable evidence suggests that such positive results are improbable among clinicians. For example, a recent study revealed large examiner effects among 448 examiners who tested 2,783 children with the WISC–IV (McDermott, Watkins, & Rhoad, 2014), and there is a long history of examiner inaccuracy, especially on the verbal portions of Wechsler scales (Babad, Mann, & Mar-Hayim, 1975; Moon, Blakey, Gorsuch, &

Fantuzzo, 1991; Oakland, Lee, & Axelrod, 1975; Slate, Jones, Murray, & Coulter, 1993).

Validity

The *WISC–V Technical and Interpretive Manual* chapter on validity references *Standards for Educational and Psychological Testing* (American Educational Research Association [AERA], American Psychological Association [AP], & National Council on Measurement in Education [NCME], 1999), although the new edition of the *Standards* (AERA, APA, & NCME, 2014) preceded the WISC–V in publication and could have been used. Presentation of evidence for WISC–V validity was structured around the *Standards*, which reflect Messick's (1995) unified validity theory that prescribes evidence based on test content, response processes, internal structure, relations with other variables, and consequences of testing.

Validity evidence based on test content is a nonempirical approach. In the WISC–V, test content was reportedly informed through review of literature and item and subtest review by experts and advisory panel members (specialists in child psychology, neuropsychology, and/or learning disabilities), a list of which is provided in the *WISC–V Technical and Interpretive Manual*. Discussion of evidence based on response processes in the manual highlighted both retention of subtests from previous versions for which such evidence was claimed as well as interviewing children regarding their rationale for selecting responses or problem-solving strategies used to complete various items. Modifications to item content and instructions were noted as a result of these procedures.

Evidence based on internal structure is one of the most important aspects for construct validity in order to understand relations between subtests and their correspondence to theoretical and latent constructs. Two approaches to examination of the internal structure are exploratory factor analysis (EFA) and confirmatory factor analysis (CFA). EFA is the method of extracting latent factors from the correlation matrix of the indicators based on their convergent and divergent relationships and allows "the data to speak for themselves" (J. B. Carroll, 1995, p. 436). CFA is a method of proposing various theoretical measurement models and empirically testing which model (or models) best fits the data. EFA and CFA are considered complementary procedures, each answering somewhat different questions, and greater confidence in the latent factor structure is achieved when EFA and CFA are in agreement (Gorsuch, 1983). Further, J. B. Carroll (1995) and Reise (2012) noted that EFA procedures are particularly useful in suggesting possible models to be tested in CFA.

The *WISC–V Technical and Interpretive Manual* describes data supporting a priori hypotheses regarding subtest correlations reflecting convergent and divergent (discriminant) validity as evidence of construct validity within the internal structure section. The average correlations (Fisher transformations) and descriptive statistics for the total normative sample are presented in Table 5.1 of the manual. Several pages in the manual are devoted to description of how various subtests within the five primary factor indexes are moderately to highly correlated with each other, suggesting construct validity (convergent validity). Descriptions of lower correlations between subtests from different primary factors also illustrate construct validity (discriminant validity). However, regardless of the a priori hypotheses regarding these relationships and their differential correlations, full understanding of the complex relationships between all the subtests at the same time requires multivariate methods, such as EFA and CFA.

CFA reported in the *WISC–V Technical and Interpretive Manual* includes specification of numerous models starting with a one-factor model. All other models were higher order with a general intelligence factor indirectly influencing subtests via full mediation through two through five first-order factors. All CFA models are illustrated with subtest assignments to latent factors in Table 5.3 of the manual. Contemporary fit statistics were described and their meaning explained.

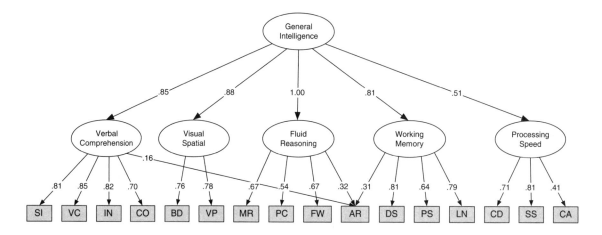

Figure 20.1 Higher-Order Measurement Model   Adapted from Figure 5.1 (Wechsler, 2014), with standardized coefficients for WISC–V normative sample (*N* = 2,200) , ages 6-16, for 16 primary and secondary subtests.
Note: SI = Similarities, VC = Vocabulary, IN = Information, CO = Comprehension, BD = Block Design, VP = Visual Puzzles, MR = Matrix Reasoning, PC = Picture Concepts, FW = Figure Weights, AR = Arithmetic, DS = Digit Span, PS = Picture Span, LN = Letter–Number Sequencing, CD = Coding, SS = Symbol Search, CA = Cancellation.

The standardized measurement model for the preferred five-factor higher-order (hierarchical) model for WISC–V primary and secondary subtests for the total normative sample is presented in Figure 5.1 of the WISC–V *Technical and Interpretive Manual* and adapted here as Figure 20.1. This "best-fitting" model includes a higher-order general intelligence dimension with five first-order factors (Verbal Comprehension, Visual Spatial, Fluid Reasoning, Working Memory, Processing Speed). The 16 subtest indicators are uniquely associated with one latent first-order factor except for Arithmetic, which was cross-loaded on Verbal Comprehension, Fluid Reasoning and Working Memory. This preferred measurement model includes a standardized path coefficient of 1.00 between the higher-order general intelligence factor and the Fluid Reasoning factor, which indicates that they are redundant. This final model was also reported to fit five different age groupings (6–7, 8–9, 10–11, 12–13, 14–16) equally well.

Finally, Figure 5.2 in the *WISC–V Technical and Interpretive Manual* illustrates the five-factor higher-order (hierarchical) model as applied to

only the 10 primary subtests. In this model there are no cross-loadings, and each first-order factor has two subtest indicators. Like the 16-subtest CFA, the standardized path coefficient of .99 between the higher-order general intelligence factor and the fluid reasoning factor indicates redundant dimensions.

Regardless of factor structure suggested by either EFA or CFA, models must be evaluated by comparisons to external criteria. Evidence based on relations with other variables presents numerous comparisons of the WISC–V with other measures of intelligence (WISC–IV [*n* = 242], WPPSI–IV [*n* = 105], WAIS–IV [*n* = 112], Kaufman Assessment Battery for Children–Second Edition [KABC–II; A. S. Kaufman & Kaufman, 2004; *n* = 89]), measures of academic achievement (Kaufman Test of Educational Achievement–Third Edition [KTEA–3; A. S. Kaufman & Kaufman, 2004; *n* = 207], Wechsler Individual Achievement Test–Third Edition [WIAT–III; Pearson, 2009a; *n* = 211]), a measure of adaptive behavior (Vineland Adaptive Behavior Scales–Second Edition [Vineland–II; Sparrow, Cicchetti, & Balla, 2005; *n* = 61]), and a measure of child behavior (Behavior Assessment System for Children–Second Edition Parent Rating Scales [BASC–2 PRS; Reynolds & Kamphaus, 2004; $n = 2,302$]) using nonclinical samples. With respect to comparisons of the WISC–V to other measures of intelligence, there appears to be good correspondence with moderate to high correlations between similar composite scores. The highest uncorrected correlations were observed between the WISC–V FSIQ and the WISC–IV FSIQ (.81), WPPSI–IV FSIQ (.74), WAIS–IV FSIQ (.84), and KABC–II MPI (.77). Comparisons between the WISC–V FSIQ and academic achievement tests (KTEA–3 and WIAT–III) produced zero-order Pearson correlations with achievement composite scores that were typically in the .60s and .70s and consistent with those reported by Naglieri and Bornstein (2003).

Correlations between the WISC–V and the Vineland–II were largely low to near zero, indicating divergent validity because the WISC–V and Vineland measure different psychological constructs (intelligence versus adaptive behavior). Comparisons of the WISC–V with the BASC–2 PRS were somewhat limited given that Resiliency, Conduct Problems, Executive Functioning, and Attention Problems were the only BASC scales reported. Like the Vineland–II, correlations between the WISC–V and BASC–2 scores on these four scales were low to near zero and supportive of divergent validity. This finding also was expected, given the different psychological constructs the WISC–V and BASC–2 measure. Canivez, Neitzel, and Martin (2005) found similar results with the Wechsler Intelligence Scale for Children–Third Edition (WISC–III; Wechsler, 1991) in comparisons with the Adjustment Scales for Children and Adolescents (ASCA; McDermott, Marston, & Stott, 1993).

WISC–V performance among 13 special groups is summarized in the *WISC–V Technical and Interpretive Manual* (pp. 112–147). Groups included intellectually gifted, intellectual disability–mild severity, intellectual disability–moderate severity, borderline intellectual functioning, specific learning disorder–reading, specific learning disorder–reading and written expression, specific learning disorder–mathematics, attention-deficit/hyperactivity disorder, disruptive behavior, traumatic brain injury, English language learner, autism spectrum disorder with language impairment, and autism spectrum disorder without language impairment. Most are small groups of 20 to 30 individuals who were then compared to a randomly selected and demographically matched standardization subsample. Acknowledged limitations included small sample sizes, nonrandom selection of special group participants, data collected by independent examiners and researchers, and special group participants had predetermined classifications that might have been based on different selection criteria. For these reasons, these results must be considered preliminary and require replication with well-designed and controlled studies.

Generally, results indicated various WISC–V scores that were significantly different between the special group and the control participants and in expected directions. For example, individuals with intellectual giftedness scored higher than the control group, but individuals with specific disabilities scored lower than the control group. Such distinct group differences provide some preliminary evidence for construct validity.

The *WISC–V Technical and Interpretive Manual* noted that results from these studies "demonstrate the differential sensitivity of the WISC–V to specific and general cognitive deficits exhibited by children commonly evaluated in clinical settings" (p. 112).

The manual further asserted that this information about group mean differences "provides evidence for the clinical utility and discriminant validity of the WISC–V subtests and composites" (p. 112). Unfortunately these conclusions are insufficiently supported by comparisons of distinct groups, which provide necessary *but not sufficient* evidence for clinical utility. Differences between groups (discriminative validity) do not automatically translate into accurate decisions about individuals (clinical utility).

Rather, methods and analyses examining conditional probabilities of diagnostic efficiency statistics are required for accurate clinical (individual) decisions (Kessell & Zimmerman, 1993; Swets, 1996; Treat & Vicken, 2012; Wasserman & Bracken, 2013). It has long been known that the base rates of clinical disorders, cut scores used for individual decisions, and the like are all vital for determining clinical utility (Meehl & Rosen, 1955). The distinction between classical validity and clinical utility has been repeatedly demonstrated with Wechsler scores (Devena & Watkins, 2012; Watkins, 2005; Watkins, Glutting, & Youngstrom, 2005); its absence in the WISC–V *Technical and Interpretive Manual* (other than a somewhat confusing presentation under the rubric of consequential validity) is disappointing.

COMMENTARY

As might have been expected, the foreword of the *WISC–V Technical and Interpretive Manual* was enthusiastically positive about the WISC–V. Such unbridled enthusiasm without regard to the psychometric limitations and past failures when numerous subtest and composite score comparisons were put to the empirical test is perhaps premature. Although there are a number of positive changes and elements in the WISC–V, there continue to remain glaring omissions previously pointed out in reviews of the WAIS–IV (Canivez, 2010), WPPSI–IV (Canivez, 2014b), and WISC–IV (Canivez & Kush, 2013) that must be examined.

Failure to Provide Results from EFA

The *WISC–V Technical and Interpretive Manual* explicitly preferred CFA over EFA methods rather than taking advantage of both methods. EFA and CFA are considered complementary procedures, each answering somewhat different

questions, and greater confidence in the latent factor structure is achieved when EFA and CFA are in agreement (Gorsuch, 1983). Further, J. B. Carroll (1995) and Reise (2012) both noted that EFA procedures are particularly useful in suggesting possible models to be tested in CFA. In fact, J. B. Carroll (1998) suggested that "CFA should derive its initial hypotheses from EFA results, rather than starting from scratch or from a priori hypotheses ... [and] CFA analyses should be done to check my EFA analyses" (p. 8).

The fact that two WISC–IV subtests were deleted (Word Reasoning and Picture Completion), three new subtests were added (Visual Puzzles, Figure Weights, and Picture Span), and items in all WISC–V subtests were new or revised suggests that relationships among retained and new subtests might result in associations and latent structure unanticipated by a priori conceptualizations (Strauss, Spreen, & Hunter, 2000). The absence of EFA results is most disappointing, given prior criticism of their absence in other Wechsler manuals (Canivez, 2010, 2014b). Because of this lacuna in the WISC–V *Technical and Interpretive Manual*, EFA results for the total WISC–V normative sample are included later in this chapter.

CFA Methods

Figure 5.1 and 5.2 in the *WISC–V Technical and Administration* mislabel the latent construct of general intelligence. What is labeled "Full Scale" in these figures should be General Intelligence, which is the name of the latent construct. The Full Scale IQ is an observed variable and an estimate of the latent construct general intelligence. Also, there is no FSIQ utilizing all 16 subtests; in fact, only seven WISC–V subtests are used to produce the FSIQ.

Unfortunately, reports of the CFA analyses in the *WISC–V Technical and Administration Manual* were not adequately informative (Boomsma, 2000). For example, there was no indication of the method used to scale the models for identification. A brief footnote to Table 5.4 indicated that weighted least squares (WLS) estimation was applied. However, "use of an estimation method other than ML [maximum likelihood] requires explicit justification" (Kline, 2011, p. 154), and no explanation was provided for the choice of WLS. WLS typically is used for categorical or nonnormal data and may not produce chi-square values nor approximate fit indices equivalent to those produced by ML estimation (Yuan & Chan, 2005). Further, WLS requires very large sample sizes (Hu, Bentler, & Kano, 1992) and may be more sensitive to model misspecification than ML estimation (Olsson, Foss, Troye, & Howell, 2000). For these and other reasons, Brown (2006) concluded that WLS is "not a good estimator choice" (p. 388). We were unable to replicate these analyses because raw data are needed for WLS estimation.

Figure 5.1 in the *WISC–V Technical and Interpretive Manual* (modified and presented as Figure 20.1 in this chapter) presents the final and publisher-preferred standardized measurement model for the hierarchical five-factor model for the 16 primary and secondary subtests with the total normative sample (ages 6–16 years). This complex model (due to cross-loadings included for the Arithmetic subtest) is problematic for several reasons. First, the standardized path of 1.00 between the latent general intelligence (Full Scale) factor and Fluid Reasoning factor means that fluid reasoning is isomorphic with the hierarchical *g* factor. This is a major threat to discriminant validity and an indication that the WISC–V may be overfactored when five group factors are included.

The relationship between fluid reasoning and general intelligence is a long-standing puzzle, and there are practical and theoretical issues remaining to be resolved (M. R. Reynolds, Keith, Flanagan, & Alfonso, 2013). Both Vernon (1965) and J. B. Carroll (2003) questioned whether general and fluid factors could be distinguished. However, Golay, Reverte, Rossier, Favez, and Lecerf (2013) used Bayesian structural equation modeling (BSEM) rather than traditional CFA methods with the French WISC–IV and found that the fluid reasoning factor *did not* load at unity on the general intelligence factor when allowing small nonzero subtest cross-loadings rather than fixing them to zero as is typically done in frequentist CFA. The relationship was still very high but less likely to be identical. Whether this BSEM result is unique to the French WISC–IV or is also observed in other Wechsler tests such as the WISC–V should be examined.

The *WISC–V Technical and Interpretive Manual* remarked on the propensity of the chi-square test to identify trivial differences with large samples but subsequently used chi-square difference tests of nested models to identify the preferred five-factor model. However, the same sensitivity to large samples is true for chi-square difference tests (Millsap, 2007), suggesting that the model differences reported in the manual might be trivial. For example, Table 5.4 in the manual reveals that the difference between models 4a and 5a was statistically significant but those two models exhibited identical comparative fit index (CFI) and root mean squared error of approximation (RMSEA) values. Likewise, the preferred five-factor higher-order model was significantly different from other five-factor models, but all exhibited identical CFI and RMSEA values (e.g., .98 and .04, respectively). Cheung and Rensvold (2002) demonstrated, in the context of factorial invariance, that practical differences independent of sample size and model complexity could be identified by ΔCFI > .01.

Figure 5.2 in the *WISC–V Technical and Interpretive Manual* presents the final and publisher-preferred standardized measurement model for the hierarchical five-factor model for the 10 primary subtests with the total normative sample (ages 6–16 years). Although this model does not include cross-loadings and thus represents simple structure (a desired feature of test structure), it is still problematic because the path from the latent general intelligence factor and

Fluid Reasoning factor is .99, suggesting that fluid reasoning is isomorphic with general intelligence. This likely indicates overfactoring when including five first-order factors. Again, it is possible that this result is an artifact of CFA methods and fixing cross-loadings to zero when they are actually small nonzero values (Golay et al., 2013). BSEM methods will help to determine this phenomenon in the WISC–V; however, independent analyses using BSEM requires access to the standardization raw data and cannot be based on summary data from the manual.

Variance Decomposition

Another problem is that the publisher did not provide decomposed variance estimates to illustrate how much subtest variance is due to the hierarchical g factor and how much is due to the specific group factors. This is a glaring omission because clinicians and researchers are unable to judge the adequacy of the group factors (Verbal Comprehension, Visual Spatial, Fluid Reasoning, Working Memory, and Processing Speed) based on how much unique variance they capture when purged of the effects of general intelligence. Because cross-loadings are included in the preferred measurement model for all 16 WISC–V subtests (Figure 5.1 in the *WISC–V Technical and Interpretive Manual*), it is not easy to use the standardized path coefficients to decompose the variance estimates. These problems were pointed out in reviews of the WAIS–IV (Canivez, 2010) and WPPSI–IV (Canivez, 2014b) as well as in a commentary regarding the WISC–IV and WAIS–IV (Canivez & Kush, 2013). The publisher was admonished to include such estimates and information to no avail.

Fortunately, the measurement model presented in Figure 5.2 of the manual exhibits simple structure so it is relatively straightforward to decompose the variance estimates from the standardized loadings. Table 20.1 in this chapter presents the subtest and factor variance estimates based on Figure 5.2. Table 20.1 reveals

that most subtest variance is associated with the general intelligence factor and substantially smaller portions of subtest variance are uniquely related to the first-order factors, except in the case of Processing Speed, which includes tasks little related to general intelligence.

Further inspection of Table 20.1 shows that the higher-order g factor accounted for 34.8% of the total variance and 67.6% of the common variance. Thus, WISC–V measurement is dominated by the higher-order general intelligence factor. At the first-order level, Verbal Comprehension accounted for an additional 4.0% of the total variance and 7.0% of the common variance; Visual Spatial accounted for an additional 2.3% of the total variance and 4.0% of the common variance; Fluid Reasoning accounted for an additional 0.2% of the total variance and 0.4% of the common variance; Working Memory accounted for an additional 3.2% of the total variance and 5.6% of the common variance; and Processing Speed accounted for an additional 8.7% of the total variance and 15.4% of the common variance. Given the extremely low variance attributable to Fluid Reasoning, there seems to be little justification for its inclusion.

Model-Based Reliability

It has long been known that classical estimates of reliability are biased (Raykov, 1997) and model-based estimates, such as omega-hierarchical (ω_h) and omega-subscale (ω_s), have been recommended as superior replacements (Gignac & Watkins, 2013). In a review of the WPPSI–IV, Canivez (2014b) noted that model-based reliability coefficients should have been included to allow clinicians and researchers to judge the merits and interpretability of the claimed latent factors. Based on the decomposed factor loadings in Table 20.1, ω_h and ω_s coefficients were computed to estimate latent factor reliabilities. Omega coefficients should exceed .50 at a minimum, but .75 would be preferred (Reise, 2012; Reise, Bonifay, &

Table 20.1   Decomposed Sources of Variance in the WISC–V 10 Primary Subtests for the Total Normative Sample (N = 2,200) According to the Higher-Order Model (Figure 5.2, *WISC–V Technical and Interpretive Manual*)

Subtest	General		Verbal Comprehension		Visual Spatial		Fluid Reasoning		Working Memory		Processing Speed		h^2	u^2
	b	S^2	b	S^2	b	S^2	b	S^2	b	S^2	b	S^2		
Similarities	.689	.474	0.442	0.196									.670	.330
Vocabulary	.697	.486	0.452	0.204									.690	.310
Block Design	.684	.468			.335	.112							.580	.420
Visual Puzzles	.702	.493			.342	.117							.610	.390
Matrix Reasoning	.673	.453					.082	.007					.460	.540
Figure Weights	.673	.453					.130	.017					.470	.530
Digit Span	.647	.419							.437	.191			.610	.390
Picture Span	.540	.291							.359	.129			.420	.580
Coding	.357	.127									.602	.363	.490	.510
Symbol Search	.423	.179									.715	.511	.690	.310
Total Variance		.348		.040		.023		.002		.032		.087		
Common Variance		.676		.070		.040		.004		.056		.154		
	$\omega_h =$	.823	$\omega_s =$	.238	$\omega_s =$	.144	$\omega_s =$	.015	$\omega_s =$	.210	$\omega_s =$	.548		

Note: b = standardized loading of subtest on factor, S^2 = variance explained in the subtest, h^2 = communality, u^2 = uniqueness, ω_h = omega hierarchical, ω_s = omega subscale

Haviland, 2013). The ω_h coefficient for general intelligence (.823) was high and sufficient for scale interpretation; however, the ω_s coefficients for the five WISC–V first-order factors (Verbal Comprehension, Visual Spatial, Fluid Reasoning, Working Memory, and Processing Speed) were considerably lower, ranging from .015 (Fluid Reasoning) to .548 (Processing Speed). Thus, the WISC–V first-order factors, with the possible exception of Processing Speed, likely possess too little true score variance for clinicians to interpret (Reise, 2012; Reise et al., 2013).

Continuing Problems with the Arithmetic Subtest

Examination of Figure 5.1 in the *WISC–V Technical and Interpretive Manual* illustrates

the continuing difficulties with the Arithmetic subtest with its cross-loading with Verbal Comprehension, Fluid Reasoning, and Working Memory. Canivez and Kush (2013) pointed out problems with Arithmetic in the WISC–IV and WAIS–IV due to cross-loadings modeled by Weiss, Keith, Zhu, and Chen (2013a) and by Weiss, Keith, Zhu, and Chen (2013b). Arithmetic had its origin in the Wechsler scales as a verbal subtest, but beginning with the Wechsler Intelligence Scale for Children–Revised (WISC–R; Wechsler, 1974a) factor-analytic studies found Arithmetic, Digit Span, and Coding formed a small third factor (so-called Freedom from Distractibility). The attempt to strengthen that small third factor by adding a new subtest (Symbol Search) in the WISC–III produced the opposite effect by pulling Coding away to form a new fourth factor, so-called

Processing Speed, a name both Keith (1997) and Kranzler (1997) questioned. This left Arithmetic and Digit Span to measure the small third factor renamed Working Memory. Subsequent analyses of national standardization samples of the WISC–IV found that Arithmetic loaded on a memory factor or a fluid reasoning factor or both (Cornoldi, Orsini, Cianci, Giofrè, & Pezzuti, 2013; Fina, Sánchez-Escobedo, & Hollingworth, 2012; Golay et al., 2013; Keith, Fine, Taub, Reynolds, & Kranzler, 2006; Weiss et al., 2013b). In fact, Arithmetic may be more of a quantitative reasoning task, as suggested by the CHC conceptualization, but there are no other quantitative reasoning tasks with which it can associate. That supposition was corroborated by a study that found that Arithmetic migrated to the Quantitative Reasoning factor when marker tests of quantitative reasoning and memory were included with subtests from the WISC–III (Watkins & Ravert, 2013). It might be time to abandon Arithmetic or provide more tasks that measure quantitative reasoning to adequately measure that broad ability.

Incremental Validity Considerations

Zero-order Pearson correlations between the WISC–V subtests, primary index scores, and ancillary index scores with the KTEA–3 and WIAT–III subtest and composite scores reported in the *WISC–V Technical and Interpretive Manual* do not account for the hierarchical nature of the WISC–V and resulting complex associations with academic achievement. As illustrated previously, WISC–V subtests measure both general intelligence variance *and* some group ability variance, but zero-order Pearson correlations between primary index scores or ancillary index scores with KTEA–3) or WIAT–III) scores conflate the general intelligence and specific group ability variance. Examination of incremental validity of primary index or ancillary index scores *beyond* that of the FSIQ (Haynes & Lench, 2003; Hunsley, 2003; Hunsley & Meyer, 2003) is

necessary because the WISC–V is interpreted across multiple levels and scores and primary and ancillary index scores conflate general and group factor variance.

Canivez (2010, 2014b) argued in reviews of the WAIS–IV and WPPSI–IV that hierarchical multiple regression analyses should have been included in the respective technical manuals but such analyses are absent from the *WISC–V Technical and Interpretive Manual*. Studies applying hierarchical multiple regression analyses have supported the dominance of the FSIQ in accounting for academic achievement variance and substantially less (and often trivial amounts) of achievement variance attributable to the factor index scores (e.g., Canivez, 2013a; Canivez et al., 2014; Freberg, Vandiver, Watkins, & Canivez, 2008; Glutting, Watkins, Konold, & McDermott, 2006; Glutting, Youngstrom, Ward, Ward, & Hale, 1997; J. J. Ryan, Kreiner, & Burton, 2002; Watkins, Glutting, & Lei, 2007). Interestingly, similar results have been found for the prediction of job training and work performance of adults (Ree, Earles, & Teachout, 1994). It may be that these limited portions of achievement test score variance accounted for by first-order factor index scores is related to the generally smaller portions of subtest variance apportioned to the first-order factor scores identified through hierarchical EFA and CFA.

Measurement Bias

The *Standards for Educational and Psychological Testing* (AERA, APA, & NCME, 2014) describe three ways that measurement bias might make test scores unfair for subgroups of the population. First, differential item functioning (DIF) could result when "equally able test takers differ in their probabilities of answering a test item correctly as a function of group membership" (p. 51). Second, predictive bias could be exhibited if group membership influences the prediction of a criterion. Finally, structural bias could result if the construct being measured has different meanings dependent on group membership. Test Standard 3.0 calls for test developers and users to analyze test scores to ensure the absence of item, predictive, and structural bias for relevant subgroups. Although few details were provided, DIF within the WISC–V was analyzed and dismissed. Predictive bias and structural bias were not addressed. Methods of evaluating these types of measurement bias are well known and should have been applied (C. R. Reynolds & Ramsay, 2003). It would also have been desirable to have provided descriptive statistics for WISC–V scores disaggregated by race/ethnicity and parent education level so that users would have more information regarding score variations across these groups. Similarly, reliability estimates across race/ethnicity and sex groups would have been useful (C. R. Reynolds & Milam, 2012).

Selective Reporting and Review of Scientific Literature

There is a rather selective reporting of empirical literature including omission of contradictory evidence, reliance on studies tangential to the issue at hand, dependence on methodologically flawed studies, failure to specify the limitations of the cited research, and focusing on inessential aspects of the cited research. These practices are most egregious in Chapter 6 of the *WISC–V Technical and Interpretive Manual*, which is devoted to interpretation of WISC–V scores. Similar criticisms were made about the evidence presented in the WISC–IV manual. For example, Braden and Niebling (2012) found that "extensive discussion of how to identify intraindividual strengths and weaknesses by using Index, subtest, and within-subtest responses does not include discussion of contradictory findings available in the literature" (p. 744) and that "no evidence is cited or provided in direct support of these claims" (p. 745) for basing educational and clinical interventions on an analysis of cognitive strengths and weaknesses. These criticisms were

also made in reviews of the WAIS–IV (Canivez, 2010) and WPPSI–IV (Canivez, 2014b).

The *Standards for Educational and Psychological Testing* (AERA, APA, & NCME, 2014) demand that "test users should be provided with clear explanation of the characteristics, meaning, and intended interpretation of scale scores, as well as their limitations" (p. 102) and that test documentation should disclose the "validity of recommended [score] interpretations" (p. 126). Further, "when interpretation of subscores, score differences, or profiles is suggested, the rationale and relevant evidence in support of such interpretation should be provided" (p. 27). Given that focus, the content of Chapter 6 of the manual should meet the evidential requirements of the *Standards*.

In the interest of space, only four major examples are presented to illustrate our assertion that Chapter 6 fails to meet the *Standards*. First, the manual asserts that the differences that occur between WISC–V scores from a single WISC–V administration are important considerations in interpreting a child's performance. This assertion was followed by a presentation on intersubtest scatter as well as pairwise comparisons of subtest and index scores. No evidence was presented to support the validity of these score interpretations. However, previous research often has revealed critical flaws in such ipsative measurement methods (McDermott, Fantuzzo, Glutting, Watkins, & Baggaley, 1992). Likewise, previous research has clearly shown that subtest scatter and other subtest comparisons exhibit little to no diagnostic utility (Kramer, Henning-Stout, Ullman, & Schellenberg, 1987; Watkins, 1999) and are not stable across time (Borsuk, Watkins, & Canivez, 2006; Watkins & Canivez, 2004). Given this evidence, Hunsley and Mash (2007) concluded that "an evidence-based approach to the assessment of intelligence would indicate that nothing is to be gained, and much is to be potentially lost, by considering subtest profiles" (p. 32). Similar opinions have been expressed by other assessment experts (e.g., Braden & Shaw, 2009;

Kamphaus, Reynolds, & Vogel, 2009; Kranzler & Floyd, 2013; Lilienfeld, Ammirati, & David, 2012; McDermott, Fantuzzo, & Glutting, 1990; C. R. Reynolds & Milam, 2012). Nevertheless, no limitations or cautions were provided in the *WISC–V Technical and Interpretive Manual* and no contradictory studies were reported.

Second, the *WISC–V Technical and Interpretive Manual* claims that "there is strong psychometric and clinical support for interpreting the WISC–V index scores as reliable and valid measures of the primary cognitive constructs they intend to represent" (p. 149) and concludes that analysis of primary index scores (e.g., Verbal Comprehension Index, Visual Spatial Index, etc.) "is recommended as the principal level of clinical interpretation" (p. 157). However, "no score yielded by intelligence tests (or any other measurement instrument) is a pure measure of the construct it targets" (Floyd, Reynolds, Farmer, & Kranzler, 2013, p. 399). Rather, the WISC–V index scores are "contaminated" by: (a) systematic variance of the general factor, (b) random error variance, and (c) systematic specific variance of each subtest that is not shared with any other subtest.

Sources of variance for the WISC–V have been itemized in Table I.10 in Appendix I in the downloadable resources: www.wiley.com/go/itwiscv and clearly show that general intelligence accounts for the bulk of the variance of the index scores. Using a primary index score as the principal level of interpretation ignores the contributions of general intelligence, error, and specific variance. Additionally, the factor index scores have demonstrated poor temporal stability (Watkins & Canivez, 2004; Watkins & Smith, 2013) and little incremental predictive validity of academic achievement (Canivez et al., 2014; Glutting et al., 2006; Parkin & Beaujean, 2012). At present, "there is very little evidence to suggest that the subtest or composite score differences on intelligence tests can be used to improve decisions about individuals" (Kranzler & Floyd, 2013, p. 86). This conclusion was affirmed by Schneider (2013b), who stated,

"there is little evidence that clinicians are able to measure the non-*g* portions of group factors with precision, make valid inferences about them, and use this knowledge to help individuals" (p. 187). However, the *WISC–V Technical and Interpretive Manual* provides no cautions and does not present contrary opinions regarding the appropriate level of interpretation.

The third major example in Chapter 6 of the manual is that many of the interpretive suggestions are based on the "pattern of scores on the composites and subtests" (p. 156). WISC–V scores are assumed to be "reliable and valid measures of the primary cognitive constructs they intend to represent" (p. 149). Thus, the score profile identifies cognitive strengths and weaknesses that are assumed to underlie learning problems. Logically, interventions could then be individualized to match the specific cognitive strengths and weaknesses of each examinee. This approach exemplifies an aptitude-treatment interaction (ATI) model where it is assumed that learners will differentially respond to interventions that capitalize on their cognitive strengths (Cronbach & Snow, 1977).

The *WISC–V Technical and Interpretive Manual* asserts that profiles are only hypotheses that must be "corroborated or refuted by other evaluation results, background information, or direct behavioral observations" (p. 157). However, the two references cited to support this statement are books that do not include primary research results. In essence, they are sources with similar opinions that do not contribute experimental evidence. Further, what evidence, exactly, is needed to corroborate or refute any particular hypothesis? This uncertainty leaves considerable subjectivity in interpretation of cognitive profiles, which has been shown to increase error rates (Aspel, Willis, & Faust, 1998).

The admonition to confirm or refute WISC–V score interpretations with other information also ignores the likelihood of reducing overall validity if multiple measures include some with low reliability or validity. As noted by Faust (2007), "prediction is often maximized by identifying a relatively small set of the most valid and minimally redundant predictors, rather than trying to integrate many variables" (p. 35). Likewise, the admonition to simultaneously consider a large amount of complex information implies that clinicians are able to combine multiple sources of information holistically and arrive at accurate judgments, which is unlikely (Faust, 1989; Ruscio & Stern, 2006). Thus, the belief that an ill-defined analysis by clinicians of an unspecified set of data will accurately adjudicate hypotheses ignores what is known about clinical judgment (Lilienfeld et al., 2012; Watkins, 2009), especially the power of confirmation bias (Nickerson, 1998).

Early analyses of aptitude-treatment interactions in education were negative (Kavale & Mattson, 1983). By 1990, Glutting and McDermott had concluded that "traditional IQ tests have not met the challenge of providing effective aptitude-treatment interactions (ATIs) for evaluating how children best learn, or for determining how a particular child's style of learning is different from the styles manifested by other children" (p. 296). Although ATIs are clinically popular, the evidence against them has accumulated over the past several decades. For example, Good, Vollmer, Creek, Katz, and Chowdhri (1993) conducted a study with the Kaufman Assessment Battery for Children (A. S. Kaufman & Kaufman, 1983) and found no benefit from matching instructional approaches to cognitive strengths. Other reviews of the literature found no support for ATIs (Canivez, 2013b; Gresham & Witt, 1997; Kamphaus, Winsor, Rowe, & Kim, 2012; Macmann & Barnett, 1997; McDermott et al., 1990; Reschly, 1997; Watkins, 2003, 2009; Watkins et al., 2005). One review of ATIs concluded that "the evidence showing cognitive assessment is useful for matching interventions under an ATI model is lacking, and in some cases, it is demonstrably negative.... [N]or do cognitive test developers provide evidence of ATI outcomes to support their claims that tests are valuable for this purpose" (Braden & Shaw, 2009, p. 107). None

of this contradictory evidence is mentioned in the *WISC–V Technical and Interpretive Manual.*

The final example from Chapter 6 of the manual is the presentation of PSW methods and the caution (that appears twice in the manual) that cognitive profiles are "not intended to diagnose specific disorders" (p. 149). However, there is an unmistakable implication that patterns of cognitive strengths and weaknesses can and should be used in the diagnosis of learning disabilities. For example, the final portion of the chapter is devoted to explication of a PSW model based on other PSW methods that are explicitly designed for the identification of learning disabilities (Flanagan, Ortiz, & Alfonso, 2007; Hale et al., 2008). The *WISC–V Technical and Interpretive Manual* claims that this PSW "model is a legally acceptable and clinically sound approach for helping practitioners identify SLDs [specific learning disabilities] and develop intervention plans based on a child's strengths and weaknesses. Use of this type of model is good clinical practice and adds weight to an eligibility or diagnostic decision" (p. 183). Additionally, the Pearson clinical website lists "identifying and diagnosing learning disabilities/disorders" as one application of the WISC–V (http://www.pearsonclinical.com/psychology/products/100000771/wechsler-intelligence-scale-for-childrensupsupfifth-edition--WISC-V.html#tab-details). How do such claims *not encourage* clinicians to use cognitive profiles for diagnostic purposes?

The assertion that PSW approaches have a sound legal foundation is also dubious. Zirkel (2014) noted that use of a PSW model relies on an inaccurate interpretation of Individuals with Disabilities Education Act regulations and that "the legally required evaluation does not necessarily include—per the aforementioned OSEP [Office of Special Education Programs] interpretation—an assessment of psychological or cognitive processing" (Zirkel, 2013, p. 95). Why the publisher includes legal advice, let alone *questionable* legal advice, in the *WISC–V Technical and Interpretive Manual* is a mystery (C. R. Reynolds & Milam, 2012).

The claim in the *WISC–V Technical and Interpretive Manual* that PSW models are "research-based" (p. 183) is debatable. There are three major models for using cognitive strengths and weaknesses to assist in the identification of children with learning disabilities (Flanagan et al., 2007; Hale et al., 2008; Naglieri & Das, 1997). The accuracy of those models was evaluated in a simulation study that found that all three failed to identify a large number of positive cases and falsely identified an even larger number of negative cases. Theoretically, these results suggest that an ATI paradigm would be iatrogenic because the misidentified children would not receive treatments matched to their true ability profiles (Stuebing, Fletcher, Branum-Martin, & Francis, 2012).

Subsequently, the accuracy of two of those PSW models (Flanagan et al., 2007; Hale et al., 2008) was evaluated for adolescents with a history of failure to respond to academic interventions (Miciak, Fletcher, Vaughn, Stuebing, & Tolar, 2014). Results revealed that there was poor agreement between the two models in identifying children with learning disabilities (kappa of –.05 to .31), and there was no pattern of academic skills that distinguished the children identified by these models. Based on these results, the authors concluded that "until empirical research provides more evidence for the validity, reliability, and utility of PSW methods, resources may be better allocated toward directly assessing important academic skills" (p. 35).

The only supportive evidence for PSW methods presented in the *WISC–V Technical and Interpretive Manual* was by authors of PSW models, although five specific references "that document empirically proven links between cognitive processes and achievement domains" (p. 183) were provided. However, all five sources were authored by developers of PSW models, and little experimental evidence was provided in any of them. To the contrary, a quantitative review of the evidence of the treatment validity of instruction based on putative cognitive strengths and weaknesses found that "a minority

of reviewed studies supported the efficacy of cognitive interventions; fewer still when the cognitive component was not paired with an academic intervention" (Kearns & Fuchs, 2013, p. 285). Considered in conjunction with the ATI evidence, it appears that, when put to the test, PSW approaches fail in both identification and intervention. None of this antithetical evidence is provided in the *WISC–V Technical and Interpretive Manual*.

WISC–V Review Summary

There are many positive aspects of the WISC–V. Specifically, the WISC–V includes a large, demographically representative normative sample that allows generalizability of individual WISC–V performance to the U.S. population at large. Changes to instructions, subtest discontinue (ceiling) rules, and attractive, well-constructed materials are also major advantages. In particular improvements in instructions were noted for Block Design, Picture Concepts, the Working Memory subtests, and the Processing Speed subtests. Inclusion of subtests, such as Visual Puzzles and Figure Weights, two subtests that appear better indicators of reasoning abilities, is also quite positive. Additionally, the publisher is commended for providing correlation matrices and descriptive statistics so that independent researchers can study some aspects of the WISC–V.

As described, there are also problems with the WISC–V. Many of these problems would be ameliorated if there was greater adherence to the *Standards for Educational and Psychological Testing* (AERA, APA, & NCME, 2014). Additionally, a more objective, scientific approach to the presentation of evidence regarding the WISC–V should be cultivated. Clinicians are ultimately responsible for use of the WISC–V, and they must be given complete, accurate, and objective information on which to base their judgments. It must be noted that many of the problems discussed in this chapter have been reported in prior test reviews or articles. Failure to acknowledge or deal with them is a serious mistake that will not be in the long-term interest of the publisher or clinicians.

INDEPENDENT ANALYSES

Given our criticism of the structural validity analyses reported in the *WISC–V Technical and Interpretive Manual*, the remainder of this chapter is devoted to an independent examination of the WISC–V structure using both EFA *and* CFA methods, including presentation of variance estimates for subtests and factors as well as model-based latent factor reliability estimates. These analyses and results, which should have been included in the WISC–V manual, are presented in Appendix I in the downloadable resources: www.wiley.com/go/itwiscv to allow clinicians and researchers to assess additional psychometric features of the WISC–V in order to determine if various WISC–V scores possess sufficient evidence of validity for clinical interpretations.

Whereas the complete independent analyses are only available in the downloadable resources: www.wiley.com/go/itwiscv, Canivez and Watkins's conclusions from their analyses are presented here, followed by their general summary.

CONCLUSIONS

We were unable to replicate the structural validity results reported in the *WISC–V Technical and Interpretive Manual*. A comparison of our results in Table I.9 (in downloadable resources: www.wiley.com/go/itwiscv) to results in Table 5.4 of the manual reveals discrepant chi-square values as well as divergences in the reported degrees of freedom for most models. The *WISC–V Technical and Interpretive Manual* reported approximate fit statistics with two-digit precision so it is not possible to make accurate comparisons of our approximate fit statistics with three-digit precision.

Further, it is not possible to tell if inadmissible solutions were obtained for the five-factor models (model specification errors such as negative variance) but approximate fit statistics were reported in the *WISC–V Technical and Interpretive Manual* or whether those models converged with proper statistical estimates.

Results from both EFA and CFA conducted in Appendix I (in downloadable resources: www.wiley.com/go/itwiscv) provide important considerations for clinical interpretation of basic scores from the WISC–V. Although the intention was to separate the former Perceptual Rasoning factor into separate Visual Spatial and Fluid Reasoning factors, it appears that this was not very successful, despite endorsement in the final measurement model selected by the publisher and development of standard scores for Visual Spatial and Fluid Reasoning. Had the publisher examined results from EFA or seriously considered the practical and theoretical issues created by the 1.00 loading of Fluid Reasoning on general intelligence in CFA, it would have been apparent that there were significant problems for separate Visual Spatial and Fluid Reasoning factors, given the available 16 WISC–V subtests. Results from EFA and CFA converged and suggest that the best representation of WISC–V measurement is a bifactor model with four specific group factors, but the limited portions of variance uniquely captured by the four specific group factors is low and the ω_s coefficients indicated too little true score variance associated with the four specific group factors, with the possible exception of Processing Speed, to warrant confident interpretation in clinical practice.

GENERAL SUMMARY

Professional standards (American Educational Research Association, American Psychological Association, & National Council on Measurement in Education, 2014) demand full and honest disclosure of psychometric features of all scores and comparisons, but sadly many are missing or obfuscated for the WISC–V. Given that numerous critiques and recommendations were known to the publisher (e.g., inclusion of EFA, bifactor CFA models, decomposed variance estimates for scores, provision of validity evidence for interpretations, disclosure of contradictory evidence, and model-based reliability coefficients for composite scores), there is an appearance of intentionality to the absence of these analyses from the *WISC–V Technical and Interpretive Manual*. Clinicians are unable to make evidence-based judgments regarding the psychometric fitness of WISC–V scores or the scientific soundness of interpretation schemes without complete and accurate information. Likewise, researchers cannot adequately

understand how to integrate WISC–V scores into theoretical and practical models without complete and accurate information. "Bad usage of tests" (Buros, 1965, p. xxiv) is exacerbated by the great number of score comparisons and analyses promoted for the WISC–V. Users should remember that "just because the test or its scoring software produces a score, you need not interpret it" (Kranzler & Floyd, 2013, p. 95). Furthermore, users must be mindful of the advice of Weiner (1989) that the ethical psychologist will "(a) know what their tests can do and (b) act accordingly" (p. 829). It is our hope that the information in this review and our independent analyses will provide the information necessary for clinicians and researchers to follow this sage advice.

CHAPTER 21

OVERVIEW AND INTEGRATION OF THE INDEPENDENT REVIEWS OF WISC–V

In this chapter, we integrate and organize all reviews of the WISC–V that appear in Section V of the book and also include the mini-review of the WISC–V that Joel Schneider appended to his CHC case report (Chapter 9).

In the sections that follow, we highlight the key features of the reviews. We focus on the reviewers' sense of the strengths and weaknesses of the WISC–V and offer the flavor of some of the most interesting insights made by each professional or team of professionals. We have quoted liberally from the reviews, usually eliminating references and other parenthetical phrases from the quotes and often eliminating some of the words without obscuring the meaning. We do not cite page numbers for these quotes because that would have bogged down this chapter with too much detail.

We have not altered the content of each review, other than editorial changes for grammar and clarity. By not reducing the length of the reviews, we allowed redundancy, such as the repetition of the structure and psychometric properties of the test. We preferred the repetition to imposing any type of censorship. One important point noted by most reviewers was the unique role played by public domain and test security in the choice of specific test items. Reynolds and Hadorn (Chapter 15), among others, stated: Note that all items previously published in the first three editions of the WISC have been removed because copyright laws now leave them open to public domain and vulnerable to test insecurity. The benefits of longevity made the challenge of assembling an entirely new set of items a bit daunting, especially when Alan remembers the weekly battles he had with

Dr. Wechsler to eliminate specific items from the WISC because of outdated content, violent themes, political incorrectness, or poor data. None of these arguments fared well against Dr. Wechsler's often historical or emotional attachment to certain items, usually on the social-context subtests of Picture Arrangement and Comprehension.

We have organized this chapter around six questions:

1. What are the reviewers' overall feelings and beliefs about the WISC–V?
2. Were the test developers responsive to feedback from the field?
3. Was it wise to split the Perceptual Reasoning Index into two components—Fluid Reasoning (*Gf*) and Visual Spatial (*Gv*)?
4. Is the WISC–V user-friendly?
5. How good are the WISC–V's psychometric properties and test development procedures?
6. Which aspects of the reviews are a few of our favorite things?

OVERVIEW OF EACH WISC–V TEST REVIEW

Schneider (Chapter 9): The worst thing to happen to the Wechsler tests would be for them to lose sight of David Wechsler's vision (see A. S. Kaufman, 2009, pp. 29–54). The second worst thing would be for them to remain as they are. The new WISC–V would never be mistaken for the cutting edge of cognitive assessment, but it is keeping up with the times without sacrificing the qualities that made it great in the first place.

This is no easy feat, and the authors are to be commended for their accomplishment.

Reynolds and Hadorn (Chapter 15): Everyone is likely to have an opinion about the WISC–V. We have yet to spend the amount of time with the WISC–V that we have had with the WISC–IV. But our initial thoughts are that the test is likely an upgrade, and it is even better than the WISC–IV. Yes, the WISC–V is likely the best WISC ever. Although we have made critiques throughout this review, we want to make it clear that we hold the WISC–V in high regard in terms of measuring intelligence.... . Intelligence tests, including the WISC–V, continue to set the standard for other psychoeducational measures.

The WISC–V is an intelligence test steeped in tradition. The WISC set an early standard for intelligence measurement in children. The standard has been continually raised over the years with the development of other more theory-based measures; some may even have wondered whether the WISC deserved such a high status in intellectual assessment due to its lack of responsiveness to what was happening around it in the IQ testing world. Well, make no mistake about it. The WISC–V is modernized to be consistent with contemporary theory and research. The WISC–V is undeniably an excellent measure of intelligence. That is really not up for debate.

Dumont and Willis (Chapter 16): A psychologist teleported 75 years from 1939 into the future would still recognize the WISC–V as a direct descendant of the Wechsler-Bellevue.... Having used all five editions of the WISC, we find almost all of the changes from the WISC–IV to the new edition to be improvements.... The WISC–V has a number of positive features that make it an attractive tool for assessing cognitive functioning in children and adolescents. Overall, each of the revision goals has been met, including improved psychometric properties, modifications and changes to the composites and subtests that better incorporate contemporary theories of intelligence, and the addition of several Complementary scales that further extend the breadth of the test. The test also has excellent psychometric properties and technical adequacy.... The WISC–V also has some limitations that should be noted. Although the *WISC–V Technical and Interpretive Manual* provides some basic step-by-step instructions and examples to aid examiners in how to conduct both primary and ancillary profile analysis when evaluating an examinee's cognitive strengths and weaknesses, the manual does not elaborate further on score interpretation. The five ancillary and three complementary index scores appear, on face value, to be important and relevant aspects of a child's cognitive functioning; however, research is needed to demonstrate how best to use these new scales.

Miller and McGill (Chapter 17): The WISC–V is a significant and positive revision from its predecessor. The integration of additional neuropsychological constructs...is a welcome addition to the test. The move from a four-factor model of interpretation to a five-factor model of interpretation better reflects current conceptualizations of intelligence. The test offers multiple psychometric comparisons between indices and subtests, which should enhance the test's clinical utility. The digital version of the tests is a significant advancement for the assessment field.

Naglieri (Chapter 18): Any review of the fifth edition of the Wechsler Scales has to begin by recognizing the enormous impact this tool has had on the field of psychology and education. The test's use is unsurpassed by any measure of intellectual ability, and the test name has come to represent the very definition of intelligence.... The publisher's efforts to sustain the Wechsler brand reflect the recognition that more information is needed from the test. The solution to the dilemma—make the WISC better but do not change it too much—apparently has led to reliance on factor analysis and diverse interpretive solutions. The authors of the WISC–V have made a valiant attempt to strengthen the integrity of this time-honored test. Even given all the efforts to inform users of the various ways to interpret the scores the WISC–V yields, these ideas are constrained by the historically determined content.

McCloskey (Chapter 19): Recognizing the need to provide a test that would appeal to a broad range of practitioners who hold widely varying opinions and beliefs about the nature of intelligence and the best way to interpret test results, the test developers have assembled an impressive array of 21 subtests for the fifth edition of the WISC. Each of these subtests is well developed; great attention has been paid to the drafting (or revising) of subtest directions, the development of new items or the revision of old ones, and the need for psychometric integrity. The 21 subtests are multifaceted tasks, most of which have great clinical utility from a neuropsychological perspective.... The good news here is that the WISC–V provides an exceptionally well-developed set of 21 subtests that can be used by experienced clinicians who are competent in the use of a cognitive neuropsychological approach to interpretation. [The bad news is that] clinicians cannot just rely on the *WISC–V Technical and Interpretive Manual* for much in the way of guidance when applying this interpretive perspective.

Canivez and Watkins (Chapter 20): There are many positive aspects of the WISC–V. Specifically, the WISC–V includes a large, demographically representative standardization sample that allows generalizability of individual WISC–V performance to the U.S. population at large. Changes to instructions, subtest discontinue (ceiling) rules, and attractive, well-constructed materials are also major advantages. In particular improvements in instructions were noted for Block Design, Picture Concepts, Working Memory subtests, and the Processing Speed subtests. Inclusion of subtests such as Visual Puzzles and Figure Weights, two subtests that appear better indicators of reasoning abilities are also quite positive. Additionally, the publisher is commended for providing correlation matrices and descriptive statistics so

that independent researchers can study some aspects of the WISC–V....

As might have been expected, the foreword of the *WISC–V Technical and Interpretive Manual* was enthusiastically positive about the WISC–V. Such unbridled enthusiasm without regard to the psychometric limitations and past failures when numerous subtest and composite score comparisons were put to the empirical test is perhaps premature.

WERE THE TEST DEVELOPERS RESPONSIVE TO FEEDBACK FROM THE FIELD?

YES, Reynolds and Hadorn (Chapter 15): One thing that we noticed while performing this review was the influence of previous reviews on the current WISC–IV ... Previous reviewers mentioned ... the time to obtain a FSIQ should be decreased, that the WISC–IV did not include measures of long-term retrieval or visual working memory, and that there may be a possible split in the Perceptual Reasoning Factor; some even described some flimsy test materials. The publishers of the WISC–V addressed all those listed weaknesses, along with a number of others. The process in addressing those weaknesses was particularly impressive and were well thought out and researched. Trying to attend to every comment ever made by a reviewer would result in a disaster; reviewers themselves have nowhere near the intimate knowledge of the test that the publisher has. But genuinely listening to those who often have experiences actually using the test, along with a number of other psychological instruments, is a useful step in improving measures. Kudos to the WISC–V developers....

The updated theoretical foundation section in the *WISC–V Technical and Administration Manual* was rather forceful in its rebuttal of the assertion that the Wechsler tests lack a theoretical foundation. The description of current research in intelligence and neuropsychology in the *WISC–V Technical and Administration Manual* is worth reading…. The bottom line is that the Wechsler tests have been pivotal to intelligence testing over the years, and we do not see a lack of strict allegiance and homage to CHC theory as a monumental weakness of the WISC–V.

NO, Canivez and Watkins (Chapter 20): Although there are a number of positive changes and elements in the WISC–V, there continue to remain glaring omissions previously pointed out in reviews of the WAIS-IV … and WISC–IV that must be examined. Some of these omissions include:

- Failure to provide results from exploratory factor analysis
- Regarding confirmatory factor analysis: Unfortunately, reports of the CFA analyses in the *WISC–V Technical and Administration and Manual* were not adequately informative.
- The publisher did not provide decomposed variance estimates to illustrate how much subtest variance is due to the hierarchical *g* factor and how much is due to the specific group factors.
- Zero-order Pearson correlations between the WISC–V subtests, primary indexes, and ancillary indexes with the KTEA–3 and WIAT–III subtest and composite scores reported in the *WISC–V Technical and Interpretive Manual* do not account for the hierarchical nature of the WISC–V and resulting complex associations with academic achievement.
- Regarding bias: Although few details were provided, differential item functioning (DIF) within the WISC–V was analyzed and dismissed. Predictive bias and structural bias were not addressed.
- There is a rather selective reporting of empirical literature including omission of contradictory evidence, reliance on studies tangential to the issue at hand, dependence on methodologically flawed studies, failure to specify the limitations of the cited research, or focusing on inessential aspects of the cited research.

WAS IT WISE TO SPLIT THE PERCEPTUAL REASONING INDEX INTO TWO COMPONENTS—FLUID REASONING (*GF*) AND VISUAL SPATIAL (*GV*)?

YES Reynolds and Hadorn (Chapter 15): The WISC–V is even more closely aligned with CHC theory than the WISC–IV was. Perhaps the developers should have emphasized CHC theory more in the *WISC–V Technical and Interpretive Manual*. But, in general, what they wrote was correct: Structural models have generally converged on some consensus with regard to cognitive ability factors.

YES, Dumont and Willis (Chapter 16): The division of Perceptual Reasoning into Fluid Reasoning and Visual Spatial composites brings the WISC–V into closer alignment with CHC theory (not an explicit goal of the revision process) and is, in our opinion, a significant enhancement of the test interpretation process.

NO, Canivez and Watkins (Chapter 20): Regarding the inclusion of the new Fluid Reasoning Index: Given the extremely low variance attributable to Fluid Reasoning, there seems to be little justification for its inclusion. Had the publisher examined results from exploratory factor analysis, or seriously considered the practical and theoretical issues created by the 1.00 loading of Fluid Reasoning on general intelligence in CFA, it would have been apparent that there were significant problems for separate Visual Spatial and Fluid Reasoning factors, given the available 16 WISC–V subtests.

IS THE WISC–V USER-FRIENDLY?

User-Friendly Administration and Scoring?

YES, say **Reynolds and Hadorn** (Chapter 15): Test materials were reconsidered to ensure greater durability, subtests were redistributed across stimulus books to reduce weight and increase stability, and scoring templates are now more substantial.... Simpler test instructions and scoring directions and guidelines have been provided in the most recent edition, and subtest instructions have been shortened.... Subtest instructions have been revised for greater simplicity and clarity. Added demonstration items, sample items, and teaching items provide students with more hands-on experience before their responses will count (for or against them).... Finally, specific-use prompts are included to help examiners handle relatively uncommon questions or behaviors from examinees. These prompts will come as a relief to any new graduate student or examiner who has been stumped by an examinee's creative question.... Serious attention was paid to the descriptive ranges provided by the WISC–V. Revisions made good effort to be more comprehensible to parents or lay-people unfamiliar with standardized testing.

But **Reynolds and Hadorn** also note some caveats: Although the instructions included in the *WISC–V Administration and Scoring Manual* are unquestionably essential for skilled administration, at times the sheer amount of verbiage makes it difficult to discriminate desired information when under administrative constraints, especially when instructions for samples or demonstration carry over onto another page. No audio CD was included in the WISC–V, and an opportunity to ease examiner burden and maintain standardization during subtests such as Letter–Number Sequencing and Digit Span seems lost.

NO, say **Dumont and Willis** (Chapter 16): Experienced examiners will need to be careful in adjusting to the changes from the WISC–IV to the WISC–V. There is new terminology to learn, such as primary (FSIQ), primary, secondary, complementary, and ancillary. Examiners will have to exercise impulse control to avoid summing the 10 primary subtest scaled scores to find the FSIQ instead of using only the seven primary (FSIQ) subtests. We have already observed instances of deficient impulse control.

... Given the vast amount of data entry that must be done to complete the four scoring pages (Summary, Primary Analysis, Ancillary and Complementary Analysis, and Process Analysis), we fear errors will be made. By our count, there are more than 550 entries to make on those pages. Clearly, Pearson's computer scoring software is likely to enjoy widespread use.

But **Dumont and Willis** see a bright side as well: Significant efforts were made to decrease the testing time (e.g., shortening subtest instructions, modifying discontinue rules).

YES, say **Miller and McGill** (Chapter 17): One of the most innovative features of the WISC–V is the inclusion of the full battery of tests in Pearson's digital Q-interactive platform.... Another major goal of the test revision was to increase the developmental appropriateness of the instrument. The test developers seem to have accomplished this by simplifying the test instructions for easier understanding and making the instructions more succinct. To ensure that children understand the task requirements, more practice items were added to the tests, as appropriate. Finally, the idea that quick task completion is always essential was deemphasized somewhat in the WISC–V by reducing the number of tests with time bonus points.

NO, says **McCloskey** (Chapter 19): The WISC–V also includes a General Ability Index based on the subtests of the Verbal Comprehension Index and the Fluid Reasoning Index and one subtest from the Visual Spatial Index, but the developers seem hardly able to hide their disdain for the existence of this measure, again burying it in the *WISC–V Administration and Scoring Manual Supplement* rather than featuring it prominently in the norm tables of the *WISC–V Administration and Scoring Manual*.

YES, Canivez and Watkins (Chapter 20): Test stimuli included in the stimulus books are attractive, in full color, and visually engaging. Materials also appear to be of high quality and likely to withstand the demands of frequent use without significant deterioration.

User-Friendly Clinical Utility?

YES, says **Schneider** (Chapter 9): This was my first experience with the WISC–V. and I was quite happy with it overall. The inclusion of Visual Puzzles corrects the great injustice done to Block Design in the transition from the WISC–III to the WISC–IV; it was stripped of its friend Object Assembly and pretty much was the only good measure of *Gv* on the WISC–IV. Now Block Design has a *Gv* friend again!

But **Schneider** also sees a problem: I am happy that there is a learning subtest on the WISC–V. However, I wish that a more creative choice had been made as to the format. We now have rebus learning tests on several major batteries that are quite similar to each other. I wish that Symbol Translation had a "friend" such as a story memory test so that a broad *Gl* (Learning efficiency) composite could be calculated.

YES, say **Dumont and Willis** (Chapter 16): The addition of the Fluid Reasoning Index and Visual Spatial Index and the availability of several new ancillary and complementary indices enhance the scale's clinical utility in comparison with its earlier versions. Finally, the WISC–V administration and scoring directions and repetition rules have been simplified and made more explicit for examiners.... The addition of the new Naming Speed, Symbol Translation, and Storage and Retrieval scales greatly increases the potential utility of the WISC–V for both neuropsychological and educational assessment.

YES, say **Miller and McGill** (Chapter 17): Taken as a whole, we believe the structural and design features of the WISC–V result in a more clinically useful instrument with broad applications for assessment psychologists as compared to its predecessor.... One of the major advantages of the WISC–V is the integration of this particular test into an entire family of intellectual functioning measures that span early childhood through older adult age ranges.

NO, says **Naglieri** (Chapter 18): Without a clear theory to guide the interpretation of the WISC–V, the responsibility for understanding learning success and failure, connecting the test results to legal definition of a specific learning disability in IDEA, and determining what type of instructional intervention to use, will become much more difficult.

YES, says **McCloskey** (Chapter 19): The WISC–V represents a significant advance in thinking at the index level. The four primary indexes of the WISC–IV have been expanded to five, and other clinically relevant indexes have been added.

But **McCloskey** has some qualms: Given the split in the globalist perspective on FSIQ interpretation, the developers may have better served the needs of a greater number of clinicians by viewing the traditional Wechsler FSIQ as just one of several options for providing a global estimate of general intelligence. Instead of addressing only the FSIQ as the first tier of interpretation, they could have suggested choosing the best global estimate that would fit the needs of the clinical context.

User-Friendly Test Interpretation Guidelines?

NO, say **Reynolds and Hadorn** (Chapter 15):

- The interpretation of the WISC–V at times seems overly complicated and some interpretations are not likely well supported. New terms for describing scores (e.g., primary, secondary) and the sheer number of scores and possible score differences are likely to overwhelm some users.
- The *WISC–V Technical and Interpretive Manual* outlines potential interpretations for WISC–V scores. It recommends collecting as much evidence to corroborate interpretations as possible. Although it is stated that the outline provides basic information, it is actually quite lengthy and can get rather complicated, especially if users believe it is necessary to interpret all of the possibilities with each test administration.

- Although the *WISC–V Technical and Interpretive Manual* seems to suggest that all of the steps for the primary analysis are not always necessary, it is not entirely clear, as it is with the ancillary and complementary analysis. New users would probably do well by focusing on the basics first.
- As is recommended in the *WISC–V Technical and Interpretive Manual*, future research will provide a better understanding of the response processes. Nevertheless, it would have been nice to break down the hypothesized processes by each subtest, for example, by using task analysis, or even by including what subtests required motor or verbal responses. A simple breakdown in a table could provide researchers or practitioners some hypotheses to test about the processes.

NO, say **Dumont and Willis** (Chapter 16):

- The addition of a visual memory task (Picture Span) to the Working Memory composite conforms to much of current neuropsychological research but complicates interpretation for examiners applying CHC theory and muddles comparison of WISC–V Working Memory scores with scores from the WISC–IV.
- Although the *WISC–V Technical and Interpretive Manual* provides some basic step-by-step instructions and examples to illustrate how to conduct both primary and ancillary profile analysis when evaluating an examinee's cognitive strengths and weaknesses, the manual does not elaborate further on score interpretation. The five ancillary and three complementary index scores appear, on face value, to be important and relevant aspects of a child's cognitive functioning; however, research is needed to demonstrate how best to use these new scales.

NO, say **Miller and McGill** (Chapter 17)

- It is suggested that examiners begin by describing the overall index score profile and then proceed to evaluating the level of performance and degree of variability for each measure individually. Although the implication is that profile variability and scatter is potentially clinically relevant, limited evidence is provided within the *WISC–V Technical and Interpretive Manual* to support these claims.

NO, says **Naglieri** (Chapter 18):

- The similarity in content across [intelligence and achievement tests] ensures that they will be correlated simply because of the similarity of the knowledge both demand. This is a significant conceptual and methodological issue that should be addressed in the WISC–V (or any of the traditional IQ test) manuals.
- The authors of the WISC–V should have made it clear that when this test is given to those with limited knowledge of English the Verbal Comprehension Index should be considered spoiled (or more a measure of verbal expression and comprehension of English) and not used to create a Full Scale.
- One can only conclude that there really is no clearly defined theory that was used to develop the fifth edition of this test and that users are, unfortunately, encouraged to find a model, hypothesis, or conceptualization that best fits the WISC–V scores a child or adolescent may earn.

NO, says **McCloskey** (Chapter 19):

- The interpretive approach outlined in the *WISC–V Technical and Interpretive Manual* provides much food for thought in that it raises many more questions about interpretation of test scores than it answers. Why does the test include subtests that do not contribute to any index? ... The interpretive structure outlined in the *WISC–V Technical and Interpretive Manual* makes no mention of what to do with the subtests that are not used in construction of any of the indexes.... Ignoring the potential contributions of these subtests to a comprehensive assessment battery and to index-level interpretive options is truly baffling.

- **Is** there a difference between a process and an ability? … Unfortunately, the WISC–V nomenclature obscures rather than clarifies the issue of defining these constructs.

NO, say **Canivez and Watkins** (Chapter 20):

- "Bad usage of tests" (Buros, 1965, p. xxiv) is exacerbated by the great number of score comparisons and analyses promoted for the WISC–V. Users should remember that "just because the test or its scoring software produces a score, you need not interpret it" (Kranzler & Floyd, 2013, p. 95). Furthermore, users must be mindful of the advice of Weiner (1989) that the ethical psychologist will "(a) know what their tests can do and (b) act accordingly" (p. 829). It is our hope that the information in this review and our independent analyses will provide the information necessary for clinicians and researchers to follow this sage advice.

HOW GOOD ARE THE WISC–V'S PSYCHOMETRIC PROPERTIES AND TEST DEVELOPMENT PROCEDURES?

Across reviews, there is general consensus that the WISC–V meets the basics of excellent psychometric properties in terms of norms, reliability, stability, and validity. Test development procedures are also generally praised. However, the reviewers made a number of salient points, mostly critical, on these topics.

Psychometric Properties

Reynolds and Hadorn (Chapter 15): It was laudable that all subtests were used in the CFAs rather than only the primary subtests. (Analysis with only the primary subtests were also reported, however.) Moreover, it is laudable that higher-order models were used.

Miller and McGill (Chapter 17) were less impressed with the factor analyses: The absence of several plausible measurement models (e.g., correlated factors, bifactor) from the CFA analyses is noteworthy, as are the lack of exploratory factor analysis (EFA) results. These authors also had concerns with reliability: Use of coefficient alpha to estimate the reliability of multidimensional measures is not ideal; coefficient alpha may overestimate the reliability of a measure even more when items within a measure are influenced by multiple common or group factors (e.g., WISC–V index-level abilities). In such circumstances, the use of alternative omega coefficients has been advised.

Canivez and Watkins (Chapter 20) concurred with criticisms of the CFA and use of coefficient alpha, and also objected to claims of clinical validity.

- They conducted a rigorous series of factor-analytic studies (presented in Appendix I in the downloadable resources: www.wiley.com/go/itwiscv). They stated that results from EFA and CFA converged and suggested that the best representation of WISC–V measurement is a bifactor model with four specific group factors, but the limited portions of variance uniquely captured by the four specific group factors is low.
- Regarding coefficient alpha, they stated that WISC–V reliability estimates and SEMs should be considered best-case estimates because they do not consider other major sources of error such as transient error, administration error, or scoring error that influence test scores in clinical assessments. They computed a variety of omega coefficients (also presented in Appendix I). They concluded that the w_s coefficients indicated too little true score variance associated with the four specific group factors, with the possible exception of Processing Speed, to warrant confident interpretation in clinical practice.
- Finally, regarding claims of the test's clinical validity: The *WISC–V Technical and Interpretive*

Manual further asserted that this information about group mean differences "provides evidence for the clinical utility and discriminant validity of the WISC–V subtests and composites" (p. 112). Unfortunately these conclusions are insufficiently supported by comparisons of distinct groups, which provide necessary *but not sufficient* evidence for clinical utility.

Test Development Procedures

Schneider (Chapter 9): The factor analyses of the WISC–IV suggested that Picture Concepts just did not have much in common with Matrix Reasoning, other than *g*. Figure Weights is a much better *Gf* mate to Matrix Reasoning than Picture Concepts was on the WISC–IV.

Reynolds and Hadorn (Chapter 15): The *WISC–V Technical and Interpretive Manual* mentions two approaches to item bias. The first was to use experts to identify problematic items.... Experts generally are not adept at identifying items that are biased in the statistical sense. The other step was to perform differential item functioning using samples of 54 African American and Hispanic children. Not much detail is presented about the analysis....Unless we are missing something, details seem to be lacking. We arc not suggesting a nefarious agenda, but more information would be useful.... Also: Several sources were used to guide improvement in content validity. In all, there is not much presented in the test content section.... Some more explicit links may have been helpful.

Dumont and Willis (Chapter 16): Conspicuously missing from the General Ability Index is the second Visual Spatial Index primary subtest (Visual Puzzles). We could not find an explanation for the elimination of this one subtest.... [However] we applaud the decision to limit subtest substitutions to the FSIQ and to permit only a single substitution in that calculation. We hope that examiners will follow that rule.

Naglieri (Chapter 18)**:** Is it really a good idea to measure intelligence using subtests that also require knowledge? ... It was encouraging to see that the authors of the WISC–V manual included

a section entitled "Update Theoretical Foundations." I wondered if the development of the fifth edition was actually guided by a theory. That hope was quickly dashed.

McCloskey (Chapter 19): One puzzling aspect of the construction of the primary indexes is why Similarities and Vocabulary were combined to produce an index that lacks the kind of homogeneity represented in the other four indexes ... Whether one agrees with Wechsler ... or not, it seems fitting that the test that bears his name would include an FSIQ score in keeping with his original conceptions about general intelligence. Unfortunately, the current version of the WISC represents a significant departure from the concept of FSIQ even though it offers an index with that name .... It is hard to see how the FSIQ and the [Woodcock-Johnson IV] General Intellectual Ability [composite] could ever be considered as even roughly equivalent measures of the same construct, whatever that construct might be.

A FEW OF OUR FAVORITE THINGS

- **Schneider's** (Chapter 9) turn of phrase:
  - There is a secret but widely shared pleasure in rooting for the underdog. A young and scrappy David Wechsler, armed with his namesake tests, may once have faced off against that erstwhile Goliath, the Stanford-Binet, but that was a long time ago. Underdog enthusiasts now have other tests to root for and often have a long list of gripes about King David's tests. I certainly have mine. If I am being honest, though, I must admit that, on balance, the Wechsler tests have been good stewards of the realm.
  - Although to my impatient nature, progress has been slow, it is clear that each successor in the Davidic line has been noticeably better than its predecessor. To be fair, there is considerable risk in innovating too quickly. It is easy to forget that "creative destruction" involves actual destruction, and that in the

wreckage there are things that were once cherished and beautiful. It is therefore prudent for leaders to give ground gradually to overeager radicals and at the same time patiently prod the hidebound forces of orthodoxy out of complacency.

- **Reynolds and Hadorn** (Chapter 15):
  - For their great summary and overview of confirmatory factor analyses (CFA), and their historical perspective that emphasized the WISC–IV's dramatic changes and how it deviated sharply from WISC tradition.
  - And for their wit:
    - A Verbal-Performance factor structure was implausible. No reason to bring those back!
    - Although perhaps a subtle change, it is worth a comment. The new descriptive classification system may eliminate the words *superior* and *borderline* from intelligence testing forever!
    - The WISC–V, like its predecessor, certainly contains some big changes, some of which may relieve or concern.
    - If subtests had feelings, the supplemental subtests probably always felt secondary.
- **Dumont and Willis's** (Chapter 16) clinical insight: We hope that examiners attempting to compare current and previous test scores will administer Letter–Number Sequencing and make an apples-to-apples comparison between the WISC–IV and WISC–V measures of working memory.
- **Miller and McGill's** (Chapter 17) Table 17.1, which presents a concise, detailed, insightful list of the WISC–V's strengths and weaknesses in these areas: Theoretical Foundation, Family of Related Products, Psychometric Properties, Quality of Testing Materials and Administration Issues, and Interpretive Options.
- **Naglieri's** (Chapter 18) reminiscences about his apprenticeship with Alan and Nadeen at the University of Georgia in the 1970s when he earned his PhD, had more publications than most of the faculty, helped spearhead the development of the K–ABC, and became the

staunchest supporter (more so than his mentors) of the separation of intelligence from achievement: "When Alan Kaufman described the WISC–R Verbal scale as achievement…I remember thinking 'that makes a lot of sense.'"

- **McCloskey's** (Chapter 19) ability to explain and deeply understand the nuances of the differences between processes and abilities, and between cognition and intelligence, and to reach back into history to help us understand the elusive *g* construct.
- **Also, McCloskey's pun:** "Given the statements made that qualify the nature of the complementary subtests, one wonders why they are even there. A group of surprise offerings for your enjoyment, compliments of the chef!" (Author's note: Susie often explains that the *complementary* subtests and index scores might be thought of as a *complimentary* test within the test).
- **Canivez and Watkins** (Chapter 20) going the full nine yards.
- They criticized an array of psychometric aspects of the WISC–V in their review and then attempted to back up their arguments by conducting extensive and exhaustive exploratory and confirmatory factor analyses of the WISC–V. This study is reported in Appendix I in the downloadable resources: www.wiley.com/go/itwiscv. Canivez and Watkins make elaborate arguments in defense of their position, which they buttress with statistics and logic. The three authors of *Intelligent Testing with the WISC–V* do not agree with their position. We adhere to Dr. Wechsler's frequent admonition to Alan that his scales are "first and foremost clinical instruments." Like Dr. Wechsler was, based on his training with Spearman and Pearson, we are statistically savvy. And we respect Canivez and Watkins's analyses and passion and professionalism. We just don't agree with their conclusions—but are delighted to include their perspectives and their incisive test review in the book. Without dissent and controversy, there can be no intelligent testing.

PART 6

AFTERWORD: ALAN KAUFMAN REFLECTS ON DAVID WECHSLER AND HIS LEGACY

Part I—written in 1992 and reprinted with permission of *The School Psychologist*

Part II—written in 2015 for *Intelligent Testing with the WISC–V*

AFTERWORD

ALAN S. KAUFMAN

I was invited by APA Division 16's *School Psychologist* to write about my relationship with David Wechsler about 20 years after I had worked with him on the revision of the 1949 WISC and the development of the WISC–R. "Dr. Wechsler Remembered" appeared in 1992 and was reprinted as the preface of *Intelligent Testing with the WISC–III* in 1994 and, again, as the preface of the first edition (2009) of *Essentials of WAIS–IV Assessment*. Once more it appears here. But this time it is Part I (1992) of an afterword, joined by Part II (2015). I wrote this continuation of Dr. Wechsler Remembered expressly for *Intelligent Testing with the WISC–V*, as I continue to reflect about the man I knew as a friend and ponder the power of his enduring legacy—nearly a half century after I was introduced to him in 1969.

DR. WECHSLER REMEMBERED, PART I

Reprinted with permission of *The School Psychologist* (Spring 1992, Vol. 46, No. 2), APA Division 16.

It is more than a decade since David Wechsler died in May 1981 at the age of 85, and I still miss him. More than any professor or older colleague, Dr. Wechsler was my mentor. I worked closely with him between late 1970 and early 1974 to help transform the WISC into a revised and restandardized battery—a test that was known as the WISC (Rev.) until a last-minute decision changed it to the WISC–R. The recent publication of the WISC–III represents a quiet burial for its predecessor, and for an important part of my past. But the changing of the guard has also rekindled a wealth of memories and feelings

regarding the great man who had the courage to challenge Terman's Binet, and the vision to triumph.

I originally entitled this informal paper "David Wechsler Remembered" but realized immediately that I never called him by his first name. He was always *Dr.* Wechsler, and not just to me, then a kid in his mid-20s, a few months past his PhD. Even the gray-haired men who were my bosses—esteemed psychologists all, whose offices lined the east wall and overlooked the United Nations Building—called him Dr. Wechsler. Behind closed doors, they referred to him smugly as "David" and liked to joke that the manuals should say "Despite David Wechsler" instead of "By David Wechsler." But to his face, no one ever complained, and no one ever called him David—unless it was after polishing off the second or third martini ("extra dry, straight up, with a twist of lemon") at the occasional, mandatory, ritualistic business lunches.

Dr. Wechsler possessed a rare blend of humility and grandeur. From the first day I met him, he treated me with kindness and with a respect I had not yet earned. He was soft-spoken, yet every word was carefully measured and carried authority. He was a man of unusual compassion and unflagging integrity. He lacked patience for the pomp and circumstance and protocol that permeated the first few corporate meetings that addressed the issue of a WISC revision. The meetings were tedious affairs, spiced with old recollections by Project Directors Past, and an incredible amount of weasel wording and bush circling by distinguished executives who couldn't quite mouth the words, "Dr. Wechsler, there are a number of black psychologists who don't much care for the WISC, and there have been some serious complaints with a lot of specific items."

At the end of the third meeting, when once more nothing was accomplished, Dr. Wechsler ended the meeting by stating simply that this was the last group meeting; from now on, he said, "Alan will come alone to my apartment, and we'll hammer out the revised WISC." And that's exactly what happened. I'd take a taxi to his East Side Manhattan apartment, and for two or three hours, week after week, we'd engage in friendly battle. He insisted that I be totally honest and tell him every thought and concern. I couldn't do that at first, but I soon realized it was the most prudent course of action. After the first meeting, he told me to put down my pen. He then talked for about 20 minutes, recounting his version of what had just transpired; he revealed every one of my "secret" feelings and perceptions, unraveling in intricate detail my attitudes and emotions about every issue we discussed and each decision we had made. I just stared at him, probably looking like retarded Benny of *LA Law*, and said nothing; how could I argue, when we both knew he was on the mark with every comment. I had always prided myself on my poker face, but I was face to face with the master clinician—the best one I would ever meet.

From that point on, I never held back anything. He would usually respond calmly, but occasionally I'd strike a raw nerve, and his grandfatherly smile would evaporate. His temples would start to pulse, and his entire face and scalp would turn crimson. I'd unconsciously move my chair back in self-protection, the way I did when I tested hard-core prisoners on the old WAIS and had to ask the question, "Why should we keep away from bad company?" I struck that exposed nerve when I urged him to eliminate the Comprehension item about walking away from a fight if someone much smaller starts to fight with you. The argument that you can't walk away from any fight in a black ghetto just added fuel to his rage. When I suggested, at a later meeting, that he just *had* to get rid of the item, "Why should women and children be saved first in a shipwreck?" or

incur the wrath of the new wave of militant feminists, his response was instant. With red face and pulsing head, he stood up, leaned on his desk with extended arms, and said as if he were firing a semiautomatic, "Chivalry may be dying. Chivalry may be dead. *But it will not die on the WISC.*"

So I waited a couple of weeks before bringing up those two items again. That particular battle ended in a tie; the fight item stayed, the shipwreck item was mercifully dropped. Though it was a little like going one-on-one with Michael Jordan, I relished those meetings. He had a good sense of humor, but not when it came to eliminating items. Only once did he readily agree to dropping an item: "What should you do if you see a train approaching a broken track?" I mentioned that if a 6- or 7-year-old child sees a train coming near a broken track, waving a white flag is not the brightest thing in the world to do; a 3-point answer on a 2–1–0 scale is "Run like hell." He laughed.

One Saturday, I drove to Manhattan with my then 5-year-old daughter Jennie to deliver a manual chapter to Dr. Wechsler. For 15 minutes or so, he charmed her, played with her, and joked with her, all the while maintaining his keen clinician's eye. I still remember his nod of approval when she responded to his question "In what way are a mommy and a daddy alike?" by saying, "They're the same 'cause they're both parents—and both human beans too, y' know." He looked at me, smiled broadly, and said, "Jennie is *very* smart—y' know.'" I took Jennie's hand and walked to the elevator. The elevator operator, who knew me quite well by then, tried to engage me in conversation, but I didn't hear a word. In fact, I didn't need the elevator, I could have flown down the eight stories. *Wechsler had just told me my daughter was very smart!* I couldn't have been more elated if Freud had told me she had a nice personality or if Bert Parks had said she was beautiful.

Dr. Wechsler liked to test me too. Whenever I arrived for our meetings, his wife Ruth always greeted me and ushered me into his study. He had one of those lamps that turned on and off by touching it—common now, but not then. I was biding my time by turning it on and off, experimenting to see how light a touch would trigger the mechanism. Out of the corner of my eye, I saw Dr. Wechsler standing in the hallway studying me, smiling, enjoying himself. I wondered how long this consummate clinician had been there, and hoped I hadn't done anything really inappropriate.

I especially enjoyed Dr. Wechsler's warm, human side, which emerged in casual moments when he didn't have to be "on." The serious and sometimes gruff side came out in business meetings, and the occasional animal rage was reserved for anyone who challenged the perfection of nearly any of his hand-picked, time-tested items, especially one that had its roots in his original Wechsler-Bellevue scales. But he displayed unabashed boy-like enthusiasm when he showed off materials for the new subtests he was constantly working on (at age 75!)—his favorite was a set of three Chinese dolls that had to be tapped in the right sequence—or when he sifted through a lifetime of comic strips that he saved for new Picture Arrangement items. And his eyes twinkled when he talked about his grandchildren; or reminisced about visiting Freud in Vienna; or spoke warmly about spending a week at the home of former Israeli Defense Minister Moshe Dayan and his wife; or boasted sheepishly about being greeted at the Bucharest Airport by the King of Romania (his birthplace in 1896); or played for over an hour with our son James, then 7 months old and called Jamie, when he and Ruth visited my family in Athens, Georgia, in April 1975. (Author's note—James is now Professor of Educational Psychology at University of Connecticut and an international leader in creativity.)

That visit was completely unexpected. I had called him to ask if he would speak by conference phone to my Intelligence Testing class the first year I was at the University of Georgia. I was crushed when he said he didn't want to do it; I had assured my class that my friend Dr. Wechsler would say yes (they already doubted

that I had even met the man). A couple of days later, he sent me a letter saying that he didn't like talking to people unless he could see them. "I would prefer, and would suggest instead, a face-to-face session at the University," he wrote. "No fee for talk, but reimbursement for travel." My school psychology students enjoyed a private question-and-answer session with him. Later in the day, I experienced high anxiety introducing him to a standing-room-only auditorium crowd of students and faculty.

That evening, Nadeen and I had dinner with the Wechslers, and we were looking forward to a bit of quiet relaxation. It was not to be. Dr. Wechsler had two things that were heavy on his mind. One was the true meaning of being an intelligent adult (he started to doubt the WAIS's effectiveness for measuring adult IQ when he realized that he had trouble solving Block Design items quickly). His other concern was the Dan Rather IQ special that was to air for the first time that night, and he absolutely didn't want to miss seeing it in his hotel room. He kept asking Nadeen and me how one could tell if an adult was smart, and no matter what we answered, he probed and challenged us until we were limp, until he was satisfied that we had covered every aspect of the issue. He confided to us that he was starting to work on a test called the Wechsler Intelligence Scale for the Elderly; had he published it, the test would have had the best acronym ever—W.I.S.E. Though the meal wasn't as relaxed as we had hoped, he was quick to praise our ideas and took a few notes on his napkin. (Years later, we would think back to that discussion when we began developing the Kaufman Adolescent and Adult Intelligence Test, or KAIT.)

When Dr. Wechsler relented in his questioning of us, he revealed his almost desperate sadness about the Dan Rather special. Though he wouldn't see it until it aired that night, he had been tipped off by an acquaintance from the TV station that the program was blatantly anti-IQ testing. Dr. Wechsler and Ruth recalled how Rather had come to their apartment; charmed them during the interview and videotaping, and told them how much he personally valued the IQ concept and how important the Wechsler scales were to the world. Rather's demeanor led Dr. Wechsler to say things candidly and—in retrospect—a bit recklessly. He was chastising himself during the meal, but mostly he was furious at Rather's behavior. Dr. Wechsler was honest and straightforward and just couldn't fathom duplicity in someone else. The next morning, after the TV show had confirmed Dr. Wechsler's worst fears, we drove to the airport in almost total silence. When he did speak, it was clear that Dr. Wechsler's anger was under control, but he was deeply wounded by the dishonesty, the blatant abuse of trust. And he felt that the strong anti-IQ statements by "people who should know better" were a personal attack on his life's work.

The kindness that Dr. Wechsler showed me by traveling to Georgia to meet with my students was typical of how he treated me the whole time I knew him. He was aware of the steep status hierarchy that existed at The Psychological Corporation, and he made sure to praise me in the presence of the upper echelon. He consistently treated my ideas with respect and never dismissed them—even the stupid ones—without first thinking about them carefully (unless I was suggesting deleting an item). He trusted me in all aspects of test construction and deferred to my knowledge of psychometrics; when he questioned a statistical decision, he would usually give in, saying, "I'm just a clinician." It wasn't until the WISC–R was nearing publication that I found out from someone else that Dr. Wechsler had studied statistics under Charles Spearman and Karl Pearson in London after World War I.

One day, he decided that he wanted me to coauthor a book on children's intelligence with him, and he made the announcement in front of one of my bosses. It was the first I'd heard about it, and it was lucky I was sitting down when he said it. When I took the position at the University of Georgia, just after the WISC–R was published, we still planned on writing the book together. During his visit, he told me that he just

didn't have the energy to participate too much in the writing of the book, and that he thought it would be hard to collaborate from a distance. But he made me promise to write a book devoted to the WISC–R, and I gave him my word. Those were the seeds for *Intelligent Testing with the WISC–R*.

The standardization of the WISC–R seemed to take forever to Dr. Wechsler, and he wanted the test to come out while he could still enjoy it. He would ask me in mock seriousness whether a standardization was even necessary. "After all," he'd say in a quiet voice while giving me a conspiratorial smile, "*we* know how well the children are going to perform on all those subtests, don't we? So why bother with all that standardization testing?" He was joking, but it was no joke that he believed firmly all he needed was 15 minutes or so of personal interview and a test item or two, and he could pinpoint a person's IQ within a few points and diagnose any pathology. He insisted that he could diagnose clinical patients by their answer to the question, "What is the population of the United States?" I never doubted that he could back up his boast. He didn't do too badly with his one-item, 15-minute assessment of my daughter Jennie's intelligence more than 20 years ago; she made Phi Beta Kappa in college, and has now almost completed her PhD in clinical psychology. (Author's note—Jennie Kaufman Singer is now a clinical psychologist, Associate Professor of Criminal Justice at CSU—Sacramento, and a major contributor to this book.)

And how would Dr. Wechsler evaluate the WISC–III? Well, he'd like the artwork, but he'd insist that it wasn't necessary. The black-and-white pictures worked fine before, so why mess with them? And he'd be impressed by the immaculate standardization and super-sophisticated psychometric treatment of the data, but he wouldn't admit it to anyone. Instead, he'd argue that his all–Coney Island standardization of the original Wechsler-Bellevue was pretty darned good; and he'd wonder aloud why you needed something called confirmatory factor analysis to tell the world what he knew axiomatically back in the early 1930s—that his scales primarily measured Verbal and Performance intelligence.

He wouldn't be too interested in the improved bottom and top for several subtests, most notably Arithmetic, which now gives bonus points for the six hardest items. He rejected most attempts that I made to add easy and hard items to the WISC–R, saying firmly, "My scales are meant for people with average or near-average intelligence, clinical patients who score between 70 and 130. They are *clinical* tests." When I reminded him that psychologists commonly use his scales for the extremes, and want to make distinctions within the "below 70" and "above 130" groups, he answered, "Then that is their misfortune. It's not what I tell them to do, and it's not what a good clinician ought to do. They should know better."

He wouldn't care much for the new Object Assembly item, the cut-up soccer ball. How do I know? Because when we were developing new items for the WISC–R tryout, I brought him a dozen envelopes, each with a cut-up puzzle I had made. I opened each envelope and assembled each puzzle, and he immediately said "Yes" or "No" to each one. He liked three, and hated nine. I couldn't figure out his decision rule, so he forced me to study the ones he liked and the ones he rejected, but every hypothesis I offered was wrong. Finally, with a touch of exasperation at my denseness, he said, "Don't you see. My Object Assembly items must have at least one puzzle piece that tells the person at once what the object is—like the horse's head or the front of the car. I don't want them fumbling around like one of Thorndike's cats or monkeys. I want them to know right away what they've got to put together." He also would not have permitted bonus points on the WPPSI–R for Block Design or the new Object Assembly subtest; as a clinician and grandfather he knew that even very bright young children often respond to puzzles like the fireman in the old Binet item who smoked a cigar before putting out the fire.

But the soccer ball and WPPSI–R time bonuses wouldn't have made Dr. Wechsler's temples start to pulse. That would have happened when he saw the Picture Arrangement items. He loved to expose examinees to emotion-laden situations, to watch how they solved the problems, to listen to their spontaneous comments, to study their reactions to danger, to conflict, to authority, to violence. "Where's the boxing match?" he would have stormed. "Replaced by a girl on a slide! And what happened to the burglar? And look what they did to the fire item! Instead of burning down his house, the kid's a damned hero!" And he would have been incensed at the emasculation of the bench item. In the old item, "Some poor sap gets hit by the bench and then gets clobbered in a fight. Great stuff! But now they just kiss and make up."

Dr. Wechsler also wouldn't have been too pleased with the elimination of *beer-wine* in Similarities or of *knife* and *gamble* in Vocabulary—all potent clinical stimuli. He never worried much about a person missing an item or two or three because of its clinical content. More than once, he'd chide me, until it finally sunk in, "First and foremost, the Wechsler scales are clinical tests—not psychometric tests but clinical tests." That was why he got so upset when someone complained about the unfairness of this or that item. What's a couple of items to a good clinician? He never could really accept the stupid way so many people interpreted his tests, with formulas, and cut-off points, and the like; it's not what he had ever planned for his clinical Wechsler scales.

When Nadeen and I started to develop the K-ABC back in 1978, the Wechsler influence was strong, although we differed from him in believing that tests such as Information and Vocabulary really measure achievement for schoolchildren, not IQ. (He didn't much care for my suggestion back in 1971 to pull out a few subtests from the Verbal Scale and offer the clinician a separate "Cultural Quotient.") Maybe it was because I felt a bit guilty at departing from his theory for our intelligence test, or maybe I just got too involved with too many things, but I stopped calling and writing Dr. Wechsler during the last years of his life. I didn't realize how much that hurt him until Ruth wrote to me, in response to our letter of sympathy, "I must tell you, Alan, he was very fond of you and admired you very much. I'm sorry you didn't write once in a while as he talked about you and what a pleasure it was to work with you on the WISC–R."

I can't undo it, though I wish I could, and her words still sting when I read them. But I try to focus instead on how much Dr. Wechsler taught me, both as a person and clinician. I was fortunate beyond words to have his life cross mine, to work so closely with this legend for several years, to have him as a mentor and friend. Those at The Psychological Corporation who did such a marvelous job of revising the WISC–R and assembling the WISC–III undoubtedly took for granted what I fervently wished for as a young Assistant Director two decades ago: the freedom to make objective item and subtest decisions without the interference and subjective whims of the author.

Little did I realize then that those battles with the Master would shape my own development as a test author and trainer of school psychologists, and would remain forever etched—fresh and vibrant and poignant—in my memory. The Project Directors of the "ISC–III" and the "PPSI–R" have no notion of their loss; they never knew the man behind the "W."

DR. WECHSLER REMEMBERED, PART II (2015)

Alan S. Kaufman

Dr. David Wechsler, my mentor, was one of the founders of the field of clinical psychology and one of the first to open up a private practice. His innovations began when the United States entered World War I in 1917, and his insightful approach to the clinical assessment of intelligence continues to reverberate a century later. And the Wechsler-Bellevue Intelligence Scale that he published in 1939, on the eve of

World War II, continues to produce offspring that reign supreme in virtually every civilized nation. With only slight exaggeration, WISC and WAIS are nearly household words in more than 25 languages with the "W" reminding us that he left his imprint on society.

I worked closely with Dr. Wechsler in the early 1970s, shortly after my 25th birthday, when he was just a bit older than I am now. And I can't shake the fact that he was the most important person I ever knew, perhaps the most interesting, and surely the one who cast the largest shadow on my life as a psychologist and also as a man. I wrote "Dr. Wechsler Remembered" in the early 1990s, shortly after the WISC–R had been put out to pasture and the WISC–III was the new kid in town. My beloved WISC–R was about to become a historical relic, except for the occasional psychologist who wouldn't let go of it. (Before the Flynn effect became part of the lexicon, some neuropsychologists were reluctant to part with the Wechsler Bellevue more than a half century after it was published.)

So I was somewhere in the grieving process when the WISC–III was published because I had so much of myself invested in the WISC–R. Nadeen, who worked directly with Dr. Wechsler in 1971 during the tryout phase of the WISC revision, was empathic to my grief. She suggested that I stop telling anecdotes about Wechsler when I gave keynote addresses, thinking that might help. It didn't. I soon put them back into my invited talks, and I still tell Wechsler anecdotes when I give my very occasional lectures. Many of my favorite Wechsler stories are documented in *IQ Testing 101* (A. S. Kaufman, 2009), a book written at the request of my son James, editor of Springer's wonderful Psych 101 series. For example:

> Like Alfred Binet, Wechsler met with frustration and couldn't find a publisher willing to subsidize his bold venture. So he did it himself. With several of his psychologist friends, Wechsler tested nearly 2,000 children, adolescents, and adults in Coney Island, Brooklyn, New York. The sample didn't

represent the whole country, and it was far too urban. But it was still quite good, because Wechsler knew from his own research that socioeconomic status was the key to getting a good "norms" sample.... But when the census called for farmers, farm managers, or farm laborers to be included in the norms group, Wechsler couldn't find any farmers in Brooklyn. So he tested barbers. He had done some research, and found that barbers and farmers performed about the same, on average, on his Wechsler-Bellevue test. His sample may have had too many barbers, too many people who were raised on Nathan's hotdogs and fries in Coney Island, and not enough mid-westerners. But for the 1930s, his methods were darned clever. (pp. 30–31)

As time has gone by, I have come to look at Dr. Wechsler from different perspectives. I have become more of a student of history and found out things about his life that I didn't know. He talked about his life extensively and his diverse experiences. But he never talked about the hardships he had endured and the prejudices he had faced, starting in early childhood. And I just didn't ask. It wasn't until I began to write his biography a few years ago (A. S. Kaufman, 2012), and started to collaborate with the brilliant historian John Wasserman on a second biography of Dr. Wechsler (Wasserman & Kaufman, in press), that I developed more insight into the man who brought the Wechsler-Bellevue to the world.

He emigrated with his family to the United States in 1902 at the age of 6 when famine and poor economic conditions in Romania led to "worsening the scapegoating of Jews and resulting in severe applications of existing anti-Jewish decrees" (Wasserman, 2012). The legislative act, as reported in the *Washington Post* in 1902 ("Forcing an exodus," 1902), "forbids Jews to engage in manual labor of any kind.... But that is not all; in addition to being robbed of the use of his limbs, he is muzzled. For the government, pledged to destroy the Jew, has suspended the constitution as far as he is concerned."

By the age of 10, he was an orphan. He was raised by his older brother, Israel, a kind and brilliant mentor who later became a pioneer in neurology. Dr. Wechsler once told me how much he valued a chapter that he wrote for his brother's handbook on clinical neurology (Wechsler, 1928), shortly after he earned his PhD at Columbia; but he never mentioned that he was an orphan and that his brother was his caretaker.

Dr. Wechsler revered his professors at Columbia who guided him through his graduate work, especially Robert S. Woodworth, who supervised his master's degree in 1917 and his postwar PhD in 1925, and James McKeen Cattell, who gave him his first professional job. (J. Cattell is the man who was Galton's lab assistant in England, who coined the term *mental tests* and founded the field of intelligence testing in the United States—not the Cattell from CHC theory) "Columbia and the other Ivy League universities all have well-documented records of anti-Semitism in the early twentieth century, and many of Wechsler's supervisors (e.g., J. McKeen Cattell, R. S. Woodworth, E. G. Boring at Harvard) all made statements that we would now consider anti-Semitic" (Wasserman, personal communication, January 5, 2015). Woodworth's letters of recommendation for Jewish students have been chronicled (Winston, 1996), as have E. G. Boring's correspondence (Winston, 1998). Boring, renowned at Harvard, supervised Wechsler in 1917 when the young master's student scored army intelligence tests as a World War I civilian volunteer (Winston, 1998).

What emerges from the attitude toward Jews at the time Wechsler completed his PhD in 1925 is that Jews were virtually blackballed from academic positions.

Winston (1996) wrote:

Otto Klineberg described Woodworth as "a constant source of help and encouragement." But Woodworth was not always encouraging. The unpublished diary of Daniel Harris, who received his Ph.D. at Columbia in 1931, notes in his entry for 22 November 1934, that "about May 1929, I had gotten a severe blow when Woodworth told me I couldn't be his assistant...

the following year because I was Jewish and that I shouldn't be too hopeful in an academic career." (p. 33)

And Winston (1998), quoting from a letter written by Boring in 1925 about a Jewish candidate:

He is a Jew, and on this account we have not found it so far easy to place him in a college teaching position in psychology, because of the personal prejudice that exists against Jews in many academic circles and possibly especially in psychology. (pp. 27–28)

With academic positions mostly out of reach for Jewish PhDs in psychology, Winston (1996) pondered the alternative:

the choice was obvious: find a career in the youthful and as yet amorphous field of pre–World War II clinical psychology, where antisemitism seemed less of an issue than in academe, and the possibilities for employment seemed better. Many Jewish psychologists from Columbia, such as Aaron Nadel and David B. Klein, took this path during the 1930s. The migration of many Jewish psychologists into clinical work, and their return to academia after World War II as clinical psychology faculty had important effects on the discipline. (p. 38)

Not surprisingly, "a 29-year-old David Wechsler, having completed his dissertation, had difficulty finding a job and contacted his old professor, Cattell, who hired him" (Wasserman, 2012, p. 33). It is true that Dr. Wechsler never complained about the anti-Jewish sentiments that might have pervaded his experiences with Woodworth or Boring, nor did he ever tell me that his great desire was to be a professor at a university. Yet I can't help but believe that his ethnic background led him toward clinical psychology, which wasn't even a field when he earned his graduate degrees in Woodworth's innovative experimental abnormal psychology program. But whatever led him to choose clinical psychology over academia, he was well suited to the profession. He was a natural clinician with

observational skills that were 5 or 6 standard deviations above the mean. And he moved to the beat of his own drummer, realizing that Terman's field of psychometric testing was static and had to be supplanted by the dynamic field of clinical assessment.

The essence of Terman's belief about IQ, the number itself, as the most important aspect of a person and society is the exact opposite of what Wechsler preached over his lifetime about the clinical value of IQ tests. Vintage Terman, from his famous debates with journalist Walter Lippmann in the early 1920s (Wasserman, 2012):

When our intelligence scales have become more accurate and the laws governing IQ changes have been more definitively established it will then be possible to say that there is nothing about an individual as important as his IQ, except possibly his morals. (p. 3)

And also: "The first concern of a nation should be the average IQ of its citizens" (Terman, 1922, p. 657).

Wechsler saw so much beyond the numbers, and his ideas were consistently decades, even generations, ahead of his time. Wechsler (1939) was an early advocate of measuring adaptive behavior skills, urging that daily behaviors, social demands, and functional living skills be considered alongside IQ test results before assigning a mental deficiency diagnosis. He also reflected current philosophies by urging caution and sensitivity about the consequences of applying labels such as mental deficiency and genius based solely on IQ because "too much is at stake" (Wechsler, 1971, p. 54).

When Wechsler (1939) published the first form of the Wechsler–Bellevue, he cautioned clinicians:

The kind of life one lives is itself a pretty good test of a person's intelligence. When a life history (assuming it to be accurate) is in disagreement with the "psychometric," it is well to pause before attempting a classification on the basis of tests alone. Generally it will be found that the former is a more reliable criterion of the individual's intelligence. (p. 48).

The consummate clinician even analyzed himself:

> After completing his fellowship at the Sorbonne, Wechsler traveled through France, Switzerland, and Italy, before reluctantly returning to the United States.... His ambivalence about returning, as disclosed to Edwards (Wechsler, 1974b), was reflected in his 1922 paper on the psychopathology of indecision. (Wasserman, 2012, p. 33)

Wechsler was the opposite of Terman as a psychologist and he was the antithesis of Alfred Binet as a man (Hargus & Wasserman, 1993). The great French test developer, "a reserved man with few friends" (Tuddenham, 1974, p. 1071), wrote to a friend in 1901: "I educated myself all alone, without any teachers; I have arrived at my present scientific situation by the sole force of my fists; *no one*, you understand, no one, has ever helped me" (Wasserman, 2012, p. 12).

By contrast, in a 1975 interview, Wechsler credited Woodworth and E. L. Thorndike as contributing most to his intellectual development, and he also praised Augusta Bronner and William Healy for refining his clinical skills: "they were both wonderful clinicians and they were the first, as I recall, who had discussions of every individual case at which first the social worker would present her history, then the psychiatrist, then the psychologist, and they either praised the individual and so forth on the basis of these conferences" (Wechsler, Doppelt, & Lennon, 1975, p. 42). He also spoke often to me about how much he owed to Bernard Glueck of the New York Bureau of Child Guidance (where Wechsler worked in the early 1920s) for training him in a discipline that would later be known as school psychology.

And Wechsler was a great humanitarian who believed in equality. "[T]he tendency in recent years has been rather to exaggerate and overemphasize human differences, whether in the field of psychology, government or industry.... Now every democracy and particularly our own is based on the very contrary assumption; ... for the differences between men, when the totality of the capacities is considered, is surprisingly small" (Wechsler, 1930, p. 39). Wasserman (personal communication, January 5, 2015) adds that "through most of his career, Wechsler cautioned against interpreting group mean intelligence score differences as having importance in describing individual human beings."

Whereas Wechsler and Binet had very different personalities, these two innovators were "alone among the early figures in intelligence testing in not having advocated for eugenics. Terman, E. L. Thorndike, and many others supported eugenics causes. It makes sense that Wechsler, having come from Romania and undoubtedly having seen antisemitism throughout his life, would caution about eugenics, and he associated eugenics with totalitarian societies (Wasserman, personal communication, January 5, 2015).

Regarding the importance of Wechsler's Jewish heritage to him and his brother Israel, Wasserman (personal communication, January 5, 2015) pointed out that

> both worked actively on Jewish causes and were important advocates for the founding and development of the Hebrew University of Jerusalem. Israel Wechsler corresponded with Sigmund Freud and Albert Einstein, asking them to donate their papers to Hebrew University, as well as raising money for the construction of the university. David Wechsler helped to establish the psychology department at Hebrew University and was honored by Hebrew University for his service.... Wechsler also worked to establish mental health services for Jewish survivors of the Holocaust.

But, importantly, Wasserman concludes: "While I think it is ultimately important to discuss Wechsler's identity as a Jew, he also offered a more [humanitarian] approach to things, embracing all peoples."

Of all of Dr. Wechsler's vast contributions, the two professional ones that continue to reverberate in my mind concern his respect for the intelligence of the examiners who use his tests and his insights into the assessment of adult intelligence. I addressed both of these topics in a foreword (A. S. Kaufman, 2010) of an edited book devoted to the WAIS–IV:

Regarding the respect he gave other clinicians:

David Wechsler challenged the Stanford-Binet in the 1930s when no one else had either the courage or the inspiration .... Dr. Wechsler was not intimidated by the thoroughly revised and expanded Binet, touted in its own manual as the IQ test to end all IQ tests. He had vision .... He offered the sophisticated standard score statistic to replace the antiquated and inadequate MA/CA X 100 formula. Terman and Merrill (1937) were well aware of standard scores; they provided a table that converted IQs to standard scores in the test manual, and praised the metric: "From the statistical point of view, every advantage is in favor of the standard score" (p. 27). Yet they continued to derive IQs by formula because "the majority of teachers, school administrators, social workers, physicians, and others who utilize mental test results have not learned to think in statistical terms. To such a person a rating expressed as '+2 sigma' is just so much Greek." (Terman & Merrill, 1937, pp. 27–28)

Dr. Wechsler, never condescending to test users, knew better. When he published the Wechsler-Bellevue for children and adults (Wechsler, 1939), a scant 2 years after the revised Binet became available ... he never doubted that clinicians were smart enough to "speak Greek." (p. xiii–xiv)

Regarding his impact on adult assessment:

Arguably, his most important innovation with the 1939 Wechsler-Bellevue was that *he actually tested representative samples of adults to include in the standardization sample.* For the first

Stanford-Binet, Terman's (1916) adult sample was small, haphazard, and unrepresentative ... For all practical purposes, *Dr Wechsler developed the first real test of intelligence for adults in 1939,* even though the Binet had been used to assess the mental ability of the adult population for a generation. (pp. xiv–xv)

And Dr. Wechsler's legacy continues. He published the Wechsler Individual Achievement Test (WIAT; The Psychological Corporation, 1992) 10 years after his death in 1981 and coauthored the *Wechsler Nonverbal Scale of Ability* (WNV) with my former doctoral student, Jack Naglieri (Wechsler & Naglieri, 2006), a quarter of a century after his passing. *Now, that is a mentor*!

And here it is about a century after Dr. Wechsler earned his first graduate degree with Woodworth and had his first supervised testing experience with E. B. Boring. His worldwide influence remains intact. If his impact begins to subside in the next decade or two as high technology takes over the field of clinical assessment, so be it. But it hasn't happened yet. The Binet supremacy that began in Paris in 1905, and continued in the United States with Terman's Stanford-Binet in 1916, lasted for about 60 years. Wechsler's adult scales took over from the Binet by the early 1950s, but the triumph wasn't complete until the multiscore WISC surpassed the one-score Binet sometime during the 1960s, when the fields of learning disabilities and neuropsychology erupted on the testing scene. Wechsler's reign has surpassed that of Alfred Binet and Queen Victoria and has kept pace with Queen Elizabeth. Matarazzo's (1981) statement in the *American Psychologist* obituary that he wrote for Dr. Wechsler is as true today as when he wrote it: "Probably the work of no other psychologists, including Freud or Pavlov, has so *directly* impinged upon the lives of so many people" (p. 1542).

REFERENCES

"A Consensus on the Brain Training Industry from the Scientific Community," Max Planck Institute for Human Development and Stanford Center on Longevity, accessed October 22, 2014, http://longevity3.stanford.edu/blog/2014/10/15/the-consensus-on-the-brain-training-industry-from-the-scientific-community/

Aaron, L., & Dallaire, D. H. (2010). Parental incarceration and multiple risk experiences: Effects on family dynamics and children's delinquency. *Journal of Youth and Adolescence, 39*, 1471–1484.

Achenbach, T. M. (1991). *Manual for the Child Behavior Checklist/4–18 and 1991 Profile*. Burlington: University of Vermont.

Adams, K. M. & Spencer, R. J. (2011). Parsing Luria's science in the rear view mirror: Luria's legacy in the 21st century [Review of the book *Luria's legacy in the 21st century*, by A. L. Christensen, E. Goldberg, & Bougakov, D. (Eds.)]. *The Clinical Neuropsychologist, 25*, 323–325.

Agnew, R. A. (2001). Building on the foundation of general strain theory. Specifying the types of strain most likely to lead to crime and delinquency. *Journal of Research in Crime and Delinquency, 38*, 319–361.

Agnew, R. A. (2006). *Pressured into crime: An overview of general strain theory*. Los Angeles, CA: Roxbury.

Alexander, K. L., Entwisle, D. R., & Kabbani, N. S. (2001). The dropout process in life course perspective: Early risk factors at home and school. *Teachers College Record, 103*, 760–822.

Alfonso, V. C., & Flanagan, D. P. (2008). Assessment of preschool children: A framework for evaluating the adequacy of the technical characteristics of norm-referenced instruments. In B. Mowder, F. Rubinson, & A. Yasik (Eds.), *Evidence based practice in infant and early childhood psychology* (pp. 129–166). Hoboken, NJ: Wiley.

Alfonso, V. C., Johnson, A., Patinella, L., & Rader, D. E. (1998). Common WISC-III examiner errors: Evidence from graduate students in training. *Psychology in the Schools, 35*, 119–125.

Allan, D. M., Allan, N. P, Lerner, M. D., Farrington, A. L., & Lonigan, C. J. (2015) Identifying unique components of preschool children's self-regulatory skills using executive function tasks and continuous performance tests. *Early Childhood Research Quarterly, 32*, 40–50.

Alliance for Excellent Education. (2003). *The impact of education on: The economy*. http://all4ed.org/reports-factsheets/the-impact-of-education-on-the-economy/

Allison, J., Blatt, S. J., & Zimet, C. N. (1968). *The interpretation of psychological tests*. New York, NY: Harper & Row.

American Educational Research Association, American Psychological Association, & National Council on Measurement in Education. (1999). *Standards for educational and psychological testing*. Washington, DC: American Educational Research Association.

American Educational Research Association, American Psychological Association, & National Council on Measurement in Education. (2014). *Standards for educational and psychological testing*. Washington, DC: American Educational Research Association.

American Psychiatric Association. (2013). *Diagnostic and statistical manual of mental disorders* (5th ed.). Washington, DC: Author.

American Psychological Association (2010). *Clinical neuropsychology*. Retrieved from http://www.apa.org/ed/graduate/specialize/neuro.aspx

Anastasi, A., & Urbina, S. (1997). *Psychological testing*. Upper Saddle River, NJ: Prentice Hall.

Andrews, D. A., & Bonta, J. (1994). *The psychology of criminal conduct*. Cincinnati, OH: Anderson.

Andrews, D. A., & Bonta, J. (1998). *The psychology of criminal conduct* (2nd ed.). Cincinnati, OH: Anderson.

Andrews, D. A, Bonta, J., & Wormith, S. A. (2011). The Risk-Need-Responsivity (RNR) model: Does adding the Good Lives Model contribute to effective crime prevention? *Criminal Justice and Behavior, 38*, 735–755.

Andrews, D. A., Zinger, I., Hoge, R. D., Bonta, J., Gendreau, P., & Cullen, F. T. (1990). Does correctional treatment work? A clinically relevant and psychologically informed meta-analysis, *Criminology*, *28*, 369–404.

Archibald, L. M. D., & Gathercole, S. E. (2006a). Short-term memory and working memory in specific language impairment. In T. P. Alloway & S. E. Gathercole (Eds.), *Working memory and neurodevelopmental disorders* (pp. 139–160). New York, NY: Psychology Press.

Archibald, L. M. D., & Gathercole, S. E. (2006b). Visuospatial immediate memory in specific language impairment. *Journal of Speech, Language, and Hearing Research*, *49*, 265–277. doi:10.1044/1092–4388(2006/022)

Arinoldo, C. G. (1981). Black-white differences in the general cognitive index of the McCarthy Scales and in the Full Scale IQs of Wechsler's scales. *Journal of Clinical Psychology*, *37*, 630–638.

Arnsten, A. F. T., & Robbins, T. W. (2002). Neurochemical modulation of prefrontal cortical functioning in humans and animals. In D. T. Stuss & R. T. Knight (Eds.), *Principles of frontal lobe function* (pp. 31–50). New York, NY: Oxford University Press.

Ashkenazi, S., Mark-Zigdon, N., & Henik, A. (2009). Numerical distance effect in developmental dyscalculia. *Cognitive Development*, *24*, 387–400.

Asparouhov, T., & Muthen, B. (2009). Exploratory structural equation modeling. *Structural Equation Modeling*, *16*, 397–438.

Aspel, A. D., Willis, W. G., & Faust, D. (1998). School psychologists' diagnostic decision-making processes: Objective-subjective discrepancies. *Journal of School Psychology*, *36*, 137–149.

Astone, N. M., & McLanahan, S. S. (1991). Family structure, prenatal practices and high school completion. *American Sociological Review*, *56*, 309–320.

Attar, B. K., Guerra, N. G., & Tolan, P. H. (1994). Neighborhood disadvantage, stressful life events, and adjustment in urban elementary school children. *Journal of Clinical Child Psychology*, *26*, 391–400.

Aukema, E. J., Caan, M., Oudhuis, N., Majoie, C., Vos, F. M., Reneman, L., et al., (2009). White matter fractional anisotropy correlates with speed of processing and motor speed in young childhood cancer survivors. *International Journal of Radiation: Oncology, Biology, Physics*, *74*, 837–843.

Avan, B., & Kirkwood, B. (2010). Review of the theoretical frameworks for the study of child development within public health and epidemiology. *Journal of Epidemiology and Community Health*, *64*, 388–393. doi:10.1136/jech.2008.084046

Babad, E. Y., Mann, M., & Mar-Hayim, M. (1975). Bias in scoring the WISC subtests. *Journal of Consulting and Clinical Psychology*, *43*, 268. doi:10.1037/h0076368

Baddeley, A., Eysenck, M. W., & Anderson, M. C. (2008). *Memory*. New York, NY: Psychology Press.

Banich, M. T. (2004). *Cognitive neuroscience and neuropsychology* (2nd ed.). Boston, MA: Houghton-Mifflin.

Bannatyne, A. (1971). *Language, reading, and learning disabilities*. Springfield, IL: Charles C. Thomas.

Bannatyne, A. (1974). Diagnosis: A note on recategorization of WISC scaled scores. *Journal of Learning Disabilities*, *7*, 272–273.

Barbey, A. K., Colom, R., Paul, E. J., & Grafman, J. (2014). Architecture of human intelligence and working memory revealed by lesion mapping. *Brain Structure and Function*, *219*, 485–494.

Barbey, A. K., Colom, R., Solomon, J., Krueger, F., Forbes, C., & Grafman, J. (2012). An integrative architecture for general intelligence and executive function revealed by lesion mapping. *Brain*, *135*, 1154–1164.

Baron, I. S. (2005). Test review: Wechsler Intelligence Scale for Children–Fourth Edition (WISC–IV). *Child Neuropsychology*, *11*, 471–475.

Baskin, T. W., Quintana, S. M., & Slaten, C. D. (2014). Family belongingness, gang friendships, and psychological distress in adolescent achievement. *Journal of Counseling and Development*, *92*, 398–405.

Baumeister, R. F., & Leary, M. R. (1995). The need to belong: Desire for interpersonal attachments as a fundamental human motivation. *Psychological Bulletin*, *117*, 497–529.

Bayley, N., & Jones, H. E. (1937). Environmental correlates of mental and motor development: A cumulative study from infancy to six years. *Child Development*, *8*, 329–341.

Bear, M. F., Conners, B. W., & Paradiso, M. A. (2016). *Neuroscience: Exploring the brain* (4th ed.). New York, NY: Wolters Kluwer.

Beck, J. S., Beck, A. T., & Jolly, J. B. (2005). *Beck youth inventories* (2nd ed.). Bloomington, MN: Pearson.

Belfiore, P. J., Auld, R., & Lee, D. L. (2005). The disconnect of poor urban education: Equal access and a pedagogy of risk taking. *Psychology in the Schools*, *42*, 855–863.

Belk, M. S., LoBello, S. G., Ray, G. E., & Zachar, P. (2002). WISC–III administration, clerical, and scoring errors made by student examiners. *Journal of Psychoeducational Assessment*, *20*, 290–300.

Bellair, P. E., & McNulty, T. L. (2005). Beyond the bell curve: Community disadvantage and the explanation of black-white differences in adolescent violence. *Criminology*, *43*, 1135–1168.

Belleville, S., Ménard, É., Mottron, L., & Ménard, M.-C. (2006). Working memory in autism. In T. P. Alloway & S. E. Gathercole (Eds.), *Working memory and neurodevelopmental disorders* (pp. 213–238). New York, NY: Psychology Press.

Benda, B. B., Corwyn, R. F., & Toombs, N. J. (2001). Recidivism among adolescent serious offenders: Prediction of entry into the correctional system for adults. *Criminal Justice and Behavior*, *28*, 588–613.

Benson, N., Hulac, D. M., & Kranzler, J. H. (2010). Independent examination of Wechsler Adult Intelligence Scale–Fourth Edition (WAIS-IV): What does the WAIS-IV measure? *Psychological Assessment*, *22*(1), 121–130.

Berninger, V. W. (1994). *Reading and writing acquisition: A developmental neuropsychological perspective*. Boulder, CO: Westview Press.

Berninger, V. W. (1998). *Process assessment of the learner: Diagnostic assessment for reading and writing*. San Antonio, TX: Psychological Corporation.

Berninger, V. W. (2007). *Process assessment of the learner* (2nd ed.). Bloomington, MN: Pearson.

Berninger, V. W., & Richards, T. L. (2002). *Brain literacy for educators and psychologists*. Waltham, MA: Academic Press.

Betjemann, R. S., Johnson, E. P., Barnard, H., Boada, R., Filley, C. M., Filipek, P. A., … Pennington, B. F. Genetic covariation between brain volumes and IQ, reading performance, and processing speed. *Behavioral Genetics*, *40*, 135–145.

Bilder, B. (2011). Neuropsychology 3.0: Evidence-based science and practice. *Journal of the International Neuropsychological Society*, *17*(1), 7–13.

Binet, A., & Simon, T. (1905). Methodes nouvelles pour le diagnostic du niveau intellectuel des anormaux. *L'Annee Psychologique*, *11*, 191–244.

Biscoe, B., & Harris, B. (1994). *Adolescent resiliency attitudes scale manual*. Oklahoma City, OK: Eagle Ridge Institute.

Biscoe, B., & Vincent, B. (1998). *Progress report for Eagle's Wings*. Oklahoma City, OK: Higher Horizons.

Blackboard Collaborate. (2015). http://www.blackboard.com/platforms/collaborate/overview.aspx

Blackwell, L. S., Rodriguez, S., & Guerra-Carrillo, B. (2015). Intelligence as a malleable construct. In S. Goldstein, D. Princiotta, & J. Naglieri (Eds.). *Handbook of intelligence: Evolutionary theory, historical perspective, and current concepts* (pp. 263–282). New York, NY: Springer.

Blakey, W, Fantuzzo, J., Gorsuch, R., & Moon, G. (1987). A peer-mediated, competency-based training package for administering and scoring the WAIS-R. *Professional Psychology: Research and Practice*, *18*, 17–20.

Blakey, W., Fantuzzo, J., & Moon, G. (1985). An automated competency-based model for teaching skills in the administration of the WAIS-R. *Professional Psychology: Research and Practice*, *16*, 641–647.

Blalock, L. D., & McCabe, D. P. (2011). Proactive interference and practice effects in visuospatial working memory span task performance. *Memory*, *19*, 83–91. doi:10.1080/09658211.2010.537035

Bloom, J. (2007). (Mis)reading social class in the journey towards college: Youth development in urban America. *Teachers College Record*, *109*, 343–368.

Bonci, A. (2011). *A research review: The importance of families and the home environment*. London, UK: National Literacy Trust. Retrieved March 22, 2015 from http://www.literacytrust.org.uk/assets/0000/7901/Research_review-importance_of_families_and_home.pdf

Boomsma, A. (2000). Reporting analyses of covariance structures. *Structural Equation Modeling*, 7, 461–483. doi:10.1207/S15328007SEM0703_6

Borsuk, E. R., Watkins, M. W., & Canivez, G. L. (2006). Long-term stability of membership in a Wechsler Intelligence Scale for Children–Third Edition (WISC-III) subtest core profile taxonomy. *Journal of Psychoeducational Assessment*, *24*, 52–68. doi:10.1177/0734282905285225

Bowen, G. L., Richman, J. M., Brewster, A., & Bowen, N. (1998). Sense of school coherence, perceptions of danger at school, and teacher support among youth at risk of school failure. *Child and Adolescent Social Work Journal*, *15*, 273–286.

Bracken, B. A. (2007). Creating the optimal preschool testing situation. In B. A. Bracken & R. J. Nagle (Eds.), *The psychoeducational assessment of preschool children* (4th ed., pp. 137–154). Mahwah, NJ: Erlbaum.

Braden, J. P. (2003). Accommodating clients with disabilities on the WAIS–III and WMS. In D. S. Tulsky & D. H. Saklofske (Eds.), *Clinical interpretation of the WAIS–III and WMS–III* (pp. 451–486). San Diego, CA: Academic Press.

Braden, J. P., & Niebling, B. C. (2012). Using the joint test standards to evaluate the validity evidence for intelligence tests. In D. P. Flanagan & P. L. Harrison (Eds.), *Contemporary intellectual assessment: Theories, tests, and issues* (3rd ed., pp. 739–757). New York, NY: Guilford Press.

Braden, J. P., & Shaw, S. R. (2009). Intervention validity of cognitive assessment: Knowns, unknowables, and unknowns. *Assessment for Effective Intervention*, *34*, 106–115. doi:10.1177/1534508407313013

Brassard, M. R., & Boehm, A. E. (Eds.). (2007). *Preschool assessment: Principles and practices*. New York, NY: Guilford Press.

Brehmer, Y., Westerberg, H., & Bäckman, L. (2012). Working-memory training in younger and older adults: training gains, transfer, and maintenance. *Frontiers in Human Neuroscience*, *6*(63). doi:10.3389/fnhum.2012.00063

Brenner, E. (2003). Consumer-focused psychological assessment. *Professional Psychology: Research and Practice*, *34*, 240–247.

Bridgeland, J. M., DiIulio, J. J., Jr., & Burke Morison, K. (2006). *The silent epidemic: Perspectives of high school dropouts*. A report by Civic Enterprises in association with Peter D. Hart Research Associates.

Brody, G. H., Ge, X., & Conger, R. (2001). The influence of neighborhood disadvantage, collective socialization, and parenting on African American children's affiliation with deviant peers. *Child Development*, *72*(4), 1231–1246.

Brown, T. A. (2006). *Confirmatory factor analysis for applied research*. New York, NY: Guilford Press.

Brown, T. A. (2015). *Confirmatory factor analysis for applied research* (2nd ed.). New York, NY: Guilford Press.

Brownfield, D., & Sorenson, A. M. (1993). Self-control and juvenile delinquency: Theoretical issues and an empirical assessment of selected elements of a general theory of crime. *Deviant Behavior*, *14*, 243–264.

Brunner, M., Nagy, G., & Wilhelm, O. (2012). A tutorial on hierarchically structured constructs. *Journal of Personality*, *80*, 796–846. doi:10.1111/j.1467–6494.2011.00749.x

Brunnert, K. A., Naglieri, J. A., & Hardy-Braz, S. T. (2009). *Essentials of WNV assessment*. Hoboken, NJ: Wiley.

Buckhalt, J. A., El-Sheikh, M., Keller, P. S., & Kelly, R. J. (2009). Concurrent and longitudinal relations between children's sleep and cognitive functioning: The moderating role of parent education. *Child Development*, *80*, 875–892.

Bunting, M. (2006). Proactive interference and item similarity in working memory. *Journal of Experimental Psychology: Learning, Memory, and Cognition*, *32*, 183–196. doi:10.1037/0278–7393.32.2.183

Burchinal, M. R., Roberts, J. E., Hooper, S., & Zeisel, S. A. (2000). Cumulative risk and early cognitive development: A comparison of statistical risk models. *Developmental Psychology*, *36*, 793–807.

Burgaleta, M., Head, K., Álvarez-Linera, J., Martinez, K., Escorial, S., Haier, R., & Colom, R. (2012). Sex differences in brain volume are related to specific skills, not to general intelligence. *Intelligence*, *40*, 60–68.

Burns, T. G., & O'Leary, S. D. (2004). Wechsler Intelligence Scale for Children–IV: Test review. *Applied Neuropsychology*, *11*, 233–236.

Buros, O. K. (1965). *The sixth mental measurements yearbook*. Highland Park, NJ: Gryphon Press.

Burt, C. H., Simons, R. L., & Simons, L. G. (2006). A longitudinal test of the effects of parenting and the stability of self-control: Negative evidence for the general theory of crime. *Criminology*, *44*, 353–396.

Burt, K. B., Hay, D. F., Pawlby, S., Harold, G., & Sharp, D. (2004). The prediction of disruptive behaviour disorders in an urban community sample: The contribution of person-centered analyses. *Journal of Child Psychology and Psychiatry*, *45*, 1159–1170.

Bush, W. J., & Waugh, K. W. (1976). *Diagnosing learning disabilities* (2nd ed.). Columbus, OH: Charles E. Merrill.

Calamia, M., Markon, K., & Tranel, D. (2012). Scoring higher the second time around: Meta-analyses of practice effects in neuropsychological assessment. *Clinical Neuropsychologist*, *26*, 543–570.

Calvin, C. M., Fernandes, C., Smith, P., Visscher, P. M., & Deary, I. J. (2010). Sex, intelligence and educational achievement in a national cohort of over 175,000 11-year-old schoolchildren in England. *Intelligence*, *38*, 424–432.

Camarata, S., & Woodcock, R. (2006). Sex differences in processing speed: Developmental effects in males and females. *Intelligence, 34,* 231–252.

Camerer, C., Loewenstein, G., & Weber, M. (1989). The curse of knowledge in economic settings: An experimental analysis. *Journal of Political Economy, 97,* 1232–1254.

Canivez, G. L. (2008). Orthogonal higher-order factor structure of the Stanford–Binet Intelligence Scales for children and adolescents. *School Psychology Quarterly, 23,* 533–541. doi:10.1037/a0012884

Canivez, G. L. (2010). Review of the Wechsler Adult Intelligence Test–Fourth Edition. In R. A. Spies, J. F. Carlson, and K. F. Geisinger (Eds.), *The eighteenth mental measurements yearbook* (pp. 684–688). Lincoln, NE: Buros Institute of Mental Measurements.

Canivez, G. L. (2011). Hierarchical factor structure of the Cognitive Assessment System: Variance partitions from the Schmid–Leiman (1957) procedure. *School Psychology Quarterly, 26,* 305–317. doi:10.1037/a0025973

Canivez, G. L. (2013a). Incremental validity of WAIS–IV factor index scores: Relationships with WIAT–II and WIAT–III subtest and composite scores. *Psychological Assessment, 25,* 484–495. doi:10.1037/a0032092

Canivez, G. L. (2013b). Psychometric versus actuarial interpretation of intelligence and related aptitude batteries. In D. H. Saklofske, C. R. Reynolds, & V. L. Schwean, (Eds.), *The Oxford handbook of child psychological assessments* (pp. 84–112). New York, NY: Oxford University Press.

Canivez, G. L. (2014a). Construct validity of the WISC-IV with a referred sample: Direct versus indirect hierarchical structures. *School Psychology Quarterly, 29,* 38–51. doi:10.1037/spq0000032

Canivez, G. L. (2014b). Review of the Wechsler Preschool and Primary Scale of Intelligence–Fourth Edition In J. F. Carlson, K. F. Geisinger, & J. L. Jonson (Eds.), *The nineteenth mental measurements yearbook* (pp. 732–737). Lincoln, NE: Buros Institute of Mental Measurements.

Canivez, G. L. (in press). Bifactor modeling in construct validation of multifactored tests: Implications for understanding multidimensional constructs and test interpretation. In K. Schweizer & C. DiStefano (Eds.), *Principles and methods of test construction: Standards and recent advancements.* Gottingen, Germany: Hogrefe.

Canivez, G. L., & Gaboury, A. R. (2013, June 11). Construct validity and diagnostic utility for the Cognitive Assessment System for ADHD. *Journal of Attention Disorders,* 1–11. doi:10.1177/1087054713489021

Canivez, G. L., Konold, T. R., Collins, J. M., & Wilson, G. (2009). Construct validity of the Wechsler Abbreviated Scale of Intelligence and Wide Range Intelligence Test: Convergent and structural validity. *School Psychology Quarterly, 24,* 252–265. doi:10.1037/a0018030

Canivez, G. L., & Kush, J. C. (2013). WISC–IV and WAIS–IV structural validity: Alternate methods, alternate results. Commentary on Weiss et al. (2013a) and Weiss et al. (2013b). *Journal of Psychoeducational Assessment, 31,* 157–169. doi:10.1177/0734282913478036

Canivez, G. L., Neitzel, R., & Martin, B. E. (2005). Construct validity of the Kaufman Brief Intelligence Test, Wechsler Intelligence Scale for Children—Third Edition, and Adjustment Scales for Children and Adolescents. *Journal of Psychoeducational Assessment, 23,* 15–34. doi:10.1177/073428290502300102

Canivez, G. L., & Watkins, M. W. (2010a). Exploratory and higher-order factor analyses of the Wechsler Adult Intelligence Scale–Fourth Edition (WAIS–IV) adolescent subsample. *School Psychology Quarterly, 25,* 223–235. doi:10.1037/a0022046

Canivez, G. L., & Watkins, M. W. (2010b). Investigation of the factor structure of the Wechsler Adult Intelligence Scale–Fourth Edition (WAIS–IV): Exploratory and higher-order factor analyses. *Psychological Assessment, 22,* 827–836. doi:10.1037/a0020429

Canivez, G. L., Watkins, M. W., James, T., James, K., & Good, R. (2014). Incremental validity of WISC–IVUK factor index scores with a referred Irish sample: Predicting performance on the WIAT–IIUK. *British Journal of Educational Psychology, 84,* 667–684. doi:10.1111/bjep.12056

Carlier, M., & Roubertoux, P. L. (2014). Genetic and environmental influences on intellectual disability in childhood. In D. Finkel & C. A. Reynolds (Eds.). *Behavior genetics of cognition throughout the lifespan* (pp. 69–101). New York, NY: Springer.

Carlson, M. J., & Corcoran, M. E. (2001). Family structure and children's behavioral and cognitive outcomes. *Journal of Marriage and Family, 63,* 779–792.

Carr, M. B., & Vandiver, T. A. (2001). Risk and protective factors among youth offenders. *Adolescence, 36,* 409–426.

Carroll, A., Hemingway, F., Bower, J., Ashman, A., Houghton, S., & Durkin, (2006). Impulsivity in juvenile delinquency: Differences among early-onset, late-onset, and non-offenders. *Journal of Youth and Adolescence, 35*, 519–529.

Carroll, J. B. (1968). Review of the nature of human intelligence by J. P. Guilford Press. *American Educational Research Journal, 73*, 105–112.

Carroll, J. B. (1993a). *Human cognitive abilities: A survey of factor-analytic studies*. New York, NY: Cambridge University Press.

Carroll, J. B. (1993b). What abilities are measured by the WISC–III? In B. A. Bracken & R. S. McCallum (Eds.), *Journal of Psychoeducational Assessment Monograph Series, Advances in psychoeducational assessment: Wechsler Intelligence Scale for Children—Third Edition* (pp. 134–143). Germantown, TN: Psychoeducational Corporation.

Carroll, J. B. (1995). On methodology in the study of cognitive abilities. *Multivariate Behavioral Research, 30*, 429–452. doi:10.1207/s15327906mbr3003_6

Carroll, J. B. (1997). The three-stratum theory of cognitive abilities. In D. P. Flanagan, J. L. Genshaft, & P. L. Harrison (Eds.), *Contemporary intellectual assessment: Theories, tests, and issues* (pp. 122–130). New York, NY: Guilford Press.

Carroll, J. B. (1998). Human cognitive abilities: A critique. In J. J. McArdle & R. W. Woodcock (Eds.), *Human cognitive abilities in theory and practice* (pp. 5–23). Mahwah, NJ: Erlbaum.

Carroll, J. B. (2003). The higher-stratum structure of cognitive abilities: Current evidence supports *g* and about ten broad factors. In H. Nyborg (Ed.), *The scientific study of general intelligence: Tribute to Arthur R. Jensen* (pp. 5–21). New York, NY: Pergamon Press.

Carroll, J. B. (2012). The three-stratum theory of cognitive abilities. In D. P. Flanagan & P. L. Harrison (Eds.), *Contemporary intellectual assessment: Theories, tests, and issues* (3rd ed., pp. 883–890). New York, NY: Guilford Press.

Carter, M., McGee, R., Taylor, B., & Williams, S. (2007). Health outcomes in adolescence: Associations with family, friends and school engagement. *Journal of Adolescence, 30*, 51–62.

Casillas, A., Robbins, S., Allen, J., Kuo, Y.-L., Hanson, M. A., & Schmeiser, C. (2012). Predicting early academic failure in high school from prior academic achievement, psychosocial characteristics, and behavior. *Journal of Educational Psychology, 104*, 407–420.

Caspi, A., Begg, D., Dickson, N., Harrington, H., Langley, J., Moffitt, T. E., and Silva, P. A. (1997). Personality differences predict health risk behaviors in young adulthood: Evidence from a longitudinal study. *Journal of Personality and Social Psychology, 73*, 1052–1063.

Catron, D. A., & Thompson, C. C. (1979). Test-retest gains in WAIS scores after four retest intervals. *Journal of Clinical Psychology, 35*, 352–357.

Cattell, R. B. (1941). Some theoretical issues in adult intelligence testing. *Psychological Bulletin, 38*, 592.

Cattell, R. B. (1943). The measurement of adult intelligence. *Psychological Bulletin, 40*, 153–193.

Cattell, R. B. (1963). Theory of fluid and crystallized intelligence: A critical experiment. *Journal of Educational Psychology, 54*, 1–22.

Cattell, R. B. (1966). The scree test for the number of factors. *Multivariate Behavioral Research, 1*, 245–276. doi:10.1207/s15327906mbr0102_10

Cattell, R. B. (1987). *Intelligence: Its structure, growth and action*. New York, NY: Elsevier.

Cattell, R. B., & Horn, J. L. (1978). A check on the theory of fluid and crystallized intelligence with description of new subtest designs. *Journal of Educational Measurement, 15*, 139–164. doi:10.1111/j.1745–3984.1978.tb00065.x

Chapple, C. L., Tyler, K. A., & Bersani, B. E. (2005). Child neglect and adolescent violence: Examining the effects of self-control and peer rejection. *Violence and Victims, 20*(1), 39–53.

Chauhan, P., & Reppucci, N. D. (2009). The impact of neighborhood disadvantage and exposure to violence on self-report of antisocial behavior among girls in the juvenile justice system. *Journal of Youth and Adolescence, 38*, 401–416.

Chauhan, P., Reppucci, N.D., & Turkheimer, En.N. (2009). Racial differences on the associations of neighborhood disadvantage, violence exposure, and criminal recidivism among female juvenile offenders. *Behavioral Sciences and the Law, 24*, 531–552.

Chavarría-Siles, I., Fernández, G., & Posthuma, D. (2014). Brain imaging and cognition. In D. Finkel & C. A. Reynolds (Eds.). *Behavior genetics of cognition throughout the lifespan* (pp. 235–256). New York, NY: Springer.

Chen, F. F., Hayes, A., Carver, C. S., Laurenceau, J.-P., & Zhang, Z. (2012). Modeling general and specific variance in multifaceted constructs: A comparison of the bifactor model to other approaches. *Journal of Personality*, *80*, 219–251. doi:10.1111/j.1467–6494.2011.00739.x

Cheung, G. W., & Rensvold, R. B. (2002). Evaluating goodness-of-fit indexes for testing measurement invariance. *Structural Equation Modeling*, *9*, 233–255. doi:10.1207/S15328007SEM0902_5

Chiang, M. C., McMahon, K. L., Greig, I., de Zubicaray, G. I., Martin, N. G., Hickie, I., … Thompson, P. M. (2011). Genetics of white matter development: A DTI study of 705 twins and their siblings aged 12–29. *NeuroImage*, *54*, 2308–2317.

Christensen, A. L. (1975) *Luria's neuropsychological investigation*. New York, NY: Spectrum.

Chun, C.-A., Moos, R. H., & Cronkite, R. C. (2006). Culture: A fundamental context for the stress and coping paradigm. In P. T. P. Wang & L. C. J. Wong (Eds.), *Handbook of multicultural perspectives on stress and coping* (pp. 29–53). New York, NY: Springer.

Chung, H. L., Mulvay, E. P., & Steinberg, L. (2011). Understanding the school outcomes of juvenile offenders: An exploration of neighborhood influences and motivational resources. *Journal of Youth and Adolescence*, *40*, 1025–1038.

Chung, H. L., & Steinberg, L. (2006). Relations between neighborhood factors, parenting behaviors, peer deviance, and delinquency among serious juvenile offenders. *Developmental Psychology*, *42*, 319–331.

Clare, L. (2010). "Chapter 25: Neuropsychological assessment. In M. T. Abou-Saleh, C. L. E. Katona, & A. Kumar (Eds.), *Principles and practice of geriatric psychiatry* (3rd ed., p. 139). Hoboken, NJ: Wiley-Blackwell.

Coalson, D. L., Raiford, S. E., Saklofske, D. H., & Weiss, L. G. (2010). WAIS-IV: Advances in the assessment of intelligence. In L. G. Weiss, D. H. Saklofske, D. L. Coalson, & S. E. Raiford (Eds.), *WAIS-IV clinical use and interpretation: Scientist-practitioner perspectives* (pp. 3–23). Amsterdam, The Netherlands: Elsevier Academic Press.

Cohen, B. H. (1996). *Explaining psychological statistics*. Pacific Grove, CA: Brooks & Cole.

Cohen, J. (1952a). A factor-analytically based rationale for the Wechsler-Bellevue. *Journal of Consulting Psychology*, *16*, 272–277.

Cohen, J. (1952b). Factors underlying Wechsler–Bellevue performance of three neuropsychiatric groups. *Journal of Abnormal and Social Psychology*, *47*, 359–365.

Cohen, J. (1957a). A factor-analytically based rationale for the Wechsler-Adult Intelligence Scale. *Journal of Consulting Psychology*, *6*, 451–457.

Cohen, J. (1957b). The factorial structure of the WAIS between early adulthood and old age. *Journal of Consulting Psychology*, *21*, 283–290.

Cohen, J. (1959). The factorial structure of the WISC at ages 7–6, 10–6, and 13–6. *Journal of Consulting Psychology*, *23*, 285–299.

Cohen, J. (1988). *Statistical power analysis for the behavioral sciences* (2nd ed.). Hillsdale, NJ: Erlbaum.

Cohen, M. J. (1997). *Children's Memory Scale*. San Antonio, TX: Harcourt Assessment.

Collins, F. S., Green, E. D. Guttmacher, A. E., & Guyer, M. S. (2003). A vision for the future of genomics research. *Nature*, *422*, 835–847.

Colman, R. A., Kim, D. H., Mitchell-Herzfeld, S., & Shady, T. A. (2009). Delinquent girls grown up: Young adult offending patterns and their relation to early legal, individual, and family risk. *Journal of Youth and Adolescence*, *38*, 355–366.

Colom, R., Burgaleta, M., Román, F. J., Karama, S., Álvarez-Linera, J., Abad, F. J., … Haier, R. J. (2013). Neuroanatomic overlap between intelligence and cognitive factors: Morphometry methods provide support for the key role of the frontal lobes. *Neuroimage*, *72*, 143–152.

Colom, R., Haier, R. J., Head, K., Álvarez-Linera, J., Ángeles Quiroga, M., Chun. P.-S., & Jung, R. E. (2009). Gray matter correlates of fluid, crystallized, and spatial intelligence: Testing the PFIT model. *Intelligence*, *37*, 124–135.

Compas, B. E., & Wagner, B. M. (1991). Psychosocial stress during adolescence: Intrapersonal and interpersonal processes. In M. E. Colten & S. Gore (Eds.), *Adolescent stress: Causes and consequences* (pp. 67–92). New York, NY: De Gruyter.

Compton, D. L. (2003). The influence of item composition on RAN letter performance in first-grade children. *Journal of Special Education*, *37*(2), 81–94.

Compton, D. L., Fuchs, L. S., Fuchs, D., Lambert, W., & Hamlett, C. (2012). The cognitive and academic profiles of reading and mathematics learning disabilities. *Journal of Learning Disabilities*, *45*, 79–95. doi:10.1177/0022219410393012

Conger, R. D., & Ge, X. (1994). Economic stress, coercive family process, and developmental problems of adolescents. *Child Development*, *65*, 541–561.

Cook, T. D., Church, M. B., Ajanaku, S., Shadish, W. R., Jr., Kim, J.-R., & Cohen, R. (1996).

The development of occupational aspirations and expectations among inner-city boys. *Child Development, 67,* 3368–3385.

Cooper, H., Lindsay, J. J., Nye, B., & Greathouse, S. (1998). Relationships among attitudes about homework, amount of homework assigned and completed, and student achievement. *Journal of Educational Psychology, 90,* 70–83.

Corapci, F. (2008). The role of child temperament on Head Start preschoolers' social competence in the context of cumulative risk. *Journal of Applied Developmental Psychology, 29,* 1–16.

Corkin, S., Amaral, D. G., González, R. G., Johnson, K. A., & Hyman, B. T. (1997). H. M.'s medial temporal lobe lesion: Findings from magnetic resonance imaging. *Journal of Neuroscience, 17*(10): 3964–3979.

Cornoldi, C., Orsini, A., Cianci, L., Giofrè, D., & Pezzuti, L. (2013). Intelligence and working memory control: Evidence from the WISC-IV administration to Italian children. *Learning and Individual Differences, 26,* 9–14. doi:10.1016/j.lindif.2013.04.005

Costello, E. J., Compton, S. N., Keeler, G., & Angold, A. (2003). Relationships between poverty and psychopathology: A natural experiment. *Journal of the American Medical Association, 290,* 2023–2029.

Cote, S. M., Vaillancourt, T., LeBlanc, J. C., Nagin, D. S., & Tremblay, R. E. (2006). The development of physical aggression from toddlerhood to preadolescence: A nationwide longitudinal study of Canadian children. *Journal of Abnormal Child Psychology, 34,* 71–85.

Coulton, C. J., Crampton, D. S., Irwin, M., Spilsbury, J. C., & Korbin, J. E. (2007). How neighborhoods influence child maltreatment: A review of the literature and alternative pathways. *Child Abuse & Neglect, 31,* 1117–1142.

Courtney, M. E., & Dworsky, A. (2006). Early outcomes for young adults transitioning from out-of-home care in the USA. *Child and Family Social Work, 11,* 209–219.

Covington, M. V. (2000). Goal theory, motivation, and school achievement: An integrative review. *Annual Review of Psychology, 51,* 171–200.

Crawford, J., & Allan, K. (1994). The Mahalanobis Distance index of WAIS-R subtest scatter: Psychometric properties in a healthy UK sample. *British Journal of Clinical Psychology, 33*(1), 65–69.

Crews, K. J., & D'Amato, R. C. (2009). Subtyping children's reading disabilities using a comprehensive neuropsychological measure. *International Journal of Neuroscience, 119,* 1615–1639. doi:10.1080/00207450802319960

Cronbach, L. J., & Snow, R E. (1977). *Aptitudes and instructional methods.* New York, NY: Wiley.

Cruickshank, W. M. (1977). Least-restrictive placement: Administrative wishful thinking. *Journal of Learning Disabilities, 10,* 193–194.

Crum, R., Lillie-Blanton, M., & Anthony, J. (1996). Neighborhood environment and opportunity to use cocaine and other drugs in late childhood and early adolescence. *Drug and Alcohol Dependence, 43,* 155–161.

Cusson, M., & Pinsonneault, P. (1986). The decision to give up crime. In D. B. Cornish & R. V. Clarke (Eds.), *The reasoning criminal* (pp. 72–82). New York, NY: Springer–Verlag.

Cytowic, R. E. (1996). *The neurological side of neuropsychology.* Cambridge, MA: MIT Press.

Dang, C., Braeken, J., Colom, R., Ferrer, E., & Liu, C. (2014). Why is working memory related to intelligence? Different contributions from storage and processing. *Memory, 22,* 426–441.

Daniel, M. H. (1997). Intelligence testing: Status and trends. *American Psychologist, 52,* 1038–1045.

Daniel, M. H. (2007). "Scatter" and the construct validity of FSIQ: Comment on Fiorello, et al. (2007). *Applied Neuropsychology, 14,* 291–295.

Daniel, M. H. (2009). *Subtest variability and the validity of WISC–IV composite scores.* Blue ribbon paper presented at the annual meeting of the American Psychological Association, Toronto, Canada.

Daniel, M. H. (2012a). Equivalence of Q-interactive™ administered cognitive tasks: CVLT–II and Selected D–KEFS subtests [Q-interactive Technical Report 3]. Retrieved from http://www.helloq .com/content/dam/ped/ani/us/helloq/media/Technical%20Report%203_CVLT_DKEFS_final_rev .pdf

Daniel, M. H. (2012b). Equivalence of Q-interactive™ administered cognitive tasks: WISC–IV® [Q-interactive Technical Report 2]. Retrieved from http://www.helloq.com/content/dam/ped/ani/us/helloq/media/Technical%20Report%202_WISC-IV_Final.pdf

Daniel, M. H. (2012c). Equivalence of Q-interactive™ administered cognitive tasks: WAIS–IV® [Q-interactive Technical Report 1]. Retrieved from http://www.helloq.com/content/dam/ped/ani/us/helloq/media/QinteractiveTechnical%20Report%201_WAIS-IV.pdf

Daniel, M. H. (2013). Equivalence of Q-interactive™ and paper administrations of cognitive tasks: Selected NEPSY®–II and CMS subtests [Q-interactive Technical Report 4]. Retrieved from http://www.helloq.com//content/dam/ped/ani/us/helloq/media/Technical%20Report%204_NEPSY-II_CMS.pdf

Daniel, M. H., Wahlstrom, D., & Zhang, O. (2014). Equivalence of Q-interactive™ and paper administrations of cognitive tasks: WISC®–V [Q-interactive Technical Report 8]. Retrieved from http://www.helloq.com/content/dam/ped/ani/us/helloq/media/Technical-Report_WISC-V_092514.pdf

Das, J. P. (2010). Book review: The essence of Luria's legacy. *Journal of Clinical and Experimental Psychology, 32,* 1036–1038.

Davis, O. S., Butcher, L. M., Docherty, S. J., Meaburn, E. L., Curtis, C. J., Simpson, M. A., ... Plomin, R. (2010). A three-stage genome-wide association study of general cognitive ability: Hunting the small effects. *Behavioral Genetics, 40,* 759–767.

Dean, R. S., & Woodcock, R. W. (2003). *Dean-Woodcock Neuropsychological Battery.* Itasca, IL: Riverside.

Deary, I. J., & Johnson, W. (2010). Intelligence and education: Causal perceptions drive analytic processes and therefore conclusions. *International Journal of Epidemiology, 39,* 1362–1369. doi:10.1093/ije/dyq072

Deary, I. J., Penke, L., & Johnson, W. (2010). The neuroscience of human intelligence differences. *Nature Reviews Neuroscience, 11,* 210–211.

Deary, I. J., Strand, S., Smith, P., & Fernandes, C. (2007). Intelligence and educational achievement. *Intelligence, 35,* 13–21.

Deary, I. J., Yang, J., Davies, G., Harris, S. E., Tenesa, A., Liewald, D., ... Visscher, P. M. (2012). Genetic contributions to stability and change in intelligence from childhood to old age. *Nature, 482,* 212–215. doi:10.1038/nature10781

Decker, S. L., Englund, J. A., & Roberts, A. M. (2012). Intellectual and neuropsychological assessment of individuals with sensory and physical disabilities and traumatic brain injury. In D. P. Flanagan & P. L. Harrison (Eds.), *Contemporary intellectual assessment:*

Theories, tests, and issues (3rd ed., pp. 708–725). New York, NY: Guilford Press.

Deffenbacher, J. L., Lynch, R. S., Oetting, E R., & Kemper, C. C. (1996). Anger reduction in early adolescents. *Journal of Counseling Psychology, 43,* 149–157.

DeFina, R., & Hannon, L. (2010). The impact of adult incarceration on child poverty: A county-level analysis, 1995–2007. *Prison Journal, 90,* 377–396.

Dehaene, S. (1997). *The number sense: How the mind creates mathematics.* New York, NY: Oxford University Press.

Dehaene, S. (2009). *Reading in the brain: The new science of how we read.* New York, NY: Penguin.

Dehaene, S. (2011). *The number sense: How the mind creates mathematics* (2nd ed.). New York, NY: Oxford University Press.

Dehaene, S. (2014). *Consciousness and the brain: Deciphering how the brain codes our thoughts.* New York, NY: Viking Press.

Dehaene-Lambertz, G., Hertz-Pannier, L., Dubois, J., & Dehaene, S. (2008). How does early brain organization promote language acquisition in humans. *European Review, 16,* 399–411.

Dehn, M. J. (2008). *Working memory and academic learning: Assessment and intervention.* Hoboken, NJ: Wiley.

Dehn, M. J. (2014). *Essentials of processing assessment* (2nd ed.) Hoboken, NJ: Wiley.

Delis, D. C., Kaplan, E., & Kramer, J. H. (2001). *Delis-Kaplan Executive Function System examiner's manual.* San Antonio, TX: Psychological Corporation.

Delis, D. C., Kramer, J. H., Kaplan, E., & Ober, B. A. (1994). *California Verbal Learning Test: Children's Version.* San Antonio, TX: Harcourt Assessment.

Dembo, R., Williams, L., Wothke, W., Schmeidler, J., & Brown, C. H. (1992). The role of family factors, physical abuse, and sexual victimization experiences in high risk youths' alcohol and other drug use and delinquency: A longitudinal model. *Violence and Victims, 7,* 245–266.

Dembo, R., Wothke, W., Seeberger, W., Shemwell, M., Pacheco, R., Rollie, M., ... Livingston, S. (2000). Testing a model of the influence of family problem factors on high-risk youths' troubled behavior: A three-wave longitudinal study. *Journal of Psychoactive Drugs, 32*(1) 55–65. doi:10.1080/02791072.2000.10400212

Demetriou, A., Spanoudis, G., Shayer, M., van der Ven, S., Brydges, C. R., Kroesbergen, E., Podjarny, G., & Swanson, H. L. (2014). Relations between speed, working memory, and intelligence from preschool to adulthood: Structural equation modeling of 15 studies. *Intelligence, 46,* 107–121.

Devena, S. E., & Watkins, M. W. (2012). Diagnostic utility of WISC-IV general abilities index and cognitive proficiency index reference scores among children with ADHD. *Journal of Applied School Psychology, 28,* 133–154. doi:10.1080/15377903.2012.669743

Diamond, A., Barnett, W. S., Thomas, J., & Munro, S. (2007). Preschool program improves cognitive control. *Science, 312,* 1900–1902.

Dishion, T. J., & Patterson, G. R. (2006). The development and ecology of antisocial behavior in children and adolescents. In D. Cicchetti & D. J. Cohen (Eds.), *Developmental psychopathology: Vol. 3: Risk, disorder, and adaptation* (2nd ed., pp. 503–541). Hoboken, NJ: Wiley.

Dodonova, Y. A., & Dodonov, Y. S. (2012). Processing speed and intelligence as predictors of school achievement: Mediation or unique contribution? *Intelligence, 40,* 163–171. doi:10.1016/j.intell.2012.01.003

Dombrowski, S. C., & Watkins, M. W. (2013). Exploratory and higher order factor analysis of the WJ-III full test battery: A school aged analysis. *Psychological Assessment, 25,* 442–455. doi:10.1037/a0031335

Dombrowski, S. C., Watkins, M. W., & Brogan, M. J. (2009). An exploratory investigation of the factor structure of the Reynolds Intellectual Assessment Scales (RIAS). *Journal of Psychoeducational Assessment, 27,* 494–507. doi:10.1177/0734282909333179

Donders, J. (1999). Pediatric neuropsychological reports: Do they really have to be so long? *Child Neuropsychology, 5*(1), 70–78.

Dowden, C., & Andrews, D. A. (1999). What works in young offender treatment: A meta-analysis. *Forum on Corrections Research, 1*(2), 21–24.

Duan, X., Shi, J., & Zhou, D. (2010). Developmental changes in processing speed: Influence of accelerated education for gifted children. *Gifted Child Quarterly, 54,* 85–91.

Duggan, E. C., & Garcia-Barrera, M. A. (2015). Executive functioning and intelligence. In S. Goldstein, D. Princiotta, & J. Naglieri (Eds.). *Handbook of intelligence: Evolutionary theory, historical perspective, and current concepts* (pp. 435–458). New York, NY: Springer.

Dumont, R., Viezel, K. D., Kohlhagen, J., & Tabib, S. (2014). A review of Q-interactive assessment technology. *Communiqué, 43*(1), 8–12. Retrieved from http//:www.nasponline.org

Dumont, R., & Willis, J. O. (2001). Use of the Tellegen & Briggs formula to determine the Dumont-Willis Indexes (DWI–I & DWI–II) for the WISC–IV. Retrieved from http://alpha.fdu.edu/psychology/WISCIV_DWI.htm

Dumontheil, I. (2014). Development of abstract thinking during childhood and adolescence: The role of the rostrolateral prefrontal cortex. *Developmental Cognitive Neuroscience, 10,* 57–76.

Dumontheil, I. & Klingberg, T. (2012). Brain activity during a visuospatial working memory task predicts arithmetical performance 2 years later. *Cerebral Cortex, 22,* 1078–1085.

Duncan, G. J. Brooks-Gunn, J., & Klebanov, P. K. (1994). Economic deprivation and early childhood development. *Child Development, 65,* 296–318. doi:10.1111/j.1467-8624.1994.tb00752.x

Dunn, T. J., Baguley, T., & Brunsden, V. (2013). From alpha to omega: A practical solution to the pervasive problem of internal consistency estimation. *British Journal of Psychology, 105,* 399–412. doi:10.1111/bjop.12046

Dunn, L. M., & Markwardt, F. C. (1970). *Peabody individual achievement test.* Circle Pines, MN: American Guidance Service.

Dweck, C. (2006). *Mindset: The new psychology of success.* New York, NY: Random House.

Dykiert, D., Gale, C. R., & Deary, I. J. (2009). Are apparent sex differences in mean IQ scores created in part by sample restriction and increased male variance? *Intelligence, 37,* 42–47.

Education Week. (2009). *Diplomas count 2009: Broader horizons: The challenge of college readiness for all students.* Bethesda, MD: Editorial Projects in Education Research Center. Retrieved from http://www.edweek.org/ew/toc/2009/06/11/index.html.

Edwards, R., & Edwards, J. L. (1993). The WISC–III: A practitioner's perspective. In B. A. Bracken & R. S. McCallum (Eds.), *Wechsler Intelligence Scale for Children–Third Edition* (pp. 144–150). Germantown, TN: Psychoeducational Corporation.

Eggert, L. L. & Herting, J. R. (1993) Drug involvement among potential dropouts and "typical" youth. *Journal of Drug Education, 23*, 31–55.

Elliott, C. D. (1983). *British Ability Scales*. Windsor: NFER-Nelson.

Elliott, C. D. (1990). *Differential Ability Scales*. San Antonio, TX: PsychCorp Harcourt Assessment.

Elliott, C. D. (2007). *Differential Ability Scales* (2nd ed.). San Antonio, TX: Pearson.

Elliott, D., Wilson, W. J., Huizinga, D., Sampson, R. J., Elliott, A., & Rankin, B. (1996). The effects of neighborhood disadvantage on adolescent development. *Journal of Research in Crime Delinquency, 33*, 389–426.

English, D. J., Spatz-Widom, C., & Brandford, C. (2001). *Childhood victimization and delinquency, adult criminality and violent criminal behavior: A replication and extension. Final report*. Washington, DC: National Institutes of Justice.

Epperson, D. L., Ralston, C. A., Fowers, D., DeWitt, J., & Gore, K. S. (2006). Actuarial risk assessment with juveniles who offend sexually: Development of the Juvenile Sexual Offense Recidivism Risk Assessment Tool–II (JSORRAT–II). In D. Prescott (Ed.), *Risk assessment of youth who have sexually abused: Theory, controversy, and emerging strategies* (pp. 118–169). Oklahoma City, OK: Woods 'N' Barnes.

Erdodi, L. A., Richard, D. C. S., & Hopwood, C. (2009). The importance of relying on the manual: Scoring error variance in the WISC–IV Vocabulary subtest. *Journal of Psychoeducational Assessment, 27*, 374–385.

Evans, G. W. (2004). The environment of childhood poverty. *American Psychologist, 59*, 77–92.

Evans, J. J., Floyd, R. G., McGrew, K. S., & Leforgee, M. H. (2002). The relations between measures of Cattell-Horn-Carroll (CHC) cognitive abilities and reading achievement during childhood and adolescence. *School Psychology Review, 31*, 246–262.

Ezell, M., & Cohen, L. E. (2005). Crime over the life course: The empirical implications of three theories. In M. Ezell & L. E. Cohen (Eds.), *Desisting from crime: Continuity and change in long-term crime patterns of serious chronic offenders* (pp. 12–52). New York, NY: Oxford University Press.

Fabrigar, L. R., Wegener, D. T., MacCallum, R. C., & Strahan, E. J. (1999). Evaluating the use of exploratory factor analysis in psychological research. *Psychological Methods, 4*, 272–299.

doi:10.1037/1082–989X.4.3.272

Fagan, J. R. (2000). A theory of intelligence as processing: Implications for society. *Psychology, Public Policy, and Law, 6*, 168–179.

Farnworth, M., Schweinhart, L. J., & Berrueta-Clement, J. R. (1985). Preschool intervention, school success and delinquency in a high-risk sample of youth. *American Educational Research Journal, 22*, 445–464.

Farrington, D. P. (1989). Early predictors of adolescent aggression and adult violence. *Violence and Victims, 4*, 79–100.

Farrington, D. P., Loeber, R., Elliott, D. S., Hawkins, J. D., Kandel, D. B., Klein, M. W., … Tremblay, R. E. (1990). Advancing knowledge about the onset of delinquency and crime. In B. B. Lahey and A. E. Kazdin (Eds.), *Clinical child psychology* (Vol. 13, pp. 283–342). New York, NY: Plenum Press.

Faust, D. (1989). Data integration in legal evaluations: Can clinicians deliver on their premises? *Behavioral Sciences & the Law, 7*, 469–483. doi:10.1002/bsl.2370070405

Faust, D. (2007). Some global and specific thoughts about some global and specific issues. *Applied Neuropsychology, 14*, 26–36. doi:10.1080/09084280701280411

Fava, J. L., & Velicer, W. F. (1992). The effects of overextraction on factor and component analysis. *Multivariate Behavioral Research, 21*, 387–415. doi:10.1207/s15327906mbr2703_5

Fergusson, D. M., Lynskey, M. T., & Horwood, L. J. (1996). Factors associated with continuity and changes in disruptive behavior patterns between childhood and adolescence. *Journal of Abnormal Child Psychology, 24*, 533–553.

Ferrer, E., Salthouse, T. A., McArdle, J. J., Stewart, W. F., & Schwartz, B. S. (2005). Multivariate modeling of age and retest in longitudinal studies of cognitive abilities. *Psychology and Aging, 20*, 412–422.

Ferrer, E., Salthouse, T. A., Stewart, W., & Schwartz, B. (2004). Modeling age and retest processes in longitudinal studies of cognitive abilities. *Psychology and Aging, 19*, 243–259.

Feuerstein, R. (1980). *Instrumental enrichment: An intervention program for cognitive modifiability*. Glenview, IL: Scott Foresman.

Feuerstein, R., with Rand, Y., & Hoffman, M. B. (1979). *The dynamic assessment of retarded performers:*

The learning potential assessment device, theory, instruments, and techniques. Glenview, IL: Scott Foresman.

Fina, A. D., Sánchez-Escobedo, P., & Hollingworth, L. (2012). Annotations on Mexico's WISC–IV: A validity study. *Applied Neuropsychology: Child, 1,* 6–17.

Finkel, D., & Reynolds, C. A. (Eds.). (2014). *Behavior genetics of cognition throughout the lifespan.* New York, NY: Springer.

Finn, S. E. (2007). *In our clients' shoes: Theory and techniques of therapeutic assessment.* Mahwah, NJ: Erlbaum.

Fiorello, C. A. (2014, October 25). *CHC theory and neuropsychological assessment: Strange bedfellows?* Lecture presented at the Richard Woodcock Institute, Austin, TX.

Fiorello, C. A., Hale, J. B., & Wycoff, K. L. (2012). Cognitive hypothesis testing: Linking test results to the real world. In D. P. Flanagan & P. L. Harrison (Eds.), *Contemporary intellectual assessment: Theories, tests, and issues* (3rd ed., pp. 484–496). New York, NY: Guilford Press.

Fischer, C. T. (1994). *Individualizing psychological assessment.* Hillsdale, NJ: Erlbaum.

Flanagan, D. P., & Alfonso, V. C. (in press). *Essentials of WISC–V assessment.* Hoboken, NJ: Wiley.

Flanagan, D. P., Alfonso, V. C., Mascolo, J. T., & Hale, J. B. (2011). The Wechsler Intelligence Scale for Children, Fourth Edition, in neuropsychological practice. In A. S. Davis (Ed.). *Handbook of pediatric neuropsychology* (pp. 397–414). New York, NY: Springer.

Flanagan, D. P., Alfonso, V. C., & Ortiz, S. O. (2012). The cross-battery assessment approach: An overview, historical perspective, and current directions. In D. P. Flanagan & P. L. Harrison (Eds.), *Contemporary intellectual assessment: Theories, tests, and issues* (3rd ed., pp. 459–483). New York, NY: Guilford Press.

Flanagan, D. P., Alfonso, V. C., Ortiz, S. O., & Dynda, A. M. (2010). Integrating cognitive assessment in school neuropsychological evaluations. In, D. Miller (Ed.), *Best practices in school neuropsychology: Guidelines for effective practice, assessment, and evidence-based intervention* (pp. 101–140). Hoboken, NJ: Wiley.

Flanagan, D. P., Alfonso, V. C., & Reynolds, M. R. (2013). Broad and narrow CHC abilities measured and not measured by the Wechsler scales: Moving beyond within-battery factor analysis. *Journal of Psychoeducational Assessment, 31,* 202–223.

Flanagan, D. P., & Harrison, P. L. (Eds.). (2012). *Contemporary intellectual assessment: Theories, test, and issues.* New York, NY: Guilford Press.

Flanagan, D. P., & Kaufman, A. S. (2004). *Essentials of WISC-IV assessment.* Hoboken, NJ: Wiley.

Flanagan, D. P., & Kaufman, A. S. (2009). *Essentials of WISC®–IV assessment* (2nd ed.). Hoboken, NJ: Wiley.

Flanagan, D. P., & McGrew, K. S., (1997). A cross-battery approach to assessing and interpreting cognitive abilities: Narrowing the gap between practice and cognitive science. In D. P. Flanagan & J. L. Genshaft (Eds.), *Contemporary intellectual assessment: Theories, tests, and issues* (pp. 314–325). New York, NY: Guilford Press.

Flanagan, D. P., McGrew, K. S., & Ortiz, S. O. (2000). *The Wechsler Intelligence Scales and Gf-Gc theory: A contemporary approach to interpretation.* Boston, MA: Allyn & Bacon.

Flanagan, D. P., Ortiz, S. O., & Alfonso, V. C. (2007). *Essentials of cross-battery assessment* (2nd ed.). Hoboken, NJ: Wiley.

Flanagan, D. P., Ortiz, S. O., & Alfonso, V. C. (2013). *Essentials of cross-battery assessment* (3rd ed.). Hoboken, NJ: Wiley.

Fletcher-Janzen, E. P., & Reynolds, C. R. (Eds.) (2008). *Neuropsychological perspectives on learning disabilities in the era of RTI: Recommendations for diagnosis and intervention.* Hoboken, NJ: Wiley.

Floyd, R. G., (2005). Information-processing approaches to interpretation of contemporary intellectual assessment instruments. In D. Flanagan & P. Harrison (Eds.). *Contemporary intellectual assessment* (2nd ed., pp. 203–233). New York, NY: Guilford Press.

Floyd, R. G., Clark, M. H., & Shadish, W. R. (2008). The exchangeability of IQs: Implications for professional psychology. *Professional Psychology: Research and Practice, 39,* 414–423. doi:10.1037/0735–7028.39.4.414

Floyd, R. G., & Kranzler, J. H. (2012). Processing approaches to interpretation of information from cognitive ability tests. In D. P. Flanagan & P. L. Harrison (Eds.), *Contemporary intellectual assessment: Theories, tests, and issues* (3rd ed., pp. 497–525). New York, NY: Guilford Press.

Floyd, R. G., Reynolds, M. R., Farmer, R. L., & Kranzler, J. H. (2013). Are the general factors from different child and adolescent intelligence tests the same? Results from a five-sample, six-test analysis. *School Psychology Review*, *42*, 383–401.

Flynn, J. R. (1984). The mean IQ of Americans: Massive gains 1932 to 1978. *Psychological Bulletin*, *95*, 29–51.

Flynn, J. R. (1987). Massive IQ gains in 14 nations: What IQ tests really measure. *Psychological Bulletin*, *101*, 171–191.

Flynn, J. R. (2009). *What is intelligence?* (expanded ed.). New York, NY: Cambridge University Press.

Fogel, S. J. (2004). Risks and opportunities for success: Perceptions of urban youths in a distressed community and lessons for adults. *Families in Society*, *85*(3), 335–344.

Forcing an exodus. (1902, June 1). *The Washington Post*, p. 26. Retrieved from ProQuest Historical Newspapers.

Ford, D. (2012). Culturally different students in special education: Looking backward to move forward. *Exceptional Children*, *78*, 391–405.

Ford, L., Kozey, M. L., & Negreiros, J. (2012). Cognitive assessment in early childhood: Theoretical and practice perspectives. In D. P. Flanagan & P. L. Harrison (Eds.), *Contemporary intellectual assessment: Theories, tests, and issues* (3rd ed., pp. 585–622). New York, NY: Guilford Press.

Frakowiak, R. S. J., Friston, K. J., Frith, C. D., Dolan, R. J., & Mazziotta, J. C. (1997). *Human brain function*. New York, NY: Academic Press.

Frank, G. (1983). *The Wechsler enterprise: An assessment of the development, structure, and use of the Wechsler tests of intelligence*. New York, NY: Pergamon Press.

Franklin, M., Stillman, P., Burpeau, M., & Sabers, D. (1982). Examiner error in intelligence testing: Are you a source? *Psychology in the Schools*, *19*, 563–569.

Fratello, J., Salsich, A., Mogulescu, S., (2011). Juvenile detention reform in New York City: Measuring risk through research. *Federal Sentencing Reporter*, *24*(1), 15–20.

Frazier, T. W., & Youngstrom, E. A. (2007). Historical increase in the number of factors measured by commercial tests of cognitive ability: Are we overfactoring? *Intelligence*, *35*, 169–182. doi:10.1016/j.intell.2006.07.002

Freberg, M. E., Vandiver, B. J., Watkins, M. W., & Canivez, G. L. (2008). Significant factor score variability and the validity of the WISC–III Full Scale IQ in predicting later academic achievement. *Applied Neuropsychology*, *15*, 131–139. doi:10.1080/09084280802084010

Fredricks, J. A., Blumenfeld, P. C., & Paris, A. H. (2004). School engagement: Potential of the concept, state of the evidence. *Review of Educational Research*, *74*, 59–109.

French, J. W. (1965). The relationship of problem-solving styles to the factor composition of tests. *Educational and Psychological Measurement*, *25*, 9–28.

Fried, P. J., Rushmore, R. J. III, Moss, M. B., Valero-Cabré, A., & Pascual-Leone, A. (2014). Causal evidence supporting functional dissociation of verbal and spatial working memory in the human dorsolateral prefrontal cortex. *European Journal of Neuroscience*, *39*, 1973–1981.

Fuchs, D., & Fuchs, L. S. (1986). Test procedure bias: A meta-analysis of examiner familiarity effects. *Review of Educational Research*, *56*, 243–262.

Fuligni, A. J., & Eccles, J. S. (1993). Perceived parent-child relationships and early adolescents' orientation toward peers. *Developmental Psychology*, *29*, 622–632.

Gale, C. R., O'Callaghan, F. J., Godfrey, K. M., Law, C. M., & Martyn, C. N. (2004). Critical periods of brain growth and cognitive function in children. *Brain*, *127*, 321–329.

Gardner, H. (1983). *Frames of mind: The theory of multiple intelligences*. New York, NY: Basic Books.

Gardner, H. (1999). *Reframing intelligence*. New York, NY: Basic Books.

Garlick, D. (2002). Understanding the nature of the general factor of intelligence: The role of individual differences in neural plasticity as an explanatory mechanism [Review]. *Psychological Review*, *109*(1), 116–136.

Gazzaniga, M. S. (Ed.) (2000). *The new cognitive neurosciences* (2nd ed.). Cambridge, MA: MIT Press.

Geary, D. C. (2015). Social competition and the evolution of human intelligence. In S. Goldstein, D. Princiotta, & J. Naglieri (Eds.) *Handbook of intelligence: Evolutionary theory, historical perspective, and current concepts* (pp. 105–119). New York, NY: Springer.

Geenen, S., & Powers, L. E. (2006). Are we ignoring youths with disabilities in foster care? An examination of their school performance. *Social Work*, *51*, 233–241.

Geller, A., Garfinkel, I., Cooper, C. E., & Mincy, R. B. (2009). Parental incarceration and child wellbeing: Implications for urban families. *Social Science Quarterly, 90,* 1186–1202.

Gendreau, P., Little, T., & Goggin, C. (1996). A meta-analysis of the predictors of adult offender recidivism: What works. *Criminology, 34,* 557–607.

Gibbs, J. J., Giever, D., & Higgins, G. E. (2003). A test of Gottfredson and Hirschi's general theory using structural equation modeling. *Criminal Justice and Behavior, 30,* 441–458.

Gignac, G. E. (2005). Revisiting the factor structure of the WAIS–R: Insights through nested factor modeling. *Assessment, 12,* 320–329. doi:10.1177/1073191105278118

Gignac, G. E. (2006). The WAIS–III as a nested factors model: A useful alternative to the more conventional oblique and higher-order models. *Journal of Individual Differences, 27,* 73–86. doi:10.1027/1614–0001.27.2.73

Gignac, G. E. (2008). Higher-order models versus direct hierarchical models: *g* as superordinate or breadth factor? *Psychology Science Quarterly, 50,* 21–43.

Gignac, G. E., & Watkins, M. W. (2013). Bifactor modeling and the estimation of model-based reliability on the WAIS–IV. *Multivariate Behavioral Research, 48,* 639–632. doi:10.1080/00273171.2013.804398

Gläscher, J., Tranel, D., Paul, L. K., Rudrauf, D., Rorden, C., Hornaday, A., … Adolphs, R. (2009). Lesion mapping of cognitive abilities linked to intelligence. *Neuron, 61,* 236–263.

Glueck, S., & Glueck, E. T. (1940). *Juvenile delinquents grown up.* New York, NY: Commonwealth Fund.

Glutting, J. J., & McDermott, P. A. (1990). Principles and problems in learning potential. In C. R. Reynolds & R. W. Kamphaus (Eds.), *Handbook of psychological and educational assessment of children: Intelligence and achievement* (pp. 296–347). New York, NY: Guilford Press.

Glutting, J. J., McDermott, P. A., & Stanley, J. C. (1987). Resolving differences among methods of establishing confidence limits for test scores. *Educational and Psychological Measurement, 47,* 607–614. doi:10.1177/001316448704700307

Glutting, J. J., Watkins, M. W., Konold, T. R., & McDermott, P. A. (2006). Distinctions without a difference: The utility of observed versus latent factors from the WISC–IV in estimating reading and math achievement on the WIAT–II. *Journal of Special Education, 40,* 103–114. doi:10.1177/00224669060400020101

Glutting, J. J., Youngstrom, E. A., Ward, T., Ward, S., & Hale, R. L. (1997). Incremental efficacy of WISC–III factor scores in predicting achievement: What do they tell us? *Psychological Assessment, 9,* 295–301. doi:10.1037/1040–3590.9.3.295

Godber, T., Anderson V., & Bell R. (2000). The measurement and diagnostic utility of intrasubtest scatter in pediatric neuropsychology. *Journal of Clinical Psychology, 66*(1), 101–112.

Goel, V. (2007). Anatomy of deductive reasoning. *Trends in Cognitive Sciences, 11,* 435–441.

Golay, P., & Lecerf, T. (2011). Orthogonal higher order structure and confirmatory factor analysis of the French Wechsler Adult Intelligence Scale (WAIS–III). *Psychological Assessment, 23,* 143–152. doi:10.1037/a0021230

Golay, P., Reverte, I., Rossier, J., Favez, N., & Lecerf, T. (2013). Further insights on the French WISC–IV factor structure through Bayesian structure equation modeling. *Psychological Assessment, 25,* 496–508. doi:10.1037/a0030676

Golden, C. J. (1978). *Stroop Colour and Word Test: A manual for clinical and experimental uses.* Chicago, IL: Stoelting.

Golden, C. J. (1981). A standardized version of Luria's neuropsychological tests. In S. J. Filskov & T. J. Boll (Eds.), *Handbook of clinical neuropsychology* (pp. 608–642). New York, NY: Wiley.

Goldstein, S., Princiotta, D., & Naglieri, J. A. (Eds.). (2014). *Handbook of intelligence: Evolutionary theory, historical perspective, and current concepts.* New York, NY: Springer.

Good, R. H., Vollmer, M., Creek, R. J., Katz, L. I., & Chowdhri, S. (1993). Treatment utility of the Kaufman Assessment Battery for Children: Effects of matching instruction and student processing strength. *School Psychology Review, 22,* 8–26.

Goodenough, F. L. (1927). The relation of intelligence of pre-school children to the education of their parents. *School and Society, 26,* 54–56.

Gordon, R. P., Stump, K., & Glaser, B. A. (1996). Assessment of individuals with hearing impairments: Equity in testing procedures and accommodations. *Measurement and Evaluation in Counseling and Development, 29,* 111–118.

Gore, S., & Eckenrode, J. (1994). Context and process in research on risk and resilience. In R. J.

Haggerty, L. R. Sherrod, N. Garmezy, & M. Rutter (Eds.), *Stress, risk, and resilience in children and adolescents* (pp. 19–63). New York, NY: Cambridge University Press.

Gorman-Smith, D., & Tolan, P. H. (1998). The role of community violence and developmental problems among inner city youth. *Development and Psychopathology, 10*, 101–116.

Gorman-Smith, D., Tolan, P. H., & Henry, D. B. (2000). A developmental ecological model of the relation of family functioning to patterns of delinquency. *Journal of Quantitative Criminology, 16*, 169–198.

Gorsuch, R. L. (1983). *Factor analysis* (2nd ed.). Hillsdale, NJ: Erlbaum.

Gorsuch, R. L. (1997). Exploratory factor analysis: Its role in item analysis. *Journal of Personality Assessment, 68*, 532–560. doi:10.1207/s15327752jpa6803_5

Gottfredson, L. S. (1997). Why *g* matters: The complexity of everyday life. *Intelligence, 24*, 79–132.

Gottfredson, L. S. (1998). The general intelligence factor. *Scientific American Presents*, 24–29.

Gottfredson, L. S. (2008). Of what value is intelligence? In A. Prifitera, D. H. Saklofske, & L. G. Weiss (Eds.), *WISC–IV clinical assessment and intervention* (2nd ed., pp. 545–564). Amsterdam, The Netherlands: Elsevier Academic Press.

Gottfredson, M. R. (2006). The empirical status of control theory in criminology. In F. T. Cullen, J. P. Wight, & K. R. Blevins (Eds.), *Advances in criminological theory, Vol. 15, Taking stock: The status of criminological theory* (pp. 205–230). New Brunswick, NJ: Transaction.

Gottfredson, M. R., & Hirschi, T. (1990). *A general theory of crime.* Stanford, CA: Stanford University Press.

Gover, A. R. (2002). The effects of child maltreatment on violent offending among institutionalized youth. *Violence and Victims, 17*, 655–668.

Graham, S., MacArthur, C.A., & Fitzgerald, J. (Eds.) (2007). *Best practices in writing instruction.* New York, NY: Guilford Press.

Greenberg, M. T., Speltz, M. L., DeKlyen, M., & Jones, K. (2001). Correlates of clinic referral for early conduct problems: Variable- and person oriented approaches. *Development and Psychopathology, 13*, 255–276.

Grégoire, J., Coalson, D. L., & Zhu, J. (2011). Analysis of WAIS–IV index score scatter using significant deviation from the mean index score. *Assessment, 18*(2), 168–177. doi:10.1177/1073191110386343

Greiff, S., Wustenberg, S., Csapo , Demetriou, A., Hautamaki, J., Graesser, A. C., & Martin, R. (2014). Domain-general problem solving skills and education in the 21st century. *Educational Research Review, 13*, 74–83.

Gresham, F. M. (2002). Responsiveness to intervention: An alternative approach to the identification of learning disabilities. In R. Bradley, L. Danielson, & D. Hallahan (Eds.), *Identification of learning disabilities: Research to practice* (pp. 467–519). Mahwah, NJ: Erlbaum.

Gresham, F. M., & Witt, J. C. (1997). Utility of intelligence tests for treatment planning, classification, and placement decisions: Recent empirical findings and future directions. *School Psychology Quarterly, 12*, 249–267. doi:10.1037/h0088961

Griffin, H., & Beech, A. (2004). *Evaluation of the AIM framework for the assessment of adolescents who display sexually harmful behavior: A report for the Youth Justice Board.* Retrieved from http://yjbpublications.justice.gov.uk/Resources/Downloads/AIM%20Full%20Report.pdf

Gross, D., Julion, W., & Fogg, L. (2001). What motivates participation and dropout among low-income urban families of color in a prevention intervention? *Family Relations, 50*, 246–254.

Groth-Marnat, G. (2009). The five assessment issues you meet when you go to heaven. *Journal of Personality Assessment, 91*, 303–310.

Gruber, E., & Machamer, A. M. (2000). Risk of school failure as an early indicator of other health risk behaviour in American high school students. *Health, Risk and Society, 2*(1), 59–68.

Grunwald, H. E., Lockwood, B., Harris, P. W., & Mennis, J. (2010). Influences of neighborhood context, individual history and parenting behavior on recidivism among juvenile offenders. *Journal of Youth and Adolescence, 39*, 1067–1079.

Guilford, J. P. (1954). *Psychometric methods.* New York, NY: McGraw-Hill.

Guilford, J. P. (1956). The structure of intellect. *Psychological Bulletin, 53*, 267–293.

Guilford, J. P. (1967). *The nature of human intelligence.* New York, NY: McGraw-Hill.

Gustafsson, J. E. (1984). A unifying model for the structure of intellectual abilities. *Intelligence, 8*, 179–203.

Gutman, L. M., Sameroff, A. J., & Cole, R. (2003). Academic growth curve trajectories from 1st grade to 12th grade: Effects of multiple social risk factors and preschool child factors. *Developmental Psychology*, *39*, 777–790.

Gutman, L. M., Sameroff, A. J., & Eccles, J. S. (2002). The academic achievement of African American students during early adolescence: An examination of multiple risk, promotive, and protective factors. *American Journal of Community Psychology*, *30*, 367–399.

Haig, B. D. (2005). Exploratory factor analysis, theory generation, and scientific method. *Multivariate Behavioral Research*, *40*, 303–329. doi:10.1207/s15327906mbr4003_2

Hale, J. B, Alfonso, V., Berninger, V., Bracken, C., Christo, C., Clarke, E., ... Yalof, J. (2010). Critical issues in response-to-intervention, comprehensive evaluation, and specific learning disabilities identification and intervention: An expert white paper consensus. *Learning Disability Quarterly*, *33*(1), 223–236.

Hale, J. B., & Fiorello, C. A. (2004). *School neuropsychology: A practitioner's handbook*. New York, NY: Guilford Press.

Hale, J. B., Fiorello, C. A., Miller, J. A., Wenrich, K., Teodori, A., & Henzel, J. N. (2008). WISC–IV interpretation for specific learning disabilities and intervention: A cognitive hypothesis testing approach. In A. Prifitera, D. H. Saklofske, & E. G. Weiss (Eds.), *WISC–IV clinical assessment and intervention* (2nd ed., pp. 109–171). New York, NY: Elsevier.

Hale, J. B., Kaufman, A. S., Naglieri, J. A., & Kavale, K. A. (2006). Implementation of IDEA: Using RTI and cognitive assessment methods. *Psychology in the Schools*, *43*(7), 753–770.

Hallenbeck, C. E., Fink, S. L., & Grossman, J. S. (1965). Measurement of intellectual inefficiency. *Psychological Reports*, *17*, 339–349.

Halliday-Boykins, C. A., & Graham, S. (2001). At both ends of the gun: Testing the relationship between community violence exposure and youth violent behavior. *Journal of Abnormal Child Psychology*, *29*(5), 383–402.

Halsey, P. A. (2005). Parent involvement in junior high schools: A failure to communicate. *American Secondary Education*, *34*(1), 57–69.

Hambleton, R. K., Bartram, D., & Oakland, T. (2011). Technical advances and guidelines for improving testing practices. In P. R. Martin, F. M. Cheung, M. C. Knowles, M. Kyrios, L. Littlefield, J. B. Overmier, & J. M. Prieto (Eds.), *IAAP handbook of applied psychology* (pp. 338–361). Malden, MA: Wiley-Blackwell.

Hanlon, T. E., Bateman, R. W., Simon, B. D., O'Grady, K. E., & Garswell, S. B. (2004). Antecedents and correlates of deviant activity in urban youth manifesting behavioral problems. *Journal of Primary Prevention*, *24*, 285–309.

Hanna, G. S., Bradley, F. O., & Holen, M. C. (1981). Estimating major sources of measurement error in individual intelligence tests. *Journal of School Psychology*, *19*, 370–376. doi:10.1016/0022–4405(81)90031–5

Hannay, H. J., Bieliauskas, L. A., Crosson, B. A., Hammeke, T. A., Hamsher, K. deS., & Koffler, S. P. (1998). Proceedings: The Houston Conference on Specialty Education and Training in Clinical Neuropsychology. *Archives of Clinical Neuropsychology*, *13*(2), 157–250.

Hannon, L. & DeFina, R. (2012). Sowing the seeds: How adult incarceration promotes juvenile delinquency. *Crime, Law, and Social Change*, *57*, 475–491.

Hardy, J. B., Welcher, D. W., Mellits, E. D., & Kagen, J. (1976). Pitfalls in the measurement of intelligence: Are standard measures of intelligence valid instruments for measuring the intellectual potential of urban children? *Journal of Psychology*, *94*, 43–51.

Hargus, M. E., & Wasserman, J. D. (1993). *Inside Wechsler's library: Insights, incongruities, and the "lost WAIS items."* Paper presented at the First Annual South Padre Island Interdisciplinary Conference on Cognitive Assessment of Children and Youth in School and Clinical Settings, South Padre Island, TX.

Harland, P., Reijneveld, S. A., Brugman, E., Verloove-Vanhorick, S. P., & Verhulst, R. C. (2002). Family factors and life events as risk factors for behvioural and emotional problems in children. *European Child & Adolescent Psychiatry*, *11*, 176–184.

Harlow, C. W. (2003). *Education and correctional populations*. Washington, DC: U.S. Department of Justice.

Harris, A. J., & Shakow, D. (1937). The clinical significance of numerical measures of scatter on the Stanford-Binet. *Psychological Bulletin*, *34*, 134–150.

Harris, P. W., Welsh, W. N., & Butler, F. (2000). A century of juvenile justice. In G. LaFree (Ed.),

Criminal justice 2000: The nature of crime: Continuity and change (pp. 359–426). Washington, DC: National Institute of Justice.

Harrison, P. L. (1987). Research with adaptive behavior scales. *Journal of Special Education, 21,* 37–68.

Hartlage, L. C., & Long, C. J. (2009). Development of neuropsychology as a professional psychology specialty: History, training, and credentialing. In C. Reynolds & E. Fletcher-Janzen (Eds.), *Handbook of clinical child neuropsychology* (pp. 3–18). New York, NY: Springer.

Hartmann, P., Larsen, L., & Nyborg, H. (2009). Personality as a predictor of achievement. *Journal of Individual Differences, 30,* 65–74. doi:10.1027/1614–0001.30.2.65

Harvey, V. S. (1997). Improving readability of psychological reports. *Professional Psychology: Research and Practice, 28*(3), 271–274.

Harvey, V. S. (2013). Communicating test results. In K. F. Geisinger, B. A. Bracken, J. F. Carlson, J. C. Hansen, N. R. Kuncel, S. P. Reise, & M. C. Rodriguez (Eds.), *APA handbook of testing and assessment in psychology, Vol. 2: Testing and assessment in clinical and counseling psychology* (pp. 35–50). Washington, DC: American Psychological Association.

Hass, M. R., & Carriere, J. A. (2014). *Writing useful, accessible, and legally defensible psychoeducational reports.* Hoboken, NJ: Wiley.

Hayiou-Thomas, M. E., Dale, P. S., & Plomin, R. (2012). The etiology of variation in language skills acquisition changes with development: A longitudinal twin study of language from 2 to 12 years. *Developmental Science, 15,* 233–249

Haynes, S. N., & Lench, H. C. (2003). Incremental validity of new clinical assessment measures. *Psychological Assessment, 15,* 456–466. doi:10.1037/1040–3590.15.4.456

Haynie, D. L., Silver, E., & Teasdale, B. (2006). Neighborhood characteristics, peer networks, and adolescent violence. *Journal of Quantitative Criminology, 22,* 147–169.

Hebben, N. & Milberg, W. (2009). *Essentials of neuropsychological assessment* (2nd ed.) Hoboken, NJ: Wiley.

Helsen, M., Vollebergh, W., & Meeus, W. (2000). Social support from parents and friends and emotional problems in adolescence. *Journal of Youth and Adolescence, 29,* 319–335.

Henry, B., Caspi, A., Moffitt, T. E., and Silva, P. A. (1996). Temperamental and familial predictors of violent and nonviolent criminal convictions: Age 3–age 18. *Developmental Psychology, 32,* 614–623.

Higgins, G. E. (2002). General theory of crime and deviance: A structural equation modeling approach. *Journal of Crime and Justice, 25*(2), 71–95.

Hill, G. D., & Atkinson, M. P. (1988). Gender, familial control, and delinquency. *Criminology, 26,* 127–147.

Hill, N. E., & Tyson, D. F. (2009). Parental involvement in middle school: A meta-analytic assessment of the strategies that promote achievement. *Developmental Psychology, 45,* 740–763.

Hirschfield, P. J., & Gasper, J. (2011). The relationship between school engagement and delinquency in late childhood and early adolescence. *Journal of Youth and Adolescence, 40,* 3–22.

Hirschi, T. (2004). Self-control and crime. In R. F. Baumeister & K. D. Vohs (Eds.), *Handbook of self-regulation: Research, theory and applications.* New York, NY: Guilford Press.

Hirshoren, A., & Kavale, K. (1976). Profile analysis of the WISC–R: A continuing malpractice. *Exceptional Child, 23,* 83–87.

Hodges, K., Doucette-Gates, A., & Liao, Q. (1999). The relationship between the Child and Adolescent Functional Assessment Scale (CAFAS) and indicators of functioning. *Journal of Child and Family Studies, 8*(1), 109–122.

Hodges, K., Horwitz, E., Kline, J., & Brandt, D. (1982). Comparison of various WISC–R summary scores for a psychiatric sample. *Journal of Clinical Psychology, 38*(4), 830–837.

Hodges, K., & Wong, M. M. (1996). Psychometric characteristics of a multidimensional measure to assess impairment: The Child and Adolescent Functional Assessment Scale. *Journal of Child and Family Studies, 5,* 445–467.

Hoffmann, J. P., Cerbone, F. G., & Su, S. S. (2000). A growth curve analysis of stress and adolescent drug use. *Substance Use & Misuse, 35,* 687–716.

Hofman, M. A. (2015). Evolution of the human brain: From matter to mind. In S. Goldstein, D. Princiotta, & J. Naglieri (Eds.), *Handbook of intelligence: Evolutionary theory, historical perspective, and current concepts* (pp. 65–82) New York, NY: Springer.

Holmes, J., Gathercole, S. E., & Dunning, D. L. (2009). Adaptive training leads to sustained enhancement of poor working memory in children. *Developmental Science, 12,* 9–15.

Holmes, J., Gathercole, S. E., Place, M., Dunning, D. L., Hilton, K. A., & Elliott, J. G. (2010). Working memory deficits can be overcome: Impacts of training and medication on working memory in children with ADHD. *Applied Cognitive Psychology, 24,* 827–836.

Holzinger, K. J., & Swineford, F. (1937). The bi-factor method. *Psychometrika, 2,* 41–54. doi:10.1007/BF02287965

Honzik, M. P. (1940). Age changes in the relationship between certain environmental variables and children's intelligence. *Yearbook of the National Society for the Study of Education, 39,* 185–205.

Horn, J. L. (1965). *Fluid and crystallized intelligence: A factor analytic and developmental study of the structure among primary mental abilities* (Doctoral dissertation, University of Illinois, Urbana-Champaign).

Horn, J. L. (1965). A rationale and test for the number of factors in factor analysis. *Psychometrika, 30,* 179–185. doi:10.1007/BF02289447

Horn, J. L. (1968). Organization of abilities and the development of intelligence. *Psychological Review, 75,* 242–259.

Horn, J. L. (1972). State, trait and change dimensions of intelligence: A critical experiment. *British Journal of Educational Psychology, 42,* 159–185.

Horn, J. L. (1976). Human abilities: A review of research and theory in the early 1970s. *Annual Review of Psychology, 27,* 437–485.

Horn, J. L. (1978). Human ability systems. In P. B. Baltes (Ed.), *Life-span development and behavior* (Vol. 1, pp. 211–256). New York, NY: Academic Press.

Horn, J. L. (1985). Remodeling old models of intelligence. In B. B. Wolman (Ed.), *Handbook of intelligence* (pp. 267–300). New York, NY: Wiley.

Horn, J. L. (1988). Thinking about human abilities. In J. R. Nesselroade (Ed.), *Handbook of multivariate psychology* (pp. 645–685). New York, NY: Academic Press.

Horn, J. L. (1989a). Cognitive diversity: A framework of learning. In P. L. Ackerman, R. J. Sternberg, & R. Glaser (Eds.), *Learning and individual differences* (pp. 61–116). New York, NY: Freeman.

Horn, J. L. (1989b). Measurement of intellectual capabilities: A review of theory. In K. S. McGrew, J. K. Werder, & R. W. Woodcock (Eds.), *WJ-R*

technical manual (pp. 197–245). Chicago, IL: Riverside.

Horn, J. L. (1991). Measurement of intellectual capabilities: A review of theory. In K. S. McGrew, J. K. Werder, & R. W. Woodcock (Eds.), *Woodcock-Johnson technical manual* (Rev. ed., pp. 197–232). Itasca, IL: Riverside.

Horn, J. L. (1998). A basis for research on age differences in cognitive abilities. In J. J. McArdle & R. W. Woodcock (Eds.), *Human cognitive abilities in theory and practice* (pp. 57–92). Mahwah, NJ: Erlbaum.

Horn, J. L., & Blankson, A. N. (2012). Foundations for better understanding of cognitive abilities. In D. P. Flanagan & P. L. Harrison (Eds.), *Contemporary intellectual assessment: Theories, tests, and issues* (3rd ed., pp. 73–98). New York, NY: Guilford Press.

Horn, J. L., & Cattell, R. B. (1966). Refinement and test of the theory of fluid and crystallized general intelligences. *Journal of Educational Psychology, 57*(5), 253–270.

Horn, J. L., & Cattell, R. B. (1967). Age differences in fluid and crystallized intelligence. *Acta Psychologica, 26,* 107–129.

Horn, J. L., & Hofer, S. M. (1992). Major abilities and development in the adult period. In R. J. Sternberg & C. A. Berg (Eds.), *Intellectual development* (pp. 44–99). Boston, MA: Cambridge University Press.

Horn, J. L., & McArdle, J. J. (1980). Perspectives on mathematical/statistical model building (MASMOB) in research on aging. In L. W. Poon (Ed.), *Aging in the 1980s: Psychological issues* (pp. 503–541). Washington, DC: American Psychological Association.

Horn, J. L., & Noll, J. (1997). Human cognitive capabilities: *Gf-Gc* theory. In D. P. Flanagan, J. L. Genshaft, & P. L. Harrison (Eds.), *Contemporary intellectual assessment: Theories, tests and issues* (pp. 53–91). New York: Guilford.

Horn, J. L., & Stankov, L. (1982). Auditory and visual factors of intelligence. *Intelligence, 6,* 165–185.

Horton, A. M., & Reynolds, C. R. (2015). Common and variable aspects of intelligence. In S. Goldstein, D. Princiotta, & J. Naglieri (Eds.), *Handbook of intelligence: Evolutionary theory, historical perspective, and current concepts* (pp. 367–380). New York, NY: Springer.

Howard-Jones, P., Ott, M., van Leeuwen, T., & De Smedt, B. (2014). The potential relevance of cognitive neuroscience for the development and use of technology-enhanced learning. *Learning, Media and Technology, 40,* 131–151. doi:10.1080/17439884.2014.919321

Howse, R. B., Calkins, S. D., Anastopoulos, A. D., Keane, S. P., & Shelton, T. L. (2003). Regulatory contributors to children's kindergarten achievement. *Early Education and Development, 14,* 101–119.

Hu, L.-T., & Bentler, P. M. (1999). Cutoff criteria for fit indexes in covariance structure analysis: Conventional criteria versus new alternatives. *Structural Equation Modeling, 5,* 1–55. doi:10.1080/10705519909540118

Hu, L.-T., Bentler, P. M., & Kano, Y. (1992). Can test statistics in covariance structure analysis be trusted? *Psychological Bulletin, 112,* 351–362. doi:10.1037/0033–2909.112.2.351

Hubley, A. M., & Zumbo, B. D. (2011). Validity and the consequences of test interpretation and use. *Social Indicators Research, 103,* 219–230. doi:10.1007/s11205–011–9843–4

Human intelligence. (2015). In *Encyclopaedia Brittanica.* Retrieved from http://www.britannica.com/EBchecked/topic/289766/human-intelligence

Hunsley, J. (2003). Introduction to the special section on incremental validity and utility in clinical assessment. *Psychological Assessment, 15,* 443–445. doi:10.1037/1040–3590.15.4.443

Hunsley, J., & Mash, E. J. (2007). Evidence-based assessment. *Annual Review of Clinical Psychology, 3,* 29 51. doi.10.1146/annurev.clinpsy.3.022806.091419

Hunsley, J., & Meyer, G. J. (2003). The incremental validity of psychological testing and assessment: Conceptual, methodological, and statistical issues. *Psychological Assessment, 15,* 446–455. doi:10.1037/1040–3590.15.4.446

Hunt, E., & Jaeggi, S. M. (2013). Challenges for research on intelligence. *Journal of Intelligence, 1,* 36–54.

Hunt, J. M. (1936). Psychological experiments with disordered persons. *Psychological Bulletin, 3,* 1–58.

Ingoldsby, E. M., & Shaw, D. S. (2002). The role of neighborhood contextual factors on early-starting antisocial behavior. *Clinical Child and Family Psychology Review, 6,* 21–65.

International Test Commission. (2006). International guidelines on computer-based and Internet-delivered testing. *International Journal of Testing, 6,* 143–171.

Irwin, C. E., Jr. (1989). Risk-taking behaviours in the adolescent patient: Are they impulsive? *Pediatric Annals, 18,* 122–125.

Irwin, C. E., Jr., & Millstein, S. G. (1986). Biopsychosocial correlates of risk-taking behaviors during adolescence. Can the physician intervene? *Journal of Adolescent Health Care, 7,* 825–965.

Ivry, R. B., & Robertson, L. C. (1998). *The two sides of perception.* Cambridge, MA: MIT Press.

Izard, C., Fine, S., Schultz, D., Mostow, A., Ackerman, B., & Youngstrom, E. (2001). Emotion knowledge as a predictor of social behavior and academic competence in children at risk. *Psychological Science, 12,* 18–23.

Jacobson, M. W., Delis, D. C., Hamilton, J. M., Bondi, M. W., & Salmon, D. P. (2004). How do neuropsychologists define cognitive constructs? Further thoughts on limitations of factor analysis used with normal or mixed clinical populations [Letter to the editor]. *Journal of the International Neuropsychological Society, 10,* 1020–1021. doi:10.1017/S1355617704107121

Jaeggi, S. M., Buschkuehl, M., Jonides, J., & Perrig, W. J. (2008). Improved fluid intelligence with training on working memory, *Proceedings of the National Academy of Sciences (USA), 105,* 6829–6833.

Jaffee, S. R., Caspi, A., Moffitt, T. E., & Taylor, A. (2004). Physical maltreatment victims to antisocial child: Evidence of an environmentally mediated process, *Journal of Abnormal Psychology, 113*(1), 44–55.

Jastak, J. (1949). Problems of psychometric scatter analysis. *Psychological Bulletin, 46*(3), 177–197.

Jennrich, R. I., & Bentler, P. M. (2011). Exploratory bi-factor analysis. *Psychometrika, 76,* 537–549. doi:10.1007/s11336–011–9218–4

Jensen, A. R. (1980). *Bias in mental testing.* New York, NY: Free Press.

Jensen, A. R. (1998). *The g factor: The science of mental ability.* Westport, CT: Praeger.

Jimerson, S. R., Campos, E., & Greif, J. L. (2003). Toward an understanding of definitions and measures of school engagement and related terms. *California School Psychologist, 8,* 7–27.

Jirout, J. J., & Newcombe, N. S. (2015). Building blocks for developing spatial skills: Evidence from a large, representative U.S. sample. *Psychological Science, 26,* 302–310.

Johnson, M. H. (2011). Developmental neuroscience, psychophysiology, and genetics. In M. H.

Bornstein & M. E. Lamb (Eds.), *Cognitive development: An advanced textbook* (pp. 217–255). New York, NY: Psychology Press.

Johnson, W., Deary, I. J., & Iacono, W. G. (2009). Genetic and environmental transactions underlying educational attainment. *Intelligence*, *37*, 466–478. doi:10.1016/j.intell.2009.05.006

Johnson, W., te Nijenhuis, J., & Bouchard, T. J. (2008). Still just 1 *g*: Consistent results from five test batteries. *Intelligence*, *36*, 81–95. doi:10.1016/j.intell.2007.06.001

Jolles, D. D. & Crone, E. A. (2012). Training the developing brain: a neurocognitive perspective. *Frontiers in Human Neuroscience*, *6*, 76. doi:10.3389/fnhum.2012.00076

Jonson-Reid, M., & Barth, R. P. (2000). From maltreatment report to juvenile incarceration: The role of child welfare services. *Child Abuse & Neglect*, *24*, 505–520.

Jorgenson, L. A., Newsome, W. T., Anderson, D. J., Bargmann, C. I., Brown, E. N., Deisseroth, K., … Wingfield, J. C. (2015). The BRAIN Initiative: Developing technology to catalyse neuroscience discovery. *Philosophical Transactions of the Royal Society B*, *370*(1668), 1–12. http://dx/doi.org/10.1098/rstb.2014.0164

Jung, R. E., & Haier, R. J. (2007). The parieto-frontal integration theory (P-FIT) of intelligence: Converging neuroimaging evidence. *Behavioral and Brain Sciences*, *30*, 135–187.

Juni, S., & Trobliger R. (2009). Codification of intratest scatter on the Wechsler Intelligence Scales: Critique and proposed methodology. *Canadian Journal of School Psychology*, *24*, 140–157.

Juolasmaa A, Outakoski J., Hirvenoja R., Tienari P., Sotaniemi K., & Takkunen J. (1981). *Journal of Clinical Psychology*, *3*, 181–197.

Kaiser, H. F. (1960). The application of electronic computers to factor analysis. *Educational and Psychological Measurement*, *20*, 141–151. doi:10.1177/001316446002000116

Kaiser, H. F. (1974). An index of factorial simplicity. *Psychometrika*, *39*, 31–36. doi:10.1007/BF02291575

Kamphaus, R. W., Reynolds, C. R., & Vogel, K. K. (2009). Intelligence testing. In J. L. Matson, F. Andrasik, & M. L. Matson (Eds.), *Assessing childhood psychopathology and developmental disabilities* (pp. 91–115). New York, NY: Springer.

Kamphaus, R. W., Winsor, A. P., Rowe, E. W., & Kim, S. (2012). A history of intelligence test interpretation. In D. P. Flanagan & P. L. Harrison (Eds.), *Contemporary intellectual assessment: Theories, tests, and issues* (3rd ed., pp. 56–70). New York, NY: Guilford Press.

Kaplan, E. (1988). A process approach to neuropsychological assessment. In T. Boll & B. K. Bryant (Eds.) *Clinical neuropsychology and brain functions: Research, measurement, and practice* (pp. 125–167). Washington, DC: American Psychological Association.

Kaplan, E. (1990). The process approach to neuropsychological assessment. *Journal of Neuropsychiatry*, *2*(1), 72–87.

Kaplan, E., Fein, D., Morris, R., & Delis, D. C. (1991). *WAIS–R as a neuropsychological instrument*. San Antonio, TX: Psychological Corporation.

Kaplan, E., Fein, D., Morris, R., Kramer, J. H., & Delis, D. C. (1999). *The WISC–III as a processing instrument*. San Antonio, TX: Psychological Corporation.

Kaufman, A. S. (1973a). Comparison of the performance of matched groups of Black children and White children on the Wechsler Preschool and Primary Scale of Intelligence. *Journal of Consulting and Clinical Psychology*, *41*, 186–191.

Kaufman, A. S. (1973b). The relationship of WPPSI IQs to SES and other background variables. *Journal of Clinical Psychology*, *39*, 354–357.

Kaufman, A. S. (1975). Factor analysis of the WISC–R at 11 age levels between 6 1/2 to 16 1/2 years. *Journal of Consulting and Clinical Psychology*, *43*, 135–147.

Kaufman, A. S. (1976a). Do normal children have "flat" ability profiles? *Psychology in the Schools*, *13*, 284–285.

Kaufman, A. S. (1976b). A new approach to the interpretation of test scatter on the WISC-R. *Journal of Learning Disabilities*, *9*, 160–168.

Kaufman, A. S. (1976c). Verbal-performance IQ discrepancies on the WISC–R. *Journal of Consulting and Clinical Psychology*, *44*, 739–744.

Kaufman, A. S. (1979). *Intelligent testing with the WISC–R*. New York, NY: Wiley.

Kaufman, A. S. (1981). The WISC–R and learning disabilities assessment: State of the art. *Journal of Learning Disabilities*, *14*, 520–526.

Kaufman, A. S. (1990). *Assessing adolescent and adult intelligence*. Boston, MA: Allyn & Bacon.

Kaufman, A. S. (1993). King WISC the Third assumes the throne. *Journal of School Psychology, 31*, 345–354.

Kaufman, A. S. (1994a). *Intelligent testing with the WISC–III*. New York, NY: Wiley.

Kaufman, A. S. (1994b). Practice effects. In R. J. Sternberg (Ed.), *Encyclopedia of intelligence* (Vol. 2, pp. 828–833). New York, NY: Macmillan.

Kaufman, A. S. (2009). *IQ Testing 101*. New York, NY: Springer.

Kaufman, A. S. (2010). Foreword. In L. G. Weiss, D. H. Saklofske, D. L. Coalson, & S. E. Raiford (eds.), *WAIS–IV clinical use and interpretation: Scientist-practitioner perspectives* (pp. xiii–xxi). Amsterdam, The Netherlands: Elsevier Academic Press.

Kaufman, A. S. (2012). Biography of David Wechsler. In F. Volkmar (Ed.), *Encyclopedia of autistic spectrum disorders*. New York, NY: Springer.

Kaufman, A. S. (2013a). Clinical applications II: Age and intelligence across the adult life span. In E. O. Lichtenberger & A. S. Kaufman, *Essentials of WAIS-IV Assessment* (2nd ed., pp. 254–298). Hoboken, NJ: Wiley.

Kaufman, A. S. (2013b). Intelligent testing with Wechsler's fourth editions: Perspectives on the Weiss et al. studies and the eight commentaries. *Journal of Psychoeducational Assessment, 31*, 224–234.

Kaufman, A. S., Flanagan, D. P., Alfonso, V. C., & Mascolo, J. T. (2006). Review of the Wechsler Intelligence Scale for Children, Fourth Edition (WISC IV). *Journal of Psychoeducational Assessment, 24*, 278–295. doi:10.1177/0734282906288389

Kaufman, A. S., Kaufman, J. C., Liu, X., & Johnson, C. K. (2009). How do educational attainment and gender relate to Gf, Gc, and academic skills at ages 22 to 90 years? *Archives of Clinical Neuropsychology, 24*, 153–163.

Kaufman, A. S., & Kaufman, N. L. (1973). Sex differences on the McCarthy Scales of Children's Abilities. *Journal of Clinical Psychology, 29*, 362–365.

Kaufman, A. S., & Kaufman, N. L. (1977). *Clinical evaluation of young children with the McCarthy Scales*. New York, NY: Grune & Stratton.

Kaufman, A. S., & Kaufman, N. L. (1983). *Kaufman Assessment Battery for Children*. Circle Pines, MN: American Guidance Service.

Kaufman, A. S. & Kaufman, N. L. (1985). *Kaufman Test of Educational Achievement*. Circle Pines, MN: American Guidance Service.

Kaufman, A. S., & Kaufman, N. L. (1993). *Kaufman Adolescent and Adult Intelligence Test*. Circle Pines, MN: American Guidance Service.

Kaufman, A. S., & Kaufman, N. L. (2004). *Kaufman Assessment Battery for Children* (2nd ed.). Circle Pines, MN: American Guidance Service.

Kaufman, A. S., & Kaufman, N. L. (2014). *Kaufman Test of Educational Achievement* (3rd ed.). Bloomington, MN: Pearson.

Kaufman, A. S., & Lichtenberger, E. O. (1999). *Essentials of WAIS–III assessment*. New York, NY: Wiley.

Kaufman, A. S., & Lichtenberger, E. O. (2006). *Assessing adolescent and adult intelligence* (3rd ed.). Hoboken, NJ: Wiley.

Kaufman, A. S., McLean J. E., & Kaufman, J. C. (1995). The fluid and crystallized abilities of white, black, and Hispanic adolescents and adults, both with and without an education covariate. *Journal of Clinical Psychology, 51*, 637–647.

Kaufman, A. S., & Weiss, L. G. (Eds.) (2010). Special issue on the Flynn effect. *Journal of Psychoeducational Assessment, 28(5)*. Thousand Oaks, CA: Sage.

Kaufman, J. C. (in press). *Creativity 101* (2nd ed.). New York, NY: Springer.

Kaufman, J. C., Kaufman, S. B., & Lichtenberger, E. O. (2011). Finding creativity on intelligence tests via divergent production. *Canadian Journal of School Psychology, 26*, 83–106.

Kaufman, S. B., Reynolds, M. R., Liu, X., Kaufman, A. S., & McGrew, K. S. (2012). Are cognitive *g* and academic *g* one and the same *g*? An exploration on the Woodcock–Johnson and Kaufman tests. *Intelligence, 40*, 123–138. doi:10.1016/j.intell.2012.01.009

Kausler, D. H. (1991). *Experimental psychology, cognition, and human aging*. New York, NY: Springer-Verlag.

Kavale, K., & Mattson, P. D. (1983). "One jumped off the balance beam": Meta-analysis of perceptual-motor training. *Journal of Learning Disabilities, 16*, 165–173. doi:10.1177/0022219 48301600307

Kearns, D. M., & Fuchs, D. (2013). Does cognitively focused instruction improve the academic performance of low-achieving students? *Exceptional Children, 79*, 263–290.

Keith, T. Z. (1997). What does the WISC–III measure? A reply to Carroll and Kranzler. *School Psychology Quarterly, 12*, 117–118. doi:10.1037/h0088953

Keith, T. Z., Fehrmann, P. G., Harrison, P. L., & Pottebaum, S. M. (1987). The relation between adaptive behavior and intelligence: Testing alternative explanations. *Journal of School Psychology, 25,* 31–43. doi:10.1016/0022–4405(87)90058–6

Keith, T. Z., Fine, J. G., Taub, G., Reynolds, M. R., & Kranzler, J. H. (2006). Higher order, multisample, confirmatory factor analysis of the Wechsler Intelligence Scale for Children–Fourth Edition: What does it measure? *School Psychology Review, 35*(1), 108–127.

Keith, T. Z., Kranzler, J. H., & Flanagan, D. P. (2001). Joint CFA of the CAS and the WJ III. *School Psychology Review, 29,* 203–307.

Keith, T. Z., & Reynolds, M. R. (2010). Cattell-Horn-Carroll abilities and cognitive tests: What we've learned from 20 years of research. *Psychology in the Schools, 47,* 635–650.

Keith, T. Z., & Reynolds, M. R. (2012). Using confirmatory factor analysis to aid in understanding the constructs measured by intelligence tests. In D. P. Flanagan & P. L. Harrison (Eds.), *Contemporary intellectual assessment: Theories, tests, and issues* (3rd ed., pp. 758–799). New York, NY: Guilford Press.

Keith, T. Z., Reynolds, M. R., Roberts, L. G., Winter, A. L., & Austin, C. A. (2011). Sex differences in latent cognitive abilities ages 5 to 17: Evidence from the Differential Ability Scales–Second Edition. *Intelligence, 39,* 389–404.

Keller, T. E., Spieker, S. J., & Gilchrist, L. (2005). Patterns of risk and trajectories of preschool problem behaviors: A person-oriented analysis of attachment in context. *Development and Psychopathology, 17,* 349–384.

Kellerman, H., & Burry, A. (1981). Intellectual functioning: Subtest and scatter analysis. In H. Kellerman, *Handbook of psychodiagnostic testing* (pp. 78–80). New York, NY: Grune & Stratton.

Kerlinger, F. N. (1986). *Foundations of behavioral research* (3rd ed.). San Diego, CA: Harcourt Brace.

Kessel, J. B., & Zimmerman, M. (1993). Reporting errors in studies of the diagnostic performance of self-administered questionnaires: Extent of the problem, recommendations for standardized presentation of results, and implications for the peer review process. *Psychological Assessment, 5,* 395–399. doi:10.1037/1040–3590.5.4.395

Kirchner, E. E., & Higgins, G. E. (2014). Self-control and racial disparities in delinquency: A structural equation modeling approach. *American Journal of Criminal Justice, 39,* 436–449.

Kline, R. B. (2011). *Principles and practice of structural equation modeling* (3rd ed.). New York, NY: Guilford Press.

Klove, H. (1963). Clinical neuropsychology. *Medical Clinics of North America, 47,* 1647–1658.

Konold, T. R., & Canivez, G. L. (2010). Differential relationships between WISC–IV and WIAT–II scales: An evaluation of potentially moderating child demographics. *Educational and Psychological Measurement, 70,* 613–627.

Korkman, M., Kirk, U., & Kemp, S. L. (1998). *NEPSY: A developmental neuropsychological assessment.* San Antonio, TX: Psychological Corporation.

Korkman, M., Kirk, U., & Kemp, S. (2007). *NEPSY–II* (2nd ed.). Bloomington, MN: Pearson.

Korkman, M., Kirk, U., & Kemp, S. (2007). *NEPSY–II: A developmental neuropsychological assessment.* San Antonio, TX: Psychological Corporation.

Kosslyn, S. M. & Koenig, O. (1992). *Wet Mind: The new cognitive neuroscience.* New York, NY: Macmillan.

Kotz, K. M., Watkins, M. W., & McDermott, P. A. (2008). Validity of the general conceptual ability score from the Differential Ability Scales as a function of significant and rare interfactor variability. *School Psychology Review, 37,* 261–278.

Koziol, L. F. & Budding, D. E. (2011). Pediatric Neuropsychological Assessment: Theoretical models of test interpretation. In A. Davis (Ed.), *Handbook of pediatric neuropsychology* (pp. 443–456). New York, NY: Springer.

Kramer, J. J., Henning-Stout, M., Ullman, D. P., & Schellenberg, R. P. (1987). The viability of scatter analysis on the WISC-R and the SBIS: Examining a vestige. *Journal of Psychoeducational Assessment, 5,* 37–47. doi:10.1177/073428298700500105

Kranzler, J. H. (1997). What does the WISC–III measure? Comments on the relationship between intelligence, working memory capacity, and information processing speed and efficiency. *School Psychology Quarterly, 12,* 110–116. doi:10.1037/h0088952

Kranzler, J. H., & Floyd, R. G. (2013). *Assessing intelligence in children and adolescents: A practical guide.* New York, NY: Guilford Press.

Kroneman, L., Loeber, R., & Hipwell, A. E. (2004). Is neighborhood context differently related to externalizing problems and delinquency for girls compared to boys? *Clinical Child and Family Psychology Review*, 7, 109–122.

Kucian, K., Grond, U., Rotzer, S., Henzi, B., Schonmann, C., Plangger, F., ... von Aster, M. (2011). Mental number line training in children with developmental dyscalculia. *Neuroimage*, 57, 782–795.

Kuentzel, J. G., Hetterscheidt, L. A., & Barnett, D. (2011). Testing intelligently includes double-checking Wechsler IQ scores. *Journal of Psychoeducational Assessment*, 29, 39–46.

Kuntsi, J., Wood, A. C., Rijsdijk, F., Johnson, K. A., Andreou, P., Albrecht, B., ... Asherson, P. (2010). Separation of cognitive impairments in attention-deficit/hyperactivity disorder into 2 familial factors. *Archives of General Psychiatry*, 67, 1159–1167.

LaForte, E. M., McGrew, K. S., & Schrank, F. A. (2014). *WJ IV technical abstract* (Woodcock-Johnson IV Assessment Bulletin No. 2). Rolling Meadows, IL: Riverside.

Landenberger, N. A. & Lipsey, M. W. (2005). The positive effects of cognitive-behavioral programs for offenders: A meta-analysis of factors associated with effective treatment. *Journal of Experimental Criminology*, 1, 451–476.

Lane, E. C. (2003). Correlates of female juvenile delinquency. *International Journal of Sociology and Social Policy*, 23(11), 1–14.

Lanza, S. T., Rhoades, B. L., Nix, R. L., Greenberg, M. T., & the Conduct Problems Prevention Research Group. (2010). Modeling the interplay of multilevel risk factors for future academic and behavior problems: A person-centered approach. *Development and Psychopathology*, 22, 313–335.

Laub, J. H., & Sampson, R. J. (1988). Unraveling families and delinquency: A reanalysis of the Gluecks' data. *Criminology*, 26, 355–380.

Lee, D., Reynolds, C. R., & Willson, V. L. (2003). Standardized test administration: Why bother? *Journal of Forensic Neuropsychology*, 3, 55–81. doi:10.1300/J151v03n03_04

Lee, V. E., & Burkam, D. T. (2002). *Inequality at the starting gate: Social background differences in achievement as children begin school*. Washington, DC: Economic Policy Institute.

Leech, S. L., Day, N. L., Richardson, G. A., & Goldschmidt, L. (2003). Predictors of self-reported delinquent behavior in a sample of young adolescents. *Journal of Early Adolescence*, 23, 78–106.

Lehr, C. A., Hansen, A. L., Sinclair, M. F., & Christenson, S. L. (2003). Moving beyond dropout towards school completion: An integrative review of data-based interventions. *School Psychology Review*, 32(3), 342–364.

Lei, P.-W., & Wu, Q. (2012). Estimation in structural equation modeling. In R. H. Hoyle (Ed.), *Handbook of structural equation modeling* (pp. 164–180). New York, NY: Guilford Press.

Lennon, R. T., & Doppelt, J. E (1976). *A conversation with David Wechsler*. Guilford, CT: Jeffrey Norton.

Leslie, L. K., Hurlburt, M., Landsverk, J., Barth, R., & Slymen, D. J. (2004). Outpatient mental health services for children in foster care: A national perspective. *Child Abuse & Neglect*, 28, 697–712.

Leslie, L. K., James, S., Monn, A., Kauten, M. C., Zhang, J., & Aarons, G. (2010). Health-risk behaviors in young adolescents in the child welfare system. *Journal of Adolescent Health*, 47, 26–34.

Letourneau, E. J., Schoenwald, S. K., & Sheidow, A. J. (2004). Children and adolescents with sexual behavior problems. *Child Maltreatment*, 9(1), 49–61.

Levine, M. D. (1994). *Educational care: A system for understanding and helping children with learning problems at home and in school*. Cambridge, MA: Educators Publishing Service.

Levine, M. D. (1998). *Developmental variation and learning disorders*. Cambridge: Educators Publishing Service.

Levine, M. D., Gordon, B. N., & Reed, M. S. (1998). *Developmental variation and learning disorders* (2nd ed.). Cambridge, MA: Educators Publishing Service.

Lezak, M. D. (1988). IQ: R. I. P. *Journal of Clinical and Experimental Neuropsychology*, 10, 351–361.

Lezak, M. D. (2004). *Neuropsychological assessment* (4th ed.). Hoboken, NJ: Wiley.

Lezak, M. D., & Howieson, D. B., Bigler, E. D., & Tranel, D. (2012). *Neuropsychological assessment* (5th ed.). New York, NY: Oxford University Press.

Lezak, M. D., Howieson, D. B., & Loring, D. W. (2004). *Neuropsychological assessment* (4th ed., pp. 5–10). New York, NY: Oxford University Press.

Lichtenberger, E. O., & Kaufman, A. S. (2004). *Essentials of WPPSI®–III assessment*. Hoboken, NJ: Wiley.

Lichtenberger, E. O., & Kaufman, A. S. (2013). *Essentials of WAIS®–IV assessment* (2nd ed.). Hoboken, NJ: Wiley.

Lichtenstein, R. (2013a). Writing psychoeducational reports that matter: A consumer-responsive approach. *NASP Communiqué, 42*(3), 1, 28–30.

Lichtenstein, R. (2013b). Writing psychoeducational reports that matter: A consumer-responsive approach, Part 2. *NASP Communiqué, 42*(4), 1, 10–13.

Lichtenstein, R. (2014). Writing psychoeducational reports that matter: A consumer-responsive approach, Part 3. *NASP Communiqué, 42*(6), 1, 30–32.

Lightfoot, D. (2004). "Some parents just don't care": Decoding the meanings of parental involvement in urban schools. *Urban Education, 39*(1), 91–107.

Lilienfeld, S. O., Ammirati, R., & David, M. (2012). Distinguishing science from pseudoscience in school psychology: Science and scientific thinking as safeguards against human error. *Journal of School Psychology, 50*, 7–36. doi:10.1016/j.jsp.2011.09.006

Lin, W.-H., & Mieczkowski, T. (2011). Subjective strains, conditioning factors, and juvenile delinquency: General Strain Theory in Taiwan. *Asian Criminology, 6*, 69–87.

Lipschitz, D. S., Rasmusson, A. M., Anyan, W., Cromwell, P., & Southwick, S. M. (2000). Clinical and functional correlates of posttraumatic stress disorder in urban adolescent girls at a primary care clinic. *Journal of the American Academy of Child and Adolescent Psychiatry, 39*, 1104–1111.

Lipszyc, J., & Schachar, R. (2010). Inhibitory control and psychopathology: A meta-analysis of studies using the stop signal task. *Journal of the International Neuropsychological Society, 16*, 1064–1076.

Litrownik, A. J., Lau, A., English, D. J., Briggs, E., Newton, R. R., Romney, S., & Dubowitz, H. (2005). Measuring the severity of child maltreatment. *Child Abuse & Neglect, 29*(5), 553–573.

Litt, R. A., de Jong, P. F., van Bergen, E., & Nation, K. (2013). Dissociating crossmodal and verbal demands in paired associative learning (PAL): What drives the PAL–reading relationship? *Journal of Experimental Child Psychology, 115*, 137–149. doi:10.1016/j.jecp.2012.11.012

Litt, R. A., & Nation, K. (2014). The nature and specificity of paired associative learning deficits in children with dyslexia. *Journal of Memory and Language, 71*, 71–88.

Little, M., & Steinberg, L. (2006). Psychosocial correlates of adolescent drug dealing in the inner city: Potential roles of opportunity, conventional commitments, and maturity. *Journal of Research in Crime and Delinquency, 43*, 357–386.

Little, T. D., Slegers, D. W., & Card, N. A. (2006). A non-arbitrary method of identifying and scaling latent variables in SEM and macs models. *Structural Equation Modeling, 13*, 59–72. doi:10.1207/s15328007sem1301_3

Lleras, C. (2008). Do skills and behaviors in high school matter? The contribution of noncognitive factor in explaining differences in educational attainment and earnings. *Social Science Research, 37*, 888–902.

LoBello, S. G., & Holley, G. (1999). WPPSI–R administration, clerical, and scoring errors by student examiners. *Journal of Psychological Assessment, 17*, 15–23.

Lodge, G. T. (1953). How to write a psychological report. *Journal of Clinical Psychology, 9*(4), 400–402.

Loe, S. A., Kadlubek, R. M., & Marks, W. J. (2007). Administration and scoring errors on the WISC-IV among graduate student examiners. *Journal of Psychoeducational Assessment, 25*, 237–247.

Loeber, R., Pardini, D. A., Stouthamer-Loeber, M., & Raine, A. (2007). Do cognitive, physiological, and psychosocial risk and promotive factors predict desistance from delinquency in males? *Development and Psychopathology 19*, 867–887.

Lohman, D. F. (1989). Human intelligence: An introduction to advances in theory and research. *Review of Educational Research, 59*, 333–373.

Lohman, D. F. (1994). Spatial ability. In R. J. Sternberg (Ed.), *Encyclopedia of human intelligence* (pp. 1000–1007). New York, NY: Macmillan.

Longman, R. S. (2004). Values for comparison of WAIS–III index scores with overall means. *Psychological Assessment, 16*, 323–325. doi:10.1037/1040–3590.16.3.323

Longman, R. S. (2005). Appendix A: Tables to compare WISC–IV index scores against overall means. In A. Prifitera, D. H. Saklofske, & L. G. Weiss (Eds.), *WISC–IV clinical use and interpretation* (pp. 68–89). San Diego, CA: Academic Press.

Loro, B., & Woodward, J. A. (1976) Verbal and performance IQ for discrimination among psychiatric diagnostic groups. *Journal of Clinical Psychology, 32*(1), 107–114.

Lowenkamp, C. T., Latessa, E. J., & Smith, P. (2006). Does correctional program quality really matter? The impact of adhering to the principles of effective intervention. *Criminology and Public Policy*, *5*, 575–594.

Lucio, R., Hunt, E., & Bornovalova, M. (2012). Identifying the necessary and sufficient number of risk factors for predicting academic failure. *Developmental Psychology*, *48*, 422–428.

Luria, A. R. (1966a). *Higher cortical functions in man*. New York, NY: Basic Books.

Luria, A. R. (1966b). *The working brain: An introduction to neuropsychology*. New York, NY: Basic Books.

Luria, A. R. (1973a). *Higher cortical function in man*. New York, NY: Basic Books.

Luria, A. R. (1973b). *The working brain: An introduction to neuropsychology* (trans. B. Haigh). London, UK: Penguin.

Luria, A. R. (1980). *Higher cortical functions in man* (2nd ed.). New York, NY: Basic Books.

Lutey, C. L. (1977). *Individual intelligence testing: A manual and sourcebook*. Greeley, CO: Carol L. Lutey.

Lynch, M., & Cicchetti, D. (1998). An ecological-transactional analysis of children and contexts: The longitudinal interplay among child maltreatment, community violence, and children's symptomatology. *Development and Psychopathology*, *10*(2), 235–257.

Lynn, R., & Irwing, P. (2008). Sex differences in mental arithmetic, digit span, and *g* defined as working memory capacity. *Intelligence*, *36*, 226–235.

Macklin, A. (2013). Community management of offenders: The interaction of social support and risk. *Federal Probation*, *77*(1), 17–21. Retrieved from http://www.uscourts.gov/uscourts/FederalCourts/PPS/Fedprob/2013-06/index.html

Macmann, D. W., & Barnett, D. W. (1994). Structural analysis of correlated factors: Lessons from the verbal-performance dichotomy of the Wechsler Scales. *School Psychology Quarterly*, *9*, 161–198.

Macmann, G. M., & Barnett, D. W. (1997). Myth of the master detective: Reliability of interpretations for Kaufman's "Intelligent Testing" approach to the WISC-III. *School Psychology Quarterly*, *12*, 197–234. doi:10.1037/h0088959

Mahoney, A., Donnelly, W. O., Boxer, P., & Lewis, T. (2003). Marital and severe parent-to-adolescent physical aggression in clinic-referred families: Mother and adolescent reports on co-occurrence and links to child behavior problems. *Journal of Family Psychology*, *17*(1), 3–19.

Malmgren, K. W., & Meisel, S. M. (2004). Examining the link between child maltreatment and delinquency for youth with emotional and behavioral disorders. *Child Welfare*, *83*(2), 175–188.

Manly, J. T., Cicchetti, D., & Barnett, D. (1994). The impact of subtype, frequency, chronicity, and severity of child maltreatment on social competence and behavior problems. *Development and Psychopathology*, *6*, 121–143.

Mapou, R. L., & Spector, J. (Eds.). (1995). *Clinical neuropsychological assessment: A cognitive approach* (Vol. *1*). New York, NY: Springer Science & Business Media.

March, J. S. (2012). *Multidimensional anxiety scale for children* (2nd ed.). North Tonawanda, NY: MHS.

Maricle, D. E., Johnson, W., & Avirett, E. (2010). Assessing and intervening in children with executive function disorders. In D. C. Miller (Ed.), *Best practices in school neuropsychology: Guidelines for effective practice, assessment, and evidence-based intervention* (pp. 599–640). Hoboken, NJ: Wiley.

Marks, H. M. (2000). Student engagement in instructional activity: Patterns in the elementary, middle, and high school years. *American Educational Research Journal*, *37*, 153–184.

Martin, A. J. (2009). Motivation and engagement across the academic life span. *Educational and Psychological Measurement*, *69*, 794–824.

Martinez, R., Rosenfeld, R., & Mares, D. (2008). Social disorganization, drug market activity, and neighborhood violent crime. *Urban Affairs Review*, *43*, 846–874.

Mascolo, J. T., Alfonso, V. C., & Flanagan, D. P. (2014). *Essentials of planning, selecting, and tailoring interventions for unique learners*. Hoboken, NJ: Wiley.

Mastoras, S. M., Climie, E. A., McCrimmon, A. W., & Schwean, V. L. (2011). A C.L.E.A.R. approach to report writing: A framework for improving the efficacy of psychoeducational reports. *Canadian Journal of School Psychology*, *26*(2), 127–147. doi:10.1177/0829573511409722

Matarazzo, J. D. (1972). *Wechsler's measurement and appraisal of adult intelligence* (5th ed.). New York, NY: Oxford University Press.

Matarazzo, J. D. (1981). Obituary: David Wechsler (1896–1981). *American Psychologist*, *36*, 1542–1543.

Matarazzo, J. D., Carmody, T. D., & Jacobs, L. D. (1980). Test-retest reliability and stability of the WAIS: A literature review with implications for clinical practice. *Journal of Clinical Neuropsychology*, *2*, 89–105.

Matarazzo, J. D., & Herman, D. O. (1984). Base rate data for the WAIS–R: test-retest stability and VIQ–PIQ differences. *Journal of Clinical Neuropsychology*, *6*, 351–366.

Matarazzo, R. G. , Matarazzo, J. D., Gallo, A., & Wiens, A. (1979). IQ and neuropsychological changes following carotid endarterectomy. *Journal of Clinical Neuropsychology*, 97–116.

Mather, N., & Schneider, D. (2015). The use of intelligence tests in the diagnosis of specific reading disability. In S. Goldstein, D. Princiotta, & J. Naglieri (Eds.), *Handbook of intelligence: Evolutionary theory, historical perspective, and current concepts* (pp. 415–433). New York, NY: Springer.

Mather, N., & Wendling, B. J. (2012). *Essentials of dyslexia assessment and intervention*. Hoboken, NJ: Wiley.

Mattis, S., Papolos, D., Luck, D., Cockerham, M., & Thode, H. C. (2011). Neuropsychological factors differentiating treated children with pediatric bipolar disorder from those with attention-deficit/hyperactivity disorder. *Journal of Clinical and Experimental Neuropsychology*, *33*, 74–84.

Mayes, S. D., & Calhoun, S. L. (2007). Learning, attention, writing, and processing speed in typical children and children with ADHD, autism, anxiety, depression, and oppositional-defiant disorder. *Child Neuropsychology*, *13*, 469–193. doi:10.1080/09297040601112773

Mayman, M. (1945). Review of the literature on "scatter." In D. Rapaport, M. Gill, & R. Schafer (Eds.), *Diagnostic psychological testing* (Vol. 1, pp. 548–558). Chicago, IL: Year Book.

Mayman, M., Schafer, R., & Rapaport, D. (1951). Interpretation of the WAIS in personality appraisal. In H. H. Anderson & G. L. Anderson (Eds.), *An introduction to projective techniques* (pp. 541–580). New York, NY: Prentice-Hall.

McBride, G., Dumont, R., & Willis, J. O. (2011). *Essentials of IDEA for assessment professionals*. Hoboken, NJ: Wiley.

McCabe, K. M., Lucchini, S. E., Hough, R. L., Yeh, M., & Hazen, A. (2005). The relation between violence exposure and conduct problems among adolescents: A prospective study. *American Journal of Orthopsychiatry*, *75*, 575–584.

McCarthy, D. (1972). *The McCarthy scales of children's abilities*. New York, NY: Psychological Corporation.

McLean, J. E., Kaufman, A. S., & Reynolds, C. R. (1989). Base rates of WAIS–R subtest scatter as a guide for clinical and neuropsychological assessment. *Journal of Clinical Psychology*, *45*, 919–926.

McCloskey, G. (2009a). Clinical applications I: A neuropsychological approach to interpretation of the WAIS–IV and the use of the WAIS–IV in learning disability assessments. In E. O. Lichtenberger & A. S. Kaufman. *Essentials of WAIS-IV assessment*. Hoboken, NJ: Wiley.

McCloskey, G. (2009b). The WISC–IV Integrated. In D. P. Flanagan & A. S. Kaufman. *Essentials of WISC–IV Assessment*. Hoboken, NJ: Wiley.

McCloskey, G., Gilmartin, C. & Stanco, B. (2014). Interventions for students with executive skill and executive functions difficulties. In J. Moscolo, D. Flanagan, & V. Alfonso, (Eds.), *Essentials of planning, selecting and tailoring interventions for unique learners* (pp. 314–356). Hoboken, NJ: Wiley.

McCloskey, G., Hewitt, J., Henzel, J. N., & Eusebio, E. (2009). Executive functions and emotional disturbance. In S. G. Feifer & G. Rattan (Eds.), *Emotional disorders: A neuropsychological, psychopharmacological, and educational perspective* (pp. 65–106). Middletown, MD: School Neuropsych Press.

McCloskey, G., & Maerlender, A. (2005). The WISC–IV Integrated. In A, Prifitera, D. H. Saklofske, & L. G. Weiss, *WISC–IV clinical use and interpretation: Scientist-practitioner perspectives* (pp. 101–149). New York, NY: Academic Press.

McCloskey, G., & Perkins, L. A. (2012). *Essentials of executive functions assessment* (Vol. 68). Hoboken, NJ: Wiley.

McCloskey, G., Perkins, L. A., & Van Diviner, B. (2008). *Assessment and intervention for executive function difficulties*. New York, NY: Routledge.

McCloskey, G., Whitaker, J., Murphy, R., & Rogers, J. (2012). Intellectual, cognitive, and neuropsychological assessment in three-tier service delivery systems in school. In D. P. Flanagan & P. L. Harrison (Eds.), *Contemporary intellectual assessment: Theories, tests and issues* (pp. 852–882). New York, NY: Guilford Press.

McCrae, J. S., Chapman, M. V., & Christ, S. L. (2006). Profile of children investigated for sexual abuse:

Association with psychopathology symptoms and services. *American Journal of Orthopsychiatry*, 76(4), 468–481.

McCrea, S. M. (2009). A review and empirical study of the composite scales of the DAS-Naglieri Cognitive Assessment System. *Psychology Research and Behavior Management*, 2, 59–79.

McDermott, P. A., Fantuzzo, J. W., & Glutting, J. J. (1990). Just say no to subtest analysis: A critique on Wechsler theory and practice. *Journal of Psychoeducational Assessment*, 8, 290–302. doi:10.1177/073428299000800307

McDermott, P. A., Fantuzzo, J. W., Glutting, J. J., Watkins, M. W., & Baggaley, A. R. (1992). Illusions of meaning in the ipsative assessment of children's ability. *Journal of Special Education*, 25, 504–526. doi:10.1177/002246699202500407

McDermott, P. A., Marston, N. C., & Stott, D. H. (1993). *Adjustment scales for children and adolescents*. Philadelphia, PA: Edumetric and Clinical Science.

McDermott, P. A., Watkins, M. W., & Rhoad, A. (2014). Whose IQ is it?— Assessor bias variance in high-stakes psychological assessment. *Psychological Assessment*, 26, 207–214. doi:10.1037/a0034832

McDonald, R. P. (1999). *Test theory: A unified treatment*. Mahwah, NJ: Erlbaum.

McDonald, R. P. (2010). Structural models and the art of approximation. *Perspectives on Psychological Science*, 5, 675–686. doi:10.1177/1745691610388766

McGee, C. L., Delis, D. C., & Holdnack, J. A. (2009). Cognitive discrepancies in children at the ends of the bell curve: A note of caution for clinical interpretation. *Clinical Neuropsychologist*, 23, 1160–1172.

McGrew, K. S. (1997). Analysis of the major intelligence batteries according to a proposed comprehensive Gf-Gc framework. In D. P. Flanagan, J. L. Genshaft, & P. L. Harrison (Eds.), *Contemporary intellectual assessment: Theories, tests, and issues* (pp. 151–179). New York, NY: Guilford Press.

McGrew, K. S. (2005). The Cattell-Horn-Carroll theory of cognitive abilities: Past, present, and future. In D. P. Flanagan & P. L. Harrison (Eds.), *Contemporary intellectual assessment: Theories, tests, and issues* (2nd ed., pp. 136–181). New York, NY: Guilford Press.

McGrew, K. S. (2009). CHC theory and the human cognitive abilities project: Standing on the shoulders of the giants of psychometric intelligence research. *Intelligence*, 37(1), 1–10.

McGrew, K. S., & Flanagan, D. P. (1998). *The intelligence test desk reference (ITDR): Gf-Gc cross-battery assessment*. Boston, MA: Allyn & Bacon.

McGrew, K. S., LaForte, E. M., & Schrank, F. A. (2014). *Technical manual. Woodcock Johnson–IV*. Rolling Meadows, IL: Riverside.

McGrew, K. S., & Wendling, B. J. (2010). Cattell-Horn-Carroll cognitive-achievement relations: What we have learned from the past 20 years of research. *Psychology in the Schools*, 47, 51–675.

McLean, J. E., Kaufman, A. S., & Reynolds, C. R. (1989). Base rates of WAIS–R subtest scatter as a guide for clinical and neuropsychological assessment. *Journal of Clinical Psychology*, 45, 919–926.

McLean, J. E., Reynolds, C. R., & Kaufman, A. S. (1990). WAIS–R subtest scatter using the profile variability index. *Psychological Assessment: The Journal of Consulting and Clinical Psychology*, 2, 289–292.

McLeod, J. D., & Nonnemaker, J. M. (2000). Poverty and child emotional behavioral problems: Racial/ethnic differences in processes and effects. *Journal of Health and Social Behavior*, 41(2), 137–161.

Mead, A. D., & Drasgow, F. (1993). Equivalence of computerized and paper-and-pencil cognitive ability tests: A meta-analysis. *Psychological Bulletin*, 114, 449–458.

Meehl, P. E., & Rosen, A. (1955). Antecedent probability and the efficiency of psychometric signs, patterns, or cutting scores. *Psychological Bulletin*, 52, 194–216. doi:10.1037/h0048070

Mersky, J. P., & Reynolds, A. J. (2007). Child maltreatment and violent delinquency: Disentangling main effects and subgroup effects. *Child Maltreatment*, 12(3), 246–258.

Messick, S. (1995). Validity of psychological assessment: Validation of inferences from persons' responses and performances as scientific inquiry into score meaning. *American Psychologist*, 50, 741–749. doi:10.1037/0003–066X.50.9.741

Meyer, G. J., Finn, S. E., Eyde, L., Kay, G. G., Moreland, K. L., Dies, R. R., … Reed, G. M. (2001). Psychological testing and psychological assessment: A review of evidence and issues. *American Psychologist*, 56, 128–165.

Miciak, J., Fletcher, J. M., Vaughn, S., Stuebing, K. K., & Tolar, T. D. (2014). Patterns of cognitive strengths and weaknesses: Identification rates, agreement, and validity for learning disability identification. *School Psychology Quarterly, 29,* 21–37. doi:10.1037/spq0000037

Milam, A. J., Furr-Holden, C. C. M., & Leaf, P. J. (2010). Perceived school and neighborhood safety, neighborhood violence and academic achievement in urban school children. *Urban Review, 42,* 458–467.

Milberg, W. P., Hebben, N., & Kaplan, E. (1996). The Boston process approach to neuropsychological assessment. In I. Grant & K. M. Adams (Eds.), *Neuropsychological assessment of neuropsychiatric disorders* (2nd ed., pp. 58–80). New York, NY: Oxford University Press.

Millager, R. A., Conture, E. G., Walden, T. A., & Kelly, E. M. (2014). Expressive language intratest scatter of preschool-age children who stutter. *Contemporary Issues in Communication Science Disorders, 41,* 110–119.

Miller, D. C. (2007). *Essentials of school neuropsychological assessment.* Hoboken, NJ: Wiley.

Miller, D. C. (Ed.) (2010). *Best practices in school neuropsychology: Guidelines for effective practice, assessment, and evidence-based intervention.* Hoboken, NJ: Wiley.

Miller, D. C. (2013). *Essentials of school neuropsychological assessment* (2nd ed.). Hoboken, NJ: Wiley.

Miller, D. C., & Hale, J. B. (2008). The neuropsychological applications of the Wechsler Intelligence Scale for Children–Fourth edition. In A. Prifitera, D. H. Saklofske, & L. G. Weiss (Eds.), *WISC–V Advanced Clinical Interpretation* (2nd ed., pp. 445–495). San Diego, CA: Academic Press.

Miller, D. C., & Maricle, D. E. (2012). The emergence of neuropsychological constructs into tests of intelligence. *Contemporary Intellectual Assessment* (3rd ed., pp. 800–819). New York, NY: Guilford Press.

Miller, D. C., & Maricle, D. E. (2014). Best practices in school neuropsychological assessment and intervention. In A. Thomas & P. Harrison (Eds.), *Best practices in school psychology VI* (pp. 247–260). Bethesda, MD: National Association of School Psychologists.

Millon, T., Millon, C., Davis, R., & Grossman, S. (1993). *Millon adolescent clinical inventory.* Bloomington, MN: Pearson.

Millsap, R. E. (2007). Structural equation modeling made difficult. *Personality and Individual Differences, 42,* 875–881. doi:10.1016/j.paid.2006.09.021

Minshew, N. J., & Keller, T. A. (2010). The nature of brain dysfunction in autism: Functional brain imaging studies. *Current Opinion in Neurology, 23,* 124–130.

Mischel, W. (2014). *The marshmallow test: Mastering self-control.* New York, NY: Little, Brown, and Company.

Mittenberg, W., Hammeke, T. A., & Rao, S. M. (1989). Intrasubtest scatter on the WAIS–R as a pathognomonic sign of brain injury. *Psychological Assessment: A Journal of Consulting and Clinical Psychology, 1*(4), 273–276.

Mittenberg, W., Thompson, G. B., Schwartz, J. A., Ryan, J. J., & Levitt, R. (1991). Intellectual loss in Alzheimer's dementia and WAIS–R intrasubtest scatter. *Journal of Clinical Psychology, 47*(4), 544–547.

Moffitt, T. E. (1993). Adolescence-limited and life-course persistent antisocial behavior: A developmental taxonomy. *Psychological Review, 100,* 674–701.

Moffitt, T. E., Caspi, A., Harrington, H., & Milne, B. J., (2002). Males on the life-course-persistent and adolescence-limited antisocial pathways: Follow-up at age 26 years. *Developmental Psychopathology, 14*(1), 179–207.

Moffitt, T. E., & Lynam, D. (1994). The neuropsychology of conduct disorder and delinquency: implications for understanding antisocial behavior. *Progress in Experimental Personality & Psychopathology, 18,* 233–262.

Molnar, B. E., Browne, A., Cerda, M., & Buka, S. L. (2005). Violent behavior by girls reporting violent victimization. *Pediatrics & Adolescent Medicine, 159,* 731–739.

Montague, M., Enders, C. K., & Castro, M. (2005). Academic and behavioral outcomes for students at risk for emotional and behavioral disorder. *Behavioral Disorders, 31,* 87–96.

Monzalvo, K. & Dehaene-Lambertz, G. (2013). How reading acquisition changes children's spoken language network. *Brain and Language, 127,* 356–365.

Moon, G. W., Blakey, W. A., Gorsuch, R. L., & Fantuzzo, J. W. (1991). Frequent WAIS–R administration errors: An ignored source of inaccurate measurement. *Professional Psychology: Research and Practice, 22,* 256–258. doi:10.1037/0735–7028.22.3.256

Moon, G. W., Fantuzzo, J., & Gorsuch, R. (1986). Teaching WAIS–R administration skills: Comparison of the MASTERY model to other existing clinical training modalities. *Professional Psychology: Research and Practice*, 17, 31–35.

Mrazik, M., Janzen, T. M., Dombrowski, S. C., Barford, S. W., & Krawchuk, L. L. (2012). Administration and scoring errors of graduate students learning the WISC–IV: Issues and controversies. *Canadian Journal of School Psychology*, 27, 279–290.

Muller, R. T., Goebel-Fabbri, A. E., Diamond, T., & Dinklage, D. (2000). Social support and the relationship between family and community violence exposure and psychopathology among high-risk adolescents. *Child Abuse & Neglect*, 24(4), 449–464.

Murray, J., & Farrington, D. P. (2005). Parental imprisonment: Effects on boys' antisocial behaviour and delinquency through the life-course. *Journal of Child Psychology and Psychiatry*, 46, 1269–1278.

Murray, J., & Farrington, D. P. (2008). Parental imprisonment: Long-lasting effects on boys internalizing problems through the life-course. *Development and Psychopathology*, 20, 273–290.

Murray, J., Farrington, D. P., & Eisner, M. P. (2009). Drawing conclusions about causes from systematic reviews of risk factors: The Cambridge Quality Checklists. *Journal of Experimental Criminology*, 5, 1–23.

Muthén, B. O., & Muthén, L. K. (2014). *Mplus user's guide* (7th ed.). Los Angeles, CA: Author.

Myers, P. I., & Hammill, D. D. (1976). *Methods for learning disorders* (2nd ed.). New York, NY: Wiley.

Naglieri, J. A. (1993). The role of intelligence assessment in school psychology. *School Psychologist*, 47(2), 9, 14–15, 17.

Naglieri, J. A. (1999). *Essentials of CAS assessment*. New York, NY: Wiley.

Naglieri, J. A. (2008a). *Naglieri Nonverbal Ability Test* (2nd ed.). San Antonio, TX: Pearson.

Naglieri, J. A. (2008b). Traditional IQ: 100 years of misconception and its relationship to minority representation in gifted programs. In J. VanTassel-Baska (Ed.), *Critical issues in equity and excellence in gifted education* (pp. 67–88). Waco, TX: Prufrock Press.

Naglieri, J. A. (2012). Psychological assessment by school psychologists: Opportunities and challenges of a changing landscape. In K. Geisinger & B. A. Bracken (Eds.), *APA handbook of testing and assessment in psychology*. Washington, DC: American Psychological Association.

Naglieri, J. A. (2015). Hundred years of intelligence testing: Moving from traditional IQ to second-generation intelligence tests. In S. Goldstein, D. Princiotta, & J. Naglieri (Eds.). *Handbook of intelligence: Evolutionary theory, historical perspective, and current concepts* (pp. 295–316). New York, NY: Springer.

Naglieri, J. A., & Bornstein, B. T. (2003). Intelligence and achievement: Just how correlated are they? *Journal of Psychoeducational Assessment*, 21, 244–260. doi:10.1177/073428290302100302

Naglieri, J. A., & Conway, C. (2009). The Cognitive Assessment System. In J. A. Naglieri & S. Goldstein (Eds.), *A practitioner's guide to assessment of intelligence and achievement* (pp. 3–10). Hoboken, NJ: Wiley.

Naglieri, J. A., & Das, J .P. (1997). *Cognitive Assessment System*. Itasca, IL: Riverside.

Naglieri, J. A., Das, J. P., & Goldstein, S. (2012). Planning, attention, simultaneous, successive: A cognitive-processing-based theory of intelligence. In D. P. Flanagan & P. L. Harrison (Eds.), *Contemporary intellectual assessment: Theories, tests, and issues* (3rd ed., pp. 178–194). New York, NY: Guilford Press.

Naglieri, J. A., Das, J. P., & Goldstein, S. (2014). *Cognitive assessment system—CAS2* (2nd ed.). Austin, TX: PRO-ED.

Naglieri, J. A., & Goldstein, S. (2009). *A practitioner's guide to assessment of intelligence and achievement*. Hoboken, NJ: Wiley.

Naglieri, J. A., Goldstein, S., Iseman, J. S., & Schwebach, A. (2003) Performance of children with attention deficit hyperactivity disorder and anxiety/depression on the WISC–III and Cognitive Assessment System (CAS). *Journal of Psychoeducational Assessment*, 21, 32–42.

Naglieri, J. A., & Otero, T. M. (2012a). The Cognitive Assessment system: From theory to practice. In D. P. Flanagan & P. L. Harrison (Eds.), *Contemporary intellectual assessment: Theories, tests, and issues* (3rd ed., pp. 376–399). New York, NY: Guilford Press.

Naglieri, J. A., & Otero, T. M. (2012b). The Wechsler Nonverbal Scale of Ability: Assessment of diverse populations. In D. P. Flanagan & P. L. Harrison (Eds.), *Contemporary intellectual assessment, third edition: Theories, tests, and issues* (pp. 436–455). New York, NY: Guilford Press.

Naglieri, J. A., & Paolitto, A. W. (2005). Ipsative comparisons of WISC–IV index scores. *Applied Neuropsychology*, 12(4), 208–211.

Nasser, F., Benson, J., & Wisenbaker, J. (2002). The performance of regression-based variations of the visual screen for determining the number of common factors. *Educational and Psychological Measurement, 62*, 397–419. doi:10.1177/00164402062003001

National Academy of Neuropsychology Policy & Planning Committee. (2001). *NAN definition of a clinical neuropsychologist.* Retrieved from http://www.nanonline.org/NAN/files/PAIC/PDFs/NANPositionDefNeuro.pdf

National Association for Gifted Children. (2010, March). *Use of the WISC–IV for gifted identification [NAGC Position Statement].* Retrieved from http://www.nagc.org/sites/default/files/Position%20Statement/Use%20of%20the%20WISC-IV%20for%20Gifted%20Education.pdf

National Institute of Child Health and Human Development Early Child Care Research Network. (2005). Duration and developmental timing of poverty and children's cognitive and social development from birth through third grade. *Child Development, 76*, 795–810.

Nee, D. E., Brown, J. W., Askren, M. K., Berman, M. G., Demira, E., Krawitz, A., & Jonides, J. (2013). A meta-analysis of executive components of working memory. *Cerebral Cortex, 23*, 264–282.

Neisser, U. (1966). *Cognitive Psychology.* New York, NY: Appleton-Century Crofts.

Nelson, J. M., & Canivez, G. L. (2012). Examination of the structural, convergent, and incremental validity of the Reynolds Intellectual Assessment Scales (RIAS) with a clinical sample. *Psychological Assessment, 24*, 129–140. doi:10.1037/a0024878

Nelson, J. M, Canivez, G. L, Lindstrom, W., & Hatt, C. (2007). Higher-order exploratory factor analysis of the Reynolds Intellectual Assessment Scales with a referred sample. *Journal of School Psychology, 45*, 439–456. doi:10.1016/j.jsp.2007.03.003

Nelson, J. M., Canivez, G. L., Watkins, M. W. (2013). Structural and incremental validity of the Wechsler Adult Intelligence Scale–Fourth Edition with a clinical sample. *Psychological Assessment, 25*, 618–630. doi:10.1037/a0032086

Neugarten, B. L., & Neugarten, D. A. (1996). *The meaning of age: Selected papers of Bernice L. Neugarten.* Chicago, IL: University of Chicago Press.

Nickerson, R. S. (1998). Confirmation bias: A ubiquitous phenomenon in many guises. *Review of General Psychology, 2*, 175–220. doi:10.1037/1089–2680.2.2.175

Niileksela, C. R., Reynolds, M. R., & Kaufman, A. S. (2012). An alternative Cattell-Horn-Carroll (CHC) factor structure of the WAIS–IV: Age invariance of an alternative model for ages 70–90. *Psychological Assessment.* Advance online publication. doi:10.1037/a0031175

Noyes, J. M., & Garland, K. J. (2008). Computer- vs. paper-based tasks: Are they equivalent? *Ergonomics, 51*, 1352–1375.

Nunnally, J. C., & Bernstein, I. H. (1994). *Psychometric theory* (3rd ed.). New York, NY: McGraw-Hill.

Nyborg, H. (2005). Sex-related differences in general intelligence *g*, brain size, and social status. *Personality and Individual Differences, 39*, 497–509.

Oakland, T., Lee, S. W., & Axelrod, K. M. (1975). Examiner differences on actual WISC protocols. *Journal of School Psychology, 13*, 227–233. doi:10.1016/0022–4405(75)90005–9

O'Connor, C. (1997). Dispositions toward (collective) struggle and educational resilience in the Inner city: A case analysis of six African-American high school students. *American Educational Research Journal, 34*(4), 563–629.

Odgers, C. L., & Reppucci, N. D. (2002). Female young offenders: A meta-analytic approach. Paper presented at the Vancouver Conference on Aggressive and Violent Girls: Contributing Factors and Intervention Strategies, Vancouver, Canada.

Olsson, U. H., Foss, T., Troye, S. V., & Howell, R. D. (2000). The performance of ML, GLS, and WLS estimation in structural equation modeling under conditions of misspecification and nonnormality. *Structural Equation Modeling, 7*, 557–595. doi:10.1207/S15328007SEM0704_3

Orr, D. P., Beiter, M., & Ingersoll, G. (1991). Premature sexual activity as an indicator of psychosocial risk. *Pediatrics, 87*, 141–147.

Orsini, A., Pezzuti, L., & Hulbert, S. (2014). The unitary ability of IQ in the WISC-IV and its computation. *Personality & Individual Differences, 69*, 173–175. doi:10.1016/j.paid.2014.05.023

Ortiz, S. O., Flanagan, D. P., & Alfonso, V. C. (2015). *Cross-Battery Assessment Software System X–BASS (Version. 1) [Software].* Hoboken, NJ: Wiley. Retrieved from www.wiley.com/go/XBASS

Ortiz, S. O., Ochoa, S. H., & Dynda, A. M. (2012). Testing with culturally and linguistically diverse populations: Moving beyond the verbal–performance dichotomy into evidence-based practice. In D. P. Flanagan & P. L. Harrison (Eds.), *Contemporary intellectual assessment: Theories, tests, and issues* (3rd ed., pp. 526–552). New York, NY: Guilford Press.

Otero, T. M. (2015). Intelligence: Defined as neurocognitive processing. In S. Goldstein, D. Princiotta, & J. Naglieri (Eds.). *Handbook of intelligence: Evolutionary theory, historical perspective, and current concepts* (pp. 193–208). New York, NY: Springer.

Ou, S. R., & Reynolds, A. J. (2008). Predictors of educational attainment in the Chicago Longitudinal Study. *School Psychology Quarterly, 23*, 199–229.

Ouellette, P., Briscoe, R., & Tyson, C. (2004). Parent-school and community partnerships in children's mental health: Networking challenges, dilemmas, and solutions. *Journal of Child and Family Studies, 13*(3), 295–308.

Ouellette, P., & Wilkerson, D. (2008). "They won't come": Increasing parent involvement in parent management training programs for at-risk youths in schools. *School Social Work Journal, 32*(2), 39–52.

Owen, A. M., Hampshire, A., Grahn, J. A., Stenton, R., Dajani, S., Burns, A. S., … Ballard, C. G. (2010). Putting brain training to the test. *Nature, 465*, 775–778.

Owen, A. M., McMillan, K. M., Laird, A. R., & Bullmore, E. (2005). N-back working memory paradigm: A meta-analysis of normative functional neuroimaging studies. *Human Brain Mapping, 25*, 46–59.

Oyserman, D., & Markus, H. R. (1990). Possible selves and delinquency. *Journal of Personality and Social Psychology, 59*(1), 112–125.

Palejwala, M. H., & Fine, J. G. (2014). Gender differences in latent cognitive abilities in children aged 2 to 7. *Intelligence, 48*, 96–108.

Parker, J. C., Granberg, B. W., Nichols, W. K., Jones, J. G., & Hewett, J. E. (1983). Mental status outcomes following carotid endarterectomy: A six-month analysis. *Journal of Clinical Neuropsychology, 5*, 345–353.

Parkin, J. R., & Beaujean, A. A. (2012). The effects of Wechsler Intelligence Scale for Children–Fourth Edition cognitive abilities on math achievement. *Journal of School Psychology, 50*, 113–128. doi:10.1016/j.jsp.2011.08.003

Pascual-Leone, J. (1970). A mathematical model for the transition rule in Piaget's developmental stages. *Acta Psychologica, 32*, 301–345.

Pascual-Leone, A., Freitas, C., Oberman, L., Horvath, J. C., Halko, M., Eldaief, M., … Rotenberg, A. (2011). Characterizing brain cortical plasticity and network dynamics across the age-span in health and disease with TMS-EEG and TMS-fMRI. *Brain Topography, 24*, 302–315. doi:10.1007/s10548–011–0196–8

Passolunghi, M. C. (2006). Working memory and arithmetic learning disability. In T. P. Alloway & S. E. Gathercole, (Eds.), *Working memory and neurodevelopmental disorders* (pp. 113–138). New York, NY: Psychology Press.

Patterson, C. H. (1953). Clinical diagnostic use of the scales: Assumptions and methods. In C. H. Patterson, *The Wechsler-Bellevue Scales: A guide for counselors. American lecture series: The Bannerstone division of American lectures in psychology* (pp. 38–50). Springfield, IL: Charles C. Thomas.

Pauly, H., Linkersdorfer, J., Lindberg, S., Woerner, W., Hasselhorn, M., & Lonnemann, J. (2011). Domain-specific rapid automatized naming deficits in children at risk for learning disabilities. *Journal of Neurolinguistics, 24*, 602 610. doi:10.1016/j. jneuroling.2011.02.002

Pears, K. C., Kim, H. K., Fisher, P. A., & Yoerger, K. (2013). Early school engagement and late elementary outcomes for maltreated children in foster care. *Developmental Psychology, 49*, 2201–2211.

Pearson. (2009a). *Advanced clinical solutions for the WAIS–IV and WMS–IV*. Bloomington, MN: Author.

Pearson. (2009b). *Wechsler Individual Achievement Test* (3rd ed.). Bloomington, MN: Author.

Pearson. (2014). *WISC–V technical manual supplement*. Retrieved from http://downloads.pearsonclinical.com/images/Assets/WISC-V/WISC-V-Tech-Manual-Supplement.pdf

Pelletier, S. L. F, Hiemenz, J. R., & Shapiro, M. B. (2004). The application of neuropsychology in the schools should not be called school neuropsychology: A rejoinder to Crespi and Cooke. *School Psychologist, 58*, 17–24.

Pennington, B. F. (1991). *Diagnosing learning disorders: A neuropsychological framework*. New York, NY: Guilford Press.

Pennington, B. F. (2008). *Diagnosing learning disorders: A neuropsychological framework* (2nd ed.). New York, NY: Guilford Press.

Peterson, S. E. & Posner, M. I. (2012). The attention system of the human brain: 20 years after. *Annual Review of Neuroscience, 35*, 73–89.

Piaget, J. (1970). *Genetic epistemology*. New York, NY: W. W. Norton and Company.

Pickering, S. J. (2006). Working memory in dyslexia. In T. P. Alloway & S. E. Gathercole (Eds.), *Working memory and neurodevelopmental disorders* (pp. 7–40). New York, NY: Psychology Press.

Pilowsky, D. J., & Wu, L.-T. (2006). Psychiatric symptoms and substance use disorders in a nationally representative sample of American adolescents involved with foster care. *Journal of Adolescent Health, 38*, 351–358.

Pinker, S. (2014). *The sense of style: The thinking person's guide to writing in the 21st century*. New York, NY: Penguin.

Piore, A., (2014). The master code. *Popular Science, 284*(5), 54–59, 82–84.

Piquero, A. R., and Chung, H. L. (2001). On the relationships between gender, early onset, and the seriousness of offending. *Journal of Criminal Justice, 29*, 189–206.

Plomin, R. & DeFries, J. C. (1980). Genetics and intelligence: Recent data. *Intelligence, 4*, 15–24.

Posner, M. I., & Raichle, M. E. (1994). *Images of mind* [Scientific American Library]. New York, NY: W. H. Freeman.

Posner, M. I., & Rothbart, M. K. (2007). *Educating the human brain*. Washington, DC: American Psychological Association.

Pratt, T. C., & Cullen, F. T. (2000). The empirical status of Gottfredson and Hirschi's general theory of crime: A meta-analysis. *Criminology, 38*, 931–964.

Preiss, M., & Franova, L. (2006). Depressive symptoms, academic achievement, and intelligence. *Studia Psychologica, 48*, 57–67.

Prelow, H. M., & Loukas, A. (2003). The role of resource, protective, and risk factors on academic achievement-related outcomes of economically disadvantaged Latino youth. *Journal of Community Psychology, 31*, 513–529.

Pressey, S. L., & Cole, L. W. (1918). Irregularity in a psychological examination as a measure of mental deterioration. *Journal of Abnormal Psychology, 13*, 285–294.

Prifitera, A., & Dersh. J. (1993). Base rates of WISC–III diagnostic subtest patterns among normal, learning-disabled, and ADHD samples. *Journal of Psychoeducational Assessment Monograph Series, Advances in psychological assessment: Wechsler Intelligence Scale for Children–Third Edition* (pp. 43–55). Germantown, TN: Psychoeducational Corporation.

Prifitera, A., & Saklofske, D. H. (Eds.). (1998). *WISC-III Clinical use and interpretation: Scientist-practitioner perspectives*. San Diego, CA: Academic Press.

Prifitera, A., Saklofske, D. H., & Weiss, L. G. (Eds.). (2005). *WISC–IV: Clinical use and interpretation: Scientist-practitioner perspectives*. Burlington, MA: Academic Press.

Prifitera, A., Saklofske, D. H., & Weiss, L. G. (Eds.). (2008). *WISC–IV: Clinical assessment and intervention* (2nd ed.). Burlington, MA: Academic Press.

Princiotta, D., & Goldstein, S. (2015). A. R. Luria and intelligence defined as a neuropsychological construct. In S. Goldstein, D. Princiotta, & J. Naglieri (Eds.), *Handbook of intelligence: Evolutionary theory, historical perspective, and current concepts* (pp. 181–191) New York, NY: Springer.

Prino, C. T., & Peyrot, M. (1994). The effect of child physical abuse and neglect on aggressive, withdrawn, and prosocial behavior. *Child Abuse & Neglect, 18*(10), 871–884.

Puzzanchera, C. (2009, December). Juvenile Arrests 2008. *Juvenile Justice Bulletin*, U.S. Department of Justice, Office of Justice Programs, Office of Juvenile Justice and Delinquency Prevention.

Quist, R. M., & Matshazi, D. G. M. (2000). The child and adolescent functional assessment scale (CAFAS): A dynamic predictor of juvenile recidivism. *Adolescence, 35*, 181–192.

Rabbitt, P., Diggle, P., Smith, D., Holland, F., & McInnes, L. (2001). Identifying and separating the effects of practice and of cognitive ageing during a large longitudinal study of elderly community residents. *Neuropsychologia, 39*, 532–543.

Rabbitt, P., Lunn, M., Wong, D., & Cobain, M. (2008). Age and ability affect practice gains in longitudinal studies of cognitive change. *Journal of Gerontology: Psychological Sciences, 63B*(4), 235–240.

Raiford, S. E., & Coalson, D. L. (2014). *Essentials of WPPSI®–IV Assessment*. Hoboken, NJ: Wiley.

Raiford, S. E., Coalson, D. L., & Engi, M. D. (2012). WPPSI-IV score differences across demographic groups. In S. E. Raiford & D. L. Coalson, *Essentials of WPPSI–IV assessment* (pp. 215–236). Hoboken, NJ: Wiley.

Raiford, S. E., Holdnack, J., Drozdick, L., & Zhang, O. (2014). *Q-interactive special group studies: The WISC–V and children with intellectual giftedness and intellectual disability* [Q-interactive Technical Report 9]. Retrieved from http://www.helloq.com/content/dam/ped/ani/us/helloq/media/Technical_Report_9_WISC-V_Children_with_Intellectual_Giftedness_and_Intellectual_Disability.pdf

Raiford, S. E., Weiss, L. G, Rolfhus, E., & Coalson, D. (2005/2008). *General Ability Index. WISC-IV Technical Report #4* (updated December 2008). San Antonio, TX: Pearson Education. Retrieved from http://images.pearsonclinical.com/images/assets/WISC-IV/80720_WISCIV_Hr_r4.pdf

Raine, A. (1993). *The psychopathology of crime*. San Diego, CA: Academic Press.

Rapaport, D., Gill, M. M., & Schafer, R. (1945–46). *Diagnostic psychological testing*. Chicago, IL: Year Book.

Rapp, B. (Ed.). (2001). *The handbook of cognitive neuropsychology: What deficits reveal about the human mind*. New York, NY: Psychology Press.

Rauh, V. A., Parker, F. L., & Garfinkel, R. S. (2003). Biological, social, and community influences on third-grade reading levels of minority Head Start children: A multilevel approach. *Journal of Community Psychology*, *31*, 255–278.

Raykov, T. (1997). Scale reliability, Cronbach's coefficient alpha, and violations of essential tau-equivalence with fixed congeneric components. *Multivariate Behavioral Research*, *32*, 329–353. doi:10.1207/s15327906mbr3204_2

Ree, M. J., Earles, J. A., & Teachout, M. S. (1994). Predicting job performance: Not much more than g. *Journal of Applied Psychology*, *79*, 518–524. doi:10.1037/0021–9010.79.4.518

Reeve, C. L., & Charles, J. E. (2008). Survey of opinions on the primacy of g and social consequences of ability testing. *A comparison of expert and non-expert views. Intelligence*, *36*, 681–688.

Reise, S. P. (2012). The rediscovery of bifactor measurement models. *Multivariate Behavioral Research*, *47*, 667–696. doi:10.1080/00273171.2012.715555

Reise, S. P., Bonifay, W. E., & Haviland, M. G. (2013). Scoring and modeling psychological measures in the presence of multidimensionality. *Journal of Personality Assessment*, *95*, 129–140. doi:10.1080/00223891.2012.725437

Reise, S. P., Moore, T. M., & Maydeu-Olivares, A. (2011). Target rotations and assessing the impact of model violations on the parameters of unidimensional item response theory models. *Educational and Psychological Measurement*, *71*, 684–711. doi:10.1177/0013164410378690

Reitan, R. M. (1955). Investigation of the validity of Halstead's measures of biological intelligence. *AMA Archives of Neurology and Psychiatry*, *73*, 28–35.

Renn, P. (2002). The link between childhood trauma and later violent offending: The application of attachment theory in a probation setting. *Attachment & Human Development*, *4*(3), 294–317.

Reschly, D. J. (1997). Diagnostic and treatment utility of intelligence tests. In D. P. Flanagan, J. L. Genshaft, & P. L. Harrison (Eds.), *Contemporary intellectual assessment: Theories, tests, and issues* (pp. 437–456). New York, NY: Guilford Press.

Reynolds, C. R., & Bigler, E. D. (1994). *Test of memory and learning* (TOMAL). Austin, TX: Pro-Ed.

Reynolds, C., & Fletcher-Janzen, E. (Eds.) (2009). *Handbook of clinical child neuropsychology*. New York, NY: Springer.

Reynolds, C. R., & Kamphaus, R. W. (2003). *Reynolds intellectual assessment scales*. Lutz, FL: Psychological Assessment Resources.

Reynolds, C. R., & Kamphaus, R. W. (2004). *Behavior assessment system for children* (2nd ed.). Bloomington, MN: Pearson.

Reynolds, C. R., & Milam, D. A. (2012). Challenging intellectual testing results. In D. Faust (Ed.), *Coping with psychiatric and psychological testimony* (6th ed., pp. 311–334). New York, NY: Oxford University Press.

Reynolds, C. R., & Ramsay, M. C. (2003). Bias in psychological assessment: An empirical review and recommendations. In J. R. Graham & J. A. Naglieri (Eds.), *Handbook of psychology: Assessment psychology* (Vol. 10, pp. 67–93). Hoboken, NJ: Wiley.

Reynolds, C. R., & Voress, J. K. (2007). *TOMAL–2: Test of Memory and Learning* (2nd ed.). Austin, TX: Pro-Ed.

Reynolds, M. R. (2014). A few thoughts on intelligence and its measurement. *School Psychologist*, *68*. Retrieved from http://www.apadivisions.org/division-16/publications/newsletters/school-psychologist/2014/11/intelligence.aspx

Reynolds, M. R., Floyd, R. F., & Niileksela, C. R. (2013). How well is psychometric *g* indexed by global composites? Evidence from three popular intelligence tests. *Psychological Assessment, 25,* 1314–1322.

Reynolds, M. R., & Keith, T. Z. (2013). Measurement and statistical issues in child assessment research. In D. H. Saklofske, C. R. Reynolds, & V. Schwean (Eds.), *Oxford handbook of child and adolescent assessment* (pp. 48–83). New York, NY: Oxford University Press.

Reynolds, M. R., Keith, T. Z., Flanagan, D. P., & Alfonso, V. C. (2013). A cross-battery, reference variable, confirmatory factor analytic investigation of the CHC taxonomy. *Journal of School Psychology, 51,* 535–555.

Reynolds, M. R., Scheiber, C., Hajovsky, D. B., Schwartz, B., & Kaufman, A. S. (2015). Gender differences in academic achievement: Is writing an exception to the gender similarities hypothesis? *Journal of Genetic Psychology, Journal of Genetic Psychology, 176,* 1–24.

Reznick, J. S. (2009). Working memory in infants and toddlers. In M. L. Courage & N. Cowan (Eds.), *The development of memory in infancy and childhood* (pp. 343–365). New York, NY: Psychology Press.

Rice, M. E., & Harris, G. T. (2005). Comparing effect sizes in follow-up studies: ROC area, Cohen's d, and r. *Law and Human Behavior, 29,* 615–620.

Richman, J.M., Bowen, G.L., & Woolley, M.E. (2004). School failure: An eco-interactional-developmental perspective. In M.W. Frasier (Ed), *Risk and resilience in childhood: An ecological perspective* (2nd ed.) (pp. 133–160). Washington, DC: NASW Press.

Rimm, S., Gilman, B., & Silverman, L. (2008). Alternative assessments with gifted and talented students. In J. L. VanTassel-Baska (Ed.), *Nontraditional applications of traditional testing* (pp. 175–202). Waco, TX: Prufrock Press.

Robbins, S. B., Oh, I., Le, H., & Button, C. (2009). Intervention effects on college performance and retention as mediated by motivational, emotional, and social control factors: Integrated meta-analytic path analyses. *Journal of Applied Psychology, 94,* 1163–1184.

Roid, G. H. (2003). *Stanford-Binet Intelligence Scales* (5th ed.). Itasca, IL: Riverside.

Ronnlund, M., & Nilsson, L.-G. (2006). Adult life-span patterns in WAIS–R Block Design performance: Cross-sectional versus longitudinal age gradients and relations to demographic factors. *Intelligence, 34,* 63–78.

Ronnlund, M., & Nilsson, L.-G. (2008). The magnitude, generality, and determinants of Flynn effects on forms of declarative memory and visuospatial ability: Time-sequential analyses of data from a Swedish cohort study. *Intelligence, 36,* 192–209.

Ronnlund, M., Nyberg, L., Backman, L., & Nilsson, L. (2005). Stability, growth, and decline in adult life span development of declarative memory: Cross-sectional and longitudinal data from a population-based study. *Psychology and Aging, 20,* 3–18. doi:10.1037/0882- 7974.20.1.3.

Roodenrys, S. (2006). Working memory function in attention deficit hyperactivity disorder. In T. P. Alloway & S. E. Gathercole (Eds.), *Working memory and neurodevelopmental disorders* (pp. 187–211). New York, NY: Psychology Press.

Rosenthal, J. A. (1996) Qualitative descriptors of strength of association and effect size. *Journal of Social Service Research, 21*(4), 37–59.

Rosseel, Y. (2012). lavaan: An R package for structural equation modeling. *Journal of Statistical Software, 48*(2), 1–36. Retrieved from http://www.jstatsoft.org/v48/i02/

Rothbart, M. K. & Posner, M. I. (2015). The developing brain in a multitasking world. *Developmental Review, 35,* 42–63.

Rotheram-Borus, M. J., Mahler, K. A., Koopman, C., & Langabeer, K. (1996). Sexual abuse history and associated multiple risk behavior in adolescent runaways. *American Journal of Orthopsychiatry, 66*(3), 390–400.

Rourke, B. P. (1982). Central processing deficits in children: Toward a developmental neuropsychological model. *Journal of Clinical Neuropsychology, 4,* 1–18.

Rowe, E. W., Kingsley, J. M., & Thompson, D. F. (2010). Predictive ability of the general ability index (GAI) versus the full scale IQ among gifted referrals. *School Psychology Quarterly, 25,* 119–128. doi:10.1037/ a0020148

Rugel, R. P. (1974). WISC subtest scores of disabled readers: A review with respect to Bannatyne's recategorization. *Journal of Learning Disabilities, 7,* 48–55.

Rumberger, R. W., & Lim, S. A. (2008). *Why students drop out of school: A review of 25 years of research.* Santa Barbara, CA: California Dropout

Research Project. Retrieved from http://cdrp.ucsb .edu/dropouts/pubs_reports.htm#15

Ruscio, J., & Stern, A. R. (2006). The consistency and accuracy of holistic judgment. *Scientific Review of Mental Health Practice*, 4, 52–65.

Rushton, J. P., & Ankney, C. D. (2009).Whole brain size and general mental ability: A review. *International Journal of Neuroscience*, 119(5), 692–732. doi:10.1080/00207450802325843

Rutland, A. F., & Campbell, R. N. (1996). The relevance of Vygotsky's theory of the "zone of proximal development" to the assessment of children with intellectual disabilities. *Journal of Intellectual Disability Research*, 40 (part 2), 151–158.

Ryan, J. J., Kreiner, D. S., & Burton, D. B. (2002). Does high scatter affect the predictive validity of WAIS–III IQs? *Applied Neuropsychology*, 9, 173–178. doi:10.1207/S15324826AN0903_5

Ryan, J. J., Printera, A., & Powers, L. (1983). Scoring reliability on the WAIS–R. *Journal of Consulting and Clinical Psychology*, 51, 149–150.

Ryan, J. P., & Testa, M. F. (2005). Child maltreatment and juvenile delinquency: Investigating the role of placement and placement instability. *Children and Youth Services Review*, 27, 227–249.

Ryckman, D. B. (1981). Searching for a WISC–R profile for learning disabled children: An inappropriate task? *Journal of Learning Disabilities*, 14(9), 508–511.

Saklofske, D., Prifitera, A., Weiss, L., Rolfhus, E., & Zhu, Z. (2005). Clinical interpretation of the WISC-IV FSIQ and GAI. In A. Prifitera, D. Saklofske, & L. Weiss (Eds.), *WISC-IV clinical use and interpretation*. Burlington, MA: Elsevier Academic Press.

Salthouse, T. A. (2010). Selective review of cognitive aging. *Journal of the International Neuropsychological Society*, 16, 754–760.

Salthouse, T. A. (2014a). Frequent assessments may obscure cognitive decline. *Psychological Assessment*. Advance online publication. 10.1037/pas0000007

Salthouse, T. A. (2014b). Why are there different age relations in cross-sectional and longitudinal comparisons of cognitive functioning? *Current Directions in Psychological Science*, 23(4) 252–256.

Salthouse, T. A. (in press). Aging cognition unconfounded by prior test experience. *Journal of Gerontology: Psychological Sciences*.

Salthouse, T. A., & Saklofske, D. H. (2010). Do the WAIS–IV tests measure the same aspects of cognitive functioning in adults under and over 65? In L. G. Weiss, D. H. Saklofske, D. Coalson, & S. E. Raiford (Eds.), *WAIS–IV clinical use and interpretation: Scientist-practitioner perspectives* (pp. 217–235). Amsterdam, The Netherlands: Elsevier Academic Press.

Salthouse, T. A., Schroeder, D. H., & Ferrer, E. (2004). Estimating retest effects in longitudinal assessments of cognitive functioning in adults between 18 and 60 years of age. *Developmental Psychology*, 40, 813–822. doi:10.1037/0012–1649.40.5.813

Sampson, R. J., & Groves, W. B. (1989). Neighborhood structure and crime: Testing social disorganization theory. *American Journal of Sociology*, 94, 774–802.

Sampson, R. J., & Laub, J. H. (1993). *Crime in the making pathways and turning points through life*. Cambridge, MA: Harvard University Press.

Sampson, R. J., & Laub, J. H. (2003). Life-course desisters? Trajectories of crime among delinquent boys followed to age 70. *Criminology*, 41(3), 301–340.

Sampson, R. J., Raudenbush, S., & Earls, F. (1997). Neighborhood and violent crime: A multilevel study of collective efficacy. *Science*, 277, 918–924.

Sattler, J. M. (1974). *Assessment of children's intelligence* (rev. ed.). Philadelphia, PA: Saunders.

Sattler, J. M. (2008). *Assessment of children: Cognitive foundations* (5th ed.). San Diego, CA: Author.

Schatz, J. (1981). WAIS practice effects in clinical neuropsychology. *Journal of Clinical Neuropsychology*, 3, 171–179.

Scheiber, C. (2015). *Do the Kaufman Tests of Cognitive Ability and Academic Achievement display ethnic bias for students in Grade 1 through 12?* (Doctoral dissertation, Alliant International University, San Diego, CA).

Scheiber, C., Reynolds, M. R., Hajovski, D. B., & Kaufman, A. S. (2015). Evidence of a gender difference in writing in a large, nationally representative sample of children and adolescents. *Psychology in the Schools*, 52(4), 335–348.

Schmid, J., & Leiman, J. M. (1957). The development of hierarchical factor solutions. *Psychometrika*, 22, 53–61. doi:10.1007/BF02289209

Schmithorst, V. J. (2009). Developmental sex differences in the relation of neuroanatomical connectivity to intelligence. *Intelligence*, 37, 164–173.

Schmitt, T. A. (2011). Current methodological considerations in exploratory and confirmatory factor analysis. *Journal of Psychoeducational Assessment, 29,* 304–321. doi:10.1177/0734282911406653

Schmitz-Sherzer, R., & Thomae, H. (1983). Constancy and change of behavior in old age: Findings from the Bonn Longitudinal Study on Aging. In K. W. Schaie (Ed.), *Longitudinal studies of adult psychological development* (pp. 191–221). New York, NY: Guilford Press.

Schneider, W. J. (2010). *The Compositator 1.0.* Olympia, WA: WMF Press.

Schneider, W. J. (2013a). Principles of assessment of aptitude and achievement. In D. Saklofske, C. Reynolds, & V. Schwean (Eds.), *The Oxford handbook of child psychological assessment* (pp. 286–330). New York, NY: Oxford University Press.

Schneider, W. J. (2013b). What if we took our models seriously? Estimating latent scores in individuals. *Journal of Psychoeducational Assessment, 31*(2), 186–201.

Schneider, W. J., & Flanagan, D. P. (2015). The relationship between theories of intelligence and intelligence tests. In S. Goldstein, D. Princiotta, & J. A. Naglieri (Eds.), *Handbook of intelligence: Evolutionary theory, historical perspective, and current concepts* (pp. 317–340). New York, NY: Springer.

Schneider, W. J., & McGrew, K. S. (2012). The Cattell-Horn-Carroll model of intelligence. In D. P. Flanagan & P. L. Harrison (Eds.), *Contemporary intellectual assessment: Theories, tests, and issues* (3rd ed., pp. 99–144). New York, NY: Guilford Press.

Schrank, F. A., McGrew, K. S., & Mather, N. (2014). *Woodcock-Johnson IV*. Rolling Meadows, IL: Riverside.

Schrank, F. A., & Wendling, B. J. (2012). The Woodcock-Johnson III Normative Update. In D. P. Flanagan & P. L. Harrison (Eds.), *Contemporary intellectual assessment: Theories, tests, and issues* (pp. 297–335). New York, NY: Guilford Press.

Schroeders, U. (2008). Testing for equivalence of test data across media. In Scheuermann & Bjornsson (Eds.), *The transition to computer-based assessment: New approaches to skills assessment and implications for large-scale testing*, pp. 164–170. Retrieved August 16, 2015, from http://www.gesci.org/assets/files/reporttransition.pdf

Schroeders, U., & Wilhelm, O. (2010). Testing reasoning ability with handheld computers, notebooks, and paper and pencil. *European Journal of Psychological Assessment, 26,* 284–292.

Schuck, A. M., & Widom, C. S. (2005). Understanding the role of neighborhood context in the long-term criminal consequences of child maltreatment. *American Journal of Community Psychology, 36,* 207–222.

Schwalbe, C. S. (2007). Risk assessment for juvenile justice: A meta-analysis. *Law and Human Behavior, 31,* 449–462.

Schwalbe, C. S. (2008). A meta-analysis of juvenile justice risk assessment instruments: Predictive validity by gender. *Criminal Justice and Behavior, 35,* 1367–1381.

Seashore, H. G. (1950). Differences between verbal and performance IQs on the Wechsler Intelligence Scale for Children. *Journal of Consulting Psychology, 15,* 62–67.

Segal, M. (2005). Dendritic spines and long-term plasticity. *Nature Reviews Neuroscience, 6,* 277–284. doi:10.1038/nrn1649

Sellers, A. H., Burns, W. J., & Guyrke, J. S. (1996). Prediction of premorbid intellectual functioning of young children using demographic information. *Applied Neuropsychology, 3,* 21–27.

Shamama-tus-Sabah, S., Gilani, N., & Iftikhar, R. (2012). Ravens progressive matrices: Psychometric evidence, gender and social class differences in middle childhood. *Journal of Behavioural Sciences, 22,* 120–131.

Shapiro, J. (2004). *Capturing the essence: How Herman Hall interpreted standardized test scores.* New York, NY: Joukowsy Family Foundation.

Shaw, P., Greenstein, D., Lerch, J., Clasen, L., Lenroot, R., Gogtay, N., Evans, A., Rapoport, J., & Giedd, J. (2006). Intellectual ability and cortical development in children and adolescents. *Nature, 440,* 676–679.

Shaw, S. R., Swerdlik, M. E., & Laurent, J. (1993). Review of the WISC–III. In B. A. Bracken & R. S. McCallum (Eds.), *Journal of Psychoeducational Assessment Monograph Series, Advances in psychoeducational assessment: Wechsler Intelligence Scale for Children–Third Edition* (pp. 151–160). Germantown, TN: Psychoeducational Corporation.

Shaywitz, S. E., & Shaywitz, B. A. (2013). Making a hidden disability visible: What has been learned from neurobiological studies of dyslexia. In H. L. Swanson, K. R. Harris, & S. Graham (Eds.), *Handbook of learning disabilities* (pp. 643–657). New York, NY: Guilford Press.

Sheldon, S. B. (2002). Parents' social networks and beliefs as predictors of parent involvement. *Elementary School Journal*, *104*(4), 301–316.

Sheslow, D., & Adams, W. (2003). *Wide range assessment of memory and learning* (2nd ed.). Wilmington, DE: Wide Range.

Silver, L. B. (1993). The secondary emotional, social, and family problems found with children and adolescents with learning disabilities. *Child and Adolescent Psychiatric Clinics of North America*, *2*, 181–353.

Simons-Morton, B. (2004). Prospective association of peer influence, school engagement, drinking expectancies, and parent expectations with drinking initiation among sixth graders. *Addictive Behaviors*, *29*, 299–309.

Sirois, P. A., Posner, M., Stehbens, J. A., Loveland, K. A., Nichols, S., Donfield, S. M., … Amodei, N. (2002). Hemophilia Growth and Development Study. Quantifying practice effects in longitudinal research with the WISC–R and WAIS–R: A study of children and adolescents with hemophilia and male siblings without hemophilia. *Journal of Pediatric Psychology*, *27*(2), 121–131.

Slate, J. R., & Chick, D. (1989). WISC–R examiner errors: Cause for concern. *Psychology in the Schools*, *26*, 78–84.

Slate, J. R., & Jones, C. H. (1990a). Identifying students' errors in administering the WAIS–R. *Psychology in the Schools*, *27*, 83–87.

Slate, J. R., & Jones, C. H. (1990b). Examiner errors on the WAIS–R. A source of concern. *Journal of Psychology*, *124*, 343–345.

Slate, J. R., Jones, C. H., Coulter, C., & Covert, T. L. (1992). Practitioners' administration and scoring of the WISC–R: Evidence that we do err. *Journal of School Psychology*, *30*, 77–82.

Slate, J. R., Jones, C. H., & Murray, K. A. (1991). Teaching administration and scoring of the Wechsler Adult Intelligence Scale–Revised: An empirical evaluation of practice administrations. *Professional Psychology: Research and Practice*, *22*, 375–379.

Slate, J. R., Jones, C. H., Murray, R. A., & Coulter, C. (1993). Evidence that practitioners err in administering and scoring the WAIS–R. *Measurement and Evaluation in Counseling and Development*, *25*, 156–166.

Slobogin, C. (2013). Risk assessment and risk management in juvenile justice. *Criminal Justice*, *27*(4), 10–18.

Smith, C. A., Ireland, T. O., & Thornberry, T. P. (2005). Adolescent maltreatment and its impact on young adult antisocial behavior. *Child Abuse & Neglect*, *29*, 1099–1119.

Smithgall, C., Gladden, R. M., Howard, E., Goerge, R., & Courtney, M. (2004). *Educational experiences of children in out-of-home care*. Chicago, IL: Chapin Hall Center for Children at the University of Chicago.

Smyth, M. M., & Scholey, K. A. (1992). Determining spatial span: The role of movement time and articulation rate. *Quarterly Journal of Experimental Psychology: Human Experimental Psychology*, *45A*, 479–501.

Snyder, H., & Sickmund, M. (2006). *Juvenile offenders and victims: 2006 national report*. Washington, DC: Office of Juvenile Justice and Delinquency Prevention.

Spanoudis, G., Demetriou, A., Zazi, S., Giorgala, K., & Zenonos, V. (2015). Embedding cognizance in intellectual development. *Journal of Experimental Child Psychology*, *132*, 32–50.

Sparrow, S., Cicchetti, D., & Balla, D. (2005). *Vineland Adaptive Behavior Scales* (2nd ed.). Bloomington, MN: Pearson.

Spearman, C. E. (1904). "General intelligence": Objectively determined and measured. *American Journal of Psychology*, *15*, 201–293. Retrieved from http://www.jstor.org/stable/1412107

Spearman, C. E. (1927). *The abilities of man: Their nature and measurement*. London, UK: Macmillan.

Sporns, O. (2011). *Networks of the brain*. Cambridge, MA: MIT Press.

Stanovich, K. (2004). *Thinking straight about psychology*. Boston, MA: Allyn and Bacon.

Steinhart, D. (2006). *Juvenile detention risk assessment: A practice guide to juvenile detention reform*. Baltimore, MD: Annie E. Casey Foundation.

Steinmayr, R., Dinger, F. C., & Spinath, B. (2010). Parents' education and children's achievement: The role of personality. *European Journal of Personality*, *24*, 535–550.

Sternberg, R. J. (1993). Rocky's back again: A review of the WISC–III. In B. A. Bracken & R. S. McCallum (Eds.), *Journal of Psychoeducational Assessment Monograph Series, Advances in psychoeducational assessment: Wechsler Intelligence Scale for Children–Third Edition* (pp. 161–164). Germantown, TN: Psychoeducational Corporation.

Sternberg, R. J. (2015) Human intelligence. In *Britannica*. Retrieved from http://www.britannica.com/topic/human-intelligence-psychology

Sternberg, R. J., Kaufman, J. C., & Grigorenko, E. L. (2008). *Applied intelligence*. New York, NY: Cambridge University Press.

Stillwell, R. (2009). *Public school graduates and dropouts from the common core of data: School year 2006–07* (NCES 2010–313). Washington, DC: National Center for Education Statistics, Institute of Education Sciences, U.S. Department of Education. Retrieved from http://nces.ed.gov/pubs2010/2010341.pdf

Stone, C. A., Ye, F., Zhu, X., & Lane, S. (2010). Providing subscale scores for diagnostic information: A case study when the test is essentially unidimensional. *Applied Measurement in Education, 23*, 63–86. doi:10.1080/08957340903423651

Strauss, E., Sherman, E. M. S., & Spreen O. (2006). *A compendium of neuropsychological tests: Administration, norms and commentary* (3rd ed.). New York, NY: Oxford University Press.

Strauss, E., Spreen, O., & Hunter, M. (2000). Implications of test revisions for research. *Psychological Assessment, 12*, 237–244. doi:10.1037/1040-3590.12.3.237

Stuebing, K. K., Fletcher, J. M., Branum-Martin, L., & Francis, D. J. (2012). Evaluation of the technical adequacy of three methods for identifying specific learning disabilities based on cognitive discrepancies. *School Psychology Review, 41*, 3–22.

Stuss, D. T., & Knight, R. T. (Eds.). (2002). *Principles of frontal lobe function*. New York, NY: Oxford University Press.

Stuss, D. T., & Knight, R. T. (Eds.). (2013). *Principles of frontal lobe function* (2nd ed.). New York, NY: Oxford University Press.

Styck, K. M., & Watkins, M. W. (2013). Diagnostic utility of the culture-language interpretive matrix for the Wechsler Intelligence Scale for Children–Fourth Edition with a referred sample. *School Psychology Review, 42*, 367–382. Retrieved from http://www.nasponline.org

Sullivan, C. J. (2006). Early adolescent delinquency: Assessing the role of childhood problems, family environment and peer pressure. *Youth Violence and Juvenile Justice, 4*, 291–313.

Suzuki, L. A., & Valencia, R. R. (1997). Race–ethnicity and measured intelligence. *American Psychologist, 52*, 1103–1114.

Swanson, H. L. (2006). Working memory and reading disabilities: Both phonological and executive processing deficits are important. In T. P. Alloway & S. E. Gathercole (Eds.), *Working memory and neurodevelopmental disorders* (pp. 59–88). New York, NY: Psychology Press.

Swets, J. A. (1996). *Signal detection theory and ROC analysis in psychological diagnostics: Collected papers*. Mahwah, NJ: Erlbaum.

Szarko, J. E., Brown, A. J., & Watkins, M. W. (2013). Examiner familiarity effects for children with autism spectrum disorders. *Journal of Applied School Psychology, 29*, 37–51. doi:10.1080/15377903.2013.751475

Taki Y, Hashizume H, Sassa Y, Takeuchi H, Wu K, Asano M, Asano K, Fukuda H, Kawashima R. (2011). Gender differences in partial-volume corrected brain perfusion using brain MRI in healthy children. *Neuroimage 58*, 709–715.

Tallent, N., & Reiss, W. J. (1959). Multidisciplinary views on the preparation of written clinical psychological reports: I. Spontaneous suggestions for content. *Journal of Clinical Psychology, 15*(2), 218–221.

Tanenhaus, D. S. (2004). *Juvenile justice in the making, studies in crime and public policy*. New York, NY: Oxford University Press.

Taub, G. E. (2014). An empirical investigation comparing the WISC–III and WISC–IV: Implications for the Atkins criterion. *Open Access Journal of Forensic Psychology, 6*, 1–16.

Taylor, J. L., & Teicher, A. (1946). A clinical approach to reporting psychological test data. *Journal of Clinical Psychology, 2*(4), 323–332.

Taylor, L. R., Karcher, M. J., Kelly, P. J. & Valescu, S. (2003). Resiliency, risk and substance use among Hispanic urban juvenile detainees. *Journal of Addictions and Offender Counseling, 24*(1), 46–64.

Temple, C. (1997). *Developmental cognitive neuropsychology*. East Sussex, UK: Psychology Press.

Terman, L. M. (1916). *The measurement of intelligence*. Boston, MA: Houghton Mifflin.

Terman, L. M. (1918). Errors in scoring Binet tests. *Psychological Clinic, 12*, 33–39.

Terman, L. M. (1922). Were we born that way? *World's Work, 44*, 655–660.

Terman, L. M., & Merrill, M. A. (1937). *Measuring intelligence*. Boston, MA: Houghton Mifflin.

Theisen, M. E., Rapport, L. J., Axelrod, B. N., & Brines, D. B. (1998). Effects of practice in repeated administrations of the Wechsler Memory Scale-Revised in normal adults. *Psychological Assessment, 5*, 85–92.

The Psychological Corporation. (1992). *Wechsler individual achievement test.* San Antonio, TX: Author.

Thompson, T. W., Waskom, M. L., Garel, K. A., Caredenas-Iniguez, C., Reynolds, G. O, Winter, R., ... Gabrieli, J. D. (2013) Failure of working memory training to enhance cognition or intelligence. *PLoS ONE 8*(5): e63614 doi:10.1371/journal.pone.0063614

Thorndike, R. L., Hagen, E. P., & Sattler, J. M. (1986). *Stanford–Binet Intelligence Scale* (4th ed.). Chicago, IL: Riverside.

Thurstone, L. L. (1938). Primary mental abilities. *Psychometric Monographs, 1.*

Thurstone, L. L. (1946). Theories of intelligence. *Scientific Monthly, 62*, 101–112.

Thurstone, L. L., & Thurstone, T. G. (1941). Factorial studies of intelligence. *Psychometric Monographs, 2.*

Tobin, R. M. (Ed.). (2013). The Wechsler intelligence tests: Revisiting theory and practice [Special Issue]. *Journal of Psychoeducational Assessment, 31*(2).

Todis, B., Bullis, M., Waintrup, M., Schultz, R., & D'Ambrosio, R. (2001). Overcoming the odds: Qualitative examination of resilience among formerly incarcerated adolescents. *Exceptional Children, 68*, 119–139.

Toga, A. W., Clark, K. A., Thompson, P. M., Shattuck, D. W, & Van Horn, J. D. (2012). Mapping the human connectome. *Neurosurgery, 71*, 1–5. doi:10.1227/NEU.0b013e318258e9ff

Trahan, L., Steubing, K. K., Hiscock, M K., & Fletcher, J. M. (2014). The Flynn effect: A meta-analysis. *Psychological Bulletin, 140*, 1332–1360. doi:10.1037/a0037173

Treat, T. A., & Viken, R. J. (2012). Measuring test performance with signal detection theory techniques. In H. Cooper, P. M. Camic, D. L. Long, A. T. Panter, D. Rindskopf, & K. J. Sher (Eds.), *Handbook of research methods in psychology: Foundations, planning, measures, and psychometrics* (Vol. 1, pp. 723–744). Washington, DC: American Psychological Association.

Trice, A. D., & Brewster, J. (2004). The effects of maternal incarceration on adolescent children. *Journal of Police and Criminal Psychology, 19*, 27–35.

Tucker-Drob, E. M., Johnson, K. E., & Jones, R. N. (2009). The cognitive reserve hypothesis: A longitudinal examination of age-associated declines in reasoning and processing speed. *Developmental Psychology, 45*, 431–446.

Tuddenham, R. (1974). Review: Fame and oblivion. *Science (New Series), 183*, 1071–1072.

Turkheimer, E., & Horn, E. E. (2014). Interactions between socioeconomic status and components of variation in cognitive ability. In D. Finkel & C. A. Reynolds (Eds.), *Behavior genetics of cognition throughout the lifespan* (pp. 41–68). New York, NY: Springer.

Turken, A. U., Whitfield-Gabrieli, S., Bammer, R., Baldo, J., Dronkers, N. F., & Gabrieli, J. D. E. (2008). Cognitive processing speed and the structure of white matter pathways: Convergent evidence from normal variation and lesion studies. *Neuroimage, 42*, 1032–1044.

Turner, M. G., Hartman, J. L., & Bishop, D. M. (2007). The effects of prenatal problems, family functioning, and neighborhood disadvantage in predicting life-course-persistent offending. *Criminal Justice and Behavior, 34*, 12–41.

Tzeng, O. J. L., Lee, C. Y., Lee, J. R., Wu, D. H., Juan, C.-H., Cheng, S.-K., ... Hung, D. L. (2013). Cognitive neuroscience in the 21st century: A selective review of prominent research topics and applications. *Journal of Neuroscience and Neuroengineering, 2*, 364–381.

Tzuriel, D. (2000). Dynamic assessment of young children: Educational and intervention perspectives. *Educational Psychology Review, 12*(4), 385–435

United States Bureau of the Census. (2014). Educational attainment in the United States: 2014—detailed tables. U. S. Census Bureau Current Population Survey Annual Social and Economic Supplement. Retrieved March 22, 2015 from http://www.census.gov/hhes/socdemo/education/data/cps/2014/tables.html

Unruh, D., Povenmire-Kirk, T., & Yamamoto, S. (2009). Perceived barriers and protective factors of juvenile offenders on their developmental pathway to adulthood. *Journal of Correctional Education, 60*(3), 201–224.

Unsworth, N., Fukuda, K., Awh, E., & Vogel, E. K. (2014). Working memory and fluid intelligence: Capacity, attention control, and secondary memory retrieval. *Cognitive Psychology, 71*, 1–26.

Van der Elst, W., Van Boxtel, M. P. J., Van Breukelen, G. J. P., & Jolles, J. (2008). Detecting the significance of changes in performance on the Stroop Color-Word Test, Rey's Verbal Learning

Test, and the Letter Digit Substitution Test: The regression-based change approach. *Journal of the International Neuropsychological Society*, *14*, 71–80. doi:10.10170S1355617708080028

VanDerHeyden, A., & Burns, M. (2010). *Essentials of RTI assessment*. Hoboken, NJ: Wiley.

van der Sluis, S., de Jong, P. F., & van der Leij, A. (2004). Inhibition and shifting in children with learning deficits in arithmetic and reading. *Journal of Experimental Child Psychology*, *87*(3), 239–266. doi:10.1016/j.jecp.2003.12.002

Van De Voorde, S., Roeyers, H., Verte, S., & Wiersema, J. R. (2010). Working memory, response inhibition, and within-subject variability in children with attention-deficit/hyperactivity disorder or reading disorder. *Journal of Clinical and Experimental Neuropsychology*, *32*, 366–379.

Van Hagen, J., & Kaufman, A. S. (1975). Factor analysis of the WISC–R for a group of mentally retarded children and adolescents. *Journal of Consulting and Clinical Psychology*, *43*, 661–667.

Van Luit, J. E., Kroesbergen, E. H., & Naglieri, J. A. (2005). Utility of PASS theory and cognitive assessment system for Dutch children with and without ADHD. *Journal of Learning Disabilities*, *38*, 434–439.

Vaske, J., Galyean, K., Cullen, F. T. (2011). Toward a biosocial theory of offender rehabilitation: Why does cognitive-behavioral therapy work? *Journal of Criminal Justice 39*, 90–102.

Velicer, W. F. (1976). Determining the number of components form the matrix of partial correlations. *Psychometrika*, *31*, 321–327. doi:10.1007/BF02293557

Velicer, W. F., Eaton, C. A., & Fava, J. L. (2000). Construct explication through factor or component analysis: A view and evaluation of alternative procedures for determining the number of factors or components. In R. D. Goffin & E. Helmes (Eds.), *Problems and solutions in human assessment: A festschrift to Douglas Jackson at seventy* (pp. 41–71). Norwell, MA: Kluwer Academic.

Vernon, P. E. (1965). Ability factors and environmental influences. *American Psychologist*, *20*, 723–733. doi:10.1037/h0021472

Vig, S., & Sanders, M. (2007). Cognitive assessment. In M. R. Brassard & A. E. Boehm (Eds.), *Preschool assessment: Principles and practices* (pp. 383–419). New York, NY: Guilford Press.

Viljoen, J. L., Elkovitch, N., Scalora, M. J., & Ullman, D. (2009). Assessment of reoffense risk in adolescents who have committed sexual offenses: Predictive validity of the ERASOR, PCL:YV, YLS/CMI, and Static-99. *Criminal Justice & Behavior*, *36*, 981–1000.

Vitacco, M. J., Neumann, C. S., Robertson, A. A., & Durrant, S. L. (2002). Contributions of impulsivity and callousness in the assessment of adjudicated male adolescents: A prospective study. *Journal of Personality Assessment*, *78*(1), 87–103.

Vitacco, M. J., & Rogers, R. (2001). Predictors of adolescent psychopathy: The role of impulsivity, hyperactivity, and sensation seeking. *Journal of the American Academy of Psychiatry and the Law*, *29*(4), 374–382.

Vitaro, F., Pedersen, S., & Brendgen, M. (2007). Children's disruptiveness, peer rejection, friends' deviancy, and delinquent behaviors: A process-oriented approach. *Development and Psychopathology*, *19*, 433–453.

von Stumm, S., & Plomin, R. (2015). Socioeconomic status and the growth of intelligence from infancy through adolescence. *Intelligence*, *48*, 30–36.

Wadsworth, S. J., Corley, R. P., & DeFries, J. C. (2014). Cognitive abilities in childhood and adolescence. In D. Finkel & C. A. Reynolds (Eds.). *Behavior genetics of cognition throughout the lifespan* (pp. 3–40). New York, NY: Springer.

Wagner, R. K., Torgeson, J. K., Rashotte, C. A., & Pearson, N. A. (2013). *Comprehensive test of phonological processing* (2nd ed.). Austin, TX: Pro-Ed.

Walhovd, K. B., Tamnes, C. K., & Fjell, A. M. (2014). Brain structural maturation and he foundations of cognitive behavioral development. *Current Opinions in Neurology*, *27*(2), 176–184.

Wang, M.-T., & Holcombe, R. (2010). Adolescents' perceptions of school environment, engagement, and academic achievement in middle school. *American Educational Research Journal*, *47*, 633–662.

Wang, M.-T., Willett, J. B., & Eccles, J. S. (2011). The assessment of school engagement: Examining dimensionality and measurement invariance by gender and race/ethnicity. *Journal of School Psychology*, *49*, 465–480.

Wang, Z., Katz, B., & Shah, P. (2014). New directions in intelligence research: Avoiding the mistakes of the past. *Journal of Intelligence*, *2*, 16–20.

Ward, L. C., Bergman, M. A., & Hebert, K. R. (2012). WAIS–IV subtest covariance structure: Conceptual and statistical considerations. *Psychological Assessment, 24,* 328–340.

Warren, S. A., & Brown, W. G. (1972). Examiner scoring errors on individual intelligence tests. *Psychology in the Schools, 9,* 118–122.

Wasserman, J. D. (2012). A history of intelligence assessment: The unfinished tapestry. In D. P. Flanagan & P. L. Harrison (Eds.), *Contemporary intellectual assessment: Theories, tests, and issues* (3rd ed., pp. 2–55). New York, NY: Guilford Press.

Wasserman, J. D., & Bracken, B. A. (2013). Fundamental psychometric considerations in assessment. In J. R. Graham & J. A. Naglieri (Eds.), *Handbook of psychology: Assessment psychology* (Vol. 10, 2nd ed., pp. 50–81). Hoboken, NJ: Wiley.

Wasserman, J. D., & Kaufman, A. S. (in press). Biography of David Wechsler. In R. Cautin & S. O. Lilienfeld (Eds.). *Encyclopedia of Clinical Psychology.* Malden, MA: Wiley-Blackwell.

Watkins, M. W. (1999). Diagnostic utility of WISC–III subtest variability among students with learning disabilities. *Canadian Journal of School Psychology, 15,* 11–20. doi:10.1177 /082957359901500102

Watkins, M. W. (2000). *Monte Carlo PCA for parallel analysis* [Computer software]. State College, PA: Ed & Psych Associates.

Watkins, M. W. (2003). IQ subtest analysis: Clinical acumen or clinical illusion? *Scientific Review of Mental Health Practice, 2,* 118–141.

Watkins, M. W. (2004). *MacOrtho [Computer Software].* State College, PA: Ed & Psych Associates.

Watkins, M. W. (2005). Diagnostic validity of Wechsler subtest scatter. *Learning Disabilities: A Contemporary Journal, 3,* 20–29.

Watkins, M. W. (2006). Orthogonal higher-order structure of the Wechsler Intelligence Scale for Children–Fourth Edition. *Psychological Assessment, 18,* 123–125.

Watkins, M. W. (2007). *SEscree* [Computer software]. State College, PA: Ed & Psych Associates.

Watkins, M. W. (2009). Errors in diagnostic decision making and clinical judgment. In T. B. Gutkin & C. R. Reynolds (Eds.), *Handbook of school psychology* (4th ed., pp. 210–229). Hoboken, NJ: Wiley.

Watkins, M. W. (2010). Structure of the Wechsler Intelligence Scale for Children–Fourth Edition among a national sample of referred students. *Psychological Assessment, 22,* 782–787. doi:10.1037 /a0020043

Watkins, M. W. (2013). *Omega* [Computer software]. Phoenix, AZ: Ed & Psych Associates.

Watkins, M. W., & Beaujean, A. A. (2014). Bifactor structure of the Wechsler Preschool and Primary Scale of Intelligence–Fourth Edition. *School Psychology Quarterly, 29,* 52–63. doi:10.1037 /spq0000038

Watkins, M. W., & Canivez, G. L. (2004). Temporal stability of WISC–III subtest composite strengths and weaknesses. *Psychological Assessment, 16,* 133–138. doi:10.1037/1040–3590.16.2.133

Watkins, M. W., Canivez, G. L., James, T., James, K., & Good, R. (2013). Construct validity of the WISC–IV UK with a large referred Irish sample. *International Journal of School & Educational Psychology, 1,* 102–111. doi:10.1080/2168 3603.2013.794439

Watkins, M. W., Glutting, J. J., & Lei, P.-W. (2007). Validity of the Full Scale IQ when there is significant variability among WISC–III and WISC–IV factor scores. *Applied Neuropsychology, 14,* 13–20. doi:10.1080/09084280701280353

Watkins, M. W., Glutting, J. J., & Youngstrom, E. A. (2005). Issues in subtest profile analysis. In D. P. Flanagan & P. L. Harrison (Eds.), *Contemporary intellectual assessment: Theories, tests, and issues* (2nd ed., pp. 251–268). New York, NY: Guilford Press.

Watkins, M. W., & Ravert, C. M. (2013). Subtests, factors, and constructs: What is being measured by tests of intelligence? In J. C. Kush (Ed.), *Intelligence quotient: Testing, role of genetics and the environment and social outcomes* (pp. 55–68). New York, NY: Nova Science.

Watkins, M. W., & Smith, L. (2013). Long-term stability of the Wechsler Intelligence Scale for Children–Fourth Edition. *Psychological Assessment, 25,* 477–483. doi:10.1037/a0031653

Weaver, C. M., Borkowski, J. G., & Whitman, T. L. (2008). Violence breeds violence: Childhood exposure and adolescent conduct problems. *Journal of Community Psychology, 36*(1), 96–112.

Wechsler, D. (1922). Quelques remarques sur la Psycho-Pathologie de l'Indecision [Some remarks on the psychopathology of indecision]. *Journal de Psychologie, 19,* 47–54.

Wechsler, D. (1928). Psychometric tests. In I. S. Wechsler (Ed.), *A textbook of clinical neurology* (pp. 104–116). Philadelphia, PA: W. B. Saunders.

Wechsler, D. (1930). The range of human capacities. *Scientific Monthly, 31*(1), 35–39.

Wechsler, D. (1939). *The measurement of adult intelligence*. Baltimore, MD: Williams & Wilkins Co.

Wechsler, D. (1944). *The measurement of adult intelligence*. Baltimore, MD: Williams & Wilkins.

Wechsler, D. (1949). *Wechsler Intelligence Scale for Children*. New York, NY: Psychological Corporation.

Wechsler, D. (1950). Cognitive, conative and non-intellective intelligence. *American Psychologist, 5*, 78–83.

Wechsler, D. (1958). *Measurement and appraisal of adult intelligence* (4th ed.). Baltimore, MD: Williams & Wilkins.

Wechsler, D. (1967). *Wechsler Preschool and Primary Scale of Intelligence*. New York, NY: Psychological Corporation.

Wechsler, D. (1971). Intelligence: Definition, theory, and the I.Q. In R. Cancro (Ed.), *Intelligence: Genetic and environmental influences* (pp. 50–55). New York: Grune and Stratton.

Wechsler, D. (1974a). *Manual for the Wechsler Intelligence Scale for Children–Revised (WISC–R)*. New York, NY: Psychological Corporation.

Wechsler, D. (1974b). *Selected papers of David Wechsler*. Ed. A. E. Edwards. New York, NY: Academic Press.

Wechsler, D. (1975). Intelligence defined and undefined: A relativistic appraisal. *American Psychologist, 30*(2), 135–139.

Wechsler, D. (1981). *Manual for the Wechsler Adult Intelligence—Revised*. San Antonio, TX: Psychological Corporation.

Wechsler, D. (1989). *Wechsler Preschool and Primary Scale of Intelligence—Revised*. San Antonio, TX: Psychological Corporation.

Wechsler, D. (1991). *Wechsler Intelligence Scale for Children* (3rd ed.). San Antonio, TX: Psychological Corporation.

Wechsler, D. (2001). *Wechsler Individual Achievement Test* (2nd ed.). San Antonio, TX: Psychological Corporation.

Wechsler, D. (2002). *Wechsler Preschool and Primary Scale of Intelligence* (3rd ed.). San Antonio, TX: Pearson.

Wechsler, D. (2003). *Wechsler Intelligence Scale for Children* (4th ed.). San Antonio, TX: Pearson.

Wechsler, D. (2008). *Wechsler Adult Intelligence Scale* (4th ed.). San Antonio, TX: Pearson.

Wechsler, D. (2009). *Wechsler Memory Scale* (4th ed.). Bloomington, MN: Pearson.

Wechsler, D. (2012). *Wechsler Preschool and Primary Scale of Intelligence* (4th ed.). Bloomington, MN: Pearson.

Wechsler, D. (2014). *Wechsler Intelligence Scale for Children* (5th ed.). Bloomington, MN: Pearson.

Wechsler, D., Doppelt, J. E., & Lennon, R. T. (1975). *A conversation with David Wechsler* (Unpublished transcript of interview). San Antonio, TX: The Psychological Corporation.

Wechsler, D., & Kaplan, E., Fein, D., Kramer, J., Morris, R., Delis, D., & Maerlender, A. (2004). *Wechsler Intelligence Scale for Children–Fourth Edition Integrated*. Bloomington, MN: Pearson.

Wechsler, D., & Kaplan, E. (2015). *Wechsler Intelligence Scale for Children–Fifth Edition Integrated*. Bloomington, MN: Pearson.

Wechsler, D., & Naglieri, J. A. (2006). *Wechsler Nonverbal Scale of Ability*. San Antonio, TX: Pearson.

Weiner, I. B. (1989). On competence and ethicality in psychodiagnostic assessment. *Journal of Personality Assessment, 53*, 827–831. doi:10.1207/s15327752jpa5304_18

Weiss, L. G., Chen, H., Harris, J. G., Holdnack, J. A., & Saklofske, D. H. (2010). WAIS–IV use in societal context. In L. G. Weiss, D. H. Saklofske, D. Coalson, & S. E. Raiford (Eds.), *WAIS–IV clinical use and interpretation: Scientist-practitioner perspectives* (pp. 97–139). Amsterdam, The Netherlands: Elsevier Academic Press.

Weiss, L. G., Harris, J. G., Prifitera, A., Courville, T., Rolfhus, E., Saklofske, D. H., & Holdnack, J. A. (2006). WISC–IV interpretation in societal context. In L. G. Weiss, D. H. Saklofske, A. Prifitera, & J. A. Holdnack, *WISC–IV advanced clinical interpretation* (pp. 1–57). Amsterdam, The Netherlands: Elsevier Academic Press.

Weiss, L. G., Keith, T., Zhu, J., & Chen, H. (2013a). WAIS–IV and clinical validation of the four- and five-factor interpretive approaches. *Journal of Psychoeducational Assessment, 31*, 94–113. doi:10.1177/0734282913478030

Weiss, L. G., Keith, T., Zhu, J., & Chen, H. (2013b). WISC–IV and clinical validation of the four- and five-factor interpretive approaches. *Journal of Psychoeducational Assessment, 31*, 114–131. doi:10.1177/0734282913478032

Weiss, L. G., Locke, V., Pan, T., Harris, J. G., Saklofske, D. H., & Prifitera, A. (2016). WISC–V use in societal context. In L. G. Weiss, D. H. Saklofske, J. A. Holdnack, & A. Prifitera

(Eds.), *WISC–V clinical use and interpretation: Scientist-practitioner perspectives* (pp. 123–185). Amsterdam, The Netherlands: Elsevier Academic Press.

Weiss, L. G., & Prifitera, A. (1995). An evaluation of differential prediction of WIAT achievement scores from WISC–III FSIQ across ethnic and gender groups. *Journal of School Psychology, 33,* 297–304.

Weiss, L. G., Saklofske, D. H. Coalson, D. L., & Raiford, S. E. (Eds.). (2010). *WAIS–IV clinical use and interpretation* (pp. 217–235). San Diego, CA: Academic Press.

Weiss, L. G., Saklofske, D. H., Prifitera, A., & Holdnack, J. A. (Eds.). (2006). *WISC–IV: Advanced clinical interpretation.* Burlington, MA: Academic Press.

Wendling, B. J., & Mather, N. (2009). *Essentials of evidence-based academic interventions.* Hoboken, NJ: Wiley.

Wentworth-Rohr, I. & Macintosh, R. (1972). Psychodiagnosis with WAIS intrasubtest scatter of scores. *Journal of Clinical Psychology, 28*(1), 68.

Wesman, A. G. (1968). Intelligent testing. *American Psychologist, 23,* 261–214.

Western, B., & Beckett, K. (1999). How unregulated is the U.S. labor market? The penal system as a labor market institution. *American Journal of Sociology, 104,* 1030–1060.

White, J. L., Moffitt, T. E., Caspi, A., Bartusch, D. J., Needles, D. J., & Stouthamer-Loeber, M. (1994). Measuring impulsivity and examining its relationship to delinquency. *Journal of Abnormal Psychology, 103*(2), 192–205.

Widom, C. S. (1989). Child abuse, neglect, and adult behavior: Research design and findings on criminality, violence, and child abuse. *American Journal of Orthopsychiatry, 59*(3), 355–367.

Wigfield, A., Eccles, J. S., Schiefele, U., Roeser, R. W., & Davis-Kean, P. (2006). Development of achievement motivation. In N. Eisenberg, W. Damon, & R. M. Lerner (Eds.), *Handbook of child psychology: Social, emotional, and personality development* (Vol. 3, 6th ed., pp. 933–1002). Hoboken, NJ: Wiley.

Wildeman, C. (2010). Paternal incarceration and children's physically aggressive behaviors: Evidence from the fragile families and child wellbeing study. *Social Forces, 89*(1), 285–309.

Willburger, E., Fussenegger, B., Moll, K., Wood, G., & Landerl, K. (2008). Naming speed in dyslexia and dyscalculia. *Learning and Individual Differences, 18,* 224–236.

Williams, J. E., & McCord, D. M. (2006). Equivalence of standard and computerized versions of the Ravens Progressive Matrices Test. *Computers in Human Behavior, 22,* 791–800.

Williams, R. L. (1974a). From dehumanization to black intellectual genocide: A rejoinder. In G. J. Williams & S. Gordon (Eds.), *Clinical child psychology* (pp. 320–323). New York, NY: Behavioral Publications.

Williams, R. L. (1974b). Scientific racism and IQ: The silent mugging of the black community. *Psychology Today, 7,* 33.

Willis, J. O., & Dumont, R. P. (1998). *Guide to identification of learning disabilities.* Acton, MA: Copley Custom Publishing. Also available at http://alpha.fdu.edu/psychology/test_score_descriptions.htm.

Willis, J. O., & Dumont, R. P. (2002). *Guide to Identification of learning disabilities* (3rd ed.). Peterborough, NH: Author.

Willis, J. O., Dumont, R. & Kaufman, A. S. (2011). Intelligence testing. In R. L. Cautin & S. O. Lilienfeld (Eds.), *The encyclopedia of clinical psychology* (pp. 39–57). New York, NY: Wiley-Blackwell.

Willis, J. O., Dumont, R., & Kaufman, A. S. (2013). Assessment of intellectual functioning in children. In K. F. Geisinger (Ed.), *APA handbook of testing and assessment in psychology* (vol. 3, pp. 39–70). Washington, DC: American Psychological Association.

Wilson, R. S., Li, Y., Bienias, J. L. & Bennett, D. A. (2006). Cognitive decline in old age: Separating retest effects from the effects of growing older. *Psychology and Aging, 21,* 774–789.

Winfree, L. T., & Bernat, F. P. (1998). Social learning, self-control, and substance abuse by eighth grade students: A tale of two cities. *Journal of Drug Issues, 28,* 539–558.

Winston, A. S. (1996). "As his name indicates": R. S. Woodworth's letters of reference and employment for Jewish psychologists in the 1930s. *Journal of the History of the Behavioral Sciences, 32,* 30–43.

Winston, A. S. (1998). "The defects of his race": E. G. Boring and antisemitism in American psychology, 1923–1953. *History of Psychology, 1,* 27–51.

Witt, J. C., & Gresham, F. M. (1985). Review of the Wechsler Intelligence Scale for Children—Revised. In J. V. Mitchell (Ed.), *Ninth mental measurements yearbook* (pp. 1716–1719). Lincoln, NE: University of Nebraska Press.

Wolfle, D. (1940). *Factor analysis to 1940. Number 3.* Psychometric Monographs. Chicago, IL: University of Chicago Press.

Wood, J. M., Tataryn, D. J., & Gorsuch, R. L. (1996). Effects of under- and over-extraction on principal axis factor analysis with varimax rotation. *Psychological Methods, 1,* 354–365. doi:10.1037/1082–989X.1.4.354

Woodcock, R. W. (1990). Theoretical foundations of the WJ–R measures of cognitive ability. *Journal of Psychoeducational Assessment, 8,* 231–258.

Woodcock, R. W., & Johnson, M. B. (1989). *Woodcock-Johnson Psycho-Educational Battery— Revised.* Itasca, IL: Riverside.

Woodcock, R. W., Mather, N., & McGrew, K. S. (2001). *Woodcock-Johnson III Tests of Achievement.* Itasca, IL: Riverside.

Woodcock, R. W., McGrew, K. S., & Mather, N. (2001). *Woodcock-Johnson III.* Itasca, IL: Riverside.

World Health Organization. (1980). *International classification of impairments, disabilities, and handicaps: A manual of classification relating to the consequences of disease, published in accordance with resolution WHA29.35 of the Twenty-ninth World Health Assembly, May 1976.* Geneva, Switzerland: Author.

World Health Organization. (2004). *International statistical classification of diseases and related health problems* (Vol. 1). Geneva, Switzerland: Author.

Worling, J. R., & Curwen, T. (2001). *Estimate of Risk of Adolescent Sexual Offense Recidivism, Version 2.0.* Toronto, Canada: Ontario Ministry of Community and Social Services

Xu, J. (2006). Middle school homework management and attitudes. *Academic Exchange Quarterly, 10*(4). Downloaded August 25, 2015 from: https://www .questia.com/library/journal/1G1-159921067/ middle-school-homework-management-and- attitudes.

Yampolskaya, S., Armstrong, M. I., & McNeish, R. (2011). Children placed in out-of-home care: Risk factors for involvement with the juvenile justice system. *Violence and Victims, 26*(2), 231–245.

Yang Y., & Green, S. B. (2011). Coefficient alpha: A reliability coefficient for the 21st century? *Journal of Psychoeducational Assessment, 29,* 377–392. doi:10.1177/0734282911406668

Yoakum, C. S., & Yerkes, R. M. (1920). *Army mental tests.* New York, NY: Henry Holt.

Yuan, K.-H., & Chan, W. (2005). On nonequivalence of several procedures of structural equation modeling. *Psychometrika, 70,* 791–798. doi:10.1007/s11336-001-0930-9

Yung, Y.-F., Thissen, D., & McLeod, L. (1999). On the relationship between the higher-order factor model and the hierarchical factor model. *Psychometrika, 64,* 113–128. doi:10.1007/BF02294531

Žebec, M., Demetriou, A., & Kotrla-Topić, M. (2015). Changing expressions of general intelligence in development: A 2-wave longitudinal study from 7 to 18 years of age. *Intelligence, 49,* 94–109.

Zhu, J. J., & Cayton, T. (2013). *Substitution, proration, or retest: The best strategy when a core subtest score is missing. Symposium presented at the annual meeting of the American Psychological Association,* Honolulu, Hawaii.

Zhu, J. J., Cayton, T. C., & Chen, H. (under review). *Substitution, proration, or a retest? The optimal strategy when standard administration is infeasible.* Manuscript under review.

Zhu, J. J., Cayton, T. C., Raiford, S. E., & Chen, H. (in preparation). *Substitution, proration, or retest approaches to compensating for missing subtests in the WISC–V.*

Zhu, J., & Chen, H. (2011). Utility of inferential norming with smaller sample sizes. *Journal of Psychoeducational Assessment, 29,* 57–580. doi:10.1177/0734282910396323

Zimmer, C. (2014). Secrets of the brain. *National Geographic, 225*(2), 28–56.

Zinbarg, R. E., Revelle, W., & Yovel, I. (2007). Estimating for structures containing two group factors: Perils and prospects. *Applied Psychological Measurement, 31,*135–157. doi:10.1177/ 0146621606291558

Zinbarg, R. E., Revelle, W., Yovel, I., & Li, W. (2005). Cronbach's α, Revelle's β, and McDonald's ω_h: Their relations with each other and two alternative conceptualizations of reliability. *Psychometrika, 70,* 123–133. doi:10.1007/s11336–003–0974–7

Zinbarg, R. E., Yovel, I., Revelle, W., & McDonald, R. P. (2006). Estimating generalizability to a latent variable common to all of a scale's indicators: A comparison of estimators for ω_h. *Applied Psychological Measurement, 30,* 121 144. doi:10.1177/0146621605278814

Zirkel, P. A. (2013). The Hale position for a "third method" for specific learning disabilities identification: A legal analysis. *Learning Disability Quarterly, 36,* 93–96. doi:10.1177/0731948713477850

Zirkel, P. A. (2014). The legal quality of articles published in school psychology journals: An initial report card. *School Psychology Review, 43,* 318–339.

Zoski, K. W., & Jurs, S. (1996). An objective counterpart to the visual scree test for factor analysis: The standard error scree. *Educational and Psychological Measurement, 56,* 443–451. doi:10.1177/0013164496056003006

Zwick, W. R., & Velicer, W. F. (1986). Comparison of five rules for determining the number of components to retain. *Psychological Bulletin, 117,* 253–269. doi:10.1037/0033–2909.99.3.432

ABOUT THE AUTHORS

Alan S. Kaufman, PhD, is Clinical Professor of Psychology at Yale University Child Study Center (since 1997). He is a Penn graduate who earned his PhD under Robert Thorndike at Columbia University. Alan worked closely with David Wechsler in the development of the WISC-R and has published, with Nadeen Kaufman, numerous tests, including the recent KTEA–3, KTEA–3 Brief, Japanese KABC–II, and German KABC–II. They authored the influential 1983 K-ABC and the second-generation KABC–II and KBIT–2 (with more than 20 foreign versions of their cognitive tests in use around the world). Alan has published widely on the clinical and neuropsychological assessment of intelligence and has greatly impacted interpretation of IQ tests, especially Wechsler's. His books include the 1979 landmark *Intelligent Testing with the WISC-R* and, more recently, *IQ Testing 101* (2009) and *Essentials of WAIS-IV Assessment—Second Edition* (with Elizabeth Lichtenberger; 2013). Alan and Nadeen co-edit the influential Wiley book series *Essentials of Psychological Assessment*. Alan, a fellow of four divisions of APA and of APS, is recipient of APA Division 16's Senior Scientist Award (1997) and Division 5's Samuel J. Messick Distinguished Scientific Contributions Award (2012). Since 2012, first Fordham University, and now Gonzaga University, has presented the Alan S. Kaufman Intelligent Testing Award at its annual Spring Assessment Conference. (The 2015 recipient is Dawn Flanagan.)

Susan (Susie) Engi Raiford is a senior research director and manager of the Wechsler Team for Pearson in San Antonio, Texas. In her 12 years with Pearson, she has served as a lead research director for numerous Wechsler intelligence scales, including the Wechsler Adult Intelligence Scale–Fourth Edition (WAIS–IV, 2008), the Wechsler Preschool and Primary Intelligence Scale–Fourth Edition (WPPSI–IV, 2012), the Wechsler Intelligence Scale for Children–Fifth Edition (WISC–V), and the Wechsler Intelligence Scale for Children Fifth Edition–Integrated (WISC–V Integrated). She conceptualized and planned the research program for the Wechsler Abbreviated Intelligence Scale–Second Edition (WASI–II; 2011) and was an active part of development of the Wechsler Intelligence Scale for Children–Fourth Edition Spanish (WISC–IV Spanish, 2005) and the Wechsler Intelligence Scale for Children–Fourth Edition Integrated (WISC–IV Integrated, 2004) and has consulted on numerous international adaptations of the scales. She served as an editor for the book *WAIS–IV Clinical Use and Interpretation* (2010) and authored the book *Essentials of WPPSI–IV Assessment*. She received her PhD in clinical psychology from Palo Alto University, with research interests in cognition and emotion and clinical specialization in child and adolescent assessment and cognitive-behavioral psychotherapy.

Diane L. Coalson is a cognitive assessment expert, research psychologist, author, and clinician. From 2000 to 2014, she served as a senior research director and manager of the Wechsler team for Pearson in San Antonio, Texas. During that time, she was intimately involved with the development of all Wechsler intelligence scales in the United States and also consulted on numerous international adaptations. In addition to serving as a research director during development of the Wechsler Intelligence Scale for Children–Fifth Edition (WISC–V) and the Wechsler Intelligence Scale for Children–Fifth Edition Integrated (WISC–V Integrated), she also contributed to the successful publication of the Wechsler Preschool and Primary Scale of Intelligence–Fourth Edition (WPPSI–IV), Wechsler Adult Intelligence Scale–Fourth Edition (WAIS–IV), the Wechsler Nonverbal Scale of Intelligence (WNV), and the Wechsler

Intelligence Scale for Children–Fourth Edition Spanish (WISC–IV Spanish). She was a coauthor on *Essentials of WPPSI–IV Assessment* (2014) and served as a coeditor on *WAIS–IV Clinical Use and Interpretation* (2010). She received her doctorate in clinical psychology from Texas A&M University, with special research interests in test development, neuropsychology, and geropsychology.

ABOUT THE CONTRIBUTORS

Joan Axelrod, MEd, is an Adjunct Faculty Member in the School Psychology program and the Coordinator of the Academic Resource Center at William James College (formerly Massachusetts School of Professional Psychology). She has worked for many years as a psychoeducational diagnostician evaluating school-age children with learning and developmental disabilities and consulting to local school systems on assessment and programming for students with special needs. From 1976 to 1989, she was the Clinical Director of the Medical Educational Evaluation Center at North Shore Children's Hospital (currently Mass General for Children at North Shore Medical Center). Her evaluations integrate cognitive, neuropsychological, and educational assessment data to develop instructional recommendations.

Kristina C. Breaux, PhD, is a licensed special educator, learning disabilities specialist, author, and clinician. In her current role as Senior Research Director at Pearson, she manages the achievement team in clinical assessment and leads the development of diagnostic achievement tests and assessment solutions for dyslexia and learning disabilities. She has served as Lead Research Director for the Wechsler Individual Achievement Test, Third Edition (WIAT–III) and the Kaufman Test of Educational Achievement, Third Edition (KTEA–3). She has coauthored book chapters and articles on assessment as well as the following books: *Essentials of WIAT–III and KTEA–II Assessment* and *Essentials of KTEA–3 and WIAT–III Assessment* (in press). She received her doctorate from Northwestern University in Communication Sciences and Disorders with special emphasis in learning disabilities.

Gary L. Canivez, PhD, was a school psychologist for 8 years in the Phoenix metropolitan area before entering academia. He is presently Professor of Psychology at Eastern Illinois University, principally involved in the Specialist in School Psychology program; he previously taught as an adjunct faculty for Arizona State University and Northern Arizona University. Dr. Canivez is a Fellow of the APA Division of Quantitative and Qualitative Methods, a Charter Fellow of the Midwestern Psychological Association, a member of the Society for the Study of School Psychology, and past president of the Arizona Association of School Psychologists. He is an associate editor for *Psychological Assessment* and is an editorial board member for *School Psychology Quarterly* and the *Journal of Psychoeducational Assessment.* He has also served as a grant reviewer for the Israel Science Foundation, the Swiss National Science Foundation, and the Kuwait Foundation for the Advancement of Sciences. The author of over 50 research and professional publications and over 200 professional presentations and continuing education/professional development workshops, Dr. Canivez has research interests in applied psychometrics in evaluating psychological and educational tests (including international applications); and his research has been supported by the National Institutes of Health/National Institute of Mental Health.

Troy Courville, PhD, is the Assistant Provost and the Associate Vice President of Academic Affairs at Texas A&M University-Central Texas. He is also an Assistant Professor in the College of Education at Texas A&M University-Central Texas. Prior to his tenure at A&M-Central Texas, Dr. Courville served as the Associate Director of Institutional Studies & Policy Analysis at the University of Texas System Office (2008–2009) and as a Psychometrician and Research Scientist at Pearson (2004–2008). While with Pearson, he contributed to the publication of the Wechsler Preschool and Primary Scale of Intelligence–Fourth Edition (WPPSI–IV), the Wechsler Nonverbal Scale of Intelligence (WNV), and several international adaptations and also served as the lead psychometrician for the English edition of the Texas Assessment of Knowledge and Skills (TAKS). He received his PhD in Educational Psychology from Texas A&M University, with a specialization in research, measurement, and statistics.

Carlea Dries, MA, MEd, NCC, is a doctoral candidate in the Advanced PsyD program at Fairleigh Dickinson University. She has been a School Psychologist in northern New Jersey for the past decade. She continued her postgraduate education to earn certifications in Educational Leadership and an additional Master of Education degree in Counseling, with certification in Professional School Counseling. Ms. Dries has been a reviewer of multiple chapters of the WPPSI–IV text in the Jerome M. Sattler series (in process) and *Assessment of Children: WISC–IV and WPPSI–III Supplement* by Jerome M. Sattler and Ron Dumont, as well as the strengths and weaknesses chapter of the WPPSI–IV text authored by Ron Dumont and John Willis (in process). She was a coauthor of the Test Descriptions and Reviews chapter of *The Special Education Almanac*.

Ron Dumont, EdD, NCSP, is a Professor of Psychology and the Director of the School of Psychology at Fairleigh Dickinson University. Dr. Dumont's areas of research interest include problems with the diagnosis of learning problems, assessment of serious emotional disturbance, and differences found between assessment tools. He is the author or coauthor of over 20 book chapters as well as over 100 journal articles and test reviews. He is coauthor, with John Willis and Colin Elliott, of *Essentials of DAS–II Assessment*; with John Willis and Guy McBride,

of *Essentials of IDEA for Assessment Professionals*; and with John Willis, of the *Guide to Identification of Learning Disabilities Third Edition* (2002). With Dr. Jerome Sattler, he coauthored the *Assessment for Children WISC–IV and WPPSI–III Supplement* (2004).

Dawn P. Flanagan, PhD, is Professor of Psychology at St. John's University in Queens, New York, and Assistant Clinical Professor at Yale Child Study Center, Yale University School of Medicine. In addition to her teaching responsibilities in the areas of cognitive assessment, specific learning disabilities, and professional issues in school psychology, she serves as an expert witness, SLD consultant, and test/measurement consultant and trainer for organizations both nationally and internationally. She is a widely published author of books, book chapters, and articles. Her most recent books include *Essentials of Cross-Battery Assessment* (3rd ed.); *Essentials of Specific Learning Disability Identification*; *Contemporary Intellectual Assessment: Theories, Tests, and Issues* (3rd ed.) and *Essentials of Planning, Selecting and Tailoring Interventions for Unique Learners*. Dr. Flanagan is a fellow of the APA and a diplomate of the American Board of Psychological Specialties. Dr. Flanagan recently received the national *Outstanding Contributions to Training* award from Trainers in School Psychology in recognition of her widespread and influential training that she continues to do for school psychologists throughout the country and abroad. Dr. Flanagan is best known for the development of the Cross-Battery Assessment (XBA) approach and the development of an operational definition of specific learning disability, known as the Dual Discrepancy/Consistency "PSW" approach to SLD identification (or DD/C model).

Katie Eklund, PhD, is an Assistant Professor in the School Psychology Program at the University of Arizona. She received her doctorate in Counseling, Clinical, and School Psychology from the University of California, Santa Barbara. Dr. Eklund has worked in public education for 14 years as a school administrator, school psychologist, and school social worker. She is a nationally certified school psychologist and licensed psychologist. She has authored a number of publications on childhood risk and resiliency factors, including early identification and intervention for behavioral and emotional concerns, school climate, and positive psychology. Her teaching interests include school-based academic and behavioral interventions, crisis response and intervention, as well as school-based consultation and problem-solving skills.

Elaine Fletcher-Janzen, **EdD, NCSP, ABPdN,** has been a school psychologist in the public schools and in neuropsychiatric inpatient and university settings for the past 32 years. Dr. Fletcher-Janzen received her Diplomate in Pediatric Neuropsychology in 2010. She is currently a Professor of School Psychology at the Chicago School of Professional Psychology and immediate past president of the American Academy of Pediatric Neuropsychology. She has coedited or authored 16 books and reference works, including the *Encyclopedia of Special Education* and the *Diagnostic Desk Reference of Childhood Disorders*. She has recently published the *Neuropsychology of Women*, the *Handbook of Clinical Child Neuropsychology* (3rd ed.), and *Neuropsychological Perspectives on the Diagnosis of Learning Disabilities in the Era of RTI*. Dr. Fletcher-Janzen's research interests address cross-cultural aspects of cognitive abilities, the impact of socioeconomic status on intelligence scores and the identification of learning disabilities, neurodevelopment models of psychological assessment and intervention, neuropsychological aspects of chronic illness, and the systematic management of pediatric chronic illness in school and clinical settings.

Megan Hadorn, EdS, received undergraduate degrees in English and Anthropology from Kansas State University in 2011. After working as a substitute teacher and school psychology aide in Wellington, Kansas, for 2 years, she decided to pursue a graduate degree. She received her Education Specialist degree from the University of Kansas School Psychology program in 2015.

Her school psychology internship is in Topeka, Kansas.

Jill Hartmann, MEd, is a Specialist in Assessment of Intellectual Functioning in SAU 24 and Director of the Hartmann Learning Center (www.hartmannlearning.com) in Chester, New Hampshire, and is currently a doctoral candidate in the Leadership and Learning program at Rivier University. She is an experienced teacher, tutor, and educational evaluator and has been directly involved in the field of education for 15 years. She has taught most grade levels from first grade through eighth grade and holds multiple certifications. As an educational evaluator, Ms. Hartmann has worked with children of all ages to help recognize their academic strengths and weaknesses. Making the connection between evaluation results and appropriate educational interventions is a priority for Ms. Hartmann. She has worked with some leading test publishers as a field researcher and participated in the norming process of several evaluation tools such as the KABC–II and KeyMath 3. Her certifications include Elementary Education (K–8), Specialist in the Assessment of Intellectual Functioning, General Special Education, Intellectual and Developmental Disabilities, and Specific Learning Disabilities in New Hampshire, and Elementary Education (1–6), Mathematics (5–8), and Moderate Disabilities (PreK–8) in Massachusetts.

Emily S. Hartz, PsyD, is a school psychologist employed by a Philadelphia charter school and is professionally affiliated with the Philadelphia College of Osteopathic Medicine, where she assists with assessment courses, and Temple University, where she supervises a social skills clinic for children with autism. Her research focus has been on culturally sound methods for identifying specific learning disabilities within a bilingual population.

Alicia M. Jones, BA, is a doctoral student in the School Psychology program at Texas Woman's University. She has been in the field of education for 6 years as a teacher, trainer, and consultant. She received her Bachelor of Arts degree in Psychology from the University of Texas at Austin in 2008. Shortly after completing her undergraduate degree, she was accepted into Teach for America as a corps member in Houston, Texas, where she taught fifth- and sixth-grade mathematics from 2009 to 2012. After completing her corps experience and teaching, she transitioned to consultation while working with a nonprofit algebra preparation company where she supported administrators, teachers, parents, and students. As a doctoral student, she has worked on several research projects and poster presentations related to children with learning disabilities and deficits in executive functions.

Nadeen L. Kaufman, **EdD,** is Lecturer, Clinical Faculty, at the Yale University School of Medicine (since 1997). Dr. Kaufman, who earned graduate degrees in psychology, reading and learning disabilities, and special education (neuroscience) from Columbia University, has been a teacher of children with learning disabilities, school psychologist, learning disabilities specialist, university professor, and founder-director of several psychoeducational clinics. She was a direct participant in the development and standardization of the *McCarthy Scales* and WISC–R and has published, with her husband, Alan, an array of intelligence and achievement tests, including the K-ABC, K-TEA, K-BIT, and next generations of these tests (KABC–II, KTEA–II, KTEA–3, KBIT–2). The Kaufmans' tests, including their adult intelligence test and neuropsychological screener, have been adapted and translated for more than 20 countries worldwide; the German KABC–II was published in 2015. The Kaufmans coedit the popular *Essentials of Psychological Assessment* series. Also, she has authored, coauthored, or coedited numerous books, chapters, articles, test manuals, and case reports; and she coedited, with Nancy Mather, two special issues of *Psychology in the Schools* on the integration of cognitive assessment and response to intervention.

Elizabeth O. Lichtenberger, PhD, is a licensed clinical psychologist in California and an author whose works have focused on psychological assessment. In addition to her current professional roles, she has worked as an adjunct faculty member at Alliant International University in San Diego and a researcher at the Laboratory for Cognitive Neuroscience at The Salk Institute for Biological Studies in La Jolla, California. Her work at The Salk Institute focused on the cognitive and neuropsychological patterns in children with genetic developmental disorders. Because of her expertise in psychological, psychoeducational, and neuropsychological assessment, Dr. Lichtenberger also serves as an editor, a psychoeducational test/measurement consultant, a trainer for organizations, and consultant to individual psychologists. Her publications include books, book chapters, and articles on assessment and assessment instruments, some of which include *Assessing Adolescent and Adult Intelligence* (3rd ed.), *Essentials of Assessment Report Writing*, *Essentials of WAIS-IV Assessment* (2nd ed.), *Essentials of KABC–II Assessment*, and *Essentials of WIAT–III and KTEA–II Assessment*. In addition, she served as a consulting editor of the second edition of the *Encyclopedia of Special Education* and is currently on the editorial board of *Psychology in the Schools*.

Robert Lichtenstein, PhD, NCSP, directs the School Psychology PsyD Program at William James College (formerly Massachusetts School of Professional Psychology). He has worked as a school psychologist, school district director of school psychological services (for New Haven Public Schools), director of training at a hospital-based evaluation clinic (North Shore Children's Hospital, Salem, Massachusetts), and consultant for school psychology for the Connecticut State Department of Education. His recent publications and presentations have been on identification of learning disabilities and consumer-responsive assessment reports. He represents the National Association of School Psychologists (NASP) on the National Joint Committee on Learning Disabilities, and received a NASP President's Award for his contributions to the organization's policy work on students with specific learning disabilities.

Michelle Lurie, **PsyD, ABPdN,** is a pediatric neuropsychologist in private practice in Dallas, Texas. She earned her PsyD in clinical psychology under Nadeen Kaufman, EdD, with research interests in neuropsychology. She is board certified in pediatric neuropsychology through the American Academy of Pediatric Neuropsychology. Dr. Lurie is a member of the Society for Clinical Neuropsychology division of the APA, the Texas Psychological Association, the National Academy of Neuropsychology and the International Neuropsychological Society.

Jennifer T. Mascolo, PsyD, NCSP, is a nationally certified school psychologist and a licensed psychologist in New York and New Jersey. Dr. Mascolo offers direct client services including assessment, consultation, and intervention planning. In conjunction with her goal of bridging assessment and intervention to create meaningful learner outcomes, she also offers professional development training and consultation services to school districts and other professionals (e.g., psychologists, teachers, administrators). Since 2002, she has taught assessment and consultation at the graduate level and has supervised doctoral and master's level students in fieldwork experiences. Currently she teaches at Teacher's College, Columbia University. Her research interests include intelligence, the relationship between academic and cognitive functioning, and assessing and intervening with specific learning disabilities. Dr. Mascolo has coauthored four books, including the first and second editions of the *Achievement Test Desk Reference*, *Essentials of the WJ III Tests of Cognitive Abilities*, and *Essentials of Planning, Selecting, and Tailoring Interventions for Unique Learners* as well as several book chapters and peer-reviewed journal articles focused on using and interpreting

specific cognitive and academic measures as well as assessing, diagnosing, and intervening with SLD.

Nancy Mather, PhD, is a Professor of Special Education at the University of Arizona in the Department of Disability and Psychoeducational Studies. She has served as a learning disabilities teacher, a diagnostician, a university professor, and an educational consultant. She has published numerous articles and books and conducts workshops on assessment and instruction both nationally and internationally. Dr. Mather was a coauthor of the Woodcock-Johnson III and is a coauthor of the Woodcock-Johnson IV; she coauthored the *Examiner's Manual* for the WJ IV Tests of Cognitive Abilities and Tests of Achievement and also coauthored two books on interpretation and application of the WJ IV. Other recent books are *Comprehensive Evaluations*, *Essentials of Dyslexia: Assessment and Intervention*, and *Learning Disabilities and Challenging Behaviors*.

George McCloskey, PhD, is a Professor and Director of School Psychology Research in the Psychology Department of the Philadelphia College of Osteopathic Medicine. He frequently presents at national, regional, and state meetings on cognitive and neuropsychological assessment and intervention topics. Dr. McCloskey is the lead author of *Assessment and Intervention for Executive Function Difficulties* and author of *Essentials of Executive Functions Assessment*. He also has been involved in test development and publishing activities for more than 30 years. He directed the development of the WISC–IV Integrated and was a Senior Research Director and the Clinical Advisor to the Wechsler Test Development Group for The Psychological Corporation (now part of Pearson) and Associate Director of Test Development for AGS (now Pearson). He has authored chapters on neuropsychological approaches to test interpretation in sources such as *Essentials of WISC-IV Assessment*, *Essentials of WAIS-IV Assessment*, and *Contemporary Intellectual Assessment* and will be authoring chapters in the upcoming *Essentials of WISC–V Assessment*.

Ryan J. McGill, PhD, BCBA-D, NCSP, is Assistant Professor of Psychology and a core school psychology faculty member at Texas Woman's University. His primary research interests are psychological assessment and test development, the science of cognitive abilities, and the identification of specific learning disability. Prior to receiving his doctorate in School Psychology from Chapman University, he practiced as a school psychologist in Southern California from 2009 to 2014.

Daniel C. Miller, PhD, ABPP, is a Professor Emeritus in the Department of Psychology and Philosophy at Texas Woman's University. He is also the Executive Director of the Woodcock Institute for the Advancement of Neurocognitive Research and Applied Practice. He is a leading expert in school neuropsychology and a past president of the National Association of School Psychologists. He is the author or editor of a wide variety of influential publications, including *Best Practices in School Neuropsychology* and *Essentials of School Neuropsychological Assessment* (2nd ed.).

Jack A. Naglieri, PhD, is Research Professor at the Curry School of Education at the University of Virginia, Senior Research Scientist at the Devereux Center for Resilient Children, and Emeritus Professor of Psychology at George Mason University. He earned a PhD under Alan S. Kaufman at the University of Georgia. His test development career began in the late 1970s when he worked closely with Alan and Nadeen Kaufman on the K-ABC. Since that time he has published many measures of ability, such as the CAS, CAS2, Naglieri Nonverbal Ability Test, GAMA, Wechsler Nonverbal Scale of Ability, the Autism Spectrum Rating Scales, and Devereux Elementary Student Strength Assessment. Many of these measures are published in countries around the world. Dr. Naglieri has published extensively in areas such as SLD, ID, giftedness, ADHD, fair assessment, and cognitive interventions. He has published various books, including *Essentials*

of CAS Assessment; *Assessment of Cognitive Processes: The PASS Theory of Intelligence*; *Helping Children Learn: Intervention Handouts for Use at School and Home*; *Essentials of WNV Assessment*; *Handbook of Assessment Psychology*; *Assessment of Autism Spectrum Disorders*; *Executive Function Handbook*; and *A Practitioner's Guide to Assessment of Intelligence and Achievement*. Dr. Naglieri is a fellow of APA and recipient of the APA Division 16 Senior Scientist Award (2002), the 2011 Italian American Psychology Assembly Award for Distinguished Contributions to Psychology, and the Fordham University Alan S. Kaufman Intelligent Testing Award (2014).

Elizabeth M. Power, EdS, NCSP, ABSNP, is currently pursuing a doctorate in school psychology with an emphasis in pediatric neuropsychology at the Chicago School of Professional Psychology (TCS). She obtained her BA from Saint Joseph's College in 2008 and earned her Education Specialist degree in school psychology from TCS in 2011. Ms. Power, who has practiced as a school psychologist, is currently completing her doctoral internship at CHSD218 INSPiRE in Oak Lawn, Illinois. She is interested in applying clinical neuropsychology services within the schools. The focus of her doctoral research is on cardiac coherence training for students with Autism Spectrum Disorder.

Matthew R. Reynolds, PhD, is an Associate Professor in the Department of Educational Psychology at the University of Kansas. He received his doctoral degree in educational psychology (school psychology and quantitative methods) from the University of Texas at Austin. His research interests are in latent-variable modeling, with particular interest in the application of such models to structure and study the development of human cognitive abilities. He has published a wide variety of articles on individual differences in children's and adolescents' cognitive functioning and has consistently used state-of-the-art methodology in his publications.

W. Joel Schneider, PhD, grew up in Southern California and completed his undergraduate education at the University of California at

Berkeley. While working toward his doctorate in clinical psychology from Texas A&M University, he met and married Renée M. Tobin. They are currently Professors of Psychology at Illinois State University, where they have the good fortune to be able to follow their scholarly interests wherever they lead. Dr. Schneider divides his time between both the Clinical/Counseling and Quantitative Psychology programs, teaching courses in statistics, cognitive assessment, and psychotherapy. His research interests are diverse but are primarily centered on the validity of psychological assessment. He develops new psychometric methods and writes clinician-friendly software to help clinicians make better inferences about individuals. He supervises a psychological assessment service and leads a dialectical behavior therapy group. He writes essays, makes multimedia presentations, and sometimes sings about psychology, psychometrics, and software at his blog, *AssessingPsyche*.

Jennie Kaufman Singer, PhD, is an Associate Professor in the Division of Criminal Justice at California State University, Sacramento, who earned her doctorate in clinical psychology. She has worked in several clinical settings, with children, adolescents, and adults in both outpatient and inpatient settings. Additionally, she has worked as a staff psychologist and a trauma psychologist for the Federal Bureau of Prisons and as a correctional psychologist, contract psychologist, Mental Health Program Supervisor for Paroles, and Senior Psychologist Supervisor for the California Department of Corrections and Rehabilitation. She has experience in intellectual, achievement, and forensic assessment, from a clinical, teaching, and a research standpoint. Dr. Singer worked as a key researcher for the California Sex Offender Management Board from 2007 to 2009 and published several government reports on sex offender management. Additionally, Dr. Singer has published articles and chapters on corrections, intelligence assessment, the mentally ill in the criminal justice system, and sex offender policy. Dr. Singer has worked as an editor for books on international

trends in policing and corrections and is currently working on a longitudinal evaluation of a cognitive-behavioral life skills rehabilitation program for offenders in the community.

Jaime E. Slonim, EdS, is a doctoral student and graduate teaching assistant in Psychology at the Philadelphia College of Osteopathic Medicine, where she is involved in a number of multidisciplinary research initiatives related to concussion and Alzheimer's disease. Professionally, she is employed as a school psychologist at the Montgomery County Intermediate Unit, where she provides a wide range of psychological services to students enrolled in nonpublic schools across Montgomery County, Pennsylvania. She is slated to complete a specialty predoctoral internship in pediatric and adult neuropsychology at Jefferson Hospital for Neuroscience in Philadelphia.

Marsha Vasserman, PsyD, **ABPP.** is a board-certified neuropsychologist and a board-certified specialist in pediatric neuropsychology. She is a clinical neuropsychologist at the NYU Child Study Center, Institute for Learning and Academic Achievement. She conducts neuropsychological and educational evaluations for children, adolescents, and young adults with a variety of neurological and psychiatric conditions that affect cognitive functioning and learning. Her interests include assessment of ADHD, learning disorders, concussion, genetic disorders, impact of early stress on brain development, as well as working with children with hearing impairment and cochlear implants. After completing her doctorate degree, she completed a postdoctoral fellowship in neuropsychology at the NYU Child Study Center, where she focused on neuropsychological assessment of children with various disorders of learning and cognition. She also completed a 1-year rotation at Rockland Children's Psychiatric Center, where she conducted neuropsychological evaluations of children with behavioral and emotional disorders.

Marley W. Watkins, PhD, was a practicing school psychologist for 15 years before entering academia. He is currently Non-Resident Scholar in the Department of Educational Psychology at Baylor University. Previous academic positions include Professor and Chairman of the Department of Educational Psychology at Baylor University and Training Director and Professor in the doctoral school psychology programs at Arizona State University and Pennsylvania State University. Dr. Watkins is a Diplomate of the American Board of Professional Psychology and a Fellow of the School Psychology Division of the APA. His research interests include professional issues, the psychometrics of assessment and diagnosis, individual differences, and computer applications. Dr. Watkins has published more than 135 peer-reviewed journal articles and made more than 100 presentations at professional conferences.

John O. Willis, EdD, is Senior Lecturer in Assessment at Rivier University, where he has taught part time since 1980, has been the instructor for the Specialist in Assessment of Intellectual Functioning certification program since 1984, and teaches in the Psy.D. Program in Counseling and School Psychology. He has been an Assessment Specialist at the Regional Services and Education Center, in Amherst, New Hampshire, since 1974 and was also Director of Psychoeducational Services for 10 years and Acting Executive Director for 1 year. He was a teacher, administrator, and evaluator at the Crotched Mountain School in Greenfield, New Hampshire, from 1969 to 1974. He received his AB magna cum laude in psychology from Cornell University and his EdD in program and staff development from Peabody College of Vanderbilt University. Dr. Willis is coauthor of the *Guide to Identification of Learning Disabilities* (3rd ed.), *Essentials of DAS–II Assessment,* and *Essentials of IDEA for Assessment Professionals,* and author or coauthor of more than 50 chapters and articles. He has been presenting workshops in the United States and Canada since 1976. His research interest is educational evaluation of students with disabilities.

ABOUT THE ONLINE RESOURCES

Thank you for choosing *Intelligent Testing with the WISC–V*. This book includes downloadable resources designed to enhance your education and practice.

To access your resources, please follow these steps:

Step 1. Go to www.wiley.com/go/itwiscv

Step 2. Enter your email address, the password provided below, and click "submit."

Password: WISCV2016

Step 3. Select and download the listed resources.

If you need any assistance, please contact Wiley Customer Care 800-762-2974 (U.S.), 317-572-3994 (International) or visit www.wiley.com.

CONTENT INCLUDED IN THE ONLINE RESOURCES

WISC–V Interpretive Assistant 1.0: Enter the WISC-V subtest scaled and standard scores to automatically derive new index scores and process scores discussed in Chapter 8 (basic interpretation), Chapter 9 (Cattell-Horn-Carroll model), and Chapter 11 (neuropsychological perspective). The interpretive assistant also automatically completes recommended comparisons, applies critical values for significance testing, and outputs relevant base rates.

Appendixes

Appendix A: Normative Tables for New Scores (Chapters 8, 9, and 11)

Table A.1 Verbal (Expanded Crystallized) Index (Also referred to as Expanded Gc in Chapter 9) Equivalents of Sums of Scaled Scores

Table A.2 General Verbal Information (Gc-K0) Equivalents of Sums of Scaled Scores

Table A.3 Expanded Fluid Index (Also Referred to as Expanded Gf in Chapter 9) Equivalents of Sums of Scaled Scores

Table A.4 Induction (Gf-I) Equivalents of Sums of Scaled Scores

Table A.5 Working Memory Capacity (MW) Equivalents of Sums of Scaled Scores

Table A.6 Perceptual Speed (Gs-P) Equivalents of Sums of Scaled Scores

Table A.7 Scaled Score Equivalents of Total Raw Scores for Matrix Reasoning Successive and Matrix Reasoning Simultaneous Process Scores, by Age Group

Table A.8 Successive Processing Index Equivalents of Sums of Scaled Scores

Table A.9 Simultaneous Processing Index Equivalents of Sums of Scaled Scores

Appendix B: Sample Tables for Reports (Chapter 8)

Table B.1 Sample Table for Step 1b: Report and Describe the Global Composite Score(s), and Step 3b: Report and Describe the Index Scores

Table B.2: Sample Table for Step 4 Report and Describe the Subtest Scaled and Standard Scores

Appendix C: Critical Values and Base Rates for Selected WISC–V Score Comparisons (Chapter 8)

Table C.1 Critical Values for Statistically Significant Differences at the .05 Level of Significance between the Full Scale IQ and the Symbol Translation Index, by Age Group and Overall Normative Sample

Table C.2 Differences between Each Index Score and the Full Scale IQ Obtained by Various Base Rates of the Normative Sample

Table C.3 Differences between Symbol Search and Cancellation Obtained by Various Base Rates of the Normative Sample

Appendix D: Forms, Scoring Keys, and Norms for the The Child and Adolescent Academic Questionnaire (Academic-Q) and the The Child and Adolescent Behavior Questionnaire (Behavior-Q) (Chapter 6)

Jennie Kaufman Singer, Alan S. Kaufman, Susan Engi Raiford, and Diane L. Coalson

Figure D.1 The Child and Adolescent Academic Questionnaire (Academic-Q)

Figure D.2 The Child and Adolescent Behavior Questionnaire (Behavior-Q)

Figure D.3 Scoring Key for the Child and Adolescent Academic Questionnaire (Academic-Q)

Figure D.4 Scoring Key for the Child and Adolescent Behavior Questionnaire (Behavior-Q)

Table D.1 *T* Score Equivalents of Total Raw Scores for the Child and Adolescent Academic Questionnaire (Academic-Q)

Table D.2 *T* Score Equivalents of Total Raw Scores for the Child and Adolescent Behavior Questionnaire (Behavior-Q)

Appendix E: Does WISC–V Scatter Matter? (Chapter 7) by Troy Courville, Diane L. Coalson, Alan S. Kaufman, and Susan Engi Raiford

Scatter: Strengths, Weaknesses, Assets, and Deficits—Subtest Level (chapter 7)

Troy Courville, Diane L. Coalson, Alan S. Kaufman, and Susan Engi Raiford

Table E.1 Percentages of Normative, Nonclinical, and Select Special Groups Obtaining 0–5 Subtest-Level Strengths

Table E.2 Percentages of Normative, Nonclinical, and Select Special Groups Obtaining 0–5 Subtest-Level Assets

Table E.3 Percentages of Normative, Nonclinical, and Select Special Groups Obtaining 0–5 Subtest-Level Weaknesses

Table E.4 Percentages of Normative, Nonclinical, and Select Special Groups Obtaining 0–5 Subtest-Level Deficits

Appendix F: Four New Process Scores (Chapter 11)

Table F.1 Critical Values for Statistically Significant Differences at the .05 Level between Successive and Simultaneous Processing Scores, by Age Group and Overall Normative Sample

Table F.2 Differences between Successive and Simultaneous Processing Scores Obtained by Various Base Rates of the Normative Sample

Appendix G: George McCloskey Case Report Details (Chapter 13)

Appendix H: WJ IV Score Report for Patrick (Chapter 14, Case 17)

Appendix I: Factor Analyses (Chapter 20), Gary L. Canivez and Marley W. Watkins

Table I.1 WISC–V Exploratory Factor Analysis: Five Oblique Factor Solution for the Total Standardization Sample ($N = 2,200$)

Table I.2 Sources of Variance in the WISC–V for the Total Standardization Sample ($N = 2,200$) According to an Exploratory Bifactor Model (Orthogonalized Higher-Order Factor Model) with Five First-Order Factors

Table I.3 WISC–V Exploratory Factor Analysis: Four Oblique Factor Solution for the Total Standardization Sample ($N = 2,200$)

Table I.4 Sources of Variance in the WISC–V for the Total Standardization Sample ($N = 2,200$) According to an Exploratory Bifactor Model (Orthogonalized Higher-Order Factor Model) with Four First-Order Factors

Table I.5 WISC–V Exploratory Factor Analysis of the 10 Primary Subtests: Five Oblique Factor Solution for the Total Standardization Sample ($N = 2,200$)

Table I.6 Sources of Variance in the WISC–V 10 Primary Subtests for the Total Standardization Sample ($N = 2,200$) According to an Exploratory Bifactor Model (Orthogonalized Higher-Order Factor Model) with Five First-Order Factors

Table I.7 WISC–V Exploratory Factor Analysis of the 10 Primary Subtests: Four Oblique Factor Solution for the Total Standardization Sample ($N = 2,200$)

Table I.8 Sources of Variance in the WISC–V 10 Primary Subtests for the Total Standardization Sample ($N = 2,200$) According to an Exploratory Bifactor Model (Orthogonalized Higher-Order Factor Model) with Four First-Order Factors

Table I.9 CFA Fit Statistics for the WISC–V 16 Primary and Secondary Subtests and 10 Primary Subtests for the Total Standardization Sample ($N = 2,200$)

Table I.10 Sources of Variance in the WISC–V 16 Subtests for the Total Standardization Sample ($N = 2,200$) According to a CFA Bifactor Model

Table I.11 Sources of Variance in the WISC–V 10 Primary Subtests for the Total Standardization Sample ($N = 2,200$) According to a CFA Bifactor Model

AUTHOR INDEX

Page references followed by *fig* indicate an illustrated figure; followed by *t* indicate a table.

Aaron, L., 188
Achenbach, T. M., 186
Adams, K. M., 406
Adams, W., 459
Agnew, R. A., 186
Alexander, K. L., 180
Alfonso, V. C., 13, 15, 17, 21, 38, 91, 212,
    229, 234, 251, 304, 460, 615, 616,
    625, 643, 651, 685, 693, 699
Allison, J., 7
Ammirati, R., 698
Anastasi, A., 663
Anastopoulos, A. D., 177
Anderson, M. C., 467
Anderson, V., 224
Andrews, D. A., 176, 192
Angold, A., 177
Ankney, C. D., 160, 161
Anthony, J., 190
Anyan, W., 190
Archibald, L. M. D., 230
Arinoldo, C. G., 167
Aristotle, 6, 11
Armstrong, M. I., 186
Arnsten, A. F. T., 493
Asherson, P., 155
Ashkenazi, S., 155
Asparouhov, T., 659
Aspel, A. D., 698
Astone, N. M., 178
Atkinson, M. P., 186
Attar, B. K., 188, 190
Aukema, E. J., 343
Auld, R., 182
Austin, C. A., 160
Avan, B., 173
Avirett, F., 466
Awh, E., 254
Axelrod, B. N., 421
Axelrod, J., 550, 554, 555, 578
Axelrod, K. M., 689

Babad, E. Y., 688
Backman, L., 421
Baddeley, A., 467
Baggaley, A. R., 8, 697
Baguley, T., 660

Baldo, J., 343
Balla, D., 629, 642, 661, 690
Bammer, R., 343
Banich, M. T., 676
Bannatyne, A., 8, 643
Barbey, A. K., 25, 343
Barford, S. W., 38t, 117
Barnett, D., 117, 186
Barnett, D. W., 9, 699
Barnett, W. S., 339
Baron, I. S., 615, 616, 633
Barth, R., 180
Barth, R. P., 186
Bartram, D., 141
Baskin, T. W., 179
Bateman, R. W., 184
Baumeister, R. F., 179
Bear, M. F., 331, 332
Beaujean, A. A., 660, 698
Beckett, K., 188
Beech, A., 192
Beiter, M., 180
Belfiore, P. J., 182
Belk, M. S., 38t
Bellair, P. E., 189, 190
Belleville, S., 230
Bell, R., 224
Benda, B. B., 189
Bennett, D. A., 422
Bentler, P. M., 693
Bergman, M. A., 15
Bernat, F. P., 185
Berninger, V. W., 493, 494, 677
Bernstein, I. H., 641, 659
Berrueta-Clement, J. R., 176, 180
Bersani, B. E., 186
Betjemann, R. S., 343
Bienas, J. L., 422
Bigler, E. D., 407, 467
Bilder, B., 406
Binet, A., 15, 673
Biscoe, B., 191
Bishop, D. M., 188
Blackwell, L. S., 338
Blakey, W., 688
Blakey, W. A., 37, 38t, 86
Blalock, L. D., 230

Blankson, A. N., 23, 43, 460, 469, 684
Blatt, S. J., 7
Bloom, J., 183
Blumenfeld, P. C., 183
Boehm, A. E., 173, 174fig
Bonci, A., 173, 174fig
Bondi, M. W., 228
Bonifay, W. E., 659, 694
Bonta, J., 176, 192
Boomsma, A., 692
Borkowski, J. G., 190
Bornovalova, M., 177, 178
Bornstein, B. T., 24, 666, 691
Borsuk, E. R., 697
Bouchard, T. J., 685
Bowen, G. L., 178, 180, 181
Bowen, N., 180
Boxer, P., 186
Bracken, B. A., 655, 684, 686, 687, 692
Braden, J. P., 45, 661, 667, 697, 699
Bradley, F. O., 656, 688
Braeken, J., 254
Brandford, C., 190
Brandt, D., 210
Branum-Martin, L., 700
Brassard, M. R., 173, 174fig
Breaux, K., 336, 347, 372, 551
Brendgen, M., 180
Brewster, A., 180
Brewster, J., 188
Bridgeland, J. M., 180
Brines, D. B., 421
Briscoe, R., 181
Brody, G. H., 190
Brooks-Gunn, J., 187
Brown, A. J., 688
Brown, C. H., 186
Browne, A., 190
Brownfield, D., 185
Brown, T. A., 657, 693
Brown, W. G., 38
Brugman, E., 178
Brunnert, K. A., 663
Brunsden, V., 660
Buckhalt, J. A., 164
Budding, D. E., 342, 409
Buka, S. L., 190

Bullis, M., 190
Bunting, M., 230
Burchinal, M. R., 178
Burgaleta, M., 160, 343
Burke Morison, K., 180
Burns, M., 9
Burns, T. G., 615, 624, 633
Burns, W. J., 164
Buros, O. K., 702, 710
Burpeau, M., 37
Burry, A., 224
Burt, C. H., 185
Burt, K. B., 178, 184
Burton, D. B., 696
Bush, W. J., 8
Butler, F., 187
Button, C., 182

Calamia, M., 421
Calhoun, S. L., 230
Calkins, S. D., 177
Calvin, C. M., 161
Camarata, S., 161
Camerer, C., 265
Campbell, R. N., 27
Campos, E., 183
Canivez, G. L., 9, 173, 217, 266, 657, 660, 661, 683, 691, 692, 694, 695, 696, 697, 698, 699, 705, 706, 707, 710–711, 712
Carlier, M., 333
Carlson, M. J., 178
Carmody, T. D., 420
Carriere, J. A., 265
Carr, M. B., 191
Carroll, A., 185
Carroll, J. B., 10, 23, 29, 43, 251, 252, 254, 255, 282, 495, 616, 672, 676, 678, 684, 689, 692, 693
Carter, M., 183
Casillas, A., 175, 180, 182
Caspi, A., 177, 184, 185, 186
Castro, M., 184
Catron, D. A., 421
Cattell, R. B., 43, 251, 252, 282, 672, 684
Cayton, T. C., 123
Cerbone, F. G., 186
Cerda, M., 190
Chan, W., 693
Chapman, M. V., 186
Chapple, C. L., 186
Charles, J. E., 228
Chauhan, P., 188, 189, 190
Chavarría-Siles, L., 333, 334, 336, 337, 341, 344
Chen, H., 15, 123, 159, 281, 616, 654, 657, 686, 695
Cheung, G. W., 693
Chiang, M. C., 333
Chick, D., 38

Chowdhri, S., 699
Christensen, A.-L., 406
Christenson, S. L., 177
Christ, S. L., 186
Chun, C. -A., 187
Chung, H. L., 183, 184, 187
Cianci, L., 696
Cicchetti, D., 186, 629, 642, 661, 690
Clare, L., 417
Clark, M. H., 685
Climie, E. A., 265
Coalson, D. L., 5, 6, 12, 15, 20, 34, 54fig, 160, 175, 209, 236, 241, 245, 549, 550, 643, 648, 674
Cobain, M., 422
Cockerham, M., 155
Cohen, J., 15, 205t, 643
Cohen, L. E., 189
Cohen, M. J., 651
Cole, L. W., 224
Cole, R., 178
Collins, F. S., 334, 335
Colman, R. A., 189
Colom, R., 25, 254, 337, 342, 343
Compas, B. E., 186
Compton, D. L., 82, 230
Compton, S. N., 177
Conger, R. D., 178
Conners, B. W., 331
Conture, E. G., 225
Conway, C., 665
Cook, T. D., 183
Cooper, C. E., 188
Cooper, H., 182
Corapci, F., 178
Corcoran, M. E., 178
Corley, R. P., 332
Cornoldi, C., 696
Corwyn, R. F., 189
Costello, E. J., 177
Cote, S. M., 178
Coulter, C., 38, 38t, 689
Coulton, C. J., 190
Courtney, M. E., 180
Courville, T., 209
Covert, T. L., 38
Covington, M. V., 182
Crampton, D. S., 190
Creek, R. J., 699
Crews, K. J., 653
Cromwell, P., 190
Cronbach, L. J., 698
Crone, E. A., 338, 339
Cronkite, R. C., 187
Cruickshank, W. M., 32
Crum, R., 190
Cullen, F. T., 185, 191
Curwen, T., 192
Cusson, M., 184
Cytowic, R. E., 493

Dale, P. S., 333
Dallaire, D. H., 188
D'Amato, R. C., 653
D'Ambrosio, R., 190
Dang, C., 254
Daniel, M. H., 140, 141, 217, 228, 252
Das, J. P., 11, 15, 407, 410, 412, 664, 668, 700
David, M., 698
Davis-Kean, P., 184
Davis, O. S., 333
Day, N. L., 177
Dean, R. S., 464
Deary, I. J., 161, 228, 333, 343
Decker, S. L., 45
Deffenbacher, J. L., 179
DeFina, R., 188
DeFries, J. C., 332
Dehaene-Lambertz, G., 342
Dehaene, S., 342, 493, 676
Dehn, M. J., 214, 338, 342, 344, 345, 410, 411, 412, 413, 414, 415, 467
de Jong, P. F., 85, 653
DeKlyen, M., 181
Delis, D. C., 213, 224, 228, 414, 465, 466, 493
Dembo, R., 186, 187
Demetriou, A., 345
Dersh, J., 643
De Smedt, B., 340
Devena, S. E., 692
DeWitt, J., 192
Diamond, T., 190, 339
Diggle, P., 422
DiIulio, J. J., Jr., 180
Dinger, F. C., 164
Dinklage, D., 190
Dishion, T. J., 190
Dodonova, Y. A., 230
Dodonov, Y. S., 230
Dolan, R. J., 676
Dombrowski, S. C., 38t, 117
Donders, J., 265
Donnelly, W. O., 186
Doppert, J. E., 13
Doucette-Gates, A., 185
Dowden, C., 192
Dowling, C., 192
Drasgow, F., 139
Dries, C., 550, 552, 553, 554, 555, 587
Dronkers, N. F., 343
Drozdick, L., 140
Duan, X., 235
Dubois, J., 342
Duggan, E. C., 337, 343, 344
Dumontheil, I., 335, 343
Dumont, R. P., 17, 19, 20, 30, 33, 34, 297t, 550, 552, 553, 554, 555, 587, 637, 643, 651, 704, 706, 707, 708, 709, 711, 712
Duncan, G. J., 187, 190
Dunn, L. M., 664

Dunn, T. J., 660
Durrant, S. L., 185
Dworksy, A., 180
Dykiert, D., 161
Dynda, A. M., 46, 230

Earles, J. A., 696
Earls, F., 188
Eccles, J. S., 178, 183, 184, 201
Eckenrode, J., 190
Edwards, J. L., 10
Edwards, R., 10
Eggert, L. L., 180
Eisner, M. P., 178
Eklund, K., 550, 551, 552, 556, 600
Elkovitch, N., 192
Elliott, C. D., 11, 32, 253, 677
Elliott, D., 188
El-Sheikh, M., 164
Enders, C. K., 184
English, D. J., 190
Englund, J. A., 45
Engri, M. D., 160
Entwisle, D. R., 180
Epperson, D. L., 192
Erdodi, L. A., 57, 91
Evans, G. W., 178
Evans, J. J., 467
Exner, J. E., Jr., 54*fig*
Eysenck, M. W., 467
Ezell, M., 189

Fagan, J. R., 668
Falanagan, D., 251, 253, 420
Fantuzzo, J. W., 5, 8, 37, 38*t*, 86, 689, 697, 698
Farmer, R. L., 698
Farnworth, M., 176, 180
Farrington, D. P., 178, 180, 185, 188
Faust, D., 698, 699
Favez, N., 658, 693
Fehrmann, P. G., 661
Fein, D., 224, 414, 493
Fergusson, D. M., 185
Fernandes, C., 161, 228
Fernández, G., 333
Ferrer, E., 254, 421, 422
Feuerstein, R., 27
Feurerstein, R., 493
Fina, A. D., 696
Fine, J. G., 15, 160, 161, 616, 657, 696
Finkel, D., 332, 333
Fink, S. L., 224
Finn, S. E., 265
Fiorello, C. A., 217, 265, 342, 414, 415, 416, 417
Fischer, C. T., 265
Fisher, P. A., 180
Fjell, A. M., 335
Flanagan, D. P., 12, 13, 14, 15, 16, 17, 18, 21, 26, 28, 29, 34, 43, 212, 217, 227,

228, 234, 235, 251, 254, 255, 256, 257, 258, 262, 263, 304, 413, 414, 460, 552, 553, 556, 615, 616, 625, 633, 643, 644, 651, 685, 693, 699, 700
Fletcher-Janzen, E. P., 17, 21, 31, 336, 346, 348, 554, 555, 556
Fletcher, J. M., 424, 700
Fletch-Janzen, E., 419
Floyd, R. G., 412, 414, 415, 417, 467, 494, 620, 627, 685, 686, 687, 688, 698, 702, 710
Flynn, J. R., 419, 423
Fogel, S. J., 183
Fogg, L., 181
Forbes, C., 343
Ford, D., 173
Ford, L., 173
Foss, T., 693
Fowers, D., 192
Frakowiak, R. S. J., 676
Francis, D. J., 700
Frank, G., 10
Franklin, M., 37
Franova, L., 161
Franzler, J. H., 415
Fratello, J., 193
Freberg, M. E., 696
Fredricks, J. A., 183
French, J. W., 495, 627
Fried, P. J., 343
Friston, K. J., 676
Frith, C. D., 676
Fuchs, D., 230, 688, 700
Fuchs, L. S., 230, 688
Fukuda, K., 254
Fuligni, A. J., 201
Furr-Holden, C. C. M., 180
Fussenegger, B., 85, 469

Gaboury, A. R., 661
Gabrieli, J. D. E., 343
Gale, C. R., 161, 337
Gallo, A., 421
Galyean, K., 191
Garcia-Barriera, M. A., 337, 343, 344
Gardner, H., 12, 30, 252
Garfinkel, I., 188
Garfinkel, R. S., 178
Garland, K. J., 139
Garlick, D., 338
Garswell, S. B., 184
Gasper, J., 183
Gathercole, S. E., 230
Gazzaniga, M. S., 676
Geenen, S., 180
Geller, A., 188
Gendreau, P., 192
Ge, X., 178
Gibbs, J. J., 185
Gignac, G. E., 660, 694
Gilani, N., 161

Gilchrist, L., 181
Gill, M. M., 7, 224
Giofrè, D., 696
Giorgala, K., 345
Gladden, R. M., 180
Gläscher, J., 342, 343
Glaser, B. A., 45
Glueck, E. T., 184
Glueck, S., 184
Glutting, J. J., 5, 8, 217, 654, 656, 688, 692, 696, 697, 698, 699
Godber, T., 224, 225
Godfrey, K. M., 337
Goebel-Fabbri, A. E., 190
Goel, V., 343
Goerge, R., 180
Goggin, C., 192
Golay, P., 658, 660, 693, 694, 696
Golden, C. J., 185, 406
Goldschmidt, L., 177
Goldstein, S., 11, 14, 407, 410, 411, 664, 668
Goodenough, F. L., 163
Good, R., 683
Good, R. H., 699
Gordon, B. N., 493
Gordon, R. P., 45
Gore, K. S., 192
Gore, S., 190
Gorman-Smith, D., 181, 190
Gorsuch, R. L., 37, 38*t*, 86, 657, 688, 689, 692
Gottfredson, L. S., 228, 671, 673–674
Gottfredson, M. R., 184, 185
Gover, A. R., 186
Grafman, J., 25, 343
Graham, S., 190
Granberg, B. W., 421
Greathouse, S., 182
Greenberg, M. T., 181
Green, E. D., 334
Green, S. B., 659, 660
Grégoire, J., 209, 210, 241, 244
Greif, J. L., 183
Gresham, F. M., 9, 10
Gresham, F. M, 699
Griever, D., 185
Griffin, H., 192
Grigorenko, E. L., 27
Gross, D., 181
Grossman, J. S., 224
Groth-Marnat, G., 224
Groves, W. B., 178
Gruber, E., 179
Grunwald, H. E., 177, 187
Guerra-Carrillo, B., 338
Guerra, N. G., 188
Guilford, J. P., 15, 251, 641
Gustafsson, J. E., 628
Gutman, L. M., 178
Guttmacher, A. E., 334

Guyer, M. S., 334
Guyrke, J. S., 164

Hadorn, M. B., 615, 703, 704, 705, 706–707, 708–709, 710, 711, 712
Hagen, E. P., 8
Haier, R. J., 336, 342
Haig, B. D., 657
Hajovsky, D. B., 161
Hale, J. B., 217, 342, 414, 415, 416, 417, 459, 464, 467, 468, 667, 696, 699, 700
Hallenbeck, C. E., 224
Halliday-Boykins, C. A., 190
Halsey, P. A., 181
Hambleton, R. K., 141
Hamilton, J. M., 228
Hamlett, C., 230
Hammeke, T. A., 224
Hammill, D. D., 8
Hanlon, T. E., 184
Hanna, G. S., 656, 688
Hannay, H. J., 408
Hannon, L., 188
Hansen, A. L., 177
Hardy-Braz, S. T., 663
Hardy, J. B., 27
Harland, P., 178
Harlow, C. W., 177
Harold, G., 178
Harrington, H., 177
Harris, A. J., 224
Harris, B., 191
Harris, G. T., 192
Harris, J. G., 159
Harrison, P. L., 28, 661
Harris, P. W., 177, 187
Hartlage, L. C., 406
Hartman, J. L., 188
Hartmann, J., 263, 283, 552, 554
Hartmann, P., 228
Hartz, E., 493
Harvey, V. S., 265
Hass, M. R., 265
Haviland, M. G., 659, 695
Hay, D. F., 178
Hayiou-Thomas, M. E., 333
Haynes, S. N, 696
Haynie, D. L., 188, 190
Hazen, A., 178
Hebben, N., 406, 417, 418, 466
Hebert, K. R., 15
Helsen, M., 179
Henik, A., 155
Henning-Stout, M., 697
Henry, B., 184
Henry, D. B., 181
Herman, D. D., 422
Herting, J. R., 180
Hertz-Pannier, L., 342
Hetterscheidt, L. A., 117
Hewett, J. E., 421

Hiemenz, J. R., 419
Higgins, G. E., 185
Hill, G. D., 186
Hill, N. E., 178
Hipwell, A. E., 178
Hirschfield, P. J., 183
Hirschi, T., 184, 185
Hirshoren, A., 8
Hirvenoja, R., 421
Hiscock, M. K., 424
Hodges, K., 185, 193, 210
Hofer, S. M., 252, 422
Hoffmann, J. P., 186
Hofman, M. A., 336
Holcombe, R., 183
Holdnack, J. A., 140, 159, 213, 643
Holen, M. C., 656, 688
Holland, F., 422
Holley, G., 38*t*
Hollingworth, L., 696
Holmes, J., 339
Holzinger, K. J., 660
Honzik, M. P., 163
Hooper, S., 178
Hopwood, C., 57, 91
Horn, J. L., 29, 43, 69, 251, 252, 253, 255, 333, 422, 460, 672, 684
Horton, A. M., 334, 411
Horwitz, E., 210
Horwood, L. J., 185
Hough, R. L., 178
Howard, E., 180
Howard-Jones, P., 340, 346
Howell, R. D., 693
Howieson, D. B., 467
Howse, R. B., 177
Hubley, A. M., 661
Hulbert, S., 212, 228
Hu, L.-T., 693
Hunsley, J., 696, 697
Hunt, E., 25, 177, 178, 332, 337, 338, 339
Hunter, M., 692
Hunt, J. McV., 224
Hurlburt, M., 180

Iacono, W. G., 228
Iftikhar, R., 161
Ingersoll, G., 180
Ingoldsby, E. M., 178
Ireland, T. O., 186
Irwin, C. E., Jr., 180
Irwing, P., 161
Irwin, M., 190
Iseman, J. S., 14
Ivry, C. F., Jr., 493
Izard, C., 177

Jacobs, L. D., 420
Jacobson, M. W., 228
Jaeggi, S. M., 25, 332, 337, 338, 339
Jaffee, S. R., 186

James, K., 683
James, T., 683
Janzen, T. M., 38*t*, 117
Jastak, J., 209, 210, 220
Jensen, A., 670–671, 672–673, 674
Jimerson, S. R., 183
Jirout, J. J., 161
Johnson, A., 38, 91
Johnson, C. K., 161
Johnson, K. E., 422
Johnson, M. B., 8
Johnson, M. H., 335, 336, 338
Johnson, W., 228, 343, 466, 685
Jolles, D. D., 338, 339
Jolles, J., 421
Jones, A. M., 459, 471, 551, 554, 556
Jones, C. H., 37, 38, 38*t*, 689
Jones, J. G., 421
Jones, K., 181
Jones, R. N., 422
Jonson-Reid, M., 186
Jorgenson, L. A., 341, 346
Julion, W., 181
Jung, R. E., 336, 342
Juni, S., 224, 225
Juolasmaa, A., 421

Kabbani, N. S., 180
Kadlubek, R. M., 38*t*, 91
Kagen, J., 27
Kamphaus, R. W., 11, 193, 234, 492, 629, 642, 651, 691, 698, 699
Kano, Y., 693
Kant, I., 6
Kaplan, E., 15, 27, 224, 225, 406, 414, 459, 465, 466, 493, 553, 651
Karcher, M. J., 191
Katz, B., 25
Katz, L. I., 699
Kaufman, A. S., 5, 6, 7, 8, 9, 10, 11, 13, 15, 16, 17, 18, 19, 20, 24, 25, 26, 28, 29, 32, 33, 54*fig*, 85, 128, 160, 161, 163, 164, 166, 167, 168, 169, 175, 209, 210, 211, 212, 217, 220, 221, 228, 229, 235, 236, 238, 245, 252, 253, 256, 332, 411, 415, 416, 420, 421, 422, 424, 493, 553, 615, 616, 629, 633, 637, 642, 643, 648, 651, 661, 663, 664, 667, 668, 699, 703, 712
Kaufman, J. C., 21, 24, 27, 161
Kaufman, N. L., 8, 9, 10, 11, 23, 32, 85, 128, 160, 161, 164, 167, 168, 169, 236, 238, 253, 411, 420, 493, 549, 550, 553, 629, 642, 651, 661, 664, 668, 690, 699, 712
Kaufman, S. B., 21, 228
Kausler, D. H., 422
Kavale, K., 8
Kavale, K. A., 667, 699
Keane, S. P., 177
Kearns, D. M., 700

Keeler, G., 177
Keith, T. Z., 14, 15, 160, 161, 281, 460, 616,
    621, 622, 627, 629, 633, 657, 660,
    661, 693, 695, 696
Kellerman, H., 224
Keller, P. S., 164
Keller, T. E., 181
Kelley, E. M., 225
Kelly, P. J., 191
Kelly, R. J., 164
Kemper, C. C., 179
Kemp, S. L., 15, 407, 409, 464, 493, 651
Kerlinger, F. N., 11
Kessel, J. B, 692
Kim, D. H., 189
Kim, H. K., 180
Kim, K. H., 139
Kim, S., 234, 699
Kingsley, J. M., 230, 235
Kirchner, E. E., 185
Kirk, U., 15, 407, 409, 464, 493, 651
Kirkwood, B., 173
Klebanov, P. K., 187
Kleppman, M., 284
Kline, J., 210
Kline, R. B., 693
Klingberg, T., 343
Klove, H., 406
Knight, R. T., 493
Koenig, O., 493, 494
Kohlhagen, J., 651
Konold, T. R., 173, 217, 696
Koopman, C., 186
Korbin, J. E., 190
Korkman, M., 15, 407, 409, 464, 468,
    493, 651
Kosslyn, S. M., 493, 494
Kotria-Topić, 345
Kotz, K. M., 228
Kozey, M. L., 173
Koziol, L. F., 342, 409
Kramer, J. H., 414, 465, 466, 493
Kramer, J. J., 697
Kranzler, J. H., 14, 15, 412, 414, 417, 616,
    627, 657, 686, 687, 688, 696, 698,
    702, 710
Krawchuk, L. L., 38t, 117
Kreiner, D. S., 696
Kroesbergen, E. H., 14
Kroneman, L., 178, 190
Krueger, F., 343
Kucian, K., 339
Kuentzel, J. G., 117
Kuntsi, J., 155
Kush, J. C., 9, 692, 694, 695
Kyllonen, P. C., 495

LaForte, E. M., 14, 254
Lambert, W., 230
Landenberger, N. A., 191
Landerl, K., 85, 469

Landsverk, J., 180
Lane, E. C., 189
Lane, S., 687
Langabeer, K., 186
Lanza, S. T., 181
Larsen, L., 228
Latessa, E. J., 176
Laub, J. H., 177, 184, 186, 189
Laurent, J., 10
Law, C. M., 337
Leaf, P. J., 180
Leary, M. R., 179
LeBlanc, J. C., 178
Lecerf, T., 658, 693
Leech, S. L., 177
Lee, D., 688
Lee, D. L., 182
Lee, S. W., 689
LeForgee, M. H., 467
Le, H., 182
Lehr, C. A., 177
Lei, P. -W., 217
Lei, P.-W., 696
Lench, H. C., 696
Lennon, R. T., 12–13
Leslie, L. K., 180
Letourneau, E. J., 186
Levine, M. D., 493, 494
Levitt, R., 224
Lewis, T., 186
Lezak, M. D., 10, 224, 409, 467
Liao, Q., 185
Lichtenberger, E. O., 9, 17, 19, 21, 28,
    54fig, 161, 236, 245, 251, 252, 347,
    362, 415, 416, 420, 421, 422, 550,
    552, 554, 555, 578
Lightfoot, D., 181
Lilienfeld, S. O., 698, 699
Lillie-Blanton, M., 190
Lim, S. A., 178, 182
Lindsay, J. J., 182
Lin, W.-H, 186, 187
Lipschitz, D. S., 190
Lipsey, M. W., 191
Lipszyc, J., 155
Litrownik, A. J., 186
Little, M., 187
Little, T., 192
Litt, R. A., 465, 653
Liu, C., 254
Liu, X., 24, 161
Li, Y., 422
Lleras, C., 182
LoBello, S. G., 38t
Locke, V., 159
Lockwood, B., 177, 187
Lodge, G. T., 265
Loeber, R., 178, 184
Loe, S. A., 38, 91
Loewenstein, G., 265
Lohman, D. F., 6, 256, 495

Long, C. J., 406
Longman, R. S., 210, 241
Loro, B., 210
Loukas, A., 178
Lowenkamp, C. T., 176
Lucchini, S. E., 178
Lucio, R., 177, 178, 182
Luck, D., 155
Lunn, M., 422
Luria, A. R., 411, 414, 424, 448, 493, 553,
    648, 676, 680
Lurie, M., 347, 362, 549, 552, 554, 556
Lutey, C. L., 8
Lynam, D., 185
Lynch, M., 186
Lynch, R. S., 179
Lynn, R., 161
Lynskey, M. T., 185

McArdle, J. J., 252, 422
McBride, G., 17, 20, 32
McCabe, D. P., 230
McCabe, K. M., 178
McCarthy, D., 7, 167
McCloskey, G., 15, 21, 22, 26, 231, 238,
    331, 405, 414, 493, 494, 495, 497,
    523, 553, 554, 556, 669, 677, 705,
    707, 708, 709–710, 711, 712
McCord, D. M., 139, 140
McCrae, J. S., 186
McCrea, J. S., 411, 412
McCrimmon, A. W., 265
McDermott, P. A., 5, 8, 9, 228, 656, 688,
    691, 696, 697, 698, 699
McDonald, R. P., 656
McGee, C. L., 213
McGee, R., 183
McGill, R. J., 645, 704, 707, 708, 709,
    710, 712
McGrew, K. S., 11, 14, 15, 17, 20, 23, 26,
    29, 43, 190, 234, 251, 253, 254, 255,
    262, 265, 460, 467, 468, 616, 644,
    648, 651, 653, 684
Machamer, G. M., 179
McInnes, L., 422
Macintosh, R., 224
Macklin, A., 191
McLanahan, S. S., 178
McLean, J. E., 221
McLeod, J. D., 190
Macmann, D. W., 9
Macmann, G. M., 699
McNeish, R., 186
McNulty, T. L., 189, 190
Maerlender, A., 494, 495
Mahler, K. A., 186
Mahoney, A., 186
Malmgren, K. W., 186
Manly, J. T., 186
Mann, M., 688
Mapou, R. L., 494

Mares, D., 187
Mar-Hayim, M., 688
Maricle, D. E., 413, 414, 460, 465
Markon, K., 421
Marks, H. M., 180
Marks, W. J., 38*t*, 91
Markus, H. R., 183
Markwardt, F. C., 664
Mark-Zigdon, N., 155
Marston, N. C., 691
Martin, B. E., 691
Martinez, R., 187
Martyn, C. N., 337
Mascolo, J. T., 17, 23, 27, 33, 263, 304, 552, 553, 556, 615, 685
Mash, E. J., 697
Mastoras, S. M., 265
Matarazzo, J. D., 8, 15, 420, 421, 422, 423, 663
Mather, N., 11, 17, 30, 31, 32, 33, 190, 253, 550, 551, 552, 556, 600, 651
Matshazi, D. G. M., 176, 193
Mattis, S., 155
Mattson, P. D., 699
Mayes, S. D., 230
Mayman, M., 7, 209
Mazziotta, J. C., 676
Mead, A. D., 139
Meehl, P. E., 692
Meeus, W., 179
Meisel, S. M., 186
Mellits, E. D., 27
Ménard, É., 230
Ménard, M.-C., 230
Mennis, J., 177, 187
Mersky, J. P., 186
Messick, S., 689
Meyer, G. J., 20, 696
Miciak, J., 700
Milam, A. J., 180
Milam, D. A., 697, 698, 699
Milberg, W. P., 406, 466
Millager, R. A., 225
Millberg, W., 417, 418
Miller, D. C., 19, 217, 238, 331, 405, 406, 407, 408, 409, 413, 414, 419, 459, 460, 464, 466, 467, 468, 469, 471, 492, 551, 554, 556, 645, 653, 704, 707, 708, 709, 710, 712
Millsap, R. E., 693
Millstein, S. G., 180
Milne, B. J., 177
Mincy, R. B., 188
Mischel, W., 680
Mitchell-Herzfeld, S., 189
Mittenberg, W., 224
Moffitt, T. E., 177, 184, 185, 186, 201
Mogulescu, S., 193
Moll, K., 85, 469

Molnar, B. E., 190
Montague, M., 184
Monzalvo, K., 342
Moon, G., 37, 38*t*, 86
Moon, G. W., 688
Moos, R. H., 187
Morris, R., 224, 414, 493
Moss, M. B., 343
Mottron, L., 230
Mrazik, M., 38*t*, 85, 117, 119
Muller, R. T., 190
Mulvay, E. P., 183
Munro, S., 339
Murphy, R., 15, 26, 494, 677
Murray, J., 178, 179, 188, 207
Murray, R. A., 38, 38*t*, 689
Muthen, B., 659
Myers, P. I., 8

Nagin, D. S., 178
Naglieri, J. A., 10, 11, 14, 15, 19, 24, 26, 210, 214, 241, 407, 411, 412, 663, 664, 665, 666, 667, 668, 691, 700, 704–705, 709, 711, 712
Nation, K., 465, 653
Nee, D. E., 343
Negreiros, J., 173
Neisser, U., 493
Neitzel, R., 691
Nelson, J. M., 660
Neugarten, B. L., 184
Neugarten, D. A., 184
Neumann, C. S., 185
Newcombe, N. S., 161
Nicholas, W. K., 421
Nickerson, R. S., 699
Niebling, B. C., 661, 667, 697
Niileksela, C. R., 15, 620
Nilsson, L., 421
Nix, R. L., 181
Noll, J., 252, 253
Nonnemaker, J. M., 190
Noyes, J. M., 139
Nunnally, J. C., 641, 659
Nyberg, L.-G., 421
Nyborg, H., 161, 228
Nye, B., 182

Oakland, T., 141, 689
Ober, B. A., 465
O'Callaghan, F. J., 337
Ochoa, S. H., 46, 230
O'Connor, C., 183
Odgers, C. L., 190
Oetting, E. R., 179
O'Grady, K. E., 184
Oh, I., 182
O'Leary, S. D., 615, 633
Olsson, U. H., 693
Orr, D. P., 180
Orsini, A., 212, 228, 696

Ortiz, S. O., 13, 15, 21, 46, 230, 234, 251, 255, 304, 460, 643, 651, 699
Otero, T. M., 339, 410, 414, 663, 665, 667
Ott, M., 340
Ouellette, P., 181
Ou, S. R., 182
Outakoski, J., 421
Owen, A. M., 343
Oyserman, D., 183

Palejwala, M. H., 160, 161
Pan, T., 159
Paolitto, A. W., 210, 241
Papolos, D., 155
Paradiso, M. A., 331
Pardini, D. A., 184
Paris, A. H., 183
Parker, F. L., 178
Parker, J. C., 421
Parkin, J. R., 698
Pascual-Leone, A., 337, 343, 345
Passolunghi, M. C., 230
Patinella, L., 38, 91
Patterson, C. H., 209
Patterson, G. R., 190
Paul, E. J., 25
Pauly, H., 85
Pawlby, S., 178
Pears, K. C., 180
Pearson, K., 712
Pearson, N. A., 464
Pedersen, S., 180
Pelletier, S. L. F., 419
Penke, L., 343
Pennington, B. F., 523
Perkins, L. A., 494
Petersen, S. E., 344
Peyrot, M., 186
Pezzuti, L., 212, 228, 696
Piaget, J., 27, 345
Pickering, S. J., 230
Pilowsky, D. J., 180
Pinker, S., 265
Pinsonneault, P., 184
Piore, A., 346
Piquero, A. R., 184
Plomin, R., 162, 164, 332
Polomin, R., 333
Posner, M. I., 339, 343, 344, 493, 494
Posthuma, D., 333
Pottebaum, S. M., 661
Povenmire-Kirk, T., 191
Power, E., 336, 346, 348, 354, 555, 556
Powers, L., 37
Powers, L. E., 180
Pratt, T. C., 185
Preiss, M., 161
Prelow, H. M., 178
Pressey, S. L., 224
Prifitera, A., 37, 159, 173, 217, 494, 643

Princiotta, D., 410, 411
Prino, C. T., 186

Quintana, S. M., 179
Quist, R. M., 176, 193

Rabbitt, P., 422, 423
Rader, D. E., 38, 91
Raichle, M. E., 493
Raiford, S. E., 5, 6, 12, 15, 54*fig*, 123, 140,
    160, 164, 168, 172, 175, 209, 236,
    245, 643, 648, 674
Raine, A., 184
Ralston, C. A., 192
Ramsay, M. C., 697
Rao, S. M., 224
Rapaport, D., 7, 224
Rapp, B., 676
Rapport, L. J., 421
Rashotte, C. A., 464
Rasmusson, A. M., 190
Raudenbush, S., 188
Rauh, V. A., 178
Ravert, C. M., 696
Ray, G. E., 38*t*
Raykov, T., 694
Reed, M. S., 493
Ree, M. J., 696
Reeve, C. L., 228
Reijneveld, S. A., 178
Reise, S. P., 659, 660, 689, 692, 694, 695
Reiss, W. J., 265
Reitan, R. M., 406
Renn, P., 186
Rensvold, R. B., 693
Reppucci, N. D., 188, 189, 190
Reschly, D. J., 699
Revelle, W., 659
Reverte, I., 658, 693
Reynolds, A. J., 182, 186
Reynolds, C. A., 332, 333
Reynolds, C. R., 11, 17, 19, 21, 193, 221,
    253, 334, 407, 411, 459, 492, 629,
    642, 651, 688, 691, 697, 698, 699,
    708–709
Reynolds, M. R., 15, 21, 24, 160, 161, 251,
    460, 616, 620, 622, 627, 628, 629,
    693, 696, 703, 704, 705, 706–707,
    710, 711, 712
Rhoad, A., 688
Rhoades, B. L., 181
Rice, M. E., 192
Richard, D. C. S., 57, 91
Richardson, G. A., 177
Richards, T. L., 493, 494
Richman, J. M., 178, 180
Rimm, S., 235
Robbins, S. B., 182
Robbins, T. W., 493
Roberts, A. M., 45
Roberts, J. E., 178

Roberts, L. G., 160
Robertson, A. A., 185
Robertson, L. C., 493
Rodriguez, S., 338
Roeser, R. W., 184
Roeyers, H., 155
Rogers, J., 15, 26, 494, 677
Rogers, R., 185
Roid, G. H., 11, 29, 253
Rolfhus, E., 494, 643, 674
Ronnlund, M., 421
Roodenrys, S., 230
Rosen, A., 692
Rosenfeld, R., 187
Rosenthal, J. A., 205*t*
Rosseel, Y., 281
Rossier, J., 658, 693
Rothbart, M. K., 339, 343, 344, 493, 494
Rotheram-Borus, M. J., 186
Roubertoux, P. L., 333
Rourke, B. P., 406
Rowe, E. W., 230, 234, 235, 699
Rugel, R. P., 643
Rumberger, R. W., 178, 182
Ruscio, J., 699
Rushmore, R. J., III, 343
Rushton, J. P., 160, 161
Rutland, A. F., 27
Ryan, J. J., 37, 224, 696
Ryan, J. P., 186

Sabers, D., 37
Saklofske, D. H., 15, 159, 161, 217, 494,
    643, 648
Salmon, D. P., 228
Salsich, A., 193
Salthouse, T. A., 161, 252, 421, 422, 423
Sameroff, A. J., 178
Sampson, R. J., 177, 178, 184, 186, 188, 189
Sánchez-Escobedo, P., 696
Sanders, M., 173
Sattler, J. M., 8, 18, 217, 238, 240, 244
Scalora, M. J., 192
Schachar, R., 155
Schafer, R., 7, 224
Schatz, J., 421
Scheiber, C., 161, 173
Schellenberg, R. P., 697
Schiefele, U., 184
Schmeidler, J., 186
Schmithorst, V. J., 160
Schmitt, T. A., 657
Schmitz-Scherzer, R., 422
Schneider, J., 253, 551, 554, 555
Schneider, W. J., 12, 17, 18, 20, 21, 22, 23,
    24, 28, 29, 34, 43, 234, 251, 256, 262,
    263, 265, 281, 460, 468, 616, 644,
    648, 698, 703–704, 708, 711–712
Schoenwald, S. K., 186
Schrank, F. A., 11, 14, 253, 254, 460, 651
Schroeder, D. H., 421

Schroeders, U., 139, 140
Schuck, A. M., 188
Schultz, R., 190
Schwalbe, C. S., 177, 192, 207
Schwartz, B., 161
Schwartz, B. S., 422
Schwartz, J. A., 224
Schwean, V. L., 265
Schwebach, A., 14
Schweinhart, L. J., 176, 180
Seashore, H. G., 210, 211
Sellers, A. H., 164, 167
Shadish, W. R., 685
Shady, T. A., 189
Shah, P., 25
Shakow, D., 224
Shamama-tus-Sabah, S., 161
Shapiro, M. B., 419
Sharp, D., 178
Shaw, D. S., 178
Shaw, P., 342
Shaw, S. R., 10, 697, 699
Shaywitz, B. A., 17, 26, 339, 340, 341
Shaywitz, S. E., 17, 26, 339, 340, 341
Sheidow, A. J., 186
Sheldon, S. B., 181
Shelton, T. L., 177
Sheslow, D., 459
Shi, J., 235
Sholey, K. A., 467
Sickmund, M., 189
Silva, P. A., 184
Silver, E., 188
Silver, L. B., 414, 415, 416
Simon, B. D., 184
Simons, L. G., 185
Simons-Morton, B., 183
Simons, R. L., 185
Sinclair, M. F., 177
Singer, J. K., 173, 175, 206, 424, 425, 555
Sioris, P. A., 423
Slate, J. R., 37, 38, 38*t*, 689
Slaten, C. D., 179
Slobogin, C., 176, 177, 192
Slonim, J., 493
Slymen, D. J., 180
Smith, C. A., 186
Smith, D., 422
Smithgall, C., 180
Smith, L., 698
Smith, P., 161, 176, 228
Smyth, M. M., 467
Snow, R. E., 698
Snyder, H., 189
Solomon, A. K., 343
Sorenson, A. M., 185
Sotaniemi, K., 421
Southwick, S. M., 190
Spanoudis, G., 345
Sparrow, S., 629, 642, 661, 690
Spatz-Widom, C., 190

Spearman, C. E., 13, 15, 251, 252, 656–657, 672, 673, 674, 680, 684, 712
Spector, J., 494
Speltz, M. L., 181
Spencer, R. J., 406
Spieker, S. J., 181
Spilsbury, J. C., 190
Spinath, B., 164
Sporns, O., 493, 494
Spreen, O., 692
Stankov, L., 252
Stanley, J. C., 656, 688
Stanovich, K., 190
Steinberg, L., 183, 187
Steinhart, D., 192
Steinmayr, R., 164
Stern, A. R., 699
Sternberg, R. J., 10, 27
Steubing, K. K., 424
Stewart, W. F., 422
Stillman, P., 37
Stone, C. A., 687
Stott, D. H., 691
Stouthamer-Loeber, M., 184
Strand, S., 228
Strauss, E., 692
Stuebing, K. K., 700
Stump, K., 45
Stuss, D. T., 493
Styck, K. M., 661
Sullivan, C. J., 177
Su, S. S., 186
Suzuki, L. A., 668
Swanson, H. L., 230
Swerdlik, M. E., 10
Swets, J. A., 692
Swineford, F., 660
Szarko, J. E., 688

Tabib, S., 651
Taki, Y., 160
Takkunen, J., 421
Tallent, N., 265
Tammes, C. K., 335
Tanenhaus, D. S., 187
Taub, G., 15
Taub, G. E., 616, 657, 685, 696
Taylor, A., 186
Taylor, B., 183
Taylor, J. L., 265
Taylor, L. R., 191
Teachout, M. S., 696
Teasdale, B., 188
Teicher, A., 265
Temple, C., 493, 676
te Nijenhuis, J., 685
Terman, L. M., 13, 688
Testa, M. F., 186
Teuber, H.-L., 680
Theisen, M. E., 421
Thode, H. C., 155

Thomas, H., 422
Thomas, J., 339
Thompson, C. C., 421
Thompson, D. E., 230, 235
Thompson, G. B., 224
Thompson, T. W., 338
Thornberry, T. P., 186
Thorndike, E., 6
Thorndike, R. L., 6, 7, 8, 13
Thurstone, L. L., 13, 15, 210, 251, 253
Thurstone, T. G., 15
Tienari, P., 421
Tobin, R. M., 251, 635
Todis, B., 190
Tolan, P. H., 181, 188, 190
Tolar, T. D., 700
Toombs, N. J., 189
Torgeson, J. K., 464
Trahan, L., 424
Tranel, D., 421, 467
Treat, T. A., 692
Tremblay, R. E., 178
Trice, A. D., 188
Trobliger, R., 224, 225
Troye, S. V., 693
Tucker-Drob, E. M., 422
Turken, A. U., 343
Turkheimer, En.N., 190, 333
Turner, M. G., 188
Tyler, K. A., 186
Tyson, C., 181
Tyson, D. F., 178
Tzeng, O.J.L., 340
Tzuriel, D., 27

Ullman, D. P., 192, 697
Unruh, D., 191
Unsworth, N., 254
Urbina, S., 663

Vaillancourt, T., 178
Valencia, R. R., 668
Valero-Cabré, A., 343
Valescu, S., 191
van Bergen, E., 653
Van Boxtel, M. P. J., 421
Van Breukelen, G. J. P., 421
Van der Elst, W., 421
VanDerHeyden, A., 9
van der Leij, A., 85
van der Sluis, S., 85
Van De Voorde, S., 155
Vandiver, B. J., 696
Vandiver, T. A., 191
Van Diviner, B., 494
Van Hagen, J., 7
van Leeuwen, T., 340
Van Luit, J. E., 14
Vaske, J., 191
Vasserman, M., 424, 437, 549, 551, 552, 553, 554, 555, 568

Vaughn, S., 700
Verhulst, R. C., 178
Verloove-Vanhorick, S. P., 178
Vernon, P. E., 693
Verte, S., 155
Vicken, R. J., 692
Viezel, K. D., 651
Vig, S., 173
Viljoen, J. L., 192
Vincent, B., 191
Visscher, P. M., 161
Vitacco, M. J., 185
Vitaro, F., 180
Vogel, E. K., 354
Vogel, K. K., 698
Vollebergh, W., 179
Vollmer, M., 699
von Stumm, S., 162, 164
Voress, J. K., 459
Vygotsky, L., 27

Wadsworth, S. J., 332, 333, 334
Wagner, B. M., 186
Wagner, R. K., 464
Wahlstrom, D., 140
Waintrup, M., 190
Walden, T. A., 225
Walhovd, K. B., 335
Wang, M. -T., 183
Wang, Z., 25
Ward, L. C., 15
Ward, S., 696
Ward, T., 696
Warren, S. A., 38
Wasserman, J. D., 684, 686, 687, 692
Watkins, M. W., 8, 9, 217, 228, 266, 616, 654, 657, 660, 661, 683, 688, 692, 694, 696, 697, 698, 699, 705, 706, 707, 710–711, 712
Waugh, K. W., 8
Weaver, C. M., 190
Weber, M., 265
Wechsler, D., 1, 5, 6, 7, 8, 11, 12, 13, 15, 16, 26, 32, 38, 43, 46, 122, 159, 161, 163, 164, 167, 187, 209, 210, 211, 224, 229, 234, 237, 237fig, 241, 342, 343, 420, 423, 459, 468, 615, 616, 617, 618, 620, 624, 631, 635, 637, 638, 639, 640, 643, 644, 645, 648, 651, 652, 655, 663–664, 665, 666, 671–672, 674–675, 677, 680, 683, 684, 690fig, 691, 695, 703, 711, 712
Weiner, I. B., 702, 710
Weiss, L. G., 15, 159, 164, 168, 169, 172, 173, 217, 281, 424, 494, 616, 621, 622, 628, 643, 648, 657, 674, 695, 696
Welcher, D. W., 27
Welsch, W. N., 187
Wendling, B. J., 17, 460, 653
Wentworth-Rohr, I., 224
Wesman, A. G., 24

Western, B., 188
Whitaker, J., 15, 26, 494, 677
White, J. L., 185
Whitfield-Gabrieli, S., 343
Whitman, T. L., 190
Widom, C. S., 186, 188
Wiens, A., 421
Wiersema, J. R., 155
Wigfield, A., 184
Wildeman, C., 188
Wilhelm, O., 139, 140
Wilkerson, D., 181
Willburger, E., 85, 469
Willett, J. B., 183
Williams, J. E., 139, 140
Williams, L., 186
Williams, R. L., 8
Williams, S., 183
Willis, J. O., 17, 20, 21, 22, 26, 30, 33, 263,
    283, 297*t*, 552, 554, 637, 643, 704,
    706, 707, 708, 709, 711, 712
Willis, W. G., 698
Willson, V. L., 688
Wilson, R. S., 422
Winfree, L. T., 185

Winsor, A. P., 234, 699
Winter, A. L., 160
Witt, J. C., 10, 699
Wolfle, D., 633
Woltz, D. J., 495
Wong, D., 422
Wong, M. M., 193
Woodcock, R. W., 8, 11, 29, 161, 190, 253,
    464, 629
Wood, G., 85, 469
Woodward, J. A., 210
Woolley, M. E., 178
Worling, J. R., 192
Wormith, S. A., 192
Wothke, W., 186
Wu, L.-T., 180
Wycoff, K. L., 416

Xu, J., 182

Yamamoto, S., 191
Yampolskaya, S., 186
Yang, Y., 659, 660
Ye, F., 687

Yeh, M., 178
Yerkes, R. M., 663–664
Yoakum, C. S., 663–664
Yoerger, K., 180
Youngstrom, E. A., 654, 692, 696
Yovel, I., 659
Yuan, K.-H., 693

Zachar, P., 38*t*
Zazi, S., 345
Žebec, M., 345
Zeisel, S. A., 178
Zenonos, V., 345
Zhang, O., 140
Zhou, D., 235
Zhu, J. J., 15, 123, 209, 241, 281, 494, 616,
    654, 657, 686, 695
Zhu, X., 687
Zimet, C. N., 7
Zimmer, C., 331, 333, 334, 336, 341, 346
Zimmerman, M., 692
Zinbarg, R. E., 659
Zirkel, P. A., 699
Zumbo, B. D., 661

SUBJECT INDEX

Page references followed by *fig* indicate an illustrated figure; followed by *t* indicate a table.

The Abilities of Man: Their Nature and Measurement (Spearman), 673

Academic failure. *See* School failure risk factors

Academic–Q (Child and Adolescent Academic Questionnaire)
- conclusions on using the, 206–207
- examining the process of creating the, 175, 194
- form used for the, 195*fig*–197*fig*
- reliability of, 200, 201*t*–202
- validity of the, 202*t*–206

ADHD (attention-deficit/hyperactivity disorder), 140–141, 155, 177, 230

ADHD–IV Rating Scale, 499

ADHD–related case reports
- Case 1–Liam, Age 9, 265–282, 551
- Case 6–Tom, Age 8, 372–403*t*, 551
- Case 9–Isabella, Age 13, 448–458*t*, 551

Administration (WISC–V test kit format)
- changes from the WISC–IV, 623–624
- common errors, 85–88
- complementary subtests, 80–85
- digital administration and scoring, 139–155
- Fluid Reasoning subtests, 63–68*t*
- frequently asked questions on subtest administration, 88–89
- general information, 46–55
- most frequent errors, 37–38*t*
- pre-administration considerations, 38–46
- Processing Speed subtests, 74–80
- Quick Reference on frequently asked questions, 88–89
- selection of the subtests, 43
- standard order and domain membership of the subtests, 42*t*
- subtest-by-subtest, 55–88
- Verbal Comprehension subtests, 55–61
- Visual Spatial subtests, 61–63
- Working Memory subtests, 69–74
- *See also WISC–V Administration and Scoring Manual*

Administration–general information (WISC–V test kit version)
- discontinue rules and stop points, 47, 49–51*t*
- qualifying, demonstration, sample, and teaching items, 51–52
- queries, 53
- recording responses and commonly used abbreviations, 53–55
- repetitions, 52–53
- reverse rule, 47, 48*t*–49*t*
- start points by age, 46–48*t*
- subtest-specific prompts, 53
- subtest time limits, 50–51, 52*t*

Adolescent limited (AL) offenders, 184

Adolescent Resiliency Attitudes Scale (ARAS), 191

Adolescents
- general strain theory on behavior of, 186
- limited research on youth risk assessment, 177
- review of research on youth risk assessment, 192–193
- *See also* Juvenile delinquency risk factors; School failure risk factors

African Americans. *See* Racial/ethnic differences

AL (adolescent limited) offenders, 184

Alicia, Age 13 case report
- background, 283–284
- conclusions, 292–293
- current evaluation, 284–292*t*
- listed with other cases, 551
- recommendations, 293–296
- summary, 283
- tests taken, 302–303

American Board of Clinical Neuropsychology (ABCN), 408

American Board of Professional Neuropsychology (ABPN), 408

American Board of School Neuropsychology (ABSNP), 408

American Educational Research Association (AERA), 44, 140, 625, 689, 701

American Psychological Association (APA), 44, 140, 405, 407–408, 625, 689, 701

Ancillary index scales (WISC–V)
- Auditory Working Memory subtests, 2*fig*
- Cognitive Proficiency subtests, 2*fig*
- description and list of, 1
- General Ability subtests, 2*fig*
- McCloskey's review of, 675–676
- Nonverbal subtests, 2*fig*
- Quantitative Reasoning subtests, 2*fig*
- review of the WISC–V composite scores, 622
- review of the WISC–V organizational framework, 649*t*
- scores and scoring of, 120–121, 631
- *See also specific case report; subtest*

Anti-IQ-testing
- Dan Rather and, 717–718
- post-IDEA sentiment of, 5

Anxiety
- Case 9–Isabella, Age 13, 448–458*t*, 551
- Case 10–John, Age 12, 471–492, 551

ARAS (Adolescent Resiliency Attitudes Scale), 191

Arithmetic subtest scoring (WISC–V)
- comparing WISC–IV scoring and, 98*t*
- scoring key, 99

Arithmetic subtest (WISC–V)
- administration of, 67–68*t*
- ancillary index scores and, 120

Arithmetic subtest (*Continued*)
  behavioral observations for, 68
  Canivez and Watkins on continuing problems with, 695–696
  Cohen's factor-analytic research on, 15
  common errors made in administration of, 86
  comparing WISC–IV administration and, 68*t*
  discontinue rule for, 50*t*
  process observation base rates for, 116
  reverse rules by age, 49*t*
  scoring the, 98*t*, 99, 116, 120
  start points by age, 47*t*
  timing rules for, 52*t*
Army Alpha test, 663
Army Beta test, 663
ASCA (Adjustment Scales for Children and Adolescents), 691
Asian Americans. *See* Racial/ethnic differences
Assessment instruments
  Academic–Q (Child and Adolescent Academic Questionnaire), 175, 194, 195–197, 201*t*–202*t*, 203*t*, 204*t*–207
  ADHD–IV Rating Scale, 499
  Adolescent Resiliency Attitudes Scale (ARAS), 191
  Army Alpha test, 663
  Army Beta test, 663
  ASCA (Adjustment Scales for Children and Adolescents), 691
  ATIs (aptitude-treatment interactions), 699, 700
  BASC–2 (Behavior Assessment Scale for Children–Second Edition), 193, 651, 691
  Behavior Rating Inventory of Executive Function (BRIEF), 499
  Behavior–Q (Child and Adolescent Behavior Questionnaire) rating scale for, 175, 197, 198–200, 201*t*–202*t*, 203*t*, 204*t*, 205*t*, 206–207
  Child and Adolescent Functional Assessment Scale (CAFAS), 193
  Child Behavior Checklist, 186
  Children's Memory Scale (CMS), 651
  Cognitive Assessment System (CAS), 11, 14
  Cognitive Assessment System–Second Edition (CAS2), 11, 14, 412
  Development and validation of new, 193–206
  Differential Ability Scales, 677
  Halsted-Reitan Neuropsychological Test Battery, 406, 407
  HEQ (Home Environment Questionnaire), 193–194
  Kaufman Adolescent and Adult Intelligence Test (KAIT), 717
  Kaufman Assessment Battery for Children (K–ABC), 8, 11, 163–164, 407, 664, 719
  Kaufman Assessment Battery for Children–Second Edition (KABC–II), 10, 164, 411–412, 660–661, 690
  Kaufman Test of Educational Achievement–Third Edition (KTEA-3), 85, 632, 690, 691, 696, 706
  Luria–Nebraska Neuropsychological Test Battery, 406, 407
  McCloskey Executive Functions Scales (MEFS), 499
  most popular juvenile delinquent risk assessment instruments, 192
  Naglieri Nonverbal Ability Test, 663
  NEPSY: A Developmental Neuropsychological Assessment, 407
  NEPSY–II: A Developmental Neuropsychological Assessment, Second Edition 409, 415, 418, 651
  Overview of the clinical validity of the Academic–Q and Behavior–Q, 206
  Peabody Individual Achievement Test, 664
  Process Assessment of the Learner–Second Edition (PAL–II), 677
  Risk Assessment Instrument (RAI), 193
  Stroop Color and Word Test, 185

Task-analysis approaches in contemporary neuropsychological assessment, 415
Test of Memory and Learning, 407
Vineland Adaptive Behavior Scales–Second Edition (Vineland–II), 690, 691
WJ III (Woodcock-Johnson–Third Edition), 11
  WJ IV (Woodcock-Johnson–Fourth Edition), 11, 12, 14, 672*t*
  WJ-R (Woodcock-Johnson Tests of Cognitive Ability–Revised), 8, 11
  See also Child assessment; *specific WISC–V interpretation case reports*; Wechsler test products
Assessment, Intervention and Moving on (AIMA), 192
ATIs (aptitude-treatment interactions), 699, 700
Attention difficulties
  Case 3–Luke, Age 9, 304–329*t*, 551
  Case 5–Tawna, Age 13, 362–371, 551
Auditory Working Memory Index
  Digit Span subtest, 120
  Letter–Number Sequencing subtest, 1210
  See also specific subtest
  Author commentary
  favorite things about the WISC–V reviews, 711–712
  overview of the WISC–V reviews, 703–705
  reviews summary on whether WISC–V is user-friendly, 707–710
  reviews summary on WISC–V test development procedures, 711
Autism spectrum disorder
  Case 7–Jaime, Age–10, 425–436
  processing speed sensitivity to, 230
Axelrod, Joan (Case 15–Jane, Age 8 report), 551, 578–586*t*

BASC–2 (Behavior Assessment Scale for Children–Second Edition), 193, 651, 691
Behavioral difficulties (Case 7–Jaime, Age 10), 425–436
Behavioral observations. *See specific subtest*
Behavior Rating Inventory of Executive Function (BRIEF), 499
Behavior–Q (Child and Adolescent Behavior Questionnaire)
  conclusions on using, 206–207
  examining the process of creating, 175, 194
  reliability of, 197, 201*t*
  validity of, 202*t*–204*t*, 205*t*, 206
Best Practices in Writing Instruction (Graham & MacArthur), 205
Bias in Mental Testing (Jensen), 673
Binet, Alfred, 720, 723, 724
Block Design subtest scoring (WISC–V)
  comparing WISC–IV scoring and, 95*t*
  scoring key, 96–98
Block Design subtest (WISC–V)
  ancillary index scores and, 120, 121
  administration of, 61*t*–62
  behavioral observations for, 61–62
  Cohen's factor-analytic research on, 15
  common errors made in the administration of, 86
  comparing WISC–IV administration and, 61*t*
  discontinue rule for, 50*t*
  primary index scores and, 120
  process observation base rates for, 116
  reverse rule, 48*t*
  scoring, 95*t*–98, 116, 120, 121
  start points by age, 47*t*
  timing rules for, 52*t*
BOLD (blood-oxygen-level-dependent) signals, 340
Boring, E. G., 721, 724

Boston Process Approach, 408–409
Brain imaging studies
    on cognitive neuroscience, 340–341
    description of, 339–340
Brain Research through Advancing Innovative Neurotechnologies
        (BRAIN) initiative, 341, 346
British Ability Scales (BAS), 11
Bronner, Augusta, 723

Canadian Psychological Association, 405
Cancellation subtest scoring (WISC–V)
    comparing WISC–IV scoring and, 103
    scoring key, 106
Cancellation subtest (WISC–V)
    administration of the, 78–80
    behavioral observations for, 79
    comparing WISC–IV administration and, 78t
    discontinue rule for, 50t
    errors in administration of, 87
    reverse rules by age, 49t
    scoring, 103t, 106, 116, 117
    start points by age, 48t
    timing rules for, 52t
Canivez, Gary L.
    review of the WISC–V by Watkins and, 683–702
Carroll's Human Cognitive Abilities (Carroll), 676
Carroll's Stratum I (Narrow), 252
Carroll's Stratum II (Broad), 252
Carroll's Stratum III (General), 252
Carroll's three-stratum theory, 252
Cattell, James McKeen, 721, 722
CFA (confirmatory factor analysis), 15, 689–694, 701
CHC-based WISC–V interpretation
    CHC broad abilities measured, 255–256
    CHC narrow abilities measured, 256–258
    interpreting narrow abilities, 260–262
    making pair–wise comparisons involving the six broad abilities,
        258–260t
    narrow abilities and academic achievement, 262–263
CHC-based WISC–V interpretation case reports
    Case 1–Liam, Age 9, 265–282, 551
    Case 2–Alicia, Age 13, 283–303, 551
    Case 3–Luke, Age 9, 304–329, 551
    introduction to the, 263–264
CHC (Cattell-Horn-Carroll) theory
    applied to profile interpretation, 15–16
    a brief history of, 251–253
    Cognitive Assessment System–Second Edition (CAS2)
        application of, 14
    contemporary, 253–255
    description of, 12
    as an effective neuropsychological processing approach, 21, 24, 28
    introduction to the *Gc, Gv, Gsm, Gf,* and *Gs* factors in, 16, 46, 251,
        252, 416
    as theoretical foundation of WISC–V, 648
    Wechsler Intelligence Scale for Children–Fifth Edition (WISC–V)
        application of, 12–15, 255–263, 414, 415, 417, 678
    See also Cognitive functioning; SNP/CHC (Integrated School
        Neuropsychological/Cattell-Horn-Carroll) model
Child abuse risk factor, 185, 186, 189, 190
Child and Adolescent Functional Assessment Scale (CAFAS), 193

Child assessment
    Case 1–Liam, Age 9, 265–282, 551
    Case 2–Alicia, Age 13, 283–303, 551
    Case 3–Luke, Age 9, 304–329t, 551
    Case 4–Josh, Age 8, 348–361, 551
    Case 5–Tawna, Age 13, 362–371, 551
    Case 6–Tom, Age 8, 372–403t, 551
    Case 7–Jaime, Age 10, 425–436
    Case 8–Christopher, Age 11, 437–447t, 551
    Case 9–Isabella, Age 13, 448–458t, 551
    Case 10–John, Age 12, 471–492, 551
    Case 11–Colin, Age 8, 497–522t, 551
    Case 12–Derek, Age 13, 523–547t, 551
    Case 13–Ellie, Age 10, 551, 557–567t
    Case 14–Jordan, Age 15, 551, 568–577t
    Case 15–Jane, Age 8, 551, 578–586t
    Case 16–Lizzie, Age 8, 551, 587–599t
    Case 17–Patrick, Age 9, 551, 600–612t
    Clinical applications of score differences, 173
    Conceptual and clinical integration of all 17 case reports, 550–556
    multiple assessments and practice effects on Wechsler's scales,
        419–424
    multiple assessments and progressive error on Wechsler's scales,
        422–423
    Quick Reference on malleable risk and protective factors for, 174
    See also Intelligent testing; Rating scales; WISC–V (Wechsler
        Intelligence Scale for Children–Fifth Edition)
Child Behavior Checklist, 186
Childhood brain development
    cognitive neuroscience on, 335–337
    P-FIT (Parieto-Frontal Integration Theory) on development of
        the neural network, 336–337
Child poverty, 187
Child protective factors, 174
Children's Memory Scale (CMS), 651
Children with special needs
    ADHD (attention-deficit/hyperactivity disorder), 140–141, 155,
        177, 230
    deaf or hard of hearing, 46
    digital administration and scoring for clinical populations and,
        140–141
    English-language learners (ELLs), 45–46, 668
    limited motor skills, 45
    serious language difficulties, 45–46
    visual impairment, 46
    WISC–V administration fairness to, 44–45
    See also Preschool children; School age children
Child risk
    Academic–Q (Child and Adolescent Academic Questionnaire)
        rating scale for, 175, 194, 195–197, 201t–202t, 203t, 204t–207
    Behavior–Q (Child and Adolescent Behavior Questionnaire)
        rating scale for, 175, 197, 198–200, 201t–202t, 203t, 204t, 205t,
        206–207
    HEQ (Home Environment Questionnaire) rating scale for,
        193–194
    Quick Reference on malleable risk and protective factors for, 174
    review of research on school failure and delinquency, 175193
Child sexual abuse, 186
Christopher, Age 11 case report
    behavioral observations, 438
    evaluation results, 439–441

Christopher, Age 11 case report (*Continued*)
   instruments used, 438
   listed with other reports, 551
   reason for referral, 437
   recommendations, 442–443
   relevant background, 437–438
   resources used, 443
   summary of, 441–442
   test scores, 443*t*–447*t*
Clinical neuropsychological evaluation
   contemporary approaches to, 409
   Integrated School Neuropsychological/Cattell-Horn-Carroll
     (SNP/CHC) model of, 414
   interpretation of WISC–V from a Lurian perspective, 410–415
   processing-based approaches to, 409–415
   task-analysis approaches to contemporary, 415
Clinical neuropsychologists
   credentialing of, 408
   definition and limited regulation of, 407–408
Clinical neuropsychology
   case report content, 417–419
   Hale and Fiorello's demands analysis, 415, 417
   history of, 405–407
   rating scales used in, 406–407
   Silver's (1993) information-processing model, 415–417
   training requirements for, 407–408
Clinical neuropsychology-based case reports
   Case 7–Jaime, Age 10, 425–436, 551
   Case 8–Christopher, Age 11, 437–447*t*, 551
   Case 9–Isabella, Age 13, 448–458*t*
   introductions to, 424
Clinical neuropsychology-based WISC–V interpretation
   case reports on using, 424–458*t*
   examining process of the, 405
   practice effects on Wechsler's scales considered in the, 419–424
   report content of the, 417–419
Coalson, Diane
   on the conceptual and clinical integration of all 17 case reports,
     550–556
   introducing the case reports on children with reading or language
     problems, 549–550
   predictions on the future of intelligent testing by, 34
   on the present state and future of intelligence testing, 20
Coding subtest scoring (WISC–V)
   comparing WISC–IV scoring and, 103
   scoring key, 103–104
Coding subtest (WISC–V)
   administration of, 74–76
   ancillary index scores and, 120, 121
   Cohen's factor-analytic research on, 16
   common errors made in the administration of, 87
   discontinue rule for, 50*t*
   do not reverse, 49*t*
   primary index scores and, 120
   scoring, 103*t*–104, 116, 120, 121
   start points by age, 48*t*
   timing rules for, 52*t*
Cognitive ability test. *See* Intelligence testing (IQ testing)
Cognitive Assessment System (CAS), 11, 407, 412, 664
Cognitive Assessment System–Second Edition (CAS2), 11, 14, 412
Cognitive-behavioral therapy (CBT), 191

Cognitive functioning
   Cognitive Assessment System (CAS) approach to, 11
   differentiating between WISC–V measurement of intelligence
     and, 678–681
   WISC–V assessment under fixed experimental conditions,
     27–28
   See also CHC (Cattell-Horn-Carroll) theory
Cognitive hypothesis testing (CHT), 414
Cognitive neuroscience
   brain imaging used to study, 339–341
   broad definition and description of, 331–332
   on childhood brain development, 335–337
   on complicated emergence of cognitive abilities, 344–345
   examining WISC–V interpretation using, 331
   future potential of, 346–347
   on genetic and environmental influences on intelligence, 332–335
   on neural plasticity, 337–339
   on neuroanatomical correlates of cognitive abilities, 341–344
Cognitive neuroscience-based WISC–V interpretation case studies
   Case 4–Josh, Age 8, 348–361*t*, 551
   Case 5–Tawna, Age 13, 362–371*t*, 551
   Case 6–Tom, Age 8, 372–403*fig*, 551
   introduction to, 346–347
Cognitive Proficiency index
   Coding subtest, 120, 121
   Digit Span subtest, 120, 121
   Picture Span subtest, 120, 121
   Symbol Search subtest, 120, 121
   See also specific subtest
Cognitive Psychology (Neisser), 493
Cohen's factor-analytic research, 15–16
Colin, Age 8 case report
   background and reason for referral, 497
   conclusions, 503–505
   listed with other reports, 551
   psychoeducational evaluation report, 497–499
   recommendations, 506–510
   summary, 499*t*–503*t*
   WISC–V scores, 510*t*–522*t*
Columbia University, 721
Community
   child protective factors of the, 174
   juvenile delinquency neighborhood risk factor, 187–188, 190
   school and neighborhood safety risk factor, 180–181, 183, 187
Complementary index scales (WISC–V)
   changes from the WISC–IV to, 623
   description and list of, 3
   McCloskey's review of the, 675–676
   Naming Speed subtests, 2*fig*
   review of the WISC–V composite scores and, 623
   review of the WISC–V organizational framework of, 650*t*
   scoring of the, 631
   Storage and Retrieval subtests, 2*fig*
   Symbol Translation subtests, 2*fig*
   See also specific case report; subtest
Complementary subtests (WISC–V)
   created specifically for the WISC–V, 619
   Delayed Symbol Translation, 48*t*, 49*t*, 51*t*, 52*t*, 83–84, 85, 88, 111,
     112, 116
   Immediate Symbol Translation, 48*t*, 49*t*, 52*t*, 82–83, 85, 88, 111,
     112, 116, 117

Naming Speed Literacy, 48*t*, 49*t*, 50*t*, 52*t*, 80–81, 85, 87, 107–110, 116

Naming Speed Quantity, 48*t*, 49*t*, 51*t*, 52*t*, 81–82, 85, 87, 110, 116

Recognition Symbol Translation, 48*t*, 49*t*, 51*t*, 52*t*, 84–85, 88, 111, 112, 116, 117

scoring, 107–112, 116, 117

Composite scores (WISC–V)

Q-global Composite Results screen, 154*fig*

Q-global summary of, 129*fig*

Quick Reference on acceptable number of total raw scores of 0 for each, 124

review of the scales and, 619–623

scoring WISC–V subtest step of obtaining, 125

sums of scaled and standard scores and invalidation of, 124–125

understanding how to apply to WISC–V interpretation, 227–232*t*

WISC–V normative sample composite score means and standard deviations by parent education levels, 165*t*–166*t*

See also Global composite scores (WISC–V); Scores (WISC–V); Specific composite scores (WISC–V)

Comprehension subtest scoring (WISC–V)

comparing WISC–IV scoring and, 92*t*

scoring key, 95

Comprehension subtest (WISC–V)

administration of, 59–61

behavioral observations for, 60–61

common errors in administration of, 85

comparing WISC–IV administration and, 60*t*

discontinue rule for, 50*t*

process observation base rates, 116

reverse rule, 48*t*

scoring, 92*t*, 95, 116

start points by age, 47*t*

timing rules for, 52*t*

Confirmatory factor analysis (CFA), 15, 689–694, 701

A Consensus on the Brain Training Injury from the Scientific Community (2014), 338

Contemporary Intellectual Assessment (McCloskey, Whitaker, Murphy, & Rogers), 677

Contrast scores, 116–117

Criminal behavior. *See* Juvenile delinquency risk factors

Crystallized intelligence (*Gc*), 252

Dayan, Moshe, 717

Deaf or hard of hearing, 46

Delayed Symbol Translation subtest (WISC–V)

administration of, 83–84, 85

behavioral observations for, 84

common errors in administration of, 88

discontinue rule for, 51*t*

do not reverse, 49*t*

scoring, 111, 112, 116

start points by age, 48*t*

timing rules for, 52*t*

Demands analysis, 415, 417

Demonstration items (WISC–V), 52

Depression

Case 9–Isabella, Age 13, 448–458*t*, 551

Case 10–John, Age 12, 471–492, 551

Derek, Age 13 case report

CMS scores, 538*t*

conclusions, 526, 530–531

findings and interpretation of assessment results, observations, and student interview, 533–534

introduction, 523–525

listed with other reports, 551

MEFS scores, 540*t*–547*t*

Psychoeducational evaluation report, 525–526

recommendations, 531–533

summary, 527*t*–529*t*

WCST scores, 537*t*

WIAT–III scores, 539*t*

WISC–V and KTEA-3 scores, 538*t*–539*t*

WISC–V scores, 535*t*–537*t*

WJ III scores, 540*t*

Differential Abilities Scale (DAS), 11

Differential Abilities Scale–II (DAS–II), 11

Differential Ability Scales, 677

Digital version (WISC–V Q-interactive)

advantages and challenges of, 139

equivalence of traditional and digital mediums, 139–140

introduction to, 1

testing special and clinical populations, 140–141

Tom, Age 8 case report, 372–403*t*, 551

WISC–IV Q-interactive users survey, 140

Digit Span subtest scoring (WISC–V)

comparing WISC–IV scoring and, 100

scoring key, 100–101

Digit Span subtest (WISC–V)

administration of, 69–70*t*

ancillary index scores and, 120

behavioral observations for, 69–70

Cohen's factor-analytic research on, 15

common errors in administration of, 87

comparing WISC–IV administration and, 70*t*

discontinue rule for, 50*t*

do not reverse, 49*t*

primary index scores and, 120

scoring, 100*t*–101, 116, 117

timing rules for, 52*t*

Discontinue rules (WISC–V)

overview of, 47, 49–50

Quick Reference on, 51

subtest discontinue rules, 50*t*–51*t*

Dries, Carlea (Case 16–Lizzie, Age 8 report), 550, 551, 587–599*t*

"Dr. Wechsler Remembered" (Kaufman), 715–720

"Dr. Wechsler Remembered Part II" (Kaufman), 720–724

DSM–5 (Diagnostic and Statistical Manual of Mental disorders, Fifth Edition), 234

DTI (diffusion tensor imaging), 340–341

Dumont, Ron

Case 16–Lizzie, Age 8 report by, 550, 551, 587–599*t*

on having multiple sources of data to support hypotheses generated from WISC–V profiles, 30–31

predictions on the future of intelligent testing by, 34

on the present state and future of intelligence testing, 19, 20

WISC–V review by Willis and, 637–644, 704

Dynamic risk factors, 176

Dyslexia

Case 6–Tom, Age 8 on, 372–403*fig*, 551

Case 8–Christopher, Age 11 on phonological, 437–447*t*, 551

Case 12–Derek, Age 13 on phonological, 523–547*t*, 551

Early childcare Research Network, 178
Educational interventions
    results from WISC–V profiles must be tied to, 32–34
    score differences and clinical applications and, 173
    See also specific WISC–V interpretation case reports
Educational Longitudinal Study (ELS), 182
Education Week, 177
EFA (exploratory factor analysis)
    Canivez and Watkins' criticism on failure to provide results of, 692
    Canivez and Watkins' review on the WISC–V validity and, 689, 690, 701
Eklund, Katie (Case 17–Patrick, Age 9), 551, 600–612*t*
Electroencephalography (EEG)
    cognitive neuroscience studies using, 340–341
    description of, 339–340
Ellie, Age 10 case report
    background, 557–558
    behavioral observations, 558
    listed with other reports, 551
    psychometric summary, 564*t*–567*t*
    reason for evaluation, 557
    recommendations, 563–564
    test results, 559–563
    tests administered, 558–559
Encyclopedia Britannica human intelligence entry, 12
English-language learners (ELLs), 45–46, 668
Error scores, 116
Estimate of Risk of Adolescent Sexual Offense Recidivism Version 2.0 (ERASOR), 192
Ethnic differences. *See* Racial/ethnic differences
Executive function difficulties
    Case 11–Colin, Age 8, 497–522*t*, 551
    Case 12–Derek, Age 13, 523–547*t*, 551
Expanded Fluid Index, 232*t*, 233*t*, 246*t*, 259*t*

Factor–analytic model of intelligence
    CFA (confirmatory factor analysis), 15, 689–694, 701
    Cohen's factor-analytic research, 15–16
    EFA (exploratory factor analysis), 689, 690, 692, 701
    Liam, Age 9 case report on WISC–V five-factor approach to, 281*fig*
    McCloskey on domains in the, 679*fig*
    Miller and McGill's review of five-factor WISC–V validation model for subtests, 657–659*fig*
    WISC–V Technical and Interpretive Manual's illustration of the five-factor model of, 690
Fairness issues
    assessing children at the extremes of the age range, 43–44*t*
    assessing children with special needs, 44–46
Family
    protective factors, 174
    risk factors, 174
    as school failure risk factor, 180, 181–182
    Youth Support Project on delinquent behavior and, 187
    See also Parent education levels; Parents
Fletcher-Janzen, Elaine, 21, 31, 249, 336, 346, 348, 419, 551, 554, 555, 556
Feuerstein, Reuven, 27
Figure Weights subtest (WISC–V)
    administration of, 64–66
    ancillary index scores and, 120, 121

    behavioral observations for, 65–66
    common errors made in administration, 86
    discontinue rule, 50*t*
    primary index scores and, 120
    reverse rules by age, 49*t*
    scoring the, 98*t*, 99, 116, 120, 121
    start points by age, 47*t*
    timing rules for, 52*t*
Five–factor model. *See* Factor–analytic model of intelligence
Flanagan, Dawn P.
    Case 3–Luke, Age 9 report by, 304–329*t*, 551
    predictions on the future of intelligent testing by, 34
    on WISC–V being optimally useful when interpreted from a theoretical basis, 29
Fletcher-Janzen, Elaine
    case report 4–Josh, age 8 by, 348–360*t*, 551
    on having multiple sources of data to support hypotheses generated from WISC–V profiles, 31
Fluid intelligence (*Gf*), 16, 46, 251, 252, 416
Fluid Reasoning subtests (WISC–V)
    Arithmetic, 15, 47*t*, 49*t*, 50*t*, 52*t*, 67–68*t*, 86, 98*t*, 99, 116, 695–696
    common errors in administration of, 86
    Figure Weights, 47*t*, 49*t*, 50*t*, 52*t*, 64–66, 86, 99, 116
    Matrix Reasoning, 47*t*, 49*t*, 50*t*, 52*t*, 63–64*t*, 86, 98*t*, 99, 116
    Picture Concepts, 47*t*, 49*t*, 50*t*, 52*t*, 66*t*–67, 86, 98*t*, 99, 116
    primary index scores and, 120
    scoring, 98*t*–102, 116, 120–121
    See also Scoring subtests (WISC–V)
    Fluid Reasoning Index index scores applied to WISC–V interpretation, 244–245
    primary index scores and, 120
    WISC–V reviewers on Perceptual Reasoning Index split into Visual Spatial and, 706
FMRI (functional MRI) studies, 340–341
Foster children, 180, 186
Freedom from Distractibility, 15, 16, 210, 220, 615, 642, 695
Freud, Sigmund, 717, 724
FSIQ (Full Scale IQ)
    changes from the WISC–IV to WISC–V, 616, 619–620
    comparing substitution, proration, and retest replacement approaches, 122–124
    comparing WISC–V FSIQ with WJ IV GIA subtests for, 672*t*
    description and what is included in, 670–675
    global interpretation options for, 675*t*
    influence of unusual index-level scatter on predictive validity of, 217
    invalidation of composite scores, 124–125
    parental education levels and, 160*t*, 165*t*–166*t*, 170*t*–171*t*
    Quick Reference on acceptable substitutions for FSIQ subtests, 122
    Quick Reference on acceptable number of total raw scores of 0 for each composite score, 124
    review of the General Ability Index (WISC–V) and, 631–632
    socioeconomic status (SES) and, 159, 160, 162–166*t*
    step-by-step process of obtaining the, 117–125
    as a type of composite score applied to WISC–V interpretation, 227–299
    using Q-global to obtain the WISC–V report, 125–132
    WISC–IV's new look on, 16
    WISC–V's seven-subtest, 16
    See also Racial/ethnic differences; Scoring subtest steps (WISC–V)

Full scale (WISC–V)
  changes from the WISC–IV to, 616
  description, 1
  Fluid Reasoning subtests, 2fig
  Processing Speed subtests, 2fig
  review of the WISC–V Composite scores and, 620
  Verbal Comprehension subtests, 2fig
  Visual Spatial subtests, 2fig
  Working Memory subtests, 2fig
  See also specific case report; subtest
Functional MRI (fMRI) studies, 340–341
Future learning predictions (WISC–V measure), 24–25

Gardner, Howard
  on asking "how" are you smart?, 30
  multiple intelligences theory by, 12
General Ability Index (WISC–V)
  Block Design subtest, 120, 121
  Figure Weights subtest, 120, 121
  as global composite score applied to WISC–V interpretation, 230, 243
  McCloskey's review on the, 674–675t
  Matrix Reasoning subtest, 120, 121
  review of the FSIQ versus, 631–632
  Similarities subtest, 120, 121
  Vocabulary subtest, 120, 121
  WISC–V interpretation and issues related to, 238–239
  See also specific subtest
General strain theory, 186
Gf (fluid intelligence), 16, 46, 251, 252, 416
Gf-Gc theory, 251–253, 416
Global composite scores (WISC–V)
  FSIQ as, 227–229
  General Ability Index as, 230
  Nonverbal Index as, 229–230
  step-by-step score analysis to inform WISC–V interpretation using, 232, 234–237
  See also Composite scores (WISC–V)
Glr (Symbol Translation), 416
Glueck, Bernard, 723
GPA (grade point average) risk factor, 177, 182, 183
Gsm (Working Memory), 16, 416
g theory, 15
GWAS (genome-wide association studies), 332–333

Hadorn, Magan B.
  final thoughts on the WISC–V by, 635
  WISC–V review by Reynolds and, 615–634, 704
Hale and Fiorello's demands analysis, 415, 417
Halsted-Reitan Neuropsychological Test Battery, 406, 407
Harris, Daniel, 721–722
Hartmann, Jill, case report 2–Alicia, age 13 by, 283–303, 551
Healy, William, 723
Hearing problems
  Case 14–Jordan, Age 15, 551, 568–577t
  WISC–V administration considerations for, 46
HEQ (Home Environment Questionnaire), 193–194
Higher Cortical Functions in Man (Luria), 406
Hispanics. See Racial/ethnic differences
Holistic view of risk, 176–177
Home Environment Questionnaire (HEQ), 193–194

Human Cognitive Abilities (Carroll), 495
"Hundred Years of Intelligence Testing: Moving from Traditional IQ to Second-Generation Intelligence Tests" (Naglieri), 668
Hypotheses
  addition checks on good quantitative reasoning of, 32
  applied to the score analyses to inform WISC–V interpretation, 239, 244–245
  multiple sources of data to support WISC–V profile generated, 29–32
  WISC–V Technical and Interpretive Manual on using WISC–V scores to generate, 667

Immediate Symbol Translation subtest (WISC–V)
  administration of, 82–83, 85
  behavioral observations for, 83
  common errors made in administration, 88
  discontinue rule for, 51t
  do not reverse, 49t
  scoring, 111, 112, 116, 117
  start points by age, 48t
  timing rules for, 52t
Index-level scatter
  concluding that it does matter for PSW analyses, 225
  influence of unusual index-level scatter on FSIQ predictive validity, 217
  overview of the issue of, 209–211
  PSW (strengths and weaknesses) approaches to, 214
  in the WISC–V, 211t–214
  WISC–V strengths and weaknesses, 214, 215t–216t, 217, 218t–220t
  See also Item-level scatter; Subtest-level scatter
Index scores (WISC–V)
  additional index and process scores in this book, 231–232t–233t
  applied to WISC–V interpretation, 239–247
  basic descriptions of, 231t
  evaluating index-level pairwise comparisons, 244–246t
  published, 230–231t
Individualized Education Program (IEP)
  Case 2–Alicia, Age 13 on, 283, 551
  Case 3–Luke, Age 9 on, 304, 320
  Case 4–Josh, Age 8 on, 348
  Case 7–Jaime, Age 10 on, 426
  Case 8–Christopher, Age 11 on, 442, 551
  Case 16–Lizzie, Age 8 on, 550, 590
Individuals with Disabilities Education Act (IDEA)
  anti-IQ-testing sentiment post-, 5
  nondiscriminatory scales requirement by, 664
  WISC–V and eligibility determination under, 667
Infant Health and Development program, 187
Information-processing model (Silver's 1993), 415–417
Information subtest scoring (WISC–V)
  comparing WISC–IV scoring and, 92t
  scoring key, 95
Information subtest (WISC–V)
  administration of, 58–59t
  behavioral observations for, 58–59
  Cohen's factor-analytic research on, 15
  common errors made in administration of, 85
  comparing WISC–IV administration and, 59t
  comparing WISC–IV scoring and, 92t
  discontinue rule for, 50t

Information subtest (*Continued*)
  process observation base rates, 116
  reverse rule, 48*t*
  scoring, 92*t*, 95, 116
  start points by age, 47*t*
  timing rules for, 52*t*
Integrated School Neuropsychological/Cattell-Horn-Carroll model.
    See SNP/CHC (Integrated School
    Neuropsychological/Cattell-Horn-Carroll) model
Intelligence
  cognitive neuroscience on the genetic and environmental
      influences on, 332–335
  crystallized intelligence (*Gc*), 252
  differentiating between cognition and WISC–V measurement of,
      678–681
  Encyclopedia Britannica entry on human, 12
  fluid intelligence (*Gf*), 16, 46, 251, 252, 416
  importance of understanding how the components function
      together, 13–14
Intelligence testing expert opinions
  Alan Kaufman, 29, 33–34
  Cecil Reynolds, 19
  Dan Miller, 19–20
  Dawn Flanagan, 26, 34
  Diane Coalson, 20, 34
  Elaine Fletcher-Janzen, 21, 31
  George McCloskey, 22
  Jack Naglieri, 19
  Jennifer Mascolo, 23–24, 27, 33
  Joel Schneider, 20–21, 22, 24–25, 29, 34
  John Willis, 20, 21, 22–23, 26, 30
  Kevin McGrew, 20, 26, 29
  Nadeen Kaufman, 23, 24
  Nancy Mather, 30, 31, 32, 33
  Ron Dumont, 19, 20, 30–31, 34
  Susan Raiford, 5, 6
Intelligence testing (IQ testing)
  contemporary thoughts about, 18–34
  criticisms of subtest profile interpretation, 8–9
  Criticisms of the WISC–R and the WISC–III (1980s),
      10–11
  current state of, 11
  Dan Rather TV special on issue of, 717–718
  evolution during the 1970s, 7–8
  evolution during the 1980s and early 1990s, 8
  Wechsler's caution to clinicians regarding, 6
  Wechsler's credo of, 6–7
  See also Child assessment
Intelligent testing basic tenets
  1: intelligence testing with the WISC–V requires training,
      experience, and flexibility, 20–24
  2: the WISC–V measures what the individual has learned and
      predicts future learning, 24–25
  3: the WISC–V subtests are samples of behavior and are not
      exhaustive, 25–27
  4: the WISC–V assesses cognitive functioning under fixed
      experimental conditions, 27–28
  5: the WISC–V is optimally useful when it is interpreted from a
      theoretical basis, 28–29
  6: hypotheses generated from WISC–V profiles should be
      supported with data from multiple sources, 29–32

  7: results from WISC–V profiles must be tied to educational
      interventions, 32–34
Intelligent Testing (Matarazzo, Bannatyne, Sattler, & Kaufman), 8
Intelligent Testing with the WISC-R (Kaufman), 5, 663, 718
Intelligent Testing with the WISC–III (Kaufman), 5, 8
Intelligent Testing with the WISC–V (Kaufman, Raiford, &
    Coalson), 5
iPad test version. *See* WISC–V Q-interactive
IQ Testing 101 (Kaufman), 720–721
IQ testing. *See* Intelligence testing (IQ testing)
Isabella, Age 13 case report
  background, 448–449
  behavioral observations, 449
  psychometric summary, 456*t*–458*t*
  reason for evaluation, 448
  recommendations, 455–456
  test results, 450–455
  tests administered, 449–450
Item-level scatter
  description of, 223–224
  history of evaluating and need for a user-friendly method of
      measuring, 224–225
  intrasubtest scatter (ISS) or, 223
  testing in the WISC–V, 225
  See also Index-level scatter; Subtest-level scatter
Item response theory (IRT), 224
Item scores, 113

Jaime, Age 10 case report
  background, 425–427
  behavioral observations, 428–429
  diagnostic impressions, 432–433
  evaluation procedures, 425
  listed with other reports, 551
  prior cognitive assessments, 427*t*–428*t*
  profile of cognitive and academic strengths and weaknesses,
      430–432
  reason for referral, 425
  recommendations, 433–436
  summary, 433
  test results, 429*t*–430*t*
Jane, Age 8 case report
  assessment findings, 579
  behavioral observations, 579–580
  clinical impressions, 582
  listed with other reports, 551
  psychoeducational assessment, 578–579
  score summaries, 583*t*–586*t*
  summary and recommendations, 582–583
  test results, 580–582
John, Age 12 case report
  background, 472–475
  comments on the case study, 492
  current assessment instruments and procedures, 475
  evaluation results, 475–483
  intervention strategies and recommendations, 484–486
  listed with other reports, 551
  reason for referral, 471–472
  school neuropsychological evaluation, 471
  summary, 483–484, 492
  test scores, 486*t*–491*t*

Jones, Alicia M.
    Case 10–John, Age 12 WISC–V report by, 471–492, 551
    on SNP/CHC model for interpreting the WISC–V, 459470
Jordan, Age 15 case report
    background, 568–569
    behavioral observations, 569
    instruments used, 569
    listed with other reports, 551
    reason for referral, 568
    recommendations, 573–575
    summary and clinical impressions, 572–573
    test results, 569–572, 575t–577t
Josh, Age 8 case report
    background, 348–349
    evaluation procedures, 349
    evaluation results, 350–356
    listed with other reports, 551
    psychometric results, 358t–361t
    reason for referral, 348
    recommendations, 356–358
    testing observations, 350
Journal of Psychoeducational Assessment, 635
Juvenile delinquency risk factors
    AL (adolescent limited) offenders, 184
    child abuse as, 185, 186, 190
    foster children, 186
    holistic view of risk and, 176–177
    influencing adolescent delinquent behavior, 184–192
    LCP (life-course persistent) offenders, 184
    neighborhood context of, 187–188, 190
    neuropsychological deficits as, 185
    protective factors interacting with, 190–191
    racial/ethnic differences, 189
    reviewing the research on, 175–193
    risk assessment research on youth and, 192–193
    self-control theory on, 185
    sex differences, 189–190
    sexual child abuse of, 186, 189
    static and dynamic, 176
    See also Adolescents; Youth risk assessment
Juvenile Detention Risk Assessment 91, 192
Juvenile Sexual Offense Recidivism Risk Assessment Tool–II
    (JSORRAT–II), 192

Kaplan, Edith, process approach of, 27
Kaufman Adolescent and Adult Intelligence Test (KAIT), 717
Kaufman, Alan S.
    "Dr. Wechsler Remembered" by, 715–720
    "Dr. Wechsler Remembered Part II" on influence of Wechsler on his own career, 720–724
    on importance of WISC–V interpretation from a theoretical basis, 29
    predictions on the future of intelligent testing by, 33–34
    on working with Wechsler on the revised WISC, 715–716, 720
Kaufman Assessment Battery for Children (K–ABC), 8, 11, 163–164, 407, 664, 719
Kaufman Assessment Battery for Children–Second Edition
    (KABC–II), 10, 164, 411–412, 660, 690
Kaufman, James, 717, 720

Kaufman method
    description of the, 5
    Hirshoren and Kavale's criticism of the, 9
    Joel Schneider's thoughts on, 17–18
    McDermott-Glutting critique of the, 9
    as the target of anti-IQ forces (1980s and 1990s), 8
    See also Subtest profile interpretation
Kaufman, Nadeen L.
    on approach to take during the evaluation, 23
    on approach to writing the evaluation report, 24
    on the conceptual and clinical integration of all 17 case reports, 550–556
    dinner with the David and Ruth Wechsler and Alan, 717–718
    introducing the case reports on children with reading or language problems, 549–550
    K–ABC developed by Alan Kaufman and, 719
    on the training, experience, and flexibility required for intelligent testing, 23
Kaufman Test of Educational Achievement–Third Edition
    (KTEA– 3), 85, 632, 690, 691, 696, 706

Language considerations
    deaf or hard of hearing, 46
    difficulties with language, 45–46
    English-language learners, 45–46, 668
Language difficulties case reports
    Case 4–Josh, Age 8, 348–361, 551
    Case 13–Ellie, Age 10, 551, 557–567t
    Case 14–Jordan, Age 15, 551, 568–577t
    Case 15–Jane, Age 8, 551, 578–586t
    Case 16–Lizzie, Age 8, 551, 587–599t
    Case 17–Patrick, Age 9, 551, 600–612t
    introduction to the five case reports on children with reading or language problems, 549–550
LCP (life-course persistent) offenders, 184
Learning
    ATIs (aptitude-treatment interactions) for evaluating child's style of, 699, 700
    Case 7–Jaime, Age 10 on autism spectrum and struggling with, 425–436, 551
    WISC–V measure of what has been learned and predictive of future, 24–25
Letter–Number Sequencing subtest scoring (WISC–V)
    comparing WISC–IV scoring and, 100
    scoring key, 101
Letter–Number Sequencing subtest (WISC–V)
    administration of, 72–74
    ancillary index scores and, 120
    behavioral observations for, 73–74
    common errors in administration of, 87
    comparing WISC–IV administration and, 73t
    discontinue rule for, 50t
    reverse rules by age, 49t
    scoring, 100t, 102, 116
    start points by age, 48t
    timing rules for, 52t
Liam, Age 9 case report
    academic skills, 271–273
    background, 265–266
    behavioral and emotional functioning, 273–274
    cognitive abilities, 268–270

Liam, Age 9 case report (*Continued*)
  critical decision points in the report-writing process, 278–281
  listed with other cases, 551
  memory, 270–271
  procedures for evaluation, 267
  psychological evaluation report, 266–267
  relevant behavioral observations, 267–268
  summary, 274–275
  test scores, 275*t*–278*t*
Lichtenberger, Elizabeth (Case 5–Tawna, age 13), 362–371, 551
Lichtenberger, Robert (Case 15–Jane, Age 8), 551, 578–586*t*
Life-course persistent (LCP) offenders, 184
Limited motor skills, 45
Lippmann, Walter, 722
Lizzie, Age 8 case report
  case formulation, 590–597
  listed with other reports, 551
  reason for referral, 587
  recommendations, 588–590
  score summaries, 598*t*–599*t*
  summary, 587–588
Longest span and sequence scores, 114–115
Low achievement (Case 2–Alicia, Age 13), 283–303, 551
Low cognitive ability
  Case 2–Alicia, Age 13, 283–303, 551
  Case 7–Jaime, Age 10, 425–436
  Case 9–Isabella, Age 13, 448–458*t*, 551
  Case 16–Lizzie, Age 8, 551, 587–599*t*
LTP (long-term potentiation), 337–338
Luke, Age 9 case report
  academic functioning, 314–318
  background, 304–305
  behavior and classroom observations, 306–307
  consideration of exclusionary factors as primary cause of Luke's weaknesses, 318–319
  evaluation procedures and tests administered, 305–306
  evaluation results, 307–314
  functional manifestations of cognitive weaknesses, 318
  listed with other reports, 551
  processing strengths and weaknesses analysis, 319
  psychometric data summary, 326*t*–329*t*
  reason for referral, 304
  recommendations, 321–326
  summary and diagnostic impressions, 319–321
Luria–Nebraska Neuropsychological Test Battery, 406, 407
Lurie, Michele
  Case 13–Ellie, Age 10 report by, 551, 557–567*t*
  case report 5–Tawna, age 13 by, 362–371, 551

McCloskey Executive Functions Scales (MEFS), 499
McCloskey, George
  Case 11–Colin, Age 8 case report by, 497–522*t*, 551
  Case 12–Derek, Age 13 case report by, 523–547*t*, 551
  NOPA (neuropsychologically oriented process approach) to psychoeducational evaluations, 493–495
  review of the WISC–V by, 669–681, 705
  on the training, experience, and flexibility required for intelligent testing, 22
McGill, Ryan J.
  WISC–V review by Miller and, 645–662

McGrew, Kevin
  importance of WISC–V interpretation from a theoretical basis, 29
  on WISC–V subtest interpretation, 26
Magnetic resonance imaging (MRI), 340
Mascolo, Jennifer
  Case 3–Luke, Age 9 report by, 304–329*t*, 551
  on targeting your observations during the evaluation, 23–24
  on tied WISC–V profile results to educational interventions, 33
  on assessment of cognitive functioning under fixed experimental conditions, 27
Math difficulties (Case 6–Tom, Age 8), 372–403*t*, 551
Mather, Nancy
  Case 17–Patrick, Age 9 report by, 551, 600–612*t*
  on having multiple sources of data to support hypotheses generated from WISC–V profiles, 30, 31
  on tying WISC–V profile results to educational interventions, 32, 33
Matrix Reasoning subtest scoring (WISC–V)
  comparing WISC–IV scoring and, 98*t*
  scoring key, 99
Matrix Reasoning subtest (WISC–V)
  administration of, 63–64*t*
  ancillary index scores and, 120, 121
  behavioral observations for, 63
  common errors made in administration of, 86
  comparing WISC–IV administration and, 64*t*
  discontinue rule for, 50*t*
  primary index scores and, 120
  process observations base rates for, 116
  reverse rules by age, 49*t*
  scoring the, 98*t*, 99, 116, 120, 121
  start points by age, 47*t*
  timing rules for, 52*t*
Max Planck Institute for Human Development (Berlin), 338
Mazes subtest (WISC–III), 15
MEG (magnetoencephalography), 340–341
Memory difficulties (Case 16–Lizzie, Age 8), 551, 587–599*t*
Middle school student school failure survey
  Midwest and South, 182–183
  San Francisco Bay, 179–180
Miller, Daniel C.
  Case 10–John, Age 12 WISC–V report by, 471–492, 551
  Integrated School Neuropsychological/Cattell-Horn-Carroll (SNP/CHC) model of, 414, 459–470
  on the present state and future of intelligence testing, 19–20
  WISC–V review by McGill and, 645–662, 704
Minnesota Department of Education, 179
MIS (mean of all primary index scores), 227
Motor skills limitations, 45
Multiple intelligences theory, 12

Naglieri, Jack
  "Hundred Years of Intelligence Testing: Moving from Traditional IQ to Second-Generation Intelligence Tests" by, 668
  Naglieri Nonverbal Ability Test by, 663
  on the present state and future of intelligence testing, 19
  WISC–V test review by, 663–668, 704–705
  WNV (Wechsler Nonverbal Scale of Ability) co-authored by Wechsler and, 724
Naglieri Nonverbal Ability Test, 663

Naming Speed Literacy subtest (WISC–V)
    administration of, 81–82, 85
    behavioral observations for, 82
    common errors made in administration, 87
    do not reverse, 49t
    scoring, 107–110, 116
    start points by age, 48t
    stop point for, 50t
    timing rules for, 52t
Naming Speed Quantity subtest (WISC–V)
    administration of, 81–82, 85
    common errors made in administration, 87
    do not reverse, 49t
    scoring, 110, 116
    start points by age, 48t
    stop point for, 51t
    timing rules for, 52t
National Academy of Neuropsychology Policy and Planning
        Committee, 405–406
National Council on Measurement in Education (NCME), 45, 140,
        625, 700, 701
National Institute of Child Health and Human Development, 178
National Longitudinal Study of Adolescent Health, 188
National Longitudinal Survey of Youth, 185
Neighborhood risk factor
    juvenile delinquency, 187–188, 190
    school failure and, 180–181, 183
NEPSY: A Developmental Neuropsychological Assessment, 407
NEPSY II: A Developmental Neuropsychological
        Assessment–Second Edition, 409, 415, 418, 651
Neural plasticity
    cognitive training and, 338–339
    definition of, 337
    LTP (long-term potentiation) form of, 337–338
Neurocognitive constructs (WISC–V, WISC–V Integrated, and
        WIAT–III)
    acquired knowledge: acculturation knowledge, 462t, 469
    acquired knowledge: language abilities, 463t, 469–470
    acquired knowledge: reading, writing, and math achievement,
        463t, 470
    basic sensorimotor functions, 460, 461t, 464
    cognitive processes: auditory/phonological, 461t, 464
    cognitive processes: executive functions, 461t, 465–466
    cognitive processes: learning and memory, 461t, 464–465
    cognitive processes: visuospatial, 461t, 464
    facilitators/inhibitors: allocating and maintaining attention, 462t,
        466–467
    facilitators/inhibitors: speed, fluency, and efficiency of processing,
        462t, 468–469
    facilitators/inhibitors: working memory, 462t, 467–468
Neurodevelopmental theory, 12
Neuropsychological deficits, 185
Neuropsychology. See Clinical neuropsychology
New York Bureau of Child Guidance, 723
Nonverbal Index (WISC–V)
    Block Design subtest, 120, 121
    Coding subtest, 120, 121
    Figure Weights subtest, 120, 121
    as global composite score applied to WISC–V interpretation,
        229–230, 243
    Matrix Reasoning subtest, 120, 121

    Picture Span subtest, 120, 121
    Visual Puzzles subtest, 120, 121
    See also Ancillary index scales
NOPA (neuropsychologically oriented process approach)
    case reports using, 496–547t
    overview of, 493–494
    six basic conceptions of, 494
    WISC–V interpretation using, 494–495
NOPA–based WISC–V interpretation case reports
    Case 11–Colin, Age 8, 497–522t, 551
    Case 12–Derek, Age 13, 523–547t, 551
    introduction to, 496

Object Assembly subtest, 13, 15, 17, 281, 708, 719

Parent education level
    as not able to compensate entirely for SES differences across racial
        groups, 172
    as school failure risk factor, 183–184
    summary of findings on WISC–V mean score differences cross
        sex, racial/ethnic differences, and, 173
    WISC–V normative sample composite score means and standard
        deviations by, 165t–166t
    WISC–V scores adjusted for sex and racial/ethnic differences by,
        170t–171t
    WISC–V scores from selected racial/ethnic groups at various, 160t
    See also Family
Parents
    juvenile delinquent risk and incarceration of, 188
    juvenile delinquent risk factors related to relationship with,
        186–187
    See also Family, Parent education level
PASS model of intellectual function, 14, 412
Pathways to Desistance Study, 183
Patrick, Age 9 case report
    background, 600–601
    listed with other reports, 551
    prior evaluations, 601
    reason for referral, 600
    recommendations, 608–610
    results from the current evaluation, 601–608
    score summaries, 611t–612t
Pavlov, Ivan, 724
Peabody Individual Achievement Test, 664
Pearson, Karl, 718
P-FIT (Parieto-Frontal Integration Theory), 336–337
Phonological dyslexia
    Case 8–Christopher, Age 11, 437–447t, 551
    Case 12–Derek, Age 13, 523–547t, 551
Physical environment administration issue, 40–41
Piaget, Jean, 27
Piaget's development theory, 12
Picture Completion subtest, 7, 16, 618, 639, 653, 684, 692
Picture Concepts subtest scoring (WISC–V)
    comparing WISC–IV scoring and, 98t
    scoring key, 99
Picture Concepts subtest (WISC–V)
    administration of, 66t–67
    behavioral observations for, 67
    common errors made in administration of, 86
    comparing WISC–IV administration and, 66t

Picture Concepts subtest (*Continued*)
  discontinue rule for, 50*t*
  reverse rules by age, 49*t*
  scoring the, 98*t*, 99, 116
  start points by age, 47*t*
  timing rules for, 52*t*
Picture Span subtest (WISC–V)
  administration of, 70–72
  ancillary index scores and, 120, 121
  behavioral observations for, 71–72
  common errors made in administration of, 87
  discontinue rule for, 50*t*
  primary index scores of, 120
  reverse rules by age, 49*t*
  scoring, 101
  start points by age, 48*t*
  timing rules for, 52*t*
Positron emission tomography (PET), 340
Power, Elizabeth (Case 4–Josh, age 8), 348–361*t*, 551
Practice effects
  the bottom line about, 423–424
  how clinicians should deal with, 422
  multiple assessments taking into account Wechsler's scales and, 419–424
  residual, 421–422
Pre-administration considerations (WISC–V)
  establishing and maintaining rapport, 41–42
  fairness issues, 43–46
  physical environment, 40–41
  selection of subtests, 43
  standard subtest administration order, 42*t*–43
  test materials, 38–40*fig*
Preschool children
  socioeconomic status (SES) and test outcomes of, 162–164
  WPPSI–III (Wechsler Preschool and Primary Scale of Intelligence–Third Edition), 5
  WPPSI–IV (Wechsler Preschool and Primary Scale of Intelligence–Fourth Edition), 43–44, 45, 122–123, 160, 164, 229, 618, 651, 696, 697
  WPPSI–R (Wechsler Preschool and Primary Scale of Intelligence–Revised Edition), 164
  See also Children with special needs; School age children
Primary Index scales (WISC–V)
  deriving primary index scores from, 120, 125, 631
  description and list of, 1
  Fluid Reasoning subtests, 2*fig*
  McCloskey's review on the, 675–676
  Processing Speed subtests, 2*fig*
  review of the WISC–V composite scores and, 620–622
  review of the WISC–V organizational framework of, 649*t*
  review on changes from the WISC–IV to, 620–622
  Verbal Comprehension subtests, 2*fig*
  Visual Spatial subtests, 2*fig*
  Working Memory subtests, 2*fig*
  See also specific case report; subtest
Process Assessment of the Learner–Second Edition (PAL–II), 677
Processing speed difficulties (Case 5–Tawna, Age 13), 362–371, 551
Processing Speed subtests (WISC–V)
  behavioral observations for, 75–76
  Cancellation, 48*t*, 49*t*, 78*t*–80, 87, 103*t*, 106, 116, 117
  Coding, 16, 48*t*, 49*t*, 50*t*, 52*t*, 74–76, 87, 103*t*–104, 116

  comparing WISC–IV administration and, 75*t*
  index scores applied to WISC–V interpretation, 245
  primary index scores and, 120
  scoring the, 102–106, 116, 117, 120–121
  Symbol Search, 16, 48*t*, 49*t*, 50*t*, 52*t*, 76–78, 87, 104–106, 116
  See also Scoring subtests (WISC–V)
Process observations
  description of, 115
  various base rates available by subtest, 116
Process-oriented approaches, 414–415
Profile interpretation
  CHC factors, 16
  Cohen's CHC-based factors, 15–16
  criticism of subtest, 8–9
  theory applied to, 15–16
  WISC–V factors, 16
Progressive error (or "test experience effects"), 422–423
Prompts (WISC–V), 53
Proration (WISC–V scoring)
  comparing substitution, retest, and, 122
  description of, 121
  how to use and record, 121–122
  limits on substitution and, 122
  WPPSI–IV replacement approach comparison studies of, 122–123
Protective factors
  child, 174
  community, 174
  family, 174
  juvenile delinquency risk factors interacting with, 190–191
PSW (pattern of strengths and weaknesses) analyses
  concluding the WISC–V scatter does matter for, 225
  for index-level scatter, 214
  putting information into a child's profile for, 16
  subtest level of, 223*t*
  WISC–V Technical and Interpretive Manual on, 699–700
The Psychological Corporation, 7, 13, 718, 720, 724

Q-global (software)
  ability-achievement discrepancy analysis, 131*fig*
  ancillary and complementary summary, 130*fig*
  composite score summary, 129*fig*
  demographics entry pages of, 126*fig*
  description and access to, 125–126
  index-level strengths and weaknesses and pairwise comparisons, 129*fig*
  pattern of strengths and weaknesses analysis, 132*fig*
  primary subtest summary, 128*fig*
  Quick Reference on FAQs (frequently asked questions on scoring), 132–137
  report configuration entry page, 127*fig*
  subtest level strengths and weaknesses and pairwise comparisons, 130*fig*
  total raw score entry page, 127*fig*
Q-interactive iPad to iPad format. *See* WISC–V Q-interactive
Qualifying items (WISC–V), 51–52
Quantitative Reasoning Index
  Arithmetic subtest, 120
  Figure Weights subtest, 120
  See also specific subtest
Queries (WISC–V), 53

Quick References (WISC–V)

  acceptable substitutions for FSIQ subtests, 122

  acceptable number of total raw scores of 0 for each composite score, 124

  commonly used recording abbreviations, 54

  examples of appropriate uses of the General Ability Index, 236

  examples of appropriate uses of the Nonverbal Index, 236

  frequently asked questions on subtest administration, 88–89

  on malleable risk and protective factors for child assessment and intervention, 174

  new and traditional descriptors of composite scores, 237

  Q-global software FAQs (frequently asked questions on scoring), 132–137

  racial/ethnic differences on the WISC–V, 172

  remembering discontinue roles, 51

  scaled and standard score metrics, 114

  Similarities general scoring principles, 93

  Vocabulary general scoring principles, 93

  on the WISC–V and as developmental trends, 163

Racial/ethnic differences

  impacting WISC–V outcomes, 159–160, 667–668

  juvenile delinquency risk factor, 189

  parent education level cannot compensate alone for SES differences across racial groups, 172

  percentage of adults from selecting groups and various levels of education, 160t

  Quick Reference on the WISC–V and, 172

  remember that there is great variance in the, 159

  school failure risk factor of, 181, 182

  scores of children who are African American, 169

  scores of children who are Hispanic, 169–170, 172

  scores of preschool children and, 166–168

  scores of school age children and, 168–169

  socioeconomic status (SES) and, 159, 160

  summary of findings on WISC–V mean score differences across sex, parent education level, and, 173

  U.S. Census Bureau data on education levels and, 160

  WISC–V scores adjusted for sex and parent education level for, 170t–171t

  See also FSIQ (Full Scale IQ)

Rather, Dan, 717–718

Raw process scores

  description of, 114

  error scores, 116

  longest span and sequence scores, 114–115

  process observations, 115–116

Reading difficulties

  Case 3–Luke, Age 9, 304–329t, 551

  Case 4–Josh, Age 8, 348–361, 551

  Case 6–Tom, Age 8, 372–403t, 551

  Case 13–Ellie, Age 10, 551, 557–567t

  Case 15–Jane, Age 8, 551, 578–586t

  Case 17–Patrick, Age 9, 551, 600–612t

Receiver operating characteristics (ROC) curve, 182

Recognition Symbol Translation subtest (WISC–V)

  administration of, 84–85

  behavioral observations for, 84

  common errors made in administration of, 88

  discontinue rule for, 51t

  do not reverse, 49t

  scoring, 111, 112, 116, 117

  start points by age, 48t

  timing rules for, 52t

Record Form

  making a requested repetition by recording RR, 53

  teaching items' dagger symbol, 52

  See also specific subtest

Recording responses/abbreviations (WISC–V), 54–55

Reliability

  Academic–Q (Child and Adolescent Academic Questionnaire), 197, 200–201t

  Behavior–Q (Child and Adolescent Behavior Questionnaire), 197, 201t

  model–based, 694–695

  WISC–V Technical and Interpretive Manual on WISC–V's validity and, 228, 623, 624–625, 625, 627, 628, 629, 631, 633, 634, 645, 653, 654, 655–656, 660, 661, 687–692, 696

Repetitions of items (WISC–V), 52–53

Replacement approaches

  comparing substitution, proration, or retest, 122

  WISC–V comparison study on, 123–124

  WPPSI–IV comparison studies on, 122–123

Response to Intervention (RTI) philosophy, 550

Responsivity Principle, 176

Retest

  comparing substitution, proration, or, 122

  WPPSI–IV replacement approach comparison studies of, 122–123

Reverse rules (WISC–V)

  overview of the, 47

  subtest reserve rule by age, 48t–49t

Reynolds Intellectual Assessment Scales (RIAS), 11

Reynolds, Matthew R.

  final thoughts on the WISC–V by, 635

  WISC–V review by Hadorn and, 615–634, 704

Risk assessment

  limited research on youth, 177

  review of research on youth, 192–193

Risk Assessment Instrument (RAI), 193

Risk factors

  holistic view of, 176–177

  influencing adolescent delinquent behavior, 184–192

  influencing school failure, 177–184

  research on youth risk assessment and, 192–193

  reviewing research on school failure and delinquency, 175–193

  static and dynamic, 176

Risk Needs Responsivity (RNR) model, 176

RNR model, 192

Scaled scores

  common errors in obtaining, 119

  description of, 113, 114

  obtaining, 118–119

  obtaining sums of standard and, 120–125

Schneider, Joel

  on approach to writing the evaluation report, 24–25

  case report 1–Liam, age 9 by, 265–282, 551

  his thoughts on the Kaufman method, 17–18

  predictions on the future of intelligent testing by, 34

  on the training, experience, and flexibility required for intelligent testing, 20–21, 22

School age children
    racial/ethnic differences and test outcomes of, 168–169
    socioeconomic status (SES) and test outcomes of,
        164, 166
    See also Children with special needs; Preschool children
School and neighborhood safety risk factor, 180–181, 183
School failure risk factors
    ADHD (attention-deficit/hyperactivity disorder), 177
    family as a, 180, 181–182
    foster children at additional risk, 180
    GPA (grade point average) and, 177, 182, 183
    holistic view of, 176–177
    influencing school failure, 177–184
    parent education level as a, 183–184
    racial/ethnic differences in, 181, 182
    reviewing the research on, 175–193
    risk assessment research on youth and, 192–193
    self-reported school and community neighborhood safety,
        180–181, 183
    socioeconomic status (SES) as a, 182
    static and dynamic risk, 176
    See also Adolescents; Youth risk assessment
School Response to Intervention (RTI) philosophy, 550
Score analysis (WISC–V)
    changes from the WISC–IV to, 624
    five principles of our approach to, 232–233
    step 1a: select appropriate global composite score to describe
        overall intellectual ability, 234–235
    step 1b: report and describe the global composite score,
        235–237
    step 2a: report and describe the Cognitive Proficiency
        Index, 237
    step 2b: evaluate pairwise discrepancy comparisons with FSIQ and
        Cognitive Proficiency Index, 237–239
    step 3a: select the index scores (specific composite scores),
        239–240
    step 3b: report and describe the index scores, 240
    step 4: report and describe the subtest scaled and standard scores,
        240–241
    step 5: evaluate index–level strengths and weaknesses, 241–243
    step 6: evaluate subtest–level strengths and weaknesses
        comparisons, 243–244
    step 7: evaluate index–level pairwise comparisons, 244–246*t*
    step 8: evaluate subtest–level pairwise comparisons, 246–247
Scores (WISC–IV Q-interactive)
    advanced scoring output, 152–153
    basic scoring output, 152
    Complementary Subtest Results screen, 153*fig*
    Composite Results screen, 154*fig*
    Primary and Secondary Subtest Results screen, 152*fig*
Scores (WISC–V)
    ancillary index, 120–121
    changes from the WISC–IV to, 624
    contrast, 116–117
    error, 115
    item, 113
    longest span and sequence, 114–115
    primary index, 120
    process observations, 115–116
    raw process, 114
    reviews on standardization of, 686–687

    scaled, 113, 114, 118–125
    standard, 113–114, 118–125
    sums of scaled and standard, 120–125
    total raw, 113, 117–118
    using Q-global to obtain the WISC–V report, 125–132
    See also Composite scores (WISC–V)
Scoring steps (WISC–V)
    1: obtain total raw scores, 117–118
    2: obtain scaled or standard subtest scores, 118–119
    3: obtain sums of scaled and standard scores, 120–125
    4: obtain composite scores, 125
    See also FSIQ (Full Scale Intelligence Quotient)
Scoring subtests (WISC–V)
    changes from the WISC–IV to, 624
    digital administration and scoring, 139–155
    Fluid Reasoning subtests, 98*t*–99
    Naming Speed subtests, 107–110
    Processing Speed subtests, 102–106
    step-by-step process of, 117–125
    Symbol Translation subtests, 111–112
    Verbal Comprehension subtests, 91–95
    Visual Spatial subtests, 95*t*–98
    Working Memory subtests, 100–102
    See also Fluid Reasoning subtests (WISC–V); Processing Speed
        subtests (WISC–V); Verbal Comprehension subtests
        (WISC–V); Working Memory subtests (WISC–V)
Self-control theory, 185
Sex differences
    impacting WISC–V outcomes, 160–162*t*
    juvenile delinquency risk factor, 189–190
    Quick Reference on the WISC–V and developmental trends, 163
    summary of findings on WISC–V mean score differences cross
        parent education level, racial/ethnic differences, and, 173
    WISC–V normative sample composite score means and standard
        deviations by, 162*t*
    WISC–V scores adjusted for racial/ethnic differences, parent
        education levels by, 170*t*–171*t*
    WPPSI–IV outcomes are often no sex difference in some young
        children, 160
Silver's (1993) information-processing model, 415–417
Similarities subtest scoring (WISC–V)
    comparing WISC–IV scoring and, 92*t*
    Quick Reference on, 93
    scoring key, 94
Similarities subtest (WISC–V)
    ancillary index scores and, 120, 121
    behavioral observations for administration, 55–56
    Cohen's factor-analytic research on, 15
    common errors made in administration of, 85
    comparing WISC–IV administration and, 55, 56*t*
    discontinue rule for, 50*t*
    overview of, 55
    primary index scores and, 120
    process observation base rates, 116
    reverse rule, 48*t*
    scoring, 92*t*, 93, 94, 116
    start points by age, 47*t*
    timing rules for, 52*t*
Singer, Jennie Kaufman
    Case 7–Jaime, Age 10, 425–436, 551
    David Wechsler's informal intelligence assessment of, 716, 718

SNP/CHC (Integrated School Neuropsychological/
    Cattell-Horn-Carroll) model
    Case 10–John, Age 12 on WISC–V interpretation using the,
        471–492, 551
    as a process-oriented approach, 414
    the WISC–V, WISC–V Integrated, and WIAT–III neurocognitive
        constructs basis of, 460–470
    See also CHC (Cattell-Horn-Carroll) theory
Socioeconomic status (SES)
    infancy and preschool test outcomes and, 162–164
    influence on intelligence, 333
    parent education level as not able to compensate entirely for racial
        differences, 172
    racial/ethnic differences and factor of, 159, 160
    school age test outcomes and, 164, 166
    as school failure risk factor, 182
    strongly associated with children's intellectual ability test scores,
        162–166
    WISC–V normative sample composite score means and standard
        deviations by parent education level, 165t–166t
Spearman, Charles, 718
Special needs populations
    ADHD (attention-deficit/hyperactivity disorder), 140–141, 155,
        177, 230
    autism spectrum disorder, 230
    deaf or hard of hearing, 46, 551, 568–577t
    digital administration and scoring for clinical and, 140–141
    English-language learners, 45–46, 668
    limited motor skills, 45
    serious language difficulties, 45–46
    visual impairment, 46
    WISC–V administration fairness to, 44–45
    See also specific case report
Specific composite scores (WISC–V)
    additional index and process scores in this book, 231–233t
    step-by-step score analysis to inform WISC V interpretation,
        239–247
    WISC–V published index scores, 230–231t
    See also Composite scores (WISC–V)
Specific learning disabilities (SLDs)
    Case 11–Colin, Age 8 mild executive function difficulties but no,
        497–522t, 551
    IDEA requirements on nondiscriminatory scales and, 664
    processing speed sensitivity to, 230
    WISC–V and eligibility determination on, 667
    WISC–V Technical and Interpretive Manual on using WISC–V to
        identify, 667
Standard scores
    common errors in obtaining, 119
    description of, 113–114
    obtaining, 118–119
    obtaining sums of scaled and, 120–125
Standards for Educational and Psychological Testing, 44–45, 140, 625,
    696–697, 700
Stanford-Binet Intelligence Scale (1916), 724
Stanford-Binet Intelligence Scales, Fifth Edition (SB5), 11
Stanford–Binet Intelligence Scale–Fourth Edition (SB IV), 8, 11
Stanford Center on Longevity, 338
Start points (WISC–V)
    overview of, 46–47
    subtest start points by age, 47t–48t

Static risk factors, 176
Stop points (WISC–V)
    overview of, 47, 49–50
    subtest discontinue rules/stop points, 50t–51t
Stopwatch use (WISC–V), 53
Stroop Color and Word Test, 185
Substitution (WISC–V scoring)
    comparing proration, retest, or, 122
    limits on proration and, 122
    Quick Reference on acceptable substitutions for FSIQ, 122
    subtests used to calculate index scores without, 120–121
    WPPSI–IV replacement approach comparison studies of, 122–123
Subtest-by-subtest administration (WISC–V)
    common errors in the, 85–88
    complementary subtests, 80–85
    Fluid Reasoning subtests, 63–68t
    Processing Speed subtests, 74–80
    Quick Reference on frequently asked questions on, 88–89
    selection of the subtests, 43
    standard order and domain membership of the, 42t
    Verbal Comprehension subtests, 55–63
    Working Memory subtests, 69–74
    See also WISC–V interpretation
Subtest discontinue rules (WISC–V)
    discontinue rules/stop points, 50t–51t
    overview of, 47, 49–50
    Quick Reference on, 51
Subtest-level scatter
    concluding that it does matter for PSW analyses, 225
    Kaufman's two methods for evaluating, 220
    past research on, 220
    strengths, weaknesses, assets, and deficits, 223t
    in the WISC–V, 220–223t
    See also Index-level scatter; Item-level scatter
Subtest profile interpretation
    criticism of, 8–9
    as the target of anti-IQ forces (1980s and 1990s), 8
    See also Kaufman method
Subtest profile interpretation (WISC–V)
    educational interventions must be tied to results from, 32–34
    hypotheses generated from profiles should be supported with
        multiple sources of data, 29–32
    importance of using a theoretical basis for, 28–29
    subtests as samples of behavior and not exhaustive, 25–27
    Wechsler's notion of "shared abilities" grouping in, 17
Subtests (WISC–V)
    interpretation of, 17, 25–34
    Q-interactive digital administration and scoring, 139–155
    test kit administration of, 41–43, 63–89
    test kit scoring of, 91–125
    See also specific subtest
Subtests (WISC–V reviews)
    changes from the WISC–IV subtests to, 617–619
    new ones adapted from other Wechsler tests, 628
    on including subtests that do not contribute to any index score, 676
    WISC–V subtests and subtest categories, 648t, 653
    See also specific subtest
Sums of scaled and standard scores
    ancillary index scores, 121
    invalidation of composite scores, 124–125
    proration, 121–122

Sums of scaled and standard scores (*Continued*)
  replacement approach comparison studies of WPPSI–IV, 122–123
  replacement approach comparison study of WISC–V, 123–124
  substitution, 120–121, 122
  subtests used to calculate index scores (no substitution allowed), 120–121
  See also specific score
Symbol Search subtest scoring (WISC–V)
  comparing WISC–IV scoring and, 103
  scoring key, 104–106
Symbol Search subtest (WISC–V)
  administration of, 76–78
  ancillary index scores and, 120, 121
  behavioral observations for, 77–78
  Cohen's factor-analytic research applied to, 16
  common errors made in the administration of, 87
  comparing WISC–IV administration and, 77t
  discontinue rule for, 50t
  do not reverse, 49t
  primary index scores and, 120
  scoring the, 104–106, 116
  start points by age, 48t
  timing rules for, 52t
Syndrome analysis, 411

Tawna, Age 13 case report
  background, 362–363
  behavioral observations, 363
  listed with other reports, 551
  neuropsychological implications and diagnostic impression, 367–368
  psychometric summary of, 369t–371t
  reason for evaluation, 362
  recommendations, 368–369
  test results, 364–367
  tests administered, 364
Teaching items (WISC–V), 52
Terman, L. M., 722, 723, 724
"Test experience effects," 422–423
Test-kit version. *See* Administration (WISC–V test kit version)
Test materials (WISC–V)
  changes from the WISC–IV to, 623
  list of, 39
  overview of, 38–40
  remember to shield the Record Form behind free-standing manual, 40fig
  remember what materials are not included in the test kit, 39
Test of Memory and Learning, 407
Theory
  applied to profile interpretation, 15–16
  applied to test construction, 12
  applied to WISC–V construction, 12–15
  Cattell-Horn-Carroll (CHC) theory, 12–13
  definition and meaning of, 11
  Gardner's multiple intelligences theory, 12
  g theory, 15
  neurodevelopmental theory, 12
  PASS model of intellectual function, 14
  Piaget's development theory, 12
Thorndike, E. L., 723

Time limits (WISC–V)
  overview of, 50–51
  subtest timing rules, 52t
Tom, Age 8 case report (digital administration)
  assessment instruments, 375
  diagnoses, 382–383
  gross motor skills, 379
  history and background, 372–374
  iPad administration of the tests in, 553
  listed with other reports, 551
  mathematics, 381–382
  oral language, 379–380
  phonological processing, 379
  rapid automatic naming (RAN), 379
  reading, 380–381
  reason for referral, 372
  recommendations on specific behavior and cognitive learning areas, 383–389
  score summary and reports of the, 389–403fig
  socioemotional functioning, 377–379
  spelling and written expression, 381
  summary of findings and analyses for the identification of a specific learning disorder, 382
  test behaviors and observations, 374–375
  test results and clinical impressions, 375–377
  vision and hearing screenings, 374
  visual-motor integration and graphomotor skills, 381
TOMAL–2 (Test of Memory and Learning–Second Edition), 459
Total raw scores
  acceptable number of total raw scores of 0 for each composite score, 124
  common errors in obtaining, 118
  description of, 113
  obtaining, 117–118

University of Connecticut, 717
University of Georgia, 717
U.S. Bureau of Labor Statistics, 185

Validity
  Academic–Q (Child and Adolescent Academic Questionnaire), 202t–207
  Behavior–Q (Child and Adolescent Behavior Questionnaire), 202t–204t, 205t, 206
  influence of unusual index-level scatter on predictive FSIQ of WISC–V, 217
  WISC–V Technical and Interpretive Manual on WISC–V's reliability and, 623, 624–625, 625, 627, 628, 629, 631, 633, 634, 645, 653, 654, 655–656, 660, 661, 687–692, 696
Vasserman, Marsha
  Case 8–Christopher, Age 11, 437–447
  Case 14–Jordan, Age 15, 551, 568–577t
Verbal Comprehension subtests (WISC–V)
  ancillary index scores and, 120–121
  Cohen's factor-analytic research on, 15
  common errors made in the administration of, 85
  comparing WISC–IV scoring and, 92t
  Comprehension, 47t, 48t, 50t, 52t, 59–61, 85, 92t, 95, 116
  Information, 15, 47t, 48t, 50t, 52t, 58–59t, 85, 92t, 95, 116
  primary index scores and, 120
  scoring, 91–95, 116, 120–121

Similarities, 47*t*, 48*t*, 50*t*, 52*t*, 55–56*t*, 85, 92*t*, 93, 94, 116
Vocabulary, 47*t*, 48*t*, 50*t*, 52*t*, 56–58, 85, 92*t*, 93, 94–95, 116
Verbal (Expanded Crystallized) Index, 232, 233, 246, 259
Vineland Adaptive Behavior Scales–Second Edition (Vineland–II), 690, 691
Visual impairment considerations, 46
Visual perceptual disorder (Case 8–Christopher, Age 11), 437–447*t*, 551
Visual Puzzles subtest (WISC–V)
    administration of, 56–58
    ancillary index scores and, 120
    behavioral observations for, 63
    common errors made in the administration of, 86
    discontinue rule for, 50*t*
    primary index scores and, 120
    reverse rule, 48*t*
    scoring, 98, 116
    start points by age, 47*t*
    timing rules for, 52*t*
Visual Spatial subtests (WISC–V)
    ancillary index scores and, 120
    Block Design, 47*t*, 48*t*, 52*t*, 61*t*–62, 86, 95*t*, 96–98
    common errors made in the administration of, 85–86
    index scores applied to WISC–V interpretation, 244–245
    primary index scores and, 120
    scoring, 95*t*–98
    Visual Puzzles, 47*t*, 48*t*, 52*t*, 62–63, 86, 95*t*, 98
    Visual Spatial Index
    WISC–V reviewers on Perceptual Reasoning Index split into Fluid Reasoning and, 706
Vocabulary subtest scoring (WISC–V)
    comparing WISC–IV scoring and, 92*t*
    Quick Reference on, 93
    scoring key, 94–95
Vocabulary subtest (WISC–V)
    administration of, 56–58
    ancillary index scores and, 120, 121
    behavioral observations for, 57–58
    Cohen's factor-analytic research on, 15
    common errors made in administration of, 85
    comparing WISC–IV administration and, 57*t*
    comparing WISC–IV scoring and, 92*t*
    discontinue rule for, 50*t*
    primary index scores and, 120
    process observation base rates, 116
    reverse rule, 48*t*
    scoring, 92*t*, 93, 94–95, 116
    start points by age, 47*t*
    timing rules for, 52*t*

WAIS (Wechsler Adult Intelligence Scale), 209, 716
WAIS–IV (Wechsler Adult Intelligence Scale–Fourth Edition), 5, 229, 695, 696, 706
Wasserman, John, 721, 723
Watkins, Marley W.
    review of the WISC–V by Canivez and, 683–702
Wechsler-Bellevue Intelligence Scale (1939), 6, 717, 720, 721, 722–723
Wechsler, David
    anti-Semitism faced by, 721–722
    "Dr. Wechsler Remembered" (Kaufman) on, 715–720

"Dr. Wechsler Remembered Part II" (Kaufman) on, 720–724
    early life and education of, 721
    his conversion of the Binet-Terman psychometric testing approach, 6, 724
    his credo of intelligence testing, 6–7
    his genius in measuring intelligence, 5–6
    on his identity as a Jew, 723
    his impact on adult assessment and continued legacy of, 724
    his response to Dan Rather's anti-IQ-testing TV special, 717–718
    on his scales being "first and foremost clinical instruments," 712
    Kaufman's description of the compassion and integrity of, 715, 716–718, 723
    Kaufman's recollections on working on the revised WISC with, 715–716, 720
    the respect he gave other clinicians, 724
    speculating on how he would have responded to the WISC–III, 718–719
Wechsler Intelligence Scale for Children–Revised (WISC–R)
    criticisms of the, 10–11
    as psychometrically sound IQ test for children during the late 1970s, 7–8, 86
Wechsler, Israel, 721, 723
Wechsler Nonverbal Scale of Ability (Wechsler & Naglieri), 663
Wechsler Nonverbal Scale of Ability (WNV) *Administration Manual* (Wechsler & Naglieri), 664
Wechsler's Measurement and Appraisal of Adult Intelligence (Matarazzo), 663
Wechsler, Ruth, 717, 719–720
Wechsler tests
    Cohen's factor-analytic research on Wechsler's scales, 15
    Lezak's criticism of the Wechsler's scales, 10
    overview of, 459
    review of WISC–V and related, 651
    theory-based test interpretation of Wechsler's scales, 15–16
    WAIS–IV (Wechsler Adult Intelligence Scale–Fourth Edition), 5, 229, 695, 706
    Wechsler-Bellevue Intelligence Scale (1939), 6, 717, 720, 721, 722–723
    Wechsler Nonverbal Scale of Ability, 663, 664
    WIAT (Wechsler Individual Achievement Test), 724
    WIAT–III (Wechsler Individual Achievement Test–Third Edition), 85, 459, 460–470, 632, 651, 661, 690, 691
    WISC (Wechsler Intelligence Scale for Children) [1949], 663, 715
    WISC–III (Wechsler Intelligence Scale for Children–Third Edition), 8, 10–11, 17, 691, 695, 719
    WISC–IV Integrated (Wechsler Intelligence Scale for Children–Fourth Edition Integrated), 5, 414
    WISC–IV (Wechsler Intelligence Scale for Children–Fourth Edition), 5, 9, 15, 16–17, 44, 91
    WISC–R (Wechsler Intelligence Scale for Children–Revised), 10–11, 16, 17, 663, 695, 715–716, 720
    WISC–V Integrated (Wechsler Intelligence Scale for Children–Fifth Edition Integrated), 5, 459–470
    WMS–IV (Wechsler Memory Scale–Fourth Edition), 459
    WNV (Wechsler Nonverbal Scale of Ability), 724
    WPPSI–III (Wechsler Preschool and Primary Scale of Intelligence–Third Edition), 5
    WPPSI–IV (Wechsler Preschool and Primary Scale of Intelligence–Fourth Edition), 43–44, 45, 122–123, 160, 164, 229, 618, 651, 696, 697

Wechsler tests (*Continued*)
WPPSI–R (Wechsler Preschool and Primary Scale of Intelligence–Revised), 164
See also Rating scales; WISC–V Q-interactive; WISC–V (Wechsler Intelligence Scale for Children–Fifth Edition)
Whites. *See* Racial/ethnic differences
WIAT (Wechsler Individual Achievement Test), 724
WIAT–III (Wechsler Individual Achievement Test–Third Edition), 85, 459, 460–470, 632, 651, 661, 690, 691
Willis, John O.
case report 2–Alicia, age 13 by, 283–303, 551
on having multiple sources of data to support hypotheses generated from WISC–V profiles, 30
on the training, experience, and flexibility required for intelligent testing, 20, 22–23
WISC–V review by Dumont and, 637–644, 704
on WISC–V subtest interpretation, 26
Winston, A. S., 721
WISC–V Q-interactive
administration of, 141–155
advantages and challenges of, 139
equivalence of traditional and digital mediums for, 139–140
introduction to, 1
testing special and clinical populations, 140–141
Tom, Age 8 case report on the use of, 372–403*t*, 551
WISC–IV Q-interactive users survey on, 140
WISC (Wechsler Intelligence Scale for Children) [1949], 663, 715
WISC–III PI (WISC–III as a Process Instrument) [Kaplan, et al.], 414
WISC–III (Wechsler Intelligence Scale for Children–Third Edition), 8, 10–11, 17, 691, 695, 719
WISC–IV Integrated (Wechsler Intelligence Scale for Children–Fourth Edition Integrated), 5, 414
WISC–IV Q-interactive survey, 140
WISC–IV (Wechsler Intelligence Scale for Children–Fourth Edition)
changes to scoring in the WISC–V from the, 91
comparing it to WISC–V, 16–17
confirmatory factor analysis (CFA) for, 15, 689–694
criticism of the, 9
description of, 5
problems with the Arithmetic subtest in, 695
Reynolds and Hadorn on major changes made in WISC–V from, 615–616
WISC–Revised (Wechsler Intelligence Scale for Children–Revised), 10–11, 16, 17, 663, 695, 715–716, 720
WISC–V Administration and Scoring Manual
concealing the Record Form behind, 40*fig*
estimated true score confidence intervals reported in, 687–688
importance of adhering to, 37
introduce the test using the verbatim directions provided in, 41
reviews on WISC–V standardization information in, 686
sample responses indicated with a Q should be queried, 83
scoring information in, 118
tables to derive the primary index scores in, 125
teaching items designated with a dagger symbol in, 52
WISC–V reviews on, 623, 656, 683, 684, 685
See also Administration (WISC–V test kit version); *specific subtest*
WISC–V Administration and Scoring Manual Supplement, 39, 45, 46, 114, 118–119, 125, 238, 623, 674, 683, 687
WISC–V Integrated (Wechsler Intelligence Scale for Children–Fifth Edition Integrated), 5, 459–470

WISC–V interpretation
Cattell–Horn–Carroll theory used for three cases of, 251–329*t*
CHC-based WISC–V interpretation and case reports, 255–264, 265–283, 265–329, 283–303, 304–329*t*
for children with reading or language problems: five illustrative case reports, 549–612*t*
cognitive neuroscience perspective used for case reports, 331–347, 348–371*t*, 372–403*fig*
McCloskey's neuropsychologically oriented process approach to psychoeducational evaluations, 493–547*t*
Miller's integrated school neuropsychological/Cattell–Horn–Carroll model used for case reports, 459–492
neuropsychological perspective used for case reports, 405–458*t*
overview of the theoretical frameworks for the 17 sample case reports on, 249–250
reviews on the new options for, 653–654, 685–686
step-by-step score analysis to inform, 232–247
of the subtests, 17, 25–34
understanding the composite scores, 227–232*t*
WISC–V Technical and Interpretive Manual's staged approach to, 669–670*fig*, 676, 681
See also WISC–V (Wechsler Intelligence Scale for Children–Fifth Edition)
WISC–V interpretation case reports
Case 1–Liam, Age 9, 265–282, 551
Case 2–Alicia, Age 13, 283–303, 551
Case 3–Luke, Age 9, 304–329*t*, 551
Case 4–Josh, Age 8, 348–361, 551
Case 5–Tawna, Age 13, 362–371, 551
Case 6–Tom, Age 8, 372–403*t*, 551
Case 7–Jaime, Age 10, 425–436, 551
Case 8–Christopher, Age 11, 437–447*t*, 551
Case 9–Isabella, Age 13, 448–458*t*, 551
Case 10–John, Age 12, 471–492, 551
Case 11–Colin, Age 8, 497–522*t*, 551
Case 12–Derek, Age 13, 523–547*t*, 551
Case 13–Ellie, Age 10, 551, 557–567*t*
Case 14–Jordan, Age 15, 551, 568–577*t*
Case 15–Jane, Age 8, 551, 578–586*t*
Case 16–Lizzie, Age 8, 551, 587–599*t*
Case 17–Patrick, Age 9, 551, 600–612*t*
conceptual and clinical integration of all 17 of the, 550–556
WISC–V Interpretive Assistant 1.0, 43, 44, 237, 241, 242, 246, 247
WISC–V Q-interactive administration
access to manuals in Central, 153
advanced scoring output, 152–153
audio recording use during, 146–147
basic scoring output, 152
potential clinical applications and digital enhancements, 153, 155
practitioner–client device interaction during, 148–149
practitioner tablet functions, 142–143
sample administration and scoring features, 142
swiping backward during, 147
WISC–V Q-interactive administration screens
Assess Discontinue Popovers on Practitioner's Screen, 148*fig*
Assess Start Popover on Practitioner's Screen, 147*fig*
assess "Swiping Backward" Popover on Practitioner's Screen, 149*fig*
Clients List screen, 142*fig*
Complementary Subtest Results, 153*fig*

Composite Results, 154*fig*
Information Text Popover on Practitioner's Screen, 150*fig*
Instructions Text Popover on Practitioner's Screen, 150*fig*
List of Assessments screen, 143*fig*
Manual Links in Central, 154*fig*
Practitioner's Screen View of an Item, Example A, 151*fig*
Practitioner's Screen View of an Item, Example B, 151*fig*
Primary and Secondary Subtest Results, 152*fig*
Q-interactive web portal, 141–142
Tutorial and Training in Central, 144*fig*
Typical Assess Buttons on Practitioner's, 145*fig*
Typical Assess Features on Practitioner's Screen for Verbal
    Items, 146*fig*
WISC–V Q-interactive
    administration of the, 141–155
    Case 6–Tom, Age 8 using, 372–403*t*, 551
    introduction to, 1
    Quick Reference on technical requirements, 141
    review of WISC–V and, 651
    structure of, 1–3
    See also Wechsler test products; WISC–V reviews
WISC–V structure
    ancillary index scales, 1, 2*fig*
    complementary index scales, 2*fig*, 3
    full scale, 1, 2*fig*
    primary index scales, 1, 2*fig*
    scores, 3
    See also specific index scale
WISC–V review (Canivez & Watkins)
    CFA methods used in WISC–V, 692–694, 701
    continuing problems with the arithmetic subtest, 695–696
    description of WISC–V, 683–684
    development of WISC–V, 684–685
    failure to provide results from EFA, 692, 701
    general summary on the WISC–V by the, 701–702
    how to access the complete independent analyses of the, 701
    incremental validity considerations, 696
    on lack of responsiveness to feedback by the test
        developers, 706
    measurement bias, 696–697
    model–based reliability of WISC–V, 694–695
    review summary of the, 700–701
    selective reporting and review of scientific literature, 697–700
    standardization, reliability, and validity of WISC–V, 686–692
    variance decomposition, 694, 695*t*
    WISC–V interpretation, 685–686
WISC–V review (Dumont & Willis)
    commentary, limitations, and recommendations, 642–644
    general description of WISC–V, 637–639
    scoring system of WISC–V, 639–640
    specific description of WISC–V, 639
    subtest modifications, 653
    technical adequacy of WISC–V, 640–642
WISC–V review (McCloskey)
    on difference and WISC–V measurement of cognition and
        intelligence, 678–681
    on difference between an ability and a process, 676–678
    on differences between primary, ancillary, and complementary
        indexes, 675–676
    domains in the factor–analytic model of intelligence, 679*fig*
    on Full Scale IQ and what it should encompass, 670–675*t*

possible index structure based on the 16 subtests, 676*t*
    on subtests that do not contribute to any of the indexes, 676
    WISC–V Technical and Interpretive Manual's staged approach to
        WISC–V interpretation, 669–670*fig*, 676
WISC–V review (Miller & McGill)
    contributions the WISC–V will make to the field, 661–662
    family of related products, 651
    five-factor WISC–V validation model for subtests, 657–659*fig*
    interpretative options, 653–654
    organization of the WISC–V, 645–647
    psychometric adequacy of the WISC–V, 654–661
    quality of testing materials, 652
    strengths and weakness of the WISC–V, 646*t*–647*t*
    theoretical foundation of WISC–V, 647–648, 651
    WISC–V subtests and subtest categories, 648*t*, 652–653
WISC–V review (Naglieri)
    on the evolution of WISC–V, 663–665
    impact of WISC–V on field of psychology and education, 668
    WISC–V and achievement, 666
    WISC–V and eligibility determination, 667
    WISC–V and race/ethnicity differences, 667–668
    WISC–V and theory, 665
WISC–V review (Reynolds & Hadorn)
    approach to item bias, 625
    on changes made from WISC–IV to, 615–616
    commentary and final thoughts on the, 632–635
    general description of WISC–V, 616–624
    norming sample of the WISC–V, 625
    reliability and validity evidence, 625–630
    scores differences and test interpretation, 630–632
    technical information on WISC–V, 624–630
    test criteria of, 630
WISC–V test reviews
    by Canivez and Watkins, 683–702, 705, 706
    comments on responsiveness to feedback by the test developers,
        705–706
    by Dumont and Willis, 637–644, 704, 706
    on if the WISC–V is user-friendly or not, 706–710
    by McCloskey, 669–681, 705
    by Miller and McGill, 645–662, 704
    by Naglieri, 663–668, 704–705
    overview and integration of the independent, 703–712
    on Perceptual Reasoning Index split into Fluid Reasoning and
        Visual Spatial, 706
    by Reynolds and Hadorn, 615–635, 704, 706
WISC–V Technical and Interpretive Manual
    Appendix C to derive the contrast scores, 116
    "Consequences of Testing" section on WISC–V score differences
        for diverse populations, 667–668
    on continuing problems with the Arithmetic subtest, 695–696
    description of, 683
    explanations for inclusion of five specific subtests, 677
    not required for administration of test, 39
    on PSW (pattern of strengths and weaknesses) analyses,
        699–700
    qualitative descriptors listed in, 236
    review on preference of CFA method used in WISC–V, 692–694,
        701
    review on selective reporting and review of scientific literature in,
        697–700
    review on variance decomposition in WISC–V, 694

WISC–V Technical and Interpretive Manual (*Continued*)
    reviews on WISC–V score reliability and validity, 623, 624–625, 625, 627, 628, 629, 631, 633, 634, 645, 653, 654, 655–656, 660, 661, 687–692, 696
    reviews on WISC–V standardization information in, 686, 687
    on revision of the goals of WISC–V, 684
    on deriving the Nonverbal Index, 230
    staged approach for interpretation of the test results in, 669–670*fig*, 676, 681, 697
    subtest reliability coefficients for special groups table in, 228
    tables on composite scores in the, 655
    on WISC–V scores used to generate hypotheses, 667
    on WISC–V used to identify specific learning disabilities (SLDs), 667
WISC–V Technical and Interpretive Manual Supplement, 626, 653
WISC–V structure
    introduction to the ancillary index scales, 1, 2*fig*
    introduction to the complementary index scales, 2*fig*, 3
    introduction to the Full scale, 1, 2*fig*
    introduction to the primary index scales, 1, 2*fig*
    scores, 3
    See also specific index scale
WISC–V (Wechsler Intelligence Scale for Children–Fifth Edition)
    administration of the subtests, 41–43, 63–89, 139–155
    applying CHC theory to construction of the, 12–15
    basic neurocognitive constructs of WISC–V Integrated, WIAT–III, and, 460–470
    basic steps for interpretation of the, 227–247
    CHC (Cattell-Horn-Carroll) theory application by, 12–15, 255–263, 414, 415, 417, 678
    compared to earlier editions, 16–17
    confirmatory factor analysis (CFA) for, 15, 689–694, 701
    description and overview of, 5, 15–17
    examining the scatter issue of, 209–225
    intertwining theoretical foundations of the CAS2, WJ IV, and, 11
    list of subtests of, 17
    multiple assessment and practice effects on, 419–424
    normative sample composite score means and standard deviations by parent education level, 165*t*–166*t*
    ongoing terminology changes evident in, 12
    Q-interactive iPad to iPad format (digital) format of, 1, 139–155
    Q-global software to obtain the score report, 125–137
    scoring, 91–125
    selecting between WISC–V and other batteries when testing children at the extremes of the age range, 44*t*
    sex, ethnic, and socioeconomic status (SES) differences in, 159–174
    three complementary index scores measuring CHC abilities, 16–17
    traditional "test kit" format of, 1, 37–137
    See also Child assessment; *specific subtest*; Wechsler test products; WISC–V interpretation

WJ III (Woodcock-Johnson–Third Edition), 11
WJ IV (Woodcock-Johnson–Fourth Edition)
    comparing WISC–V FSIQ with GIA subtests of, 672*t*
    description of the, 11
    functional emphasis of the, 14
    ongoing terminology evident in the, 12
WJ–R (Woodcock-Johnson Tests of Cognitive Ability–Revised), 8, 11
WMS–IV (Wechsler Memory Scale–Fourth Edition), 459
WNV (Wechsler Nonverbal Scale of Ability), 724
Woodworth, R. S., 721–722, 723, 724
Word Reasoning subtest (WISC–IV), 618–619, 639, 653, 684, 692
The Working Brain (Luria), 406
Working memory (*Gsm*) measure, 16, 416
Working Memory subtests (WISC–V)
    ancillary index scores and, 120
    common errors made in administration of, 86–87
    Digit Span, 15, 69–70*t*, 87, 100*t*–101, 116, 117
    index scores applied to WISC–V interpretation, 245
    Letter–Number Sequencing, 48*t*, 72–74, 87, 100*t*, 102, 116
    Picture Span, 48*t*, 70–72, 87, 101, 116
    primary Index scores and, 120
    scoring the, 100–102, 116, 120–121
    See also Scoring subtests (WISC–V)
WPPSI–IV (Wechsler Preschool and Primary Scale of Intelligence–Fourth Edition)
    Canivez's arguments on need for hierarchical multiple regression analyses in, 696
    consistency of the FSIQ composition with related scales of, 229
    development of the, 5
    new WISC–V subtests adapted from the, 618
    often no sex difference in some young children, 160
    replacement approach comparison studies of, 122–123
    review comparing WISC–V and, 651
    for testing children at the younger extreme of the age range, 43–44
    for testing children with limited motor skills, 45
WPPSI–R (Wechsler Preschool and Primary Scale of Intelligence–Revised Edition), 164
WRAML–2 (Wide Range Assessment of Memory and Learning–Second Edition), 459
Writing difficulties
    Case 1–Liam, Age 9, 265–282, 551
    Case 6–Tom, Age 8, 372–403*t*
    Case 10–John, Age 12, 471–492

Youth Level of Service/Case Management Inventory (YLS/CMI), 192
Youth risk assessment
    limited research on, 177
    review of research on, 192–193
    See also Juvenile delinquency risk factors; School failure risk factors
Youth Support Project, 187